# Business Programming Logic and Design

## Second Edition

Jack P. Russell

Tarleton State University

 HarperCollins*CollegePublishers*

Dedication

To Barbara and Jenny
and
my mother and dad,
Paul and Laura Russell

Sponsoring Editor: John Lenchek
Design Administrator: Jess Schaal
Cover Design: Fulton Design, Kay D. Fulton
Production Administrator: Randee S. Wire
Project Coordination and Text Design: Elm Street Publishing Services, Inc.
Compositor: Weimer Graphics, Inc.
Printer and Binder: R. R. Donnelley and Sons Co.
Cover Printer: R. R. Donnelley and Sons Co.

*Business Programming Logic and Design,* Second Edition
Copyright © 1994 by HarperCollins College Publishers

**Library of Congress Cataloging-in-Publication Data**

**Russell, Jack (Jack P.)**
　　Business programming logic and design / Jack Russell. —
　　　　2nd ed. p.　　cm.
　　Includes index.
　　ISBN 0-673-46840-2
　　　1. Electronic digital computers—Programming.
2. Structured programming.　　3. Business—Data processing.
I. Title.
QA76.6.R874　　　1994
0051—dc20　　　　　　　　　　　　　93-43817

7 8 9 10-ML-01 00 99

# Contents

# Preface

Students continue to need more help understanding problem analysis and design prior to writing code. Programmers must clearly understand a business problem before they can reach a concise and implementable solution. This text provides a systematic method for analyzing and designing business applications and assumes the student has little background in computer programming. The book's structured and modular approach enables the student to see the relationship between a simple design solution and a more complex one. The instructor can guide the student one step at a time through the design concepts.

*Business Programming Logic and Design,* second edition, is intended for the programming design or programming logic course at two-year or four-year colleges. The only prerequisite to this text is a general introduction to computers. Because of its ability to cover both introductory and advanced concepts adequately, the book would be ideal for upper-level study in a graduate program or as an in-depth workshop for programmer/analysts or systems professionals. The book also fills the void for primary reference material that government agencies and businesses find for workshops in programming design, programming logic, structured programming, COBOL, and BASIC. Instructors of COBOL and BASIC can use the text as either a primary or secondary reference. Although the text does not cover language syntax, it does cover the hardest part—design. The syntax can be taught easily from the teacher's favorite COBOL book or from a vendor publication.

*Business Programming Logic and Design,* second edition, can be taught in two parts. The first part, consisting of Chapters 1–10, addresses introductory logic concepts such as accumulation, comparison, data validation, control breaks, table handling, and interactive programming logic. The second part, Chapters 11–14, addresses more advanced logic

topics that include sorting, sequential file maintenance, interactive file maintenance, and computer-aided systems engineering (CASE).

Chapter 1 covers basic terminology, such as the processing cycle, data representation, the functions of data processing, and the steps in writing a computer program. Chapter 2 introduces basic design ideas: structured programming is discussed; a brief history and rationale is provided; and the three main constructs are explained. The concept of modularity is emphasized by showing hierarchy charts as the first step in the design process, and the student learns a standard method of program design and module decomposition by using flowcharts, pseudocode, and action diagrams. Chapter 3 covers the subject of accumulation of totals. Chapter 4 discusses comparison of values using IF . . . THEN . . . ELSE and the CASE structures, nested comparisons, compound AND and compound OR comparisons, and a more advanced discussion of the evaluation of expressions that involve both AND and OR operators.

Chapter 5 covers the data validation process, independent data validation routines, and built-in validation modules. Chapter 6 discusses single-level, two-level, and three-level control breaks. Chapter 7 discusses the concept of table handling, the use of subscripts, definite iteration or count-controlled loops, and positionally addressing elements within a table. Chapter 8 discusses various techniques for both loading and searching a single-dimensional table. More applications are added to show both data validation and data extraction from tables. Chapter 9 covers two-dimensional table handling. Chapter 10 discusses simple interactive logic by introducing the basic logic involved in presenting menus to the user, validating that which is keyed-in by the user (error trap routines), and a simple menu-driven application.

Chapter 11 deals with sorting of data internally in memory. Chapter 12 covers sequential file maintenance, and Chapter 13 picks up where Chapter 10 left off on the discussion of interactive logic and delves into indexed file maintenance and reporting using interactive screens. Chapter 14 describes a modern systems development methodology—computer-aided systems engineering. The leading-edge nature of this information and its relation to program design is quite an appropriate summation to this text.

Since the first edition, many teachers and trainers have switched to COBOL 85 and/or QBASIC. The update to COBOL 85 and QBASIC was a must. The reader will find improved consistency in module naming reference between the hierarchy charts, flowcharts, and pseudocode. All hierarchy chart boxes are now represented as module calls in the program flowchart and pseudocode. A balanced use of both module calls (to enforce and highlight the importance of modularity) and also "in-line" sequence of commands within a repetition structure to show the importance of coding efficiency has been used. Increased coverage of table handling with more examples and programming design problems is provided. The types of table problems and applications have been expanded as well.

The use of COBOL 85 instead of COBOL 74 and the use of QBASIC instead of GWBASIC is a significant update. Chapter 10 makes use of microcomputer COBOL II (MicroFocus COBOL) to allow students to compare it with what they may use. Another significant improvement is the addition of elementary interactive programming logic. Chapter 10 does not require any advanced file handling concepts. It carefully leads the student into screen-driven, interactive logic.

A new Chapter 14 on Computer-Aided Systems Engineering (CASE) describes new methods for systems development. Action diagrams are discussed as a design tool that is rapidly gaining acceptance in CASE environments. Another major improvement is the addition of more laboratory problems at the ends of chapters.

Single dimensional tables are now addressed in two chapters rather than one. Chapter 7 discusses table concepts, and Chapter 8 now discusses the table loading and searching process in greater depth. This edition includes discussions and examples on alternate methods for loading and searching tables. The first edition only addressed loading and searching tables with a known number of elements. This edition now addresses variable-sized tables. An introductory chapter on interactive logic, as well as a chapter that uses interactive programming logic to maintain indexed files, will permit the student a more progressive learning process. Chapter 10 introduces the student to the idea and use of interactive programming without wading out too deeply, while Chapter 13 continues to cover interactive logic and file maintenance in greater depth.

As stated previously, all COBOL examples use COBOL 85/COBOL II. The greatest differences to note in the code are: 1) the use of END-IF with all IF statements; 2) the use of END-PERFORM with the "in-line" PERFORMS; and 3) the use of the EVALUATE statement when using some CASE structures. Chapter 4 shows both the manual use of the IF . . . THEN . . . ELSE . . . IF approach to handling CASE structure logic as well as the EVALUATE command to accomplish the same thing. These parallel illustrations hopefully clarify the use and advantage of the EVALUATE statement in COBOL or the SELECT CASE command in QBASIC.

With CASE technology rapidly finding its place in the application development process, the design aspect of application development is further highlighted. CASE technology demands a sound knowledge of software design logic. CASE packages such as KnowledgeWare's Application Development Workbench (ADW) generate COBOL code from action diagrams. The Texas Instruments Information Engineering Facility (IEF) also generates code from an action diagram that resembles pseudocode. Action diagrams are rapidly becoming a standard design tool when using CASE packages; therefore, action diagrams are also covered in Chapter 14. It is likely that prospective graduates of CIS programs will soon be required to be competent in the use of such tools, since they will be working within a CASE-oriented development environment. This new environment is not magical—to develop action diagrams with a CASE tool, the developer must have a strong knowledge of program design logic.

## Acknowledgments

I wish to thank several people who made substantial contributions to this second edition. I especially appreciate the comments of Paula Funkhauser from Truckee Meadows Community College. At Harper Collins, I wish to thank Maureen Hull for serving as editor and having faith in the project. At Elm Street Publishing, I wish to thank Nancy Shanahan for meticulously managing the final stages of the project. Thanks also is extended to Danny Johnson, Computer Laboratory Supervisor at Tarleton State University, for his laboratory cooperation during program development of material reproduced in the text.

I wish to especially thank a colleague, Bev Hargrave, for assisting in the final editing of the art work and final proofs. As a teacher of a design course, his comments were very helpful. I wish to thank my wife, a systems development consultant and instructor of CIS at Tarleton State, for inspiring me to write the first edition as well as the second edition. Her comments and suggestions are appreciated. Thanks go to Ms. Pat Cude at Tarleton State for her many suggestions and for helping me identify weaknesses in the "table" chapters of the first edition. I wish to thank my daughter, Tammi, for her computer assistance and support; and to Billy, for being my inspiration and helper during it all.

I also thank the following for their technical expertise in helping make this text the best on the market.

Tom Athey, California State Polytechnic University
Paula Funkhauser, Truckee Meadows Community College
Shari Barker, Rockhurst College
Richard Fleming, North Lake College
Judy V. Humphrey, Tarrant County Junior College
Barbara Russell, Tarleton State University
Pat Cude, Tarleton State University
Bev Hargrave, Tarleton State University
Peter Welcher, United States Naval Academy
Carolyn Budd, University of North Carolina—Greensboro
David Wen, Diablo Valley College
Don Dershem, Mountain View College

Finally, let me thank the students and former students at TSU, who helped ferret out many errors and ambiguities and who also kept me "fired up" enough to finish the project.

Jack P. Russell
December, 1993

# 1

# Computer Programming Concepts: A Review

## OBJECTIVES

After completing this chapter, the students will be able to:

1. Describe the four basic functions of a computer.
2. Define *data*.
3. Describe the four main units of a computer system.
4. Describe main memory and the byte, explain how data is addressed, and recognize high- and low-level languages.
5. Describe a typical business application and how the components of a computer are used to produce output.
6. Explain the processing cycle.
7. Identify three secondary methods of storing data for processing.
8. Define the following terms and describe how they are used: *file, record, field*.
9. Identify three types of data and differentiate between them.
10. Describe the functions of data processing.
11. List the fundamental steps in writing a computer program and explain each one.
12. Be able to explain why flowcharting is an important tool in program design.
13. Understand the system development process and comprehend how modern systems development tools are being used.

## BASIC FUNCTIONS OF A COMPUTER

In order to develop computer programs, the student must be familiar with the four basic functions of the modern-day computer. Although the computer can assist in a lunar landing and can keep track of hundreds of thousands of airline passengers each day, it is actually limited to these four main operations:

1. **Arithmetic operations** addition, subtraction, multiplication, division, and exponentiation.
2. **Logical operations** comparing a value with another value. The comparison can determine whether the values are equal or unequal. It can also determine if one number is greater than or less than another.
3. **Input/Output operations** accepting or reading data for processing and printing data on an output device such as a printer or terminal screen. This includes the transfer of data to a peripheral device.
4. **Storage operation** saving data at another memory location.

Computers are able to (1) input data, (2) perform calculations and/or compare one value with another to determine whether or not they are equal, as well as perform special processing steps based on the result of the comparison, (3) store data at another place in memory if necessary, and (4) display or print out useful information resulting from the calculation or comparison.

## WHAT ARE DATA?

**Data** are the organized facts (numbers, letters, and special symbols) about a person, place, or thing. In a business organization, for example,

```
452112680BOB ARNOLD 00500
```

could represent the data from a sales receipt; however, certain data processing steps must be performed before useful results are obtained—such as a bill for Bob Arnold in the amount of $5.00.

## WHAT IS INFORMATION?

**Information** is data organized into a usable form. The sales receipt (data) is processed and a customer bill is produced. The customer bill is the usable document (information).

## THE FOUR MAIN UNITS OF A COMPUTER

In order to program a computer, it is necessary to understand the functions of a computer's four main types of units. These units are:

1. **Input units** transfer data to the computer's main memory for processing.
2. **Processor unit** accepts the instructions and data into the memory unit and processes the data according to the instructions.
3. **Output units** print or display the results of the processing.
4. **Peripheral units** store data permanently on tape or disk.

Figure 1.1 illustrates these units and their relationship. The **CPU (central processing unit)** is the part of the processor responsible for interpreting and executing the instructions to the computer. **Main memory** is where the instructions are held during the execution process.

## THE COMPUTER PROGRAM

The operations a computer can perform must be directed before useful results can be produced. This direction is accomplished by a **computer program,** a set of instructions given to a computer to solve a specific problem or set of problems. As mentioned, before the instructions can be executed, the pro-

gram must be stored in the computer's memory. (You may wish to consult an introductory textbook on computer concepts for a more complete explanation of how a computer carries out these instructions.)

The following is a small segment of a computer program written in a language called COBOL (Common Business Oriented Language).

```
COMPUTE DISC = SALES * .10.
COMPUTE NET = GROSS - DISC.
COMPUTE TOTAL = TOTAL + NET.
```

## MAIN MEMORY AND THE BYTE

The previous discussions about data and the computer program pointed out that both must be held in main memory of the computer before processing can occur. Each character (letter, digit, or special symbol) needed for either the data or the instructions themselves is stored at a particular place in memory called a byte. The **byte** is a sort of "pigeon-hole" in which characters are stored. Figure 1.2 illustrates the computer byte in memory and how the computer can access it.

Notice the labels beneath the pigeon holes. Each label is an **address** for a byte, and the addressing starts at zero. On most computers, each byte is addressable, which means that an individual byte can be manipulated by most computers. The illustration shows that the digit 5 is found at address 48 in memory, a digit 6 is found at address 49 in memory, etc. This concept will become more significant as this chapter progresses.

## HIGH-LEVEL AND LOW-LEVEL LANGUAGES

Computer languages can be categorized as high-level or low-level. COBOL (COmmon Business Oriented Language) and PASCAL are examples of **high-level languages.** Their instructions are written in a language very much like standard English that allows the programmer to concentrate on the problems to be solved rather than on the complexities of the machine and what it is doing. High-level languages are *machine independent*; that is, it does not matter on which computer one runs the program. Instructions like

```
COMPUTE NET = GROSS - TAX.
```

mean to the programmer exactly what they say and require very little interpretation. A computer, however, is unable to understand high-level instructions (at this time, anyway). It can execute only **machine language** instructions; therefore, the high-level computer program must be compiled (or translated) into machine language before execution can occur.

A **low-level language** is, on the other hand, much like the language of the machine itself. **Assembly language** is an example of a low-level language and is *machine dependent*; that is, it will execute on only one kind of computer system. The assembly language instructions often resemble the actual machine language instructions. A one-to-one relationship exists between the assembly language instruction set and the machine language instruction set. Every assembly language command equates to a corresponding machine language command. Assembly language is often referred to as symbolic machine language because it is easier to read and understand than pure machine language.

## THIRD, FOURTH, FIFTH, AND SIXTH-GENERATION LANGUAGES

Procedural languages such as COBOL, BASIC, and C are called third-generation languages. This was a big step up from the first- and second-generation languages that required either machine or assembly language coding. Third-generation programming still strong in the software development process although fourth-generation languages such as RBASE, DBASE, CLIPPER, and Natural are also very popular tools. File maintenance and Query commands allow the programmer to quickly develop computer applications that once took much longer in third-generation language programming. Report and screen output can be produced rapidly allowing almost immediate prototyping with the end-user. Prototyping is building a small model of the actual application or system. The user can quickly ascertain the usefulness and decision support nature of various forms of output. Fifth-generation languages include Com-

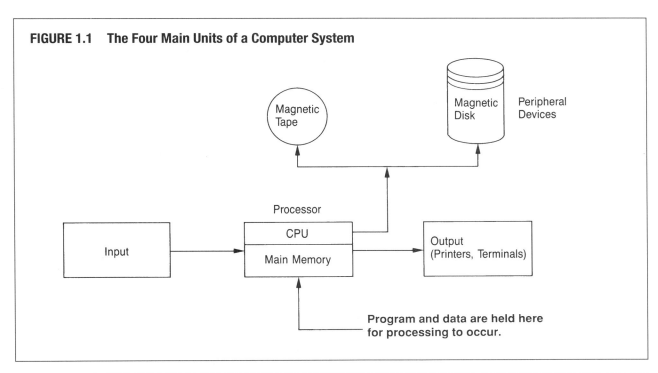

**FIGURE 1.1   The Four Main Units of a Computer System**

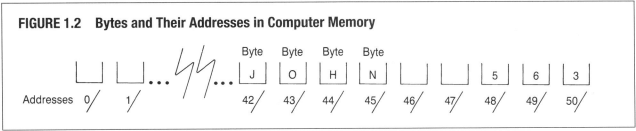

**FIGURE 1.2   Bytes and Their Addresses in Computer Memory**

puter-Aided Systems Engineering products that allow an automated approach to the engineering of business systems through the planning, analysis, design, and code generation phases. Sixth-generation languages include Executive Support Systems. This product often embodies many of the features of fourth- and fifth-generation languages in that the ESS often uses a relational data base with SQL, spreadsheet and graphics capability, and may even contain expert system capabilities.

## THE COMPUTER INSTRUCTION

The **computer instruction** in machine language consists of two main parts, the operation code and the operand. The **operation code** tells the computer what operation, or function, to perform, and the **operand** tells the computer the location (address) of the data upon which the operation will be performed. For example, a COBOL command (panel A) and the resultant machine language equivalent (panel C) are shown in Figure 1.3. An assembly language command (panel B) and its associated machine language equivalent (panel C) are shown in the same figure.

It is important that the reader understand that the business programmer will not write programs in machine language. He or she will write programs in a high-level language such as COBOL or BASIC. Sometimes programmers who are writing specialized system software *programs* will use a low-level language to decrease program execution time, but normally it is not a frequently used system development tool. Instead, a program called a compiler handles the process of translating high-level language instructions into machine language.

This will be elaborated in a later section on explaining the steps in writing a program.

Figure 1.4 illustrates that both the program and data are held in main memory. It is important to recognize the distinction between the program and the data. The computer program reads only one record (or block) at a time into the computer's main memory. Figure 1.4 illustrates how both instructions and data might appear in the individual bytes of main memory.

The circled instruction in Figure 1.4 illustrates how the computer is able to subtract the tax amount from the gross salary. The gross salary of "50060" is read into memory at the address location 7010, and the tax amount of "10621" is read into memory at address location 7020.

The FB of this instruction tells the computer to subtract. The next two positions (55) tell the computer that both numbers involved in the subtraction are five positions (bytes) in length. The next two values (7010 and 7020) are the addresses of the two numbers to be used in the subtraction process. Thus, the computer knows to subtract 10621 from 50060.

## A TYPICAL BUSINESS APPLICATION— THE PROCESSING CYCLE

A customer billing application in Figure 1.5 illustrates how the components of a computer can produce bills to customers. The following operations are performed:

1. The data from a customer's sales invoice are entered to tape or disk.

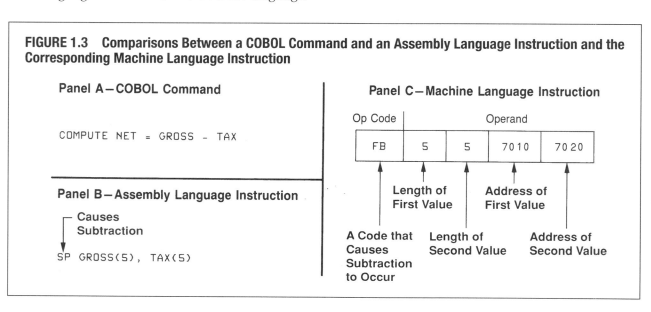

**FIGURE 1.3    Comparisons Between a COBOL Command and an Assembly Language Instruction and the Corresponding Machine Language Instruction**

### Panel A — COBOL Command

```
COMPUTE NET = GROSS - TAX
```

### Panel B — Assembly Language Instruction

Causes Subtraction

```
SP GROSS(5), TAX(5)
```

### Panel C — Machine Language Instruction

| Op Code | | | Operand | |
|---|---|---|---|---|
| FB | 5 | 5 | 7010 | 7020 |

A Code that Causes Subtraction to Occur
Length of First Value
Length of Second Value
Address of First Value
Address of Second Value

2. Each record is read into computer memory for processing one at a time.
3. The computer program written to generate the bills calculates the respective bill amount.
4. The bill is printed on a printer

## DATA REPRESENTATION

Three major devices, or media, for data storage are magnetic tape, magnetic disk, and floppy disk. The process of recording data on the media is called, quite appropriately, data entry.

**FIGURE 1.4   A Close-up Look at a Program Excerpt and Data Located in Memory**

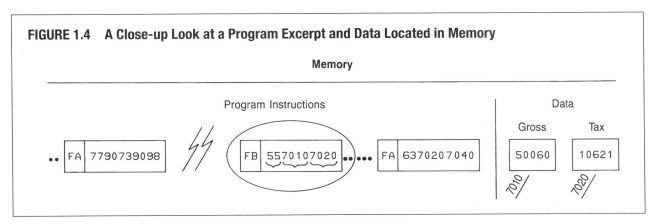

**FIGURE 1.5   The Processing Cycle: Input, Process, Output**

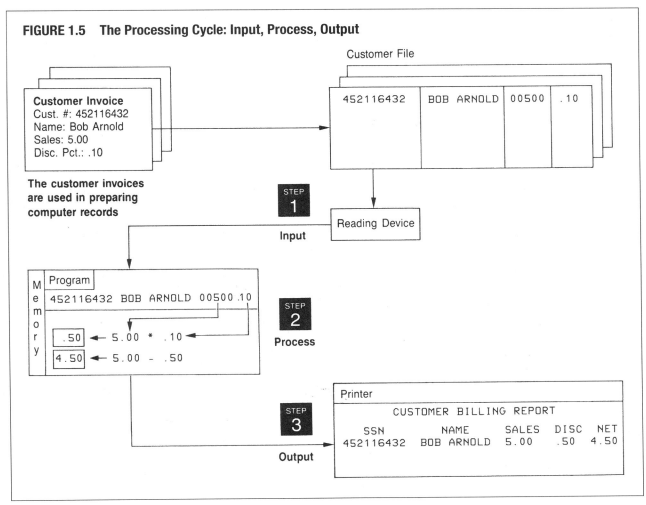

## Magnetic Tape and Disk

The most frequently used media for recording data are magnetic tape and magnetic disk. Data is usually stored on the disk or tape in special computer code, either ASCII (American Standard Code for Information Interchange) or EBCDIC (Extended Binary Coded Decimal Interchange Code). These codes are shown in Appendix D. Each character on the record is represented by a particular configuration of magnetic spots within a given area, or frame, of the tape or disk. The characters can be any digit, letter of the alphabet, or special symbol.

## FILE, RECORD, AND FIELD

Usually, several individual collections of data are recorded about a person, place, or thing in an organization. This unit of data is called a **record.** The record contains the necessary data to produce useful results. The record is subdivided into **fields,** or **attributes.** Each field (or attribute) is a specific area on the record reserved to store a specific category of data about the person, place, or thing. A person's social security number, for example, may be recorded in a specific position on a record, thus becoming one of the fields on that record. Usually, in the data processing function, a record is processed for every person, place, or thing; therefore, a multitude of records must be prepared—one for each person, place, or thing. This collection of records constitutes a **file.** Figure 1.6 illustrates the concept of files, records, and fields.

## TYPES OF DATA

When data are stored in a field on a record, the data are usually classified as numeric, alphabetic, or alphanumeric. In COBOL, **numeric data** consist of only the digits 0 through 9. **Alphabetic data** consist of only the letters of the alphabet and the space, which is created when the space bar is pressed and looks like a character to the computer. In BASIC, numeric data include the decimal point. **Alphanumeric data** consist of any combination of digits, letters, and special characters. Special characters are all the symbols on the keyboard, including the space. Some of these symbols are: ! @ # $ % ^ & * ( ) _ + | < > ? : " { } [ ] ; ' . , / .

Numeric data are recorded in the field on the record in a **right-justified** position, which means that the numbers are placed in the field as far to the right as possible (or are aligned by a decimal point), and the preceding empty spaces are filled with zeros. If you wished to record the value 500 in a field that has five positions, the field would appear as in Figure 1.7.

## PROCESSING STEPS REVISITED

Once the data are properly recorded on the appropriate media, they must be transferred to the computer for processing. This process has been previously defined as *input*. Once the necessary processing takes place, the computer will produce useful results. These useful results are called *output*, commonly produced in the form of a printed report. Figure 1.8 illustrates the processing steps of (1) input, (2) process, and (3) output.

## THE PROCESSING CYCLE FROM A PROGRAMMING PERSPECTIVE

The previous illustration (Figure 1.8) shows the processing of a single record. One customer record is input, the discount (10 percent of sales) and net amount are calculated, and a report line is printed. In a real application, there would be an entire file of customer records. Records would be input to the computer one at a time, the discount calculated for each record, and a billing invoice printed for each record. A new line of data would be printed for every customer record. This process is called **looping.** Panel A of Figure 1.9 (see pg. 8) illustrates the processing cycle with looping: input, process, output, repeat.

Panel B of Figure 1.9 is a graphic illustration of the major functions that the computer must perform to produce this report. Notice that the basic steps of input, process, and output must be repeated as many times as there are records. This, again, is looping.

## FUNCTIONS OF DATA PROCESSING

Concerning the previous example, you might ask, "Who would initiate this project?" A data processing project is often initiated by a person outside the actual data processing department. This person is referred to as the **end user** of the computer. The end user might request that a computer be used to help solve a problem in order to meet specific departmental or company objectives, such as finding a more efficient way of generating bills to send to customers or a report that breaks down company sales by department.

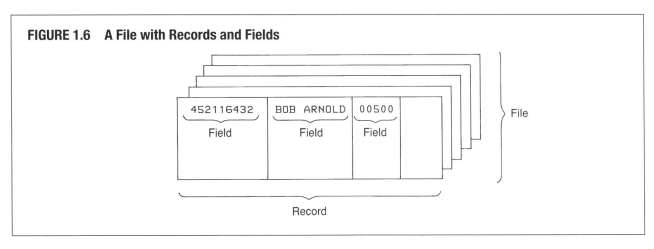

**FIGURE 1.6  A File with Records and Fields**

452116432    BOB ARNOLD    00500

Field        Field         Field

File

Record

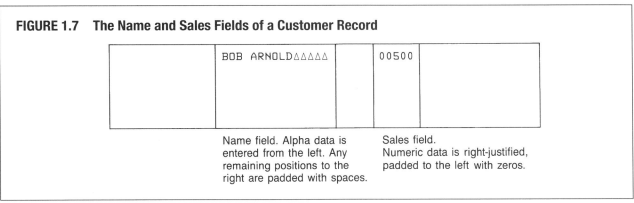

**FIGURE 1.7  The Name and Sales Fields of a Customer Record**

BOB ARNOLD△△△△△          00500

Name field. Alpha data is         Sales field.
entered from the left. Any         Numeric data is right-justified,
remaining positions to the         padded to the left with zeros.
right are padded with spaces.

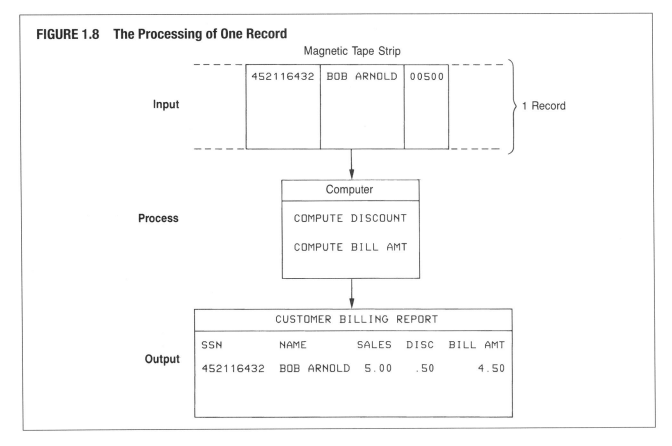

**FIGURE 1.8  The Processing of One Record**

Magnetic Tape Strip

**Input**

452116432    BOB ARNOLD    00500

1 Record

**Process**

Computer

COMPUTE DISCOUNT

COMPUTE BILL AMT

**Output**

CUSTOMER BILLING REPORT

SSN          NAME        SALES   DISC   BILL AMT

452116432    BOB ARNOLD   5.00    .50      4.50

In order to produce useful results (information) for the end user, the normal data processing operations would consist of (1) data entry, (2) data validation, (3) sorting, (4) updating, (5) calculation, and (6) reporting.

## Data Entry

The process of transferring data from a source document (the document that originally contained the data) to a computer record is called **data entry.**

## Data Validation

Once the data have been entered on magnetic tapes, magnetic disks, or floppy disks, the next step is to validate the data, that is, make sure the data

that was previously recorded are reasonably correct. A programmer might need to ensure, for example, that the data entered are numeric and that the numeric values are within a predefined range of valid values. Or the programmer may want to ensure that the number of hours worked by an employee is between 1 and 40. Much more will be discussed in Chapter 5 about testing for reasonable values. The main idea here is that keying errors frequently occur that, in turn, create invalid data for the computer to process. To avoid as much invalid data as possible, a **data validation** function is of the utmost importance in data processing.

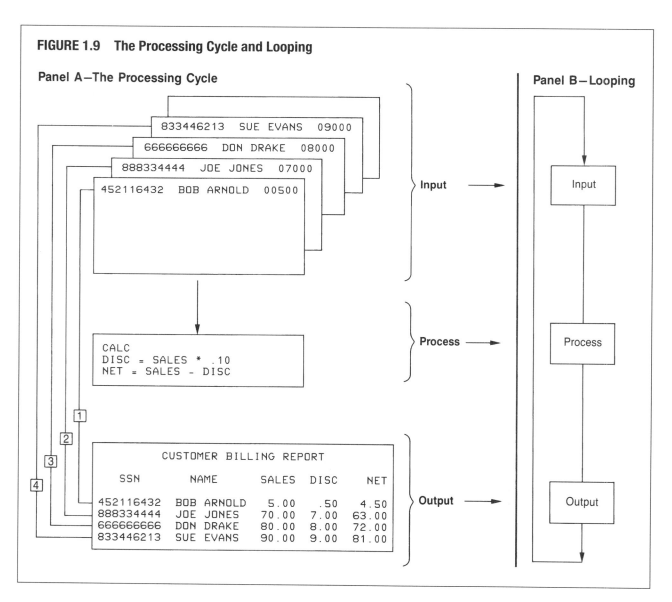

**FIGURE 1.9    The Processing Cycle and Looping**

**Panel A—The Processing Cycle**

```
833446213   SUE EVANS    09000
666666666   DON DRAKE    08000
888334444   JOE JONES    07000
452116432   BOB ARNOLD   00500
```

Input

```
CALC
DISC = SALES * .10
NET = SALES - DISC
```

Process

```
           CUSTOMER BILLING REPORT

  SSN          NAME       SALES   DISC    NET

452116432   BOB ARNOLD    5.00    .50    4.50
888334444   JOE JONES    70.00   7.00   63.00
666666666   DON DRAKE    80.00   8.00   72.00
833446213   SUE EVANS    90.00   9.00   81.00
```

Output

**Panel B—Looping**

Input

Process

Output

## Sorting

Once data are validated, records in a file can be arranged according to a key field, or fields, on the record. The user may wish to arrange the records according to the SSN field or to alphabetize them by the name field. This process of arranging or alphabetizing is called sorting. The selected field(s) becomes the **sort key.** Often, in data processing operations, a sort key is composed of several combined fields from the record. Chapter 11 is devoted to the subject of **sorting** data and the programming logic necessary for the computer to perform this function.

## Updating

Once the data records are in the proper sequence for processing, the file can be brought up-to-date. One or more of the fields on some of the records may require changes. Or new records must be added to the existing file. In other cases, some of the existing records must be removed or deleted.

The record that contains relatively permanent information about a person, place, or thing is called a **master record.** These data are frequently used in producing the kind of information management needs in order to make decisions. A file of these records is called a **master file.** For example, a master customer record might contain an SSN, customer name, billing address, phone, ship-to address, ship-via, terms of discount, and customer balance due. This information is relatively permanent but will require periodic update.

The update procedure will also include a **transaction file.** Each transaction record in this file contains the necessary data to bring the master record up-to-date. For example, if a customer's address changes, a transaction record is created that contains the new address. The program will use the information from the transaction record to alter the data on the master record. Also, as sales transactions occur, the master file will require additional updating. The transaction record may contain the sales transaction number, register number, salesman, items sold, and price. A calculation then determines the sales amount, and the update procedure brings the balance due on the master record up-to-date by adding the new sales amount to the old balance due amount. The process of changing, adding, and deleting records is called **updating.** Chapter 12 is devoted to the concept of updating files and to the necessary programming logic to accomplish this task.

## Calculation and Reporting

Once the file is brought up-to-date, values such as an employee's net salary or a customer's billing amount can be **calculated.** After the calculations are complete, the end result, or output, is usually printed in the form of a **report.** The report might be a payroll register listing each employee's SSN, name, and net salary, or it might be a customer billing report depicting customer data together with a billing amount. The terminal screen is another type of computer output. If an accountant should inquire about the status of a customer, the screen output could quickly display that customer's record.

## BATCH VS. ON-LINE PROCESSING

The process of collecting records over a period of time to create a file and then processing the entire file periodically is called **batch processing.** A teacher, for example, might use batch processing to produce a student report, a report that needs to be printed only periodically.

**On-line (interactive) processing** is a method by which the computer constantly has access to the file. The processing is ongoing. With the help of a computer program, a teacher could inquire about the status of student's test scores anytime and could make immediate changes, deletions, or additions to the class file by simply responding to certain prompts from an on-line monitor program. Much more will be said about on-line processing in Chapter 13.

## STEPS IN WRITING A COMPUTER PROGRAM

The various data processing functions that have been previously discussed are actually implemented in most cases by specifically tailored computer programs. In other words, computer programs will be written to sort records, update a file, or generate a report for management.

The necessary steps in writing a computer program are:

1. Defining the problem.
2. Designing a structure and logic hierarchy chart, a flowchart, and/or the pseudocode.
3. Coding in a programming language.
4. Keying-in the code to the computer.
5. Compiling or interpreting.
6. Debugging.

7. Executing.
8. Testing.
9. Documenting.

## Problem Definition

The first step in writing a computer program is to determine clearly just what the problem is that you are trying to solve with the help of a computer. A programmer is normally given a set of program specifications that include:

1. Program requirements and objectives.
2. Printer spacing charts for report design.
3. Screen layout forms for screen design for use with interactive programs.
4. Record layout forms depicting input design.

**Program Requirements.**   These will vary based upon the complexity of the problem. For example, to produce a grade report for a teacher, the computer program must be able to:

1. Access the student master file.
2. Print headings where appropriate.
3. Print each student's SSN, name, first exam score, second exam score, third exam score, and the arithmetic average of the three scores on a single line.

The specifications shown above are quite brief compared to more advanced examples presented later. The objective here is not to overwhelm the reader with too elaborate and rigorous an example, but instead to show a simple and realistic list of program requirements for a relatively simple problem to be solved with a computer.

**Problem definition** also includes the conceptualization and design of the output (and its related inputs). First, the programmer normally sketches or draws an output design, which may resemble Figure 1.10.

**Printer Spacing Charts.**   Using this basic design, the programmer can fill in a **printer spacing chart.** A printer spacing chart enables the programmer to visualize the actual print positions that each value will occupy on the printed page of the report. Computer printers print 80, 120, or 132 characters per line. The actual print position can range from 1 to 150 on some printers.

The printer spacing chart (Figure 1.11) indicates the precise locations in which the data is to be printed. Normally a report contains three types of lines: heading lines, detail lines, and summary lines. The headings serve to tell the user what the data represent. The detail lines contain the desired information, the result of the computer's having read and processed an input record. The summary lines summarize the detail information. More will be said about total lines in Chapter 3.

**Screen Design.**   Screen layout forms will be discussed in Chapters 10 and 13. The design of screen layout forms is virtually identical to the design of printer spacing charts, except that they are used in designing output for an on-line processing application where the output media is the terminal screen (CRT, or cathode ray tube) instead of a sheet of paper.

**Input Design.**   Having thoroughly understood and completed the output report, the programmer/analyst is ready to design the input record that will be read to produce a detail line on the printed report. Often the file already exists, and the programmer must simply know the input format. If the programmer must design the format, a **record layout form** is useful. Figure 1.12 shows the record format for the student record.

The record layout form has two main purposes. First, it provides a document from which the programmer can describe the input format to the computer when he or she writes the computer program; second, the form is used in designing the data entry form to be used in keying-in records. Figure 1.13 illustrates how records might appear as a result of using the record layout in Figure 1.12.

## Designing Structure and Logic

Once the programmer has defined the problem and carefully reviewed all the specifications, the next phase begins—designing the structure and logic of the computer program. This design is one of the most important steps. If a program is designed carefully it will (1) be coded easily, (2) be debugged easily, (3) run or execute correctly, and (4) be easy to maintain. Designing a program normally requires the use of a hierarchy chart, a flowchart, and/or pseudocode.

A **hierarchy chart** is a hierarchical representation of the various modules or possible functions within a program. The chart in Figure 1.14 shows how major modules are decomposed into lower-level modules (submodules). The purpose of the hierarchy chart is to show the overall program makeup. Hierarchy charts may include function boxes that do not represent formal module calls. However, typically a box does represent a module call. It doesn't show the detailed programming logic, only a generalized outline of the relationship of modules. On the other hand, a **flowchart** is a diagram or a graphical representation of the instructions to the computer that describes the program logic in greater detail. It is a picture in block diagram form of the path of execution that the computer is to follow. (The mechanics of constructing charts are discussed in Chapter 2.) Since people conceptualize in the form of pictures, graphs, and diagrams, it logically follows that they can better understand a program if it is graphically represented before the actual program coding begins. A picture really *is* worth a thousand words! Figure 1.15 illustrates a flowcharting segment within a program.

**Pseudocode** is sometimes used as an alternative to flowcharting. It consists of short commands in English that permit the programmer to concentrate on the problem instead of the programming language. Figure 1.16 illustrates the use of pseudocode. The program design illustrations in this text show both the flowchart and pseudocode designs.

A detailed study of flowcharting is presented in Chapter 2. The flowchart shown in Figure 1.15 will give you a global picture of the programming process before you delve into the details of the various steps.

**FIGURE 1.10    Sketch of Output Design**

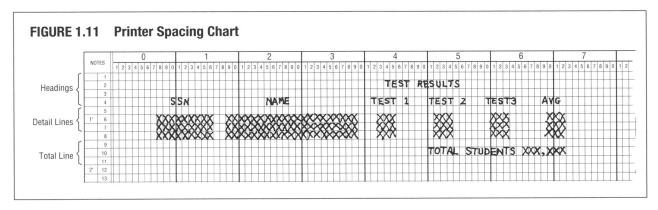

**FIGURE 1.11    Printer Spacing Chart**

**FIGURE 1.12    Record Layout for Student Records**

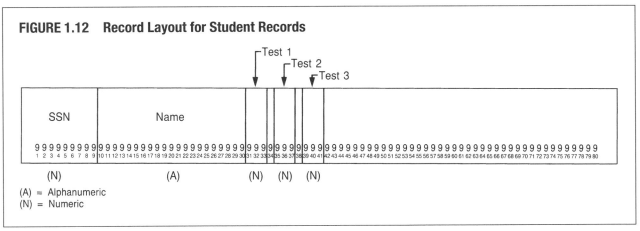

(A) = Alphanumeric
(N) = Numeric

## Coding

Once the flowchart is finished and the programmer is satisfied that it accurately represents the logical steps that the computer is to follow, the next step is to **code** the program in a specific computer language. Some programming languages available include COBOL, BASIC, Pascal, FORTRAN, PL/I,

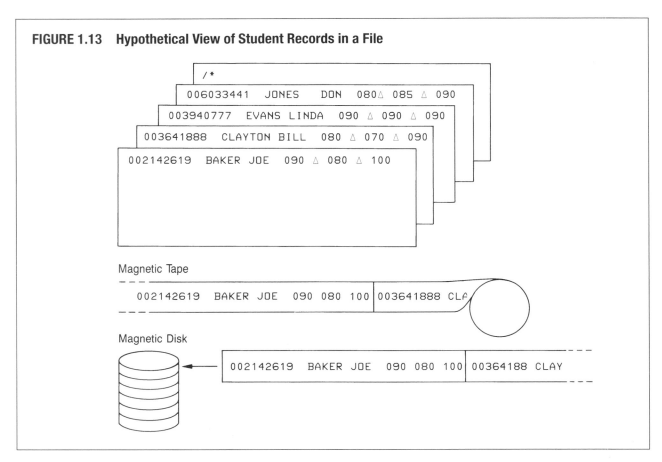

**FIGURE 1.13   Hypothetical View of Student Records in a File**

Magnetic Tape

Magnetic Disk

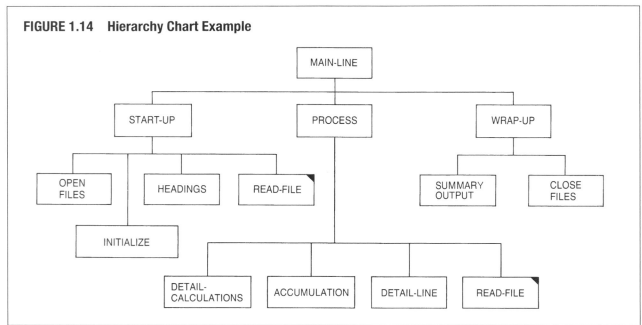

**FIGURE 1.14   Hierarchy Chart Example**

and assembly language. Specific computer languages have been developed to solve particular types of problems or applications. COBOL, for example, was developed primarily to provide the programmer with a language that lends itself to the solution of business-oriented problems. Figure 1.17 shows, as an example, part of a COBOL program.

Notice the similarities and correspondence between the flowchart in Figure 1.15 and the partial program in Figure 1.17.

### Keying-In

Once the code is developed from the flowchart, the next step is to key the coding lines into the computer's memory. The programmer types the lines of code using a computer terminal or PC monitor (see Figure 1.18, panel A). Panel B shows the code on the terminal screen. Once entered, the computer language program is called the source program.

### Compiling

The previous discussion about high- and low-level languages pointed out that a computer cannot execute a high-level instruction such as

```
COMPUTE NET = GROSS - TAX.
```

The high-level instructions must be translated, or compiled, into a machine language instruction before execution can occur. The programmer uses a special computer program called a **compiler** to translate the instructions. The input to the COBOL compiler could be the programmer's COBOL program, for example. The output is the machine language program, also referred to as the object program. See Figure 1.19 and a source listing. (Figure 1.17 shows a partial source listing.)

### Debugging

After the program is compiled, the next step is to check it for errors. Some of the errors will be "typos" or syntax errors. Others may be less obvious, such as logic errors that result from the mistaken inclusion or exclusion of particular instructions. A program containing logic errors will execute, but it will come up with incorrect results.

The programmer's efforts to correct these errors is called **debugging** the program.

### Execution

Once the various errors have been removed from the source program and the program has been successfully compiled, the computer can **execute** the resulting object program. When the program has finished executing, the program and output go to the computer printer.

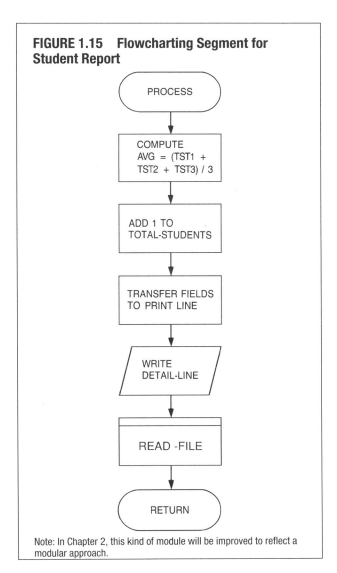

### FIGURE 1.15    Flowcharting Segment for Student Report

PROCESS

COMPUTE
AVG = (TST1 +
TST2 + TST3) / 3

ADD 1 TO
TOTAL-STUDENTS

TRANSFER FIELDS
TO PRINT LINE

WRITE
DETAIL-LINE

READ -FILE

RETURN

Note: In Chapter 2, this kind of module will be improved to reflect a modular approach.

### FIGURE 1.16    Pseudocode Segment for Student Report

*process-routine
    calculate avg = (tst1 + tst 2 + tst3) / 3
    add 1 to total-students
    transfer input and calculated fields to print line
    write detail line
    read-file
    return

## Testing

Although the program seems to be working properly and producing valid results, questions still remain. How robust is the program? Will it work with any data record? What happens if it attempts to process an invalid record? An earlier discussion briefly reviewed data validation as a function of data processing. The programmer must remember an old programming axiom, "A program is only as good as its test cases." Thorough program testing is *vital* if we are to rely on the program's ability to produce correct results every time it is run with a new set of data.

## Documentation

Before the program is turned over to the user to be used with "real" data, the programmer must prepare a set of documents that describe how the user will use the computer program. These documents will become the user's manual, which will include such items as:

1. User specifications.
2. Technical specifications describing the overall program design from a technical viewpoint, with answers to such questions as the following: What are the files and databases to be

---

**FIGURE 1.17    COBOL Program Segment for Student Report**

```
200-PROCESS.

    COMPUTE AVG = (TST1 + TST2 + TST3) / 3.
    ADD 1 TO TOTAL-STUDENTS.
    MOVE SSN TO SSN-OUT.
    MOVE NAME TO NAME-OUT.
    MOVE TST1 TO TST1-OUT.
    MOVE TST2 TO TST2-OUT.
    MOVE TST3 TO TST3-OUT.
    MOVE AVG TO AVG-OUT.
    WRITE STUDENT-RPT-REC FROM DETAIL-LINE AFTER
        ADVANCING 2 LINES.
    PERFORM 500-READ-STUDENT-FILE.
```

---

**FIGURE 1.18    Keying-in the Lines of Code—An Excerpt of the Program**

Panel A

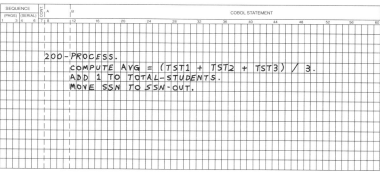

Panel B

```
200-PROCESS.
    COMPUTE AVG = (TST1 + TST2 + TST3) / 3.
    ADD 1 TO TOTAL-STUDENTS.
    MOVE SSN TO SSN-OUT.
```

processed? What documents are necessary to produce desired results? What data processing functions are performed in producing desired results?

3. Report descriptions that estimate the frequency, volume, and distribution of the report(s).
4. A list of specific types of transactions that can occur and specific files or data bases affected.
5. Program flowcharts, pseudocode, and module descriptions.
6. Examples of test cases used in testing the program(s).

A fuller description of these forms of **documentation** can be found in most systems analysis and design textbooks. A final note: Documentation is not just a single activity that occurs at the end of the systems development process; it is an ongoing activity. The entire systems development process is accompanied by a constant evolution of documentation.

## THE SOFTWARE DEVELOPMENT REVOLUTION

Traditional programming philosophies and methods are rapidly being challenged by those who believe that systems can be engineered. Straightforward design philosophies as well as revolutionary systems development tools such as Computer-Aided Systems Engineering, Object-Oriented Programming, and improved fourth-generation languages will rapidly improve the systems development process. These new systems development tools will be briefly discussed in this chapter. As a result of the rapid integration of Executive Support Systems, Decision Support Systems, and various kinds of application software tailored to meet the needs of management, from the outset the user will be the center of the software development universe in all software development projects where software applications expand around corporate goals, strategies, and critical success factors. The gradual decline in the number of computer programmer/analysts in the United States and the booming rise in demand for computer software systems will require corporate leaders to shift toward the use of more productive software development tools. The great demand for new and innovative techniques to develop highly reliable and cost-effective systems hinges on "working smart" using the latest systems and program design techniques and tools.

In the past, once the high-level analysis and system design had been completed, the programmer would first design an application using design tools discussed in this text (or similar tools), and then subsequently begin the process of hand coding the design in the application languages such as COBOL, C, or BASIC. While this still remains a viable method for implementing business systems, there is a definite trend toward computer-aided methodologies. Whether processes and data are modeled using automated or manual techniques, it is important to note that management is making their point that the emphasis must be placed on the *design* of cost-effective and maintainable business systems.

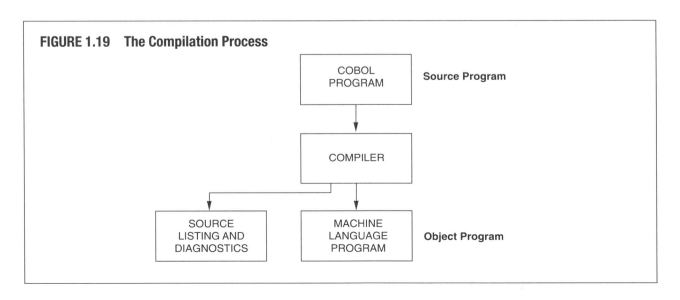

**FIGURE 1.19  The Compilation Process**

COBOL PROGRAM — **Source Program**

COMPILER

SOURCE LISTING AND DIAGNOSTICS

MACHINE LANGUAGE PROGRAM — **Object Program**

## COMPUTER-AIDED SYSTEMS ENGINEERING (CASE)

Computer-Aided Systems Engineering (**CASE**) is an automated systems development strategy in which the systems analyst/programmer uses the microcomputer (directed by the CASE product) to develop critical documentation for the planning, analysis, design, and automatic construction of application programs. The analyst develops high-level planning diagrams such as Decomposition Diagrams that portray a company's organizational structure, goals, major functional areas, and major processes. The use of Decomposition Diagrams allows one to hierarchically break down various objects within the company, creating a framework for the remainder of the project. Figure 1.20 illustrates this decomposition using functions and processes. Analysts often develop various matrices of corporate information allowing the study of relationships between object categories. For example, an **Association Matrix** may be developed that shows the relationship between corporate goals

and corporate functional areas, or possibly the relationship between various corporate functional areas and the various entities of data within the company. The latter case is illustrated in Figure 1.21. The rows are the goals and the columns are the functions. A differentiating feature of this method is that it is accomplished by using pull-down windows, and mouse strokes. **Entity Diagrams** are easily developed using the automated tool that depicts the various relationships between the various entities. For example, an entity diagram (FIG 1.22—Panel A) may show the relationship between a Customer and an Order, or it may show how the Order is related to a Product. Once the enterprise, data, and processes are modeled the CASE tool augments the application design process with workstations that include Data Structure Diagrams, Structure Charts (FIG 1.22—Panel B), and Action Diagrams (FIG 1.22—Panel C). Once again, these diagrams are developed from the CASE workstation using pull-down windows, mouse strokes, and default settings rather than pencil and paper as was done in the past.

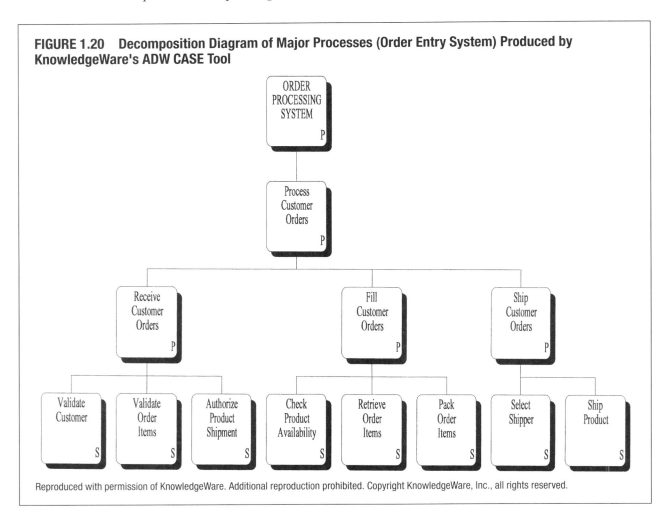

**FIGURE 1.20 Decomposition Diagram of Major Processes (Order Entry System) Produced by KnowledgeWare's ADW CASE Tool**

The major underlying philosophy of CASE tools is for the company to develop software applications that give the company an edge on the competition by carefully planning, analyzing, and designing the steps along the way. With powerful knowledge engines, these CASE packages are able to update application encyclopedias constantly on all objects in the system application. The pencil, erasure (with emphasis on erasure), and paper techniques of the past took too long to draw various diagrams, were very difficult to update without completely redrawing them, and required manual cross-verifying. On the average, people are not as good as computers at doing these tedious tasks. As we move to the fifth-generation of programming, let us watch for even more powerful design tools. One should also expect a rapid increase in the number of professionals trained in the areas of systems design and program design rather than in the knowledge of any particular programming language or other software application tool.

## Object-Oriented Programming

**Object-Oriented Programming** is a significant departure from traditional programming languages that require operations and operands. On the other hand, Object-Oriented programming languages such as Smalltalk, pioneered by Alan Kay at the University of Utah in the late 1960s, consists of objects and messages. The user points to graphical icons and text options on the screen during processing. Files can be retrieved by simply pointing to a specific icon or message prompt. Definition of data structures or entities can be similarly created or manipulated. Procedures along with the data that relate to that procedure can be used to create new applications by simply pointing to the appropriate pull-down menu, message prompt, or graphical icon. The basic idea is to create objects that consist of procedures and data. These objects provide the interface for accessing the data. These procedures-linked-to-data objects are invoked or called upon by messages sent by the programmer or even other objects. Many believe that Object-Oriented Programming is the wave of the future. We are likely to see this technology dovetailing with Computer-Aided Systems Engineering, with the design phase becoming even more object-oriented.

## Executive Support Systems

**Executive Support Systems** represent the next dimension in decision support systems. This kind of decision support system is tailored to an individual executive's managerial style and approach to management. Traditionally, high-level managers and computers have not mixed well. Managers have claimed that decision makers do not need a computer on their desks since the clerks and secretaries should be able to supply needed information to them. Although some managers have toyed around with various decision support tools such as Lotus 123 and the like, only now with the advent of tailor-made executive support systems have man-

**FIGURE 1.21   KnowledgeWare's ADW CASE Tool Association Matrix Showing Relationship Between Goals and Functions**

## Goal is supported by Function

| | Assure Product Quality | Manage Money | Market and Sell the Product | Market the Product | Pay Accounts Payable | Plan Strategic Direction | Plan the Product | Sell The Product | Support the Company | Support the Product |
|---|---|---|---|---|---|---|---|---|---|---|
| Be The Market Leader | ✓ | | ✓ | | | | | | | |
| Control Inventory | | | | | | | | | | |
| Expand The Product Line | | | ✓ | | | | | | | |
| Improve Cashflow Management | | | | | | | | | | |
| Improve Customer Satisfaction | | | ✓ | | | | | | | |
| Improve Product Quality | | | | | | | | | | |

# FIGURE 1.22 Summary of Case Diagrams by KnowledgeWare ADW Case Tool

## Panel A Entity-Relationship Diagrams—The Entity Model (by KnowledgeWare's ADW)

## Panel C Module Action Diagram (By KnowledgeWare's ADW CASE TOOL)

Application Development Workstation

```
*RECEIVE CUSTOMER ORDERS
M1-MAINLINE SECTION
*PROGRAM INITIALIZATION
        OPS MAIN MENU
Get

*PFKEY ASSIGNMENTS
  IF CNAME-NUM-SELECT = '1' OR CNAME-ACTIONBAR = '1'

        Call Asynch        Validate
                           Customer        %NEXT TASK

  Else IF CNAME-NUM-SELECT-2 = '2' OR CNAME-ACTIONBAR = '2'

        Call Asynch        Maintain
                           Customer
                           Data            %NEXT TASK

  Else If CNAME-NUM-SELECT-3 = '3' OR CNAME-ACTIONBAR = '3'

        Call Asynch        PRODUCT
                           MAINTENANCE     %NEXT TASK

  Else
        MOVE 'INVALID FUNCTION'
        TO CNAME-ERROR-MESSAGE
                           OPS
        Put                MAIN
                           MENU

        NEXT TASK MYSELF

  ENDIF
... *THE FOLLOWING IS A BATCH PROGRAM.
```

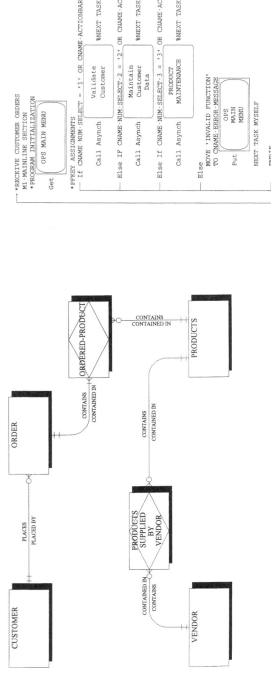

## Panel B Structure Chart (by KnowledgeWare ADW CASE TOOL)

Structure Chart Diagrammer - RECEIVE CUSTOMER ORDERS

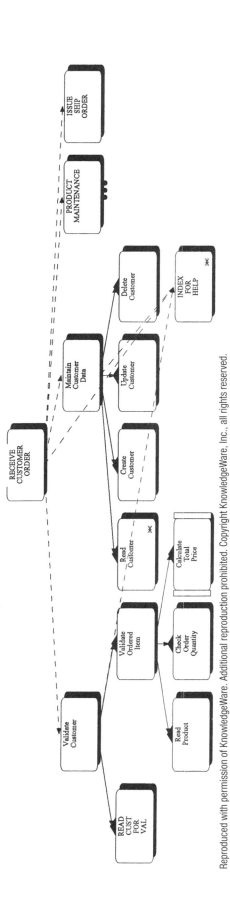

agement shown a real interest in personally using a computer. Executives have come to realize that they can no longer function successfully without top-notch automation to provide the competitive edge in today's corporate "shark tank" of fast-paced, progressive competitors. Any competitive edge is essential, and this EDS technology is just one more corporate equalizer. EDS allows a versatile retrieval of information about many different objects within the company. "What if" questions are quickly answered in many different graphical formats and character forms. The executive can work through statistical analysis quickly without knowing how the statistical test will actually be performed on the data. Using a mouse pointer the manager can quickly retrieve specific records of a file or a complete histogram chart of sales information for the quarter. Systems Development professionals will continue to be in demand by aggressive, progressive corporations well into the twenty-first century.

### Traditional Versus Information Engineering Approach to Systems Development of Business Systems

Over the years, the process for developing business systems has been an arduous task indeed. The traditional methodology involves the following: 1) preliminary investigation, 2) detailed systems analysis, 3) general design of alternative or candidate systems, 4) detailed design, 5) systems implementation, 6) testing, and 7) production. This traditional method often takes many weeks or months to complete because of the lengthy implementation and testing period. The preliminary investigation involves formal interviews with management to determine the initial feasibility of the project. A feasibility report is prepared that evaluates the general benefits, costs, and problems with the current system and delves into some general recommendations to either continue on to the detailed analysis or terminate the project. The detailed analysis phase concerns understanding the processes of the current system, the cost-effectiveness of the current system, the cost-effectiveness of two or more proposed alternative systems, and a recommendation of an alternative system. If management agrees, the project continues to the design phase. The major processes and subprocesses are further refined along with screen layouts, report layouts, and so on. This is normally accomplished through a technique known as structured systems analysis, which employs data flow diagrams. The data flow diagrams are useful in understanding and conveying the meaning of the functions and

processes of the company. Using the data flow diagrams to describe the overall picture, developers design computer programs for each process or function within the DFD.

The painstaking task of converting data flow diagrams into, let's say, COBOL provides a useful example of the complexities involved. In the mid-to late 1980s, the science of Information Engineering began to replace the traditional method for developing systems. Informing engineering was observed to be a much faster and systematic method, employing automated planning, analysis, design, and automatic code generation tools. The impressive aspect of information engineering methodology lay also in its utilization of prototyping methods with the end-user. At the heart of information engineering is a Computer-Aided Systems Engineering (CASE) tool. The CASE tool requires that the analyst follow exactly the same process in developing a new system as was employed in the previous systems project. Systems are truly engineered following proved information engineering methods such as Enterprise Modeling and Data Modeling as well as the traditional Process Modeling. This method focuses on important issues such as corporate structure, goals, plans, critical-success factors, critical assumptions, projects, and the data needed to carry out these projects to a successful completion and accomplish stated goals. Business systems must be developed with the user at the very heart of the development process. Data and processes must be modeled with full user participation, if the system is ever to be used by the user. Employment of quality CASE products can quickly involve the user in prototyping and developing a business system with a built-in documentation trail.

## SUMMARY

A problem must be clearly defined and understood before a correct and concise solution can be developed. Two important competencies are needed by the programmer/analyst. They are (1) problem analysis and (2) program design.

The basic functions of a computer are (1) arithmetic, (2) logical, (3) input/output, and (4) data storage. Data are the formalized facts about a person, place, or thing.

The four main types of units of a computer are (1) input units, (2) processor unit, (3) output units, and (4) peripheral units. The input units transfer data to the computer's main memory. The processor accepts the instructions and data into the memory unit and processes the data according to the instructions. The output unit prints or displays the results. The peripheral units store data permanently on tape or disk.

A computer program is a set of instructions given to a computer to solve a specific problem or set of problems. Programs and data are placed into memory temporarily while program execution is in progress. Memory in the computer consists of storage areas called bytes. A byte of memory can hold one digit, letter, or special symbol. Each byte in memory has an associated address. Through the use of the address the computer is able to locate a specific piece of data for processing.

Computer languages are classified as either high-level or low-level. Today, the vast majority of the programs being developed for business applications are coded in high-level languages such as COBOL (Common Business Oriented Language).

In the basic processing cycle, the computer (1) inputs the data into memory, (2) processes the data (performs calculations, etc.), and (3) outputs results.

The various media for storing data for permanent keeping are (1) magnetic tape, (2) magnetic disk (hard disk), and (3) magnetic diskettes (floppy disks). A unit of data about a person, place, or thing is called a record. A record consists of fields that hold specific information about the record (facts about a person, place, or thing). A file is a collection of records.

Data are basically classified as (1) numeric, (2) alphabetic, and (3) alphanumeric. Classification is important because the computer stores numeric data in a field in a right-justified format and stores alphabetic/alphanumeric data in a left-justified format.

The basic functions of data processing consist of (1) data entry, (2) data validation, (3) sorting, (4) updating, (5) calculation, and (6) reporting. Today most of these functions are carried out through the use of specifically tailored computer programs.

Programs are implemented according to (1) problem definition, (2) program design, (3) coding, (4) program code entry, (5) compiling, (6) debugging, (7) execution, (8) testing, and (9) documentation. Programs can execute in one of two basic modes, either (1) batch or (2) on-line.

Computer-Aided Systems Engineering (CASE) is rapidly becoming a systems development alternative to the traditional method. Using CASE tools, applications can be typically developed and modified faster and with precision. The stages of CASE development include planning, analysis, design, and construction.

## VOCABULARY

data
information
input unit
processor unit
output unit
peripheral unit
computer program
main memory
(CPU) central
    processing unit
byte
address
high-level languages
machine language
low-level language
assembly language
computer instruction
op code/operation
    code
operand
processing cycle
record
field
file
attribute
numeric data
alphabetic data
alphanumeric data
association matrix
entity diagram
right-justified
left-justified

looping
end user
data entry
data validation
sorting
sort key
master record
master file
transaction file
updating
calculating
reporting
batch processing
on-line (interactive)
    processing
problem definition
printer spacing chart
record layout form
hierarchy chart
flowchart
pseudocode
code
compiler
debugging
execute
documentation
C.A.S.E.
Executive Support
    system
Object-Oriented
    programming

## EXERCISES/QUESTIONS

1. What are the four main units of a basic computer system?

2. Where are programs and data held for processing?

3. Compare and contrast high- and low-level languages.

4. What are the two parts of an instruction?

5. What are the three types of data? Give examples of each.

6. What are the functions of data processing? Explain each.

7. What kinds of data validation checks are usually made?

8. Compare and contrast on-line and batch processing.

9. List and explain the steps in writing a computer program.

10. Why is it necessary for a high-level computer program to be compiled before execution?

11. On a separate piece of paper, draw a diagram illustrating the processing cycle.

12. What is CASE? What are its advantages?

## PROBLEM

**1-1.** Using Figures 1.23 and 1.24, prepare a printer spacing chart and a record layout form for the sample report shown below.

```
                        TEXTBOOK REQUISITION
    COURSE       TEACHER        AUTHOR        PUBLISHER    QUANTITY    DATE
    CIS 2123   MARY   SMITH   JON ANDERSON   ABC PUBL.       100      12/87
    CIS 2121   DONALD  RAY    RONALD BAKER   DEF PUBL.        50      12/87
    CIS 3133   BOB JOHNSON    DONALD SMART   GHI PUBL.        50      11/88
    XXXXXXX    XXXXXXXXXX     XXXXXXXXXXX    XXXXXXXXX       XXX      XXXXX
    XXXXXXX    XXXXXXXXXX     XXXXXXXXXXX    XXXXXXXXX       XXX      XXXXX
```

**FIGURE 1.23  Printer Spacing Chart for Problem 1.1**

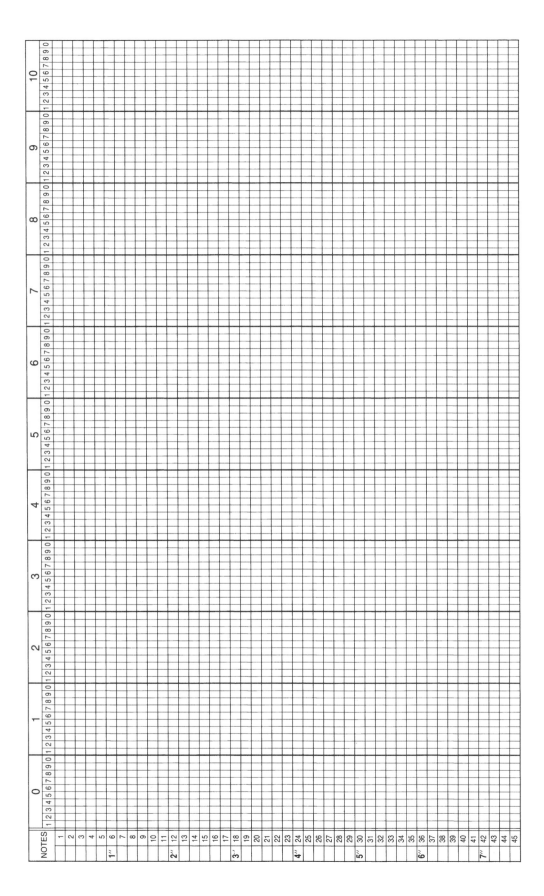

**FIGURE 1.24 Record Layout for Problem 1.1**

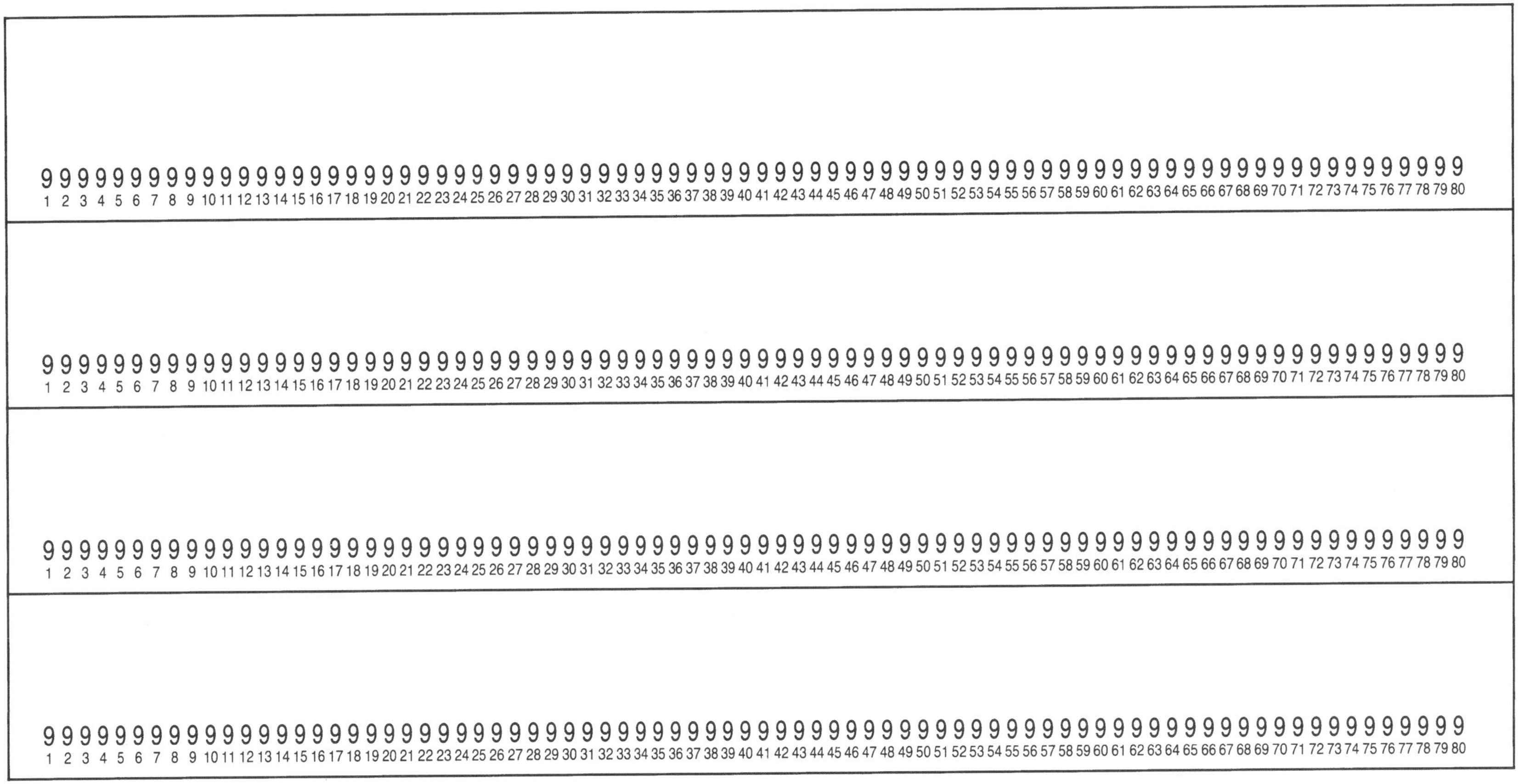

# 2

# Introduction to Program Design—
# A Structured Approach

## OBJECTIVES

As a result of having read and studied this chapter, the student will be able to:

1. Draw hierarchy charts for a simple problem and recognize the rules and constraints for drawing them.

2. Describe the purpose of flowcharting and draw the various flowcharting symbols.

3. Describe how a record is read and define the concepts of automatic-destroy-read-in and non-automatic-destroy-read-out.

4. Draw and describe the predefined process block.

5. Define structured programming and draw the three main logic structures.

6. Explain the concept of modular design.

7. Draw a hierarchy chart of the general structure of a simple business report problem.

8. Develop a structured flowchart and pseudocode for a simple business report problem.

9. Explain the use of an end-flag or end-of-file switch in a structured program.

As discussed in Chapter 1, once the program specifications, input design, and output design have been accomplished, the programmer must design the program logic. Program logic design can take many forms—hierarchy charts, pseudocode, structured flowcharts, and other specialized diagramming methods. The three primary methods discussed here are hierarchy charts, structured flowcharts, and pseudocode.

## HIERARCHY CHARTS— AN INTRODUCTION

The first step in program design is to draw a hierarchy chart that represents the overall structural breakdown of the various modules. The hierarchy chart serves as a logic development tool, using block diagramming or boxes and connecting lines to show the program structure and the flow of program logic. The only two symbols used in drawing hierarchy charts are the rectangle and the flowline (see Figure 2.1).

### Characteristics of Hierarchy Charts

The rectangle in a hierarchy chart represents a module, whereas in a program flowchart (discussed next) a rectangle can represent a single instruction to the computer. The flowline in a hierarchy chart moves in only two directions, from top to bottom or left to right. The line does not have an attached arrow (as in a flowchart) showing direction, since the direction, as previously stated, can always be determined. Another characteristic of hierarchy charts is that the boxes that represent major functions are also labeled with descriptive names that identify those functions. The logical flow starts at the top block, which represents the driving or controlling module often referred to as the "driver." The execution progression continues with the boxes at the second level of the hierarchy (see Figure 2.2) in order from left to right. Of course, a box at the second level could also represent a major function that requires decomposition into a third level. Again, if a major module is decomposed into third-level modules, execution flows from left to right, just as it does at the second level. Once all the submodules (subordinate modules) of a given module have been performed on a left-to-right basis, the flow of control passes to the next rightmost module on the second level. This same progression continues from left to right until all modules have finished executing.

## STRUCTURED FLOWCHARTING

In Chapter 1, a flowchart was defined as a diagram or a graphical representation of the commands to a computer to solve a particular problem or set of problems. The flowcharting process has worked for thousands of programmers over the years, since it

seems to be a natural activity to conceptualize solutions to problems in pictorial form. Travelers often use maps to find the way to their destinations. Lines and arrows seem to stick in their minds better than a wordy explanation of how to get from one place to another. The process of conceptualizing a problem to be solved with a computer is much the same. To think through the path of execution that the computer needs to follow can become rather complex; and in order to simplify the task as much as possible, the programmer will draw a flowchart before attempting to code the instructions.

A flowchart consists of a set of flowcharting symbols, whose shapes represent the different categories of computer processing. *Flowlines* connect the flowcharting symbols. These symbols are often referred to as flowcharting blocks, or boxes, since they hold the commands that are to be executed at particular stages in the program.

### Flowcharting Symbols

The flowcharting symbols used in drawing structured and modular flowcharts are (1) terminal, (2) predefined process (external), (3) flowline, (4) input/output, (5) predefined process (internal), (6) preparation, (7) process, (8) decision, (9) connector, and (10) subscript increment. Figure 2.3 identi-

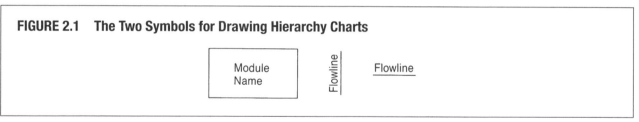

**FIGURE 2.1** The Two Symbols for Drawing Hierarchy Charts

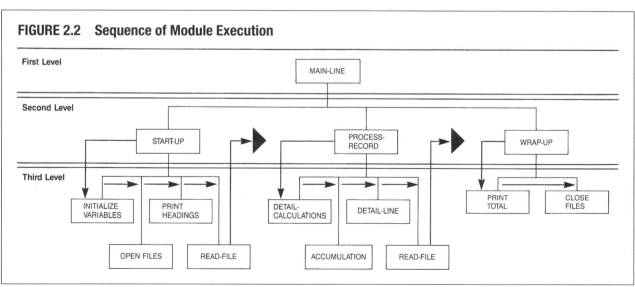

**FIGURE 2.2** Sequence of Module Execution

fies these symbols and illustrates a flowcharting template used for drawing flowcharts.

**Terminal Symbol.**    The **terminal symbol** marks both the beginning and the end of programming segments, or modules. When the terminal symbol is the first symbol in a flowcharting segment, it contains the module name (see Figure 2.4). If it is the last symbol in the flowcharting segment, it contains either the word "STOP" or the word "RETURN."

**Input/Output Symbol.**    The **input/output** (I/O) **symbol** indicates the reading of a record or the writing of the contents of variables. Figure 2.5 shows how an I/O block might appear. This I/O

block symbolizes the reading of one record into an input area of main memory. Sometimes the programmer will specify the fields of the record that is to be read. Panel A of Figure 2.6 displays an I/O block with more detail. Panel B of Figure 2.6 illustrates what actually takes place when the read instruction is executed by the computer. The read command transfers the data character by character from the input device to the input area of memory. In other words, an exact copy of the record can now be found in the input area of memory. Figure 2.6 also illustrates the memory input area.

The programmer can name the separate fields that comprise the record according to the rules for naming variables of the computer programming language he or she has chosen to use. A **variable** is

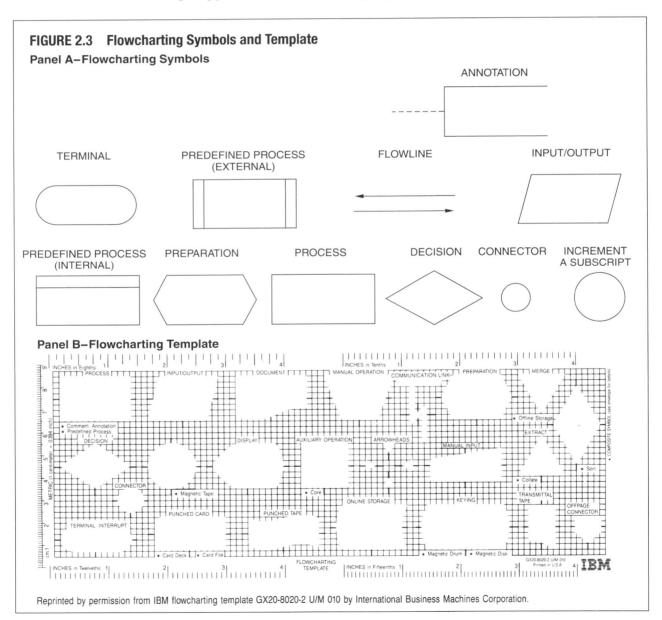

**FIGURE 2.3    Flowcharting Symbols and Template**

Reprinted by permission from IBM flowcharting template GX20-8020-2 U/M 010 by International Business Machines Corporation.

the field into which data is read or in which it is stored. By definition, a variable is a memory area whose contents can vary during the execution of the computer program. It can be referenced in a programming command by its variable name. In Figure 2.6, the first field on the record is referred to as SN, the second field is referred to as NAME, and so on.

In all high-level programming languages, these areas of data can be referred to conveniently by their variable names; the programmer doesn't have to know the actual byte address of the locations in main memory.

At this point, it may not yet be clear to you how the data in the variables will vary. As stated in Chapter 1, data records are read and processed one at a time. After the first record has been processed, the second record is read into the same variables. Panel A of Figure 2.7 illustrates the reading of the first record. After record 1 is read, the contents of the variables would appear as shown below it. After record 2 is read, the contents of the same variables would appear as depicted in panel B.

As you can see, the contents of the variable NAME, for example, is now different. It has changed from BAKER JOE to CLAYTON BILL. Note that new record information has replaced, or overlaid, the previous record data. This operation is called **automatic-destroy-read-in.** When a record is read into memory, it automatically destroys whatever else is there at the time.

The input/output symbol, besides standing for the reading of data into memory for processing, can also be used to symbolize the writing of information from a memory area in the computer to an output device such as a printer. Figure 2.8 illustrates the transfer and writing of a line.

In Figure 2.8, notice that after the data from the input area has been moved to the respective output fields, the data in the input area remains intact. The term "move" is not strictly accurate, since the data is really not moved at all, only copied. This is sometimes called **non-automatic-destroy-read-out.**

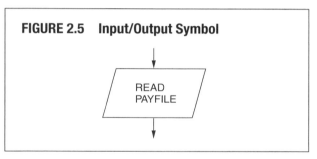

FIGURE 2.4 Terminal Symbol

FIGURE 2.5 Input/Output Symbol

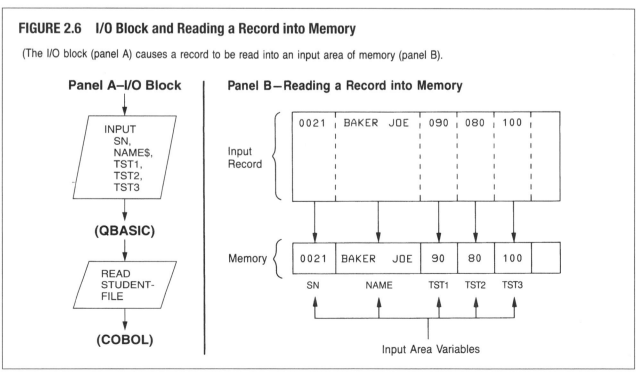

FIGURE 2.6 I/O Block and Reading a Record into Memory

(The I/O block (panel A) causes a record to be read into an input area of memory (panel B).

The work area, AVG, is a variable used to store the computed average. A work area variable is a variable used to store results of computations, intermediate results, etc. It is independent of, and separate from, input area variables, which are filled during the reading of a record.

**Process Symbol.** The **process symbol** is used to represent processing steps such as computations and data movement. Figure 2.9 shows how the process symbol might be used in a computer program flowchart.

In some programming languages, such as COBOL, the programmer must first transfer the

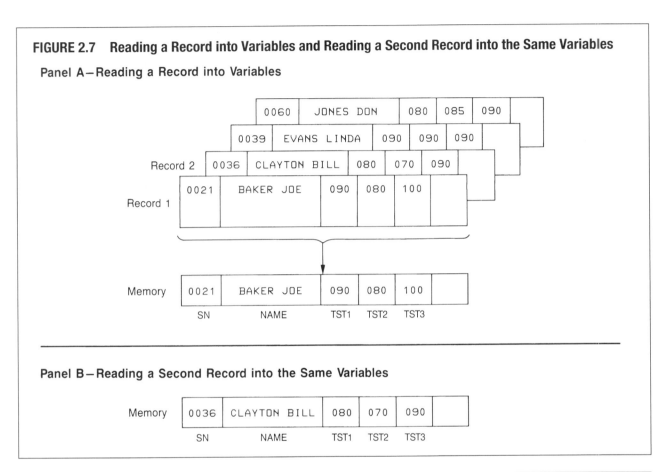

**FIGURE 2.7   Reading a Record into Variables and Reading a Second Record into the Same Variables**

Panel A—Reading a Record into Variables

Panel B—Reading a Second Record into the Same Variables

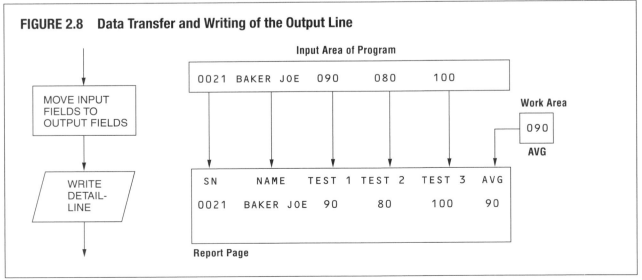

**FIGURE 2.8   Data Transfer and Writing of the Output Line**

data from the input area and work areas of his or her program to the output area of the program before writing the line. Figure 2.10 shows the use of the process symbol for this purpose.

Figure 2.11 illustrates yet another use of the process symbol. Here it is used to initialize a variable to a particular value. The variable, END-FLAG, is set to the constant, "NO."

**Predefined Process Symbol.** The **predefined process symbol** is used for the purpose of calling (invoking) a segment of the program that has been or will be defined elsewhere. A segment of the program that performs a single function is often referred to as a module, and it is often represented by the use of the predefined process block. Figure 2.12 shows how the internal predefined process

works. The predefined process block indicates that a module will be invoked. The label on the predefined process block is the name of the module to be used. Using the predefined processing block, we are able to segment a large, complicated problem into smaller, solvable submodules. Breaking a problem down into subcomponents can involve the use of subprograms that are not a part of the calling program. The subprograms have been compiled separately and entered into a subroutine library on disk. As the subprograms are needed, they are loaded into memory along with the calling program, which receives control at the appropriate processing time. The use of subroutine linkage is a common programming practice, since the smart programmer will use existing running programs to carry out certain functions. It is certainly more effi-

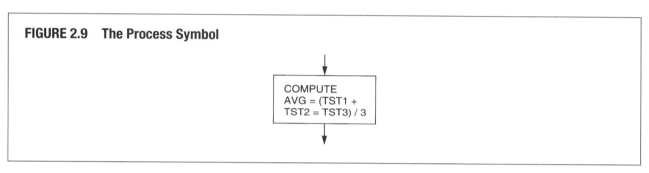

**FIGURE 2.9    The Process Symbol**

COMPUTE
AVG = (TST1 +
TST2 = TST3) / 3

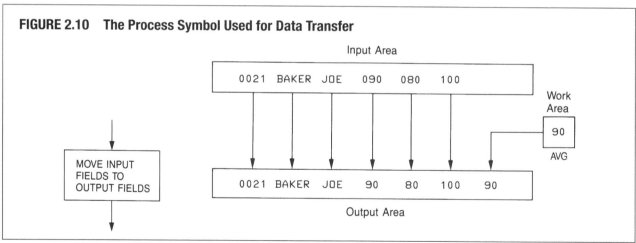

**FIGURE 2.10    The Process Symbol Used for Data Transfer**

Input Area

0021   BAKER   JOE    090    080    100

Work Area

90

AVG

MOVE INPUT FIELDS TO OUTPUT FIELDS

0021   BAKER   JOE    90    80    100    90

Output Area

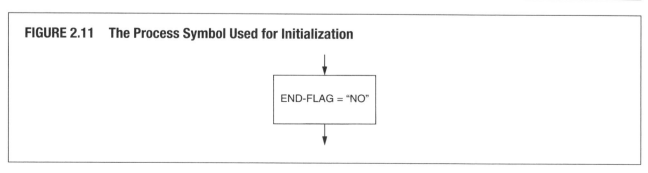

**FIGURE 2.11    The Process Symbol Used for Initialization**

END-FLAG = "NO"

cient than duplicating the code. The section on modular design will describe the program module in greater detail.

The primary reason for flowcharting the predefined process block is to specify that a processing step is to occur, without distracting the programmer's attention from the major steps or overall solution. In other words, it reminds the programmer that this step must be programmed later. It keeps the programmer from becoming sidetracked with details pertaining to an isolated aspect of the problem.

**Decision Symbol.**    In Chapter 1, one of the functions of the computer that was discussed was its ability to perform comparison operations. The computer can compare values and determine if the values are equal, unequal, or if one value is larger or smaller than the other. The diamond-shaped **decision symbol** is used to denote that two values are being compared. Figure 2.13 illustrates the use of the decision symbol.

**Connector.**    The **connector symbol** has two uses. It serves as a focal point to illustrate that two or more flowlines are merging. (Flowlines should never cross one another.) Figure 2.14 illustrates the second use of connectors—to continue a flowchart module on the same page.

**Flowline.**    An extremely important symbol in flowcharting is the **flowline,** which represents the execution path of the program. Flowlines are always straight, never curved, and usually marked with arrowheads to eliminate any confusion as to their direction of movement.

## STRUCTURED PROGRAMMING LOGIC— THE MAIN STRUCTURES

Now that each flowcharting symbol has been described as representing a particular function to be performed by the computer, it is important at this point to emphasize that program logic can be expressed in terms of three main structures:

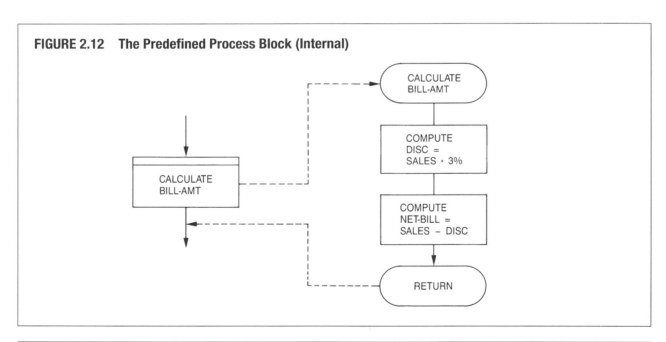

**FIGURE 2.12    The Predefined Process Block (Internal)**

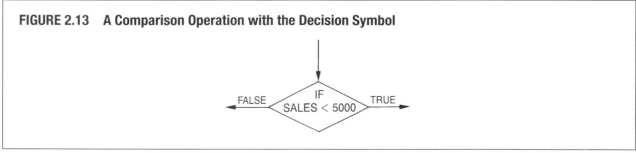

**FIGURE 2.13    A Comparison Operation with the Decision Symbol**

(1) sequence, (2) selection (If . . . Then . . .Else), and (3) repetition (DoWhile). These structures are illustrated in flowcharting form in Figure 2.15.

## HISTORY OF STRUCTURED PROGRAMMING

The use of the three main structures was first introduced by Bohn and Jacopini.[1] The basic philosophy of the type of computer programming universally

[1]Gary B. Shelly and Thomas J. Cashman, *Introduction to Computer and Data Processing*, 1980: 6, 11

known as **structured programming** hinges on the consistent use of these three main structures.

In the early sixties, computer programming was an undisciplined expression of each individual programmer's idea of how to go about solving a problem. Every programmer had his or her own style (good or bad) for developing program logic; thus every program was unique in its construction. Debugging was difficult because of each program's unique style and lack of standard organization. Because of inconsistent and unstructured programming techniques, programmers were seldom successful at helping a fellow programmer correct program errors. The inability of programmers to work successfully as a team toward the solution of complex and lengthy programming projects

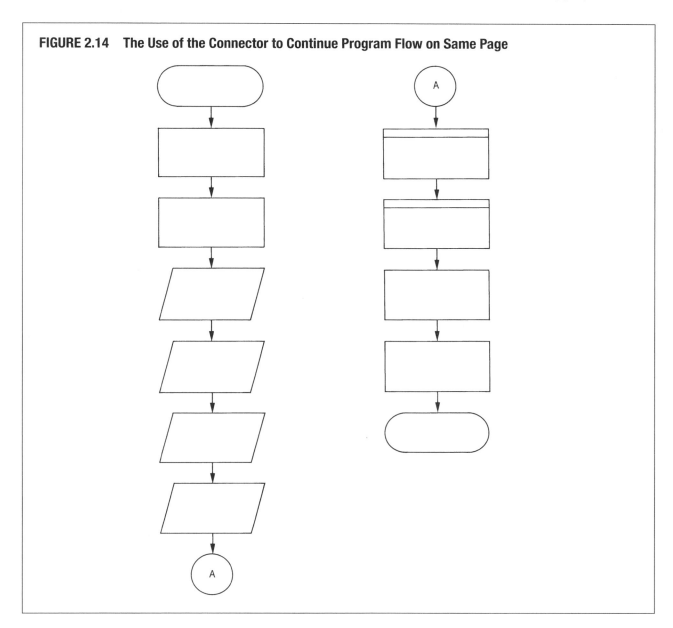

**FIGURE 2.14    The Use of the Connector to Continue Program Flow on Same Page**

rapidly became a major concern of corporate management. Delays in the timely completion of such projects often depleted company resources—time, manpower, and money. By 1966, some programmers were recognizing the importance of writing computer programs according to a set of relatively rigid rules in order to increase programming productivity and program maintainability and to decrease program testing problems.

## BASIC THEORIES OF STRUCTURED PROGRAMMING

A basic theory of structured programming is this: If a programmer is limited to the same programming structures as every other programmer, then programs written by one programmer are more easily understood and maintained by another. As program size and complexity increase, several programmers must work concurrently on a programming project. With concurrent programming tasks, it is vital that the programmers closely adhere to the use of these three structures.

A second theory of structured programming was introduced by Professor Edgar W. **Dijkstra** of the University of Eindhoven in the Netherlands. In a letter to the editor of the *Communications of the ACM*

in March, 1968,[2] he denounced the use of the GOTO command (not formally discussed in this book). This primitive command allowed the programmer to arbitrarily branch or jump to another instruction in the computer program. Dijkstra was quite persuasive in discouraging its use, claiming that the vast majority of programming errors were the result of erroneous branching (going to the wrong place in the program).

When programmers were free to branch from one place in the program to another, it became an arduous task to track down an erroneous branch or jump. In structured programming, the repetition structure eliminates the need for the GOTO command. (The repetition structure will be explained later.) The programming method Dijkstra advocated was called **"GOTOless" programming.**

### Sequence Structure

The **sequence structure** represents the sequential execution of any unconditional command given to the computer, whether it is an input, output, store,

[2]Edgar W. Dijkstra, "GOTO Statement Considered Harmful," *Communications of the ACM*, Vol. II, No. 3 (March 1968): 147.

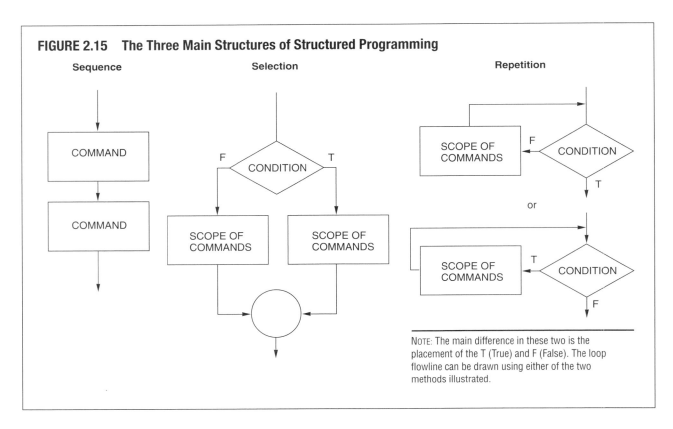

**FIGURE 2.15    The Three Main Structures of Structured Programming**

NOTE: The main difference in these two is the placement of the T (True) and F (False). The loop flowline can be drawn using either of the two methods illustrated.

or arithmetic command. An unconditional command is executed every time, without exception.

## Selection Structure

The purpose of the **selection structure** (often called If . . . Then . . . Else) is to compare two values in order to determine if one value is less than, greater than, or equal to the other value. If the condition test is "true," the computer takes a certain path of execution; if the condition is "false," the computer takes an alternate path of execution.

The important thing to note about this structure is the fact that no matter which of the two paths the computer takes, both paths merge back into the main flow of the program at exactly the same point. This fact will become significant as we look at the repetition structure.

## Repetition Structure

The purpose of the **repetition structure** is to provide the programmer with a mechanism that will cause automatic looping. Chapter 1 presented the concepts of the processing cycle and looping. The repetition (DoWhile) structure handles the task of looping. While some textbooks explore unstructured programming techniques that use GOTO commands to cause looping, this author prefers not to encourage poor programming habits by delving into the subject.

When the repetition structure is executed, a condition is tested. If the condition is true, a segment of code is executed by the computer and then transfers back to the condition being tested. This looping continues as long as the condition remains true. When the condition tests false, the repetition of the loop ceases and the computer executes the instruction after the repetition structure. In other words, it "falls through" to the next instruction.

Here again we see that the decision symbol has two paths—one for the condition being true and one for the condition being false. The two paths in the repetition structure, unlike those in the selection structure, do not merge back to the same point. The path taken when the condition is true causes looping to occur, while the path taken when the condition is false causes an exit from the loop.

Another point should be made about this structure. Since the decision symbol is diagrammed first—we say that the decision is "at the top of the loop"—transposing the decision and process blocks will cause major changes to the logic and should be avoided.

When the programmer is limited to using these three structures of programming, the behavior of any computer program becomes easier to predict, given a specific set of input data; furthermore, the debugging and maintenance of the program is greatly simplified. An important characteristic of each of these structures is that there is only *one entry point* into it and only *one exit point* from it. Thus control of a program can be tightly maintained.

# MODULAR DESIGN— STEP-WISE REFINEMENT

As a complement to structured programming logic, the concept of **step-wise refinement** was devised. This concept incorporates the use of **top-down,** or **modular, design.**

## Module Decomposition

Fundamental to modular design is the idea that a large problem can be decomposed into smaller and more manageable submodules. The process of decomposing is repeated until an isolated function can be stated in the form of a coding segment, or module. The segment of code, when executed, performs a specific task that can be identified by a single action word. For example, refer to the flowcharting module in Figure 2.16. This module has only one purpose—to calculate the federal tax. The module has only one entry point at the top and only one exit point at the bottom. By allowing access to a module from only one entry point and by allowing only one outlet from the module, the programmer significantly reduces the program's complexity. Outdated programming techniques allowed multiple outlets from a module through the use of the GOTO command. Those techniques should be avoided.

## Characteristics of a Module

In order for the programmer to become effective at designing modules within the program, he or she should be aware of the essential characteristics of a program module.

1. A module is a unique set of commands referred to by a descriptive name.
2. A module must return to its caller. Once finished executing, a module must relinquish control back to the module that invoked it.
3. A module may call, (or invoke), other modules (and usually does).
4. As previously mentioned, a module should

have only one point of entry and only one exit.

5. A module should perform only one function. It should not attempt to accomplish several unrelated tasks.

6. A module should be relatively small in size. Literature on the subject indicates that, on the average, easily maintained programs have modules no longer than a single page of code.

## A RATIONALE FOR MODULAR PROGRAM DESIGN

Normally, to enhance the concept of step-wise refinement, modules are invoked (or called) from a module on a higher level in the program. The subordinate modules that have been invoked from higher-level modules can themselves invoke still lower-level modules. This process of calling subordinate modules becomes the rule rather than the exception for designing maintainable computer programs. An underlying rationale for writing modules that call other routines is that it forces the programmer to create an outline, or "laundry list," of functions that the computer program must perform. This approach forces the programmer to develop an orderly programming plan for problem solution and discourages the programmer from taking programming shortcuts and creating hard-to-follow code. Modular programming received a lot of attention following an experimental project in which Dr. **Harlan Mills** of IBM was assigned a 30 man-year project to be completed in six months. Only through using top-down design was he able to accomplish work that would have otherwise required two groups of programmers.[3] The superiority of modular (top-down) programming design was also emphasized by IBM's information retrieval project for the *New York Times*.[4] The productivity of the programmers using structured programming and modular program design in this project was five times greater than that of the group using the unstructured methods. The adage "Divide and conquer" became the motto of modular programming.

## A STANDARD PROGRAMMING DESIGN

Figure 2.17 illustrates a **standard program design** approach that fits the vast majority of applications in the business environment. This approach is based on the idea that the three primary programming tasks are (1) START-UP, (2) PROCESS-RECORD, and (3) WRAP-UP. The first, START-UP, generates the headings of a report. The second major task, PROCESS-RECORDS, generates the detail (data) lines of a report; and finally, WRAP-UP generates the total lines of a report. The subac-

---

[3]Edward Yourdon, *Techniques of Program Structure and Design*, Prentice Hall, 138.
[4]Ibid., 83–88, 138.

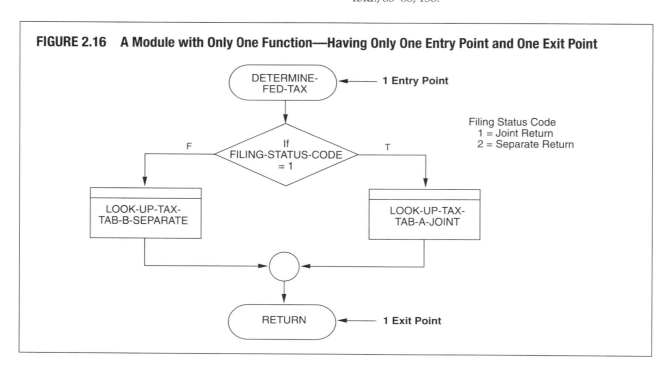

**FIGURE 2.16    A Module with Only One Function—Having Only One Entry Point and One Exit Point**

tivities are also shown in Figure 2.17. Notice the shaded corner on the READ-FILE. The shaded corner means that module is called from multiple places in the program, but exists only once.

## A PROTOTYPE

The structure in Figure 2.17 is rapidly being adopted as a prototype for future batch programming projects. While some more advanced on-line applications use a slightly more complex form of this general design, the vast majority of all batch-oriented applications can follow this logic. This method prevents the programmer from introducing a web of details too soon into the thought process and losing sight of the global problem. As the saying goes, the programmer might not see the forest for the trees.

## A RATIONALE FOR THE THREE MAIN MODULES

In Chapter 1, you learned that the three basic processing steps in the processing cycle consist of (1) input, (2) process, and (3) output. Let's apply this processing cycle to the solution of business application problems by using flowcharting symbols. Let's also incorporate the generalized logic described in the hierarchy chart in Figure 2.17. We can see that the basic logic for most business reporting problems can be decomposed into three major modules, since a report consists of three kinds of report lines,

(1) heading lines, (2) detail (or data) lines, and (3) total lines.

The START-UP module is actually responsible for more than just printing the headings, but the printing of headings is the most visible function of the START-UP routine. The PROCESS-RECORD module generates the detail lines of the report. Each detail line represents the output that results from the processing of an input record. The WRAP-UP module is responsible for those functions related to the printing of all information following the detail lines, such as totals, etc. Figure 2.18 shows the relationship between the three modules and the three types of report lines in a business report.

## DESIGNING PROGRAM LOGIC USING MODULARITY AND STRUCTURED PROGRAMMING
### Problem Definition

So that you can apply the concepts you have learned about structured programming and modularity, a problem statement is presented in this section. Remember that in Chapter 1 you learned that the first step in writing a program is to determine exactly what the problem is that you are trying to solve with the help of the computer. As you recall, the programmer is normally given a set of program specifications that include (1) program requirements and objectives, (2) report design, and (3) record layout. The problem statements presented throughout this text will be in this format.

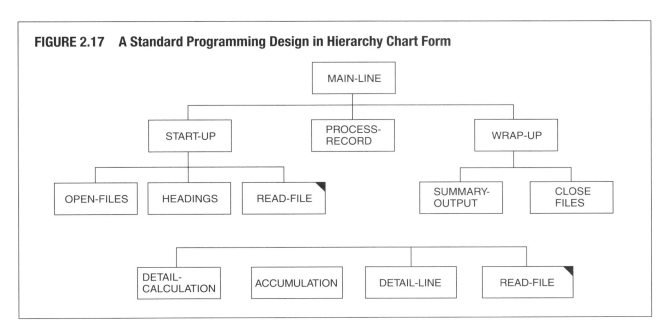

FIGURE 2.17    A Standard Programming Design in Hierarchy Chart Form

## Program Requirements

We are being asked to produce a test results report for a professor from a file of student records called STUDENT-FILE. The report is to contain each student's SN (student number), name, three test scores, and the average of the test scores. The input record for each student contains the SN, name, and three test scores. At the end of the report, the message "End of Report" will be printed. Figure 2.19 (panel A) illustrates the output design in print chart format, and panel B illustrates the record layout.

## Program Design

The next step involves developing the hierarchy chart, the structured flowchart, and pseudocode. The hierarchy chart will resemble the previous

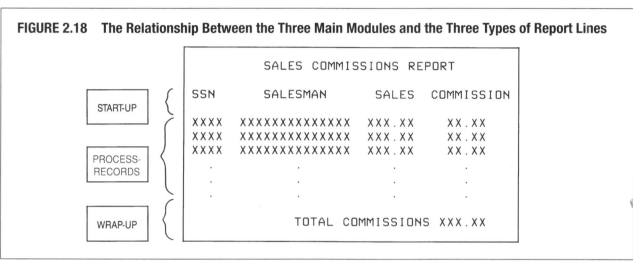

**FIGURE 2.18    The Relationship Between the Three Main Modules and the Three Types of Report Lines**

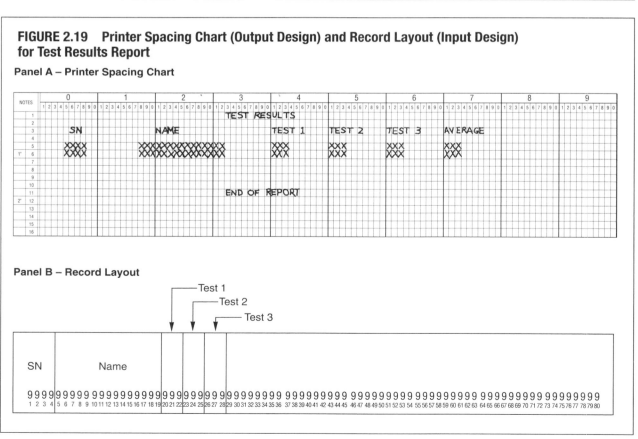

**FIGURE 2.19    Printer Spacing Chart (Output Design) and Record Layout (Input Design) for Test Results Report**

**Panel A – Printer Spacing Chart**

**Panel B – Record Layout**

hierarchy chart shown in Figure 2.17. The main difference is that in this programming problem there is no accumulation and printing of totals. Figure 2.20 shows the structure chart for this problem. The shaded corners on the READ-FILE blocks indicate that, although the module actually occurs only once, it is invoked from two different places in the program.

The programmer develops the program flowchart structure by closely adhering to the hierarchy chart in Figure 2.20. The flowchart in its entirety is presented in Figure 2.21.

The MAIN-LINE module is the starting point of the logic. It consists of three parts, (1) the **START-UP module,** (2) the **PROCESS-RECORD module,** and (3) the **WRAP-UP module.** Using the predefined process block (internal) and the repetition structure, the MAIN-LINE flowcharting segment would appear as shown in Figure 2.21.

The first predefined process block indicates that the computer is to perform, or execute, a set of code found elsewhere in the program that is identified as START-UP. When the START-UP module has finished executing, program control is to be passed back to the next block in the MAIN-LINE module, the diamond-shaped decision symbol. Please note that this decision symbol is a part of the repetition

structure. The repetition structure in the MAIN-LINE module symbolizes the executing of a module of the program called PROCESS-RECORD *repeatedly* until a variable called **END-FLAG** (a program switch or control variable) is equal to YES. This part of the flowchart is what is controlling the looping process.

The student usually wants to know how the variable called **END-FLAG** will eventually become equal to YES. When the end of the student file (STUDENT-GRADES) is sensed in the PROCESS-RECORD module, the constant YES is moved to this variable called END-FLAG. When control is passed back to the repetition structure, the first thing that happens is that the condition is retested. If the variable called END-FLAG is equal to YES, the computer then begins to execute the third part of the MAIN-LINE module called WRAP-UP. When control passes on to the next block in the MAIN-LINE module, processing terminates.

Now let's develop the second level of modules as defined by the MAIN-LINE routine.

**The START-UP Module**   Figure 2.21 also illustrates the second-level modules of the flowchart. The components of these modules will remain virtually the same throughout this text.

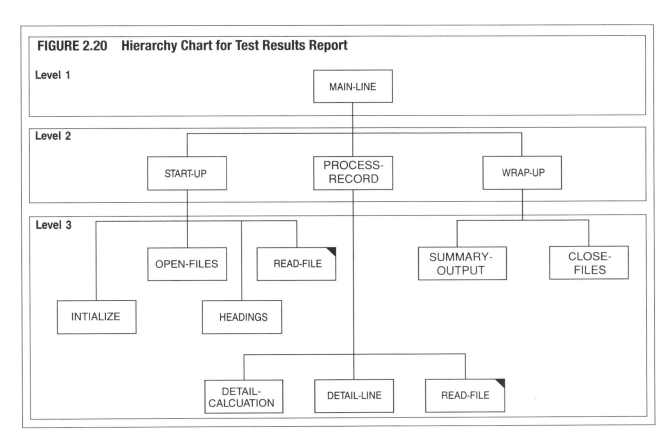

**FIGURE 2.20   Hierarchy Chart for Test Results Report**

Level 1 — MAIN-LINE

Level 2 — START-UP, PROCESS-RECORD, WRAP-UP

Level 3 — OPEN-FILES, READ-FILE, SUMMARY-OUTPUT, CLOSE-FILES, INTIALIZE, HEADINGS, DETAIL-CALCULATION, DETAIL-LINE, READ-FILE

The START-UP module, as previously explained, is responsible for the printing of the report headings as well as a few other equally important activities. In any program certain variables must be initialized—set to some initial value—as shown in the first block of the START-UP module. This is the initialize block. For example, the END-FLAG variable must be initialized to some value other than

YES. The variable was initialized to NO. It could have just as easily been initialized to STOP or NAY. The important point here is that it must be set equal to something other than YES, or the programmer runs the risk, however unlikely, that the value YES could be found in this variable. Many computer language compilers do not generate machine language code that will automatically initialize mem-

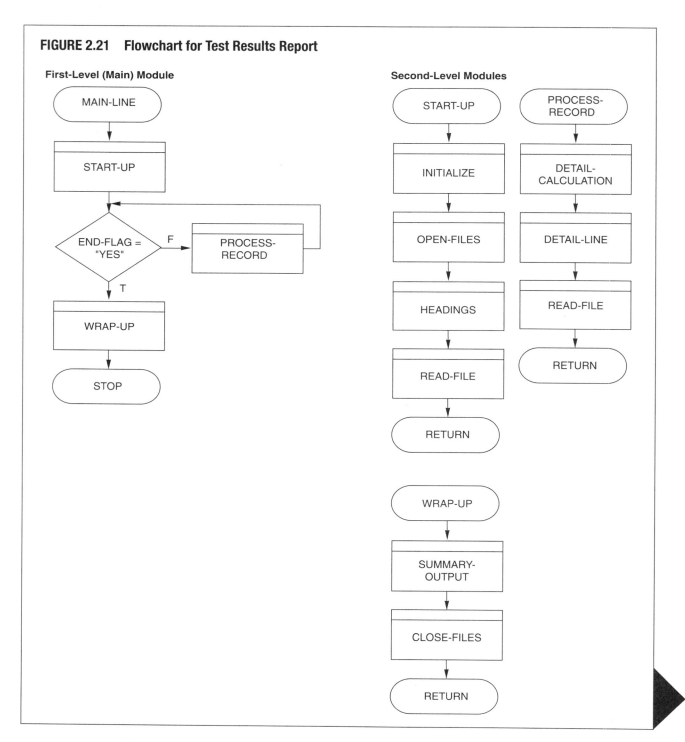

**FIGURE 2.21   Flowchart for Test Results Report**

ory (BASIC does, COBOL does not); therefore, whatever was in memory previously (the previous program and its associated work areas) is still there. Figure 2.22 (Panel A) illustrates.

The next block in START-UP indicates that the program is to call the open-files module. Some computer languages require that, before an input file can be read or before an output file can be written to, it must be opened. The OPEN command, in general, readies the file for processing. Figure 2.22 (Panel B) depicts this process.

The next task is to perform the printing of the headings. Figure 2.23 (Panel A) illustrates the procedure.

Notice that the predefined process blocks are used in the START-UP Module to symbolize the fact that the actual module for initializing, opening files, writing headings, and reading the first record are found elsewhere. They are simply called upon to execute at the appropriate time. The **Initialize Module** has only one task in this simple application and that is to set the end-flag variable to "NO." In subsequent chapters, the contents of this module

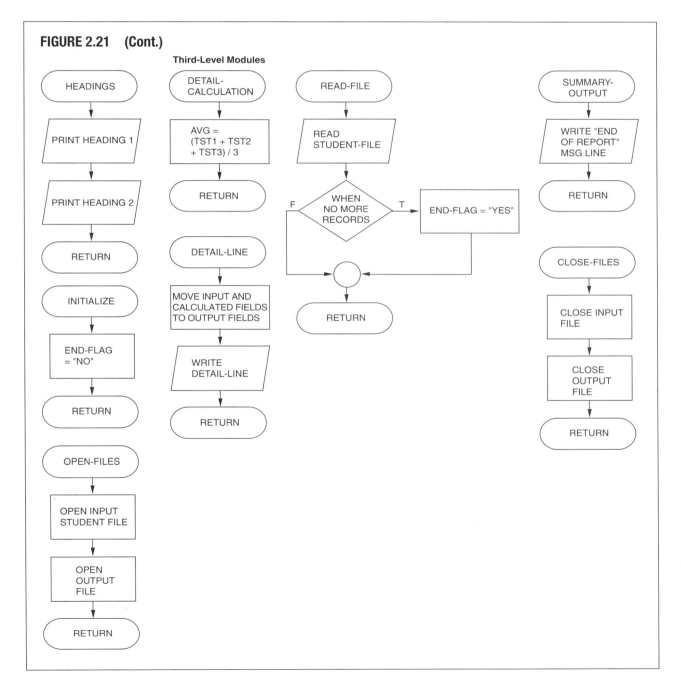

**FIGURE 2.21 (Cont.)**

Third-Level Modules

will expand. The **Open-Files** Modules are responsible for opening the input and output files. The next call in the START-UP handles the details of writing the headings on the first page, followed by the calling of the module that reads the first record. Figure 2.23 illustrates the modules for printing the headings and reading the first record. The function of this block at this point in the logic is called **preread** or **prime-read.** Its purpose is to read the first record. All subsequent records will be read from the bottom of PROCESS-RECORD.

The next symbol encountered is the terminal block labelled RETURN. RETURN simply provides the return linkage back to the calling module. This symbol should be drawn at the bottom of any module that has been invoked by another. In other words, all modules except MAIN-LINE ends with a RETURN. MAIN-LINE ends with a STOP.

**The PROCESS-RECORD Module.**   This module contains the heart of the processing activity for the program. In this problem, it represents the three processing steps that are to occur for each and every record in the file. Figure 2.24 reviews these steps.

Notice that the three blocks in Figure 2.24 are all predefined process blocks. By now, you know that these blocks indicate that the actual modules are found elsewhere. As your programming expertise develops, you will probably question the necessity of using modules at this level in a simple report problem; however, in more difficult programming problems, this level of development is extremely important. It is better to develop a good habit now rather than have to unlearn a bad habit later.

## The DETAIL-CALCULATION Module

Think of the **DETAIL-CALCULATION module** as the pigeonhole into which all calculation activities related to the record itself will be placed. If the calculation to be made is used either as an intermediate result or as a final result and is usually printed on the detail line, it is classified as a detail calculation. Adding to final totals (accumulation) is not included here. Figure 2.25 illustrates the detail calculations to be performed for this problem definition.

The calculation needed here requires us to sum the three test scores, divide by three, then place the answer in a separate variable so we can access the

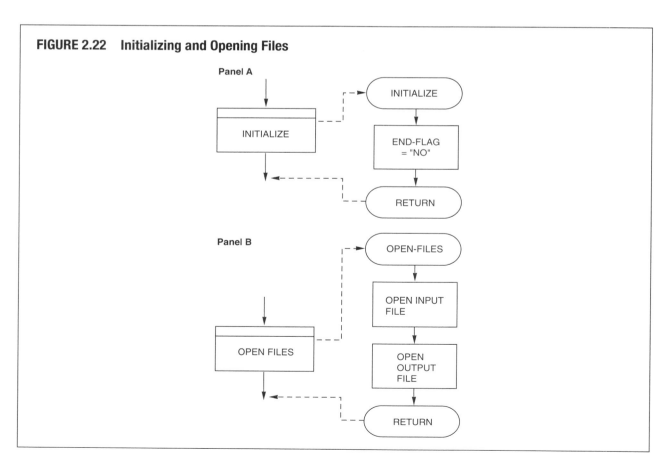

**FIGURE 2.22    Initializing and Opening Files**

value. The average is stored in the variable named AVG. In future chapters, as program complexity grows, you will see flowcharts that depict the DETAIL-CALCULATIONS module further subdivided into a fourth level of submodules.

## The DETAIL-LINE Module

Figure 2.26 illustrates the logic of writing a detail line. After the appropriate calculations have been done, let's print the detail line that contains the SN (student number), name, test score 1, test score 2, test score 3, and the average. The printing of the **DETAIL-LINE** is primarily a two-step process. Before the input and calculated variables can be printed, they must be transferred to an output storage area.

This output area is usually set up to be exactly the same length in bytes as there are print positions on the output medium, such as a printer. For example, if the printer has 132 print positions, then the output area is established with 132 print positions. Figure 2.27 illustrates the two-step process of writing a detail line.

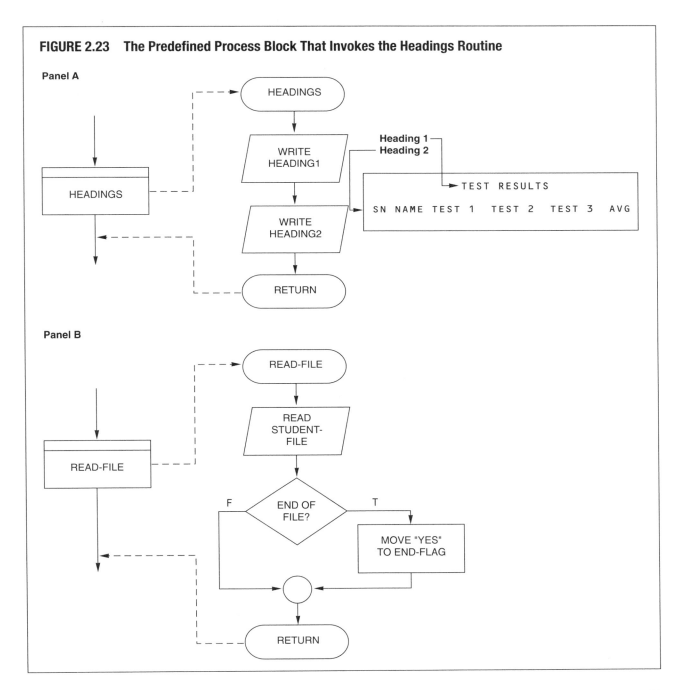

**FIGURE 2.23    The Predefined Process Block That Invokes the Headings Routine**

## The READ-FILE Module

The process of reading the next record is exactly the same as previously described in Figure 2.23. Here, the function of the **READ-FILE module** is to input the remaining records of the file, one at a time, until no more records are remaining. The decision block following the input block tests if the end of the file has been reached. If so, a control variable called END-FLAG is set to the value YES.

## The WRAP-UP Module

Once all the detail lines have been printed on the report, the message "End of Report" is specified to be printed. The first block in the WRAP-UP module indicates that this message is to be printed. The second block indicates that the input and output files are to be closed. Any files that have been opened for processing to occur must be closed in the WRAP-UP module.

**End-of-File and END-FLAG.** The purpose of a **program switch,** or **control variable,** is to control the execution path of the program. A special case of the program switch is the end-flag. The end-flag is used in determining when the program has finished processing all the records in the file.

The repetition structure, as shown in the MAIN-LINE module in Figure 2.21, causes the PROCESS-RECORDS module to be executed repeatedly until END-FLAG = "YES". What is the purpose of a program's automatically testing a condition called END-FLAG to see if it is equal to YES? END-FLAG serves as a signaling device, or message box; it communicates to the MAIN-LINE module when **end-of-file (EOF)** occurs. The READ-FILE module is aware of when EOF occurs but cannot communicate this to the MAIN-LINE module without a message box (END-FLAG). So the programmer creates a message box (END-FLAG) to give the rest of the program access to the state of the end-of-file condition.

Figure 2.28 helps to show the significance of END-FLAG. It illustrates four data records with a fifth end-of-file record placed at the end. This record is placed at the end to show that it is signalling to the program that at this point no records remain in the file. This last record is certainly not a normal record to be processed like the others; therefore, when the program reads this record and determines that it is the end-of-file signal, the program will store the constant, "YES", in the special control variable called END-FLAG. The end-of-file signal occurs during the execution of the READ-FILE module.

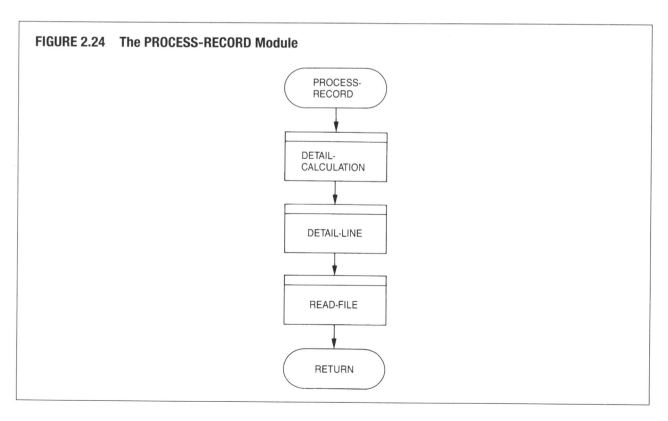

**FIGURE 2.24   The PROCESS-RECORD Module**

At this point, the MAIN-LINE routine is not yet informed of the fact that the last record was read. When the READ-FILE module is finished, control is passed back to the bottom of the PROCESS-RECORD module. Subsequently, the RETURN at the bottom of the PROCESS-RECORD module passes control back to the point immediately after the predefined block in the repetition structure. The next program event is the retesting of the control variable, END-FLAG. This time, the condition will test to be true, END-FLAG will equal "YES", and control will pass to the predefined process block labelled WRAP-UP. At this point, the repetition structure has been informed of the fact that all the records have been processed.

Figure 2.28 illustrates the file with an end-of-file record. Figure 2.29 correlates the READ-FILE block from the START-UP module with the reading of the first record, and the READ-FILE block from the PROCESS-RECORD module with the reading of the remainder of the records.

Figure 2.30 traces in tabular form the reading of each record in the file through the end-of-file record. The first column indicates the module that causes the record to be read; the second column depicts the actual record read when the read command is executed; the third column shows the current contents of the control variable, END-FLAG. At the beginning of the START-UP module, END-FLAG is initialized to "NO". The fourth column

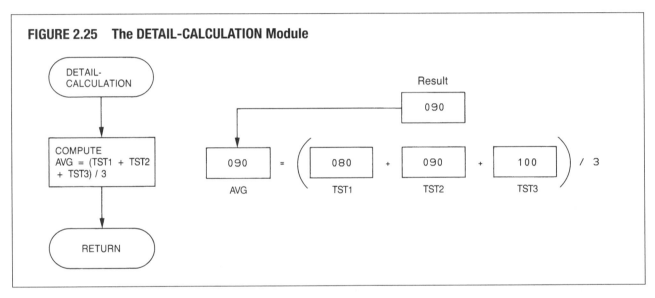

FIGURE 2.25    The DETAIL-CALCULATION Module

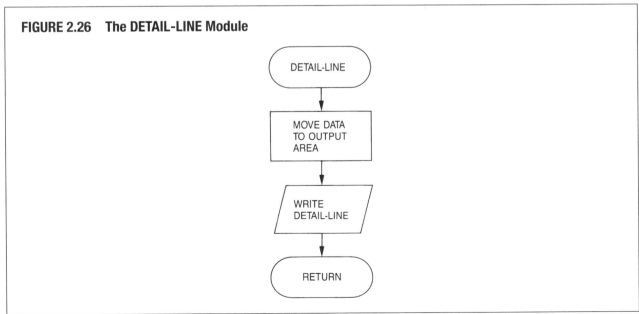

FIGURE 2.26    The DETAIL-LINE Module

indicates the condition being tested. At the risk of being redundant, the same condition is placed in each cell of this column to make sure the reader is aware that the condition is being tested prior to the execution of the PROCESS-RECORD module. The fifth column discloses the result of the test as either

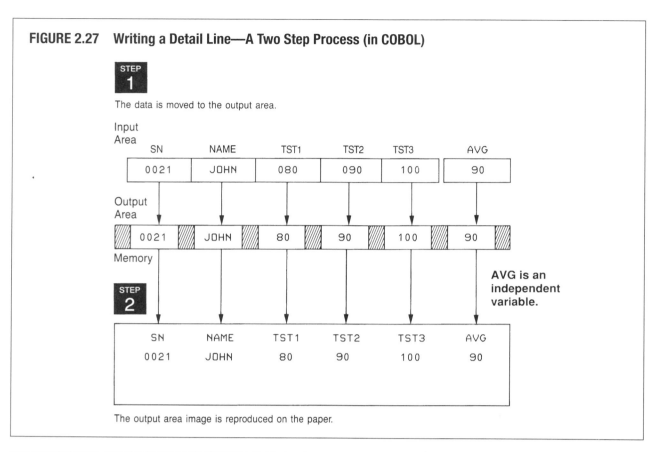

**FIGURE 2.27   Writing a Detail Line—A Two Step Process (in COBOL)**

**STEP 1**

The data is moved to the output area.

Input Area

| SN | NAME | TST1 | TST2 | TST3 | AVG |
|------|------|------|------|------|-----|
| 0021 | JOHN | 080 | 090 | 100 | 90 |

Output Area

| 0021 | JOHN | 80 | 90 | 100 | 90 |

Memory

**AVG is an independent variable.**

**STEP 2**

| SN | NAME | TST1 | TST2 | TST3 | AVG |
|------|------|------|------|------|-----|
| 0021 | JOHN | 80 | 90 | 100 | 90 |

The output area image is reproduced on the paper.

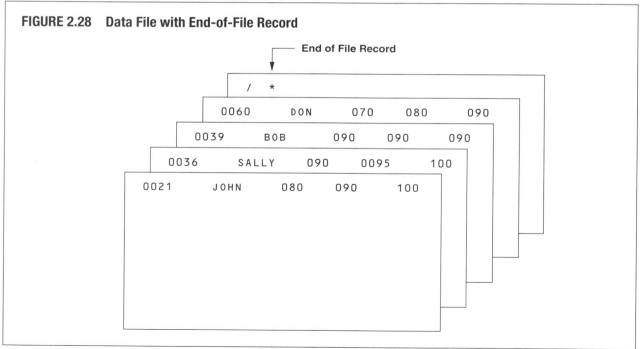

**FIGURE 2.28   Data File with End-of-File Record**

End of File Record

| / | * |

| 0060 | DON | 070 | 080 | 090 |

| 0039 | BOB | 090 | 090 | 090 |

| 0036 | SALLY | 090 | 0095 | 100 |

| 0021 | JOHN | 080 | 090 | 100 |

true or false. The sixth column shows which course of action the program will take depending on the result of the test. If the test is false, the PROCESS- RECORD module is executed; if the test is true, the WRAP-UP module is executed instead.

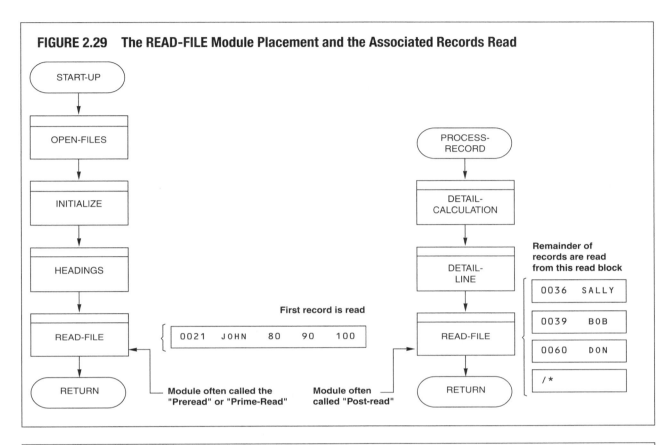

**FIGURE 2.29    The READ-FILE Module Placement and the Associated Records Read**

**FIGURE 2.30    Trace of the Selection Structure Execution**

| | Read Invoked By Module | Record Image After Read Command | Contents of END-FLAG After Read | Condition Tested | Result of Test | Program Action | |
|---|---|---|---|---|---|---|---|
| 1 | START-UP | 0021   JOHN | No | IS END-FLAG = "YES" | False | Invoke PROCESS-RECORD | 2 |
| 2 | PROCESS-RECORD | 0036   SALLY | No | IS END-FLAG = "YES" | False | Invoke PROCESS-RECORD | 3 |
| 3 | PROCESS-RECORD | 0039   BOB | No | IS END-FLAG = "YES" | False | Invoke PROCESS-RECORD | 4 |
| 4 | PROCESS-RECORD | 0060   DON | No | IS END-FLAG = "YES" | False | Invoke PROCESS-RECORD | 5 |
| 5 | PROCESS-RECORD | / * | Yes | IS END-FLAG = "YES" | True | Invoke WRAP-UP | |

## CAUTION! The BASIC and Pascal Test for EOF Differs from That in COBOL and PL/I

The explanation previously given for determining end-of-file and setting END-FLAG is based on the COBOL and PL/I languages. The rationale for using the COBOL and PL/I method for testing EOF is that this technique can be made to work for all languages. The choice of technique is arbitrary. In COBOL, the end-of-file is not determined until the EOF marker (/* on IBM computers) at the end of the data file is actually read. Unfortunately, there is a lack of consistency in the way in which some other languages test for the end-of-file. (A lot of confusion would have been avoided if all compilers had been designed to handle EOF testing the same way.) In BASIC and Pascal, for example, when a record is read, the program looks forward one record in the file to determine if this *next* one is the end-of-file record. (COBOL does not do this.) If this *next* record is the end-of-file record, a special compiler-generated switch called (EOF) is turned on. This (EOF) setting will occur before the last real data record has been processed. This means that the subsequent condition test for (EOF) will be true, and the logic will continue at the WRAP-UP module. Therefore, with a post-read technique (reading at the bottom of the PROCESS-RECORD module), the last record is never processed.

In BASIC or Pascal, however, *the logic design can be modified, or the data file can be slightly altered to include a dummy record.* Either method can resolve the problem. The programmer can alter the program logic by (1) eliminating the preread in the START-UP module, (2) placing the READ-FILE module call at the top of the PROCESS-RECORD module instead of at the bottom (post-read) as previously illustrated.

If the programmer is using the EOF() indicator and prefers to use the same logic as in Figure 2.21 and continue to use the preread and post-read logic, then the data file can be altered to include a *dummy record* at the end of the data records (test cases). In BASIC and Pascal, when using the pre-read in the START-UP module and the post-read in the PROCESS-RECORD module, *place the dummy record at the end of the data file. The dummy record does not contain real data. It simply prevents a premature signaling of end-of-file that would result in the last record not getting processed.* Why is this? Remember, the READ-FILE block is at the bottom of the PROCESS-RECORD module. For the last real record to be processed, *one more iteration through the PROCESS-RECORD module is needed.* At this point, the last record has only been read, not processed. Without the dummy record to prevent the prema-

ture EOF signal, the last real data record of the file would never get processed. To the beginner, this is often unclear until he or she has written programs using both methods. If they use their own **end-flag** variable, then there is no need for this; simply use a delimiter record.

This text pursues only one logic design—the use of preread in the START-UP module and post-read in the PROCESS-RECORD module; therefore, when using BASIC or Pascal, *one should always add an additional dummy record to all data files (or test cases) when following the logic method emphasized in this text.* This should not be done when using COBOL. The dummy record may contain any series of characters as long as the fields are of the proper data type (numeric or alphanumeric). Since this record will never get processed, it does not matter what values are in the record. Programmers normally place a series of Xs in alphanumeric fields and zeros in numeric fields. Now, this dummy record really *looks* like a dummy record. For example, the following record could be added to the data file.

00000,XXXXXXXXXXXXXXX,000,000,000
[Note: only used if using EOF()]

In this record, the SN is all zeros, the fifteen-position name field is all Xs, and the three test scores are all zeros. The reason each field of the record must contain some kind of data rather than remain blank is that a blank numeric field would cause an "out of data" message in BASIC. The BASIC examples in this text do not use the EOF indicator. Instead, the examples illustrate the use of a programmer supplied end-flag (control variable) and the use of a delimiter record.

## PSEUDOCODE

As a compliment or replacement to flowcharting, the next step is to develop pseudocode. Pseudocode was discussed in Chapter 1 as an alternate program design. Pseudocode was defined in Chapter 1 as a set of commands in English with a very limited set of keywords. The use of pseudocode allows the programmer to concentrate on developing program logic rather than focus on writing the specific syntax of the computer language. The rationale for using pseudocode is that it allows the program design to be reduced to a level that resembles the program itself without having to follow a specific language syntax.

Each pseudocode command identifies a particular processing step. To illustrate the use of pseudocode, let's consider the test results report from Figure 2.19. You'll follow both the hierarchy chart in Figure 2.20 and the program flowchart in Figure 2.21 in writing the necessary pseudocode.

## Guidelines for Writing Pseudocode

Unlike programming languages, which have a multitude of commands, syntax, and keywords, pseudocode has a restricted set of commands and keywords. The basic pseudocode structures are the same as those used in flowcharting. They are (1) sequence, (2) repetition, and (3) selection (If . . . Then . . . Else). A substructure of the If . . . Then . . . Else is called the CASE, which will be discussed in Chapter 4. The following brief samples of pseudocode highlight how the commands are used.

**Sequence**
open-customer-file
print-headings
read-customer-file
**Repetition**
dowhile end-flag is off
    process-routine
enddo
**Selection**
if customer is not on-time
    increment overdue-total by 1
endif

      or

if customer is on-time
    null*
else
increment overdue-total by 1
endif
Case (a substructure of the If . . . Then . . . Else)

If a computer language has a formal CASE command, then the following method seems to correlate more closely with the language.

when freshman
    increment freshman-total by 1
when sophomore
    increment sophomore-total by 1
when junior
    increment junior-total by 1
when senior
    increment senior-total by 1
error-message
endcase

If the language does not have a formal CASE command, then the following pseudocode seems to correlate more closely to the actual language.

If freshman
    increment freshman-total by 1
else
If sophomore
    increment sophomore-total by 1
else
If junior
    increment junior-total by 1
else
If senior
    increment senior-total by 1
endif

## Basic Rules for Writing Pseudocode

Before the pseudocode is developed, let's examine some of the basic guidelines or rules for using pseudocode.

1. The main-line logic is presented first, then followed by the various modules that are invoked, or called, from the mainline. The modules are listed in the code according to the order in which they are invoked, i.e., in a hierarchical manner.
2. The *if* command will have an associated ENDIF.
3. The *case* will have an associated *endcase* when using WHEN.
4. The *read* will have an associated *endread*.
5. The pseudocode commands are in lower-case.
6. Modules that are invoked are named using lowercase and are *underlined*.
7. Module names are preceded by an asterisk.
8. The null command is normally used to avoid negative comparisons (the use of the NOT operator can often be confusing).

Figure 2.31 depicts the pseudocode that is associated with the flowcharting logic shown in Figure 2.21. Figures 2.32 and 2.33 illustrate the COBOL 85 and QBASIC programs and output.

## THEORETICAL FOUNDATION OF STRUCTURED AND MODULAR DESIGN—COHESION, COUPLING, AND SPAN OF CONTROL

Before leaving Chapter 2, you should become acquainted with three important concepts that form a theoretical frame of reference about structured

---

*null command equates to NEXT SENTENCE clause in COBOL.

programming and modular design. You may be able to design relatively simple programs without knowing a great deal about the theory of structured programming, but as the problems grow more complex, understanding these three concepts becomes more important. They are (1) **cohesion,** (2) **coupling,** and (3) **span of control.**

## Cohesion

Cohesion is a measure of the degree of relationship that exists between commands in the same module. By definition, cohesion is "that which binds together"; therefore, module cohesion is what holds the pieces of the module together. The stronger this relationship, the closer the module comes to being a single unit designed to accomplish a single function. A module with high cohesiveness is the ideal. It is desirable to have a module with statements that relate only to the achievement of the function at hand. Figure 2.34 illustrates a module with strong cohesion in panel A and a module with weak cohesion in panel B. Avoid designing a module that includes commands unrelated to its function simply because it would be convenient to place them there.

## Coupling

The concept of module coupling relates to the interconnectedness of the modules themselves. Module coupling is a measure of the relationships that exist between modules. The ideal program is a program where modules are able to stand by themselves without depending much on the output from other modules. In general, the more one module must know about another, the tighter the coupling. Tightly coupled modules are often a source of debugging and testing problems. Normally, the programmer attempts to write program modules that are *loosely coupled.*

The three types of coupling are (1) content, (2) control, and (3) data. Content coupling refers to the manner in which one module calls, or invokes, another. Ideally, a module will invoke an entire module, not a segment of a module. The programmer should avoid calling a portion of a module simply because the module contains some commands that need to be performed to accomplish some other task. Sometimes a programmer must create redundant code in a module to avoid having to invoke a portion of another module. If the programmer knows that the needed code exists in another module, he or she should resist the tempta-

---

**FIGURE 2.31  Pseudocode for Flowchart in Figure 2.21**

```
*mainline                                  *read-file
    startup                                    read student-file
    dowhile end-flag = "no"                    when no more records set end-flag = "yes"
        process-record                         endread
    enddo                                      return
    wrap-up                                *process-record
    stop                                       detail-calculation
*start-up                                      detail-line
    initialize                                 read-file
    open-files                                 return
    headings                               *detail-calculation
    read-file                                  calculate avg = (tst1 + tst2 + tst3) / 3
    return                                     return
*initialize                                *detail-line
    end-flag = "no"                            move input and calculated fields to output field
    return                                     write the detail line
*open-files                                    return
    open input student-file                *wrap-up
    open output report-file                    summary-output
    return                                     close-files
*headings                                      return
    advance to top of page                 *summary-output
    write page heading                         write "end of report" message
    write field heading                        return
    return                                 *close-files
                                               close student-file
                                               return
```

**FIGURE 2.32    COBOL 85 Program for Application 2.1**

```
1             IDENTIFICATION DIVISION.
2             PROGRAM-ID. CH2APL1.
3
4         ****ANS COBOL 85****
5
6         * REMARKS:    THIS PROGRAM PRODUCES A TEST RESULTS REPORT FROM
7         *             A  GRADE FILE.
8
9          ENVIRONMENT DIVISION.
10
11         CONFIGURATION SECTION.
12
13         SOURCE-COMPUTER.  CYBER.
14         OBJECT-COMPUTER.  CYBER.
15
16         INPUT-OUTPUT SECTION.
17
18         FILE-CONTROL.
19
20             SELECT STUDENT-FILE ASSIGN TO DTA21.
21             SELECT STUDENT-REPORT ASSIGN TO OUTFILE.
22
23
24         DATA DIVISION.
25
26         FILE SECTION.
27
28         FD   STUDENT-FILE.
29
30         01   STUDENT-REC.
31
32             05 SN                    PIC 9(4).
33             05 NAME                  PIC X(15).
34             05 TEST1                 PIC 999.
35             05 TEST2                 PIC 999.
36             05 TEST3                 PIC 999.
37
38
39         FD   STUDENT-REPORT.
40
41         01   REPORT-REC              PIC X(133).
42
43
44         WORKING-STORAGE SECTION.
45
46         01   END-FLAG                PIC XXX VALUE "NO".
47         01   AVG-TEST-SCORE          PIC 999.
48
49         01   PAGE-HEADING.
50
51             05                       PIC X(32) VALUE SPACES.
52             05                       PIC X(13) VALUE "TEST RESULTS".
53             05                       PIC X(88) VALUE SPACES.
54
55         01   COLUMN-HEADING.
56
57             05                       PIC X(5) VALUE SPACES.
58             05                       PIC XX    VALUE "SN".
59             05                       PIC X(13) VALUE SPACES.
60             05                       PIC X(4)  VALUE "NAME".
61             05                       PIC X(16) VALUE SPACES.
62             05                       PIC X(6)  VALUE "TEST 1".
63             05                       PIC X(4)  VALUE SPACES.
64             05                       PIC X(6)  VALUE "TEST 2".
65             05                       PIC X(4)  VALUE SPACES.
66             05                       PIC X(6)  VALUE "TEST 3".
```

**FIGURE 2.32   COBOL 85 Program for Application 2.1** *(cont.)*

```
67                05                                PIC X(4)  VALUE SPACES.
68                05                                PIC X(7)  VALUE "AVERAGE".
69                05                                PIC X(12) VALUE SPACES.
70
71         01   DETAIL-LINE.
72
73                05                                PIC X(4) VALUE SPACE.
74                05  SN-OUT                        PIC ZZZ9.
75                05                                PIC X(9) VALUE SPACES.
76                05  NAME-OUT                      PIC X(15).
77                05                                PIC X(8)  VALUE SPACES.
78                05  TEST1-OUT                     PIC Z99.
79                05                                PIC X(7)  VALUE SPACES.
80                05  TEST2-OUT                     PIC Z99.
81                05                                PIC X(7)  VALUE SPACES.
82                05  TEST3-OUT                     PIC Z99.
83                05                                PIC X(7) VALUE SPACES.
84                05  TEST-AVG-OUT                  PIC Z99.
85                05                                PIC X(59) VALUE SPACES.
86
87
88        /
89         PROCEDURE DIVISION.
90
91         000-MAINLINE.
92
93             PERFORM 100-START-UP.
94             PERFORM 200-PROCESS-RECORD  UNTIL END-FLAG = "YES".
95             PERFORM 300-WRAP-UP.
96             STOP RUN.
97
98         100-START-UP.
99
100            PERFORM 102-INITIALIZE.
101            PERFORM 105-OPEN-FILES.
102            PERFORM 110-HEADINGS.
103            PERFORM 120-READ-FILE.
104
105        102-INITIALIZE.
106
107            MOVE "NO" TO END-FLAG.
108
109        105-OPEN-FILES.
110
111            OPEN INPUT STUDENT-FILE.
112            OPEN OUTPUT STUDENT-REPORT.
113
114        110-HEADINGS.
115
116            WRITE REPORT-REC FROM PAGE-HEADING AFTER ADVANCING PAGE.
117            WRITE REPORT-REC FROM COLUMN-HEADING AFTER ADVANCING 2 LINES.
118            MOVE SPACES TO REPORT-REC.
119            WRITE REPORT-REC.
120
121        120-READ-FILE.
122
123            READ STUDENT-FILE AT END MOVE "YES" TO END-FLAG.
124
125        200-PROCESS-RECORD.
126
127            PERFORM 210-DETAIL-CALCULATIONS.
128            PERFORM 220-DETAIL-LINE.
129            PERFORM 120-READ-FILE.
130
131        210-DETAIL-CALCULATIONS.
132
133            COMPUTE AVG-TEST-SCORE ROUNDED = (TEST1 + TEST2 + TEST3) / 3.
```

**FIGURE 2.32    COBOL 85 Program for Application 2.1** *(cont.)*

```
134
135         220-DETAIL-LINE.
136
137             MOVE SN TO SN-OUT.
138             MOVE NAME TO NAME-OUT.
139             MOVE TEST1 TO TEST1-OUT.
140             MOVE TEST2 TO TEST2-OUT.
141             MOVE TEST3 TO TEST3-OUT.
142             MOVE AVG-TEST-SCORE TO TEST-AVG-OUT.
143             WRITE REPORT-REC FROM DETAIL-LINE.
144
145
146
147         300-WRAP-UP.
148
149             PERFORM 310-SUMMARY-OUTPUT.
150             PERFORM 320-CLOSE.
151
152         310-SUMMARY-OUTPUT.
153
154             MOVE "                              END OF REPORT"
155                 TO REPORT-REC.
156             WRITE REPORT-REC AFTER ADVANCING 2 LINES.
157
158         320-CLOSE.
159
160             CLOSE STUDENT-FILE  STUDENT-REPORT.
```

```
                        TEST RESULTS

SN              NAME               TEST 1    TEST 2    TEST 3    AVERAGE

21              JOHN                 80        90       100        90
36              SALLY                90        95       100        95
39              BOB                  90        90        90        90
60              DON                  70        80        90        80

                    END OF REPORT
```

**FIGURE 2.33    QBASIC for Application 2.1**

```
'****************************************************************
'*                   PROGRAM IDENTIFICATION                    *
'****************************************************************
'* PROGRAM NAME: CH2APL1                                       *
'* REMARKS:  THIS PROGRAM PRODUCES A TEST RESULTS REPORT FROM A GRADE *
'*           FILE.  THIS REPORT LISTS A STUDENT'S THREE TEST SCORES   *
'*           AND AVG                                           *
'****************************************************************
'*                       MAIN-LINE                            *
'****************************************************************
GOSUB START.UP                      'PERFORM START-UP          *
DO UNTIL END.FLAG$ = "YES"
    GOSUB PROCESS.RECORD            'PERFORM PROCESS           *
LOOP
GOSUB WRAP.UP                       'PERFORM WRAP-UP           *
END
    '****************************************************************
    '*                       START-UP                         *
    '****************************************************************
```

**FIGURE 2.33    QBASIC for Application 2.1 *(cont.)***

```
START.UP:
    GOSUB INITIALIZE
    GOSUB OPEN.FILES
    GOSUB HEADINGS                          'PERFORM HEADINGS          *
    GOSUB READ.FILE                         'PERFORM READ-FILE         *
    RETURN


    '****************************************************************
    '*                         INITIALIZE                          *
    '****************************************************************

INITIALIZE:

    WIDTH LPRINT 132
    DETAIL.LINE$ = "    ####         \          \       ###     ###     ###     ###"
    END.FLAG$ = "NO"
    RETURN


    '****************************************************************
    '*                         OPEN-FILES                          *
    '****************************************************************
OPEN.FILES:

    OPEN "I", #1, "CH2ILL1.DAT"
    RETURN

    '****************************************************************
    '*                         HEADINGS                            *
    '****************************************************************

HEADINGS:

    LPRINT CHR$(12)
    LPRINT : LPRINT
    LPRINT TAB(33); "TEST  RESULTS"
    LPRINT
    LPRINT TAB(6); "SN"; TAB(21); "NAME"; TAB(41); "TEST 1"; TAB(51); "TEST 2"; TAB(61); "TEST 3"; TAB(71); "AVG"
    LPRINT
    RETURN

    REM ************************************************************
    REM *                       READ-FILE                         *
    REM ************************************************************

READ.FILE:

    INPUT #1, SN, STD.NAME$, TEST1, TEST2, TEST3
    IF STD.NAME$ = "EOF" THEN END.FLAG$ = "YES"
    RETURN
    REM ************************************************************
    REM *                       PROCESS                           *
    REM ************************************************************

PROCESS.RECORD:

    GOSUB DETAIL.CALCULATIONS           'PERFORM DETAIL-CALCULATIONS    *
    GOSUB DETAIL.LINE                   'PERFORM DETAIL-LINE            *
    GOSUB READ.FILE                     'PERFORM READ-FILE             *
    RETURN
```

## FIGURE 2.33    QBASIC for Application 2.1 *(cont.)*

```
'*********************************************************************
'*                          DETAIL-CALCULATIONS                      *
'*********************************************************************

DETAIL.CALCULATIONS:

    AVG = (TEST1 + TEST2 + TEST3) / 3
    RETURN

        '*****************************************************************
        '*                          DETAIL-LINE                          *
        '*****************************************************************

DETAIL.LINE:
    LPRINT USING DETAIL.LINE$; SN; STD.NAME$; TEST1; TEST2; TEST3; AVG
    RETURN

        '*****************************************************************
        '*                          WRAP-UP                              *
        '*****************************************************************

WRAP.UP:

    LPRINT
    LPRINT TAB(33); "END OF REPORT"
    CLOSE
    RETURN
```

```
                        TEST   RESULTS


SN              NAME            TEST 1    TEST 2    TEST 3    AVG


21              JOHN              80        90       100       90
36              SALLY             90        95       100       95
39              BOB               90        90        90       90
60              DON               70        80        90       80


                        END OF REPORT
```

## FIGURE 2.34    Routine with Strong Cohesion and Routine with Weak Cohesion

**Panel A—Routine with Strong Cohesion**

```
*compute-pay
    lookup-tax-amount
    calculate-fica
    calculate net = gross - (fica + tax)
    return
```

NOTE: All statements support the computation of pay.

**Panel B—Routine with Weak Cohesion**

```
*compute-pay
    lookup-tax-amount
    calc-fica
    calculate net = gross - (tax + fica)
    store net to print-line
    accumulate 1 into total-employees
    if fica > 0
        then add 1 to total-fica employees
    endif
    return
```

NOTE: The last three commands have nothing to do with computing pay. The fourth line of pseudocode belongs in the DETAIL-LINE module; the fifth and remaining lines belong in the ACCUMULATION module since they deal with accumulating into totals.

tion to invoke that segment of code rather than rewrite it.

**Control Coupling.**  **Control coupling** exists when a control variable is passed from one module to the other. A control variable determines the action to be taken within a module. An END-FLAG is a common example of a control variable. In many cases, control coupling cannot be avoided and can actually be advantageous; however, the passing of too many control variables can become very unwieldy and create program maintenance problems. In later chapters you will see numerous examples where the author has used control variables (VALID-REC-SWITCH, FOUND-SWITCH, etc.) appropriately. You will probably find that control coupling makes more sense once you've read Chapters 5 and 7.

## Span of Control

Just as there's a limit to the number of employees a manager can effectively supervise, so there's a limit to the number of subordinate modules that a given module should directly control. It's important that a module have a reasonable span of control over subordinate modules. Judging from the author's experience, the span of control for any given module should rarely exceed three to five submodules. Of course, there are exceptions. But when a given module attempts to accomplish too many tasks, the module becomes complex and hard to debug. It's also likely that a module with a very large span of control is attempting to accomplish too much *too soon*. The programmer should always avoid introducing detail into the design prematurely and instead should constantly strive to see the "big picture" first.

## SUMMARY

Once the program specifications are understood, the programmer develops a hierarchy chart of the overall basic design of the program. From the hierarchy chart, the programmer draws a structured flowchart that represents in symbolic form the logical steps of the program.

Since programmers conceptualize and think through problems in terms of pictures, the hierarchy chart and the structured flowchart have become ideal tools for program design. The flowcharting symbols include (1) terminal, (2) input/output, (3) process, (4) predefined process (external), (5) predefined process (internal), (6) decision, (7) preparation, (8) flowline, (9) connector, and (10) subscript increment.

A very important process to understand is the way in which a computer reads a record by transferring the image of the record into a main memory input area.

Before data can be printed, it must first be moved or transferred from the input area and various other calculation fields into an output area, from which the data is actually printed.

Structured programming logic can be expressed in terms of (1) sequence, (2) selection, and (3) repetition. These three main structures are used for the most part in writing structured programs. The sequence structure represents the sequential execution of commands. The selection structure is used to compare two values. The execution path the computer takes is determined by this comparison. The repetition structure provides the programmer with a mechanism that will cause automatic looping when a set of code needs to be repeated a number of times.

Modular design complements the idea of structured programming through the use of step-wise refinement, decomposition of a large problem into smaller and more manageable subproblems.

A hierarchical program design that is rapidly becoming accepted by the programming community is the MAIN-LINE module that is decomposed into three second-level modules, which are (1) START-UP, (2) PROCESS-RECORD, and (3) WRAP-UP. For simple reports, the START-UP module is further decomposed into third-level modules, (1) INITIALIZE, (2) OPEN-FILES, (3) HEADINGS and (4) READ-FILE. The PROCESS-RECORD module is normally decomposed into (1) DETAIL-CALCULATION, (2) ACCUMULATION, (3) DETAIL-LINE, and (4) READ-FILE. The WRAP-UP module normally consists of a SUMMARY-OUTPUT module and CLOSE-FILES module.

Before a file can be processed, it must be opened. After a file is opened, the headings are printed, and the first record is read from the START-UP module.

The PROCESS-RECORD module is subsequently performed. This module is responsible for calculating results, accumulating necessary totals, printing the detail line, and reading the next record. These activities are repeated until all of the records have been processed, at which time the necessary total lines are printed and the files are closed. Either as an adjunct to flowcharting or (sometimes) as a replacement for flowcharting, pseudocode is an important design tool. Pseudocode uses the same design constructs as flowcharting.

The theoretical frame of reference for modularity is based on three main concepts—module cohesion, coupling, and span of control. Module cohesion has to do with the homogeneity of commands within the module itself. Coupling measures the strength of relationships or interconnectedness of the various modules in a program. We are looking for modules with high cohesion, that is, modules whose commands all relate to the same function. But we are also looking for modules with low coupling, that is, modules relatively independent of the output from another module. Span of control means the number of submodules for which a module is responsible.

## VOCABULARY

terminal symbol
input/output (I/O)
    symbol
variable
automatic-destroy-
    read-in
non-automatic-destroy-
    read-out
process symbol
predefined process
    symbol
decision symbol
connector symbol
flowline
structured
    programming
Dijkstra
GOTOless
    programming
sequence structure
selection structure
repetition structure
step-wise refinement
top-down design

modular design
    (modular
    programming)
module
Harlan Mills
standard program
    design
START-UP module
PROCESS-RECORD
WRAP-UP module
END-FLAG
DETAIL-
    CALCULATION
    module
DETAIL-LINE module
READ-FILE module
program switch
control variable
EOF or end-of-file
cohesion
coupling
control coupling
span of control
open files module
initialize module

## EXERCISES/QUESTIONS

**True-False:**

Write T next to each true statement. Write F next to each false statement.

———— 1. In a flowchart, the terminal symbol is used to indicate a stopping point only.

———— 2. The selection structure is sometimes called the If . . . Then . . . Else, or decision structure.

———— 3. The repetition structure is sometimes referred to as the DoWhile.

———— 4. Structures may have several entry points but only one exit.

———— 5. The predefined process block indicates that the commands are found elsewhere.

———— 6. Structured programming usually prohibits the use of the GOTO command.

———— 7. The main idea of modular programming is to allow the programmer a shortcut for finishing sooner.

———— 8. When a second record is read, the image of this second record replaces, or overlays, the image of the first record.

———— 9. Decision symbols always provide for two or more alternative paths of execution or transfer of control.

———— 10. A program switch is often associated with the repetition structure.

**Fill-in-the Blanks:**
Label the symbols in Figure 2.35 by placing the symbol name in the blank provided.

---

## PROBLEMS

**2-1.** Produce a hierarchy chart, a structured flowchart, and pseudocode to generate the Sales Commission Report shown in Figure 2.36. The input record layout is presented in Figure 2.37. The commission is calculated as 3% of sales.

---

**2-2.** Produce a hierarchy chart, a structured flowchart, and pseudocode to generate the Sales Analysis Report shown in Figure 2.38. The input record layout is presented in Figure 2.39. Sales is computed as Quantity multiplied by Unit Price. The Discount is 3% of Sales. The Net Sales is computed as Sales-Discount.

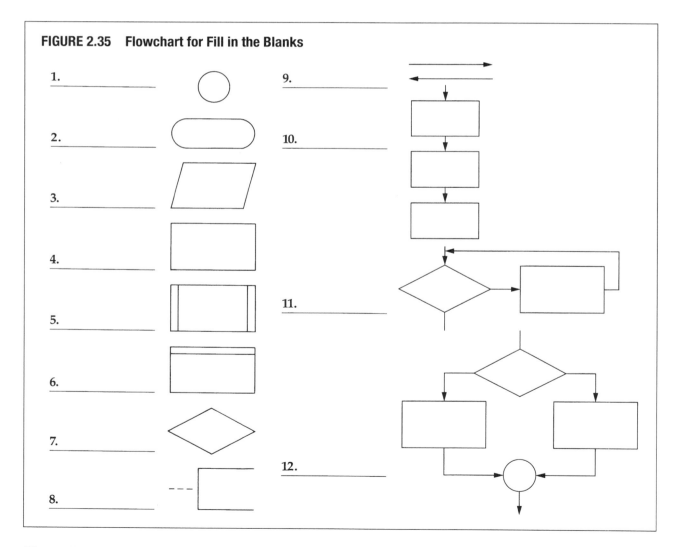

**FIGURE 2.35    Flowchart for Fill in the Blanks**

1. _____
2. _____
3. _____
4. _____
5. _____
6. _____
7. _____
8. _____
9. _____
10. _____
11. _____
12. _____

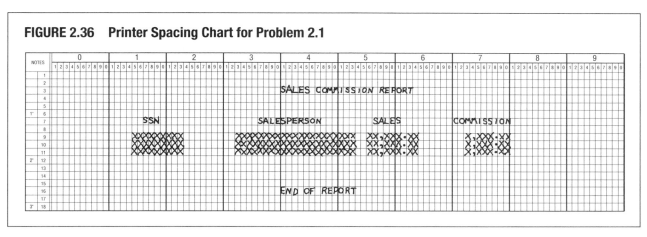

**FIGURE 2.36    Printer Spacing Chart for Problem 2.1**

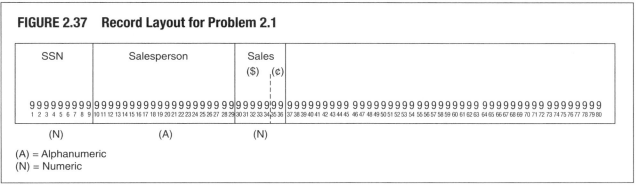

**FIGURE 2.37    Record Layout for Problem 2.1**

(A) = Alphanumeric
(N) = Numeric

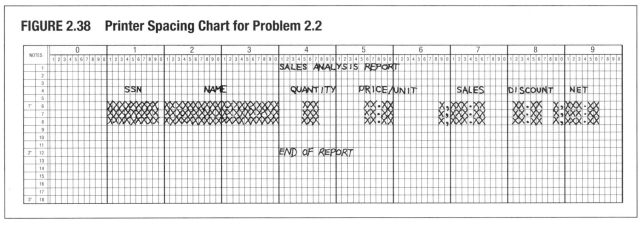

**FIGURE 2.38    Printer Spacing Chart for Problem 2.2**

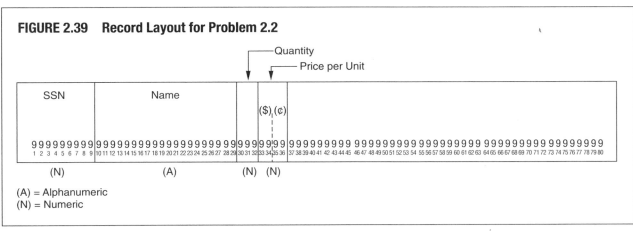

**FIGURE 2.39    Record Layout for Problem 2.2**

(A) = Alphanumeric
(N) = Numeric

**2-3.** ACE Savings and Loan wishes to generate a report listing the loan number, customer, number of payments, principal, annual interest rate, and the maturity value. The maturity value of the note is calculated as the principal of the note multiplied by (1 + Annual Interest Rate) raised to an exponent that is equal to the number of yearly payments. Draw a hierarchy chart, flowchart, and pseudocode for this problem. A sample report is shown below. For example on the third detail line we see the principal amount of 1000 which is multiplied by 1.331 (which is 1 + .10)$^3$. The maturity value is thus equal to \$1331.00. To notate exponents on flowcharts or pseudocode, you may use either the carat $^\wedge$ or the ** double asterisk. Example: I**2 means $I^2$ or I^2 is $I^2$.

**Input Record Format**

| Field | Type | Column |
|---|---|---|
| Loan-Number | N | 1–5 |
| Cust-Name | A/N | 6–25 |
| Principal | N | 26–32 ($$$$$.¢¢) |
| Annual-Int-Rate | N | 33–35 (.XXX) |
| No-of-Paymts | N | 36–37 |

```
                        ACE SAVINGS AND LOAN
                 MATURITY AMOUNTS ON CUSTOMER NOTES
     LOAN          CUSTOMER        PRINCIPAL      ANNUAL        NUMBER OF      MATURITY
    NUMBER           NAME           AMOUNT       INTEREST        ANNUAL         AMOUNT
                                                  RATE         PAYMENTS
    XXXXX        XXXXXXXXXXXX      XXXXX.XX        XX.X%           XX         XXXXXX.XX
    XXXXX        XXXXXXXXXXXX      XXXXX.XX        XX.X%           XX         XXXXXX.XX
    03468        JOHN ROBINSON     1000.00        10.0%            3          1331.00
    98765        SUE JOHNSON       5000.00        10.0%            1          5500.00
```

**2-4.** Art Briles, Head Coach of the 1990 Region I Texas Football Quarter Final Champions wishes to produce a report that lists his opponents and vital statistics about each one. Draw the flowchart for the report shown below. The Total Yards is the sum of Total Yards Rushing plus the Total Yards Passing. The Net Yards Gained is simply the difference in the Total Yards and the Defensive Yards Allowed.

**Input Record Format**

| Field | Type | Column |
|---|---|---|
| School | A/N | 1–8 |
| Coach | A/N | 9–15 |
| Set | A/N | 16–23 |
| Yds-Rush | N | 24–27 |
| Yds-Pass | N | 28–31 |
| Def-Yds-Allowed | N | 32–35 |

```
                  STEPHENVILLE HIGH SCHOOL FOOTBALL REPORT
                       OPPONENT STATISTICS FOR SEASON
  SCHOOL      COACH      OFFENSIVE     YARDS       YARDS      TOTAL     DEFENSIVE    NET YARDS
                            SET       RUSHING     PASSING     YARDS    YARDS ALWD     GAINED
  BRNWOOD    JOHNSON     PRO           3000        2000       5000       4000         1000
  EVERMAN    BALES       WISHBONE      2500        4000       6500       4500         2000
  GRANBURY   JONES       PRO           2000        2000       4000       6000        -2000
  BURK       HICKS       I             4000        3000       7000       1000         6000
  SVILLE     BRILES      PRO           3500        4000       7500       1000         6500
  XXXXXXXX   XXXXX       XXXXXXXX      XXXX        XXXX       XXXX       XXXX         XXXX
  XXXXXXXX   XXXXX       XXXXXXXX      XXXX        XXXX       XXXX       XXXX         XXXX
```

# 3

# Accumulating and Printing Final Totals

## OBJECTIVES

As a result of having read and studied this chapter, the student will be able to design the program logic to:

1. Accumulate grand totals.

2. Increment an accumulator (or counter) by a constant value.

3. Perform calculations in the WRAP-UP module.

4. Print final totals and WRAP-UP calculations.

## INTRODUCTION

Often reports will contain **final** (or grand) **totals** that represent the summation of the values in a column of numbers. For example, a report for a teacher who wishes to know the class average on a given test requires the accumulation of individual test scores and the number of students in the class. A manager may request a report that lists individual sales amounts for each salesperson and, at the end of the report, prints the final total of each sales representative's sales amounts.

# A Test Results Program with Multiple Totals

## Program Requirements

A teacher wishes to produce a test results report similar to the one depicted in Figure 2.19 except that he or she also wishes to know the class average and the total number of students. First, the student number, name, test 1, test 2, test 3, and test average for each student are to print on the detail lines. Afterwards, a **total line** is to print with the class average and the total number of students.

## Output Design

In Exhibit 3.1, panel A illustrates the sample report that is to be produced, and panel B depicts the associated printer spacing chart.

## Input Design

Exhibit 3.2 shows the input record format. The input record layout sheet shows the locations of student number (the last four digits of the student's SSN), student name, test 1, test 2, and test 3 in record positions 1–4, 5–19, 20–22, 23–25, and 26–28, respectively. All fields on the record are numeric except the name. The letter N below the field indicates the field is numeric, and the letter A below the field indicates the field is either alphabetic or alphanumeric.

## Test Cases

The test cases (sample records) used to determine if the computer program executes properly are illustrated in Exhibit 3.3.

---

**EXHIBIT 3.1    Output Design**

**Panel A—Sample Report**

```
                              TEST   RESULTS

        SN                NAME          TEST 1     TEST 2    TEST 3       AVERAGE

        21        JOHN                    80         90       100           90
        36        SALLY                   90         95       100           95
        39        BOB                     90         90        90           90
        60        DON                     70         80        90           80


        TOTAL STUDENTS    4                                CLASS AVERAGE 88.75

                              END OF REPORT
```

**Panel B—Printer Spacing Chart**

## Logic Considerations

So that a **total line** can print with the class average, it is necessary to add the individual student's test score average to an **accumulator.** An accumulator is a memory area for the purpose of adding, or accumulating, a total. Prior to use in a program, this memory area should be initialized to zeros. At the end of the program, the contents of the accumulator (the total of the averages) will be divided by the total number of students and the result (the class average) printed on the report.

This brings us around to the question, "How do we know the number of students?" For any particular execution of the program, we could predetermine the number of students in the class and divide by this constant value. This would certainly work for a *constant* class size, but what happens when the class size changes? What if some students drop out and others join the class? How can we make our computer program divide the accumulated averages by the value that represents the true class size? Assuming that each separate record in the file represents a student, we can reduce the task to the process of simply counting the records. How? By simply adding the value 1 to an accumulator after each record is read. When it's used to count the occurrence of something, it is often referred to as a **counter.** Let's take a look at what must take place in the computer in order to cause accumulation.

## THE ACCUMULATION PROCESS

Exhibit 3.4 (Panel A) illustrates the step-by-step procedure for accumulating the total of the individual student test averages. As mentioned, this total is an intermediate total to be used in calculating the class average. Before processing occurs for the first record, the accumulator variable is initialized to zero (see step 1). When using most compilers, such as COBOL, for example, the programmer must ensure that the accumulators are cleared to zero.

After record 1 is read and the average is calculated for this record, step 2 from Exhibit 3.4 shows the student's average (AVG) added to the grand total (TOTAL-AVG). At this point, TOTAL-AVG is equal to 090.

After record 2 is read and the average calculated, step 3 adds the second average to the grand total (TOTAL-AVG). Now TOTAL-AVG equals 185. Steps 4 and 5 repeat the procedure for record 3 and record 4. Panel B of Exhibit 3.4 also illustrates this process in a tabular format.

The second part of the accumulation process in this program counts the number of records as previously described. As you recall, each record in the file represents an individual student, and the sum can be determined by simply adding the constant value 1 to the total every time a record is read. This total is called TOT-STUDENTS. Exhibit 3.5 (Panel A) shows this counting process. Note that before

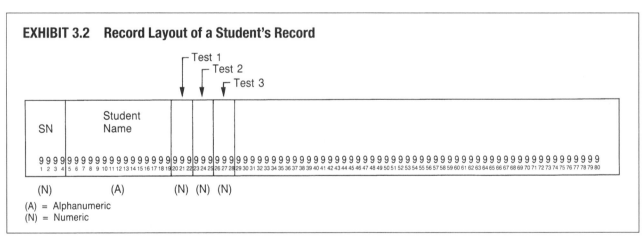

**EXHIBIT 3.2    Record Layout of a Student's Record**

(A) = Alphanumeric
(N) = Numeric

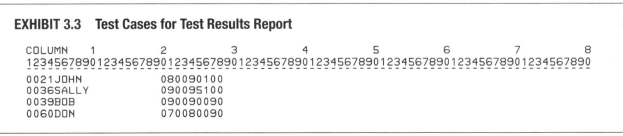

**EXHIBIT 3.3    Test Cases for Test Results Report**

```
COLUMN    1         2         3         4         5         6         7         8
12345678901234567890123456789012345678901234567890123456789012345678901234567890
0021JOHN           080090100
0036SALLY          090095100
0039BOB            090090090
0060DON            070080090
```

**EXHIBIT 3.4   Step-by-Step Accumulation of a Total**

Panel A

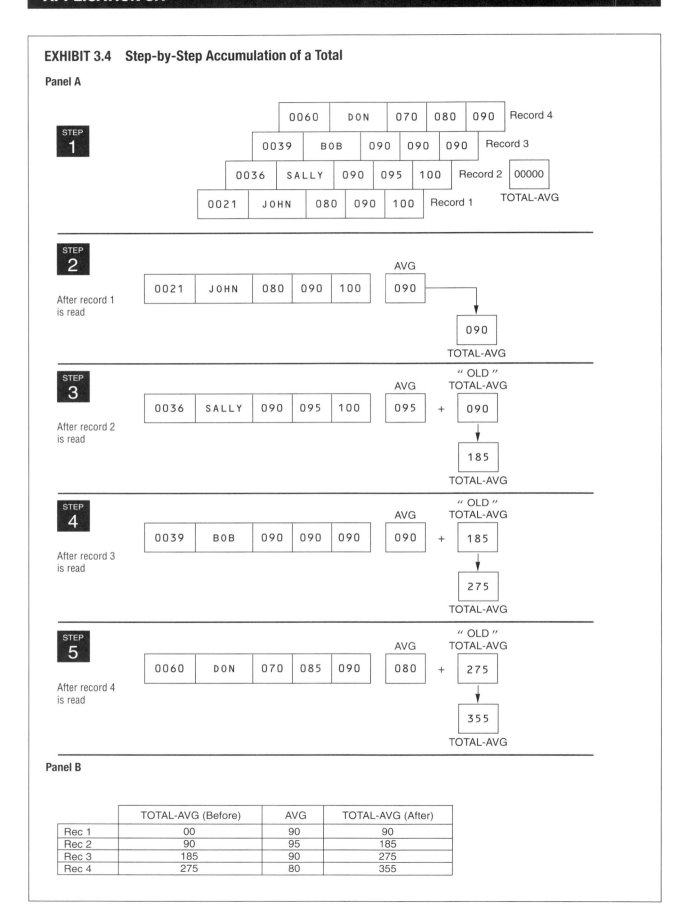

Panel B

|  | TOTAL-AVG (Before) | AVG | TOTAL-AVG (After) |
|---|---|---|---|
| Rec 1 | 00 | 90 | 90 |
| Rec 2 | 90 | 95 | 185 |
| Rec 3 | 185 | 90 | 275 |
| Rec 4 | 275 | 80 | 355 |

**EXHIBIT 3.5    Counting Records as They Are Read**

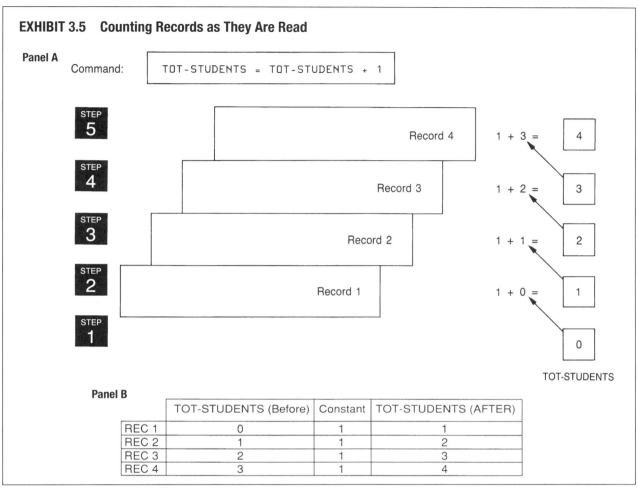

Panel A

Command:    `TOT-STUDENTS = TOT-STUDENTS + 1`

STEP 5    Record 4    1 + 3 =    4

STEP 4    Record 3    1 + 2 =    3

STEP 3    Record 2    1 + 1 =    2

STEP 2    Record 1    1 + 0 =    1

STEP 1    0

TOT-STUDENTS

Panel B

|        | TOT-STUDENTS (Before) | Constant | TOT-STUDENTS (AFTER) |
|--------|-----------------------|----------|----------------------|
| REC 1  | 0                     | 1        | 1                    |
| REC 2  | 1                     | 1        | 2                    |
| REC 3  | 2                     | 1        | 3                    |
| REC 4  | 3                     | 1        | 4                    |

**EXHIBIT 3.6    The Calculation of a Class Average**

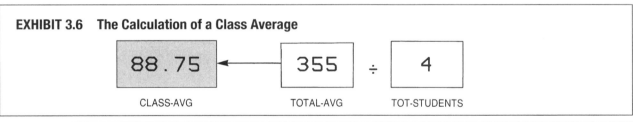

88.75    ←    355    ÷    4

CLASS-AVG        TOTAL-AVG        TOT-STUDENTS

**EXHIBIT 3.7    Transferring and Printing the Contents of the Accumulators on the Total Line**

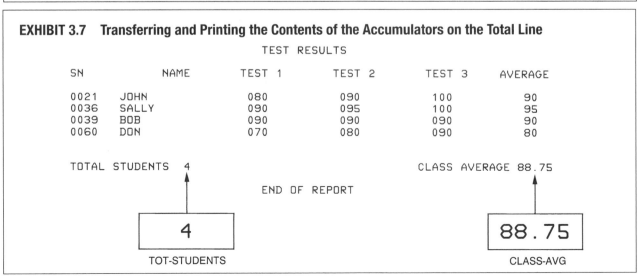

```
                         TEST RESULTS

SN           NAME        TEST 1      TEST 2      TEST 3     AVERAGE

0021    JOHN             080         090         100          90
0036    SALLY            090         095         100          95
0039    BOB              090         090         090          90
0060    DON              070         080         090          80


TOTAL STUDENTS   4                               CLASS AVERAGE 88.75

                         END OF REPORT
```

4

TOT-STUDENTS

88.75

CLASS-AVG

the first record is read, the variable called TOT-STUDENTS is equal to zero. Panel B also shows the process in tabular form.

Notice also that the new contents of the accumulator called TOT-STUDENTS becomes the old contents for the subsequent step in Exhibit 3.5.

Finally, after all records are read and END-FLAG is encountered, the next step is to calculate the class average. Exhibit 3.6 illustrates this procedure. This calculation divides the accumulator TOT-STUDENT into the accumulator TOTAL-AVG. The quotient (answer) is then placed in a variable called CLASS-AVG.

On the last line of the report, the contents of the variables TOT-STUDENTS and CLASS-AVG are to be printed. Exhibit 3.7 depicts the contents of these two accumulators being moved to the appropriate output print line prior to printout.

## Program Design

Now that you have an idea of what the computer needs to do, let's develop the programming logic to tell the computer how to produce the accumulations we need. Descriptions of the individual modules follow.

**Hierarchy Chart.** The MAIN-LINE routine will remain virtually constant throughout this text, and the second-level modules (START-UP, PROCESS-RECORD, and WRAP-UP) will only occasionally contain small changes. The hierarchy chart in Exhibit 3.8 depicts the general design of the program. The PROCESS-RECORD module decomposes into four separate submodules: (1) DETAIL-CALCULA-TION, (2) ACCUMULATION, (3) DETAIL-LINE,

and (4) READ-FILE. The modules, SUMMARY-CALC, SUMMARY-OUTPUT, and CLOSE-FILES make up the WRAP-UP Module.

**Structured Program Flowchart.** The structured program flowchart in Exhibit 3.9 shows the program design in greater detail. Comparing this flowchart with the one developed in Chapter 2, you'll note that the initializing of the two accumulators to zero in the START-UP module is the only modification required in this module. Initialization is analogous to pressing the clear button on a calculator prior to adding a column of numbers.

The PROCESS-RECORD module looks almost the same as before, but now it includes an accumulation module. Once the DETAIL-CALCULATION process of computing the average (AVG) is done, the task of accumulation should be assigned to a module by itself. Since accumulation is present in a great number of programming applications and, in some cases, constitutes a major portion of a program's logic development, it's a good idea to set this process apart from any other processing activity. The invoking (calling) of the accumulation module follows the DETAIL-CALCULATION call. Logically, though, it would not matter if it were placed after the DETAIL-LINE module.

The accumulation process is further subdivided into two events: adding AVG to TOTAL-AVG and adding 1 to TOT-STUDENTS.

The DETAIL-LINE and READ-FILE modules remain the same as the ones in Chapter 2. The DETAIL-LINE module again handles the transfer of data to the detail line and the printing of the line. The READ-FILE module causes the reading of the next record.

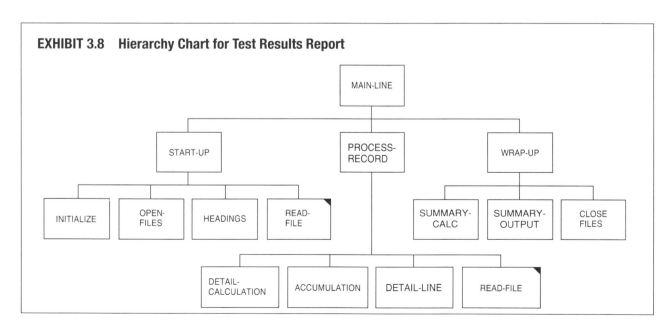

**EXHIBIT 3.8 Hierarchy Chart for Test Results Report**

You'll note that all four of the submodules in the PROCESS-RECORD module are themselves predefined modules, which means that the actual code for these functions is found elsewhere. The programming technique that establishes the PROCESS-RECORD module as a driving module that simply calls other lower-level modules is partly based on the concept of step-wise refinement. The other reason is that in this position it provides a pattern, or template, for solving busi-

**EXHIBIT 3.9  Structured Flowchart for Test Results Report**

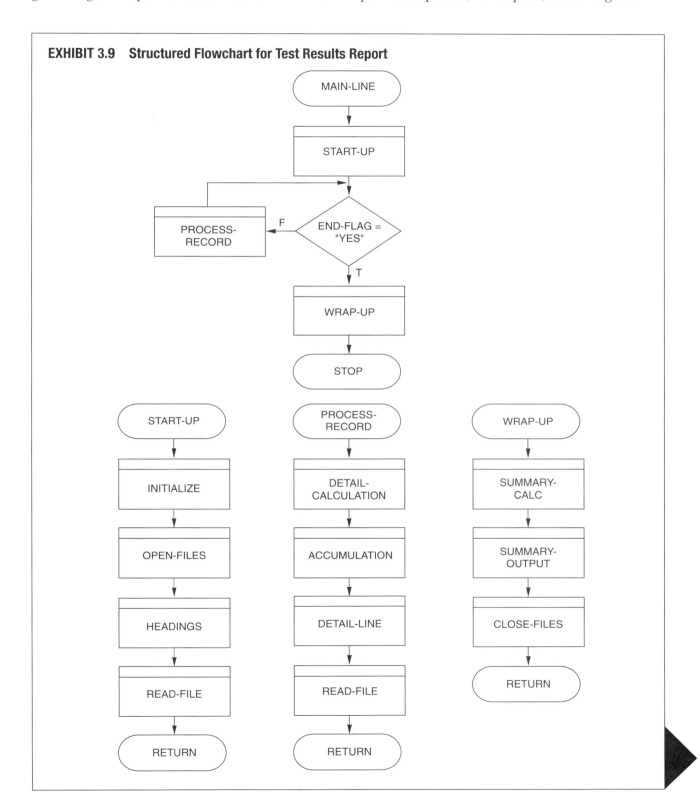

ness problems with a computer. The next program we write and the next one after that will very likely include the four major functions of (1) detail calculations, (2) accumulation, (3) detail line, and (4) read next record. If we invoke separate modules designed for these specific purposes, the programmer is more likely to remember to develop the logic for each function, just as a list helps one remember to perform certain household chores. In subsequent programs that illustrate more advanced programming concepts, additional submodules will be added to the PROCESS-RECORD module; but in

**EXHIBIT 3.9 (Cont.)**

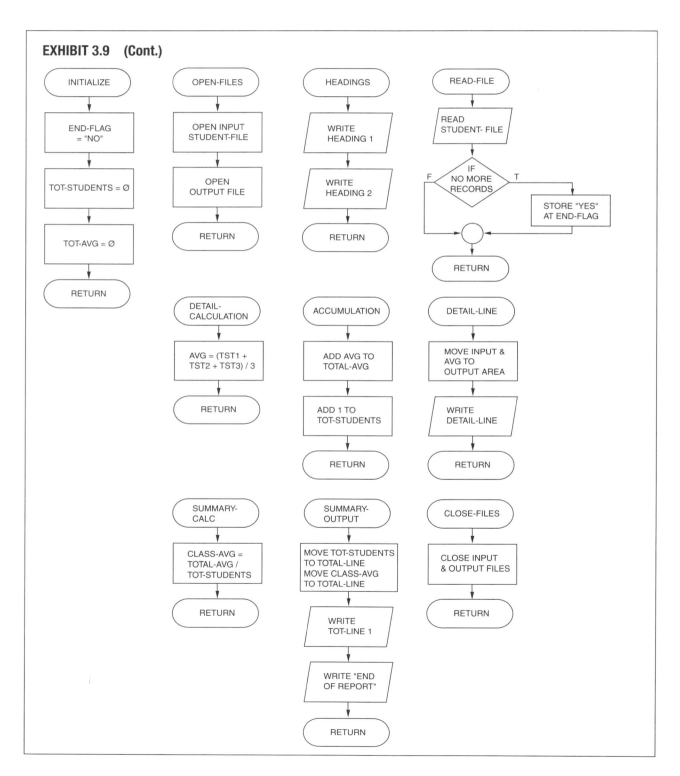

many cases, the four submodules previously mentioned will reappear.

The WRAP-UP module includes a computation to divide TOT-STUDENTS into TOTAL-AVG, yielding a quotient called CLASS-AVG. The contents of TOT-STUDENTS and TOTAL-AVG are then moved into their respective output fields and printed on the first total line. The message END OF REPORT is then moved and printed and the files are closed.

**Pseudocode.**   Exhibit 3.10 depicts the necessary pseudocode for the student grade report with total lines.

**Program Development.**   Exhibits 3.11 and 3.12 are the associated COBOL 85 and QUICKBASIC programs, respectively.

---

**EXHIBIT 3.10    Pseudocode for Application 3.1**

```
*mainline
    start-up
    dowhile end-flag = "no"
        process-record
    enddo
    wrap-up
    stop
*start-up
    initialize
    open-files
    headings
    read-file
    return
*initialize
    set end-flag = "no"
    set tot-students = 0
    set tot-avg = 0
    return
*open-files
    open input student-file
    open output file
    return
*headings
    advance to top of page
    write page heading
    write field headings
    return
*read-file
    read student-file
    when no more records set end-flag = "yes"
    endread
    return
```

```
*process-record
    detail-calculation
    accumulation
    detail-line
    read-file
    return
*detail-calculation
    calculate avg = (tst1 + tst2 + tst3) / 3
    return
*accumulation
    add avg to the TOT-AVG
    add 1 to tot-students
    return
*detail-line
    transfer input fields and avg to output fields
    write the detail-line
    return
*wrap-up
    summary-calc
    summary-output
    return
*summary-calc
    calculate class-avg = TOT-AVG / tot-students
    close files
    return
*summary-output
    move class-avg to the total print line
    move tot-students to the total print line
    write total line
    close files
    return
```

**EXHIBIT 3.11    COBOL 85 Program for Application 3.1**

```
1          IDENTIFICATION DIVISION.
2          PROGRAM-ID. CH3APL1.
3
4         ****ANS COBOL 85****
5
6         * REMARKS:    THIS PROGRAM PRODUCES A TEST RESULTS REPORT FROM
7         *             A  GRADE FILE.  SPECIAL PROCESSING INCLUDES:
8         *                1) COUNT OF STUDENT RECORDS PROCESSED
9         *                2) CLASS AVERAGE.
10
11         ENVIRONMENT DIVISION.
12
13         CONFIGURATION SECTION.
14
15         SOURCE-COMPUTER.  CYBER.
16         OBJECT-COMPUTER.  CYBER.
17
18         INPUT-OUTPUT SECTION.
19
20         FILE-CONTROL.
21
22             SELECT STUDENT-FILE ASSIGN TO DTA31.
23             SELECT STUDENT-REPORT ASSIGN TO OUTFILE.
24
25
26         DATA DIVISION.
27
28         FILE SECTION.
29
30         FD   STUDENT-FILE.
31
32         01   STUDENT-REC.
33
34             05 SN                      PIC 9(4).
35             05 NAME                    PIC X(15).
36             05 TEST1                   PIC 999.
37             05 TEST2                   PIC 999.
38             05 TEST3                   PIC 999.
39
40
41         FD   STUDENT-REPORT.
42
43         01   REPORT-REC               PIC X(133).
44
45
46         WORKING-STORAGE SECTION.
47
48         01   END-FLAG                 PIC XXX VALUE "NO".
49         01   TOT-AVG                  PIC 999 VALUE ZERO.
50         01   TOT-STUDENTS             PIC 999 VALUE ZERO.
51         01   CLASS-AVG                PIC 999V99.
52         01   TEST-AVG                 PIC 999.
53
54
55         01   PAGE-HEADING.
56
57             05                        PIC X(40) VALUE SPACES.
58             05                        PIC X(13) VALUE "TEST RESULTS".
59             05                        PIC X(79) VALUE SPACES.
60
61         01   COLUMN-HEADING.
62
63             05                        PIC X(14) VALUE SPACES.
64             05                        PIC XX    VALUE "SN".
65             05                        PIC X(13) VALUE SPACES.
66             05                        PIC X(4)  VALUE "NAME".
```

**EXHIBIT 3.11  (Cont.)**

```
 67            05                              PIC X(11) VALUE SPACES.
 68            05                              PIC X(6)  VALUE "TEST 1".
 69            05                              PIC X(5)  VALUE SPACES.
 70            05                              PIC X(6)  VALUE "TEST 2".
 71            05                              PIC X(4)  VALUE SPACES.
 72            05                              PIC X(6)  VALUE "TEST 3".
 73            05                              PIC X(6)  VALUE SPACES.
 74            05                              PIC X(7)  VALUE "AVERAGE".
 75            05                              PIC X(38) VALUE SPACES.
 76
 77     01  DETAIL-LINE.
 78
 79            05                              PIC X(13) VALUE SPACE.
 80            05 SN-OUT                       PIC ZZZ9.
 81            05                              PIC X(5)  VALUE SPACES.
 82            05 NAME-OUT                     PIC X(15).
 83            05                              PIC X(8)  VALUE SPACES.
 84            05 TEST1-OUT                    PIC Z99.
 85            05                              PIC X(8)  VALUE SPACES.
 86            05 TEST2-OUT                    PIC Z99.
 87            05                              PIC X(7)  VALUE SPACES.
 88            05 TEST3-OUT                    PIC Z99.
 89            05                              PIC X(10) VALUE SPACES.
 90            05 TEST-AVG-OUT                 PIC Z99.
 91            05                              PIC X(50) VALUE SPACES.
 92
 93     01  TOTAL-LINE.
 94
 95            05                              PIC X(13) VALUE SPACES.
 96            05                              PIC X(15) VALUE "TOTAL STUDENTS".
 97            05 TOT-STUDENTS-OUT             PIC ZZ9.
 98            05                              PIC X(35) VALUE SPACES.
 99            05                              PIC X(13) VALUE "CLASS AVERAGE".
100            05 CLASS-AVG-OUT               PIC ZZ9.99.
101            05                              PIC X(48) VALUE SPACES.
102
103     /
104      PROCEDURE DIVISION.
105
106      000-MAINLINE.
107
108          PERFORM 100-START-UP.
109          PERFORM 200-PROCESS-RECORD UNTIL END-FLAG = "YES".
110          PERFORM 300-WRAP-UP.
111          STOP RUN.
112
113      100-START-UP.
114
115    *     INITIALIZE VARIABLES (WORKING-STORAGE SECTION)
116          PERFORM 105-OPEN-FILES.
117          PERFORM 110-HEADINGS.
118          PERFORM 120-READ-FILE.
119
120      105-OPEN-FILES.
121
122          OPEN INPUT STUDENT-FILE.
123          OPEN OUTPUT STUDENT-REPORT.
124
125
126      110-HEADINGS.
127
128          WRITE REPORT-REC FROM PAGE-HEADING AFTER ADVANCING PAGE.
129          WRITE REPORT-REC FROM COLUMN-HEADING AFTER ADVANCING 2 LINES.
130          MOVE SPACES TO REPORT-REC.
131          WRITE REPORT-REC.
132
```

**EXHIBIT 3.11   (Cont.)**

```
133          120-READ-FILE.
134
135              READ STUDENT-FILE AT END MOVE "YES" TO END-FLAG.
136
137          200-PROCESS.
138
139              PERFORM 210-DETAIL-CALCULATION.
140              PERFORM 220-ACCUMULATION.
141              PERFORM 230-DETAIL-LINE.
142              PERFORM 120-READ-FILE.
143
144          210-DETAIL-CALCULATION.
145
146              COMPUTE TEST-AVG ROUNDED = (TEST1 + TEST2 + TEST3) / 3.
147
148          220-ACCUMULATION.
149
150              ADD TEST-AVG TO TOT-AVG.
151              ADD 1 TO TOT-STUDENTS.
152
153          230-DETAIL-LINE.
154
155              MOVE SN TO SN-OUT.
156              MOVE NAME TO NAME-OUT.
157              MOVE TEST1 TO TEST1-OUT.
158              MOVE TEST2 TO TEST2-OUT.
159              MOVE TEST3 TO TEST3-OUT.
160              MOVE TEST-AVG TO TEST-AVG-OUT.
161              WRITE REPORT-REC FROM DETAIL-LINE.
162
163
164
165          300-WRAP-UP.
166
167              PERFORM 310-SUMMARY-CALC.
168              PERFORM 320-SUMMARY-OUTPUT.
169              PERFORM 330-CLOSE-FILES.
170
171          310-SUMMARY-CALC.
172
173              COMPUTE CLASS-AVG ROUNDED = TOT-AVG / TOT-STUDENTS.
174
175          320-SUMMARY-OUTPUT.
176
177              MOVE TOT-STUDENTS TO TOT-STUDENTS-OUT.
178              MOVE CLASS-AVG TO CLASS-AVG-OUT.
179              WRITE REPORT-REC FROM TOTAL-LINE AFTER ADVANCING 3 LINES.
180              MOVE "                                      END OF REPORT"
181                  TO REPORT-REC.
182              WRITE REPORT-REC AFTER ADVANCING 2 LINES.
183
184          330-CLOSE-FILES.
185
186              CLOSE STUDENT-FILE  STUDENT-REPORT.

    **** NO DIAGNOSTICS
total cp time (in microsec) = 1015541    822347    193194
```

**EXHIBIT 3.11    (Cont.)**

```
                        TEST RESULTS

SN              NAME          TEST 1    TEST 2    TEST 3      AVERAGE

  21      JOHN                  80        90       100          90
  36      SALLY                 90        95       100          95
  39      BOB                   90        90        90          90
  60      DON                   70        80        90          80


TOTAL STUDENTS    4                               CLASS AVERAGE 88.75

                        END OF REPORT
```

**EXHIBIT 3.12    Quick BASIC Program and Output for Application 3.1**

```basic
'*********************************************************************
'*                 PROGRAM IDENTIFICATION                          *
'*********************************************************************
'* PROGRAM NAME: CH3APL1                                           *
'* REMARKS: THIS PROGRAM PRODUCES A TEST RESULTS REPORT FROM A GRADE *
'*          FILE.  SPECIAL PROCESSING INCLUDES:                    *
'*             1) COUNT OF STUDENT RECORDS PROCESSED               *
'*             2) CLASS AVERAGE                                    *
'*********************************************************************
'*                      MAIN-LINE                                  *
'*********************************************************************

   GOSUB STARTUP                        'PERFORM START-UP          *
   DO UNTIL END.FLAG$ = "YES"
      GOSUB PROCESS.RECORD              'PERFORM PROCESS-RECORD    *
   LOOP
   GOSUB WRAPUP                         'PERFORM WRAP-UP           *
   END
      '*********************************************************************
      '*                    START-UP                                  *
      '*********************************************************************

STARTUP:

   GOSUB INITIALIZE
   GOSUB OPEN.FILES
   GOSUB HEADINGS                       'PERFORM HEADINGS          *
   GOSUB READ.FILE                      'PERFORM READ-FILE         *
   RETURN
```

**EXHIBIT 3.12    (Cont.)**

```
'*********************************************************************
'*                          INITIALIZE                          *
'*********************************************************************

INITIALIZE:

    WIDTH LPRINT 132
    DETAIL.LINE$ = "            ####        \            \      ###      ###      ###      ###"
    TOT.STUDENT = 0
    TOT.AVE = 0
    END.FLAG$ = "NO"
    RETURN

        '*****************************************************************
        '*                      OPEN.FILES                  *              *
        '*****************************************************************
OPEN.FILES:
        OPEN "I", #1, "CH3ILL1.DAT"
        RETURN

        '*****************************************************************
        '*                      HEADINGS                    *
        '*****************************************************************

HEADINGS:

    LPRINT CHR$(12)
    LPRINT TAB(41); "TEST  RESULTS"
    LPRINT
    LPRINT TAB(15); "SN"; TAB(31); "NAME"; TAB(45); "TEST 1"; TAB(56); "TEST 2"; TAB(66); "TEST 3"; TAB(78); "AVERAGE"
    LPRINT
    RETURN


    REM ***************************************************************
    REM *                      READ-FILE                        *
    REM ***************************************************************
READ.FILE:

    INPUT #1, SN, STD.NAME$, TST1, TST2, TST3
    IF STD.NAME$ = "EOF" THEN
        END.FLAG$ = "YES"
    END IF
    RETURN

        '*****************************************************************
        '*                      PROCESS-RECORD                  *
        '*****************************************************************
PROCESS.RECORD:

    GOSUB DETAIL.CALCULATION        'PERFORM DETAIL-CALCULATION    *
    GOSUB ACCUMULATION              'PERFORM ACCUMULATION          *
    GOSUB DETAIL.LINE               'PERFORM DETAIL-LINE           *
    GOSUB READ.FILE                 'PERFORM READ-FILE             *
    RETURN
```

**EXHIBIT 3.12    (Cont.)**

```
'********************************************************************
'*                        DETAIL-CALCULATION                       *
'********************************************************************


DETAIL.CALCULATION:

    AVG = (TST1 + TST2 + TST3) / 3
    RETURN


    '********************************************************************
    '*                          ACCUMULATION                          *
    '********************************************************************


ACCUMULATION:

    TOT.AVE = TOT.AVE + AVG
    TOT.STUDENT = TOT.STUDENT + 1
    RETURN


    '********************************************************************
    '*                          DETAIL-LINE                           *
    '********************************************************************


DETAIL.LINE:

    LPRINT USING DETAIL.LINE$; SN; STD.NAME$; TST1; TST2; TST3; AVG
    RETURN


    '********************************************************************
    '*                            WRAP-UP                             *
    '********************************************************************


WRAPUP:

    GOSUB SUMMARY.CALC
    GOSUB SUMMARY.OUTPUT
    GOSUB CLOSE.FILES
    RETURN


    '********************************************************************
    '*                          SUMMARY-CALC                          *
    '********************************************************************


SUMMARY.CALC:

    CLASS.AVE = TOT.AVE / TOT.STUDENT
    RETURN
```

**EXHIBIT 3.12   (Cont.)**

```
'*********************************************************************
'*                          SUMMARY-OUTPUT                          *
'*********************************************************************

SUMMARY.OUTPUT:

    LPRINT : LPRINT
    LPRINT TAB(14); "TOTAL STUDENTS   "; TOT.STUDENT; TAB(67); "CLASS AVERAGE"; CLASS.AVE
    LPRINT
    LPRINT TAB(41); "END OF REPORT"
    RETURN


'*********************************************************************
'*                           CLOSE-FILES                            *
'*********************************************************************

CLOSE.FILES:

    CLOSE
    RETURN
```

---

                            TEST   RESULTS

| SN | NAME | TEST 1 | TEST 2 | TEST 3 | AVERAGE |
|----|------|--------|--------|--------|---------|
| 21 | JOHN | 80 | 90 | 100 | 90 |
| 36 | SALLY | 90 | 95 | 100 | 95 |
| 39 | BOB | 90 | 90 | 90 | 90 |
| 60 | DON | 70 | 80 | 90 | 80 |

TOTAL STUDENTS   4                              CLASS AVERAGE 88.75

                    END OF REPORT

## A Sales Report with Multiple Totals

More often than not, reports contain a plurality of totals. So let's consider a typical programming application.

### Program Requirements

The sales manager of a company wants to know how well her sales representatives are doing in selling a product. The report will list the name, weekly sales, and total monthly sales of each sales rep in the company. At the end of the report will be printed a total line that includes totals for each weekly column and monthly total column as well as a separate total line for the number of sales transactions and the average sales amounts for each salesperson.

### Output Design

Exhibit 3.13 shows the final report. The accompanying printer spacing chart is shown in Exhibit 3.14.

---

### EXHIBIT 3.13 Sales Analysis Report with Total Lines

```
                      ACME COMPANY
                 SALES ANALYSIS REPORT

SALES REP         WEEK 1    WEEK 2    WEEK 3    WEEK 4   MONTHLY TOTAL

JOHN JOHNSON      1,000     2,000     1,000     3,000       7,000
BILLY DICKSON     2,000     1,000     3,000     2,000       8,000
SUSAN GREEN       1,500     1,500     3,000     4,000      10,000
JANE BAKER        1,000     1,000     1,500     3,000       6,500

TOTAL             5,500     5,500     8,500    12,000      31,500

   NUMBER OF SALES          4
   SALESPERSON AVERAGE SALES   7,875

                    END OF REPORT
```

---

### EXHIBIT 3.14 Printer Spacing Chart for Sales Analysis Report

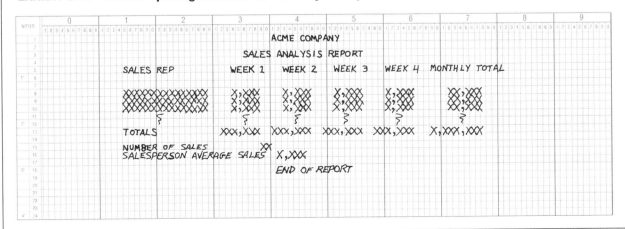

### Input Design

Exhibit 3.15 illustrates the various input fields of the sales file. The sales representative's name is found in positions 1 through 15, the four sales amounts are found in adjacent fields starting in position 16 and ending in position 31. Each weekly sales amount (whole dollars) is four positions in length and is numeric.

### Test Cases

Exhibit 3.16 depicts the test data for this program.

### Logic Considerations

In this problem application, the programmer must write a program that will accumulate grand totals for week 1, week 2, week 3, week 4, and monthly totals. Also, the total number of sales representatives will be needed at the end of the run in order to calculate their average sales; therefore, a counter is needed to hold this total.

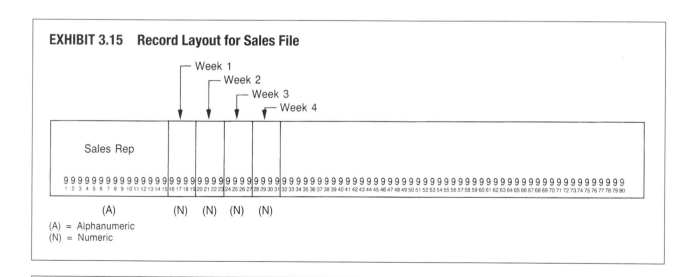

**EXHIBIT 3.15  Record Layout for Sales File**

**EXHIBIT 3.16  Test Data for Sales Analysis Program**

```
COLUMN     1          2          3          4          5          6          7          8
1234567890123456789012345678901234567890123456789012345678901234567890123456789 0
JOHN JOHNSON    1000200010003000
BILLY DICKSON   2000100030002000
SUSAN GREEN     1500150030004000
JANE BAKER      1000100015003000
```

## Program Design

**Hierarchy Chart.** The hierarchy chart shown in Exhibit 3.17 looks very similar to the one in Exhibit 3.8 for the test results report. Again, the big pieces of the puzzle remain the same. This problem requires a calculation for monthly sales, so the chart includes a detail-calculation module. Since several totals are to be printed on the report, an accumulation module will also be needed to handle the accumulation process.

**Structured Program Flowchart.** Exhibit 3.18 (see pgs. 74–75) displays the structured program flowchart logic for this problem. In the START-UP module, each of these accumulators will be initialized to zero before further processing takes place. The assignment command "TOT-WK1 = 0" assigns zeros to the variable. The PROCESS-RECORD module looks the same as it did in Exhibit 3.9 in the test results program. The DETAIL-CALCULATION submodule contains a computation (MONTHLY-SUM) to sum the four weekly sales amounts. The ACCUMULATION module includes the accumulation of grand totals for each of the weekly columns and the monthly sum. The first accumulation (TOT-WK1 = TOT-WK1 + WK1) says to add WK1 to TOT-WK1. The next accumulation says to add WK2 to TOT-WK2, etc. Also, the total number of employees is determined by adding 1 to an accumulator each time a record is processed (TOT-SALES-REP = TOT-SALES-REP + 1). The *logic* of the DETAIL-LINE and READ-FILE modules remains the same. The only differences in the DETAIL-LINE module are the names of the fields that are assigned and other variables that are to be moved to the print line area. The only difference in the READ-FILE module is the file name that is being read.

In the WRAP-UP module, the sales rep's sales average is computed by dividing TOT-SALES-REP into TOT-MONTHLY-SUM and placing the quotient in AVG-SALES. After the total calculation (a calculation made in the WRAP-UP module) is performed, the next steps print the three total lines. The first total line is prepared for writing by first moving TOT-WK1, TOT-WK2, TOT-WK3, TOT-WK4, and TOT-MONTHLY-SUM to the appropriate output print line area. Once the first print line is written, the next step moves the number of sales representatives (TOT-SALES-REP) to the appropriate print line area and writes the output. Next, AVG-SALES is moved to its respective output field of a print line and written. The "END OF REPORT" message is then printed on a line by itself, and the files are closed. Exhibit 3.19 shows the associated pseudocode for this problem.

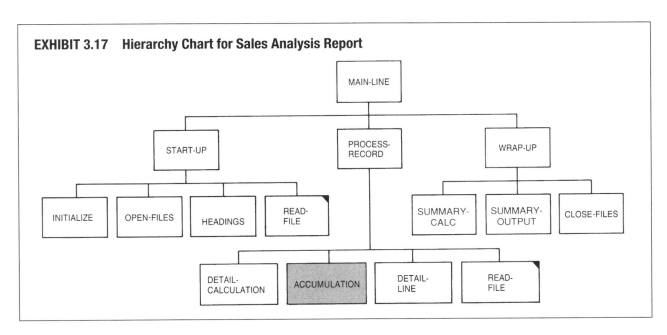

**EXHIBIT 3.17 Hierarchy Chart for Sales Analysis Report**

**EXHIBIT 3.18    Structured Flowchart for Sales Analysis Report**

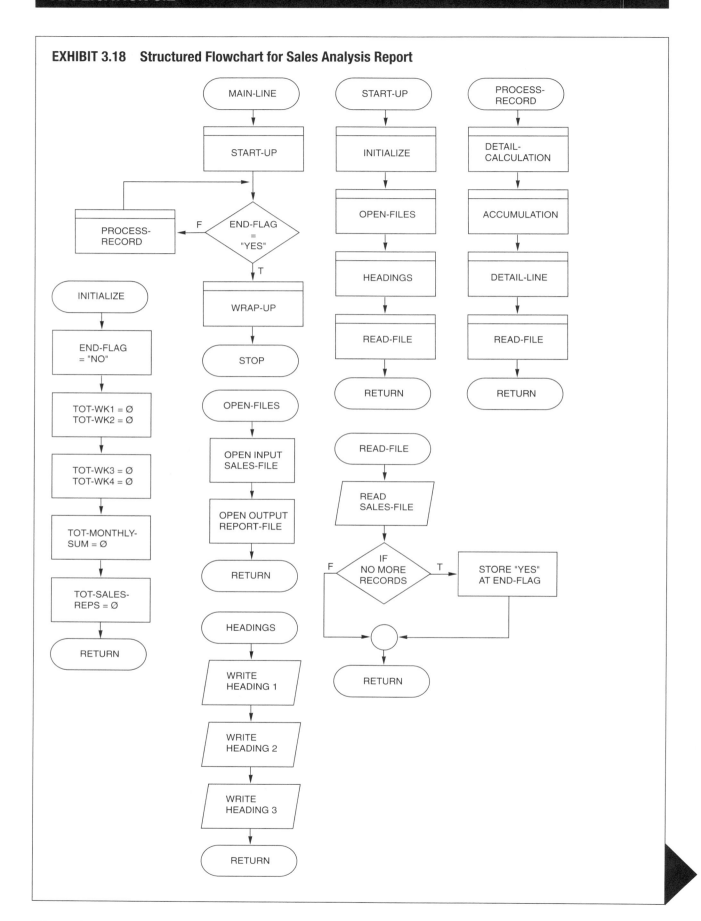

**EXHIBIT 3.18   (Cont.)**

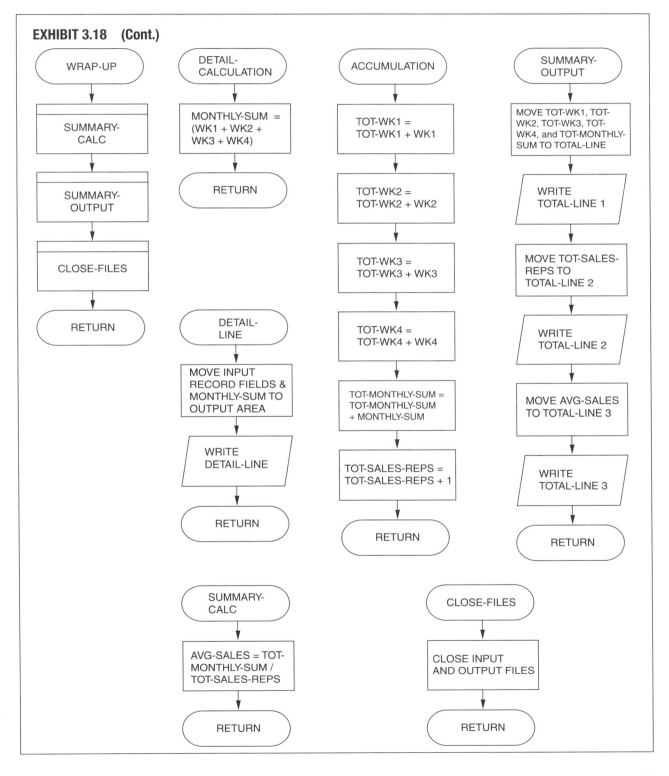

### EXHIBIT 3.19    Pseudocode for Application 3.2

*mainline
  start-up
  dowhile end-flag = "no"
    process-record
  enddo
  wrap-up
  stop
*start-up
  initialize
  open-files
  headings
  read-file
  return
*initialize
  set tot-wk1 = 0
  set tot-wk2 = 0
  set tot-wk3 = 0
  set tot-wk4 = 0
  set tot-sales-rep = 0
  return
*open-files
  open input file
  open output file
  return
*process-record
  detail-calculation
  accumulation
  detail-line
  read-sales-file
  return
*headings
  advance to top of the page
  write page headings
  write field headings
  return
*read-file
  read sales-file
  when no more records set end-flag = "yes"
  endread
  return

*detail-calculation
  calculate monthly-sum = (wk1+wk2+wk3+wk4)/4
  return
*accumulation
  tot-wk1 = tot-wk1 + wk1
  tot-wk2 = tot-wk2 + wk2
  tot-wk3 = tot-wk3 + wk3
  tot-wk4 = tot-wk4 + wk4
  tot-monthly-sum = tot-monthly-sum + monthly-sum
  tot-sales-rep = tot-sales-rep + 1
  return
*detail-line
  transfer input fields and monthly-sum to print line
  write detail line
  return
*wrap-up
  summary-calc
  summary-output
  close-files
  return
*summary-calc
  avg-sales = tot-monthly-sum / tot-sales-rep
  return
*summary-output
  transfer week totals to print-line1
  write the total-line1
  transfer tot-sales-rep to total-line2
  write total-line2
  transfer avg-sales to total-line3
  write total-line3
  write "end-of-report" line
  return
*close-files
  close files
  return

### EXHIBIT 3.20    COBOL 85 Program for Application 3.2

```
1        IDENTIFICATION DIVISION.
2        PROGRAM-ID. CH3APL2.
3
4        ****ANSI COBOL 85 ******
5
6        AUTHOR. JACK RUSSELL.
7
8        *REMARKS:   THIS PROGRAM PRODUCES A SALES ANALYSIS REPORT
9        *           FROM A SALES REP. FILE. THE REPORT LISTS THE
10       *           FOUR WEEK SALES AMOUNTS AND THE MONTHLY TOTAL.
11       *           TOTALS ARE PRINTED FOR EACH WEEK SALES, THE
12       *           NUMBER OF SALES, AND THE SALES REP AVERAGE SALES.
13
14       ENVIRONMENT DIVISION.
15       CONFIGURATION SECTION.
16       SOURCE-COMPUTER. CYBER.
17       OBJECT-COMPUTER. CYBER.
```

**EXHIBIT 3.20**   **(Cont.)**

```
18          *
19            INPUT-OUTPUT SECTION.
20            FILE-CONTROL.
21                SELECT SALES1 ASSIGN TO DTA32.
22                SELECT SALES-RPT ASSIGN TO OUTFILE.
23          *
24            DATA DIVISION.
25            FILE SECTION.
26            FD  SALES1.
27            01  SALES-REC.
28                05   SALES-REP   PIC X(15).
29                05   WK1         PIC 9(4).
30                05   WK2         PIC 9(4).
31                05   WK3         PIC 9(4).
32                05   WK4         PIC 9(4).
33          *
34            FD  SALES-RPT  LABEL RECORDS OMITTED.
35            01  SALES-LIST-REC  PIC  X(132).
36          *
37            WORKING-STORAGE SECTION.
38            01 MONTHLY-SUM       PIC  9(5).
39            01 TOT-WK1           PIC  9(6)  VALUE ZERO.
40            01 TOT-WK2           PIC  9(6)  VALUE ZERO.
41            01 TOT-WK3           PIC  9(6)  VALUE ZERO.
42            01 TOT-WK4           PIC  9(6)  VALUE ZERO.
43            01 TOT-MONTHLY-SUM PIC 9(7)  VALUE ZERO.
44            01 TOT-SALES-REP     PIC  9(2)  VALUE ZERO.
45            01 AVG-SALES         PIC  9(4).
46            01 END-FLAG          PIC  XXX    VALUE "NO".
47          *
48            01  HEADING1.
49                05              PIC X(40)   VALUE SPACES.
50                05              PIC X(93)   VALUE "ACME COMPANY".
51          *
52            01  HEADING2.
53                05              PIC X(35)  VALUE SPACES.
54                05              PIC X(97)  VALUE "SALES ANALYSIS REPORT".
55          *
56            01  HEADING3.
57                05              PIC X(14)   VALUE SPACES.
58                05              PIC X(9)    VALUE "SALES-REP".
59                05              PIC X(10)   VALUE SPACES.
60                05              PIC X(27)   VALUE "WEEK 1   WEEK 2    WEEK 3".
61                05              PIC X(72)   VALUE "WEEK 4   MONTHLY TOTAL".
62          *
63          *
64            01  DETAIL-LINE.
65                05              PIC X(14)  VALUE SPACES.
66                05   SALES-REP-OUT   PIC  X(15).
67                05              PIC  X(4)   VALUE SPACES.
68                05   WK1-OUT     PIC  Z,ZZ9.
69                05              PIC  X(4)   VALUE SPACES.
70                05   WK2-OUT     PIC  Z,ZZ9.
71                05              PIC  X(4)   VALUE SPACES.
72                05   WK3-OUT     PIC  Z,ZZ9.
73                05              PIC  X(4)   VALUE SPACES.
74                05   WK4-OUT     PIC  Z,ZZ9.
75                05              PIC  X(6)   VALUE SPACES.
76                05   MONTHLY-SUM-OUT  PIC  ZZZ,ZZ9.
77                05              PIC  X(54)  VALUE SPACES.
78          *
79            01  TOT-LINE-1.
80                05              PIC  X(14)  VALUE SPACES.
81                05              PIC  X(16)  VALUE "TOTALS".
82                05   TOT-WK1-OUT     PIC  ZZZZ,ZZ9.
83                05              PIC  X     VALUE SPACES.
84                05   TOT-WK2-OUT     PIC  ZZZZ,ZZ9.
```

**EXHIBIT 3.20 (Cont.)**

```
85                05                   PIC  X       VALUE SPACES.
86                05   TOT-WK3-OUT     PIC  ZZZZ,ZZ9.
87                05                   PIC  X       VALUE SPACES.
88                05   TOT-WK4-OUT     PIC  ZZZZ,ZZ9.
89                05                   PIC  X(3)    VALUE SPACES.
90                05   TOT-MONTHLY-SUM-OUT  PIC  ZZ,ZZZ,ZZ9.
91                05                   PIC  X(55)    VALUE SPACES.
92        *
93         01  TOT-LINE-2.
94                05                   PIC  X(14)  VALUE SPACES.
95                05                   PIC  X(23)  VALUE
96                     "NUMBER OF SALESPERSONS".
97                05   TOT-SALES-REP-OUT  PIC  Z9.
98                05                   PIC  X(93)  VALUE SPACES.
99        *
100        01  TOT-LINE-3.
101               05                   PIC  X(14)  VALUE SPACES.
102               05                   PIC  X(28)  VALUE
103                   "SALESPERSON AVERAGE SALES".
104               05  AVG-SALES-OUT     PIC  Z,ZZ9.
105               05                   PIC  X(87)  VALUE SPACES.
106        *
107        01  TOT-LINE-4.
108               05                   PIC  X(40)   VALUE SPACES.
109               05                   PIC  X(93)   VALUE "END OF REPORT".
110        *
111        ***
112        /
113         PROCEDURE DIVISION.
114        ***
115         000-MAIN-LINE.
116             PERFORM 100-START-UP.
117             PERFORM 200-PROCESS-RECORD
118                 UNTIL END-FLAG = "YES".
119             PERFORM 300-WRAP-UP.
120             STOP RUN.
121        *
122         100-START-UP.
123
124             PERFORM 105-OPEN-FILES.
125             PERFORM 110-HEADINGS.
126             PERFORM 120-READ-FILE.
127
128         105-OPEN-FILES.
129
130             OPEN INPUT SALES1.
131             OPEN OUTPUT SALES-RPT.
132
133
134        *
135         110-HEADINGS.
136             WRITE SALES-LIST-REC FROM HEADING1 AFTER PAGE.
137             WRITE SALES-LIST-REC FROM HEADING2 AFTER 2.
138             WRITE SALES-LIST-REC FROM HEADING3 AFTER 2
139             MOVE SPACES TO SALES-LIST-REC.
140             WRITE SALES-LIST-REC AFTER 2.
141        *
142         120-READ-FILE.
143             READ SALES1 AT END MOVE "YES" TO END-FLAG.
144        *
145         200-PROCESS-RECORD.
146             PERFORM 210-DETAIL-CALCULATIONS.
147             PERFORM 220-ACCUMULATION.
148             PERFORM 230-DETAIL-LINE.
149             PERFORM 120-READ-FILE.
150        *
```

**EXHIBIT 3.20    (Cont.)**

```
151        210-DETAIL-CALCULATIONS.
152            COMPUTE MONTHLY-SUM =  WK1 + WK2 + WK3 + WK4.
153      *
154        220-ACCUMULATION.
155            ADD WK1 TO TOT-WK1.
156            ADD WK2 TO TOT-WK2.
157            ADD WK3 TO TOT-WK3.
158            ADD WK4 TO TOT-WK4.
159            ADD MONTHLY-SUM TO TOT-MONTHLY-SUM.
160            ADD 1 TO TOT-SALES-REP.
161      *
162        230-DETAIL-LINE.
163            MOVE SALES-REP TO SALES-REP-OUT.
164            MOVE WK1 TO WK1-OUT.
165            MOVE WK2 TO WK2-OUT.
166            MOVE WK3 TO WK3-OUT.
167            MOVE WK4 TO WK4-OUT.
168            MOVE MONTHLY-SUM TO MONTHLY-SUM-OUT.
169            WRITE SALES-LIST-REC FROM DETAIL-LINE AFTER 1.
170      *
171        300-WRAP-UP.
172            PERFORM 310-SUMMARY-CALC.
173            PERFORM 320-SUMMARY-OUTPUT.
174            PERFORM 330-CLOSE-FILES.
175
176        310-SUMMARY-CALC.
177
178            COMPUTE AVG-SALES ROUNDED = TOT-MONTHLY-SUM / TOT-SALES-REP.
179
180        320-SUMMARY-OUTPUT.
181
182            MOVE TOT-WK1 TO TOT-WK1-OUT.
183            MOVE TOT-WK2 TO TOT-WK2-OUT.
184            MOVE TOT-WK3 TO TOT-WK3-OUT.
185            MOVE TOT-WK4 TO TOT-WK4-OUT.
186            MOVE TOT-MONTHLY-SUM TO TOT-MONTHLY-SUM-OUT.
187            WRITE SALES-LIST-REC FROM TOT-LINE-1 AFTER 2.
188      *
189            MOVE TOT-SALES-REP TO TOT-SALES-REP-OUT.
190            WRITE SALES-LIST-REC FROM TOT-LINE-2 AFTER 2.
191      *
192            MOVE AVG-SALES TO AVG-SALES-OUT.
193            WRITE SALES-LIST-REC FROM TOT-LINE-3 AFTER 1.
194            WRITE SALES-LIST-REC FROM TOT-LINE-4 AFTER 2.
195
196        330-CLOSE-FILES.
197
198            CLOSE SALES1  SALES-RPT.
```

```
                         ACME COMPANY

                      SALES ANALYSIS REPORT

SALES-REP          WEEK 1    WEEK 2    WEEK 3   WEEK 4   MONTHLY TOTAL


JOHN JOHNSON        1,000     2,000     1,000    3,000      7,000
BILLY DICKSON       2,000     1,000     3,000    2,000      8,000
SUSAN GREEN         1,500     1,500     3,000    4,000     10,000
JANE BAKER          1,000     1,000     1,500    3,000      6,500

TOTALS              5,500     5,500     8,500   12,000     31,500

NUMBER OF SALESPERSONS   4
SALESPERSON AVERAGE SALES     7,875

                      END OF REPORT
```

**EXHIBIT 3.21   Quick BASIC Program for Application 3.2**

```
'*********************************************************************
'                     PROGRAM IDENTIFICATION                        *
'*********************************************************************
'* PROGRAM NAME: CH3APL2                                            *
'*********************************************************************
'* REMARKS: THIS PROGRAM PRODUCES A SALES ANALYSIS REPORT FROM A SALES *
'*         FILE.   THE REPORT LISTS THE FOUR WEEK SALES AMOUNTS      *
'*         AND THE MONTHLY TOTAL.   TOTALS ARE PRINTED FOR EACH      *
'*         WEEK SALES, THE NUMBER OF SALESPERSONS, AND THE SALES REP *
'*         AVERAGE SALES.                                            *
'*********************************************************************
'*                        MAIN-LINE                                 *
'*********************************************************************
     GOSUB STARTUP                          'PERFORM START-UP
     DO UNTIL END.FLAG$ = "YES"
        GOSUB PROCESS RECORD:               'PERFORM PROCESS-RECORD
     LOOP
     GOSUB WRAPUP                           'PERFORM WRAP-UP
     END


     '*********************************************************************
     '*                        START-UP                                  *
     '*********************************************************************

STARTUP:
     GOSUB INITIALIZE
     GOSUB OPEN.FILES
     GOSUB HEADINGS                         'PERFORM HEADINGS
     GOSUB READFILE                         'PERFORM READ-FILE
     RETURN

     '*********************************************************************
     '*                        INITIALIZE                                *
     '*********************************************************************

INITIALIZE:

     WIDTH LPRINT 132
     TOT.WK1 = 0: TOT.WK2 = 0: TOT.WK3 = 0: TOT.WK4 = 0: TOT.MONTHLY.SUM = 0
     TOT.SALES = 0: END.FLAG$ = "NO"
     DET.LINE$ = "              \              \   #,###    #,###    #,###    #,###      ##,###"
     TOT.LINE1$ = "            TOTALS          ###,### ###,### ###,### ###,###  #,###,###"
     RETURN

     '*********************************************************************
     '*                        OPEN-FILES                                *
     '*********************************************************************

OPEN.FILES:

     OPEN "I", #1, "CH3ILL2.DAT"
     RETURN

     '*********************************************************************
     '*                        HEADINGS                                  *
     '*********************************************************************

HEADINGS:

     LPRINT CHR$(12)
     LPRINT TAB(41); "ACME COMPANY"
     LPRINT
     LPRINT TAB(36); "SALES ANALYSIS REPORT"
     LPRINT
     LPRINT TAB(15); "SALES REP"; TAB(34); "WEEK 1"; TAB(43); "WEEK 2"; TAB(52); "WEEK 3"; TAB(61); "WEEK 4"; TAB(69); "MONTHLY TOTAL"
     LPRINT : LPRINT
     RETURN
```

## APPLICATION 3.2

### EXHIBIT 3.21    (Cont.)

```
'******************************************************************
'*                       READ-FILE                               *
'******************************************************************

READFILE:
    INPUT #1, SALES.REP$, WK1, WK2, WK3, WK4
    IF SALES.REP$ = "EOF" THEN END.FLAG$ = "YES"
    RETURN


    '******************************************************************
    '*                     PROCESS-RECORD                            *
    '******************************************************************
PROCESS RECORD:
    GOSUB DETAIL.CALCULATION           'PERFORM DETAIL-CALCULATION
    GOSUB ACCUMULATION                 'PERFORM ACCUMULATION
    GOSUB DETLINE                      'PERFORM DETAIL-LINE
    GOSUB READFILE                     'PERFORM READ-FILE
    RETURN

    '**********************************************************************
    '*                     DETAIL-CALCULATION                            *
    '**********************************************************************

DETAIL.CALCULATION:

    MONTHLY.SUM = WK1 + WK2 + WK3 + WK4
    RETURN


    '**********************************************************************
    '*                        ACCUMULATION                              *
    '**********************************************************************

ACCUMULATION:

    TOT.WK1 = TOT.WK1 + WK1
    TOT.WK2 = TOT.WK2 + WK2
    TOT.WK3 = TOT.WK3 + WK3
    TOT.WK4 = TOT.WK4 + WK4
    TOT.MONTHLY.SUM = TOT.MONTHLY.SUM + MONTHLY.SUM
    TOT.SALES.REP = TOT.SALES.REP + 1
    RETURN


    '**********************************************************************
    '*                        DETAIL-LINE                               *
    '**********************************************************************

DETLINE:

    LPRINT USING DET.LINE$; SALES.REP$; WK1; WK2; WK3; WK4; MONTHLY.SUM
    RETURN


    '**********************************************************************
    '*                         WRAP-UP                                  *
    '**********************************************************************

WRAPUP:
    GOSUB SUMMARY.CALC
    GOSUB SUMMARY.OUTPUT
    GOSUB CLOSE.FILES
    RETURN
```

**EXHIBIT 3.21    (Cont.)**

```
'**********************************************************************
'                          SUMMARY-CALC                               *
'**********************************************************************

SUMMARY.CALC:
    AVE.SALES = TOT.MONTHLY.SUM / TOT.SALES.REP
    RETURN


    '******************************************************************
    '*                       SUMMARY-OUTPUT                          *
    '******************************************************************

SUMMARY.OUTPUT:

    LPRINT
    LPRINT USING TOT.LINE1$; TOT.WK1; TOT.WK2; TOT.WK3; TOT.WK4; TOT.MONTHLY.SUM
    LPRINT
    LPRINT TAB(15); "NUMBER OF SALESPERSONS"; TAB(39); TOT.SALES.REP
    LPRINT TAB(15); "SALESPERSON AVERAGE SALES"; TAB(42);
    LPRINT USING "##,###"; AVE.SALES
    LPRINT : LPRINT TAB(42); "END OF REPORT"
    RETURN


    '******************************************************************
    '*                         CLOSE-FILES                           *
    '******************************************************************

CLOSE.FILES:

    CLOSE
    RETURN
```

```
                         ACME COMPANY

                      SALES ANALYSIS REPORT

SALES REP          WEEK 1   WEEK 2   WEEK 3   WEEK 4   MONTHLY TOTAL


JOHN JOHNSON        1,000    2,000    1,000    3,000       7,000
BILLY DICKSON       2,000    1,000    3,000    2,000       8,000
SUSAN GREEN         1,500    1,500    3,000    4,000      10,000
JANE BAKER          1,000    1,000    1,500    3,000       6,500

TOTALS              5,500    5,500    8,500   12,000      31,500

NUMBER OF SALESPERSONS    4
SALESPERSON AVERAGE SALES    7,875

                      END OF REPORT
```

## SUMMARY

Accumulation is an integral part of almost all computer programming problems. Many reporting applications require the printing of grand totals or of values that depend on the accumulation of intermediate total results.

A professor wishes to print a test results report that includes each student's SSN, name, test scores, and an average. At the end of the report, the professor wants to print the total number of students in the class and the class average. To calculate the class's average grade, the total of the students' averages must be accumulated. At the end of the run, the total of the student averages is divided by the total number of students. Assuming that the class size will vary from time to time, the total number of students must also be accumulated by adding a constant, 1, to an accumulator or counter each time a record is processed. An accumulator is a memory area, or variable, that is used to accumulate a total.

To illustrate the accumulation process, the assignment statement TOT-WK1-SALES = TOT-WK1-SALES + WK1-SALES will cause the computer to take the current contents of WK1-SALES and add it to the current contents of TOT-WK1-SALES. The result of this addition is then stored into the variable to the left of the equal sign. In this case, that variable is TOT-WK1-SALES. The current contents of TOT-WK1-SALES is now the sum of the previous TOT-WK1-SALES plus WK1-SALES. The assignment statement notation is used almost universally since it easily transfers into practically any computer programming language. In COBOL, the programmer may choose to use a more English-like notation, such as ADD WK1-SALES TO TOT-WK1-SALES. This notation is neither required nor recommended over the assignment notation; it is simply a flowcharting option.

The process of accumulation should be formalized as a separate module within the PROCESS-RECORD module. The author has chosen to place the predefined process block that involves the accumulation module immediately after the DETAIL-CALCULATION module. The module *could* be placed, however, *after* the DETAIL-LINE module. Logically, it makes no difference which of the two it follows.

## VOCABULARY

final totals          accumulator
total line            counter
accumulation

## EXERCISES/QUESTIONS

1. Consider the initial values of the following three variables; what will be the value of TOT after the execution of the respective three assignment statements that follow?

```
TOT = 0
C = 5
D = 2
```

   Assume that the following commands are executed independently of one another.

   a.   TOT = C + D          _____
   b.   TOT = TOT + C + D    _____
   c.   TOT = TOT + C        _____

2. Assume that the following commands are treated as one segment of code, so that the content of any variable is the value placed there from the previously executed command. This value is to be assumed when executing the next command.

   a.   TOT = 0          _____
   b.   TOT = TOT + 1    _____
   c.   TOT = TOT + 2    _____
   d.   TOT = TOT + 1    _____

# PROBLEMS

**3-1.** Produce the hierarchy chart, structured flowchart, and pseudocode for the following problem statement. The report layout is depicted in Figure 3.1 and the input record layout is shown in Figure 3.2. A sales manager wishes to produce a report that lists the salesperson's number and name along with the number of subscriptions each salesperson sold for various categories of magazines. A total number of subscriptions for all magazines sold by each salesperson is also to print on the same line. A final total is to print for each of the categories of magazines, and the average number sold for each category should be printed on the subsequent line.

**3-2.** An inventory manager wishes to produce a report that lists the inventory number, item description, dollar values of merchandise on-hand, on-order, and the sum of on-hand and on-order (called merchandise available). A total line is to print that lists the grand totals of on-hand, on-order, and merchandise available. A separate total line is to print that lists the stock ratio (stock ratio = total on hand / total available).

Produce the printer spacing chart, record layout, hierarchy chart, structured flowchart, and pseudocode for this problem.

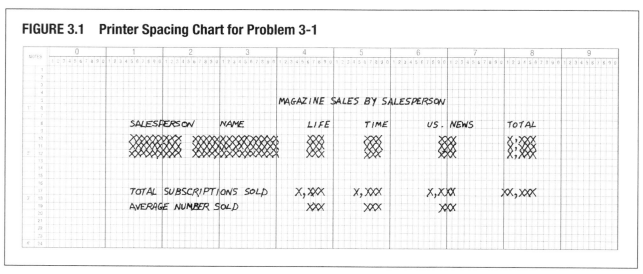

**FIGURE 3.1    Printer Spacing Chart for Problem 3-1**

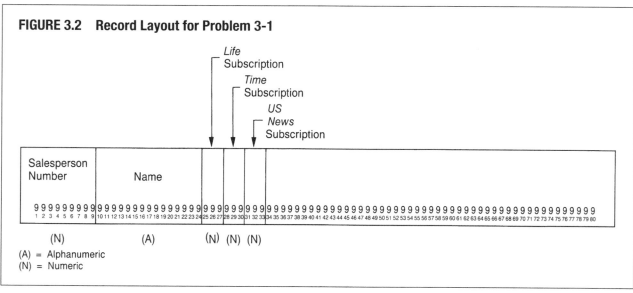

**FIGURE 3.2    Record Layout for Problem 3-1**

**3-3.** The University wishes to produce a report as shown below that lists grade point totals for each course taken by each student. (see Figure 3.3.) The total grade points for each student record is the product of the credit hours multiplied by grade points for the respective letter grade. The records are arranged by student number; therefore, all the courses for each student are grouped for convenience. A university grade point average is to be printed at the end of the report. The input record description layout is also described in Figure 3.4.

---

**FIGURE 3.3   Grade Point Average Report for Problem 3.3**

```
                              THE UNIVERSITY
                        GRADE POINT AVERAGE REPORT

    STUDENT #        NAME          COURSE      CREDIT      LTR      GRADE       TOTAL
                                               HOURS       GRD      POINTS    GRADE PTS

       4502      CHARLES BAKER    ACCT 2013      4          A         4          16
       XXXX      XXXXXXXXXXXXX    XXXXXXXXX      X          X         X          XX

       XXXX      XXXXXXXXXXXXX    XXXXXXXXX      X          X         X          XX

                       TOTAL CREDIT HOURS       XXX
                       TOTAL GRADE POINTS       XXXXX
                       UNIVERSITY GPA           X.XX
```

---

**FIGURE 3.4   Input Record Layout for Problem 3.3**

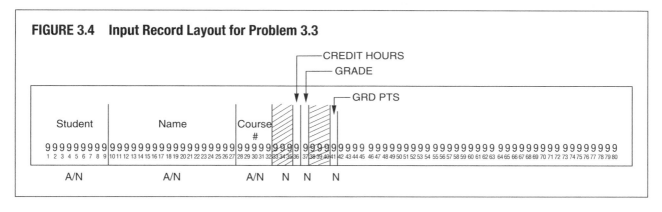

---

**3-4.** Acme Discount Department Stores desires a profit report on sales transactions for the week. The report (Fig. 3.6) lists the item number, merchandise description, wholesale price of the item, markup amount, retail price, discount, net amount, and profit margin on the item. Figure 3.5 illustrates the record layout. Markup amount is determined by multiplying the wholesale price by markup-pct. Retail price is sum of wholesale price and markup amount. Discount is the product of retail price and discount-pct. Net is difference between retail and discount. Profit margin is calculated by subtracting the wholesale from the net price. Totals are to print for the wholesale amounts, retail amounts, net amounts, and profit margins. Additional summary lines are needed to disclose the weekly profit ratio and the average markup per item. The profit ratio is determined by dividing total profit margin by the total wholesale amount. Average markup per item is calculated by dividing the number of items sold into the total markup amount.

Produce a printer spacing chart and record layout sheet for this problem first. Then develop the hierarchy chart, flowchart, and pseudocode for this problem.

**FIGURE 3.5   Input Record Layout:**

| Field | Location | Type | |
|---|---|---|---|
| Item # | 1–4 | A/N | |
| Description | 5–15 | A/N | |
| Wholesale | 16–21 | N | ($$$$.¢¢) |
| Markup-Pct | 22–23 | N | (.XX) |
| Discount-Pct | 24–25 | N | (.XX) |

**3-5.** Develop the hierarchy chart, flowchart, and pseudocode for a university budget (Fig. 3.7) as shown below. The budget is to list the budget item, allocated amounts and actual amounts for the three month period which includes January, February, and March. Columns are included which represent totals of the three months (allocated and actual). At the end of the run, print columnar totals for each month, and a summary report that lists the three months, their respective allocated and actual totals, and the differential (the difference between allocated and actual—allocated-actual). Figure 3.8 illustrates the record layout.

---

**3-6.** Design the hierarchy chart, flowchart, and pseudocode to produce the report in Figure 3.9. The weather bureau requires the statistics shown in Figure 3.9. Convert Fahrenheit to Centigrade by subtracting 32 from the Fahrenheit temperature and multiplying the difference by 5/9. Figure 3.10 illustrates the record layout.

```
┌─────────────────────────────────────────────────────────────────────────────────────────────────┐
│  FIGURE 3.7   Report for Problem 3.5                                                               │
│                                    UNIVERSITY BUDGET REPORT                                        │
│                                        FIRST QUARTER                                               │
│                                                                                                   │
│  BUDGET        JANUARY           FEBRUARY            MARCH              TOTAL                       │
│   ITEM     ALLOC    ACTUAL    ALLOC    ACTUAL    ALLOC    ACTUAL    ALLOC    ACTUAL                 │
│                                                                                                   │
│  LABOR     5000     4000      5000     6000      4000     5000      14000    15000                 │
│  XXXXXXX   XXXX     XXXX      XXXX     XXXX      XXXX     XXXX      XXXXX    XXXXX                  │
│  XXXXXXX   XXXX     XXXX      XXXX     XXXX      XXXX     XXXX      XXXXX    XXXXX                  │
│                                                                                                   │
│  TOTALS    XXXXX    XXXXX     XXXXX    XXXXX     XXXXX    XXXXX     XXXXXX   XXXXXX                 │
│  ─────────────────────────────────────────────────────────────────────────────────────────────  │
│                          ALLOCATED        ACTUAL          DIFFERENTIAL                             │
│                                                                                                   │
│               JANUARY     XXX,XXX        XXX,XXX          XX,XXX +                                 │
│               FEBRUARY    XXX,XXX        XXX,XXX          XX,XXX -                                 │
│               MARCH       XXX,XXX        XXX,XXX          XX,XXX +                                 │
└─────────────────────────────────────────────────────────────────────────────────────────────────┘
```

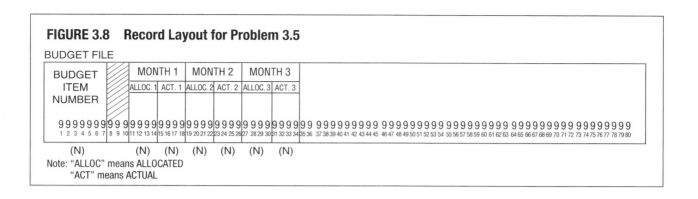

**FIGURE 3.8   Record Layout for Problem 3.5**

BUDGET FILE

| BUDGET ITEM NUMBER | | MONTH 1 | | MONTH 2 | | MONTH 3 | |
|---|---|---|---|---|---|---|---|
| | | ALLOC. 1 | ACT. 1 | ALLOC. 2 | ACT. 2 | ALLOC. 3 | ACT. 3 |

999999999 99 99999 99999 99999 99999 99999 99999 99 9999999999 9999999999 9999999999 9999999999 9999999999
1 2 3 4 5 6 7 8 9 10 11 12 13 14 15 16 17 18 19 20 21 22 23 24 25 26 27 28 29 30 31 32 33 34 35 36  37 38 39 40 41 42 43 44 45  46 47 48 49 50 51 52 53 54  55 56 57 58 59 60 61 62 63  64 65 66 67 68 69 70 71 72 73 74 75 76 77 78 79 80

(N)      (N)   (N)   (N)   (N)   (N)   (N)

Note: "ALLOC" means ALLOCATED
      "ACT" means ACTUAL

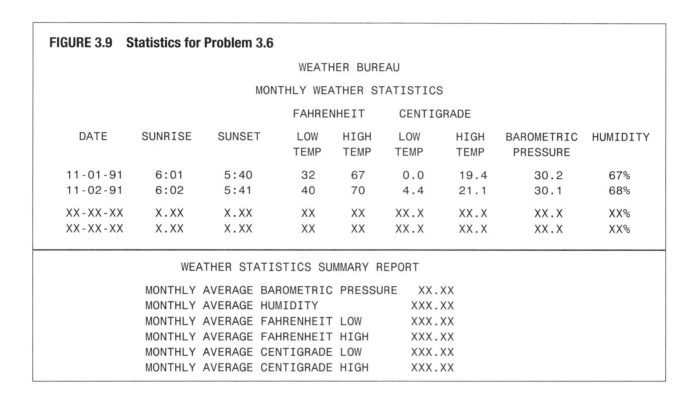

**FIGURE 3.9   Statistics for Problem 3.6**

WEATHER BUREAU

MONTHLY WEATHER STATISTICS

| | | | FAHRENHEIT | | CENTIGRADE | | | |
|---|---|---|---|---|---|---|---|---|
| DATE | SUNRISE | SUNSET | LOW TEMP | HIGH TEMP | LOW TEMP | HIGH TEMP | BAROMETRIC PRESSURE | HUMIDITY |
| 11-01-91 | 6:01 | 5:40 | 32 | 67 | 0.0 | 19.4 | 30.2 | 67% |
| 11-02-91 | 6:02 | 5:41 | 40 | 70 | 4.4 | 21.1 | 30.1 | 68% |
| XX-XX-XX | X.XX | X.XX | XX | XX | XX.X | XX.X | XX.X | XX% |
| XX-XX-XX | X.XX | X.XX | XX | XX | XX.X | XX.X | XX.X | XX% |

WEATHER STATISTICS SUMMARY REPORT

MONTHLY AVERAGE BAROMETRIC PRESSURE    XX.XX
MONTHLY AVERAGE HUMIDITY               XXX.XX
MONTHLY AVERAGE FAHRENHEIT LOW         XXX.XX
MONTHLY AVERAGE FAHRENHEIT HIGH        XXX.XX
MONTHLY AVERAGE CENTIGRADE LOW         XXX.XX
MONTHLY AVERAGE CENTIGRADE HIGH        XXX.XX

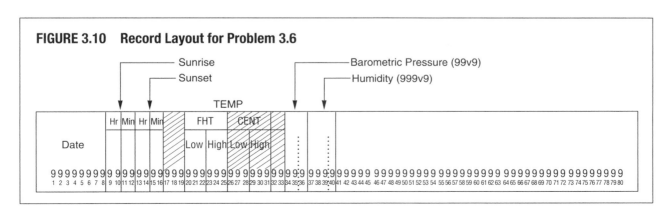

**FIGURE 3.10   Record Layout for Problem 3.6**

— Sunrise
— Sunset
— Barometric Pressure (99v9)
— Humidity (999v9)
TEMP

| Date | | Hr | Min | Hr | Min | | FHT | | CENT | | | | | |
|---|---|---|---|---|---|---|---|---|---|---|---|---|---|---|
| | | | | | | | Low | High | Low | High | | | | |

999999999 99 99999 99999 99999 99999 99999 99999 99 999 99 9999 9999999999 9999999999 9999999999 9999999999
1 2 3 4 5 6 7 8 9 10 11 12 13 14 15 16 17 18 19 20 21 22 23 24 25 26 27 28 29 30 31 32 33 34 35 36  37 38 39 40 41 42 43 44 45  46 47 48 49 50 51 52 53 54  55 56 57 58 59 60 61 62 63  64 65 66 67 68 69 70 71 72 73 74 75 76 77 78 79 80

# 4

# Comparing and Branching

## OBJECTIVES

As a result of having read and studied this chapter, the student will be able to:

1. Develop the flowchart and pseudocode logic that perform a simple comparison between two values using the If . . . Then . . . Else structure; and then, based on the true or false outcome of the comparison operation, draw the alternative flowcharting steps that will occur.

2. Develop the flowchart and pseudocode steps that cause the printer to advance to the top of the next page once a page has finished printing.

3. Develop the flowchart and pseudocode steps for a CASE structure where a series of comparison operations are to be made; and, for each comparison, flowchart the necessary alternative processing steps.

4. Develop the flowchart and pseudocode steps for a nested IF (nested comparison).

5. Develop and draw a decision table.

6. Draw the flowchart and pseudocode steps for compound conditional expressions.

An important characteristic of the computer is its ability to compare two values and, based on the results of the comparison, perform alternative processing operations. The **comparison** determines if one value is less than, equal to, or greater than the other value. When the computer has finished comparing the two values, the result of the comparison will be either true or false. If the result of the comparison is true, the computer program may direct the computer to follow a particular execution path; if the result of the comparison is false, the program may direct the computer to follow an alternate execution path. The comparison operation uses the If . . . Then . . . Else control structure.

## SIMPLE COMPARISONS

### Selection (If . . . Then . . . Else) Control Structure

Chapter 2 alludes to the selection structure as the appropriate control structure for comparing two values. The unique feature of the selection structure is that there is only one entry point and only one exit point.

### Using the Selection Structure

A teacher wishes to produce a report that lists each student's two test scores on a detail line. At the end of the report, a class average is to be printed. In determining the class average, however, the teacher wants to drop the lesser and use only the greater of each student's two test scores. Figure 4.1 illustrates the sample report.

### Logic Considerations

Figure 4.2 illustrates the reading of the student record and the subsequent comparison process that determines the greater of the two student test scores. Step 2 of Figure 4.2 shows the comparison of the value (080) of SCORE1 and the value (090) of SCORE2. The condition being tested is as follows:

```
IF SCORE1 > SCORE2 . . .
```

**FIGURE 4.1    Test Results Report**

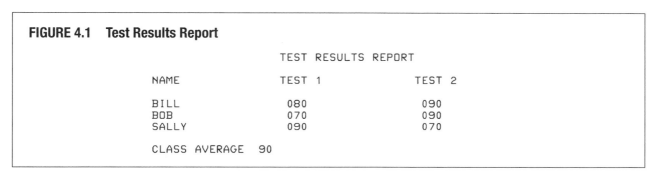

```
                    TEST RESULTS REPORT

    NAME            TEST 1              TEST 2

    BILL            080                 090
    BOB             070                 090
    SALLY           090                 070

    CLASS AVERAGE   90
```

**FIGURE 4.2    Comparison of Two Test Scores Being Read to Memory and Processing Steps Being Determined**

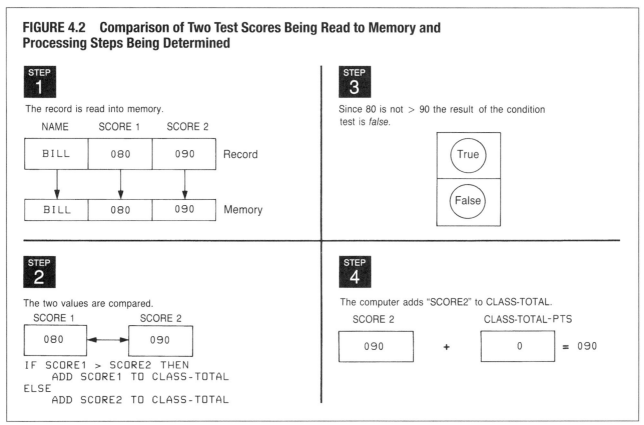

**STEP 1**

The record is read into memory.

| NAME | SCORE 1 | SCORE 2 | |
|------|---------|---------|--------|
| BILL | 080 | 090 | Record |
| BILL | 080 | 090 | Memory |

**STEP 2**

The two values are compared.

SCORE 1 [ 080 ] ←→ SCORE 2 [ 090 ]

```
IF SCORE1 > SCORE2 THEN
    ADD SCORE1 TO CLASS-TOTAL
ELSE
    ADD SCORE2 TO CLASS-TOTAL
```

**STEP 3**

Since 80 is not > 90 the result of the condition test is *false*.

True
False

**STEP 4**

The computer adds "SCORE2" to CLASS-TOTAL.

SCORE 2 [ 090 ]  +  CLASS-TOTAL-PTS [ 0 ]  = 090

In step 3 of Figure 4.2, the computer program decides that the result of this comparison is false, i.e., that the value of 80 is not greater than 90. Since the result of the condition test is false, the execution path the computer takes is the adding of SCORE2 (the larger of the two scores in this case) to the total (step 4 of Figure 4.2). Figure 4.3 illustrates the comparison of the two test scores in flowcharting form. As mentioned, this is called a selection (or If . . . Then . . . Else) structure. If the condition is *true*, the instruction in the box to the *right* of the decision symbol is executed; otherwise (indicating the condition is *false*), the instruction to the *left* of the decision symbol is executed. Normally, it is standard practice to place the commands that are to be executed if the condition is true on the right side and the commands that are to be executed if the condition is false on the left. However, it is permissible to reverse the two.

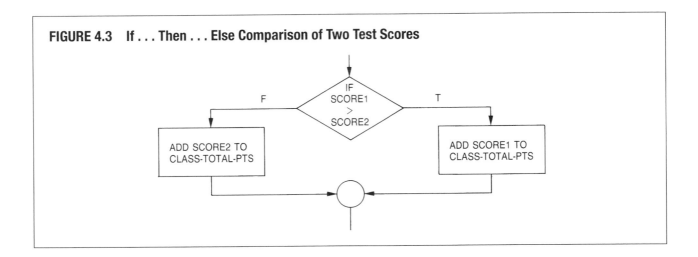

**FIGURE 4.3    If . . . Then . . . Else Comparison of Two Test Scores**

# Customer Sales Report Using Comparison

## Program Requirements

The following business application also illustrates the use of the comparison operation. A manager wishes to produce a Customer Sales Report that discloses the customer number, customer name, sales amount, sales discount, and net sales. The sales discount is calculated as a percentage of

sales, which is based on the sales volume, as discussed later.

## Output Design

Exhibit 4.1 illustrates the sample customer sales report, and Exhibit 4.2 shows the associated printer spacing chart. Total net sales is to print at the bottom.

---

**EXHIBIT 4.1   An Example of a Customer Sales Report**

```
                    CUSTOMER SALES REPORT

    CUST #       CUSTOMER NAME        SALES      DISCOUNT       NET

     2001        BAKER, BOB           400.00       4.00       396.00
     2007        CARLTON, MARY       1000.00      30.00       970.00
     2009        DICKSON, DON         150.00       1.50       148.50
     6000        DONALDSON, JOE       999.00      29.97       969.03

                                    TOTAL NET SALES  $2,483.53
```

---

**EXHIBIT 4.2   Printer Spacing Chart for a Customer Sales Report**

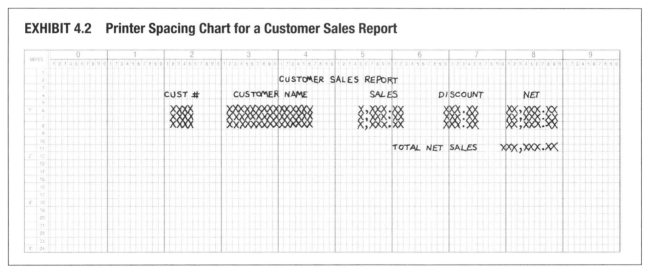

---

**EXHIBIT 4.3   Record Layout of a Customer Sales Record**

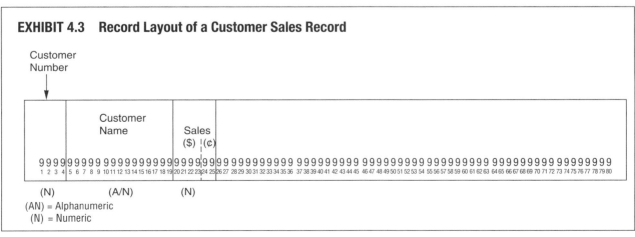

## Input Design

The input record layout is shown in Exhibit 4.3. The three input fields are the customer number (1-4), customer name (5-19), and sales (20-25). The sales are entered in a dollars-and-cents format.

## Test Data

Exhibit 4.4 depicts the test data used to execute the computer program.

## Logic Considerations

Exhibit 4.5 shows the schedule of sales discounts to be used in computing the discount. If the sales amount is less than $500, the discount is computed

as one percent of sales. If the sales amount is equal to or greater than $500, the discount is computed as three percent of sales. For example, the first record in the file of test cases has a sales amount of $400. This amount is less than $500; therefore, the rate used is one percent. The discount for Bob Baker is $4 (400 x .01 = 4), and the net amount is $396 (400 – 4 = 396).

The sales amount for the second record in the file, May Carlton, exceeds $499.99; therefore, the discount for Mary's record will be calculated at the three percent rate (1000 x .03 = $30). The DETAIL-CALCULATION module appears in the flowchart in Exhibit 4.10. If the sales amount is less than $500, the variable PCT is assigned the value of .01. If the sales amount is $500 or greater, then the variable

---

**EXHIBIT 4.4    Test Data**

```
COLUMN   1         2         3         4         5         6         7         8
1234567890123456789012345678901234567890123456789012345678901234567890123456789012345678901234567890

2001BAKER, BOB      040000
2007CARLTON, MARY   100000
2009DICKSON, DON    015000
6000DONALDSON, JOE  099900
```

---

**EXHIBIT 4.5    Schedule of Sales Discounts**

| Sales Range | Discount Percent |
|-------------|------------------|
| < 500.00 | 1% |
| 500.00 or > | 3% |

---

**EXHIBIT 4.6    Pseudocode for DETAIL-CALCULATION Module**

```
*detail-calculation module
if sales < 500.00
        then store .01 at pct
else store .03 at pct
endif
calculate disc = sales * pct
calculate net = sales - disc
return
```

---

**EXHIBIT 4.7    COBOL Code for DETAIL-CALCULATION Module**

```
210-DETAIL-CALCULATION.

IF SALES < 500.00
        THEN MOVE .01 TO PCT
ELSE
        MOVE .03 TO PCT
END-IF
COMPUTE DISC = SALES * PCT.
COMPUTE NET = SALES — DISC.
```

PCT is assigned the value of .03. This technique of assigning to the PCT variable the constant value of .01 or .03 avoids an otherwise redundant calculation of the DISC variable. In other words, the program would otherwise have to contain a discount calculation at the one percent rate and another at the three percent rate. Exhibit 4.6 illustrates the pseudocoding segment for the discount calculation module, while Exhibits 4.7 and 4.8 show the COBOL and BASIC codes, respectively.

## Program Design

**Hierarchy Chart.** The hierarchy chart for this problem is shown in Exhibit 4.9. The RECORD-PROCESS module this time does contain detail calculations; therefore, a DETAIL-CALCULATION module is included. The inclusion of alternative processing steps to select the proper discount rate

is the only significant difference in this detail calculation module from those in previous programs.

**Structure Program Flowchart.** Exhibits 4.10 and 4.11 illustrate the structured program flowchart and pseudocode for the customer sales report. The START-UP module handles the functions of initializing TOT-NET-SALES to zero and END-FLAG = "NO," opening the files, printing the headings, and reading the first record. The PROCESS module invokes the typical four submodules (DETAIL-CALCULATION, ACCUMULATION, DETAIL-LINE, and READ-FILE). The WRAP-UP module prints TOT-NET-SALES and closes the files. Exhibits 4.12 and 4.13 illustrate the COBOL and QBASIC programs for this problem, respectively.

---

**EXHIBIT 4.8    BASIC Code for DETAIL-CALCULATION Module**

```
REM DETAIL-CALCULATION MODULE
IF SALES < 500.00    THEN
        LET PCT = .01
     ELSE LET PCT = .03
END IF
LET DISC = SALES * PCT
LET NET = SALES — DISC
RETURN
```

---

**EXHIBIT 4.9    Hierarchy Chart for a Customer Sales Report**

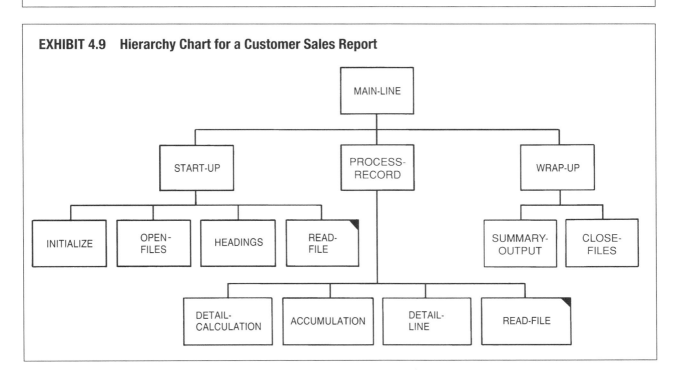

**EXHIBIT 4.10    Flowchart for a Customer Sales Report**

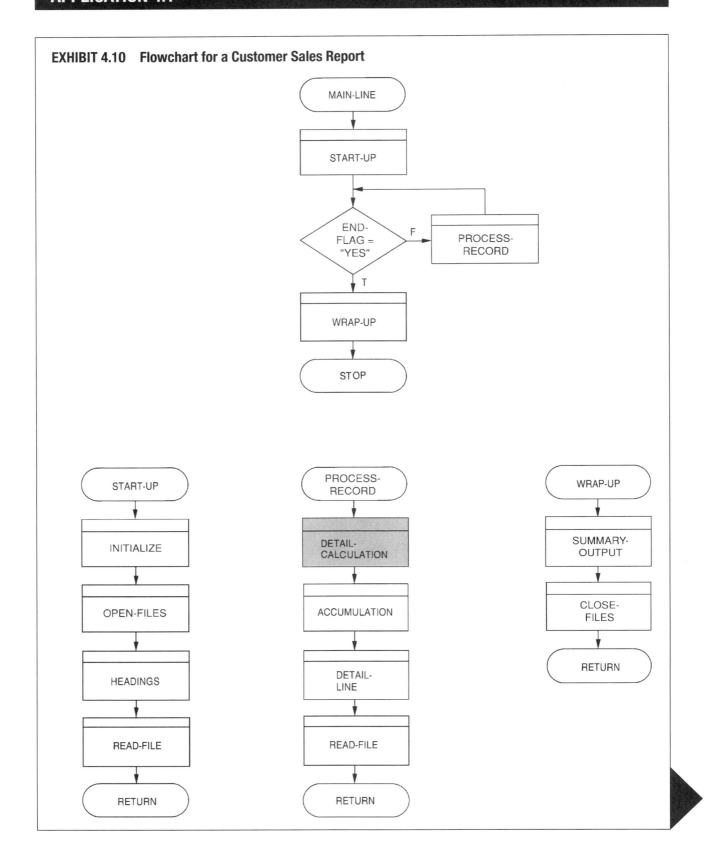

**EXHIBIT 4.10 (Cont.)**

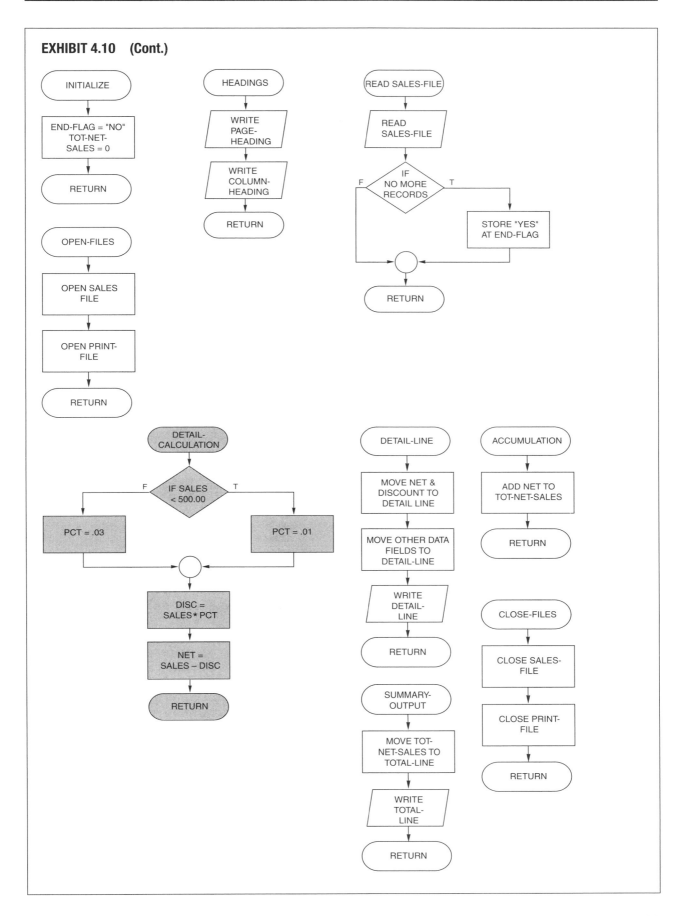

## EXHIBIT 4.11    Pseudocode for Application 4.1, Customer Sales Report

```
*mainline
     start-up
        dowhile end-flag = "no"
           process-record
        enddo
     wrap-up
     stop
*start-up
     initialize
     open-files
     headings
     read-file
     return
*initialize
     end-flag="no"
     tot-net-sales = 0
     return
*open-files
     open customer-file
     open print-file
     return
*headings
     write page heading
     write column heading
     return
*read-file
     read customer-file
        when out of records
           end-flag = "yes"
     endread
     return

*process-record
     detail-calculation
     accumulation
     detail-line
     read-file
     return
*detail-calculation
     if sales < 500
        then
              pct = .01
        else
              pct = .03
     endif
     calculate discount = sales * pct
     calculate net = sales − discount
     return
*accumulation
     add net to tot-net-sales
     return
*detail-line
     transfer input data to detail-line
     transfer net and discount to detail-line
     write detail-line
     return
*wrap-up
     summary-output
     close-files
     return
*summary-output
     move tot-net-sales to total-line
     write total-line
     return
*close-files
     close files
     return
```

## EXHIBIT 4.12    COBOL 85 Program for Application 4.1, Customer Sales Report

```
 1          IDENTIFICATION DIVISION.
 2
 3       ****ANSI COBOL 85****
 4
 5        PROGRAM-ID. CH4ILL1.
 6        DATE-WRITTEN. AUGUST 19, 1993.
 7        DATE-COMPILED. 1993-06-28.
 8
 9       *REMARKS:   THIS PROGRAM PRODUCES A CUSTOMER SALES REPORT
10       *           FROM A SALES FILE. THE REPORT LISTS THE CUST.
11       *           NUMBER, NAME, SALES, DISCOUNT, AND NET.  SPECIAL
12       *           PROCESSING INCLUDES:
13       *
14       *              1)  SALES DISCOUNT CALCULATIONS.
15       *              2)  TOTAL NET SALES LINE.
16
17        ENVIRONMENT DIVISION.
18        CONFIGURATION SECTION.
19        SOURCE-COMPUTER. CYBER.
20        OBJECT-COMPUTER. CYBER.
```

**EXHIBIT 4.12    (Cont.)**

```
21         INPUT-OUTPUT SECTION.
22         FILE-CONTROL.
23             SELECT SALES-FILE ASSIGN TO DTA41.
24             SELECT SALES-REPORT ASSIGN TO OUTFILE.
25         DATA DIVISION.
26         FILE SECTION.
27
28         FD  SALES-FILE.
29         01  RECORD-DESCR.
30             05 CUST-NO              PIC 9(4).
31             05 NAME                 PIC X(15).
32             05 SALES                PIC 9(4)V99.
33
34         FD  SALES-REPORT.
35         01  SALES-PRINT-REC         PIC X(133).
36
37         WORKING-STORAGE SECTION.
38
39         01 PCT                      PIC V99 VALUE ZERO.
40         01 END-FLAG                 PIC XXX VALUE "NO".
41         01 DISC                     PIC 9(3)V99 VALUE ZERO.
42         01 NET                      PIC 9(3)V99 VALUE ZERO.
43         01 TOT-NET-SALES            PIC 9(6)V99 VALUE ZERO.
44
45         01 PAGE-HEADING.
46             05                      PIC X(40) VALUE SPACES.
47             05                      PIC X(21) VALUE
48                 "CUSTOMER SALES REPORT".
49             05                      PIC X(72) VALUE SPACES.
50
51         01 COLUMN-HEADING.
52             05                      PIC X(20) VALUE SPACES.
53             05                      PIC X(13) VALUE "CUST #".
54             05                      PIC X(23) VALUE "CUSTOMER NAME".
55             05                      PIC X(12) VALUE "SALES".
56             05                      PIC X(15) VALUE "DISCOUNT".
57             05                      PIC X(50) VALUE "NET".
58
59         01 DETAIL-LINE.
60             05                      PIC X(21) VALUE SPACES.
61             05 CUST-NO-OUT          PIC 9999.
62             05                      PIC X(7) VALUE SPACES.
63             05 NAME-OUT             PIC X(15).
64             05                      PIC X(7) VALUE SPACES.
65             05 SALES-OUT            PIC Z,ZZ9.99.
66             05                      PIC X(7) VALUE SPACES.
67             05 DISC-OUT             PIC ZZ9.99.
68             05                      PIC X(8) VALUE SPACES.
69             05 NET-OUT              PIC ZZ9.99.
70             05                      PIC X(44) VALUE SPACES.
71         01 TOTAL-LINE.
72             05                      PIC X(60) VALUE SPACES.
73             05                      PIC X(15) VALUE
74                 "TOTAL NET SALES".
75             05                      PIC X(4) VALUE SPACES.
76             05 TOT-NET-SALES-OUT    PIC ZZZ,ZZ9.99.
77             05                      PIC X(44) VALUE SPACES.
78     /
79       PROCEDURE DIVISION.
80
81       000-MAIN-LINE.
82           PERFORM 100-START-UP.
83           PERFORM 200-PROCESS-RECORD UNTIL END-FLAG = "YES".
84           PERFORM 300-WRAP-UP.
85           STOP RUN.
86
```

**EXHIBIT 4.12   (Cont.)**

```
87          100-START-UP.
88              PERFORM 105-OPEN-FILES.
89              PERFORM 110-HEADINGS.
90              PERFORM 120-READ-SALES-FILE.
91
92          105-OPEN-FILES.
93              OPEN INPUT SALES-FILE
94                  OUTPUT SALES-REPORT.
95
96          110-HEADINGS.
97              WRITE SALES-PRINT-REC FROM PAGE-HEADING AFTER PAGE.
98              WRITE SALES-PRINT-REC FROM COLUMN-HEADING AFTER 2.
99              MOVE SPACES TO SALES-PRINT-REC.
100             WRITE SALES-PRINT-REC AFTER 1.
101
102         120-READ-SALES-FILE.
103             READ SALES-FILE AT END MOVE "YES" TO END-FLAG.
104
105         200-PROCESS-RECORD.
106             PERFORM 210-DETAIL-CALCULATION.
107             PERFORM 220-ACCUMULATION.
108             PERFORM 230-WRITE-DETAIL-LINE.
109             PERFORM 120-READ-SALES-FILE.
110
111         210-DETAIL-CALCULATION.
112
113             IF SALES < 500
114                 THEN COMPUTE PCT = .01
115                 ELSE COMPUTE PCT = .03
116             END-IF.
117
118             COMPUTE DISC ROUNDED = SALES * PCT.
119             COMPUTE NET = SALES - DISC.
120
121         220-ACCUMULATION.
122
123             ADD NET TO TOT-NET-SALES.
124
125         230-WRITE-DETAIL-LINE.
126
127             MOVE CUST-NO TO CUST-NO-OUT.
128             MOVE NAME TO NAME-OUT.
129             MOVE SALES TO SALES-OUT.
130             MOVE DISC TO DISC-OUT.
131             MOVE NET TO NET-OUT.
132             WRITE SALES-PRINT-REC FROM DETAIL-LINE.
133
134         300-WRAP-UP.
135             PERFORM 310-SUMMARY-OUTPUT.
136             PERFORM 320-CLOSE-FILES.
137
138         310-SUMMARY-OUTPUT.
139             MOVE TOT-NET-SALES TO TOT-NET-SALES-OUT.
140             WRITE SALES-PRINT-REC FROM TOTAL-LINE AFTER 2.
141
142         320-CLOSE-FILES.
143             CLOSE SALES-FILE
144                   SALES-REPORT.
145
```

## EXHIBIT 4.12   (Cont.)

```
                 CUSTOMER SALES REPORT

CUST #        CUSTOMER NAME        SALES        DISCOUNT        NET

 2001        BAKER, BOB          400.00          4.00        396.00
 2007        CARLTON, MARY     1,000.00         30.00        970.00
 2009        DICKSON, DON        150.00          1.50        148.50
 6000        DONALDSON, JOE      999.00         29.97        969.03

                                        TOTAL NET SALES    2,483.53
```

## EXHIBIT 4.13   QBASIC Program for Application 4.1, Customer Sales Report

```
'*******************************************************************
'*                    PROGRAM IDENTIFICATION                      *
'*******************************************************************
'* PROGRAM NAME: CUSTOMER SALES REPORT (CH4APL1)                  *
'*******************************************************************

'REMARKS:    THIS PROGRAM PRODUCES A CUSTOMER SALES REPORT
'            FROM A SALES FILE.  THE REPORT LISTS THE CUSTOMER
'            NUMBER, NAME, SALES, DISCOUNT, AND NET.  SPECIAL
'            PROCESSING INCLUDES:
'               1.  SALES DISCOUNT CALCULATIONS.
'               2.  TOTAL NET SALES LINE.


'*******************************************************************
'*                         MAIN-LINE                              *
'*******************************************************************
GOSUB STARTUP                         'PERFORM START-UP           *
DO UNTIL END.FLAG$ = "YES"
    GOSUB PROCESS.RECORD               'PERFORM PROCESS            *
LOOP
GOSUB WRAPUP                           'PERFORM WRAP-UP            *
END
    '*************************************************************
    '                       START-UP                            *
    '*************************************************************

STARTUP:

    GOSUB INITIALIZE
    GOSUB OPEN.FILES
    GOSUB HEADINGS                    'PERFORM HEADINGS
    GOSUB READFILE                    'PERFORM READ-FILE
    RETURN
```

**EXHIBIT 4.13  (Cont.)**

```
'*********************************************************************
'*                         INITIALIZE                               *
'*********************************************************************


INITIALIZE:

    WIDTH LPRINT 120
    END.FLAG$ = "NO"
    TOT.NET.SALES = 0
    RETURN


        '*****************************************************************
        '*                     OPEN-FILES                               *
        '*****************************************************************
OPEN.FILES:

        OPEN "I", #1, "CH4ILL1.DAT"
        RETURN


        '*****************************************************************
        '                      HEADINGS                                 *
        '*****************************************************************


HEADINGS:

    LPRINT CHR$(12)
    LPRINT
    LPRINT TAB(41); "CUSTOMER SALES REPORT"
    LPRINT
    LPRINT TAB(21); "CUST #"; TAB(33); "CUSTOMER NAME"; TAB(57); "SALES"; TAB(69); "DISCOUNT"; TAB(84); "NET"
    LPRINT
    RETURN
        ' ***************************************************************
        ' *                     READ-FILE                              *
        ' ***************************************************************


READFILE:
    INPUT #1, CUST.NUMB, CUST.NAME$, SALES
    IF CUST.NAME$ = "EOF" THEN END.FLAG$ = "YES"
    RETURN


    '*****************************************************************
    '*                        PROCESS                               *
    '*****************************************************************
PROCESS.RECORD:

    GOSUB DETAIL.CALCULATION          'PERFORM DETAIL-CALCULATION
    GOSUB ACCUMULATION                'PERFORM ACCUMULATION
    GOSUB DETAIL.LINE                 'PERFORM DETAIL-LINE
    GOSUB READFILE                    'PERFORM READ-FILE
    RETURN
```

**EXHIBIT 4.13   (Cont.)**

```
'**********************************************************************
'*                      DETAIL-CALCULATION                           *
'**********************************************************************

DETAIL.CALCULATION:

    IF SALES < 500 THEN
        PCT = .01
    ELSE
        PCT = .03
    END IF
    DISC = SALES * PCT
    NET = SALES - DISC
    RETURN


    '**********************************************************************
    '*                        ACCUMULATION                             *
    '**********************************************************************

ACCUMULATION:

    TOT.NET.SALES = TOT.NET.SALES + NET
    RETURN
    '**********************************************************************
    '*                        DETAIL-LINE                              *
    '**********************************************************************

DETAIL.LINE:

    LPRINT TAB(22); CUST.NUMB; TAB(32); CUST.NAME$; TAB(55);
    LPRINT USING "#,###.##"; SALES;
    LPRINT TAB(70); USING "###.##"; DISC;
    LPRINT TAB(81); USING "##,###.##"; NET
    RETURN
    '**********************************************************************
    '*                         WRAP-UP                                 *
    '**********************************************************************

WRAPUP:

    GOSUB SUMMARY.OUTPUT
    GOSUB CLOSE.FILES
    RETURN
```

**EXHIBIT 4.13   (Cont.)**

```
'**********************************************************************
'*                         SUMMARY.OUTPUT                             *
'**********************************************************************

SUMMARY.OUTPUT:

    LPRINT : LPRINT
    LPRINT TAB(61); "TOTAL NET SALES";
    LPRINT TAB(80); USING "###,###.##"; TOT.NET.SALES
    RETURN

    '**********************************************************************
    '*                         CLOSE.FILES                               *
    '**********************************************************************

CLOSE.FILES:

    CLOSE
    RETURN
```

```
                     CUSTOMER SALES REPORT

CUST #     CUSTOMER NAME        SALES       DISCOUNT        NET

 2001      BAKER BOB           400.00         4.00        396.00
 2007      CARLTON MARY      1,000.00        30.00        970.00
 2009      DICKSON DON         150.00         1.50        148.50
 6000      DONALDSON JOE       999.00        29.97        969.03


                             TOTAL NET SALES     2,483.53
```

## CHECKING FOR BOTTOM-OF-PAGE (FORMS ADVANCING)

In most reporting applications, the finished report will consist of more than one page. The records in the file will probably be so numerous that they won't list on one page.

The simple If . . . Then . . . Else structure usually provides the logic that enables the computer to determine when the printer is printing the last line on a page. Then the computer can stop the printing, cause the printer to advance the paper, and restart printing at the top of the next page. This is called **checking for bottom-of-page**. In printing a typical business report, a computer should, of course, allow for both top and bottom margins as well as left and right margins. But unless the computer is provided with the necessary instructions to check for the bottom of the page and perform the appropriate actions, the printer will continue to print across the bottom margin, over the perforation, and into the top margin of the next page as well. The computer on its own doesn't know when to cease printing on one page and skip to the next.

The programmer analyst determines the number of lines that will print on a page by inspecting the continuous form and counting the number of lines between the top and bottom margins that he or she plans to use. In Figure 4.4, the report output is often designed long before the program is written. The programmer/analyst may design a customer bill as shown on the printer spacing chart in Fig. 4.5. This design contains 20 lines; therefore, the Programmer/analyst will design the bottom-of-page-check module to allow page advance after printing the twentieth line.

**FIGURE 4.4 Continuous Form**

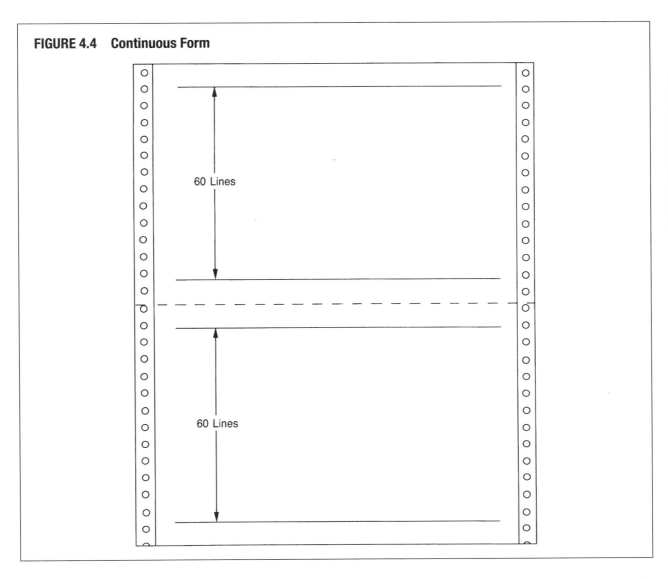

### Bottom-of-Page Checking Routine

A sound programming technique for handling page advancement is to provide programming logic to count the report lines as the program instructs the computer to print them. Figure 4.6 shows the flowchart for the page check, and Figure 4.7 illustrates the associated pseudocode. Prior to the printing of a line, a constant value, 1, is added to an accumulator. After the constant 1 has been added to the accumulator, the next step is to determine if the cumulative total of lines printed (represented by the variable, LINES-PRINTED) is equal to the predetermined number of lines (here represented by the constant 59) that are to print on a single page. If the cumulative total is *not greater than* the predetermined value, no special processing has to occur. If, on the other hand, the cumulative total of the current number of lines printed *is greater than* the predetermined value of 59, the commands to the computer are:

1. Advance the paper to the top of the next page.
2. Print the column-headings.
3. Clear the accumulator that is holding the number of lines that have been printed.

More will be said in Chapter 6 about the rationale for placing the bottom-of-page-checking module at the top of the processing loop.

## CASE STRUCTURE

For simple comparison operations where one value is compared with another, the If . . . Then . . . Else structure is the most appropriate one to use. The program design, however, may require a structure that allows for several consecutive comparisons to be made in which each comparison involves the same variable or set of variables. Furthermore, the design may require that after a dependent set of code is executed, control will jump to the very end of the series of comparison blocks instead of passing to the next condition test. Dependent code will be executed only if a specific condition test is satisfied. The **CASE structure** *(a special "case" of If . . . Then . . . Else)* allows for this kind of logic. When a condition tests true, a dependent set of code or a separate module is executed, and program control passes to the bottom of the series of comparison blocks.

With the CASE structure, the Else is followed by another If statement rather than an imperative command. (An imperative command, such as "COMPUTE" in COBOL or "LET" in BASIC, is any command other than a conditional command.)

The unique characteristic of the CASE structure is that once a given condition test is true and a separate module or set of dependent code has been executed, execution is resumed at the *bottom* of the structure. All other comparison operations are bypassed. Figure 4.8 illustrates the general logic of a CASE structure in flowchart form. Frame A shows the flowcharting form for the "CASE" command used by various languages. Frame B shows the flowcharting form when the "If . . . Then . . . Else" structure must be employed. Figure 4.9 shows the corresponding pseudocode. Examples of both dependent coding segments (not formal modules) and dependent, "callable," modules are shown, in order to emphasize the fact that the CASE structure can contain both types.

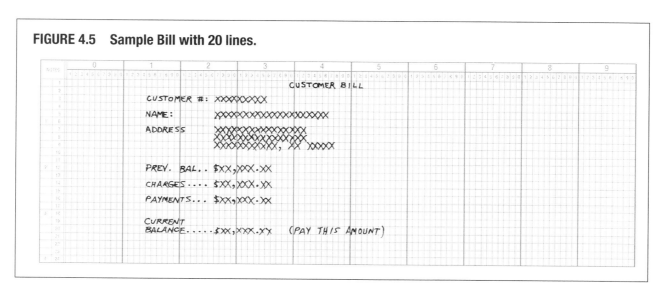

**FIGURE 4.5    Sample Bill with 20 lines.**

**FIGURE 4.6　A Flowchart Modified for Page Advancement**

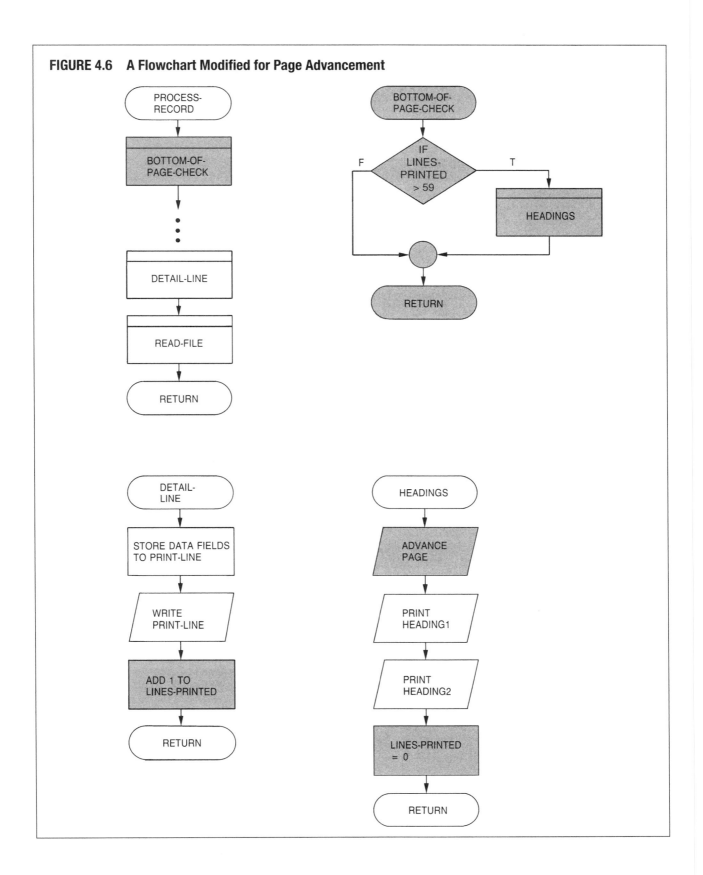

Some programming languages (Pascal and C, for example) that have a formal CASE command limit the programmer to using a simple conditional expression for each decision block in the CASE structure. With COBOL, however, the comparison can be either a simple or compound condition and may even be a comparison that determines if a variable is within a range of values, all because the programmer is not limited by a formal CASE structure. ANS 74 COBOL doesn't have a CASE statement, but it emulates one by using If . . . Then . . . Else. A universal limitation of the CASE is that only a single variable is involved in the series of comparisons.

---

**FIGURE 4.7   Pseudocode for Bottom-of-Page Check**

```
*process-record                          *detail-line
    bottom-of-page-check                     store data fields to print-line
    .                                        write print-line
    .                                        add 1 to lines-printed
    .                                        return
    detail-line                          *headings
    read-file                                advance page
    return                                   print heading1
*bottom-of-page-check                        print heading2
    if lines-printed > 59                    lines-printed = 0
        headings                             return
    endif
    return
```

---

**FIGURE 4.8   CASE Structure (General Logic)**

(Frame A)

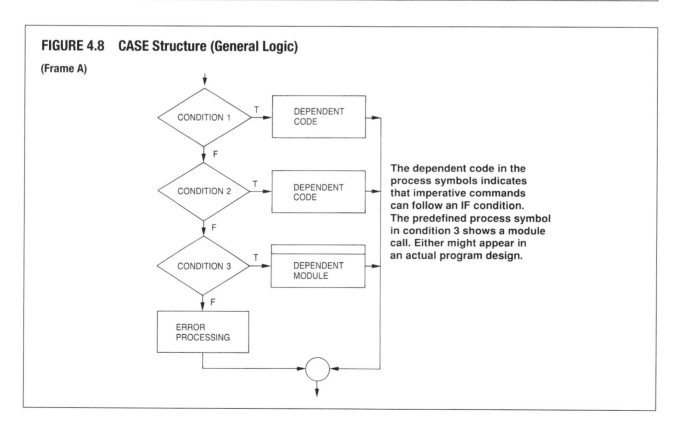

The dependent code in the process symbols indicates that imperative commands can follow an IF condition. The predefined process symbol in condition 3 shows a module call. Either might appear in an actual program design.

## FIGURE 4.8   CASE Structure (Alternate Method)

(Frame B) A Nested If . . . Then . . . Else . . . If

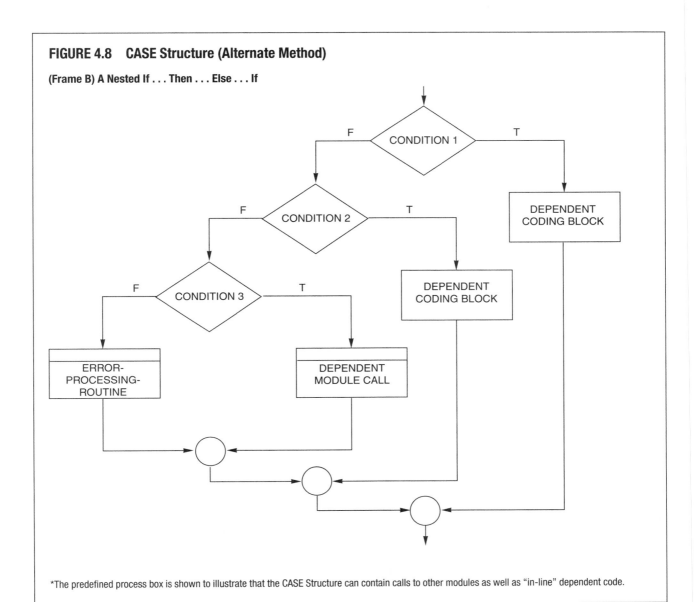

*The predefined process box is shown to illustrate that the CASE Structure can contain calls to other modules as well as "in-line" dependent code.

## FIGURE 4.9   Pseudocode for General Logic of CASE Structure

**(Frame A) When using an actual CASE command**

```
CASE . . . comments
when condition 1 is true
     execute dependent coding block 1
when condition 2 is true
     execute dependent coding block 2
when condition 3 is true
     dependent module
error-processing-routine
ENDCASE
```

**(Frame B) — Using the "If . . . Then . . . Else" to implement**

```
if conditional expression 1
     then imperative command 1
else
if conditional expression 2
     then imperative command2
else
if conditional expression 3
     then dependent module call
else
     error-processing-routine
endif
endif
endif
```

## Customer Report with Expanded Discount Schedule

Many business applications need the CASE structure. The customer report application shown below is one of them.

### Program Requirements

A manager wishes to offer discounts to his customers based on *four* different sales ranges instead of the two ranges previously discussed. This report will be similar to the one in Exhibit 4.1 in Application 4.1 and will be produced from the same input file.

### Output Design

Exhibit 4.1 in Application 4.1 illustrates the required report.

### Input Design

Exhibit 4.3 in Application 4.1 depicts the input file format for this report also.

### Test cases

Exhibit 4.4 in Application 4.1 illustrates the records to be used to test this program as well.

### Logic Considerations

Exhibit 4.14 depicts the schedule of discount rates. When the same field is compared with a multitude of values, the CASE control structure is often the most appropriate if a particular course of action will be performed as a result of each comparison, with the transfer of control passing to a point beyond the series of comparison operations. Precisely this kind of logic is needed to determine the appropriate discount percentage in this example of a customer report.

### EXHIBIT 4.14 Discount Schedule for Four Sales Ranges

| Sales Range | Percent Discount |
| --- | --- |
| 0 . . . . . . . . 199.99 | 0% |
| 200.00 . . . . 499.99 | 1% |
| 500.00 . . . . 999.99 | 2% |
| >999.99 | 3% |

### Program Design

Since all modules remain the same except the DETAIL-CALCULATION module, it would be redundant to present them again. Only the DETAIL-CALCULATION module will be reillustrated. Exhibits 4.15 and 4.16 depict the structured flowchart module and pseudocode, respectively. Frame A of Fig. 4.16 shows a method previously illustrated in Fig. 4.9. Frame B shows the "If . . . Then . . . else . . . if method."

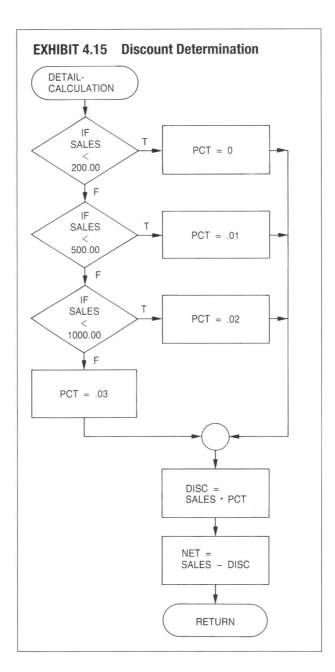

**EXHIBIT 4.15 Discount Determination**

If the sales amount is less than $200, the variable PCT is assigned a value of zero, and an automatic transfer of control occurs that will cause program execution to resume at the point of the connector (just above the calculation of DISC). If the result of this first comparison is *true*, the computer computes PCT = 0; if the resulting test is *false*, the computer executes the next comparison operation. The next comparison compares SALES to determine if SALES is less than $500. If the result of this comparison is *true*, it will store the value of .01 in the PCT variable, and transfer of control will pass to the connector at the end of the structure. If the result of this comparison is *false*, the program proceeds to determine if SALES is less than $10000. If this condition is *true*, it stores .02 in the PCT variable and transfers control to the connector; if, however, this condition is *false*, the PCT variable is assigned the value .03 and proceeds to the next instruction after the connector symbol. For clarity, a programmer will often establish compound "AND" conditions for determining if the value of a variable falls within a range of values. For example, IF SALES > 199.99 AND < 500.00 THEN . . . could be one of the condition tests in a CASE structure. COBOL handles this admirably through the use of 88 condition names also. A student of COBOL should consult a COBOL reference. The compound AND is discussed later in Exhibits 4.35 and 4.36. When comparing to see if a given value falls within a range of values, it is important to note that, using the CASE structure, the array of comparisons in the CASE structure (whether compound conditions or simple conditions) should involve only a single variable. In our example, the single variable involved in the CASE structure is SALES.

**Program Coding.** Exhibit 4.17 illustrates the COBOL program for this problem. Exhibit 4.18, Panel A, shows the QBASIC program and Panel B depicts the output.

**A Common Logic Design Fallacy.** Notice that a series of If . . . Then . . . Else structures would not be appropriate in this particular problem. Exhibit 4.19 illustrates this fallacy in logic. The error can best be described with the following example: If we are processing the third record in the data file shown in Exhibit 4.1, the sales amount is less than 200 (150 < 200); therefore, PCT is assigned the value zero. The next operation then compares the same 150 with 500. Again it is true that 150 < 500; therefore, PCT will be assigned the value of .01. This process continues all the way down the series of comparisons. Each time the sales amount is less than the upper limit constant; therefore, the PCT variable will be changed at each If . . . Then . . . Else block.

---

### EXHIBIT 4.16  Pseudocode for Customer Report

**(Frame A)**

```
*detail-calculation
    CASE
    when sales < 200
        store 0 at pct
    when sales < 500
        store .01 at pct
    when sales < 1000
        store .02 at pct
    otherwise store .03 at pct
    ENDCASE
    calculate disc = sales * pct
    calculate net = sales – disc
    return
```

**(Frame B)**

```
*detail-calculation
    if sales < 200
        then pct = 0
    else
    if sales < 500
        then pct = .01
    else
    if sales < 1000
        then pct = .02
    else
            pct = .03
    endif
    endif
    endif
    disc = sales * pct
    net = sales – disc
    return
```

Note:
Notice that there is a matching "endif" for each "if" using this method

**EXHIBIT 4.17   COBOL 85 Program Excerpt for Application 4.2**

```
1            IDENTIFICATION DIVISION.
2            PROGRAM-ID. CH4ILL2.
3
4        ****ANS COBOL 85****
5
6        *REMARKS:      THIS PROGRAM PRODUCES A CUSTOMER SALES REPORT
7        *              FROM A SALES FILE.  THE REPORT LISTS THE CUSTOMER
8        *              NUMBER, NAME, SALES, DISCOUNT AND NET AS FROM THE
9        *              PREVIOUS APPLICATION.  SPECIAL PROCESSING INCLUDES:
10       *
11       *                 1) CALCULATION OF DISCOUNT USING CASE STRUCTURE.
12       *                 2) CALCULATION OF TOTAL NET SALES.
13
14
15           ENVIRONMENT DIVISION.
16           CONFIGURATION SECTION.
17           SOURCE-COMPUTER.  CYBER.
18           OBJECT-COMPUTER.  CYBER.
19
20           INPUT-OUTPUT SECTION.
21           FILE-CONTROL.
22               SELECT SALES-FILE ASSIGN TO DTA42.
23               SELECT SALES-REPORT ASSIGN TO OUTFILE.
24
25           DATA DIVISION.
26           FILE SECTION.
27           FD SALES-FILE.
28           01 RECORD-DESCR.
29                   05 CUST-NO              PIC 9999.
30                   05 NAME                 PIC X(15).
31                   05 SALES                PIC 9(4)V99.
32           FD SALES-REPORT.
33           01 SALES-PRINT-REC              PIC X(133).
34
35           WORKING-STORAGE SECTION.
36           01 PCT                          PIC V99.
37           01 END-FLAG                     PIC XXX VALUE "NO".
38           01 DISC                         PIC 9(3)V99 VALUE ZERO.
39           01 NET                          PIC 9(5)V99 VALUE ZERO.
40           01 TOT-NET-SALES                PIC 9(6)V99 VALUE ZERO.
41
42           01 PAGE-HEADING.
43                   05                      PIC X(40) VALUE SPACES.
44                   05                      PIC X(21) VALUE
45                       "CUSTOMER SALES REPORT".
46                   05                      PIC X(62) VALUE SPACES.
47
48           01 COLUMN-HEADING.
49                   05                      PIC X(20) VALUE SPACES.
50                   05                      PIC X(13) VALUE "CUST #".
51                   05                      PIC X(23) VALUE "CUSTOMER NAME".
52                   05                      PIC X(12) VALUE "SALES".
53                   05                      PIC X(15) VALUE "DISCOUNT".
54                   05                      PIC X(50) VALUE "NET".
55
56           01 DETAIL-LINE.
57                   05                      PIC X(21) VALUE SPACES.
58                   05 CUST-NO-OUT           PIC 9999.
59                   05                      PIC X(7) VALUE SPACES.
60                   05 NAME-OUT              PIC X(15).
61                   05                      PIC X(6) VALUE SPACES.
62                   05 SALES-OUT             PIC Z,ZZZ9.99.
63                   05                      PIC X(7) VALUE SPACES.
64                   05 DISC-OUT              PIC ZZ9.99.
65                   05                      PIC X(5) VALUE SPACES.
66                   05 NET-OUT               PIC ZZ,ZZ9.99.
```

**EXHIBIT 4.17    (Cont.)**

```
67              05                       PIC X(44) VALUE SPACES.
68
69      01 TOTAL-LINE.
70              05                       PIC X(60) VALUE SPACES.
71              05                       PIC X(15) VALUE
72                  "TOTAL NET SALES".
73              05                       PIC X(4) VALUE SPACES.
74              05 TOT-NET-SALES-OUT      PIC ZZZ,ZZ9.99.
75              05                       PIC X(44) VALUE SPACES.
76      /
77       PROCEDURE DIVISION.
78       000-MAIN-LINE.
79           PERFORM 100-START-UP.
80           PERFORM 200-PROCESS-RECORD UNTIL END-FLAG = "YES".
81           PERFORM 300-WRAP-UP.
82           STOP RUN.
83
84       100-START-UP.
85           PERFORM 105-OPEN-FILES.
86           PERFORM 110-HEADINGS.
87           PERFORM 120-READ-FILE.
88
89       105-OPEN-FILES.
90           OPEN INPUT SALES-FILE.
91           OPEN OUTPUT SALES-REPORT.
92
93       110-HEADINGS.
94           WRITE SALES-PRINT-REC FROM PAGE-HEADING AFTER PAGE.
95           WRITE SALES-PRINT-REC FROM COLUMN-HEADING AFTER 2.
96           MOVE SPACES TO SALES-PRINT-REC.
97           WRITE SALES-PRINT-REC AFTER 1.
98
99       120-READ-FILE.
100          READ SALES-FILE
101             AT END MOVE "YES" TO END-FLAG.
102
103      200-PROCESS-RECORD.
104          PERFORM 210-DETAIL-CALCULATION.
105          PERFORM 220-ACCUMULATION.
106          PERFORM 230-DETAIL-LINE.
107          PERFORM 120-READ-FILE.
108
109      210-DETAIL-CALCULATION.
110          IF SALES < 200
111             THEN  COMPUTE PCT = 0
112          ELSE
113          IF SALES < 500
114             THEN  COMPUTE PCT = .01
115          ELSE
116          IF SALES < 1000
117             THEN COMPUTE PCT = .02
118          ELSE
119             COMPUTE PCT = .03.
120          COMPUTE DISC ROUNDED = SALES * PCT.
121          COMPUTE NET = SALES - DISC.
122
123      220-ACCUMULATION.
124          ADD NET TO TOT-NET-SALES.
125
126      230-DETAIL-LINE.
127          MOVE CUST-NO TO CUST-NO-OUT.
128          MOVE NAME TO NAME-OUT.
```

**EXHIBIT 4.17    (Cont.)**

```
129              MOVE SALES TO SALES-OUT.
130              MOVE DISC TO DISC-OUT.
131              MOVE NET TO NET-OUT.
132
133              WRITE SALES-PRINT-REC FROM DETAIL-LINE AFTER 1.
134
135          300-WRAP-UP.
136
137              PERFORM 310-SUMMARY-OUTPUT.
138              PERFORM 320-CLOSE-FILES.
139
140          310-SUMMARY-OUTPUT.
141              MOVE TOT-NET-SALES TO TOT-NET-SALES-OUT.
142              WRITE SALES-PRINT-REC FROM TOTAL-LINE AFTER 3.
143
144          320-CLOSE-FILES.
145              CLOSE SALES-FILE  SALES-REPORT.
146
147
```

```
                   CUSTOMER SALES REPORT

CUST #        CUSTOMER NAME        SALES       DISCOUNT        NET

 2001         BAKER, BOB           400.00         4.00        396.00
 2007         CARLTON, MARY       1000.00        30.00        970.00
 2009         DICKSON, DON         150.00         0.00        150.00
 6000         DONALDSON, JOE       999.00        19.98        979.02


                                        TOTAL NET SALES    2,495.02
```

**EXHIBIT 4.18    QBASIC Program for Application 4.2**

```
' *****************************************************************
' *                  PROGRAM IDENTIFICATION                      *
' *****************************************************************
' * PROGRAM NAME: CUSTOMER REPORT (CASE STRUCTURE) (CH4APL2)      *
' *****************************************************************
' REMARKS:  THIS PROGRAM PRODUCES CUSTOMER SALES REPORT
'           FROM A SALES FILE.  THE REPORT LISTS THE CUSTOMER
'           NUMBER, NAME, SALES, DISCOUNT, AND NET AS FROM THE
'           PREVIOUS APPLICATION.  SPECIAL PROCESSING INCLUDES:
'           1) CALCULATION OF DISCOUNT USING NESTED IF
'           2) CALCULATION OF TOTAL NET SALES
' *****************************************************************
' *                      MAIN-LINE                               *
' *****************************************************************
GOSUB STARTUP                      'PERFORM START-UP
DO UNTIL END.FLAG$ = "YES"
    GOSUB PROCESS.RECORD           'PERFORM PROCESS
LOOP
GOSUB WRAPUP                       'PERFORM WRAP-UP
END
```

**EXHIBIT 4.18 (Cont.)**

```
' *********************************************************************
' *                         START-UP                              *
' *********************************************************************

STARTUP:
     GOSUB INITIALIZE
     GOSUB OPEN.FILES
     GOSUB HEADINGS                        'PERFORM HEADINGS
     GOSUB READFILE                        'PERFORM READ-FILE
     RETURN


     '*******************************************************************
     '*                    INITIALIZE                               *
     '*******************************************************************

INITIALIZE:

     WIDTH LPRINT 120
     END.FLAG$ = "NO"
     TOT.NET.SALES = 0
     RETURN

     '*******************************************************************
     '*                    OPEN-FILES                              *
     '*******************************************************************

OPEN.FILES:

     OPEN "I", #1, "CH4ILL2.DAT"
     RETURN

     ' *****************************************************************
     ' *                     HEADINGS                              *
     ' *****************************************************************

HEADINGS:

     LPRINT CHR$(12)
     LPRINT
     LPRINT TAB(41); "CUSTOMER SALES REPORT"
     LPRINT
     LPRINT TAB(21); "CUST #"; TAB(33); "CUSTOMER NAME"; TAB(57); "SALES"; TAB(69); "DISCOUNT"; TAB(84); "NET"
     LPRINT
     RETURN

     ' *****************************************************************
     ' *                     READ-FILE                             *
     ' *****************************************************************

READFILE:

     INPUT #1, CUST.NUMB, CUST.NAME$, SALES
     IF CUST.NAME$ = "EOF" THEN END.FLAG$ = "YES"
     RETURN
```

**EXHIBIT 4.18 (Cont.)**

```
' **********************************************************************
' *                          PROCESS                                  *
' **********************************************************************
PROCESS.RECORD:

     GOSUB DETAIL.CALCULATION          'PERFORM DETAIL-CALCULATION
     GOSUB ACCUMULATION                'PERFORM ACCUMULATION
     GOSUB DETAIL.LINE                 'PERFORM DETAIL-LINE
     GOSUB READFILE                    'PERFORM READ-FILE
     RETURN


     ' *******************************************************************
     ' *                     DETAIL-CALCULATION                         *
     '*******************************************************************

DETAIL.CALCULATION:

     IF SALES < 200 THEN
         PCT = 0
     ELSE
         IF SALES < 500 THEN
           PCT = .01
         ELSE
             IF SALES < 1000 THEN
               PCT = .02
             ELSE PCT = .03
             END IF
         END IF
     END IF
     DISC = SALES * PCT
     NET = SALES - DISC
     RETURN


     '*******************************************************************
     '*                      ACCUMULATION                              *
     ' *****************************************************************

ACCUMULATION:

     TOT.NET.SALES = TOT.NET.SALES + NET
     RETURN


     ' *****************************************************************
     ' *                       DETAIL-LINE                             *
     ' *****************************************************************

DETAIL.LINE:

     LPRINT TAB(22); CUST.NUMB; TAB(32); CUST.NAME$; TAB(55);
     LPRINT USING "#,###.##"; SALES;
     LPRINT TAB(70); USING "###.##"; DISC;
     LPRINT TAB(81); USING "##,###.##"; NET
     RETURN
```

**EXHIBIT 4.18   (Cont.)**

```
' ***********************************************************************
' *                          WRAP-UP                                   *
' ***********************************************************************

WRAPUP:
     GOSUB SUMMARY.TOTAL
     GOSUB CLOSE.FILES
     RETURN


' ***********************************************************************
'*                        SUMMARY-TOTAL                                *
' ***********************************************************************

SUMMARY.TOTAL:

     LPRINT : LPRINT
     LPRINT TAB(61); "TOTAL NET SALES";
     LPRINT TAB(80); USING "$$#,###.##"; TOT.NET.SALES
     RETURN


' ***********************************************************************
'*                        CLOSE-FILES                                  *
' ***********************************************************************

CLOSE.FILES:
     CLOSE
     RETURN
```

```
                      CUSTOMER SALES REPORT

CUST #      CUSTOMER NAME      SALES      DISCOUNT      NET

  2001     BAKER BOB          400.00        4.00      396.00
  2007     CARLTON MARY     1,000.00       30.00      970.00
  2009     DICKSON DON        150.00        0.00      150.00
  6000     DONALDSON JOE      999.00       19.98      979.02


                               TOTAL NET SALES    $2,495.02
```

**EXHIBIT 4.18    (Cont.)   ILLUSTRATIVE OUTPUT FOR BOTH COBOL 85 and BASIC**
**Panel B**

```
                         CUSTOMER SALES REPORT
        CUST #       CUSTOMER NAME      SALES     DISCOUNT      NET
        2001        BAKER BOB          400.00       4.00      396.00
        2007        CARLTON MARY     1,000.00      30.00      970.00
        2009        DICKSON DON        150.00       0.00      150.00
        6000        DONALDSON JOE      999.00      19.98      979.02
                               TOTAL NET SALES    $2,495.02
```

**EXHIBIT 4.19   A Common Fallacy in Logic**

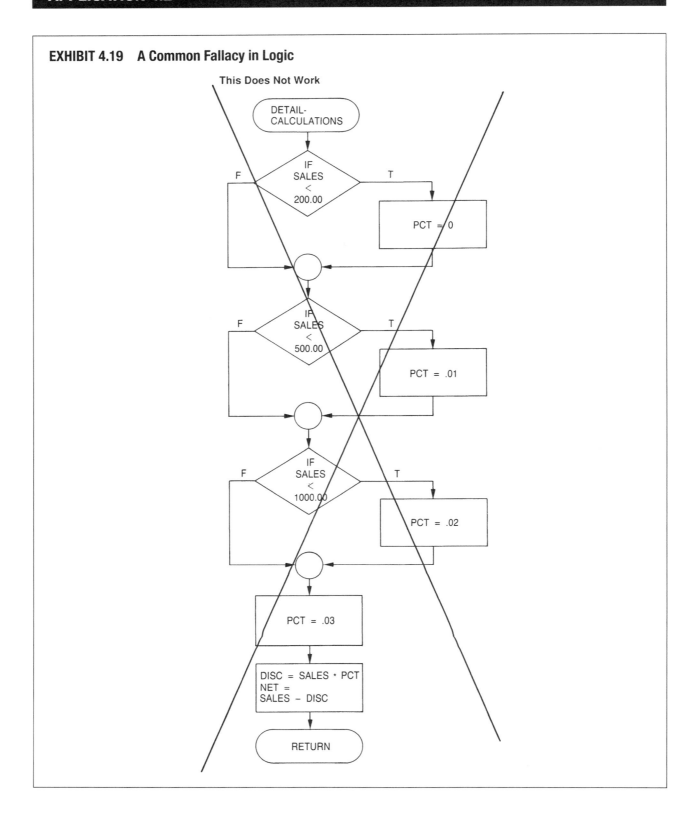

## A Student Grade Report Using Both If . . . Then . . . Else and CASE

The following Student Grade Report problem illustrates the use of both the If . . . Then . . . Else and CASE structures.

### Program Requirements

A teacher wishes to produce a class grade report that prints each student's number (SN), name, three test scores (TEST1, TEST2, TEST3), and their average (AVG), as well as the student's letter grade. At the bottom of the report, the teacher wishes to print the number of students in the class and the number of students who failed the test.

### Output Design

Exhibit 4.20 illustrates the class grade report, and Exhibit 4.21 depicts the associated printer spacing chart.

### Input Design

The record layout for this problem is the same input file illustrated in Exhibit 3.2.

### Logic Considerations

The average test score (AVG) is computed by summing the three test scores and dividing by 3. Once AVG is determined, the appropriate letter grade, which is based on the average grade range for the test, must be transferred to the print line. A student receives a letter grade of F for an average grade less than 60, a D for an average grade between 60.00 and 69.99, a C for an average grade between 70.00 and 79.99, a B for an average grade between 80.00 and 89.99, and an A for an average grade between 90.00 and 100.00

Also, the number of failures (averages less than 60) must be accumulated.

### Program Design

**Hierarchy Chart.**   The hierarchy chart remains unchanged from Exhibit 3.8, except that there is no computation to be made in the WRAP-UP module.

**Structured Flowchart.**   Exhibit 4.22 (Frame A) shows the structured flowchart for the student grade report. The MAIN-LINE module, of course, remains the same in all the program logic found in this text. The START-UP module contains initialization blocks that set the TOT-STUDENTS and TOT-FAILURES variables equal to zero. The files are opened, the headings are printed, and the first record from the file is read (that is the *preread*).

The PROCESS module looks the same as in the previous problem, since it serves as a subdriver or intermediate level control module that invokes other subordinate level modules. The PROCESS module invokes the DETAIL-CALCULATION, ACCUMULATION, DETAIL-LINE, and READ-STUDENT-FILE modules-in that order.

The DETAIL-CALCULATION (Frame B) module first calculates the average (AVG) by summing the three test scores and dividing by 3. The next step is to determine which letter grade to assign to the student. If the student's average (AVG) is less than 60.00, the constant F is stored or moved into an outfield (GRADE-OUT) of the detail line. If the result of this condition test is false, it then tests to see if AVG is less than 70. If this condition test is true, then AVG must be equal to or greater than 60.00 and less than 70 (that is, between 60 and 69.99). If AVG is within this range, the constant D is stored into GRD-OUT of the detail line. If the condition test is false, then the next step is to determine if AVG is less than 80. If this test is true, then AVG is within the range of 70 to 79.99. In this case, the constant C is stored into GRD-OUT. This process of comparing AVG with the next higher grade level

---

**EXHIBIT 4.20   Sample Class Grade Report**

```
                         CLASS GRADE REPORT

     SN         NAME        TEST 1   TEST 2   TEST 3   AVG   LTR GRD

    4502    CARL BAKER        100       90       80     90     A
    6011    DON CROCKER        90       85       80     85     B
    XXXX    XXXXXXXXXXXX       XX       XX       XX     XX     X


                         TOTAL STUDENTS       XXX
                        NUMBER OF FAILURES    XXX
```

boundary (the upper limit) continues for both the B and the A letter grades. If AVG is within the range of 80 to 89.99, then the constant B is stored into GRD-OUT. If AVG is within the range of 90 to 100, the constant A is stored into GRD-OUT. This flowchart shows the "straight down" approach. See Frame C for a "nested" approach to the CASE.

The ACCUMULATE module includes a command that accumulates the total students (TOT-STUDENTS) and an If . . . Then . . . Else command that allows the accumulation of all students who failed the exam (TOT-FAILURES). It is true that this accumulation step could have been included in the DETAIL-CALCULATIONS module at the first deci-

sion block; but the program becomes much easier to maintain when all accumulation steps are kept in a separate accumulation block of the flowchart, even if it requires a redundant comparison operation. Thus the programmer is never in doubt as to where he or she will find code related to the accumulation of a total; it will always be found in the ACCUMU-LATION module except for certain counters.

**Pseudocode.** Exhibit 4.23 depicts the associated pseudocode for this problem.

**Program Coding.** Exhibits 4.24 and 4.25 illustrate the COBOL 85 and QBASIC codes respectively.

**EXHIBIT 4.21** Printer Spacing Chart for Student Grade Report

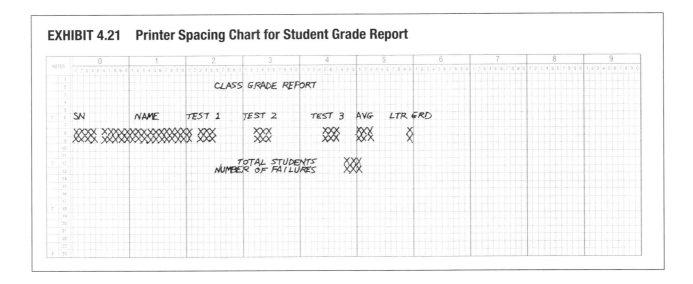

# APPLICATION 4.3

**EXHIBIT 4.22    Flowchart for Student Grade Report**

(Frame A)

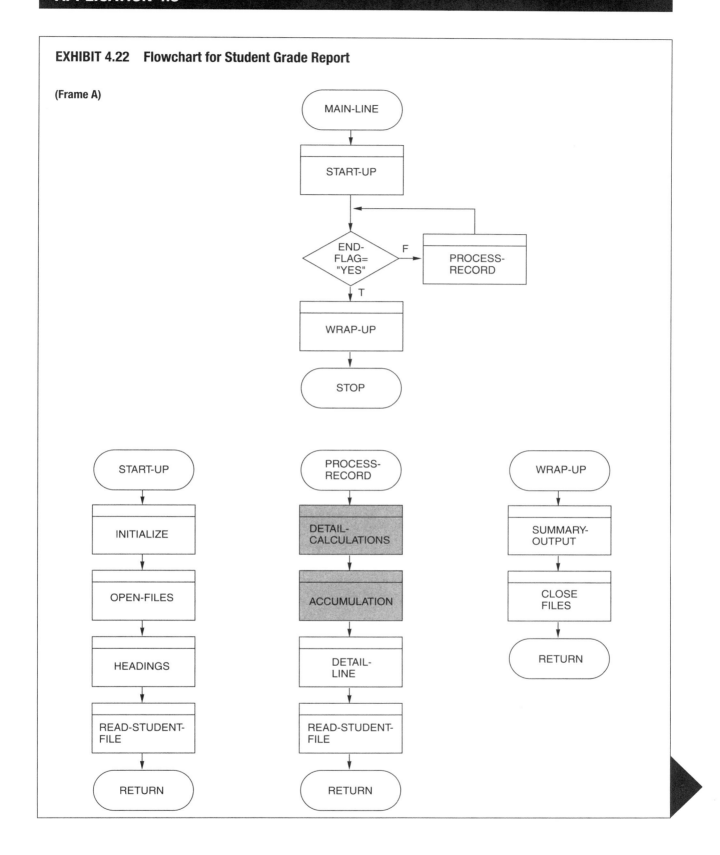

**EXHIBIT 4.22    (Cont.)**

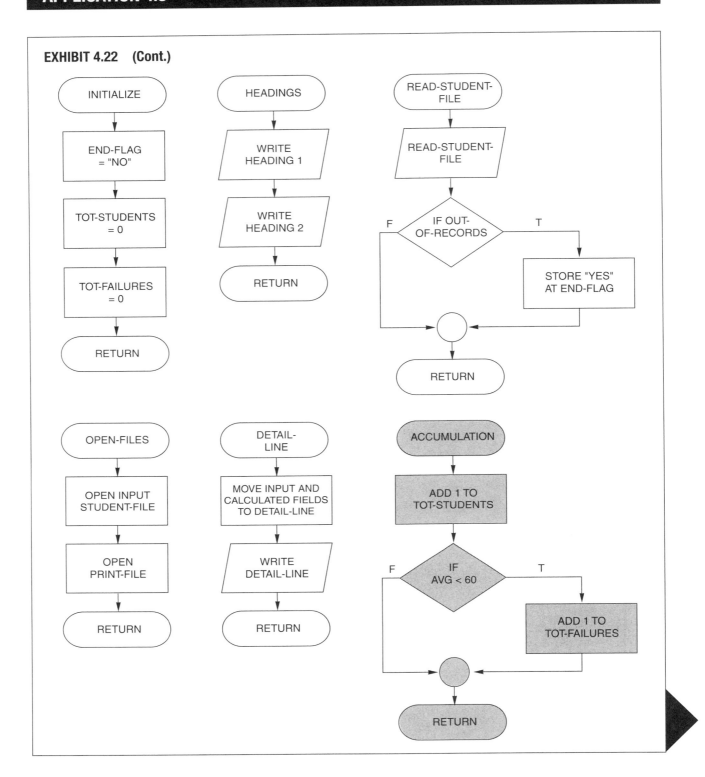

**EXHIBIT 4.22    (Cont.)**

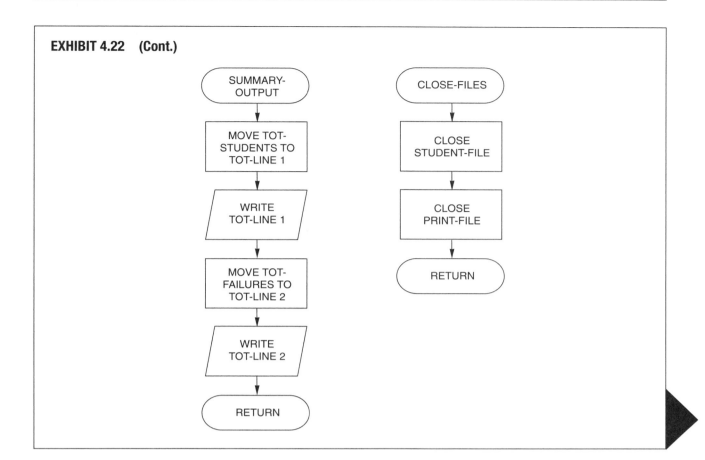

**EXHIBIT 4.22    "Straight down" approach**

(Frame B)

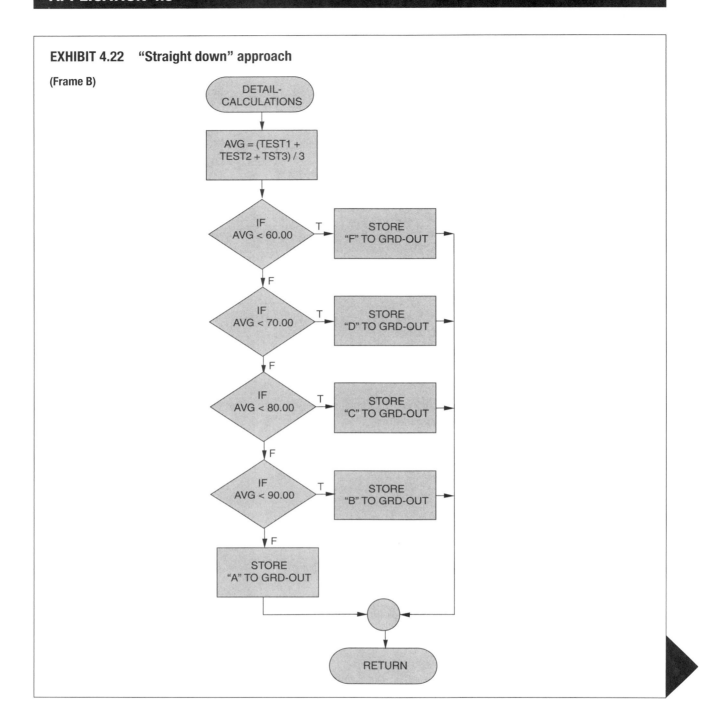

**EXHIBIT 4.22  Alternate Nested Method**

**(Frame C)**

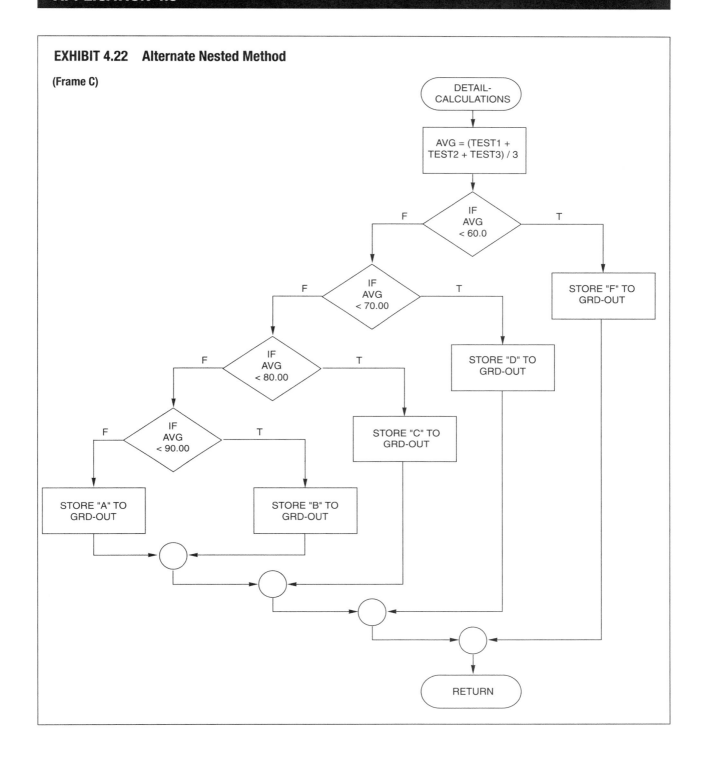

**EXHIBIT 4.23   Pseudocode for Application 4.3, Student Grade Report**

*mainline
    start-up
      dowhile end-flag = "no"
        process-record
    enddo
    wrap-up
    stop
*start-up
    initialize
    open-files
    headings
    read-file
    return
*initialize
    end-flag = "no"
    tot-students = 0
    tot-failures = 0
    return
*open-files
    open student-file
    open print-file
    return
*headings
    write page heading
    write column heading
    return
*read-file
    read student-file
      when out of records
        end-flag = "yes"
    endread
    return
*process-record
    detail-calculations
    accumulation
    detail-line
    read-file
    return

*detail-calculations
    avg = (test1 + test2 + test3) /3
    if avg < 60
      then
        grd-out = "f"
    else
      if avg < 70
        then
          grd-out = "d"
        else
          if avg < 80
            then
              grd-out = "c"
            else
              if avg < 90
                then
                  grd-out = "b"
              else
                grd-out = "a"
              endif
            endif
          endif
        endif
      endif
    return
*accumulation
    add 1 to tot-students
    if avg < 60
      then add 1 to tot-failures
    endif
    return
*detail-line
    transfer input data to detail-line
    transfer calculated fields to detail-line
    write detail-line
    return
*wrap-up
    summary-output
    close-files
    return
*summary-output
    move tot-students to total-line1
    write total-line1
    move tot-failures to total-line2
    write total-line2
    return
*close-files
    close files
    return

**EXHIBIT 4.24    COBOL 85 for Application 4.3 Student Grade Report**

```
1          IDENTIFICATION DIVISION.
2          PROGRAM-ID. CH4ILL3.
3
4         ****ANS COBOL 85****
5         ****USES END-IF METHODOLOGY WITH CASE STRUCTURE USING IF THEN ELSE****
6
7
8         *REMARKS:   THIS PROGRAM PRODUCES A CLASS GRADE REPORT FROM A
9         *              STUDENT FILE.  IN ADDITION TO INDIVIDUAL GRADE
10        *              AVERAGES, IT ALSO PROCESSES THE TOTAL STUDENT
11        *              COUNT, NUMBER OF FAILURES, AND ASSIGNS A LETTER
12        *              GRADE FOR EACH STUDENT.  TOTALS ARE PRINTED FOR
13        *              TOTAL STUDENTS AND  NUMBER OF FAILURES.
14
15         ENVIRONMENT DIVISION.
16
17         CONFIGURATION SECTION.
18
19         SOURCE-COMPUTER.  CYBER.
20         OBJECT-COMPUTER.  CYBER.
21
22         INPUT-OUTPUT SECTION.
23
24         FILE-CONTROL.
25             SELECT STUDENT-FILE ASSIGN TO DTA43.
26             SELECT STUDENT-REPORT ASSIGN TO OUTFILE.
27
28
29         DATA DIVISION.
30
31         FILE SECTION.
32
33         FD   STUDENT-FILE.
34
35         01   STUDENT-REC.
36
37             05 SN                 PIC 9(4).
38             05 NAME               PIC X(15).
39             05 TEST1              PIC 999.
40             05 TEST2              PIC 999.
41             05 TEST3              PIC 999.
42
43         FD   STUDENT-REPORT LABEL RECORDS ARE OMITTED.
44
45         01   REPORT-REC               PIC X(133).
46
47
48         WORKING-STORAGE SECTION.
49
50         01   END-FLAG                 PIC XXX VALUE "NO".
51         01   TOT-STUDENTS             PIC 999 VALUE ZERO.
52         01   TOT-FAILURES             PIC 999 VALUE ZERO.
53         01   TEST-AVG                 PIC 999.
54
55         01   PAGE-HEADING.
56
57             05                       PIC X(25) VALUE SPACES.
58             05                       PIC X(18) VALUE
59                                        "CLASS GRADE REPORT".
60             05                       PIC X(89) VALUE SPACES.
61
62         01   COLUMN-HEADING.
63             05                       PIC X     VALUE SPACES.
64             05                       PIC XX    VALUE "SN".
65             05                       PIC X(9) VALUE SPACES.
66             05                       PIC X(4) VALUE "NAME".
```

**EXHIBIT 4.24   (Cont.)**

```
67              05                          PIC X(4) VALUE SPACES.
68              05                          PIC X(6) VALUE "TEST 1".
69              05                          PIC X(5) VALUE SPACES.
70              05                          PIC X(6) VALUE "TEST 2".
71              05                          PIC X(6) VALUE SPACES.
72              05                          PIC X(6) VALUE "TEST 3".
73              05                          PIC X(2) VALUE SPACES.
74              05                          PIC X(3) VALUE "AVG".
75              05                          PIC X(3) VALUE SPACES.
76              05                          PIC X(7) VALUE "LTR GRD".
77              05                          PIC X(68) VALUE SPACES.
78
79
80         01   DETAIL-LINE.
81              05                          PIC X VALUE SPACES.
82              05 SN-OUT                   PIC 9(4).
83              05                          PIC X    VALUE SPACES.
84              05 NAME-OUT                 PIC X(15).
85              05                          PIC X    VALUE SPACES.
86              05 TEST1-OUT                PIC Z99.
87              05                          PIC X(8) VALUE SPACES.
88              05 TEST2-OUT                PIC Z99.
89              05                          PIC X(9) VALUE SPACES.
90              05 TEST3-OUT                PIC Z99.
91              05                          PIC X(3) VALUE SPACES.
92              05 TEST-AVG-OUT             PIC Z99.
93              05                          PIC X(6) VALUE SPACES.
94              05 LETTER-GRADE-OUT         PIC X.
95              05                          PIC X(71) VALUE SPACES.
96
97         01   TOT-LINE1.
98
99              05                          PIC X(29) VALUE SPACES.
100             05                          PIC X(17) VALUE
101                                            "TOTAL STUDENTS    ".
102             05 TOT-STUDENTS-OUT          PIC ZZ9.
103             05                          PIC X(83) VALUE SPACES.
104
105
106        01   TOT-LINE2.
107
108             05                          PIC X(25) VALUE SPACES.
109             05                          PIC X(21) VALUE
110                                            "NUMBER OF FAILURES    ".
111             05 TOT-FAILURES-OUT          PIC ZZ9.
112             05                          PIC X(83) VALUE SPACES.
113
114    /
115      PROCEDURE DIVISION.
116
117      000-MAIN-LINE.
118
119          PERFORM 100-START-UP.
120          PERFORM 200-PROCESS-RECORD UNTIL END-FLAG = "YES".
121          PERFORM 300-WRAP-UP.
122          STOP RUN.
123
124      100-START-UP.
125
126    *     INITIALIZATION FROM W-S
127          PERFORM 105-OPEN-FILES.
128          PERFORM 110-HEADINGS.
129          PERFORM 120-READ-FILE.
130
131      105-OPEN-FILES.
132          OPEN INPUT STUDENT-FILE.
```

**EXHIBIT 4.24   (Cont.)**

```
133            OPEN OUTPUT STUDENT-REPORT.
134
135
136        110-HEADINGS.
137
138            WRITE REPORT-REC FROM PAGE-HEADING AFTER ADVANCING PAGE.
139            WRITE REPORT-REC FROM COLUMN-HEADING AFTER ADVANCING 2 LINES.
140            MOVE SPACES TO REPORT-REC.
141            WRITE REPORT-REC.
142
143        120-READ-FILE.
144
145            READ STUDENT-FILE AT END MOVE "YES" TO END-FLAG.
146
147        200-PROCESS-RECORD.
148
149            PERFORM 210-DETAIL-CALCULATIONS.
150            PERFORM 220-ACCUMULATION.
151            PERFORM 230-DETAIL-LINE.
152            PERFORM 120-READ-FILE.
153
154        210-DETAIL-CALCULATIONS.
155
156            COMPUTE TEST-AVG ROUNDED = (TEST1 + TEST2 + TEST3) / 3.
157
158            IF TEST-AVG < 60.00
159               THEN MOVE "F" TO LETTER-GRADE-OUT
160               ELSE
161                  IF TEST-AVG < 70.00
162                    THEN MOVE "D" TO LETTER-GRADE-OUT
163                    ELSE
164                       IF TEST-AVG < 80.00
165                          THEN MOVE "C" TO LETTER-GRADE-OUT
166                          ELSE
167                          IF TEST-AVG < 90.00
168                             THEN MOVE "B" TO LETTER-GRADE-OUT
169                             ELSE
170                                MOVE "A" TO LETTER-GRADE-OUT
171                          END-IF
172                       END-IF
173                  END-IF
174            END-IF.
175
176        220-ACCUMULATION.
177
178            ADD 1 TO TOT-STUDENTS.
179            IF TEST-AVG < 60
180               THEN ADD 1 TO TOT-FAILURES
181            END-IF.
182
183        230-DETAIL-LINE.
184
185            MOVE SN TO SN-OUT.
186            MOVE NAME TO NAME-OUT.
187            MOVE TEST1 TO TEST1-OUT.
188            MOVE TEST2 TO TEST2-OUT.
189            MOVE TEST3 TO TEST3-OUT.
190            MOVE TEST-AVG TO TEST-AVG-OUT.
191            WRITE REPORT-REC FROM DETAIL-LINE.
192
193        300-WRAP-UP.
194            PERFORM 310-SUMMARY-OUTPUT.
195            PERFORM 320-CLOSE-FILES.
196
197        310-SUMMARY-OUTPUT.
198            MOVE TOT-STUDENTS TO TOT-STUDENTS-OUT.
```

---

**EXHIBIT 4.24   COBOL 85 for Application 4.3 Class Grade Report**

```
199              MOVE TOT-FAILURES TO TOT-FAILURES-OUT.
200              WRITE REPORT-REC FROM TOT-LINE1 AFTER ADVANCING 3 LINES.
201              WRITE REPORT-REC FROM TOT-LINE2.
202
203          320-CLOSE-FILES.
204              CLOSE STUDENT-FILE   STUDENT-REPORT.
```

```
                      CLASS GRADE REPORT

SN         NAME      TEST 1      TEST 2      TEST 3   AVG    LTR GRD

4502  CARL BAKER       100         90          80      90      A
6011  DON CROCKER       90         85          80      85      B
7053  SALLY SMITH       50         60          60      57      F
8464  DANA JACKSON      75         70          80      75      C


                        TOTAL STUDENTS      4
                        NUMBER OF FAILURES  1
```

---

**EXHIBIT 4.25   QBASIC Program for Application 4.3.**

```
'**********************************************************************
'*                     PROGRAM IDENTIFICATION                        *
'**********************************************************************
'* PROGRAM NAME: CH4APL3                                             *
'**********************************************************************
'   REMARKS:    THIS PROGRAM PRODUCES A CLASS GRADE REPORT FROM A
'               STUDENT FILE.  IN ADDITION TO INDIVIDUAL GRADE
'               AVERAGES, IT ALSO COMPUTES THE TOTAL STUDENT COUNT, NUMBER
'               OF FAILURES, AND ASSIGNS A LETTER GRADE FOR EACH STUDENT.
'               TOTALS ARE PRINTED FOR TOTAL STUDENTS AND NUMBER OF FAILURE
'**********************************************************************
'*                         MAIN-LINE                                 *
'**********************************************************************
GOSUB STARTUP                     '   PERFORM START-UP
DO UNTIL END.FLAG$ = "YES"
    GOSUB PROCESS                 '   PERFORM PROCESS
LOOP
GOSUB WRAPUP                      '   PERFORM WRAP-UP
END
'**********************************************************************
'*                          START-UP                                 *
'**********************************************************************



STARTUP:
    GOSUB INITIALIZE
    GOSUB OPEN.FILES
    GOSUB HEADINGS                '  PERFORM HEADINGS
    GOSUB READFILE                '  PERFORM READ-STUDENT-FILE
    RETURN
```

---

## EXHIBIT 4.25   (Cont.)

```
'**********************************************************************
'*                         INITIALIZE                                *
'**********************************************************************

INITIALIZE:

    WIDTH LPRINT 132
    END.FLAG$ = "NO"
    TOT.STUDENTS = 0
    TOT.FAILURES = 0
    RETURN
        '****************************************************************
        '*                    OPEN FILES                      *
        '****************************************************************

OPEN.FILES:

    OPEN "I", #1, "CH4ILL3.DAT"
    RETURN


        '****************************************************************
        '*                     HEADINGS                       *
        '****************************************************************
HEADINGS:
    LPRINT CHR$(12)
    LPRINT
    LPRINT TAB(26); "CLASS GRADE REPORT"
    LPRINT
    LPRINT TAB(1); "SN"; TAB(12); "NAME"; TAB(21); "TEST 1"; TAB(31); "TEST 2"; TAB(43); "TEST  3"; TAB(51); "AVG"; TAB(57); "LTR GRD"
    LPRINT
    RETURN




        '****************************************************************
        '*                  READ-STUDENT-FILE                 *
        '****************************************************************
READFILE:

    INPUT #1, STUD.NUMB, STUD.NAME$, TEST1, TEST2, TEST3
    IF STUD.NAME$ = "EOF" THEN END.FLAG$ = "YES"
    RETURN

        '****************************************************************
        '*                     PROCESS                        *
        '****************************************************************
PROCESS:

    GOSUB DETAIL.CALCULATION          ' PERFORM DETAIL-CALCULATION
    GOSUB ACCUMULATION                ' PERFORM ACCUMULATION
    GOSUB DETAIL.LINE                 ' PERFORM DETAIL-LINE
    GOSUB READFILE                    ' PERFORM READ-STUDENT-FILE
    RETURN
```

**EXHIBIT 4.25 (Cont.)**

```
'****************************************************************************
'*                          DETAIL-CALCULATION                           *
'****************************************************************************
DETAIL.CALCULATION:

    TEST.AVG = (TEST1 + TEST2 + TEST3) / 3

    IF TEST.AVG < 60 THEN
        GRD.OUT$ = "F"
    ELSE
      IF TEST.AVG < 70 THEN
          GRD.OUT$ = "D"
      ELSE
          IF TEST.AVG < 80 THEN
              GRD.OUT$ = "C"
          ELSE
              IF TEST.AVG < 90 THEN
                  GRD.OUT$ = "B"
              ELSE GRD.OUT$ = "A"
              END IF
          END IF
      END IF
    END IF

    RETURN
'.
    ' ****************************************************************************
    ' *                          ACCUMULATION                                *
    ' ****************************************************************************

ACCUMULATION:

    TOT.STUDENTS = TOT.STUDENTS + 1
    IF TEST.AVG < 60 THEN
        TOT.FAILURES = TOT.FAILURES + 1
    END IF
    RETURN

    '****************************************************************************
    '*                          DETAIL-LINE                                 *
    '****************************************************************************

DETAIL.LINE:
    LPRINT USING "####"; STUD.NUMB;
    LPRINT TAB(6); STUD.NAME$;
    LPRINT TAB(23); USING "###"; TEST1;
    LPRINT TAB(33); USING "###"; TEST2;
    LPRINT TAB(45); USING "###"; TEST3;
    LPRINT TAB(51); USING "##"; TEST.AVG;
    LPRINT TAB(60); GRD.OUT$
    RETURN
```

**EXHIBIT 4.25   (Cont.)**

```
'**********************************************************************
'*                         WRAP-UP                                    *
'**********************************************************************

WRAPUP:

    GOSUB SUMMARY.OUTPUT
    GOSUB CLOSE.FILES
    RETURN

SUMMARY.OUTPUT:

    LPRINT : LPRINT
    LPRINT TAB(30); "TOTAL STUDENTS      "; TOT.STUDENTS
    LPRINT TAB(26); "NUMBER OF FAILURES     "; TOT.FAILURES

CLOSE.FILES:

    CLOSE
    RETURN
```

```
                     CLASS GRADE REPORT

SN        NAME        TEST 1    TEST 2      TEST 3 AVG   LTR GRD

4502 CARL BAKER        100        90          80   90       A
6011 DON CROCKER        90        85          80   85       B
7053 SALLY SMITH        50        60          60   57       F
8564 DANA JACKSON       75        70          80   75       C


                     TOTAL STUDENTS      4
                     NUMBER OF FAILURES  1
```

## IDENTIFICATION CODES

Often a code is used to classify data according to a certain variable or attribute. For example, a one-byte field on a master pay record could be established to record the sex of an employee. The letter F in the designated field could represent a female, and the letter M could represent a male. The use of **identification codes** (or **classification codes**) reduces the amount of record storage space and often reduces errors in entering data, since there is less to key in, using codes.

Figure 4.10 shows a student record with two codes—a sex code and a class code. The sex code in this record is an M, which means that the student is a male, and the class code is a 4, which means the student is a senior.

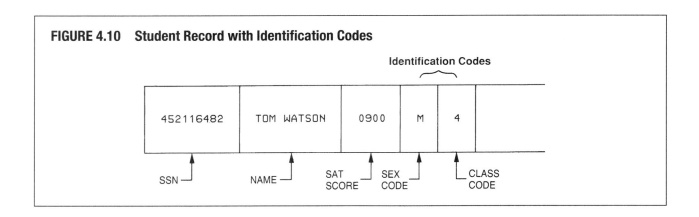

**FIGURE 4.10  Student Record with Identification Codes**

## Student Summary Report Using Identification Codes

### Program Requirements

To illustrate the use of identification codes, let's suppose than an administrator wants to know the total number of students in each of the class categories (freshman, sophomore, junior, and senior). A report can summarize this tally.

### Output Design

Exhibit 4.26 illustrates the summary report of student classification. The report is nothing more than a series of total lines. Exhibit 4.27 describes the associated print chart.

### Input Design

Exhibit 4.28 illustrates the record layout for the file.

### Test Data

Exhibit 4.29 shows the test data for program execution.

---

**EXHIBIT 4.26   Summary Report of Student Classification**

```
                    TOTALS BY STUDENT CLASSIFICATION

              TOTAL FRESHMEN...........X,XXX
              TOTAL SOPHOMORES.........X,XXX
              TOTAL JUNIORS............X,XXX
              TOTAL SENIORS............X,XXX

              TOTAL STUDENTS..........XX,XXX
```

---

**EXHIBIT 4.27   Printer Spacing Chart for Student Classification**

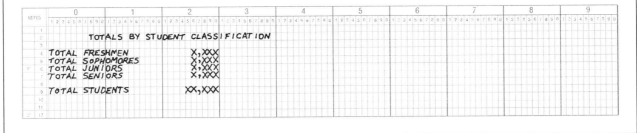

---

**EXHIBIT 4.28   Record Layout for Student Record**

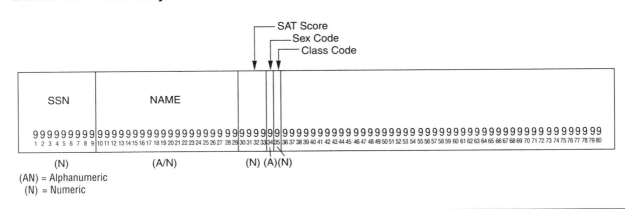

## Logic Considerations

Printing will occur only after all records have been read and the appropriate accumulators have been incremented. Exhibits 4.30 and 4.31 illustrate the respective meanings of the class and sex codes in the record.

## Program Design

**Hierarchy Chart.**   Exhibit 4.32 illustrates the hierarchy chart for this problem. The PROCESS-RECORD module includes only ACCUMULATION and READ-FILE modules. The WRAP-UP module, however, contains five write commands to print the five totals.

**Structured Flowchart.**   Exhibit 4.33 describes the various program modules in structured flowchart form. The ACCUMULATION module contains a CASE structure similar to the one found in Exhibit 4.15 or Exhibit 4.22 for the DETAIL-CALCULATION module. If the class-code = 1, then the constant value 1 is added to an accumulator (TOT-FRESHMEN) specifically designated to hold the total number of freshmen. If the class-code = 2, then the constant value 1 is added to TOT-SOPHO-MORE. The comparisons and their respective de-

---

### EXHIBIT 4.29    Test Data for Student Record

```
COLUMN   1         2         3         4         5         6         7         8
12345678901234567890123456789012345678901234567890123456789012345678901234567890
123456789TOM WATSON           0900M4
458994256KATHY JOHNSON        0750F1
988624893BOB CARSON           0800M3
478522469TERRY WARNER         1000M2
788513579THERESA JONES        1200F1
155798525BOBBI CARTER         0650F3
579369874TOMMIE COLLINS       0855M4
786213997RENEE THOMAS         1300F3
```

---

### EXHIBIT 4.30    Class Codes and Their Corresponding Meaning

| Code | Meaning |
|------|---------|
| 1 | Freshman |
| 2 | Sophomore |
| 3 | Junior |
| 4 | Senior |

pendent processing steps are next performed for junior and senior students. An unconditional command at the end adds a constant of 1 to the accumulator (TOT-STUDENT) designated to hold the total number of students.

**Pseudocode.** Exhibit 4.34 illustrates the associated pseudocode.

**Program Coding.** Exhibit 4.35 and 4.36 depict the respective COBOL 85 and QBASIC Program exerpts. Frame B of Exhibit 4.35 shows the use of the EVALUATE command in COBOL 85 as an alternative to the If . . . Then . . . Else . . . If. Frame B of Exhibit 4.36 shows the use of the SELECT COMMAND in QBASIC as an alternative method.

---

**EXHIBIT 4.31    Sex Codes and Their Meanings**

| Code | Meaning |
|------|---------|
| M | Male |
| F | Female |

---

**EXHIBIT 4.32    Student Summary Report**

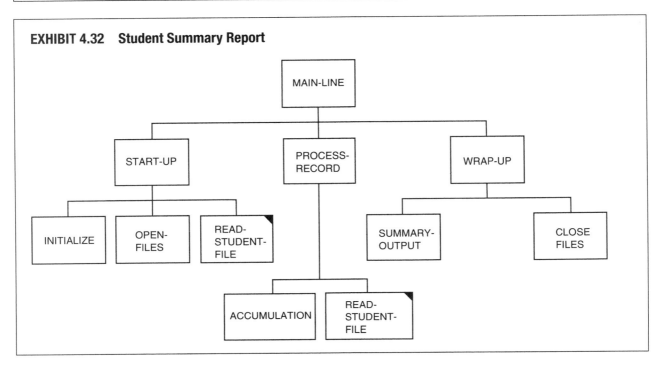

**EXHIBIT 4.33    Flowchart for Student Summary Report**

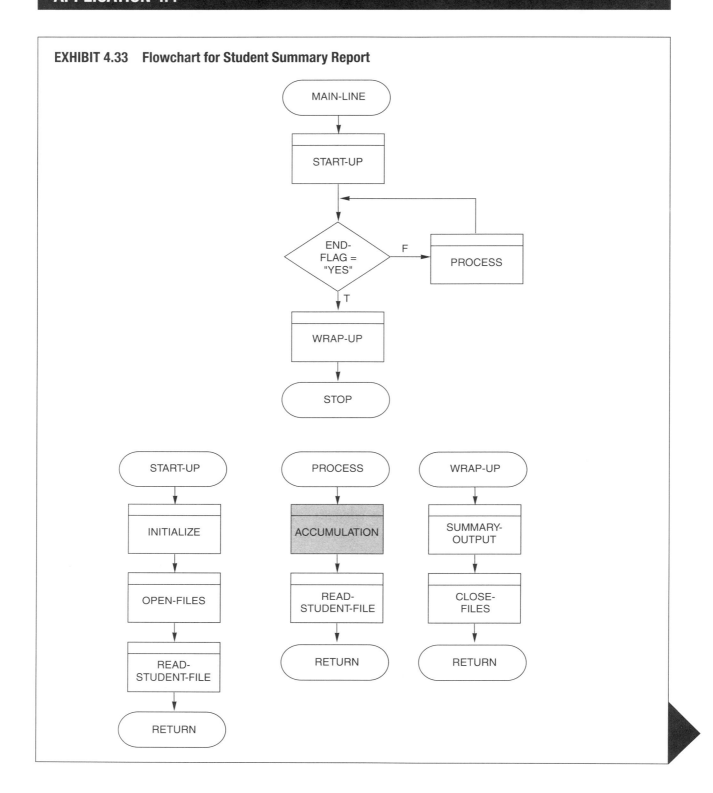

**EXHIBIT 4.33 (Cont.)**

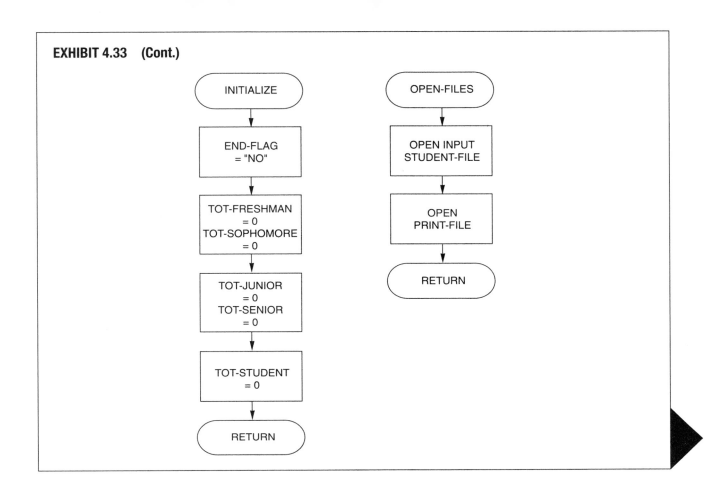

**EXHIBIT 4.33   (Cont.)**

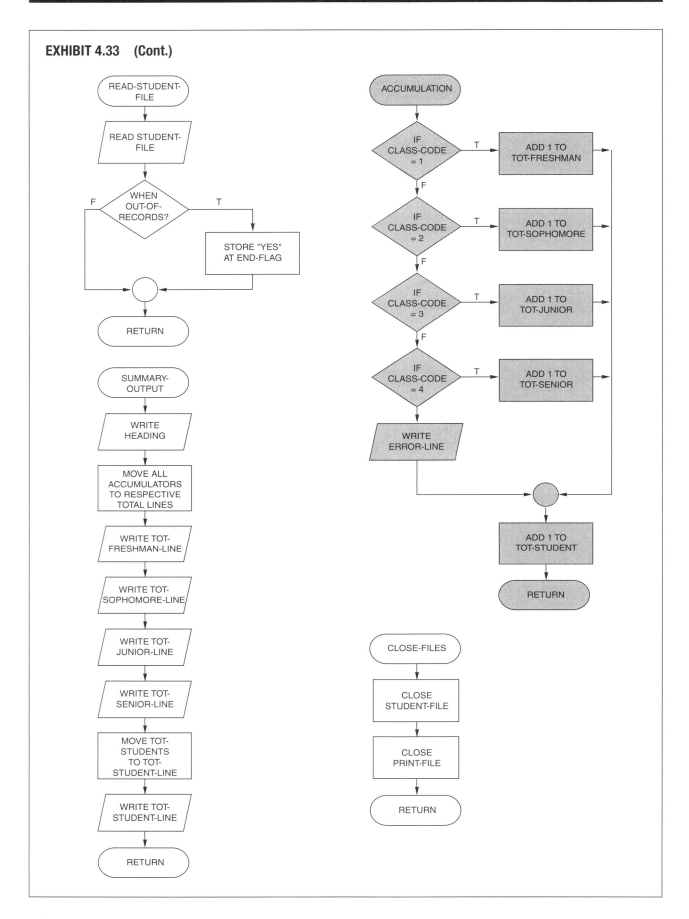

## Exhibit 4.34 Pseudocode for Application 4.4 (Summary Report)

*mainline logic
    start-up
    dowhile end-flag = "no"
        process-record
    enddo
    wrap-up
    stop
*start-up
    initialize
    open-files
    read student-file
    return
*initialize
    end-flag = "no"
    tot-freshman = 0
    tot-sophomore = 0
    tot-junior = 0
    tot-senior = 0
    tot-student = 0
    return
*open-files
    open input student-file, print file
    return
*read-student-file
    read student-file
    when out of records end-flag = "yes"
    return
*process-record
    accumulation
    read-student-file
    return

*accumulation
    if class-code = 1 then add 1 to tot-freshman
    else
    if class-code = 2 then add 1 to tot-sophomore
    else
    if class-code = 3 then add 1 to tot-junior
    else
    if class-code = 4 then add 1 to tot-senior
    else write error-line
    endif, endif, endif, endif
    add 1 to tot-student
*wrap-up
    summary-output
    close-files
    return
*summary-output
    move all accumulators to respective total lines
    write total freshmen line
    write total sophomore line
    write total junior line
    write total senior line
    move tot-student to total student line
    write total student line
    return
*close-files
    close student-file, print-file
    return

## EXHIBIT 4.35 COBOL 85 Program for Application 4.4

(Frame A)

```
 1        IDENTIFICATION DIVISION.
 2        PROGRAM-ID. CH4ILL4.
 3
 4     ****ANS COBOL 85 ****
 5
 6
 7     *REMARKS:  THIS PROGRAM PRINTS A SUMMARY OF THE TOTAL NUMBER
 8     *          OF FRESHMEN, SOPHOMORES, JUNIORS, SENIORS, AND TOTAL
 9     *          NUMBER OF STUDENTS.
10
11      ENVIRONMENT DIVISION.
12      CONFIGURATION SECTION.
13      SOURCE-COMPUTER.  CYBER.
14      OBJECT-COMPUTER.  CYBER.
15
16      INPUT-OUTPUT SECTION.
17      FILE-CONTROL.
18          SELECT STUDENT-FILE ASSIGN TO DTA44.
19          SELECT REPORT-REC ASSIGN TO OUTFILE.
20
21      DATA DIVISION.
22      FILE SECTION.
23      FD STUDENT-FILE.
24
25      01 STUDENT-RECORD.
26             05 SSN              PIC 9(9).
27             05 NAME             PIC X(20).
28             05 SAT-SCORE        PIC 9(4).
```

**EXHIBIT 4.35   (Cont.)**

```
29               05 SEX-CODE                   PIC X.
30               05 CLASS-CODE                 PIC 9.
31
32       FD REPORT-REC
33          LABEL RECORDS OMITTED.
34       01 REC                                PIC X(133).
35
36       WORKING-STORAGE SECTION.
37       01 END-FLAG                           PIC XXX VALUE "NO".
38       01 TOT-FRESH                          PIC 9(4) VALUE ZERO.
39       01 TOT-SOPH                           PIC 9(4) VALUE ZERO.
40       01 TOT-JUNIOR                         PIC 9(4) VALUE ZERO.
41       01 TOT-SENIOR                         PIC 9(4) VALUE ZERO.
42       01 TOT-STUDENT                        PIC 9(5) VALUE ZERO.
43
44       01 PAGE-HEADING.
45          05                                 PIC X(7) VALUE SPACES.
46          05                                 PIC X(32) VALUE
47             "TOTALS BY STUDENT CLASSIFICATION".
48          05                                 PIC X(93) VALUE SPACES.
49
50       01 TOT-FRESH-LINE.
51          05                                 PIC X(26) VALUE
52             " TOTAL FRESHMEN...........".
53          05 TOT-FRESH-OUT                   PIC Z,ZZ9.
54          05                                 PIC X(101) VALUE SPACES.
55
56       01 TOT-SOPH-LINE.
57          05                                 PIC X(26) VALUE
58             " TOTAL SOPHOMORES.........".
59          05 TOT-SOPH-OUT                    PIC Z,ZZ9.
60          05                                 PIC X(101) VALUE SPACES.
61
62       01 TOT-JUNIOR-LINE.
63          05                                 PIC X(26) VALUE
64             " TOTAL JUNIORS............".
65          05 TOT-JUNIOR-OUT                  PIC Z,ZZ9.
66          05                                 PIC X(101) VALUE SPACES.
67
68       01 TOT-SENIOR-LINE.
69          05                                 PIC X(26) VALUE
70             " TOTAL SENIORS............".
71          05 TOT-SENIOR-OUT                  PIC Z,ZZ9.
72          05                                 PIC X(101) VALUE SPACES.
73
74       01 TOTAL-LINE.
75          05                                 PIC X(25) VALUE
76             " TOTAL STUDENTS..........".
77          05 TOT-STUDENT-OUT                 PIC ZZ,ZZ9.
78          05                                 PIC X(101) VALUE SPACE.
79
80       01 ERROR-LINE1.
81          05                                 PIC X VALUE SPACES.
82          05 ERR-SSN                         PIC 9(4).
83          05                                 PIC XX VALUE SPACES.
84          05                                 PIC X(8) VALUE "BAD CODE".
85          05                                 PIC X(119) VALUE SPACES.
86    /
87       PROCEDURE DIVISION.
88
89       000-MAIN-LINE.
90           PERFORM 100-START-UP.
91           PERFORM 200-PROCESS UNTIL END-FLAG = "YES".
92           PERFORM 300-WRAP-UP.
93           STOP RUN.
94
```

**EXHIBIT 4.35** (Cont.)

```
95          100-START-UP.
96     *        INTIALIZATION FROM WORKING-STORAGE
97              PERFORM 105-OPEN-FILES.
98              PERFORM 120-READ-STUDENT-FILE.
99
100         105-OPEN-FILES.
101             OPEN INPUT STUDENT-FILE.
102             OPEN OUTPUT REPORT-REC.
103
104         120-READ-STUDENT-FILE.
105             READ STUDENT-FILE
106                 AT END MOVE "YES" TO END-FLAG.
107
108         200-PROCESS.
109             PERFORM 210-ACCUMULATE.
110             PERFORM 120-READ-STUDENT-FILE.
111
112         210-ACCUMULATE.
113             IF CLASS-CODE = 1
114                 THEN ADD 1 TO TOT-FRESH
115             ELSE
116             IF CLASS-CODE = 2
117                 THEN ADD 1 TO TOT-SOPH
118             ELSE
119             IF CLASS-CODE = 3
120                 THEN ADD 1 TO TOT-JUNIOR
121             ELSE
122             IF CLASS-CODE = 4
123                 THEN ADD 1 TO TOT-SENIOR
124             ELSE
125                 MOVE SSN TO ERR-SSN
126                 WRITE REC FROM ERROR-LINE1.
127
128             ADD 1 TO TOT-STUDENT.
129
130         300-WRAP-UP.
131             PERFORM 310-SUMMARY-OUTPUT.
132             PERFORM 320-CLOSE-FILES.
133
134         310-SUMMARY-OUTPUT.
135             WRITE REC FROM PAGE-HEADING AFTER PAGE.
136             MOVE TOT-FRESH TO TOT-FRESH-OUT.
137             WRITE REC FROM TOT-FRESH-LINE AFTER 2.
138             MOVE TOT-SOPH TO TOT-SOPH-OUT.
139             WRITE REC FROM TOT-SOPH-LINE.
140             MOVE TOT-JUNIOR TO TOT-JUNIOR-OUT.
141             WRITE REC FROM TOT-JUNIOR-LINE.
142             MOVE TOT-SENIOR TO TOT-SENIOR-OUT.
143             WRITE REC FROM TOT-SENIOR-LINE.
144             MOVE TOT-STUDENT TO TOT-STUDENT-OUT.
145             WRITE REC FROM TOTAL-LINE AFTER 2.
146
147         320-CLOSE-FILES.
148             CLOSE STUDENT-FILE
149                 REPORT-REC.
150


        TOTALS BY STUDENT CLASSIFICATION

TOTAL FRESHMEN...........    2
TOTAL SOPHOMORES..........   1
TOTAL JUNIORS.............   3
TOTAL SENIORS.............   2

TOTAL STUDENTS...........    8
```

**EXHIBIT 4.35** **(Cont.) Repeated Code to Show Use of COBOL Evaluate Command Below**

**(Frame B)**

```
85
86          PROCEDURE DIVISION.
87
88          000-MAIN-LINE.
89              PERFORM 100-START-UP.
90              PERFORM 200-PROCESS UNTIL END-FLAG = "YES".
91              PERFORM 300-WRAP-UP.
92              STOP RUN.
93
94          100-START-UP.
95              OPEN INPUT STUDENT-FILE.
96              OPEN OUTPUT REPORT-REC.
97              PERFORM 120-READ-STUDENT-FILE.
98
99          120-READ-STUDENT-FILE.
100             READ STUDENT-FILE
101                 AT END MOVE "YES" TO END-FLAG.
102
103         200-PROCESS.
104             PERFORM 210-ACCUMULATE.
105             PERFORM 120-READ-STUDENT-FILE.
106
107         210-ACCUMULATE.
108             EVALUATE CLASS-CODE
109                 WHEN 1
110                     ADD 1 TO TOT-FRESH
111                 WHEN 2
112                     ADD 1 TO TOT-SOPH
113                 WHEN 3
114                     ADD 1 TO TOT-JUNIOR
115                 WHEN 4
116                     ADD 1 TO TOT-SENIOR
117                 WHEN OTHER
118                     MOVE SSN TO ERR-SSN
119                     WRITE REC FROM ERROR-LINE1
120             END-EVALUATE.
121             ADD 1 TO TOT-STUDENT.
122
123         300-WRAP-UP
124             WRITE REC FROM PAGE-HEADING AFTER PAGE.
125             MOVE TOT-FRESH TO TOT-FRESH-OUT.
126             WRITE REC FROM TOT-FRESH-LINE AFTER 2.
127             MOVE TOT-SOPH TO TOT-SOPH-OUT.
128             WRITE REC FROM TOT-SOPH-LINE.
129             MOVE TOT-JUNIOR TO TOT-JUNIOR-OUT.
130             WRITE REC FROM TOT-JUNIOR-LINE.
131             MOVE TOT-SENIOR TO TOT-SENIOR-OUT.
132             WRITE REC FROM TOT-SENIOR-LINE.
133             MOVE TOT-STUDENT TO TOT-STUDENT-OUT.
134             WRITE REC FROM TOTAL-LINE AFTER 2.
135             CLOSE STUDENT-FILE
136                 REPORT-REC.
```

Lines 108–120 (the EVALUATE ... END-EVALUATE block) are marked:

**AN ALTERNATE METHOD USING THE COBOL EVALUATE COMMAND**

**EXHIBIT 4.36    QBASIC Program for Application 4.4**

```
'********************************************************************
'*                    PROGRAM IDENTIFICATION                      *
'********************************************************************
'* PROGRAM NAME: CH4APL4                                          *
'* REMARKS:   THIS PROGRAM PRINTS A SUMMARY OF THE TOTAL NUMBER OF *
'*            FRESHMEN, SOPHOMORES, JUNIORS, AND SENIORS AND TOTAL *
'*            NUMBER OF STUDENTS                                  *
'********************************************************************
'********************************************************************
'*                         MAIN-LINE                             *
'********************************************************************
    GOSUB STARTUP                          'PERFORM START-UP
    DO UNTIL END.FLAG$ = "YES"
       GOSUB PROCESS                       ' PERFORM PROCESS
    LOOP
    GOSUB WRAPUP                           'PERFORM WRAP-UP
    END


    '********************************************************************
    '*                        START-UP                               *
    '********************************************************************

STARTUP:

    GOSUB INITIALIZE
    GOSUB OPEN.FILES
    GOSUB HEADINGS                         'PERFORM HEADINGS
    GOSUB READFILE                         'PERFORM READ-STUDENT-FILE
    RETURN

    '********************************************************************
    '*                        INITIALIZE                             *
    '********************************************************************

INITIALIZE:

    END.FLAG$ = "NO": TOT.FRESHMAN = 0: TOT.SOPHOMORE = 0: TOT.JUNIOR = 0:
    TOT.SENIOR = 0: TOT.STUDENT = 0
    RETURN

    '********************************************************************
    '                        OPEN-FILES                             *
    '********************************************************************

OPEN.FILES:

        OPEN "I", #1, "CH4ILL4.DAT"
        RETURN
```

**EXHIBIT 4.36    (Cont.)**

```
'********************************************************************
'*                            HEADINGS                             *
'********************************************************************

HEADINGS:

     LPRINT CHR$(12)
     LPRINT
     LPRINT TAB(24); "TOTALS BY STUDENT CLASSIFICATION"
     LPRINT
     RETURN


     '********************************************************************
     '*                      READ-STUDENT-FILE                          *
     '********************************************************************

READFILE:

     INPUT #1, STUD.NUMB$, STUD.NAME$, SAT, SEX.CODE$, CLASS.CODE
     IF STUD.NAME$ = "EOF" THEN
             END.FLAG$ = "YES"
     END IF
     RETURN



     '********************************************************************
     '*                           PROCESS                               *
     '********************************************************************

PROCESS:

     GOSUB ACCUMULATE                      '* PERFORM ACCUMULATE
     GOSUB READFILE                        '* PERFORM READ-STUDENT-FILE
     RETURN
```

**EXHIBIT 4.36   (Cont.)**

```
'**********************************************************************
'*                          ACCUMULATE                               *
'**********************************************************************

ACCUMULATE:

    IF CLASS.CODE = 1 THEN
         TOT.FRESHMAN = TOT.FRESHMAN + 1
    ELSE
         IF CLASS.CODE = 2 THEN
              TOT.SOPHOMORE = TOT.SOPHOMORE + 1
         ELSE
              IF CLASS.CODE = 3 THEN
                     TOT.JUNIOR = TOT.JUNIOR + 1
              ELSE
                   IF CLASS.CODE = 4 THEN

                      TOT.SENIOR = TOT.SENIOR + 1
                   ELSE
                      LPRINT STUD.NUMB; "BAD CODE"
                   END IF
              END IF
         END IF
    END IF

TOT.STUDENT = TOT.STUDENT + 1
RETURN

'**********************************************************************
'*                          WRAP-UP                                  *
'**********************************************************************

WRAPUP:

    GOSUB SUMMARY.OUTPUT
    GOSUB CLOSE.FILES
    RETURN
    '**********************************************************************
    '*                       SUMMARY.OUTPUT                              *
    '**********************************************************************

SUMMARY.OUTPUT:

    LPRINT "TOTAL FRESHMEN........."; USING "#,###"; TOT.FRESHMAN
    LPRINT "TOTAL SOPHOMORES......."; USING "#,###"; TOT.SOPHOMORE
    LPRINT "TOTAL JUNIORS.........."; USING "#,###"; TOT.JUNIOR
    LPRINT "TOTAL SENIORS.........."; USING "#,###"; TOT.SENIOR
    LPRINT
    LPRINT "TOTAL STUDENTS........"; USING "##,###"; TOT.STUDENT
```

**EXHIBIT 4.36  (Cont.)**

```
'*********************************************************************
'*                          CLOSE.FILES                             *
'*********************************************************************
```

```
CLOSE.FILES:

    CLOSE
    RETURN
```

```
                    TOTALS BY STUDENT CLASSIFICATION

TOTAL FRESHMEN.........    2
TOTAL SOPHOMORES.......    1
TOTAL JUNIORS..........    3
TOTAL SENIORS..........    2

TOTAL STUDENTS........    8
```

**EXHIBIT 4.36  (Cont.)**

**Panel B**

```
SELECT CASE CLASS.CODE
  CASE IS = 1
    TOT.FRESHMAN = TOT.FRESHMAN + 1
  CASE IS = 2
    TOT.SOPHOMORE = TOT.SOPHOMORE + 1
  CASE IS = 3
    TOT.JUNIOR = TOT.JUNIOR + 1
  CASE IS = 4
    TOT.SENIOR = TOT.SENIOR + 1
  CASE ELSE
    PRINT STUD.NUMB; "BAD CODE"
  END SELECT
```

## COMPOUND *AND* CONDITIONS

Computer programming applications often specify that processing will occur only if two or more conditions are true or false. As an example, let's suppose that a researcher wishes to produce the report shown in Figure 4.11. He is interested in determining the number of both male and female Democrats as well as the number of both male and female Republicans. Summary totals will be printed to represent the number for each category. In order to determine which accumulator to increase, a **compound AND condition** is tested. A compound AND condition is a condition test in which two or more internal simple conditions are tested together. If all the simple conditions test true, then the compound condition is true. If any one of the simple conditions in the compound condition is false, then the compound condition is also false. The diagram in Figure 4.12 describes how the compound AND condition works. The flowcharting and pseudocode logic for the Accumulation module for this problem is shown in Figures 4.13 and 4.14, respectively. The two different methods for pseudocoding the problem are shown in Panel A and Panel B of Figure 4.14.

## COMPOUND *OR* CONDITIONS

Frequently a programmer must perform a particular operation based on either of two simple conditions being true. In this case, a **compound OR condition** is used. For example, in an accounting application, a program must increase an accumula-

tor if an account number is less than 100 (asset) or greater than 150 (expense); otherwise it decreases the accumulator. To increase the accumulator requires that only *one* of the two simple conditions be true. In this case, it is possible only that one of the two conditions is true. Consider the illustration in Figure 4.15.

You'll find the flowcharting logic of the DETAIL-CALCULATION module for this condition test in panel A of Figure 4.16.

Let's consider one more example to illustrate the compound OR logic. An administrator wishes to send a congratulatory letter to computer majors who have either an *overall* GPA of 3.5 or greater in all their classes or a GPA of 3.8 or greater in only their computer-related courses. The conditional expression in panel B of Figure 4.16 is used to depict this logic. One important observation is that *either* of the simple conditions being tested as true will result in a true compound OR condition. Another important observation is that *both* simple conditions can be true, resulting in a true compound condition. The only way that the compound will test false is if both of the simple conditions test false (see Figure 4.17).

## NESTED COMPARISONS

Many computer programming problems require that comparisons be made that are dependent on the outcome of a previous comparison. This type of comparison is called a **nested comparison** or a **nested IF**.

---

**FIGURE 4.11    Summary Report: The Number of Democrats and Republicans Broken Down by Gender**

```
              DEMOGRAPHIC REPORT

                      MALE        FEMALE
          DEMOCRAT    XXX         XXX
          REPUBLICAN  XXX         XXX
```

---

**FIGURE 4.12    The Compound AND**

| Simple Condition 1 | AND | Simple Condition 2 | Compound Condition |
|---|---|---|---|
| IF SEX-CODE = 1 | AND | POL-PARTY = "D" | RESULT |
| TRUE | AND | TRUE ⟶ | TRUE |
| TRUE | AND | FALSE ⟶ | FALSE |
| FALSE | AND | TRUE ⟶ | FALSE |
| FALSE | AND | TRUE ⟶ | FALSE |

To illustrate the nested IF logic, let's suppose that ABC Company wishes to produce a sales commission report (Figure 4.18) from a file of sales records (Figure 4.19). The schedule in Figure 4.20 shows how the sales commission is to be calculated. The sales rep's number, name, sales amount, and commission are to be printed for each record in the sales file. The commission is determined from a schedule of commission rates based on sales rep class and sales range.

The schedule in Figure 4.20 indicates that the commission will be calculated at the rate of one percent for the first $5000 of sales if the class code is a 1. Sales in *excess* of $5000 are computed at three percent of sales if the class code is also a 1. However, if the class code is 2, the commission on the first $5000 is computed at the two percent rate. Sales in excess of $5000 are calculated at the four percent rate if the class code is 2.

Figures 4.21 and 4.22 illustrate the respective flowchart and pseudocode representations for the DETAIL-CALCULATIONS module. The module starts off by comparing the sales rep class code with the value 1. If the condition tests true, the next decision block is encountered, which determines if the sales amount is greater than $5000. If the result of this condition test is false, then the commission is computed by multiplying the sales amount by .01.

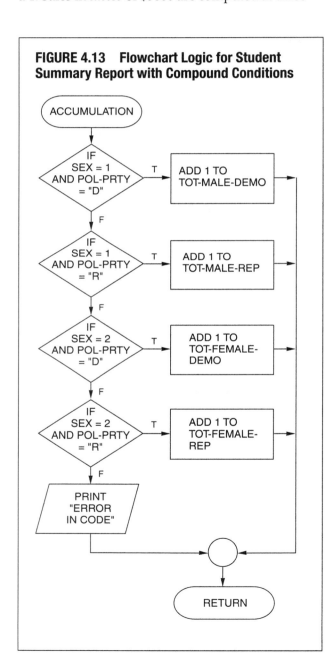

**FIGURE 4.13  Flowchart Logic for Student Summary Report with Compound Conditions**

**FIGURE 4.14  Pseudocode Logic for Student Summary Report with Compound Conditions**

**PANEL A (When using a CASE command)**

```
*accumulation
    CASE (sex and political party type)
    when sex = 1 and pol-prty = "d"
        add 1 to tot-male-demo
    when sex = 1 and pol-prty = "r"
        add 1 to tot-male-rep
    when sex = 2 and pol-prty = "d"
        add 1 to tot-female-demo
    when sex = 2 and pol-prty = "r"
        add 1 to tot-female-rep
    print error message
    ENDCASE
    return
```

**PANEL B (When no CASE command available)**

```
*accumulation
    if sex = 1 and pol-prty = "d"
        then add 1 to tot-male-demo
    else
    if sex = 1 and pol-prty = "r"
        then add 1 to tot-male-rep
    else
    if sex = 2 and pol-prty = "d"
        then add 1 to tot-female-demo
    else
    if sex = 2 and pol-prty = "r"
        then add 1 to tot-female-rep
    else print "error in code"
    endif
    endif
    endif
    endif
    return
```

## FIGURE 4.15 The Compound OR

| Simple Condition 1 | OR | Simple Condition 2 | Compound Condition |
|---|---|---|---|
| IF  TR-CODE  <  50 | OR | TR-CODE  >  150 | RESULT |
| TRUE | OR | FALSE ⟶ | TRUE |
| FALSE | OR | TRUE ⟶ | TRUE |
| TRUE | OR | TRUE ⟶ | TRUE |
| FALSE | OR | FALSE ⟶ | FALSE |

## FIGURE 4.16 If . . . Then . . . Else with Compound OR

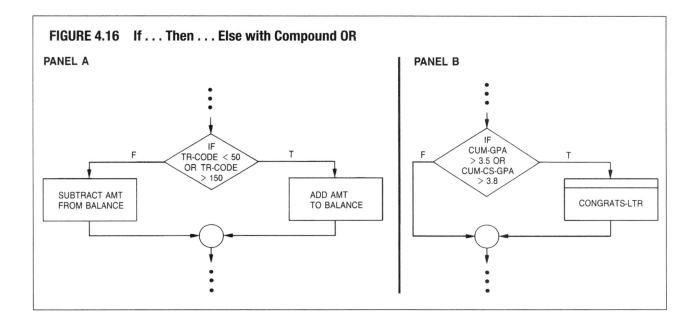

PANEL A

PANEL B

## FIGURE 4.17 Testing Compound OR Conditions

| Simple Condition 1 | OR | Simple Condition 2 | Compound Condition |
|---|---|---|---|
| IF  CUM-GPA  >  3.5 | OR | CUM-CS-GPA  >  3.8 | RESULT |
| TRUE | OR | FALSE ⟶ | TRUE |
| FALSE | OR | TRUE ⟶ | TRUE |
| TRUE | OR | TRUE ⟶ | TRUE |
| FALSE | OR | FALSE ⟶ | FALSE |

## FIGURE 4.18 A Sales Commission Report

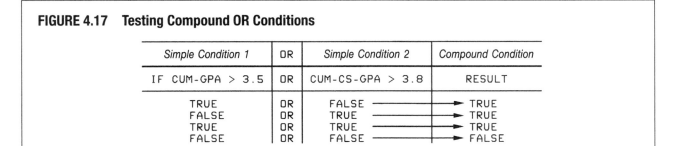

```
                    SALES COMMISSION REPORT

    SALES-REP          NAME              SALES       COMMISSION

      XXXX      XXXXXXXXXXXXXXXXX      XX,XXX.XX       XXX.XX
      XXXX      XXXXXXXXXXXXXXXXX      XX,XXX.XX       XXX.XX
      XXXX      XXXXXXXXXXXXXXXXX      XX,XXX.XX       XXX.XX
```

## FIGURE 4.19 Record Layout for Sales Commission Report

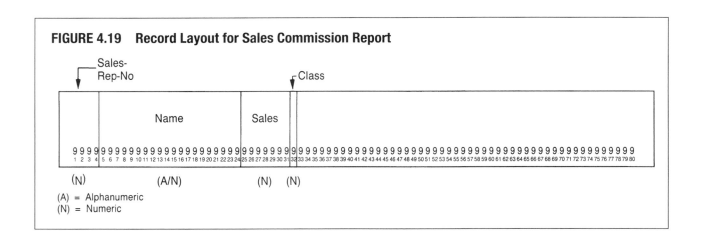

## FIGURE 4.20 Schedule of Commission Rates

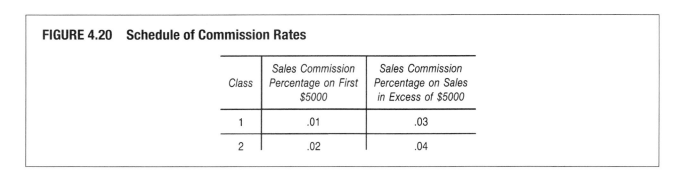

| Class | Sales Commission Percentage on First $5000 | Sales Commission Percentage on Sales in Excess of $5000 |
|-------|--------------------------------------------|---------------------------------------------------------|
| 1 | .01 | .03 |
| 2 | .02 | .04 |

## FIGURE 4.21 Nested IF Flowchart Module

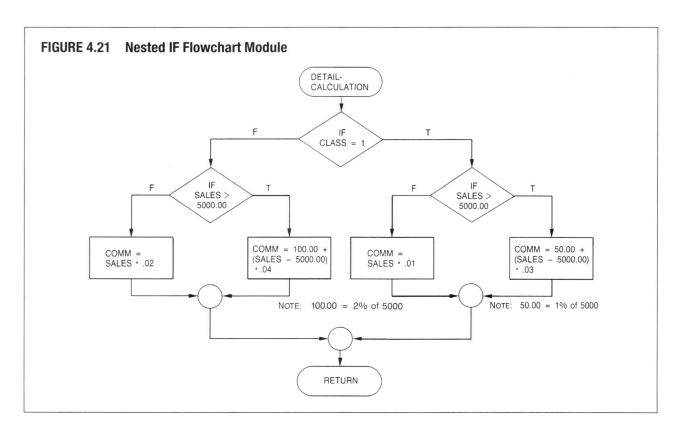

However, if the result of this nested condition is false, then the commission is calculated by determining the excess over $5000, multiplying it by .03, and adding $50 (the commission for the first $5000).

Now, what if the first condition tested is false? If this is the case (class code = 2), then the nested IF on the left side is executed. The condition is tested to determine if the sales amount is greater than $5000. If the condition tests false, the commission is computed as two percent of sales. If, however, the results of the nested condition test is true, then the commission is determined by multiplying the amount in excess of $5000 by four percent and adding it to $100 (the commission for the first $5000).

## The "AND" and "OR" Operator Hierarchy

The use of compound conditions where both AND and OR operators are used in the same conditional expression can sometimes be tricky. For example, what does the following conditional expression say?

```
IF CLASS-CODE = 3 OR CLASS-CODE = 4 AND
   CUM-GPA > 3.25
      THEN
            INVITATION-TO-JOIN-HONOR-SOCIETY
ELSE LETTER-OF-REJECTION
ENDIF
```

Note: A class-code of 3 represents a JUNIOR.
A class-code of 4 represents a SENIOR.

At first glance, one might think that the pseudocode above says to send out a letter inviting students who are either a junior or senior and have a cumulative GPA of 3.25 or greater. Since AND operators take precedence over OR operators, the computer evaluates that the student must be a junior OR must be a senior with a 3.25 GPA or better. This is hardly what one may have intended when coding this statement. The following command and the use of parentheses helps clarify what is meant.

```
IF (CLASS-CODE = 3 OR CLASS-CODE = 4) AND
   GPA > 3.25
      THEN . . . . . . .
ENDIF
```

Without the presence of the set of parentheses as shown above, what the computer does is to evaluate the simple conditions on each side of an AND operator and determine whether this part of the conditional is true or false. The computer then evaluates the only remaining simple condition (IF CLASS-CODE = 3) as true or false. It would only require that the simple condition, IF CLASS-CODE = 3, be true to cause the entire compound conditional to be evaluated as true. An easy way to solve this problem is always to use parentheses to clarify the conditional expression.

The following illustrates a more complex example. Suppose a college is planning to generate a list of qualified graduating seniors. The student master record contains the following:

STUDENT-NO, NAME, CLASS, CUM-HRS, YEAR-ENTERED, APPROVED-DEGREE-PLAN-CODE

A student can graduate with senior status (class code = 4), with at least 128 semester hours, and an approved degree plan (approved degree plan code must equal "A"). This is true *unless* the student entered before the 1987 school year. If

---

**FIGURE 4.22    Structured Pseudocode for Nested IF**

```
*detail-calculation
 if class = 1
      if sales > 5000.00
            comm = 50.00 + (sales − 5000.00) * .03
      else
            comm = sales * .01
      endif
 else
      if sales > 5000.00
            comm = 100.00 + (sales − 5000.00) * .04
      else
            comm = sales * .02
      endif
 endif
```

he or she entered prior to the 1987 term, then the student must have at least 120 semester hours and an approved degree plan to graduate

The pseudocode below illustrates how this must be coded.

```
IF CLASS-CODE = 4 AND (CUM-HRS > 127 OR
    YEAR-ENTERED < 87 AND CUM-HRS > 119)
    AND APPROVED-DEGREE-PLAN-CODE = "A"
        THEN ADD-STUDENT-TO-GRADUATION-LIST
ENDIF
```

Do you see the significance of the parentheses in this statement? What would happen if the set of parentheses were missing? The entire conditional could be evaluated as true, if the student was a senior with cumulative hours greater than 127, regardless of whether or not the degree plan was approved. This would hardly be what the dean and the registrar want! One can also observe from this example how critical the placement of parentheses are in expressions that involve both AND and OR operators. The truth table in Figure 4.23 helps clarify this example. The following explanation relates to the circled steps in Figure 4.23.

Steps:

1. Since this comparison test is an "AND", it takes both simple conditions to be TRUE; therefore, the result of this first test is "FALSE".
2. Next, a TRUE result "ORed" with a FALSE result yield a TRUE result.
3. A TRUE simple condition and a TRUE result from Step 2 above yield a TRUE result.
4. A TRUE and a TRUE yield a TRUE result of the compound test.

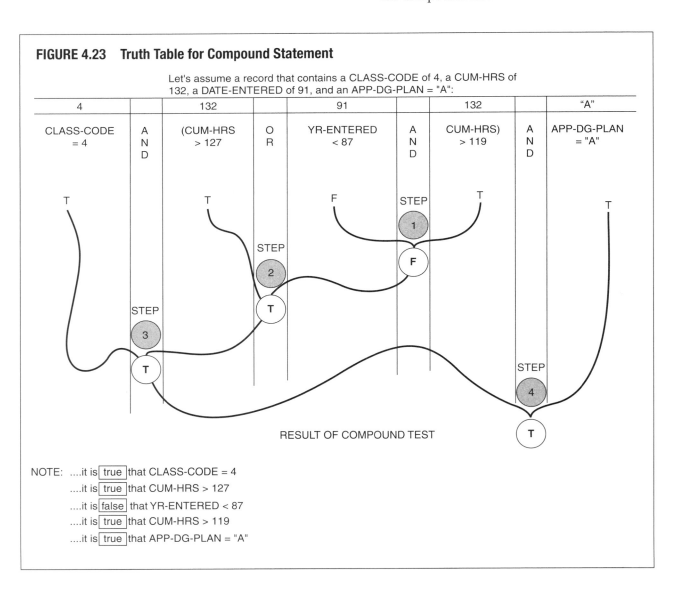

**FIGURE 4.23    Truth Table for Compound Statement**

Let's assume a record that contains a CLASS-CODE of 4, a CUM-HRS of 132, a DATE-ENTERED of 91, and an APP-DG-PLAN = "A":

| 4 | | 132 | | 91 | | 132 | | "A" |
|---|---|---|---|---|---|---|---|---|
| CLASS-CODE = 4 | AND | (CUM-HRS > 127 | OR | YR-ENTERED < 87 | AND | CUM-HRS) > 119 | AND | APP-DG-PLAN = "A" |

RESULT OF COMPOUND TEST

NOTE: ....it is [true] that CLASS-CODE = 4
....it is [true] that CUM-HRS > 127
....it is [false] that YR-ENTERED < 87
....it is [true] that CUM-HRS > 119
....it is [true] that APP-DG-PLAN = "A"

# Customer Account Status Report Using Nested and Compound Conditions

## Program Requirements

Let us illustrate the use of both nested and compound conditions by supposing that management wants to know the status of their customer accounts. A Customer Account Status Report is to be produced that lists the customer number, customer name, customer's balance forward from the last period, payments received during the period, finance charge, new purchases during the period, the new balance at the end of the period (including finance charge), and the minimum payment. This report will also summarize the billing procedure (not a part of this application).

## Output Design

Exhibit 4.37 illustrates the Customer Account Status Report. Each line represents a single customer's account information.

## Input Design

Exhibit 4.38 depicts the associated record layout for the customer master record.

## Logic Considerations

The minimum payment that a customer will pay is based on the Balance Forward amount and whether or not the customer paid on the account during the period. If the Balance Forward amount is zero and if New Purchases is greater than zero, then the minimum payment is simply 12% of New Purchases.

If the Balance Forward is zero and no new purchases were made during the period, then the minimum payment is zero. However, if the Balance Forward amount is greater than zero, and if the Payment Received is also zero, then the Minimum Payment is 12% of the sum of New Purchases and Balance Forward. Also a message should print indicating that no payment was received from the customer for the period. On the other hand, if payment was received from the customer and is an amount less than 12% of the Balance Forward, then the Minimum Payment should reflect the amount the customer should have paid last period plus 12% of any New Purchases (that is, 12% of the New Purchases are added to the difference between 12% of the Balance Forward and the Payment Received). A message is to print that indicates that the payment

## Exhibit 4.37 Print Chart for Application 4.5, Customer Account Status Report

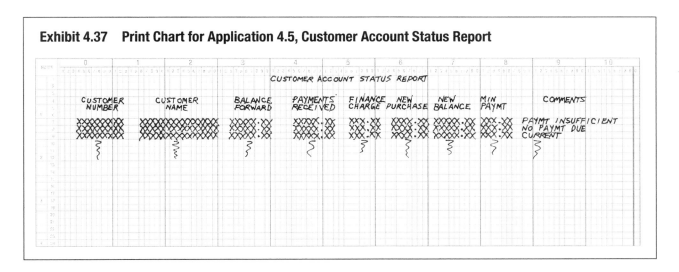

## Exhibit 4.38 Record Layout for Application 4.5

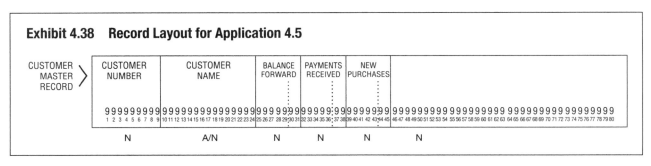

was insufficient. Now, if the Payment Received is equal or greater than 12% of Balance Forward, then let us calculate the Minimum Payment as 12% of New Purchases and print a message indicating the account is "current."

## Decision Tables

Since the "IF . . . Then" logic of this problem is non-trivial, the introduction of a new design tool may be helpful. This tool is called a **decision table**. Figure 4.24 illustrates. *Decision tables are especially helpful when nested if and compound if logic becomes complex.* Without the decision table it is difficult to sort out the conditions and associated actions. The decision table is constructed in row/column format and illustrates the various conditions and associated actions. The top row segment of the table shows the various **conditions**. The bottom row segment depicts the various **actions** to be taken based on the existence of certain conditions. The columns of the table illustrate the various **rules** that may exist. A rule represents a specific set of conditions that result in a specific **action**. A decision table will often accommodate a number of rules. Exhibit 4.39 represents a generic depiction of a decision table.

Notice that the letter T is used to represent that a condition is true and the letter F is employed to show that a condition is false. The letter X is placed at the row/column intersect to represent the action to be performed.

Exhibit 4.39 illustrates how the decision table is used to help break down a web of conditions and actions. Now the decision table can easily be converted to flowchart form.

For example, for Rule 1, the table says if bal-fwd = 0 and new.purch > 0 then the min-payment is equal to new.purch * .12. Furthermore, if balance = 0 and new.purch is *NOT* > 0 then the min-paymt = 0, says Rule 2. Do you see how to read it? Let us try one more rule. For example, Rule 5 says that if Balance is *NOT* = 0 and payment received is *NOT* = 0 and the paymt-rec is *NOT* < 12% of Bal-Fwd, then the min-paymt = new-bal * .12.

Exhibit 4.40 represents the flowchart logic for this problem, and Exhibit 4.41 depicts the matching pueudocode. Exhibit 4.42 highlights the COBOL 85 for this problem, and Exhibit 4.43 shows the associated Quick Basic Code.

**FIGURE 4.24    General Structure of Decision Table**

| CONDITIONS | RULE 1 | RULE 2 | RULE 3 | RULE 4 | RULE 5 | RULE 6 |
|---|---|---|---|---|---|---|
| CONDITION STATEMENT 1 | T | T | T | F | F | F |
| CONDITION STATEMENT 2 | T | T | F | F | T | F |
| CONDITION STATEMENT 3 | T | F | T | T | F | F |
| | | | | | | |
| ACTION STATEMENT 1 | X | | | | | X |
| ACTION STATEMENT 2 | | X | | | X | |
| ACTION STATEMENT 3 | | | X | | X | X |
| ACTION STATEMENT 4 | | | | X | | |

CONDITIONS: CONDITION STATEMENT 1, 2, 3
ACTIONS: ACTION STATEMENT 1, 2, 3, 4

**EXHIBIT 4.39    Decision Table for Application 4.5**

| CONDITIONS | RULE 1 | RULE 2 | RULE 3 | RULE 4 | RULE 5 |
|---|---|---|---|---|---|
| BAL-FWD = 0? | T | T | F | F | F |
| NEW-PURCH > 0? | T | F | | | |
| PAYMT-REC = 0? | | | T | F | F |
| PAYMT-REC > OR = 12% OF BAL-FWD? | | | | T | F |
| MIN-PAYMT = NEW-PURCH *.12 | X | | | | |
| MIN-PAYMT = Ø | | X | | | |
| MIN-PAYMT = (.12 *BAL-FWD) −PAYMT-REC) + NEW−PURCH *.12 | | | | X | |
| MIN-PAYMT = NEW-BAL *.12 | | | X | | X |
| FORMAT "NO PAYMT RECEIVED" | | | X | | |
| FORMAT "PAYMT INSUFFICIENT" | | | | X | |
| FORMAT "CURRENT" | | | | | X |

CONDITIONS / ACTIONS

- The T means that a condition is true.
- The F means that a condition is false.
- The X means that the action is to take place.

For any particular Rule (represented by 1 column)
there can be a combination of true and false
conditions and at least one action.

**EXHIBIT 4.40    Flowchart for Application 4.5**

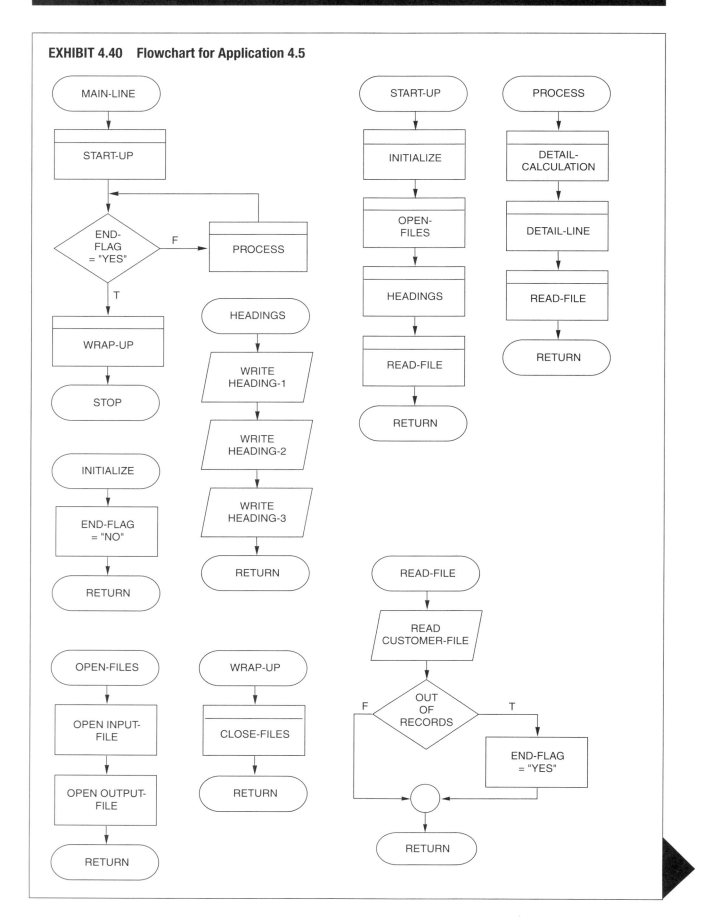

**EXHIBIT 4.40 (Cont.)**

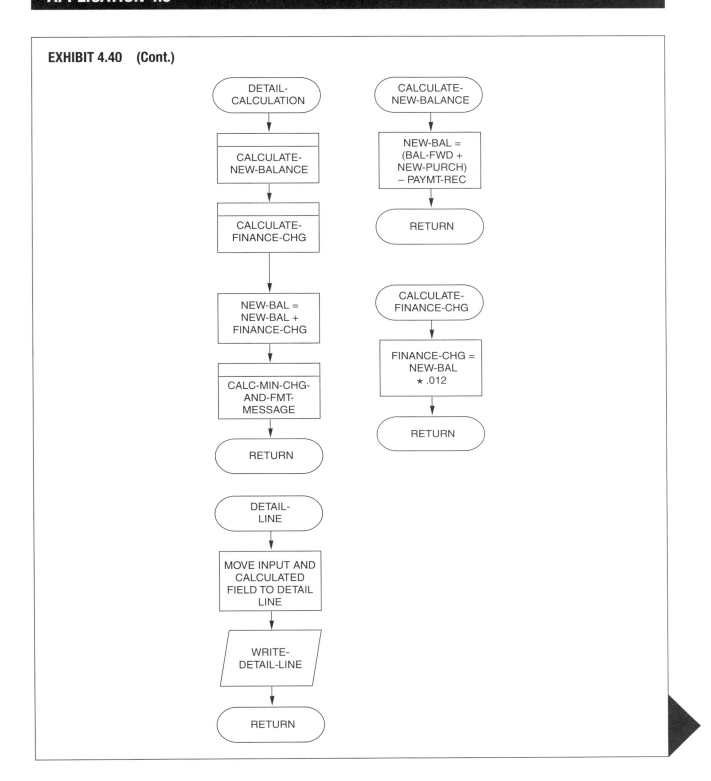

**EXHIBIT 4.40    Application 4.5 Flowchart – Customer Account Status**

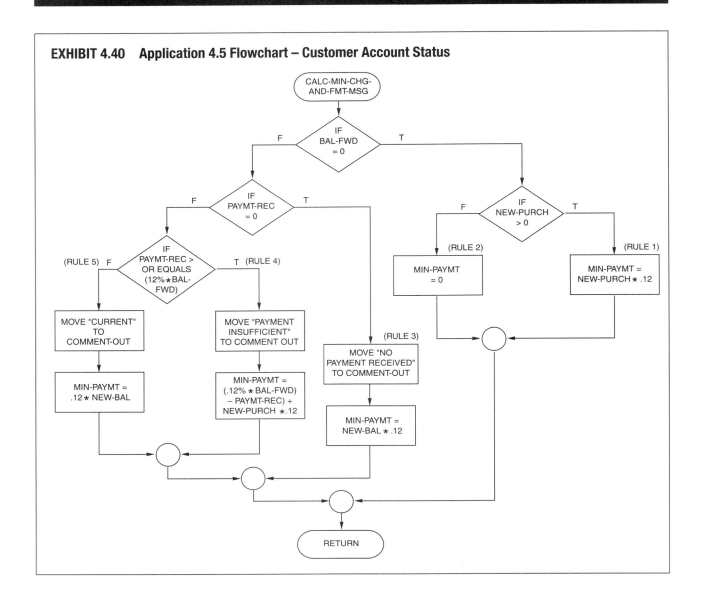

## EXHIBIT 4.41   Pseudocode for Customer Account Status Report

*mainline
    start-up
    dowhile end-flag = "no"
        process module
    enddo
    wrap-up
    stop
*start-up
    initialize
    open-files
    headings
    read-customer-file
    return
*initialize
    end-flag = "no"
    return
*open-files
    open input customer-file
    open output print-file
    return
*headings
    write page heading
    write column heading
    return
*read-file
    read customer-file
        when out of records set end-flag = "yes"
    endread
    return
*process
    detail-calculations
    detail-line
    read-customer-file
    return
*detail calculations
    calculate-new-balance
    calculate-finance-charge
    new-bal = new-bal + finance-chg
    calc-min-chg-and-fmt-message
    return
*calculate-new-balance
  new-bal = (bal-fwd + new-purch) − paymt-rec
  return

*calculate-finance-chg
    finance-chg = new-bal * .012
    return
*calc-min-chg-and-fmt-message
    if bal-fwd = 0
      then
        if new-purch > 0
          then
            min-paymt = new-purch * .12
        else min-paymt = 0
      else
      if paymt-rec = 0
        then
          move "no paymt received" to msg-out
          min-paymt = new-bal * .12
        else
        if paymt-rec > or = (.12 * bal.fwd)
          then
            move "paymt insufficient" to comment-out
            min-paymt = (.12 * bal-fwd − paymt-rec)
             + new-purch * .12
          else
            move "current" to msg-out
            min-paymt = .12 * new-bal
          endif
        endif
      endif
    return
*detail-line
    transfer input data to print line
    write print line
    return
*wrap-up module
    close files
    return

**EXHIBIT 4.42    COBOL 85 for Application 4.5**

```
1          IDENTIFICATION DIVISION.
2          PROGRAM-ID. CH4APL5.
3
4      ****ANS COBOL 85****
5
6      * REMARKS:     THIS PROGRAM PRODUCES A CUSTOMER ACCOUNT STATUS REPORT
7      *              USING NESTED AND COMPOUND CONDITIONS.  THIS REPORT LISTS
8      *              THE CUSTOMER NUMBER, CUSTOMER NAME, BALANCE FORWARD
9      *              FROM LAST PERIOD, PAYMENTS RECEIVED DURING THE PERIOD
10     *              THE NEW BALANCE AT THE END OF THE PERIOD, AND THE MINIMUM
11     *              PAYMENT.
12
13       ENVIRONMENT DIVISION.
14
15       CONFIGURATION SECTION.
16
17       SOURCE-COMPUTER.  CYBER.
18       OBJECT-COMPUTER.  CYBER.
19
20       INPUT-OUTPUT SECTION.
21
22       FILE-CONTROL.
23
24           SELECT CUSTOMER-FILE ASSIGN TO DTA45.
25           SELECT CUSTOMER-REPORT ASSIGN TO OUTFILE.
26
27
28       DATA DIVISION.
29
30       FILE SECTION.
31
32       FD   CUSTOMER-FILE.
33
34       01   CUSTMER-REC.
35
36            05 CUST-NO             PIC 9(9).
37            05 CUST-NAME           PIC X(15).
38            05 BAL-FWD             PIC 9(5)V99.
39            05                     PIC X.
40            05 PAYMT-REC           PIC 9(5)V99.
41            05                     PIC X.
42            05 NEW-PURCH           PIC 9(5)V99.
43
44       FD   CUSTOMER-REPORT.
45
46       01   REPORT-REC            PIC X(133).
47
48
49       WORKING-STORAGE SECTION.
50
51       01   END-FLAG             PIC XXX VALUE "NO".
52       01   NEW-BAL              PIC 9(5)V99.
53       01   MIN-PAYMT            PIC 9(3)V99.
54       01   FINANCE-CHG          PIC 9(5)V99.
55
56       01   PAGE-HEADING.
57
58            05      PIC X(40) VALUE SPACES.
59            05      PIC X(30) VALUE "CUSTOMER ACCOUNT STATUS REPORT".
60            05      PIC X(63) VALUE SPACES.
61
62       01   COLUMN-HEADING1.
63
64            05      PIC X(4)  VALUE SPACES.
65            05      PIC X(30) VALUE "CUSTOMER        CUSTOMER       ".
66            05      PIC X(29) VALUE "BALANCE     PAYMENTS    FINANCE".
```

**EXHIBIT 4.42    (Cont.)**

```
67           05                              PIC X(4)  VALUE SPACES.
68           05                              PIC X(6)  VALUE "TEST 1".
69           05                              PIC X(5)  VALUE SPACES.
70           05                              PIC X(6)  VALUE "TEST 2".
71           05                              PIC X(6)  VALUE SPACES.
72           05                              PIC X(6)  VALUE "TEST 3".
73           05                              PIC X(2)  VALUE SPACES.
74           05                              PIC X(3)  VALUE "AVG".
75           05                              PIC X(3)  VALUE SPACES.
76           05                              PIC X(7)  VALUE "LTR GRD".
77           05                              PIC X(68) VALUE SPACES.
78
79
80      01   DETAIL-LINE.
81           05                              PIC X VALUE SPACES.
82           05  SN-OUT                      PIC 9(4).
83           05                              PIC X     VALUE SPACES.
84           05  NAME-OUT                    PIC X(15).
85           05                              PIC X     VALUE SPACES.
86           05  TEST1-OUT                   PIC Z99.
87           05                              PIC X(8)  VALUE SPACES.
88           05  TEST2-OUT                   PIC Z99.
89           05                              PIC X(9)  VALUE SPACES.
90           05  TEST3-OUT                   PIC Z99.
91           05                              PIC X(3)  VALUE SPACES.
92           05  TEST-AVG-OUT                PIC Z99.
93           05                              PIC X(6)  VALUE SPACES.
94           05  LETTER-GRADE-OUT            PIC X.
95           05                              PIC X(71) VALUE SPACES.
96
97      01   TOT-LINE1.
98
99           05                              PIC X(29) VALUE SPACES.
100          05                              PIC X(17) VALUE
101     /
102       PROCEDURE DIVISION.
103
104       000-MAINLINE.
105
106           PERFORM 100-START-UP.
107           PERFORM 200-PROCESS UNTIL END-FLAG = "YES".
108           PERFORM 300-WRAP-UP.
109           STOP RUN.
110
111       100-START-UP.
112
113           PERFORM 102-INITIALIZE.
114           PERFORM 105-OPEN-FILES.
115           PERFORM 110-HEADINGS.
116           PERFORM 120-READ-FILE.
117
118       102-INITIALIZE.
119
120           MOVE "NO" TO END-FLAG.
121
122       105-OPEN-FILES.
123
124           OPEN INPUT CUSTOMER-FILE.
125           OPEN OUTPUT CUSTOMER-REPORT.
126
127       110-HEADINGS.
128
129           WRITE REPORT-REC FROM PAGE-HEADING AFTER ADVANCING PAGE.
130           WRITE REPORT-REC FROM COLUMN-HEADING1 AFTER ADVANCING 2 LINES.
131           WRITE REPORT-REC FROM COLUMN-HEADING2 AFTER ADVANCING 1 LINES.
132           MOVE SPACES TO REPORT-REC.
```

**EXHIBIT 4.42    (Cont.)**

```
133            WRITE REPORT-REC.
134
135        120-READ-FILE.
136
137            READ CUSTOMER-FILE AT END MOVE "YES" TO END-FLAG.
138
139        200-PROCESS.
140
141            PERFORM 210-CALCULATIONS.
142            PERFORM 220-DETAIL-LINE.
143            PERFORM 120-READ-FILE.
144
145        210-CALCULATIONS.
146
147            PERFORM 211-CALCULATE-NEW-BALANCE.
148            PERFORM 212-CALCULATE-FINANCE-CHARGE.
149            ADD FINANCE-CHG TO NEW-BAL.
150            PERFORM 213-CALC-MIN-CHG-AND-FMT-MESSAGE.
151
152        211-CALCULATE-NEW-BALANCE.
153
154            COMPUTE NEW-BAL = (BAL-FWD + NEW-PURCH) - PAYMT-REC.
155
156        212-CALCULATE-FINANCE-CHARGE.
157
158            COMPUTE FINANCE-CHG ROUNDED = NEW-BAL * .012.
159
160
161        213-CALC-MIN-CHG-AND-FMT-MESSAGE.
162
163            IF BAL-FWD = 0
164               THEN
165                  IF NEW-PURCH > 0
166                     THEN
167                        COMPUTE MIN-PAYMT ROUNDED = NEW-PURCH * .12
168                     ELSE
169                        COMPUTE MIN-PAYMT = 0
170                  END-IF
171
172               ELSE
173                  IF PAYMT-REC = 0
174                     THEN
175                        MOVE "NO PAYMENT RECEIVED" TO COMMENT-OUT
176                        COMPUTE MIN-PAYMT ROUNDED =
177                                        NEW-BAL * .12
178                     ELSE
179                        IF PAYMT-REC < (.12 * BAL-FWD)
180                           THEN
181                              MOVE "PAYMENT INSUFFICIENT" TO COMMENT-OUT
182                              COMPUTE MIN-PAYMT ROUNDED = ((.12 * BAL-FWD)
183                                      - PAYMT-REC) + NEW-PURCH * .12
184                           ELSE
185                              MOVE "CURRENT" TO COMMENT-OUT
186                              COMPUTE MIN-PAYMT ROUNDED =
187                                        .12 * NEW-BAL
188                        END-IF
189                  END-IF
190            END-IF.
191
192
193
194        220-DETAIL-LINE.
195
196            MOVE CUST-NO TO CUST-NO-OUT.
197            MOVE CUST-NAME TO NAME-OUT.
198            MOVE BAL-FWD TO  BAL-FWD-OUT.
```

**EXHIBIT 4.42    (Cont.)**

```
199              MOVE PAYMT-REC TO PAYMT-REC-OUT.
200              MOVE FINANCE-CHG TO FIN-CHG-OUT.
201              MOVE NEW-PURCH TO NEW-PURCH-OUT.
202              MOVE NEW-BAL TO NEW-BAL-OUT.
203              MOVE MIN-PAYMT TO MIN-PAY-OUT.
204
205              WRITE REPORT-REC FROM DETAIL-LINE.
206
207
208
209      300-WRAP-UP.
210
211          PERFORM 310-CLOSE.
212
213      310-CLOSE.
214
215          CLOSE CUSTOMER-FILE CUSTOMER-REPORT.
```

```
                      CUSTOMER ACCOUNT STATUS REPORT

   CUSTOMER    CUSTOMER       BALANCE    PAYMENTS   FINANCE  NEW        NEW       MIN      COMMENTS
   NUMBER      NAME           FORWARD    RECEIVED   CHARGE   PURCHASE   BALANCE   PAYMT

   123456792   BILL BAKER      500.00     100.00     7.20    200.00     607.20    72.86   CURRENT
   234567888   MARY JONES        0.00       0.00     3.60    300.00     303.60    36.00   CURRENT
   345678912   SUE BLACK       100.00      10.00     1.68     50.00     141.68     8.00   PAYMENT INSUFFICIENT
   456789024   JOE MCCOY       100.00      20.00     1.56     50.00     131.56    15.79   CURRENT
   567890112   BOB DOBSON        0.00       0.00     0.00      0.00       0.00     0.00   CURRENT
   678901248   SUE ROBISON    1000.00     300.00    14.40    500.00    1214.40   145.73   CURRENT
   888888896   TOM DICKSON     100.00       0.00     2.40    100.00     202.40    24.29   NO PAYMENT RECEIVED
```

**EXHIBIT 4.43    QBASIC Program for Application 4.5**

```
'************************************************************
'*                  PROGRAM IDENTIFICATION                 *
'************************************************************
'* PROGRAM NAME: CH4APL5                                   *
'************************************************************
'* REMARKS:    THIS PROGRAM PRODUCES A CUSTOMER ACCOUNT STATUS REPORT
'*             USING NESTED AND COMPOUND CONDITIONS.  THIS REPORT LISTS
'*             THE CUSTOMER NUMBER, CUSTOMER NAME, BALANCE FORWARD
'*             FROM LAST PERIOD, PAYMENTS RECEIVED DURING THE PERIOD,
'*             THE NEW BALANCE AT THE END OF THE PERIOD, AND THE MINIMUM
'*              PAYMENT.
'************************************************************
'************************************************************
'*                     MAIN-LINE                           *
'************************************************************
GOSUB STARTUP                        'PERFORM START-UP
DO UNTIL END.FLAG$ = "YES"
   GOSUB PROCESS                     ' PERFORM PROCESS
LOOP
GOSUB WRAPUP                         'PERFORM WRAP-UP
END


    '************************************************************
    '*                     START-UP                            *
    '************************************************************

STARTUP:

   GOSUB INITIALIZE
   GOSUB OPEN.FILES
   GOSUB HEADINGS                    'PERFORM HEADINGS
   GOSUB READFILE                    'PERFORM READ-CUSTOMER-FILE
   RETURN
```

**APPLICATION 4.5**

**EXHIBIT 4.43   (Cont.)**

```
'******************************************************************
'*                      INITIALIZE                               *
'******************************************************************
INITIALIZE:
   WIDTH LPRINT 120
     END.FLAG$ = "NO"
     DET.LINE$ = "   #########   \            \ #####.##   #####.##   ###.## ####.## #####.## ###.## \                          \"
     NEW.BAL = 0
     RETURN
          '******************************************************************
          '*                      OPEN FILES                               *
          '******************************************************************

OPEN.FILES:


     OPEN "I", #1, "CH4ILL6.DAT"
     RETURN


          '******************************************************************
          '*                       HEADINGS                                *
          '******************************************************************


HEADINGS:


     LPRINT CHR$(12)
     LPRINT
     LPRINT TAB(39); "CUSTOMER ACCOUNT STATUS REPORT"
     LPRINT
     LPRINT TAB(5); "CUSTOMER      CUSTOMER        BALANCE    PAYMENTS";
     LPRINT TAB(56); "FINANCE  NEW       NEW        MIN        COMMENTS"
     LPRINT TAB(6); "NUMBER          NAME          FORWARD    RECEIVED";
     LPRINT TAB(56); "CHARGE PURCHASE  BALANCE  PAYMT"
     LPRINT
     RETURN


          '******************************************************************
          '*                    READ-CUSTOMER-FILE                         *
          '******************************************************************

READFILE:

     INPUT #1, CUST.NUMB, CUST.NAME$, BAL.FWD, PAYMT.REC, NEW.PURCH
     IF CUST.NAME$ = "EOF" THEN END.FLAG$ = "YES"
     RETURN
```

# APPLICATION 4.5

**EXHIBIT 4.43   (Cont.)**

```
'*********************************************************************
'*                          PROCESS                                  *
'*********************************************************************

PROCESS:

    GOSUB DETAIL.CALCULATION              '* PERFORM DETAIL-CALC
    GOSUB DETAIL.LINE                     '* PERFORM DET-LINE
    GOSUB READFILE                        '* PERFORM READ-CUST-FILE
    RETURN


    '*********************************************************************
    '*                      DETAIL-CALCULATION                       *
    '*********************************************************************
DETAIL.CALCULATION:

    GOSUB CALC.NEW.BALANCE               '*PERFORM CALCULATE NEW BALANCE
    GOSUB CALC.FIN.CHG                   '*PERFORM CALCULATE FINANCE CHARGE
    NEW.BAL = NEW.BAL + FIN.CHG          '*ADD FINANCE CHARGE TO NEW BALANCE
    GOSUB CALC.MIN.CHG.AND.FMT.MESSAGE   '*PERFORM CALCULATE MINIMUM CHARGE
    RETURN


    '*********************************************************************
    '*                      CALC-NEW-BALANCE                         *
    '*********************************************************************

CALC.NEW.BALANCE:

    NEW.BAL = (BAL.FWD + NEW.PURCH) - PAYMT.REC
    RETURN


    '*********************************************************************
    '*                      CALC-FIN-CHG                             *
    '*********************************************************************

CALC.FIN.CHG:

    FIN.CHG = NEW.BAL * .012
    RETURN
```

**EXHIBIT 4.43    (Cont.)**

```
'*******************************************************************
'*                    CALC-MIN-CHG-AND-FMT-MESSAGE                 *
'*******************************************************************

CALC.MIN.CHG.AND.FMT.MESSAGE:

        IF BAL.FWD = 0 THEN
            IF NEW.PURCH > 0 THEN
                MIN.PAYMT = NEW.PURCH * .12
            ELSE
                MIN.PAYMT = 0
            END IF
        ELSE
            IF PAYMT.REC = 0 THEN
                COMMENT.OUT$ = "NO PAYMENT RECEIVED"
                MIN.PAYMT = NEW.BAL * .12
            ELSE
                IF PAYMT.REC < (.12 * BAL.FWD) THEN
                    COMMENT.OUT$ = "PAYMENT INSUFFICIENT"
                    MIN.PAYMT = ((.12 * BAL.FWD) - PAYMT.REC) + NEW.PURCH * .12
                ELSE
                    COMMENT.OUT$ = "CURRENT           "
                    MIN.PAYMT = .12 * NEW.BAL
                END IF
            END IF
        END IF
        RETURN


'*******************************************************************
'*                           DETAIL-LINE                           *
'*******************************************************************

DETAIL.LINE:

        LPRINT USING DET.LINE$; CUST.NUMB; CUST.NAME$; BAL.FWD; PAYMT.REC; FIN.CHG; NEW.PURCH; NEW.BAL; MIN.PAYMT; COMMENT.OUT$
        RETURN


'*******************************************************************
'*                            WRAP-UP                              *
'*******************************************************************

WRAPUP:
        CLOSE
        RETURN
```

CUSTOMER ACCOUNT STATUS REPORT

| CUSTOMER NUMBER | CUSTOMER NAME | BALANCE FORWARD | PAYMENTS RECEIVED | FINANCE CHARGE | NEW PURCHASE | NEW BALANCE | MIN PAYMT | COMMENTS |
|---|---|---|---|---|---|---|---|---|
| 123456792 | BILL BAKER | 500.00 | 100.00 | 7.20 | 200.00 | 607.20 | 72.86 | CURRENT |
| 234567888 | MARY JONES | 0.00 | 0.00 | 3.60 | 300.00 | 303.60 | 36.00 | CURRENT |
| 345678912 | SUE BLACK | 100.00 | 10.00 | 1.68 | 50.00 | 141.68 | 8.00 | PAYMENT INSUFFICIENT |
| 456789024 | JOE MCCOY | 100.00 | 20.00 | 1.56 | 50.00 | 131.56 | 15.79 | CURRENT |
| 567890112 | BOB DOBSON | 0.00 | 0.00 | 0.00 | 0.00 | 0.00 | 0.00 | CURRENT |
| 678901248 | SUE ROBISON | 1000.00 | 300.00 | 14.40 | 500.00 | 1214.40 | 145.73 | CURRENT |
| 888888896 | TOM DICKSON | 100.00 | 0.00 | 2.40 | 100.00 | 202.40 | 24.29 | NO PAYMENT RECEIVED |

## SUMMARY

An important characteristic of the computer is its ability to compare two values and, based on the results of the comparison, perform alternative processing operations. The key to making comparisons is the If . . . Then . . . Else structure. Until Chapter 4, all the processing steps in the DETAIL-CALCULATION module were imperative commands. This chapter introduced the If . . . Then . . . Else structure into the DETAIL-CALCULATION module in one example and into the ACCUMULATE module in a second example.

The CASE structure was introduced to show how a field can be tested for a number of different values and, based on the presence of a particular value, a specific course of action can be taken. A different course of action would be specified for every decision block. The key difference between the CASE structure and If . . . Then . . . Else is that the CASE structure allows control to pass to the end of the structure once an alternative series of commands have been executed. The CASE structure is handy when you want to compare a variable with a series of values where each value represents the ceiling (or upper limit) for an associated range of values. If the ranges were 0-10, 11-20, and 21-30, the first comparison value (ceiling) would be 10, the second comparison value would be 20, and the third comparison value would be 30.

## VOCABULARY

comparison
checking for bottom-of-page
CASE structure
identification codes (classification codes)
compound AND condition
compound OR condition
nested comparison (or nested IF)
decision table

## EXERCISES/QUESTIONS

1. What are the three kinds of comparison operations? Give an example of the use of each one.

2. Draw the general flowchart structure for the If . . . Then . . . Else.

3. Draw the general flowchart structure for the CASE structure.

4. Give an example of how the If . . . Then . . . Else would be used.

5. Give an example of how the CASE structure would be used.

## PROBLEMS

Develop the hierarchy chart, structured flowchart, and pseudocode for the following problems.

**4-1.** Bill's Lawnmower Shop needs a report to help them keep track of how much they charge for repair. The repair charge rate is based on the type of lawnmower. The schedule of repair charges follows.

| Code | Description | Charge per Minute |
|------|-------------|-------------------|
| 1 | Rider | .30 |
| 2 | Self-Propelled | .25 |
| 3 | Manual | .20 |

The input record layout appears as follows:

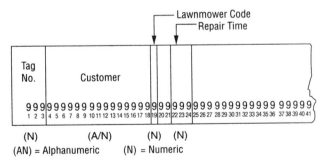

The report is illustrated here

```
                    BILL'S LAWNMOWER SHOP
                    CUSTOMER BILLING REPORT

TAG#    CUSTOMER      LAWNMOWER CODE    RATE    REPAIR TIME (MIN)    CHARGE

021     MARY JONES          1           .30          100            30.00
445     BILL SMITH          2           .25          200            50.00
XXX     XXXXXXXXXX          X           .XX          XXX            XX.XX
XXX     XXXXXXXXXX          X           .XX          XXX            XX.XX
XXX     XXXXXXXXXX          X           .XX          XXX            XX.XX
```

**4-2**  A teacher wishes to produce a summary report that shows the total number of students with a passing and failing average, broken down into male and female. The students' average is the sum of three test scores divided by three

```
            STUDENT  TEST  RESULTS

            PASSED      FAILED

 MALE         XXX        XXX
 FEMALE       XXX        XXX
 TOTALS      XXXX       XXXX
```

A passing test average is > 59.99.

The input record layout is as follows:

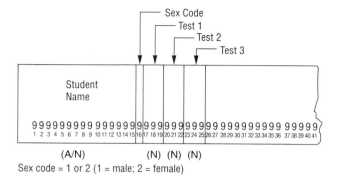

Sex code = 1 or 2 (1 = male; 2 = female)

Notice that in this problem no detail line is to be printed, only total lines.

**4-3.**  Acme Sports wants to produce a payroll register containing each employee's number, name, gross salary, federal tax, and net salary. The federal tax deduction is calculated according to the tax schedule below.

| Monthly Salary Range | Tax Percentage of Gross |
|---|---|
| 0 – 2000.00 | 18% |
| 2000.01 – 4000.00 | 22% |
| >4000 | 28% |

The first $2000 is to be taxed at 18 percent. The next $2000 (2000.01 through 4000.00) is to be taxed at the 22 percent rate, and any income in excess of $4000 is to be taxed at the 28 percent rate. The report appears as follows.

The input consists of a file of master pay records. The format of the sample record layout appears as follows:

For example, in the preceding sample record format, a salary of $5000 would be taxed as follows:

First 2000 @ .18 = 360
Next 2000 @ .22 = 440
Next 1000 @ .28 = 280
           Total Tax = 1080

```
                    ACME  SPORTS

        SSN          NAME        GROSS      TAX        NET

    452368114   JOHN DICKSON    5000.00   1080.00    3920.00
    XXXXXXXXX   XXXXXXXXXXX     XXXX.XX   XXXX.XX    XXXX.XX
    XXXXXXXXX   XXXXXXXXXXX     XXXX.XX   XXXX.XX    XXXX.XX
```

**4-4.** A manager is preparing a sales commission report. The sales commission percentages are determined from the schedule that follows. No commission is offered for sales amounts less than $500. A two percent commission rate is used if sales are between $500 and $750, and a three percent rate is used if sales are greater than $750.

| Sales Range | Commission Percent |
|---|---|
| 0 – 499.99 | NO COMMISSION |
| 500.00 – 750.00 | 2% |
| > 750.00 | 3% |

The following report is to be produced

The input record layout is shown as follows.

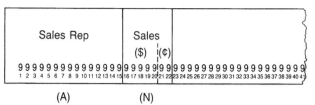

(A) = Alphanumeric
(N) = Numeric

```
                     SALES COMMISSIONS
    SALES REP       SALES AMOUNT    COMMISSION RATE    COMMISSION

XXXXXXXXXXXXXXX      XX,XXX.XX          X %             XXX.XX
XXXXXXXXXXXXXXX      XX,XXX.XX          X %             XXX.XX
XXXXXXXXXXXXXXX      XX,XXX.XX          X %             XXX.XX

                                   TOTAL COMMISSION   $ X,XXX.XX
```

**4.5** Produce the same report shown in Problem 3.4 except use the schedules below for determining the markup amount and the discount. The modified input record layout also follows.

Determination of Markup

| Merchandise Code | Markup |
|---|---|
| 1 | 12% |
| 2 | 18% |
| 3 | 22% |
| 4 | 30% |
| 5 | 50% |

Determination of Discount

| Price Range | Discount % |
|---|---|
| 0 – 99.99 | 0.0% |
| 100.00 – 500.00 | 4.0% |
| 500.01 – 1000.00 | 4.5% |
| 1000.01 – 2000.00 | 5.2% |
| > 2000.00 | 6.3% |

Input Record Layout for Ace Discount Department Stores Inventory Master.

| Field | Location | Type |
|---|---|---|
| Item # | 1 – 4 | A/N |
| Description | 5 – 15 | A/N |
| Wholesale | 16 – 21 | N ($$$.CC) |
| Merch-code | 22 | N |

4.6 Woody's Lumber Materials Company wishes to produce the report shown below which lists the material type, the material grade, description length, width, thickness, board feet, cost per board foot, and extended cost for this piece of material. To compute the board feet for a piece of material, first convert the length of the material from feet to inches. Then multiply the length X width X thickness to compute the volume in inches. Then divide the volume by 144 to convert to board feet. A board foot is a piece of material one foot in length by one foot in width by one inch thick (144 cu. inches).

Draw the hierarchy chart, flowchart, and pseudocode for this problem. Print 45 detail lines per page. Each page will have identical heading information.

```
                          WOODY'S LUMBER MATERIALS
                            STOCK STATUS REPORT

   ITEM #    GRADE     DESC      LGTH     WIDTH    THICKNESS   BD FT   COST/BF   EXTENDED
                                 (FT)     (IN)      (IN)

    P304       A      PLYWOOD      8       48"       .5         16      2.00      32.00
    L405       A      FR.LUMBER   10        6"      2.0         10       .85       8.50
    XXXX       X      XXXXXXXXX   XX        X"        X         XX      X.XX      XX.XX
    XXXX       X      XXXXXXXXX   XX        X"        X         XX      X.XX      XX.XX
```

Material Cost Per Board Foot

| | Material Type | |
|---|---|---|
| Grade | Plywood | Framing Lumber |
| GRADE A | 2.00 | .85 |
| GRADE B | 1.40 | .65 |
| GRADE C | 1.20 | .55 |

The input record format is illustrated below for Inventory Master File

| Field | Location | Type | Comment |
|---|---|---|---|
| Item # | 1 – 4 | A/N | |
| Grade | 5 | A/N | values are "A", "B", or "C" |
| Material-type | 6 | N | 1=plywood, |
| Description | 7 – 15 | A/N | 2=framing lumber |
| Length (ft) | 16 – 17 | N | |
| Width (in) | 18 – 20 | N | |
| Thickness (in) | 21 – 23 | N | (X.XX) |

**4.7** Design the program that will produce a Customer Report as shown below for Woody's Lumber Materials, which prints the customer date, item, material type, board feet, cost shipweight, distance, freight, and total. The weights of the materials are determined from the weight chart below.

The freight charges below describe the freight charges. Use nested or compound IF . . . THEN . . . ELSE where appropriate to solve this problem.

Draw the flowchart and develop the pseudocode for this problem.

## MATERIAL WEIGHT/BOARDFEET

| Material Type | Weight/Board Feet Weight in lbs. |
|---|---|
| Plywood | 1.2 |
| Framing Lumber | 1.0 |

## CHARGES TABLE

| Distance (Miles) | Weight of Freight (Pounds) | |
|---|---|---|
| | 1–20 | Over 20 |
| 1–15 | 1.20 | 2.10 |
| 15–50 | 2.40 | 3.40 |
| > 50 | 5.00 | 8.00 |

```
                         CUSTOMER ORDERS REPORT

CUSTOMER      DATE      ITEM      MAT      BD.    COST      SHIP     SHIP       FRGHT    TOTAL
                                 TYPE     FOOT             WT.      DISTANCE

BILL JONES    11/91     3454     PLYWOOD  32     64.00     38.4     20         3.40     67.40
SUE BAKER     11/91     4433     FR.LUM.  10      8.50     10.0      5         1.20      9.70
XXXXXXXXXX    XX/XX     XXXX     XXXXX    XX     XX.XX     XX.X      X         X.XX      X.XX
XXXXXXXXXX    XX/XX     XXXX     XXXXX    XX     XX.XX     XX.X      X         X.XX      X.XX
-------------------------------------------------------------------------------------------------
```

Input Record Layout of Customer Sales Transaction file.

| Field | Location | Type |
|---|---|---|
| Customer # | 1–9 | N |
| Cust-Name | 10–30 | A/N |
| Item | 31–34 | N |
| Board Feet | 35–36 | N* |
| Cost/Board Ft. | 37–40 | N* |
| Distance | 41–45 | N |
| Material Type | 46 | A/N (A = Plywood, B = Fr.Lumber) |
| Date | 47–54 | |

*The board feet and cost/board feet are manually extracted from the inventory master record at the time of the transaction and recorded in these fields respectively. While it is more realistic to electronically extract this information from the inventory file, the data processing technique and logic for this is more advanced. To simplify this procedure, assume that the board feet and cost/board feet are on the transaction record.

**4.8** Bob's Casual Clothing Store is having problems controlling their inventory due to a manual reordering procedure. Bob wishes to convert to an automated reorder system. Design a program that will produce an Inventory Control Report as shown below. The report should list the branch code and name, merchandise code, merchandise description, quantity available for sale inventory classification (i.e., the kind of merchandise), the reorder point, the standard reorder point, the amount to reorder, unit cost, and the reorder cost for this line item.

The quantity available for sale is computed as quantity on hand plus quantity on order. Of course, if the quantity available is greater than the reorder point, then the amount to reorder is zero. If the quantity available for sale is exactly equal to the reorder point, then the amount to reorder is precisely the standard reorder amount (the standard reorder amount is the amount to order assuming the reorder point is equal to the quantity available); how-

ever, if the quantity available is *less* than the reorder point then the amount to reorder is equal to the difference between the reorder point and the quantity available *plus* the standard reorder quantity from record.

Let's consider the first line of output on the report below. If quantity available is 90, then the quantity available is greater than the reorder point, so no order is needed. The amount to order is zero.

Now, let's consider the second line of output where the quantity available is 80. The value, 80, is ten less than the reorder point (the difference in the reorder quantity of 90 and the quantity available of 80 is = ten). Ten plus the standard order quantity of 40 is equal to 50. We always add the amount we are currently short of the reorder point to standard reorder quantity.

A second report is to summarize the reorder quantities by branch and product class.

*Hint:* use decision table.

```
                        BOB'S CASUAL CLOTHING STORES
                         INVENTORY CONTROL REPORT

                                                STANDARD   AMOUNT
 BRANCH   BRANCH   MERCH              QTY      REORDER   REORDER     TO      UNIT    REORDER
  CODE    (CITY)   CODE     DESC     AVAIL.    POINT     POINT    REORDER    COST     COST

    3     DALLAS     1    LEVIS501      90        80        50        0      21.00      0.00
    4     FT WTH     1    LEVISRF       80        90        40       50      20.00   1000.00
    2     AUSTIN     2    WRANG.SL      60        80        60       80      18.00   1440.00
    X     XXXXXX     X    XXXXXXXXX     70        70       135      135     XX.XX    XXXX.XX
    X     XXXXXX     X    XXXXXXXXX     XX        XX       XXX      XXX     XX.XX    XXXX.XX

                                                       TOTAL . . . . . . . . $XX,XXX.XX
```

```
      REORDER QUANTITY BY BRANCH AND PRODUCT

      BRANCH       LEVIS     WRANGLER      LEE

      AUSTIN        XXX        XXX        XXX
      DALLAS        XXX        XXX        XXX
      FT. WORTH     XXX        XXX        XXX
```

Input Record Layout for Master Inventory Record

| FIELD | LOCATION | TYPE |
|---|---|---|
| *Branch Code | 1 | N |
| Branch City | 2–7 | A/N |
| *Merch Code (1, 2, or 3) | 10 | N |
| Description | 14–27 | A/N |
| Qty-on-hand | 28–30 | N |
| Qty-on-order | 31–33 | N |
| Merch-class | 34 | N |
| Reorder-point | 35–37 | N |
| Amt-to-reorder | 38–40 | N |
| Unit-cost | 41–45 | N ($$$.cc) |

| *Branch Code | Merch. Code |
|---|---|
| 1 = WACO | 1 = LEVI'S |
| 2 = AUSTIN | 2 = WRANGLER |
| 3 = DALLAS | 3 = LEE |
| 4 = FT. WORTH | |
| 5 = HOUSTON | |

# 5

# Data Validity Checking
# Before Processing

## OBJECTIVES

After completing this chapter, the student will be able to:

1. List and describe the types of validity checking common to data processing.

2. List the types of data errors that occur during processing.

3. Explain the difference between errors that cause interrupts and errors that cause incorrect results.

4. Distinguish between an independent edit program and a processing program with built-in validity checking.

5. Develop the hierarchy chart, program flowchart, and pseudocode for a processing program with a built-in validity-checking function. The validity checking should handle any of the four validity tests (class, reasonableness, sign, and code).

6. Develop the hierarchy chart, program flowchart, and pseudocode for an independent edit program that tests each field for class, reasonableness, sign, or code.

One of the major problem areas in data processing is the presence of erroneous input data. Despite various controls, data are sometimes erroneously entered on the record. Characters are often miskeyed during data input to tapes, disks, diskettes, cards, or other storage media.

Because programmers expect the unwanted, but inevitable, presence of erroneous data in file records, the programs they write will contain some type of routine that checks for invalid fields to determine if important fields contain valid data. It is not usually possible to determine that the data are precisely correct, but the program can determine whether the data in the important fields satisfy certain prescribed criteria.

## VALIDITY CHECKING

The kinds of validity checking that are often established in a program include the following:

1. Class tests
2. Limit or reasonableness tests
3. Code tests
4. Sign tests

A **class test** determines whether the content of a field is numeric or alphabetic. A **limit test (reasonableness test)** determines if a particular value is within a prescribed range of acceptable values. Often this type of test is used to eliminate unreasonable values before processing occurs. A **valid code test** ensures that the content of the identification code field contains one of the valid codes. A sign test tells whether a value is positive or negative. Figure 5.1 shows a student input record previously presented in Chapter 4. The only valid codes in the student classification field are 1, 2, 3, or 4. Any other values would be meaningless. The valid sex codes in the same example are M or F, so a 3 or a J in this field would be erroneous.

From a pragmatic perspective, however, regardless of the degree of sophistication we build into our validity-checking routines, all that can be done is reduce the probability of erroneous data being processed as valid data. We can never be absolutely certain that the data are error-free. For example, although our program can make sure that only values of 1, 2, 3, and 4 are accepted as valid codes, it cannot detect if the 2 value in a field should have actually been a 3.

## TYPES OF ERRORS

The programmer soon discovers that the two major types of errors that occur during processing are (1) errors that cause program interrupts and (2) errors that cause incorrect results.

## Errors That Cause Program Interrupts

What is an interrupt? An **interrupt** is an abrupt halt in a program's execution that occurs when, for some reason, the operating system of the computer can no longer process the user's program. A number of causes exist for program interrupts. The one that relates to validity checking is called the **data exception**. Some manufacturers' operating systems (IBM's, for example) will not attempt to do arithmetic or numeric comparisons with a field that the computer doesn't recognize as numeric, that is, as having a valid sign. The two ways a programmer can be sure that the contents of a field contain a valid sign is to make sure that (1) the field contains only numbers and (2) it is declared as a numeric value in the programming language. (See Appendix B for details regarding data representation in storage.) Certainly, the program should use a class test to check any field involved in arithmetic or numeric comparisons in order to determine if its contents are numeric. Failure to perform class tests often leads to needless compiles, project delays, and cost overruns.

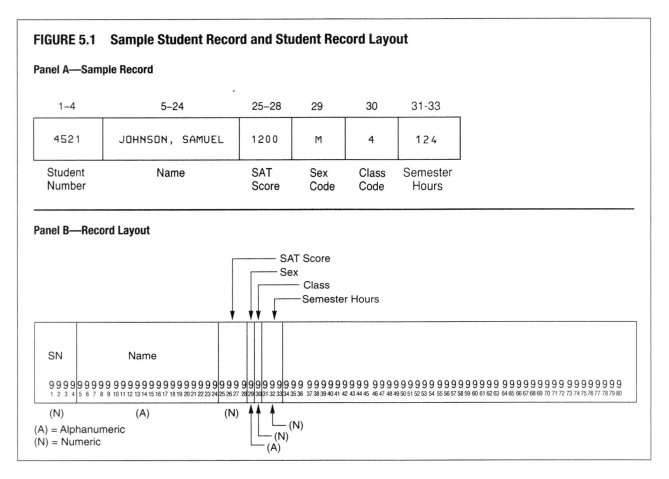

FIGURE 5.1   Sample Student Record and Student Record Layout

## Errors That Cause Incorrect Results

These errors are usually caused by miskeying a value that is properly numeric but is simply not the correct value. The value keyed in may be within an acceptable range and possess all the right attributes, but it is *not* the number the operator intended to key into the computer.

## VALIDITY-CHECKING PROGRAMS— EDIT PROGRAM AND BUILT-IN VALIDITY-CHECKING PROGRAM

The two major kinds of validity-checking programs are (1) the edit program and (2) the processing program with built-in validity checking.

The sole purpose of an independent **edit program** is to check the validity of all, or at least a significant portion of, the fields in the various records of a file. The edit program, in theory, is the best kind of validity checking, for it screens out invalid records before the processing program ever reads a single record of the file. (The processing program is the program that performs calculations and produces a report.) Nevertheless, due to the dynamic nature of an information system and the brief time frame in which programs are often developed in order to meet critical system development deadlines, it is not always possible to write an edit program for every file that a given program will access. Therefore, the program must contain **built-in validity-checking routines** that check the validity of critical fields in a record that are used by the processing modules of the program. Even when generalized edit programs are used, sometimes special built-in validity-checking programs are also needed for particular applications.

## ERROR ROUTINES
### Edit Program

The edit program normally produces an *edit report*, which is a listing of appropriate messages that identify which field(s) within a record is (are) in error. Figure 5.2 illustrates the edit program output. The program reads and interrogates each and every record in the file. If a record contains an invalid field, the appropriate message is printed. In some instances, a number of messages print for a given record that is found to contain numerous errors. A key characteristic of an edit program is that it interrogates all records in the file. Once the edit program is complete, the edit report is often used in creating a transaction file. The transaction file represents the changes to be made to the master file. The concept of file update will be addressed in Chapter 12. Today, an alternative method for making minor repairs to a record in a file can be accomplished through the use of the full-screen editor, which allows the file to be listed on the terminal screen and modified by the user. The use of the full-screen editor for making *major* changes to a file, however, would be too time-consuming and would lend itself to the propagation of additional data entry errors in an attempt to correct others.

### Built-In Validity Checking

A processing program with built-in validity-checking routines may contain two different kinds of error routines.

1. The job is aborted if a record contains bad data (often the case).
2. The job continues, but an error message is printed either as a part of an exception report or as a part of the user report.

---

### FIGURE 5.2  A Typical Data Validation Edit Report*

(Generated from Independent Edit Program)

```
                    EDIT RUN, STUDENT AUGUST 12, 1992

         SN        NAME        I N V A L I D  F I E L D S MESSAGES

        0211     ABLES, J      CLASS CODE INVALID
                               SEMESTER HOURS UNREASONABLE
                               SEX CODE INVALID
        1346     BROWN, M      SEX CODE INVALID
        3421     J/*.732       NAME NOT ALPHA
                               CLASS CODE INVALID
```

*The SN and Name fields of each record print for each invalid record regardless of which field is in error.

An error message is simply an alphanumeric constant or a string of characters that prints in some area of a print line to indicate that a record or a field is in error.

Figure 5.3 illustrates sample output that could be generated in case of an error routine that allows the program to run but causes an error message to be printed on an exception report. An **exception report** is a report that contains the unusual cases. Sometimes the exception report is a report of only records in error; at other times the report may contain only correct data, but correct data that meet a prescribed criteria. For example, a manager may wish to produce a report of only salesmen who sold more than 100,000 dollars worth of merchandise last month. Those selling less than this amount would not appear on the report.

Figure 5.3 represents essentially the same kind of report shown in Figure 5.2. The erroneous data are simply depicted in a slightly different way. Which method of reporting to use is usually the decision of the systems analyst and/or the programmer/ analyst. The key point to note here is that the erroneous data are not included in the user report but form a separate document to be used for file main-

tenance purposes only. The character X identifies a particular field in the record as invalid.

Figure 5.4 is a sample of output that might be generated when an error routine allows the program to continue to run and prints the error message(s) on the detail line in the user report itself. This technique of printing error messages in the user report is used infrequently because it distracts the user. Certainly, reports intended for management should not contain error messages. Such indications of errors in the files might give managers a poor impression of the computer system. Note that Figure 5.4 is an operational (or functional) level report used by clerical, warehouse, and data processing personnel.

## PROGRAM DESIGN

A separate program design will be presented for each kind of validity-checking program that follows. The first problem will require a program designed with a built-in validity-checking routine; the second will call for the design of an edit program that produces a report of invalid records only.

---

**FIGURE 5.3    An Exception Report Depicting Invalid Records and Specific Fields in the Record That Are Invalid**

(Generated Using Built-in Validity Checking Program)

```
            EXCEPTION REPORT OF ERRONEOUS RECORDS -- PAYFILE 8/12/92
                        (AN "X" INDICATES BAD DATA)

      SSN         NAME            ADDRESS      JOB CODE     SEX      RATE/HOUR

      1136         X                              X
      3642                          X
      6421                                                  X          X
```

---

**FIGURE 5.4    An Operational Report with Error Messages**

```
                    INVENTORY LISTING, AUG. 13, 1992

      INVENTORY #      DESCRIPTION          QUANTITY          MESSAGE

          4502         STEEL ROD 1/4"          10
          8211         U-BOLT, 3 3/4"           8
          4211         4,,.J23.                 3        INVALID DESCRIPTION
          8217         I-BEAM 4"               10
          3114         STEEL JOIST             J?        INVALID QUANTITY
```

## Inventory Report Using a Built-In Validity-Checking Routine

### Program Requirements

Omni Industries needs an inventory report that lists each inventoried item, with its inventory description, price per unit, quantity on hand, and cost. At the end of the inventory report, the total cost is to be printed. The program that prints this report must also include a built-in routine that will eliminate records with invalid values from the processing modules.

### Output Design

Exhibit 5.1 illustrates the user report that is to be generated from the valid records. Exhibit 5.2 shows the exception report that identifies erroneous data records in the file.

### Input Design

Exhibit 5.3 depicts the input record format for the inventory field, and Exhibit 5.4 contains the associated test cases.

### Logic Considerations

The validity-checking routine should provide for the following checks:

1. The PART-NO field should be numeric.
2. The PART-DESC field should be alphabetic.
3. The PRICE-PER-UNIT field should be numeric and between 1 and 750.
4. The QTY should be numeric.

In the exception report shown in panel A of Exhibit 5.2, you will see Xs in various columns opposite the part numbers on each line. The column headings indicate the kinds of invalid data a particular record contains. For example, the first invalid record in the file, shown on the first line of the exception report, is identified as PART-NO 46092. price-per-unit, the only invalid field in this record, has been flagged with an X. The next record shown to be in error is 82134. The QTY and PART-DESC fields are the only fields in this record identified as incorrect. The third record in the exception report is

---

**EXHIBIT 5.1    User Inventory Report Sample and Associated Printer Spacing Chart**

**Panel A—User Report Sample**

```
                          OMNI INDUSTRIES

        PART NO     PART DESCRIPTION        PRICE/UNIT   QTY   COST

        45036       APPLES                       2.35    10    23.50
        82113       PECANS                      10.00    80   800.00

                                             TOTAL COST       $823.50
```

**Panel B—Printer Spacing Chart**

the one identified as part number ZZZZZ. Every field in this record is marked as invalid.

## Program Design of a Built-in Validity-Checking Program

Exhibit 5.5 illustrates the hierarchy chart phase of program design that checks the validity of the file and produces the two reports shown in Exhibits 5.1 and 5.2. In Exhibit 5.5, you'll note the inclusion of one additional third-level module called VALIDATE-ROUTINE. The DETAIL-CALCULA-TION, ACCUMULATION, AND DETAIL-LINE-INVENTORY lines remain much the same as in previous examples. This validation program intro-duces two important new concepts. The first is that more than one report file can be generated from the same processing program. This is possible because the operating system can "spool" the print files to a disk. When the program instructs the computer to print a line, it actually writes images of the print lines as records on a disk file instead. Why does it do this? Since writing a record to a disk is many

times faster than writing a line to a printer, **spool-ing** allows a greater degree of throughput to the system. And, of course, it enables the processing program to generate more than one print file. More will be said about disk processing in Chapter 12. Second, this validation program will introduce you to a new function of, or purpose for, a control vari-able. In Chapter 2, you encountered a control vari-able, END-FLAG, that was used in the MAIN-LINE routine with a repetition structure (DoWhile). END-FLAG has appeared in every program exam-ple since and will continue to appear in subsequent examples. This chapter introduces an additional control variable that flags the presence or absence of a valid record. We will refer to this variable as **VALIDITY-SWITCH**. VALIDITY-SWITCH will be initially set to the value "YES". If the record cur-rently being read is found to be invalid, the value "NO" will be moved to the control variable. When the content of VALIDITY-SWITCH is "NO", the record is considered invalid, normal processing is bypassed, and an appropriate line is printed on the exception report.

After the hierarchy chart is complete, the next step is to draw the structured program flowchart

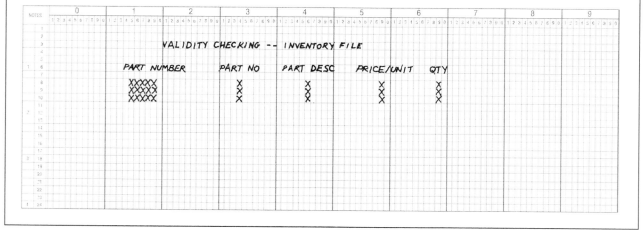

**EXHIBIT 5.2    Exception Report for Inventory Report Run and Associated Printer Spacing Chart**

**Panel A—Exception Report**

```
     VALIDITY CHECKING -- INVENTORY FILE

PART NUMBER        PART NO      PART DESC      PRICE/UNIT      QTY

46092                                              X
82134                            X                              X
ZZZZZ               X            X                 X            X
```

"X" indicates field invalid

**Panel B—Printer Spacing Chart**

shown in Exhibit 5.6. The flowchart for this program looks a lot like the flowchart for the last problem except for the inclusion of logical steps to handle the validation process.

Let's discuss the modules in our program flowchart (Exhibit 5.6). Again the main-line routine remains unchanged. The START-UP module initializes TOT-COST to zero and opens the appropriate input and output files. Because two separate and distinct reports are to be printed during the same processing program, two different print files are opened. The headings for both reports are then printed, and the first record of the file is read.

The VALIDATE-PROCESS module first invokes the VALIDATE-ROUTINE submodule. If the contents of the control variable, VALIDITY-SWITCH, change during the execution of VALIDATE-ROUTINE, an exception line prints on the exception report. If the contents of the control variable remain unchanged, the DETAIL-CALCULATION, ACCUMULATION, and DETAIL-LINE-INVEN-

TORY submodules execute instead. In either case, after the inventory report line or the exception report line is printed, the next record is read. This module, of course, repeats until all records have been read.

VALIDATE-ROUTINE is the built-in module that checks the validity of each record. The first command in the module initializes the VALID-SWITCH variable to the constant YES. The second step clears the exception report's print line. The third step determines if the contents of the PART-NO field are numeric. The COBOL programming language provides for such class tests. See Exhibit 5.8 for the COBOL conditional expression that tests a field for all numeric characters. In 210-VALI-DATE-ROUTINE of the COBOL procedure division, if the PART-NO field is not numeric, the alphanumeric constant X is moved to the print line variable called PART-NO-EXC-RPT and the constant NO is moved to the control variable, VALID-SWITCH. Whether the PART-NO field is numeric or

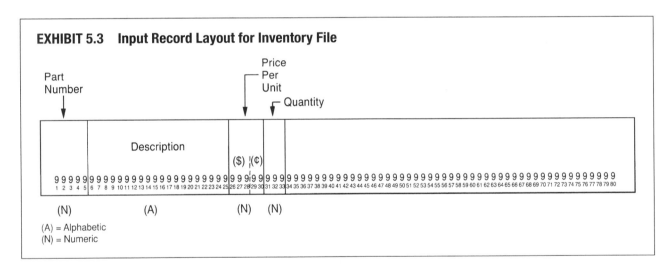

**EXHIBIT 5.3    Input Record Layout for Inventory File**

Part Number

Price Per Unit

Quantity

Description

($)  (¢)

9 9 9 9 9 | 9 9 9 9 9 9 9 9 9 9 9 9 9 9 9 9 9 9 9 9 | 9 9 9 9 | 9 9 9 | 9 9 9 9 9 9 9 9 9 9 9 9 9 9 9 9 9 9 9 9 9 9 9 9 9 9 9 9 9 9 9 9 9 9 9 9 9 9 9 9 9 9 9 9 9 9 9 9

1 2 3 4 5 | 6 7 8 9 10 11 12 13 14 15 16 17 18 19 20 21 22 23 24 25 | 26 27 28 | 29 30 | 31 32 33 | 34 35 36 37 38 39 40 41 42 43 44 45 46 47 48 49 50 51 52 53 54 55 56 57 58 59 60 61 62 63 64 65 66 67 68 69 70 71 72 73 74 75 76 77 78 79 80

(N)        (A)              (N)   (N)

(A) = Alphabetic
(N) = Numeric

**EXHIBIT 5.4    Input File Test Case for the Program Run**

INPUT FILE TEST DATA

| PART NO | DESCRIPTION | PRICE/UNIT | QUANTITY |
|---------|-------------|------------|----------|
| 45036 | APPLES | 00235 | 010 |
| 46092 | ORANGES | JJKKK | 020 |
| 82134 | BANANAS34 | 00222 | MMN |
| ZZZZZ | 821346211 | MMMMM | XXX |
| 82113 | PECANS | 01000 | 080 |
| 11111 | TELEVISION | 0500 | 500 |
| 22222 | VCR | 0400 | 300 |
| 33333 | CAMERA | 0300 | 200 |
| 77777 | TRI POD | XYZ | 010 |
| 88888 | MINICAM | JMK | 010 |
| 99999 | MAXI CAM | DDD | XX |
| 00000 | BINOCULARS | YYY | ZZZ |

otherwise, execution resumes with the next comparison operation. The fourth step tests to see if the contents of the DESC variable consist of all alphabetic characters (letters of the alphabet or spaces). If this condition tests false, the constant X is moved to the print line variable called DESC-EXC-RPT, and the constant NO is moved to the control variable, VALIDITY-SWITCH. The next two decision steps of the flowchart test the contents of the two remaining fields to determine if they are numeric. If the conditional tests are false, an X is moved to each of the

appropriate print line variables, and NO is moved to VALIDITY-SWITCH.

It is important to note that this module consists of a series of If . . . Then . . . Else structures—*not* the CASE structure. In this example, the programmer wants execution to resume at the next decision block, not go to the end of the structure as it would with the CASE structure.

Exhibit 5.7 illustrates the pseudocode for this problem, and Exhibits 5.8 and 5.9 depict the respective COBOL and BASIC programs.

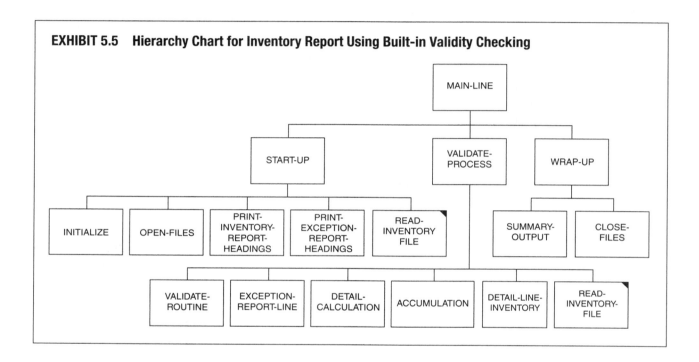

**EXHIBIT 5.5 Hierarchy Chart for Inventory Report Using Built-in Validity Checking**

**EXHIBIT 5.6   Structured Flowchart for Inventory Report Using Built-in Validity Checking**

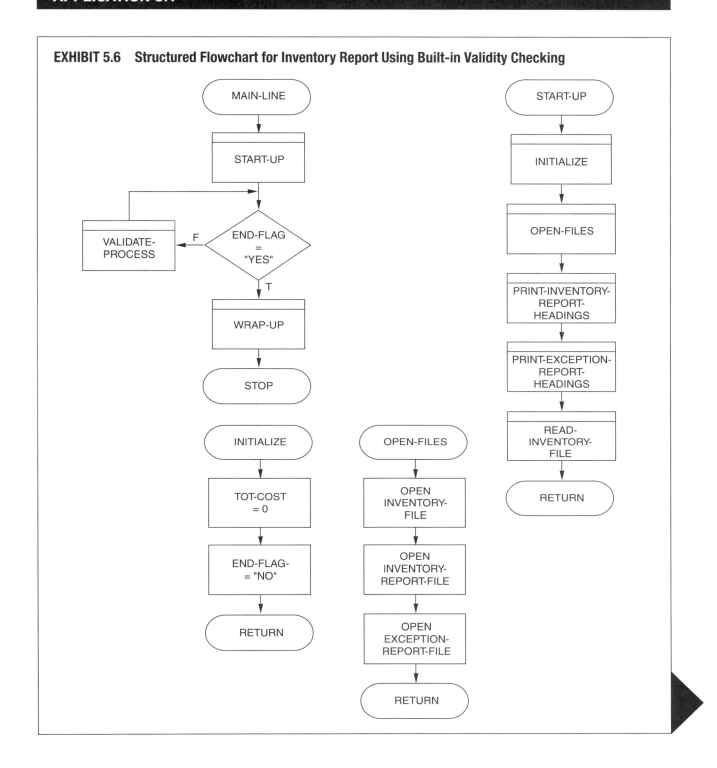

**EXHIBIT 5.6** (Cont.)

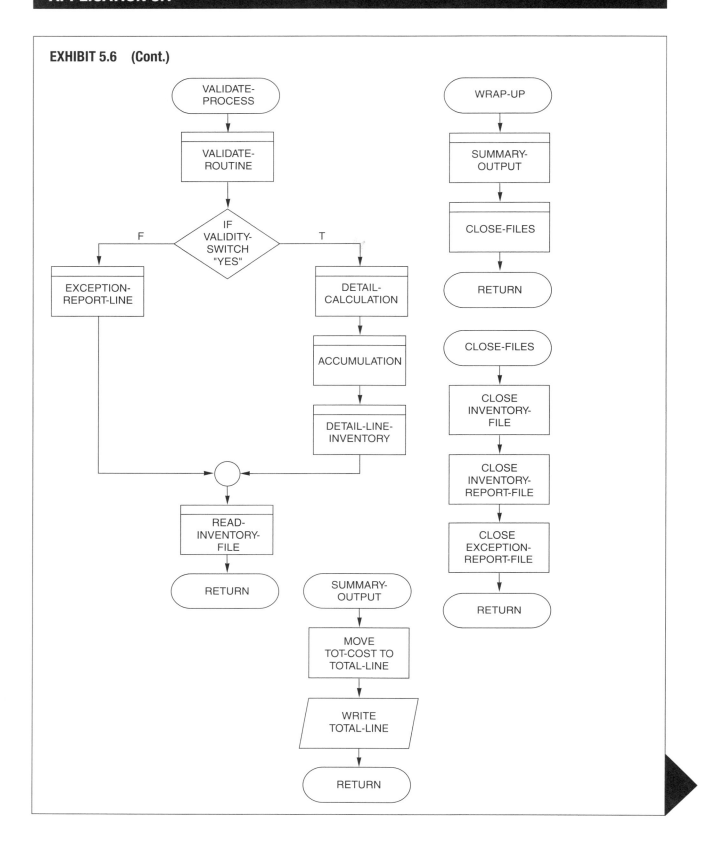

**EXHIBIT 5.6    (Cont.)**

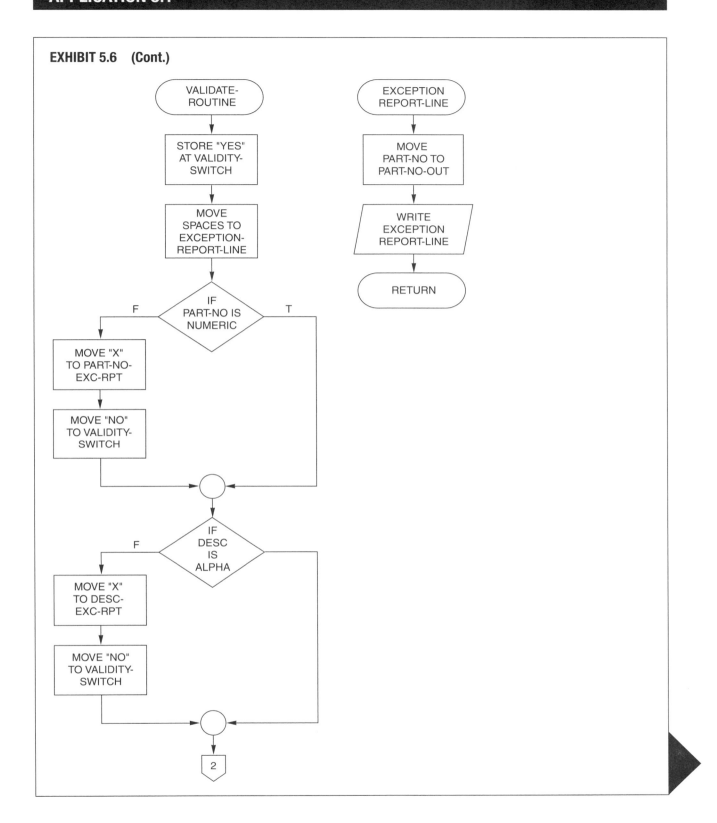

# APPLICATION 5.1

**EXHIBIT 5.6    (Cont.)**

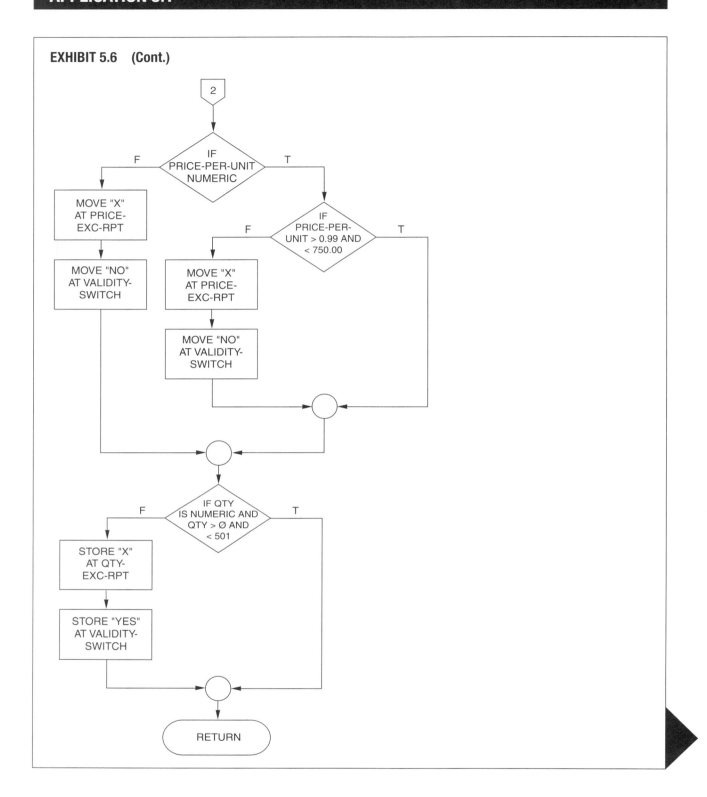

**EXHIBIT 5.6  (Cont.)**

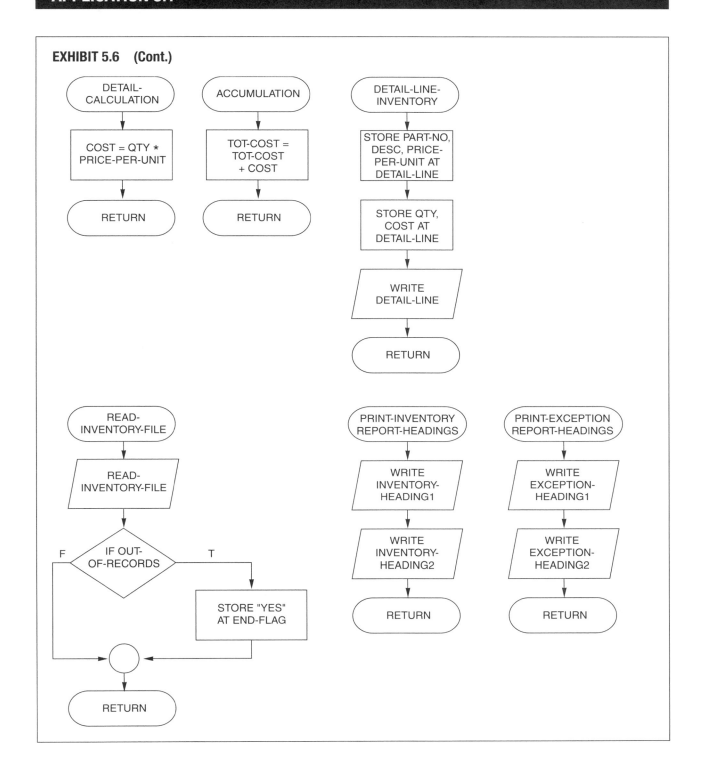

## EXHIBIT 5.7    Pseudocode for Built-in Validity Checking Program

```
*main-line
    start-up
    dowhile end-flag = "no"
        validate-process
    enddo
    wrap-up
    stop
*start-up
    initialize
    open-files
    print-inventory-report-headings
    print-exception-report-headings
    read-inventory-file
    return
*initialize
    tot-cost = 0
    end-flag = "no"
    return
*open-files
    open input inventory-file
    open output inventory-report-file
    open output exception-report-file
    return
*print-inventory-report-headings
    write inventory-heading1
    write inventory-heading2
    return
*print-exception-report-headings
    write exception-heading1
    write exception-heading2
    return
*read-inventory-file
    read inventory-file
    when no more records set endflag = "yes"
    endread
    return
*validate-process
    validate-routine
    if validity-switch = "yes"
        then
            detail-calculation
            accumulation
            detail-line-inventory
        else
            exception-report-line
    endif
    read-inventory-file
    return
*validate-routine
    validity-switch = "yes"
    move spaces to exception-report-line
    if part-no is numeric
        then
            null
        else
            transfer "X" to part-no-exc-rpt
            validity-switch = "no"
```

```
    endif
    if desc is alphabetic
        then
            null
        else
            store "X" at desc-exc-rpt
            store "no" at validity-switch
    endif
    if price-per-unit is numeric
        then
            if price-per-unit > .99 and < 750.00
                then
                    null
                else
                    move "X" to price-exc-rpt
                    move "no" to validity-switch
            endif
        else
            move "X" to price-exc-rpt
            move "no" to validity-switch
    endif
    if qty is numeric and (qty > 0 and qty < 500.01)
        then
            move "X" to qty-exc-rpt
            move "yes" to validity-switch
    endif
    return
*detail-calculation
    calculate cost = qty * price-per-unit
    return
*accumulation
    tot-cost = tot-cost + cost
    return
*detail-line-inventory
    format and transfer input and calculated fields to their
        respective output fields
    write detail-line
    return
*exception-report-line
    store part-no to part-no-out
    write exception-report-line
    return
*wrap-up
    summary output
    close-files
    return
*close-files
    close inventory-file
    close inventory-report-file
    close exception-report-file
    return
*summary output
    move tot-cost to total-line
    write total-line
    return
```

**EXHIBIT 5.8 COBOL 85 Program for Application 5.1, Inventory Report, Built-in Validation**

```
1          IDENTIFICATION DIVISION.
2
3          PROGRAM-ID.  CH5ILL1.
4        * ANS COBOL 85
5        *          THE FOLLOWING PROGRAM GENERATES AN INVENTORY
6        *          REPORT AND AN EDIT REPORT OF INVALID DATA.
7        *     USES END-IF STATEMENTS WITH IF..THEN..ELSE
8        *     USES DATA CLASS (NUMERIC AND ALPHABETIC) TESTS
9        *     USES NESTED IF STATEMENTS FOR DATA VALIDATION
10
11         ENVIRONMENT DIVISION.
12         CONFIGURATION SECTION.
13
14         SOURCE-COMPUTER.  CYBER.
15         OBJECT-COMPUTER.  CYBER.
16
17         INPUT-OUTPUT SECTION.
18
19         FILE-CONTROL.
20             SELECT INVENTORY-MASTER ASSIGN TO DTA51.
21             SELECT INVENTORY-REPORT ASSIGN TO OUTFILE.
22             SELECT EDIT-REPORT ASSIGN TO INRPT.
23
24         DATA DIVISION.
25
26         FILE SECTION.
27
28         FD   INVENTORY-MASTER.
29
30         01   INVENTORY-RECORD.
31
32             05 PART-NO-INV           PIC 9(5).
33             05 DESC-INV              PIC X(20).
34             05 PRICE-PER-UNIT-INV    PIC 9(3)V99.
35             05 QTY-INV               PIC 999.
36
37         FD   INVENTORY-REPORT.
38         01   INVENTORY-REPORT-REC    PIC X(133).
39
40         FD   EDIT-REPORT.
41         01   EDIT-REPORT-REC         PIC X(133).
42
43         WORKING-STORAGE SECTION.
44
45         01   TOT-COST                PIC 9(7)V99 VALUE ZERO.
46         01   COST                    PIC 9(6)V99 VALUE ZERO.
47         01   END-FLAG                PIC XXX VALUE "NO".
48         01   VALIDITY-SWITCH         PIC XXX VALUE "YES".
49
50         01   INVENTORY-REPORT-HEADING1.
51
52             05                       PIC X(30) VALUE SPACES.
53             05                       PIC X(15) VALUE
54                                           "OMNI INDUSTRIES".
55             05                       PIC X(87) VALUE SPACES.
56
57
58         01   INVENTORY-REPORT-HEADING2.
59
60             05                       PIC X(11) VALUE SPACES.
61             05                       PIC X(7) VALUE "PART-NO".
62             05                       PIC X(6) VALUE SPACES.
63             05                       PIC X(16) VALUE
64                                           "PART DESCRIPTION".
65             05                       PIC X(6) VALUE SPACES.
66             05                       PIC X(10) VALUE "PRICE/UNIT".
```

**EXHIBIT 5.8    (Cont.)**

```
67              05                           PIC X(3) VALUE SPACES.
68              05                           PIC X(3) VALUE "QTY".
69              05                           PIC X(3) VALUE SPACES.
70              05                           PIC X(4) VALUE "COST".
71              05                           PIC X(63) VALUE SPACES.
72
73      01   INVENTORY-REPORT-DETAIL-LINE.
74
75              05                           PIC X(12) VALUE SPACES.
76              05 PART-NO-INV-OUT           PIC ZZZZ9.
77              05                           PIC X(6) VALUE SPACES.
78              05 DESC-INV-OUT              PIC X(20).
79              05                           PIC X(5) VALUE SPACES.
80              05 PRICE-PER-UNIT-OUT        PIC ZZ9.99.
81              05                           PIC X(5) VALUE SPACES.
82              05 QUANTITY-OUT              PIC ZZ9.
83              05                           PIC X(02) VALUE SPACES.
84              05 COST-OUT                  PIC ZZZ,ZZZ.99.
85              05                           PIC X(58) VALUE SPACES.
86
87      01   INVENTORY-REPORT-TOTAL-LINE.
88
89              05                           PIC X(49) VALUE SPACES.
90              05                           PIC X(13) VALUE "TOTAL COST".
91              05 TOT-COST-OUT              PIC Z,ZZZ,ZZ9.99.
92              05                           PIC X(59) VALUE SPACES.
93
94      01   EDIT-REPORT-HEADING1.
95
96              05                           PIC X(20) VALUE SPACES.
97              05                           PIC X(36) VALUE
98                      "VALIDITY CHECKING -- INVENTORY FILE".
99              05                           PIC X(76) VALUE SPACES.
100
101     01   EDIT-REPORT-HEADING2.
102
103             05                           PIC X(14) VALUE SPACES.
104             05                           PIC X(16) VALUE "PART NUMBER".
105             05                           PIC X(11) VALUE "PART-NO".
106             05                           PIC X(13) VALUE "PART-DESC".
107             05                           PIC X(13) VALUE "PRICE/UNIT".
108             05                           PIC X(82) VALUE "QTY".
109
110     01   EDIT-DETAIL.
111
112             05                           PIC X(15) VALUE SPACE.
113             05 PART-NO-OUT               PIC X(5).
114             05                           PIC X(13) VALUE SPACES.
115             05 PART-NO-EXC-RPT           PIC X     VALUE SPACES.
116             05                           PIC X(11) VALUE SPACES.
117             05 DESC-EXC-RPT              PIC X     VALUE SPACES.
118             05                           PIC X(12) VALUE SPACES.
119             05 PRICE-EXC-RPT             PIC X     VALUE SPACES.
120             05                           PIC X(9)  VALUE SPACES.
121             05 QTY-EXC-RPT               PIC X     VALUE SPACES.
122             05                           PIC X(63) VALUE SPACES.
123
124     /
125      PROCEDURE DIVISION.
126
127      000-MAIN-LINE.
128
129          PERFORM 100-START-UP.
130          PERFORM 200-VALIDATE-PROCESS UNTIL END-FLAG = "YES".
131          PERFORM 300-WRAP-UP.
132          STOP RUN.
```

**EXHIBIT 5.8   (Cont.)**

```
133
134        100-START-UP.
135
136    *       INITIALIZATION - W-S
137           PERFORM 105-OPEN-FILES.
138           PERFORM 110-PRINT-INVENTORY-HEADINGS.
139           PERFORM 120-PRINT-EDIT-HEADINGS.
140           PERFORM 130-READ-INVENTORY-FILE.
141
142       105-OPEN-FILES.
143           OPEN INPUT INVENTORY-MASTER.
144           OPEN OUTPUT INVENTORY-REPORT   EDIT-REPORT.
145
146       110-PRINT-INVENTORY-HEADINGS.
147
148           WRITE INVENTORY-REPORT-REC FROM INVENTORY-REPORT-HEADING1
149              AFTER ADVANCING PAGE.
150           WRITE INVENTORY-REPORT-REC FROM INVENTORY-REPORT-HEADING2
151              AFTER 2.
152           MOVE SPACES TO INVENTORY-REPORT-REC.
153           WRITE INVENTORY-REPORT-REC AFTER 1.
154
155       120-PRINT-EDIT-HEADINGS.
156
157           WRITE EDIT-REPORT-REC FROM EDIT-REPORT-HEADING1
158              AFTER ADVANCING PAGE.
159           WRITE EDIT-REPORT-REC FROM EDIT-REPORT-HEADING2
160              AFTER 3.
161           MOVE SPACES TO EDIT-REPORT-REC.
162           WRITE EDIT-REPORT-REC AFTER 1.
163
164       130-READ-INVENTORY-FILE.
165
166           READ INVENTORY-MASTER AT END MOVE "YES" TO END-FLAG.
167
168
169       200-VALIDATE-PROCESS.
170
171           PERFORM 210-VALIDATE-ROUTINE.
172           IF VALIDITY-SWITCH = "YES"
173              PERFORM 220-DETAIL-CALCULATION
174              PERFORM 230-ACCUMULATE-TOTAL
175              PERFORM 240-DETAIL-LINE-INVENTORY
176           ELSE
177              MOVE PART-NO-INV TO PART-NO-OUT
178              PERFORM 250-EDIT-REPORT-LINE
179           END-IF.
180
181           PERFORM 130-READ-INVENTORY-FILE.
182
183       210-VALIDATE-ROUTINE.
184
185           MOVE "YES" TO VALIDITY-SWITCH.
186
187           IF PART-NO-INV IS NUMERIC
188              NEXT SENTENCE
189           ELSE
190              MOVE "X" TO PART-NO-EXC-RPT
191              MOVE "NO" TO VALIDITY-SWITCH
192           END-IF.
193
194           IF DESC-INV IS ALPHABETIC
195              NEXT SENTENCE
196           ELSE
197              MOVE "X" TO DESC-EXC-RPT
198              MOVE "NO" TO VALIDITY-SWITCH
```

**EXHIBIT 5.8 (Cont.)**

```
199            END-IF.
200
201            IF PRICE-PER-UNIT-INV IS NUMERIC
202               THEN
203                  IF PRICE-PER-UNIT-INV > 0.99 AND < 750.00
204                     THEN NEXT SENTENCE
205                  ELSE
206                     MOVE "X" TO PRICE-EXC-RPT
207                     MOVE "NO" TO VALIDITY-SWITCH
208                  END-IF
209               ELSE
210                  MOVE "X" TO PRICE-EXC-RPT
211                  MOVE "NO" TO VALIDITY-SWITCH
212            END-IF.
213
214            IF QTY-INV IS NUMERIC AND (QTY-INV > 0 AND < 501)
215               THEN NEXT SENTENCE
216            ELSE
217               MOVE "X" TO QTY-EXC-RPT
218               MOVE "NO" TO VALIDITY-SWITCH
219            END-IF.
220
221        220-DETAIL-CALCULATION.
222
223            COMPUTE COST ROUNDED = QTY-INV * PRICE-PER-UNIT-INV.
224
225        230-ACCUMULATE-TOTAL.
226
227            COMPUTE TOT-COST = TOT-COST + COST.
228
229        240-DETAIL-LINE-INVENTORY.
230
231            MOVE PART-NO-INV TO PART-NO-INV-OUT.
232            MOVE DESC-INV TO DESC-INV-OUT.
233            MOVE PRICE-PER-UNIT-INV TO PRICE-PER-UNIT-OUT.
234            MOVE QTY-INV TO QUANTITY-OUT.
235            MOVE COST TO COST-OUT.
236            WRITE INVENTORY-REPORT-REC FROM INVENTORY-REPORT-DETAIL-LINE
237               AFTER 1.
238
239        250-EDIT-REPORT-LINE.
240               WRITE EDIT-REPORT-REC FROM EDIT-DETAIL
241                  AFTER 1.
242               MOVE SPACES TO EDIT-DETAIL.
243
244        300-WRAP-UP.
245            PERFORM 310-SUMMARY-OUTPUT.
246            PERFORM 320-CLOSE-FILES.
247
248        310-SUMMARY-OUTPUT.
249            MOVE TOT-COST TO TOT-COST-OUT.
250            WRITE INVENTORY-REPORT-REC FROM INVENTORY-REPORT-TOTAL-LINE
251               AFTER 3.
252
253        320-CLOSE-FILES.
254            CLOSE INVENTORY-MASTER  INVENTORY-REPORT   EDIT-REPORT.
255
```

**EXHIBIT 5.8   (Cont.)**

```
                        OMNI INDUSTRIES

     PART-NO      PART DESCRIPTION      PRICE/UNIT   QTY    COST

      45036       APPLES                    2.35     10        23.50
      82113       PECANS                   10.00     80       800.00
      11111       TELEVISION              500.00    500   250,000.00
      22222       VCR                     400.00    300   120,000.00
      33333       CAMERA                  300.00    200    60,000.00


                                      TOTAL COST     430,823.50
```

```
            VALIDITY CHECKING -- INVENTORY FILE


     PART NUMBER      PART-NO     PART-DESC     PRICE/UNIT     QTY

        46092                                       X
        82134                        X                          X
        ZZZZZ           X            X              X           X
        77777                                       X
        88888                                       X
        99999                                       X           X
        00000                                       X           X
```

**EXHIBIT 5.9   QBASIC Program for Application 5.1, Inventory Report, Built-in Validation**

```
'******************************************************************
'                   PROGRAM IDENTIFICATION               *
'******************************************************************
'*   PROGRAM NAME: CH5APL1                                *
'******************************************************************
'*   REMARKS:    THE FOLLOWING PROGRAM GENERATES AN INVENTORY REPORT  *
'*               AND AN EDIT REPORT OF INVALID DATA.                  *
'*                                                                    *
'*               IN BASIC, IT IS POSSIBLE TO PRINT MORE THAN ONE OUTPUT  *
'*               REPORT WITHIN THE SAME PROCESSING MODULE WHEN A "PRINT  *
'*               SPOOLING" PACKAGE EXISTS; OTHERWISE, THE SECOND OUTPUT  *
'*               REPORT MUST BE SEQUENTIALLY GENERATED. THEREFORE, THE   *
'*               DATA FOR THE SECOND REPORT MUST BE SAVED DURING NORMAL  *
'*               PROCESSING. THE PROCESS OF SAVING THE DATA CAN BE       *
'*               HANDLED EITHER BY CREATING A SEQUENTIAL FILE OR IN A    *
'*               TABLE(S). THIS PROGRAM USES TABLES TO SAVE THE DATA FOR *
'*               THE SECOND REPORT. TABLES ARE DISCUSSED IN CHAPTER 7.   *
'******************************************************************
'*                      MAIN-LINE                        *
'******************************************************************
GOSUB STARTUP                   '* PERFORM START-UP
DO UNTIL END.FLAG$ = "YES"
   GOSUB VALIDATE.PROCESS       '* PERFORM VALIDATE-PROCESS
LOOP
GOSUB WRAPUP                    ' * PERFORM WRAP-UP
END
```

**EXHIBIT 5.9    (Cont.)**

```
'**********************************************************************
'*                             START-UP                              *
'**********************************************************************
STARTUP:
    GOSUB INITIALIZE                          'OPEN FILES
    GOSUB OPEN.FILES
    GOSUB PRINT.INVENTORY.REPORT.HEADINGS               ' * PERFORM INVENTORY-HEADINGS
    'COMMENT: UNABLE TO PERFORM OR CALL A MODULE CALLED
    '          PRINT.EXCEPTION.REPORT.HEADINGS SINCE
    '          SPOOLING TO TWO OUTPUT FILES IS NOT FEASIBLE.
    GOSUB READ.INVENTORY.FILE                           ' * PERFORM READ-INVENTORY-FILE
    RETURN
INITIALIZE:
    WIDTH LPRINT 132
    OUTPUT.LINE$ = "          \  \    \              \   ###.##    ### ###,###.##"
    END.FLAG$ = "NO"
    TOT.COST = 0
    SUB1 = 1
    DIM EDIT.PART.TABLE$(65):          ' SET UP EDIT REPORT TABLE
    DIM BAD.PART.TABLE$(65)
    DIM BAD.DESC.TABLE$(65)
    DIM BAD.PRICE.TABLE$(65)
    DIM BAD.QTY.TABLE$(65)
    DIM A$(20)
    RETURN

OPEN.FILES:

    OPEN "I", #1, "CH5ILL1.DAT"
    RETURN


    '********************************************************************
    '*                     INVENTORY HEADINGS                    *
    '********************************************************************

PRINT.INVENTORY.REPORT.HEADINGS:

    LPRINT CHR$(12)
    LPRINT
    LPRINT TAB(31); "OMNI INDUSTRIES"
    LPRINT
    LPRINT TAB(12); "PART NO"; TAB(24); "PAR'   CRIPTION"; TAB(46); "PRICE/UNIT"; TAB(59); "QTY"; TAB(65); "COST"
    LPRINT
    RETURN


    '********************************************************************
    '*                    READ-INVENTORY-FILE                    *
    '********************************************************************

READ.INVENTORY.FILE:

    INPUT #1, PART.NUMBER$, DESCRIPTION$, PRICE.PER.UNIT$, QTY$
    IF DESCRIPTION$ = "EOF" THEN END.FLAG$ = "YES"
    RETURN
```

**EXHIBIT 5.9    (Cont.)**

```
'*******************************************************************
'*                      VALIDATE-PROCESS                          *
'*******************************************************************

VALIDATE.PROCESS:

    GOSUB VALIDATE.ROUTINE                * PERFORM VALIDATE-ROUTINE
    IF VALIDITY.SWITCH$ = "YES" THEN
        GOSUB DETAIL.CALCULATION
        GOSUB ACCUMULATION
        GOSUB DETAIL.LINE.INVENTORY
    ELSE GOSUB SAVE.ERROR.LINE.DATA       ' THIS IS A NECESSARY DEVIATION FROM THE FLOWCHART/HIERARCHY CHART
                                          ' WITHOUT HAVING TO DRAW SPECIAL VERSION FOR QBASIC

    END IF
    GOSUB READ.INVENTORY.FILE             ' * PERFORM READ-INVENTORY-FILE
    RETURN


        '*******************************************************************
        '*                    SAVE.ERROR.LINE.DATA                        *
        '*******************************************************************

SAVE.ERROR.LINE.DATA:

    EDIT.PART.TABLE$(SUB1) = PART.NUMBER$
    BAD.PART.TABLE$(SUB1) = BAD.PART$
    BAD.DESC.TABLE$(SUB1) = BAD.DESC$
    BAD.PRICE.TABLE$(SUB1) = BAD.PRICE$
    BAD.QTY.TABLE$(SUB1) = BAD.QTY$
    SUB1 = SUB1 + 1
    PART.NUMBER$ = ""
    BAD.PART$ = ""
    BAD.DESC$ = ""
    BAD.PRICE$ = ""
    BAD.QTY$ = ""
    RETURN
        '*******************************************************************
        '*                      VALIDATE-ROUTINE                          *
        '*******************************************************************

VALIDATE.ROUTINE:

    VALIDITY.SWITCH$ = "YES"

    IF PART.NUMBER$ < "0" OR PART.NUMBER$ > "99999" THEN
        BAD.PART$ = "X"
        VALIDITY.SWITCH$ = "NO"
    END IF

    LENGTH = LEN(DESCRIPTION$)
    FOR N = 1 TO LENGTH
        C$ = MID$(DESCRIPTION$, N, 1)
            IF (C$ < "A" OR C$ > "Z") AND C$ <> " " THEN
                BAD.DESC$ = "X"
                VALIDITY.SWITCH$ = "NO"
            END IF
    NEXT N
```

**EXHIBIT 5.9   (Cont.)**

```
IF PRICE.PER.UNIT$ < "0" OR PRICE.PER.UNIT$ > "999.99" THEN
    BAD.PRICE$ = "X"
    VALIDITY.SWITCH$ = "NO"
END IF


IF QTY$ < "0" OR QTY$ > "999" THEN
    BAD.QTY$ = "X"
    VALIDITY.SWITCH$ = "NO"
END IF
RETURN
        '*********************************************************************
        '*                      DETAIL-CALCULATION                        *
        '*********************************************************************


DETAIL.CALCULATION:

    QTY = VAL(QTY$)
    PRICE.PER.UNIT = VAL(PRICE.PER.UNIT$)
    COST = QTY * PRICE.PER.UNIT
    RETURN


        '*********************************************************************
        '*                      ACCUMULATION                              *
        '*********************************************************************


ACCUMULATION:

        TOT.COST = TOT.COST + COST
        RETURN



        '*********************************************************************
        '*                      DETAIL-LINE-INVENTORY                     *
        '*********************************************************************


DETAIL.LINE.INVENTORY:

    LPRINT USING OUTPUT.LINE$; PART.NUMBER$; DESCRIPTION$; PRICE.PER.UNIT; QTY; COST
    RETURN


        '*********************************************************************
        '*                      WRAP-UP                                   *
        '*********************************************************************

WRAPUP:

    GOSUB SUMMARY.OUTPUT
    GOSUB CLOSE.FILES
    RETURN
```

**EXHIBIT 5.9    (Cont.)**

SUMMARY.OUTPUT:

```
    LPRINT : LPRINT
    LPRINT TAB(50); "TOTAL COST  "; TAB(62);
    LPRINT USING "$$,###,###.##"; TOT.COST
    GOSUB EDIT.HEADINGS              '* PERFORM EDIT-HEADINGS
    MAX.PRINT = SUB1 - 1
    FOR SUB1 = 1 TO MAX.PRINT
        LPRINT TAB(25); EDIT.PART.TABLE$(SUB1); TAB(43);
        LPRINT BAD.PART.TABLE$(SUB1); TAB(55);
        LPRINT BAD.DESC.TABLE$(SUB1); TAB(68);
        LPRINT BAD.PRICE.TABLE$(SUB1); TAB(78);
        LPRINT BAD.QTY.TABLE$(SUB1)
    NEXT SUB1
    RETURN

    '**********************************************************************
    '*                          EDIT HEADINGS                            *
    '**********************************************************************

EDIT.HEADINGS:

    LPRINT CHR$(12)
    LPRINT
    LPRINT
    LPRINT "                          VALIDITY CHECKING -- INVENTORY RUN"
    LPRINT
    LPRINT
    LPRINT "                 PART NUMBER    PART-NO    PART-DESC    PRICE/UNIT    QTY"
    LPRINT
    RETURN

CLOSE.FILES:
    CLOSE
    RETURN
```

```
            OMNI INDUSTRIES

PART NO    PART DESCRIPTION    PRICE/UNIT   QTY    COST

 45036     APPLES                   2.35    10       23.50
 82113     PECANS                  10.00    80      800.00
 11111     TELEVISION             500.00   500  250,000.00
 22222     VCR                    400.00   300  120,000.00
 33333     CAMERA                 300.00   200   60,000.00


                        TOTAL COST    $430,823.50
```

**EXHIBIT 5.9   (Cont.)**

```
       VALIDITY CHECKING -- INVENTORY RUN


PART NUMBER    PART-NO    PART-DESC    PRICE/UNIT    QTY

  46092                                     X
  82134                      X                         X
  ZZZZZ          X           X              X          X
  77777                                     X
  88888                                     X
  99999                                     X          X
  00000                                     X          X
```

## Student Master File with an Independent Data Validation Edit Program

Now that built-in validation programming logic has been discussed, let us look at the second type of validation—the independent edit program. This program can only determine the validity of a file and generate a report. The independent data validation edit program will be dealt with first, using the example application that follows.

### Program Requirements

The data processing department at a university wishes to produce a data validation edit report of the master student file before it attempts to generate the student grade report for the semester. The edit report is a listing of records that contain invalid data. A basic difference between the edit report to be produced here and the reports shown in Exhibits 5.1 and 5.2 is that this will be a single report that flags the erroneous fields in the records. No further processing will occur.

### Output Design

Exhibit 5.10 illustrates the edit report that will be generated from the invalid records. It lists the student number and a message or series of messages describing the kind of invalidity found in each record.

### Input Design

The input record format for the inventory file is shown in Exhibit 5.11.

The input test cases for the program run are given in Exhibit 5.12.

---

**EXHIBIT 5.10  Edit Report and Printer Spacing Chart for Student Master File**

**Panel A—Edit Report**

```
                    ABC UNIVERSITY

            EDIT REPORT OF STUDENT MASTER FILE

        STUDENT NO.          ERROR MESSAGE

          4502           NAME NOT ALPHABETIC
          4708           CLASS CODE IS INVALID
          9321           CLASS CODE IS INVALID
                         CUMULATIVE HOURS ARE INVALID
          9372           SEX CODE IS INVALID
                         CUMULATIVE HOURS ARE INVALID

       NUMBER OF INVALID RECORDS IN RUN IS 4    **JOB IS COMPLETE**
```

**Panel B—Printer Spacing Chart**

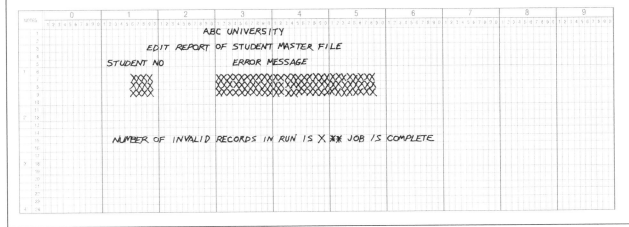

## Logic Considerations

The edit routine should provide a validity check for the following fields:

1. Student number (numeric)
2. Student name (alphabetic)
3. Student classification (numeric range from 1 to 4)
4. Major-Code (1 through 20)
5. Cumulative hours (1 through 199)
6. Sex-code (1, 2)

## Program Design of the Data Validation Edit Program

Exhibit 5.13 depicts the generalized logic in hierarchy chart form. Exhibit 5.14 illustrates the program design in structured flowchart form to validate the test data and produce the report illustrated in Exhibit 5.10. Exhibit 5.15 depicts the pseudocode logic, and Exhibit 5.16 illustrates the associated COBOL program. Since BASIC is a cumbersome tool for data validation—it has no data class test capability—there is no associated BASIC program for this problem. The main difference between the design of this program and the design shown in the hierarchy chart in Exhibit 5.5 of a program with built-in data validation is that this design only prints a line of output for the records that are invalid. There is no processing or output of the valid records.

The MAIN-LINE module remains unchanged except for the name of the module in the DoWhile structure. The START-UP and WRAP-UP modules contain no new additions. The START-UP module performs the following activities:

1. Sets the END-FLAG control variable to NO.
2. Opens both input and output files.
3. Prints the headings.
4. Reads the first record of the file.

The RECORD-VALIDATE-PROCESS module is executed repeatedly until there are no more records in the file. This routine controls the validity-checking portion of the program. The RECORD-

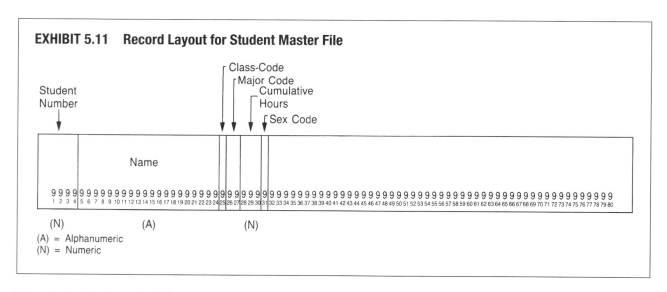

**EXHIBIT 5.11   Record Layout for Student Master File**

**EXHIBIT 5.12   Test Cases for Validity Checking Edit Program**

| TEST CASES -- EDIT RUN | | | | | |
|---|---|---|---|---|---|
| STUDENT NUMBER | NAME | CLASS CODE | MAJOR CODE | CUM HRS | SEX CODE |
| 4502 | JOE 5621/? | 3 | 6 | 060 | 2 |
| 4708 | BOB SMITH | 9 | 3 | 080 | 1 |
| 9321 | SALLY BROWN | 7 | 8 | 270 | 1 |
| 9372 | MARY WHITE | 2 | 4 | 300 | 8 |
| 8888 | DONNA JONES | 1 | 21 | 150 | 2 |

VALIDATE-PROCESS module performs the following functions:

1. Determines the validity of the various fields and prints an appropriate error message.
2. Reads another record.

The RECORD-VALIDATE-PROCESS module consists of two modules. The first one to perform is called VALIDATE-FIELDS. This module consists of a series of submodule calls that invoke respective validation submodules to check for the validity or invalidity of specific fields. Within the respective submodules, if a field is invalid, an appropriate

error message is moved to a message line and a check made to determine if the student number needs to be reprinted or not. Subsequently, the detail line is written, and the entire RECORD-VALIDATE-PROCESS is repeated.

RECORD-VALIDATE-PROCESS also contains a programming technique that involves bypassing the printing of a portion of a detail line when subsequent detail lines are associated with the same input record. In other words, if one record has several different error lines to be printed, the report is more readable if the SN is printed only on the first of the associated error lines. If the SN field were reprinted for the same record on the second error

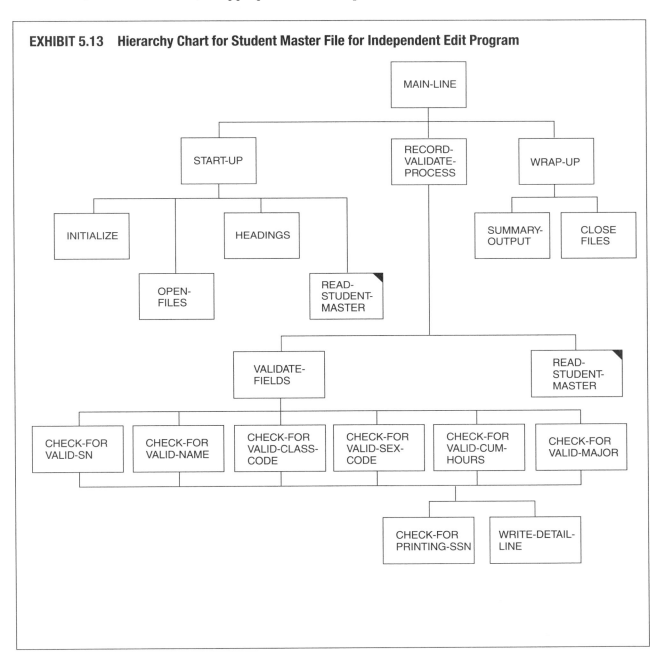

**EXHIBIT 5.13 Hierarchy Chart for Student Master File for Independent Edit Program**

**EXHIBIT 5.14   Structured Flowchart for Student-Master-File Using Independent Edit Program**

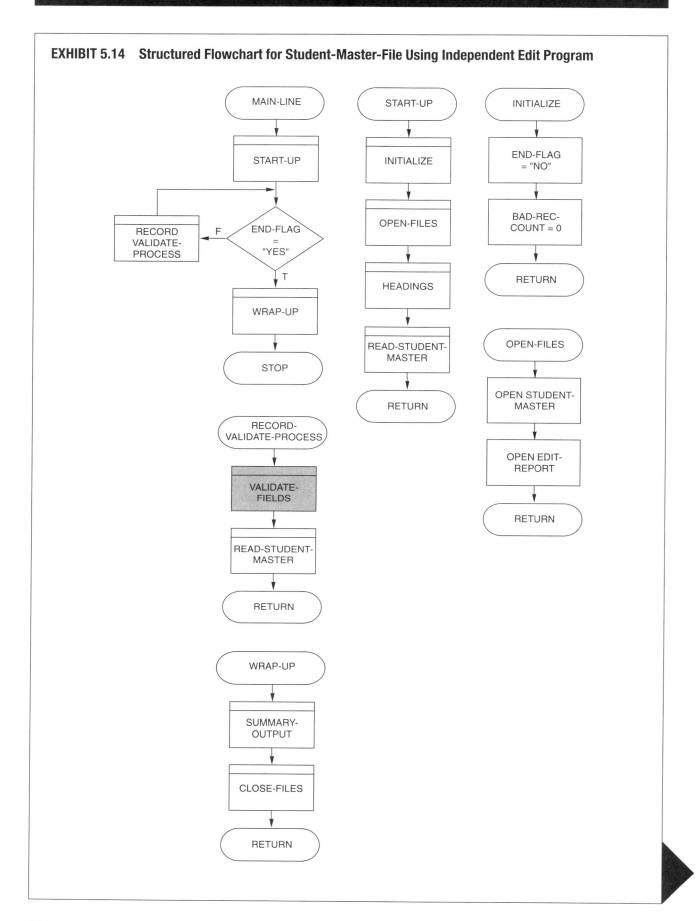

line, it would be difficult to detect which messages belonged to which record.

The programming technique for handling the print suppression of a portion of a detail line involves the use of another control variable, which is referred to as NEW-RECORD-SWITCH (see the VALIDATE-FIELDS module in Exhibit 5.14). The purpose of NEW-RECORD-SWITCH is to control whether or not the SSN of a record will print on the detail line. If NEW-RECORD-SWITCH contains a "YES," it indicates that a record has just been read and no fields have been found to be invalid at this point. When a field within a record is found to be

invalid, and NEW-RECORD-SWITCH = "YES" (indicating a brand new record), then the SN should be printed along with the message that identifies the kind of invalid field. Once the line is printed, the control variable, NEW-RECORD-SWITCH, is turned off, or reinitialized to the value "NO" (see submodule labeled CHECK-FOR-PRINTING-SN in Exhibit 5.14). Reinitializing the control variable, NEW-RECORD-SWITCH, equal to the value "NO" will allow the bypassing of the printing of SSN and allow the printing of possible subsequent messages related to the same record.

**EXHIBIT 5.14 (Cont.)**

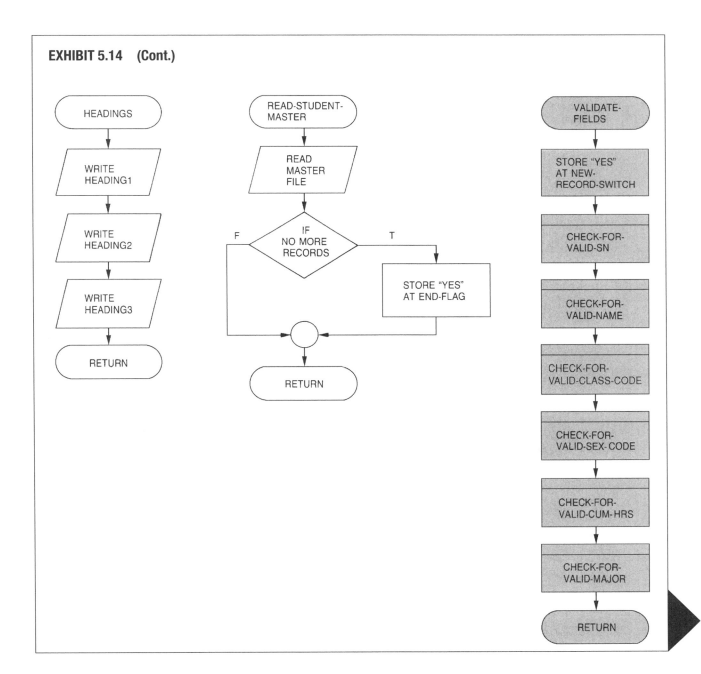

**EXHIBIT 5.14    (Cont.)**

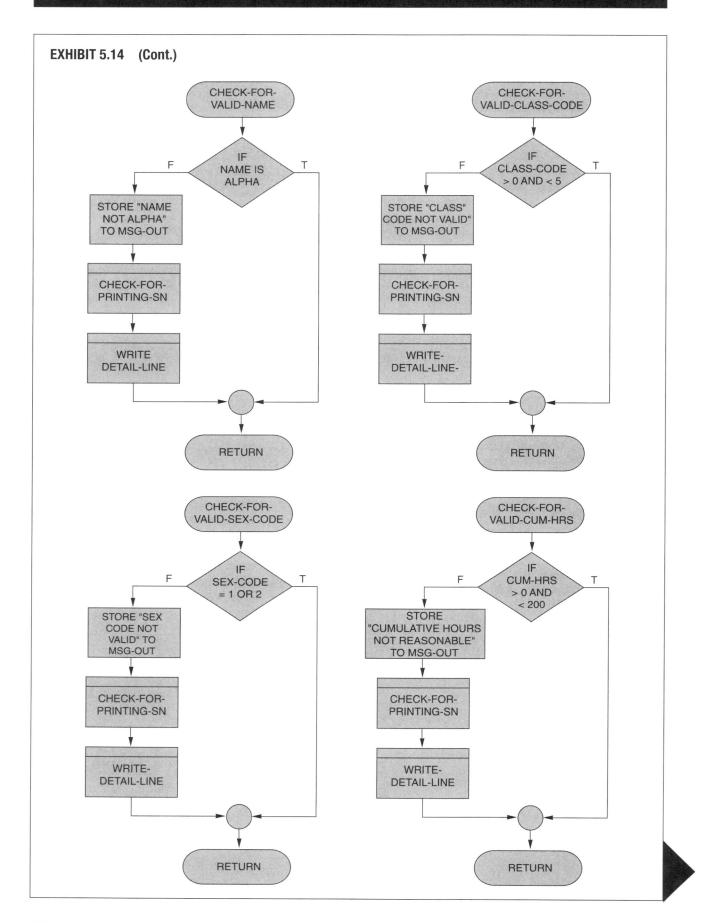

Each submodule that is invoked from within the VALIDATE-FIELDS module is responsible for three main tasks:

1. Move the appropriate message to the message portion of the detail line.
2. Check to see whether to print the SN as well as the message. This will be necessary only if it is the first line or the only message to print for a record.
3. Write the detail line.

It is necessary to have a module for performing the writing of a detail line for each of the submodules, since the report could contain up to five message lines per invalid record.

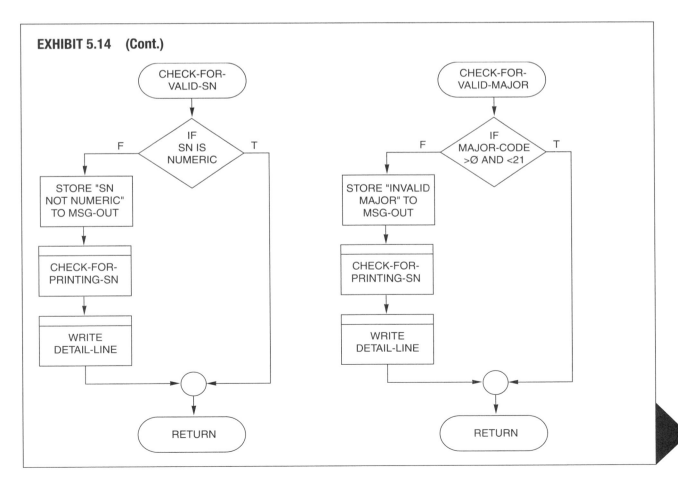

**EXHIBIT 5.14    (Cont.)**

**EXHIBIT 5.14    (Cont.)**

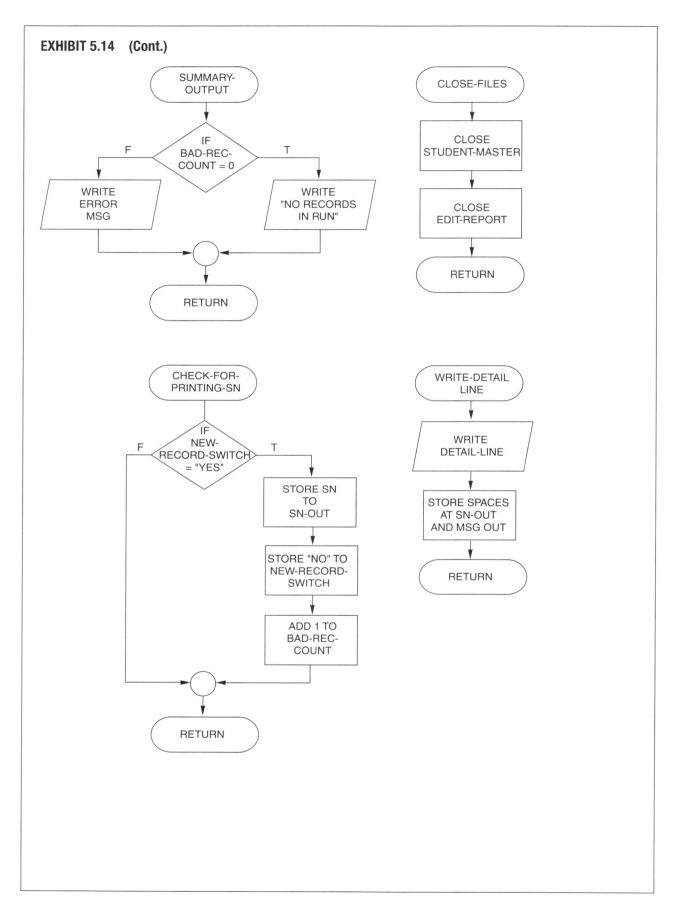

## EXHIBIT 5.15    Pseudocode for Validity Checking

*main-line
  start-up module
  dowhile end-flag="no"
    record-validate-process
  enddo
  wrap-up module
  stop
*start-up module
  initialize
  open-files
  headings
  read-student-master
  return
*record-validate-process
  validate-fields
  read-student-master
  return
*wrap-up module
  summary-output
  close-files
  return
*initialize
  end-flag = "no"
  bad-rec-count = 0
  return
*open-file
  open input student-master
  open output edit-report
  return
*headings
  write heading1
  write heading2
  write heading3
  return
*read-student-master
  read student master file
  when no more records set end-flag = "yes"
  endread
  return
*validate-fields
  initialize new-record-switch = "yes"
  check-for-valid-sn
  check-for-valid-name
  check-for-valid-class-code
  check-for-valid-sex-code
  check-for-valid-cum-hrs
  check-for-valid-major
  return
*check-for-valid-sn
  if sn is numeric then
  then
    null
  else
    transfer "sn not numeric" to message-out
    check-for-printing-sn
    write-detail-line
  endif
  return

*summary-output
  if bad-rec-count = 0
    then write "no records in run"
  else write "number of bad records is"
    bad-rec-count
  endif
  return
*close-files
  close student-master
  close edit-report
  return
*check-for-valid-name
  if name is alphabetic
  then
    null
  else
    transfer "name not alphabetic" to message-out
    check-for-printing-sn
    write-detail-line
  endif
  return
*check-for-valid-class-code
  if class-code > 0 and < 5
  then
    null
  else
    transfer "class code not valid" to message-out
    check-for-printing-sn
    write-detail-line
  endif
  return
*check-for-valid-sex-code
  if sex-code = 1 or 2
  then
    null
  else
    transfer "sex code invalid" to message-out
    check-for-printing-sn
    write-detail-line
  endif
  return
*check-for-valid-cum-hrs
  if cum-hrs > 0 and < 200
  then
    null
  else
    transfer "cumulative hours invalid" to message-out
    check-for-printing-sn
    write-detail-line
  endif
  return

**EXHIBIT 5.15    (Cont.)**

*check-for-valid-major
    if major-code > 0 and < 21 then
    then  null
    else
        store "invalid major" to message-out
        check-for-printing-sn
        write-detail-line
    endif
    return
*check-for-printing-sn
    if new-record-switch = "yes"

        then
            transfer sn to sn-out
            transfer "no" to new-record-switch
            add 1 to bad-record-count
        endif
        return
*write-detail-line
        write detail line
        clear the sn-out and message-out fields
        return

**EXHIBIT 5.16    COBOL 85 Program for Application 5.2, Student Master File, Independent Edit**

```
1          IDENTIFICATION DIVISION.
2          PROGRAM-ID. CH5ILL2.
3       *      ANS COBOL 85
4       *              THE FOLLOWING PROGRAM CREATES AN EDIT REPORT
5       *              WHICH LISTS THE STUDENT IDENTIFICATION NUMBER
6       *              AND A MESSAGE OR A SERIES OF MESSAGES FOR
7       *              EACH INVALID INPUT RECORD FROM THE STUDENT-
8       *              MASTER FILE.  NO FURTHER PROCESSING OF DATA
9       *              OCCURS IN THIS PROGRAM.
10      *   USES BOTH NESTED IF LOGIC AND COMPOUND CONDITIONAL TESTS
11
12         ENVIRONMENT DIVISION.
13         CONFIGURATION SECTION.
14
15         SOURCE-COMPUTER.  CYBER.
16         OBJECT-COMPUTER.  CYBER.
17
18         INPUT-OUTPUT SECTION.
19
20         FILE-CONTROL.
21             SELECT STUDENT-MASTER ASSIGN TO DTA52.
22             SELECT EDIT-REPORT ASSIGN TO OUTFILE.
23
24         DATA DIVISION.
25
26         FILE SECTION.
27
28         FD   STUDENT-MASTER.
29
30         01   STUDENT-RECORD.
31
32              05 SN               PIC 9(4).
33              05 NAME             PIC X(20).
34              05 CLASS-CODE       PIC 9.
35              05 MAJOR-CODE       PIC 99.
36              05 CUM-HRS          PIC 999.
37              05 SEX-CODE         PIC 9.
38
39         FD   EDIT-REPORT.
40
41         01   REPORT-REC         PIC X(133).
42
43         WORKING-STORAGE SECTION.
44
45         01   END-FLAG           PIC XXX VALUE "NO".
46         01   NEW-RECORD-SWITCH  PIC XXX VALUE "YES".
47         01   BAD-REC-CT         PIC 999 VALUE ZERO.
```

**EXHIBIT 5.16   (Cont.)**

```
48
49        01   HEADING1.
50
51             05                          PIC X(28) VALUE SPACES.
52             05                          PIC X(14) VALUE "ABC UNIVERSITY".
53             05                          PIC X(91) VALUE SPACES.
54
55        01   HEADING2.
56
57             05                          PIC X(18) VALUE SPACES.
58             05                          PIC X(34) VALUE
59                                         "EDIT REPORT OF STUDENT-MASTER FILE".
60             05                          PIC X(81) VALUE SPACES.
61
62        01   HEADING3.
63
64             05                          PIC X(11) VALUE SPACES.
65             05                          PIC X(11) VALUE "STUDENT NO.".
66             05                          PIC X(12) VALUE SPACES.
67             05                          PIC X(13) VALUE "ERROR MESSAGE".
68             05                          PIC X(86) VALUE SPACES.
69
70        01   DETAIL-LINE.
71
72             05                          PIC X(14) VALUE SPACES.
73             05  SN-OUT                  PIC X(4) VALUE SPACES.
74             05                          PIC X(12) VALUE SPACES.
75             05  MSG-OUT                 PIC X(30) VALUE SPACES.
76             05                          PIC X(73) VALUE SPACES.
77        01   END-OF-JOB-MESSAGE.
78
79             05                          PIC X(2) VALUE SPACES.
80             05  EOJ-MESSAGE-OUT         PIC X(38) VALUE SPACES.
81             05  BAD-REC-CT-OUT          PIC ZZZ VALUE SPACES.
82             05                          PIC X(16) VALUE SPACES.
83             05                          PIC X(17) VALUE "**JOB IS COMPLETE**".
84             05                          PIC X(57) VALUE SPACES.
85
86        /
87         PROCEDURE DIVISION.
88
89         000-MAINLINE.
90
91             PERFORM 100-START-UP.
92             PERFORM 200-RECORD-VALIDATE-PROCESS UNTIL END-FLAG = "YES".
93             PERFORM 300-WRAP-UP.
94             STOP RUN.
95
96         100-START-UP.
97
98             PERFORM 105-OPEN-FILES.
99             PERFORM 110-HEADINGS.
100            PERFORM 120-READ-STUDENT-MASTER.
101
102        105-OPEN-FILES.
103            OPEN INPUT STUDENT-MASTER
104                 OUTPUT EDIT-REPORT.
105
106
```

**EXHIBIT 5.16   (Cont.)**

```
107        110-HEADINGS.
108
109            WRITE REPORT-REC FROM HEADING1 AFTER ADVANCING PAGE.
110            WRITE REPORT-REC FROM HEADING2.
111            WRITE REPORT-REC FROM HEADING3 AFTER ADVANCING 3 LINES.
112            MOVE SPACES TO REPORT-REC.
113            WRITE REPORT-REC.
114
115        120-READ-STUDENT-MASTER.
116
117            READ STUDENT-MASTER AT END MOVE "YES" TO END-FLAG.
118
119        200-RECORD-VALIDATE-PROCESS.
120
121            PERFORM 210-VALIDATE-FIELDS.
122            PERFORM 120-READ-STUDENT-MASTER.
123
124        210-VALIDATE-FIELDS.
125
126            MOVE "YES" TO NEW-RECORD-SWITCH.
127            PERFORM 220-CHECK-FOR-VALID-SN.
128            PERFORM 230-CHECK-FOR-VALID-NAME.
129            PERFORM 240-CHECK-FOR-VALID-CLASS-CODE.
130            PERFORM 250-CHECK-FOR-VALID-SEX-CODE.
131            PERFORM 260-CHECK-FOR-VALID-CUM-HRS.
132            PERFORM 265-CHECK-FOR-VALID-MAJOR.
133
134        220-CHECK-FOR-VALID-SN.
135
136            IF SN IS NUMERIC
137                THEN   NEXT SENTENCE
138            ELSE
139               MOVE "STUDENT NUMBER NOT NUMERIC" TO MSG-OUT
140               PERFORM 270-CHECK-FOR-PRINTING-SN
141               PERFORM 280-WRITE-DETAIL-LINE
142            END-IF.
143
144        230-CHECK-FOR-VALID-NAME.
145
146            IF NAME IS ALPHABETIC
147                THEN NEXT SENTENCE
148            ELSE
149               MOVE "NAME NOT ALPHABETIC" TO MSG-OUT
150               PERFORM 270-CHECK-FOR-PRINTING-SN
151               PERFORM 280-WRITE-DETAIL-LINE
152            END-IF.
153
154        240-CHECK-FOR-VALID-CLASS-CODE.
155
156            IF CLASS-CODE IS NUMERIC
157                THEN
158                  IF CLASS-CODE > 0 AND CLASS-CODE < 5
159                      THEN NEXT SENTENCE
160                  ELSE
161                      MOVE "CLASS CODE IS OUT OF RANGE" TO MSG-OUT
162                      PERFORM 270-CHECK-FOR-PRINTING-SN
163                      PERFORM 280-WRITE-DETAIL-LINE
164                  END-IF
165            ELSE
166               MOVE "CLASS CODE IS NOT NUMERIC" TO MSG-OUT
167               PERFORM 270-CHECK-FOR-PRINTING-SN
168               PERFORM 280-WRITE-DETAIL-LINE
169            END-IF.
170
```

**EXHIBIT 5.16   (Cont.)**

```
171         250-CHECK-FOR-VALID-SEX-CODE.
172
173             IF SEX-CODE = 1 OR SEX-CODE = 2
174                 NEXT SENTENCE
175             ELSE
176                 MOVE "SEX CODE IS INVALID" TO MSG-OUT
177                 PERFORM 270-CHECK-FOR-PRINTING-SN
178                 PERFORM 280-WRITE-DETAIL-LINE.
179
180         260-CHECK-FOR-VALID-CUM-HRS.
181
182             IF CUM-HRS IS NUMERIC
183                 THEN
184                     IF CUM-HRS > 0 AND CUM-HRS < 200
185                         THEN NEXT SENTENCE
186                       ELSE
187                           MOVE "CUMULATIVE HOURS OUT OF RANGE" TO MSG-OUT
188                           PERFORM 270-CHECK-FOR-PRINTING-SN
189                           PERFORM 280-WRITE-DETAIL-LINE
190                     END-IF
191             ELSE
192                           MOVE "CUMULATIVE HOURS NOT NUMERIC" TO MSG-OUT
193                           PERFORM 270-CHECK-FOR-PRINTING-SN
194                           PERFORM 280-WRITE-DETAIL-LINE
195             END-IF.
196
197         265-CHECK-FOR-VALID-MAJOR.
198             IF MAJOR-CODE > 1 AND MAJOR-CODE < 21
199                 NEXT SENTENCE
200             ELSE
201                 MOVE "INVALID MAJOR" TO MSG-OUT
202                 PERFORM 270-CHECK-FOR-PRINTING-SN
203                 PERFORM 280-WRITE-DETAIL-LINE.
204
205         270-CHECK-FOR-PRINTING-SN.
206
207             IF NEW-RECORD-SWITCH = "YES"
208                 MOVE SN TO SN-OUT
209                 MOVE "NO" TO NEW-RECORD-SWITCH
210                 ADD 1 TO BAD-REC-CT.
211
212         280-WRITE-DETAIL-LINE.
213
214             WRITE REPORT-REC FROM DETAIL-LINE.
215             MOVE SPACES TO SN-OUT.
216
217         300-WRAP-UP.
218             PERFORM 310-SUMMARY-OUTPUT.
219             PERFORM 320-CLOSE-FILES.
220
221         310-SUMMARY-OUTPUT.
222             IF BAD-REC-CT = 0
223                 MOVE "NO ERRORS IN RUN" TO EOJ-MESSAGE-OUT
224             ELSE
225                 MOVE "NUMBER OF INVALID RECORDS IN RUN IS "
226                 TO EOJ-MESSAGE-OUT
227                 MOVE BAD-REC-CT TO BAD-REC-CT-OUT.
228             WRITE REPORT-REC FROM END-OF-JOB-MESSAGE
229                 AFTER ADVANCING 2 LINES.
230
231         320-CLOSE-FILES.
232             CLOSE STUDENT-MASTER  EDIT-REPORT.
```

**EXHIBIT 5.16   (Cont.)**

```
                        ABC UNIVERSITY
              EDIT REPORT OF STUDENT-MASTER FILE


        STUDENT NO.                  ERROR MESSAGE

           4502              NAME NOT ALPHABETIC
           4708              CLASS CODE IS OUT OF RANGE
           9321              CLASS CODE IS OUT OF RANGE
                             CUMULATIVE HOURS OUT OF RANGE
           9372              SEX CODE IS INVALID
                             CUMULATIVE HOURS OUT OF RANGE
           5555              CUMULATIVE HOURS OUT OF RANGE
                             INVALID MAJOR
           7777              CLASS CODE IS NOT NUMERIC
                             CUMULATIVE HOURS OUT OF RANGE
           8888              CUMULATIVE HOURS NOT NUMERIC
           9999              NAME NOT ALPHABETIC
                             CLASS CODE IS NOT NUMERIC
                             SEX CODE IS INVALID
                             CUMULATIVE HOURS NOT NUMERIC
                             INVALID MAJOR

NUMBER OF INVALID RECORDS IN RUN IS     8            **JOB IS COMPLETE
```

# Ace Auto Parts Sales Report with Built-in Data Validation—(Error Messages on the Sales Report)

Ace Auto wishes to produce a sales report that lists the department, salesperson, part description, cost per unit, quantity, cost, markup, retail amount, discount, and net amount on each sale for the month. Data validation messages are to print on the report for records with invalid fields. One or more validation message lines may appear for any record in error.

## Output Design

Exhibit 5.17 illustrates the printer spacing chart and sample report for Ace Auto's Sales Report. Notice that two kinds of detail lines are present on the chart. The first two detail lines represent the detail data that will print if the record is valid. The next two lines (further down) represent data validation error lines that would print if a field or fields are invalid. The report represents a user report with possible data validation error lines on the same report.

To illustrate how Application 5.3 is unique, let us review the previous applications. Application 5.1 illustrated a built-in validation program that generated both a user report (OMNI INDUSTRIES) and a validation report (VALIDITY CHECKING, INVENTORY RUN). Application 5.2 showed an independent edit program that generated only a validation report listing the records that were invalid with their associated error messages (showing the field(s) in error).

This application is different since it shows built-in validity checking like in 5.1, but generates error lines much like those done in Application 5.2. This is much more practical for built-in validity checking since a record may have many fields to test for validity. Generating multiple error lines works better than using the reporting method in Application 5.1. Using columns for each field with an X to mark the field as invalid works well if there are not too

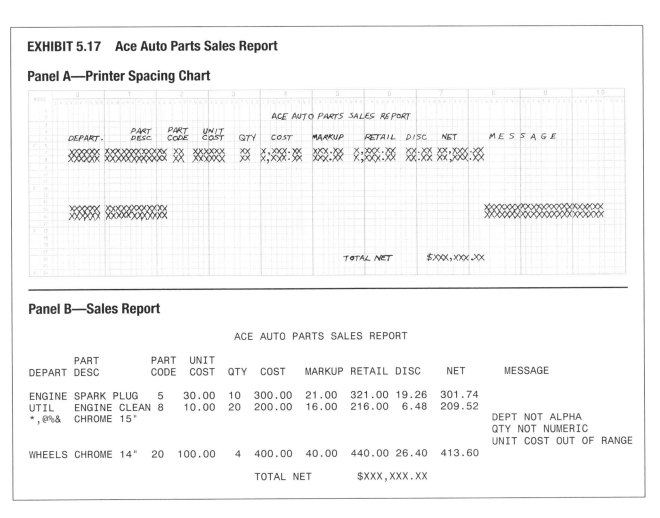

**EXHIBIT 5.17    Ace Auto Parts Sales Report**

**Panel A—Printer Spacing Chart**

**Panel B—Sales Report**

```
                      ACE AUTO PARTS SALES REPORT

        PART         PART  UNIT
DEPART  DESC         CODE  COST  QTY  COST    MARKUP RETAIL DISC   NET       MESSAGE

ENGINE  SPARK PLUG    5    30.00  10  300.00  21.00  321.00 19.26  301.74
UTIL    ENGINE CLEAN  8    10.00  20  200.00  16.00  216.00  6.48  209.52
*,@%&   CHROME 15"                                                          DEPT NOT ALPHA
                                                                            QTY NOT NUMERIC
                                                                            UNIT COST OUT OF RANGE

WHEELS  CHROME 14"   20   100.00   4  400.00  40.00  440.00 26.40  413.60

                          TOTAL NET         $XXX,XXX.XX
```

many fields to test. Otherwise, this Application 5.3 is far superior.

## Input Design

Exhibit 5.18 details the record layout for the sales file for Ace Auto. The record contains a department description, part description, part-code, unit-cost, and quantity.

## Logic Considerations

The cost is the product of quantity and unit cost. The markup is the product of the cost and the markup percent. Markup percent is determined from Exhibit 5.19 (Frame A). The retail amount is the sum of the cost and the markup. The discount is the product of the retail amount and the discount percent. The discount percent is determined from Exhibit 5.19 (Frame B). The net is the difference in the retail amount and the discount.

The following validation criteria apply for the different fields.

DEPARTMENT—Alphabetic
DESCRIPTION—Must be present
   (Alphanumeric)
PART-CODE—Numeric and in the range
   of 1–20
UNIT COST—Numeric and in the range
   of 1–750.00
QUANTITY—Positive, Numeric and in the
   range of 1 to 999

## Program Design of Built-in Validation Logic (Sales Report with Error Messages)

The hierarchy chart for the design is shown in Exhibit 5.20 and the flowchart for this problem is shown in Exhibit 5.21. The flowcharting logic resembles the logic from both Application 5.1 and 5.2. Notice, however, that the PROCESS-RECORD module also includes a Bottom-of-Page-Check module call and a Validate-Fields call. Only if the Valid-Switch equals "YES" (which means the record is valid), will the normal processing activities occur. Also notice that there is no "error" processing steps on the "else" side of the IF. To produce multiple error lines for any given record, the error processing and error output line generation must be part of each individual field validity check. The Validate-Fields module initializes the Valid-Switch to "YES" just as in Application 5.1. The detail-line is cleared to spaces, and the new-record-switch is set equal to "YES." The use of new-record-switch technique was used in Application 5.2. to detect whether the computer needs to print the key fields on the first line of a group of lines that pertain to this key field. For multiple error messages for the same record, the computer should print only the department and description on the first line with an error message. All subsequent error lines will print without the department and descriptions. This enhances the readability of the report. The remaining "call modules" in the Validate-Fields module pertain to the checking of each field in the record to determine the validity of each. For example, the Check-Department Module checks the department field for alphabetic characters. If this condition is false, a message is formatted, a determination is made whether the department and description is to reprint (CHK-FOR-PRT-DEPT-AND-DESC), and the error line is generated (ERROR-LINE).

As another illustration of the validate-checking process, the CHECK-UNIT-COST illustrates the process of making sure that the field is numeric before even testing for a range. If the program is

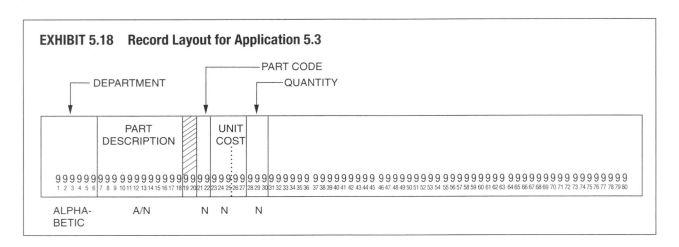

**EXHIBIT 5.18    Record Layout for Application 5.3**

being executed on an IBM mainframe or Plug compatible, the need to test for data class is imperative prior to doing either arithmetic or comparison operations. If the data are *not* numeric and there is an attempt to compare the field with other numeric data or perform arithmetic with the nonnumeric field, the program will abort with what is called a "data exception interrupt." Another reason for the "nested if" approach is to allow for a separate error message for nonnumeric data and an alternate message for data that is out of range.

The CHECK-FOR-PRT-DEPT-AND-DESC module is the mechanism whereby the program is able to print the department and description on the first error line but not on subsequent error lines. Upon initial entry into the Process-Record module, the New-Record-Switch is initialized to "YES." In the first validation check (CHECK-DEPARTMENT), the test is made to determine if the department is numeric. If the department is not numeric the appropriate message is formatted to the detail line, the CHK-FOR-PRT-DEPT-AND-DESC is executed, which looks to see if the NEW-RECORD-SWITCH is "YES." If this is true, the department and description are moved to the line, and the NEW-RECORD-SWITCH is set off (NEW-RECORD-SWITCH = "NO"). Subsequent tests of NEW-RECORD-SWITCH while processing the same record will result in a false condition; thus, the department and description are not moved to the detail line for these successive lines that belong to the same record.

The markup determination is illustrated in the DETERMINE-MARKUP. A CASE structure is used to compare the Part-Code with a set of value ranges. If the Part-Code falls into a particular range, an associated markup percent is assigned. The discount is determined in a similar manner.

## EXHIBIT 5.19 Schedule of Markup Percentages for Associated Part Codes

**Panel A**

| Part Code Values | Markup % |
|---|---|
| 1–5 | 7% |
| 6–10 | 8% |
| 11–15 | 9% |
| 16–20 | 10% |
| > 20 | 11% |

**Panel B**

| Retail Price Range | Discount % |
|---|---|
| < 10.00 | 0% |
| 10.00–49.99 | 3% |
| 50.00–100.00 | 5% |
| > 100 | 6% |

**EXHIBIT 5.20**  Hierarchy Chart for Application 5.3, Ace Auto Parts Report, Built-in Validation

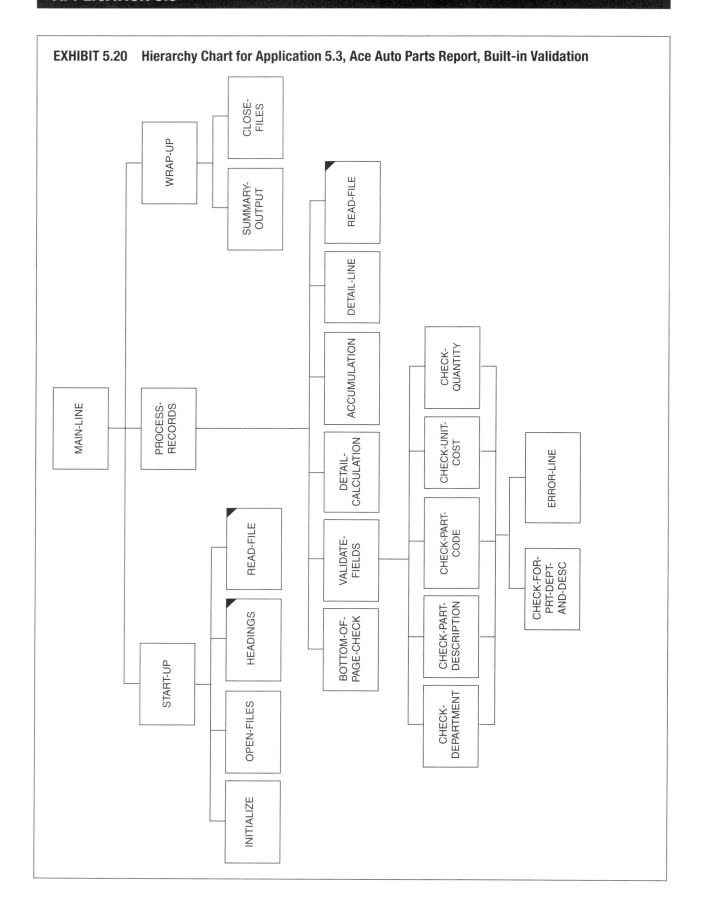

**EXHIBIT 5.21   Flowchart for Application 5.3, Ace Auto Parts, Built-in Validation**

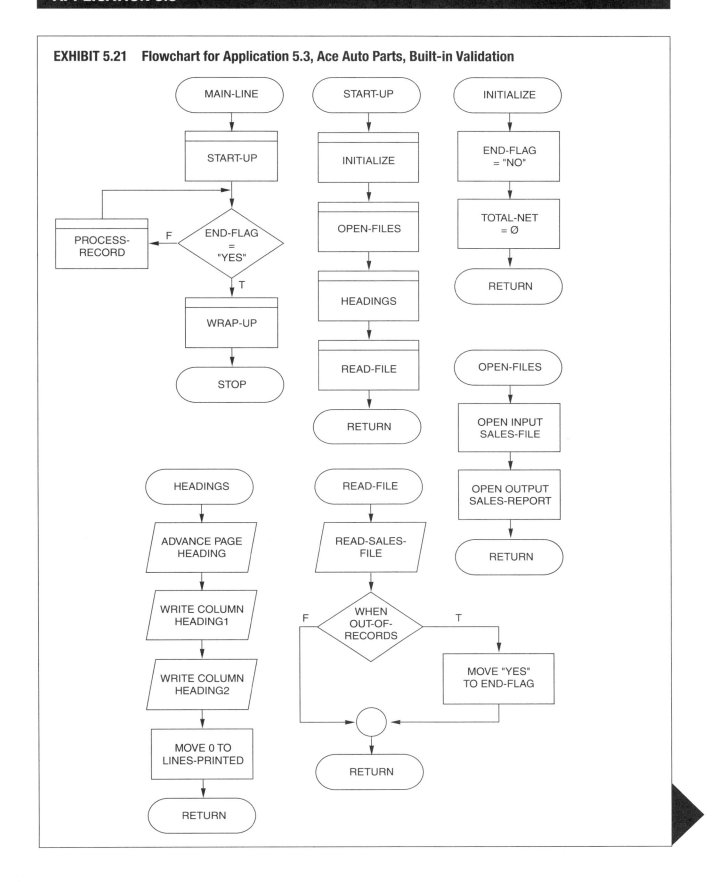

**EXHIBIT 5.21    (Cont.)**

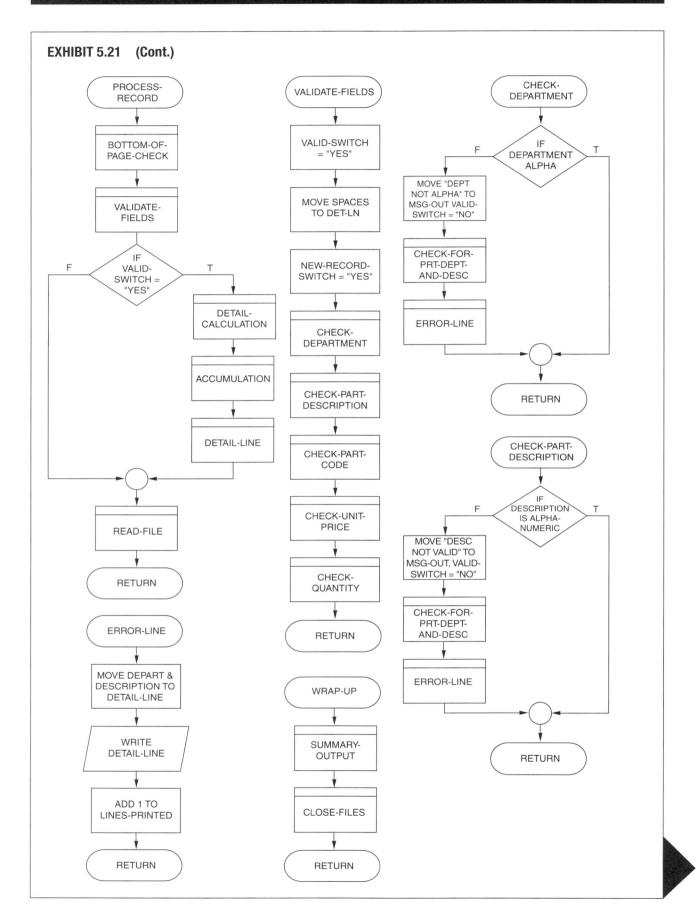

**EXHIBIT 5.21    (Cont.)**

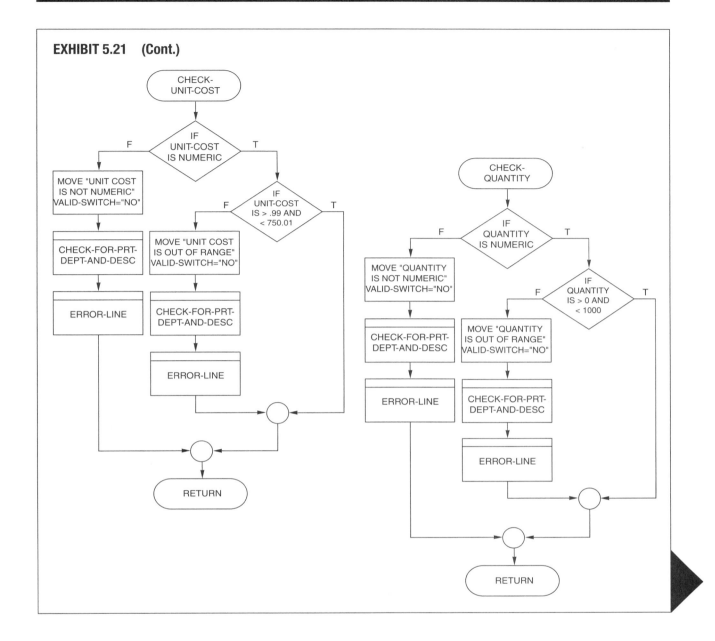

**EXHIBIT 5.21   (Cont.)**

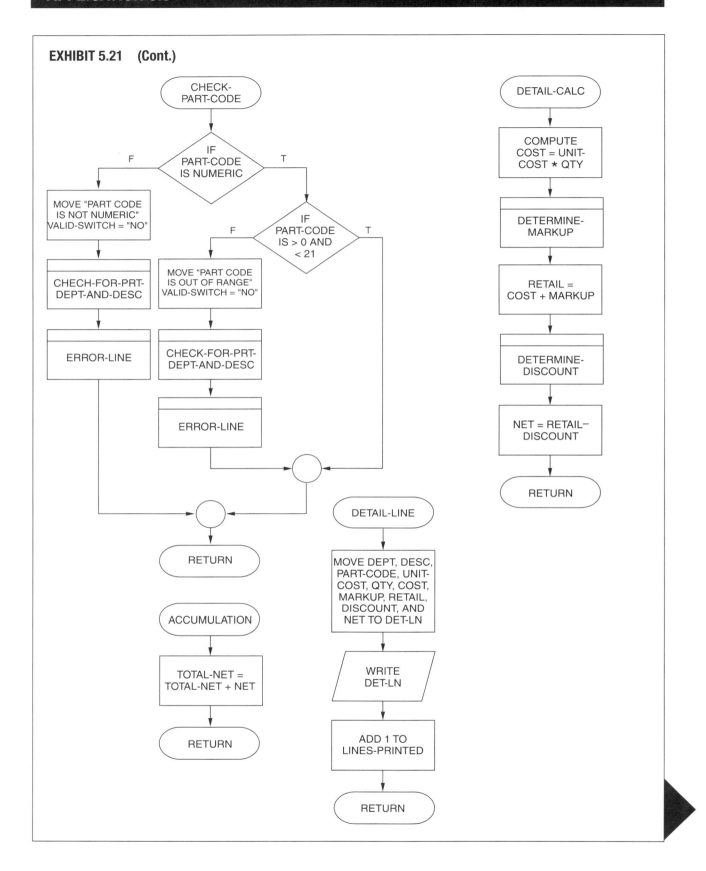

**EXHIBIT 5.21    (Cont.)**

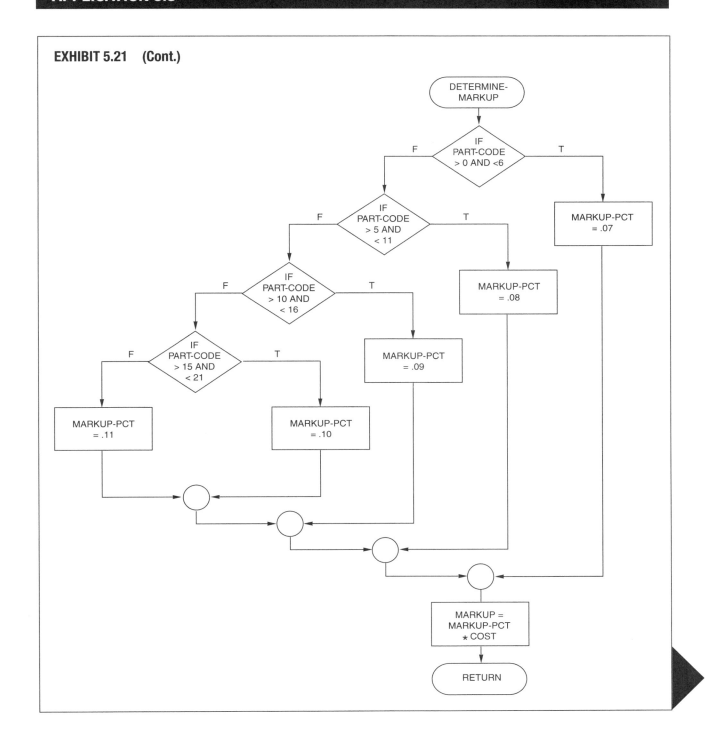

**EXHIBIT 5.21    (Cont.)**

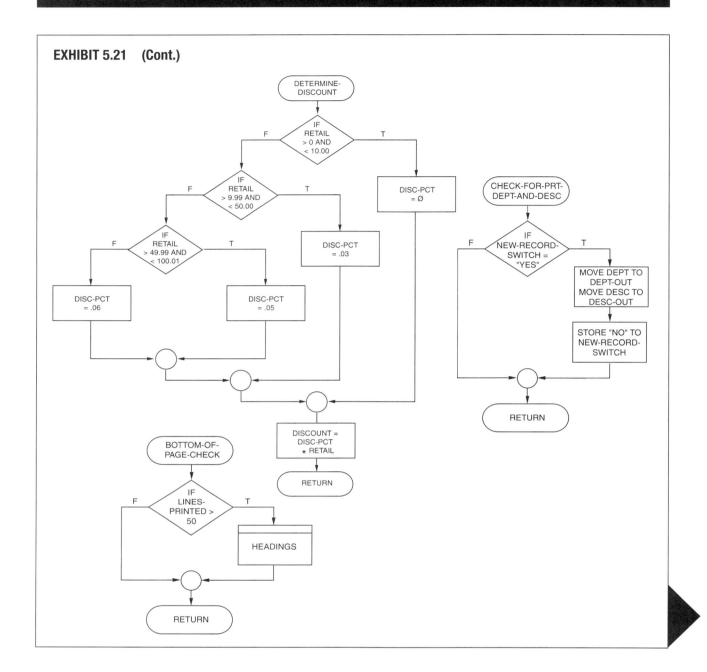

**EXHIBIT 5.21    (Cont.)**

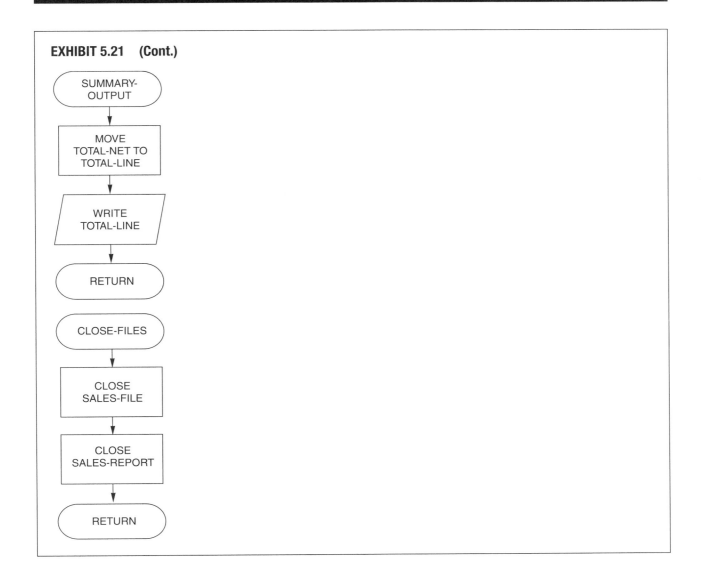

## SUMMARY

Erroneously recorded input data cause many a problem in the information processing world. Often, the data are simply miskeyed. Since programmers are conditioned to *expect* invalid data, they wisely incorporate validity-checking routines into their processing programs. A common procedure in data processing installations is to implement and utilize independent edit programs whose sole purpose is to validate a file. In addition, programmers frequently need to install built-in edit routines in their processing programs.

The four kinds of validity-checking tests that are routinely included in a program are (1) class tests, (2) limit tests, (3) code tests, and (4) sign tests. The two major kinds of validity checking programs are (1) the edit program and (2) the processing program with built-in validity-checking routines. The edit program normally produces an edit report, a listing of erroneous records. The key characteristic of the edit program is that it produces only a report of invalid records. The processing program with a built-in validity-checking routine, however, normally produces a user's information report as well as an exception report of invalid records. The typical edit report contains the key field of the record and a message listing the invalid field name and the type of invalidity present.

The program design of a built-in error-checking program that will produce two reports—a user report and an edit report—requires opening two separate report files. This production of two reports with one program is possible only because large systems can spool the output to disk first. This type of program has another significant feature—the inclusion of a separate module that handles the validity checking of the records. If a record passes the various validity tests, the record-processing module performs the necessary steps to print a detail line on the user report; if, however, the record fails the various validity tests, the record-processing module performs an alternative set of steps and prints a message on an exception report instead.

The logic of the edit program is essentially the same as that of the built-in validity-checking module, except that there is no validity switch to be manipulated. The logic of the edit program contains one other addition—the use of a switch to suppress the printing of a key field (SN) when multiple error lines are to be printed for a given record.

## VOCABULARY

class test
limit test
  (reasonableness
  test)
code test
sign test
interrupt
data exception

independent edit
  program
built-in validity-
  checking routine
edit report
exception report
spooling
VALIDITY-SWITCH

## EXERCISES/QUESTIONS

1. Compare and contrast the independent edit program with the processing program with a built-in validity-checking routine.

2. List and explain the four kinds of validity tests.

3. Explain how the following data accepted for input might be validated using independent edit.

   a. A valid class code consists of the values 1, 2, 3, or 4.
   b. A student's name must be alphabetic.
   c. A student's cumulative semester hours must be within the range of 0–200.
   d. An employee's pay rate code must be within the range of 1 through 10.

## PROBLEMS

**5–1.** ABC Hardware wishes to produce an edit report generated from its master inventory file, which follows. Prepare a printer spacing chart that lists invalid records in the file. In addition, create a hierarchy chart, a structured program flowchart, and pseudocode for this problem.

### INPUT RECORD FORMAT:

#### MASTER INVENTORY FILE

| Columns | Field Description | Format |
|---------|-------------------|--------|
| 1–5 | Stock Number | Numeric |
| 6–9 | Item Number | Numeric (1–5000) |
| 10–30 | Description | Alphabetic |
| 31–33 | Quantity on Hand | Numeric (500–999) |
| 34–36 | Quantity on Order | Numeric (500–999) |
| 37–41 | Price per Unit | Numeric (10–1000) |
| 42–45 | Inventory Reorder Level | Numeric (50–500) |

## LOGIC CONSIDERATIONS:

1. Interrogate the various input fields for invalid data. Some records may contain multiple errors.
2. If a field is not numeric, there is no need to check for a range of values.

Print an independent edit report similar to the one that follows depicting all the records found to be in error. The first detail line representing a record with multiple errors should contain the stock number, item number, and message. The message should describe the kind of invalidity found. A separate message should print for each invalid field found in the record.

```
┌─────────────────────────────────────────────────────────────────────┐
│                   DATA VALIDATION EDIT REPORT                         │
│                                                                       │
│   STOCK NUMBER        ITEM NUMBER              MESSAGE                 │
│                                                                       │
│      00742               4003         QUANTITY-ON-HAND OUT OF RANGE    │
│                                       QUANTITY-ON-ORDER OUT OF RANGE   │
│      00932               1007         PRICE-PER-UNIT NOT NUMERIC       │
│                                       REORDER LEVEL NOT VALID          │
└─────────────────────────────────────────────────────────────────────┘
```

**5-2.** Create a printer spacing chart, a hierarchy chart, a structured program flowchart, and pseudocode for the following problem.

Acme company wishes to produce an accounts receivable report from customer sales records. Unfortunately, there is not yet an independent edit program for the customer file. The various fields need to be validated within the processing program with a built-in validation routine. This validation process needs to occur before the records are processed any further. The program must produce two reports, (1) a validation report listing the records found to be invalid and (2) an accounts receivable report, similar to those that follow. The input record format is also presented.

### PROCESSING:

Determine the validity of the various fields shown in the columns of the validation report. There is no need to validate the fields not shown in the preceding output record format.

### TEST DATA:

Make up a set of test data or use ancillary test data that will produce both the preceding validation report and an accounts receivable report.

### INPUT RECORD FORMAT:

| Field Name | Location | Data Class |
|---|---|---|
| Customer Number | 1–9 | Numeric |
| Customer Name | 10–28 | Alphabetic |
| Address | 29–38 | Not Numeric |
| City | 39–46 | Alphabetic |
| State Code | 47–48 | Numeric (range = 1 to 50) |
| Zip | 49–53 | Numeric |
| Phone | 54–63 | Numeric |
| Balance Due | 64–70 | Numeric (dollars and cents) |
| Credit Limit | 71–77 | Numeric (dollars and cents) |

### OUTPUT REQUIRED:

```
┌──────────────────────────────────────────────────────────────────────────────┐
│                     VALIDATION REPORT, CUST. FILE                              │
│                                                                                │
│   CUSTOMER NUMBER      CUST.    CUST.    ADDR   CITY   STATE   BALANCE          │
│                        NUM.     NAME                                           │
│      000234534                                   X              X              │
│      002349877                   X                                             │
│      120384753                   X       X                                     │
│      56J/33#%*          X                               X                      │
└──────────────────────────────────────────────────────────────────────────────┘
```

```
┌──────────────────────────────────────────────────────────────────────────────┐
│                        ACCOUNTS RECEIVABLE REPORT                              │
│                                                                                │
│   CUSTOMER        CUSTOMER           ADDRESS        CITY        STATE  BALANCE  │
│   XXXXXXXXX       XXXXXXXXXXXXXXX    XXXXXXXXX       XXXXXXXXX    XX   XX,XXX.XX │
│   XXXXXXXXX       XXXXXXXXXXXXXXX    XXXXXXXXX       XXXXXXXXX    XX   XX,XXX.XX │
│   XXXXXXXXX       XXXXXXXXXXXXXXX    XXXXXXXXX       XXXXXXXXX    XX   XX,XXX.XX │
│                                                                                │
│   TOTAL VALID CUSTOMERS XXX                                                    │
│   TOTAL BALANCE $XXX,XXX.XX                                                    │
└──────────────────────────────────────────────────────────────────────────────┘
```

**5–3.** Prestige Gifts, Inc. wants to produce an Inventory Analysis File Listing that depicts the gift number, description, item cost, suggested retail price, the investment in the item, potential profit associated with the item, over/under minimum stock level, and markup percent on the item. Print grand totals for investment in the item and potential profit. The printer spacing chart and record layout are shown in Figure 5.5 and 5.6, respectively.

1. The *over-under-minimum-inventory* amount should be calculated using the *quantity-on-hand* and the *minimum-inventory* amounts in the Inventory Master Record (quantity-on-hand—minimum-inventory).
2. The *investment-in-item* amount should be calculated by multiplying the *quantity-on-hand* by the *item-cost*.
3. The *markup-percent* should be calculated by subtracting the *item-cost* from the suggested-retail, and then determining what percentage of the *item-cost* this difference represents.
4. Potential-profit should be calculated by multiplying the *suggested-retail* by the *quantity-on-hand*, and then calculating the difference between this result and the total investment in the item.
5. Print 42 lines on each page.
6. Print the page number on each page starting at 1.
7. In the over-under-minimum column on the report, print "over" if the value represents an amount greater than or equal to the item's minimum inventory and "under" if the amount is less than the minimum inventory.
8. The Data Validation Report depicting records in error is to print next. This report lists the record images that were found to have some type of problem.
9. The validity testing should include a test that tests each field for valid class tests (either numeric or alphabetic).
10. Check to make sure that the quantity-on-hand field is both numeric and positive before processing. A zero balance may indicate a discontinued item. Simply, print "quantity-on-hand is zero."

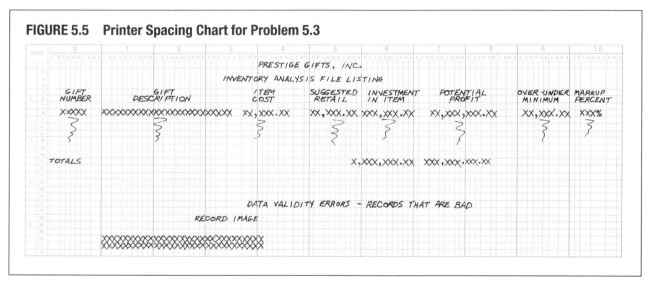

**FIGURE 5.5   Printer Spacing Chart for Problem 5.3**

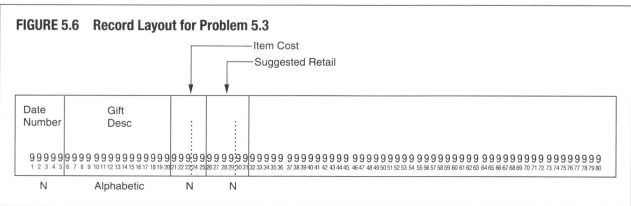

**FIGURE 5.6   Record Layout for Problem 5.3**

**5–4.** The sales manager calculates commissions based on quota and variances. This report will determine the rate of sales based on the current month and then develop a comparative quota amount. The variance is positive, if the rate of sales = or exceeds the quota; it is negative if the sales are less than the quota. Commissions are based on current month sales multiplied by a percentage. Negative variances reduce the amount of commission. Data in the sales file also need to be examined and validated. The report should indicate all errors found.

The printer spacing chart and record layout follow.

## PROCESSING SPECIFICATIONS:

Process each record in the file, in the same sequence as stored in the file, until the end of the file.

Print the report title and column headings at the top of each page of the report.

Print "error lines" for each error encountered in the record. Only records that have all valid fields will contain a regular detail line as shown on the printer spacing chart.

Notice that the error line only lists the Sales ID, the Salesperson's Name, and the error message. If multiple errors occur in a record, multiple lines will appear on the report.

Print 28 detail/error lines per page.

## DATA VALIDATION REQUIREMENTS

A. Sales ID must be present. If not present, print the message:
   "MISSING SALES ID."

B. Salesperson's name must be present, not numeric and left-justified. Print the message:
   "SALESPERSON MISSING."

C. Commission rate must be present, numeric, and within the range of 5% to 40%. If incorrect, print an appropriate error message for each possible error. If the commission rate is not present, print "COMMISSION RATE IS NOT PRESENT." If the commission rate is not numeric, then print "COMMISSION RATE IS NOT NUMERIC"; and if the value is not in the appropriate range, then print, "COMMISSION RATE IS OUT OF RANGE."

D. Annual quota may be zero, must be numeric, and may *not* be negative. If incorrect, print the appropriate message.

E. Sales, both year-to-date and current month, must be present, may be zero, and may be a negative amount. If incorrect, print the appropriate message.

## CALCULATIONS:

A. Number of months of sales is the current month minus 1.

B. Equivalent quota = annual quota * (number-of-months-of-sales / 12).

C. Quota variance = sales-to-date − equivalent quota.

D. The commission rate is stored as a decimal.

E. Commission amount = commission rate * sales this month. Negative quota variances reduce commission amount by one-half. Commission calculations are not to be performed on negative monthly sales amounts.

Accumulate a final total for commission amount.

# FIGURE 5.7 Gold Direct Sales Monthly Commission Report

| SALES ID | SALESPERSON NAME | ANNUAL QUOTA | SALES YEAR-TO-DATE | SALES THIS MONTH | NO. OF MONTHS | EQUIV. QUOTA | QUOTA VARIANCE | COMM. RATE | COMMISSION AMOUNT | VALIDATION MESSAGE |
|---|---|---|---|---|---|---|---|---|---|---|
| XXXXX | XXXXXXXXXXXXXX | XXX,XXX | XXX,XXX.XX | XXX,XXX.XX | XX | XXX,XXX | ++++,++9 | XXX% | XXXX,XXX.XX | |
| XXXX | XXXXXXXXXXXX | | | | | | | | | XXXXXXXXXXXXXXXXXX |

REPORT DATE: 29/29/99    GOLD DIRECT SALES MONTHLY COMMISSION REPORT    PAGE 29

## MULTIPLE-CARD LAYOUT FORM

Company ___GOLD 2___

Application _____ by _____ Date ____ Job. No. _____ Sheet No. ____

| SALES ID A/N | SALESMAN NAME A/N | CRATE N | SSN A/N | ANNUAL QUOTA N | NOT USED | SALES YTD N | SALES CUR N | PHONE NUMBER N | |
|---|---|---|---|---|---|---|---|---|---|
| 99999 | 999999999999999 | 99 | 99999999999 | 999999 | 9 | 999999 | 9999999 | 99999 99 | 999999999999999 |
| 1 2 3 4 5 | 6 7 8 9 10 11 12 13 14 15 16 17 18 19 20 | 21 22 | 23 24 25 26 27 28 29 30 31 | 32 33 34 35 36 | 37 | 38 39 40 41 42 43 | 44 45 46 47 48 49 50 51 | 52 53 54 55 56 57 58 | 59 60 61 62 63 64 65 66 67 68 69 70 71 72 73 74 75 76 77 78 79 80 |

# 6

# Control Break Reports

## OBJECTIVES

As a result of having read and studied this chapter, the student will be able to:

1. Explain the purpose of a control field.

2. Explain the purpose of sorting the file prior to generating a control break report.

3. Draw a hierarchy chart, design a structured flowchart, and write the pseudocode for the following:
   a. A single-level (detail-printed) control break report.
   b. A single-level (group-indicated) control break report.
   c. A two-level control break report.
   d. A three-level control break report.

In previous chapters, we processed each record as a separate entity having no relationship with the other records except that they all belonged to the same file. However, managers are often interested in more than grand totals; they may be interested in control totals (subtotals) for various groups or subgroups of records. Reports with subtotals are often referred to as **control break reports**. For example, a company's sales manager wishes to know the total sales for each store in the company. Figure 6.1 illustrates that sort of sales report, showing subtotals for each store, that will be later referred to as a **single-level control break report**.

A store's sales manager, however, may be interested in more than subtotals for the various stores; he or she may want the subtotals for each department in the store. Figure 6.2 illustrates a store sales report with both major subtotals for each store in the company and a further breakdown into department totals within each store. This will be referred to later as a **two-level control break report**.

A department sales manager may even request a report that shows a breakdown of sales totals not only by store and department but also by salesperson within each department. Figure 6.3 illustrates such a report. This type of report will be referred to later as a **three-level control break report**.

## Sorting the File

Before control break reports can be produced, the input file must be ordered, or sorted, into an appropriate sequence. All the records, for example, of Store 100 should precede the records for Store 200. The field on the record used for sorting the file is called the **sort key field**. The sort key field on a record is a unique identifier; it differentiates this record from any other record in the file. In this example, the sort key field is the store number. The actual process of writing programs that can sort files into a particular sequence according to one or more specified keys will be discussed in Chapter 11. But for now, in this chapter, the student may assume that the files are properly ordered.

## The Control Field

When generating control break reports, the programmer uses a unique identifier called a **control field** to distinguish between groups of records. It is called a control field because its contents *control* the

kinds of calculations and output that are done. For example, if several records with the same store number are read and processed, and then a subsequent record with a different store number is read, it is at this point—when a different store number is detected—that the program has to switch to an alternate set of commands that cause the printing of a subtotal as well as the execution of other needed activities (to be explained later). The point at which the new control field value is detected is often referred to as a **control break**.

## THE SINGLE-LEVEL CONTROL BREAK

By now you can recognize some of the kinds of reports that control break programs produce. To write a program that will produce such a report requires an understanding of the step-by-step processing of an ordered file. Let us discuss single-level control breaks first.

You have learned that there are three main parts to any computer program. The steps involved in generating a control break report are divided into the same three main categories, namely (1) the initial processing steps that occur in the START-UP module, (2) the record-by-record processing steps for the file that occur in the PROCESS-RECORD module, and (3) the printing of the last subtotal and the final total that occur in the WRAP-UP module.

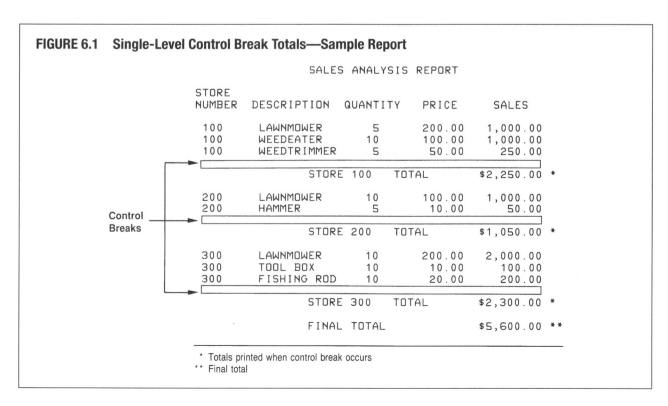

**FIGURE 6.1    Single-Level Control Break Totals—Sample Report**

```
                          SALES ANALYSIS REPORT

        STORE
        NUMBER   DESCRIPTION   QUANTITY    PRICE      SALES

         100     LAWNMOWER         5       200.00    1,000.00
         100     WEEDEATER        10       100.00    1,000.00
         100     WEEDTRIMMER       5        50.00      250.00

                         STORE  100     TOTAL      $2,250.00  *

         200     LAWNMOWER        10       100.00    1,000.00
         200     HAMMER            5        10.00       50.00

                         STORE  200     TOTAL      $1,050.00  *

         300     LAWNMOWER        10       200.00    2,000.00
         300     TOOL BOX         10        10.00      100.00
         300     FISHING ROD      10        20.00      200.00

                         STORE  300     TOTAL      $2,300.00  *

                         FINAL   TOTAL             $5,600.00  **
```
Control Breaks

 * Totals printed when control break occurs
** Final total

## Step-by-Step Processing

In the START-UP module, the following activities must occur:

1. Variables are initialized.
2. Files are opened.
3. Report headings are printed.
4. The first record is read.
5. *The control field of the first record is moved to a work area variable.*

The only addition to this module from START-UP in previous examples is the transfer of the control field to a work area variable. In Figure 6.4, a sales file is illustrated, showing the reading of the first record into the input areas as the first step. The first field in the record is also the control field called STORE-NUMBER. The second step shows the storing of the STORE-NUMBER value, 100, in the **PREVIOUS-NUMBER work area** variable. Why is this done? It sets up a copy of the current control field value with which subsequent control fields will be compared. As long as subsequent control fields match the value in the PREVIOUS-NUMBER field, the records belong to the same control group and therefore will require only normal detail record processing. When the computer program detects that the content of the current record's control field is different from that of the PREVIOUS-NUMBER field, it switches to an alternate set of steps that essentially provide for the printing of the

---

**FIGURE 6.2    Two-Level Control Break Totals**

```
                    SALES ANALYSIS REPORT

      STORE
      NUMBER   DEPARTMENT   DESCRIPTION   QUANTITY    PRICE      SALES

       100       005        LAWNMOWER         5       200.00    1,000.00
       100       005        WEEDEATER        10       100.00    1,000.00
       100       005        WEEDTRIMMER       5        50.00      250.00

                            DEPARTMENT 005   TOTAL           $2,250.00  *

       100       007        SHIRT             1        10.00       10.00
       100       007        TIE              10         5.00       50.00

                            DEPARTMENT 007   TOTAL           $   60.00  *
                                    STORE 100   TOTAL        $2,310.00  **


       200       005        LAWNMOWER        10       100.00    1,000.00
       200       005        HAMMER            5        10.00       50.00

                            DEPARTMENT 005   TOTAL           $1,050.00  *

       200       009        DIAMOND RING      2       500.00    1,000.00
       200       009        NECKLACE          3       100.00      300.00

                            DEPARTMENT 009   TOTAL           $1,300.00  *
                                    STORE 200   TOTAL        $2,350.00  **


       300       005        LAWNMOWER        10       200.00    2,000.00
       300       005        TOOL BOX         10        10.00      100.00
       300       005        FISHING ROD      10        20.00      200.00

                            DEPARTMENT 005   TOTAL           $2,300.00  *
                                    STORE   300   TOTAL      $2,300.00  **
                                    FINAL TOTAL              $6,960.00  ***
```

  \*    Minor total
 \*\*   Major total
\*\*\*  Final total

---

**FIGURE 6.3  Three-Level Control Break Totals**

```
                    SALES ANALYSIS REPORT

STORE     DEPART-   SALES-
NUMBER    MENT      PERSON    DESCRIPTION    QUANTITY    PRICE    SALES

100       005       0056      LAWNMOWER         5        200.00   1,000.00
100       005       0056      WEEDEATER        10        100.00   1,000.00

                              SALESPERSON 0056       TOTAL   $2,000.00 *

100       005       0098      WEEDTRIMMER       5         50.00     250.00
100       005       0098      LAWN FERTILIZER 1           10.00      10.00

                              SALESPERSON 0098       TOTAL     $260.00 *
                              DEPARTMENT   005       TOTAL   $2,260.00 **

100       007       4000      SHIRT             1         10.00      10.00
100       007       4000      TIE              10          5.00      50.00

                              SALESPERSON  4000      TOTAL      $60.00 *

100       007       4500      JEANS             1         15.00      15.00
100       007       4500      SHIRT             2         20.00      40.00

                              SALESPERSON  4500      TOTAL      $55.00 *
                              DEPARTMENT    007      TOTAL     $115.00 **
                              STORE         100      TOTAL   $2,375.00 ***

200       005       2356      LAWNMOWER        10        100.00   1,000.00
200       005       2356      HAMMER            5         10.00      50.00

                              SALESPERSON  2356      TOTAL   $1,050.00 *

200       005       2560      SAW               1         20.00      20.00
200       005       2560      RULER             1         10.00      10.00

                              SALESPERSON  2560      TOTAL      $30.00 *
                              DEPARTMENT    005      TOTAL   $1,080.00 **

200       009       6700      DIAMOND RING      2        500.00   1,000.00
200       009       6700      NECKLACE          3        100.00     300.00

                              SALESPERSON  6700      TOTAL   $1,300.00 *
                              DEPARTMENT    009      TOTAL   $1,300.00 **
                              STORE         200      TOTAL   $2,380.00 ***

300       005       2300      LAWNMOWER        10        200.00   2,000.00
300       005       2300      TOOL BOX         10         10.00     100.00

                              SALESPERSON  2300      TOTAL $2,100.00 *

300       005       2340      FISHING ROD      10         20.00     200.00

                              SALESPERSON  2340      TOTAL     $200.00 *
                              DEPARTMENT    005      TOTAL $2,300.00 **
                              STORE         300      TOTAL $2,300.00 ***
                                  FINAL TOTAL          $7,055.00 ****
```

```
   * Minor total
  ** Intermediate total
 *** Major total
**** Final total
```

subtotal (STORE-TOTAL). The control break processing steps will be discussed later.

The major modules in the PROCESS-RECORD module accomplish the following tasks:

1. CONTROL-BREAK-CHECK determines if a control break has occurred.
2. DETAIL-CALCULATION calculates the sales amount.
3. ACCUMULATION accumulates the sales amount into the store total.
4. DETAIL-LINE writes the detail line.
5. READ-FILE reads the next record into the input area.

The steps in the WRAP-UP module include:

1. Printing the subtotal.
2. Adding the subtotal to the final total.
3. Printing the final total.
4. Closing the files.

Figure 6.5 illustrates the processing of the first record. STORE-NUMBER is compared with PREVIOUS-NUMBER. Since these two values are equal, SALES is calculated (in the DETAIL-CALCULATION module). SALES, 1000, is added to STORE-TOTAL. Since this is the first record processed, STORE-TOTAL is now also 1000. The input and cal-

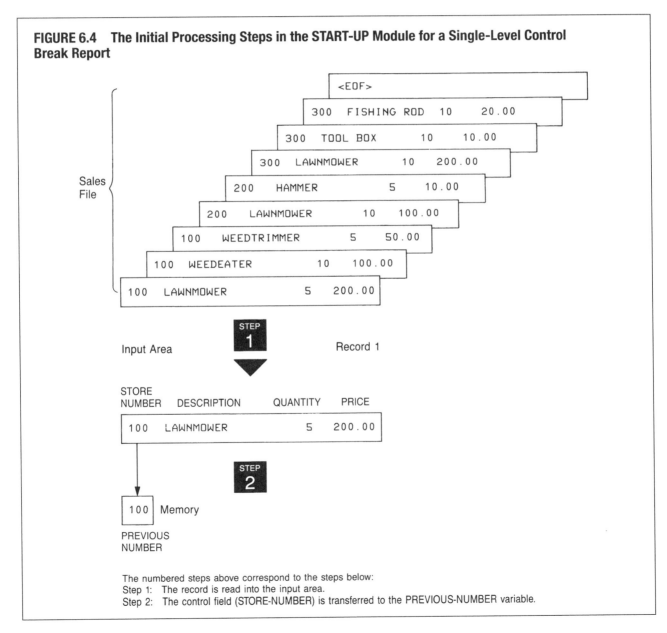

**FIGURE 6.4    The Initial Processing Steps in the START-UP Module for a Single-Level Control Break Report**

Sales File

| | | | |
|---|---|---|---|
| | | <EOF> | |
| 300 | FISHING ROD | 10 | 20.00 |
| 300 | TOOL BOX | 10 | 10.00 |
| 300 | LAWNMOWER | 10 | 200.00 |
| 200 | HAMMER | 5 | 10.00 |
| 200 | LAWNMOWER | 10 | 100.00 |
| 100 | WEEDTRIMMER | 5 | 50.00 |
| 100 | WEEDEATER | 10 | 100.00 |
| 100 | LAWNMOWER | 5 | 200.00 |

Input Area                                    Record 1

**STEP 1**

| STORE NUMBER | DESCRIPTION | QUANTITY | PRICE |
|---|---|---|---|
| 100 | LAWNMOWER | 5 | 200.00 |

**STEP 2**

100  Memory

PREVIOUS NUMBER

The numbered steps above correspond to the steps below:
Step 1:  The record is read into the input area.
Step 2:  The control field (STORE-NUMBER) is transferred to the PREVIOUS-NUMBER variable.

culated fields are then transferred to the printer output area, where the detail line is printed.

Figure 6.6 and 6.7 illustrate the processing for the next two records. The first three records, each with a control field of 100, all belong to the same control group.

Figure 6.8 illustrates what happens when the fourth record read has a control field different from the first group's control field. STORE-NUMBER, 200, is compared with PREVIOUS-NUMBER, 100. Since the result of this comparison is false, the CONTROL-BREAK steps are performed. PREVIOUS-NUMBER and STORE-TOTAL are transferred to the subtotal line where they are both printed

(steps 1 and 2). STORE-TOTAL is then added to FINAL-TOTAL (step 3). The subtotal line is then printed (step 4). Next, STORE-TOTAL is initialized to zero (step 5), and PREVIOUS-NUMBER is set to STORE-NUMBER, 200 (step 6), to prepare for the processing of the next group of records with a control field of 200.

Figure 6.9 illustrates the steps to print the last STORE-TOTAL and the FINAL-TOTAL. PREVIOUS-NUMBER, 300, and STORE-TOTAL, 2300, are transferred to the subtotal line and printed. STORE-TOTAL, 2300, is then added to FINAL-TOTAL. The FINAL-TOTAL, 5600, is transferred to the final total line and printed.

**FIGURE 6.5   Processing Steps for the First Record (PROCESS-RECORD Module)**

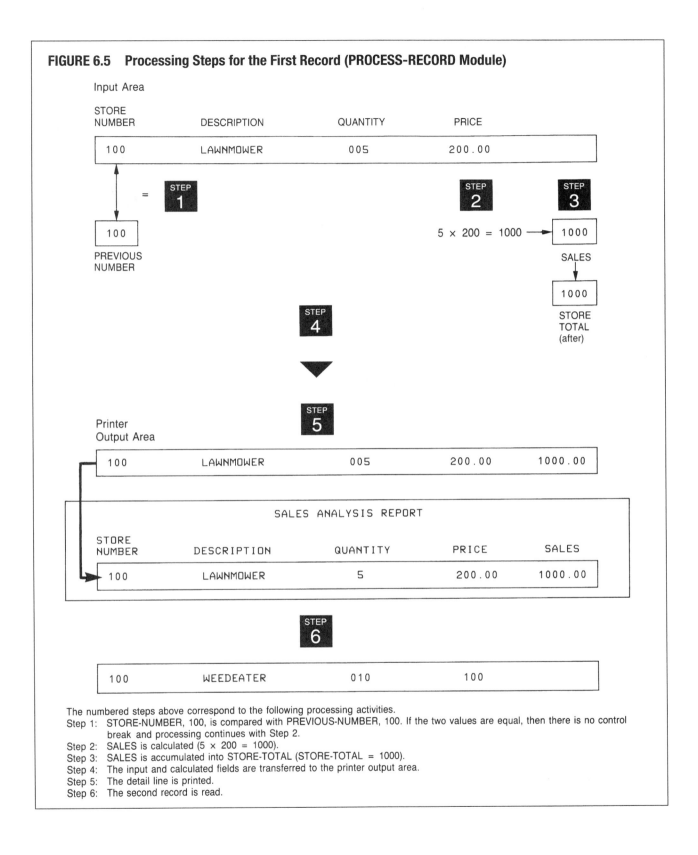

Input Area

| STORE NUMBER | DESCRIPTION | QUANTITY | PRICE |
|---|---|---|---|
| 100 | LAWNMOWER | 005 | 200.00 |

STEP **1**    STEP **2**    STEP **3**

= 

100

PREVIOUS NUMBER

5 × 200 = 1000 → 1000

SALES

1000

STORE TOTAL (after)

STEP **4**

STEP **5**

Printer Output Area

| 100 | LAWNMOWER | 005 | 200.00 | 1000.00 |
|---|---|---|---|---|

SALES ANALYSIS REPORT

| STORE NUMBER | DESCRIPTION | QUANTITY | PRICE | SALES |
|---|---|---|---|---|
| 100 | LAWNMOWER | 5 | 200.00 | 1000.00 |

STEP **6**

| 100 | WEEDEATER | 010 | 100 |
|---|---|---|---|

The numbered steps above correspond to the following processing activities.

Step 1:  STORE-NUMBER, 100, is compared with PREVIOUS-NUMBER, 100. If the two values are equal, then there is no control break and processing continues with Step 2.

Step 2:  SALES is calculated (5 × 200 = 1000).

Step 3:  SALES is accumulated into STORE-TOTAL (STORE-TOTAL = 1000).

Step 4:  The input and calculated fields are transferred to the printer output area.

Step 5:  The detail line is printed.

Step 6:  The second record is read.

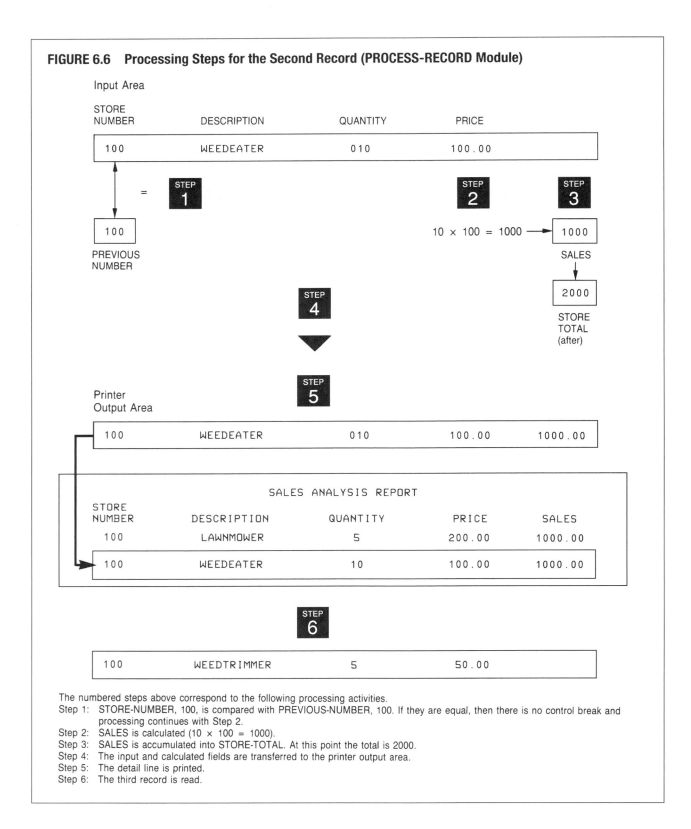

**FIGURE 6.6   Processing Steps for the Second Record (PROCESS-RECORD Module)**

Input Area

| STORE NUMBER | DESCRIPTION | QUANTITY | PRICE |
|---|---|---|---|
| 100 | WEEDEATER | 010 | 100.00 |

**STEP 1**  **STEP 2**  **STEP 3**

= 

100

PREVIOUS NUMBER

10 × 100 = 1000 ⟶ 1000

SALES

2000

STORE TOTAL (after)

**STEP 4**

**STEP 5**

Printer Output Area

| 100 | WEEDEATER | 010 | 100.00 | 1000.00 |
|---|---|---|---|---|

SALES ANALYSIS REPORT

| STORE NUMBER | DESCRIPTION | QUANTITY | PRICE | SALES |
|---|---|---|---|---|
| 100 | LAWNMOWER | 5 | 200.00 | 1000.00 |
| 100 | WEEDEATER | 10 | 100.00 | 1000.00 |

**STEP 6**

| 100 | WEEDTRIMMER | 5 | 50.00 |
|---|---|---|---|

The numbered steps above correspond to the following processing activities.
Step 1:  STORE-NUMBER, 100, is compared with PREVIOUS-NUMBER, 100. If they are equal, then there is no control break and processing continues with Step 2.
Step 2:  SALES is calculated (10 × 100 = 1000).
Step 3:  SALES is accumulated into STORE-TOTAL. At this point the total is 2000.
Step 4:  The input and calculated fields are transferred to the printer output area.
Step 5:  The detail line is printed.
Step 6:  The third record is read.

## FIGURE 6.7 Processing Steps for the Third Record (PROCESS-RECORD Module)

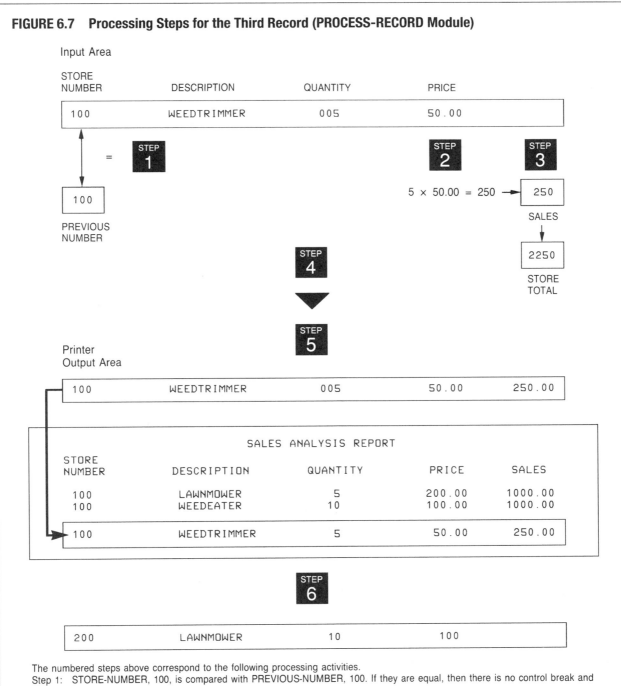

The numbered steps above correspond to the following processing activities.

Step 1: STORE-NUMBER, 100, is compared with PREVIOUS-NUMBER, 100. If they are equal, then there is no control break and processing continues with Step 2.

Step 2: SALES is calculated (5 × 50 = 250).

Step 3: SALES is accumulated into STORE-TOTAL. At this point the total is 2250.

Step 4: The input and calculated fields are transferred to the printer output area.

Step 5: The detail line is printed.

Step 6: The fourth record is read.

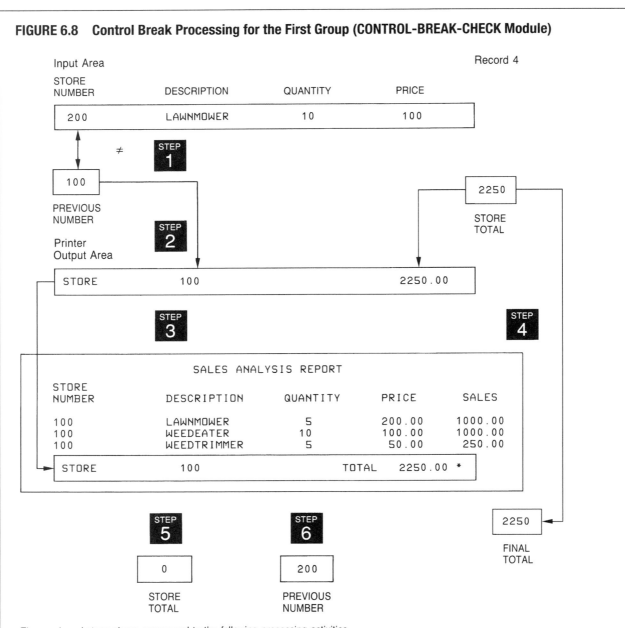

**FIGURE 6.8   Control Break Processing for the First Group (CONTROL-BREAK-CHECK Module)**

The numbered steps above correspond to the following processing activities.

Step 1: The record 4 control field (STORE-NUMBER) value of 200 is compared to PREVIOUS-NUMBER, 100. Since these two values are unequal, Step 2 is carried out.

Step 2: PREVIOUS-NUMBER and STORE-TOTAL are transferred to print area.

Step 3: The subtotal line is printed.

Step 4: STORE-TOTAL is accumulated into FINAL-TOTAL.

Step 5: STORE-TOTAL is initialized to zero.

Step 6: STORE-NUMBER of the fourth record (200) is transferred to PREVIOUS-NUMBER. Future control break checks will key off the value 200.

# FIGURE 6.9 Final Total Processing (WRAP-UP Module)

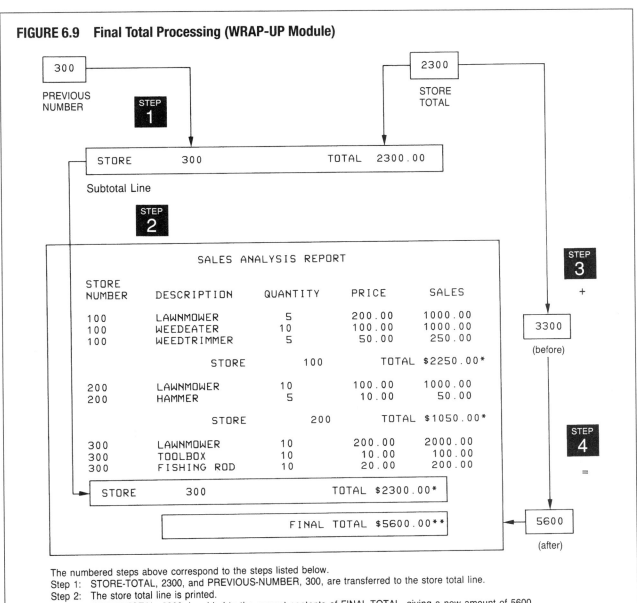

The numbered steps above correspond to the steps listed below.

Step 1:  STORE-TOTAL, 2300, and PREVIOUS-NUMBER, 300, are transferred to the store total line.

Step 2:  The store total line is printed.

Step 3:  STORE-TOTAL, 2300, is added to the current contents of FINAL-TOTAL, giving a new amount of 5600.

Step 4:  FINAL-TOTAL is transferred and printed on the report.

## A Sales Analysis Report Using a Single-Level Control Break Program

### Program Requirements

J-Mart Stores owns and operates a number of retail stores and wishes to produce a sales analysis report with sales subtotals for each store and a final total of sales for all stores.

### Output Design

Figure 6.1 shows the report to be produced. The same output was illustrated in Figures 6.4 through 6.9 to explain the concept of control break processing. The associated print chart is Exhibit 6.1.

### Input Design

The input record format of the sales record is shown in Exhibit 6.2. The fields include STORE-NUMBER (the control key), DESCRIPTION, QUANTITY, and PRICE per unit.

Exhibit 6.3 lists a representative set of test case records for testing the program.

### Logic Considerations

The control break program should provide for the following logic:

1. A control break check to determine if a subtotal is to be printed.

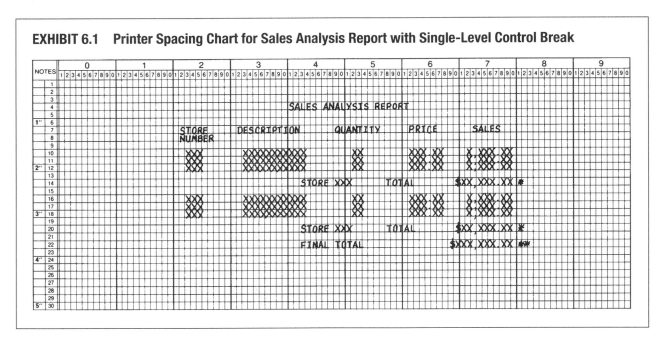

**EXHIBIT 6.1    Printer Spacing Chart for Sales Analysis Report with Single-Level Control Break**

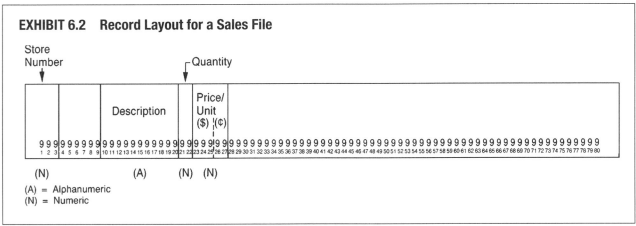

**EXHIBIT 6.2    Record Layout for a Sales File**

2. The printout of a detail line for every record in the file.
3. The printout of a subtotal for every control group in the file.
4. The printout of a final company total for sales at the end of the report.

## Designing a Single-Level Control Break Program

Exhibit 6.4 shows the hierarchy chart for the general design of the single-level control break program. The basic three main modules are shown as usual. Note the addition to the START-UP module

---

**EXHIBIT 6.3    Single-Level Control Break—Test Data**

| STORE | DESCRIPTION | QUANTITY | PRICE |
|-------|-------------|----------|--------|
| 100 | LAWNMOWER | 5 | 200.00 |
| 100 | WEEDEATER | 10 | 100.00 |
| 100 | WEEDTRIMMER | 5 | 50.00 |
| 200 | LAWNMOWER | 10 | 100.00 |
| 200 | HAMMER | 5 | 10.00 |
| 300 | LAWNMOWER | 10 | 200.00 |
| 300 | TOOL BOX | 10 | 10.00 |
| 300 | FISHING ROD | 10 | 20.00 |

---

**EXHIBIT 6.4    Hierarchy Chart for Sales Analysis Report with Single-Level Control Break**

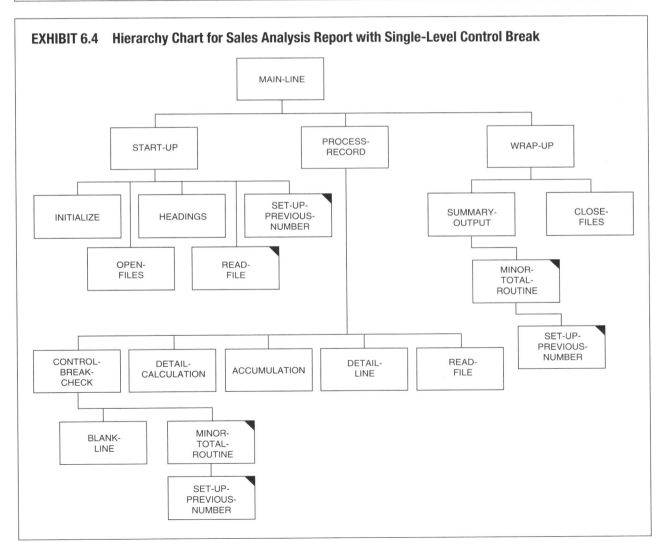

of one additional module called SET-UP-PREVI-OUS-NUMBER. The PROCESS-RECORD module also has one additional module, positioned at the beginning, called CONTROL-BREAK-CHECK. The purpose of this module was explained previously in the discussion of the steps for processing records (control break processing). Since this chapter deals with control breaks, it is worth repeating that the function of this module is to determine whether or not the current control field is the same as the previous record's control key. If they are equal, detail record processing continues as usual; but if the fields are unequal, special control break processing must occur in order to handle the printing of the subtotal (STORE-TOTAL) and other special processing tasks preparatory to processing the next group. These tasks are performed in the routine called MINOR-TOTAL-ROUTINE, just below the CONTROL-BREAK-CHECK module. The remainder of the hierarchy chart modules—DETAIL-CALCULATIONS, ACCUMULATION, DETAIL-LINE, and READ-FILE—appear the same as in previous examples.

Exhibit 6.5 illustrates the structure program flowchart for this problem. The START-UP module, as previously stated, contains one additional module called SET-UP-PREVIOUS-NUMBER. The PROCESS-RECORD module depicts one additional predefined process block at the beginning of the PROCESS-RECORD routine. Notice that PROCESS-RECORD is a control module—all the blocks are predefined process blocks that invoke other subordinate modules found elsewhere in the program. The WRAP-UP module starts off by calling SUMMARY-OUTPUT module. SUMMARY-OUTPUT module calls MINOR-TOTAL-ROUTINE in order to take care of the printing of the last STORE-TOTAL and the adding of the last STORE-TOTAL to FINAL-TOTAL before printing it. The WRAP-UP calls the CLOSE-FILES module.

## The CONTROL-BREAK-CHECK Module

The first module invoked by the PROCESS-RECORD module is the CONTROL-BREAK-CHECK module, shown highlighted in Exhibit 6.5 It consists of an If . . . Then . . . Else structure that tests to determine if STORE-NUMBER is equal to PREVIOUS-NUMBER. If the two numbers are equal, there is no control break; control simply falls through to Return. However, if the condition test is false (if the two values are not equal), a submodule called MINOR-TOTAL-ROUTINE is invoked. The purpose of this routine has already been explained in the previous discussions of the hierarchy chart and step-by-step processing of the fourth record of

the file. Since the minor total logic is needed in both the CONTROL-BREAK-CHECK and WRAP-UP modules, it is established as a separate module called MINOR-TOTAL-ROUTINE and then called where appropriate. One of the main purposes of modular programming is to reduce redundant code in the program where the same set of code must be performed at different places in the program.

The purpose of the MINOR-TOTAL-ROUTINE is to:

1. Transfer the necessary data to the subtotal line. (In this case, PREVIOUS-NUMBER and STORE-TOTAL are transferred to the subtotal line.)
2. Print the subtotal line.
3. Accumulate STORE-TOTAL into FINAL-TOTAL.
4. Store zeros in STORE-TOTAL.
5. Call the SET-UP-PREVIOUS-NUMBER module.

These five steps, described in the step-by-step discussion of the control break concept in Figure 6.8 (steps 2–6), equate to the five blocks in the flowcharting segment of MINOR-TOTAL-ROUTINE. SET-UP-PREVIOUS-NUMBER has been formalized into a module, since it is invoked from two different places. While it appears only once in the program, it can be invoked from either the START-UP module or the MINOR-TOTAL-ROUTINE module.

**Pseudocode.** Exhibit 6.6 depicts the associated pseudocode for this problem.

**Program Code.** Exhibits 6.7 and 6.8 illustrate the associated COBOL and BASIC programs.

**EXHIBIT 6.5    Structured Flowchart for Sales Analysis Report with Single-Level Control Break**

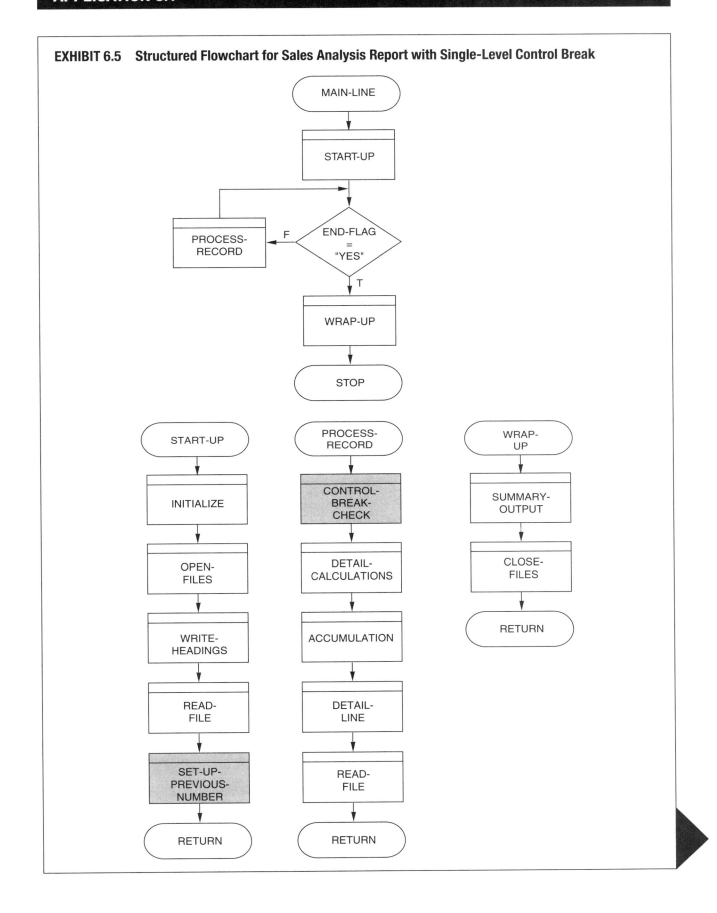

**EXHIBIT 6.5    (Cont.)**

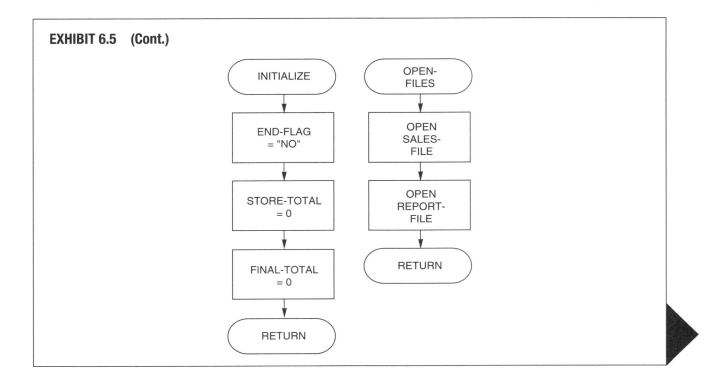

**EXHIBIT 6.5    (Cont.)**

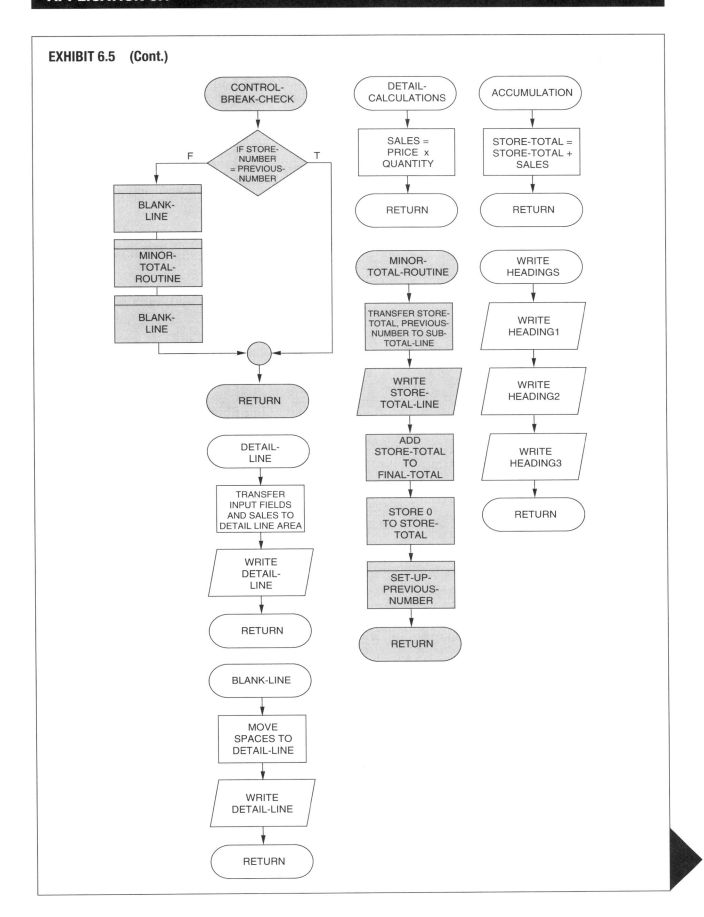

APPLICATION 6.1

**EXHIBIT 6.5 (Cont.)**

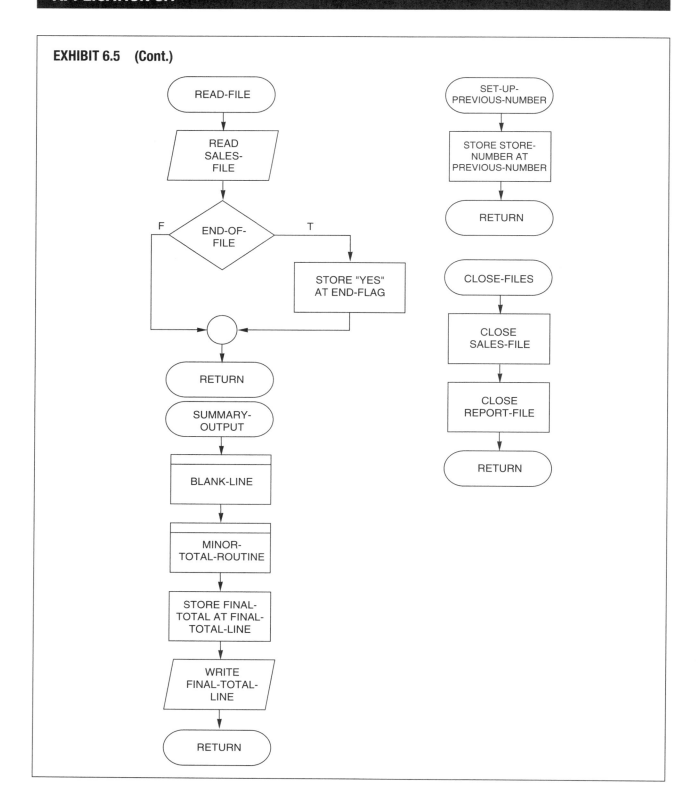

## EXHIBIT 6.6   Pseudocode for Single-Level Control Break

*mainline
    start-up
    dowhile end-flag = "no"
        process-record
    enddo
    wrap-up
    stop
*start-up
    initialize
    open-files
    headings
    read-file
    set-up-previous-number
    return
*initialize
    end-flag = "no"
    store-total = 0
    final-total = 0
    return
*open-files
    open sales-file
    open report-file
    return
*process-record module
    control-break-check
    detail-calculation
    accumulation
    detail-line
    read-file
    return
*wrap-up module
    summary-output
    close-files
    return
*summary-output
    minor-total-routine
    format final-total-line
    print final-total-line
    return
*close-files
    close sales-file
    close report-file
    return

*headings
    print heading1
    print heading2
    return
*read-file
    read sales-file
    when no more records store "yes" at end-flag
    endread
    return
*set-up-previous-number
    store store-number at previous-number
    return
*control-break-check module
    if store-number = previous-number
        then null
    else
        blank-line
        minor-total-routine
        blank-line
    endif
    return
*detail-calculation
    sales = quantity $\times$ price
    return
*accumulation
    add sales to store-total
    return
*detail-line
    transfer input fields and sales to output area
    print detail-line
    return
*minor-total routine
    transfer store-total and previous-number to output area
    print sub-total-line
    accumulate store-total into final-total
    store zeros into store-total
    set-up-previous-number
    return
*blank-line
    move spaces to detail-line
    write detail-line
    return

**EXHIBIT 6.7    COBOL 85 for Appl. 6.1, Sales Analysis Report with Single-Level Control Break**

```
1          IDENTIFICATION DIVISION.
2          PROGRAM-ID.  CH6ILL1.
3          DATE-WRITTEN.  APRIL 16, 1993.
4          DATE-COMPILED. 1993-06-28.
5
6
7       *REMARKS:   COBOL 85 PROGRAM
8       *              THIS PROGRAM PRODUCES A SALES ANALYSIS REPORT
9       *              FROM A SALES FILE.  IT LISTS THE STORE NUMBER,
10      *              DESCRIPTION, QUANTITY, PRICE, AND SALES.  CONTROL
11      *              TOTALS ARE TAKEN AND PRINTED  FOR EACH STORE.
12      *              A FINAL TOTAL IS PRINTED AT THE END OF THE REPORT.
13
14       ENVIRONMENT DIVISION.
15       CONFIGURATION SECTION.
16       SOURCE-COMPUTER. CYBER.
17       OBJECT-COMPUTER. CYBER.
18       INPUT-OUTPUT SECTION.
19       FILE-CONTROL.
20           SELECT SALES-FILE ASSIGN TO DTA61.
21           SELECT OUT-FILE ASSIGN TO OUTFILE.
22      *
23       DATA DIVISION.
24       FILE SECTION.
25
26       FD   SALES-FILE.
27
28       01   IN-REC.
29            05   STORE-NUMBER PIC 9(03).
30            05   FILLER       PIC X(06).
31            05   DESCRIPTION  PIC X(11).
32            05   QUANTITY     PIC 9(02).
33            05   PRICE        PIC 9(03)V99.
34
35
36       FD   OUT-FILE.
37
38       01   OUT-REC          PIC X(133).
39      *
40       WORKING-STORAGE SECTION.
41
42       01   END-FLAG         PIC X(3)          VALUE "NO".
43
44       01   PAGE-HEADING.
45            05               PIC X(40)         VALUE SPACES.
46            05               PIC X(21)         VALUE
47                             "SALES ANALYSIS REPORT".
48            05               PIC X(72)         VALUE SPACES.
49
50       01   COLUMN-HEADING1.
51            05               PIC X(21)         VALUE SPACES.
52            05               PIC X(05)         VALUE "STORE".
53            05               PIC X(05)         VALUE SPACES.
54            05               PIC X(11)         VALUE "DESCRIPTION".
55            05               PIC X(06)         VALUE SPACES.
56            05               PIC X(08)         VALUE "QUANTITY".
57            05               PIC X(05)         VALUE SPACES.
58            05               PIC X(05)         VALUE "PRICE".
59            05               PIC X(06)         VALUE SPACES.
60            05               PIC X(05)         VALUE "SALES".
61            05               PIC X(56)         VALUE SPACES.
62
63       01   COLUMN-HEADING2.
64            05               PIC X(21)         VALUE SPACES.
65            05               PIC X(06)         VALUE "NUMBER".
66            05               PIC X(106)        VALUE SPACES.
```

**EXHIBIT 6.7    (Cont.)**

```
67
68        01   DETAIL-LINE.
69             05                  PIC X(22)         VALUE SPACES.
70             05   STORE-NUM-OUT PIC 9(03).
71             05                  PIC X(07)         VALUE SPACES.
72             05   DESCRIPT-OUT  PIC X(11).
73             05                  PIC X(08)         VALUE SPACES.
74             05   QUANTITY-OUT  PIC Z9.
75             05                  PIC X(08)         VALUE SPACES.
76             05   PRICE-OUT     PIC ZZ9.99.
77             05                  PIC X(04)         VALUE SPACES.
78             05   SALES-OUT     PIC Z,ZZ9.99.
79             05                  PIC X(54)         VALUE SPACES.
80
81        01   STORE-TOTAL-LINE.
82             05                  PIC X(42)         VALUE SPACES.
83             05                  PIC X(06)         VALUE "STORE ".
84             05   SUB-STORE-NUM PIC 9(03).
85             05                  PIC X(06)         VALUE SPACES.
86             05                  PIC X(05)         VALUE "TOTAL".
87             05                  PIC X(07)         VALUE SPACES.
88             05   STORE-TOTAL-OUT PIC  $$$,$$9.99.
89             05                  PIC X(02)         VALUE " *".
90             05                  PIC X(51)         VALUE SPACES.
91
92        01   FINAL-TOTAL-LINE.
93             05                  PIC X(42)         VALUE SPACES.
94             05                  PIC X(11)         VALUE "FINAL TOTAL".
95             05                  PIC X(15)         VALUE SPACES.
96             05   FINAL-TOTAL-OUT PIC $$$$,$$9.99.
97             05                  PIC X(03)         VALUE " **".
98             05                  PIC X(49)         VALUE SPACES.
99
100       01   PREVIOUS-NUMBER   PIC 9(03)       VALUE 0.
101       01   SALES             PIC 9(04)V99    VALUE 0.
102       01   STORE-TOTAL       PIC 9(05)V99    VALUE 0.
103       01   FINAL-TOTAL       PIC 9(06)V99    VALUE 0.
104
105
106       /
107        PROCEDURE DIVISION.
108        ********************
109        000-MAIN-LINE.
110           PERFORM 100-START-UP.
111           PERFORM 200-PROCESS-RECORD UNTIL END-FLAG = "YES".
112           PERFORM 300-WRAP-UP.
113           STOP RUN.
114
115        100-START-UP.
116       *    INITIALIZATION - W-S
117           PERFORM 105-OPEN-FILES.
118           PERFORM 110-HEADINGS.
119           PERFORM 120-READ-FILE.
120           PERFORM 130-SET-UP-PREVIOUS-NUMBER.
121
122        105-OPEN-FILES.
123           OPEN INPUT SALES-FILE  OUTPUT OUT-FILE.
124
125
126        110-HEADINGS.
127           WRITE OUT-REC FROM PAGE-HEADING AFTER ADVANCING PAGE.
128           WRITE OUT-REC FROM COLUMN-HEADING1 AFTER ADVANCING 2 LINES.
129           WRITE OUT-REC FROM COLUMN-HEADING2 AFTER ADVANCING 1 LINE.
130           MOVE SPACES TO OUT-REC.
131           WRITE OUT-REC AFTER ADVANCING 1 LINE.
```

**EXHIBIT 6.7    (Cont.)**

```
132
133          120-READ-FILE.
134               READ SALES-FILE AT END MOVE "YES" TO END-FLAG.
135
136          130-SET-UP-PREVIOUS-NUMBER.
137               MOVE STORE-NUMBER TO PREVIOUS-NUMBER.
138
139          200-PROCESS-RECORD.
140               PERFORM 210-CONTROL-BREAK-CHECK.
141               PERFORM 220-DETAIL-CALCULATIONS.
142               PERFORM 230-ACCUMULATION.
143               PERFORM 240-DETAIL-LINE.
144               PERFORM 120-READ-FILE.
145
146          210-CONTROL-BREAK-CHECK.
147               IF STORE-NUMBER NOT = PREVIOUS-NUMBER
148                  THEN
149                     PERFORM 20X-BLANK-LINE
150                     PERFORM 211-MINOR-TOTAL-ROUTINE
151                     PERFORM 20X-BLANK-LINE
152               END-IF.
153
154          20X-BLANK-LINE.
155
156               MOVE SPACES TO OUT-REC.
157               WRITE OUT-REC.
158
159          211-MINOR-TOTAL-ROUTINE.
160               MOVE PREVIOUS-NUMBER TO SUB-STORE-NUM.
161               MOVE STORE-TOTAL TO STORE-TOTAL-OUT.
162               WRITE OUT-REC FROM STORE-TOTAL-LINE.
163               ADD STORE-TOTAL TO FINAL-TOTAL.
164               MOVE ZERO TO STORE-TOTAL.
165               PERFORM 130-SET-UP-PREVIOUS-NUMBER.
166
167          220-DETAIL-CALCULATIONS.
168               COMPUTE SALES ROUNDED = PRICE * QUANTITY.
169
170          230-ACCUMULATION.
171               COMPUTE STORE-TOTAL  = STORE-TOTAL + SALES.
172
173          240-DETAIL-LINE.
174               MOVE STORE-NUMBER TO STORE-NUM-OUT.
175               MOVE DESCRIPTION TO DESCRIPT-OUT.
176               MOVE QUANTITY TO QUANTITY-OUT.
177               MOVE PRICE TO PRICE-OUT.
178               MOVE SALES TO SALES-OUT.
179               WRITE OUT-REC FROM DETAIL-LINE AFTER ADVANCING 1 LINE.
180
181          300-WRAP-UP.
182
183               PERFORM 310-SUMMARY-OUTPUT.
184               PERFORM 320-CLOSE-FILES.
185
186          310-SUMMARY-OUTPUT.
187
188               PERFORM 20X-BLANK-LINE.
189               PERFORM 211-MINOR-TOTAL-ROUTINE.
190               MOVE FINAL-TOTAL TO FINAL-TOTAL-OUT.
191               WRITE OUT-REC FROM FINAL-TOTAL-LINE AFTER 1.
192
193          320-CLOSE-FILES.
194               CLOSE SALES-FILE  OUT-FILE.
```

**EXHIBIT 6.7 (Cont.)**

```
                    SALES ANALYSIS REPORT

STORE       DESCRIPTION       QUANTITY       PRICE        SALES
NUMBER

100         LAWNMOWER            5          200.00      1,000.00
100         WEEDEATER           10          100.00      1,000.00
100         WEEDTRIMMER          5           50.00        250.00

                      STORE 100      TOTAL      $2,250.00 *

200         LAWNMOWER           10          100.00      1,000.00
200         HAMMER               5           10.00         50.00

                      STORE 200      TOTAL      $1,050.00 *

300         LAWNMOWER           10          200.00      2,000.00
300         TOOL BOX            10           10.00        100.00
300         FISHING ROD         10           20.00        200.00

                      STORE 300      TOTAL      $2,300.00 *
                      FINAL TOTAL               $5,600.00 **
```

**EXHIBIT 6.8  QBASIC Program and Output for Appl. 6.1**

```
' ***********************************************************************
' *                    PROGRAM IDENTIFICATION                          *
' ***********************************************************************
' *   PROGRAM NAME: CH6APL1                                            *
' *   REMARKS:    THIS PROGRAM PRODUCES A SALES ANALYSIS REPORT FROM A *
' *               SALES FILE.  IT LISTS THE STORE NUMBER, DESCRIPTION, *
' *               QUANTITY, PRICE, AND SALES. CONTROL TOTALS ARE TAKEN *
' *               AND PRINTED FOR EACH STORE.  A FINAL TOTAL IS PRINTED*
' *               AT THE END OF THE REPORT.                            *
' ***********************************************************************
' *                    MAIN-LINE                                       *
' ***********************************************************************
GOSUB STARTUP                        ' PERFORM START-UP
DO UNTIL END.FLAG$ = "YES"
    GOSUB PROCESS.RECORD             ' PERFORM PROCESS-RECORD
LOOP
GOSUB WRAPUP                         ' PERFORM WRAP-UP
END
   ' ********************************************************************
   ' *                    START-UP                                     *
   ' ********************************************************************

STARTUP:

    GOSUB INITIALIZE
    GOSUB OPEN.FILES
    GOSUB HEADINGS                   'PERFORM HEADINGS
    GOSUB READFILE                   'PERFORM READ-FILE
    GOSUB SET.UP.PREVIOUS.NUMBER     'PERFORM SET-UP-PREVIOUS-NUMBER
    RETURN
```

**EXHIBIT 6.8    (Cont.)**

```
      ' ***********************************************************************
      ' *                         INITIALIZE                              *
      ' ***********************************************************************

INITIALIZE:
      END.FLAG$ = "NO": STORE.TOTAL = 0: TOTAL = 0
      DETAIL.LINE$ = "                         ###        \        \        ##        ###.##    #,###.##"
      SUBTOTAL.LINE$ = "                                        STORE ###      TOTAL        $$#,###.## *"
      FINAL.TOTAL.LINE$ = "                                        FINAL TOTAL              $$##,###.## *_*"
      RETURN



      '  ***********************************************************************
      '  *                         OPEN.FILES                              *
      '  ***********************************************************************

OPEN.FILES:
      OPEN "I", #1, "CH6ILL1.DAT"
      RETURN



      '  ***********************************************************************
      '  *                         HEADINGS                                *
      '  ***********************************************************************

HEADINGS:

      LPRINT CHR$(12)
      LPRINT : LPRINT
      LPRINT TAB(41); "SALES ANALYSIS REPORT"
      LPRINT : LPRINT
      LPRINT TAB(22); "STORE"; TAB(32); "DESCRIPTION"; TAB(49); "QUANTITY"; TAB(62); "PRICE"; TAB(73); "SALES"
      LPRINT TAB(22); "NUMBER"
      LPRINT
      RETURN

      '  ***********************************************************************
      '  *                         READ-FILE                               *
      '  ***********************************************************************

READFILE:

      INPUT #1, STORE.NUMBER, DESCRIPTION$, QUANTITY, PRICE
      IF DESCRIPTION$ = "EOF" THEN END.FLAG$ = "YES"
      RETURN

      REM ***********************************************************************
      REM *                     SET-UP-PREVIOUS-FIELD                        *
      REM ***********************************************************************

SET.UP.PREVIOUS.NUMBER:
    PREVIOUS.NUMBER = STORE.NUMBER
    RETURN
```

**EXHIBIT 6.8    (Cont.)**

```
'*******************************************************************
'*                      PROCESS-RECORD                            *
'*******************************************************************
PROCESS.RECORD:

    GOSUB CONTROL.BREAK.CHECK            ' * PERFORM CONTROL-BREAK-CHECK
    GOSUB DETAIL.CALCULATIONS             ' * PERFORM DETAIL-CALCULATIONS
    GOSUB ACCUMULATION                   ' * PERFORM ACCUMULATION
    GOSUB DETAIL.LINE                    ' * PERFORM DETAIL-LINE
    GOSUB READFILE                       ' * PERFORM READ-FILE
    RETURN


    ' ****************************************************************
    ' *                    CONTROL-BREAK-CHECK                      *
    ' ****************************************************************


CONTROL.BREAK.CHECK:
    IF STORE.NUMBER <> PREVIOUS.NUMBER THEN
       GOSUB BLANK.LINE
       GOSUB MINOR.TOTAL.ROUTINE         'PERFORM MINOR-TOTAL-LINE
       GOSUB BLANK.LINE
       '**CANNOT GOSUB BLANK.LINE HERE AS IN COBOL--QBASIC LPRINT
       '**USING ADVANCES BEFORE PRINT AND RESULTS IN ONE TOO MANY BLANK LINES

    END IF
    RETURN



    ' ****************************************************************
    ' *                    MINOR-TOTAL-ROUTINE                      *
    ' ****************************************************************



  MINOR.TOTAL.ROUTINE:

    LPRINT USING SUBTOTAL.LINE$; PREVIOUS.NUMBER; STORE.TOTAL
    TOTAL = TOTAL + STORE.TOTAL
    STORE.TOTAL = 0
    GOSUB SET.UP.PREVIOUS.NUMBER                '* PERFORM SET-UP-PREVIOUS-NUMBER
    RETURN


    '****************************************************************
    '*                    DETAIL-CALCULATIONS                      *
    '****************************************************************

DETAIL.CALCULATIONS:

    SALES = PRICE * QUANTITY
    RETURN
```

**EXHIBIT 6.8    (Cont.)**

```
'*********************************************************************
'*                         ACCUMULATION                             *
'*********************************************************************


ACCUMULATION:

    STORE.TOTAL = STORE.TOTAL + SALES
    RETURN


    '*********************************************************************
    '*                         DETAIL-LINE                              *
    '*********************************************************************

DETAIL.LINE:

    LPRINT USING DETAIL.LINE$; STORE.NUMBER; DESCRIPTION$; QUANTITY; PRICE; SALE
    RETURN


    '*********************************************************************
    '*                           WRAP-UP                                *
    '*********************************************************************

WRAPUP:

    GOSUB SUMMARY.OUTPUT
    GOSUB CLOSE.FILES
    RETURN


    '*********************************************************************
    '*                         BLANK-LINE                               *
    '*********************************************************************
BLANK.LINE:
    LPRINT
    RETURN


    '*********************************************************************
    '*                        SUMMARY-OUTPUT                            *
    '*********************************************************************


SUMMARY.OUTPUT:
    GOSUB BLANK.LINE
    GOSUB MINOR.TOTAL.ROUTINE                   'PERFORM MINOR-TOTAL-ROUTINE
    LPRINT USING FINAL.TOTAL.LINE$; TOTAL


    '*********************************************************************
    '*                         CLOSE FILES                              *
    '*********************************************************************
CLOSE.FILES:
    CLOSE
    RETURN
```

**EXHIBIT 6.8 (Cont.)**

```
                    SALES ANALYSIS REPORT


STORE      DESCRIPTION      QUANTITY      PRICE      SALES
NUMBER


100        LAWNMOWER             5       200.00    1,000.00
100        WEEDEATER            10       100.00    1,000.00
100        WEEDTRIMMER           5        50.00      250.00

                    STORE 100      TOTAL      $2,250.00 *


200        LAWNMOWER            10       100.00    1,000.00
200        HAMMER                5        10.00       50.00

                    STORE 200      TOTAL      $1,050.00 *


300        LAWNMOWER            10       200.00    2,000.00
300        TOOL BOX             10        10.00      100.00
300        FISHING ROD          10        20.00      200.00

                    STORE 300      TOTAL      $2,300.00 *
                    FINAL TOTAL               $5,600.00 **
```

## GROUP-INDICATED SINGLE-LEVEL CONTROL BREAK REPORTS

Figure 6.1 described a single-level control break report. Such reports are called **detail-printed reports**, since the control field(s) print on each detail line. Reports such as this contain relatively few records and are not difficult to read; but when a multitude of lines are written for each control group, the groups become less distinguishable from one another. It's hard to tell where one group stops and the next one starts.

Figure 6.10 illustrates a group-indicated report that uses a single-level control break. In a **group-indicated report**, the control key prints on only the first detail line of a given control group. The subsequent detail lines in the group contain all the other fields except the control key. This technique allows the control groups to be easily distinguished. Notice that STORE-NUMBER prints on only the first detail line of each control group.

### Print Suppression of the Control Field

Figure 6.11 illustrates the necessary logic modification to make the control field print only on the first detail line of each control group. The procedure is as follows:

1. The STORE-NUMBER from the record is initially moved to the detail line.
2. The following modifications are made to the DETAIL-LINE routine:
   a. All input fields *except* STORE-NUMBER are moved to the detail line.
   b. The detail line is written as before.
   c. Spaces or blanks are moved to the detail line.
3. In the MINOR-TOTAL routine, STORE-NUMBER is moved back into the detail line.

## A TWO-LEVEL CONTROL BREAK

In the previous examples, which introduced you to single-level control break logic, we developed logic that allowed only a single breakdown of subtotals. Figure 6.1 and Figure 6.10 both illustrate this type of reporting. Now, suppose a manager of J-Mart Stores needs a report that shows not only a breakdown by store total but also a breakdown of sales by each department in every J-Mart store. Figure 6.2 illustrates the sales analysis report with two levels of totals—one level for each department total in a single store and a second level for each store total. This report, then, is referred to as a two-level control break report. For producing two-level control break reports, *two control fields* are required—a **major control field** and a **minor control field**. The major control field for the sales file is STORE-NUMBER. The minor control field for the sales file is DEPARTMENT-NUMBER. Figure 6.12 illustrates the company structure and clarifies the concepts of major and minor control fields and control totals.

As previously explained, before a single-level control break program can execute, the file must be sorted by the control field. To produce a report with two levels of subtotals, the sales file must be sorted into an ascending sequence according to *both* control fields. Basically, what happens here is that the

---

**FIGURE 6.10    Single-Level Control Break Totals (Group-Indicated) Sample Report**

```
                         SALES ANALYSIS REPORT
    STORE        DESCRIPTION      QUANTITY      PRICE        SALES
    NUMBER

     100         LAWNMOWER            5         200.00       1,000.00
                 WEEDEATER           10         100.00       1,000.00
                 WEEDTRIMMER          5          50.00         250.00

                     STORE 100 TOTAL                        $2,250.00 *

     200         LAWNMOWER           10         100.00       1,000.00
                 HAMMER               5          10.00          50.00

                     STORE 200 TOTAL                        $1,050.00 *

     300         LAWNMOWER           10         200.00       2,000.00
                 TOOL BOX            10          10.00         100.00
                 FISHING ROD         10          20.00         200.00

                     STORE 300 TOTAL                        $2,300.00 *

                     FINAL TOTAL                            $5,600.00 **
```

major and minor control fields combine into one sort key. You'll read more about this in the chapter on sorting (Chapter 9). For now, the key point to note is that the records are ordered so that department numbers of 005 precede department numbers of 007 for Store 100 and all records for Store 100 precede all records for Store 200, and so on.

Figure 6.13 depicts the same two-level sales analysis report, except that its labels show both minor and major totals. Note how the sequence of records is governed by the values in the first two columns. Notice that if the two control fields (the major listed first and the minor listed second) are perceived as a single value, then the single values are arrayed in order of increasing magnitude (ascending sequence).

The programming logic development for a two-level control break program is quite similar to that of a single-level control break program. As before, the main steps for generating a two-level control break report are (1) the initial processing steps that occur in the START-UP module, (2) the record-by-record file-processing steps in the PROCESS-RECORD module, (3) the printing of the last minor and major subtotals, and the printing of the final total in the WRAP-UP module.

## Step-by-Step Processing

In the START-UP module, the following activities must occur:

1. Variables are initialized.
2. Files are opened.
3. Report headings are printed.
4. The first record is read.

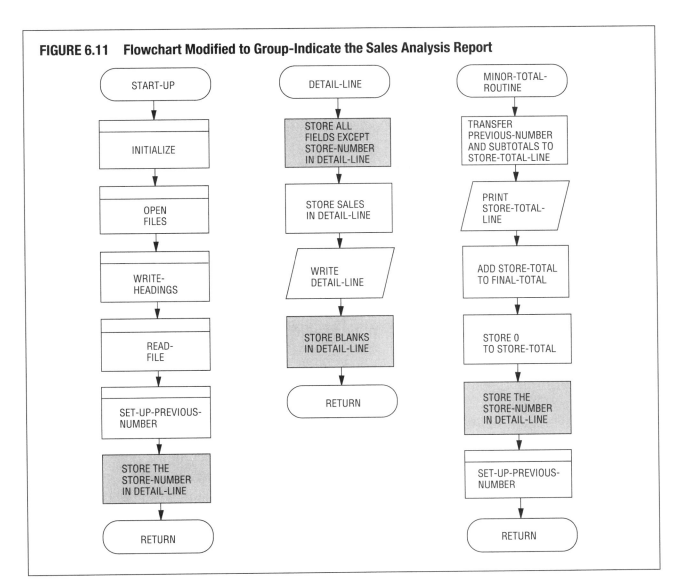

**FIGURE 6.11    Flowchart Modified to Group-Indicate the Sales Analysis Report**

5. *The major and minor control fields are moved to their respective work area variables (PREVIOUS-STORE and PREVIOUS-DEPARTMENT).*

The only other addition to the previous single-level control break examples is the transfer of *two* control fields to their respective work area variables

instead of only one. In Figure 6.14, a sales file illustrates the reading of the first record into the input area as the first step. The first two fields listed are STORE-NUMBER and DEPARTMENT-NUMBER—the major and minor keys, respectively. The second step illustrates the storing of the STORE-NUMBER value, 100, into the PREVIOUS-STORE variable

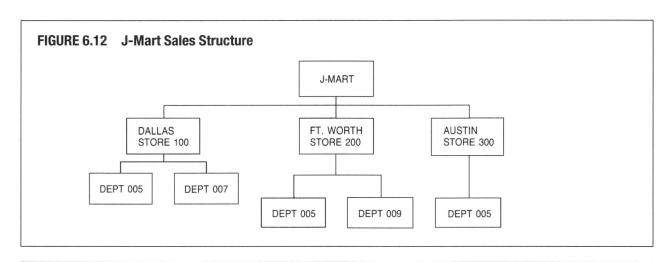

**FIGURE 6.12    J-Mart Sales Structure**

**FIGURE 6.13    Two-Level Control Break Report Highlighting Control Totals**

```
                          SALES ANALYSIS REPORT

        STORE
        NUMBER    DEPARTMENT    DESCRIPTION    QUANTITY    PRICE       SALES

         100        005         LAWNMOWER         5        200.00    1,000.00
         100        005         WEEDEATER        10        100.00    1,000.00
         100        005         WEEDTRIMMER       5         50.00      250.00
                                                                                    Minor
                         DEPARTMENT  005   TOTAL            $2,250.00  *            Total
                                                                                    Line
         100        007         SHIRT             1         10.00       10.00
         100        007         TIE              10          5.00       50.00

                         DEPARTMENT  007   TOTAL             $ 60.00   *            Major
                               STORE  100   TOTAL           $2,310.00  **           Total
                                                                                    Line
         200        005         LAWNMOWER        10        100.00    1,000.00
         200        005         HAMMER            5         10.00       50.00

                         DEPARTMENT  005   TOTAL           $1,050.00  *

         200        009         DIAMOND RING      2        500.00    1,000.00
         200        009         NECKLACE          3        100.00      300.00

                         DEPARTMENT  009   TOTAL           $1,300.00  *
                               STORE  200   TOTAL          $2,350.00  **

         300        005         LAWNMOWER        10        200.00    2,000.00
         300        005         TOOL BOX         10         10.00      100.00
         300        005         FISHING ROD      10         20.00      200.00

                         DEPARTMENT  005   TOTAL           $2,300.00  *
                               STORE  300   TOTAL          $2,300.00  **
                               FINAL  TOTAL                $6,960.00  ***
```

and the DEPARTMENT-NUMBER value, 005, into the PREVIOUS-DEPARTMENT variable. Both the major and minor control fields are stored in their respective work variables because (1) the program must not only be able to compare the current store number to the previous store number in order to detect a *major* control break, but (2) it must be able to compare the current department number to the previous department number in order to detect a *minor* control break.

The PROCESS-RECORD module for a two-level control break is identical to that of a single-level control break; in other words, it (1) invokes a CONTROL-BREAK-CHECK module, (2) performs the DETAIL-CALCULATIONS module, (3) calls the ACCUMULATION module, (4) executes the DETAIL-LINE module, and (5) performs the READ-FILE module.

The WRAP-UP module:

1. Writes the minor total line.
2. Accumulates the minor total into the major total.
3. Writes the major total line.
4. Accumulates the major total into the final total.
5. Writes the final total.
6. Closes the files.

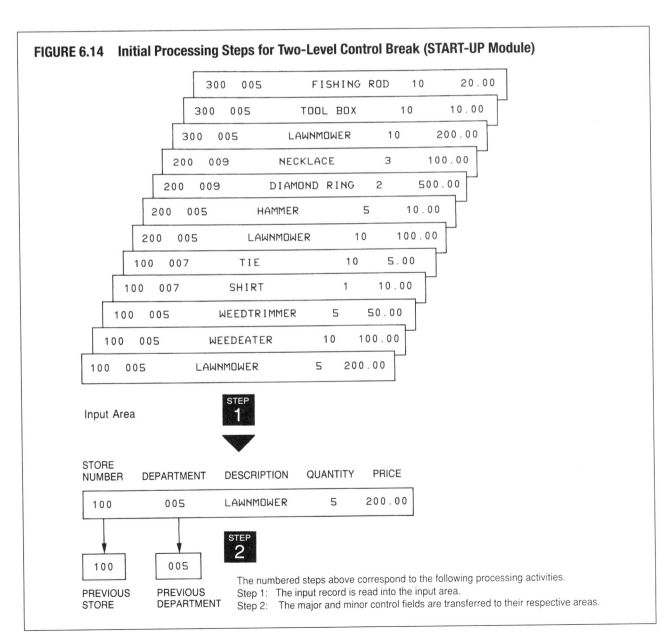

**FIGURE 6.14   Initial Processing Steps for Two-Level Control Break (START-UP Module)**

The numbered steps above correspond to the following processing activities.
Step 1:   The input record is read into the input area.
Step 2:   The major and minor control fields are transferred to their respective areas.

The major difference between this WRAP-UP and the previous one for a single-level control break is that this one prints both the last minor and major totals prior to printing the final total. Also, when the minor total is printed, it has not yet been carried forward and added to the major total; therefore, this step needs to be accomplished. The same is true, in turn, of the major total; it too needs to be carried forward and added to the final total.

## Comparison Sequence for Control Fields

Once the initial values of the control fields are established in the PREVIOUS-STORE and PREVIOUS-DEPARTMENT variables, the next important consideration is the sequence by which the control fields are compared. Does it matter which control field is compared with its respective "previous" variable first? The answer is, Yes, it does matter. The comparison always starts with the *major* control field first, followed by the next lower control field. For example, in the sales analysis report problem, STORE-NUMBER would be compared with PREVIOUS-STORE number first; if the values are unequal, both DEPARTMENT TOTAL and STORE TOTAL must print. If STORE-NUMBER is equal to its previous number, then the program compares DEPARTMENT-NUMBER with PREVIOUS-DEPARTMENT; if the values are unequal, then only

DEPARTMENT-TOTAL prints. Note an important point here: if a higher level control break occurs, it *forces lower level control breaks to occur also*. The reason is that if the file is sequenced by both major and minor control fields, and if the current STORE-NUMBER is different from PREVIOUS-STORE, then certainly this would indicate an automatic change in department number. Even if the following record of the next group should contain a department number that is the same as the previous one, it would be solely coincidental; the department number would have to belong to a different store. Also, at the end of the file (END-FLAG = "YES"), before the final total prints, all control breaks are forced to occur, starting at the lower level and progressing to the higher level. Finally, after all subtotals (from lower to higher) have printed, the final total prints.

## Processing the Sales File

**Detail Processing of Input Records.** As previously referenced, Figure 6.14 illustrates the reading of the first record into the input area and the subsequent transferring of both the major and minor control fields to their respective work areas—PREVIOUS-STORE and PREVIOUS-DEPARTMENT.

The first three records that belong to DEPARTMENT-NUMBER 005 are processed and a DE-

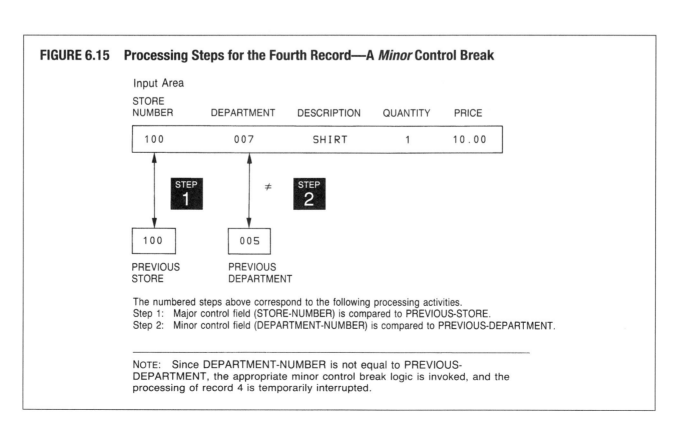

FIGURE 6.15    Processing Steps for the Fourth Record—A *Minor* Control Break

Input Area

| STORE NUMBER | DEPARTMENT | DESCRIPTION | QUANTITY | PRICE |
|---|---|---|---|---|
| 100 | 007 | SHIRT | 1 | 10.00 |

STEP 1    ≠    STEP 2

PREVIOUS STORE: 100

PREVIOUS DEPARTMENT: 005

The numbered steps above correspond to the following processing activities.
Step 1:   Major control field (STORE-NUMBER) is compared to PREVIOUS-STORE.
Step 2:   Minor control field (DEPARTMENT-NUMBER) is compared to PREVIOUS-DEPARTMENT.

NOTE:   Since DEPARTMENT-NUMBER is not equal to PREVIOUS-DEPARTMENT, the appropriate minor control break logic is invoked, and the processing of record 4 is temporarily interrupted.

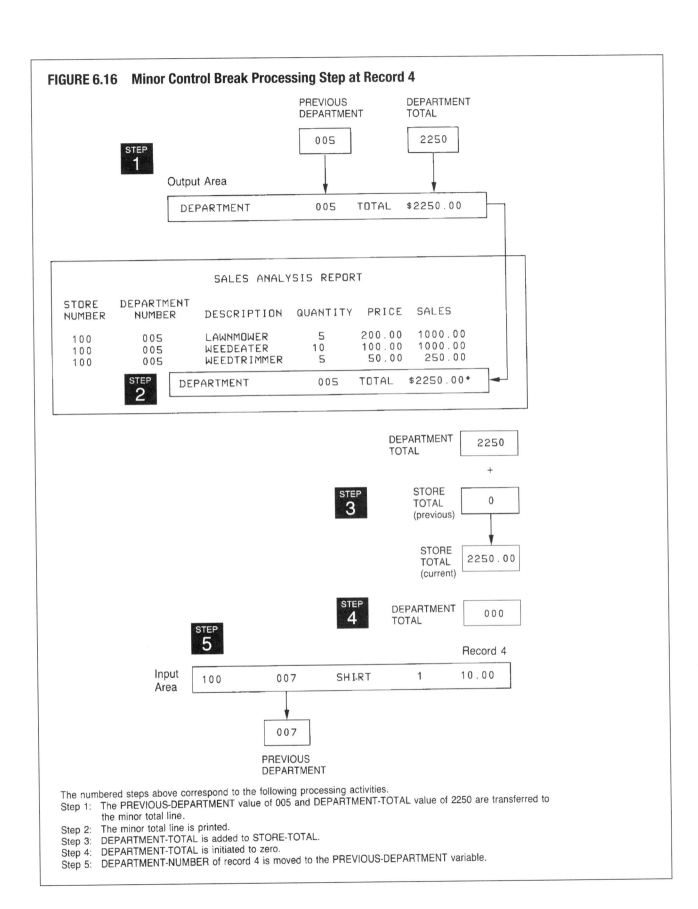

**FIGURE 6.16    Minor Control Break Processing Step at Record 4**

The numbered steps above correspond to the following processing activities.

Step 1:  The PREVIOUS-DEPARTMENT value of 005 and DEPARTMENT-TOTAL value of 2250 are transferred to the minor total line.

Step 2:  The minor total line is printed.

Step 3:  DEPARTMENT-TOTAL is added to STORE-TOTAL.

Step 4:  DEPARTMENT-TOTAL is initiated to zero.

Step 5:  DEPARTMENT-NUMBER of record 4 is moved to the PREVIOUS-DEPARTMENT variable.

PARTMENT-TOTAL is accumulated. This detail processing is similar to that found in Figures 6.5 through 6.7.

Figure 6.15 illustrates the control break checking that takes place for the fourth record. In this case, DEPARTMENT-NUMBER is unequal to PREVIOUS-DEPARTMENT, and a minor control break results. Figure 6.16 illustrates the minor control break steps that result from a break on the fourth record. PREVIOUS-DEPARTMENT and DEPARTMENT-TOTAL are transferred to the minor total line and printed on the report (steps 1 and 2). DEPARTMENT-TOTAL, 2250, is added to STORE-TOTAL (step 3), and DEPARTMENT-TOTAL is then zeroed (step 4). The DEPARTMENT-NUMBER of 007 from the fourth record is then moved to the PREVIOUS-DEPARTMENT variable (step 5).

After the first minor total line is printed, processing of record four resumes. Records four and five belong to the same minor control group (007); therefore, they receive normal detail processing.

Figure 6.17 illustrates the processing of record six, which results in a major control break. STORE-NUMBER, 200, is unequal to the PREVIOUS-STORE value, 100; therefore, logic relating to the major total is invoked, and the processing of record six is temporarily suspended. Panels A and B of Figure 6.18 depict the processing of the major control break processing steps. Panel A shows how the logic that produces the minor total is performed

first, and Panel B depicts the major total logic that is executed next. If a major control break is encountered, the minor control break steps are performed first, and then the major control break steps are executed. The minor control break segment (panel A) shows the formatting and printing of the minor total line. Then DEPARTMENT-TOTAL, 60.00, is added to STORE-TOTAL, bringing the latter to 2310.00. DEPARTMENT-TOTAL is next cleared to zeros, and PREVIOUS-DEPARTMENT is updated to 005 (the department number of record six).

Once the minor total logic is taken care of, the major control break is performed (panel B). The nature of this logic is the same as that of the minor control break, except that it deals with STORE-NUMBER and STORE-TOTAL rather than DEPARTMENT-NUMBER and DEPARTMENT-TOTAL. In steps 6 through 9, the major total line is formatted with the proper values and printed; STORE-TOTAL is added forward into FINAL-TOTAL; STORE-TOTAL is zeroed and STORE-NUMBER, 200, is moved to PREVIOUS-STORE.

At this point, the processing of record six resumes, and the remainder of the minor and major control groups would be processed in the same manner as previously described.

Next, program design will be presented for the two-level control break problem. The basic logic differences will be highlighted.

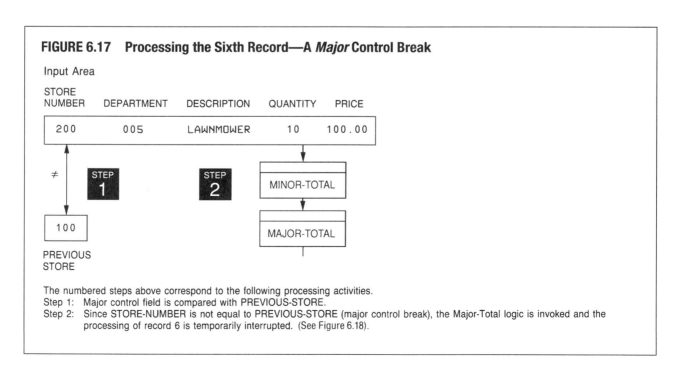

**FIGURE 6.17   Processing the Sixth Record—A *Major* Control Break**

Input Area

| STORE NUMBER | DEPARTMENT | DESCRIPTION | QUANTITY | PRICE |
|---|---|---|---|---|
| 200 | 005 | LAWNMOWER | 10 | 100.00 |

The numbered steps above correspond to the following processing activities.
Step 1:  Major control field is compared with PREVIOUS-STORE.
Step 2:  Since STORE-NUMBER is not equal to PREVIOUS-STORE (major control break), the Major-Total logic is invoked and the processing of record 6 is temporarily interrupted. (See Figure 6.18).

## FIGURE 6.18  Major Control Break Processing Steps

A major control break requires that the minor control break steps be done first, then followed by major control break steps. (Interrupting detail processing of record 6)

**Panel A — Minor Control Break Steps Invoked First**

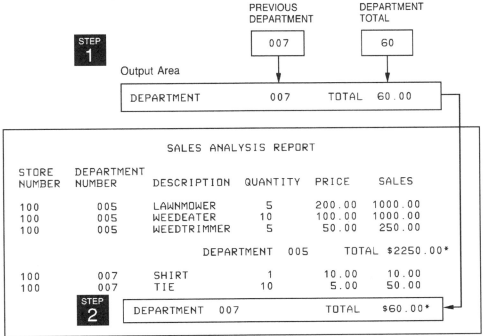

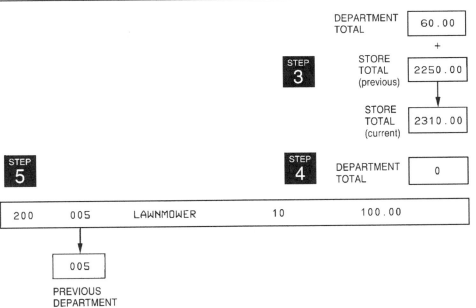

The numbered steps above correspond to the following processing activities.

Step 1:  The minor total line is formatted.
Step 2:  The minor total line is printed.
Step 3:  DEPARTMENT-TOTAL, 60, is added to STORE-TOTAL.
Step 4:  DEPARTMENT-TOTAL is zeroed out.
Step 5:  DEPARTMENT-NUMBER, 005, from the sixth record is transferred to PREVIOUS-DEPARTMENT.

**FIGURE 6.18 (Cont.)**

**Panel B—Major Control Break Steps Performed Next**

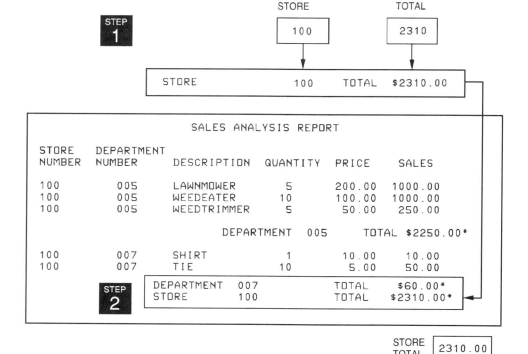

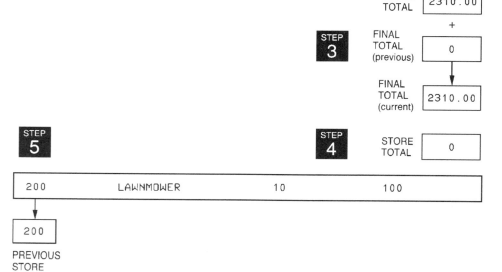

At this point, the processing of record 6 resumes. The remainder of the minor and major control groups would be processed in the same manner as previously discussed.

The numbered steps above correspond to the following processing activities.
Step 1: PREVIOUS-STORE and STORE-TOTAL are transferred to the Major-Total line.
Step 2: The major total line is printed.
Step 3: STORE-TOTAL is accumulated into FINAL-TOTAL.
Step 4: STORE-TOTAL is zeroed out.
Step 5: STORE-NUMBER from the sixth record is moved to PREVIOUS-STORE.

# A Sales Analysis Report Using a Two-Level Control Break Program

## Program Requirements

The department managers of several J-Mart stores have requested a sales analysis report that breaks down total sales by individual department as well as by each store in the company. The report will also include a final company total.

## Output Design

As previously noted, Figure 6.13 illustrates the two-level sales analysis report to be produced. Exhibit 6.9 depicts the associated print chart.

## Input Design

The input record format of the sales record is illustrated in Exhibit 6.10. The fields are: STORE-NUMBER and DEPARTMENT-NUMBER (the major and minor control fields), DESCRIPTION, QUANTITY and PRICE.

## Test Data

Exhibit 6.11 lists a representative set of test case records for testing the program.

**EXHIBIT 6.9    Printer Spacing Chart for Two-Level Control Break**

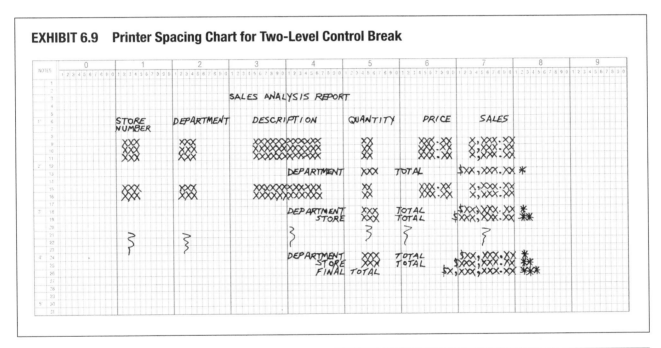

**EXHIBIT 6.10    Record Layout for Sales File That Includes Department Number**

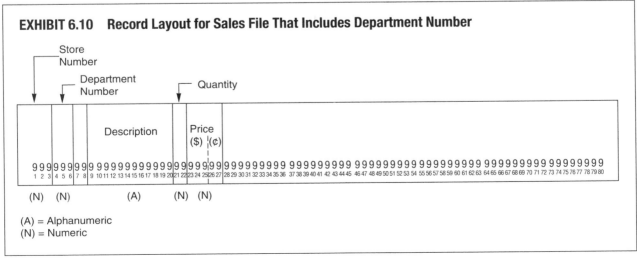

## Logic Considerations

The control break program logic should:

1. Provide for a control break check to determine if subtotals are to be taken.
   a. Check for a control field change for the major control field. If there is a change, print both a department total and a store total.
   b. Check for a control field change for the minor control field. If there is a change, print only a department total.
2. Print a detail line for every record in the file.
3. Print a final total.

## Program Design

**Hierarchy Chart.** Exhibit 6.12 illustrates the hierarchy chart for the general design of the two-level control break program. The basic three modules are shown, as usual. Under the START-UP module, as you can see, there are two modules for handling previous numbers. One is called SET-UP-PREVIOUS-DEPARTMENT and the second is called SET-UP-PREVIOUS-STORE.

The PROCESS-RECORD module is decomposed into the same five modules shown in the previous example—CONTROL-BREAK-CHECK, DETAIL-CALCULATION, ACCUMULATION, DETAIL-LINE, and READ-FILE. The significant difference is found in the CONTROL-BREAK-CHECK module, which is here further decomposed into two functional areas—a check for a major control field change and a check for a minor control field change. If there is a major control break, MINOR-TOTAL-ROUTINE and MAJOR-TOTAL-ROUTINE are executed. If there is not a major control break

but there is a minor control break, only MINOR-TOTAL-ROUTINE is performed.

The WRAP-UP module, compared to the same module in the single-level problem previously presented, has one addition: Both MINOR-TOTAL-ROUTINE and MAJOR-TOTAL-ROUTINE must be invoked prior to printing FINAL-TOTAL for the same reason previously discussed in the single-level control break problem.

**Structured Program Flowchart.** Exhibit 6.13 illustrates the two-level control break logic in structured flowcharting form. The MAIN-LINE module appears as usual. The START-UP module includes predefined process blocks for both the SET-UP-PREVIOUS-STORE and the SET-UP-PREVIOUS-DEPARTMENT modules. These are established as callable modules, since they will be invoked from not only the START-UP module but also from the minor and major total routines. Once again, the PROCESS-RECORD module appears as it did for a single-level control break, and the WRAP-UP module includes both MINOR-TOTAL-ROUTINE and MAJOR-TOTAL-ROUTINE prior to printing final totals. As previously explained, at the end of the file, neither of the two subtotal lines have been printed, nor have the subtotals been accumulated forward into the next higher level total. Those two routines will accomplish these tasks.

**The CONTROL-BREAK-CHECK Module.** Except for this module, the third-level modules remain basically the same. First, a comparison determines if STORE-NUMBER is equal to PREVIOUS-STORE. If this condition test is true, no processing takes place; processing simply resumes at the next connector symbol. On the other hand, if the condition test is false, then MINOR-TOTAL-ROUTINE and

---

**EXHIBIT 6.11    Two-Level Control Break—Test Data**

| STORE | DEPARTMENT | DESCRIPTION | QUANTITY | PRICE |
|-------|------------|-------------|----------|-------|
| 100 | 005 | LAWNMOWER | 5 | 200.00 |
| 100 | 005 | WEEDEATER | 10 | 100.00 |
| 100 | 005 | WEEDTRIMMER | 5 | 50.00 |
| 100 | 007 | SHIRT | 1 | 10.00 |
| 100 | 007 | TIE | 10 | 5.00 |
| 200 | 005 | LAWNMOWER | 10 | 100.00 |
| 200 | 005 | HAMMER | 5 | 10.00 |
| 200 | 009 | DIAMOND RING | 2 | 500.00 |
| 200 | 009 | NECKLACE | 3 | 100.00 |
| 300 | 005 | LAWNMOWER | 10 | 200.00 |
| 300 | 005 | TOOL BOX | 10 | 10.00 |
| 300 | 005 | FISHING ROD | 10 | 20.00 |

MAJOR-TOTAL-ROUTINE are invoked in that order. If no change in the store number occurs, the next processing step compares DEPARTMENT-NUMBER with PREVIOUS-DEPARTMENT. If this condition test is true, then no processing takes place; it simply resumes at the next connector symbol. Otherwise, if the condition is false, then only MINOR-TOTAL-ROUTINE is executed. A noteworthy point is that if the major control break occurs and both MINOR-TOTAL-ROUTINE and MAJOR-TOTAL-ROUTINE are executed, the minor control break check will always test to be true and will simply cause processing to resume at the RETURN. Why will it always test to be true? The reason is that, at this point, DEPARTMENT-NUMBER must equal PREVIOUS-DEPARTMENT, since PREVIOUS-DEPARTMENT would have been previously stored with DEPARTMENT-NUMBER during MINOR-TOTAL-ROUTINE. Look at the last step of MINOR-TOTAL-ROUTINE. The CONTROL-BREAK-CHECK module is thus established without nesting the check for a *minor* control break within the check for a *major* control break. This sim-

plifies the logic. Anytime the programmer can reduce program complexity, he or she should do so. Another strong justification for this method is that it simplifies the logic significantly when the programmer is faced with, let's say, a *seven*-level control break. A programmer runs out of room on the coding sheet if he or she attempts to indent for each new nested IF. In the "real world," the programmer will encounter a number of reports that require a multiplicity of control break events.

MINOR-TOTAL-ROUTINE symbolizes (1) the transfer of DEPARTMENT-TOTAL and PREVIOUS-DEPARTMENT to the output area, (2) the printing of the minor total line, (3) the accumulation of DEPARTMENT-TOTAL into STORE-TOTAL, (4) the storing of zero in DEPARTMENT-TOTAL, and (5) the invoking of SET-UP-PREVIOUS-DEPARTMENT.

MAJOR-TOTAL-ROUTINE depicts (1) the transfer of STORE-TOTAL and PREVIOUS-STORE to the output area, (2) the printing of the major subtotal line, (3) the accumulation of STORE-TOTAL into the FINAL-TOTAL, (4) the initializing of STORE-

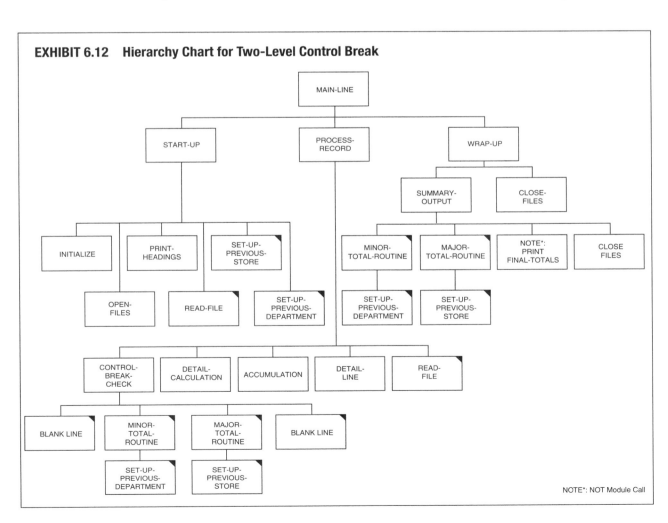

**EXHIBIT 6.12  Hierarchy Chart for Two-Level Control Break**

NOTE*: NOT Module Call

**EXHIBIT 6.13  Structured Flowchart for Sales Analysis Report with Two-Level Control Break**

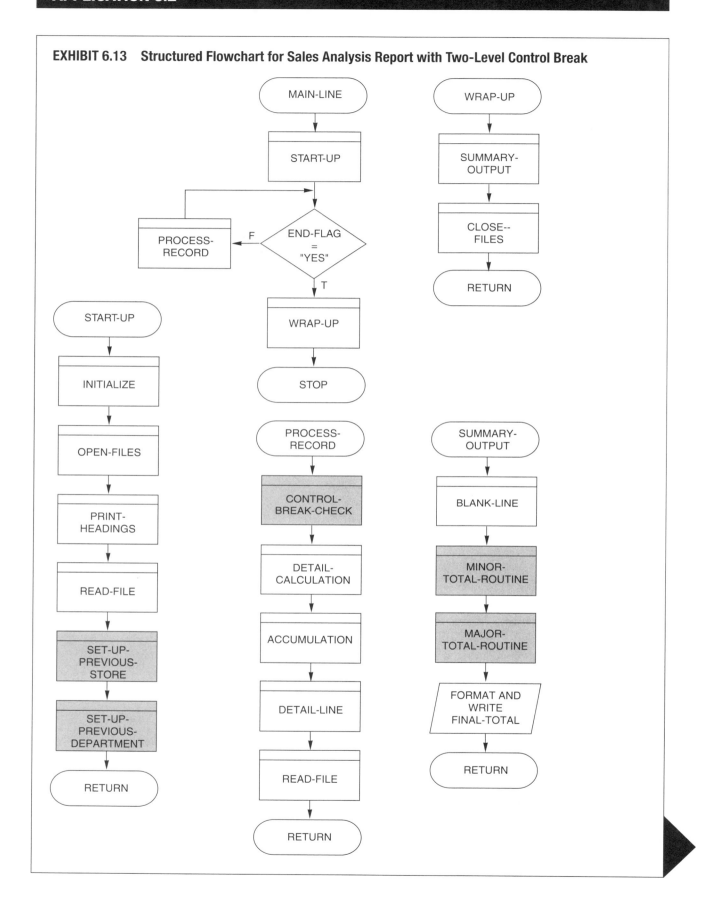

**EXHIBIT 6.13    (Cont.)**

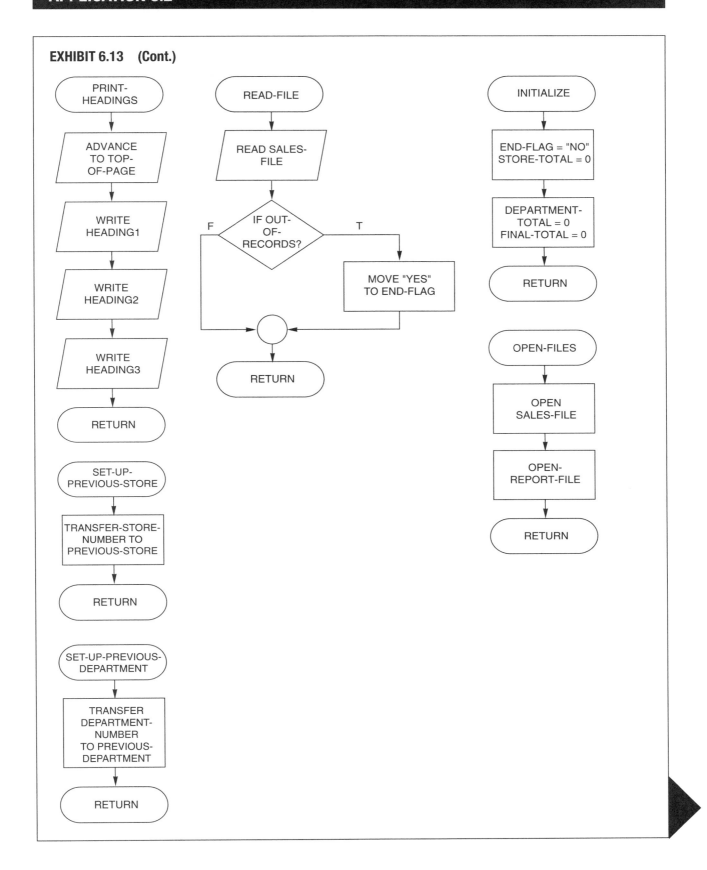

**EXHIBIT 6.13   (Cont.)**          **2 Alternate Methods**

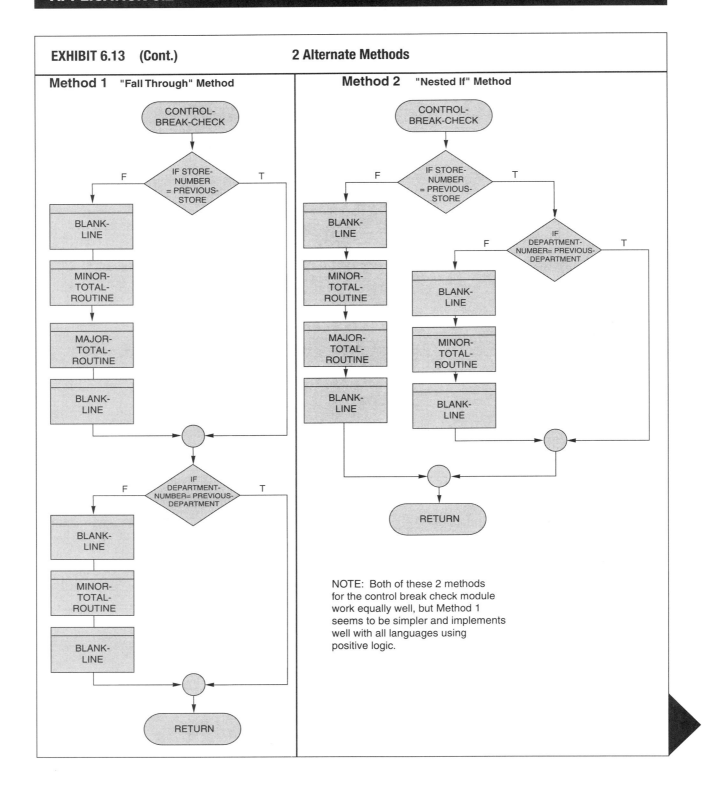

**Method 1**  "Fall Through" Method

**Method 2**  "Nested If" Method

NOTE:  Both of these 2 methods
for the control break check module
work equally well, but Method 1
seems to be simpler and implements
well with all languages using
positive logic.

**EXHIBIT 6.13    (Cont.)**

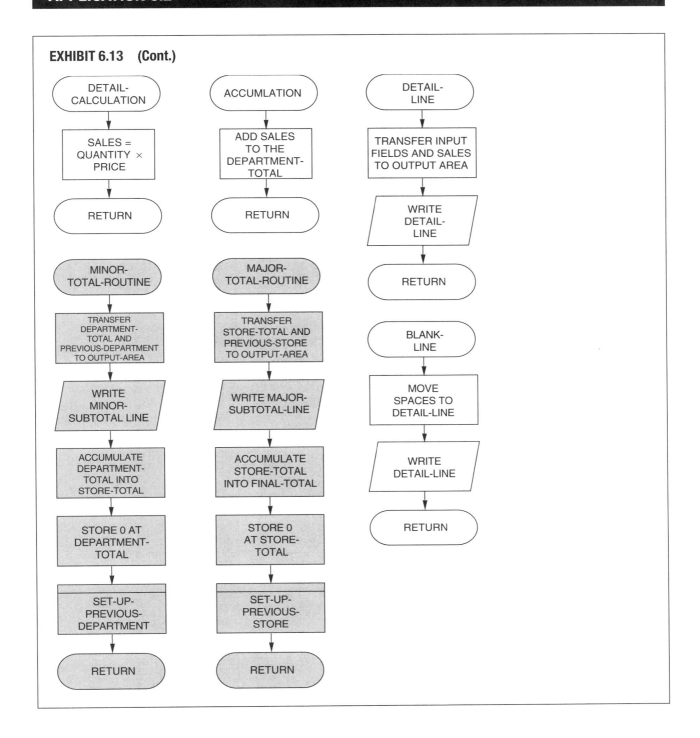

TOTAL to zero, and (5) the performing of the SET-UP-PREVIOUS-STORE module.

The accumulation process in the minor and major total routines is sometimes called "rolling totals forward," since the minor total is "rolled" into the major total and the major total is "rolled" forward into the final total. The rationale for rolling totals forward rather than adding the value into all three totals from the ACCUMULATION routine in the PROCESS-RECORD module is to save execution time. This technique requires fewer calculations. The only time the program adds is when

there is a change in a control group, as opposed to the alternative of adding SALES into all three totals (DEPARTMENT-TOTAL, STORE-TOTAL, and FINAL-TOTAL) every time a record is read. When the computer is processing very large files with a multitude of subtotals to be accumulated at numerous control breaks, the execution time saved can become significant.

**Pseudocode.**   Exhibit 6.14 illustrates the pseudocode for this two-level control break problem.

---

**EXHIBIT 6.14    Pseudocode for Two-Level Control Break (Appl. 6.2)**

```
*mainline
     start-up
     dowhile end-flag = "no"
          process-record
     enddo
     wrap-up
     stop
*start-up
     initialize
     open-files
     headings
     read-file
     set-up-previous-store
     set-up-previous-department
     return
*initialize
     end-flag = "no"
     store-total = 0
     department-total = 0
     final-total = 0
     return
*open-files
     open sales-file
     open report-file
     return
*process-record
     control-break-check
     detail-calculation
     accumulation
     detail-line
     read-file
     return
*wrap-up
     summary-output
     close-files
     return
*summary-output
     blank-line
     minor-total-routine
     major-total-routine
     move final-total to final-total-line
     print final-total
     return
```

```
*close-files
     close sales-file
     close report-file
     return
*headings
     print page heading
     print column heading1
     print column heading2
     return
*read-file
     read sales-file
     when no more records store "yes" at end-flag
     endread
     return
*set-up-previous-store
     move store-number to previous-store
     return
*set-up-previous-department
     move department-number to previous-department
     return
*control-break-check
     if store-number = previous-store
          then null
     else
          blank-line
          minor-total-routine
          major-total-routine
          blank-line
     endif
     if department-number = previous-department
          then null
     else
          blank-line
          minor-total-routine
          blank-line
     endif
     return
*detail-calculation
     sales = quantity × price
     return
```

---

**EXHIBIT 6.14     (Cont.)**

*accumulation
    add sales to department-total
    return
*detail-line
    transfer input fields and sales to output area
    print detail-line
    return
*minor-total-routine
    transfer department-total and previous-department to
        output area
    print minor-total-line
    add department-total into store-total
    store zeros into department-total
    set-up-previous-department
    return
*major-total-routine
    transfer store-total and previous-store to output area
    print major-total-line
    add store-total into final-total
    store zeros into store-total
    set-up-previous-store
    return
*blank-line
    move spaces to detail-line
    write detail-line
    return

**Alternate "Nested if" Method**

```
*control-break-check
    If store-number = previous-number
        then
                if department-number = previous-department
                    then null
                else
                        blank-line
                        minor-total-routine
                        blank-line
        endif
    else
                blank-line
                minor-total-routine
                major-total-routine
                blank-line
    endif
    return
```

## Program Logic to Handle Printing Subtotals at Page Breaks

A common problem in printing control break reports is the occurrence of a page break when the last record of the group is being processed and written. Unless the logic is handled carefully, the subtotals are printed at the top of the next page—something to avoid. Subtotals should appear together with their records even if it means printing beyond the last line that would normally print on a page of the report. You must be careful to allow a bottom margin wide enough to permit the printing of the required number of subtotal lines without printing across the perforation. Figure 6.19 illustrates the structured flowchart modifications that will handle this.

notice that the BOTTOM-OF-PAGE-CHECK module is placed after the CONTROL-BREAK-CHECK module. This sequence ensures that the following steps occur in the proper order:

1. The last detail line of a group prints as the last line of a control group. This line is also assumed to be the *last line* to normally print on a page. LINE-COUNT is incremented by 1 to reflect that one more line has been printed.
2. The next record is read (the first record of the next control group).
3. The bottom of the PROCESS-RECORD module is encountered, and program control passes back to MAIN-LINE.
4. An end-of-file test is made; if false, the program control passes back to the PROCESS-RECORD module.
5. The first thing that happens now is that CONTROL-BREAK-CHECK is performed. It senses that a control break exists; therefore, MINOR-TOTAL ROUTINE and MAJOR-TOTAL-ROUTINE are executed, *thus producing the two subtotal lines at the bottom of the same page as the control group.* LINE-COUNT is incremented to reflect the inclusion of the subtotal lines.
6. The next module executed is BOTTOM-OF-PAGE-CHECK. At this point,the condition test is made that determines that a page break has occurred. Next, the PRINT-HEADINGS module is invoked, causing the paper to advance to the next page and the headings to be printed.

The only peculiarity in the construction of the modules to handle this situation is that the line increments in MINOR-TOTAL-ROUTINE and in MAJOR-TOTAL-ROUTINE cause the number of lines in LINE-COUNT to be incremented *beyond* the line count needed to invoke the PRINT-HEADINGS module. The reason for this is that the line count is incremented to 50 when the last detail line for the page is printed. Then, during the minor and major total routines, LINE-COUNT is incremented by 4 more lines (2 are added subsequent to the writing of each of the two subtotal lines), making a total of 54 in LINE-COUNT. This makes no difference, from a programming logic perspective, since this condition (if $54 > 50$) is just as *true* as the other condition (if $51 > 50$).

## A THREE-LEVEL CONTROL BREAK

The management of J-Mart wants to generate a report that depicts an even further breakdown in sales that shows a subtotal for each salesperson in each department. This new report will show (1) a major breakdown in sales by each store, (2) sales by each department, and (3) sales by each salesperson in the company. This type of report is called a three-level control break report and is illustrated in Figure 6.3. Figure 6.20 depicts the hierarchical breakdown of J-Mart stores that reflects the relationship of the various stores, departments, and salespersons.

## FIGURE 6.19  Two-Level Control Break Modified

(Allows subtotals to print on same page as detail record group in the event of a page break occurring concurrently with last record of a control group)

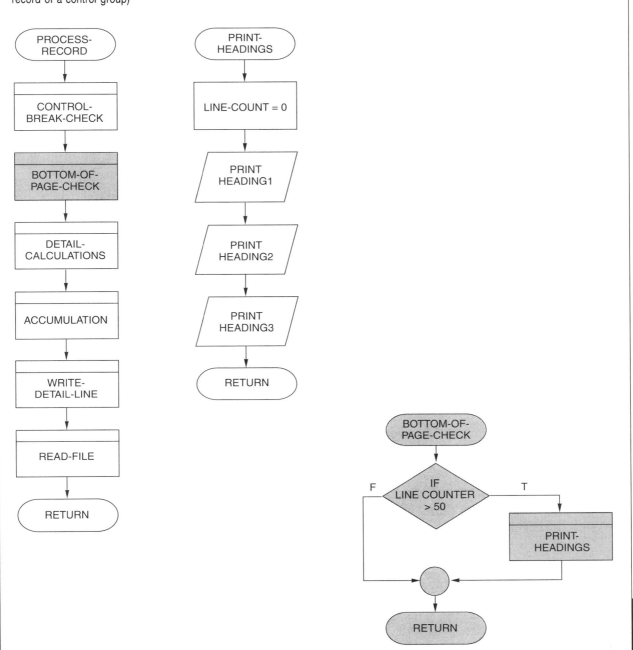

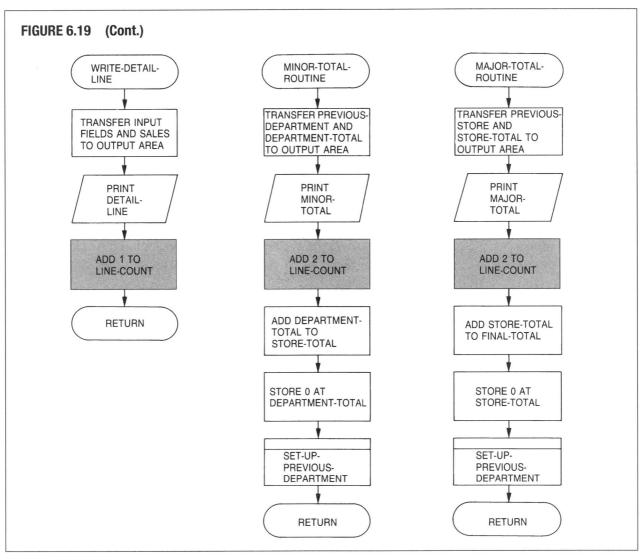

**FIGURE 6.19  (Cont.)**

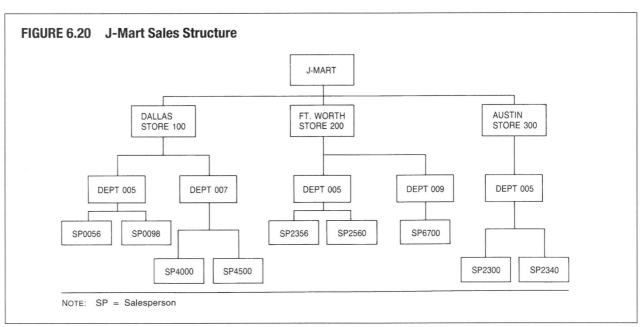

**FIGURE 6.20   J-Mart Sales Structure**

NOTE:  SP = Salesperson

# A Sales Analysis Report Using a Three-Level Control Break Program

## Program Requirements

The management of J-Mart Stores wants to produce a three-level control break sales analysis report with the following specifications:

1. The heading line is to contain the page number and the date.
2. The report is to be detail-printed; that is, each detail line is to be printed.
3. A subtotal is to be accumulated and printed for each salesperson in each department.
4. A subtotal is to be accumulated and printed for each department in each store.
5. A subtotal is to be accumulated and printed for each store in the company.
6. A grand total is to be accumulated and printed at the end of the report.

The J-Mart sales structure is depicted in Figure 6.20.

## Output Design

Figure 6.3 illustrates the modified sales analysis report to be produced, and Exhibit 6.15 illustrates the print chart to be completed prior to designing the logic and writing the program.

## Input Design

The input record format of the sales record is illustrated in Exhibit 6.16. One additional field is shown—Salesperson Number.

Exhibit 6.17 lists a representative set of test case records for testing the program.

## Logic Considerations

The program must provide one additional level of accumulation and printing not included in the previous two-level control break example. The minor total routine should handle the accumulation process of the department total and printing of the salesperson total; *the store accumulation and the printing of the department total should be handled by an* **intermediate total routine:** (invoked by an **intermediate control field** *change)*, and the major total routine will handle the accumulation of the final total and the printing of the store total. Also, prior to printing the final total, the program must handle the printing of the three subtotals and rolling the last set of subtotals forward into their respective next higher level subtotals.

## Program Design

**Hierarchy Chart.** Exhibit 6.18 illustrates the general logic of a three-level control break program in hierarchy chart form. The MAIN-LINE module appears unchanged. The START-UP module contains

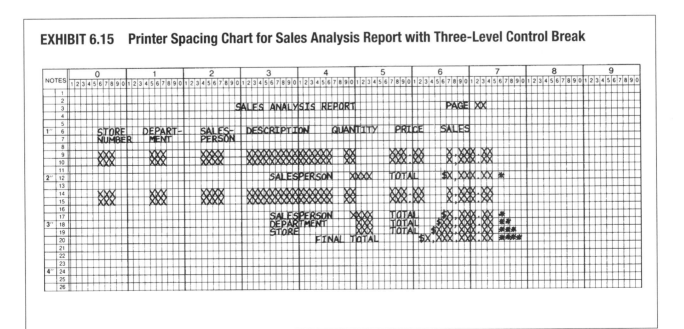

**EXHIBIT 6.15    Printer Spacing Chart for Sales Analysis Report with Three-Level Control Break**

the quite familiar first four steps—initializing the variables, opening the files, printing the headings, and reading the first record. The next three modules are SET-UP-PREVIOUS-STORE, SET-UP-PREVIOUS-DEPARTMENT, and SET-UP-PREVIOUS-SALESPERSON. The PROCESS-RECORD module is shown with a BOTTOM-OF-PAGE-CHECK module to handle the printing of subtotals, as discussed in the previous section.

The CONTROL-BREAK-CHECK module is decomposed into three levels in order to reflect the three levels of subtotals to be printed. The three comparison steps detect whether a *major* control break, an *intermediate* control break, or a *minor* control break has occurred. The comparison sequence is from higher level control break toward lower level control break. The major break is tested first,

the intermediate break is tested second, followed by the test for a minor break.

When a major control break occurs, the routines are invoked in the following order: (1) MINOR-TOTAL-ROUTINE, (2) INTERMEDIATE-TOTAL-ROUTINE, and (3) MAJOR-TOTAL-ROUTINE. If an intermediate control break occurs, MINOR-TOTAL-ROUTINE and INTERMEDIATE-TOTAL-ROUTINE are invoked, in that order. If only a minor control break occurs, only MINOR-TOTAL-ROUTINE is called.

The WRAP-UP module shows the inclusion of MINOR-TOTAL-ROUTINE, INTERMEDIATE-TOTAL-ROUTINE, and MAJOR-TOTAL-ROUTINE, in that order. As they did in the two-level control breaks when the end of the file was encountered, these modules print and roll forward the subtotals prior to printing the final total.

---

**EXHIBIT 6.16 Record Layout for Sales File That Includes Salesperson Number as Minor Control Field**

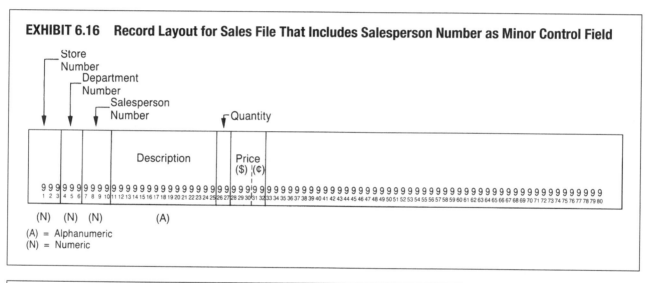

---

**EXHIBIT 6.17 Three-Level Control Break—Test Cases**

| STORE | DEPARTMENT | SALESPERSON | DESCRIPTION | QUANTITY | PRICE |
|-------|------------|-------------|-------------|----------|-------|
| 100 | 005 | 0056 | LAWNMOWER | 5 | 200.00 |
| 100 | 005 | 0056 | WEEDEATER | 10 | 100.00 |
| 100 | 005 | 0098 | WEEDTRIMMER | 5 | 50.00 |
| 100 | 005 | 0098 | LAWN FERTILIZER | 1 | 10.00 |
| 100 | 007 | 4000 | SHIRT | 1 | 10.00 |
| 100 | 007 | 4000 | TIE | 10 | 5.00 |
| 100 | 007 | 4500 | JEANS | 1 | 15.00 |
| 100 | 007 | 4500 | SHIRT | 2 | 20.00 |
| 200 | 005 | 2356 | LAWNMOWER | 10 | 100.00 |
| 200 | 005 | 2356 | HAMMER | 5 | 10.00 |
| 200 | 005 | 2560 | SAW | 1 | 20.00 |
| 200 | 005 | 2560 | RULER | 1 | 10.00 |
| 200 | 009 | 6700 | DIAMOND RING | 2 | 500.00 |
| 200 | 009 | 6700 | NECKLACE | 3 | 100.00 |
| 300 | 005 | 2300 | LAWNMOWER | 10 | 200.00 |
| 300 | 005 | 2300 | TOOL BOX | 10 | 10.00 |
| 300 | 005 | 2340 | FISHING ROD | 10 | 20.00 |

**Structured Flowchart.** Exhibit 6.19 illustrates the structured programming flowchart logic for this problem. MAIN-LINE remains unchanged. The only new addition to the START-UP module is SET-UP-PREVIOUS-SALESPERSON. The only major change to the PROCESS-RECORD module is the inclusion of the BOTTOM-OF-PAGE-CHECK routine. The WRAP-UP module includes one additional

predefined process block called INTERMEDIATE-TOTAL-ROUTINE.

As in the two-level control break program, the first step of the CONTROL-BREAK-CHECK module is to test for a major control field change. If a change has accurred, MINOR-TOTAL-ROUTINE, INTERMEDIATE-TOTAL-ROUTINE, and MAJOR-TOTAL-ROUTINE are executed. If the control break does not occur, then program execution con-

---

**FIGURE 6.21   COBOL II or COBOL 85 for Implementing Nested Method for Three-Level Control Break Check**

**Panel A**

```
IF STORE-NUMBER = PREVIOUS-STORE-NUMBER
  THEN
      IF DEPARTMENT-NUMBER = PREVIOUS-DEPARTMENT-NUMBER
        THEN
            IF SALESPERSON-NUMBER = PREVIOUS-SALESPERSON
               THEN CONTINUE
            ELSE   PERFORM BLANK-LINE
                   PERFORM MINOR-TOTAL-ROUTINE
                   PERFORM BLANK-LINE
            END-IF
        ELSE
            PERFORM BLANK-LINE
            PERFORM MINOR-TOTAL-ROUTINE
            PERFORM INTERMEDIATE-TOTAL-ROUTINE
            PERFORM BLANK-LINE
      END-IF
ELSE
        PERFORM BLANK-LINE
        PERFORM MINOR-TOTAL-ROUTINE
        PERFORM INTERMEDIATE-TOTAL-ROUTINE
        PERFORM STORE-TOTAL-ROUTINE
        PERFORM BLANK-LINE


END-IF.
```

**Panel B**

```
IF STORE-NUMBER = PREVIOUS-STORE-NUMBER
  THEN
      IF DEPARTMENT-NUMBER = PREVIOUS-DEPARTMENT-NUMBER
        THEN
            IF SALESPERSON-NUMBER NOT = PREVIOUS-SALESPERSON
               THEN
                   PERFORM BLANK-LINE
                   PERFORM MINOR-TOTAL-ROUTINE
                   PERFORM BLANK-LINE
             END-IF
        ELSE
            PERFORM BLANK-LINE
            PERFORM MINOR-TOTAL-ROUTINE
            PERFORM INTERMEDIATE-TOTAL-ROUTINE
            PERFORM BLANK-LINE
      END-IF
ELSE
        PERFORM BLANK-LINE
        PERFORM MINOR-TOTAL-ROUTINE
        PERFORM INTERMEDIATE-TOTAL-ROUTINE
        PERFORM MAJOR-TOTAL-ROUTINE
        PERFORM BLANK-LINE
END-IF.
```

tinues at the next connector symbol. The second condition is now tested to determine if DEPART-MENT-NUMBER is equal to PREVIOUS-DEPART-MENT. If false, then MINOR-TOTAL-ROUTINE and INTERMEDIATE-TOTAL-ROUTINE are executed. If no break occurs for the department, the program resumes execution at the next connector symbol. If SALESPERSON-NUMBER is not equal to PREVIOUS-SALESPERSON, then only MINOR-TOTAL-ROUTINE is executed; else, execution continues at the bottom of the CONTROL-BREAK-CHECK routine.

Exhibit 6.19 also includes a Method II for the control break check (see page 287). Method II uses a nested approach for checking for the three possible control breaks. (Note: While I normally avoid this method in my own programming projects, the technique is frequently shown in various programming textbooks and for this reason is demonstrated.)

The method tests to see if store-number is equal to previous-store. If the condition is true, the nested condition is then tested to determine if the department number is equal to the previous-department. If this second, nested condition is true, the third nested condition is then tested to determine whether the salesperson number is equal to the previous salesperson number. If this condition is also true, then no processing takes place, else the minor total routine is invoked. Frame B uses negative logic in the third nested IF to get rid of the NEXT SENTENCE, allowing the coding of the matching END-IF statement. (While this may seem rhetorical it illustrates more clearly why the author uses the "Fall Through" Method I rather than Method II. Programmers can take their pick as long as they are aware of the pitfalls.)

Exhibit 6.20 illustrates even a third method for handling control breaks. This **"embedded" control break method** becomes especially attractive when the report will include many levels of subtotals. Three-level, four-level, five-level (and so on) control break report logic will be much easier to develop using the method illustrated in Exhibit 6.20. This technique embeds the call to the next lower level reducing redundancy in flowcharting, pseudocoding, and program code. Notice, for example, that in the first major control break condition test only the MAJOR-TOTAL-ROUTINE is invoked. This works fine since the MAJOR-TOTAL-ROUTINE contains a call to the INTERMEDIATE-TOTAL-ROUTINE, and in turn, the INTERMEDIATE-TOTAL-ROUTINE contains a call to the MINOR-TOTAL-ROUTINE. Also for example, if there was only a change in the Department-number, this would invoke the INTERMEDIATE-TOTAL-ROUTINE module which, in turn, invokes the MINOR-TOTAL-ROU-TINE. Neat, huh? Well, for the most part this method can save time, but can get confusing, especially to the novice programmer. The logic is not readily apparent to the casual reader.

**EXHIBIT 6.18  Hierarchy Chart for Three-Level Control Break**

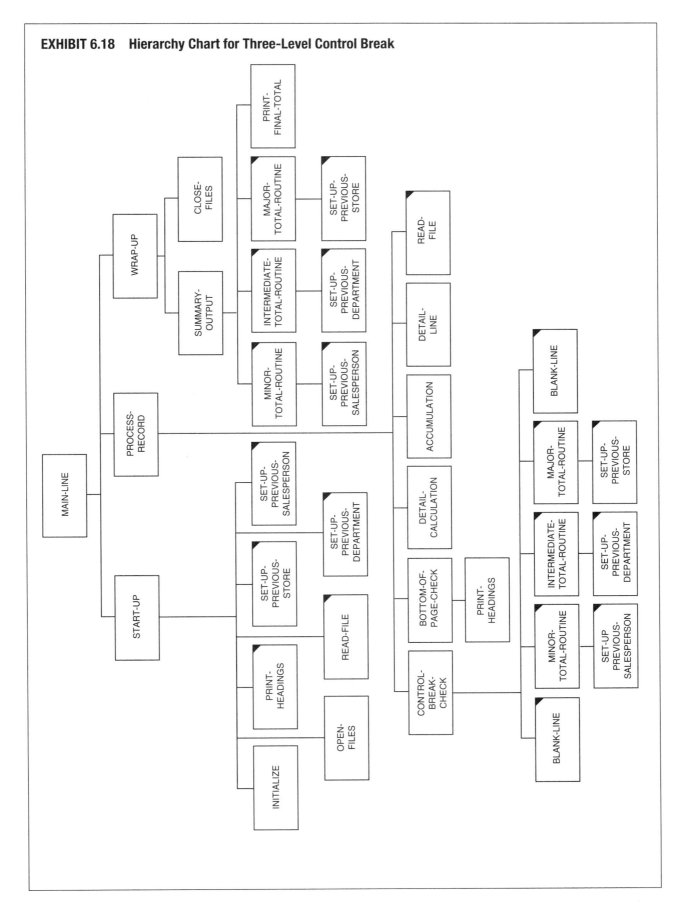

**EXHIBIT 6.19  Structured Flowchart for Three-Level Control Break**

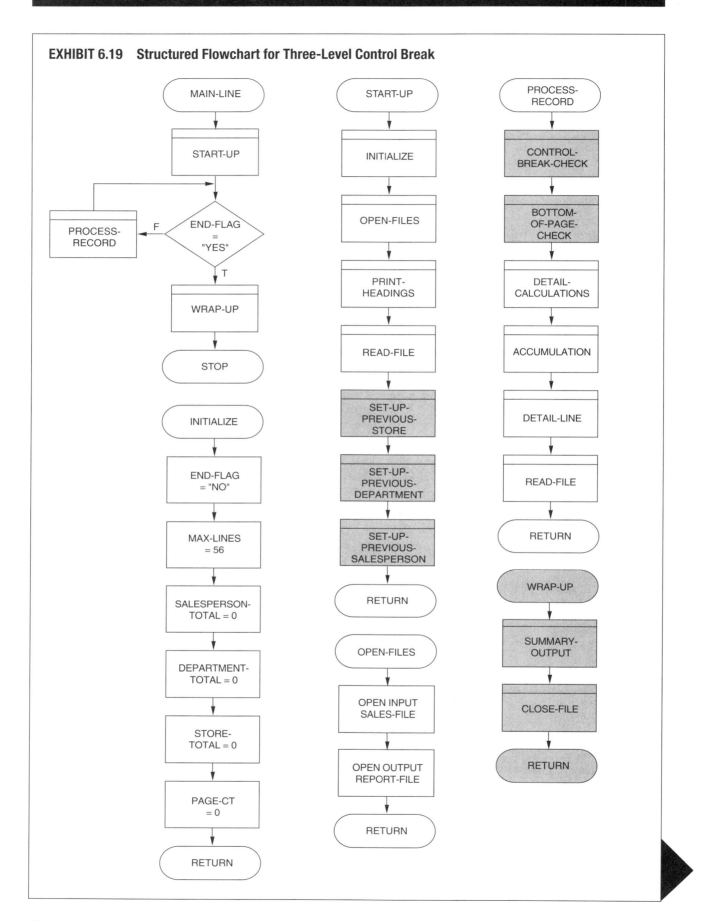

**EXHIBIT 6.19   (Cont.)**

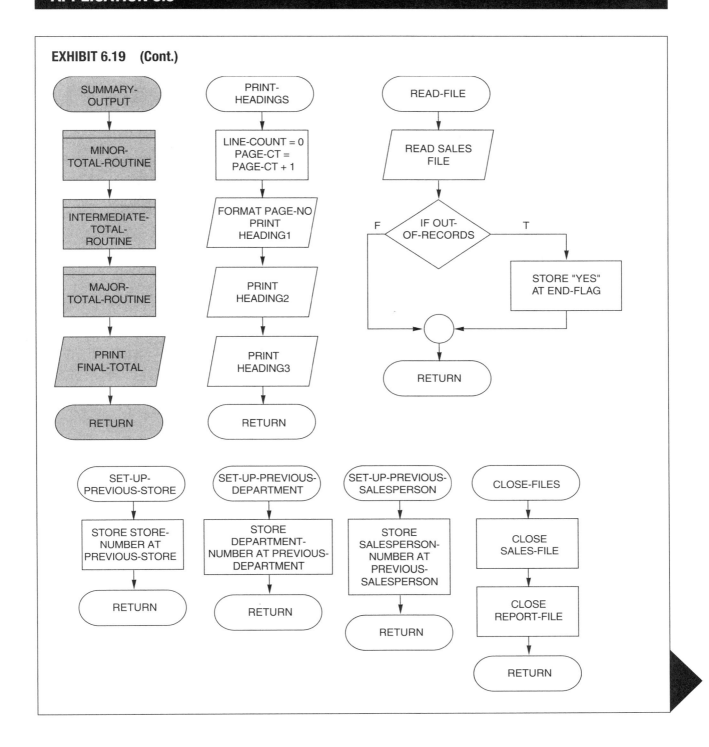

**EXHIBIT 6.19 (Cont.) Use of Method 1**

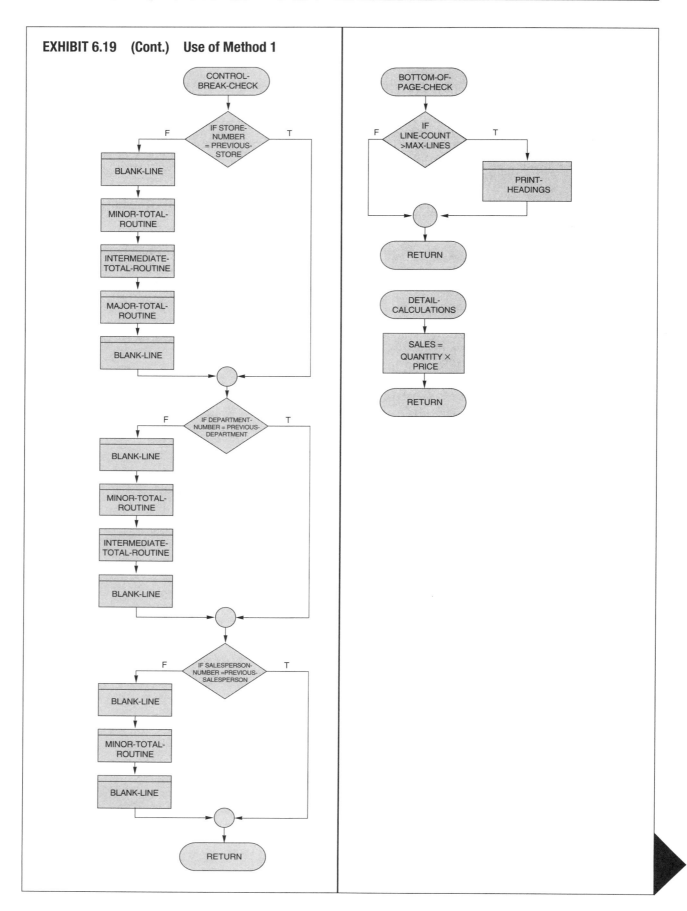

**EXHIBIT 6.19   (Cont.)   Use of Method 2**

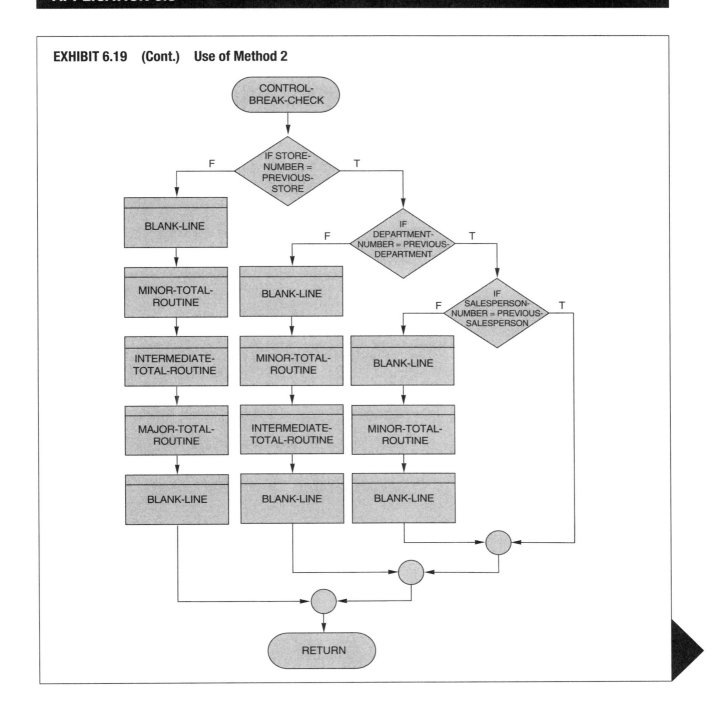

**EXHIBIT 6.19   (Cont.)**

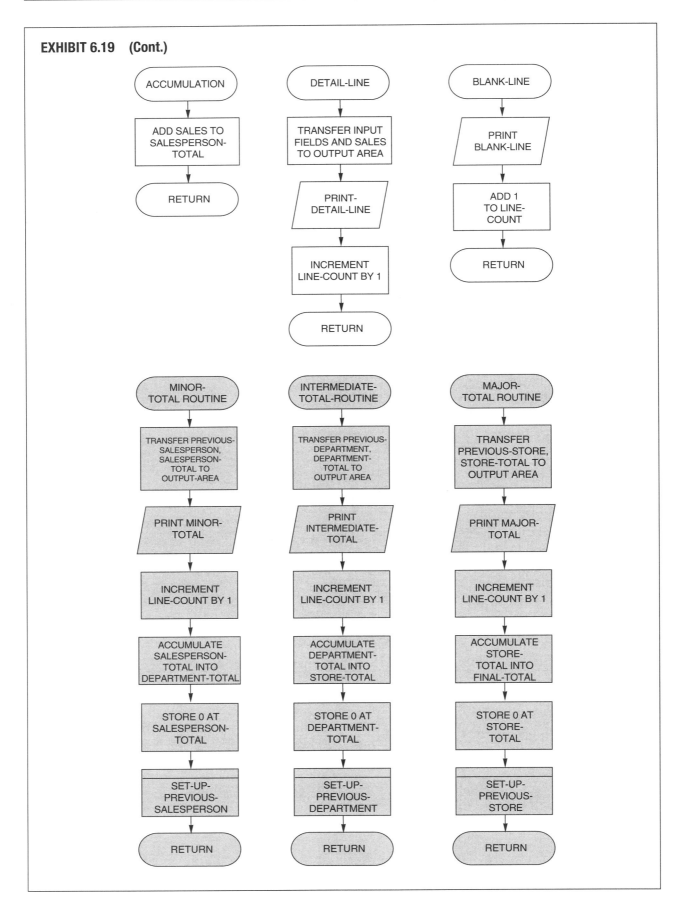

**EXHIBIT 6.20    The *Embedded* Logic Method for Control Breaks
When There Are Many Control-Break Levels**

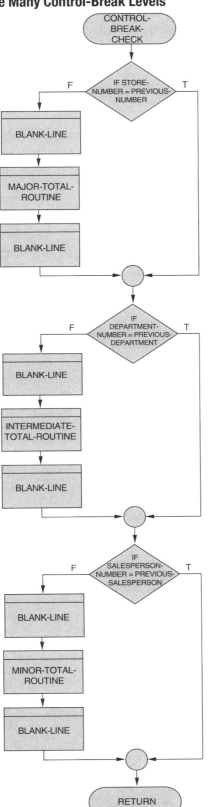

NOTE:
By calling the MAJOR-TOTAL-ROUTINE,
this will include the "embedded call" to
the intermediate-total-routine. The
intermediate-total-routine-in-turn calls
the minor-total-routine. The embedded
method works best and is easiest to
flowchart and code with 3 or more
control breaks.

NOTE:
This condition will always be true if
MAJOR-TOTAL-ROUTINE is executed.

NOTE:
This condition will always be true if
Intermediate-Total-Routine is executed.

NOTE:
Notice that this method requires
modification of major and intermediate
total routines *to include embedded calls*.

EXHIBIT 6.20    (Cont.)

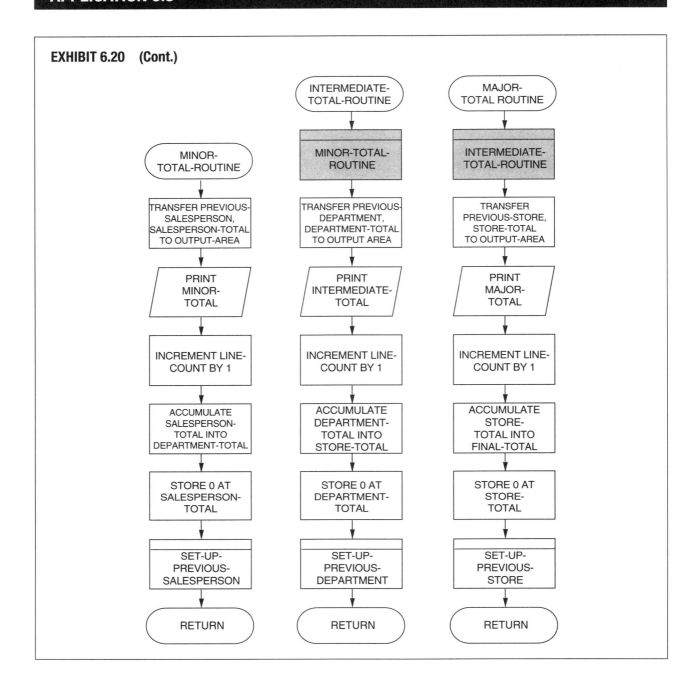

## Pseudocode and Programs

Exhibit 6.21, 6.22, and 6.23 illustrate the pseudocode, COBOL 85, and QUICK BASIC, respectively. Frame A of Exhibit 6.21 illustrates the entire pseudocode using Method I (straight-down method) and Frame B shows only the CONTROL-BREAK-CHECK module for Method II (nested method). The COBOL 85 program uses the embedded method (Method III) for handling three-level control break while the QUICK BASIC program uses Method I.

---

**EXHIBIT 6.21 Pseudocode for Three-Level Control Break (Appl. 6.3)**
**Panel A**

```
*mainline
    start-up
    dowhile end-flag = "no"
        process-record
    enddo
    wrap-up
    stop
*start-up
    initialize
    open-files
    headings
    read-file
    set-up-previous-store
    set-up-previous-department
    set-up-previous-salesperson
    return
*initialize
    max-lines = 56
    end-flag = "no"
    pg.ct = 0
    store-total = 0
    department-total = 0
    salesperson-total = 0
    final-total = 0
    return
*open-files
    open sales-files
    open report-file
    return
*process-records
    control-break-check
    bottom-of-page-check
    detail-calculation
    accumulation
    detail-line
    read-file
    return
*wrap-up
    summary-output
    close-files
    return
```

```
*summary-output
    minor-total-routine
    intermediate-total-routine
    major-total-routine
    move final-total to final-total-line
    print final-total-line
    return
*close-files
    close sales-file
    close report-file
    return
    return
*headings
    advance top-of-page
    line-ct = 0
    pg.ct = pg.ct + 1
    print page heading
    print column-heading1
    print column-heading2
    return
*read-file
    read sales-file
    when no more records store "yes" at end-flag
    endread
    return
*set-up-previous-store
    move store-number to previous-store
    return
*set-up-previous-department
    move department-number to previous-department
    return
*set-up-previous-salesperson
    move salesperson-number to previous-salesperson-number
    return
```

**EXHIBIT 6.21    (Cont.)**

```
*control-break-check
    if store-number = previous-store
        then null
    else
        blank-line
        minor-total-routine
        intermediate-total-routine
        major-total-routine
        blank-line
    endif
    if department-number = previous-department
        then null
    else
        blank-line
        minor-total-routine
        intermediate-total-routine
        blank-line
    endif
    if salesperson-number = previous-salesperson
        then null
    else
        blank-line
        minor-total-routine
        blank-line
    return
*bottom-of-page-check
    if line-ct > max-lines
        headings
    endif
    return
*detail-calculation
    sales = quantity times price
    return
*accumulation
    add sales into salesperson-total
    return
```

```
*detail-line
    transfer input fields and sales to output area
    print detail-line
    add 1 to line-ct
    return
*minor-total-routine
    transfer salesperson-total and previous-salesperson to
        output area
    print minor-total-line
    add 1 to line-ct
    add salesperson-total into department-total
    move zeros into salesperson-total
    set-up-previous-salesperson
    return
*intermediate-total-routine
    transfer department-total and previous-department to
        output area
    print intermediate-total-line
    add 1 to line-ct
    add department-total into store-total
    move 0 to department-total
    set-up-previous-department
    return
*major-total-routine
    transfer store-total and previous-store to output area
    print major-total-line
    add 1 to line-ct
    add store-total into final-total
    move zeros into store-total
    set-up-previous-store
    return1
*blank-line
    move spaces to detail-line
    write detail-line
    add 1 to line-ct
```

**EXHIBIT 6.21    (Cont.)**

**Panel B NESTED METHOD**

```
*control-break-check
     if store-number = previous-store
        then
           if department-number = previous-department
                then
                   if salesperson number = previous-salesperson
                        then
                                null
                   else
                        blank-line
                        minor-total-routine
                        blank-line
                   endif
           else
                blank-line
                minor-total-routine
                intermediate-total-routine
                blank-line
           endif
     else
           blank-line
           minor-total-routine
           intermediate-total-routine
           major-total-routine
           blank-line
     endif
     return
```

### EXHIBIT 6.22 COBOL 85 Code and Output for Three-Level Control Break (Appl. 6.3)

```
1          IDENTIFICATION DIVISION.
2          PROGRAM-ID. CH6APL3.
3          DATE-WRITTEN.  APRIL 15, 1993.
4          DATE-COMPILED. 1993-06-24.
5
6
7      *REMARKS:      ***COBOL 85***
8      *              THIS PROGRAM PRODUCES A THREE-LEVEL CONTROL BREAK
9      *              REPORT.  IT PRINTS STORE NUMBER, DEPARTMENT,SALES-
10     *              PERSON, DESCRIPTION, QUANTITY, PRICE, AND SALES.
11     *              CONTROL TOTALS ARE BROKEN DOWN BY SALESPERSON WITHIN
12     *              DEPARTMENT, DEPARTMENT WITHIN STORE, AND STORE.  A
13     *              FINAL TOTAL IS PRINTED AT THE END OF THE REPORT.
14
15         ENVIRONMENT DIVISION.
16         CONFIGURATION SECTION.
17         SOURCE-COMPUTER. CYBER.
18         OBJECT-COMPUTER. CYBER.
19         INPUT-OUTPUT SECTION.
20         FILE-CONTROL.
21             SELECT SALES-FILE ASSIGN TO DTA63.
22             SELECT OUT-FILE ASSIGN TO OUTFILE.
23         DATA DIVISION.
24         FILE SECTION.
25         FD  SALES-FILE.
26
27         01  IN-REC.
28             05  STORE-NUMBER      PIC 9(03).
29             05  DEPARTMENT-NUMBER PIC 9(03).
30             05  SALESPERSON-NUM   PIC 9(04).
31             05  DESCRIPTION       PIC X(15).
32             05  QUANTITY          PIC 9(02).
33             05  PRICE             PIC 9(03)V99.
34
35
36         FD  OUT-FILE.
37
38         01  OUT-REC               PIC X(133).
39
40         WORKING-STORAGE SECTION.
41
42         01  END-FLAG        PIC X(3)         VALUE "NO".
43
44         01  PAGE-HEADING.
45             05  FILLER      PIC X(29)         VALUE SPACES.
46             05              PIC X(21)         VALUE
47                             "SALES ANALYSIS REPORT".
48             05              PIC X(15)         VALUE SPACES.
49             05              PIC X(05)         VALUE "PAGE ".
50             05  PAGE-OUT    PIC Z9.
51             05              PIC X(61).
52
53         01  COLUMN-HEADING1.
54             05              PIC X(05)         VALUE SPACES.
55             05              PIC X(05)         VALUE "STORE".
56             05              PIC X(03)         VALUE SPACES.
57             05              PIC X(07)         VALUE "DEPART-".
58             05              PIC X(03)         VALUE SPACES.
59             05              PIC X(06)         VALUE "SALES-".
60             05              PIC X(02)         VALUE SPACES.
61             05              PIC X(11)         VALUE "DESCRIPTION".
62             05              PIC X(04)         VALUE SPACES.
63             05              PIC X(08)         VALUE "QUANTITY".
64             05              PIC X(03)         VALUE SPACES.
65             05              PIC X(05)         VALUE "PRICE".
66             05              PIC X(03)         VALUE SPACES.
```

EXHIBIT 6.22 (Cont.)

```
67          05                 PIC X(05)      VALUE "SALES".
68          05                 PIC X(63)      VALUE SPACES.
69
70    01    COLUMN-HEADING2.
71          05                 PIC X(05)      VALUE SPACES.
72          05                 PIC X(06)      VALUE "NUMBER".
73          05                 PIC X(03)      VALUE SPACES.
74          05                 PIC X(04)      VALUE "MENT".
75          05                 PIC X(05)      VALUE SPACES.
76          05                 PIC X(06)      VALUE "PERSON".
77          05                 PIC X(104)     VALUE SPACES.
78
79    01    DETAIL-LINE.
80          05                 PIC X(05)      VALUE SPACES.
81          05    STORE-NUM-OUT PIC 9(03).
82          05                 PIC X(06)      VALUE SPACES.
83          05    DEPARTMENT-OUT PIC 9(03).
84          05                 PIC X(06)      VALUE SPACES.
85          05    SALESPERSON-OUT PIC 9(04).
86          05                 PIC X(04)      VALUE SPACES.
87          05    DESCRIPT-OUT  PIC X(15).
88          05                 PIC X(02)      VALUE SPACES.
89          05    QUANTITY-OUT  PIC Z9.
90          05                 PIC X(06)      VALUE SPACES.
91          05    PRICE-OUT      PIC ZZ9.99.
92          05                 PIC X(04)      VALUE SPACES.
93          05    SALES-OUT      PIC Z,ZZ9.99.
94          05                 PIC X(58)      VALUE SPACES.
95
96    01    SALES-TOTAL-LINE.
97          05                 PIC X(35)      VALUE SPACES.
98          05                 PIC X(11)      VALUE "SALESPERSON".
99          05                 PIC X(03)      VALUE SPACES.
100         05    SALES-NUM-OUT PIC 9(04).
101         05                 PIC X(03)      VALUE SPACES.
102         05                 PIC X(05)      VALUE "TOTAL".
103         05                 PIC X(03)      VALUE SPACES.
104         05    SALES-TOT-OUT PIC  $$$,$$9.99.
105         05                 PIC X(02)      VALUE " *".
106         05                 PIC X(56)      VALUE SPACES.
107
108   01    DEPARTMENT-TOTAL-LINE.
109         05                 PIC X(35)      VALUE SPACES.
110         05                 PIC X(10)      VALUE "DEPARTMENT".
111         05                 PIC X(05)      VALUE SPACES.
112         05    DEPARTMENT-NUM-OUT PIC 9(03).
113         05                 PIC X(03)      VALUE SPACES.
114         05                 PIC X(05)      VALUE "TOTAL".
115         05                 PIC X(02)      VALUE SPACES.
116         05    DEPT-TOTAL-OUT PIC  $$$$,$$9.99.
117         05                 PIC X(03)      VALUE " **".
118         05                 PIC X(55)      VALUE SPACES.
119
120   01    STORE-TOTAL-LINE.
121         05                 PIC X(35)      VALUE SPACES.
122         05                 PIC X(05)      VALUE "STORE".
123         05                 PIC X(10)      VALUE SPACES.
124         05    SUB-STORE-NUM PIC 9(03).
125         05                 PIC X(03)      VALUE SPACES.
126         05                 PIC X(05)      VALUE "TOTAL".
127         05    STORE-TOTAL-OUT PIC $$,$$$,$$9.99.
128         05                 PIC X(04)      VALUE " ***".
129         05                 PIC X(54)      VALUE SPACES.
130
131   01    FINAL-TOTAL-LINE.
132         05                 PIC X(44)      VALUE SPACES.
```

**EXHIBIT 6.22** (Cont.)

```
133              05                  PIC X(11)       VALUE "FINAL TOTAL".
134              05                  PIC X(6)        VALUE SPACES.
135              05    FINAL-TOTAL-OUT PIC $$,$$$,$$9.99.
136              05                  PIC X(05)       VALUE " ****".
137              05                  PIC X(53)       VALUE SPACES.
138
139         01   PREVIOUS-DEPARTMENT      PIC 9(03)      VALUE 0.
140         01   PREVIOUS-STORE           PIC 9(03)      VALUE 0.
141         01   PREVIOUS-SALESPERSON     PIC 9(04)      VALUE 0.
142         01   SALES                    PIC 9(04)V99   VALUE 0.
143         01   SALES-PERSON-TOTAL       PIC 9(05)V99   VALUE 0.
144         01   STORE-TOTAL              PIC 9(07)V99   VALUE 0.
145         01   DEPT-TOTAL               PIC 9(06)V99   VALUE 0.
146         01   FINAL-TOTAL              PIC 9(08)V99   VALUE 0.
147         01   PAGE-COUNT               PIC 9(03)      VALUE 0.
148         01   LINE-COUNT               PIC 9(03)      VALUE 0.
149         01   MAX-LINES                PIC 9(03)      VALUE 35.
150
151       /
152       PROCEDURE DIVISION.
153       *********************
154
155       000-MAIN-LINE.
156           PERFORM 100-START-UP.
157           PERFORM 200-PROCESS-RECORD UNTIL END-FLAG = "YES".
158           PERFORM 300-WRAP-UP.
159           STOP RUN.
160
161       100-START-UP.
162       *     INITIALIZATION - W-S
163           PERFORM 105-OPEN-FILES.
164           PERFORM 110-PRINT-HEADINGS.
165           PERFORM 120-READ-FILE.
166           PERFORM 150-SET-UP-PREVIOUS-STORE.
167           PERFORM 130-SET-UP-PREVIOUS-DEPARTMENT.
168           PERFORM 140-SET-UP-PREVIOUS-SALESPERSON.
169
170       105-OPEN-FILES.
171           OPEN INPUT SALES-FILE  OUTPUT OUT-FILE.
172
173       110-PRINT-HEADINGS.
174           MOVE ZERO TO LINE-COUNT.
175           ADD 1 TO PAGE-COUNT.
176           MOVE PAGE-COUNT TO PAGE-OUT.
177           WRITE OUT-REC FROM PAGE-HEADING AFTER ADVANCING PAGE.
178           WRITE OUT-REC FROM COLUMN-HEADING1 AFTER ADVANCING 2 LINES.
179           WRITE OUT-REC FROM COLUMN-HEADING2 AFTER ADVANCING 1 LINES.
180           MOVE SPACES TO OUT-REC.
181           WRITE OUT-REC AFTER ADVANCING 1 LINES.
182
183       120-READ-FILE.
184           READ SALES-FILE AT END MOVE "YES" TO END-FLAG.
185
186       130-SET-UP-PREVIOUS-DEPARTMENT.
187           MOVE DEPARTMENT-NUMBER TO PREVIOUS-DEPARTMENT.
188
189       140-SET-UP-PREVIOUS-SALESPERSON.
190           MOVE SALESPERSON-NUM TO PREVIOUS-SALESPERSON.
191
192       150-SET-UP-PREVIOUS-STORE.
193           MOVE STORE-NUMBER TO PREVIOUS-STORE.
194
195       200-PROCESS-RECORD.
196           PERFORM 210-CONTROL-BREAK-CHECK.
197           PERFORM 220-BOTTOM-OF-PAGE-CHECK.
198           PERFORM 230-DETAIL-CALCULATIONS.
```

**EXHIBIT 6.22    (Cont.)**

```
199              PERFORM 240-ACCUMULATE.
200              PERFORM 250-DETAIL-LINE.
201              PERFORM 120-READ-FILE.
202
203         210-CONTROL-BREAK-CHECK.
204              IF STORE-NUMBER = PREVIOUS-STORE THEN
205                NEXT SENTENCE
206              ELSE
207                  PERFORM 21X-BLANK-LINE
208                  PERFORM 213-MAJOR-TOTAL-ROUTINE
209                  PERFORM 21X-BLANK-LINE
210              END-IF.
211
212              IF DEPARTMENT-NUMBER = PREVIOUS-DEPARTMENT THEN
213                NEXT SENTENCE
214              ELSE
215                  PERFORM 21X-BLANK-LINE
216                  PERFORM 212-INTERMEDIATE-TOTAL-ROUTINE
217                  PERFORM 21X-BLANK-LINE
218              END-IF.
219
220              IF SALESPERSON-NUM = PREVIOUS-SALESPERSON THEN
221                NEXT SENTENCE
222              ELSE
223                  PERFORM 21X-BLANK-LINE
224                  PERFORM 211-MINOR-TOTAL-ROUTINE
225                  PERFORM 21X-BLANK-LINE
226              END-IF.
227
228         211-MINOR-TOTAL-ROUTINE.
229              MOVE PREVIOUS-SALESPERSON TO SALES-NUM-OUT.
230              MOVE SALES-PERSON-TOTAL TO SALES-TOT-OUT.
231              WRITE OUT-REC FROM SALES-TOTAL-LINE.
232              ADD 1 TO LINE-COUNT.
233              ADD SALES-PERSON-TOTAL TO DEPT-TOTAL.
234              MOVE ZEROES TO SALES-PERSON-TOTAL.
235              PERFORM 140-SET-UP-PREVIOUS-SALESPERSON.
236
237         212-INTERMEDIATE-TOTAL-ROUTINE.
238              PERFORM 211-MINOR-TOTAL-ROUTINE.
239              MOVE PREVIOUS-DEPARTMENT TO DEPARTMENT-NUM-OUT.
240              MOVE DEPT-TOTAL TO DEPT-TOTAL-OUT.
241              WRITE OUT-REC FROM DEPARTMENT-TOTAL-LINE.
242              ADD 1 TO LINE-COUNT.
243              ADD DEPT-TOTAL TO STORE-TOTAL.
244              MOVE ZEROES TO DEPT-TOTAL.
245              PERFORM 130-SET-UP-PREVIOUS-DEPARTMENT.
246
247         213-MAJOR-TOTAL-ROUTINE.
248              PERFORM 212-INTERMEDIATE-TOTAL-ROUTINE.
249              MOVE PREVIOUS-STORE TO SUB-STORE-NUM.
250              MOVE STORE-TOTAL TO STORE-TOTAL-OUT.
251              WRITE OUT-REC FROM STORE-TOTAL-LINE.
252              ADD 1 TO LINE-COUNT.
253              ADD STORE-TOTAL TO FINAL-TOTAL.
254              MOVE ZEROES TO STORE-TOTAL.
255              PERFORM 150-SET-UP-PREVIOUS-STORE.
256
257         21X-BLANK-LINE.
258              MOVE SPACES TO OUT-REC.
259              WRITE OUT-REC.
260              ADD 1 TO LINE-COUNT.
261
262         220-BOTTOM-OF-PAGE-CHECK.
263              IF LINE-COUNT > MAX-LINES THEN
264                  PERFORM 110-PRINT-HEADINGS
```

**EXHIBIT 6.22** (Cont.)

```
266              ELSE
267                 NEXT SENTENCE.
268
269       230-DETAIL-CALCULATIONS.
270           COMPUTE SALES ROUNDED = PRICE * QUANTITY.
271
272       240-ACCUMULATE.
273           ADD SALES TO SALES-PERSON-TOTAL.
274
275       250-DETAIL-LINE.
276           MOVE STORE-NUMBER TO STORE-NUM-OUT.
277           MOVE DEPARTMENT-NUMBER TO DEPARTMENT-OUT.
278           MOVE SALESPERSON-NUM TO SALESPERSON-OUT.
279           MOVE DESCRIPTION TO DESCRIPT-OUT.
280           MOVE QUANTITY TO QUANTITY-OUT.
281           MOVE PRICE TO PRICE-OUT.
282           MOVE SALES TO SALES-OUT.
283           WRITE OUT-REC FROM DETAIL-LINE AFTER ADVANCING 1 LINES.
284           ADD 1 TO LINE-COUNT.
285
286       300-WRAP-UP.
287           PERFORM 310-SUMMARY-OUTPUT.
288           PERFORM 320-CLOSE-FILES.
289
290       310-SUMMARY-OUTPUT.
291           PERFORM 21X-BLANK-LINE
292           PERFORM 213-MAJOR-TOTAL-ROUTINE.
293           MOVE FINAL-TOTAL TO FINAL-TOTAL-OUT.
294           WRITE OUT-REC FROM FINAL-TOTAL-LINE AFTER 1.
295
296       320-CLOSE-FILES.
297           CLOSE SALES-FILE  OUT-FILE.
```

**EXHIBIT 6.22   (Cont.)**

```
                    SALES ANALYSIS REPORT              PAGE   1

STORE      DEPART-    SALES-    DESCRIPTION    QUANTITY   PRICE    SALES
NUMBER     MENT       PERSON

100        005        0056      LAWNMOWER         5       200.00   1,000.00
100        005        0056      WEEDEATER        10       100.00   1,000.00

                                SALESPERSON    0056      TOTAL    $2,000.00 *

100        005        0098      WEEDTRIMMER       5        50.00     250.00
100        005        0098      LAWN FERTILIZER   1        10.00      10.00

                                SALESPERSON    0098      TOTAL      $260.00 *
                                DEPARTMENT      005      TOTAL    $2,260.00 **

100        007        4000      SHIRT             1        10.00      10.00
100        007        4000      TIE              10         5.00      50.00

                                SALESPERSON    4000      TOTAL       $60.00 *

100        007        4500      JEANS             1        15.00      15.00
100        007        4500      SHIRT             2        20.00      40.00

                                SALESPERSON    4500      TOTAL       $55.00 *
                                DEPARTMENT      007      TOTAL      $115.00 **
                                STORE           100      TOTAL    $2,375.00 ***

200        005        2356      LAWNMOWER        10       100.00   1,000.00
200        005        2356      HAMMER            5        10.00      50.00

                                SALESPERSON    2356      TOTAL    $1,050.00 *

200        005        2560      SAW               1        20.00      20.00
200        005        2560      RULER             1        10.00      10.00

                                SALESPERSON    2560      TOTAL       $30.00 *
                                DEPARTMENT      005      TOTAL    $1,080.00 **

200        009        6700      DIAMOND RING      2       500.00   1,000.00
200        009        6700      NECKLACE          3       100.00     300.00

                                SALESPERSON    6700      TOTAL    $1,300.00 *
                                DEPARTMENT      009      TOTAL    $1,300.00 **
                                STORE           200      TOTAL    $2,380.00 ***

                    SALES ANALYSIS REPORT              PAGE   2

STORE      DEPART-    SALES-    DESCRIPTION    QUANTITY   PRICE    SALES
NUMBER     MENT       PERSON

300        005        2300      LAWNMOWER        10       200.00   2,000.00
300        005        2300      TOOL BOX         10        10.00     100.00

                                SALESPERSON    2300      TOTAL    $2,100.00 *

300        005        2340      FISHING ROD      10        20.00     200.00

                                SALESPERSON    2340      TOTAL      $200.00 *
                                DEPARTMENT      005      TOTAL    $2,300.00 **
                                STORE           300      TOTAL    $2,300.00 ***
                                    FINAL TOTAL          $7,055.00 ****
```

**EXHIBIT 6.23    QBASIC for Application 6.3 Three-Level Control Break**

```
'****************************************************************+**
'*    QUICK BASIC ---    PROGRAM IDENTIFICATION                    *
'*****************************************************************
'* PROGRAM NAME: CH6APL3                                           *
'*****************************************************************
'* REMARKS: THIS PROGRAM PRODUCES A THREE-LEVEL CONTROL BREAK REPORT.  *
'*          IT PRINTS THE STORE NUMBER, DEPARTMENT, SALESPERSON,   *
'*          PRICE, AND SALES. CONTROL TOTALS ARE BROKEN DOWN BY SALES- *
'*          PERSON WITHIN DEPARTMENT, DEPARTMENT WITHIN STORE, AND     *
'*          STORE. A FINAL TOTAL IS PRINTED AT THE END OF THE REPORT.  *
'*****************************************************************
'*                        MAIN-LINE                               *
'*****************************************************************
    GOSUB STARTUP                   '* PERFORM START-UP
    DO UNTIL END.FLAG$ = "YES"
        GOSUB PROCESS.RECORD        '* PERFORM PROCESS-RECORD
    LOOP
    GOSUB WRAPUP                    '* PERFORM WRAP-UP
    END


    '*****************************************************************
    '*                        START-UP                              *
    '*****************************************************************

STARTUP:

    GOSUB INITIALIZE
    GOSUB OPEN.FILES
    GOSUB HEADINGS                  '* PERFORM PRINT-HEADINGS
    GOSUB READFILE                  '* PERFORM READ-FILE
    GOSUB SET.UP.PREV.STORE         '* PERFORM SET-UP-PREVIOUS-STORE
    GOSUB SET.UP.PREV.DEPT          '* PERFORM SET-UP-PREVIOUS-DEPART
    GOSUB SET.UP.PREV.SLSMN         '* PERFORM SET-UP-PREVIOUS-SLSMN
    RETURN


    '*****************************************************************
    '*                        INITIALIZE                            *
    '*****************************************************************
INITIALIZE:
    END.FLAG$ = "NO"
    STORE.TOTAL = 0
    DEPT.TOTAL = 0
    PERSON.TOTAL = 0
    FINAL.TOTAL = 0
    MAX.LINES = 40
    PAGE.COUNT = 0
    DETAIL.LINE$ = "    \ \    \ \    \ \ \              \ ##     ###.##   #,###.##"
    DEPT.LINE$ = "                                  DEPARTMENT    \ \ TOTAL $$##,###.## *_*"
    SALES.LINE$ = "                                  SALESPERSON  \   \ TOTAL $$###,###.## *"
    STORE.LINE$ = "                                  STORE        \   \ TOTAL $$###,###.## *_*_*"
    FINAL.LINE$ = "                                      FINAL TOTAL    $$#,###,###.## *_*_*_*"
    RETURN
```

**EXHIBIT 6.23    (Cont.)**

```
'**********************************************************************
'*                          OPEN FILES                              *
'**********************************************************************
OPEN.FILES:
      OPEN "I", #1, "CH6ILL3.DAT"
      RETURN


      '**********************************************************************
      '*                      PRINT-HEADINGS                               *
      '**********************************************************************

HEADINGS:

      LINE.COUNT = 0
      PAGE.COUNT = PAGE.COUNT + 1
      LPRINT CHR$(12)
      LPRINT TAB(30); "SALES ANALYSIS REPORT"; TAB(66); "PAGE:"; PAGE.COUNT
      LPRINT : LPRINT
      LPRINT TAB(6); "STORE"; TAB(14); "DEPART-"; TAB(24); "SALES-"; TAB(32); "DESCRIPTION";
      LPRINT TAB(47); "QUANTITY"; TAB(58); "PRICE"; TAB(66); "SALES"
      LPRINT TAB(6); "NUMBER"; TAB(15); "MENT"; TAB(24); "PERSON"
      LPRINT
      RETURN


      '**********************************************************************
      '*                        READ-FILE                                 *
      '**********************************************************************

READFILE:
      INPUT #1, STORE.NUMBER$, DEPT.NUMBER$, SALESPERSON$, DESCRIPTION$, QUANTITY, PRICE
      IF DESCRIPTION$ = "EOF" THEN END.FLAG$ = "YES"
      RETURN


      '**********************************************************************
      '*                   SET-UP-PREVIOUS-STORE                          *
      '**********************************************************************

SET.UP.PREV.STORE:

      PREVIOUS.STORE$ = STORE.NUMBER$
      RETURN


      '**********************************************************************
      '*                 SET-UP-PREVIOUS-DEPARTMENT                       *
      '**********************************************************************

SET.UP.PREV.DEPT:

      PREVIOUS.DEPT$ = DEPT.NUMBER$
      RETURN
```

## EXHIBIT 6.23   (Cont.)

```
'**********************************************************************
'*                     SET-UP-PREVIOUS-SALESPERSON                    *
'**********************************************************************

SET.UP.PREV.SLSMN:

    PREVIOUS.PERSON$ = SALESPERSON$
    RETURN


    '**********************************************************************
    '*                         PROCESS-RECORD                          *
    '**********************************************************************

PROCESS.RECORD:

    GOSUB CONTROL.BREAK.CHECK            ' PERFORM CONTROL-BREAK-CHECK
    GOSUB BOTTOM.OF.PAGE.CHECK           ' PERFORM BOTTOM-OF-PAGE-CHECK
    GOSUB DETAIL.CALCULATION             ' PERFORM DETAIL-CALCULATIONS
    GOSUB ACCUMULATION                   ' PERFORM ACCUMULATION
    GOSUB DETAIL.LINE                    ' PERFORM DETAIL-LINE
    GOSUB READFILE                       ' PERFORM READ-FILE
    RETURN



    '**********************************************************************
    '*                       CONTROL-BREAK-CHECK                       *
    '**********************************************************************

CONTROL.BREAK.CHECK:

    IF STORE.NUMBER$ <> PREVIOUS.STORE$ THEN
       GOSUB BLANK.LINE
       GOSUB MINOR.TOTAL.ROUTINE
       GOSUB INTERMEDIATE.TOTAL.ROUTINE
       GOSUB MAJOR.TOTAL.ROUTINE
       GOSUB BLANK.LINE
    END IF
    IF DEPT.NUMBER$ <> PREVIOUS.DEPT$ THEN
       GOSUB BLANK.LINE
       GOSUB MINOR.TOTAL.ROUTINE
       GOSUB INTERMEDIATE.TOTAL.ROUTINE
       GOSUB BLANK.LINE
    END IF

    IF SALESPERSON$ <> PREVIOUS.PERSON$ THEN
       GOSUB BLANK.LINE
       GOSUB MINOR.TOTAL.ROUTINE
       GOSUB BLANK.LINE
    END IF
    RETURN
```

## APPLICATION 6.3

**EXHIBIT 6.23 (Cont.)**

```
'********************************************************************
'*                     MINOR-TOTAL-ROUTINE                         *
'********************************************************************

MINOR.TOTAL.ROUTINE:

    LPRINT USING SALES.LINE$; PREVIOUS.PERSON$; SALES.TOTAL
    LINE.COUNT = LINE.COUNT + 3
    DEPT.TOTAL = DEPT.TOTAL + SALES.TOTAL
    SALES.TOTAL = 0
    GOSUB SET.UP.PREV.SLSMN              'PERFORM SET-UP-PREVIOUS-SALES
    RETURN
    '********************************************************************
    '*                 INTERMEDIATE-TOTAL-ROUTINE                      *
    '********************************************************************

INTERMEDIATE.TOTAL.ROUTINE:

    LPRINT USING DEPT.LINE$; PREVIOUS.DEPTS$; DEPT.TOTAL
    LINE.COUNT = LINE.COUNT + 1
    STORE.TOTAL = STORE.TOTAL + DEPT.TOTAL
    DEPT.TOTAL = 0
    GOSUB SET.UP.PREV.DEPT                    'PERFORM SET-UP-PREVIOUS-DEPART
    RETURN


    '********************************************************************
    '*                     MAJOR-TOTAL-ROUTINE                         *
    '********************************************************************

MAJOR.TOTAL.ROUTINE:

    LPRINT USING STORE.LINE$; PREVIOUS.STORE$; STORE.TOTAL
    LINE.COUNT = LINE.COUNT + 1
    FINAL.TOTAL = FINAL.TOTAL + STORE.TOTAL
    STORE.TOTAL = 0
    GOSUB SET.UP.PREV.STORE                   'PERFORM SET-UP-PREVIOUS-STORE
    RETURN


    '********************************************************************
    '*                     BOTTOM-OF-PAGE-CHECK                        *
    '********************************************************************

BOTTOM.OF.PAGE.CHECK:

    IF LINE.COUNT > MAX.LINES THEN
       GOSUB HEADINGS
    END IF
    RETURN
```

**EXHIBIT 6.23    (Cont.)**

```
'**********************************************************************
'*                       DETAIL-CALCULATIONS                         *
'**********************************************************************

DETAIL.CALCULATION:

    SALES = QUANTITY * PRICE
    RETURN

    ' **********************************************************************
    ' *                        ACCUMULATION                              *
    ' **********************************************************************

ACCUMULATION:

    SALES.TOTAL = SALES.TOTAL + SALES
    RETURN

    '**********************************************************************
    '*                         DETAIL-LINE                              *
    '**********************************************************************

DETAIL.LINE:

    LPRINT USING DETAIL.LINE$; STORE.NUMBER$; DEPT.NUMBER$; SALESPERSON$; DESCRIPTION$; QUANTITY; PRICE; SALES
    LINE.COUNT = LINE.COUNT + 1
    RETURN

    '**********************************************************************
    '*                          BLANK-LINE                              *
    '**********************************************************************

BLANK.LINE:

    LPRINT
    LINE.COUNT = LINE.COUNT + 1
    RETURN

    '**********************************************************************
    '*                           WRAP-UP                                *
    '**********************************************************************

WRAPUP:

    GOSUB SUMMARY.OUTPUT
    GOSUB CLOSE.FILES
    RETURN
```

**EXHIBIT 6.23   (Cont.)**

```
'*****************************************************************
'*                        SUMMARY-OUTPUT                        *
'*****************************************************************
SUMMARY.OUTPUT:

    GOSUB BLANK.LINE
    GOSUB MINOR.TOTAL.ROUTINE            '* PERFORM MINOR-TOTAL-ROUTINE
    GOSUB INTERMEDIATE.TOTAL.ROUTINE     '* PERFORM INTERMEDIATE-TOTAL-ROUT
    GOSUB MAJOR.TOTAL.ROUTINE            '* PERFORM MAJOR-TOTAL-ROUTINE
    LPRINT USING FINAL.LINE$; FINAL.TOTAL
    RETURN


    '*****************************************************************
    '*                        CLOSE-FILES                          *
    '*****************************************************************
CLOSE.FILES:
    CLOSE
    RETURN
```

```
                    SALES ANALYSIS REPORT            PAGE: 2


STORE     DEPART-   SALES-   DESCRIPTION   QUANTITY   PRICE    SALES
NUMBER    MENT      PERSON

200       009       6700     DIAMOND RING      2      500.00   1,000.00
200       009       6700     NECKLACE          3      100.00     300.00

                             SALESPERSON    6700    TOTAL    $1,300.00 *
                             DEPARTMENT      009    TOTAL    $1,300.00 **
                             STORE           200    TOTAL    $2,380.00 ***


300       005       2300     LAWNMOWER        10      200.00   2,000.00
300       005       2300     TOOL BOX         10       10.00     100.00

                             SALESPERSON    2300    TOTAL    $2,100.00 *


300       005       2340     FISHING ROD      10       20.00     200.00

                             SALESPERSON    2340    TOTAL      $200.00 *
                             DEPARTMENT      005    TOTAL    $2,300.00 **
                             STORE           300    TOTAL    $2,300.00 ***
                                   FINAL TOTAL      $7,055.00 ****
```

# SUMMARY

An extremely valuable use of data processing is in the production of reports, including reports with significant subtotals. To generate a report giving a subtotal for each group of records requires that the file be initially sorted into ascending sequence by the control field(s). A control field is the field that is used in the comparison process to determine when a control break occurs. A control break is the point during processing where there is a change in control group—a group of records containing the same control field.

Reports can be printed so that the detail lines of one group are followed by a subtotal; more detail lines are then printed, followed by another subtotal, and so on. A sales analysis report broken down only by sales for each store in the company, using a single control field, is called a single-level control break report. If the sales of the company were further broken down to show sales both by store and by individual departments within each store, then it is called a two-level control break report. A sales analysis report with sales broken down by store within company, department within store, and salesperson within department is a three-level control break report.

The major difference between the logic of a detail-printed report without subtotals and one with a single-level control break is the inclusion of a CONTROL-BREAK-CHECK module. This module is responsible for determining if a control field is equal to the contents of a previously established work area that contains the control field value. When the control field of a control group proves unequal to the previous number value, a module is executed that (1) transfers the subtotal to the subtotal line, (2) prints the subtotal line, (3) accumulates the subtotal to the next higher level total, (4) clears the subtotal to zero, and (5) sets up for the next control group. This routine simply moves the current control field of the record being processed into the previous number variable.

After all records have been processed and the WRAP-UP module is invoked, the last subtotal must be printed and rolled forward into the final total. The final total is then printed and the files closed.

Two-level control breaks involve initially storing away both a minor and a major key in their respective previous number fields. The PROCESS-RECORD module appears the same as in a single-level control break program. The CONTROL-BREAK-CHECK module now consists of two different comparison tests—a major control break check and a minor control break check. The major control break check compares the major control field with the major control field's previous number. If the values are unequal, it performs two modules—MINOR-TOTAL-ROUTINE and MAJOR-TOTAL-ROUTINE. MINOR-TOTAL-ROUTINE is responsible for printing the minor total (DEPARTMENT-TOTAL), rolling the subtotal forward into a major total (STORE-TOTAL), clearing the minor subtotal, and reestablishing the next previous number. MAJOR-TOTAL-ROUTINE is responsible for transferring the major subtotal to the output area, printing it, rolling it forward into a final total, clearing it, and setting up for the next previous major control field.

This same process is repeated for three-level control breaks, except that here an INTERMEDIATE-TOTAL-ROUTINE is involved. In three-level control break programs, CONTROL-BREAK-CHECK includes three different control break checks—a minor control break check, an intermediate control break check, and a major control break check. The major control break check determines, for example, whether a store number is different from its predecessor; the intermediate control break check determines if a department number is different from its predecessor; and the minor control break check determines if the salesperson number has changed.

Method II shows a nesting approach for checking for control breaks. Method III, the embedded method for control breaks is preferred for a problem with many control break totals. This method embeds the call to the next lower level total logic, thus removing much of the redundancy necessary in either Method I or Method II.

# VOCABULARY

control break report
single-level control
  break report
two-level control
  break report
three-level control
  break report
sort key field
control field
control break

PREVIOUS-NUMBER
  work area
detail printed report
group-indicated
  report
major control field
minor control field
intermediate control
  field
embedded control
  break method
nested control break
  method

## EXERCISES/QUESTIONS

1. What is the purpose of the CONTROL-BREAK-CHECK module?

2. What two fields or variables, are compared during the one-level CONTROL-BREAK-CHECK module? If the result of the comparison test is true, what action should the program take? If the result of the comparison test is false, what action should the program take?

3. What is the purpose of MINOR-TOTAL-ROUTINE in a single-level control break program? What are the five major activities, or steps, that must be accomplished?

4. What is the purpose of MAJOR-TOTAL-ROUTINE in a two-level control break program? What are the five major activities, or steps, that must be accomplished?

5. What two comparisons are made during the two-level CONTROL-BREAK-CHECK module? What happens if there is a major control break? A minor control break?

6. In what order must control break comparisons be made when there are multiple control fields?

7. What is the purpose of "rolling totals forward"? What is the advantage of this technique?

8. Explain the difference between the three methods for control-break processing.

## PROBLEMS

**6–1.** Jennifer's Dress Shop wishes to produce an inventory report as follows. Group totals should be taken for quantity and total price when the style number changes. Final totals should also be printed. The input record format is also presented. Create a printer spacing chart, hierarchy chart, structured program flowchart, and pseudocode for this problem.

**INPUT RECORD FORMAT:**

| Field Description | Column Locations | Type |
|---|---|---|
| Style number | 1–6 | N |
| Size | 7–8 | N |
| Quantity | 9–11 | N |
| Unit price | 12–16 | N ($.¢¢) |

```
                INVENTORY REPORT        PAGE XXXX

  STYLE    SIZE  QUANTITY   UNIT           TOTAL
  NO.                       PRICE          PRICE

  XXXXXX    XX     XXX     XXX.XX        XX,XXX.XX
  XXXXXX    XX     XXX     XXX.XX        XX,XXX.XX
  XXXXXX    XX     XXX     XXX.XX        XX,XXX.XX

           TOTAL  X,XXX                $X,XXX,XXX.XX  *

  XXXXXX    XX     XXX     XXX.XXX       XX,XXX.XX
  XXXXXX    XX     XXX     XXX.XXX       XX,XXX.XX
  XXXXXX    XX     XXX     XXX.XXX       XX,XXX.XX
           TOTAL  X,XXX                $X,XXX,XXX.XX  *

    FINAL TOTAL  XX,XXX                $XX,XXX,XXX.XX **
```

**6–2.** A major university wishes to produce a bidding report (as follows) that indicates the bids on various proposed building projects. The report is to list the construction project number, bidding number, bidder name, and bid amount for each proposed construction project and then print the number of bids and the average bid for each project. Allow for a multiple page report. The input record format is also presented. Create a printer spacing chart, hierarchy chart, structured program flowchart, and pseudocode for this problem.

**INPUT RECORD FORMAT:**

| Field Description | Column Locations | Type |
|---|---|---|
| Construction project | 1–5 | N |
| Bid. I.D. | 6–9 | N |
| Bidding company | 10–25 | A |
| Bid amount | 26–32 | N ($.¢¢) |

```
XX/XX/XX           UNIVERSITY BIDDING REPORT        PAGE XXXX

CONSTRUCTION    BID           BIDDING            BID
   PROJECT      I.D.          COMPANY            AMOUNT

   XXXXX        XXXX   XXXXXXXXXXXXXXX        XXX,XXX.XX
   XXXXX        XXXX   XXXXXXXXXXXXXXX        XXX,XXX.XX
   XXXXX        XXXX   XXXXXXXXXXXXXXX        XXX,XXX.XX

TOTAL NUMBER OF BIDS   XXX     AVERAGE BID $ XX,XXX.XX *

   XXXXX        XXXX   XXXXXXXXXXXXXXX        XXX,XXX.XX
   XXXXX        XXXX   XXXXXXXXXXXXXXX        XXX,XXX.XX
   XXXXX        XXXX   XXXXXXXXXXXXXXX        XXX,XXX.XX

TOTAL NUMBER OF BIDS   XXX     AVERAGE BID $ XX,XXX.XX *

                   END OF REPORT.
```

**6–3.** The management of Dale's Auto Service wishes to produce an invoice register as follows. The register is to list the customer number, invoice date, invoice number, rate per hour, job duration, and invoice amount. A total is to be printed when there is a change in the invoice date or the customer number. A final total is to print also. The input record format is also presented. Create a printer spacing chart, hierarchy chart, structured program flowchart, and pseudocode for this problem.

**INPUT RECORD FORMAT:**

| Field Description | Column Locations | Type |
|---|---|---|
| Customer number | 1–5 | N |
| Invoice date | 6–11 | N |
| Invoice number | 12–16 | N |
| Rate per hour | 17–20 | N ($$.¢¢) |
| Job duration (hrs.) | 21–22 | N |

Calculate invoice amount = Rate per hour × job duration (in hours).

```
XX/XX/XX              DALE'S AUTO SERVICE        PAGE XXXX
                       INVOICE REGISTER

CUSTOMER    INVOICE    INVOICE   RATE/HR   JOB      INVOICE
NUMBER      DATE       NUMBER              HRS

 XXXXX     XX/XX/XX   XXXXX      XX.XX     XX       XXX.XX
 XXXXX     XX/XX/XX   XXXXX      XX.XX     XX       XXX.XX

       TOTAL CUSTOMER INVOICE FOR XX/XX/XX     $X,XXX.XX *

 XXXXX     XX/XX/XX   XXXXX      XX.XX     XX       XXX.XX
 XXXXX     XX/XX/XX   XXXXX      XX.XX     XX       XXX.XX

        TOTAL CUSTOMER INVOICES FOR XX/XX/XX    $X,XXX.XX *
 TOTAL CUSTOMER INVOICES FOR CUSTOMER XXXXX    $XX,XXX.XX **
                     FINAL TOTAL               $XXX,XXX.XX ***
```

**6–4.** In the report you produced for problem 6–3, group-indicate both the major and minor control fields. Use the embedded logic method discussed in Exhibit 6.20.

---

**6–5.** A university wishes to produce a teacher information report (as follows) that indicates the courses each teacher teaches and the total number of credit hours for each teacher. Totals are to be printed when there is a change in teacher number, department number, or college number. The input record format is also presented. Create a printer spacing chart, hierarchy chart, structured flowchart, and pseudocode for this problem.

**INPUT RECORD FORMAT:**

| Field Description | Column Locations | Type |
|---|---|---|
| College number | 1–3 | N |
| Department number | 4–5 | N |
| Teacher number | 7–10 | N |
| Course title | 11–21 | A/N |
| Credit hours | 22–23 | N |
| Class size | 25–26 | N |

Contact hours = credit hours × class size.

```
                          ABC UNIVERSITY

                    TEACHER INFORMATION REPORT

COLLEGE   DEPARTMENT   TEACHER   COURSE          CREDIT     CLASS       CONT.
NUMBER    NUMBER       NUMBER    TITLE           HOURS      SIZE        HRS.

XXX       XX           XXXX      XXXXXXXXXXX      XX         XX          XXX
                                 XXXXXXXXXXX      XX         XX          XXX
                                 XXXXXXXXXXX      XX         XX          XXX

                       CONTACT HOURS FOR TEACHER XXXX                    X,XXX*

                       XXXX      XXXXXXXXXXX      XX         XX          XXX
                                 XXXXXXXXXXX      XX         XX          XXX

                       CONTACT HOURS FOR TEACHER XXXX                    X,XXX*
                       CONTACT HOURS FOR DEPT.    XX                    XX,XXX**

          XX           XXXX      XXXXXXXXXXX      XX         XX          XXX
                                 XXXXXXXXXXX      XX         XX          XXX
                                 XXXXXXXXXXX      XX         XX          XXX
                                 XXXXXXXXXXX      XX         XX          XXX

                       CONTACT HOURS FOR TEACHER XXXX                    X,XXX*

                       XXXX      XXXXXXXXXXX      XX         XX          XXX
                                 XXXXXXXXXXX      XX         XX          XXX

                       CONTACT HOURS FOR TEACHER   XXXX                  X,XXX*
                       CONTACT HOURS FOR DEPT.     XX                   XX,XXX**
                       CONTACT HOURS FOR COLLEGE   XXX                 XXX,XXX*

XXX       XX           XXX       XXXXXXXXXXX      XX         XX          XXX
                                 XXXXXXXXXXX      XX         XX          XXX

                       CONTACT HOURS FOR TEACHER   XXXX                  X,XXX*
                       CONTACT HOURS FOR DEPT.     XX                   XX,XXX**
                       CONTACT HOURS FOR COLLEGE   XXX                XXX,XXX***
                       CONTACT HOURS FOR UNIVERSITY              X,XXX,XXX****
```

# 7
# Table Handling Concepts

## OBJECTIVES

As a result of having read and studied this chapter, the student will be able to do the following activities:

1. Define a table.

2. List the various uses of tables.

3. Contrast internal and external tables.

4. Describe the logic of the definite iteration.

5. Describe the process of loading a single-dimensional table.

6. Describe the general logic of a table search.

7. Describe what is meant by positional addressing.

8. Draw a hierarchy chart, design a structured flowchart, and write the pseudocode that will:
   a. load a single-dimensional table.
   b. search a single-dimensional table.
   c. access data from the single-dimensional table using positional addressing.

Frequently, a computer program will access data that are not part of the input record itself. In many cases, these data are the kind that must be frequently accessed and would be redundant if included on the input records. Data that are common to more than one record in the input file are often placed in a **table** in memory (sometimes called a **memory table**) prior to processing the input records. During the processing of the input records and when needed, certain table values are extracted in order to complete a calculation. Just as a tax accountant refers to tax tables to determine an employee's tax deduction, a programmer must develop programs that access tables of commonly used data to complete the necessary processing for each record. Sometimes a table is referred to as an **array**.

## A TABLE DEFINED

A table is a list of related items—ones with common attributes—that is placed into main memory for fast access during record processing. The table is normally loaded with values prior to the actual record processing activity. The program then searches the table from the beginning toward the end until it finds a specific value of interest. To continue the example above, a tax accountant might search sequentially through a list of salary ranges until discovering the one that includes the employee's salary amount. Then the accountant can extract from the table a corresponding tax amount. Figure 7.1 illustrates this procedure. Here, the employee has a salary of $272. The accountant searches through a tax table and locates the salary range (201–300) that includes the employee's salary. The accountant then extracts the corresponding tax amount of $27.80, which is subsequently used in calculating the employee's net pay.

## Table Uses

Tables, or arrays, have many uses. They can store tax amounts, commission rates, discount percentages, product descriptions, product prices, etc., for later use. Normally, tables are used in the following ways:

1. A table is searched to validate a record key value, a classification code, or other value prior to processing the input records.

2. A table is searched or otherwise accessed for a value to be used in a subsequent calculation.

3. A table is searched for a value that would be redundant to include on every record in order to complete a processing step.

Figure 7.2 illustrates the first listed use of tables. Before it computes an employee's salary and writes a paycheck, the program searches a table of valid employee numbers (SSNs) in order to validate this particular employee's number. This search, along with many other processing safeguards, prevents attempts by unscrupulous employees from making up bogus pay records for processing in order to receive pay more than once during a single pay period.

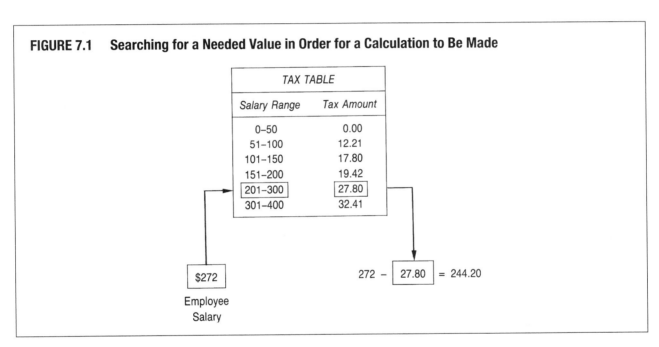

**FIGURE 7.1    Searching for a Needed Value in Order for a Calculation to Be Made**

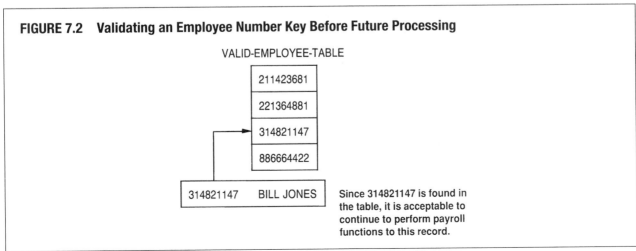

**FIGURE 7.2    Validating an Employee Number Key Before Future Processing**

Figure 7.3 illustrates the second listed use of tables. Here, the search takes place during the processing of an inventory record in order to extract an item description. The program locates the item description by using the item number from the input record as the **search key**. The search key is the value on the input record for which you are looking in the table. The value in the table that corresponds to the item number is the actual value we're after. This type of table access is often used because it would be time-consuming to key in, for example, the word BANANAS on a transaction record every time a customer purchased bananas. The idea is to create a table with the word BANANAS in it only once and then locate the word BANANAS by its item number when processing transactions that involve bananas. In Figure 7.3, you can see the word BANANAS being extracted from the table and placed into the print line for reporting purposes.

Figure 7.4 depicts both the second and third uses of tables listed above. The word BANANAS is extracted from the table and placed into the appropriate area of the print line, while the price, $1.46, is extracted and used in a calculation to determine the sales amount. It is common for a table to be used for a dual purpose.

# POINTING TO A SPECIFIC TABLE VALUE
## Using a Subscript

Locating a value in a table is similar to locating a person in a hotel. First, you must know the room number of the person for whom you are searching. To locate a value in a table, you need to locate the compartment, or pigeonhole, in which the value is stored. Such a compartment in a table is called an **element**. Figure 7.5 illustrates the various elements in the VALID-EMPLOYEE-TABLE. Figure 7.6 shows an element with subcompartments. Here, a subcompartment consists of a **table key** (or **table argument**) called PRODUCT-NUMBER and a corresponding value (or **table function**) called PRODUCT-DESCRIPTION. A table argument is the value you are trying to locate in the table. The table function is the item of interest that corresponds to its respective table argument. An element is a subset of a table, in which one or more values are placed. To refer to a specific value in a table requires that the table have a name and a **subscript**. A subscript can be either a constant or a variable number, placed in parentheses immediately following the table name, that establishes the relative location of a value in a table. Figure 7.7 shows how a table name and a

**FIGURE 7.3  Searching for a Value That Would Be Redundant to Include on Every Sales Record**

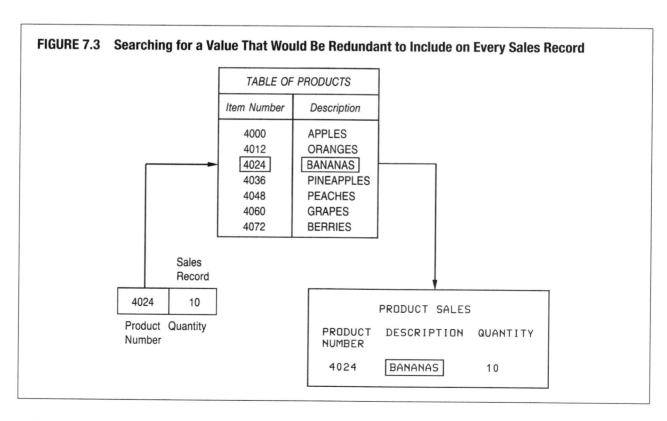

subscript are used to point to a specific element in the table. The subscript in this case is a constant. For example, the subscript (1) indicates that the element referenced is the first one in the set; the subscript (2) indicates that the element referenced is the second, and so on. In COBOL, the subscript must be a non-zero, positive integer. But in BASIC and several other computer languages, the subscript *may* be zero, because the first element in these tables is located at element zero. It is a good idea to avoid the use of the subscript value zero, however, and start with the subscript value 1 instead. Notice in Figure 7.7 that every reference requires both a table name and an associated subscript. VALID-EMPLOYEE-TABLE (1) points to

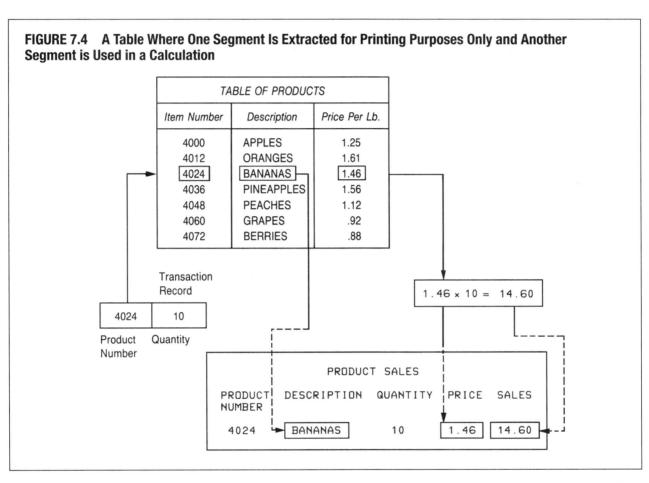

**FIGURE 7.4   A Table Where One Segment Is Extracted for Printing Purposes Only and Another Segment is Used in a Calculation**

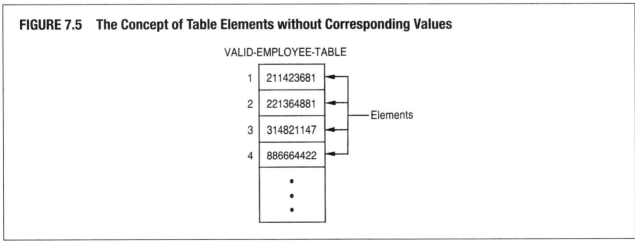

**FIGURE 7.5   The Concept of Table Elements without Corresponding Values**

the first element; VALID-EMPLOYEE-TABLE (2) points to the second element, and so on.

A subscript can also be, and usually is, a variable. Panel A of Figure 7.8 illustrates that the contents of the subscript determine the elements pointed to. Panel B of Figure 7.8 illustrates the use of a subscript variable referred to as a SUB. In this example, a change in SUB will result in a reference to a different element. If the value of SUB = 1, a reference to PRODUCTS-TAB (SUB) points to the first element of the table. On the other hand, if the value of SUB = 2, a reference to PRODUCTS-TAB (SUB) points to the second element of the table. In other words, which element the table reference points to will depend on the contents of the subscript. Panel B of Figure 7.8 shows that the third element, 4024 BANANAS, is referenced when the content of the subscript called (SUB) is equal to 3. It is important

to note that a single subscript can be used in conjunction with *more than one* table name. In other words, the same contents of SUB can serve as a pointer to PRODUCTS-TAB as well as a pointer to, let's say, PRICE-TAB. This is extremely important where the elements of two physically separate tables correspond to each other, that is, where the first element of PRODUCTS-TAB corresponds to the first element of PRICE-TAB. This is discussed later and also referenced in Figure 7.6.

## LOADING TABLES

Tables can be created in either of two ways. The first type of table can be set up as a part of the computer program work area and is often referred to as an **internal table** or **hard-coded** table. Here, the

---

**FIGURE 7.6    The Concept of Table Elements with Corresponding Values**

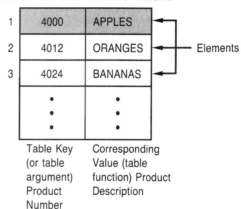

NOTE:    A table of corresponding values can be handled with the COBOL language.
    In BASIC, this type of table concept is physically treated as two separate tables. The table argument forms one table and the table function is the second table.

---

**FIGURE 7.7    Referencing a Table Using a Table Name and a Subscript**

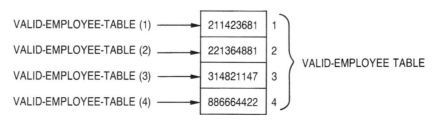

A table name and an associated subscript are necessary in order to point to an element.

table values are coded directly into the computer program itself. Another term for this type of table is **compile-time table**, since the table is actually in existence once the compilation process is complete. The second type of table is often referred to as an **external table**. It is first created as a file, an external set of data that is later read and loaded into the memory table area for processing. This type of table is also referred to as an **execution-time table**, since it is not created until the program module responsible for the loading process has finished executing.

## A Rationale for Table Usage

A table is usually created as a separate file, often called the **table file**. In some cases, tables are made by extracting data from various fields in an existing file or from various fields in a number of different files. Here we will concentrate on the creation of a separate table file. In order to drastically decrease the computer time required for searching tables, the table data file is loaded into main memory of the computer. This is called a **table load**. This method reduces computer time because data can be manip-

ulated in memory in microseconds as opposed to the much slower process of accessing data stored on peripheral devices such as tape and disk. For example, while it might take less than a millionth of a second to locate a value in a memory table once it has been loaded, it could take as long as 30 thousandths of a second to access the same piece of data in a disk file. This means it is more than 30,000 times faster to access the data from a memory table than from a direct access device. The process of locating an element in a table is called a **table lookup** or **table search**.

Before a table search can occur in a memory table, the table data have to get there somehow; a table-loading process has to occur at some point. Fortunately, the table file must be loaded to the table only once each time the program is executed. After the loading process is complete, an unlimited number of accesses can be made to the table, each at virtually the speed of electric current (that is, close to the speed of light). In most cases, the processing time devoted to loading tables is time well spent.

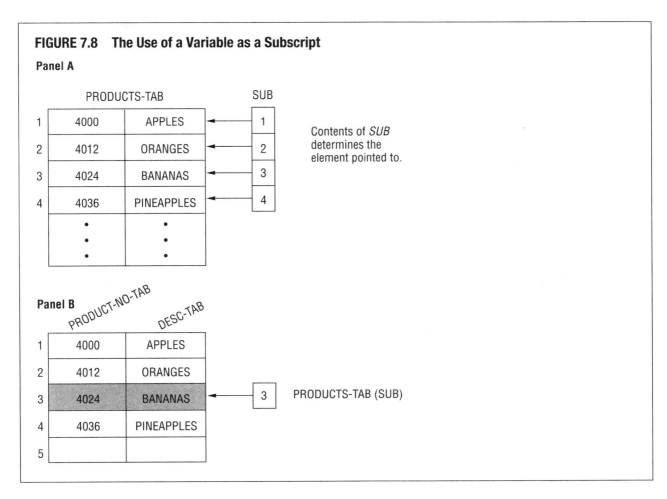

**FIGURE 7.8    The Use of a Variable as a Subscript**

**Panel A**

PRODUCTS-TAB     SUB

| | | | |
|---|---|---|---|
| 1 | 4000 | APPLES | 1 |
| 2 | 4012 | ORANGES | 2 |
| 3 | 4024 | BANANAS | 3 |
| 4 | 4036 | PINEAPPLES | 4 |

Contents of *SUB* determines the element pointed to.

**Panel B**

PRODUCT-NO-TAB    DESC-TAB

| | | |
|---|---|---|
| 1 | 4000 | APPLES |
| 2 | 4012 | ORANGES |
| 3 | 4024 | BANANAS |
| 4 | 4036 | PINEAPPLES |
| 5 | | |

3    PRODUCTS-TAB (SUB)

Figure 7.9 illustrates the table-loading process from a programming perspective. Here, a table of valid employee numbers is created from a table file. In all likelihood, the table would be loaded from a master employee file, but for illustrative purposes, let's assume that the only field on the table is the SSN. Each SSN is a separate record in the file; therefore, a new record is read prior to storing the SSN in the appropriate element of the table. Figure 7.9 also illustrates how the subscript SUB is initialized to 1 and subsequently increased by 1 as each element is loaded. Prior to the reading of the first table record, the content of SUB is equal to 1. After the record is read and the SSN, 211422681, is transferred to the first table element, the subscript SUB is increased by 1. Now, because the value of SUB is 2, the second record's SSN, 221364881, is transferred to the second element of the table. Each time an element is loaded, the subscript is increased so that it points to the next element. Then the next record is read, and the process is repeated until all SSNs have been stored in the table.

## Programming Logic for Loading Tables

The programming logic in flowchart form for loading a table is illustrated in Figure 7.10. As previously explained, the table-loading process has to occur prior to the actual processing of the input (transaction) records; therefore, a separate module must be established to load the table. In the START-UP module, the table file is opened and the first table record is read. Next, the TABLE-LOAD module is invoked. The table-load logic shown in the TABLE-LOAD module is the *manual manipulation of a subscript to load a table using a counting loop*. In a subsequent flowchart (Figure 7.15), you will see a more sophisticated method for handling the table-load process, but for illustrative purposes at this time, let us pursue the manual technique shown in Figure 7.10. Figure 7.11 illustrates the step-by-step execution of the flowchart shown in Figure 7.10.

In step 1A of Figure 7.11, the first record of the file is read into the input area. Step 1B depicts the TABLE-LOAD module invoked from the START-UP module; the subscript SUB is initialized to 1 in step 1C. Then, step 1D shows the comparison test (while SUB not > 4). The value 1 is less than 4; thus the result of the test is *false*. The resulting program path stores the SSN at the first element of the table (step 1E). In step 1F, the second record of the table file is read into the input area. Next, step 1G shows the subscript SUB is increased by 1 (SUB = 2). Now the logic has established the proper element location to house the SSN for the second record.

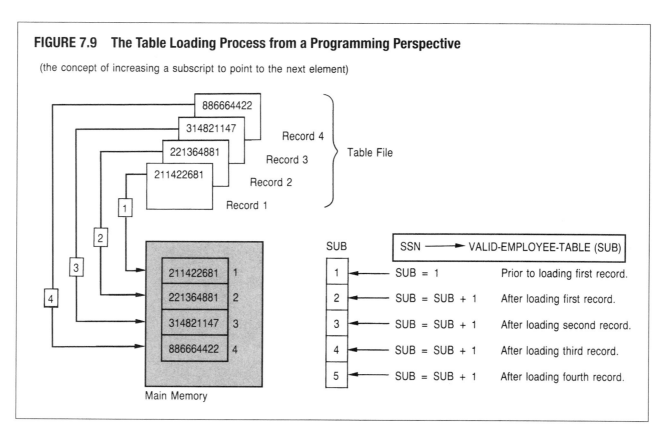

**FIGURE 7.9   The Table Loading Process from a Programming Perspective**

(the concept of increasing a subscript to point to the next element)

**FIGURE 7.10  A Manual Manipulation of a Subscript to Load a Table Using a Counting Loop***
(not the best method)

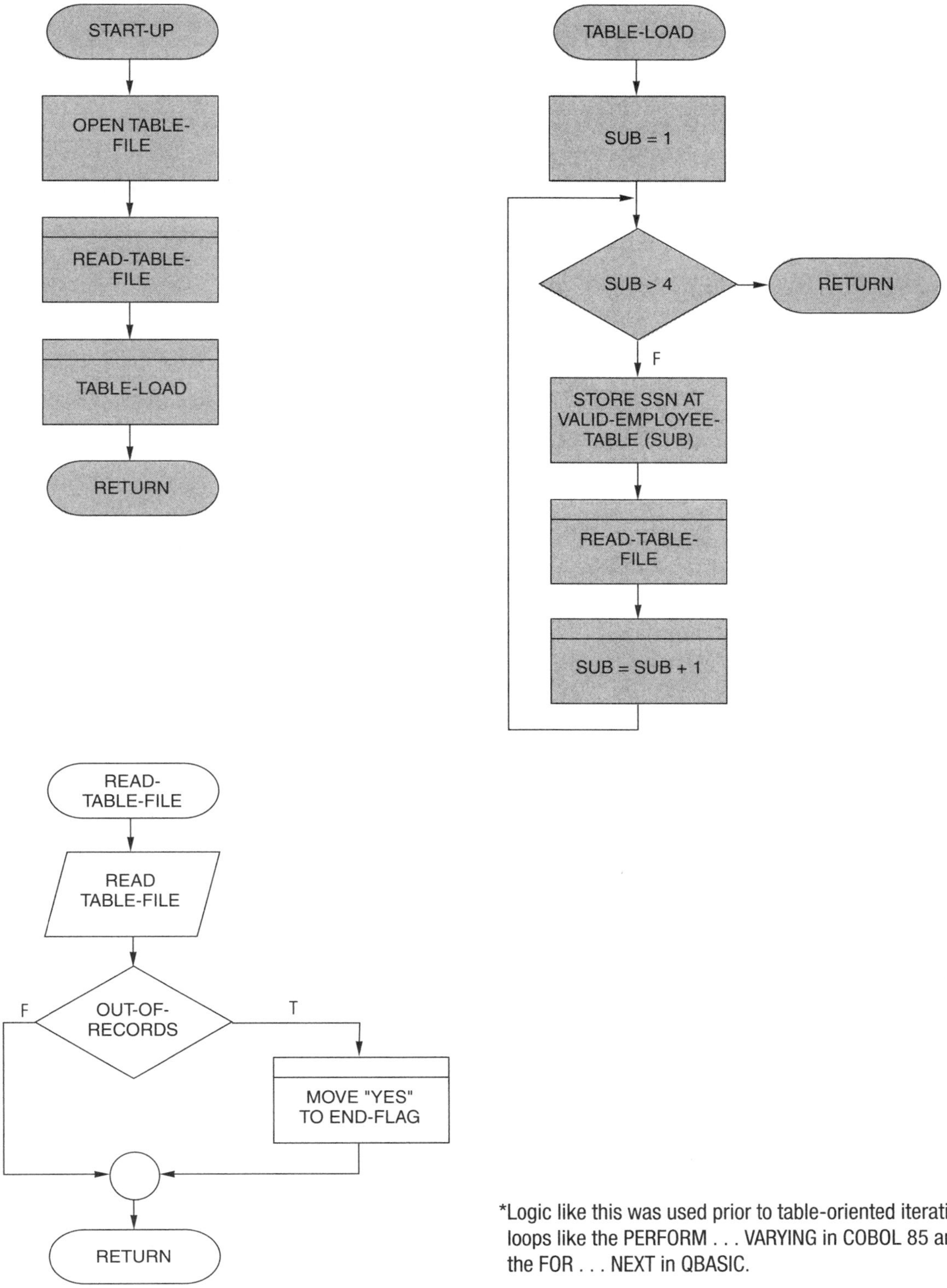

*Logic like this was used prior to table-oriented iteration loops like the PERFORM . . . VARYING in COBOL 85 and the FOR . . . NEXT in QBASIC.

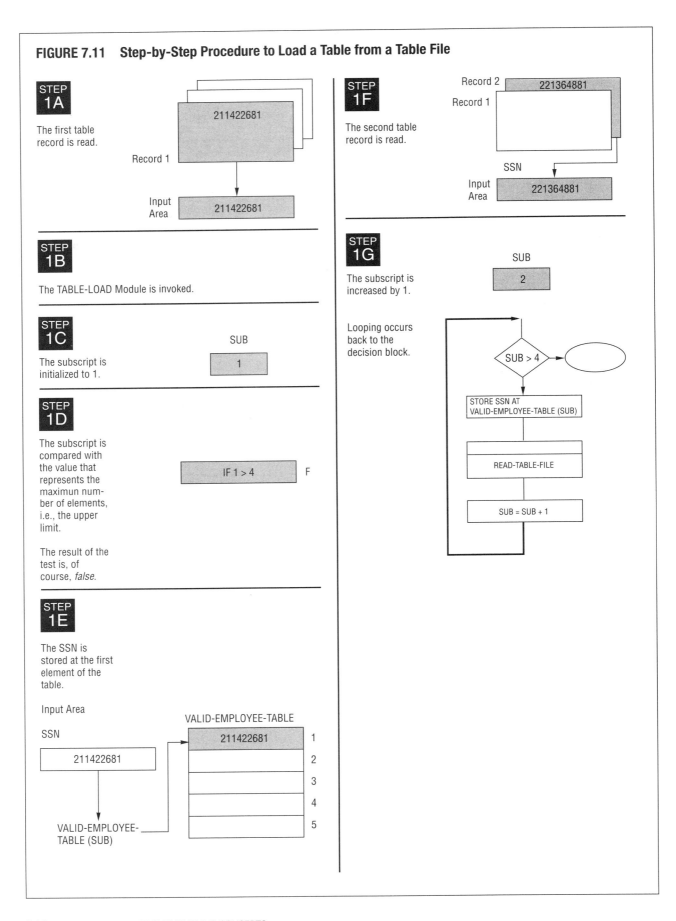

**FIGURE 7.11    Step-by-Step Procedure to Load a Table from a Table File**

**STEP 1A**

The first table record is read.

Record 1

211422681

Input Area    211422681

**STEP 1B**

The TABLE-LOAD Module is invoked.

**STEP 1C**

The subscript is initialized to 1.

SUB

1

**STEP 1D**

The subscript is compared with the value that represents the maximun number of elements, i.e., the upper limit.

IF 1 > 4    F

The result of the test is, of course, *false*.

**STEP 1E**

The SSN is stored at the first element of the table.

Input Area

SSN

211422681

VALID-EMPLOYEE-TABLE (SUB)

VALID-EMPLOYEE-TABLE

| 211422681 | 1 |
| | 2 |
| | 3 |
| | 4 |
| | 5 |

**STEP 1F**

The second table record is read.

Record 2    221364881
Record 1

SSN

Input Area    221364881

**STEP 1G**

The subscript is increased by 1.

SUB

2

Looping occurs back to the decision block.

SUB > 4

STORE SSN AT VALID-EMPLOYEE-TABLE (SUB)

READ-TABLE-FILE

SUB = SUB + 1

**FIGURE 7.11    (Cont.)**

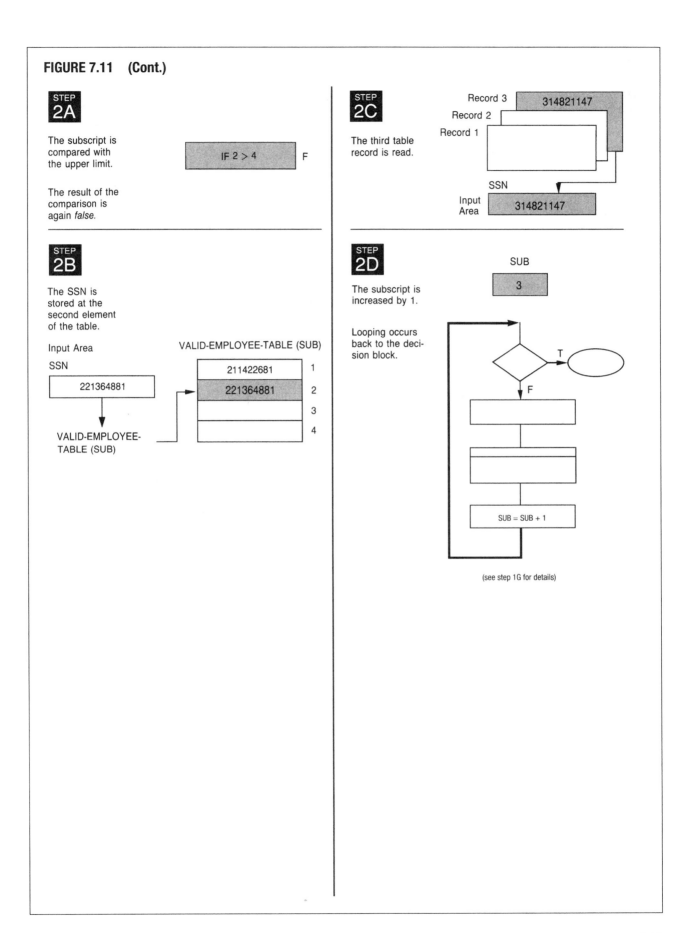

**STEP 2A**

The subscript is compared with the upper limit.

The result of the comparison is again *false*.

IF 2 > 4     F

**STEP 2B**

The SSN is stored at the second element of the table.

Input Area

SSN

221364881

VALID-EMPLOYEE-TABLE (SUB)

VALID-EMPLOYEE-TABLE (SUB)

| | |
|---|---|
| 211422681 | 1 |
| 221364881 | 2 |
| | 3 |
| | 4 |

**STEP 2C**

The third table record is read.

Record 3     314821147
Record 2
Record 1

SSN

Input Area     314821147

**STEP 2D**

The subscript is increased by 1.

Looping occurs back to the decision block.

SUB

3

T

F

SUB = SUB + 1

(see step 1G for details)

**FIGURE 7.11    (Cont.)**

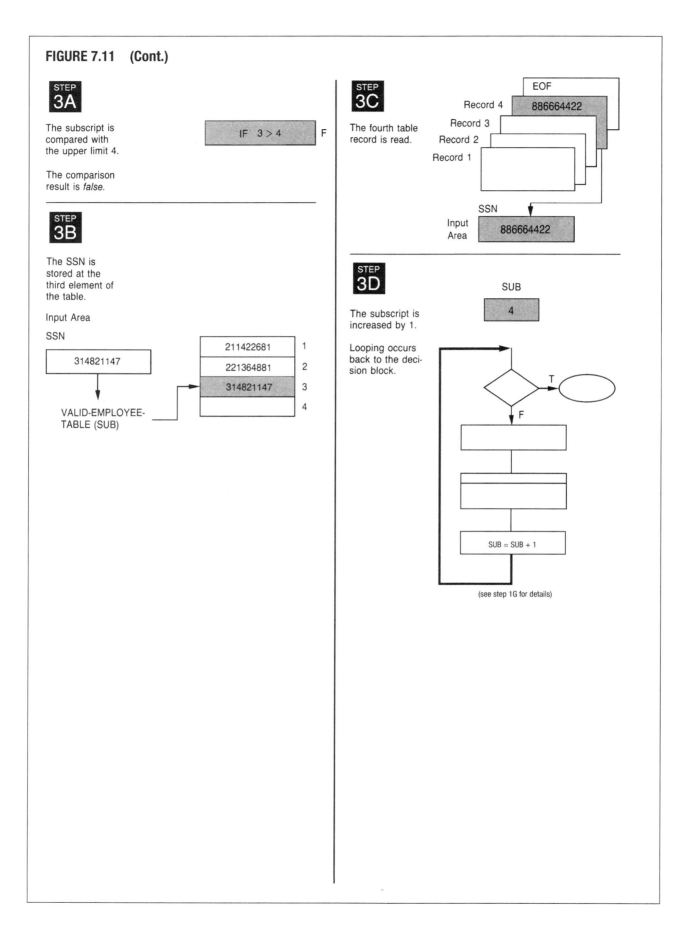

**STEP 3A**

The subscript is compared with the upper limit 4.

IF  3 > 4     F

The comparison result is *false*.

**STEP 3B**

The SSN is stored at the third element of the table.

Input Area

SSN

314821147

VALID-EMPLOYEE-TABLE (SUB)

| | |
|---|---|
| 211422681 | 1 |
| 221364881 | 2 |
| 314821147 | 3 |
| | 4 |

**STEP 3C**

The fourth table record is read.

EOF

Record 4    886664422
Record 3
Record 2
Record 1

SSN

Input Area    886664422

**STEP 3D**

The subscript is increased by 1.

Looping occurs back to the decision block.

SUB

4

SUB = SUB + 1

(see step 1G for details)

**FIGURE 7.11    (Cont.)**

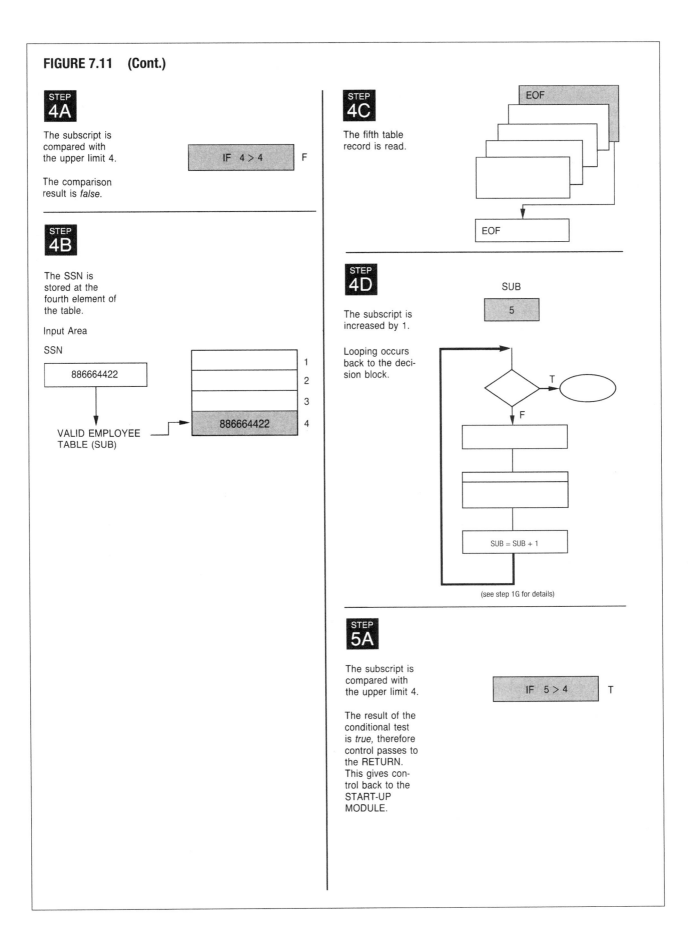

**STEP 4A**

The subscript is compared with the upper limit 4.

IF  4 > 4     F

The comparison result is *false*.

**STEP 4B**

The SSN is stored at the fourth element of the table.

Input Area

SSN

886664422

VALID EMPLOYEE TABLE (SUB)

886664422

1
2
3
4

**STEP 4C**

The fifth table record is read.

EOF

EOF

**STEP 4D**

The subscript is increased by 1.

Looping occurs back to the decision block.

SUB

5

T

F

SUB = SUB + 1

(see step 1G for details)

**STEP 5A**

The subscript is compared with the upper limit 4.

IF  5 > 4     T

The result of the conditional test is *true*, therefore control passes to the RETURN. This gives control back to the START-UP MODULE.

Next, looping occurs, passing control back to the decision block of the DoWhile structure. Once again, a comparison determines whether the current content of the subscript is greater than the upper limit (the value that represents the maximum number of elements in the table).

Step 2A of Figure 7.11 illustrates this comparison process. The result of this test is once again *false*, because 2 is not greater than 4. The execution path leads to step 2B. Here the SSN is stored at the second element of the table. The value, 221364881, is stored at VALUE-EMPLOYEE-TABLE (SUB) where SUB = 2. Step 2C illustrates the reading of the third record into the input area, and step 2D depicts the increment of SUB to the value 3. At this point, the control once again passes to the decision block.

Step 3A of Figure 7.11 notes the comparison process that occurs at the decision block. The content of SUB (the value 3) is compared with the upper limit, 4. The result of the comparison is *false* ; therefore, the path the program takes leads to step 3B. Step 3B shows that the SSN, 314821147, is moved to the third element of the table. After the third record's SSN is transferred, the fourth record is read in step 3C; and step 3D depicts the variable SUB increased to the value 4. Looping occurs once again back to the decision block.

Steps 4A through 4D of Figure 7.11 represent the comparison of SUB with 4, the loading of the fourth record to the fourth element, the reading of the next record (EOF record), and the incrementing of the subscript to 5. Looping occurs back to the decision block.

Step 5A of Figure 7.11 depicts the comparison of the contents of SUB (the value 5) with the upper limit of 4. The result of the comparison (If SUB > 4) is not *true*; therefore, control passes this time to RETURN. This, in turn, gives control back to the START-UP module. The loading process is now complete.

An important feature of this loading method is that the process of reading the record is separate from that of storing the data in the table. While many languages allow direct-read transfer to a table, you should know how to perform the loading process as a separate function. Why is it necessary to know both methods? A direct-read transfer is fine. However, if the formats of the record and the table should differ, as they often do in real-world applications, a separate store operation is required. You should be aware that in COBOL the Read . . . Into command transfers data to the table on a left-to-right basis and thus requires that the formats of the table record and the table element agree identically.

## The Built-in Logic of Two Definite Iteration Commands

You have seen how a table is loaded through a step-by-step manual flowcharting procedure, where every step is a separate block in the flowchart—including the subscript increment. COBOL and BASIC, like most languages, have looping commands with *built-in logic* to handle automatic increasing of a subscript or variable. The COBOL command, Perform . . . Varying, and the BASIC command, For . . . Next, both possess this valuable capability. Either of these commands, used with the appropriate compiler or interpreter software, enables the programmer to develop programming loops *without* having to manually initialize, test, or increase subscripts through the use of conditional or arithmetic commands.

Figure 7.12 illustrates the built-in logic of these two "definite iteration" commands. The term **definite iteration** means that the loop will be executed a definite, or predefined, number of times. Panel A of Figure 7.12 depicts the use of the **Perform . . . Varying** command in flowchart form in COBOL, and Panel B of Figure 7.12 shows the **For . . . Next** logic in BASIC. Subscript adjusting is built into both of these commands; that is, the subscript is automatically initialized, tested, and increased each time the body of the loop is processed. In panel A, Perform . . . Varying, in the *first step* the subscript is initialized; *second*, the condition is tested; *third*, the module (or paragraph) is performed; and *fourth*, the subscript is automatically increased. The actual COBOL command is shown beneath the flowchart: Perform paragraph name Varying subscript From 1 By 1 Until subscript > 4. In the Perform . . . Varying command in COBOL, the From value represents the initial value of the subscript. The By value represents the increment amount. The From or By values can be any positive, zero, or negative integer values, but manipulation of the subscript must not result in a negative value.

Panel B demonstrates the built-in logic of the For . . . Next statement. Essentially, the logic of For . . . Next is the same as Perform . . . Varying, except that Perform actually causes a module to be invoked, whereas this is not always the case with For . . . Next. In For . . . Next, statements to be executed usually immediately follow the For command. Another major difference between the two commands is that Perform . . . Varying allows *any* condition to be tested, whereas the For . . . Next statement tests only the subscript (or index) to determine if it is greater than the upper limit. But the two commands function basically the same in processing tables.

## FIGURE 7.12  Built-in Logic of Two Definite Iteration Commands

When the Varying option is used with the Perform command, this logic (panel A) is automatically executed. The same appl
the For . . . Next commands (panel B).

### Panel A—COBOL 85
PERFORM . . . VARYING

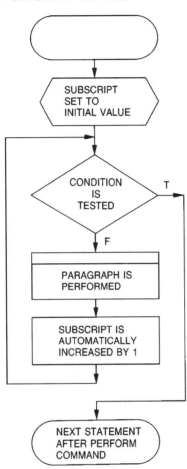

```
COBOL
PERFORM paragraph name
VARYING SUB FROM 1
BY 1 UNTIL SUB > 4
```

### Panel B—QBASIC
FOR . . . NEXT

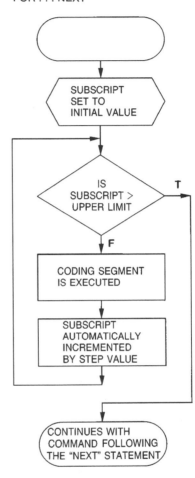

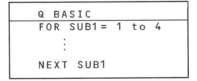

```
Q BASIC
FOR SUB1 = 1 to 4
   ⋮
NEXT SUB1
```

## Flowchart Model of the Definite Iteration Structure

Figure 7.13 illustrates how one goes about flow-charting either the For . . . Next or the Perform . . . Varying statements. It would be a mistake to draw a flowchart similar to the one in Figure 7.10 if you plan to use FOR . . . NEXT or Perform . . . Varying, because both of these statements have looping and automatic subscript incrementing built into their commands. A flowchart that shows separate blocks for each of the steps might lead you to believe that there is a one-to-one correspondence between the flowchart boxes and the program commands. This is not so when you're dealing with these two commands. Figure 7.13 illustrates the four basic parts of a programming structure with *definite iteration*. To cause a loop to be executed a fixed number of times requires the use of a counter. (Panel A of Figure 7.13 illustrates this four-step process.) Therefore, the first part of the structure is the *initialization of the counter* to 1. Second, the *counter is tested* to determine if it is greater than some predetermined value, which normally represents the maximum number of iterations to be made; third, the *body of commands is executed*; and fourth, the *counter is increased* by some value (probably 1). The transfer of control is back to the condition test. Once again the condition is tested to determine if the counter is greater than the predetermined value. If the result of the condition test is false, then the loop is repeated. This process continues until the value in the loop counter is greater than the upper limit. When this happens, the looping ceases and processing contin-

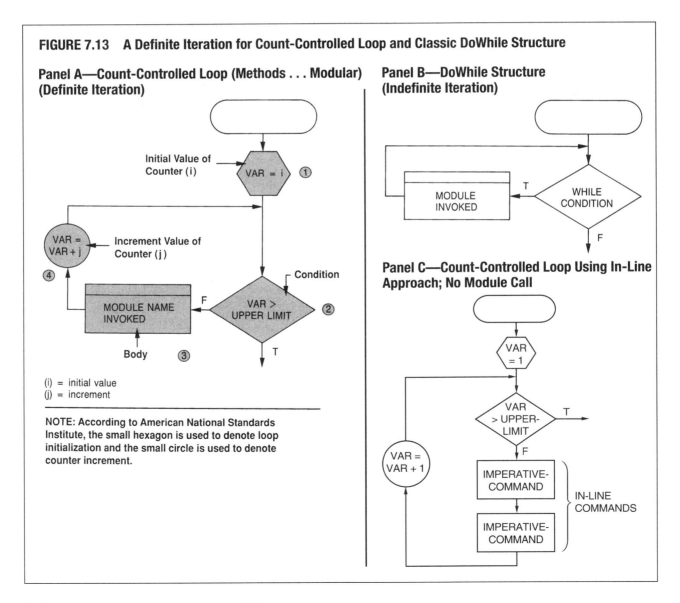

**FIGURE 7.13    A Definite Iteration for Count-Controlled Loop and Classic DoWhile Structure**

Panel A—Count-Controlled Loop (Methods . . . Modular) (Definite Iteration)

Initial Value of Counter (i)    VAR = i    ①

VAR = VAR + j    Increment Value of Counter (j)    ④

MODULE NAME INVOKED    F    VAR > UPPER LIMIT    ②

Body    ③    T

Condition

(i) = initial value
(j) = increment

NOTE: According to American National Standards Institute, the small hexagon is used to denote loop initialization and the small circle is used to denote counter increment.

Panel B—DoWhile Structure (Indefinite Iteration)

MODULE INVOKED    T    WHILE CONDITION    F

Panel C—Count-Controlled Loop Using In-Line Approach; No Module Call

VAR = 1

VAR = VAR + 1    VAR > UPPER-LIMIT    T    F

IMPERATIVE-COMMAND    IN-LINE COMMANDS

IMPERATIVE-COMMAND

ues with the next command beneath the structure. Panel B shows, for the purpose of comparison, the simple DoWhile logic.

Panel C of Figure 7.13 illustrates an alternative (Method 2) to the count-controlled loop previously discussed. This technique places the commands "in line" or within the loop itself. No module is called. In very simple functions, this method may be preferred.

Figure 7.14 (panel A) illustrates the definite iteration structure. Panels B and C show the associated COBOL and BASIC code.

### Loading a Table Using the Definite Loop Structure

The concept of loading a table was previously discussed and the step-by-step process of loading a table was illustrated using the flowchart segment in Figure 7.10 and the step-by-step illustration in Figure 7.11. The table load process can be depicted in flowchart form to adhere to the definite iteration methodology previously discussed. Figure 7.15 best illustrates the definite iteration that will match the implementing command (either Perform . . . Varying or For . . . Next). Since VALID-EMPLOYEE-TABLE has four elements, the ELEMENT-LOAD module will need to loop four times to complete

the load process. The first step is to initialize the subscript SUB to 1. Then SUB is compared with 4. If the result of the condition is *false*, the ELEMENT-LOAD module is invoked. The invoking of the ELEMENT-LOAD module causes SSN to be stored at the first element of the table and the second record to be read. Linkage then occurs back to the increment block, where the subscript is automatically increased by 1, in order to point to the second element of the table. Since the content of SUB is less than 4, this loop is repeated a second, a third, and a fourth time. However, the next time through the loop, the increment block causes SUB to be increased to 5. When the subsequent comparison is made, the condition tests *true*, since the content of SUB (the value 5) is greater than 4. The program execution continues with the RETURN block, which in turn gives control back to the invoking module, START-UP.

## SEARCHING TABLES

After the table has been created, using either an internal or an external load process, the next step is to search it for a particular value. As mentioned, this procedure is often called a table lookup or a table search. The two main searching techniques are

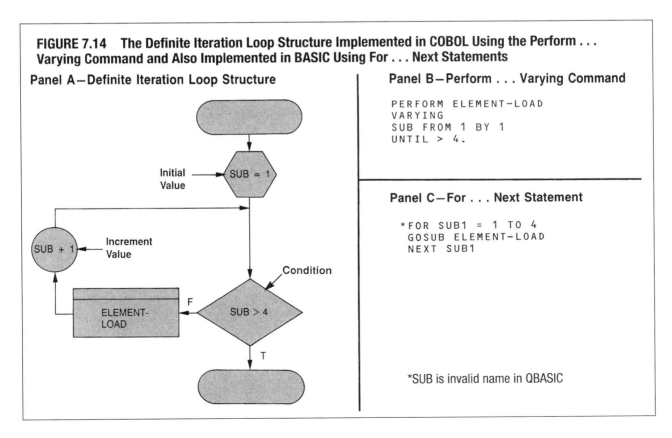

**FIGURE 7.14  The Definite Iteration Loop Structure Implemented in COBOL Using the Perform . . . Varying Command and Also Implemented in BASIC Using For . . . Next Statements**

Panel A—Definite Iteration Loop Structure

Initial Value → SUB = 1

Increment Value → SUB + 1

ELEMENT-LOAD

Condition → SUB > 4

F

T

Panel B—Perform . . . Varying Command

```
PERFORM ELEMENT-LOAD
VARYING
SUB FROM 1 BY 1
UNTIL > 4.
```

Panel C—For . . . Next Statement

```
*FOR SUB1 = 1 TO 4
 GOSUB ELEMENT-LOAD
 NEXT SUB1
```

*SUB is invalid name in QBASIC

(1) the **sequential** (or **serial**) **search** and (2) the **binary search**. The sequential search is by far the more popular method for searching tables with less than 50 records, since it is easier to design and code. Also, with such small files, the techniques are equally efficient. The Binary Search is discussed in Chapter 8.

Figure 7.16 illustrates the sequential searching process, which starts with the first element of the VALID-EMPLOYEES-TABLE and progresses one by one through the table, comparing the SSN from the input transaction record (search key, or search argument) with the SSN in the VALID-EMPLOYEES-TABLE (table key, or table argument) until a matching condition occurs. If a match occurs, normal record processing continues; but if all the elements of the table are searched and a matching condition does not exist, an error message prints, indicating that this particular SSN is invalid and will not be processed. In Figure 7.16, the searching process ceases when the search key becomes equal to the fourth value in the table.

Next, how do we design programs for searching? As Figure 7.16 shows, a search key from a transaction record is normally read into the program. This key becomes the value for which the search is made, the value that the program must try to locate in the table. Just as in the preceding section a subscript was manipulated to *load* a table, here a subscript will be manipulated to *search for a value* in a table.

For the comparison process to start at the top of the table, the subscript must be initialized to 1. If the search key is not equal to the table key, then the subscript is increased by 1. This will cause the SSN from the input record to be compared with the second element of the table VALID-EMPLOYEE-TABLE (SUB), where SUB = 2. The process of increasing the subscript and comparing continues until one of two events occurs—either the value is found or the end of the table is sensed. Figure 7.17 illustrates the searching process when no matching condition exists. The sensing of the end of the table occurs when the last element is still not equal to the search value and the subscript is increased by 1; hence, this subscript becomes larger than the table size of 4. When the subscript value, 5, tests greater than the maximum table size, 4, it means that the SSN is not found in the table.

## Sequential Search Logic

Figure 7.18 illustrates the basic logic of a table search. For every record read, a table lookup operation is performed. The START-UP module is shown simply to depict the presence of the READ-TRANS-

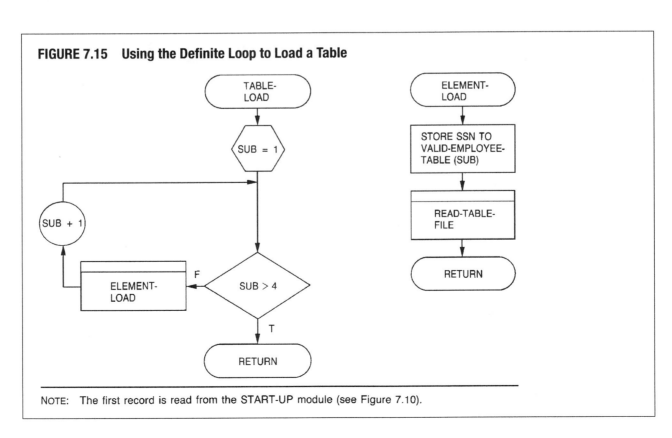

**FIGURE 7.15  Using the Definite Loop to Load a Table**

NOTE:   The first record is read from the START-UP module (see Figure 7.10).

FILE module, from which the first transaction record is read. The model logic of a table lookup operation begins by invoking a separate module that contains all the necessary logic to handle the table lookup function. Here the module is called TABLE-LOOKUP. Just as a control variable was used in Chapter 5 to handle the validation of a record, a control variable called **FOUND-SWITCH** is used here to detect whether or not a specific search key is found in the table. If the search key is found in the table, the FOUND-SWITCH is turned on; and if the FOUND-SWITCH is turned on, normal processing occurs. But if the FOUND-SWITCH remains off (FOUND-SWITCH = "NO"), some type of error message is printed. In either case, after one of the alternative steps is performed, the next record is read and the entire record processing activity repeats until all the records are processed.

The TABLE-LOOKUP module consists of an initialization step to set the FOUND-SWITCH control variable to an off position (FOUND-SWITCH = "NO"). The remainder of the module is a definite iteration structure that (1) initializes the subscript

to 1, (2) compares the current contents of the subscript with the upper limit of the table and, if the result of the comparison is false, (3) invokes and executes the ELEMENT-COMPARE module and (4) increments the subscript by 1 so as to point to the next element in the table. The table lookup process is repeated until the subscript, SUB, is greater than the upper limit of the table.

The ELEMENT-COMPARE module is the heart of the searching process. Its first operation is to compare the search key from the input transaction record with the table key from the element in the table. If the result of the comparison test is true, then three important commands are executed. The first turns on the control variable, FOUND-SWITCH. The constant "YES" is stored at FOUND-SWITCH. For reasons that will be clarified shortly, the second command transfers the contents of the subscript to a holding area variable called SAVE-SUB. And the third stores the constant that represents the size of the table being searched into SUB. If the table size is four, the constant 4 is stored at the variable SUB. What is the reason for these last

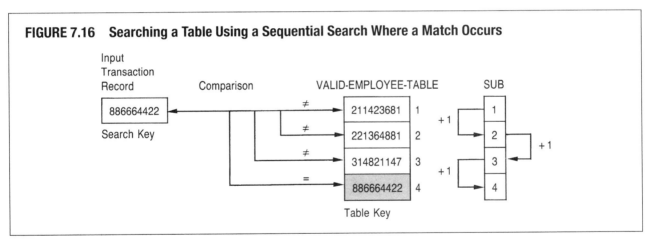

**FIGURE 7.16    Searching a Table Using a Sequential Search Where a Match Occurs**

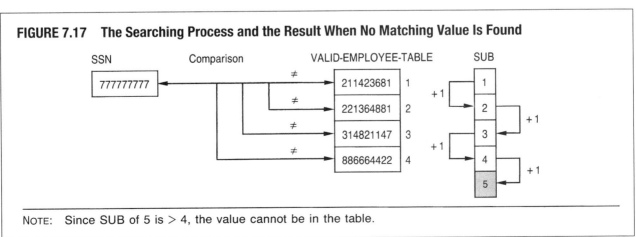

**FIGURE 7.17    The Searching Process and the Result When No Matching Value Is Found**

NOTE:    Since SUB of 5 is > 4, the value cannot be in the table.

two steps? In order to have a simple conditional in the TABLE-LOOKUP module (Until SUB > upper-limit value), you need a way to "trip the switch" when the element is found in the table. This is how it works: If a matching element is *not* found in the table, the subscript becomes 5 after the last element of the table is searched, and the searching process stops. Here is the case of not finding a matching value. If the only way to get out of the definite iteration loop is for SUB to be greater than the maximum table size, then in order to end the looping process when a value is found, you must *force the contents of the subscript to be greater than the maximum table size*. However, one thing must happen before you change the value of the subscript; the subscript must be stored away in another variable (called SAVE-SUB), if the subscript is to be subsequently referenced in a command. Failure to do so would result in the loss of the pointer to the element in the table that is equal to the search key. *Now it is SAVE-SUB—not SUB—that will be used as the subscript to point to the value in the table.* In other words, to point to a certain element in the table now requires the following table reference: table name (SAVE-SUB).

There are a number of different searching techniques for the sequential search; but for now it is important that you learn *one way* and later explore other methods (not covered here). The method just presented allows for only one simple conditional expression. Many other acceptable table search algorithms can be used, some of which, however, require compound conditional expressions. Variations of the sequential search in this book can be found in practically any programming language text in COBOL, BASIC, PL/I, and so on.

## A Step-by-Step Trace of a Table Search

The last section gave you an overview of the basic logic of a table search. Now, here is a more in-depth discussion of the actual trace of the program instructions for searching a table. Figure 7.19 (panel A) illustrates the transaction records. Panel B de-

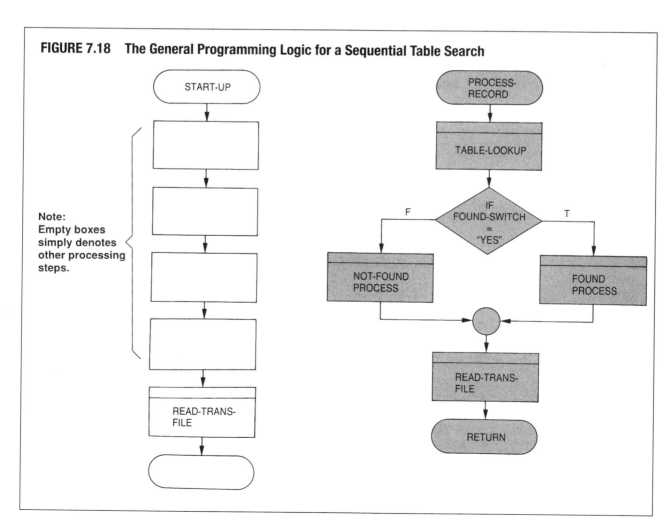

**FIGURE 7.18    The General Programming Logic for a Sequential Table Search**

Note: Empty boxes simply denotes other processing steps.

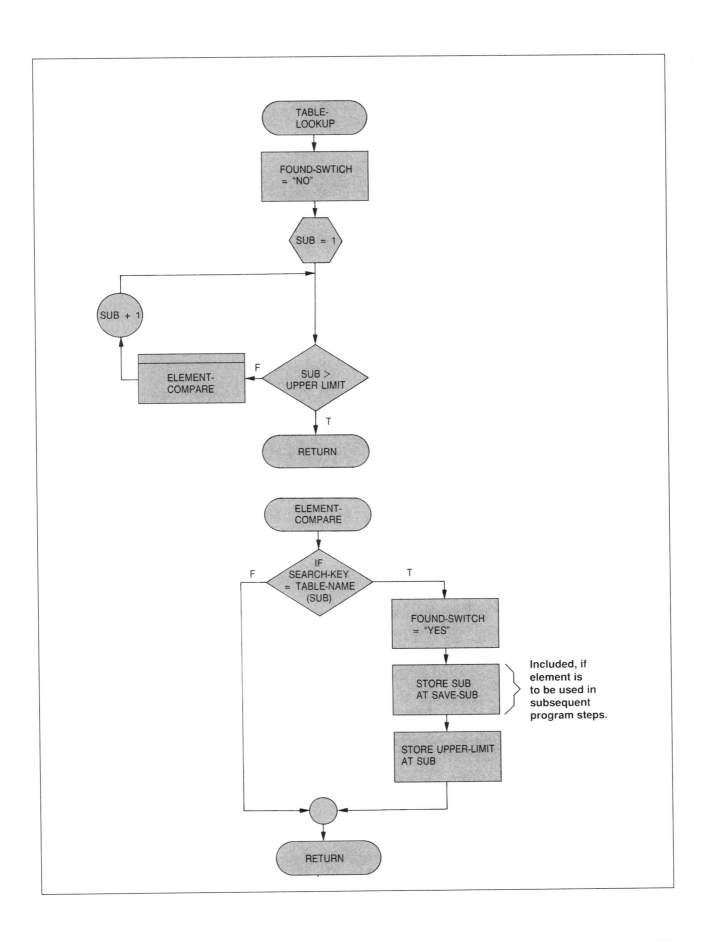

picts the table, and panel C shows the report to be printed.

Figure 7.20 illustrates the step-by-step trace of two table-searching operations to locate a valid employee number. The figure also depicts the logic trace chart for the two input records. Panel A represents the first input case where the search key of 777777777 is *not found* in the table. Panel B of Figure 7.20 shows a second input record where the SSN 211423681 *is found* in the table. Panel C summarizes the search logic for the unsuccessful lookup opera-

tion in the form of a trace table. The trace table tracks the logic that compares the search key of 777777777 to all three of the table values. Panel D shows a trace of the logic that compares the search key of 211423681 with the first search argument of 211423681. Since the values are equal, the lookup operation terminates. Study panels C and D of Figure 7.20 for a better understanding of the flowchart logic in Figure 7.18.

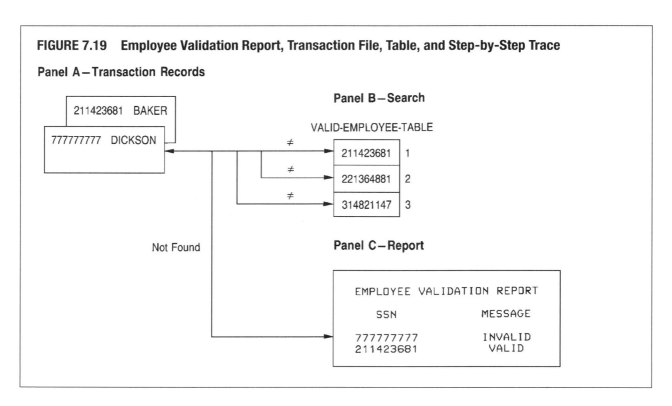

FIGURE 7.19   Employee Validation Report, Transaction File, Table, and Step-by-Step Trace

Panel A—Transaction Records

Panel B—Search

VALID-EMPLOYEE-TABLE

211423681   BAKER
777777777   DICKSON

≠   211423681   1
≠   221364881   2
≠   314821147   3

Not Found

Panel C—Report

```
EMPLOYEE VALIDATION REPORT

     SSN              MESSAGE

  777777777          INVALID
  211423681           VALID
```

## FIGURE 7.20   A Step-by-Step Trace of a Table Search Process

### Panel A—A Trace of an Unsuccessful Search

**STEP 1**

START-UP Module

The first transaction record is read from the START-UP module.

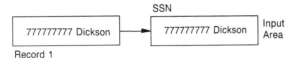

| 777777777 Dickson | → | SSN<br>777777777 Dickson | Input Area |

Record 1

**STEP 2**

RECORD-PROCESS Module → TABLE-LOOK-UP Module

The TABLE-LOOK-UP module is invoked.

**STEP 3**

NO

FOUND-SWITCH

The FOUND-SWITCH is initialized to NO.

**STEP 4**

1

SUB

The subscript SUB is initialized to 1.

**STEP 5**

IF 1 > 3    False

The subscript value 1 is compared to the upper limit 3.

**STEP 6**

ELEMENT-COMPARE Module

Since the result of this comparison is *false*, the program path leads to the invoking of the ELEMENT-COMPARE module, which is invoked the first time for the first record.

**STEP 7**

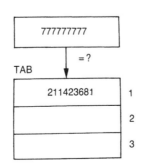

The SEARCH KEY SSN is compared to the first element of the table to determine equality.

Since 777777777 is unequal to the first element, the result of the comparison is false, therefore the program path leads to the RETURN, and subsequently back to the statement after the ELEMENT-COMPARE module call in the TABLE-LOOK-UP module (see Figure 7.18).

**STEP 8**

TABLE-LOOK-UP Module

The subscript is increased by 1.

2

SUB

**STEP 9**

If 2 > 3?

False

The value of SUB is compared to the upper limit 3.

**STEP 10**

ELEMENT-COMPARE Module

The ELEMENT-COMPARE Module is invoked for the second time.

**STEP 11**

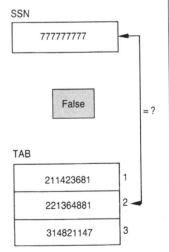

The SSN is compared with the second element. Since the condition is *false*, control passes to the RETURN and then links back to the TABLE-LOOK-UP Module.

**STEP 12**

3

SUB

The subscript is increased by 1.

The lookup process would continue for the third element in the same manner as

## FIGURE 7.20 (Cont.)

### Panel B—A Trace of a Successful Search

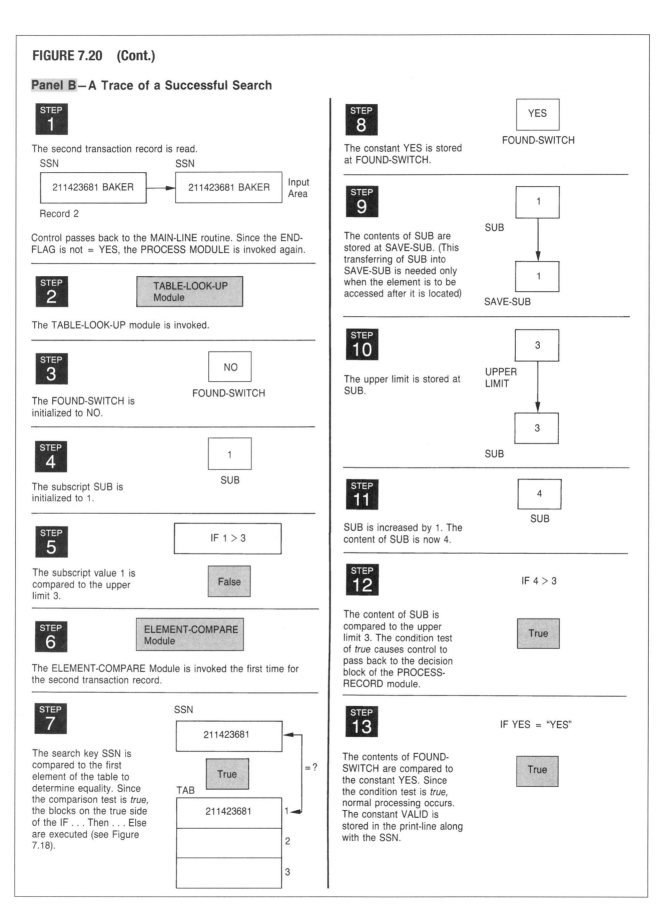

**STEP 1**

The second transaction record is read.

SSN                       SSN

| 211423681 BAKER | → | 211423681 BAKER | Input Area |

Record 2

Control passes back to the MAIN-LINE routine. Since the END-FLAG is not = YES, the PROCESS MODULE is invoked again.

**STEP 2**

TABLE-LOOK-UP Module

The TABLE-LOOK-UP module is invoked.

**STEP 3**

NO

FOUND-SWITCH

The FOUND-SWITCH is initialized to NO.

**STEP 4**

1

SUB

The subscript SUB is initialized to 1.

**STEP 5**

IF 1 > 3

The subscript value 1 is compared to the upper limit 3.

False

**STEP 6**

ELEMENT-COMPARE Module

The ELEMENT-COMPARE Module is invoked the first time for the second transaction record.

**STEP 7**

SSN

| 211423681 |

True

TAB

| 211423681 | 1 |
| | 2 |
| | 3 |

= ?

The search key SSN is compared to the first element of the table to determine equality. Since the comparison test is *true*, the blocks on the true side of the IF . . . Then . . . Else are executed (see Figure 7.18).

**STEP 8**

YES

FOUND-SWITCH

The constant YES is stored at FOUND-SWITCH.

**STEP 9**

| 1 |

SUB

↓

| 1 |

SAVE-SUB

The contents of SUB are stored at SAVE-SUB. (This transferring of SUB into SAVE-SUB is needed only when the element is to be accessed after it is located)

**STEP 10**

| 3 |

UPPER LIMIT

↓

| 3 |

SUB

The upper limit is stored at SUB.

**STEP 11**

| 4 |

SUB

SUB is increased by 1. The content of SUB is now 4.

**STEP 12**

IF 4 > 3

True

The content of SUB is compared to the upper limit 3. The condition test of *true* causes control to pass back to the decision block of the PROCESS-RECORD module.

**STEP 13**

IF YES = "YES"

True

The contents of FOUND-SWITCH are compared to the constant YES. Since the condition test is *true*, normal processing occurs. The constant VALID is stored in the print-line along with the SSN.

# FIGURE 7.20 (Cont.)

## Panel C—Logic Trace Chart for the Unsuccessful Search

Compare

| | Executing Module | Record Image | SUB (Contents) | FOUND-SWITCH Contents | SSN (Search Key) | TAB (SUB) (Table Argument) | Condition Tested | Result of Test | Program Action | |
|---|---|---|---|---|---|---|---|---|---|---|
| 1 | START-UP | 777777777 Dickson | 0 | NO | | | | | PROCESS-RECORD | ►2 |
| 2 | PROCESS-RECORD / TABLE-LOOKUP | 777777777 Dickson | 1 | NO | | | SUB > 3? | False | Invoke ELEMENT-COMPARE | ►3 |
| 3 | ELEMENT-COMPARE | 777777777 Dickson | 1 | NO | 777777777 | 211423681 | SSN = TAB (SUB) | False | Link back to TABLE-LOOKUP | ►4 |
| 4 | TABLE-LOOKUP | 777777777 Dickson | 2 | NO | | | SUB > 3? | False | Invoke ELEMENT-COMPARE | ►5 |
| 5 | ELEMENT-COMPARE | 777777777 Dickson | 2 | NO | 777777777 | 221364881 | SSN = TAB (SUB) | False | Link back to TABLE-LOOKUP | ►6 |
| 6 | TABLE-LOOKUP | 777777777 Dickson | 3 | NO | | | SUB > 3? | False | Invoke ELEMENT-COMPARE | ►7 |
| 7 | ELEMENT-COMPARE | 777777777 Dickson | 3 | NO | 777777777 | 314821147 | SSN = TAB (SUB) | False | Link back to TABLE-LOOKUP | ►8 |
| 8 | TABLE-LOOKUP | 777777777 Dickson | 4 | NO | | | SUB > 3 | True | Link back to PROCESS-RECORD | |

Content of FOUND-SWITCH still equals NO at end of searching process.

When SUB is greater than upper limit of table linkage occurs to the PROCESS-RECORD module.

## Panel D—Logic Trace Chart for the Successful Search

Compare

| | Executing Module | Record Image | SUB (Contents) | FOUND-SWITCH Contents | SSN (Search Key) | TAB (SUB) (Table Argument) | Condition Tested | Result of Test | Program Action | |
|---|---|---|---|---|---|---|---|---|---|---|
| 1 | START-UP | 211423681 Jones | 0 | NO | | | | | RECORD-PROCESS | ►2 |
| 2 | PROCESS-RECORD / TABLE-LOOKUP | 211423681 Jones | 1 | NO | | | SUB > 3? | False | Invoke ELEMENT-COMPARE | ►3 |
| 3 | ELEMENT-COMPARE | 211423681 Jones | 1 | NO | 211423681 | 211423681 | SSN = TAB (SUB) | True | TABLE-LOOKUP | |
| 4 | TABLE-LOOKUP | 211423681 Jones | 4 | YES | | | SUB > 3? | True | Link back to RECORD-PROCESS | |

Content of FOUND-SWITCH is YES since value was found in table.

# A Payroll Listing Using Single-Dimensional Table Search and Positional Addressing
(Table Search Used for Employee Validation Only)

## Program Requirements

A company wishes to produce a payroll list of its employees. The report is to contain the employee's SSN, name, hours worked, pay code, pay rate, and gross pay. Before the employee information is printed on a line, the employee's SSN is validated by searching for a matching SSN in a table of valid employee numbers. The pay rate is extracted from a table of pay rates based on pay codes found in the payroll record. A detail line is to print for every record in the file. If the employee number is not found, an appropriate message is to print on the line, indicating that the record is invalid.

## Output Design

Exhibit 7.1 illustrates the sample report to be produced, and Exhibit 7.2 shows the associated print chart.

## Input Design

The input record format is illustrated in Exhibit 7.3. The record layout sheet shows three different record formats. The transaction input record (payroll) format is shown first, followed by the record descriptions for the valid employee table file and the pay rate table file. The last two record layouts illustrate records that are used only for the purpose of loading tables. The transaction pay file is the actual file to be processed.

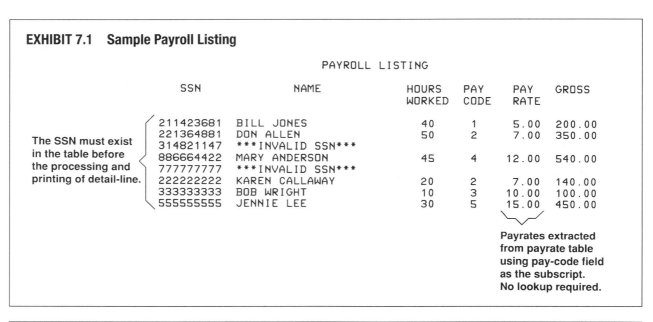

**EXHIBIT 7.1    Sample Payroll Listing**

```
                              PAYROLL LISTING

             SSN              NAME             HOURS    PAY    PAY     GROSS
                                               WORKED   CODE   RATE

           211423681    BILL JONES               40      1     5.00    200.00
           221364881    DON ALLEN                50      2     7.00    350.00
           314821147    ***INVALID SSN***
           886664422    MARY ANDERSON            45      4    12.00    540.00
           777777777    ***INVALID SSN***
           222222222    KAREN CALLAWAY           20      2     7.00    140.00
           333333333    BOB WRIGHT               10      3    10.00    100.00
           555555555    JENNIE LEE               30      5    15.00    450.00
```

The SSN must exist in the table before the processing and printing of detail-line.

Payrates extracted from payrate table using pay-code field as the subscript. No lookup required.

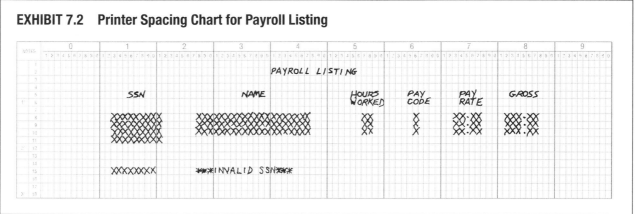

**EXHIBIT 7.2    Printer Spacing Chart for Payroll Listing**

PAYROLL LISTING

SSN    NAME    HOURS WORKED    PAY CODE    PAY RATE    GROSS

XXXXXXXX    ***INVALID SSN***

## Tables

Exhibit 7.4 illustrates the tables for this problem. Panel A depicts the valid employee table; panel B shows the payrate table.

## Test Cases

The test cases used are shown in Exhibit 7.5. There are eight records. The third and fifth records are invalid.

## Logic Considerations

The table search procedure should:

1. Provide a table search operation that uses the SSN from the transaction payroll record as the search key and the valid SSNs from the table as the table key.
2. Permit normal processing to continue when a matching condition exists between the search key and the table key. However, if the search key (SSN) is compared with all the table keys in the table and no matching condition is found, an error message is to print beside the SSN.
3. Compute the gross salary by multiplying the pay rate by the hours worked. *The pay rate is to be extracted from the pay rate table using **positional addressing**. This type of addressing uses a field from an input transaction record as the subscript value.* Positional addressing is discussed later in the section on modules.

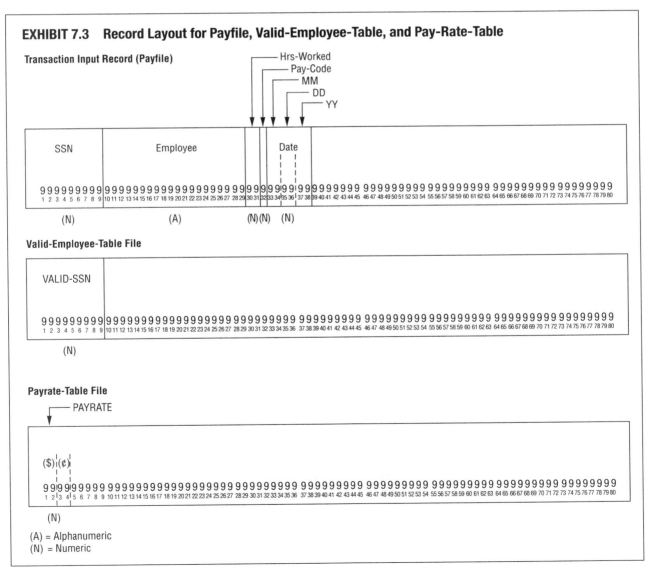

**EXHIBIT 7.3    Record Layout for Payfile, Valid-Employee-Table, and Pay-Rate-Table**

(A) = Alphanumeric
(N) = Numeric

EXHIBIT 7.4   Tables for Payroll Listing

Panel A — Valid-Employee-Table

| | |
|---|---|
| 1 | 211423681 |
| 2 | 221364881 |
| 3 | 314821477 |
| 4 | 886664422 |
| 5 | 222222222 |
| 6 | 333333333 |
| 7 | 555555555 |

Panel B — Payrate-Table

| | |
|---|---|
| 05 00 | 1 |
| 07 00 | 2 |
| 10 00 | 3 |
| 12 00 | 4 |
| 15 00 | 5 |

EXHIBIT 7.5   Test Cases for Payroll Listing

Panel A — Test Cases for Pay File

```
COLUMN    1         2         3         4         5         6         7         8
12345678901234567890123456789012345678901234567890123456789012345678901234567890
211423681JENNY BETH RUSSELL  401081287
221364881TAMMI GEORGE        502081387
314821147BILLY GEORGE
886664422JAMES RUSSELL       454081687
777777777BROOKE SLEMMONS
222222222CRISTA RUSSELL      202081387
333333333MANDY RUSSELL       103081887
555555555JON CHUMBLEY        305081287
```

Panel B — Test Cases for Valid Employee SSNs

```
COLUMN    1         2         3         4         5         6         7         8
12345678901234567890123456789012345678901234567890123456789012345678901234567890
211423681
221364881
314821477
886664422
222222222
333333333
555555555
```

Panel C — Cases for Valid Pay Rates

```
COLUMN    1         2         3         4         5         6         7         8
12345678901234567890123456789012345678901234567890123456789012345678901234567890
0500
0700
1000
1200
1500
```

## Program Design

**Hierarchy Chart.**   Exhibit 7.6 illustrates the general program design for a payroll listing problem that requires a table search. The chart shows, as usual, three main modules. The START-UP module comprises the usual modules, but the reader should notice the addition of a module called LOAD-TABLES. The PROCESS-RECORDS module also includes one additional module called LOOK-UP-SSN, the purpose of which is to validate the employee number prior to processing the record. The DETAIL-CALCULATION module is included because the gross pay must be calculated. The PRINT-DETAIL-LINE module is needed to print a detail line for

each valid record. In any case, the READ TRANS-ACTION-FILE module reads the next record to be processed, while the WRAP-UP module prints the end-of-file message and closes the files.

**Structured Flowchart/Pseudocode.**   Exhibit 7.7 depicts the structured flowchart and Exhibit 7.8 shows the pseudocode for this problem. The MAIN-LINE module appears as always. The START-UP module initializes variables, opens the files (TRANSACTION-FILE, PAYRATE-FILE, VALID-SSN-FILE, and REPORT FILE), loads the two tables (VALID-EMPLOYEE-TABLE and PAYRATE-TABLE), prints the headings, and reads the first transaction record from TRANSACTION-FILE.

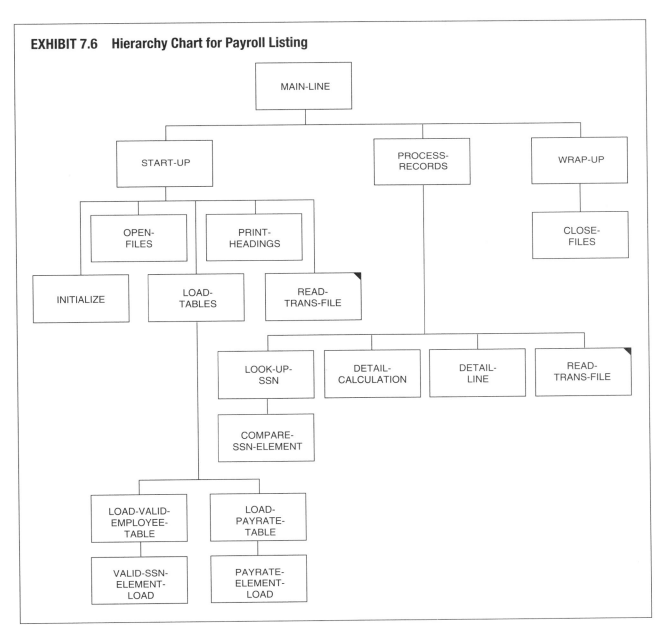

**EXHIBIT 7.6   Hierarchy Chart for Payroll Listing**

**EXHIBIT 7.7  Structured Flowchart for Payroll Listing**

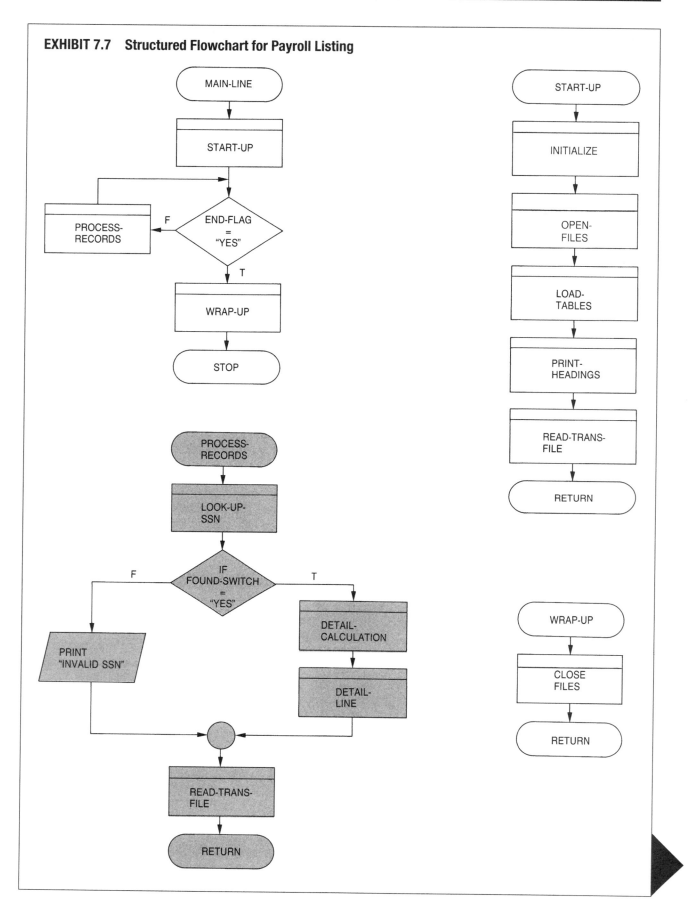

The PROCESS-RECORDS module begins with the invoking of the LOOK-UP-SSN module. The LOOK-UP-SSN module's function is to determine if the SSN of the transaction file is valid. In other words, it checks to make sure that the SSN is located in the table of valid employee numbers. During execution of the LOOK-UP-SSN module, FOUND-SWITCH is initialized to an *off* position (FOUND-SWITCH = "NO") before each search and is turned *on* (FOUND-SWITCH = "YES") if the value is found. The key event in the LOOK-UP-SSN module is to either turn on or turn off FOUND-SWITCH. It is through the setting of this control variable that the table lookup operation can be established as a separate module within the program. In the PROCESS-RECORDS module, if FOUND-SWITCH = "YES", then the DETAIL-CALCULATION and DETAIL-LINE modules are invoked. If FOUND-SWITCH is not equal to "YES", an error message prints on the detail line, indicating that the record is invalid. The last step reads the next transaction record in order to repeat the processing steps. The WRAP-UP module simply prints the end-of-file message and closes the files.

Next, look at the third-level modules. The LOAD-TABLES module consists of two steps. The first loads VALID-EMPLOYEE-TABLE, and second loads PAYRATE-TABLE. LOAD-VALID-EM-PLOYEE-TABLE (p. 340, Technique 1) requires the use of the *definite iteration* structure. The first step is to read the first record from the VALID-SSN-FILE. Second, the subscript SUB is initialized to 1; third, SUB is compared with 7, the upper limit of the table. Fourth, if the condition test is false, then the VALID-SSN-ELEMENT-LOAD module is invoked (*Technique 1*) and fifth, the subscript is increased by 1. As previously explained, the process is repeated until all seven of the elements are loaded into the memory table (that is, until the maximum table limit is reached). The VALID-SSN-ELEMENT-LOAD module takes care of storing the value into the table element and reading the next valid SSN table record.

See the shaded module labeled *Technique B,* p. 341 for an alternate way of handling the loading process. Technique B, for the LOAD-VALID-EM-PLOYEE-TABLE, uses an "in-line" approach of moving the SSN field to the valid-employee-table element and for reading the next record. The code is physically placed in the count-controlled loop—*not* in a separate module.

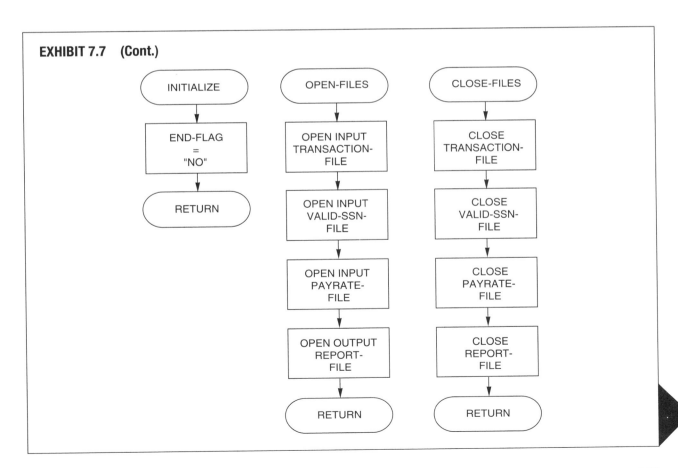

**EXHIBIT 7.7    (Cont.)**

**EXHIBIT 7.7    (Cont.)**

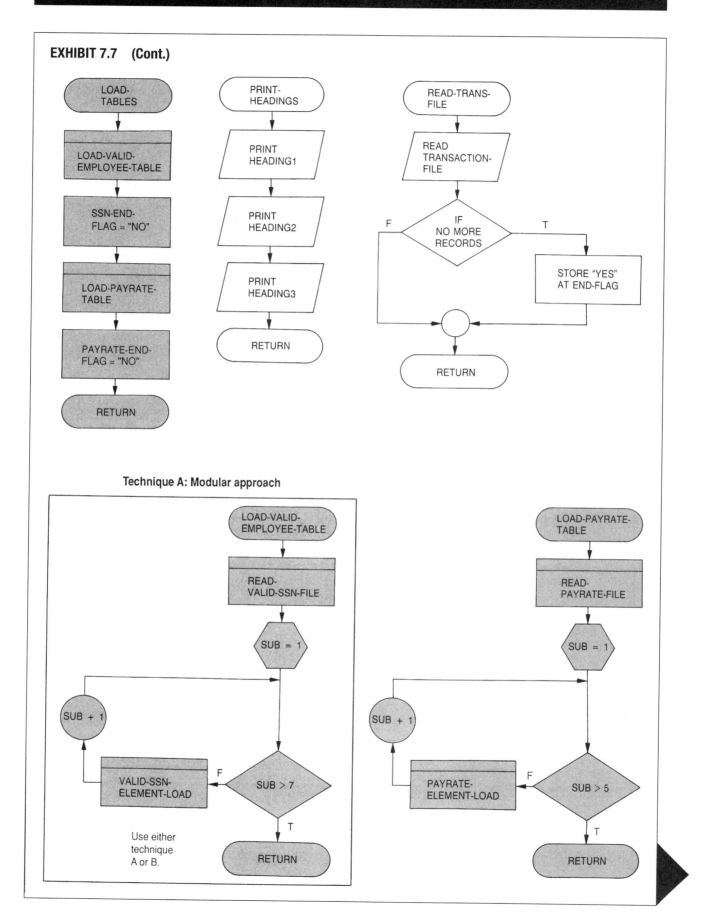

Technique A: Modular approach

Use either technique A or B.

LOAD-PAYRATE-TABLE is handled in the same manner as LOAD-VALID-EMPLOYEE-TABLE, except that SUB is compared to the upper limit of 5, since there are only 5 elements in the table.

The LOOK-UP-SSN module consists of two initialization steps. First, FOUND-SWITCH is initialized to NO, and SUB is set to 1. The same type of definite iteration structure used in loading a table is once again utilized for the searching function. Here the DoUntil structure compares SUB with 7 (the upper limit). If the comparison result is false, then the COMPARE-SSN-ELEMENT module is invoked when using Method 1. As its module name implies, its function is to determine if the current SSN is equal to the table element at which the subscript is currently pointing. If this comparison is unequal, the subscript is increased and the searching process is repeated until either the value is found or the value is not found (that is, the end of the table is reached without a match occurring). Referring back to the COMPARE-SSN-ELEMENT module, as previously illustrated in Figure 7.18, if the SSN is equal to the SSN in the table of valid employee numbers, the following events occur. The first event is the storing of the constant YES at FOUND-SWITCH; and second, the value 7 is stored at SUB. As previously explained, this last step allows the simple condition of the DoWhile command in the LOOK-UP-SSN module to suffice in preventing future searches for the value once it is found. The storing of 7 at SUB trips the switch and allows an exit from a loop that would otherwise loop 7 times.

Method 2 for handling the look-up process (LOOK-UP-SSN) incorporates the function of com-

**EXHIBIT 7.7    (Cont.)**

**Technique B:  Loading valid employee-table using "IN-LINE" logic rather than calling a module.**

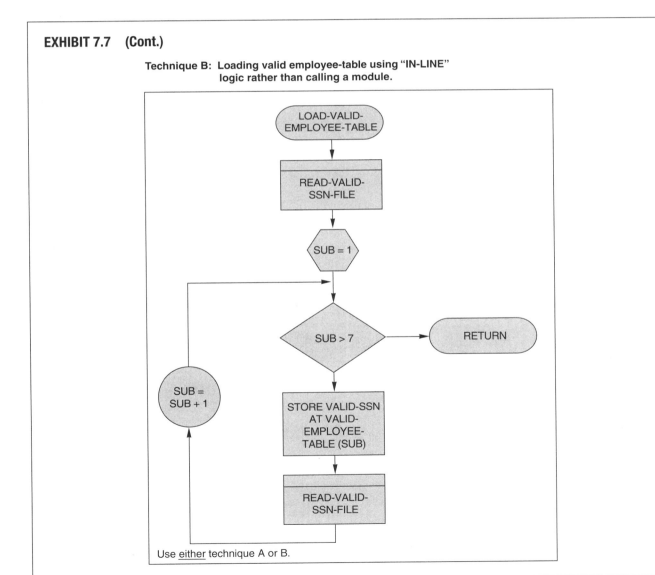

Use either technique A or B.

**EXHIBIT 7.7 (Cont.)**

**Method 1: MODULAR SEARCHING**

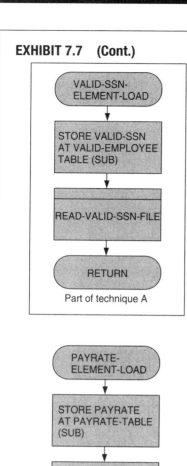

Part of technique A

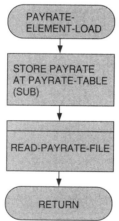

Note: Use either this Method 1 or use Method 2 also shown highlighted.

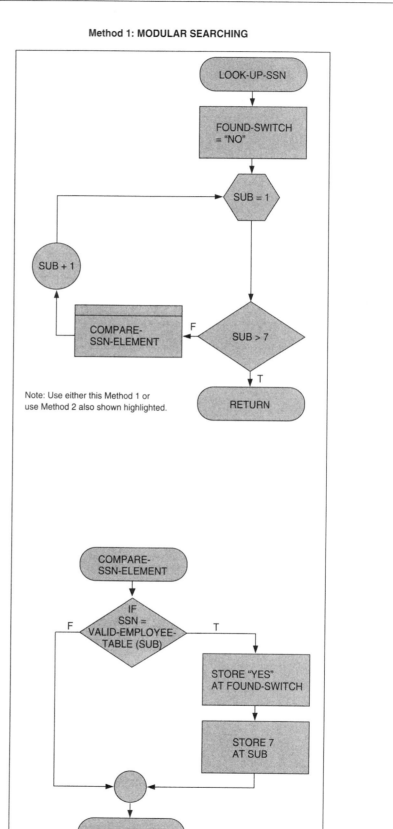

NOTE: Storing SUB in SAVE-SUB is not necessary in this problem, since the element located is not used for either printing or calculation purposes.

paring the SSN from the transaction record with the valid-employee-table element within the same count-controlled loop. The comparison process is placed "in-line" as a sequence of commands. No actual module is performed with this method. This method can reduce code and will execute a little faster. A major disadvantage is that it is not modular and goes against the concept of module-decomposition. In complex problems, we prefer to use the modular method (Method 1).

Once the table-searching procedure is complete and control passes back to the PROCESS-RECORDS module at the decision block, the determination is made whether the FOUND-SWITCH was turned *on* (YES) or *off* (NO). If the switch is now on, then the DETAIL-CALCULATION and DETAIL-LINE modules are executed in the order listed. If the switch is off the message "INVALID SSN" is printed.

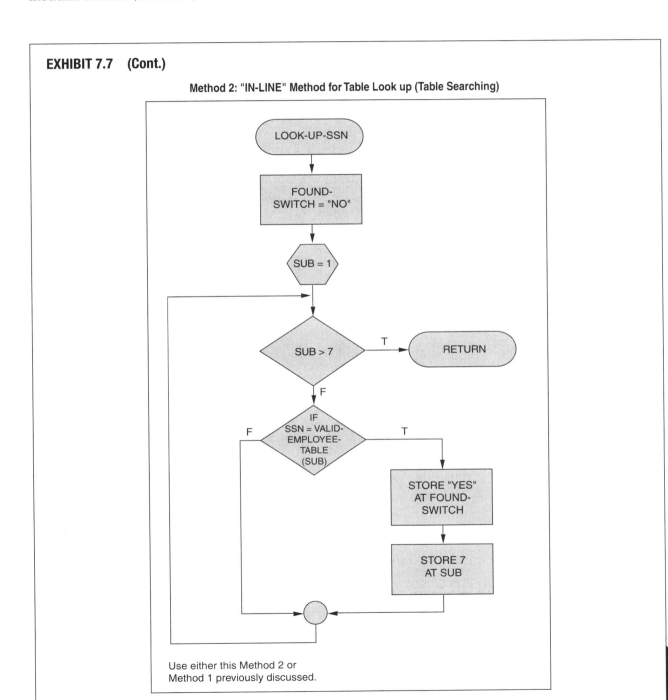

**EXHIBIT 7.7     (Cont.)**

Method 2: "IN-LINE" Method for Table Look up (Table Searching)

Use either this Method 2 or Method 1 previously discussed.

## COBOL 85/QBASIC Programs

The COBOL 85 and QBASIC programs for Application 7.1 are found in Exhibit 7.9 and 7.10, respectively. Exhibit 7.9 demonstrates modular Method 1 for Table Look Up using COBOL 85. Exhibit 7.10 depicts Method 2 for handling Table Look Up (In-Line Method).

**EXHIBIT 7.7   (Cont.)**

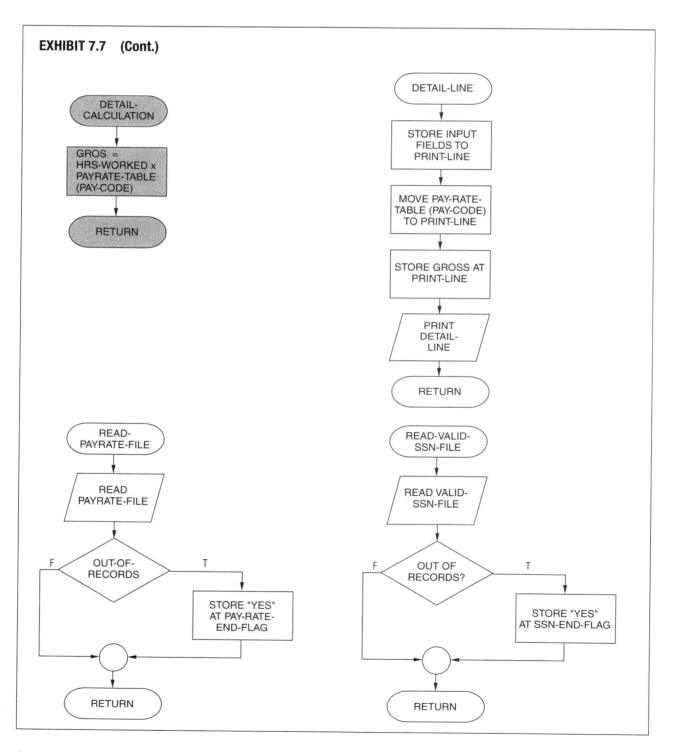

## EXHIBIT 7.8   Pseudocode for Payroll Listing (Application 7.1)

```
*main-line
    start-up
    dountil end-flag = "yes"
        process-record
    enddo
    wrap-up
    stop
*start-up
    initialize
    open-files
    load-tables
    print-headings
    read-trans-file
    return
*initialize
    initialize end-flag = "no"
    return
*open-files
    open transaction-file as input
    open valid-ssn-file as input
    open payrate-file as input
    open report-file as output
    return
*process-records
    look-up-ssn
    if found-switch = "yes"
        then
            detail-calculations
            detail-line
        else
            print "invalid ssn"
    endif
    read-trans-file
    return
*wrap-up
    close-files
    return
*close-files
    close transaction-file
    close valid-ssn-file
    close payrate-file
    close report-file
    return
*load-tables
    load-valid-employee-table
    end-flag = "NO"
    load-payrate-table
    end-flag = "NO"
    return
*print-headings
    print heading1
    print heading2
    print heading3
    return
*read-trans-file
    read transaction-file
        when no more records store "yes" at end-flag
    endread
    return
```

```
*load-valid-employee-table
    read-valid-ssn-file
    store 1 at sub
    dountil sub > 7
        valid-ssn-element-load
        increase sub by 1
    enddo
    return
*load-payrate-table
    read-payrate-file
    store 1 at sub
    dountil sub > 5
        payrate-element-load
        increase sub by 1
    enddo
    return
*valid-ssn-element-load
    store valid-ssn at valid-employee-table (sub)
    read-ssn-file
    return
*payrate-element-load
    store payrate at payrate-table (sub)
    read-payrate-file
    return
*look-up-ssn
    store "no" at found-switch
    store 1 at sub
    dountil sub > 7
        compare-ssn-element
        increase sub by 1
    enddo
    return
*compare-ssn-element
    if ssn = valid-employee-table (sub)
        then
            store "yes" at found-switch
            store 7 at sub
    endif
    return
*detail-calculations
    calculate gross = hrs-worked X payrate-table (paycode)
    return
*detail-line
    store input and gross located fields to print line
    move pay rate-table (paycode) to print-line
    print the detail line
    return
*read-payrate-file
    read payrate-file
        when out of records store "yes" at end-flag
    endread
    return
*read-valid-ssn-file
    read valid-ssn-file
        when out of records store "yes" at end-flag
    endread
    return
```

**EXHIBIT 7.9   COBOL 85 Program for Application 7.1, Payroll Listing**

```
1          IDENTIFICATION DIVISION.
2          PROGRAM-ID. CH7ILL1.
3          DATE-WRITTEN.  APRIL 19, 1993.
4          DATE-COMPILED. 1993-06-28.
5
6
7         *REMARKS:   ****COBOL 85****
8          *************************************************************
9         *                 USES BOTH IN-LINE AND MODULE CALL PERFORM       *
10        *                 IN-LINE PERFORM USES END-PERFORM STATEMENT      *
11         *************************************************************
12
13        *             THIS PROGRAM PRODUCES A PAYROLL LISTING.  BEFORE
14        *             AN EMPLOYEE'S GROSS SALARY IS COMPUTED AND DETAIL
15        *             INFO IS PRINTED, HIS OR HER SOCIAL SECURITY NUMBER IS
16        *             FIRST LOOKED UP IN A TABLE OF VALID SOCIAL SECURITY
17        *             NUMBERS.  IF THE SSN IS NOT FOUND IN THE TABLE AN
18        *             ERROR MESSAGE IS PRINTED ON THE DETAIL LINE WHERE
19        *             THE EMPLOYEE NAME WOULD HAVE APPEARED OTHERWISE.
20
21         ENVIRONMENT DIVISION.
22         CONFIGURATION SECTION.
23         SOURCE-COMPUTER.  CYBER.
24         OBJECT-COMPUTER.  CYBER.
25         INPUT-OUTPUT SECTION.
26         FILE-CONTROL.
27             SELECT TRANSACTION-FILE ASSIGN TO DTA71.
28             SELECT PAYRATE-FILE     ASSIGN TO DTA71PAY.
29             SELECT VALID-SSN-FILE   ASSIGN TO DTA71SSN.
30             SELECT OUT-FILE         ASSIGN TO OUTFILE.
31
32         DATA DIVISION.
33         FILE SECTION.
34         FD   TRANSACTION-FILE.
35         01   TRANS-REC.
36             05   SSN           PIC 9(09).
37             05   EMPLOYEE      PIC X(20).
38             05   HOURS-WORKED  PIC 9(02).
39             05   PAY-CODE      PIC 9.
40             05   DATE-IN.
41                 10   MM-IN     PIC 99.
42                 10   DD-IN     PIC 99.
43                 10   YY-IN     PIC 99.
44
45         FD   PAYRATE-FILE.
46         01   PAY-REC.
47             05   PAYRATE       PIC 99V99.
48
49         FD   VALID-SSN-FILE.
50         01   SSN-REC.
51             05   VALID-SSN     PIC 9(09).
52
53         FD   OUT-FILE.
54         01   OUT-REC           PIC X(133).
55
56         WORKING-STORAGE SECTION.
57
58         01   END-FLAG              PIC X(03)    VALUE "NO".
59         01   FOUND-SWITCH          PIC X(03)    VALUE "NO".
60         01   SUB                   PIC 99       VALUE 0.
61         01   GROSS                 PIC 9(04)V99 VALUE 0.
62
63         01   SSN-TAB.
64             05   SSN-TABLE OCCURS 7 TIMES.
65                 10   VALID-SSN-TABLE    PIC 9(09).
66
```

**EXHIBIT 7.9**   **(Cont.)**

```
67
68
69       01   PAYRATE-TAB.
70            05   PAYRATE-TABL OCCURS 5 TIMES.
71                 10   PAYRATE-TABLE              PIC 99V99.
72
73
74
75       01   PAGE-HEADING.
76            05                       PIC X(40)    VALUE SPACES.
77            05                       PIC X(15)    VALUE "PAYROLL LISTING".
78            05                       PIC X(77)    VALUE SPACES.
79
80       01   COLUMN-HEADING1.
81            05                       PIC X(15)    VALUE SPACES.
82            05                       PIC X(03)    VALUE "SSN".
83            05                       PIC X(17)    VALUE SPACES.
84            05                       PIC X(04)    VALUE "NAME".
85            05                       PIC X(15)    VALUE SPACES.
86            05                       PIC X(05)    VALUE "HOURS".
87            05                       PIC X(05)    VALUE SPACES.
88            05                       PIC X(03)    VALUE "PAY".
89            05                       PIC X(06)    VALUE SPACES.
90            05                       PIC X(03)    VALUE "PAY".
91            05                       PIC X(06)    VALUE SPACES.
92            05                       PIC X(05)    VALUE "GROSS".
93            05                       PIC X(45)    VALUE SPACES.
94
95       01   COLUMN-HEADING2.
96            05                       PIC X(54)    VALUE SPACES.
97            05                       PIC X(06)    VALUE "WORKED".
98            05                       PIC X(04)    VALUE SPACES.
99            05                       PIC X(04)    VALUE "CODE".
100           05                       PIC X(05)    VALUE SPACES.
101           05                       PIC X(04)    VALUE "RATE".
102           05                       PIC X(55)    VALUE SPACES.
103
104      01   DETAIL-LINE.
105           05                       PIC X(12)    VALUE SPACES.
106           05   SSN-OUT             PIC 9(09).
107           05                       PIC X(06)    VALUE SPACES.
108           05   NAME-OUT            PIC X(20).
109           05                       PIC X(09)    VALUE SPACES.
110           05   HOUR-WORKED-OUT     PIC Z9.
111           05                       PIC X(07)    VALUE SPACES.
112           05   PAY-CODE-OUT        PIC 9.
113           05                       PIC X(06)    VALUE SPACES.
114           05   PAY-RATE-OUT        PIC Z9.99.
115           05                       PIC X(04)    VALUE SPACES.
116           05   GROSS-OUT           PIC ZZZ9.99.
117           05                       PIC X(44)    VALUE SPACES.
118
119      /
120       PROCEDURE DIVISION.
121       *********************
122
123       000-MAIN-LINE.
124           PERFORM 100-START-UP.
125           PERFORM 200-PROCESS-RECORDS UNTIL END-FLAG = "YES".
126           PERFORM 300-WRAP-UP.
127           STOP RUN.
128
129       100-START-UP.
130      *    INTIALIZATION PROCESS IN W-S
131           PERFORM 105-OPEN-FILES.
132           PERFORM 110-LOAD-TABLES.
```

EXHIBIT 7.9 (Cont.)

```
133            PERFORM 120-PRINT-HEADINGS.
134            PERFORM 130-READ-TRANS-FILE.
135
136        105-OPEN-FILES.
137            OPEN INPUT   TRANSACTION-FILE
138                         VALID-SSN-FILE
139                         PAYRATE-FILE
140            OUTPUT OUT-FILE.
141
142        110-LOAD-TABLES.
143            PERFORM 111-LOAD-VALID-EMPLOYEE-TABLE.
144            MOVE "NO" TO END-FLAG.
145            PERFORM 112-LOAD-PAYRATE-TABLE.
146            MOVE "NO" TO END-FLAG.
147
148        111-LOAD-VALID-EMPLOYEE-TABLE.
149            PERFORM 111-A-READ-VALID-SSN-FILE.
150            PERFORM
151                    VARYING SUB FROM 1 BY 1 UNTIL SUB > 7
152
153     **IN-LINE CODE FOR ELEMENT LOAD BELOW
154
155            MOVE VALID-SSN TO VALID-SSN-TABLE (SUB)
156            PERFORM 111-A-READ-VALID-SSN-FILE
157            END-PERFORM.
158
159        111-A-READ-VALID-SSN-FILE.
160            READ VALID-SSN-FILE AT END MOVE "YES" TO END-FLAG.
161
162
163        112-LOAD-PAYRATE-TABLE.
164            PERFORM 112-A-READ-PAYRATE-FILE.
165            PERFORM
166                    VARYING SUB FROM 1 BY 1 UNTIL SUB > 5
167
168     **IN-LINE CODE APPEARS BELOW FOR THE COBOL 85 OPTION**
169
170            MOVE PAYRATE TO PAYRATE-TABLE (SUB)
171            PERFORM 112-A-READ-PAYRATE-FILE
172            END-PERFORM.
173
174
175
176        112-A-READ-PAYRATE-FILE.
177            READ PAYRATE-FILE AT END MOVE "YES" TO END-FLAG.
178
179        120-PRINT-HEADINGS.
180            WRITE OUT-REC FROM PAGE-HEADING AFTER ADVANCING PAGE.
181            WRITE OUT-REC FROM COLUMN-HEADING1  AFTER ADVANCING 3 LINES.
182            WRITE OUT-REC FROM COLUMN-HEADING2 AFTER ADVANCING 1 LINES.
183            MOVE SPACES TO OUT-REC.
184            WRITE OUT-REC AFTER ADVANCING 1 LINES.
185
186        130-READ-TRANS-FILE.
187            READ TRANSACTION-FILE AT END MOVE "YES" TO END-FLAG.
188
189        200-PROCESS-RECORDS.
190            PERFORM 210-LOOK-UP-SSN.
191            IF FOUND-SWITCH = "YES" THEN
192              PERFORM 220-DETAIL-CALCULATIONS
193              PERFORM 230-DETAIL-LINE
194            ELSE
195              MOVE SPACES TO DETAIL-LINE
196              MOVE SSN TO SSN-OUT
197              MOVE "*** INVALID SSN ***" TO NAME-OUT
198              WRITE OUT-REC FROM DETAIL-LINE AFTER ADVANCING 1 LINES.
```

**EXHIBIT 7.9** (Cont.)

```
199            PERFORM 130-READ-TRANS-FILE.
200
201      ***********MODULAR PERFORM..VARYING -- using paragraph name****
202       210-LOOK-UP-SSN.
203            MOVE "NO" TO FOUND-SWITCH.
204            PERFORM 211-COMPARE-ELEMENT
205                    VARYING SUB FROM 1 BY 1 UNTIL SUB > 7.
206       211-COMPARE-ELEMENT.
207                IF SSN = VALID-SSN-TABLE (SUB) THEN
208                  MOVE "YES" TO FOUND-SWITCH
209                  MOVE 7 TO SUB
210                END-IF.
211
212       220-DETAIL-CALCULATIONS.
213            COMPUTE
214            GROSS ROUNDED = HOURS-WORKED * PAYRATE-TABLE (PAY-CODE).
215
216       230-DETAIL-LINE.
217            MOVE SSN TO SSN-OUT.
218            MOVE EMPLOYEE TO NAME-OUT.
219            MOVE HOURS-WORKED TO HOUR-WORKED-OUT.
220            MOVE PAY-CODE TO PAY-CODE-OUT.
221            MOVE PAYRATE-TABLE (PAY-CODE) TO PAY-RATE-OUT.
222            MOVE GROSS TO GROSS-OUT.
223            WRITE OUT-REC FROM DETAIL-LINE AFTER ADVANCING 1 LINES.
224
225       300-WRAP-UP.
226            PERFORM 310-CLOSE.
227
228       310-CLOSE.
229            CLOSE TRANSACTION-FILE
230                  PAYRATE-FILE
231                  VALID-SSN-FILE
232                  OUT-FILE.
```

## PAYROLL LISTING

| SSN | NAME | HOURS WORKED | PAY CODE | PAY RATE | GROSS |
|-----|------|--------------|----------|----------|-------|
| 211423681 | JENNY BETH RUSSELL | 40 | 1 | 5.00 | 200.00 |
| 221364881 | TAMMI GEORGE | 50 | 2 | 7.00 | 350.00 |
| 314821147 | *** INVALID SSN *** | | | | |
| 886664422 | JAMES RUSSELL | 45 | 4 | 12.00 | 540.00 |
| 777777777 | *** INVALID SSN *** | | | | |
| 222222222 | CRISTA RUSSELL | 20 | 2 | 7.00 | 140.00 |
| 333333333 | MANDY RUSSELL | 10 | 3 | 10.00 | 100.00 |
| 555555555 | JON CHUMBLEY | 30 | 5 | 15.00 | 450.00 |

**EXHIBIT 7.10    QBASIC Code and Output for Application 7.1**

```
'************************************************************************
'*                      PROGRAM IDENTIFICATION                         *
'************************************************************************
'* PROGRAM NAME: CH7APL1                                               *
'* REMARKS: THIS PROGRAM PRODUCES A PAYROLL LISTING. BEFORE AN         *
'*          EMPLOYEE'S GROSS SALARY IS COMPUTED AND DETAIL INFO IS     *
'*          PRINTED, HIS OR HER SOCIAL SECURITY NUMBER IS FIRST LOOKED *
'*          UP IN A TABLE OF VALID SOCIAL SECURITY NUMBERS. IF THE SSN *
'*          IS NOT FOUND IN THE TABLE AN ERROR MESSAGE IS PRINTED ON   *
'*          THE DETAIL LINE WHERE THE EMPLOYEE NAME WOULD HAVE APPEARED*
'*          OTHERWISE.                                                 *
'************************************************************************
'*                         MAIN-LINE                                   *
'************************************************************************
GOSUB STARTUP                       '* PERFORM START-UP
DO UNTIL END.FLAG$ = "YES"
    GOSUB PROCESS.RECORDS           '* PERFORM PROCESS-RECORDS
LOOP
GOSUB WRAPUP                        '* PERFORM WRAP-UP
END


'************************************************************************
'*                         START-UP                                    *
'************************************************************************

STARTUP:
    GOSUB INITIALIZE
    GOSUB OPEN.FILES
    GOSUB LOAD.TABLES               '* PERFORM TABLE-LOAD
    GOSUB PRINT.HEADINGS            '* PERFORM PRINT-HEADINGS
    GOSUB READ.TRANSACTION.FILE     '* PERFORM READ-TRANS-FILE
    RETURN
    '********************************************************************
    '*                       INITIALIZE                                *
    '********************************************************************

INITIALIZE:
    WIDTH LPRINT (132)
    END.FLAG$ = "NO"
    DIM PAY.RATE.TAB(5)
    DIM EMPLOYEE.TAB$(7)
    ERROR.LINE$ = "          \          \    *_*_* INVALID SSN *_*_*"
    DETAIL.LINE$ = "          \         \        \                   \        ##      #     ##.##    ###.##"
    RETURN


    '************************************************************************
                              OPEN.FILES                                  *
    '************************************************************************

OPEN.FILES:
    OPEN "I", #1, "CH7ILL1A.DAT"
    OPEN "I", #2, "CH7ILL1B.DAT"
    OPEN "I", #3, "CH7ILL1C.DAT"
    RETURN
```

**EXHIBIT 7.10 (Cont.)**

```
'*********************************************************************
'*                        TABLE-LOAD                              *
'*********************************************************************

LOAD.TABLES:

    GOSUB LOAD.VALID.EMPLOYEE.TABLE      '* PERFORM LOAD-VALID-EMPLOYEE
    GOSUB LOAD.PAYRATE.TABLE             '* PERFORM LOAD-PAYRATE-TABLE
    RETURN


    '*********************************************************************
    '*                 LOAD-VALID-EMPLOYEE-TABLE                      *
    '*********************************************************************

LOAD.VALID.EMPLOYEE.TABLE:

    GOSUB READ.VALID.SSN.FILE            '* READ-VALID-SSN-FILE
    FOR SUB1 = 1 TO 7
        GOSUB VALID.SSN.ELEMENT.LOAD     '* PERFORM VALID-SSN-ELEMENT-LOAD
    NEXT SUB1
    RETURN


    '*********************************************************************
    '*                    READ-VALID-SSN-FILE                         *
    '*********************************************************************

READ.VALID.SSN.FILE:

    INPUT #2, VALID.SSN$
    RETURN


    '*********************************************************************
    '*                  VALID-SSN-ELEMENT-LOAD                        *
    '*********************************************************************

VALID.SSN.ELEMENT.LOAD:

    EMPLOYEE.TAB$(SUB1) = VALID.SSN$
    GOSUB READ.VALID.SSN.FILE            ' READ-VALID-SSN-FILE
    RETURN


    '*********************************************************************
    '*                    LOAD-PAYRATE-TABLE                          *
    '*********************************************************************

LOAD.PAYRATE.TABLE:

    GOSUB READ.PAYRATE.FILE              '* READ-PAYRATE-FILE
    FOR SUB1 = 1 TO 5
        GOSUB PAYRATE.ELEMENT.LOAD       '* PERFORM PAYRATE-ELEMENT-LOAD
    NEXT SUB1
    RETURN
```

**EXHIBIT 7.10    (Cont.)**

```
'*********************************************************************
'*                         READ-PAYRATE-FILE                       *
'*********************************************************************

READ.PAYRATE.FILE:

    INPUT #3, PAY.RATE
    RETURN


    '*****************************************************************
    '*                    PAYRATE-ELEMENT-LOAD                   *
    '*****************************************************************

PAYRATE.ELEMENT.LOAD:

    PAY.RATE.TAB(SUB1) = PAY.RATE
    GOSUB READ.PAYRATE.FILE                    '* READ-PAYRATE-FILE
    RETURN


    '*****************************************************************
    '*                       PRINT-HEADINGS                      *
    '*****************************************************************

PRINT.HEADINGS:

    LPRINT CHR$(12)
    LPRINT TAB(41); "PAYROLL LISTING"
    LPRINT : LPRINT
    LPRINT TAB(16); "SSN"; TAB(36); "NAME"; TAB(55); "HOURS"; TAB(65); "PAY"; TAB(74); "PAY"; TAB(83); "GROSS"
    LPRINT TAB(54); "WORKED"; TAB(64); "CODE"; TAB(73); "RATE"
    LPRINT
    RETURN


    '*****************************************************************
    '*                      READ-TRANS-FILE                      *
    '*****************************************************************

READ.TRANSACTION.FILE:

    INPUT #1, SSN$, EMPLOYEE$, HOURS, PAY.CODE, DOE$
      IF EMPLOYEE$ = "EOF" THEN END.FLAG$ = "YES"
    RETURN


    '*****************************************************************
    '*                      PROCESS-RECORDS                      *
    '*****************************************************************

PROCESS.RECORDS:

    GOSUB LOOK.UP.SSN                       PERFORM LOOK-UP-SSN
    IF FOUND.SW$ = "YES" THEN
        GOSUB DETAIL.CALCULATIONS
        GOSUB DETAIL.LINE
      ELSE LPRINT USING ERROR.LINE$; SSN$
    END IF
    GOSUB READ.TRANSACTION.FILE             'PERFORM READ-TRANS-FILE
    RETURN
```

**EXHIBIT 7.10    (Cont.)**

```
'***************************************************************
'*                      LOOK-UP-SSN                            *
'***************************************************************


LOOK.UP.SSN:

    FOUND.SW$ = "NO"
    FOR SUB1 = 1 TO 7
        GOSUB COMPARE.SSN.ELEMENT        '* PERFORM COMPARE-SSN-ELEMENT
    NEXT SUB1
    RETURN



    '***************************************************************
    '*                  COMPARE-SSN-ELEMENT                        *
    '***************************************************************


COMPARE.SSN.ELEMENT:

    IF SSN$ = EMPLOYEE.TAB$(SUB1) THEN
        FOUND.SW$ = "YES"
        SUB1 = 7
    END IF
    RETURN


    '***************************************************************
    '*                  DETAIL-CALCULATIONS                        *
    '***************************************************************


DETAIL.CALCULATIONS:

    GROSS = HOURS * PAY.RATE.TAB(PAY.CODE)
    RETURN


    '***************************************************************
    '*                      DETAIL-LINE                            *
    '***************************************************************


DETAIL.LINE:

    LPRINT USING DETAIL.LINE$; SSN$; EMPLOYEE$; HOURS; PAY.CODE; PAY.RATE.TAB(PAY.CODE); GROSS
    RETURN


    '***************************************************************
    '*                        WRAP-UP                             *
    '***************************************************************


WRAPUP:
    GOSUB CLOSE.ROUTINE
    RETURN
```

## EXHIBIT 7.10 (Cont.)

```
'****************************************************************
'*                     CLOSE-ROUTINE                          *
'****************************************************************

CLOSE.ROUTINE:
    CLOSE
    RETURN
```

PAYROLL LISTING

| SSN | NAME | HOURS WORKED | PAY CODE | PAY RATE | GROSS |
|-----|------|--------------|----------|----------|-------|
| 211423681 | JENNY BETH RUSSELL | 40 | 1 | 5.00 | 200.00 |
| 221364881 | TAMMI GEORGE | 50 | 2 | 7.00 | 350.00 |
| 314821147 | *** INVALID SSN *** | | | | |
| 886664422 | JAMES RUSSELL | 45 | 4 | 12.00 | 540.00 |
| 777777777 | *** INVALID SSN *** | | | | |
| 222222222 | CRISTA RUSSELL | 20 | 2 | 7.00 | 140.00 |
| 333333333 | MANDY RUSSELL | 10 | 3 | 10.00 | 100.00 |
| 555555555 | JON CHUMBLEY | 30 | 5 | 15.00 | 450.00 |

**EXHIBIT 7.11    Program Excerpt: In-Line Perform Varying (Method 2) for a Table Search**

**Panel A**

```
112-A-READ-PAYRATE-FILE.
    READ PAYRATE-FILE AT END MOVE "YES" TO END-FLAG.

120-PRINT-HEADINGS.
    WRITE OUT-REC FROM PAGE-HEADING AFTER ADVANCING PAGE.
    WRITE OUT-REC FROM COLUMN-HEADING1 AFTER ADVANCING 3 LINES.
    WRITE OUT-REC FROM COLUMN-HEADING2 AFTER ADVANCING 1 LINES.
    MOVE SPACES TO OUT-REC.
    WRITE OUT-REC AFTER ADVANCING 1 LINES.

130-READ-TRAN-FILE.
    READ TRANSACTION-FILE AT END MOVE "YES" TO END-FLAG.

200-PROCESS-RECORDS.
    PERFORM 210-LOOK-UP-SSN.
    IF FOUND-SWITCH = "YES" THEN
       PERFORM 220-DETAIL-CALCULATIONS
       PERFORM 230-DETAIL-LINE
    ELSE
       MOVE SPACES TO DETAIL-LINE
       MOVE SSN TO SSN-OUT
       MOVE "*** INVALID SSN ***" TO NAME-OUT
       WRITE OUT-REC FROM DETAIL-LINE AFTER ADVANCING 1 LINES.
    PERFORM 130-READ-TRANS-FILE.

210-LOOK-UP-SSN.
    MOVE "NO" TO FOUND-SWITCH.
    PERFORM
              VARYING SUB FROM 1 BY 1 UNTIL SUB > 7
*IN-LINE COMPARE
         IF SSN = VALID-SSN-TABLE (SUB) THEN
            MOVE "YES" TO FOUND-SWITCH
            MOVE 7 TO SUB
         END-IF
    END-PERFORM.
```

← METHOD 2
IN-LINE PERFORM

```
220-DETAIL-CALCULATIONS.
    COMPUTE
    GROSS ROUNDED = HOURS-WORKED * PAYRATE-TABLE (PAY-CODE).

230-DETAIL-LINE.
    MOVE SSN TO SSN-OUT.
    MOVE EMPLOYEE TO NAME-OUT.
    MOVE HOURS-WORKED TO HOURS-WORKED-OUT.
    MOVE PAY-CODE TO PAY-CODE-OUT.
    MOVE PAYRATE-TABLE (PAY-CODE) TO PAY-RATE-OUT.
    MOVE GROSS TO GROSS-OUT.
    WRITE OUT-REC FROM DETAIL-LINE AFTER ADVANCING 1 LINES.

300-WRAP-UP.
    CLOSE TRANSACTION-FILE
          PAYRATE-FILE
```

**Panel B Quick Basic Excerpt for In-Line (For . . . Next Loop) To Search Table**

```
FOR SUB1 = 1 TO 7
    IF SSN = SSN.TAB (SUB1) THEN
       FOUND.SW$ = "YES"
       SAVE.SUB = SUB1
    END IF
NEXT SUB1
```

## SUMMARY

Few major application programs are written without the manipulation of tables. A table is a list of related items with common attributes that is placed into main memory for fast access during record processing. Tables are used to validate input records prior to processing and to locate needed values in order to complete a computation or other processing step.

To reference a table element requires both a table name and an associated subscript. A subscript can be either a constant or a variable. Its content represents the actual relative element location. In other words, if the subscript contains a 2, it points to the second element of the table. If the subscript contains a 3, it points to the third element of the table, etc.

Before a table can be used in a program, it must first reside in memory. The table can be either an internal table or an external table. An internal table is created during its compilation. An external table is loaded into memory from a table file as a part of program execution. When table data change frequently and occupy a large amount of space, it is a good idea to load a table from a file. If the data in the table rarely change and the table is relatively small, then the table can be created as an internal table (using the COBOL language) or as an external table by storing literals into the table (using BASIC).

The programming logic for loading tables consists of (1) initializing the subscript to 1, (2) comparing the subscript with the upper limit and, if the comparison result is false, then (3) performing the routine that actually loads the input value into the table, and (4) increasing the subscript by 1 in order to point to the next element. This process is repeated until all table records are loaded into the table. The routine that actually loads the input value into the table consists of (1) storing the input value into the table, and (2) reading the next record.

The logic for searching a table is essentially the same as the logic for loading a table, except that, in a search, a comparison must be made between the key in the input transaction record and the table key. A serial search through the table compares the search key from the input record with the table key found in each table element. If the comparison result between two keys is true, then FOUND-SWITCH is turned on. The content of the subscript is transferred to a save area, and the value that represents the upper limit is moved to SUB. Storing the upper limit value in SUB will cause the table search definite iteration to terminate. Since the content of SUB was saved previously, the new variable in which the content of SUB was stored will be used as the subscript in future references to the table element that was found. Both modular and "in-line" searching are discussed.

## VOCABULARY

| | |
|---|---|
| table | external table |
| memory table | execution-time table |
| array | table load |
| search key | table lookup |
| element | table search |
| table key | definite iteration |
| table argument | Perform . . . Varying |
| table file | For . . . Next |
| table function | sequential (serial) |
| subscript | search |
| internal table | binary search |
| hard-coded table | FOUND-SWITCH |
| compile-time table | positional addressing |

## EXERCISES/QUESTIONS

1. What is a table?

2. What is the purpose of a table?

3. Why is it better to access data stored in a table than to access the same information from a file?

4. List three different ways that tables can be used.

5. Compare and contrast *internal* tables and *external* tables. What other names are used for these two types of tables?

6. Describe the logic of the definite iteration. What are the four steps or activities that occur in the definite iteration?

7. Describe the process of loading a single-dimensional table from a file of four records where a single field from each record is loaded into separate elements of the table using the definite iteration structure.

8. Describe the general logic of performing a table search.

9. What is meant by positional addressing? Give an example of a table to be accessed using positional addressing.

10. In the table search logic, what is the purpose of storing the contents of SUB into a save area (SAVE-SUB)?

## LAB PROBLEMS

**7–1.** ACME University wishes to generate a registration report. A detail line will only print for a student record if the Course-ID is located in the Table of Valid Courses. An error message is to print on the detail line instead. The lab fee is to be lifted from the Lab Fees Table using positional addressing—not using a table search. The registration report, record layout, and tables are shown below. Draw a structured flowchart and write the pseudocode for this problem.

```
                            ACME UNIVERSITY
                      STUDENT REGISTRATION REPORT

    STUDENT       STUDENT           COURSE-ID    CREDIT    REG.      LAB      CHARGE/
    NUMBER        NAME                           HOURS     TUITION   FEE      COURSE

    111111111     BAKER, JOE        CIS2023      3         60.00     15.00    75.00
    222222222     COLLINS, D        HIS2043      3         60.00      0.00    60.00
    222222222     COLLINS, D        BUS3013      3         60.00     20.00    80.00
    222222222     COLLINS, D        ENG2013      3         60.00      0.00    60.00
    222222222     INVALID COURSE    X*$@#&0
    XXXXXXXXX     XXXXXXXXX,X        XXXXXXX     X         XX.XX     XX.XX    XX.XX
    XXXXXXXXX     INVALID COURSE
    XXXXXXXXX     XXXXXXXXX,X        XXXXXXX     X         XX.XX     XX.XX    XX.XX

                                                STUDENT   TOTAL    $ XXX.XX*
```

### RECORD LAYOUT:

| | | |
|---|---|---|
| STUDENT # | 1–9 | (N) |
| NAME | 10–25 | (A/N) |
| COURSE-ID | 26–31 | (A/N) |
| CREDIT HRS | 32–33 | (N) |
| LAB CODE | 34 | (VALUES = 1 THRU 9) Code values match up with relative positions of lab fee table (that is, a lab code of 1 means 0.00, a lab code of 2 means 10.00) |

### VALID COURSES TABLE
#### (only representative courses)

| |
|---|
| AGR2011 |
| AGR3073 |
| BUS2003 |
| BUS3013 |
| CIS2003 |
| CIS2023 |
| ENG2013 |
| ENG2123 |
| HIS2043 |
| HIS3024 |
| HIS4034 |
| GOV2013 |
| GOV2023 |
| GOV3044 |
| GEO1003 |
| GEO2023 |
| AST2013 |
| AST3033 |
| ACC1043 |
| ACC2023 |
| ACC3034 |

### LAB FEES TABLE

| |
|---|
| 0.00 |
| 10.00 |
| 15.00 |
| 15.00 |
| 20.00 |
| 25.00 |
| 30.00 |
| 35.00 |

**7–2.** ACME University wishes to generate a registration report similar to the one in Problem 7–1 but the report should have subtotals for each group of courses a student takes. This represents the total charge for each student. A student can have multiple records in the file. In other words, each student has a logical record which represents the entire group of physical records where each physical record represents a particular course for which he or she is registering. The records are sorted by student number (SSN) so that they are grouped by each student. A detail line will only print for a student record if the Course-ID is located in the Table of Valid Courses. Otherwise, an error message is to print on the detail line. The lab fee is to be lifted from the Lab Fees Table using positional addressing—*not* using a table search. The registration report, record layout, and tables are shown below.

Note: The same input record and table data apply to this problem as well.

```
                            ACME UNIVERSITY
                      STUDENT REGISTRATION REPORT
                        BROKEN DOWN BY STUDENT
    STUDENT      STUDENT           COURSE-ID    CREDIT    REG.        LAB      COURSE
    NUMBER       NAME                           HOURS     TUITION     FEE      TOTAL

    111111111    BAKER, JOE        CIS2123        3       60.00      15.00     75.00

                                            STUDENT 111111111 TOTAL    $   75.00*

    222222222    COLLINS, D        HIS2043        3       60.00       0.00     60.00
    222222222    COLLINS, D        BUS3013        3       60.00      20.00     80.00
    222222222    COLLINS, D        ENG2013        3       60.00       0.00     60.00
    222222222    INVALID COURSE    X*$@#&0

                                            STUDENT 222222222 TOTAL    $  200.00*

    XXXXXXXX     XXXXXXXXX,X       XXXXXXX        X       XX.XX      XX.XX     XX.XX
    XXXXXXXX     INVALID COURSE
    XXXXXXXX     XXXXXXXXX,X       XXXXXXX        X       XX.XX      XX.XX     XX.XX

                                            STUDENT XXXXXXXX TOTAL    $ XXX.XX*
```

358 CHAPTER 7 TABLE HANDLING CONCEPTS

**7–3.** A daily medical charge report is to be prepared. The design logic for this problem is to include a hierarchy chart, flowchart, and pseudocode.

The report is to print patient ID, patient name, charge, lab test type. The input consists of patient ID, patient name, and charge code. Use positional addressing for this problem.

```
                    MEDICAL CHARGES

    PATIENT ID      PATIENT NAME      CHARGE      SERVICE

       6093         ABLES, AARON      250.00      CHECKUP
       7055         BOYD, JIM         155.00      INJECTION
       4444         CARLTON, CARL     400.00      X-RAY
       3333         DOBSON, SUE       125.00      BLOOD TEST

    TOTAL PATIENTS          XX
    TOTAL CHARGES      XX,XXX.XX
    AVERAGE CHARGE     XX,XXX.XX
```

DATA:

```
PATIENT ID    1–5     NUMERIC
NAME          6–25    ALPHA
CHARGE CODE   27      NUMERIC (VALUES 1–5)
```

TABLE DATA

| CHARGE CODE | EXAM TYPE | CHARGE |
|---|---|---|
| 1 | CHECKUP | 250.00 |
| 2 | BLOOD TEST | 125.00 |
| 3 | INJECTION | 155.00 |
| 4 | X-RAY | 400.00 |
| 5 | MEDICATION | 100.00 |

---

**7–4.** Modify the design in Problem 7.3 so that the table data are also printed out on a separate page after the Medical Charges Report. Print appropriate field headings. The sample report appears below.

| Code | Service | Charge |
|---|---|---|
| 1 | CHECKUP | 250.00 |
| 2 | BLOOD TEST | 125.00 |
| . | . | . |
| . | . | . |
| . | . | . |

# 8

# Intermediate and Advanced Single-Dimensional Table Processing

## OBJECTIVES

As a result of having read and studied this chapter, the student will be able to do the following activities:

1. Design a program that looks up and extracts applicable table data for calculation and output purposes.

2. Design a program that both validates that a value exists in one table and looks up and extracts data from a second table that is used for calculation and output purposes.

3. Design a program that uses various alternate design methods for both loading and searching tables.

4. Design a program that:
   a. uses a table load and search where the number of table records to be loaded are unknown at execution time;
   b. uses a table value from one table as the subscript or pointer for a different table;
   c. uses control break logic;
   d. uses positional addressing as well as table searching;
   e. saves data in a summary table that is to be printed at the end of the run.

Chapter 7 covered the basics of table handling. You learned the concepts of loading and searching a single-dimensional table. The chapter application (Application 7.1) used a table lookup to validate the presence (or absence) of an employee's social security number in a table of valid employee numbers (SSNs). Positional addressing was also introduced in the application, using a pay code as a subscript to access an applicable pay rate in a pay rate table.

In this chapter, Application 8.1 illustrates how the table lookup process is used to *look up and extract* applicable product information. A produce wholesale report is produced. Application 8.2 expands on Application 8.1 from this chapter and uses what was learned from Chapter 7. A sales commission report is produced involving a *table search for validation purposes* (to ensure the SSN is in the table of valid SSNs) and also a table search to *locate and extract* the appropriate product description and product price. *Positional addressing* is used to locate and extract the appropriate commission rate for calculating the salesperson's commission.

These two applications simply expand on the concepts from Chapter 7. Both applications assume a fixed number of record values are loaded to the table. The programmer knows how many elements there will be in the table and how many actual values are being loaded.

An *alternate searching method* (Method II) is also presented. Some programmers prefer this method to the method (Method I) used in all previous applications. Next, an *alternate loading method* is presented that takes care of the possibility that the *number of loaded values may vary* from one computer run to the next. Its effect on both loading and searching is discussed and illustrated.

Also, a searching method (Method III) is discussed which is sometimes called an "in-line" PERFORM . . . VARYING technique. This technique embeds the element comparison process inside the decision block of the count-controlled loop. This method only works with COBOL 85. COBOL 74 does not support in-line Perform Varying; and, QBasic's FOR NEXT statement does not permit programmer-supplied conditional expressions (that is, one could not use a compound expression as one can with COBOL 85).

Application 8.3 uses many of the concepts presented. This application assumes a variable number of records to be loaded to COMPUTER-PARTS-TABLE; therefore, the alternate loading method is used. Method II is used for searching this table.

Computer parts information is extracted for both printing and computational purposes. A new concept illustrated in this application is the use of an element value from the computer parts table (PART-MARKUP-TAB) as a subscript to be used to point to an appropriate markup from the MARKUP-TABLE. The concept could be called *the use of a subscripted table item as a subscript with a second table*. Straight positional addressing is also used in extracting discount percentages. Moreover, this application illustrates the use of control breaks from Chapter 6.

Application 8.4 illustrates a more efficient manner of searching when the table size is very large. This method is called the binary search and is essential in on-line applications, especially where multiple, large tables must be searched prior to refreshing a screen with new information.

## A Single-Dimensional Table Search with Positional Addressing and Use of Table Elements in Calculations (Data Extraction)

Produce Wholesale Report

### PROGRAM REQUIREMENTS

The management of a grocery chain wishes to produce a report that lists the product number, description, price, and quantity, and the sales amount for each product sold during a given month. Appropriate headings are to be printed, as well as a final sales total at the end of the report. The product description and price are to be extracted from a product table. The price from the table is to be used in calculating the sales amount (quantity * price = sales). The month of the year is to be extracted from a table of months through positional addressing and is to be printed as a part of the first heading line. The MM sub-field of DATE (the month field in the first record) is to be used as the subscript as the actual value of the MM field points positionally to the appropriate alphanumeric description of the

month. A further discussion of this is presented later in **Logic Considerations.**

### OUTPUT DESIGN

Exhibit 8.1 illustrates the sample report which is to be produced, and Exhibit 8.2 depicts the printer spacing chart.

### INPUT DESIGN

The input record formats are illustrated in Exhibit 8.3; the sales transaction input record is shown first. Beneath the transaction record is illustrated the product table file. The sole purpose of this file is to serve as input to the product table. The third illus-

---

**EXHIBIT 8.1    Sample of Produce Wholesale Report**

```
                    PRODUCE WHOLESALE REPORT              MONTH:    AUGUST

    PRODUCT             DESCRIPTION        PRICE      QUANTITY          SALES
    NUMBER

     4024             BANANAS              1.46          10            14.60
     4060             GRAPES               0.92           5             4.60
     4000             APPLES               1.25          20            25.00
     4072             BERRIES              0.88          10             8.80
     5000             PRODUCT NUMBER INVALID

                                           TOTAL SALES               $53.00
```

---

**EXHIBIT 8.2    Printer Spacing Chart for Application 8.1, Produce Wholesale Report**

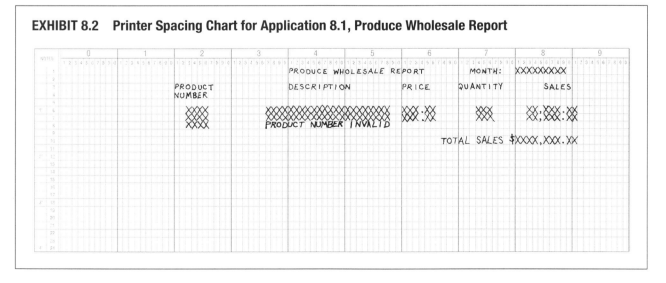

trated record layout is the month table. The only field to be loaded into the memory table is the alphanumeric description of the month; therefore, this record only contains one field.

## TABLES

Exhibit 8.4 illustrates the tables for this problem. Frame A depicts the products table of corresponding values, and Frame B shows the month table.

## TEST DATA

The test data for the various files are illustrated in Exhibit 8.5. Frame A depicts the sales transaction input file; Frame B shows the test cases for the product table and illustrated in Frame C are the test cases for the month table. For the product table file and the month table file the term test cases may be a misnomer in that the data being loaded to the table are not validated. The record is simply read and loaded to its respective memory table element.

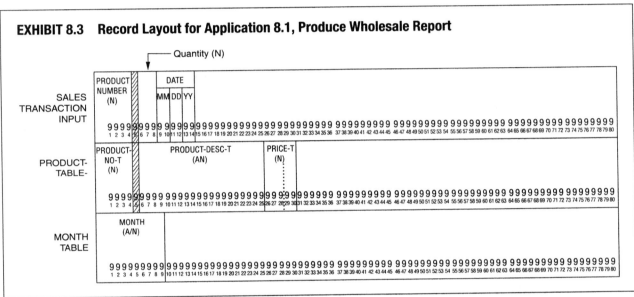

**EXHIBIT 8.3** Record Layout for Application 8.1, Produce Wholesale Report

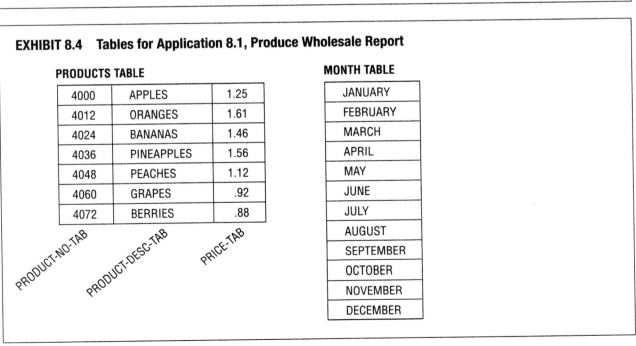

**EXHIBIT 8.4** Tables for Application 8.1, Produce Wholesale Report

### PRODUCTS TABLE

| | | |
|---|---|---|
| 4000 | APPLES | 1.25 |
| 4012 | ORANGES | 1.61 |
| 4024 | BANANAS | 1.46 |
| 4036 | PINEAPPLES | 1.56 |
| 4048 | PEACHES | 1.12 |
| 4060 | GRAPES | .92 |
| 4072 | BERRIES | .88 |

PRODUCT-NO-TAB    PRODUCT-DESC-TAB    PRICE-TAB

### MONTH TABLE

| |
|---|
| JANUARY |
| FEBRUARY |
| MARCH |
| APRIL |
| MAY |
| JUNE |
| JULY |
| AUGUST |
| SEPTEMBER |
| OCTOBER |
| NOVEMBER |
| DECEMBER |

## LOGIC CONSIDERATIONS

In order to print the date on the right side of the first heading, a table must be loaded to memory that contains the months of the year in alphanumeric form. In some languages such as COBOL it is easier to set up an internal (compile time) table to handle the task. In this application, to accommodate any programming language as the implementing tool the data to be loaded are set up as a file and subsequently loaded to a memory table. The technique for handling this varies depending upon the language the programmer is using. After the first record—which contains the date in a month-date-year format (MMDDYY)—is read, the MM subfield is used as the subscript to positionally reference the appropriate alphanumeric month description. No table search is required, because the contents of the MM field correspond with the element number where the associated month of the year is found. For example, MONTH-TAB (MM), where MM = 3, points to the third element of the table, which contains MARCH.

In order to extract the appropriate product description and price from the product table, a sequential table search is to be performed starting with the first product number and progressing one at a time through the PRODUCT-NO-TAB until a product number from the table matches that of the product number in the transaction record. When a match is found in the table, the corresponding product description [PRODUCT-DESC-TAB (SUB)] is to be moved to the output area for printing purposes. The second corresponding value in the table is the price. This corresponding price is to be used in the calculation of sales.

## PROGRAM DESIGN

### Hierarchy Chart

The general program design of this problem is close to that of Application 7.1 in Chapter 7, with one major difference. This difference is shown in Exhibit 8.6, the hierarchy chart. The main difference in this logic is found in the START-UP module, where the execution of the LOAD-TABLES module precedes the execution of the READ-TRANS-FILE module and the PRINT-HEADINGS module. In the previous illustration the PRINT-HEADINGS appeared prior to the loading of the table. The sequence of the modules in that program was not important from a programming logic perspective. In this second problem, however, the alphanumeric form of the date must appear on the heading. In order to accomplish this, the table must be resident in a memory table prior to printing the headings; therefore the loading process must precede the printing of headings.

---

### EXHIBIT 8.5  Test Cases for Sales Transactions

**Sales Transaction Records**

```
          1         2
12345678901234567890
- - - - - - - - - - - - - - - - - - - -
4024 010081293
4060 005081393
4000 020081493
4072 010081493
5000 008081593
- - - - - - - - - - - - - - - - - - - -
```

**Product Table Data**

```
          1         2         3
12345678901234567890123456789012345678901234567890
- - - - - - - - - - - - - - - - - - - - - - - - -
4000 APPLES         00125
4012 ORANGES        00161
4024 BANANAS        00146
4036 PINEAPPLES     00156
4048 PEACHES        00112
4060 GRAPES         00092
4072 BERRIES        00088
- - - - - - - - - - - - - - - - - - - - - - - - -
```

**Month Table Data**

```
          1         2         3         4
12345678901234567890123456789012345678901234567890
- - - - - - - - - - - - - - - - - - - - - - - - - - - - - -
JANUARY
FEBRUARY
MARCH
APRIL
MAY
JUNE
JULY
AUGUST
SEPTEMBER
OCTOBER
NOVEMBER
DECEMBER
- - - - - - - - - - - - - - - - - - - - - - - - - - - - - -
```

The PROCESS-RECORD module is decomposed into a LOOK-UP-PRODUCT-INFO module, DETAIL-CALCULATIONS module, ACCUMULATION module, PRINT-DETAIL-LINE module, and a READ-TRANS-FILE module. As previously discussed, *the purpose of the LOOK-UP-PRODUCT-INFO module is to locate the appropriate product description and price.* The DETAIL-CALCULATIONS module calculates the sales amount by multiplying the quantity from the transaction record by the corresponding price from the product table. In this illustration it is observed that table values are to be used in computations. The ACCUMULATION module adds the sales amount to the total sales amount. The PRINT-DETAIL-LINE module is responsible for the data transfer from the input transaction record into the output area. This includes the transfer of the description and price from the Products table and the calculated sales value into the output area as well.

## Structured Flowchart

Exhibit 8.7 illustrates the structured flowchart logic for this problem. In the START-UP module the END-FLAG is set equal to "NO." The TOTAL-SALES is initialized to zero. The three input files are opened (as many files as required can be opened at once in any programming language). After the files are opened the LOAD-TABLES module is invoked. The LOAD-TABLES module serves as a control module which invokes separate and subordinate modules to load the two tables. The first block invokes the LOAD-PRODUCT-TABLE and the second module invokes the LOAD-MONTHS-TABLE. The next instruction shown is designed to reinitialize the END-FLAG, because the same END-FLAG switch is used for the READ-PRODUCTS-TABLE-FILE and READ-MONTHS-TABLE. If the program executes properly, the END-FLAG will never be turned on because the loop is actually a definite iteration and is to be repeated precisely the number of times as there are elements. The two table read modules contain a check for end of file because in some languages, such as COBOL (COBOL 68), sequential read command requires an AT END clause that handles the testing for the end of file status. If the AT END is left off of the READ command, where access is assumed sequential, a diagnostic will be generated. So, even if the programming logic dictates that end of file will not be encountered, it is better to provide for the end of file check in the read modules unless the COBOL compiler in use by the programmer does not require the AT END clause. ANS COBOL 74 (IBM Extension), for example, does not

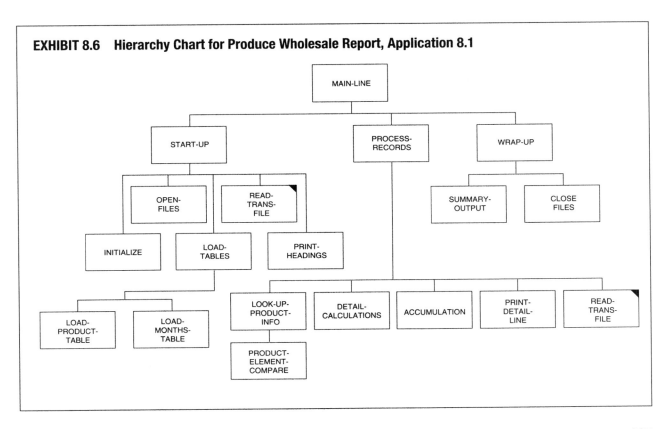

**EXHIBIT 8.6    Hierarchy Chart for Produce Wholesale Report, Application 8.1**

require the AT END, but ANS COBOL 68 does require it.

When loading an exact number of values to a table with an ELEMENT LOAD module that contains the READ statement before the data transfer to the table, it would be satisfactory to leave off the AT END clause because the count-controlled logic would prevent an EOF from ever being encountered. On the other hand, with the pre-read, post-read logic used throughout this book, there is a problem if one leaves the AT END off the READ statement. After the last table record is loaded, the post-read statement reads the EOF marker. If there is no AT END clause, COBOL generates a run time error message, "END OF FILE ENCOUNTERED AND NO END OF FILE PROCESSING SPECIFIED." In the language BASIC or Quick BASIC, there is no need to provide for the end of file check when under the control of a definite iteration module.

The logic of the LOAD-PRODUCT-TABLE and LOAD-MONTHS-TABLE modules is the same as presented in the load modules from the first illustration, except for the "do until" condition test. The LOAD-PRODUCT-TABLE module "do until" tests to determine whether SUB is greater than seven as it must load exactly seven into the table. The LOAD-MONTHS-TABLE "do until" tests to determine whether SUB is greater than 12 as it must load precisely twelve months into the table. For both load routines the SUB is initialized to one, and the condition is tested; if the condition is false, the routine that loads the element is invoked (PRODUCT-ELEMENT-LOAD or MONTHS-ELEMENT-LOAD, depending upon which table is being loaded). Here the input values are loaded to the respective table element, and the next table record is read. Subsequently, the SUB is increased by 1, and the entire definite iteration is repeated until the respective table is loaded.

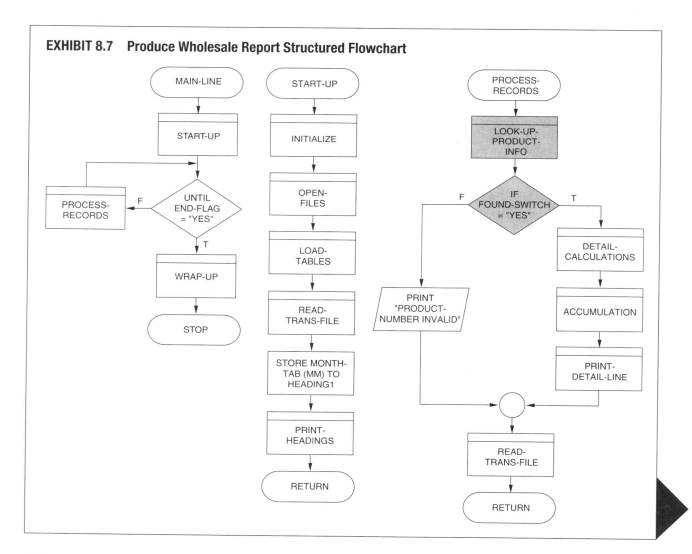

EXHIBIT 8.7 Produce Wholesale Report Structured Flowchart

The LOOK-UP-PRODUCT-INFO routine contains the same search logic that was presented in the prior example, except that the PRODUCT-ELEMENT-COMPARE module contains a third block that stores the contents of SUB into a SAVE-SUB variable. The reason for this was previously referenced in Chapter 7 in the discussion pertaining to the concept of table searching. In this example, after a product number has been found, the corresponding description and price must be referenced in subsequent program steps. To reference these corresponding values the contents of the subscript that existed at the time the product number was found must be stored away for future use. In other words, SAVE-SUB will be used as the subscript instead of SUB. The reader may recall from the prior discussion about the concept of table searching that this is done to "trip the switch" and make the value of SUB greater than the upper limit in order for the repetition condition to be true. Once the condition is true (or false, depending upon the implementing iteration command), the iteration process ceases and the table lookup module terminates.

In this structured flowchart observe the DETAIL-CALCULATIONS module. The SALES is computed by multiplying the QUANTITY by the PRICE-TAB (SAVE-SUB). It is important for the reader to understand that it would *not* work to compute SALES = QUANTITY X PRICE-TAB (SUB). Why is this true? SUB contains an 8 when the LOOK-UP-PRODUCT-INFO module is complete. In attempting to reference PRICE-TAB (SUB) the programmer will try to reference the eighth element of the table (which only contains 7). This will result in a subscripting error. The computer is unable to reference an element in the table that does not exist. The use of SAVE-SUB as the subscript is also shown in the PRINT-DETAIL-LINE module. The use of the SAVE-SUB approach allows *future* reference to the appropriate table element while other techniques may not provide this flexibility. This method allows for strong module cohesion by keeping table-searching activities separate from other functions.

## Pseudocode

Exhibit 8.8 illustrates the associated pseudocode for this problem.

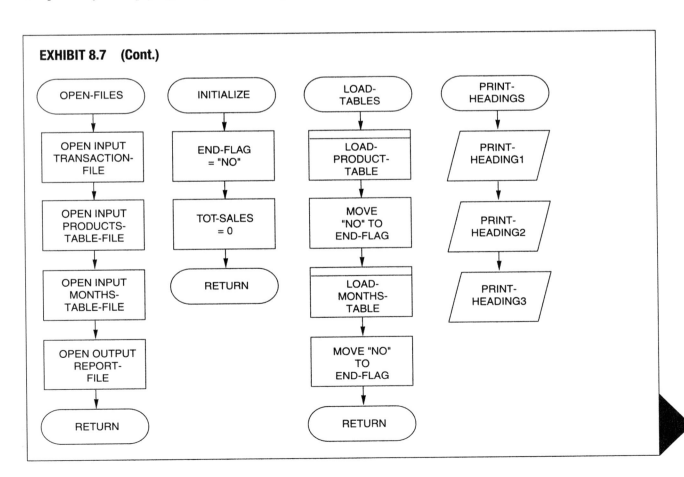

**EXHIBIT 8.7 (Cont.)**

## Programs

Exhibits 8.9 and 8.10 illustrate the COBOL 85 and Quick BASIC programs for this problem, respectively.

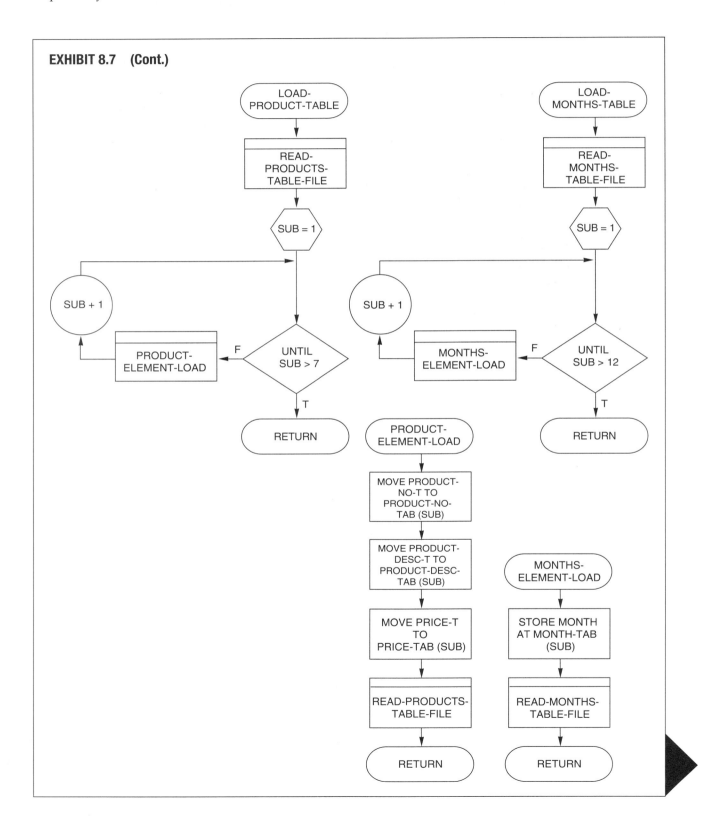

EXHIBIT 8.7 (Cont.)

**EXHIBIT 8.7    (Cont.)**

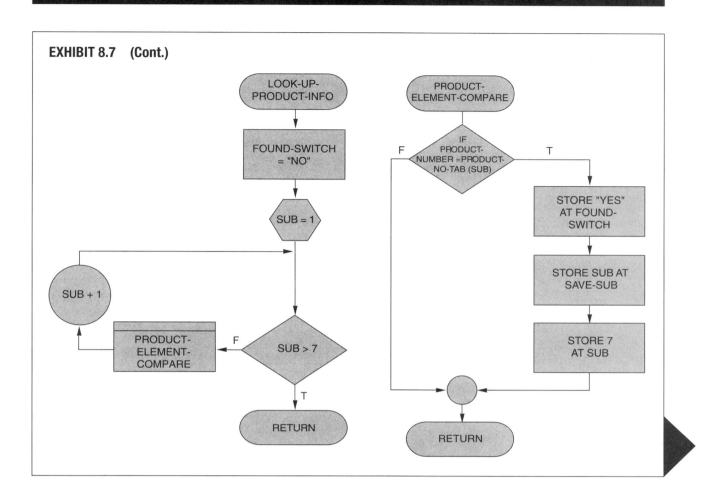

**EXHIBIT 8.7** (Cont.)

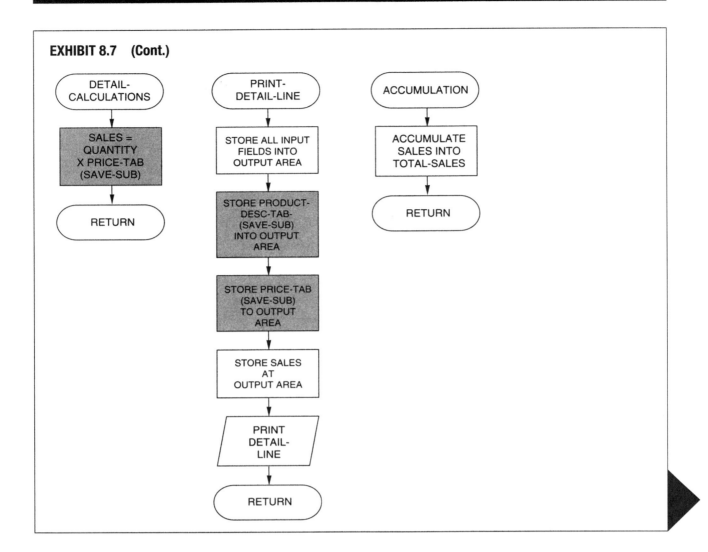

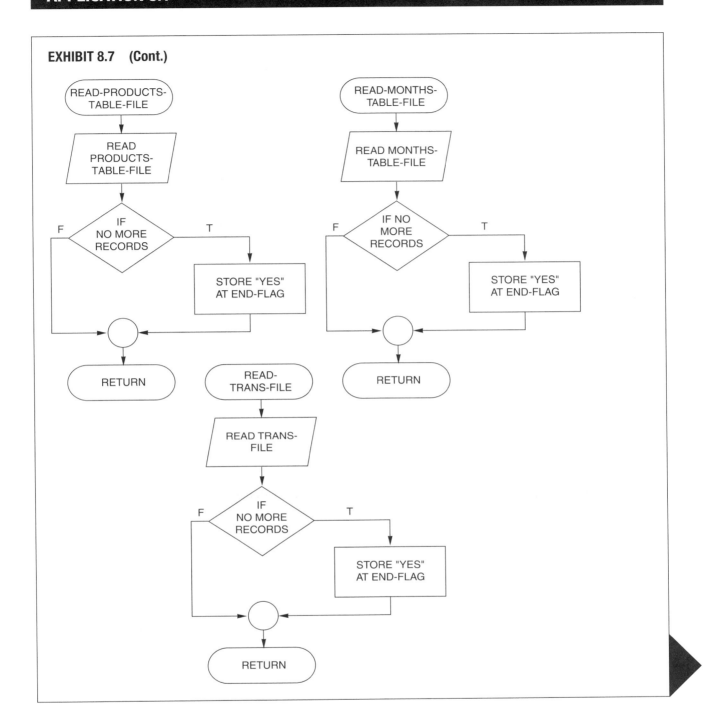

**EXHIBIT 8.7     (Cont.)**

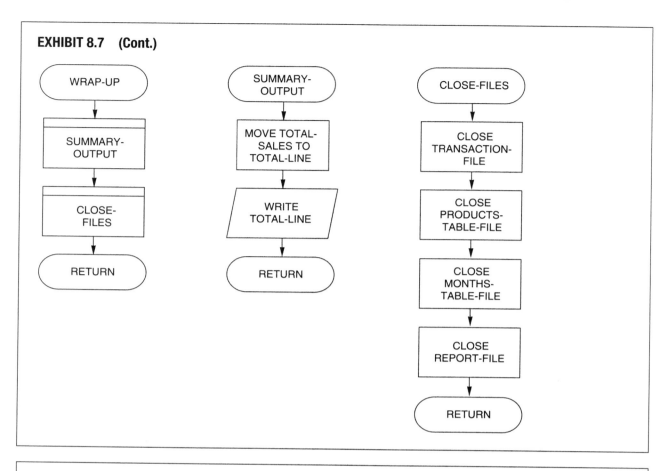

**EXHIBIT 8.7    (Cont.)**

**EXHIBIT 8.8    Pseudocode for Application 8.1 (Produce Wholesale Report)**

```
*main-line
    start-up
    dountil end-flag = "yes"
        process-records
    enddo
    wrap-up
    stop
*start-up
    initialize
    open-files
    load-tables
    read-trans-file
    store month-tab (mm) to heading 1
    print-headings
    return
*initialize
    end-flag = "no"
    total-sales = 0
    return
*open-files
    open transaction-file
    open products-table-file
    open months-table-file
    open report-file
    return
```

```
*process-records
    look-up-product-info
    if found-switch = "yes"
        then
            detail-calculations
            accumulation
            detail-line
        else
            print "product number invalid"
    endif
    read-trans-file
    return
*load-tables
    load-product-table
    store "no" at end-flag
    load-months-table
    store "no" at end-flag
    return
*print-headings
    print heading1
    print heading2
    print heading3
    return
*read-trans-file
    read transaction-file
    when no more records store "yes" at end-flag
    endread
    return
```

**EXHIBIT 8.8    (Cont.)**

*load-product-table
    <u>read product-table-file</u>
    store 1 at sub
    dountil sub > 7
        <u>product-element-load</u>
            increase sub by 1
    enddo
    return
*load-months-table
    <u>read-months-table-file</u>
    store 1 at sub
    dountil sub > 5
        <u>months-element-load</u>
            increase sub by 1
    enddo
    return
*product-element-load
    store product-no-t at product-no-tab (sub)
    store product-desc-t at product-desc-tab (sub)
    store price-t at price-tab (sub)
    <u>read-product-table-file</u>
    return
*months-element-load
    store month at month-tab (sub)
    <u>read-months-table-file</u>
    return
*look-up-product-info
    store "no" at found-switch
    store 1 at sub
    dountil sub > 7
        <u>product-element-compare</u>
            increase sub by 1
    enddo
    return
*product-element-compare
    if product-number = product-no-tab (sub)
        then
            store "yes" at found-switch
            store sub at save-sub
            store 7 at sub
    endif
    return

*detail-calculations
    calculate sales = quantity × price-tab (save-sub)
    return
*accumulation
    accumulate sales into total-sales
    return
*detail-line
    store input fields to print line
    store product-desc-tab (save-sub) at print line
    store price-tab (save-sub) at print line
    store sales at print line
    print the detail line
    return
*read-products-table-file
    read products-table-file
        when out of records store "yes" at end-flag
    endread
    return
*read-months-table-file
    read months-table-file
        when out of records store "yes" at end-flag
    endread
    return
*wrap-up
    <u>summary-output</u>
    <u>close-files</u>
    return
*summary-output
    move total-sales to total-line
    write total-line
    return
*close-files
    close transaction-file
    close products-table-file
    close months-table-file
    close report-file
    return

```
1           IDENTIFICATION DIVISION.
2           PROGRAM-ID.  CHAPTER8-ILL1.
3           AUTHOR.  JACK RUSSELL.
4           DATE-WRITTEN.  APRIL 17, 1993.
5           DATE-COMPILED. 1993-06-24.
6          *REMARKS:
7          *  THIS PROGRAM PRODUCES A WHOLESALE SALES REPORT.  BOTH
8          *  TRANSACTION DATA AND TABLE DATA IS NEEDED TO PRODUCE THE
9          *  REPORT.
10         *  BOTH THE PRODUCT DESCRIPTION AND PRICE IS EXTRACTED FROM
11         *  A PRODUCTS TABLE.  THE PRICE FROM THE PRODUCTS TABLE IS USED
12         *  IN CALCULATING THE SALES AMOUNT FOR THE SALES TRANSACTION
13         *  RECORD.
14
15          ENVIRONMENT DIVISION.
16          CONFIGURATION SECTION.
17          SOURCE-COMPUTER.  CYBER.
18          OBJECT-COMPUTER.  CYBER.
19          INPUT-OUTPUT SECTION.
20          FILE-CONTROL.
21              SELECT TRANSACTION-FILE ASSIGN TO DTA81.
22              SELECT PRODUCTS-TABLE-FILE ASSIGN TO DTA81PRO.
23              SELECT MONTHS-TABLE-FILE ASSIGN TO DTA81MOS.
24              SELECT OUT-FILE ASSIGN TO OUTFILE.
25
26          DATA DIVISION.
27          FILE SECTION.
28          FD  TRANSACTION-FILE.
29          01  TRANS-REC.
30              05   PRODUCT-NUMBER PIC 9(04).
31              05   FILLER         PIC X.
32              05   QUANTITY       PIC 9(03).
33              05   DATE-IN.
34                   10   MM        PIC 99.
35                   10   DD        PIC 99.
36                   10   YY        PIC 99.
37              05   FILLER         PIC X(66).
38
39          FD  PRODUCTS-TABLE-FILE.
40          01  PRODUCTS-REC.
41              05   PRODUCT-NO-T   PIC 9(04).
42              05   FILLER         PIC X.
43              05   PRODUCT-DESC-T PIC X(20).
44              05   PRICE-T        PIC 9(03)V99.
45              05   FILLER         PIC X(52).
46
47          FD  MONTHS-TABLE-FILE.
48          01  MONTHS-REC.
49              05   MONTH          PIC X(09).
50              05   FILLER         PIC X(71).
51
52          FD  OUT-FILE.
53          01  OUT-REC            PIC X(133).
```

**EXHIBIT 8.9    (Cont.)**

```
54
55          WORKING-STORAGE SECTION.
56
57          01   END-FLAG            PIC X(03)          VALUE "NO".
58
59          01   NO-MORE-RECORDS     PIC X(03)          VALUE "NO".
60
61          01   PRODUCTS-TAB.
62               05   PRODUCTS-TABLE OCCURS 7 TIMES.
63                    10   PRODUCT-NO-TAB     PIC 9(04).
64                    10   PRODUCT-DESC-TAB   PIC X(20).
65                    10   PRICE-TAB          PIC 9(03)V99.
66
67          01   MONTH-TABLE.
68               05   MONTH-TABL   OCCURS 12 TIMES.
69                    10   MONTH-TAB          PIC X(09).
70
71          01   PAGE-HEADING.
72               05                   PIC X(40)   VALUE SPACES.
73               05                   PIC X(24)   VALUE
74                                    "PRODUCE WHOLESALE REPORT".
75               05                   PIC X(08)   VALUE SPACES.
76               05                   PIC X(09)   VALUE "MONTH:    ".
77               05   MONTH-OUT       PIC X(09).
78               05                   PIC X(42)    VALUE SPACES.
79
80          01   COLUMN-HEADING1.
81               05                   PIC X(20)   VALUE SPACES.
82               05                   PIC X(07)   VALUE "PRODUCT".
83               05                   PIC X(13)   VALUE SPACES.
84               05                   PIC X(11)   VALUE "DESCRIPTION".
85               05                   PIC X(09)   VALUE SPACES.
86               05                   PIC X(05)   VALUE "PRICE".
87               05                   PIC X(05)   VALUE SPACES.
88               05                   PIC X(08)   VALUE "QUANTITY".
89               05                   PIC X(07)   VALUE SPACES.
90               05                   PIC X(05)   VALUE "SALES".
91               05                   PIC X(42)   VALUE SPACES.
92
93          01   COLUMN-HEADING2.
94               05                   PIC X(20)   VALUE SPACES.
95               05                   PIC X(06)   VALUE "NUMBER".
96               05                   PIC X(106)  VALUE SPACES.
97
98          01   DETAIL-LINE.
99               05                   PIC X(22)   VALUE SPACES.
100              05   NUMBER-OUT      PIC 9(04).
101              05                   PIC X(10)   VALUE SPACES.
102              05   DESC-OUT        PIC X(23).
103              05                   PIC X(01)   VALUE SPACES.
104              05   PRICE-OUT       PIC ZZ9.99.
105              05                   PIC X(07)   VALUE SPACES.
106              05   QUANTITY-OUT    PIC ZZ9.
107              05                   PIC X(06)   VALUE SPACES.
108              05   SALES-OUT       PIC ZZ,ZZ9.99.
109              05                   PIC X(41)   VALUE SPACES.
110
111         01   TOTAL-LINE.
112              05                   PIC X(68)   VALUE SPACES.
113              05                   PIC X(11)   VALUE "TOTAL SALES".
114              05                   PIC X(02)   VALUE SPACES.
115              05   TOT-SALES-OUT   PIC $$$$,$$9.99.
116              05                   PIC X(41)   VALUE SPACES.
117
```

EXHIBIT 8.9   (Cont.)

```
118         01   FOUND-SWITCH              PIC X(03)      VALUE "NO".
119         01   SUB                       PIC 99         VALUE 0.
120         01   SAVE-SUB                  PIC 99         VALUE 0.
121         01   TOTAL-SALES               PIC 9(06)V99   VALUE 0.
122         01   SALES                     PIC 9(05)V99   VALUE 0.
123
124         PROCEDURE DIVISION.
125         *********************
126
127         0000-MAIN-LINE.
128             PERFORM 1000-START-UP.
129             PERFORM 2000-PROCESS-RECORDS UNTIL END-FLAG = "YES".
130             PERFORM 3000-WRAP-UP.
131             STOP RUN.
132
133         1000-START-UP.
134     *       INITIALIZE-VARIABLES (W-S)
135             PERFORM 1050-OPEN-FILES.
136             PERFORM 1100-LOAD-TABLES.
137             PERFORM 1200-READ-TRANS-FILE.
138             MOVE MONTH-TAB (MM) TO MONTH-OUT.
139             PERFORM 1300-PRINT-HEADINGS.
140
141         1050-OPEN-FILES.
142             OPEN INPUT   TRANSACTION-FILE
143                          PRODUCTS-TABLE-FILE
144                          MONTHS-TABLE-FILE.
145             OPEN OUTPUT OUT-FILE.
146
147
148
149         1100-LOAD-TABLES.
150             PERFORM 1110-LOAD-PRODUCT-TABLE.
151             MOVE "NO" TO END-FLAG.
152             PERFORM 1120-LOAD-MONTHS-TABLE.
153             MOVE "NO" TO END-FLAG.
154
155         1110-LOAD-PRODUCT-TABLE.
156             PERFORM 1111-READ-PRODUCTS-TABLE-FILE.
157             PERFORM 1112-PRODUCT-ELEMENT-LOAD VARYING SUB
158                        FROM 1 BY 1 UNTIL SUB > 7.
159
160         1111-READ-PRODUCTS-TABLE-FILE.
161             READ PRODUCTS-TABLE-FILE AT END MOVE "YES"
162                    TO END-FLAG.
163
164         1112-PRODUCT-ELEMENT-LOAD.
165             MOVE PRODUCT-NO-T TO PRODUCT-NO-TAB (SUB).
166             MOVE PRODUCT-DESC-T TO PRODUCT-DESC-TAB (SUB).
167             MOVE PRICE-T TO PRICE-TAB (SUB).
168             PERFORM 1111-READ-PRODUCTS-TABLE-FILE.
169
170         1120-LOAD-MONTHS-TABLE.
171             PERFORM 1121-READ-MONTHS-TABLE-FILE.
172             PERFORM 1122-MONTHS-ELEMENT-LOAD VARYING SUB
173                    FROM 1 BY 1 UNTIL SUB > 12.
174
175         1121-READ-MONTHS-TABLE-FILE.
176             READ MONTHS-TABLE-FILE AT END MOVE "YES" TO END-FLAG.
177
178         1122-MONTHS-ELEMENT-LOAD.
179             MOVE MONTH TO MONTH-TAB (SUB).
180             PERFORM 1121-READ-MONTHS-TABLE-FILE.
181
```

**EXHIBIT 8.9   (Cont.)**

```
182        1200-READ-TRANS-FILE.
183            READ TRANSACTION-FILE AT END MOVE "YES" TO END-FLAG.
184
185        1300-PRINT-HEADINGS.
186            WRITE OUT-REC FROM PAGE-HEADING AFTER ADVANCING PAGE.
187            WRITE OUT-REC FROM COLUMN-HEADING1  AFTER ADVANCING 2 LINES.
188            WRITE OUT-REC FROM COLUMN-HEADING2 AFTER ADVANCING 1 LINES.
189            MOVE SPACES TO OUT-REC.
190            WRITE OUT-REC AFTER ADVANCING 1 LINES.
191
192        2000-PROCESS-RECORDS.
193            PERFORM 2100-LOOK-UP-PRODUCT-INFO.
194            IF FOUND-SWITCH = "YES" THEN
195               PERFORM 2200-DETAIL-CALCULATIONS
196               PERFORM 2300-ACCUMULATION
197               PERFORM 2400-DETAIL-LINE
198            ELSE
199               MOVE SPACES TO DETAIL-LINE
200               MOVE PRODUCT-NUMBER TO NUMBER-OUT
201               MOVE "PRODUCT NUMBER INVALID" TO DESC-OUT
202               WRITE OUT-REC FROM DETAIL-LINE AFTER ADVANCING 1 LINES.
203            PERFORM 1200-READ-TRANS-FILE.
204
205        2100-LOOK-UP-PRODUCT-INFO.
206
207            MOVE "NO" TO FOUND-SWITCH.
208            PERFORM 2110-PRODUCT-ELEMENT-COMPARE
209                        VARYING SUB FROM 1 BY 1 UNTIL SUB > 7.
210
211        2110-PRODUCT-ELEMENT-COMPARE.
212            IF PRODUCT-NUMBER = PRODUCT-NO-TAB (SUB) THEN
213               MOVE "YES" TO FOUND-SWITCH
214               MOVE SUB TO SAVE-SUB
215               MOVE 7 TO SUB
216            ELSE
217               NEXT SENTENCE.
218
219        2200-DETAIL-CALCULATIONS.
220            COMPUTE SALES ROUNDED = QUANTITY * PRICE-TAB (SAVE-SUB).
221
222        2300-ACCUMULATION.
223            ADD SALES TO TOTAL-SALES.
224
225        2400-DETAIL-LINE.
226            MOVE PRODUCT-NUMBER TO NUMBER-OUT.
227            MOVE PRODUCT-DESC-TAB (SAVE-SUB) TO DESC-OUT.
228            MOVE PRICE-TAB (SAVE-SUB) TO PRICE-OUT.
229            MOVE QUANTITY TO QUANTITY-OUT.
230            MOVE SALES TO SALES-OUT.
231            WRITE OUT-REC FROM DETAIL-LINE AFTER ADVANCING 1 LINES.
232
233        3000-WRAP-UP.
234            PERFORM 3050-SUMMARY-OUTPUT.
235            PERFORM 3100-CLOSE-FILES.
236
237        3050-SUMMARY-OUTPUT.
238            MOVE TOTAL-SALES TO TOT-SALES-OUT.
239            WRITE OUT-REC FROM TOTAL-LINE AFTER ADVANCING 3 LINES.
240
241        3100-CLOSE-FILES.
242            CLOSE TRANSACTION-FILE
243                  PRODUCTS-TABLE-FILE
244                  MONTHS-TABLE-FILE
245                  OUT-FILE.
```

**EXHIBIT 8.9   (Cont.)**

```
              PRODUCE  WHOLESALE  REPORT        MONTH:    AUGUST

PRODUCT              DESCRIPTION        PRICE    QUANTITY        SALES
NUMBER

   4024             BANANAS             1.46         10        14.60
   4060             GRAPES              0.92          5         4.60
   4000             APPLES              1.25         20        25.00
   4072             BERRIES             0.88         10         8.80
   5000             PRODUCT  NUMBER  INVALID


                                              TOTAL SALES     $53.00
```

**EXHIBIT 8.10   QBasic Program and Output for Application 8.1, Produce Wholesale Report**

```
'*********************************************************************
'*                      PROGRAM-IDENTIFICATION                      *
'*********************************************************************
'*   PROGRAM NAME: CH8APL1                                          *
'*   REMARKS: THIS PROGRAM PRODUCES A WHOLESALE SALES REPORT.  BOTH *
'*   TRANSACTION DATA AND TABLE DATA ARE NEEDED TO PRODUCE THE      *
'*   REPORT.                                                        *
'*   BOTH THE PRODUCT DESCRIPTION AND PRICE IS EXTRACTED FROM       *
'*   A PRODUCTS TABLE.  THE PRICE FROM THE PRODUCTS TABLE IS USED   *
'*   IN CALCULATING THE SALES AMOUNT FOR THE SALES TRANSACTION RECORD. *
'*********************************************************************


'*********************************************************************
'*                           MAIN-LINE                              *
'*********************************************************************


    GOSUB START.UP                    'PERFORM START-UP
    DO UNTIL END.FLAG$ = "YES"
        GOSUB PROCESS.RECORDS         'PERFORM PROCESS.RECORDS
    LOOP
    GOSUB WRAP.UP                     'PERFORM WRAP-UP
    END


    '*********************************************************************
    '*                         START-UP                               *
    '*********************************************************************

START.UP:
    DIM MONTHTAB$(12)
    DIM PRODUCTNOTAB$(7): DIM DESCRIPTIONTAB$(7): DIM PRICETAB(7)


    GOSUB INITIALIZE
    GOSUB OPEN.FILES
    GOSUB LOAD.TABLES
```

**EXHIBIT 8.10    (Cont.)**

```
      GOSUB READ.TRANS.FILE                    '* PERFORM READ-TRANS-FILE
      HEADMONTH$ = MONTHTAB$(DATEMONTH)
      GOSUB PRINT.HEADINGS                      '* PERFORM PRINT-HEADINGS
      RETURN

       '*******************************************************************
       '*                         INITIALIZE                            *
       '*******************************************************************
INITIALIZE:

      WIDTH LPRINT (132)
      END.FLAG$ = "NO"
      ERRORLINE$ = "                  \     \      *_*_* INVALID RECORD *_*_*"
      DETAILLINE$ = "                 \      \       \           \    ###.##     ###     ##,###.##"
      TOT.LINE$ = "                                                        TOTAL SALES  $###,###.##"
      TOT.SALES = 0
      RETURN


       '*******************************************************************
       '*                       OPEN FILES                              *
       '*******************************************************************
OPEN.FILES:
      OPEN "I", #3, "CH8ILL2C.DAT"       '* OPEN MONTHS-TABLE-FILE
      OPEN "I", #2, "CH8ILL2B.DAT"       '* OPEN PRODUCTS-TABLE-FILE
      OPEN "I", #1, "CH8ILL2A.DAT"       '* OPEN TRANSACTION FILE
      RETURN



       '*******************************************************************
       '*                       LOAD TABLES                             *
       '*******************************************************************

LOAD.TABLES:

      GOSUB LOAD.PRODUCT.TABLE           '* PERFORM LOAD-PRODUCT-TABLE
      END.FLAG$ = "NO"
      GOSUB LOAD.MONTHS.TABLE            '* PERFORM LOAD-MONTHS-TABLE
      END.FLAG$ = "NO"
      RETURN
       '*******************************************************************
       '*                     LOAD PRODUCT TABLE                        *
       '*******************************************************************

LOAD.PRODUCT.TABLE:

      GOSUB READ.PRODUCTS.TABLE.FILE           '* READ-PRODUCTS-TABLE-FILE
      FOR SUB1 = 1 TO 7
        GOSUB PRODUCT.ELEMENT.LOAD             '* PERFORM PRODUCT-ELEMENT-LOAD
      NEXT SUB1
      RETURN
```

## EXHIBIT 8.10    (Cont.)

```
'**********************************************************************
'*                    READ-PRODUCT-TABLE-FILE                        *
'**********************************************************************

READ.PRODUCTS.TABLE.FILE:

    INPUT #2, PRODUCTNO$, DESCRIPTION$, PRICE
    RETURN




    '**********************************************************************
    '*                    PRODUCT-ELEMENT-LOAD                          *
    '**********************************************************************

PRODUCT.ELEMENT.LOAD:

    PRODUCTNOTAB$(SUB1) = PRODUCTNO$
    DESCRIPTIONTAB$(SUB1) = DESCRIPTION$
    PRICETAB(SUB1) = PRICE
    GOSUB READ.PRODUCTS.TABLE.FILE              '* READ-PRODUCT-TABLE-FILE
    RETURN

        ' **********************************************************************
        ' *                    LOAD MONTH TABLE                              *
        ' **********************************************************************

LOAD.MONTHS.TABLE:

    GOSUB READ.MONTHS.TABLE.FILE                ' READ-MONTHS-TABLE-FILE
    FOR SUB1 = 1 TO 12
      GOSUB MONTHS.ELEMENT.LOAD                 '* PERFORM MONTHS-ELEMENT-LOAD
    NEXT SUB1
    RETURN

        '**********************************************************************
        '*                    READ-MONTH-TABLE-FILE                         *
        '**********************************************************************

READ.MONTHS.TABLE.FILE:

    INPUT #3, MONTHNAME$
    RETURN

        '**********************************************************************
        '*                    MONTHS-ELEMENT-LOAD                           *
        '**********************************************************************

MONTHS.ELEMENT.LOAD:

    MONTHTAB$(SUB1) = MONTHNAME$
    GOSUB READ.MONTHS.TABLE.FILE                ' READ-MONTH-TABLE-FILE
    RETURN
```

**EXHIBIT 8.10 (Cont.)**

```
'*********************************************************************
'                          READ-TRANS-FILE                          *
'*********************************************************************


READ.TRANS.FILE:

    INPUT #1, PRODUCTNUMBER$, QUANTITY, DATEMONTH, DATEDAY, DATEYEAR, SSN$, CLASS
    IF PRODUCTNUMBER$ = "9999" THEN END.FLAG$ = "YES"
    RETURN


    '*********************************************************************
    '*                       PRINT HEADINGS                             *
    '*********************************************************************


PRINT.HEADINGS:

    LPRINT CHR$(12): LPRINT
    LPRINT TAB(40); "PRODUCE WHOLESALE REPORT"; TAB(72); "MONTH:"; TAB(81); HEADMONTH$
    LPRINT
    LPRINT TAB(20); "PRODUCT"; TAB(40); "DESCRIPTION"; TAB(60); "PRICE"; TAB(70); "QUANTITY";
    LPRINT TAB(83); "SALES"
    LPRINT TAB(20); "NUMBER"
    LPRINT
    RETURN




    '*********************************************************************
    '*                       PROCESS RECORDS                            *
    '*********************************************************************


PROCESS.RECORDS:
    GOSUB LOOK.UP.PRODUCT.INFO
    IF PRODUCTFOUNDSW$ = "YES" THEN
      GOSUB DETAIL.CALCULATIONS
      GOSUB ACCUMULATION
      GOSUB PRINT.DETAIL.LINE
     ELSE LPRINT USING ERRORLINE$; PRODUCTNUMBER$
     END IF
    GOSUB READ.TRANS.FILE                    '* PERFORM READ-TRANS-FILE
    RETURN
    '*********************************************************************
    '*                    LOOK-UP-PRODUCT-INFO                          *
    '*********************************************************************


 LOOK.UP.PRODUCT.INFO:

    PRODUCTFOUNDSW$ = "NO"
    FOR SUB1 = 1 TO 7
        GOSUB PRODUCT.ELEMENT.COMPARE        '* PERFORM PRODUCT-ELEMENT-COMPARE
    NEXT SUB1
    RETURN
```

**EXHIBIT 8.10  (Cont.)**

```
'*******************************************************************
'*                    PRODUCT-ELEMENT-COMPARE                      *
'*******************************************************************


PRODUCT.ELEMENT.COMPARE:

    IF PRODUCTNUMBER$ = PRODUCTNOTAB$(SUB1) THEN
       PRODUCTFOUNDSW$ = "YES"
       SUBSAVE = SUB1
       SUB1 = 7
    END IF
    RETURN




    ' *****************************************************************
    ' *                      DETAIL-CALCULATIONS                     *
    ' *****************************************************************


DETAIL.CALCULATIONS:

    SALES = QUANTITY * PRICETAB(SUBSAVE)
    RETURN
    '*****************************************************************
    '*                      ACCUMULATION                            *
    '*****************************************************************

ACCUMULATION:
    TOT.SALES = TOT.SALES + SALES
    RETURN



    '*****************************************************************
    '*                    PRINT DETAIL LINE                         *
    '*****************************************************************

PRINT.DETAIL.LINE:

  LPRINT USING DETAILLINE$; PRODUCTNUMBER$; DESCRIPTIONTAB$(SUBSAVE); PRICETAB(SUBSAVE); QUANTITY; SALES
  RETURN



    '***************************************************************
    '*                      WRAP-UP                               *
    '***************************************************************

WRAP.UP:
    GOSUB SUMMARY.OUTPUT
    GOSUB CLOSE.FILES
    RETURN



    '***************************************************************
    '*                    SUMMARY-OUTPUT                          *
    '***************************************************************

SUMMARY.OUTPUT:
    LPRINT USING TOT.LINE$; TOT.SALES
    RETURN
```

**EXHIBIT 8.10   (Cont.)**

```
'*******************************************************************
'*                        ACCUMULATION                            *
'*******************************************************************

ACCUMULATION:
     TOT.SALES = TOT.SALES + SALES
     RETURN


     '*******************************************************************
     '*                      PRINT DETAIL LINE                         *
     '*******************************************************************

PRINT.DETAIL.LINE:

     LPRINT USING DETAILLINE$; PRODUCTNUMBER$; DESCRIPTIONTAB$(SUBSAVE); PRICETAB(SUBSAVE); QUANTITY; SALES
     RETURN


     '*******************************************************************
     '*                        WRAP-UP                                 *
     '*******************************************************************

WRAP.UP:
     GOSUB SUMMARY.OUTPUT
     GOSUB CLOSE.FILES
     RETURN


     '*******************************************************************
     '*                      SUMMARY-OUTPUT                            *
     '*******************************************************************

SUMMARY.OUTPUT:
     LPRINT USING TOT.LINE$; TOT.SALES
     RETURN
     '*******************************************************************
     '*                       CLOSE-FILES                              *
     '*******************************************************************
CLOSE.FILES:
     CLOSE
     RETURN
```

```
                    PRODUCE WHOLESALE REPORT      MONTH:    AUGUST

PRODUCT             DESCRIPTION        PRICE     QUANTITY      SALES
NUMBER


  4024             BANANAS            1.46        10         14.60
  4060             GRAPES             0.92         5          4.60
  4000             APPLES             1.25        20         25.00
  4072             BERRIES            0.88        10          8.80
  5000          *** INVALID RECORD ***
                                      TOTAL SALES  $      53.00
```

## Two Table Search Operations and Positional Addressing in Two Tables
(Sales Commission Report)

### PROGRAM REQUIREMENTS

The management of Grocery Produce Company wishes to produce a sales commission report. This report is an extension of the one produced in Application 8.1. The report is to list the salesperson number, the product number, the product description, price, quantity, sales, and the commission. The sales is to be calculated in the same manner as in Application 8.1.

Only records with valid salesperson numbers are to be processed. The salesperson number is validated by searching a table of valid SSNs. If the SSN from the sales transaction record matches a SSN from the table of valid SSNs, then the record is valid and can be processed. The quantity from the transaction sales record is to be multiplied by the appropriate price from the product table. *The appropriate price is determined by performing a table search.*

When a product number from the table matches that from the transaction record, the corresponding price in the table is used. The commission is computed by multiplying the sales amount from the previous computation by the appropriate commission percentage. This percentage rate depends upon the classification of the salesman. *A table of commission rates is used in determining the correct rate for any particular salesperson classification.* Grand totals are to print for sales and commission.

### OUTPUT DESIGN

Exhibit 8.11 depicts the sample report and Exhibit 8.12 illustrates the associated printer spacing chart.

---

**EXHIBIT 8.11   Sample Sales Commission Report**

```
                    SALES COMMISSION REPORT      MONTH:      AUGUST

   SALES-         PRODUCT      DESCRIPTION      PRICE     QUANTITY           SALES        COMMISSION
   PERSON         NUMBER

   333445555        4024        BANANAS          1.46         10             14.60            .44
   333442222        4060        GRAPES            .92          5              4.60            .18
   172348114        4000        APPLES           1.25         20             25.00           1.25
   211684888        4072        BERRIES           .88         10              8.80            .44
   999887777        5000        ***INVALID RECORD***

                                                              TOTALS        $53.00          $2.31
```

---

**EXHIBIT 8.12   Printer Spacing Chart Sales Commission Report**

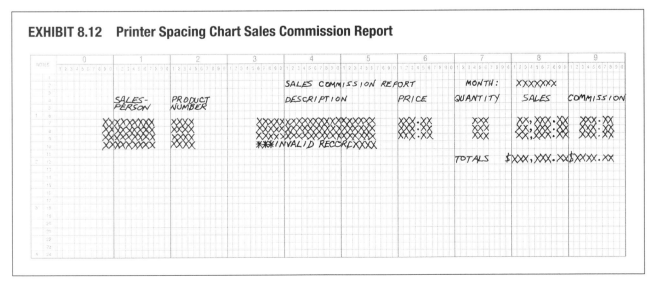

## INPUT DESIGN

Exhibit 8.13 shows the four different record layouts for this problem. Four files are needed. A sales transaction input file is the file to be processed. Three other files are to be used for loading tables. A product table file is used to load a product table just like the one loaded in the previous illustration. The same month table file illustrated in the previous example is once again used. The only new file is the VALID-SALESPERSON-TABLE-FILE.

## TABLES

Exhibit 8.14 shows the three tables needed for this problem. Frame A depicts the table of valid salespersons. Frame B shows the previously illustrated table of products, and Frame C illustrates the commission table to be used through positional addressing.

## TEST DATA

Exhibit 8.15 depicts the test data for the various files.

## PROGRAM DESIGN

The general design of this program is illustrated in the hierarchy chart in Exhibit 8.16. The only modification from the previous illustration is found in the LOAD-TABLES module and the TABLE-LOOK-UPS module.

Exhibit 8.17 illustrates the structured flowchart. The LOAD-TABLES module includes a LOAD-VALID-SALESPERSON-TABLE module. The logic of this module is identical to previously discussed load modules, except that the dountil condition allows for the loading of twenty sales transaction records.

The fourth noteworthy difference in the LOAD-TABLES module is found in the fourth and last block. The actual literal decimal value is stored at a specific element in the table using literal subscripting. Literal subscripting means using the actual literal value as the subscript to point to a particular element of the table. The use of literals as subscripts was previously described in the introductory discussion of referencing a table using a table name and a subscript (Figure 7.7). In this fourth block of the TABLE-LOAD module three values (0.03, 0.04, and 0.05) are stored at consecutive elements in the COM-RATE-TAB. When tables are very small (say, 3 elements) and the data found in the tables remain

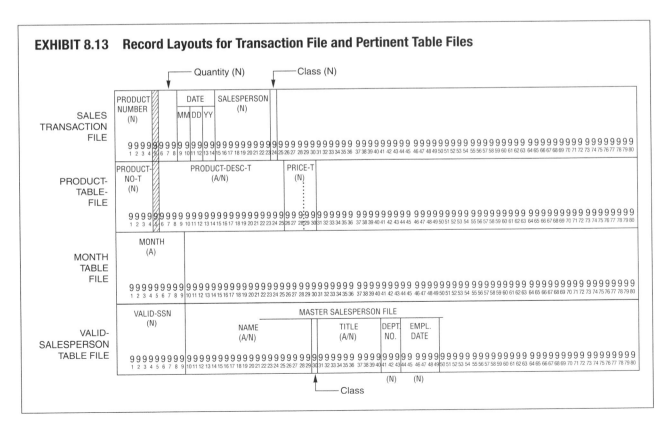

**EXHIBIT 8.13   Record Layouts for Transaction File and Pertinent Table Files**

relatively constant, it is normally much faster to initialize data into the table using literals for values and subscripts rather than load tables as previously explained. However, this technique would be unwieldy with large tables. To fill a table with 50 elements would require 50 separate store operations!

The TABLE-LOOKUPS module, as the name implies, performs two separate table searches. The TABLE-LOOKUP module is further decomposed into a LOOK-UP-VALID-SALESPERSON module and a LOOK-UP-PRODUCT-INFO module. Basically, the program from the previous illustration is being expanded. Before a record is valid and subsequent processing steps can be taken, two successful table searches must be performed. The first table search determines whether the salesperson's SSN is valid. The second table search locates the appropriate product number in order to extract the associated description and price. Both of these search operations must be successful before further processing may occur. This is controlled by the decision block shown in the PROCESS-RECORDS module. A compound condition is found in the block; it requires that the VALID-SSN-SWITCH = "YES" *and* the PRODUCT-NO-FOUND-SWITCH =

"YES." If the comparison result of this compound condition is TRUE, then normal processing occurs; otherwise, the message "INVALID RECORD" is printed.

In the LOOK-UP-VALID-SSN module the same search logic exists as shown in previous table search operations except that the SSN-ELEMENT-COMPARE module does not require that the subscript be saved because the table elements will not be further referenced. The logic here resembles the logic shown in Exhibit 8.17 (COMPARE-SSN-ELEMENT). The logic of the LOOK-UP-PRODUCT-INFO remains unchanged from the previous application.

The DETAIL-CALCULATIONS module shows the calculation of SALES by multiplying QUANTITY by PRICE-TAB (SUB-SAVE). The COMMISSION is calculated by multiplying the SALES by the COM-RATE-TAB (CLASS). The subscript used here is the CLASS field from the sales transaction record. This again demonstrates the use of positional subscripting. If the value of CLASS were 3, COM-RATE-TAB (SUB) would point to the third element in the table, and the contents of the table would be 8.14.

---

**EXHIBIT 8.14    Tables for Application 8.2 Sales Commission Report**

**A.    VALID SALESPERSON TABLE**

| |
|---|
| 172348114 |
| 211684888 |
| 333445555 |
| 222334444 |
| 111223333 |
| 666778888 |
| 999887777 |
| 333442222 |

**COMMISSION TABLE**

| |
|---|
| .03 |
| .04 |
| .05 |

**MONTH TABLE**

| |
|---|
| JANUARY |
| FEBRUARY |
| MARCH |
| APRIL |
| MAY |
| JUNE |
| JULY |
| AUGUST |
| SEPTEMBER |
| OCTOBER |
| NOVEMBER |
| DECEMBER |

**B.    PRODUCTS TABLE**

| PRODUCT-NO-TAB | PRODUCT-DESC-TAB | PRICE-TAB |
|---|---|---|
| 4000 | APPLES | 1.25 |
| 4012 | ORANGES | 1.61 |
| 4024 | BANANAS | 1.46 |
| 4036 | PINEAPPLES | 1.56 |
| 4048 | PEACHES | 1.12 |
| 4060 | GRAPES | .96 |
| 4072 | BERRIES | .88 |

## Pseudocode

Exhibit 8.18 shows the associated pseudocode.

## Programs

Exhibits 8.19 and 8.20 show the COBOL 85 and Quick BASIC, respectively.

## AN ALTERNATE SEARCHING METHOD—METHOD II COMPOUND CONDITION IN THE SEARCH LOOP

Figure 8.1 (on page 411) illustrates a modified version of the table searching technique illustrated in Chapter 7 and in Applications 8.1 and 8.2 in this chapter. This modified version of Method I allows the future use of SUB as the pointer to the located element rather than SAVE-SUB. To refresh your memory, if needed, refer back to Exhibit 8.7 and review how the LOOK-UP-PRODUCT-INFO module is set up. Pay special attention to the conditional in the count-controlled loop (Perform . . . Varying loop) of this first application. Notice that there is only a *simple condition*. Using this first method (Method I), if the value is located, the program

module, ELEMENT-COMPARE, will force SUB to become greater than 7 by assigning a value equal to the maximum number of elements in the table to the subscript called SUB. Only a simple condition is needed to terminate the loop in the case of locating the matching value or where the value is not located.

## AN ALTERNATIVE SEARCHING METHOD—METHOD II

We will now examine an alternate method (Method II) that uses a compound conditional. The first simple condition in the compound expression tests to determine whether SUB is greater than 7 (the physical table size in elements). The purpose of this first test is to determine **if the value is not located**. The second simple condition in the compound expression tests to determine **if the value is located** (by the content of the FOUND-SW being equal to "YES"). The ELEMENT-COMPARE module now only contains two activities if the value is located in the table. As before, FOUND-SW is set equal to "YES." Next, observe that the contents of SUB is being decreased by one. This is done, because SUB will be increased by one when control goes back to

---

### EXHIBIT 8.15   Test Data for Application 8.2

**Sales Transaction File**
```
         1         2         3         4
1234567890123456789012345678901234567890
4024 01008129333334455551
4060 00508139333334422222
4000 02008149317234811 43
4072 01008149321168488 83
5000 00008159399998877772
```

**Products Table**
```
1234567890123456789012345678901234567890
----------------------------------------
4000 APPLES            00125
4012 ORANGES           00161
4024 BANANAS           00146
4036 PINEAPPLES        00156
4048 PEACHES           00112
4060 GRAPES            00092
4072 BERRIES           00088
----------------------------
```

**Months Table**
```
         1         2         3         4
1234567890123456789012345678901234567890
----------------------------------------
JANUARY
FEBRUARY
MARCH
APRIL
MAY
JUNE
JULY
AUGUST
SEPTEMBER
OCTOBER
NOVEMBER
DECEMBER
```

**Valid Salesperson Table Data (Master Salesperson File)**
```
1234567890123456789012345678901234567890123456789012345678901234567890
----------------------------------------------------------------------
172348114ALEX ALEXANDER      1SALES REP1001092978
211684888MARIA SHRIVER       2SALES REP3002081477
333445555DAN COLLINS         3SALES REP3001122377
222334444TONY PENNINGTON     2SALES REP2001052676
111223333CHAIWAT KHEMTHONG    3SALES REP3001031283
666778888CHINTANA KHEMTHONG   3SALES REP3001031283
999887777CHARLES LAMBETH     2SALES REP2001031186
333442222FRANCIS WALKER      1SALES REP1002042376
```

the calling module, ELEMENT-COMPARE. The next "built in" command increases SUB by 1. If SUB were to be used as the pointer to the table, it would point to an element one beyond where the actual value was found. This would result in the wrong data being used by the program, or result in an out-of-range subscript (where the last table element is the matching value). In the latter case where the match occurs on the last element and SUB is increased by 1, this makes SUB contain a value that is one unit greater than the number of elements in the table. If SUB is used as the subscript, this attempts to point one beyond the end of the table. The result will be an "addressing" interrupt or an "out-of-range" subscript.

An advantage of Method II is that it eliminates the use of a SAVE-SUB variable. A disadvantage of the method is that it is somewhat esoteric. Having to modify variable contents this way to offset the effect of a command can be confusing to maintenance programmers who have to be able to read and modify the program. Then there are those who believe that an index or subscript used in a count-controlled loop should never be altered within the code itself. I agree that such "tricks" should be used very sparingly.

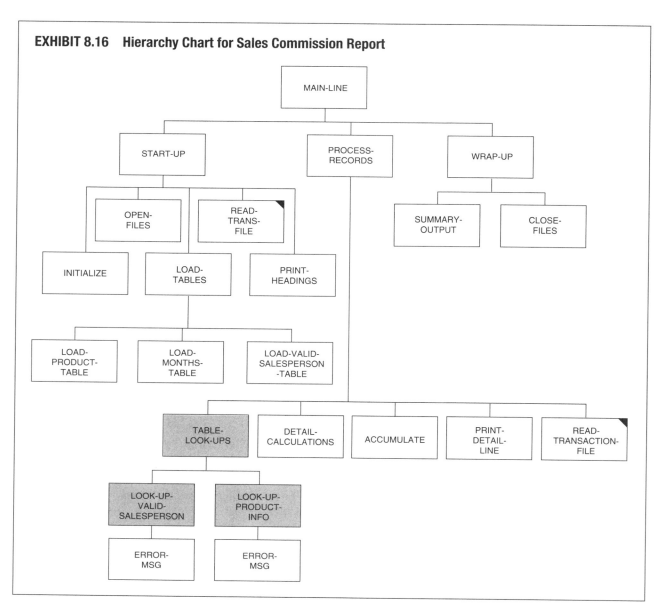

**EXHIBIT 8.16    Hierarchy Chart for Sales Commission Report**

## A Table Where The Number Of Loaded Values May Vary—Its Effect on *Both* Loading and Searching

We rarely know how many values are to be loaded!

Realistically, the programmer cannot assume that the same number of records will be loaded to the table each time the program runs, for most table information will be variable in nature. These tables are called **variable sized tables**. For example, we do not know how many products will be loaded to a table for any given computer run, because the company may add or delete product line-items from one computer run to the next. Another example is the loading of a customer master table from a customer information file. Customers are created or added and deleted in an ongoing fashion. At the moment the computer application is to run, there is no way for the programmer to know how many customers will be in the customer information file;

thus, there is no way to predict how many customer items will be added to the customer master table. Applications 8.1 and 8.2 assume a fixed number of records (regardless of the lack of realism) so that the logic facets of table handling can be introduced gradually, keeping them as simple and straightforward as possible.

### Table Load Modifications

We will now add the necessary logic to handle tables with a variable number of values depending upon the computer run. The LOAD-TABLE module in Figure 8.2 (Frame A), on page 412, looks almost like the ones from Application 8.1 and 8.2 except it includes a compound condition test that determines whether the subscript called SUB is greater than 7 (the maximum size of the table) or END-FLAG = "YES". If SUB becomes greater than 7, the program should not attempt loading more values

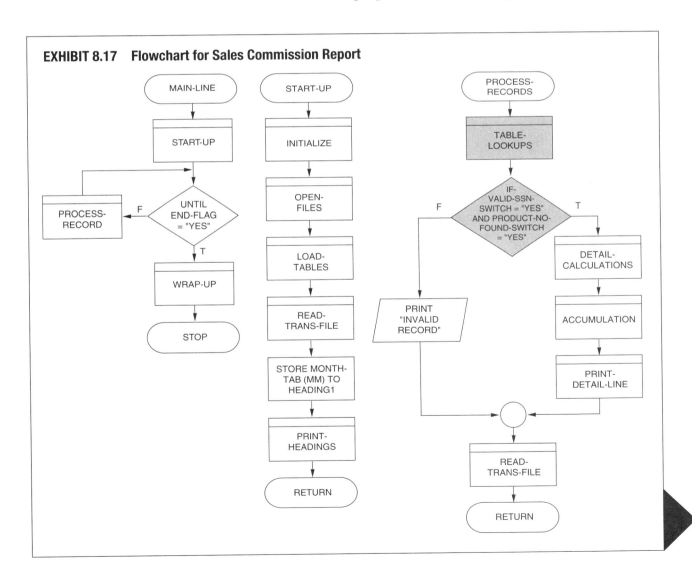

**EXHIBIT 8.17    Flowchart for Sales Commission Report**

**EXHIBIT 8.17    (Cont.)**

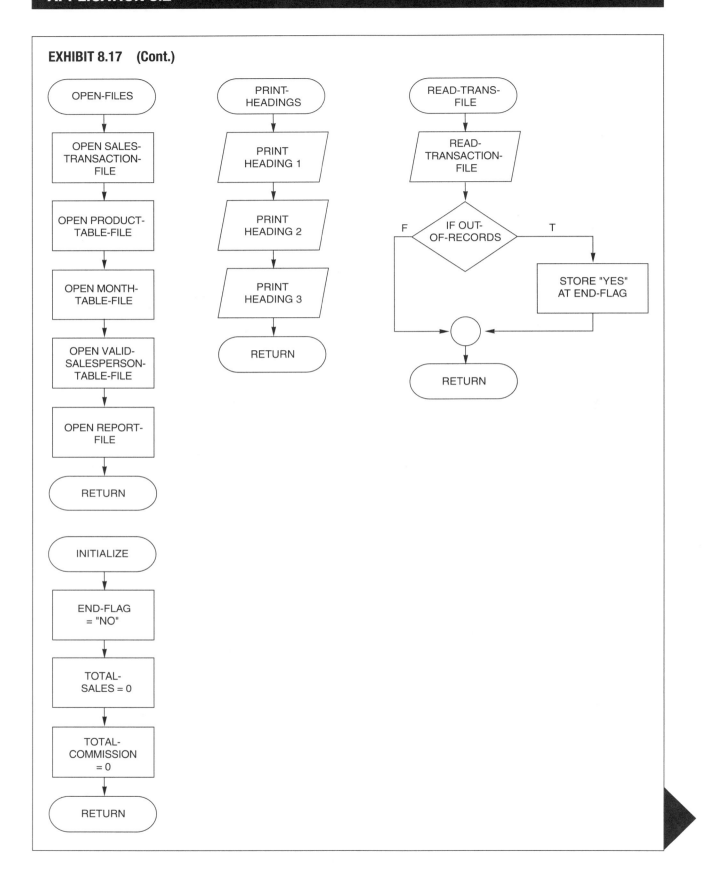

**EXHIBIT 8.17** **(Cont.)**

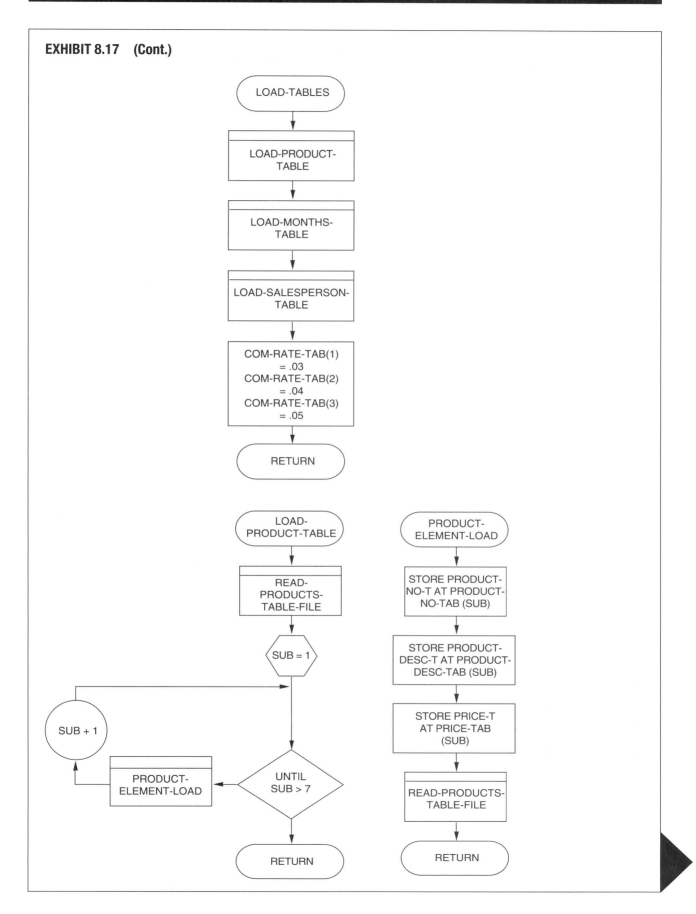

because no more room exists in the table. Or, if END-FLAG = "YES," there are no more record values to load to the table. The next change in the logic is reflected in the statement after the compound condition—the assignment of one less than the content of SUB into the variable called MAX-ELEMENTS. This assignment statement captures the number of actual values loaded to the table. Why SUB - 1? Why not SUB? Remember that when using PERFORM . . . VARYING (COBOL) or the FOR . . . NEXT (BASIC) the count-controlled looping struc-

ture will add a unit to SUB after the last value is stored in the table. So, after the condition tests TRUE, the program must decrease SUB by 1 to bring it back to the number of values loaded. MAX-ELEMENTS now contains the actual number of values loaded.

Notice that if there are fewer than seven records to load to the table the END-FLAG control variable will be assigned the value of YES when the table file is exhausted. No additional attempts are made to load values to the table once all records have

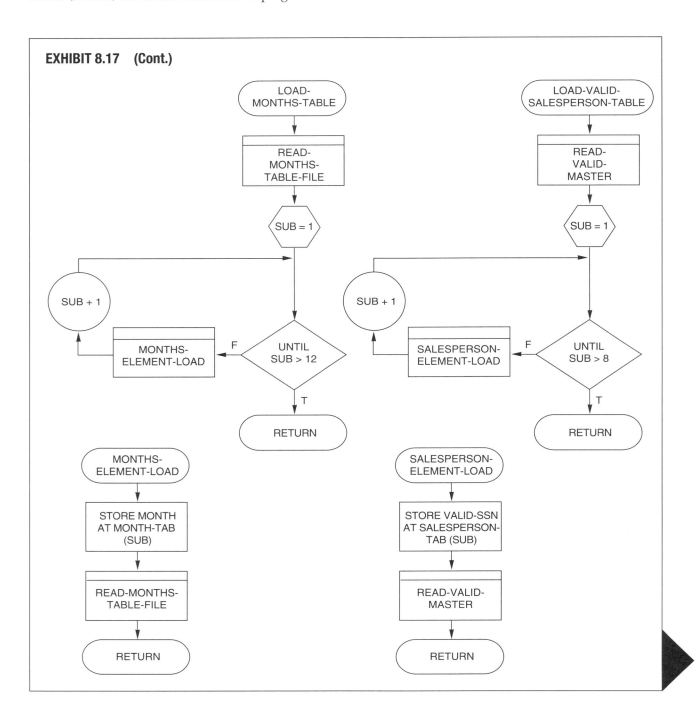

EXHIBIT 8.17    (Cont.)

been read. One may ask why we preserved the number of records loaded. The answer: we need to know this in our table searching process so that we look through exactly the right number of values that were loaded. The computer program should not look beyond the last table value loaded, nor should the program prematurely quit searching possible matching values.

## Table Searching Modifications

We will now examine the TABLE-LOOKUP-PARTS-INFO module in Figure 8.2 (p. 412). Notice that the conditional in the count-controlled loop may become TRUE by either SUB becoming greater than MAX-ELEMENTS or the FOUND-SWITCH becoming equal to YES. the essence of the condition means that the program continues to look for a

**EXHIBIT 8.17 (Cont.)**

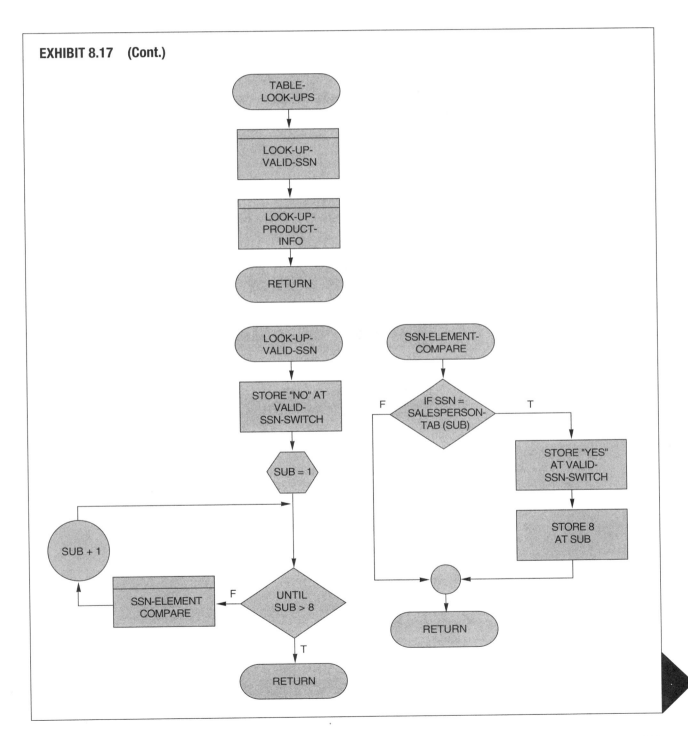

value until all elements of the table that contain actual values (some elements may be empty) are searched (SUB > MAX-ELEMENTS), or until the end of the physical limit of the table is reached (FOUND-SW = "YES"). Observe that SUB is compared with a variable, MAX-ELEMENTS, rather than with a constant as in previous applications. Notice that the ELEMENT-COMPARE module uses Searching Method II as was illustrated in Figure 8.1. (This was an arbitrary choice to demonstrate one of these methods in actual use.) An advantage of this method is to allow the continued use of SUB as the pointer to the matching value. (Note: Do you recall why SUB is decremented by one unit in the ELEMENT-COMPARE module? This is a second opportunity to exercise your understanding of the searching Method II. If necessary, go and look at Figure 8.1 again.)

## SEARCHING METHOD III—EMBEDDING THE ELEMENT COMPARISON INSIDE THE DECISION BLOCK OF THE COUNT-CONTROLLED LOOP

### A Cobol 85 In-line Perform Method: a Short-Cut Method for Cobol 85

Since the PERFORM . . . VARYING (or the Perform . . . Until—for that matter) allows the condition to be either a simple or compound condition involving any valid conditional expression or condition name, an alternate method for the search is to place the element comparison test inside the same decision block of the count-controlled loop. Frame A of Figure 8.3 shows how this loop is modified. The FOUND-SWITCH is set to "NO" as previously illustrated. Notice that the count-controlled loop does *not* contain a "call" to a module that takes care of the comparison process. Also notice that the conditional compound OR causes looping to continue until either SUB > 7 or PARTS-NO = PARTS-NO-TAB (SUB). This technique allows the lookup process to be embedded in the decision box of the count-controlled loop. There is no longer an

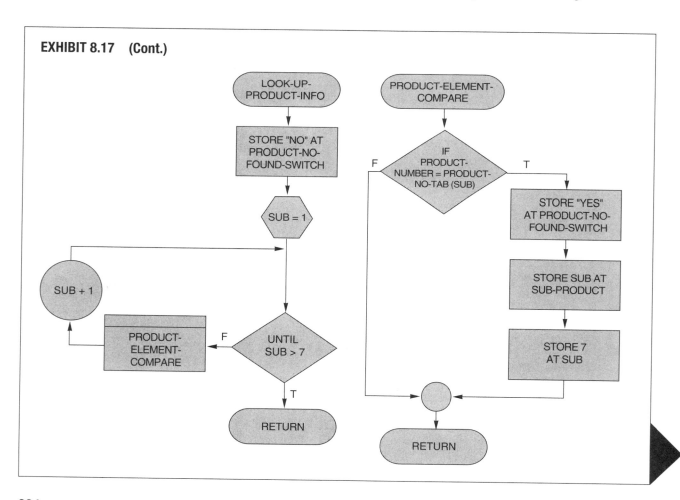

**EXHIBIT 8.17   (Cont.)**

**EXHIBIT 8.17    (Cont.)**

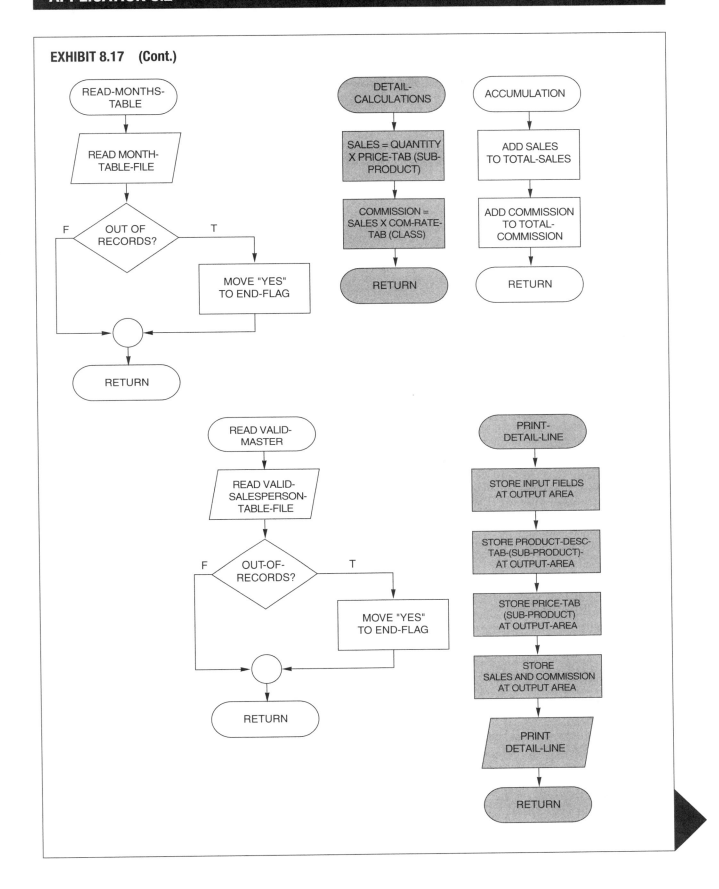

ELEMENT-COMPARE module. *An advantage of this method is that SUB contains the correct value upon leaving the loop.* This allows the programmer to use SUB as the subscript pointer (thus eliminating the need for a SAVE-SUB variable, as used in Method 1 or an arithmetic command to decrease it by one as in Method II). Frame B of Figure 8.3 illustrates the

COBOL 85 code for the "in-line" PERFORM . . . VARYING to accomplish the flowchart logic in Frame A. Observe that the entire table lookup process is contained in the PERFORM . . . VARYING command. The element comparison activity is a part of the conditional expression.

**EXHIBIT 8.17 (Cont.)**

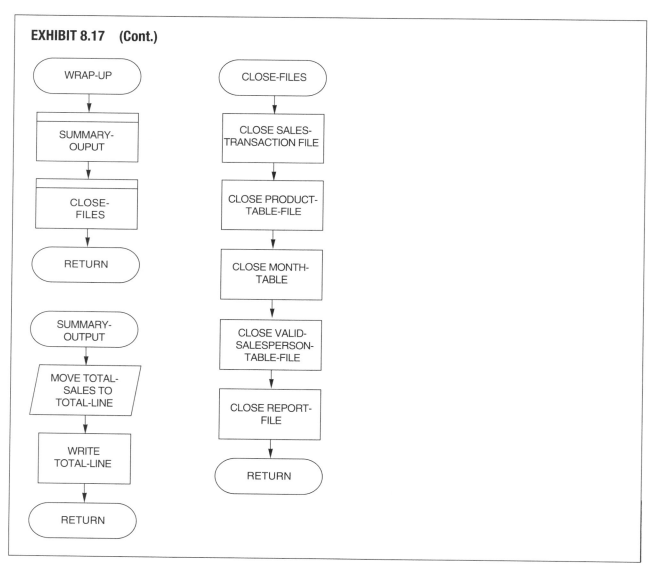

**EXHIBIT 8.18   Pseudocode for Application 8.2 (Sales Commission Report)**

\*main-line
    start-up
    dountil end-flag = "yes"
        process-record
    enddo
    wrap-up
    stop
\*start-up
    initialize
    open-files
    load-tables
    read-trans-file
    store month-tab (mm) at heading1
    print-headings
    return
\*initialize
    store "no" at end-flag
    store 0 at total-sales
    store 0 at total-commissions
    return
\*open-files
    open input transaction-file
    open input products-table-file
    open input months-table-file
    open input valid-master-file
    open output report-file
    return
\*process-records
    table-lookups
    if valid-ssn-switch = "yes" and
        product-no-found-switch = "yes"
        detail-calculations
        accumulation
        print-detail-line
    else
        print "invalid-record"
    endif
        read-trans-file
    return
\*print-headings
    print heading1
    print heading2
    print heading3
    return
\*read-trans-file module
    read transaction-file
    when out of records store "no" at end-flag
    endread
    return

\*load-tables
    load-product-table
    store "no" at end-flag
    load-months-table
    store "no" at end-flag
    load-valid-salesperson-table
    store "no" at end-flag
    store .03 at com-rate-tab (1)
    store .04 at com-rate-tab (2)
    store .05 at com-rate-tab (3)
    return
\*load-product-table
    read-product-table-file
    initialize sub to 1
    dountil sub > 7
        product-element-load
        increase sub by 1
    enddo
    return
\*read-products-table-file
    read products-table-file
    when no-more-records move "yes" to end-flag
    endread
    return
\*product-element-load
    store product-no-t at product-no-tab (sub)
    store product-desc-t at product-desc-tab (sub)
    store price-t at price-tab (sub)
    read-products-table-file
    return
\*load-months-table
    read-months-table-file
    initialize sub to 1
    dountil sub > 12
        months-element-load
        increase sub by 1
    enddo
    return
\*read-months-table-file
    read months-table-file
    when no-more-records move "yes" to end-flag
    endread
    return
\*months-element-load
    store month at month-tab (sub)
    read-months-table-file
    return

**EXHIBIT 8.18   (Cont.)**

*load-valid-salesperson-table
   read-valid-master
   initialize sub to 1
   dountil sub > 8
      salesperson-element-load
      increase sub by 1
   endo
   return
*read-valid-master
   read transaction-file
   when no-more-data move "yes" to end-flag
   endread
   return
*salesperson-element-load
   store ssn at salesperson-tab (sub)
   read-valid-master
   return
*table-look ups
   look-up-valid-ssn
   look-up-product-info
   return
*look-up-valid-ssn
   store "no" at valid-ssn-switch
   initialize sub to 1
   dountil sub > 8
      ssn-element-compare
      increase sub by 1
   enddo
   return
*ssn-element-compare
   if ssn = salesperson-tab (sub)
      store "yes" at valid-ssn-switch
      store 8 at sub
   endif
   return
*look-up-product-info
   store "no" at product-no-found-switch
   initialize sub to 1
   dountil sub > 7
      product-element-compare
      increase sub by 1
   enddo
   return

*product-element-compare
   if product-number = product-no-tab (sub)
      store "yes" at product-no-found-switch
      store sub at sub-product
      store 7 at sub
   endif
   return
*detail-calculations
   calculate sales = quantity times price-tab (sub-product)
   calculate commission = sales times com-rate-tab (class)
   return
*accumulation
   add sales to total-sales
   add commission to total-commission
   return
*print-detail-line
   store input fields at output area
   store product-desc-tab (sub-product) at output area
   store price-tab (sub-product) at output area
   store sales and commission at output area
   print the detail-line
   return
*wrap-up
   summary-output
   close-files
   return
*summary-output
   move total-sales, total-commission to total-line
   print total-line
   return
*close-files
   close transaction-file
   close products-table-file
   close months-table-file
   close valid-master-file
   close report-file
   return

**EXHIBIT 8.19   COBOL 85 Program and Report for Application 8.2 (Sales Commission Report)**

```
1          IDENTIFICATION DIVISION.
2          PROGRAM-ID. CHAPTER8-APL2.
3          AUTHOR. JACK RUSSELL.
4          DATE-WRITTEN.  APRIL 18, 1992.
5          DATE-COMPILED. 1993-06-28.
6          ****REMARKS****
7          ****THIS PROGRAM PRODUCES A SALES COMMISSION REPORT.  FOR
8          ****PRINTING AND CALCULATION PURPOSES, DATA IS EXTRACTED FROM
9          ****A PRODUCTS TABLE, ALPHABETIC DATE TABLE, AND A COMMISSION
10         ****TABLE.   A TABLE LOOKUP IS ALSO MADE TO VALIDATE THE SALES-
11         ****PERSON PRIOR TO ANY PROCESSING.  AN ERROR MESSAGE IS PRODUCED
12         ****IF EITHER THE SALESPERSON NUMBER OR PRODUCT NUMBER IS INVALID
13         ****(OR NOT FOUND IN THE RESPECTIVE TABLES).  THE SALES IS THE
14         ****PRODUCT OF QUANTITY (FROM THE TRANSACTION RECORD) * PRICE (FROM
15         ****THE PRODUCTS TABLE.  THE COMMISSION IS THE PRODUCT OF SALES
16         ****TIMES THE APPROPRIATE COMMISSION RATE FROM THE COMMISSION RATE
17         ****TABLE.   THIS RATE WHICH IS EXTRACTED IS BASED ON THE COMMISSION
18         ****CODE FOUND IN THE TRANSACTION RECORD.  THE COMMISSION CODE
19         ****VALUE AGREES WITH THE RELATIVE POSITION IN THE COMMISSION TABLE.
20
21         ENVIRONMENT DIVISION.
22         CONFIGURATION SECTION.
23         SOURCE-COMPUTER.  CYBER.
24         OBJECT-COMPUTER.  CYBER.
25         INPUT-OUTPUT SECTION.
26         FILE-CONTROL.
27             SELECT SALES-TRANSACTION-FILE ASSIGN TO DTA82.
28             SELECT PRODUCTS-TABLE-FILE ASSIGN TO DTA82PRO.
29             SELECT MONTHS-TABLE-FILE ASSIGN TO DTA82MOS.
30             SELECT VALID-SALESPERSON-TABLE-FILE ASSIGN TO DTA82SSN.
31             SELECT OUT-FILE ASSIGN TO OUTFILE.
32
33         DATA DIVISION.
34         FILE SECTION.
35         FD   SALES-TRANSACTION-FILE.
36         01   TRANS-REC.
37             05   PRODUCT-NUMBER PIC 9(04).
38             05   FILLER         PIC X.
39             05   QUANTITY       PIC 9(03).
40             05   DATE-IN.
41                 10   MM         PIC 99.
42                 10   DD         PIC 99.
43                 10   YY         PIC 99.
44             05   SALESPERSON    PIC 9(09).
45             05   CLASS1         PIC 9.
46             05   FILLER         PIC X(56).
47
48         FD   PRODUCTS-TABLE-FILE.
49         01   PRODUCTS-REC.
50             05   PRODUCT-NO-T   PIC 9(04).
51             05   FILLER         PIC X.
52             05   PRODUCT-DESC-T PIC X(20).
53             05   PRICE-T        PIC 9(03)V99.
54             05   FILLER         PIC X(50).
55
56         FD   MONTHS-TABLE-FILE  LABEL RECORDS OMITTED.
57         01   MONTHS-REC.
58             05   MONTH          PIC X(09).
59             05   FILLER         PIC X(71).
60
61         FD   VALID-SALESPERSON-TABLE-FILE.
62         01   SALES-REC.
63             05   VALID-SSN      PIC 9(09).
64             05   NAME           PIC X(20).
65             05   CLASS-V        PIC X.
66             05   TITLE          PIC X(10).
```

EXHIBIT 8.19 (Cont.)

```
67              05  DIST-NO        PIC X(03).
68              05  EMPL-DATE      PIC X(06).
69              05  FILLER         PIC X(31).
70
71      FD  OUT-FILE.
72      01  OUT-REC            PIC X(133).
73
74      WORKING-STORAGE SECTION.
75
76      01  END-FLAG           PIC X(03)          VALUE "NO".
77      01  VALID-SSN-SWITCH   PIC X(03)          VALUE "NO".
78      01  PRODUCT-NO-FOUND-SWITCH PIC X(03)     VALUE "NO".
79      01  PRODUCTS-TAB.
80          05  PRODUCTS-TABLE OCCURS 7 TIMES.
81              10  PRODUCT-NO-TAB    PIC 9(04).
82              10  PRODUCT-DESC-TAB  PIC X(20).
83              10  PRICE-TAB         PIC 9(03)V99.
84
85      01  MONTH-TABLE.
86          05  MONTH-TAB    OCCURS 12 TIMES PIC X(09).
87
88      01  VALID-SALESPERSON-TABLE.
89          05  SALESPERSON-TAB OCCURS 20 TIMES PIC 9(09).
90
91      01  COMMISSION-TABLE.
92          05  COM-RATE-TAB OCCURS 3 TIMES PIC V99.
93
94      01  PAGE-HEADING.
95          05                     PIC X(40)    VALUE SPACES.
96          05                     PIC X(23)    VALUE
97                                 "SALES COMMISSION REPORT".
98          05                     PIC X(09)    VALUE SPACES.
99          05                     PIC X(09)    VALUE "MONTH:   ".
100         05  MONTH-OUT          PIC X(09).
101         05                     PIC X(42)    VALUE SPACES.
102
103     01  COLUMN-HEADING1.
104         05                     PIC X(10)    VALUE SPACES.
105         05                     PIC X(06)    VALUE "SALES-".
106         05                     PIC X(04)    VALUE SPACES.
107         05                     PIC X(07)    VALUE "PRODUCT".
108         05                     PIC X(13)    VALUE SPACES.
109         05                     PIC X(11)    VALUE "DESCRIPTION".
110         05                     PIC X(09)    VALUE SPACES.
111         05                     PIC X(05)    VALUE "PRICE".
112         05                     PIC X(05)    VALUE SPACES.
113         05                     PIC X(08)    VALUE "QUANTITY".
114         05                     PIC X(05)    VALUE SPACES.
115         05                     PIC X(05)    VALUE "SALES".
116         05                     PIC X(03)    VALUE SPACES.
117         05                     PIC X(10)    VALUE "COMMISSION".
118         05                     PIC X(31)    VALUE SPACES.
119
120     01  COLUMN-HEADING2.
121         05                     PIC X(10)    VALUE SPACES.
122         05                     PIC X(06)    VALUE "PERSON".
123         05                     PIC X(04)    VALUE SPACES.
124         05                     PIC X(06)    VALUE "NUMBER".
125         05                     PIC X(106)   VALUE SPACES.
126
127     01  DETAIL-LINE.
128         05                     PIC X(08)    VALUE SPACES.
129         05  SALESPERSON-OUT    PIC X(09).
130         05                     PIC X(03)    VALUE SPACES.
131         05  NUMBER-OUT         PIC ZZZZ9.
132         05                     PIC X(10)    VALUE SPACES.
```

**EXHIBIT 8.19   (Cont.)**

```
133              05    DESC-OUT             PIC X(23).
134              05                         PIC X(01)      VALUE SPACES.
135              05    PRICE-OUT            PIC ZZ9.99.
136              05                         PIC X(07)      VALUE SPACES.
137              05    QUANTITY-OUT         PIC ZZ9.
138              05                         PIC X(06)      VALUE SPACES.
139              05    SALES-OUT            PIC ZZ,ZZ9.99.
140              05                         PIC XX         VALUE SPACES.
141              05    COMM-OUT             PIC $$9.99.
142              05                         PIC X(33)      VALUE SPACES.
143
144         01   TOTAL-LINE.
145              05                         PIC X(70)      VALUE SPACES.
146              05                         PIC X(11)      VALUE "TOTAL SALES".
147              05    TOT-SALES-OUT        PIC $$$,$$9.99.
148              05                         PIC X          VALUE SPACES.
149              05    TOT-COMM-OUT         PIC $,$$9.99.
150              05                         PIC X(34)      VALUE SPACES.
151
152         01   FOUND-SWITCH              PIC X(03)      VALUE "NO".
153         01   SUB                       PIC 99         VALUE 0.
154         01   SUB-PRODUCT               PIC 99         VALUE 0.
155         01   TOTAL-SALES               PIC 9(07)V99   VALUE 0.
156         01   TOTAL-COMMISSION          PIC 9(07)V99   VALUE 0.
157         01   SALES                     PIC 9(07)V99   VALUE 0.
158         01   COMMISSION                PIC 9(07)V99   VALUE 0.
159
160
161    /
162         PROCEDURE DIVISION.
163
164         0000-MAIN-LINE.
165             PERFORM 1000-START-UP.
166             PERFORM 2000-PROCESS-RECORDS UNTIL END-FLAG = "YES".
167             PERFORM 3000-WRAP-UP.
168             STOP RUN.
169
170         1000-START-UP.
171     *       INITIALIZE-VARIABLES (WS)
172             PERFORM 1050-OPEN-FILES.
173             PERFORM 1100-LOAD-TABLES.
174             PERFORM 1200-READ-TRANS-FILE.
175             MOVE MONTH-TAB (MM) TO MONTH-OUT.
176             PERFORM 1300-PRINT-HEADINGS.
177
178         1050-OPEN-FILES.
179             OPEN INPUT  SALES-TRANSACTION-FILE
180                         PRODUCTS-TABLE-FILE
181                         MONTHS-TABLE-FILE
182                         VALID-SALESPERSON-TABLE-FILE.
183             OPEN OUTPUT OUT-FILE.
184
185
186         1100-LOAD-TABLES.
187             PERFORM 1110-LOAD-PRODUCT-TABLE.
188             MOVE "NO" TO END-FLAG.
189             PERFORM 1120-LOAD-MONTHS-TABLE.
190             MOVE "NO" TO END-FLAG.
191             PERFORM 1130-LOAD-VALID-SSN-TABLE.
192             MOVE "NO" TO END-FLAG.
193             MOVE 0.03 TO COM-RATE-TAB (1).
194             MOVE 0.04 TO COM-RATE-TAB (2).
195             MOVE 0.05 TO COM-RATE-TAB (3).
196
197
198    **********IN-LINE PERFORM VARYING USED BELOW ***
```

**EXHIBIT 8.19 (Cont.)**

```
199
200    ******************************************************************
201          1110-LOAD-PRODUCT-TABLE.
202             PERFORM 1111-READ-PRODUCTS-TABLE-FILE.
203             PERFORM        VARYING SUB
204                        FROM 1 BY 1 UNTIL SUB > 7
205
206                MOVE PRODUCT-NO-T TO PRODUCT-NO-TAB (SUB)
207                MOVE PRODUCT-DESC-T TO PRODUCT-DESC-TAB (SUB)
208                MOVE PRICE-T TO PRICE-TAB (SUB)
209                PERFORM 1111-READ-PRODUCTS-TABLE-FILE
210
211             END-PERFORM.
212    ******************************************************************
213
214          1111-READ-PRODUCTS-TABLE-FILE.
215             READ PRODUCTS-TABLE-FILE AT END MOVE "YES"
216                TO END-FLAG.
217
218    **********IN-LINE PERFORM VARYING FOR LOADING MONTHS TABLE******
219
220    ******************************************************************
221          1120-LOAD-MONTHS-TABLE.
222             PERFORM 1121-READ-MONTHS-TABLE-FILE.
223             PERFORM        VARYING SUB
224                        FROM 1 BY 1 UNTIL SUB > 12
225
226                MOVE MONTH TO MONTH-TAB (SUB)
227                PERFORM 1121-READ-MONTHS-TABLE-FILE
228
229             END-PERFORM.
230    ******************************************************************
231
232
233
234
235          1121-READ-MONTHS-TABLE-FILE.
236             READ MONTHS-TABLE-FILE AT END MOVE "YES" TO END-FLAG.
237
238          1130-LOAD-VALID-SSN-TABLE.
239             PERFORM 1131-READ-VALID-MASTER.
240             PERFORM 1132-SALESPERSON-ELEMENT-LOAD VARYING SUB
241                FROM 1 BY 1 UNTIL SUB > 8.
242
243          1131-READ-VALID-MASTER.
244             READ VALID-SALESPERSON-TABLE-FILE AT END MOVE "YES" TO
245                END-FLAG.
246
247          1132-SALESPERSON-ELEMENT-LOAD.
248             MOVE VALID-SSN TO SALESPERSON-TAB (SUB).
249             PERFORM 1131-READ-VALID-MASTER.
250
251          1200-READ-TRANS-FILE.
252             READ SALES-TRANSACTION-FILE AT END MOVE "YES" TO
253             END-FLAG.
254
255          1300-PRINT-HEADINGS.
256             WRITE OUT-REC FROM PAGE-HEADING AFTER ADVANCING PAGE.
257             WRITE OUT-REC FROM COLUMN-HEADING1  AFTER ADVANCING 2 LINES.
258             WRITE OUT-REC FROM COLUMN-HEADING2 AFTER ADVANCING 1 LINES.
259             MOVE SPACES TO OUT-REC.
260             WRITE OUT-REC AFTER ADVANCING 1 LINES.
261
262          2000-PROCESS-RECORDS.
263             PERFORM 2100-TABLE-LOOK-UPS.
264             IF VALID-SSN-SWITCH = "YES" AND
```

**EXHIBIT 8.19 (Cont.)**

```
265                     PRODUCT-NO-FOUND-SWITCH = "YES" THEN
266                     PERFORM 2200-DETAIL-CALCULATIONS
267                     PERFORM 2300-ACCUMULATION
268                     PERFORM 2400-DETAIL-LINE
269                ELSE
270                  MOVE SPACES TO DETAIL-LINE
271                  MOVE SALESPERSON TO SALESPERSON-OUT
272                  MOVE PRODUCT-NUMBER TO NUMBER-OUT
273                  MOVE "*** INVALID RECORD ***" TO DESC-OUT
274                  WRITE OUT-REC FROM DETAIL-LINE AFTER ADVANCING 1 LINES.
275              PERFORM 1200-READ-TRANS-FILE.
276
277          2100-TABLE-LOOK-UPS.
278              PERFORM 2110-LOOK-UP-VALID-SSN.
279              PERFORM 2120-LOOK-UP-PRODUCT-INFO.
280
281          2110-LOOK-UP-VALID-SSN.
282              MOVE "NO" TO VALID-SSN-SWITCH.
283              PERFORM 2111-SSN-ELEMENT-COMPARE
284                      VARYING SUB FROM 1 BY 1 UNTIL SUB > 8.
285
286          2111-SSN-ELEMENT-COMPARE.
287              IF SALESPERSON = SALESPERSON-TAB (SUB) THEN
288                MOVE "YES" TO VALID-SSN-SWITCH
289                MOVE 8 TO SUB
290              ELSE
291                NEXT SENTENCE.
292
293          2120-LOOK-UP-PRODUCT-INFO.
294              MOVE "NO" TO PRODUCT-NO-FOUND-SWITCH.
295              PERFORM 2121-PRODUCT-ELEMENT-COMPARE
296                      VARYING SUB FROM 1 BY 1 UNTIL SUB > 7.
297
298          2121-PRODUCT-ELEMENT-COMPARE.
299              IF PRODUCT-NUMBER = PRODUCT-NO-TAB (SUB) THEN
300                MOVE "YES" TO PRODUCT-NO-FOUND-SWITCH
301                MOVE SUB TO SUB-PRODUCT
302                MOVE 7 TO SUB
303              ELSE
304                NEXT SENTENCE.
305
306          2200-DETAIL-CALCULATIONS.
307              COMPUTE SALES ROUNDED = QUANTITY * PRICE-TAB (SUB-PRODUCT).
308              COMPUTE COMMISSION ROUNDED = SALES * COM-RATE-TAB (CLASS1).
309
310          2300-ACCUMULATION.
311              ADD SALES TO TOTAL-SALES.
312              ADD COMMISSION TO TOTAL-COMMISSION.
313
314          2400-DETAIL-LINE.
315              MOVE SALESPERSON TO SALESPERSON-OUT.
316              MOVE PRODUCT-NUMBER TO NUMBER-OUT.
317              MOVE PRODUCT-DESC-TAB (SUB-PRODUCT) TO DESC-OUT.
318              MOVE PRICE-TAB (SUB-PRODUCT) TO PRICE-OUT.
319              MOVE QUANTITY TO QUANTITY-OUT.
320              MOVE SALES TO SALES-OUT.
321              MOVE COMMISSION TO COMM-OUT.
322              WRITE OUT-REC FROM DETAIL-LINE AFTER ADVANCING 1 LINES.
323
324          3000-WRAP-UP.
325              PERFORM 3050-SUMMARY-OUTPUT.
326              PERFORM 3100-CLOSE-FILES.
327
328          3050-SUMMARY-OUTPUT.
329              MOVE TOTAL-SALES TO TOT-SALES-OUT.
330              MOVE TOTAL-COMMISSION TO TOT-COMM-OUT.
```

**EXHIBIT 8.19    (Cont.)**

```
331               WRITE OUT-REC FROM TOTAL-LINE AFTER ADVANCING 3 LINES.
332
333          3100-CLOSE-FILES.
334             CLOSE SALES-TRANSACTION-FILE
335                   PRODUCTS-TABLE-FILE
336                   MONTHS-TABLE-FILE
337                   VALID-SALESPERSON-TABLE-FILE
338                   OUT-FILE.
```

```
                              SALES COMMISSION REPORT      MONTH:  AUGUST
        SALES-      PRODUCT
        PERSON      NUMBER       DESCRIPTION        PRICE   QUANTITY   SALES   COMMISSION

        333445555    4024     BANANAS               1.46       10     14.60    $0.44
        333442222    4060     GRAPES                0.92        5      4.60    $0.18
        172348114    4000     APPLES                1.25       20     25.00    $1.25
        211684888    4072     BERRIES               0.88       10      8.80    $0.44
        999887777    5000     *** INVALID RECORD ***

                                                         TOTAL SALES   $53.00     $2.31
```

**EXHIBIT 8.20    QBASIC for Application 8.2, Sales Commission Report**

```
'**********************************************************************
'*                        PROGRAM-IDENTIFICATION                     *
'**********************************************************************
'PROGRAM NAME: CH8APL2
'REMARKS:   THIS PROGRAM PRODUCES A SALES COMMISSION REPORT. FOR
'PRINTING AND CALCULATION PURPOSES, DATA IS EXTRACTED FROM
'A PRODUCTS TABLE, ALPHABETIC DATE TABLE, AND A COMMISSION
'TABLE.  A TABLE LOOKUP IS ALSO MADE TO VALIDATE THE SALES-
'PERSON PRIOR TO ANY PROCESSING.  AN ERROR MESSAGE IS PRODUCED
'IF EITHER THE SALESPERSON NUMBER OR PRODUCT NUMBER IS INVALID
'(OR NOT FOUND IN THE RESPECTIVE TABLES).  THE SALES IS THE
'PRODUCT OF QUANTITY (FROM THE TRANSACTION RECORD) * PRICE (FROM
'THE PRODUCTS TABLE). THE COMMISSION IS THE PRODUCT OF SALES
'TIMES THE APPROPRIATE COMMISSION RATE FROM THE COMMISSION RATE
'TABLE.  THIS RATE WHICH IS EXTRACTED IS BASED ON THE COMMISSION
'CODE FOUND IN THE TRANSACTION RECORD.  THE COMMISSION CODE
'VALUE AGREES WITH THE RELATIVE POSITION IN THE COMMISSION TABLE.
'**********************************************************************
'*                        MAIN-LINE                                  *
'**********************************************************************
GOSUB START.UP                      'PERFORM START-UP
DO UNTIL END.FLAG$ = "YES"
    GOSUB PROCESS.RECORDS            'PERFORM PROCESS.RECORDS
LOOP
GOSUB WRAP.UP                        'PERFORM WRAP-UP
END
```

**EXHIBIT 8.20   (Cont.)**

```
'*****************************************************************
'*                          START-UP                            *
'*****************************************************************


START.UP:

    DIM PRODUCTNOTAB$(7): DIM DESCRIPTIONTAB$(7): DIM PRICETAB(7): DIM MONTHTAB$(12)
    DIM COMRATETAB(3): DIM VALIDSSNTAB$(8): DIM NAMETAB$(8): DIM CLASSTAB(8)
    DIM TITLETAB$(8): DIM DISTNOTAB$(8): DIM EMPLDATETAB$(8)
    GOSUB INITIALIZE
    GOSUB OPEN.FILES
    GOSUB LOAD.TABLES                      '* PERFORM LOAD TABLES
    GOSUB READ.TRANS.FILE                  '* PERFORM READ-TRANS-FILE
    HEADMONTH$ = MONTHTAB$(DATEMONTH)
    GOSUB PRINT.HEADINGS                   '* PERFORM PRINT-HEADINGS
    RETURN


    '*************************************************************
    '*                     INITIALIZE                           *
    '*************************************************************
INITIALIZE:

    WIDTH LPRINT (132)
    END.FLAG$ = "NO"
    TOTAL.SALES = 0
    TOTALCOMMISSION = 0
    TOTALLINE$ = "                                             TOTALS    $$##,###.##$$###.##"
    ERRORLINE$ = "  \          \ \      \       *_*_* INVALID RECORD *_*_*"
    DETAILLINE$ = "  \          \ \      \          \              \    ###.##      ###     ##,###.##  ###.##"
    RETURN


    '*************************************************************
    '*                     OPEN-FILES                           *
    '*************************************************************


OPEN.FILES:
    OPEN "I", #2, "CH8ILL2B.DAT":          '* OPEN PRODUCTS-TABLE-FILE
    OPEN "I", #3, "CH8ILL2C.DAT":          '* OPEN MONTHS-TABLE-FILE
    OPEN "I", #1, "CH8ILL2D.DAT":          '* OPEN VALID SALESPERSON FILE
    OPEN "I", #4, "CH8ILL2A.DAT":          '* OPEN TRANSACTION-FILE
    RETURN




    '*************************************************************
    '*                     LOAD TABLES                          *
    '*************************************************************


LOAD.TABLES:

    GOSUB LOAD.PRODUCT.TABLE               '* PERFORM LOAD-PRODUCT-TABLE
    GOSUB LOAD.MONTHS.TABLE                '* PERFORM LOAD-MONTHS-TABLE
    GOSUB LOAD.VALID.SALESPERSON.TABLE     '* PERFORM LOAD-VALID-SALESPERSON
    COMRATETAB(1) = .03
    COMRATETAB(2) = .04
    COMRATETAB(3) = .05
    RETURN
```

**EXHIBIT 8.20    (Cont.)**

```
'************************************************************************
'*                      LOAD PRODUCT TABLE                             *
'************************************************************************

LOAD.PRODUCT.TABLE:

    GOSUB READ.PRODUCTS.TABLE.FILE          '* READ-PRODUCTS-TABLE-FILE
    FOR SUB1 = 1 TO 7
    GOSUB PRODUCT.ELEMENT.LOAD              '* PERFORM PRODUCT-ELEMENT-LOAD
    NEXT SUB1
    RETURN


    '************************************************************************
    '*                      READ-PRODUCT-TABLE-FILE                        *
    '************************************************************************

READ.PRODUCTS.TABLE.FILE:

    INPUT #2, PRODUCTNO$, DESCRIPTION$, PRICE
    RETURN


    '************************************************************************
    '*                      PRODUCT-ELEMENT-LOAD                           *
    '************************************************************************

PRODUCT.ELEMENT.LOAD:

    PRODUCTNOTAB$(SUB1) = PRODUCTNO$
    DESCRIPTIONTAB$(SUB1) = DESCRIPTION$
    PRICETAB(SUB1) = PRICE
    GOSUB READ.PRODUCTS.TABLE.FILE          '* READ-PRODUCT-TABLE-FILE
    RETURN


    ' ************************************************************************
    ' *                      LOAD MONTH TABLE                               *
    ' ************************************************************************
LOAD.MONTHS.TABLE:

    GOSUB READ.MONTHS.TABLE.FILE            ' READ-MONTHS-TABLE-FILE
    FOR SUB1 = 1 TO 12
    GOSUB MONTHS.ELEMENT.LOAD               ' PERFORM MONTHS-ELEMENT-LOAD
    NEXT SUB1
    RETURN
```

**EXHIBIT 8.20    (Cont.)**

```
'*******************************************************************
'*                      READ-MONTH-TABLE-FILE                     *
'*******************************************************************


READ.MONTHS.TABLE.FILE:

    INPUT #3, MONTHNAME$
    RETURN


    '*******************************************************************
    '*                      MONTHS-ELEMENT-LOAD                       *
    '*******************************************************************
MONTHS.ELEMENT.LOAD:

    MONTHTAB$(SUB1) = MONTHNAME$
    GOSUB READ.MONTHS.TABLE.FILE              ' READ-MONTH-TABLE-FILE
    RETURN




    '*******************************************************************
    '*                  LOAD-VALID-SALESPERSON-TABLE                  *
    '*******************************************************************


LOAD.VALID.SALESPERSON.TABLE:

    GOSUB READ.VALID.MASTER                   ' READ-VALID-MASTER
    FOR SUB1 = 1 TO 8
    GOSUB SALESPERSON.ELEMENT.LOAD            '* PERFORM SALESPERSON-ELEMENT
    NEXT SUB1
    RETURN


    '*******************************************************************
    '*                      READ-VALID-MASTER                         *
    '*******************************************************************


READ.VALID.MASTER:

    INPUT #1, VALIDSSN$, SALESPERSON$, CLASS, TITLE$, DISTNO$, EMPLDATE$
    RETURN


    '*******************************************************************
    '*                  SALESPERSON-ELEMENT-LOAD                      *
    '*******************************************************************
SALESPERSON.ELEMENT.LOAD:

    VALIDSSNTAB$(SUB1) = VALIDSSN$
    NAMETAB$(SUB1) = SALESPERSON$
    CLASSTAB(SUB1) = CLASS
    TITLETAB$(SUB1) = TITLE$
    DISTNOTAB$(SUB1) = DISTNO$
    EMPLDATETAB$(SUB1) = EMPLDATE$
    GOSUB READ.VALID.MASTER                   '* READ-VALID-MASTER
    RETURN
```

**EXHIBIT 8.20** (Cont.)

```
'***********************************************************************
'                         READ-TRANS-FILE                             *
'***********************************************************************
READ.TRANS.FILE:

    INPUT #4, PRODUCTNUMBER$, QUANTITY, DATEMONTH, DATEDAY, DATEYEAR, SSN$, CLASS
    IF PRODUCTNUMBER$ = "9999" THEN END.FLAG$ = "YES"
    RETURN


'***********************************************************************
'*                       PRINT HEADINGS                               *
'***********************************************************************

PRINT.HEADINGS:

    LPRINT CHR$(12): LPRINT
    LPRINT TAB(35); "SALES COMMISSION REPORT"; TAB(67); "MONTH:"; TAB(76); HEADMONTH$
    LPRINT
    LPRINT TAB(5); "SALES-"; TAB(15); "PRODUCT"; TAB(35); "DESCRIPTION"; TAB(55); "PRICE"; TAB(65); "QUANTITY"; TAB(77); "SALES"; TAB(85); "COMMISSION"
    LPRINT TAB(5); "PERSON"; TAB(15); "NUMBER"
    LPRINT
    RETURN


'   **********************************************************************
'   *                        PROCESS RECORDS                            *
'   **********************************************************************

PROCESS.RECORDS:

    GOSUB TABLE.LOOKUPS                              PERFORM TABLE LOOKUPS
    IF VALIDSSNSW$ = "YES" AND PRODUCTFOUNDSW$ = "YES" THEN
       GOSUB DETAIL.CALCULATIONS
       GOSUB ACCUMULATIONS
       GOSUB PRINT.DETAIL.LINE
     ELSE LPRINT USING ERRORLINE$; SSN$; PRODUCTNUMBER$
     END IF
    GOSUB READ.TRANS.FILE                            PERFORM READ-TRANS-FILE
    RETURN


'***********************************************************************
'*                        TABLE LOOK UPS                              *
'***********************************************************************

TABLE.LOOKUPS:

    GOSUB LOOK.UP.VALID.SSN              '* PERFORM LOOK-UP-VALID-SSN
    GOSUB LOOK.UP.PRODUCT.INFO           '* PERFORM LOOK-UP-PRODUCT-INFO
    RETURN
```

**EXHIBIT 8.20 (Cont.)**

```
'*******************************************************************
'*                      LOOK UP VALID SSN                         *
'*******************************************************************


LOOK.UP.VALID.SSN:

    VALIDSSNSW$ = "NO"
    FOR SUB1 = 1 TO 8
    GOSUB SSN.ELEMENT.COMPARE                  '* PERFORM SSN-ELEMENT-COMPARE
    NEXT SUB1
    RETURN



        '*******************************************************************
        '*                  SSN ELEMENT COMPARE                          *
        '*******************************************************************


SSN.ELEMENT.COMPARE:

    IF SSN$ = VALIDSSNTAB$(SUB1) THEN
       VALIDSSNSW$ = "YES"
       SUB1 = 8
    END IF
    RETURN


        '*******************************************************************
        '*                  LOOK-UP-PRODUCT-INFO                         *
        '*******************************************************************


LOOK.UP.PRODUCT.INFO:
    PRODUCTFOUNDSW$ = "NO"
    FOR SUB1 = 1 TO 7
        GOSUB PRODUCT.ELEMENT.COMPARE          '* PERFORM PRODUCT-ELEMENT-COMPARE
    NEXT SUB1
    RETURN



        '*******************************************************************
        '*                  PRODUCT-ELEMENT-COMPARE                      *
        '*******************************************************************


PRODUCT.ELEMENT.COMPARE:

    IF PRODUCTNUMBER$ = PRODUCTNOTAB$(SUB1) THEN
       PRODUCTFOUNDSW$ = "YES"
       SUBSAVE = SUB1
       SUB1 = 7
    END IF
    RETURN
```

## EXHIBIT 8.20   (Cont.)

```
' ********************************************************************
' *                    DETAIL-CALCULATIONS                          *
' ********************************************************************

DETAIL.CALCULATIONS:

    SALES = QUANTITY * PRICETAB(SUBSAVE)
    COMMISSION = SALES * COMRATETAB(CLASS)
    RETURN


    ' ********************************************************************
    ' *                    ACCUMULATIONS                              *
    ' ********************************************************************

ACCUMULATIONS:

    TOTALSALES = TOTALSALES + SALES
    TOTALCOMMISSION = TOTALCOMMISSION + COMMISSION
    RETURN


    '********************************************************************
    '*               PRINT DETAIL LINE                               *
    '********************************************************************

PRINT.DETAIL.LINE:

    LPRINT USING DETAILLINE$; SSN$; PRODUCTNUMBER$; DESCRIPTIONTAB$(SUBSAVE); PRICETAB(SUBSAVE); QUANTITY; SALES; COMMISSION
    RETURN




    '********************************************************************
    '*                    WRAP-UP                                    *
    '********************************************************************

WRAP.UP:
    GOSUB SUMMARY.OUTPUT
    GOSUB CLOSE.FILES
    RETURN

    '************************************************************************
    '*                    SUMMARY-OUTPUT                                   *
    '  '************************************************************************

SUMMARY.OUTPUT:
    LPRINT : LPRINT
    LPRINT USING TOTALLINE$; TOTALSALES; TOTALCOMMISSION
    RETURN

CLOSE.FILES:
    CLOSE 1, 2, 3, 4
    RETURN
```

**EXHIBIT 8.20    (Cont.)**

| | | SALES COMMISSION REPORT | MONTH: | AUGUST | | |
|---|---|---|---|---|---|---|

| SALES–<br>PERSON | PRODUCT<br>NUMBER | DESCRIPTION | PRICE | QUANTITY | SALES | COMMISSION |
|---|---|---|---|---|---|---|
| 333445555 | 4024 | BANANAS | 1.46 | 10 | 14.60 | 0.44 |
| 333442222 | 4060 | GRAPES | 0.92 | 5 | 4.60 | 0.18 |
| 172348114 | 4000 | APPLES | 1.25 | 20 | 25.00 | 1.25 |
| 211684888 | 4072 | BERRIES | 0.88 | 10 | 8.80 | 0.44 |
| 999887777 | 5000 | ★★★ INVALID RECORD ★★★ | | | | |
| | | | | TOTALS | $53.00 | $2.31 |

**FIGURE 8.1    An Alternative Searching Method (A Modified Version of Method 1)**

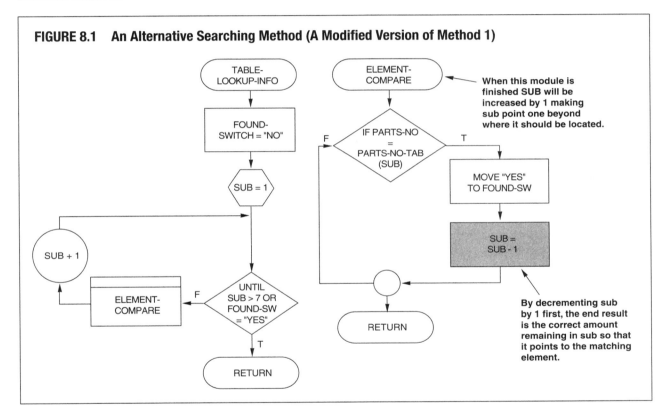

**FIGURE 8.2    Loading an Unknown Number of Values to a Table. Its Effect on the Logic of both the Table Loading Process and the Table Searching Activity.**

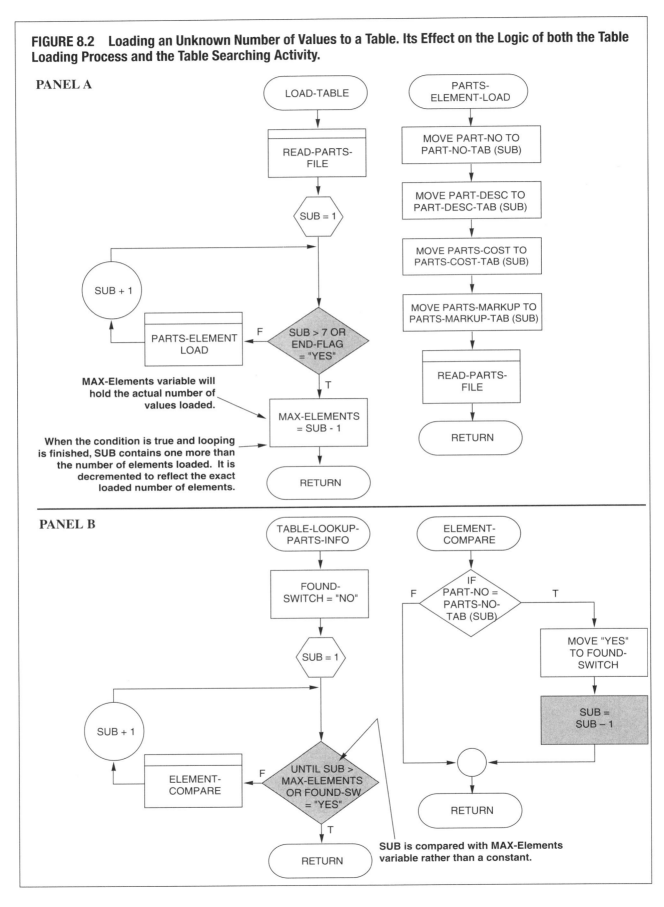

## FIGURE 8.3    Searching Method III An In-Line Perform Technique

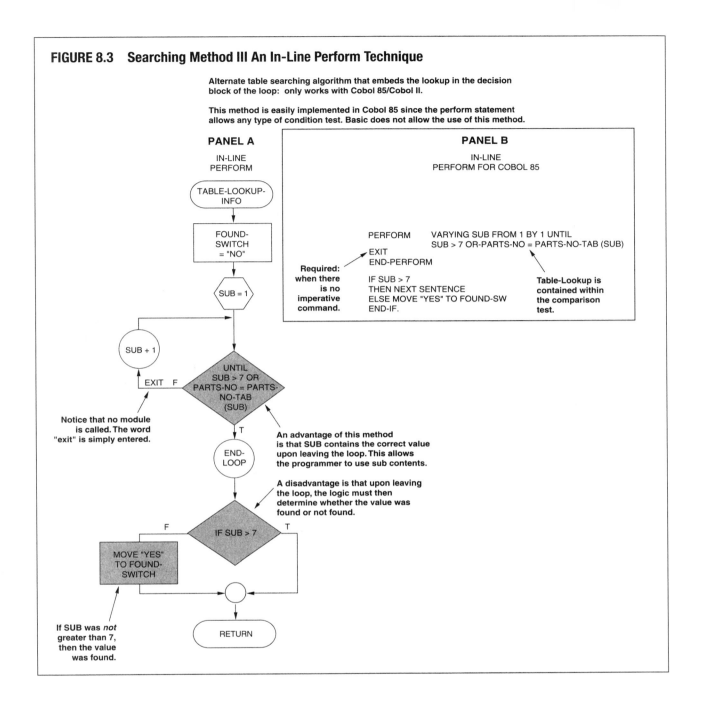

Alternate table searching algorithm that embeds the lookup in the decision block of the loop: only works with Cobol 85/Cobol II.

This method is easily implemented in Cobol 85 since the perform statement allows any type of condition test. Basic does not allow the use of this method.

**PANEL A**

IN-LINE PERFORM

TABLE-LOOKUP-INFO

FOUND-SWITCH = "NO"

SUB = 1

SUB + 1

EXIT    F

UNTIL SUB > 7 OR PARTS-NO = PARTS-NO-TAB (SUB)

Notice that no module is called. The word "exit" is simply entered.

T

END-LOOP

An advantage of this method is that SUB contains the correct value upon leaving the loop. This allows the programmer to use sub contents.

A disadvantage is that upon leaving the loop, the logic must then determine whether the value was found or not found.

F    IF SUB > 7    T

MOVE "YES" TO FOUND-SWITCH

If SUB was *not* greater than 7, then the value was found.

RETURN

**PANEL B**

IN-LINE PERFORM FOR COBOL 85

PERFORM    VARYING SUB FROM 1 BY 1 UNTIL
SUB > 7 OR PARTS-NO = PARTS-NO-TAB (SUB)

EXIT
END-PERFORM

Required: when there is no imperative command.

IF SUB > 7
THEN NEXT SENTENCE
ELSE MOVE "YES" TO FOUND-SW
END-IF.

Table-Lookup is contained within the comparison test.

## Computer Parts and Accessories

- uses table load and search where the number of table records to be loaded are unknown at execution time
- uses a table value from one table as the subscript or pointer for a different table (positional addressing used)
- includes both table searching and control break check
- uses straight positional addressing (contents of a field from the transaction record becomes the subscript for a table)

## PROGRAM REQUIREMENTS

ABC Computer Stores needs a retail sales analysis report that lists the department number, salesperson, part number, part description, cost per unit, quantity, extended cost, markup, retail, discount code, discount amount, and net. The report is to include subtotals and a final total for the net amounts.

The report information is to be extracted from the sales transaction file, parts information table, discount table, months table, and markup table. The current date is to be retrieved from the system date and the month field used as a subscript to extract the alphabetic month from the month table.

The parts description is to be extracted from the parts table using a sequential table search. The part number is the search key, and the part number from the table is the table argument (or the part number to match on). The corresponding table function is the parts description, which is to be extracted from

the table for printing purposes. The part cost (per unit cost) is also extracted from the same parts table and multiplied by the quantity from the sales transaction record to yield the extended cost. The markup percentage is determined by extracting the markup code from the parts table and using this markup code as the subscript in the markup table. This is a case of using a subscripted table item from one table (that is, parts table) as a *subscript* itself to point to data in another table (that is, the markup table). This is also a case of positional addressing as no table search is required to locate the markup percentage. In slightly different words, the percentage is determined directly by using the markup code as the pointer into the markup table. The markup amount is computed by multiplying the markup percentage from the table by the extended cost.

The retail is calculated as the sum of the extended cost and the markup amount. The discount is the retail multiplied by the discount table subscripted by the discount code. This is another case of positional addressing. The discount code is the pointer to the appropriate discount percentage in the discount table. The net is the difference in the retail and the discount.

## OUTPUT DESIGN

Exhibit 8.21 illustrates a sample report for this application. Notice that an error message "ITM NOT FND" is to print, if the part number is not found in the table.

**EXHIBIT 8.21   Sample Report for Application 8.3 (Computer Parts Retail Sales Report)**

```
                         COMPUTER PARTS AND ACCESSORIES
                                                    DATE:      XXXXXXXXXX, XX 199X
                         RETAIL SALES ANALYSIS REPORT

DEPART-    SALESPERSON    PART     PART        COST/  QTY   COST   MARKUP  RETAIL DISC. DISCOUNT  NET
MENT    FIRST    LAST    NUMBER    DESC        UNIT                              CODE

19000  JAMES    MARTIN    7009   MOUSE PAD      7.70  100  770.00  169.40  939.40   1   32.87   906.53
19000  SUSAN    SMITH     7007   KEY BD COVER   3.70   10   37.00    3.70   40.70   2    1.55    39.15
XXXXX  XXXXXXX  XXXXXXXX  XXXX   XXXXXXXXXXXX  XXX.XX  XX   XX.XX   XX.XX   XX.XX   X   XX.XX    XX.XX
XXXXX  XXXXXXX  XXXXXXXX  XXXX   XXXXXXXXXXXX  XXX.XX  XX  XXX.XX
XXXXX  XXXXXXX  XXXXXXXX  XXXX   ITM NOT FND
XXXXX  XXXXXXX  XXXXXXXX  XXXX   XXXXXXXXXXXX  XXX.XX  XX   XX.XX   XX.XX   XX.XX   X   XX.XX    XX.XX

                                               DEPARTMENT 19000    TOTAL      250,000.00*

XXXXX  XXXXXXX  XXXXXXXX  XXXX   XXXXXXXXXXXX  XXX.XX  XX   XX.XX   XX.XX   XX.XX   X   X.XX    XX.XX
XXXXX  XXXXXXX  XXXXXXXX  XXXX   XXXXXXXXXXXX  XXX.XX  XX  XXX.XX
XXXXX  XXXXXXX  XXXXXXXX  XXXX   ITM NOT FND
XXXXX  XXXXXXX  XXXXXXXX  XXXX   XXXXXXXXXXXX  XXX.XX  XX  XXX.XX   XX.XX   XX.XX   X   X.XX    XX.XX

                                               DEPARTMENT XXXXX    TOTAL       X,XXX.XX*
                                               FINAL                        XXX,XXX.XX**
```

Observe that the data are in order by department number and subtotals are printed for each department.

## INPUT DESIGN

Exhibit 8.22 depicts the record layout for the files used in this application. The SALES-FILE, PARTS-FILE, and DISCOUNT-FILE record formats are illustrated showing their respective field formats.

## TABLES

Exhibit 8.23 shows the four tables used in this application. The COMPUTER-PARTS-TABLE shows a table of corresponding values that include PART-NO-TAB, PART-DESC-TAB, PART-COST-TAB, and PART-MARKUP-TAB. This table illustrates the contents of **memory** after the PARTS-FILE is loaded to it. This is the view one takes of the table when coding COBOL. However, when coding BASIC, the programmer views this table as four separate single-dimensional tables that correspond with each other rather than as one large single dimensional table with subcompartments in each element. The DISCOUNT-TAB shows the five discount rates that will reside there after the table is loaded from the DISCOUNT-FILE. The MONTHS-TAB illustrates

the twelve alphabetic month descriptions after the data are initialized. The MARKUP-TABLE contains five markup percentages. These percentages relate to the markup codes in the PART-MARKUP-TAB.

## TEST DATA

Exhibit 8.24 depicts the SALES-FILE (transaction file), the PARTS-FILE, and DISCOUNT-FILE.

## HIERARCHY CHART

Exhibit 8.25 shows the general program logic for this application. Notice that the START-UP module contains a LOAD-TABLES module as well as a PREV-DEPT module. The LOAD-TABLES module is broken down into four submodules. Each submodule has the function of loading a respective table (LOAD-PARTS-TABLE, LOAD-DISC-TABLE, LOAD-MONTH-TABLE, LOAD-MARKUP-TABLE). The PROCESS-RECORDS module includes both a TABLE-LOOK-UP-PARTS-INFO module and a CONTROL-BREAK-CHECK module. The BOTTOM-OF-PAGE-CHECK, DETAIL-CALC, ACCUMULATION, DETAIL-LINE and READ-SALES-FILE modules are quite similar to any other program involving these same modules.

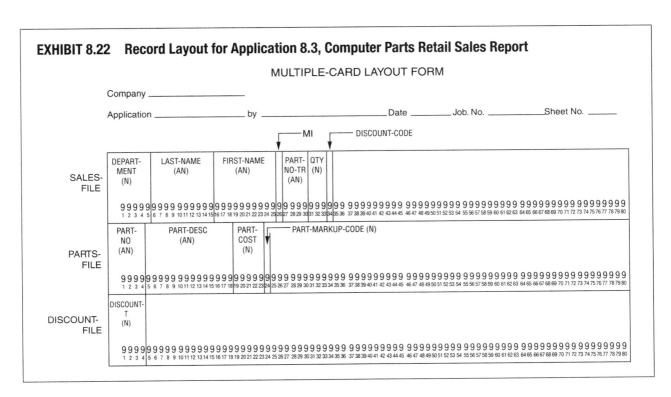

**EXHIBIT 8.22   Record Layout for Application 8.3, Computer Parts Retail Sales Report**

## STRUCTURED FLOWCHART

Exhibit 8.26 illustrates the detailed structured program logic for this application. The START-UP module acts as a sub-driver that calls a third-level set of modules. These include the OPEN-FILES, INITIALIZE-VARIABLES, LOAD-TABLES, HEADINGS, READ-SALES-FILE, and PREV-DEPT. The OPEN-FILES module opens the sales file, parts file, discount file, and sales report file. The initialize-variables module takes care of initializing the pg-ct, final-total, and dept-net variables to zero, and end-flag is set to "no." The LOAD-TABLES module handles the invoking of modules that load the parts information table, the discount table, the months table, and the markup table. Next, the READ-SALES-FILE module is invoked. This is followed by the calling of the PREV-DEPT module.

The LOAD-PARTS-TABLE routine includes the READ-PARTS-FILE (pre-read), followed by what appears to be the quite familiar count-controlled loop that is used for loading and searching tables. However, the condition test has been modified as a compound conditional that tests for sub > 11 or END-FLAG = "YES." The element loading process is terminated by either attempting to load values beyond the end of the table or by reaching the end of the table file. As this is "OR" logic, either of the simple conditions causes a TRUE condition. Regardless of which of the two simple conditions causes a TRUE condition, it is important to preserve the number of loaded elements. Because SUB will contain one more than the number of elements loaded, it is necessary to decrement SUB by one unit prior to transferring it to a new variable called MAX-ELEMENTS. MAX-ELEMENTS can be used as the upper limit rather than a constant in future searches involving this table.

The LOAD-DISC-TABLE module is handled as if there is a fixed number of five records to load to the table. The LOAD-MONTHS-TABLE demonstrates a new technique of loading data to a table. Where

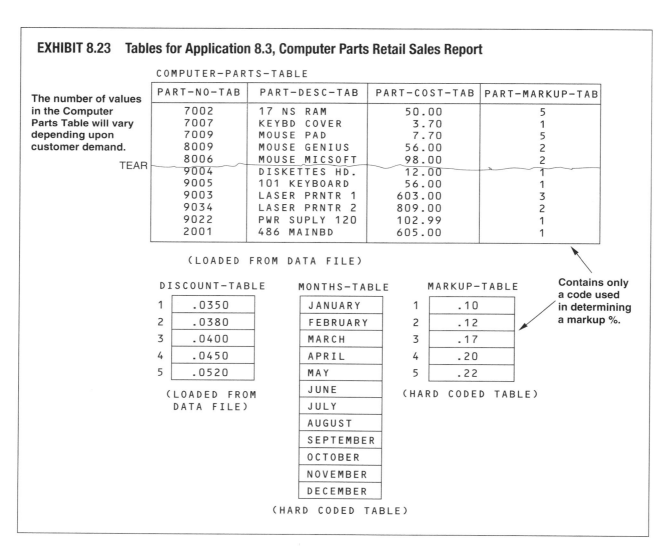

**EXHIBIT 8.23  Tables for Application 8.3, Computer Parts Retail Sales Report**

COMPUTER-PARTS-TABLE

The number of values in the Computer Parts Table will vary depending upon customer demand.

| PART-NO-TAB | PART-DESC-TAB | PART-COST-TAB | PART-MARKUP-TAB |
|---|---|---|---|
| 7002 | 17 NS RAM | 50.00 | 5 |
| 7007 | KEYBD COVER | 3.70 | 1 |
| 7009 | MOUSE PAD | 7.70 | 5 |
| 8009 | MOUSE GENIUS | 56.00 | 2 |
| 8006 | MOUSE MICSOFT | 98.00 | 2 |
| 9004 | DISKETTES HD. | 12.00 | 1 |
| 9005 | 101 KEYBOARD | 56.00 | 1 |
| 9003 | LASER PRNTR 1 | 603.00 | 3 |
| 9034 | LASER PRNTR 2 | 809.00 | 2 |
| 9022 | PWR SUPLY 120 | 102.99 | 1 |
| 2001 | 486 MAINBD | 605.00 | 1 |

TEAR

(LOADED FROM DATA FILE)

Contains only a code used in determining a markup %.

DISCOUNT-TABLE

| | |
|---|---|
| 1 | .0350 |
| 2 | .0380 |
| 3 | .0400 |
| 4 | .0450 |
| 5 | .0520 |

(LOADED FROM DATA FILE)

MONTHS-TABLE

| |
|---|
| JANUARY |
| FEBRUARY |
| MARCH |
| APRIL |
| MAY |
| JUNE |
| JULY |
| AUGUST |
| SEPTEMBER |
| OCTOBER |
| NOVEMBER |
| DECEMBER |

(HARD CODED TABLE)

MARKUP-TABLE

| | |
|---|---|
| 1 | .10 |
| 2 | .12 |
| 3 | .17 |
| 4 | .20 |
| 5 | .22 |

(HARD CODED TABLE)

data remain relatively constant (such as the MONTH-TAB), it is unnecessary to keep a file of such data. Instead, we initialize the constant data into the cells of the table. Here we see the constant "JANUARY" assigned to MONTH-TAB (1). Next, the month "FEBRUARY" is assigned to MONTH-TAB (2), and so on. If this MONTH-TABLE contained, say, thirty different values then this would be cumbersome and would take too long. A good candidate table is one that is relatively short and contains relatively constant data. While the MARKUP-TAB data may not be static, we assign values to it without loading table file data. MARKUP-TAB (1) is assigned the value of 0.10, and MARKUP-TAB (2) is assigned the value 0.12, and so on.

The PROCESS-RECORDS module is relatively traditional except that we see both a table lookup operation and a control-break check all in the same program. The part number must be found in the table before any valid processing occurs. If the value is not found, an ERROR-LINE module is performed that takes care of printing an appropriate error message on the detail line. If the value is found, a control-break-check is made to determine if a subtotal line is to print yet. Regardless of this outcome, the BOTTOM-OF-PAGE-CHECK, DE-TAIL-CALCULATION, ACCUMULATION, and DETAIL-LINE modules are performed and executed.

Notice that in the TABLE-LOOKUP-PARTS-INFO there is a compound conditional test rather than the traditional method presented in Chapter 7. This is Method II, previously discussed. Notice that the loop terminates by either SUB becoming greater than MAX-ELEMENTS (the upper limit or maxi-

mum number of elements loaded) or FOUND-SWITCH being equal to "YES." In the first case where SUB becomes greater than MAX-ELE-MENTS, the value was not found. The searching process continued all the way to the end of the table and no matching value was found. In the second case, where FOUND-SWITCH is equal to "YES," the value was found in the table. The ELE-MENT-COMPARE module contains one fewer number of boxes. Thus, the SAVE-SUB variable has been excluded and replaced by an arithmetic command that reduces the content of SUB by 1. (Why is this done? Think about what happens if we do not!) If the value is found in the table, FOUND-SWITCH is set to "YES," and program control goes back to the command after the predefined process block, the next step is to again increase SUB by one unit. Now SUB no longer points to the value that was found in the table, but, instead, points to the *next* value down in the table. To remedy this problem, we decrease SUB by one unit while in the ELE-MENT-COMPARE module, resulting in an offsetting effect. (Think about it.) Method III (previously discussed) could be a viable alternative for the one used, but it works only with COBOL 85—not BASIC. Recall in the discussion from Method III it was pointed out that this "in-line" technique does not work in BASIC since BASIC's FOR . . . NEXT loop does not provide for a programmer-supplied conditional test.

The CONTROL-BREAK-CHECK, BOTTOM-OF-PAGE-CHECK, and ACCUMULATION modules are relatively "ho hum" modules that you may be tired of hearing about by now. They were placed in the program for a realistic effect.

**EXHIBIT 8.24  Test Data for Application 8.3, Computer Parts Retail Sales Report**

```
Sales File:

         1         2         3         4         5         6
1234567890123456789012345678901234567890123456789012345678901234567890

19000MARTIN      JAMES      P70091001
19000SMITH       SUSAN      A70070102
19000JONES       JOE        J90030505
20000DONALDSON   DON        K90220903
20000BAKER       MARY       D90050202
20000WHITE       JILL       E70090304
20000ABLE        AB         A20010052
30000KNUTH       DONALD     E90030033
30000CHEN        PETER      A80090102
30000YOURDAN     ED         M70020204
30000GANE        CHRIS      A00000104
300000RR         KEN        D99990000
30000ALBORN      AL         A70090202
```

The DETAIL-CALCULATION module contains several important commands. The EXT-COST is set equal to the product of QTY and PART-COST-TAB (SUB). The PART-MARKUP-TAB (SUB) is moved to the MARKUP-PTR. In both cases we have used SUB as the subscript rather than SAVE-SUB. Why? Remember, we eliminated SAVE-SUB in the ELE-MENT-COMPARE module and replaced it with an arithmetic command that decreased the content of SUB. SUB is the variable to be used as the subscript, as it still points at the true location in the table where the value was located.

In the second box of the DETAIL-CALCULA-TION module, notice that we are transferring the PART-MARKUP-TAB (SUB) to the MARKUP-PTR. MARKUP-PTR will be used subsequently as the subscript into the PART-MARKUP table. The RE-TAIL is the sum of EXT-COST and MARKUP. The DISCOUNT is calculated as the product of the RETAIL and DISCOUNT-TAB (DISC-CODE). The DISC-CODE is a field from the input sales transaction record. This is a case of positionally addressing data from the table without having to actually search the table. Small, integer, nonzero, and positive field values (calculated or just a value of the record) can easily be used as the subscript as long as the data have been prearranged to agree by position with the value in the said field.

The key point to notice about the DETAIL-LINE module is the use of SUB instead of SAVE-SUB as the subscript when moving various fields to the detail-line. The ERROR-LINE module is relatively straightforward. The DEPT-NO, the PART-NO, and the message, "PART NOT FOUND IN PARTS TABLE" are formatted into the detail line.

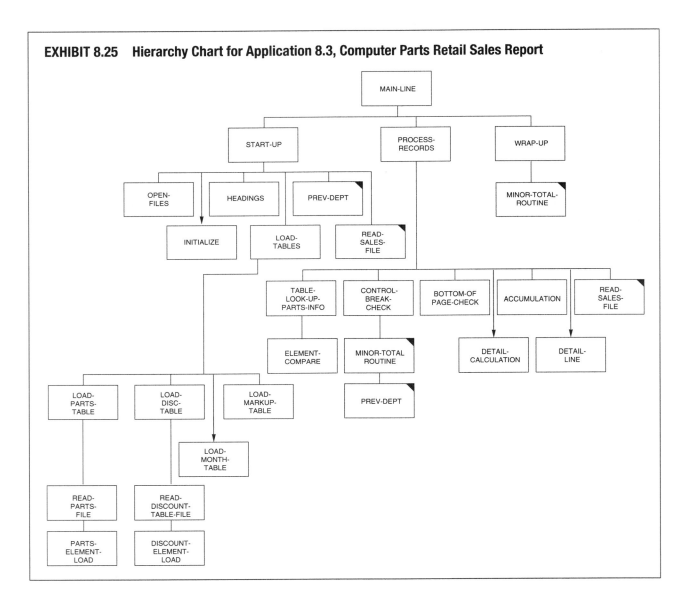

**EXHIBIT 8.25   Hierarchy Chart for Application 8.3, Computer Parts Retail Sales Report**

The WRAP-UP module shows the performing of the MINOR-TOTAL-ROUTINE prior to writing the final total and closing the files. Control is given back to the MAIN-LINE module at this point, and the program passes control back to the operating system.

## PSEUDOCODE

The pseudocode for Application 8.3 is found in Exhibit 8.27. Notice the "repeat until . . . altering" command that has been introduced to offer an equivalent pseudocode command to the perform . . . varying in COBOL and the For . . . Next command in BASIC.

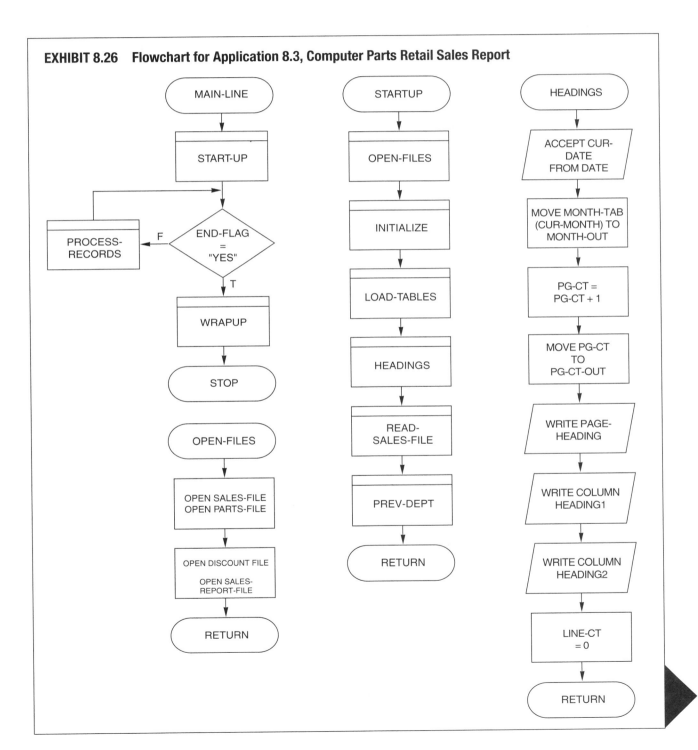

**EXHIBIT 8.26    Flowchart for Application 8.3, Computer Parts Retail Sales Report**

**EXHIBIT 8.26 (Cont.)**

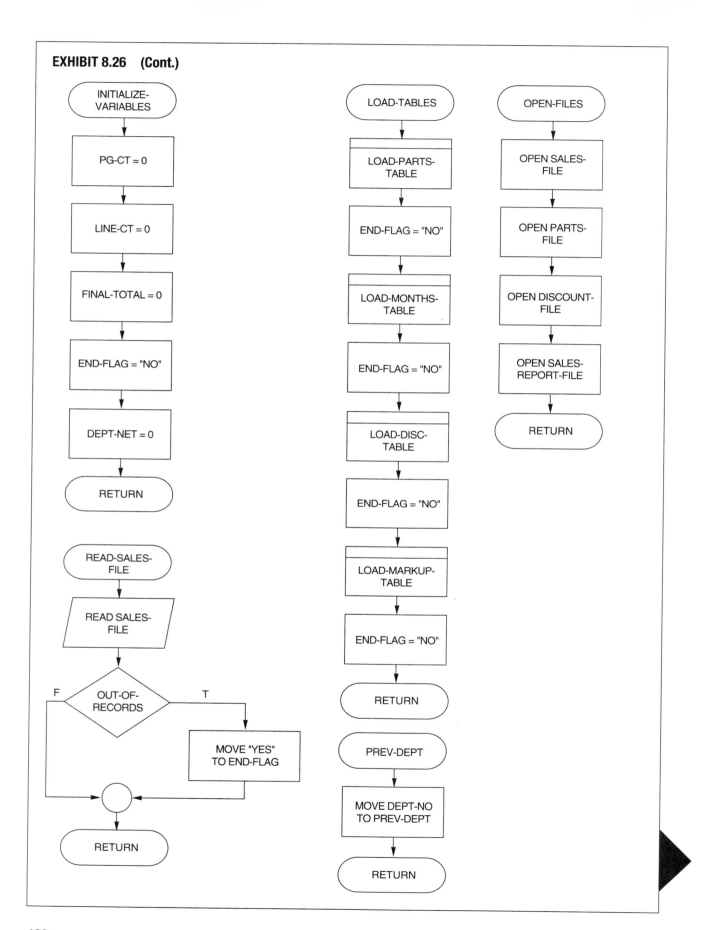

**EXHIBIT 8.26    (Cont.)**

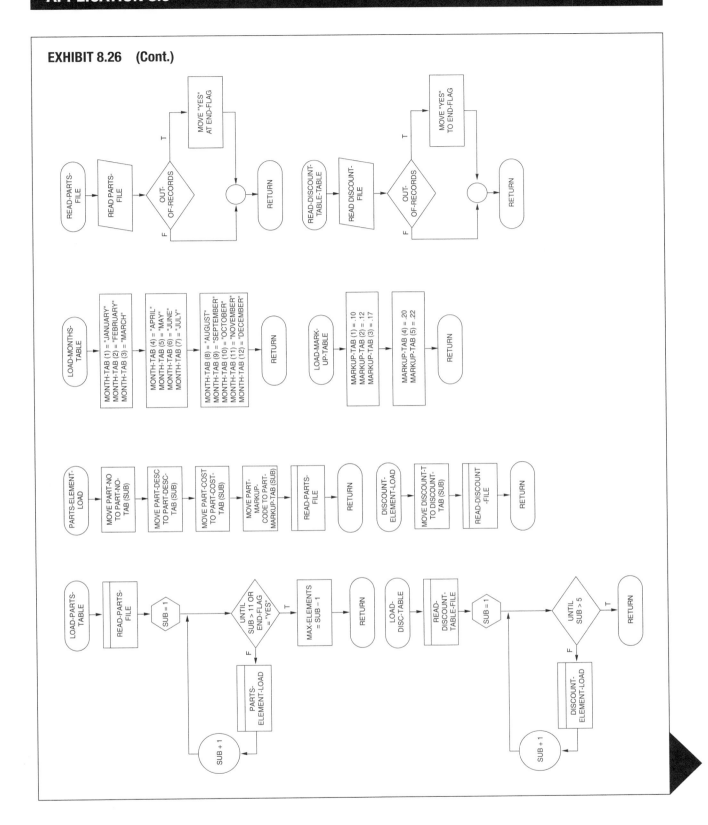

**EXHIBIT 8.26 (Cont.)**

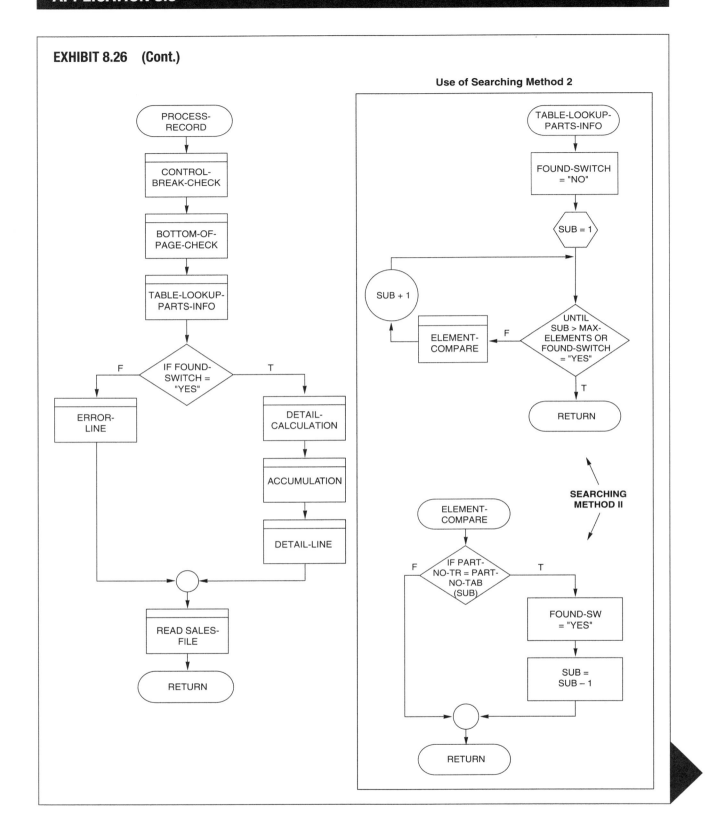

**Use of Searching Method 2**

## USING TABLES TO STORE SUMMARY REPORT INFORMATION

Suppose Application 8.3 is to produce a Departmental Bonuses Summary Report, which summarizes the net sales for each department, and an associated bonus, which is to be paid to each salesperson within the respective department. *Salespersons receive bonuses at the end of the year based on the sales history of the department.* This is done to promote team spirit within the department and to work as a team toward common corporate and departmental goals.

Figure 8.4 (page 429) illustrates the Departmental Bonuses Summary Report. Figure 8.5 shows the BONUS table that contains a search argument rep-

resenting the upper limit of departmental sales. This upper limit is associated with a specific bonus amount. In other words, the first element indicates that a sales range of 0 to 20000 receives no bonus. A sales range of 20001 through 50000 will receive a 50.00 bonus, and so on.

The structured flowchart is illustrated in Exhibit 8.28. Only modules from Application 8.3 that require modifying are shown. In the START-UP module a blank box and dots indicate that the same logic from the START-UP module in Application 8.3 is also found here. The only new box is the initializing of CTR = 1. CTR will become the subscript used for the table holding summary data (SUMMARY-TAB). SUMMARY-TAB consists of sub-elements (or slots) called DEPT-NO-TAB,

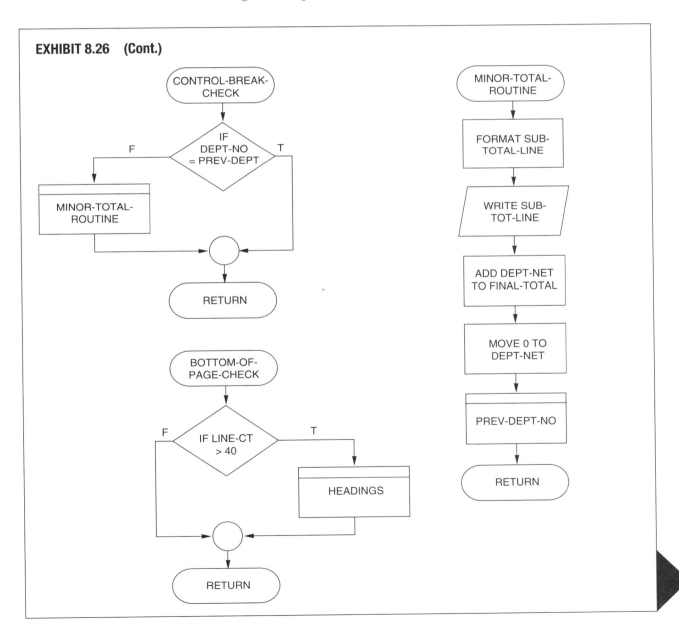

**EXHIBIT 8.26  (Cont.)**

DEPT-NET-TAB, and BONUS-DEPT-TAB. These three sub-elements will hold the department number, department net, and the appropriate bonus for this department's level of sales for the period.

An excellent way to handle a summary report application is *first to save the summary data* in a separate table, then after all transaction records are processed, *print out the summary table data as a report.* To save the departmental summary data, the transaction sales file must be ordered by DEPT-NO and there must be a change in department numbers (that is, there must be a control break). The MINOR-TOTAL-ROUTINE is where the new commands and logic should appear. Notice that the formatting and writing the subtotal line appears as before. Adding the depart-net to final-net appears as usual. Notice the next predefined process block is called LOOKUP-BONUS-AMOUNT. This mod-

ule's function is to look up the appropriate bonus amount based upon the DEPT-NET from the BONUS table. The LOOKUP-BONUS-AMOUNT module appears as most of the other lookup routines except that the count-controlled loop contains a compound condition. This is the searching Method II previously discussed. The significant difference is found in the BONUS-ELEMENT-COMPARE where the decision block contains a comparison of the DEPT-NET and the department net in the table [DEPT-NET-MAX (SUB)]. The test is to determine whether DEPT-NET *is less than or equal to* DEPT-NET-MAX (SUB). Until now, all the comparisons were based upon exact matches; here, the program is trying to determine whether the desired amount is within a prescribed range, rather than being equal to a specific value. If the condition test is true, "YES" is moved to FOUND-SWITCH

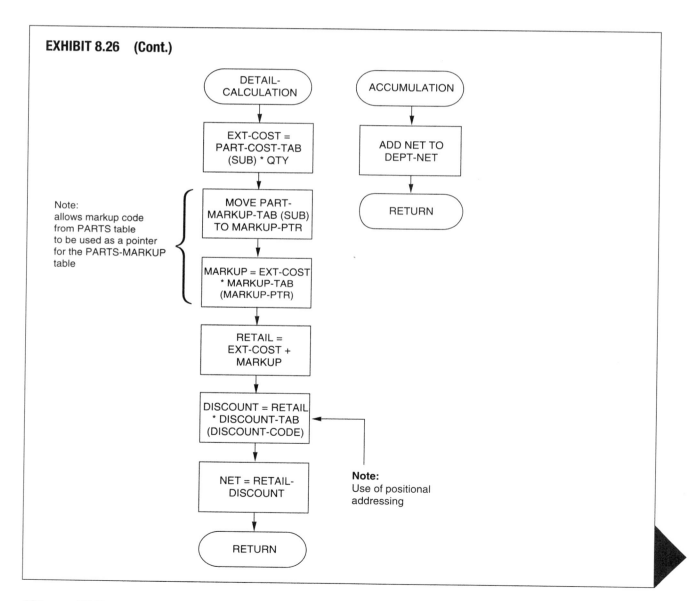

**EXHIBIT 8.26    (Cont.)**

and SUB is decreased by 1. This follows the Method II searching technique.

After the appropriate bonus has been determined from the table search, the BONUS-TAB (SUB) is moved over into the summary table—BONUS-DEPT-TAB. Also, the PREV-DEPT is moved to the DEPT-NO-TAB (SUB), and the DEPT-NET is moved to the DEPT-NET-TAB (SUB). All pertinent summary data are now stored for a par-

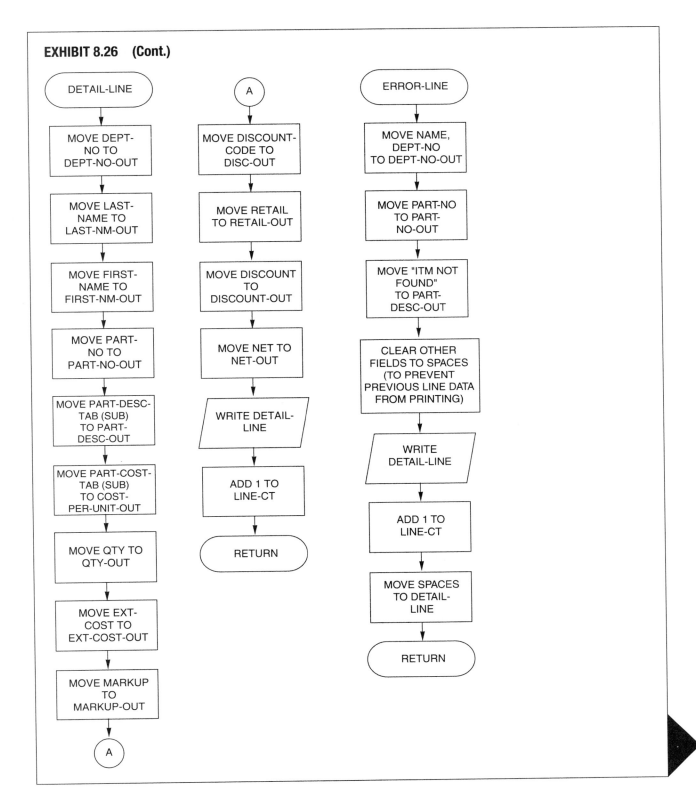

EXHIBIT 8.26    (Cont.)

ticular department. When the next control break is encountered, this process is repeated.

In the wrap-up module, after all transaction records have been processed, it is time to print the Departmental Bonuses Summary Report. The printing of the summary table information is similar to loading a table except that data are being extracted from the table and written to a print line. Observe the PRINT-SUMMARY-REPORT module. It first shows an I/O command to advance to the top of the page. This is easily handled in the WRITE command in COBOL, or the use of a CHAR(12) in BASIC. Notice that CTR is decreased by one to represent the exact number of values actually loaded during control break intervals. The count-con-

trolled loop looks just like a table load process except that the until condition causes looping until SUB becomes greater than the value in CTR. The module being performed is called PRINT-SUM-MARY-LINE instead of ELEMENT-LOAD (or something similar). The PRINT-SUMMARY-LINE module contains three move commands. One at a time, data are lifted from the summary table and printed on the summary line. This requires the programmer to MOVE DEPT-NO-TAB (SUB) to DEPT-SUMMARY-OUT (an output field in the print line). The other two move statements follow. This is all followed by a WRITE command to physically write the line on the report.

EXHIBIT 8.26   (Cont.)

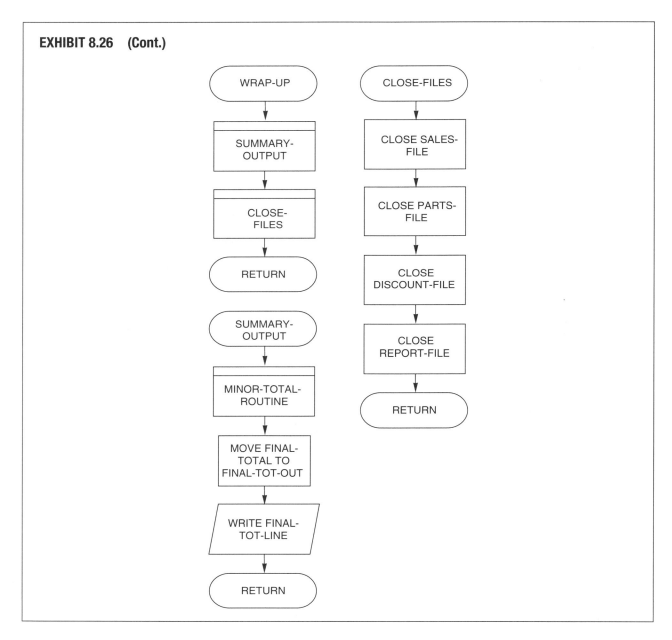

## EXHIBIT 8.27 Pseudocode for Application 8.3, Computer Parts Retail Sales Report

(Uses a "table-oriented" REPEAT command for loading tables and searching tables.)

```
*main-line
    start-up
    dowhile end-flag = "no"
        process-records
    enddo
    wrap-up
    stop
*start-up
    open-files
    initialize-variables
    load-tables
    headings
    read-sales-file
    prev-dept
    return
*open-files
    open sales-file
    open parts-file
    open discount-file
    open sales-report-file
    return
*initialize-variables
    pg-ct = 0
    line-ct = 0
    final-total = 0
    dept-net = 0
    end-flag = "no"
    return
*load-tables
    load-parts-table
    end-flag = "no"
    load-disc-table
    end-flag = "no"
    load-month-table
    end-flag = "no"
load-mark-up-table
    end-flag = "no"
    return
*headings
    accept cur-date from the system date
    store month-tab (current-month) to month-out
    pg-ct = pg-ct + 1
    store pg-ct to pg-ct-out
    write page heading
    write column heading1
    write column heading2
    line-ct = 0
    return
*read-sales-file
    read sales-file
        when out of records move "yes" to end-flag
    end-read
    return
```

```
*prev-dept
    move dept-no to prev-dept
    return
*load-parts-table
    read-parts-file
    repeat until sub > 11
            setting sub to 1
        parts-element-load
        increasing sub by 1
    endrepeat
    return
*read-parts-file
    read parts-file
        when out of records move "yes" to end-flag
    end-read
    return
*parts-element-load
    move part-no to part-no-tab (sub)
    move part-desc to part-desc-tab (sub)
    move part-cost to part-cost-tab (sub)
    move part-markup to part-markup-tab (sub)
    read-parts-file
    return
*load-disc-table
    read-discount-table-file
    repeat until sub > 11 or end-flag = "yes"
            setting sub to 1
        discount-element-load
            incrementing by 1
    endrepeat
    max-elements = sub minus 1
    return
*read-discount-table-file
    read discount-file
        when out of records move "yes" to end-flag
    endread
    return
*discount-element-load
    move discount-t to discount-tab (sub)
    read-discount-table-file
    return
*load-months-table
    month-tab (1) = "JANUARY"
    month-tab (2) = "FEBRUARY"
    month-tab (3) = "MARCH"
    month-tab (4) = "APRIL"
    month-tab (5) = "MAY"
    month-tab (6) = "JUNE"
    month-tab (7) = "JULY"
    month-tab (8) = "AUGUST"
    month-tab (9) = "SEPTEMBER"
    month-tab (10) = "OCTOBER"
    month-tab (11) = "NOVEMBER"
    month-tab (12) = "DECEMBER"
    return
```

**EXHIBIT 8.27    (Cont.)**

```
*load-mark-up-table
      markup-tab (1) = .10
      markup-tab (2) = .12
      markup-tab (3) = .17
      markup-tab (4) = .20
      markup-tab (5) = .22
      return
*process-records
      table-lookup
      if found-switch = "yes"
            then
                  control-break-check
                  bottom-of-page-check
                  detail-calculation
                  accumulation
                  detail-line
      else
                  error-line
      end-if
      read-sales-file
      return
*table-lookup
      move "no" to found-switch
      repeat until sub > max-elements or found-switch = "yes"
                  altering sub from initial value of 1
            element-compare
                  incrementing sub by 1
      endrepeat
      return
*element-compare
      if part-no = part-no-tab (sub)
            then
                  found-switch = "yes"
                  sub = sub minus 1 (note: adjusts for automatic
                              increment of sub)
      endif
      return
*control-break-check
      if dept-no = prev-dept
            then null
            else   minor-total-routine
      endif
      return
*minor-total-routine
      format sub-tot-line
      write sub-tot-line
      add dept-net to final-total
      move 0 to dept-net
      prev-dept
      return
*bottom-of-page-check
      if line-ct > 40 then
            headings
      endif
      return
```

```
*detail-calculation
      ext-cost = part-cost-tab (sub) * qty
      move markup-tab (sub) to markup-ptr
      markup = ext-cost * markup-tab (markup-ptr)
      retail = ext-cost + markup
      discount = retail * discount-tab (disc-code)
      net = retail minus discount
      return
*accumulation
      add net to dept-net
      return
*detail-line
      move dept-no to dept-no-out
      move last-name to last-name-out
      move first-name to first-name-out
      move part-no to part-no-out
      move part-desc-tab (sub) to part-desc-out
      move part-cost-tab (sub) to cost-per-unit-out
      move qty to qty-out
      move ext-cost to ext-cost-out
      move markup to markup-out
      move retail to retail-out
      move discount to discount-out
      move net to net-out
      write detail-line
      add 1 to line-ct
      return
*error-line
      move name to name-out
      move dept-no to dept-no-out
      move part-no to part-no-out
      move "Itm not found" to part-desc-out
      clear other output fields to spaces
      write detail-line
      add 1 to line-ct
      move spaces to detail-line
      return
*wrap-up
      summary-output
      close-files
      return
*summary-output
      minor-total-routine
      move final-total to final-tot-out
      write final-total-line
      return
*close-files
      close sales-file
            parts-file
            discount-file
            report-file
      return
```

# A BINARY TABLE SEARCH

The previously described methods of searching tables work fine with tables having fewer than 50 elements, but as the table size increases significantly beyond that number, the sequential search is too time-consuming. If a table contains, for example, 200 elements, it would take about 100 searches to locate any given value.

A searching technique called a binary search can drastically—in fact, exponentially—reduce the number of searches needed to locate a value in an ordered table. But the method does not become significantly faster than the sequential search until the table size goes well beyond 50 elements. In a real-world programming environment, it is common to access data in tables containing hundreds or even thousands of elements. When data are accessed from very large tables in an on-line environment, it is essential to perform binary, rather than sequential, searches. When an on-line program is execut-

ing, a user expects an immediate response from the computer, and a table must be searched as rapidly as possible. The user does not want to wait several seconds for a response while a 3000-element table is searched sequentially. In general, a response time greater than two seconds is unacceptable. (In Chapter 13, more will be said about on-line response times.)

## The Ordered Table

A binary search requires that the table be ordered into ascending sequence. In this searching technique, the *mid element (or midpoint) of the table is compared with the search key*. If the comparison is unequal, a *new midpoint* is determined for the *remaining table half* in which the value could be found. The search key is then compared with the element located at this new midpoint. Until the search key equals the table key (or no more logical elements remain for comparison), the process of locating the

---

**FIGURE 8.4 Departmental Bonuses Summary Report**

| DEPARTMENTAL BONUS SUMMARY REPORT | | |
|---|---|---|
| DEPARTMENT | MONTHLY NET SALES | BONUS/SALESPERSON |
| 19000 | $250,000.00 | 121.00 |
| 19280 | $350,000.00 | 211.00 |
| XXXXX | $XXX,XXX.XX | XXX.XX |
| XXXXX | $XXX,XXX.XX | XXX.XX |

---

**FIGURE 8.5 Bonus Table**

| SALES TO NOT EXCEED | BONUS AMOUNT |
|---|---|
| DEPT-NET-MAX | BONUS-TAB |
| 20,000 | 0.00 |
| 50,000 | 50.00 |
| 75,000 | 61.00 |
| 100,000 | 73.00 |
| 125,000 | 84.00 |
| 150,000 | 91.00 |
| 250,000 | 121.00 |
| 360,000 | 211.00 |
| 500,000 | 300.00 |
| 999,000 | 500.00 |

| | DEPT-NO-TAB | DEPT-NET-TAB $ ¢¢ | BONUS-DEPT-TAB $ ¢¢ |
|---|---|---|---|
| 1 | 19000 | 250000 00 | 121 00 |
| 2 | 19280 | 350000 00 | 211 00 |
| 3 | | | |
| 4 | | | |
| 5 | | | |
| 6 | | | |
| 7 | | | |
| 8 | | | |
| 9 | | | |
| 10 | | | |
| 11 | | | |
| 12 | | | |
| 13 | | | |

Table to store departmental bonus summary data.
Note: at wrap-up time, table data saved here is written to report above.

midpoint of the remaining table half within which the value could be found continues.

An overhead factor associated with the binary search is the fact that the table elements must initially be sorted into sequence. The concept of sorting tables will be presented in Chapter 11. For now, assume that the table data are prearranged.

## The Next Comparison at the Newly Calculated Midpoint

Figure 8.6 illustrates the binary search process. A table is shown with 16 elements arranged in ascending sequence. The search key (125) from the first transaction record is compared first with the midpoint element of the table (115). This is the eighth element. In this case, the value 115 is the table argument or key. Since 125 is not equal to

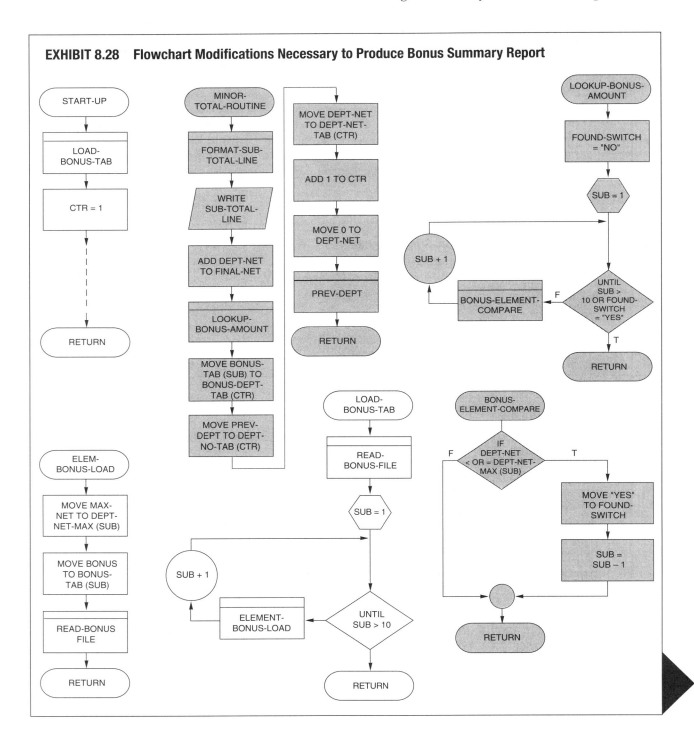

**EXHIBIT 8.28  Flowchart Modifications Necessary to Produce Bonus Summary Report**

(and is greater than) 115, the next midpoint is calculated and the comparison process resumes with the *subsequent midpoint*. The calculation of midpoints is discussed in the next section. Because the search key is greater than the table argument, this midpoint is the twelfth element of the table. In the second iteration, the search key (125) is compared with the subsequent midpoint (table argument) value (121) to determine equality. Again the comparison result is *false*. Because the search key is still greater than the table argument, for the third time a new midpoint is calculated. The midpoint this time is the fourteenth element of the table. In the third iteration, the search key (125) is compared with the latest midpoint value (123). Because 125 is not equal to 123, the comparison result is again *false*; again the search key is greater than the table argument, and the midpoint is recalculated for the fourth time. This time, the midpoint of the table is the fifteenth element. In the fourth iteration, the search

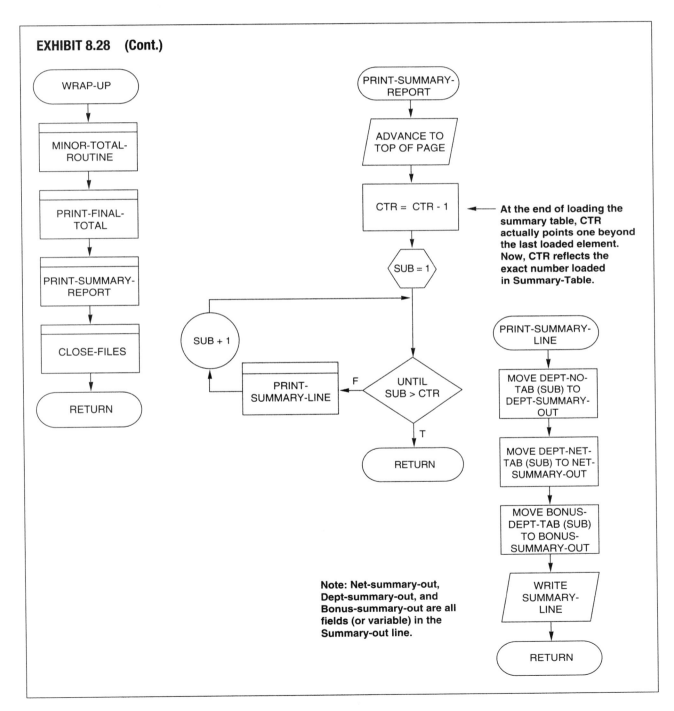

**EXHIBIT 8.28   (Cont.)**

key (125) is compared with the new midpoint value (125). This time the comparison result is *true*. Even with a table size of 16 elements, a value was found on the fourth comparison. With a sequential search, on the average, it would take eight comparisons. But in this particular example, *fifteen* comparisons would have been required to match the search key if a sequential search had been used!

## Calculating a Midpoint

Figure 8.7 illustrates the development of binary search logic from a programming perspective. The heart of the binary search is the determination of the proper midpoint element so that the next comparison can be performed. In order to always be able to calculate a midpoint for the remaining segment of the table, the program must keep track of

### FIGURE 8.6 The Binary Search

A comparison process whereby the search key is compared first with the midpoint element, and successive searches are made at the midpoints of remaining table segments until a matching value is found or no more comparisons can be made. (Figure 8.5 explains the calculation of the various midpoints.)

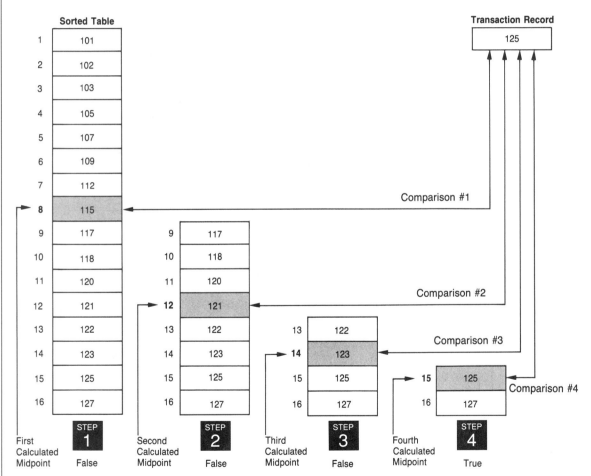

The numbered steps in this figure correspond to the comparison steps as follows:

Step 1: The first comparison is made.

Step 2: If the first comparison is false and the search key is > table argument, then a second comparison is made at the second calculated midpoint.

Step 3: If the second comparison is false, and the search key is > table argument, then a third comparison is made at the third calculated midpoint.

Step 4: If the third comparison is false, and the search key is > table argument, then a fourth comparison is made at the fourth calculated midpoint. Since the comparison is true, the search ends.

the *lower* and *upper bounds* of the table segments. In the beginning, the lower bound is simply the first element of the table, and the upper bound is the last element of the table. The midpoint at which the comparison is to take place is calculated by adding the element locations of the lower bound and upper bound together and dividing by two. Any remainder is ignored.

In step 1, this midpoint is calculated to be 5 [(1 + 9) / 2]. Since the search key, 114, is not equal to TAB (MID-POINT), 109, then the second searching iteration occurs. In step 2, before this second comparison is made, the second midpoint is calculated to be 7 [(6 + 9) / 2]. The new lower bound becomes the old midpoint plus 1 (5 + 1 = 6), and the upper bound stays the same (9). The search key value, 114, is compared this time with the value 112 [TAB (MID-POINT)]. Because the comparison result is again *false*, a subsequent midpoint is calculated and the search comparison repeated. The new lower bound becomes the old midpoint plus 1 (7 + 1 = 8). The subsequent midpoint is calculated to be 8 [(8 + 9) / 2]. The search key value of 114 is compared this time with the value 114 at TAB (MID-POINT). This time, on the fourth try, the comparison result is *true*. In this case, it took four searches to locate the value in a table size of 16. It could, however, take a

maximum of five searches to locate a value in a table with 16 elements, if the value for which the search is made is located in the last element of the table. It would require one additional search, with the new midpoint at 16 [(16 + 16) / 2].

## Binary Search Efficiency

How efficient is this search technique? In a table of only 16 elements, it may not impress you with its efficiency. However, as pointed out earlier, the table elements must number more than 50 before any significant efficiency is detected. A table with only 16 elements is used in this discussion strictly to prevent an unnecessarily long trace of search logic. Now, to answer the question. The maximum number of searches required in a binary search is represented by N + 1 (or M), where N represents the exponent in the formula that follows. Assume a table size of 32.

$$\text{Table Size (T)} = 2^N \quad \text{or } 32 = 2^5$$
$$M = N + 1 \quad \text{or } \mathbf{6} = 5 + 1$$

(The maximum number of comparisons in a table size (T) of 32 is **6**.)

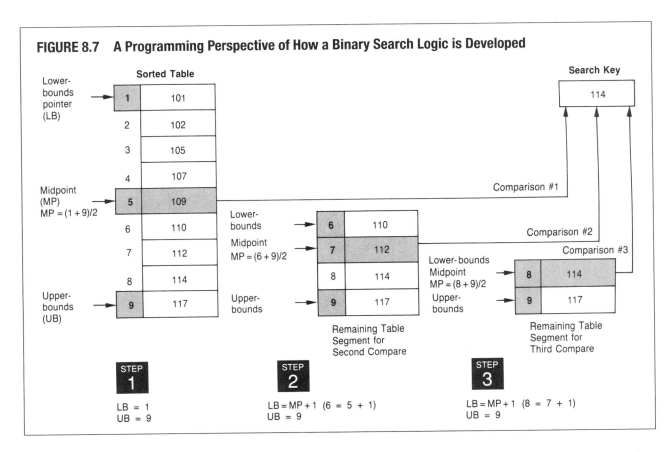

**FIGURE 8.7    A Programming Perspective of How a Binary Search Logic is Developed**

The exponent 5, plus 1, yields the actual number of comparisons, 6. Compare this with the 16 required searches (on the average) to locate the same value with a sequential search (32/2). In Figure 8.4, with 16 elements, it will require a maximum of five searches, since $16 = 2^4$, and the exponent 4, plus 1, equals 5. Just remember to add 1 to the size of the exponent to give the maximum number of searches in a binary search. The maximum number of comparisons can be expressed as:

$$M = [\log_2 N] + 1.$$

For example, $\log_2 32 = 5$; therefore, $M = N + 1$ or 6.

# A Payroll Listing Using a Binary Search of the Valid Employee Table

In Application 7.1, the Valid Employee Table has only seven elements. A small table facilitates the process of explaining the table-searching logic. But in the real business world, a company will probably have many more than seven employees! Let's suppose the company has 50 employees and wants a table of valid employees to be loaded, sorted, and searched. Because this table will be far too large for a sequential search, we will use the binary search technique instead. Fifty was chosen to make the data file a reasonable length; 500 would be a more realistic number to show the power of a binary search.

**Structured Flowchart.** For a binary search, logic modifications shown in Exhibit 8.29 would be made to the structured flowchart previously shown in Exhibit 7.7 of Chapter 7.

The only change to make in LOAD-VALID-EMPLOYEE-TABLE is to alter the upper limit in the DoWhile block from 7 to 50. The logic of LOOK-UP-SSN is the only module modification. The new binary search in Exhibit 8.29 simply replaces the old sequential table search (note the advantage of modular design!). At this point, the table would require sorting. Remember, however, you are going to assume that the file is in sequence; hence, so will the table be, once the loading process is complete.

The LOOK-UP-SSN module starts off by initializing FOUND-SWITCH equal to spaces (instead of NO). The next block establishes a LOWERBOUND = 1 and an UPPERBOUND = 50. This is followed by a DoWhile structure where FOUND-SWITCH is compared with YES or NO. If the content of FOUND-SWITCH is equal to either YES or NO, control passes to RETURN; otherwise, COMPARE-LOOP is executed. In a binary search, the program must set a switch if the value is found, but the program must also set a switch to some other value if the value is *not* found. In sequential searches, the

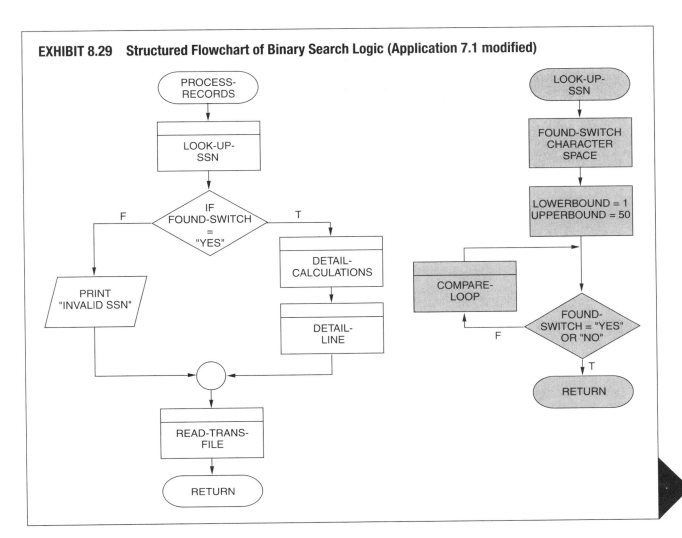

**EXHIBIT 8.29** Structured Flowchart of Binary Search Logic (Application 7.1 modified)

**EXHIBIT 8.29    (Cont.)**

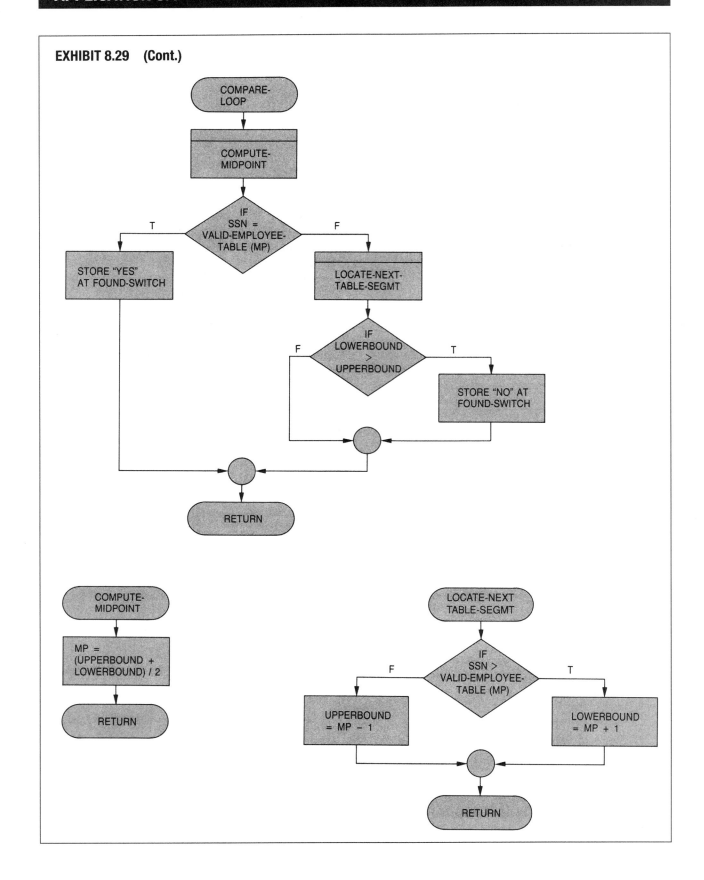

program checks to see if either the value is found or the end of the table is encountered. In a binary search, it is unlikely that the physical end of the table agrees with the logical end (that is, with the last calculated midpoint); therefore, it is necessary to set a switch regardless of whether the value is found or *not*. This will be clarified a little later in the program logic.

The COMPARE-LOOP module contains the heart of the searching process. It is here that the midpoint is calculated each time through the loop. The midpoint (MP) is calculated as the sum of the lower bound and upper bound values divided by 2. The first midpoint and all successive midpoints are calculated from the COMPUTE-MIDPOINT block in the COMPARE-LOOP module.

Once the midpoint is calculated, the search key (SSN) is compared with the table key [VALID-EM-PLOYEE-TABLE (MP)]. If the comparison result is false, then the predefined module called LOCATE-NEXT-TABLE-SEGMT is executed. It is here that the program determines in which remaining table half the search key value is to be sought. If the value is to be sought in the first half of the table, the upper bound is adjusted to the midpoint value *minus one*. On the other hand, if the value is to be sought in the second half of the table, the lower bound is adjusted to the midpoint value *plus one*.

Once the LOCATE-NEXT-TABLE-SEGMT module is finished and control is regained at the decision block beneath the call to this module, the next step is to determine whether there are more ele-

ments to be searched. This is done by determining if the calculated lower bound value is greater than the upper bound value. As long as the upper bound value is greater than the lower bound value, elements remain with which the search key can be compared. If the lower bound value becomes greater than the upper bound, then the very last remaining element in the table has been searched, and the value "NO" is stored in FOUND-SWITCH. Conversely, in the first comparison, if SSN is equal to VALID-EMPLOYEE-TABLE (MP), the value YES is stored in FOUND-SWITCH. In either case, whether FOUND-SWITCH contains a "YES," a "NO," or remains equal to spaces, control passes back to the DoWhile structure in the LOOK-UP-SSN module. The comparison is once again made to determine if the value is found or not found. If neither of these conditions exists, it means that another comparison is required; otherwise, if FOUND-SWITCH is equal to either YES or NO, control passes back to the comparison block underneath the call to LOOK-UP-SSN in the PROCESS-RECORDS module. The next block in the PROCESS-RECORDS module tests to determine if FOUND-SWITCH equals "YES." If the comparison result is *true*, the DETAIL-CALCULATION and DETAIL-LINE modules are executed; otherwise, the message "INVALID SSN" prints.

**Pseudocode.** Exhibit 8.30 depicts the associated pseudocode for this problem.

---

**EXHIBIT 8.30   Pseudocode for Binary Search Example**

```
*process-records
    look-up-ssn
    if found-switch = "yes"
        then
            detail-calculations
            detail-line
    else
        print "invalid ssn"
    endif
    read-trans-file
    return
*look-up-ssn
    store spaces at found-switch
    store 1 at lowerbound
    store 50 at upperbound
    do until found-switch = "yes" or "no"
        compare loop
    enddo
    return
```

```
*compare-loop
    compute-mid-point
    if ssn = valid-employee-table (mp)
            store "yes" at found-switch
    else
        locate-next-table-segmt
        if lowerbound > upperbound
                store "no" at found-switch
        endif
    endif
    return
*compute-mid-point
    mp = (upperbound + lowerbound)/2
    return
*locate-next-table-segmt
    if ssn > valid-employee-table (mp)
            lowerbound = mp + 1
    else
            upperbound = mp – 1
    endif
    return
```

# SUMMARY

This chapter provides a rigorous coverage of single-dimensional table handling. Application 8.1 is a Wholesale Produce Report and illustrates the logic of a single-dimensional table lookup operation where data are extracted from the table for both output and calculation purposes. Application 8.2 deals with the production of a Sales Commission Report, which requires multiple lookups to produce each line of output. One table lookup extracts data for printing and calculation purposes, and the other lookup validates the existence of the salesperson's social security number in a table of valid social security numbers. A commission is determined from a table using positional addressing rather than a lookup procedure. The uniqueness of Application 8.2 is that it performs table lookup procedures for multiple purposes: validation, data extraction for output, and data extraction for calculation purposes. Before any processing occurs, the SSN from the transaction record must be found in the table of valid SSNs and the appropriate product number must be found before any valid processing occurs. Both Application 8.1 and 8.2 use the searching method (Method I) from Chapter 7.

Alternate searching and table loading methods are presented. A searching method (Method II) eliminates the need for a subscript save area (SAVE-SUB) like the Method I previously illustrated. Reducing SUB by one unit if the value is found in the table offsets the automatic increment of SUB when the count-controlled loop automatically increments it.

An alternate table loading method is illustrated that provides for the most common situation where the number of record values to be loaded to the table is not known at run time. This number will even vary from one run to the next. The load module logic is affected as well as the search logic used to correctly search such a table.

A third searching method is called the "in-line" PERFORM . . . VARYING . . . . This method works fine with COBOL 85 but not with either COBOL 74 or QBASIC.

Application 8.3 produces a Retail Sales Analysis Report for a Computer Parts Retailer. A parts table is searched to extract the part description, cost/unit and markup code. The part description is printed on the detail line. The cost/unit is used in determining cost. The markup code from the parts table becomes a subscript to point to a specific markup percentage in the markup table. Positional addressing is used to accomplish this because the locations of the markup percentages agree by position with the value in the markup code. The cost is multiplied by markup percentage from the markup table. The retail is the sum of cost and markup. The discount is calculated as the retail multiplied by the discount percent (extracted from a discount table) using positional addressing. The discount code is on the transaction record.

A binary search is also illustrated. This searching method becomes essential when the number of record values loaded to the table exceeds 50. The need for a binary search is imperative to reduce search time, especially in cases where on-line processing is involved and response times become critical. The search time is reduced exponentially as compared with the sequential search.

## VOCABULARY LIST

Searching Method II
Searching Method III
"in-line" PERFORM varying
Variable sized tables

## PROBLEMS

**8–1.** A schoolteacher wishes to produce a student grade report that lists each student's SSN, name, and letter grade. At the end of the report, the class grade point average is to print. Create the hierarchy chart, flowchart, and pseudocode to produce the report below.

The input consists of the student's SSN, name, and letter grade (A, B, C, D, F). The record input format follows.

| Field Name | Locations | Type |
|---|---|---|
| SSN | 1–9 | Numeric |
| Name | 10–30 | Alpha |
| Letter Grade | 32 | Alpha |

A table is searched to locate the appropriate number of grade points for any given letter grade. The table is illustrated below.

| Letter Grade | Grade Points |
|---|---|
| A | 12 |
| B | 9 |
| C | 6 |
| D | 3 |
| F | 0 |

Calculate the GPA (grade point average) for the class by accumulating each student's grade points for the class into a grand total of grade points. At the end of the run, divide the total by the product of (total students X 3). (This multiplication by 3 occurs because each course has three credit hours). Use Method I for searching. Assume a fixed Table length.

**OUTPUT REQUIRED FOR PROBLEM 8–1:**

```
                        CLASS GPA REPORT

        SSN             NAME        LETTER GRADE    GRADEPOINTS

     333333333     JOHN ANDERSON         A              12
     444444444     BILL BAKER            B               9
     555555555     BROOKE CLAYTON        A              12
     666666666     JOAN DRAKE            B               9
     777777777     DON EVANS             A              12
     888888888     RAYMOND RILEY         C               6
     999999999     RICKY RAMBO           D               3
     000000000     DONNA DOLITTLE        F               0

     TOTAL STUDENTS   8            CLASS GPA 2.625
```

**8–2.** A personnel department wishes to produce a personnel report that lists each employee's SSN, name, job type, and hourly wage. Create the hierarchy chart, flowchart, and pseudocode to produce the report.

The input consists of a personnel file with the following record input format. The data will contain at least one record with a bad job code that does not match those in the job code table discussed later. Print a message if the job code is not found in the table.

| Field Name | Location | Type |
|---|---|---|
| SSN | 1–9 | Numeric |
| Name | 10–30 | Alpha |
| Job Code | 32–35 | Alphanumeric |
| Pay Code | 37–38 | Numeric |
| Hrs-Wkd | 39–40 | Numeric |

The following Job Table and the Pay Rate Table are used in producing the personnel report. The number of entries in the Job Table may vary in size from one computer run to the next. Use Searching Method I.

| JOB TABLE | |
|---|---|
| Job Code | Job Description |
| A080 | CLERKS |
| A090 | TYPIST |
| A100 | ACCOUNTANT |
| A110 | PROGRAMMER |
| A120 | SYSTEMS ANALYST |
| E130 | ENGINEER |
| E140 | SENIOR ENGINEER |
| M150 | COMPUTER CENTER DIR |
| M200 | SYSTEMS DIRECTOR |

| PAY RATE TABLE | |
|---|---|
| Pay Code | Pay Rate |
| 01 | 6.00 |
| 02 | 7.00 |
| 03 | 20.00 |
| 04 | 25.00 |
| 05 | 30.00 |
| 06 | 35.00 |
| 07 | 40.00 |
| 08 | 45.00 |
| 09 | 50.00 |
| 10 | 60.00 |

**OUTPUT REQUIRED FOR PROBLEM 8.2:**

```
                                PERSONNEL REPORT

    SSN           NAME          JOB DESCRIPTION    PAY CODE    PAY RATE    HRS    GROSS

  111111111   DONALD ROB        ACCOUNTANT             3         20.00      40    800.00
  222222222   MARY BARKER       PROGRAMMER             4         25.00      10    250.00
  333333333   JERRY JOHNSON     CLERK                  1          6.00      30    180.00
  444444444   SUSAN SAMUEL      JOB CODE NOT FOUND     -           -
  555555555   JOHN BLACK        SYSTEMS ANALYST        6         35.00      10    350.00
  666666666   BOB GRAY          SYSTEMS DIRECTOR       8         45.00      20    900.00
```

**8–3.** An accounts receivable report is to be produced for Blister Shoe Company. Blister Shoe Company allows preferred customers to charge based on their credit ratings with the store. The down payment is computed by multiplying sales by the appropriate percentage from the down payment table. Create the hierarchy chart, flowchart, and pseudocode to produce the report. Use Search Method II.

The record input format of the transaction record is as follows.

| Field Name | Location | Type |
|---|---|---|
| Customer Number | 1–4 | N |
| Sales | 11–17 | N ($$$$$.¢¢) |
| Date | 20–25 | N (MMDDYY) |
| Dept. | 26–27 | |

The following two tables are needed for this problem.

### Customer Information Table(s)

| Customer | Name | Address | Credit Rating |
|---|---|---|---|
| 1111 | Joe Adams | Rt. 3 | 1 |
| 2222 | Don James | Box 155 | 5 |
| 6333 | Mary Barker | 112 Pine | 3 |
| 4444 | Sue Driden | 444 Oak | 4 |

NOTE: This can be viewed as four separate tables for BASIC programs or as one table in COBOL with four subelements per element.

Number of table entries may vary from one computer run to the next.

The credit rating subelement becomes the search argument to be used in locating the down payment percent charges.

### DOWN PAYMENT TABLE

| Credit Rating | Down Payment (percentage of sales) |
|---|---|
| 1 | .50 |
| 2 | .40 |
| 3 | .30 |
| 4 | .20 |
| 5 | .10 |
| 6 | .05 |

**OUTPUT REQUIRED FOR PROBLEM 8.3:**

```
DATE:    MM/DD/YY              ACCOUNTS RECEIVABLE REPORT

CUST.    NAME        ADDRESS       SALES    CREDIT   DOWN      BALANCE
NUM.                                        RATING   PAYM'T    CHARGE

1111     JOE ADAMS   RT. 3         1000.00    1      500.00    500.00
2222     DON JAMES   BOX 155       2000.00    5      200.00    1800.00
XXXX     XXXXXXXXX   XXXXXXXXX     XXXX.XX    X      XXX.XX    XXXX.XX
XXXX     XXXXXXXXX   XXXXXXXXX     XXXX.XX    X      XXX.XX    XXXX.XX
```

**8–4.** The management of Acme Auto Sales wishes to produce a sales commission report that lists the salesperson, customer, Julian date, auto make, body description, color, price, and commission. Much of these data are to be extracted from tables. The report is to print the date (spelled out) and the page number on the first line of the report. Draw the print chart and create the flowchart and pseudocode to produce the report.

The transaction record input format follows.

| Field Name | Location | Type |
|---|---|---|
| Salesperson | 1–19 | Alphanumeric |
| Customer | 20–23 | N |
| Date | 25–30 | N (MMDDYY) |
| Make code | 31–35 | Alphanumeric |
| Body code | 36 | N (values = 1 to 6) |
| Color code | 37 | N (values = 1 to 6) |
| Price | 38–42 | N ($$$$$) |

The Julian date is to be partially determined by first extracting the Julian date for the *first day* of a given month from the table.

| Month | Julian Day |
|---|---|
| JANUARY | 000 |
| FEBRUARY | 031 |
| MARCH | 059 |
| APRIL | 090 |
| MAY | 120 |
| JUNE | 151 |
| JULY | 181 |
| AUGUST | 212 |
| SEPTEMBER | 243 |
| OCTOBER | 273 |
| NOVEMBER | 304 |
| DECEMBER | 334 |

The auto make, color, body style, and commission are to be extracted from the tables below. (Hint: The commission table can actually be created using only the upper limit in the table key segment of the table(s) of corresponding values, since the program will need to compare the sales price with the upper limit in the table. If the sales price is greater than the upper limit in the table, the table search continues to the next element, etc.)

| AUTO MAKE TABLE | |
|---|---|
| Make | Description |
| ZA313 | ZEBRA |
| CA314 | CHETAH |
| BA315 | BUFFALO VAN |
| RA316 | RHINO TRUCK |

| AUTO COLOR TABLE | |
|---|---|
| Color Code | Color |
| 1 | BLUE |
| 2 | RED |
| 3 | WHITE |
| 4 | GREEN |
| 5 | GRAY |
| 6 | BROWN |

| BODY TABLE | |
|---|---|
| Body Code | Body |
| 1 | 2 DR. HT |
| 2 | 4 DR. HT |
| 3 | 2 DR. HB |
| 4 | 2 DR. CVT |
| 5 | CREW CAB |
| 6 | ST. CAB. |

| COMMISSION TABLE | |
|---|---|
| Sales Range | Comm. Pct. |
| 5000–10,000 | .05 |
| 10,001–15,000 | .06 |
| 15,001–20,000 | .07 |
| 20,001–25,000 | .08 |
| 25,001–30,000 | .09 |
| 30,001–35,000 | .10 |
| 35,001–40,000 | .11 |

NOTE: Only the upper limit of the above commission table is actually placed into the memory table (alongside the commission percent table segment).

**8–5.** Problem 8-3 is to be modified in order to produce the report shown below. Notice that subtotals print for each department. Assume that the records in the sales file are first sorted in ascending order by DEPT-NO. The second report contains summary total and record count information. Assume empty tables exist called DEPT-SUM-TAB, TOT-TAB, and COUNT-TAB, which will be used to store summary data. Draw the print chart, flowchart, and pseudocode for this problem.

```
                    ACCOUNTS RECEIVABLE REPORT
   DEPARTMENT   CUST.        NAME       SALES        DOWN        BALANCE
                NUM.                                 PAYMENT     CHARGE

      01        1111     JOE ADAMS     1000.00       500.00       500.00
      01        2222     SAM JONES     2000.00       200.00      1800.00
      XX        XXXX     XXXXXXX       XXXX.XX       XXX.XX       XXXX.XX
                                             DEPT  TOTAL     $XX,XXX.XX*

      02        XXXX     XXXXXXX       XXXX.XX       XXX.XX       XXX.XX
      02        XXXX     XXXXXXX       XXXX.XX       XXX.XX       XXX.XX
                                             DEPT  TOTAL     $XX,XXX.XX*
                                             GRAND TOTAL     $XX,XXX.XX*
```

```
                        SUMMARY A/R INFO

           DEPT          TOTAL        RECORD COUNT

           01         XX,XXX.XX            3
           02         XX,XXX.XX            2
           XX         XX,XXX.XX            X
           XX         XX,XXX.XX            X
```

NOTE: Record count simply represents the number of records per departmental group.

# 9

# Two-Dimensional Tables

## OBJECTIVES

After completing this chapter, the student will be able to:

1. Define the term *two-dimensional table*.

2. Explain how a row-and-column subscript is used to refer to an element in a two-dimensional table.

3. Explain the purpose of a two-dimensional table.

4. Discuss the two methods of accessing a two-dimensional table.

5. Explain the procedure for loading a two-dimensional table.

6. Explain how to use positional addressing with both row and column subscripts to locate an element in a two-dimensional table.

7. Explain how to find an element in a two-dimensional table by first searching a top-level table argument in order to locate the row, then tell how to find the column through positional addressing.

8. Draw a hierarchy chart and flowchart and write the pseudocode to load a two-dimensional table from a table file.

9. Draw a hierarchy chart and flowchart and write the pseudocode to extract, from a two-dimensional table, data that will be used in further processing steps. Use positional addressing.

10. Draw a flowchart and write the pseudocode to search a top-level table argument with the proper key to locate the appropriate row. Identify the column, using positional addressing.

The previous examples of table processing have dealt with single-dimensional (one-level) tables, defined as an array of related items, each of which can be referenced by a table name and a subscript. The single-dimensional table normally contains single-value elements; in COBOL, however, an element can actually consist of multiple subelements or subfields. The main advantage of a single-dimensional table is that any element can be referenced with only one subscript. But in many business computer problems, it is necessary to extract data from tables with more than one level, that is, more than one point of reference.

## THE TWO-DIMENSIONAL TABLE

A **two-dimensional table** has two levels (or two points of reference). The major subdivision in such a table is called the **row**. The row is further subdivided into **columns**. This arrangement is sometimes referred to as a **chart**, or **matrix**. In order to refer to a specific element in the table, a subscript points to the row where the data is first classified, and a column subscript points to the column in the row where the specific item of data is stored.

Every day, people refer to charts for useful information. For instance, a traveler uses a mileage chart to determine the distance between two cities. The mileage chart requires two reference points in order to show a distance. The traveler first looks down the rows in the left-hand column to locate the departure city and then looks across the columns at the top of the chart to find the arrival city. In the block where the row and column cross, the traveler finds the number representing the distance in miles between the two cities.

## Examples of Two-Dimensional Tables

One use of a two-dimensional table is illustrated in Figure 9.1. A salesperson earns a commission that is based on (1) the salesperson's job classification (row) and (2) the category of merchandise (column) he or she sells. In this table of values, you can see that Sales Rep 1 (in row 1) who sells furniture (column 3), earns a commission of 4 percent. No search is required to locate the commission rate; it is found through positional addressing.

Figure 9.2 is a two-dimensional table of shipping charges. A company that ships building materials bases its shipping charges on both the weight and the category of the material. In this table, a search is first made for the weight range that includes the weight of a given shipment. This locates the appropriate row; then the merchandise category number positionally locates the column with the appropriate charges. For example, a shipment of metal weighing 800 pounds has a shipping charge of $7.00.

## Referencing Elements by Row and Column

Figure 9.3 depicts the elements of the commission rate table, which has three rows and four columns. The rows run horizontally and the columns vertically. As in the previous example, a value is located using row and column subscripts. The **row subscript** appears first and the **column subscript** appears second. Figure 9.3 shows the element addresses in (row, column) format. Look, for exam-

---

**FIGURE 9.1    A Two-Dimensional Table of Sales Commission Rates**

| | Job Class | Merchandise Category | | | |
|---|---|---|---|---|---|
| | | Garden | Sporting Goods | Furniture | Jewelry |
| 1 | Sales Rep. 1 | .02 | .03 | .04 | .05 |
| 2 | Sales Rep. 2 | .03 | .04 | .05 | .06 |
| 3 | Sales Rep. 3 | .04 | .05 | .06 | .07 |
| | | 1 | 2 | 3 | 4 |

---

**FIGURE 9.2    A Two-Dimensional Table of Shipping Charges**

| Weight (lbs.) Not to Exceed | Merchandise Category | | | |
|---|---|---|---|---|
| | Lumber 1 | Metal 2 | Concrete 3 | Glass 4 |
| 00500 | 0500 | 0400 | 0450 | 2250 |
| 01000 | 0900 | 0700 | 0850 | 4450 |
| 01500 | 1200 | 1000 | 1050 | 6650 |
| 03000 | 1900 | 1500 | 1700 | 7750 |
| 05000 | 2400 | 1800 | 1950 | 8850 |
| 10000 | 3300 | 2900 | 2700 | 9488 |

NOTE:    Shipping charges is in a $$.¢¢ format (i.e., 1800 is actually $18.00).

ple, at the subscript notation (3,4) in the lower right corner of the table; the 3 indicates the value is found in the third row, and the 4 indicates the value is found in the fourth column.

**Pointing to a Specific Element.** Figure 9.4 shows the commission rate table once again. The notation shown refers to the value found in the second row, third column. COMMISSION-TABLE (2,3) is highlighted. The percentage found here is .05. COMMISSION-TABLE (3,4) is also highlighted. The value found here is .07.

## Accessing a Two-Dimensional Table

The same two methods explained in Chapters 7 and 8 for accessing data in a single-dimensional table apply to two-dimensional tables. Data can be accessed either by *positional addressing*, using no explicit table argument, or by a *table search*, using an explicit table argument. This table argument can be either an exact value or a **range-step value** (a value that represents either the bottom or top of a range of values) that is searched for in order to locate the appropriate row. When the table argument allows access to a row, it is called a **top-level explicit search argument**. If it allows access to a particular column, it is a **bottom-level explicit search argument**. In most cases, the top-level explicit argument arrangement is used.

Panel A of Figure 9.5 shows a table element referenced with positional addressing. No explicit table key (or table argument) is used. The content of one field (JOB) on a transaction record becomes the row subscript, and the content of another field (CATEGORY) becomes the column subscript. In this case, TAB-COM (JOB, CATEGORY) references the highlighted element (the value .03) found at the intersection of row 2 and column 1.

Panel B of Figure 9.5 illustrates a two-dimensional table that uses an explicit table key (or table argument). In this case, the table row is located by first searching a list of table arguments for weights in the maximum, or upper, range in a list of weight ranges. In this type of table, also called a **range-step table**, the purpose of the search is to locate an appropriate *range* of values rather than a *specific* value. The table of functions appears next to the

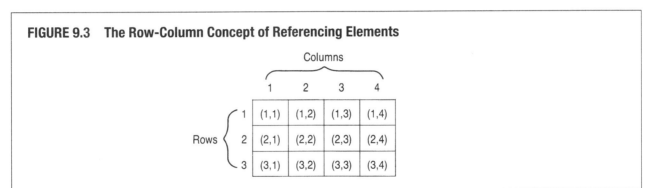

**FIGURE 9.3   The Row-Column Concept of Referencing Elements**

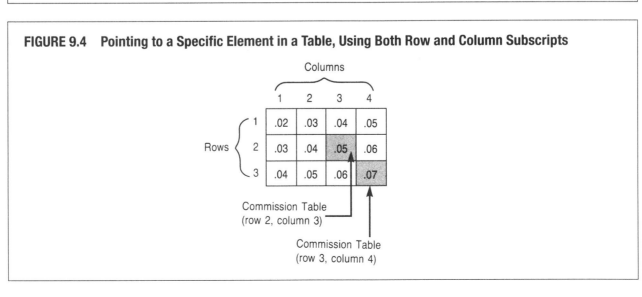

**FIGURE 9.4   Pointing to a Specific Element in a Table, Using Both Row and Column Subscripts**

FIGURE 9.5 **Categories of Two-Dimensional Tables**

**Panel A—No Explicit Key (table argument)**

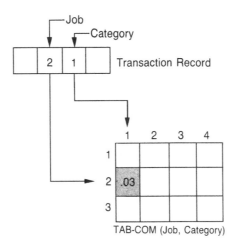

TAB-COM (Job, Category)

**Panel B—Explicit Table Key (table argument)**

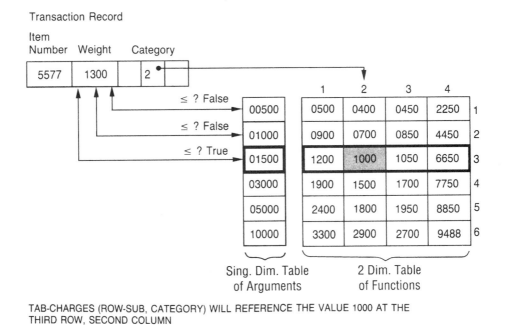

TAB-CHARGES (ROW-SUB, CATEGORY) WILL REFERENCE THE VALUE 1000 AT THE
THIRD ROW, SECOND COLUMN

table of arguments. With COBOL, both of these tables can be conceptualized and defined as just one two-dimensional table. In BASIC, the argument table is defined as a single-dimensional table separate from the two-dimensional function table.

In panel B, the weight from the transaction record (WT) is the search key. The search key is compared with the various table argument values. When it is either less than or equal to the upper limit value, the row is located that contains the appropriate shipping charge. Here the explicit argument is at the row level. It required a table search to locate the proper row. Next, the column is located, not with an explicit key, but simply through positional addressing, as in the previous example. The merchandise category field (CATEGORY) is the column subscript. In this example, TAB-CHARGES (ROW-SUB, CATEGORY) references the highlighted value of 1000.

## LOADING A TWO-DIMENSIONAL TABLE

To access data in a two-dimensional table, the data must first be either loaded from an input file or initialized with literal values. Both of these procedures resemble those in Chapters 7 and 8. Figure 9.6 illustrates the loading of the two-dimensional commission rate table. The table file consists of records that each contain only one table element value. The table file (A) consists of 12 records. The loading process occurs by the row, placing the first four records consecutively into the first four columns of the first row. The next four records are loaded one by one into the four columns of the second row, and the last four records are loaded into the four columns of the third row. This method of loading tables is referred to as **row major** and is nearly universal. [In FORTRAN, however, a table load procedure loads first by the column instead of

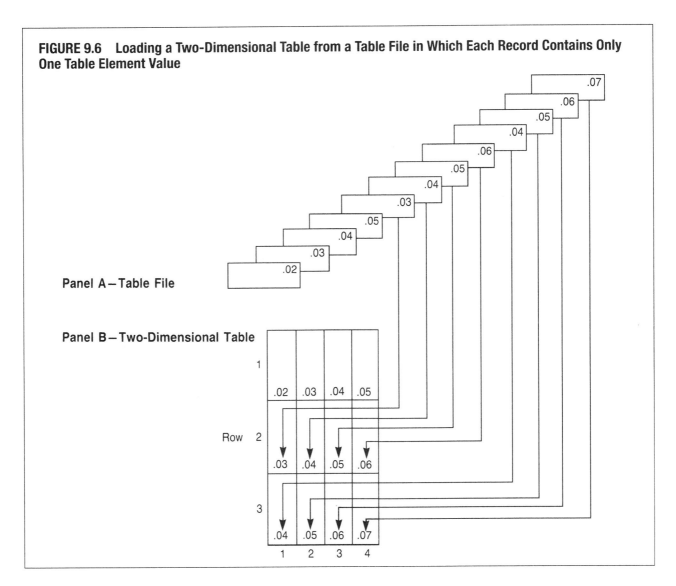

**FIGURE 9.6    Loading a Two-Dimensional Table from a Table File in Which Each Record Contains Only One Table Element Value**

Panel A—Table File

Panel B—Two-Dimensional Table

by the row. This method is called **column major**. The row and column subscripts are simply reversed, with the column subscript appearing first, followed by the row subscript. This fact is relevant only for the programmer who plans to call a FORTRAN subroutine containing two-dimensional tables.] The twelve records are loaded one by one, starting at element location (1,1). The order of the table load proceeds according to the subscript locations that follow: (1,1), (1,2), (1,3), (1,4), (2,1), (2,2), (2,3), (2,4), (3,1), (3,2), (3,3), and (3,4).

## Flowchart Logic for Loading a Two-Dimensional Table Using Nested Definite Iteration

The programming logic for loading the two-dimensional table shown in Figure 9.6 is presented in Figure 9.7 (panel A). This technique uses the **nested definite iteration method**. The TABLE-LOAD module first invokes the READ-TAB-RECORD module to read the first table record. Next, ROW-SUB (the row subscript) is initialized to 1. The logic now consists of two levels of definite iteration logic. The first level starts with a condition test to determine if ROW-SUB is greater than 3. The pur-

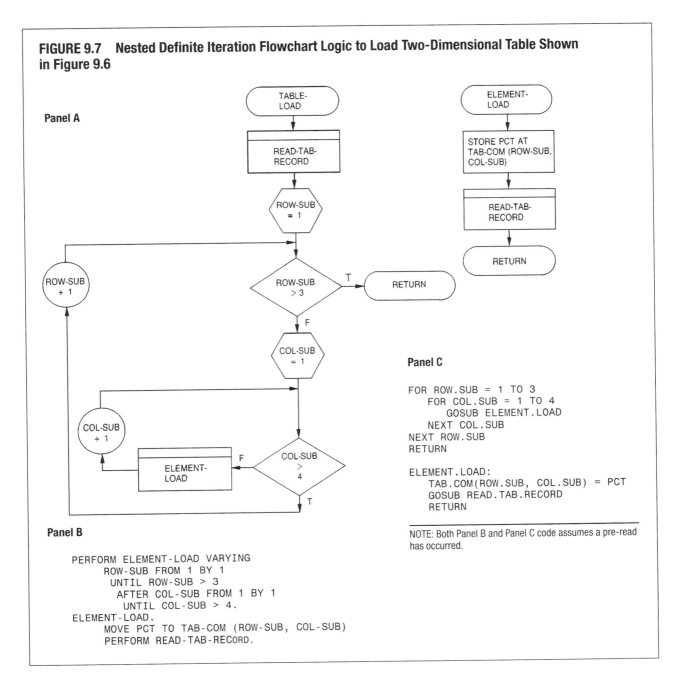

**FIGURE 9.7    Nested Definite Iteration Flowchart Logic to Load Two-Dimensional Table Shown in Figure 9.6**

**Panel A**

**Panel C**

```
FOR ROW.SUB = 1 TO 3
   FOR COL.SUB = 1 TO 4
      GOSUB ELEMENT.LOAD
   NEXT COL.SUB
NEXT ROW.SUB
RETURN

ELEMENT.LOAD:
   TAB.COM(ROW.SUB, COL.SUB) = PCT
   GOSUB READ.TAB.RECORD
   RETURN
```

NOTE: Both Panel B and Panel C code assumes a pre-read has occurred.

**Panel B**

```
PERFORM ELEMENT-LOAD VARYING
     ROW-SUB FROM 1 BY 1
       UNTIL ROW-SUB > 3
         AFTER COL-SUB FROM 1 BY 1
           UNTIL COL-SUB > 4.
ELEMENT-LOAD.
     MOVE PCT TO TAB-COM (ROW-SUB, COL-SUB)
     PERFORM READ-TAB-RECORD.
```

pose of the first DoWhile is to determine if all three rows of the table are loaded. If the condition test is false, the program path continues with the initializing of the column subscript (COL-SUB) to 1. The second level of definite iteration logic then follows. The purpose of the second DoWhile condition is to determine if all the columns of a given row are loaded. As long as the condition is false, the ELEMENT-LOAD module is repeatedly invoked; and, each time, the respective table record value (PCT) is loaded into its respective table element, TAB-COM (ROW-SUB, COL-SUB). Once the value is loaded and the next record is read, COL-SUB is increased and the loop repeated. This inside loop continues until COL-SUB is greater than 4, at which point all the elements of the first row have been loaded.

Once the first row is loaded (i.e., COL-SUB is > 4), the next step is the ROW-SUB increment. The outside definite iteration loop is repeated, as it first compares the contents of ROW-SUB with the value 3. Since the comparison result is still false (2 is not > 3), the program path continues by reinitializing COL-SUB to 1, thus setting up the correct subscript location to repeat the loading process for the second row of the table (ROW-SUB = 2 and COL-SUB = 1). The same process would be repeated to load the third row of the table. Before leaving the flowchart logic, let's recall that PCT is stored at TAB-COM (ROW-SUB, COL-SUB), as both row and column subscripts are necessary to load the elements properly.

Panel B of Figure 9.7 depicts the COBOL coding segment to accomplish this logic. This is Format 4 of the Perform command, often called **Perform . . . Varying . . . After**. Panel C shows the equivalent QBASIC commands to carry out this flowchart logic. In BASIC, **nested For . . . Next** commands are needed. The outer For . . . Next loop controls the row subscript, while the inner For . . . Next controls the column subscript increment. The body of the loop loads the table record value into the appropriate table element.

### Step-by-Step Trace of Loading a Two-Dimensional Table

The manipulation of row and column subscripts is described in the following step-by-step trace of a two-dimensional table load. Figure 9.8 illustrates the processing steps to load the first five records of the table file in Figure 9.6. By examining the execution process, you can trace the subsequent records with little difficulty.

Step 1A:   The first table record (.02) is read into the input area (PCT).

Step 1B:   ROW-SUB is initialized to 1 for the purpose of pointing to the first row.

Step 1C:   This step in the flowchart performs the condition test of the DoWhile structure. The comparison determines if the row subscript (ROW-SUB) is greater than 3. (When this condition becomes true, all three rows will have been loaded.) Here the content of ROW-SUB is 1; therefore, the comparison result (until ROW-SUB > 3) is *false.*

Step 1D:   Since the result of the first comparison test (a) is *false*, this step initializes the column subscript (COL-SUB) to 1.

Step 1E:   This phase of the flowchart handles the actual loading of the values into the table. The inner loop of the flowchart loads the value into the appropriate table element, reads the next record, and advances the column subscript pointer so that the next value will be loaded into the appropriate slot of the table. The comparison test made here determines if COL-SUB is greater than 4 (the maximum number of columns per row). If the comparison result is *true*, then program execution continues with the row subscript increment. In this case, the comparison result is *false*, since 1 is not greater than 4.

Step 1F:   Since the comparison result is false, the ELEMENT-LOAD module is invoked.

Step 1G:   In the ELEMENT-LOAD module, the PCT field from the record is stored at the (1,1) position of the table.

Step 1H:   The second command of the ELEMENT-LOAD module is to read the next record (.03) into the input area (PCT).

Step 1I:   After the ELEMENT-LOAD module has completed its execution, this step increases the column subscript (COL-SUB) by 1, thus completing the first iteration.

Step 2A:   The DoWhile condition (b) is tested to determine if COL-SUB is greater than 4. The COL-SUB value, 2, is not greater than 4; therefore, the comparison result is *false.*

Step 2B:   Since the comparison is false, the ELEMENT-LOAD module is once again invoked.

Step 2C:   The PCT field is stored at the (1,2) position of the table.

Step 2D:   The third record (.04) is read into the input area (PCT).

Step 2E:   COL-SUB is increased by 1. Now the content of COL-SUB is 3.

Step 3A: The DoWhile condition in Figure 9.7 is tested to determine if COL-SUB is greater than 4. The comparison result is once again *false*.

Step 3B: The ELEMENT-LOAD module is invoked.

Step 3C: The PCT field (.04) is stored at (1,3) of the table.

Step 3D: The fourth record (.05) is read.

Step 3E: COL-SUB is increased by 1, giving it a value of 4.

Step 4A: The DoWhile condition is tested to determine if COL-SUB is greater than 4. Since 4 is not greater than 4, the comparison result is *false*.

Step 4B: The ELEMENT-LOAD module is invoked again.

Step 4C: The PCT field (.05) is stored at the (1,4) position of the table.

Step 4D: The fifth record (.03) is read.

Step 4E: COL-SUB is increased by 1, giving it the value of 5.

Step 5A: The DoWhile condition is tested to determine if COL-SUB is greater than 4. The COL-SUB value of 5 is greater than 4; therefore, the condition test is *true*.

(Now, program control passes to the outer loop.)

**FIGURE 9.8  Step-by-Step Trace of the Loading of a Two-Dimensional Table (First five records)**

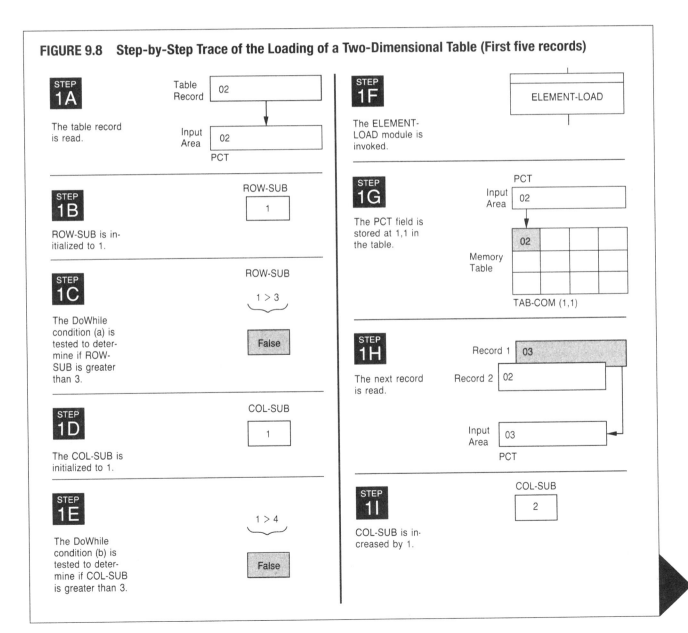

Step 5B:   ROW-SUB is increased by 1, giving it the value of 2.

Step 5C:   The DoWhile condition is tested to determine if ROW-SUB is greater than 3. The comparison result is *false*, since 2 is not greater than 3.

Step 5D:   The program execution then continues into the inner loop area where COL-SUB is initialized back to 1. This sets up the row and column subscripts to point to the element position (2,1).

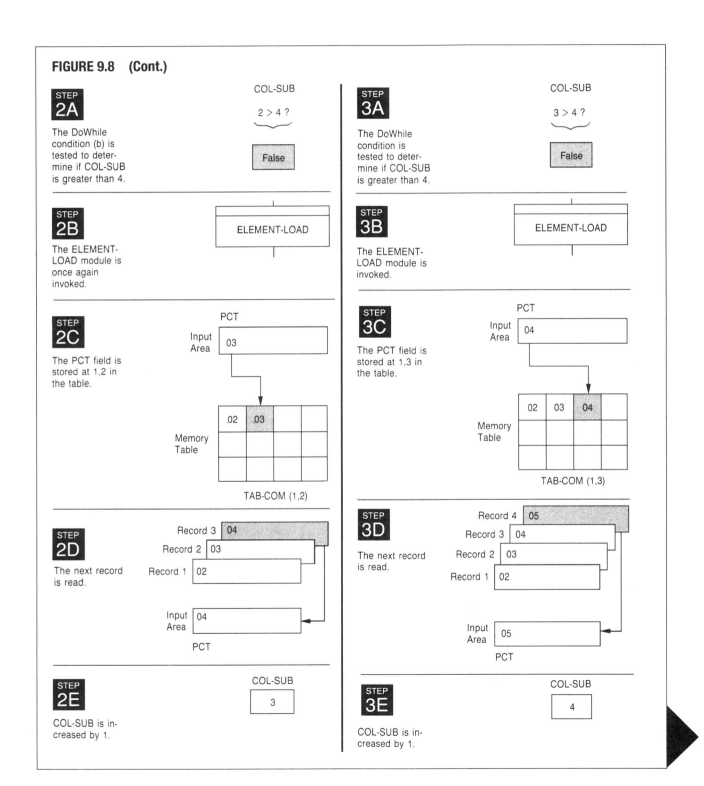

**FIGURE 9.8    (Cont.)**

**STEP 2A**
The DoWhile condition (b) is tested to determine if COL-SUB is greater than 4.

COL-SUB
2 > 4 ?
False

**STEP 2B**
The ELEMENT-LOAD module is once again invoked.

ELEMENT-LOAD

**STEP 2C**
The PCT field is stored at 1,2 in the table.

PCT
Input Area    03

Memory Table
| .02 | .03 | | |
| | | | |
| | | | |

TAB-COM (1,2)

**STEP 2D**
The next record is read.

Record 3    04
Record 2    03
Record 1    02

Input Area    04
PCT

**STEP 2E**
COL-SUB is increased by 1.

COL-SUB
3

**STEP 3A**
The DoWhile condition is tested to determine if COL-SUB is greater than 4.

COL-SUB
3 > 4 ?
False

**STEP 3B**
The ELEMENT-LOAD module is invoked.

ELEMENT-LOAD

**STEP 3C**
The PCT field is stored at 1,3 in the table.

PCT
Input Area    04

Memory Table
| 02 | 03 | 04 | |
| | | | |
| | | | |

TAB-COM (1,3)

**STEP 3D**
The next record is read.

Record 4    05
Record 3    04
Record 2    03
Record 1    02

Input Area    05
PCT

**STEP 3E**
COL-SUB is increased by 1.

COL-SUB
4

FIGURE 9.8 (Cont.)

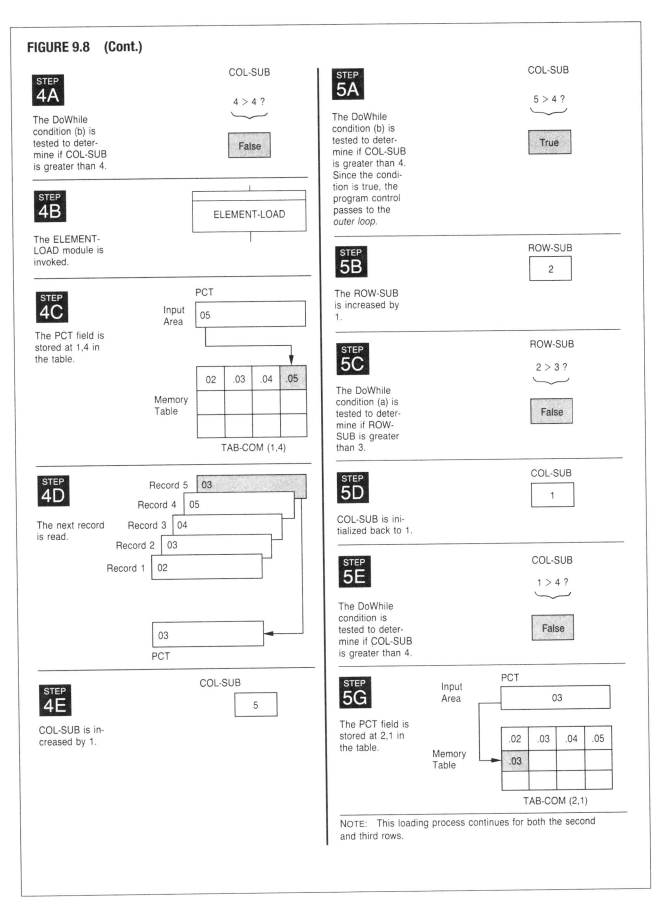

**STEP 4A**
The DoWhile condition (b) is tested to determine if COL-SUB is greater than 4.

COL-SUB
4 > 4 ?
False

**STEP 4B**
The ELEMENT-LOAD module is invoked.

ELEMENT-LOAD

**STEP 4C**
The PCT field is stored at 1,4 in the table.

PCT
Input Area  05

Memory Table

| 02 | .03 | .04 | .05 |
|----|-----|-----|-----|
|    |     |     |     |
|    |     |     |     |

TAB-COM (1,4)

**STEP 4D**
The next record is read.

Record 5  03
Record 4  05
Record 3  04
Record 2  03
Record 1  02

03
PCT

**STEP 4E**
COL-SUB is increased by 1.

COL-SUB
5

**STEP 5A**
The DoWhile condition (b) is tested to determine if COL-SUB is greater than 4. Since the condition is true, the program control passes to the *outer loop*.

COL-SUB
5 > 4 ?
True

**STEP 5B**
The ROW-SUB is increased by 1.

ROW-SUB
2

**STEP 5C**
The DoWhile condition (a) is tested to determine if ROW-SUB is greater than 3.

ROW-SUB
2 > 3 ?
False

**STEP 5D**
COL-SUB is initialized back to 1.

COL-SUB
1

**STEP 5E**
The DoWhile condition is tested to determine if COL-SUB is greater than 4.

COL-SUB
1 > 4 ?
False

**STEP 5G**
The PCT field is stored at 2,1 in the table.

PCT
Input Area  03

Memory Table

| .02 | .03 | .04 | .05 |
|-----|-----|-----|-----|
| .03 |     |     |     |
|     |     |     |     |

TAB-COM (2,1)

NOTE: This loading process continues for both the second and third rows.

Step 5E:  The DoWhile condition is tested to determine if COL-SUB is greater than 4. Since 1 is not greater than 4, the comparison result is *false*.

Step 5F:  The ELEMENT-LOAD module is invoked.

Step 5G:  The PCT field (.03) is stored at the (2,1) element in the table.

(In steps 5B through 5G, notice the manipulation of the subscript to point to a subsequent row and the sliding back of the column pointer to the first column.)

This loading process continues for the second and third rows.

---

**FIGURE 9.9    Loading a Two-Dimensional Table of Table Functions and a Single-Dimensional Table of Table Arguments**

(Using multiple fields per record—record loads one row)

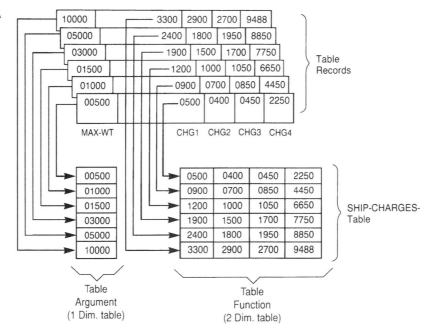

Table
Argument
(1 Dim. table)

Table
Function
(2 Dim. table)

---

**Panel B—COBOL OCCURS Clause to Define Table**

```
01 SHIP-CHARGES-TABLE.
   05 TAB-CHARGES OCCURS 6 TIMES.
      10 MAX-WT PIC 9(5)
      10 COLUMN-AMOUNT-TAB
         OCCURS 4 TIMES PIC 99V99.
```

NOTE:  In COBOL, one entire table record can be stored in one row with one move operation, using a group move. In the COBOL code, this table can be conceptualized as one table.

---

**Panel C—BASIC Dimension Statement to Define Tables**

```
DIM MAXTAB(6), CHARGETAB (6,4)
```

NOTE:  In BASIC, to load the four columns of a row requires four separate table assignments. In the BASIC code, this must be set up as two tables (one single-dimensional table of arguments, and one two-dimensional table of table functions).

## Loading a Two-Dimensional Table of Table Functions and a Single-Dimensional Table of Table Arguments

The table file shown in Figure 9.9 contains a table row in each record. Each table record contains a table argument and a corresponding set of four table functions. The first field in the record, MAX-WT (the table argument), is loaded into its respective element in a single-dimensional table. The four subsequent fields (shipping charges) in the table record are loaded into the four respective columns of the applicable row. These fields are the table functions. In COBOL, if the table is defined properly, the entire record can be stored column by column into one row of the two-dimensional table. A corresponding single-dimensional table for the table arguments would not be needed. In BASIC, however, one table must be defined for the arguments (maximum weights) and another table separately established for the two-dimensional table of table functions (shipping charges). Panel A in Figure 9.9 shows the loading procedure for the various

elements of the table argument and the various rows of the table functions.

Panel B of Figure 9.9 illustrates the OCCURS clause in COBOL needed to define the table(s). Panel C depicts the dimension (DIM) statement needed to define the tables for BASIC.

Figure 9.10 illustrates the table-load process for the program written in COBOL. This TABLE-LOAD module resembles the one shown in Chapter 7 for loading a single-dimensional table. There is only one level of definite iteration. The row subscript (ROW-SUB) is the only subscript to be altered, because the entire table record is loaded into the table row. The characters of the table record are loaded one by one, from left to right, into the row of the table. This is called a **group move** in COBOL. The group move causes the record image to be reproduced in the row of the table. Because the entire string of characters is loaded with one command, there is no need to adjust the value of the column subscript.

In BASIC, there is no such thing as a group move; each column value must be loaded with a

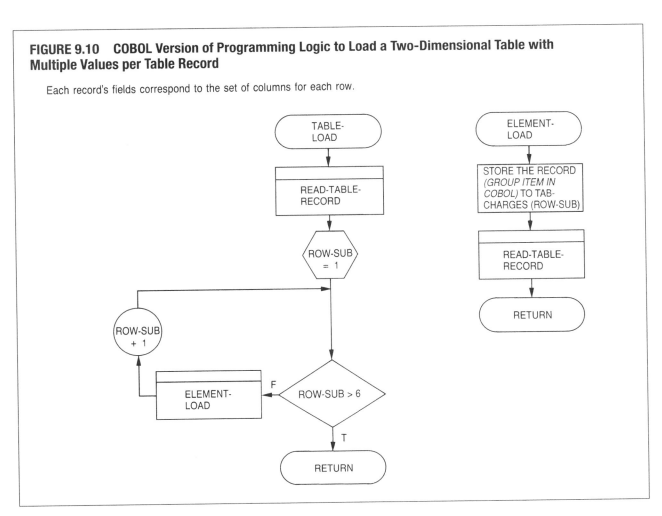

**FIGURE 9.10    COBOL Version of Programming Logic to Load a Two-Dimensional Table with Multiple Values per Table Record**

Each record's fields correspond to the set of columns for each row.

separate command. Figure 9.11 illustrates a definite iteration loop identical to that in Figure 9.10. The ELEMENT-LOAD module contains separate store commands that load the elements of the argument table and the four shipping charge amounts into the columns of the two-dimensional table of functions. In the store commands that load the four columns in a row, you will see an element that is referenced using both a variable and a literal subscript. For example, the second entry in the ELEMENT-LOAD module in Figure 9.11 is STORE CHG1 AT CHARGES-TAB (ROW-SUB, 1). CHG1

can be loaded into the appropriate row of the table, but only into the *first* column of that row.

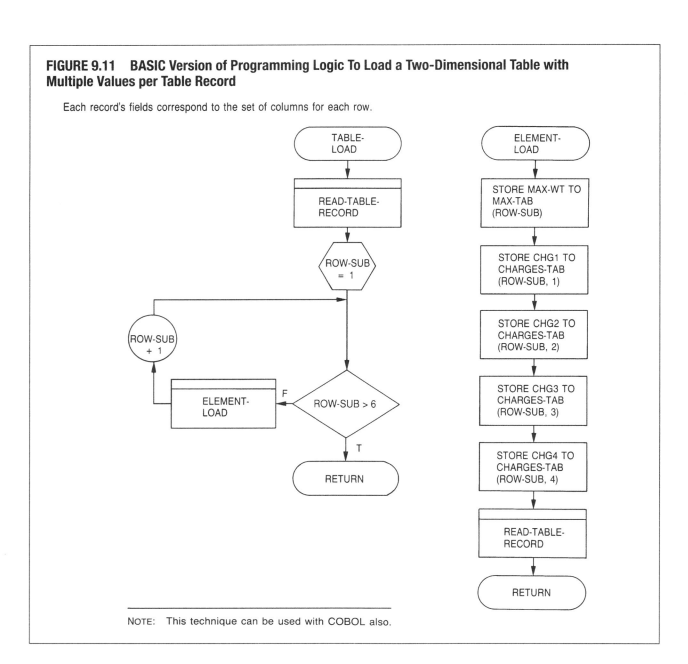

**FIGURE 9.11    BASIC Version of Programming Logic To Load a Two-Dimensional Table with Multiple Values per Table Record**

Each record's fields correspond to the set of columns for each row.

NOTE:   This technique can be used with COBOL also.

## Table Handling with Positional Addressing (Sales Commission Report)

### Program Requirements

The management of a department store chain wishes to produce a sales commission report that lists the salesperson's number (SSN), job classification, merchandise category (or department), sales amount, commission rate, and commission amount. The commission rate varies according to (1) the job classification code and (2) the category of merchandise the salesperson sells. The commission rate is to be extracted from a two-dimensional table, using these two codes as subscripts. Positional addressing will locate the element.

### Output Design

Exhibit 9.1 illustrates the sample report, and Exhibit 9.2 depicts the associated print chart.

### Input Design

Exhibit 9.3 shows the record layout for the sales transaction file and the commission rate table file.

### Tables

Exhibit 9.4 illustrates the two-dimensional sales commission table. The rows refer to the appropriate job class, and the columns refer to a specific merchandise category. The three job classifications are sales rep 1, sales rep 2, and sales rep 3. The four merchandise categories are (1) garden, (2) sporting goods, (3) furniture, and (4) jewelry.

### Test Cases

Exhibit 9.5 contains the necessary test data to be used in running this program.

**EXHIBIT 9.1  Sample Report of Sales Commission Report (Positional Addressing)**

```
                    SALES COMMISSION REPORT

   SALESPERSON  JOB CLASS   MERCHANDISE   SALES     RATE   COMMISSION
                             CATEGORY
                              (DEPT)
     444444444      1           3        5,000.00    4%      200.00
     555555555      2           4        3,000.00    6%      180.00
     666666666      3           1        1,000.00    4%       40.00
     777777777      2           2        3,500.00    4%      140.00

                              TOTALS    12,500.00            560.00
```

**EXHIBIT 9.2  Printer Spacing Chart for Sales Commission Report (Two-Dimensional Table)**

## Program Design

Exhibit 9.6 illustrates the general design of the program logic in hierarchy chart form. The general structure of the modules has not changed.

**Structured Flowchart.** Exhibit 9.7 depicts the structured flowchart logic for this problem. The START-UP module contains a LOAD-COMMISSION-RATE-TABLE module, the purpose of which is to load the commission rates into a two-dimensional table. The process records module looks the same as in previous programs. The four modules are (1) DETAIL-CALCULATIONS, to determine commission rate and compute commissions, (2) ACCUMULATION (since the sales and commission amounts are accumulated in order to print

final totals), (3) DETAIL-LINE, to print the detail line, and (4) READ-TRANS-FILE, to read the next transaction record.

LOAD-COMMISSION-RATE-TABLE, as illustrated in Figure 9.7, includes an initial read block, which reads the first table record. ROW-SUB is set to 1. The condition is tested to determine if ROW-SUB is greater than 3. If the comparison result is *false*, execution resumes with the next block. COL-SUB is then initialized to 1, and the inner loop is executed. The DoWhile condition is tested to determine if COL-SUB is greater than 4. If the comparison result is *false*, ELEMENT-LOAD is invoked. Once the element is loaded and the next record is read, COL-SUB is increased by 1 and the loop is repeated. This inner loop is repeated until all four columns of the given row are loaded. The ELE-

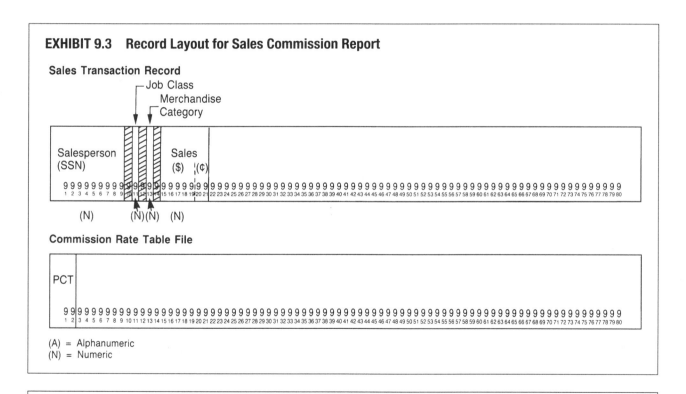

**EXHIBIT 9.3  Record Layout for Sales Commission Report**

**EXHIBIT 9.4  Sales Commission Table**

| Job Class | Merchandise Category | | | |
|---|---|---|---|---|
| | Garden | Sporting Goods | Furniture | Jewelry |
| Sales Rep. 1 | .02 | .03 | .04 | .05 |
| Sales Rep. 2 | .03 | .04 | .05 | .06 |
| Sales Rep. 3 | .04 | .05 | .06 | .07 |

### EXHIBIT 9.5 Test Cases for Sales Commission Report

**Sales Transaction File**

```
COLUMN    1         2         3         4         5         6         7         8
12345678901234567890123456789012345678901234567890123456789012345678901234567890

444444444 1 3 0500000
555555555 2 4 0300000
666666666 3 1 0100000
777777777 2 2 0350000
```

**Sales Commission Percentage Table File**

COBOL                                          BASIC

```
COLUMN    1         2         3         4       COLUMN    1         2         3         4
12345678901234567890123456789012345678901       12345678901234567890123456789012345678901
02                                              .02
03                                              .03
04                                              .04
05                                              .05
03                                              .03
04                                              .04
05                                              .05
06                                              .06
04                                              .04
05                                              .05
06                                              .06
07                                              .07
```

### EXHIBIT 9.6 Hierarchy Chart (Two-Dimensional Table) for Sales Commission Report

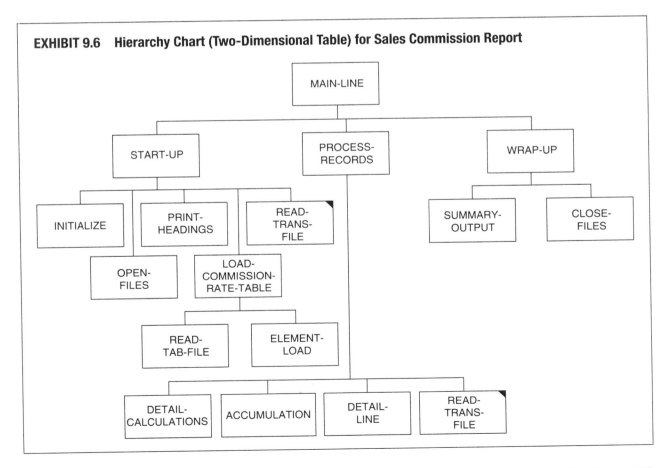

MENT-LOAD module consists of a block that stores the PCT value from the record into the TAB-COM (ROW-SUB, COL-SUB). As shown previously, the next block reads the next table record. When the comparison result of the outer condition (While ROW-SUB < 4 or Until ROW > 3) becomes *true*, the table-loading operation is complete, and control transfers back to the START-UP module.

Calculation of the commission is a noteworthy addition to the logic. The commission is equal to the sales multiplied by the commission rate from the table. The command is shown as COMMISSION = SALES × TAB-COM (JOB-CLASS, CATG). Here, both the row and column subscripts are actual fields from the transaction record. Again, this is called positional addressing. Other modules appear as usual and require no further elaboration.

**Pseudocode.**   Exhibit 9.8 depicts the associated pseudocode.

**Program Coding.**   Because the program coding for this application is so similar to that for Application 9.2, the necessary program coding can be found in Application 9.2.

**EXHIBIT 9.7    Structured Flowchart (Two-Dimensional Table) for Sales Commission Report**

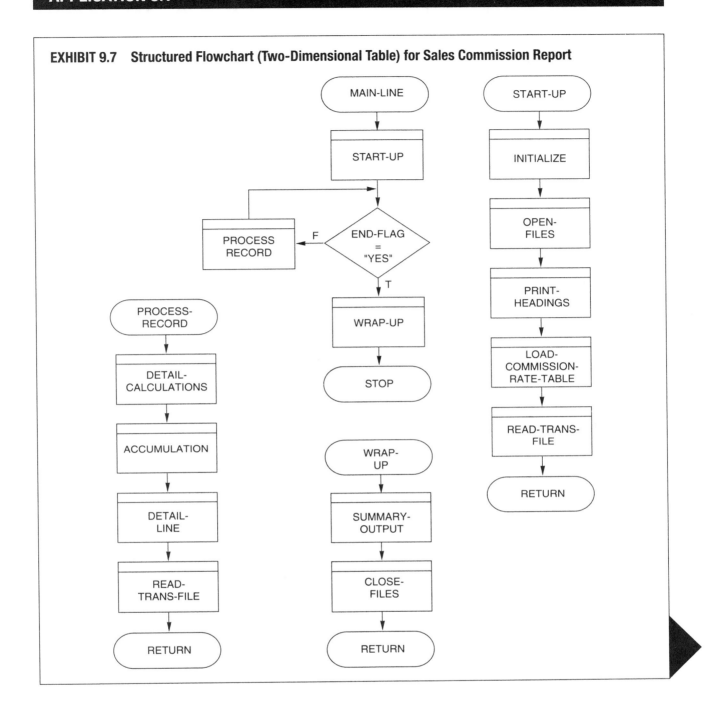

**EXHIBIT 9.7 (Cont.)**

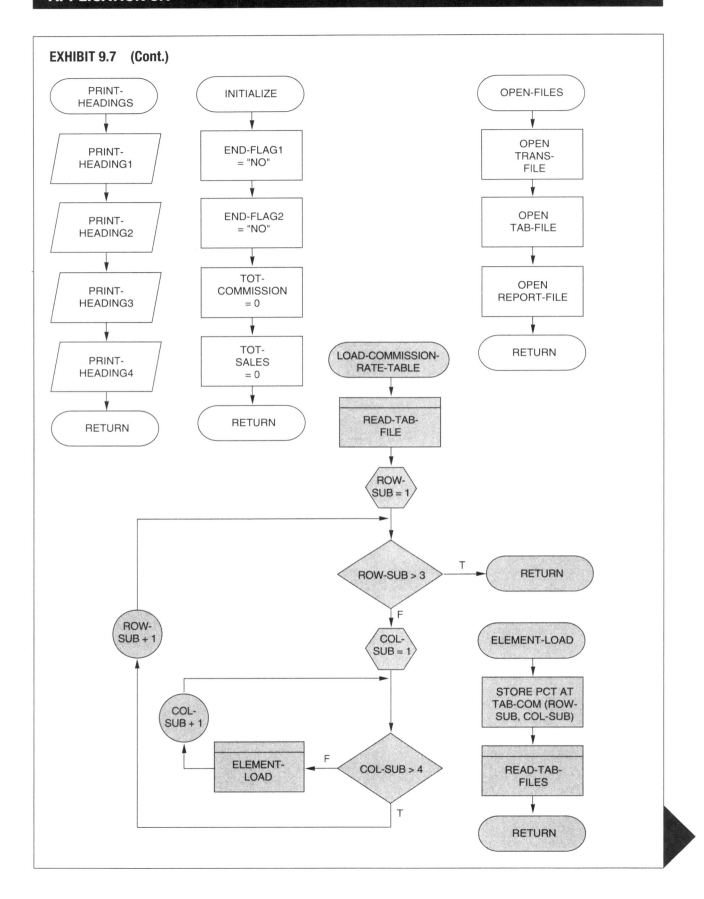

**EXHIBIT 9.7** **(Cont.)**

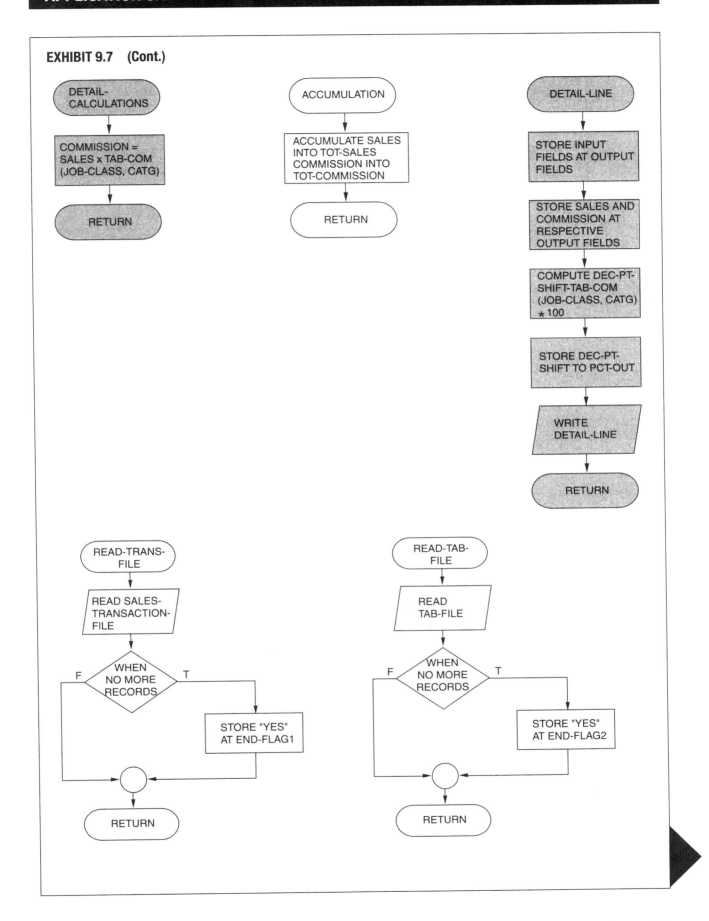

**EXHIBIT 9.7   (Cont.)**

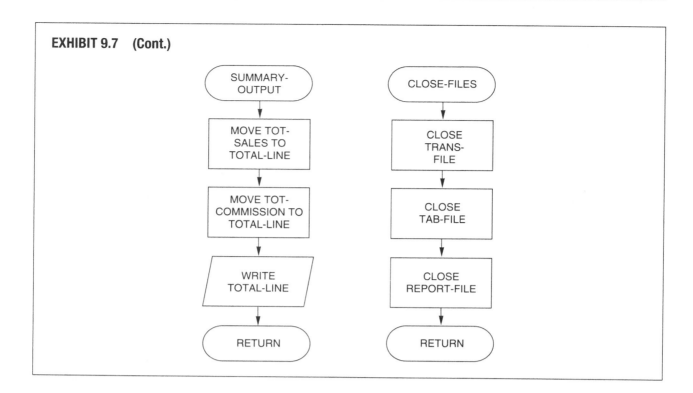

**EXHIBIT 9.8** **Pseudocode for Appl. 9.1 (Sales Commission Report)**

*main-line
 start-up
 do while end-flag1 = "no"
  process-records
 enddo
 wrap-up
 stop
*start-up
 initialize
 open-files
 print-headings
 load-commission-rate-table
 read-trans-file
 return
*initialize
 end-flag1 = "no"
 end-flag2 = "no"
 tot-commission = 0
 tot-sales = 0
 return
*open-files
 open trans-file
 open tab-file
 open report-file
 return
*print-headings
 print heading1
 print heading2
 print heading3
 print heading4
 return
*load-commission-rate-table
 read-tab-file
 set row-sub to 1
 do while row-sub < 4
  set col-sub to 1
  do while col-sub < 5
   element-load
   increase col-sub by 1
  enddo
  increase row-sub by 1
 enddo
 return
*element-load
 store pct at tab-com (row-sub, col-sub)
 read-tab-file
 return

*process-records
 detail-calculations
 accumulation
 detail-line
 read-trans-file
 return
*detail-calculations
 calculate commission = sales × tab-com (jobclass, catg)
 return
*accumulation
 add sales into tot-sales
 add commission into tot-commission
 return
*detail-line
 store input fields at respective output fields
 store sales at output field
 store commission at output field
 store tab-com (jobclass, catg) to pct-out
 dec-pt-shift = tab-com (jobclass, catg) * 100
 move dec-pt-shift to pct-out
 print detail-line
 return
*read-trans-file
 read sales-transaction-file
  when no more records
   store "yes" at end-flag1
 endread
 return
*read-tab-file
 read tab-file
  when no more records
   store "yes" at end-flag2
 endread
 return
*wrap-up
 summary-output
 close-files
 return
*summary-output
 move tot-sales to total line
 move tot-commission to total line
 print total line
 return
*close-files
 close trans-file
 close tab-file
 close report-file
 return

# Acme Shipping Report Featuring:
# Two-Dimensional Table with Top-Level Explicit Argument and Table Search

## Program Requirements

Acme Shipping Company Management requires a shipping report that lists the shipment number, item number, item description, shipment weight in pounds, material category, and shipment charge. The item description and material category are coded on the input record; therefore, the actual alphanumeric description of these two codes must be extracted from tables, using positional addressing. The shipping charge is based on the weight and category of the material being shipped, and the actual charge amount is extracted from a two-dimensional table of shipping charges. A total shipping charge prints at the end of the report.

## Output Design

The sample report is shown in Exhibit 9.9. Notice that the shipping weight of the third record is not valid. Exhibit 9.10 illustrates the print chart.

## Input Design

Exhibit 9.11 illustrates the record layout for the various file types. The shipping transaction report is shown first with shipment number, item number, shipment weight, and material category. All four fields are numeric. The table file has a maximum weight field followed by four fields that contain the charges for each of the material categories. The four charge fields are to be loaded into their respective columns in the table. The item description table record contains one alphanumeric field, as does the

---

**EXHIBIT 9.9    Sample Report for Acme Shipping Report (Two-Dimensional Table Search)**

```
                      ACME  SHIPPING  REPORT

SHIPMENT    ITEM      DESCRIPTION         WEIGHT    MATERIAL    SHIPPING
 NUMBER    NUMBER                         (LBS)     CATEGORY    CHARGE

   207       01       PLYWOOD,  GRADE  A  1200      LUMBER        12.00
   208       04       2X4,  UTILITY       2100      LUMBER        19.00
   209       07       1"  ANGLE           4010      METAL         18.00
   210       10       1"  REBAR           4070      METAL         18.00
   211       13       MORTAR  MIX         3500      CONCRETE      19.50
   212       19       PLATE  GLASS,  52"  4150      GLASS         88.50
   213       14       PURE  CONCRETE      5800      CONCRETE      27.00
   999       14       PURE  CONCRETE      ***NOT  FOUND***

                                                    TOTAL  202.00
```

---

**EXHIBIT 9.10    Printer Spacing Chart for Acme Shipping Report**

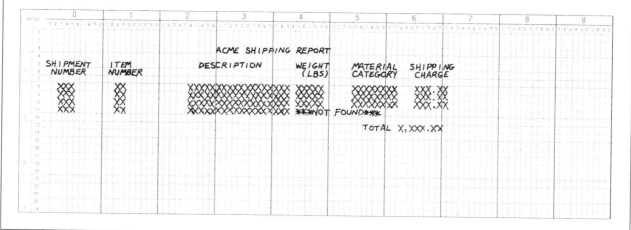

---

**EXHIBIT 9.11    Record Layout for Acme Shipping Charges Report**

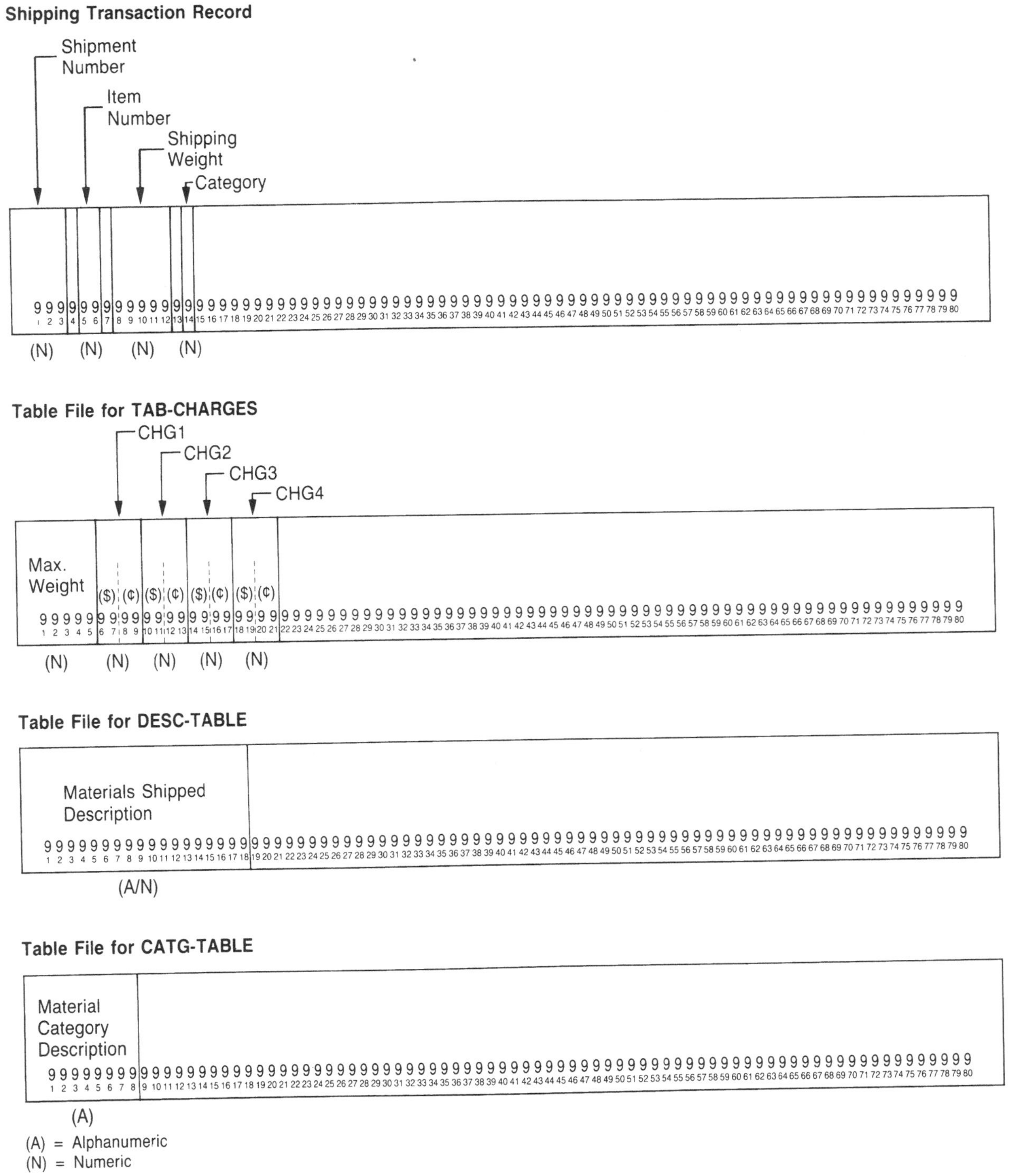

Shipping Transaction Record

Table File for TAB-CHARGES

Table File for DESC-TABLE

Table File for CATG-TABLE

(A) = Alphanumeric
(N) = Numeric

category table; these two files are to be loaded into their respective single-dimensional tables.

## Tables

Panel A of Exhibit 9.12 illustrates the two-dimensional table of shipment charges. The table contains a top-level table argument, which is searched to locate the corresponding row for the appropriate shipping charge. In COBOL, this table argument of maximum weights can be part of the same table as the charges; in BASIC, however, the argument table of maximum weights must be a separate single-dimensional table.

Panel B of Exhibit 9.12 depicts the single-dimensional table of descriptions (ITEM-DESC-TAB). Panel C shows the four material categories in a single-dimensional table (CATG-TABLE).

Exhibit 9.13 illustrates a set of test cases to be used in running this program. Here we find data for the transaction file and each of the table files that are to be loaded to their respective memory tables.

## Program Design

The general program design for this example is illustrated in the hierarchy chart in Exhibit 9.14. Its

### EXHIBIT 9.12

**Panel A—TAB-CHARGES**

| Max-Weight-<br>Tab-Arg | | 1<br>Lumber | 2<br>Metal | 3<br>Concrete | 4<br>Glass |
|---|---|---|---|---|---|
| 1 | 00500 | 0500 | 0400 | 0450 | 2250 |
| 2 | 01000 | 0900 | 0700 | 0850 | 4450 |
| 3 | 01500 | 1200 | 1000 | 1050 | 6650 |
| 4 | 03000 | 1900 | 1500 | 1700 | 7750 |
| 5 | 05000 | 2400 | 1800 | 1950 | 8850 |
| 6 | 10000 | 3300 | 2900 | 2700 | 9488 |

**Can be viewed as a field in the two-dimensional table for COBOL or as a separate one-dimensional table for BASIC.**

**Panel B—ITEM-DESC-TAB**

| | |
|---|---|
| 1 | Plywood, Grade A |
| 2 | Plywood, Grade B |
| 3 | 2 x 4, Framing |
| 4 | 2 x 4, Utility |
| 5 | 2 x 6, Framing |
| 6 | 2 x 6, Utility |
| 7 | 1" Angle |
| 8 | 2" Angle |
| 9 | 3" Angle |
| 10 | 1" Rebar |
| 11 | 2" Rebar |
| 12 | Ready Mix |
| 13 | Mortar Mix |
| 14 | Pure Concrete |
| 15 | Sand and Gravel |
| 16 | Single Pane, St |
| 17 | Double Pane, Lg |
| 18 | Plate Glass, Patio |
| 19 | Plate Glass, 52" |
| 20 | Plate Glass, 72" |

**Panel C—CATG-TABLE**

| | |
|---|---|
| 1 | Lumber |
| 2 | Metal |
| 3 | Concrete |
| 4 | Glass |

modules are common to the hierarchy chart found in previous table look-up examples, but one small exception should be noted. The PROCESS-RECORD module does not contain a calculation module, because no actual calculations will be performed. The shipping charge itself is extracted from the two-dimensional table, and no additional computation is needed.

**Structured Flowchart.** Exhibit 9.15 illustrates the specific program logic in structured flowchart form. The MAIN-LINE and START-UP modules appear as usual. Since a table-search operation is required to locate the appropriate shipping charge, the first module shown is LOOK-UP-SHIPMENT-CHARGE. The remainder of the PROCESS-RECORD module looks much the same as in previous table-search operations, except that here no calculation is performed. The LOAD-TABLES module consists of three predefined process blocks: LOAD-TAB-CHARGES, LOAD-DESC-TABLE, and LOAD-CATG-TABLE. The purpose of the LOAD-TAB-CHARGES module is to load the two-dimen-

sional table of shipment charges. This routine is different from the two-dimensional table load routines found in Application 9.2. They contained a nested definite iteration structure because each record contained only one element value. The outside loop controlled the row subscript value, and the inner loop controlled the column subscript value. To load the two-dimensional table in this problem requires only one definite iteration structure to manipulate the row subscript, since the entire row is to be loaded with multiple values from a table record. The table record contains fields that correspond to the table argument and the four table functions of a given row. In COBOL, the table argument (the maximum weight) and the four shipment charge fields can be transferred from one move command, as previously explained in Figure 9.10. As explained in Figure 9.11, the only alteration in BASIC to the above-mentioned logic is that the ROW-LOAD module includes separate store commands, one for each column in the row. This requires using a variable for the row subscript and a literal of 1, 2, 3, or 4 as the column subscript.

---

### EXHIBIT 9.13  Test Cases for Acme Shipping Report

*Transaction Test Cases for Acme Shipping Report*

```
COLUMN    1         2         3         4
1234567890123456789012345678901234567890
-----------------------------------------
207 01 01200 1
208 04 02100 1
209 07 04010 2
210 10 04070 2
211 13 03500 3
212 19 04150 4
213 14 05800 3
999 14 99999 3
```

*Table File for TAB-CHARGES*

```
COLUMN    1         2         3         4
1234567890123456789012345678901234567890
-----------------------------------------
00500050000400004502250
01000090000700008504450
01500120010001050 6650
03000190015001700 7750
05000240018001950 8850
10000330029002700 9488
```

*Materials Shipped Item Description Table Data*

```
COLUMN    1         2         3         4
1234567890123456789012345678901234567890
-----------------------------------------
PLYWOOD, GRADE A
PLYWOOD, GRADE B
2X4, FRAMING
2X4, UTILITY
2X6, FRAMING
2X6, UTILITY
1" ANGLE
2" ANGLE
3" ANGLE
1" REBAR
2" REBAR
READY MIX
MORTAR MIX
PURE CONCRETE
SAND AND GRAVEL
SINGLE PANE, ST
DOUBLE PANE, LG
PLATE GLASS, PATIO
PLATE GLASS, 52"
PLATE GLASS, 72"
```

*Category Table Data*

```
COLUMN    1         2         3         4
1234567890123456789012345678901234567890
-----------------------------------------
LUMBER
METAL
CONCRETE
GLASS
```

**EXHIBIT 9.14** **Hierarchy Chart for Acme Shipping Report (Two-Dimensional Table) Range-Step Argument Search**

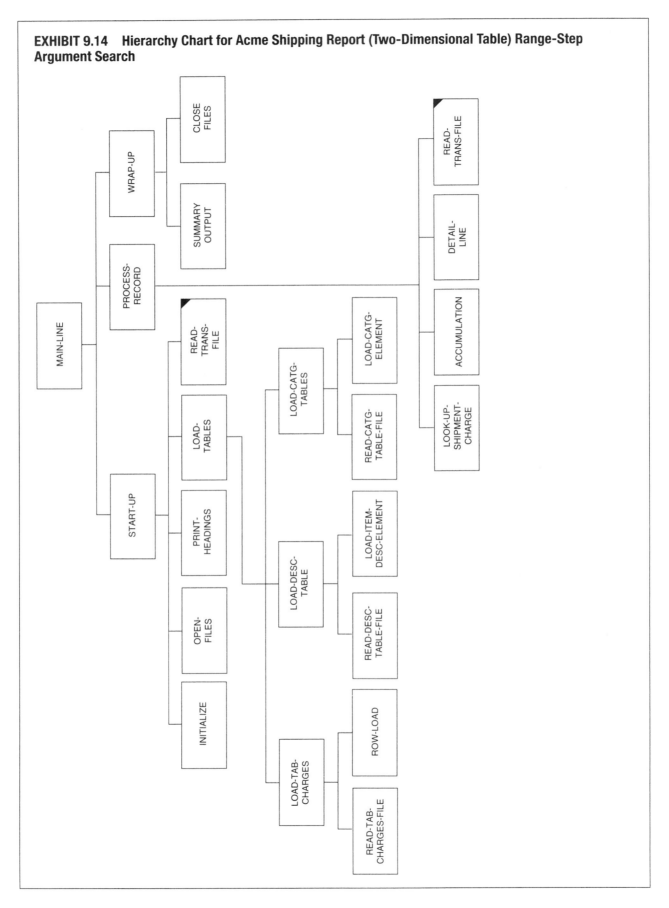

**EXHIBIT 9.15   Structured Flowchart for Acme Shipping Report**

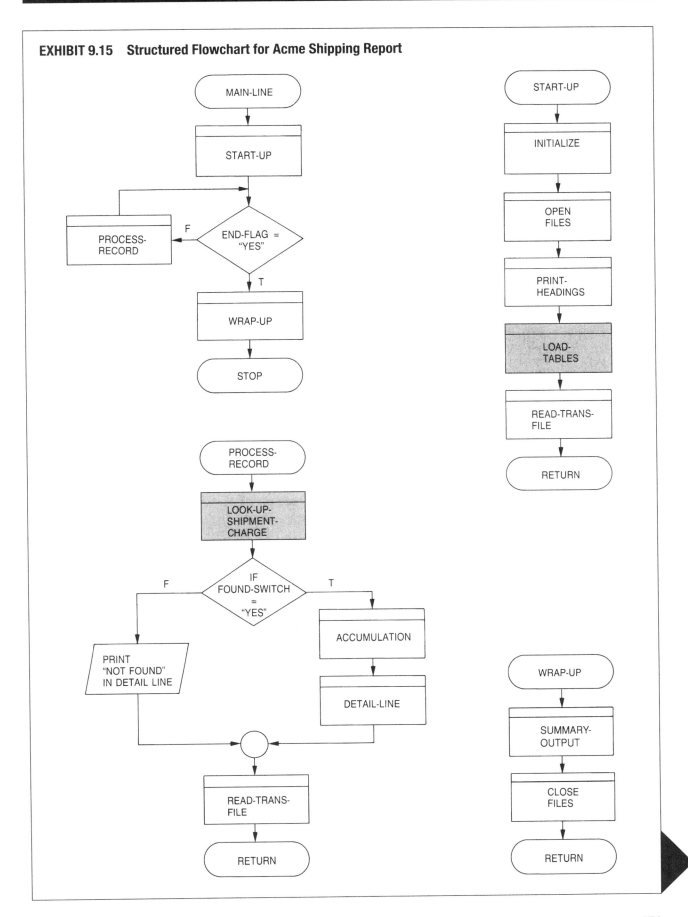

LOAD-DESC-TAB is simply a single-dimensional table load that uses a definite iteration structure. Since 20 elements are to be loaded, the DoWhile condition tests to determine if SUB is greater than 20. The purpose of the LOAD-CATG-TABLE module is to load the single-dimensional table of material category descriptions. Since four elements are to be loaded, the DoWhile condition determines if SUB is greater than four.

LOOK-UP-SHIPMENT-CHARGE resembles previous single-dimensional table searches. Since there are only six rows, the DoWhile condition determines if ROW-SUB is greater than 6. If ROW-SUB is increased one by one until it is greater than 6, it means that the value has not been found in the table. On the other hand, if the value is found in the table, then ROW-SUB is *forced* to be greater than six. The WEIGHT-LIMIT-TAB-ARG-COMPARE routine contains a condition similar to previous table-search examples, except that this one compares a search argument (SHIP-WEIGHT) with a table argument [MAX-WEIGHT-TAB-ARG (ROW-SUB)] to determine if SHIP-WEIGHT is less than or equal to the value in the table argument [MAX-WEIGHT-TAB-ARG (ROW-SUB)]. Until now, comparisons have been made to determine whether two values were equal. But in this example, the comparison is made to determine the row from which to extract the appropriate shipping charge. To do this, the shipping weight must *not* be greater than the one in the element of the argument table. As long as the shipping weight is greater than the maximum weight in the argument table element, the search continues to the next table argument element [MAX-WEIGHT-TAB-ARG (ROW-SUB)].

Once the appropriate row is located, the shipping charge is referenced through positional addressing the locate the column. The ACCUMU-LATE module adds the shipping charge in the table to TOTAL-CHARGES. The purpose of DETAIL-LINE is to store the various fields in the output fields prior to printing. It is important to note that two of the values transferred to the output fields come from DESC-TABLE and CATG-TABLE and

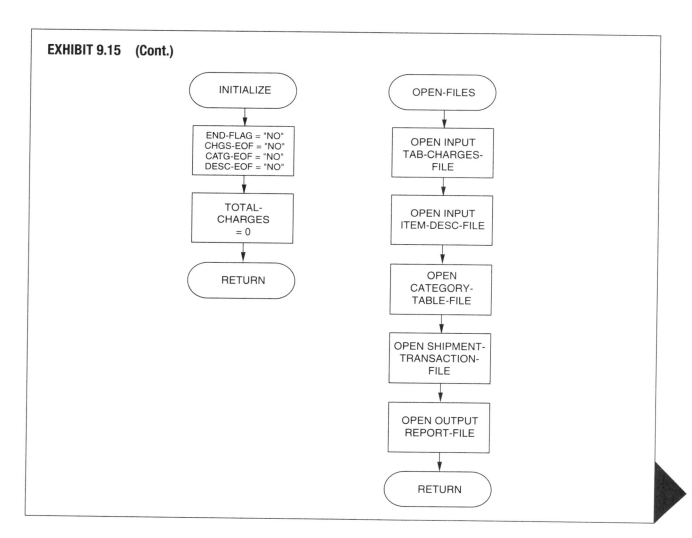

EXHIBIT 9.15 (Cont.)

are referenced using positional addressing. The codes from the transaction record are used as subscripts to reference the respective values. The ITEM-NO field from the transaction record refers to the appropriate element from DESC-TABLE, and CATEGORY from the transaction record refers to the appropriate element from CATG-TABLE.

The use of positional addressing hinges on the proper establishment of codes. When the codes start at 1 and run consecutively, they can be used as subscripts. Positional addressing would not work, for example, if CATEGORY started with the value 887. If the computer attempted to access the category description found at CATG-TABLE (CATEGORY) where the value of CATEGORY is 887, it would look for the 887th element of the table. Since the table has only four elements, it would thus attempt to point beyond the table boundary. The result would be a "subscript out of range" error.

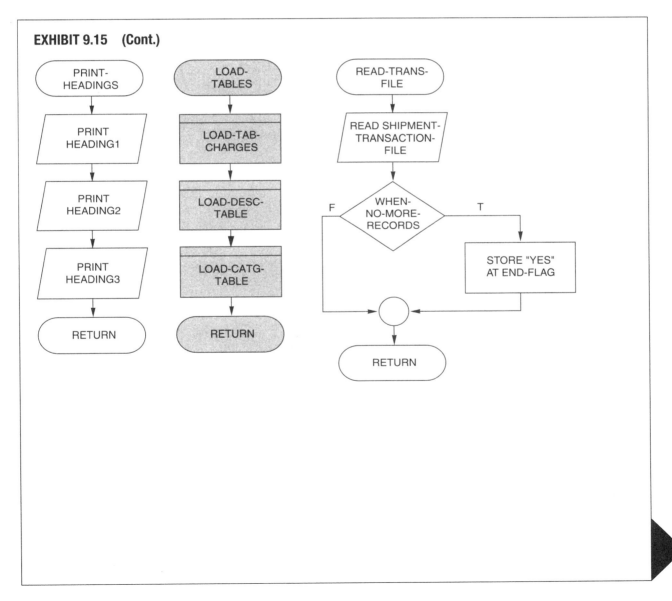

**EXHIBIT 9.15    (Cont.)**

**Pseudocode.** Exhibit 9.16 illustrates the Shipping Report logic for Application 9.2 in pseudocode form.

**Program Code.** The COBOL 85 program is illustrated in Exhibit 9.17. The interested student of COBOL 85 may observe the way the two-dimensional table is defined with OCCURS clauses on lines 68 through 72 of the program listing.

The QBASIC program is depicted in Exhibit 9.18. The student of QBASIC may observe the Dim statement for defining the various tables. The student should also observe how QBASIC is coded for loading the 2 dim table. This is found in the Row-Load module of Exhibit 9.18. The entire row cannot be loaded in one statement as it can in COBOL.

**EXHIBIT 9.15 (Cont.)**

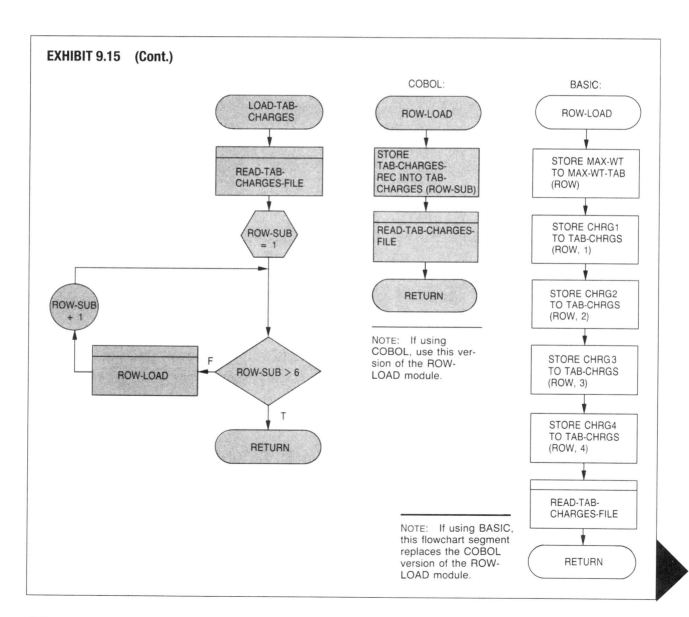

**EXHIBIT 9.15    (Cont.)**

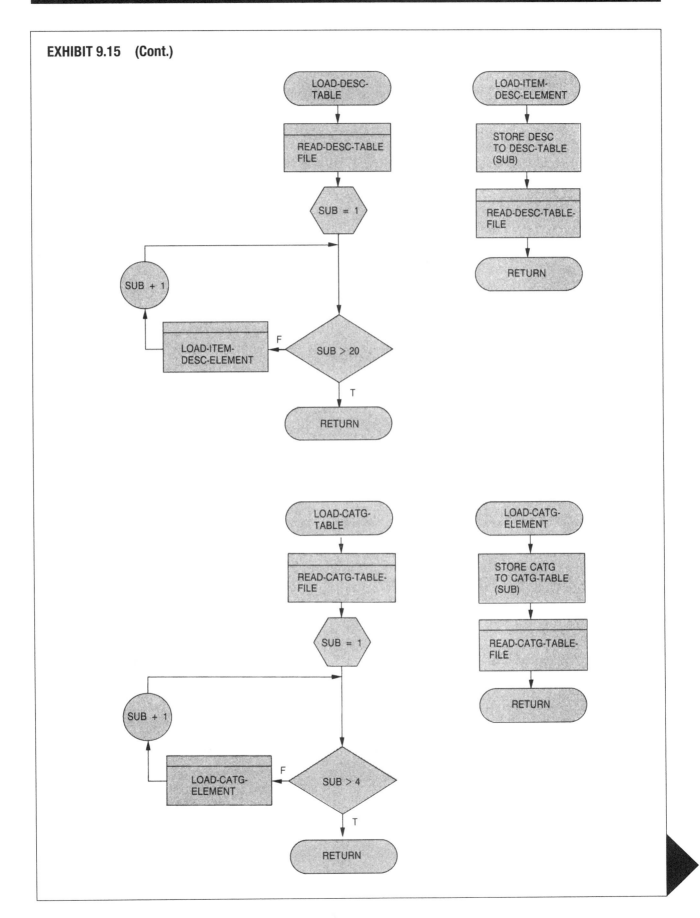

**EXHIBIT 9.15** (Cont.)

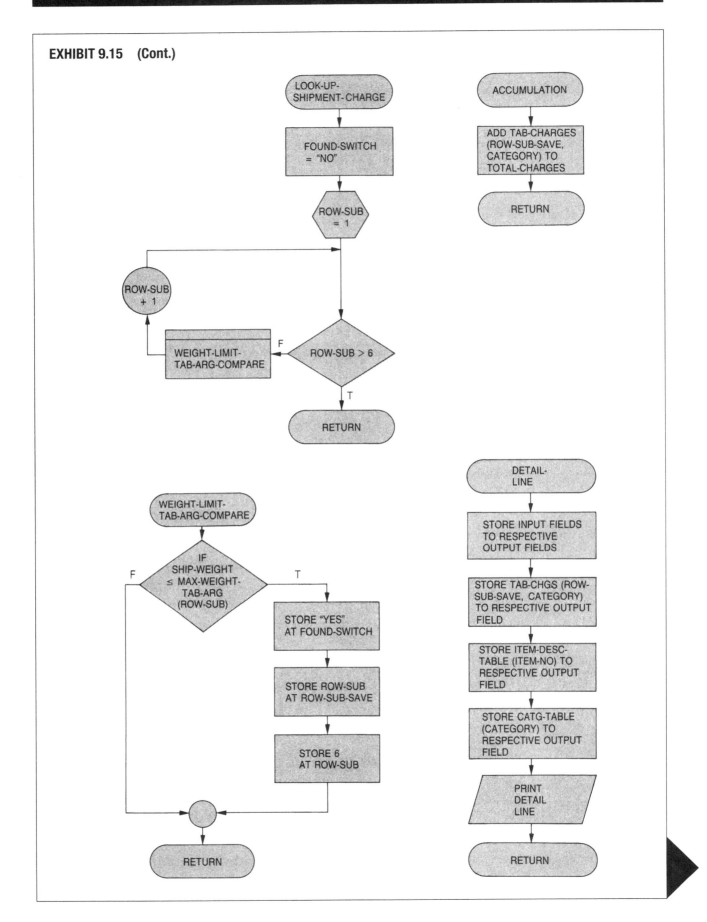

**EXHIBIT 9.15   (Cont.)**

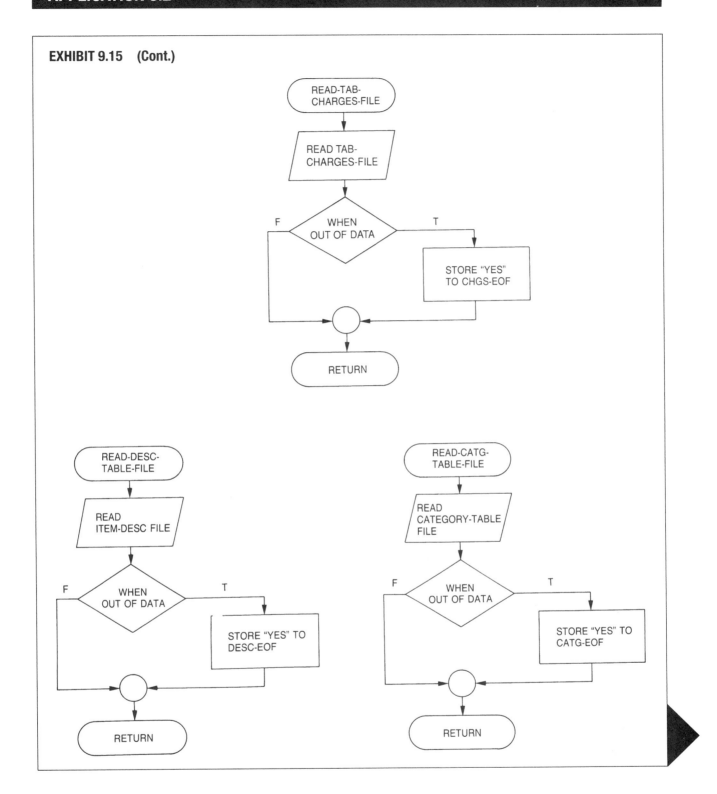

EXHIBIT 9.15 (Cont.)

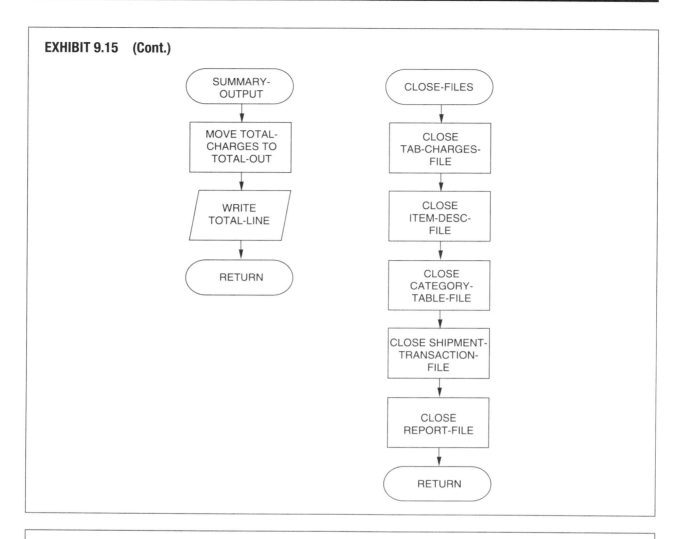

EXHIBIT 9.16 Pseudocode for Appl. 9.2

```
*main-line
     start-up
     do while end-flag1 = "no"
          process-record
     enddo
     wrap-up
     stop
*start-up
     initialize
     open-files
     print-headings
     load-tables
     read-trans-file
     return
*initialize
     end-flag = "no"
     catg-eof = "no"
     desc-eof = "no"
     chgs-eof = "no"
     total-charges = 0
     return
```

```
*open-files
     open trans-file
     open tab-charges-file
     open desc-file
     open catg-file
     open report-file
     return
*print-headings
     print heading1
     print heading2
     print heading3
     return
*load-tables
     load-tab-charges
     load-desc-table
     load-catg-table
     return
*read-trans-file
     read shipment-transaction-file
     when no more records store "yes" at end-flag1
     endread
     return
```

**EXHIBIT 9.16    (Cont.)**

```
*load-tab-charges
    read-tab-charges-file
    set row-sub = 1
    do while row-sub < 7
        row-load
        increase row-sub by 1
    enddo
    return
*read-tab-charges-file
    read tab-charges-file
        when no more records store "yes" at chgs-eof
    endread
    return
*row-load
    store tab-charges-rec to tab-charges (row-sub)
    read-tab-charges-file
    return
*load-desc-table
    read-desc-table-file
    set sub = 1
    dountil sub > 20
        load-item-desc-element
        increase sub by 1
    enddo
    return
*read-desc-table-file
    read desc-table-file
    when no more records store "yes" at desc-eof
    endread
    return
*load-item-desc-element
    store desc to desc-table (sub)
    read-desc-table-file
    return
*load-catg-table
    read-catg-table-file
    set sub = 1
    do while sub < 5
        load-catg-element
        increase sub by 1
    enddo
    return
*read-catg-table-file
    read catg-table-file
    when no more records store "yes" at catg-eof
    endread
    return
*load-catg-element
    store catg to catg-table (sub)
    read-catg-table-file
    return
```

```
*process-records
    look-up-shipment-charge
    if found-switch = "yes" then
        accumulation
        detail-line
    else
        print "not found" in detail line
    endif
    read-trans-file
    return
*look-up-shipment-charge
    initialize found-switch = "no"
    set row-sub = 1
    do while row-sub < 7
        weight-limit-tab-arg-compare
        increase row-sub by 1
    enddo
    return
*weight-limit-tab-arg-compare
    if ship-weight not greater than max-weight-tab-arg
       (row-sub) then
        store "yes" at found-switch
        store row-sub at row-sub-save
        store 6 at row-sub
    endif
    return
*accumulation
    add tab-charges (row-sub-save, category) to total-charges
    return
*detail-line
    store input fields to their respective output fields
    store tab-charges (row-sub-save, category) to respective
        output field
    store desc-table (item-no) to respective output field
    store catg-table (category) to respective output field
    print detail line
    return
*wrap-up
    summary-output
    close-files
    return
*summary-output
    move total-charges to total-line
    print total-line
    return
*close-files
    close tab-file
    close desc-file
    close catg-file
    close trans-file
    return
```

**EXHIBIT 9.17    COBOL 85 and Output for Application 9.2, Acme Shipping Report**

```
1          IDENTIFICATION DIVISION.
2          PROGRAM-ID. CH9APL1-2DIM-TABLES.
3
4      *      COBOL 85
5      *              THIS PROGRAM PRODUCES A SHIPPING REPORT FROM A
6      *              SHIPPING TRANSACTION RECORD.  THE SHIPPING CHARGE
7      *              IS DETERMINED BY LOOKING UP THE APPROPRIATE
8      *              WEIGHT FROM A TWO-DIMENSIONAL TABLE (TABLE ARGUMENT)
9      *              AND EXTRACTING THE APPROPRIATE SHIPPING CHARGE. THE
10     *              REPORT LISTS THE SHIPMENT NUMBER, ITEM, DESCRIPTION,
11     *              WEIGHT, MATERIAL CATEGORY AND SHIPPING CHARGE.
12
13
14         ENVIRONMENT DIVISION.
15         CONFIGURATION SECTION.
16         SOURCE-COMPUTER.  CYBER.
17         OBJECT-COMPUTER.  CYBER.
18
19         INPUT-OUTPUT SECTION.
20         FILE-CONTROL.
21             SELECT TRANS-FILE ASSIGN TO DTA91SHP.
22             SELECT CATEG-FILE ASSIGN TO DTA91CAT.
23             SELECT CHARGE-FILE ASSIGN TO DTA91CHG.
24             SELECT DESC-FILE ASSIGN TO DTA91DES.
25             SELECT REPORT-FILE ASSIGN TO OUTFILE.
26
27         DATA DIVISION.
28         FILE SECTION.
29         FD CHARGE-FILE.
30         01 TAB-CHARGES-RECORD.
31             05 MAX-WT                 PIC 9(5).
32             05 CH1                     PIC 9(4).
33             05 CH2                     PIC 9(4).
34             05 CH3                     PIC 9(4).
35             05 CH4                     PIC 9(4).
36
37         FD REPORT-FILE.
38         01 REC                         PIC X(133).
39
40         FD CATEG-FILE.
41         01 CATEGORY-RECORD.
42             05 CATG                    PIC X(8).
43
44         FD TRANS-FILE.
45         01 SHIPPING-RECORD.
46             05 SHIPMENT-NO             PIC 9(3).
47             05 FILLER                  PIC X.
48             05 ITEM-NO                 PIC 99.
49             05 FILLER                  PIC X.
50             05 SHIP-WEIGHT             PIC 9(5).
51             05 FILLER                  PIC X.
52             05 CATEGORY                PIC 9.
53
54         FD DESC-FILE.
55         01 DESCRIPTION-RECORD.
56             05 SHIPMENT-DESC           PIC X(18).
57
58         WORKING-STORAGE SECTION.
59         01 END-OF-FILE-FLAGS.
60             05 CHGS-EOF                PIC XXX VALUE "NO".
61             05 DESC-EOF                PIC XXX VALUE "NO".
62             05 CATEG-EOF               PIC XXX VALUE "NO".
63             05 END-FLAG                PIC XXX VALUE "NO".
64         01 SUB                         PIC 999 VALUE ZERO.
65         01 SUB-SAVE                    PIC 999 VALUE ZERO.
66         01 FOUND-SWITCH                PIC XXX VALUE "NO".
```

**EXHIBIT 9.17** **(Cont.)**

```
67        01 TOTAL-CHARGES                 PIC 9(4)V99 VALUE ZERO.
68
69        01 SHIP-CHARGES-TABLE.
70           05 TABLE-CHARGES OCCURS 6 TIMES.
71              10 MAX-WEIGHT-TAB-ARG    PIC 9(5).
72              10 TAB-CHARGES
73                    OCCURS 4 TIMES     PIC 99V99.
74
75        01 CATEGORIES-TABLE.
76           05 TAB-CATEGORIES OCCURS 4 TIMES.
77              10 TAB-MATERIAL-CATEGORY  PIC X(8).
78
79        01 DESCRIPTIONS-TABLE.
80           05 TAB-DESCRIPTIONS OCCURS 20 TIMES.
81              10 DESC-TABLE            PIC X(18).
82
83        01 PAGE-HEADING.
84           05                            PIC X(29) VALUE SPACES.
85           05                            PIC X(20) VALUE
86                   "ACME SHIPPING REPORT".
87           05                            PIC X(83) VALUE SPACES.
88
89        01 COLUMN-HEADING1.
90           05                            PIC X VALUE SPACES.
91           05                            PIC X(8) VALUE "SHIPMENT".
92           05                            PIC X(3) VALUE SPACES.
93           05                            PIC X(4) VALUE "ITEM".
94           05                            PIC X(11) VALUE SPACES.
95           05                            PIC X(11) VALUE "DESCRIPTION".
96           05                            PIC X(06) VALUE SPACES.
97           05                            PIC X(6) VALUE "WEIGHT".
98           05                            PIC X(4) VALUE SPACES.
99           05                            PIC X(8) VALUE "MATERIAL".
100          05                            PIC X(2) VALUE SPACES.
101          05                            PIC X(8) VALUE "SHIPPING".
102          05                            PIC X(60) VALUE SPACES.
103
104       01 COLUMN-HEADING2.
105          05                            PIC X(2) VALUE SPACES.
106          05                            PIC X(6) VALUE "NUMBER".
107          05                            PIC X(4) VALUE SPACES.
108          05                            PIC X(6) VALUE "NUMBER".
109          05                            PIC X(27) VALUE SPACES.
110          05                            PIC X(5) VALUE "(LBS)".
111          05                            PIC X(4) VALUE SPACES.
112          05                            PIC X(8) VALUE "CATEGORY".
113          05                            PIC X(3) VALUE SPACES.
114          05                            PIC X(6) VALUE "CHARGE".
115          05                            PIC X(61) VALUE SPACES.
116
117       01 DET-LINE.
118          05                            PIC X(2) VALUE SPACES.
119          05 SHIPMENT-NO-OUT            PIC ZZ9.
120          05                            PIC X(7) VALUE SPACES.
121          05 ITEM-NO-OUT               PIC Z9.
122          05                            PIC X(10) VALUE SPACES.
123          05 DESCRIPTION-OUT           PIC X(18).
124          05                            PIC X(01) VALUE SPACES.
125          05 SHIPMENT-WEIGHT-OUT       PIC ZZZZZ.
126          05                            PIC X(5) VALUE SPACES.
127          05 CATEGORY-OUT              PIC X(8).
128          05                            PIC X(3) VALUE SPACES.
129          05 SHIPPING-CHG-OUT          PIC ZZ9.99.
130          05                            PIC X(62) VALUE SPACES.
131
```

**EXHIBIT 9.17   (Cont.)**

```
132        01  NOT-FOUND-LINE.
133            05                      PIC X(2) VALUE SPACES.
134            05  NF-SHIPMENT-NO       PIC ZZ9.
135            05                      PIC X(7) VALUE SPACES.
136            05  NF-ITEM-NO           PIC Z9.
137            05                      PIC X(10) VALUE SPACES.
138            05  NF-DESCRIPTION       PIC X(18).
139            05                      PIC X VALUE SPACE.
140            05                      PIC X(15) VALUE "***NOT FOUND***".
141            05                      PIC X(74) VALUE SPACES.
142
143        01  TOTAL-LINE.
144            05                        PIC X(56) VALUE SPACES.
145            05                        PIC X(6) VALUE "TOTAL ".
146            05  TOTAL-CHARGES-OUT      PIC Z,ZZ9.99.
147            05                        PIC X(62) VALUE SPACES.
148        /
149         PROCEDURE DIVISION.
150         000-MAIN-LINE.
151            PERFORM 100-START-UP.
152            PERFORM 200-PROCESS-RECORD UNTIL END-FLAG = "YES".
153            PERFORM 300-WRAP-UP.
154            STOP RUN.
155
156         100-START-UP.
157      *      INITIALIZE-VARIABLES (W-S)
158            PERFORM 105-OPEN-FILES.
159            PERFORM 110-PRINT-HEADINGS.
160            PERFORM 120-LOAD-TABLES.
161            PERFORM 140-READ-TRANS-FILE.
162
163         105-OPEN-FILES.
164            OPEN OUTPUT REPORT-FILE.
165            OPEN INPUT CHARGE-FILE  CATEG-FILE  TRANS-FILE   DESC-FILE.
166
167
168         110-PRINT-HEADINGS.
169            WRITE REC FROM PAGE-HEADING AFTER PAGE.
170            WRITE REC FROM COLUMN-HEADING1 AFTER 2.
171            WRITE REC FROM COLUMN-HEADING2 AFTER 1.
172            MOVE SPACES TO REC.
173            WRITE REC.
174
175         120-LOAD-TABLES.
176            PERFORM 122-LOAD-TAB-CHARGES.
177            PERFORM 128-LOAD-DESC-TABLE.
178            PERFORM 134-LOAD-CATG-TABLE.
179
180         122-LOAD-TAB-CHARGES.
181            PERFORM 123-READ-TAB-CHARGES-FILE.
182            PERFORM 124-ROW-LOAD VARYING SUB
183                  FROM 1 BY 1 UNTIL SUB > 6.
184
185         123-READ-TAB-CHARGES-FILE.
186            READ CHARGE-FILE
187                AT END MOVE "YES" TO CHGS-EOF.
188
189         124-ROW-LOAD.
190            MOVE TAB-CHARGES-RECORD TO TABLE-CHARGES (SUB).
191            PERFORM 123-READ-TAB-CHARGES-FILE.
192
193         128-LOAD-DESC-TABLE.
194            PERFORM 130-READ-DESC-TABLE-FILE.
195            PERFORM 131-LOAD-ITEM-DESC-ELEMENT VARYING SUB
196                  FROM 1 BY 1 UNTIL SUB > 20.
197
```

**EXHIBIT 9.17  (Cont.)**

```
198          130-READ-DESC-TABLE-FILE.
199              READ DESC-FILE
200                  AT END MOVE "YES" TO DESC-EOF.
201
202          131-LOAD-ITEM-DESC-ELEMENT.
203              MOVE SHIPMENT-DESC TO DESC-TABLE (SUB).
204              PERFORM 130-READ-DESC-TABLE-FILE.
205
206          134-LOAD-CATG-TABLE.
207              PERFORM 136-READ-CATG-TABLE-FILE.
208              PERFORM 137-LOAD-CATG-ELEMENT VARYING SUB
209                      FROM 1 BY 1 UNTIL SUB > 04.
210
211          136-READ-CATG-TABLE-FILE.
212              READ CATEG-FILE
213                  AT END MOVE "YES" TO CATEG-EOF.
214
215          137-LOAD-CATG-ELEMENT.
216              MOVE CATG TO TAB-MATERIAL-CATEGORY (SUB).
217              PERFORM 136-READ-CATG-TABLE-FILE.
218
219          140-READ-TRANS-FILE.
220              READ TRANS-FILE
221                AT END MOVE "YES" TO END-FLAG.
222
223          200-PROCESS-RECORD.
224              PERFORM 210-LOOK-UP-SHIPMENT-CHARGE.
225              IF FOUND-SWITCH = "YES"
226                  PERFORM 220-ACCUMULATION
227                  PERFORM 230-DETAIL-LINE
228              ELSE
229                  MOVE SHIPMENT-NO TO NF-SHIPMENT-NO
230                  MOVE ITEM-NO TO NF-ITEM-NO
231                  MOVE DESC-TABLE (ITEM-NO) TO NF-DESCRIPTION
232                  WRITE REC FROM NOT-FOUND-LINE AFTER 1.
233              PERFORM 140-READ-TRANS-FILE.
234
235          210-LOOK-UP-SHIPMENT-CHARGE.
236              MOVE "NO" TO FOUND-SWITCH.
237              PERFORM 210-A-WEIGHT-LIMIT-COMPARE VARYING
238                  SUB FROM 1 BY 1 UNTIL SUB > 6.
239
240          210-A-WEIGHT-LIMIT-COMPARE.
241              IF SHIP-WEIGHT < MAX-WEIGHT-TAB-ARG (SUB)
242                OR SHIP-WEIGHT = MAX-WEIGHT-TAB-ARG (SUB)
243                          MOVE "YES" TO FOUND-SWITCH
244                          MOVE SUB TO SUB-SAVE
245                          MOVE 6 TO SUB
246              END-IF.
247
248          220-ACCUMULATION.
249              ADD TAB-CHARGES (SUB-SAVE, CATEGORY) TO
250                          TOTAL-CHARGES.
251
252          230-DETAIL-LINE.
253              MOVE SHIPMENT-NO TO SHIPMENT-NO-OUT.
254              MOVE ITEM-NO TO ITEM-NO-OUT.
255              MOVE SHIP-WEIGHT TO SHIPMENT-WEIGHT-OUT.
256              MOVE DESC-TABLE (ITEM-NO) TO DESCRIPTION-OUT.
257              MOVE TAB-MATERIAL-CATEGORY (CATEGORY)
258                          TO CATEGORY-OUT.
259              MOVE TAB-CHARGES (SUB-SAVE CATEGORY) TO
260                          SHIPPING-CHG-OUT.
261              WRITE REC FROM DET-LINE AFTER 1.
262
```

**EXHIBIT 9.17    (Cont.)**

```
263          300-WRAP-UP.
264               PERFORM 310-SUMMARY-OUTPUT.
265               PERFORM 320-CLOSE-FILES.
266
267          310-SUMMARY-OUTPUT.
268               MOVE TOTAL-CHARGES TO TOTAL-CHARGES-OUT.
269               WRITE REC FROM TOTAL-LINE AFTER 2.
270
271          320-CLOSE-FILES.
272               CLOSE REPORT-FILE CHARGE-FILE TRANS-FILE
273                    CATEG-FILE DESC-FILE.
```

```
                        ACME SHIPPING REPORT

SHIPMENT    ITEM          DESCRIPTION       WEIGHT    MATERIAL    SHIPPING
NUMBER      NUMBER                          (LBS)     CATEGORY    CHARGE

  207         1       PLYWOOD, GRADE A      1200      LUMBER       12.00
  208         4       2X4, UTILITY          2100      LUMBER       19.00
  209         7       1" ANGLE              4010      METAL        18.00
  210        10       1" REBAR              4070      METAL        18.00
  211        13       MORTAR MIX            3500      CONCRETE     19.50
  212        19       PLATE GLASS, 52"      4150      GLASS        88.50
  213        14       PURE CONCRETE         5800      CONCRETE     27.00
  999        14       PURE CONCRETE        ***NOT FOUND***

                                                      TOTAL       202.00
```

**EXHIBIT 9.18    QBASIC Program and Output for Application 9.2, Acme Shipping Report**

```
'*********************************************************************
'*   QUICK BASIC          PROGRAM-IDENTIFICATION                     *
'*********************************************************************
'* PROGRAM NAME: CH9APL2                                             *
'  REMARKS: THIS PROGRAM PRODUCES A SHIPPING REPORT FROM A SHIPPING  *
'*          TRANSACTION RECORD. THE SHIPPING CHARGE IS DETERMINED BY *
'*          LOOKING UP THE APPROPRIATE WEIGHT FROM A TWO-DIMENSIONAL *
'*          TABLE (TABLE ARGUMENT) AND EXTRACTING THE APPROPRIATE    *
'*          SHIPPING CHARGE. THE REPORT LISTS THE SHIPMENT NUMBER,ITEM *
'*          DESCRIPTION, WEIGHT, MATERIAL CATEGORY, AND SHIPPING     *
'*          CHARGE.                                                  *
' *
'*********************************************************************
'*                      MAIN-LINE                                    *
'*********************************************************************

MAIN.LINE:

    GOSUB STARTUP                    'PERFORM START-UP
    DO UNTIL END.FLAG$ = "YES"
        GOSUB PROCESS.RECORD         'PERFORM PROCESS-RECORD
    LOOP
    GOSUB WRAPUP                     'PERFORM WRAP-UP
    END
```

**EXHIBIT 9.18    (Cont.)**

```
'*********************************************************************
'*                          START-UP                              *
'*********************************************************************

STARTUP:
    DIM DESCRIPTION.TAB$(20): DIM CATG.TAB$(4): DIM MAX.WEIGHT(6): DIM TAB.CHARGES(6, 4)
    GOSUB INITIALIZE
    GOSUB OPEN.FILES
    GOSUB PRINT.HEADINGS                        'PERFORM LPRINT-HEADINGS
    GOSUB LOAD.TABLES                       'PERFORM LOAD-TABLES
    GOSUB READ.TRANS.FILE                   'PERFORM READ-TRANS-FILE
    RETURN


    '*********************************************************************
    '*                          INITIALIZE                            *
    '*********************************************************************

INITIALIZE:
    WIDTH LPRINT 132
    END.FLAG$ = "NO": TOTAL.CHARGES = 0
    DETAIL.LINE$ = " \    \       ##            \      \  #####   \    \  ###.##"
    ERROR.LINE$ = " \   \       ##          \          \ *_*_*NOT FOUND*_*_*"
    TOTAL.LINE$ = "                                               TOTAL #,###.##"
    RETURN


    '*********************************************************************
    '*                          OPEN FILES                            *
    '*********************************************************************

OPEN.FILES:
    OPEN "I", #1, "C:\QBASIC\cH9ILL2B.DAT":             'OPEN TAB-FILE
    OPEN "I", #2, "C:\QBASIC\CH9ILL2C.DAT":             'OPEN DESC-FILE
    OPEN "I", #3, "C:\QBASIC\CH9ILL2D.DAT":             'OPEN CATG-FILE
    OPEN "I", #4, "C:\QBASIC\CH9ILL2A.DAT":             'OPEN TRANS-FILE
    RETURN



    '*********************************************************************
    '*                          LPRINT-HEADINGS                       *
    '*********************************************************************

PRINT.HEADINGS:
    LPRINT CHR$(12)
    LPRINT TAB(30); "ACME SHIPPING REPORT"
    LPRINT
    LPRINT "SHIPMENT"; TAB(12); "ITEM"; TAB(27); "DESCRIPTION"; TAB(44); "WEIGHT"; TAB(54); "MATERIAL"; TAB(64); "SHIPPING"
    LPRINT " NUMBER"; TAB(12); "NUMBER"; TAB(45); "(LBS)"; TAB(54); "CATEGORY"; TAB(65); "CHARGE"
    LPRINT
    RETURN
```

**EXHIBIT 9.18    (Cont.)**

```
'*******************************************************************
'*                         LOAD-TABLES                            *
'*******************************************************************

LOAD.TABLES:

    GOSUB LOAD.TAB.CHARGES                'LOAD-TAB-CHARGES
    GOSUB LOAD.DESC.TABLE                 'LOAD-ITEM-DESC-TABLE
    GOSUB LOAD.CATG.TABLE                 'LOAD-CATG-TABLE
    RETURN


    '*******************************************************************
    '*                      LOAD-TAB-CHARGES                          *
    '*******************************************************************

LOAD.TAB.CHARGES:

    GOSUB READ.TAB.CHARGES.FILE       ' PERFORM READ-TAB-CHARGES-FILE
    FOR ROW.SUB = 1 TO 6
        GOSUB ROW.LOAD                ' PERFORM ROW-LOAD
    NEXT ROW.SUB
    RETURN


    '*******************************************************************
    '*                    READ-TAB-CHARGES-FILE                       *
    '*******************************************************************

READ.TAB.CHARGES.FILE:

    INPUT #1, WEIGHT, CHG1, CHG2, CHG3, CHG4
    RETURN


    '*******************************************************************
    '*                         ROW-LOAD                              *
    '*******************************************************************

ROW.LOAD:

    MAX.WEIGHT(ROW.SUB) = WEIGHT
    TAB.CHARGES(ROW.SUB, 1) = CHG1
    TAB.CHARGES(ROW.SUB, 2) = CHG2
    TAB.CHARGES(ROW.SUB, 3) = CHG3
    TAB.CHARGES(ROW.SUB, 4) = CHG4
    GOSUB READ.TAB.CHARGES.FILE             'PERFORM READ-TAB-CHARGES-FILE
    RETURN
```

**EXHIBIT 9.18    (Cont.)**

```
'*********************************************************************
'*                     LOAD-ITEM-DESC-TABLE                         *
'*********************************************************************


LOAD.DESC.TABLE:

    GOSUB READ.DESC.TABLE.FILE              'PERFORM READ-DESC-TABLE-FILE
    FOR SUB1 = 1 TO 20
        GOSUB LOAD.DESC.ELEMENT             'PERFORM LOAD-DESC-ELEMENT
    NEXT SUB1
    RETURN



    '*********************************************************************
    '*                     READ-DESC-TABLE-FILE                         *
    '*********************************************************************


READ.DESC.TABLE.FILE:

    INPUT #2, DESCRIPTION$
    RETURN


    '*********************************************************************
    '*                     LOAD-DESC-ELEMENT                            *
    '*********************************************************************


 LOAD.DESC.ELEMENT:

    DESCRIPTION.TAB$(SUB1) = DESCRIPTION$
    GOSUB READ.DESC.TABLE.FILE              'PERFORM READ-DESC-TABLE-FILE
    RETURN


    '*********************************************************************
    '*                     LOAD-CATG-TABLE                              *
    '*********************************************************************


 LOAD.CATG.TABLE:

    GOSUB READ.CATG.TABLE.FILE              'PERFORM READ-CATG-TABLE-FILE
    FOR SUB1 = 1 TO 4
        GOSUB LOAD.CATG.ELEMENT             'PERFORM LOAD-CATG-ELEMENT
    NEXT SUB1
    RETURN



    '*********************************************************************
    '*                     READ-CATG-TABLE-FILE                         *
    '*********************************************************************


 READ.CATG.TABLE.FILE:

    INPUT #3, CATG$
    RETURN
```

**EXHIBIT 9.18   (Cont.)**

```
'*************************************************************************
'*                          LOAD-CATG-ELEMENT                           *
'*************************************************************************

LOAD.CATG.ELEMENT:

    CATG.TAB$(SUB1) = CATG$
    GOSUB READ.CATG.TABLE.FILE                'PERFORM READ-CATG-TABLE-FILE
    RETURN


    '*************************************************************************
    '*                          READ-TRANS-FILE                            *
    '*************************************************************************

READ.TRANS.FILE:

    INPUT #4, SHIPMENT.NUMBER$, ITEM.NO, SHIP.WEIGHT, CATEGORY
    IF SHIPMENT.NUMBER$ = "EOF" THEN
        END.FLAG$ = "YES"
    END IF
    RETURN


    '*************************************************************************
    '*                          PROCESS-RECORD                             *
    '*************************************************************************

PROCESS.RECORD:

    GOSUB LOOK.UP.SHIPPING.CHARGE            'PERFORM LOOK-UP-SHIPMENT-CHARGES
    IF FOUND.SW$ = "YES" THEN
       GOSUB ACCUMULATION
       GOSUB DETAIL.LINE
    ELSE
       LPRINT USING ERROR.LINE$; SHIPMENT.NUMBER$; ITEM.NO; DESCRIPTION.TAB$(ITEM.NO)
    END IF
    GOSUB READ.TRANS.FILE                        'PERFORM READ-TRANS-FILE
    RETURN


    '*************************************************************************
    '*                     LOOK-UP-SHIPMENT-CHARGES                        *
    '*************************************************************************

LOOK.UP.SHIPPING.CHARGE:

    FOUND.SW$ = "NO"
    FOR ROW.SUB = 1 TO 6
        GOSUB WEIGHT.LIMIT.TAB.ARG.COMPARE   'PERFORM WEIGHT LIMIT TAB ARG COMPARE
    NEXT ROW.SUB
    RETURN
```

**EXHIBIT 9.18    (Cont.)**

```
'*****************************************************************
'*                  WEIGHT-LIMIT-TAB-ARG-COMPARE                 *
'*****************************************************************


WEIGHT.LIMIT.TAB.ARG.COMPARE:

    IF SHIP.WEIGHT < MAX.WEIGHT(ROW.SUB) OR SHIP.WEIGHT = MAX.WEIGHT(ROW.SUB) THEN
         FOUND.SW$ = "YES"
         ROW.SUB.SAVE = ROW.SUB
         ROW.SUB = 6
    END IF
    RETURN



    '*****************************************************************
    '*                       ACCUMULATION                           *
    '*****************************************************************


ACCUMULATION:

    TOTAL.CHARGES = TOTAL.CHARGES + TAB.CHARGES(ROW.SUB.SAVE, CATEGORY)
    RETURN

    '*****************************************************************
    '*                        DETAIL-LINE                           *
    '*****************************************************************


DETAIL.LINE:

    LPRINT USING DETAIL.LINE$; SHIPMENT.NUMBER$; ITEM.NO; DESCRIPTION.TAB$(ITEM.NO); SHIP.WEIGHT; CATG.TAB$(CATEGORY); TAB.CHARGES(ROW.SUB.SAVE, CATEGORY)
    RETURN



    '*****************************************************************
    '*                          WRAP-UP                             *
    '*****************************************************************


WRAPUP:
    GOSUB SUMMARY.OUTPUT
    GOSUB CLOSE.FILES
    RETURN

    '*****************************************************************
    '*                       SUMMARY-OUTPUT                         *
    '*****************************************************************


SUMMARY.OUTPUT:
    LPRINT
    LPRINT USING TOTAL.LINE$; TOTAL.CHARGES
    RETURN

    '*****************************************************************
    '*                        CLOSE FILES                           *
    '*****************************************************************


CLOSE.FILES:
    CLOSE #1, #2, #3, #4
    RETURN
```

**EXHIBIT 9.18   (Cont.)**

```
                        ACME SHIPPING REPORT

SHIPMENT    ITEM         DESCRIPTION      WEIGHT    MATERIAL   SHIPPING
NUMBER      NUMBER                        (LBS)     CATEGORY   CHARGE


  207         1       PLYWOOD GRADE A      1200     LUMBER      12.00
  208         4       2 X 4 UTILITY        2100     LUMBER      19.00
  209         7       1 INCH ANGLE         4010     METAL       18.00
  210        10       1 INCH REBAR         4070     METAL       18.00
  211        13       MORTAR MIX           3500     CONCRETE    19.50
  212        19       PLATE GLASS/ 52 I    4150     GLASS       88.50
  213        14       PURE CONCRETE        5800     CONCRETE    27.00
  999        14       PURE CONCRETE     ***NOT FOUND***

                                                   TOTAL      202.00
```

## SUMMARY

Data must often be referenced in a table with two or more reference points. Such a table is called a two-dimensional table. It is established using both rows and columns, and to refer to an element within requires both a row and a column subscript. In most cases the row is located by searching a corresponding single-dimensional table of table arguments. If the values in the single-dimensional table are associated with specific rows in the two-dimensional table, then locating the table argument automatically locates the appropriate row.

The same methods for accessing data in a single-dimensional table are used to access data in a two-dimensional table. The data can be accessed either by positional addressing using no explicit table argument or by a table search using an explicit table argument. This table argument can be either an exact value or a range-step value (a value that represents either the bottom or the top of a range of values) that is searched to locate the appropriate row. When the table argument allows access to a row, it is called a top-level explicit search argument. A bottom-level explicit search argument allows access to a specific column.

There are two methods for loading tables. The row-major concept of loading tables is the storing of values in the respective elements by the row. After one complete row is loaded, the next row is loaded, and so on. The column-major concept is just the opposite. Values are loaded by the column. When the first column fills up, values are loaded into the second column, and so on.

The loading process of a two-dimensional table can be handled in COBOL, for example, using a Perform . . . Varying . . . After command. This assumes that the design uses the nested definite iteration. This same process can also be done in BASIC using a nested For . . . Next loop.

In COBOL, a two-dimensional table can also be loaded a row at a time rather than a single element at a time if the table records are established properly. This requires only the definite iteration structure (Perform . . . Varying or simple For . . . Next).

The table-searching process normally involves the searching of a table argument list (table of table arguments). When the row has been located through a sequential search, the column is determined through positional addressing (using the actual value from an input field).

## VOCABULARY

| | |
|---|---|
| two-dimensional table | bottom-level explicit |
| row | search argument |
| column | range-step table |
| chart (matrix) | row major |
| row subscript | column major |
| column subscript | nested definite iteration |
| range-step value | Perform . . . Varying |
| top-level explicit | . . . After |
| search argument | Nested For . . . Next |
| | group move |

## EXERCISES/QUESTIONS

1. What is the major subdivision of a two-dimensional table? The minor subdivision?

2. How many subscripts are needed to reference an element in a two-dimensional table?

3. What is meant by positional addressing?

4. What basic methods are used to access data from a two-dimensional table?

5. What is meant by a top-level explicit search argument? A bottom level explicit search argument?

# PROBLEMS

**9-1.** Acme Oil and Gas Company needs a personnel salary report for its employees. The report is to print each employee's department number, SSN, name, 1988 gross salary, salary increase for 1989, and 1989 gross salary as follows. Subtotals for all three amounts are to be printed for each department. The personnel file is sorted by department. Grand totals are to print at the end of the report. The salary increase percentage (based on gross) is determined by two factors (1) peer review rating and (2) supervisor rating. This percentage is extracted from a two-dimensional table as follows and multiplied by the gross salary for 1988 to give the 1989 increase amount. The 1989 gross salary is the sum of the 1988 gross and the 1989 increase. Create a hierarchy chart, structured flowchart, and pseudocode for this problem.

## THE TABLE RECORD FORMAT:

| Field | Columns | Type |
|-------|---------|------|
| PCT | 1–3 | N |

The table file consists of records that contain only one PCT value per record.

## INPUT RECORD FORMAT:

| Field | Columns | Data Type |
|-------|---------|-----------|
| Department | 1–3 | N |
| SSN | 4–12 | N |
| Name | 13–27 | A/N |
| Date of hire | 28–33 | N |
| Address | 34–53 | A/N |
| State | 54–55 | A/N |
| Zip | 56–60 | N |
| Gross | 61–67 | N |
| Supervisor rating | 69 | N |
| Peer rating | 71 | N |

## TWO-DIMENSIONAL TABLE OF SALARY INCREASE PERCENTAGE BASED ON ANNUAL SALARY:

| Performance Rating by Peers | Performance Rating by Supervisor | | | | |
|---|---|---|---|---|---|
| | 1 | 2 | 3 | 4 | 5 |
| 1 | .010 | .015 | .017 | .020 | .022 |
| 2 | .015 | .017 | .020 | .022 | .025 |
| 3 | .017 | .020 | .022 | .025 | .027 |
| 4 | .020 | .022 | .025 | .027 | .030 |
| 5 | .022 | .025 | .027 | .030 | .040 |

## OUTPUT REQUIRED:

```
                       ACME OIL AND GAS COMPANY
                  PERSONNEL SALARY REPORT FOR 1989

DEPART-     SSN          NAME           1992        1993         1993
MENT                                    GROSS       INCREASE     GROSS

  XXX    XXXXXXXXX   XXXXXXXXXXXXXX   XX,XXX.XX    X,XXX.XX    XX,XXX.XX
  XXX    XXXXXXXXX   XXXXXXXXXXXXXX   XX,XXX.XX    X,XXX.XX    XX,XXX.XX
  XXX    XXXXXXXXX   XXXXXXXXXXXXXX   XX,XXX.XX    X,XXX.XX    XX,XXX.XX

         DEPARTMENT XXX TOTAL      XXX,XXX.XX    XX,XXX.XX    XXX,XXX.XX

  XXX    XXXXXXXXX   XXXXXXXXXXXXXX   XX,XXX.XX    X,XXX.XX    XX,XXX.XX
  XXX    XXXXXXXXX   XXXXXXXXXXXXXX   XX,XXX.XX    X,XXX.XX    XX,XXX.XX

         DEPARTMENT XXX TOTAL      XXX,XXX.XX    XX,XXX.XX    XXX,XXX.XX
         GRAND TOTALS          $X,XXX,XXX.XX   XXX,XXX.XX   X,XXX,XXX.XX
```

**9-2.** Otto's Auto Dealership needs a customer sales report. The report is to print the date of sale, customer, automobile registration number, car description, year of make, sales price, sales discount, and net sales as follows. The discount granted on an automobile is based on its age and type. The discount is extracted from a two-dimensional table as follows. The age of the car is divided into five categories (1993, 1992, 1991, 1990, and 1989), and the type of car is broken down into five categories (subcompact, compact, mid-size, full-size, and luxury). No discount is given for an automobile year prior to 1984. The car type code (1, 2, 3, 4, or 5) and year are found in the customer sales record. Create a hierarchy chart, structured flowchart, and pseudocode for this problem.

**INPUT RECORD FORMAT:**

| Field | Location | Type |
|---|---|---|
| Date of sale | 1–6 | N |
| Customer | 7–21 | A/N |
| Auto registration | 22–28 | A/N |
| Car type | 30 | N |
| Year | 31–34 | N |
| Sales price | 35–41 | N ($$.¢¢) |

**SINGLE-DIMENSIONAL TABLE:**

| Type Code | Type Description |
|---|---|
| 1 | S-COMPACT |
| 2 | COMPACT |
| 3 | MID-SIZE |
| 4 | FULL-SIZE |
| 5 | LUXURY |

**TWO-DIMENSIONAL TABLE:**

| Auto Year | Discount Percentage Based on Year and Auto Type | | | | |
|---|---|---|---|---|---|
| | SUB 1 | COMP 2 | MID 3 | FULL 4 | LUX 5 |
| 1993 | .050 | .055 | .060 | .065 | .070 |
| 1992 | .040 | .045 | .050 | .060 | .065 |
| 1991 | .030 | .035 | .040 | .050 | .055 |
| 1990 | .020 | .025 | .027 | .029 | .030 |
| 1989 | .005 | .010 | .015 | .020 | .025 |

**OUTPUT REQUIRED:**

```
                        OTTO'S AUTO DEALERSHIP

                        CUSTOMER SALES REPORT

    DATE OF    CUSTOMER     AUTO      AUTO        YR    SALES     DISCOUNT      NET
     SALE       NAME        REG.      TYPE              PRICE

    06/12/93   B. JONES     A-552-Z   S-COMPACT   92   12,000.00   480.0    11,520.00
    07/12/93   D. BAKER     A-445-Q   COMPACT     92   10,000.00   450.00    9,550.00
    07/15/93   S. WHITE     D-555-M   MID-SIZE    90    7,000.00   189.00    6,811.00
    07/17/93   B. JOHNSON   M-773-B   FULL-SIZE   91    8,000.00   400.00    7,600.00
    07/18/93   D. DOBSON    M-663-C   LUXURY      88    5,000.00     0.00    5,000.00
```

**9-3.** Acme Oil and Gas needs a payroll register that lists each employee's department, SSN, name, pay rate, regular hours, overtime hours, gross pay, federal income tax, and net pay. The regular pay rate is to be extracted from a pay rate table. The federal tax, based on gross salary and number of exemptions, is to be extracted from the table containing salary ranges and the number of exemptions claimed on the W-4 form. Examples of these tables follow. Create a hierarchy chart, structured flowchart, and pseudocode for this problem.

**REQUIRED:**

1. Obtain each employee's pay rate by extracting it from a two-dimensional table. The pay rate is based on the employee's job code and number of years of experience. The job code corresponds positionally with the rows in the table. Calculate years of experience by subtracting the year of hire from the current year.* To determine the column in which the pay rate is found, the program must determine the employee's experience range.

2. Calculate the gross pay as follows:

   Gross Pay = (Reg. Pay Rate × Reg. Hrs.)
   + (OT Hrs. × Reg. Pay Rate × 1.5)

3. Look up the appropriate federal income tax amount from the federal income tax table. The search is based on the gross salary range and the number of exemptions.

4. Calculate the net pay as follows:

   Net Pay = Gross Pay — Federal Tax.

Hint: You must establish the correct subscript value for the column subscript. Use a case structure of IF statements, or use the CASE command if the language has it.

*This calculation does not always accurately determine years of experience, but simplifies the procedure for the student. Your teacher may suggest that you alter the logic to accurately determine the years of experience as an embellishment.

**OUTPUT REQUIRED:**

```
                              ACME OIL AND GAS
                              PAYROLL REGISTER

DEPT    SSN         LAST        FIRST    PAY     REG  OT    GROSS     FIT      NET
                                INITIAL  RATE    HRS. HRS.   PAY

XXX   XXXXXXXXX XXXXXXXXX        X      XX.XX   XX   XX    XXXX.XX  XXXX.XX  XXXX.XX
XXX   XXXXXXXXX XXXXXXXXX        X      XX.XX   XX   XX    XXXX.XX  XXXX.XX  XXXX.XX
XXX   XXXXXXXXX XXXXXXXXX        X      XX.XX   XX   XX    XXXX.XX  XXXX.XX  XXXX.XX

TOTAL GROSS PAY      $XXX,XXX.XX
TOTAL FEDERAL TAX    $X,XXX.XX
TOTAL NET PAY        $XX,XXX.XX
```

## INPUT RECORD FORMAT:

| Field | Location | Type |
|---|---|---|
| Department | 1–3 | N |
| SSN | 4–12 | N |
| Last name | 13–22 | A/N |
| First initial | 24 | A/N |
| First name | 25–32 | A/N |
| Middle initial | 33 | A/N |
| Regular hours | 34–35 | N |
| Overtime hours | 36–37 | N |
| Experience code | 38–39 | N |
| Job code | 40–41 | N |
| Date of hire (DOH) | 42–47 | N (MMDDYY) |
| Exemptions | 48–49 | N |

## PAY RATE TABLE:

| Job Code | Years of Experience | | | | | | |
|---|---|---|---|---|---|---|---|
| | 1–5 | 6–10 | 11–15 | 16–20 | 21–25 | 26–35 | 36–45 |
| 1 | 15.00 | 16.00 | 18.00 | 19.00 | 20.00 | 21.00 | 23.00 |
| 2 | 7.00 | 8.00 | 8.50 | 9.00 | 9.50 | 10.00 | 10.50 |
| 3 | 15.00 | 16.00 | 10.00 | 19.00 | 20.00 | 21.50 | 25.00 |
| 4 | 20.00 | 25.00 | 27.00 | 30.00 | 33.00 | 35.00 | 38.00 |
| 5 | 22.00 | 27.00 | 29.00 | 33.00 | 36.00 | 40.00 | 42.00 |
| 6 | 22.00 | 28.00 | 30.00 | 34.00 | 37.00 | 41.00 | 43.00 |
| 7 | 24.00 | 30.00 | 32.00 | 36.00 | 39.00 | 43.00 | 45.00 |
| 8 | 30.00 | 35.00 | 38.00 | 40.00 | 45.00 | 50.00 | 52.00 |
| 9 | 31.00 | 36.00 | 39.00 | 41.00 | 46.00 | 51.00 | 53.00 |
| 10 | 10.00 | 12.00 | 14.00 | 16.00 | 18.00 | 19.00 | 20.00 |

The Pay Rate Table file used in loading the table consists of 70 records. Each record contains 1 pay rate in columns 1–4. The table is loaded using *row major*.

The Federal Income Tax Table is loaded from an Income Tax File. For COBOL, the individual record format identically matches that of the row in the table; therefore, the entire record is moved to the entire row as a group move. There are 16 records in the file, one for each of the 16 rows in the table. For BASIC, the same record format is used, but the loading process will be different, as previously explained in Application 2 of this chapter.

## FEDERAL INCOME TAX TABLE:

| If Gross Does Not Exceed | Exemptions | | | | | | | | |
|---|---|---|---|---|---|---|---|---|---|
| | 0 | 1 | 2 | 3 | 4 | 5 | 6 | 7 | 8 |
| 200 | 30 | 29 | 28 | 27 | 25 | 20 | 12 | 3 | 0 |
| 400 | 60 | 50 | 40 | 30 | 28 | 27 | 15 | 5 | 3 |
| 600 | 100 | 90 | 80 | 70 | 60 | 50 | 40 | 30 | 20 |
| 800 | 120 | 100 | 90 | 80 | 70 | 60 | 50 | 40 | 30 |
| 1000 | 150 | 130 | 120 | 110 | 100 | 90 | 80 | 70 | 60 |
| 1400 | 200 | 180 | 160 | 150 | 140 | 130 | 120 | 110 | 100 |
| 1800 | 230 | 220 | 210 | 200 | 190 | 180 | 170 | 160 | 120 |
| 2100 | 300 | 290 | 280 | 270 | 260 | 250 | 240 | 230 | 200 |
| 2500 | 350 | 340 | 330 | 320 | 310 | 300 | 280 | 270 | 230 |
| 3000 | 600 | 500 | 450 | 430 | 420 | 400 | 390 | 380 | 370 |
| 3500 | 700 | 600 | 550 | 500 | 475 | 450 | 440 | 430 | 420 |
| 4000 | 800 | 750 | 700 | 680 | 670 | 660 | 650 | 640 | 630 |
| 5000 | 1000 | 950 | 900 | 850 | 800 | 750 | 730 | 720 | 700 |
| 6000 | 1500 | 1200 | 1100 | 1000 | 900 | 850 | 800 | 750 | 700 |
| 7000 | 1750 | 1700 | 1650 | 1500 | 1400 | 1350 | 1300 | 1250 | 1200 |
| 8000 | 2000 | 1950 | 1900 | 1850 | 1800 | 1750 | 1700 | 1650 | 1600 |

# 10

# Interactive Programming Logic

## OBJECTIVES:

1. Be able to define both interactive and batch programming.

2. Be able to differentiate between interactive programming and batch programming.

3. Be able to identify advantages and disadvantages of both interactive and batch programs.

4. Be able to identify an environment or processing situation where interactive systems are superior.

5. Be able to identify systems that are characteristically developed using interactive dialogue.

6. Be able to identify the three parts to an interactive screen.

7. Be able to develop the flowchart and pseudocode for an interactive program for a simple business system.

Today's modern business systems are being developed with clients in mind. Clients (or users) of the computer are finally where they have always belonged—at the heart of the development process. Users are the center of the system universe; consequently, they want more control over the data being processed and more interactive access to information. For example, the accountants are interested in the integrity of their ledger data, and warehouse managers are concerned about the validity of their purchase orders. Billing clerks want more control over the maintenance of customer data while top management wants strategic information at the tip of their fingers that enables high-quality decision-support. In many cases today, monthly or weekly reports are unacceptable; therefore, users want to *interact* with the computer in an on-going conversational mode to receive on-the-spot information. Interactive programs provide users with these kinds of capabilities, permitting constant access to user files. An interactive program allows an ongoing dialogue to continue between the user and the program using a menu-driven approach.

## INTERACTIVE VS BATCH PROCESSING

Chapters 2 through 9 dealt with computer applications that utilized batch processing. This means that data were collected over a period of time to create a complete file that is processed periodically. The batch program is only temporarily connected to the file. The records are read and the report is printed. Then the file is closed. An example of a batch processing system is an employee payroll application. The pay data is "batched" or collected over the week, and then pay checks and pay registers are printed at the end of that week. The program is no longer connected to the file nor any longer in control of the computer.

Nevertheless, in an interactive system, there can be continuous interaction with a file. An example is an airline reservation system. Customer's reservation records are constantly being created, deleted, and changed. Thousands of queries are made to check on the status of various flights. On the other hand, using another example, in some cases the interactive program only calculates and produces information from the responses of the user without involving any file. An example is an annuity computation program or a program that computes the area of geometric figures depending upon the selection from the user. The latter application is employed in Application 10.1 of this chapter.

While both batch and interactive systems are used today, *there is an increasing demand for interactive systems.* Interactive programs should be well developed to give the user instant access to information. The time span from entering a response to receiving wanted information is called *response time.* Response time should not be more than two seconds in most cases; programs should be carefully developed to ensure acceptable response times.

## ADVANTAGES AND LIMITATIONS OF INTERACTIVE PROCESSING

### Advantages

A major advantage of interactive processing is that the interactive dialogue produced by the program puts the power of processing alternatives and file maintenance in the hands of the user. The user of the computer, whether the company president or a warehouse clerk, is able to access current, up-to-date information and make decisions with the information immediately. Compare this with batch processing where, say, the sales manager is unable to make a purchasing decision until the monthly sales forecast report arrives. By the time the report arrives it may be too late to make a prudent decision. A second advantage is that users are often able to help maintain the data files or data bases used by their functional areas. In the past, too often this data was maintained by the data processing department, as they were the only ones who had the knowhow to add, delete, and change records in the files. With interactive file maintenance systems (discussed in Chapter 13) users are able to maintain

their own data. The third advantage of interactive processing is made manifest in conversational information retrieval systems. An example is a national discount chain's automobile parts customer information system. The customer selects from a query list of optional parts categories. After this major category has been entered, the computer then prompts the customer to enter the automobile type. From there, it prompts the customer to choose from a selection of engine types for that make of automobile. Then, the computer prints a part description and part number that may be purchased in the discount store. What may have taken the customer a lengthy period to investigate manually takes only a few seconds with the interactive system. Anyone who has attempted to buy an automobile oil filter at a large discount store can appreciate such a time-saving system. The system just described is controlled by the user through a set of menus. The choice from the menu is what controls the path of program execution. These types of systems are often called menu-driven systems.

### Limitations

While users of information systems normally agree that interactive systems are generally better, the method is not without drawbacks. The systems tend to be more expensive, as they normally require expensive communications equipment and terminals as well as skilled personnel. The skill level for a programmer/analyst designing interactive systems is usually greater than that for a batch programmer. Because the programs are typically more involved and difficult to write, they require more development time than batch systems. This extra development time equates to more expense. Also, they are typically bigger interactive programs which take up more storage and must always be available to accept incoming data or responses. These programs also may require faster processors to accommodate concurrent multiple use.

Chapter 13 deals with the advanced interactive logic associated with maintaining non-sequential files. This file maintenance includes adding, deleting, and changing records in a file using an interactive dialogue with the computer.

## MENU-DRIVEN INTERACTIVE DIALOGUE

The dialogue between the user and the computer is controlled by a menu-driven interactive program. The user is presented a set of hierarchical menus. The main menu is presented with a selection of processing choices. The computer program evaluates the response from the user and determines the appropriate course of action. Sometimes this course of action is to present the user with a sub-menu of possible selections from which to choose. The user once again chooses from the sub-menu and the computer program evaluates this sub-response and determines the next course of action, and so on.

## USER PROMPTS AND RESPONSES

When presenting the user with a prompt in the form of a menu, the programmer should provide:

1. A major heading that clearly describes the functions of the processing program.
2. Clear and concise options. Use as few words as possible to describe the function.
3. A choice that allows escape from the module back to the calling module.
4. Numeric options (1, 2, 3, 4, 5, and so on). Avoid using alphabetic options such as I, C, U, H, and Q.
5. A program that traps errors keyed in by the user and requires the user to re-key the data. The technique of requiring the user to re-key erroneously entered data until a valid response is recognized by the program is called *validation loops* or *error traps*. The method repeatedly presents the user with the menu and checks the subsequent response until the user response is valid.

Figure 10.1 illustrates a main menu for a simple application. The interactive application permits a user to compute the area of various geometric figures. Based on the user's choice from the main menu, the program presents the appropriate screen prompt. Figure 10.2 shows a sample screen prompt to determine the area of a circle. This screen prompt asks the user to enter the needed dimensions of the figure so that the area computation can be made. After the responses have been received from the user, the computer program calculates the area of the selected geometric figure and displays the area on the screen. Figure 10.3 illustrates a second screen prompt to compute the area of a triangle. This program's purpose is strictly conversational. No file processing is involved in this application. One sees a simple dialogue between the user and computer program.

Application 10.1 includes the complete screen design, hierarchy chart, structured flowchart, pseudocode, COBOL 85, and Quick Basic programs for this problem.

**FIGURE 10.1   Geometric Figures**

```
*************************************
INTERACTIVE GEOMETRIC FIGURE CALCULATOR
*************************************

PRESS 1 FOR CALCULATING AREA OF CIRCLE

PRESS 2 FOR CALCULATING AREA OF TRIANGLE

PRESS 3 FOR CALCULATING AREA OF RECTANGLE

PRESS 4 FOR CALCULATING AREA OF TRAPEZOID

PRESS 5 TO QUIT


ENTER YOUR RESPONSE :□
```

**FIGURE 10.2    SUB-MENU (on screen prompt) for Interactive Geometric Figure Calculator—To Calculate Area of Circle**

```
* * * * * * * * * * * * * * * * * * * * * * * * * * * * * * * * * * *
CALCULATE AREA OF CIRCLE
* * * * * * * * * * * * * * * * * * * * * * * * * * * * * * * * * * *


WHAT IS THE DIAMETER?      :10


THE AREA OF A CIRCLE WITH
NUMBER OF 10 IS 78.5



PRESS ANY KEY TO CONTINUE
```

**FIGURE 10.3    SUB-MENU (on screen prompt) for Interactive Geometric Figure Calculator—To Calculate Area of Triangle**

```
* * * * * * * * * * * * * * * * * * * * * * * * * * * * * * * * * * * * *
CALCULATE AREA OF TRIANGLE
* * * * * * * * * * * * * * * * * * * * * * * * * * * * * * * * * * * * *


WHAT IS THE BASE?       5
WHAT IS THE HEIGHT?       4

THE AREA OF A TRIANGLE WITH A HEIGHT
OF 4 AND A BASE OF 5 IS 10



PRESS ANY KEY TO CONTINUE
```

## Interactive Geometric Figure Area Calculator

A student wishes to have an interactive computer program that will calculate the area of various geometric figures. The geometric figures to be included are the circle, triangle, rectangle, and trapezoid. The program is to be menu-driven with error traps for each of the selection responses from the main menu. Realistically, every single user-response variable entered should be checked for errors using an error trap loop, but for the sake of brevity for the first application, no other data entries include error traps. The program will prompt the user from a second-level menu or prompt screen to provide dimensions for the geometric figure and subsequently supply the area of the figure at the bottom of the screen.

### SCREEN DESIGN

Exhibits 10.1 and 10.2 depict CRT Layout Forms for the main menu and the circle calculation subscreen for this application. Actually, a CRT Layout Form is prepared for every submenu as well. To reduce redundancy, only the first two are presented. Notice the row and column locations the text is placed in. These row and column locations will be needed in

the development of the COBOL and QuickBASIC programs. Exhibit 10.3 illustrates the set of screens for this application. Frame A shows the main menu previously illustrated in Figure 10.1. Frames B, C, D, and E illustrate the various subscreens for the calculation of the area for the circle, triangle, rectangle, and trapezoid, respectively.

### PROGRAM DESIGN

Exhibit 10.4 shows the hierarchy chart for this problem. Exhibit 10.5 depicts the structured flowchart. The general design shown in the hierarchy chart in Exhibit 10.4 is structured similarly to the batch program designs from previous chapters. Notice that instead of a READ-FILE "call," which has been used in all the batch programming examples thus far, there is a repetition loop that presents a menu repeatedly until a valid response is entered. Also, instead of a PROCESS module (also used in previous batch programs), there is a SELECT-OPTIONS module.

The detailed design shown in the flowchart in Exhibit 10.5 is similar to the flowchart designs in batch programs from previous chapters but has

---

**EXHIBIT 10.1    Screen Design of Main Menu Application 10.1 on CRT Layout Form**

CRT LAYOUT FORM

PROGRAM                                                    PAGE _____ OF _____

PROGRAMMER _____ CRT NO. _____ DATE _____

```
        1 2 3 4 5 6 7 8 9 10 11 12 13 14 15 16 17 18 19 20 21 22 23 24 25 26 27 28 29 30 31 32 33 34 35 36 37 38 39 40 41 42 43 44 45 46 47 48 49 50
   1
   2
   3                * * * * * * * * * * * * * * * * * * * * * * * * * * * * * * * * * *
   4                I N T E R A C T I V E   G E O M E T R I C   F I G U R E   C A L C U L A T O R
   5                * * * * * * * * * * * * * * * * * * * * * * * * * * * * * * * * * *
   6
   7
   8                P R E S S   1   F O R   C A L C U L A T I N G   A R E A   O F   C I R C L E
   9
  10                P R E S S   2   F O R   C A L C U L A T I N G   A R E A   O F   T R I A N G L E
  11
  12                P R E S S   3   F O R   C A L C U L A T I N G   A R E A   O F   R E C T A N G L E
  13
  14                P R E S S   4   F O R   C A L C U L A T I N G   A R E A   O F   T R A P E Z O I D
  15
  16                P R E S S   5   T O   Q U I T
  17
  18
  19
  20
  21
  22
  23
  24
```

specific features to handle the presentation of interactive menus and subscreens until valid responses are received from the user.

The MAIN-MENU looks almost identical to those from previous chapters for batch processing jobs. Notice one difference in the repetition structure where the condition is testing to see if RESP (the response variable) is equal to 5. The user will choose 5 from the menu when finished; therefore, the conditional test causes the SELECT-OPTIONS module to be invoked so long as the user does not press 5. When 5 is entered, the condition becomes true and the program execution continues with the WRAP-UP module.

Let us look at the STARTUP module. What is different about this module from previous chapters? First, there are no files to open or headings to print. Nevertheless, notice that the repetition structure is performing a DISPLAY-MENU-ACCEPT-RESP module until there is a *valid response*. A valid response is a value in the range of 1 through 5. This logic prevents a user from entering an invalid value. The invalid value would probably be inadvertently entered by the user, but nonetheless would cause the computer program to invoke an unwanted module. This would be disastrous, if any value, including values out of range, could be entered. This repetition structure requires that the

value be in the range of 1 through 5 or the main menu is re-presented to the user. This technique is called error trapping or validation looping. The user is in a loop, so to speak, until he or she supplies a valid response.

The DISPLAY-MENU-ACCEPT-RESP module clears the screen, displays the main menu heading and selection choices, and accepts the response from the user into a variable called RESP.

The SELECT-OPTIONS module is the traffic cop of the program. It determines which processing module is to be invoked based upon the user's selection (contents of RESP). The various computational modules clear the screen and display a screen title. Prompts are displayed that require the user to enter the dimension (s) of the geometric figure. The area for the figure is calculated and displayed upon the screen. To hold the information on the screen, the message "PRESS ANY KEY TO CONTINUE" is displayed at the bottom of the screen, and an ACCEPT ANY-KEY (for COBOL 85) or an INPUT ANY.KEY (for Quick Basic) causes a wait state that freezes the screen. Why is this? If it were not for the ACCEPT or INPUT, the screen information would appear and vanish in a flash. To keep the screen painted with information, the user must resort to programming trickery to keep the screen alive. The screen data stay on the screen until the user presses

**EXHIBIT 10.2    Sub Screen Layout for Application 10.1 on CRT Screen Form**

CRT LAYOUT FORM

PROGRAM _____    PAGE _____ OF_____

PROGRAMMER _____ CRT NO._____    DATE_____

```
* * * * * * * * * * * * * * * * * * * * * * * * * *

CALCULATE AREA OF CIRCLE

* * * * * * * * * * * * * * * * * * * * * * * * * *

WHAT IS THE DIAMETER? XX

THE AREA OF A CIRCLE WITH DIAMETER OF XX IS XXX.X



PRESS ANY KEY TO CONTINUE
```

**EXHIBIT 10.3   Screen Designs for Application 10.1 as they would appear on the monitor**

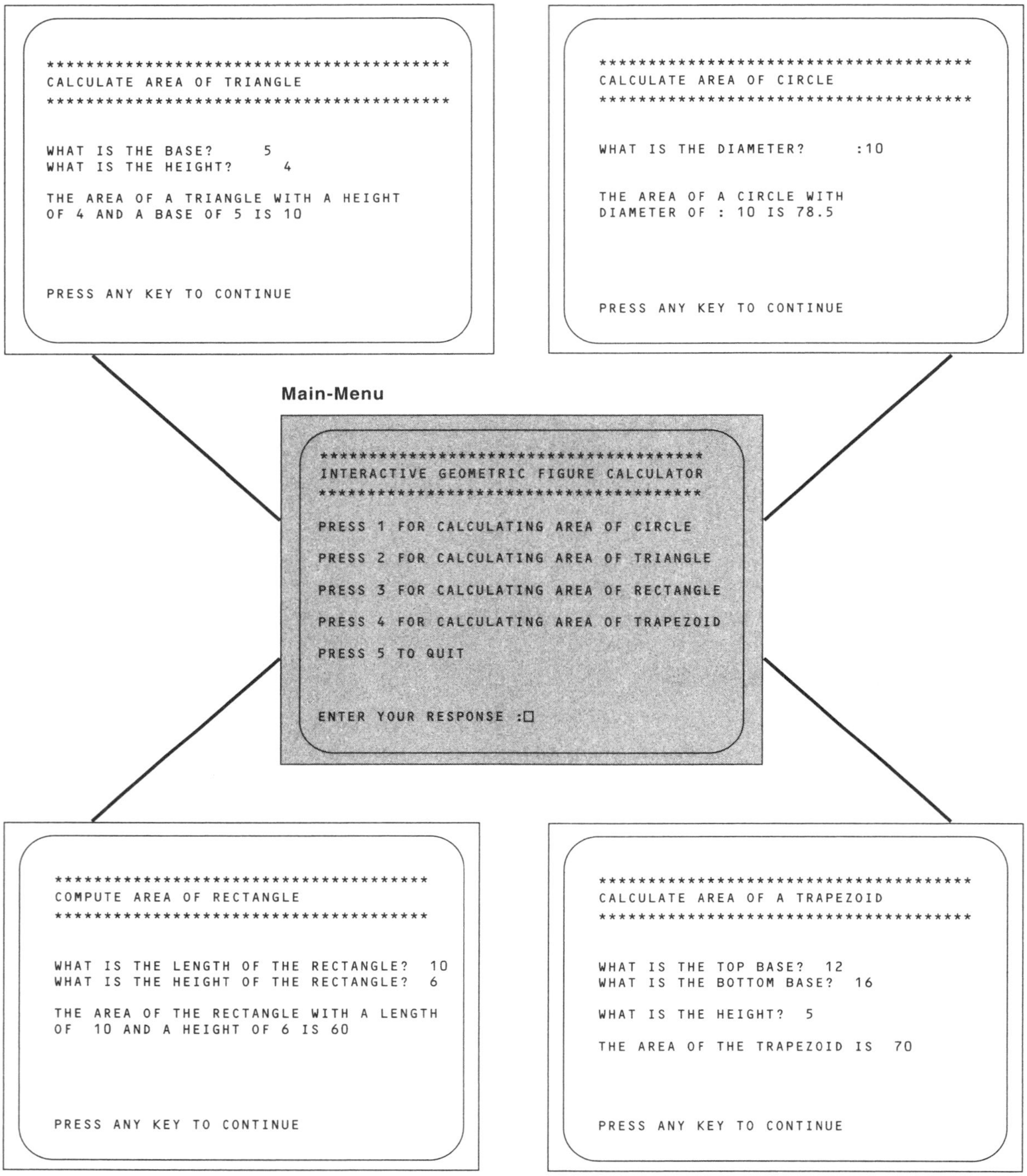

```
***********************************************
CALCULATE AREA OF TRIANGLE
***********************************************

WHAT IS THE BASE?      5
WHAT IS THE HEIGHT?       4

THE AREA OF A TRIANGLE WITH A HEIGHT
OF 4 AND A BASE OF 5 IS 10



PRESS ANY KEY TO CONTINUE
```

```
***********************************************
CALCULATE AREA OF CIRCLE
***********************************************

WHAT IS THE DIAMETER?      :10


THE AREA OF A CIRCLE WITH
DIAMETER OF : 10 IS 78.5



PRESS ANY KEY TO CONTINUE
```

**Main-Menu**

```
***********************************************
INTERACTIVE GEOMETRIC FIGURE CALCULATOR
***********************************************

PRESS 1 FOR CALCULATING AREA OF CIRCLE

PRESS 2 FOR CALCULATING AREA OF TRIANGLE

PRESS 3 FOR CALCULATING AREA OF RECTANGLE

PRESS 4 FOR CALCULATING AREA OF TRAPEZOID

PRESS 5 TO QUIT


ENTER YOUR RESPONSE :□
```

```
***********************************************
COMPUTE AREA OF RECTANGLE
***********************************************

WHAT IS THE LENGTH OF THE RECTANGLE?  10
WHAT IS THE HEIGHT OF THE RECTANGLE?  6

THE AREA OF THE RECTANGLE WITH A LENGTH
OF  10 AND A HEIGHT OF 6 IS 60



PRESS ANY KEY TO CONTINUE
```

```
***********************************************
CALCULATE AREA OF A TRAPEZOID
***********************************************

WHAT IS THE TOP BASE?  12
WHAT IS THE BOTTOM BASE?  16

WHAT IS THE HEIGHT?  5

THE AREA OF THE TRAPEZOID IS   70



PRESS ANY KEY TO CONTINUE
```

any key on the keyboard; the ACCEPT or INPUT is waiting on a user response.

The various computational modules such as AREA-OF-CIRCLE do not include validation statements. Realistically, they should. There should be a validation loop that guarantees that every value entered is within a prescribed range. In this chapter, validation loops are used only to validate the selection response to demonstrate how interactive data validation is handled. (As mentioned earlier, this was done to keep the first application elementary

rather than long and drawn out.) In Chapter 13, these error traps (or validation loops) are used wherever data are inputted. Chapter 13 expands on these concepts and deals with a real-world application where it would be unrealistic to allow a user to key in an invalid datum of any kind.

Exhibit 10.6 contains the pseudocode for Application 10.1, and Exhibits 10.7 and 10.8 show the COBOL 85 and Quick BASIC programs for this problem.

**EXHIBIT 10.4    Hierarchy Chart for Application 10.1, Geometric Figure Calculator**

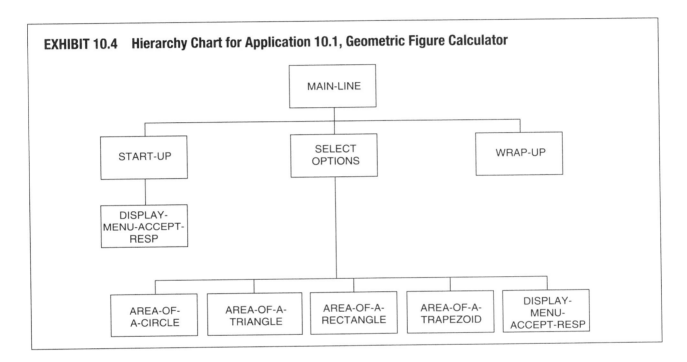

**EXHIBIT 10.5    Structured Flowchart for Application 10.1 (Geometric Figure Area Calculation)**

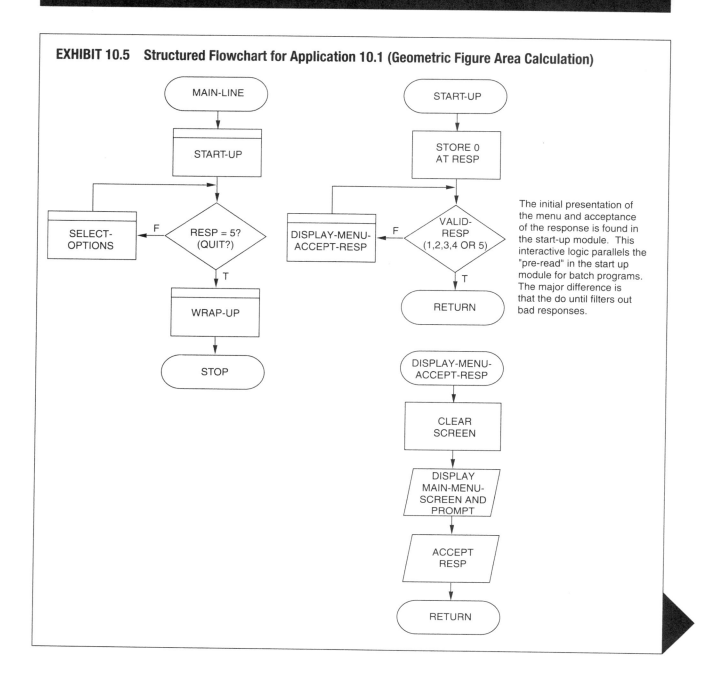

The initial presentation of the menu and acceptance of the response is found in the start-up module. This interactive logic parallels the "pre-read" in the start up module for batch programs. The major difference is that the do until filters out bad responses.

**EXHIBIT 10.5    (Cont.)**

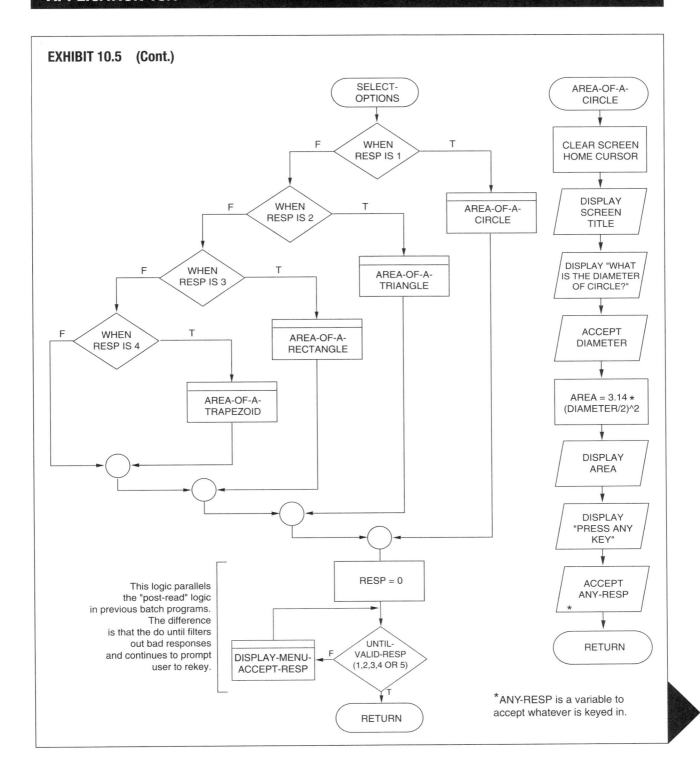

This logic parallels the "post-read" logic in previous batch programs. The difference is that the do until filters out bad responses and continues to prompt user to rekey.

*ANY-RESP is a variable to accept whatever is keyed in.

**EXHIBIT 10.5   (Cont.)**

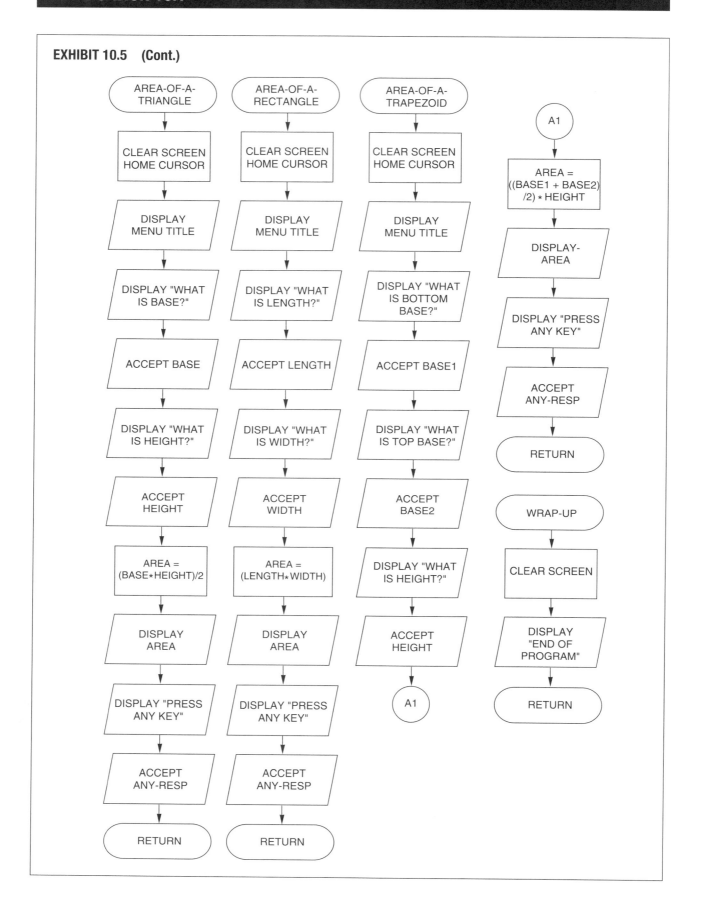

## EXHIBIT 10.6  Exhibit 10.6 Pseudocode for Application 10.1 (Geometric Figure Calculator)

```
*main-line
    startup
    do until resp = 5 (quit?)
        select-options
    end do
    wrapup
    stop
*startup
    store 0 at resp
    do until valid-resp (1 thru 5)
        display-menu-accept-resp
    end do
    return
*display-menu-accept-resp
    clear screen
    display main-menu-screen and prompt
    accept resp
    return
*select-options
    case resp
    when resp is 1
        area-of-circle
    when resp is 2
        area-of-triangle
    when resp is 3
        area-of-rectangle
    when resp is 4
        area-of-trapezoid
    end case
    resp = 0
    do until valid-resp (1, 2, 3, 4 or 5)
        display-menu-accept-resp
    end do
    return
*area-of-circle
    clear screen and home cursor
    display screen title
    display "what is the diameter?"
    accept diameter
    area = 3.14 * (diameter/2) ^ 2 (raised to power of 2)
    display area
    display "press any key to continue"
    accept any-resp
    return
```

```
*area-of-triangle
    clear screen and home cursor
    display screen title
    display "what is the base?"
    accept base
    what is the height?
    accept height
    area = (base * height) / 2
    display area
    display "press any key to continue"
    accept any-resp
    return
*area-of-rectangle
    clear screen and home cursor
    display screen title
    display "what is the length?"
    accept length
    display "what is the width?"
    accept width
    area = length * width
    display area
    display "press any key to continue"
    accept any-resp
    return
*area-of-trapezoid
    clear screen and home cursor
    display screen title
    display "what is the bottom base?"
    accept base1
    display "what is the top base?"
    accept base2
    display "what is the height?"
    accept height
    area = ((base1 + base2)/2) * height
    display area
    display "press any key to continue"
    accept any-resp
    return
*wrap-up
    clear screen
    display "end of program"
    return
```

**EXHIBIT 10.7    COBOL 85 (Interactive COBOL Program—Geometric Figure Area Calculator)**

```
1         *mainframe version
2          IDENTIFICATION DIVISION.
3          PROGRAM-ID. CH101NEW.
4         *REMARKS:   THIS IS THE MAINFRAME VERSION OF THE GEOMETRIC
5         *           FIGURE CALCULATION PROGRAM.  IT INCLUDES AN
6         *           INSPECT COMMAND AND A SPECIAL COMPUTE ALGORITHM
7         *           TO HANDLE NUMERIC DATA ENTRY FROM THE KEYBOARD
8         *           WHEN USING THE ACCEPT COMMAND.  OTHERWISE, THE ACCEPT
9         *           COMMAND WOULD REQUIRE THE USER TO ENTER LEADING ZEROS
10        *           (THE CORRECT NUMBER OF LEADING ZEROS) ON ALL NUMERIC
11        *           FIELDS.
12         ENVIRONMENT DIVISION.
13         CONFIGURATION SECTION.
14         SOURCE-COMPUTER. CYBER.
15         OBJECT-COMPUTER. CYBER.
16         INPUT-OUTPUT SECTION.
17
18         DATA DIVISION.
19         WORKING-STORAGE SECTION.
20         01   RESP     PIC    9  VALUE ZERO.
21              88 VALID-RESPONSE VALUES ARE 1 THRU 5.
22         01   ANY-KEY    PIC   XX VALUE SPACES.
23         01   BASE     PIC   999 VALUE ZEROS.
24         01   BASE1    PIC   999 VALUE ZEROS.
25         01   BASE2    PIC   999 VALUE ZEROS.
26         01   HEIGHT   PIC   999 VALUE ZEROS.
27         01   DIAMETER PIC 999 VALUE ZEROS.
28         01   AREAX      PIC    9999V99 VALUE ZEROS.
29         01   AREAX-OUT PIC Z,ZZ9.99.
30         01   LENGTHX    PIC   999 VALUE ZEROS.
31         01   WIDTH    PIC   999 VALUE ZEROS.
32         01   INSPECT-FIELD-ALPHA PIC XXX VALUE SPACES.
33         01   INSPECT-FIELD-NUMERIC REDEFINES INSPECT-FIELD-ALPHA PIC 999.
34         01   TALLY-CT   PIC   9 VALUE ZERO.
35         01   TEN   PIC 99 VALUE 10.
36         PROCEDURE DIVISION.
37         000-MAIN-LINE.
38             PERFORM 100-STARTUP-MAINMENU.
39             PERFORM 200-SELECT-OPTIONS UNTIL RESP = 5.
40             PERFORM 300-WRAPUP.
41             STOP RUN.
42
43         100-STARTUP-MAINMENU.
44
45             MOVE 0 TO RESP.
46             PERFORM 110-DISPLAY-MENU-ACCEPT-RESP
47                 UNTIL VALID-RESPONSE.
48
49         110-DISPLAY-MENU-ACCEPT-RESP.
50
51        *NOTE: INDIVIDUAL USERS OF THIS PROGRAM WILL NEED TO INSERT
52        *      THEIR OWN CLEAR SCREEN AND HOME CURSOR COMMANDS OR
53        *      CHARACTERS, DEPENDING ON HARDWARE/SOFTWARE ENVIRONMENTS.
54             DISPLAY "********************************************".
55             DISPLAY "INTERACTIVE GEOMETRIC FIGURE CALCULATOR".
56             DISPLAY "********************************************".
57             DISPLAY "PRESS 1 FOR CALCULATING AREA   OF CIRCLE".
58             DISPLAY "PRESS 2 FOR CALCULATING AREA   OF TRIANGLE".
59             DISPLAY "PRESS 3 FOR CALCULATING AREA   OF RECTANGLE".
60             DISPLAY "PRESS 4 FOR CALCULATING AREA   OF TRAPEZOID".
61             DISPLAY "PRESS 5 TO QUIT".
62             DISPLAY "ENTER YOUR RESPONSE".
63             ACCEPT RESP.
64
```

**EXHIBIT 10.7 (Cont.)**

```
65          200-SELECT-OPTIONS.
66
67              EVALUATE RESP
68                  WHEN 1
69                      PERFORM 210-AREAX-OF-CIRCLE
70                  WHEN 2
71                      PERFORM 220-AREAX-OF-TRIANGLE
72                  WHEN 3
73                      PERFORM 230-AREAX-OF-RECTANGLE
74                  WHEN 4
75                      PERFORM 240-AREAX-OF-TRAPEZOID
76              END-EVALUATE
77              MOVE 0 TO RESP.
78              PERFORM 110-DISPLAY-MENU-ACCEPT-RESP UNTIL VALID-RESPONSE.
79
80          210-AREAX-OF-CIRCLE.
81
82      *INSERT YOUR OWN CLS COMMAND HERE
83              DISPLAY "************************".
84              DISPLAY "CALULATE AREA  OF CIRCLE".
85              DISPLAY "************************".
86              DISPLAY "WHAT IS THE DIAMETER? ".
87              ACCEPT DIAMETER
88
89      *SET UP DIAMETER FOR NUMERIC INPUT
90              MOVE DIAMETER TO INSPECT-FIELD-NUMERIC.
91              PERFORM 270-FIELD-TRANSFORM.
92              MOVE INSPECT-FIELD-NUMERIC TO DIAMETER.
93              DISPLAY " ".
94              COMPUTE AREAX = 3.14 * (DIAMETER / 2)**2.
95              MOVE AREAX TO AREAX-OUT.
96              DISPLAY "THE AREA OF THE CIRCLE IS " AREAX-OUT.
97
98              DISPLAY "PRESS ANY KEY TO CONTINUE".
99              ACCEPT ANY-KEY.
100
101          220-AREAX-OF-TRIANGLE.
102
103      *INSERT YOUR OWN CLEAR SCREEN COMMAND HERE
104              DISPLAY "******************************".
105              DISPLAY "CALCULATE AREA OF TRIANGLE".
106              DISPLAY "******************************".
107              DISPLAY "WHAT IS THE BASE? ".
108              ACCEPT BASE.
109
110      *PAD ACCEPTED NUMERIC FIELDS WITH LEFT ZEROS.
111              MOVE BASE TO INSPECT-FIELD-ALPHA.
112              PERFORM 270-FIELD-TRANSFORM.
113              MOVE INSPECT-FIELD-NUMERIC TO BASE.
114
115
116              DISPLAY " ".
117              DISPLAY "WHAT IS THE HEIGHT?".
118              ACCEPT HEIGHT.
119
120      *PAD ACCEPTED NUMRIC FIELD WITH LEFT ZEROS.
121              MOVE HEIGHT TO INSPECT-FIELD-ALPHA.
122              PERFORM 270-FIELD-TRANSFORM.
123              MOVE INSPECT-FIELD-NUMERIC TO HEIGHT.
124
125
126              COMPUTE AREAX  = (BASE * HEIGHT) / 2.
127              MOVE AREAX  TO AREAX-OUT.
128              DISPLAY "THE AREA  OF THE TRIANGLE IS " AREAX-OUT.
129
```

**EXHIBIT 10.7** (Cont.)

```
130              DISPLAY "PRESS ANY KEY TO CONTINUE"
131              ACCEPT ANY-KEY.
132
133
134
135        230-AREAX-OF-RECTANGLE.
136
137     *INSERT YOUR OWN CLEAR SCREEN COMMAND HERE
138              DISPLAY "*******************************"
139              DISPLAY "CALCULATE AREA OF RECTANGLE".
140              DISPLAY "*******************************"
141              DISPLAY "WHAT IS THE WIDTH?"
142              ACCEPT WIDTH.
143
144     *PAD ACCEPTED NUMERIC FIELDS WITH ZEROS.
145              MOVE WIDTH TO INSPECT-FIELD-ALPHA.
146              PERFORM 270-FIELD-TRANSFORM.
147              MOVE INSPECT-FIELD-NUMERIC TO WIDTH.
148              DISPLAY " ".
149              DISPLAY "WHAT IS THE LENGTH ?".
150              ACCEPT LENGTHX.
151
152     *PAD ACCEPTED NUMERIC FIELDS WITH ZEROS.
153              MOVE LENGTHX TO INSPECT-FIELD-ALPHA.
154              PERFORM 270-FIELD-TRANSFORM.
155              MOVE INSPECT-FIELD-NUMERIC TO LENGTHX.
156              COMPUTE AREAX  = LENGTHX * WIDTH.
157              MOVE AREAX  TO AREAX-OUT.
158              DISPLAY "THE AREA  OF THE RECTANGLE IS " AREAX-OUT.
159              DISPLAY "PRESS ANY KEY TO CONTINUE"
160              ACCEPT ANY-KEY.
161
162
163
164        240-AREAX-OF-TRAPEZOID.
165
166     *INSERT YOUR OWN CLEAR SCREEN COMMAND HERE
167              DISPLAY "*****************************".
168              DISPLAY "CALCULATE AREA  OF TRAPEZOID".
169              DISPLAY "*****************************".
170              DISPLAY "WHAT IS THE TOP BASE? ".
171              ACCEPT BASE1.
172
173     *FIX ACCEPTED NUMERIC FIELD WITH LEFT ZEROS.
174              MOVE BASE1 TO INSPECT-FIELD-ALPHA.
175              PERFORM 270-FIELD-TRANSFORM.
176              MOVE INSPECT-FIELD-NUMERIC TO BASE1.
177              DISPLAY "  ".
178              DISPLAY "WHAT IS THE BOTTOM BASE?".
179              ACCEPT BASE2.
180
181     *FIX ACCEPTED NUMERIC FIELD WITH LEFT ZEROS.
182              MOVE BASE2 TO INSPECT-FIELD-ALPHA.
183              PERFORM 270-FIELD-TRANSFORM.
184              MOVE INSPECT-FIELD-NUMERIC TO BASE2.
185              DISPLAY "WHAT IS THE HEIGHT? ".
186              ACCEPT HEIGHT.
187     *FIX ACCEPTED NUMERIC FIELD WITH LEFT ZEROS.
188              MOVE HEIGHT TO INSPECT-FIELD-ALPHA.
189              PERFORM 270-FIELD-TRANSFORM.
190              MOVE INSPECT-FIELD-NUMERIC TO HEIGHT.
191              COMPUTE AREAX  = ((BASE1 + BASE2) / 2 * HEIGHT).
192              MOVE AREAX  TO AREAX-OUT.
193              DISPLAY "THE AREA OF THE TRAPEZOID IS " AREAX-OUT.
194              DISPLAY "PRESS ANY KEY TO CONTINUE".
```

**EXHIBIT 10.7    (Cont.)**

```
195            ACCEPT ANY-KEY.
196
197       270-FIELD-TRANSFORM.
198            MOVE 0 TO TALLY-CT.
199            INSPECT INSPECT-FIELD-ALPHA TALLYING TALLY-CT FOR
200               ALL SPACES.
201            INSPECT INSPECT-FIELD-ALPHA REPLACING ALL SPACES BY ZERO.
202            COMPUTE INSPECT-FIELD-NUMERIC =
203                           INSPECT-FIELD-NUMERIC / TEN**TALLY-CT.
204
205       300-WRAPUP.
206
207            DISPLAY "END OF PROGRAM".
208            DISPLAY "PRESS ANY KEY TO CONTINUE".
209            ACCEPT ANY-KEY.
210
211
212
```

**EXHIBIT 10.8    Quick BASIC (Interactive Program—Geometric Figure Area Calculation)**

```
'****************************************************************
'*                    PROGRAM-IDENTIFICATION                   *
'****************************************************************
'* PROGRAM NAME: CH10I1NW                                      *
'****************************************************************
'* REMARKS:                                                    *
'* THE FOLLOWING PROGRAM IS AN INTERACTIVE PROGRAM THAT ALLOWS A USER *
'* TO CALCULATE THE AREA OF FOUR GEOMETRIC FIGURES BY SELECTING THE   *
'* THE GEOMETRIC FIGURE FROM A MENU SELECTION.  IT THEN PROMPTS THE   *
'* USER FOR GEOMETRIC PARAMETERS AND PROVIDES THE APPROPRIATE AREA.   *
'* THE PROGRAM ALSO TRAPS INVALID DATA AND ASKS THE USER TO RETRY IF  *
'* FOUND TO BE INVALID.  FOR EXAMPLE, THE ONLY VALID RESPONSE FROM THE*
'* MAIN MENU IS A NUMERIC VALUE FROM 1 TO 5.                    *
'****************************************************************


'****************************************************************
'*                       MAIN-LINE                             *
'****************************************************************

MAIN.LINE:
      GOSUB STARTUP                    'PERFORM STARTUP ROUTINE
      DO UNTIL RESP = 5
            GOSUB SELECT.OPTIONS       'PERFORM SELECT-OPTIONS ROUTINE
      LOOP
      GOSUB WRAPUP                     'PERFORM WRAPUP ROUTINE
      END
```

**EXHIBIT 10.8** **(Cont.)**

```
'************************************************************************
'*                          STARTUP                                    *
'************************************************************************

STARTUP:
     RESP = 0                           'INITIALIZE RESPONSE VARIABLE

     DO UNTIL RESP > 0 AND RESP < 6        'INSURES A PROPER RESPONSE IS ENTERED
         GOSUB DISPLAY.MENU.ACCEPT.RESPONSE
     LOOP
     RETURN



     '************************************************************************
     '*                    DISPLAY-MENU-ACCEPT-RESPONSE                      *
     '************************************************************************

DISPLAY.MENU.ACCEPT.RESPONSE:
     COLOR 7, 9
     CLS
     LOCATE 4, 10: PRINT "***************************************"
     LOCATE 5, 10: PRINT "INTERACTIVE GEOMETRIC FIGURE CALCULATOR"
     LOCATE 6, 10: PRINT "***************************************"
     LOCATE 9, 10: PRINT "PRESS 1 FOR CALCULATING AREA OF CIRCLE"
     LOCATE 11, 10: PRINT "PRESS 2 FOR CALCULATING AREA OF TRIANGLE"
     LOCATE 13, 10: PRINT "PRESS 3 FOR CALCULATING AREA OF RECTANGLE"
     LOCATE 15, 10: PRINT "PRESS 4 FOR CALCULATING AREA OF TRAPEZOID"
     LOCATE 17, 10: PRINT "PRESS 5 TO QUIT"

     LOCATE 22, 10: INPUT "ENTER YOUR RESPONSE :", RESP
     RETURN


     '************************************************************************
     '*                       SELECT-OPTIONS                                *
     '************************************************************************

SELECT.OPTIONS:
     SELECT CASE RESP
     CASE 1                         'SELECT THIS OPTION IF RESP IS 1
          GOSUB AREA.OF.CIRCLE
     CASE 2                         'SELECT THIS OPTION IF RESP IS 2
          GOSUB AREA.OF.TRIANGLE
     CASE 3                         'SELECT THIS OPTION IF RESP IS 3
          GOSUB AREA.OF.RECTANGLE
     CASE 4                         'SELECT THIS OPTION IF RESP IS 4
          GOSUB AREA.OF.TRAPEZOID
     END SELECT
     RESP = 0
     DO UNTIL RESP > 0 AND RESP < 6
          GOSUB DISPLAY.MENU.ACCEPT.RESPONSE
     LOOP
     RETURN
```

**EXHIBIT 10.8 (Cont.)**

```
'*****************************************************************
'*                       AREA-OF-CIRCLE                          *
'*****************************************************************

AREA.OF.CIRCLE:
     CLS
     COLOR 2, 13
     LOCATE 5, 10: PRINT "****************************"
     LOCATE 7, 10: PRINT "CALCULATE AREA OF CIRCLE"
     LOCATE 9, 10: PRINT "****************************"
     LOCATE 12, 10: INPUT "WHAT IS THE DIAMETER?  :", DIAMETER
     AREA = 3.14 * (DIAMETER / 2) ^ 2
     LOCATE 15, 10: PRINT "THE DIAMETER OF A CIRCLE OF :"; DIAMETER; "IS "; AREA
     LOCATE 22, 10: PRINT "PRESS ANY KEY TO CONTINUE"
     ANYKEY$ = INPUT$(1)
     RETURN


'*****************************************************************
'*                      AREA-OF-TRIANGLE                         *
'*****************************************************************

AREA.OF.TRIANGLE:
     CLS
     COLOR 4, 15
     LOCATE 5, 10: PRINT "****************************"
     LOCATE 7, 10: PRINT "CALCULATE AREA OF TRIANGLE"
     LOCATE 9, 10: PRINT "****************************"
     LOCATE 12, 10: INPUT "WHAT IS THE BASE"; BASEX
     LOCATE 13, 10: INPUT "WHAT IS THE HEIGHT"; HEIGHT
     AREA = (BASEX * HEIGHT) / 2
     LOCATE 15, 10: PRINT "THE AREA OF A TRIANGLE WITH A HEIGHT OF "; HEIGHT
     LOCATE 16, 10: PRINT "AND A BASE OF "; BASEX; "IS "; AREA
     LOCATE 25, 10: PRINT "PRESS ANY KEY TO CONTINUE"
     ANYKEY$ = INPUT$(1)
     RETURN


'*****************************************************************
'*                      AREA-OF-RECTANGLE                        *
'*****************************************************************

AREA.OF.RECTANGLE:

     CLS
     COLOR 5, 11
     PRINT "**********************************"
     PRINT "COMPUTE AREA OF RECTANGLE        "
     PRINT "**********************************"
     PRINT
     INPUT "WHAT IS THE LENGTH OF THE RECTANGLE"; LENGTH
     INPUT "WHAT IS THE HEIGHT OF THE RECTANGLE"; HEIGHT
     AREA = LENGTH * HEIGHT
```

**EXHIBIT 10.8   (Cont.)**

```
      PRINT
      PRINT "THE AREA OF THE RECTANGLE WITH A LENGTH OF "; LENGTH
      PRINT "AND A HEIGHT OF "; HEIGHT; "IS "; AREA
      PRINT : PRINT : PRINT : PRINT : PRINT : PRINT : PRINT
      PRINT "PRESS ANY KEY TO CONTINUE"
      ANYKEY$ = INPUT$(1)
      RETURN


      '*******************************************************************
      '*                      AREA-OF-TRAPEZOID                         *
      '*******************************************************************


AREA.OF.TRAPEZOID:

      CLS
      COLOR 4, 15
      LOCATE 5, 10: PRINT "*****************************"
      LOCATE 7, 10: PRINT "CALCULATE AREA OF A TRAPEZOID"
      LOCATE 9, 10: PRINT "*****************************"
      LOCATE 12, 10: INPUT "WHAT IS THE TOP BASE"; BASE1
      LOCATE 13, 10: INPUT "WHAT IS THE BOTTOM BASE"; BASE2
      LOCATE 15, 10: INPUT "WHAT IS THE HEIGHT "; HEIGHT
      AREA = ((BASE1 + BASE2) / 2 * HEIGHT)
      LOCATE 17, 10: PRINT "THE AREA OF THE TRAPEZOID IS "; AREA
      LOCATE 25, 10: PRINT "PRESS ANY KEY TO CONTINUE"
      ANYKEY$ = INPUT$(1)
      RETURN


      '*******************************************************************
      '*                          WRAPUP                               *
      '*******************************************************************

WRAPUP:

      CLS
      PRINT "END OF PROGRAM"
      PRINT "PRESS ANY KEY TO CONTINUE"
      ANYKEY$ = INPUT$(1)
      RETURN
```

# Interactive File Creation and Mailing Label Generation

A file is needed periodically to generate mailing labels for employees. An interactive, menu-driven program is appropriate for this function. The program should be able to: 1) allow the entry of employee address data and the subsequent record creation into a sequential file, 2) print the file to the screen, 3) print the file to the printer, and 4) generate mailing labels for each employee in the file. Validation loops should be supplied to ensure the appropriate menu selection.

## SCREEN DESIGN

Exhibit 10.9 illustrates the main menu and its associated subscreens. Panel A depicts the main menu which allows the user to: 1) select 1 to create or append records to the file, 2) select 2 to display the records on the screen, 3) select 3 to print the file to a printer, 4) select 4 to generate mailing labels from the file, and 5) select 5 to quit. Panel B illustrates the Add Menu screen to allow records to be added. Panel C shows a data entry screen. Panel D shows a sample screen of records that have been added to the label file. Panel E illustrates a few of the labels that would be produced.

## PROGRAM DESIGN

Exhibit 10.10 shows the structured flowchart for Application 10.2. The MAIN-LINE, STARTUP, AND DISPLAY-MENU-ACCEPT-RESP modules remain virtually the same from Application 10.1. The structure of the SELECT-OPTIONS module is also almost a carbon copy of that from Application 10.1, except the module calls are to different modules. A case structure is used with four selections. When the RESP variable is equal to 1, then the ADD-RECORDS is invoked. When the RESP variable is equal to 2, then the PRINT-THE-FILE-TO-SCREEN module is invoked. When the RESP variable is equal to 3, then the PRINT-THE-FILE-TO-PRINTER module is invoked. When the RESP variable is equal to 4, then the PRINT-LABELS module is invoked. An error message prints otherwise. This message should be a double safety valve as no value other than 1 through 5 is allowed as input to this module. The validation loop at the bottom of the SELECT-OPTIONS module is also a carbon copy from Application 10.1. The main menu is re-presented until a valid response of 1 through 5 is entered by the user.

The ADD-RECORDS module clears the screen and homes the cursor. The label file is OPENed as EXTEND for the language COBOL or OPENed as APPEND for the language Quick BASIC. The RESP variable is cleared to zero the first time so that the condition will be at least false the first time; otherwise, the menu would never be displayed. A validation loop calls the PRESENT-ADD-MENU until a valid response of 1 or 2 is received. A response of 1 causes the ADD-A-SINGLE-RECORD module to be called. A user can enter a multiple number of records within the confines of this loop. Until the user keys in a response of 2, the ADD-A-SINGLE-RECORD module is repeatedly executed. This is a nice feature of the logic. Users who enter a single record and are returned to the main menu must re-select a 1 just to re-enter the ADD-RECORDS module. Users can be annoyed when this happens, especially if they must enter hundreds or thousands of records.

The PRESENT-ADD-MENU simply displays the two choices on the screen. One choice is to add a record to the file, and the second choice is to quit. The RESPonse from the user is accepted and checked for validity. If not valid, a message is displayed that the response just entered is invalid and the user should retry. An ACCEPT or INPUT command follows to create a wait state so the message stays on the screen.

The ADD-A-SINGLE-RECORD contains various pairs of displays and accepts to allow data entry for each record field. At the bottom of the module is the validation loop, which re-presents the PRESENT-ADD-MENU until a response of a 1 (add another record) or 2 (quit).

The PRINT-THE-FILE-TO-SCREEN is virtually self-explanatory. For each entry into this module, the END-FLAG is reinitialized, the label file is opened as input, and the sub-menu information is displayed. Scrolling can be a problem when more record rows that need to be displayed exist in the file than are available on the screen; when this occurs, a BOTTOM-OF-SCREEN-CHECK is made. LN-CT is initialized to 5 to reflect the counting of headings on the screen. The first record is then read. A repetition loop is established that contains the BOTTOM-OF-SCREEN-CHECK, the record fields are displayed to the screen, and the next record is read. When END-FLAG is equal to "YES" the file is closed. The PRINT-FILE-TO-PRINTER is a near duplicate of the one just discussed except that BOTTOM-OF-PAGE-CHECK tests for printing 40 lines while the BOTTOM-OF-SCREEN-CHECK tests for displaying only 15 lines (actually only ten

**EXHIBIT 10.9  The Menus and Screens for Application 10.2, Mailing Label Generation**

**Panel A Main Menu**

```
*****************************************
INTERACTIVE FILE MAINTENANCE
*****************************************

PRESS 1 TO ADD RECORDS TO THE FILE

PRESS 2 TO LIST THE FILE TO THE SCREEN

PRESS 3 TO PRINT A HARD COPY OF THE FILE

PRESS 4 TO PRINT LABELS

PRESS 5 TO QUIT

ENTER YOUR RESPONSE :
```

**Panel B The Add Records Sub Menu**

```
*********************************************
ADD RECORDS TO FILE MENU
*********************************************

TO ADD RECORD TO FILE, PRESS 1

TO EXIT THE ADD MENU, PRESS 2

WHAT IS YOUR RESPONSE?
```

**Panel C Name and Address Data Entry Screen**

```
WHAT IS THE SSN?  000000000
WHAT IS THE LAST NAME?           DOE
WHAT IS THE FIRST NAME?          JOHN
WHAT IS THE STREET?   MISTY LANE
WHAT IS THE CITY?     GOTHAM
WHAT IS THE STATE?    MAINE
WHAT IS THE ZIP?      00000

THE RECORD WAS ADDED TO THE LABELS FILE

PRESS ANY KEY TO CONTINUE
```

**Panel D Example Listing of Label Data File**

```
          SEQUENTIAL LISTING OF LABELS FILES

SSN        LAST NAME   FIRST NAME  STREET        CITY           STATE  ZIP
111111111  RUSSELL     JACK        HCR 51        STEPHENVILLE    TX    76401
222222222  RUSSELL     BARBARA     STONE CUTOFF  STEPHENVILLE    TX    76401
333333333  RUSSELL     JENNY       STONE CUTOFF  STEPHENVILLE    TX    76401
444444444  ALBORN      AL          WASHINGTON    RESTON          VA    77777
888888889  BAKER       CHARLIE     111 LEVITA    LEVITA          TX    33333
555555555  DONALDSON   SAM         222 EAST      WASHINGTON      DC    33333
393939394  COOPER      DAMON       333 RANGE     ARLINGTON       TX    33333
110101017  LAMBETH     CHARLIE     222 HELM      FORT WORTH      TX    44444
191919199  HILL        BOBBY       333 WEST      JONESBORO       TX    33333
888888888  STRICKER    ROBERT      333 MAXWELL   WARREN          MI    22222
202020222  MUSSON      BETTY       222 NORTH     WARREN          MI    33333
67676767673 DOBSON     DAVE        333 OAK       FT. WORTH       TX    44444
000000000  DOE         JOHN        MISTY LANE    GOTHAM          ME    00000


PRESS ENTER TO CONTINUE
```

**Panel E Sample Labels for Label Generation**

```
BETTY          MUSSON
222 NORTH
WARREN          , MI  33333
```

```
ROBERT         STRICKER
333 MAXWELL
WARREN          , MI  22222
```

data records). The PRINT-LABELS module is also very similar except that the record fields are formatted into three separate label lines. The first name and last name are printed on the first label line. The address is printed on the second label line, and the city, state, and zip are printed on the third label line. Two blank lines are printed to allow

proper paper advance to next blank label. WRAP-UP module once again simply handles the clearing of the screen and displaying of an end of program message.

Exhibit 10.11 illustrates the pseudocode, and Exhibits 10.12 and 10.13 show the associated COBOL 85 and Quick BASIC programs, respectively.

**EXHIBIT 10.10  Structured Flowchart for Application 10.2**

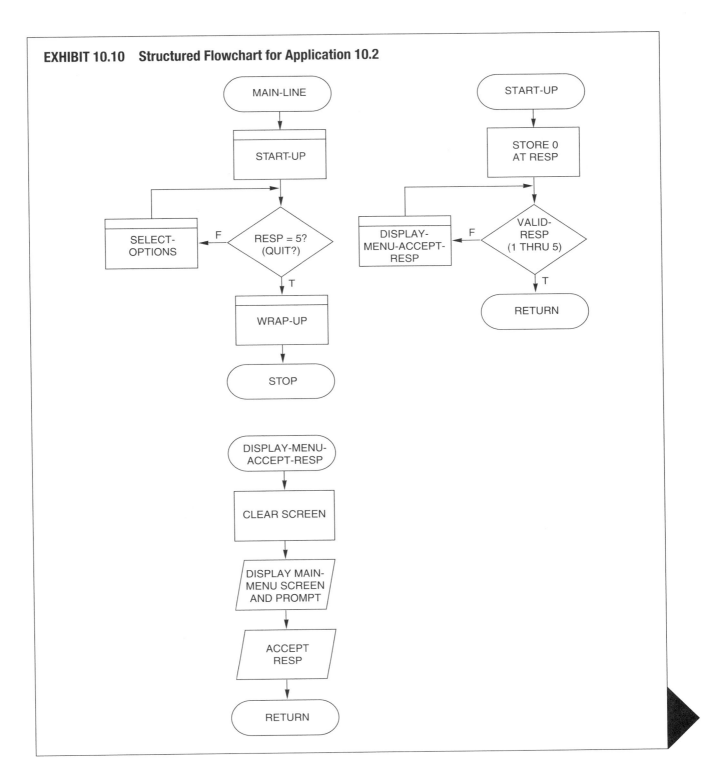

**EXHIBIT 10.10    (Cont.)**

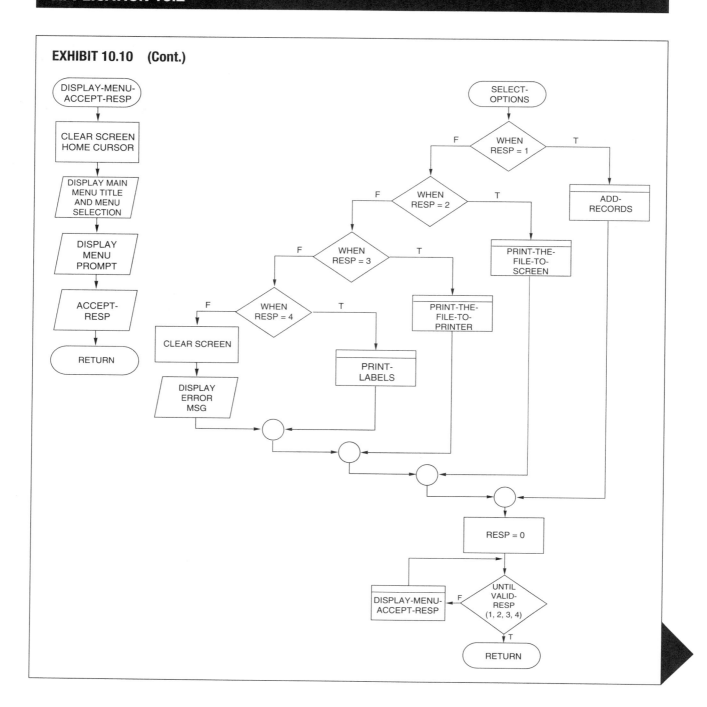

**EXHIBIT 10.10    (Cont.)**

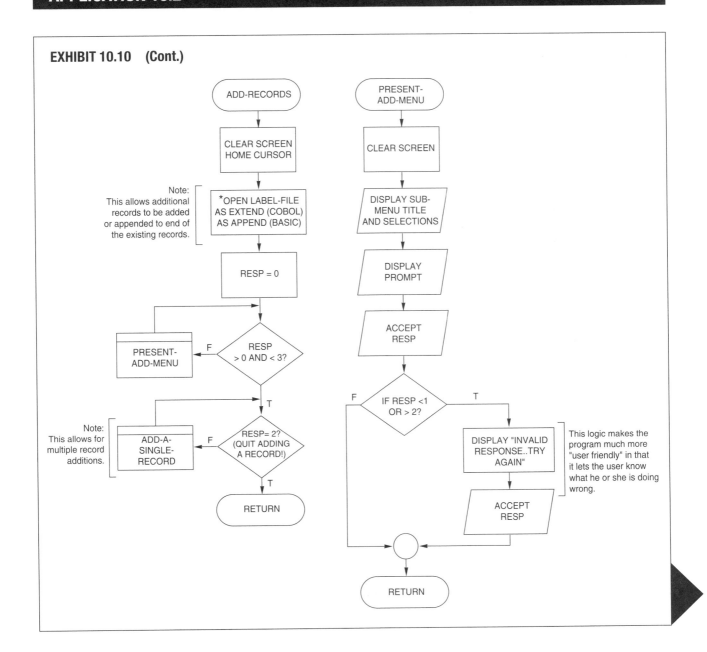

## EXHIBIT 10.10   (Cont.)

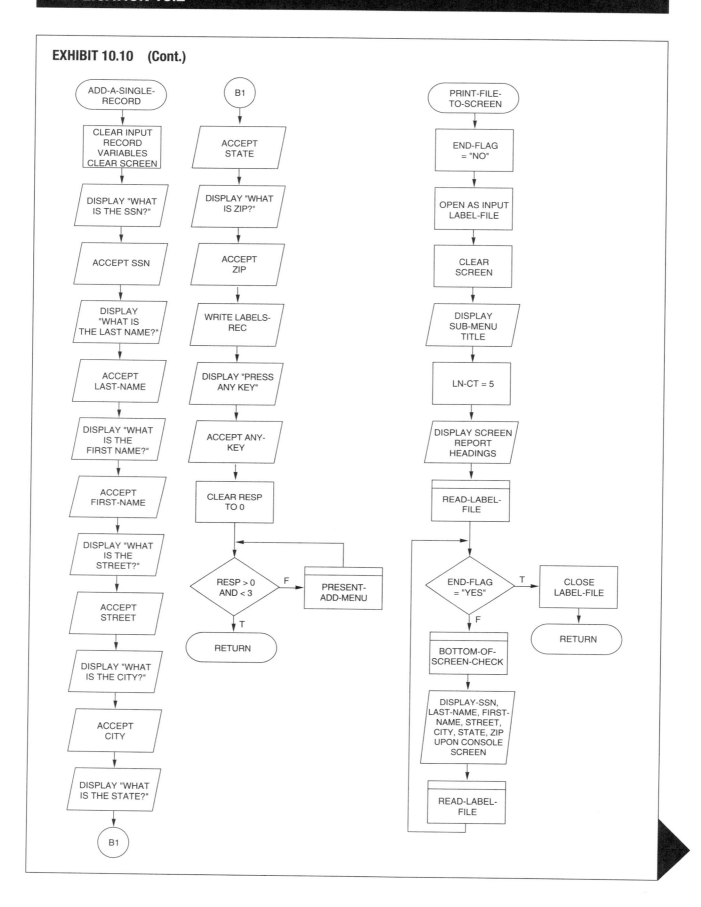

**EXHIBIT 10.10** (Cont.)

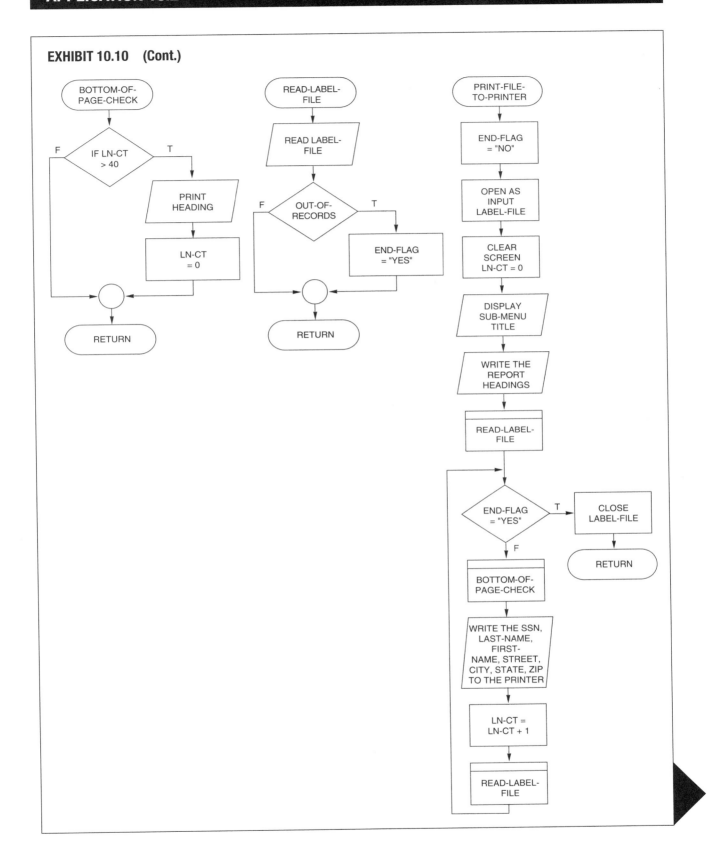

**EXHIBIT 10.10    (Cont.)**

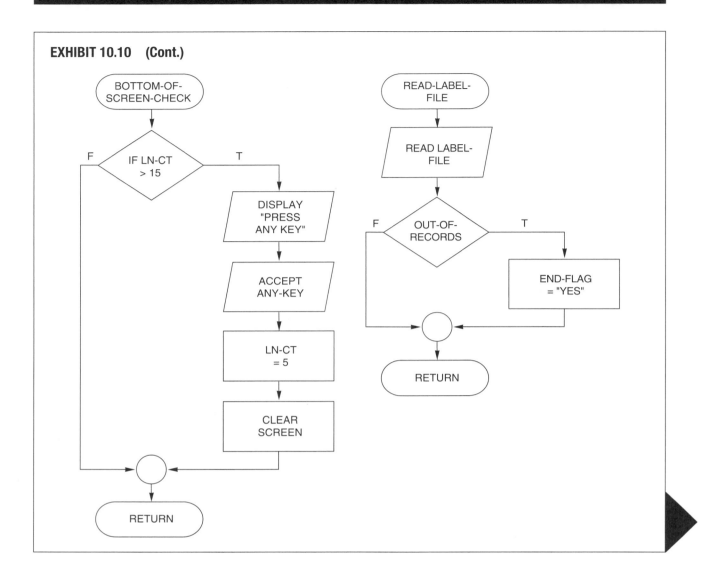

**EXHIBIT 10.10    (Cont.)**

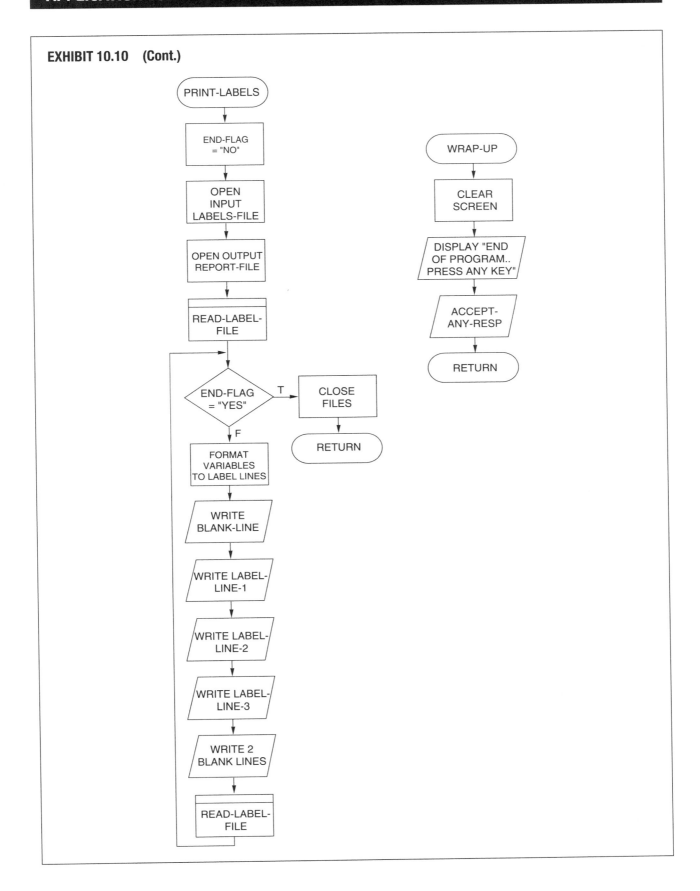

**EXHIBIT 10.11    Pseudocode for Application 10.2 (Interactive Sequential File Creation and Label Generator)**

```
*main-line
      startup
      do until resp = 5 (quit?)
            select-options
      end do
      wrapup
      stop
*startup
      store 0 at resp
      do until valid-resp (1 thru 5)
            display-menu-accept-resp
      end do
      return
*display-menu-accept-resp
      clear screen
      display main-menu-screen and prompt
      accept resp
      return
*select-options
      case resp
      when resp is 1
            add-records
      when resp is 2
            print-file-to-screen
      when resp is 3
            print-file-to-printer
      when resp is 4
            print-labels
      end case
      resp = 0
      do until valid-resp (1, 2, 3, 4 or 5)
            display-menu-accept-resp
      end do
      return
*add-records
      clear screen and home cursor
      open label-file as EXTEND (COBOL) or APPEND
        (QUICK BASIC)
      display screen title
      do until resp > 0 and < 3
            present-add-menu
      end do
      do until resp = 2 (quit?)
            add-a-single-record
      end do
      return
```

```
*present-add-menu
      clear screen
      display sub-menu title and selections
      display prompt
      accept resp
      if resp < 1 or > 2 then
              display "invalid response . . try again."
              accept resp
      end if
      return
*add-a-single-record
      clear input record variables
      clear screen
      display "what is the ssn?"
      accept ssn
      display "what is the last name?"
      accept last-name
      display "what is the first name?"
      accept first-name
      display "what is the street?"
      accept street
      display "what is the city?"
      accept city
      display "what is the state?"
      accept state
      display "what is the zip?"
      accept zip
      write labels-rec
      display "press any key to continue"
      accept any-key
      clear resp to 0
      do until resp > 0 and < 3
            present-add-menu
      end do
      return
```

**EXHIBIT 10.11    (Cont.)**

```
*print-file-to-screen
      end-flag = "no"
      open as input label-file
      clear screen
      display sub-menu title
      ln-ct = 5
      display screen report headings
      read-label-file
      do until end-flag = "yes"
            bottom-of-screen-check
            display ssn, last-name, first-name, street, city,
              state, zip
                  upon console
            read-label-file
      end do
      close label-file
      return
*read-label-file
      read label-file
         when out-of-records
            move "yes" to end-flag
      end read
      return
*bottom-of-screen-check
      if  ln-ct > 15 then
            display "press any key"
            accept any-key
            ln-ct = 5
            clear screen
      end if
      return
*print-file-to-printer
      end-flag = "no"
      open as input label-file
      clear screen
      write page heading
      ln-ct = 1
      read-label-file
      do until end-flag = "yes"
            bottom-of-page-check
            write ssn, last-name, first-name, street, city, state,
              zip to the printer
            ln-ct = ln-ct + 1
            read-label-file
      end do
      close label-file
      return
```

```
*bottom-of-page-check
      if ln-ct > 40 then
            advance to new page
            write page heading
            ln-ct = 0
      end if
      return
*print-labels
      end-flag = "no"
      open input labels-file
      open output report-file
      read-label-file
      do until end-flag = "yes"
            format variables to label lines
            write blank line
            write label-line-1
            write label-line-2
            write label-line-3
            write 2 blank lines
            read-label-file
      end do
      close files
      return
*wrap-up
      clear screen
      display "end of program"
      return
```

**EXHIBIT 10.12    Microfocus COBOL 85 Interactive Program—Sequential File Creation and Label Generation**

```
$SET ANS85 MF ALIGN(2)
*THE FOLLOWING IS AN INTERACTIVE PROGRAM THAT ALLOWS A USER
*TO INTERACTIVELY CREATE A SEQUENTIAL FILE AND PRODUCE LABELS.
*THE USER CAN SELECTIVELY PRODUCE LABELS, LIST THE RECORDS TO
*THE SCREEN OR PRINT A HARD COPY.  THE PROGRAM PROVIDES FOR SOME
*ERROR TRAPPING AND PROMPTS THE USER TO RETRY.

$SET ANS85 MF ALIGN(2)
 IDENTIFICATION DIVISION.
 PROGRAM-ID. CH101NEW.
 ENVIRONMENT DIVISION.
 CONFIGURATION SECTION.
 SOURCE-COMPUTER. IBM-PC.
 OBJECT-COMPUTER. IBM-PC.
 SPECIAL-NAMES.
     CONSOLE IS CRT.
 INPUT-OUTPUT SECTION.
 FILE-CONTROL.
     SELECT LABEL-FILE ASSIGN TO "LABELS.DAT".
     SELECT REPORT-FILE ASSIGN TO "PRN".


 DATA DIVISION.
 FILE SECTION.
 FD    LABEL-FILE.
 01    LABEL-REC.
       05  filler     pic x.
       05  SSN        PIC   X(9).
       05  LAST-NM    PIC   X(12).
       05  FIRST-NM   PIC   X(12).
       05  STREET     PIC   X(10).
       05  CITY       PIC   X(10).
       05  STATE      PIC   XX.
       05  ZIP        PIC   X(5).
       05  filler     pic   x.

 FD    REPORT-FILE.
 01    REPORT-REC.
       05                 PIC   XX  VALUES SPACES.
       05    SSN-O        PIC   X(9).
       05                 PIC   XXX VALUE SPACES.
       05    LAST-O        PIC   X(12).
       05                 PIC   XXX VALUE SPACES.
       05    FIRST-O      PIC   X(12).
       05                 PIC   XXX VALUE SPACES.
       05    STREET-O     PIC   X(10).
       05                 PIC   XXX VALUE SPACES.
       05    CITY-O       PIC   X(10).
       05                 PIC   XXX VALUE SPACES.
       05    STATE-O      PIC   XX.
       05                 PIC   XXX VALUE SPACES.
       05    ZIP-O        PIC   XXXXX.
       05                 PIC   X(44) VALUES SPACES.
```

**EXHIBIT 10.12 (Cont.)**

```cobol
WORKING-STORAGE SECTION.
01  RESP    PIC   9  VALUE ZERO.
       88  VALID-RESPONSE  VALUES ARE 1 THRU 5.
01  RESP-BLANK  REDEFINES RESP  PIC X.
01  LN-CT   PIC 99.
01  ANY-KEY    PIC   XX.
78  CLEAR-SCREEN VALUE X"E4".
01  END-FLAG    PIC  XXX  VALUE "NO".
01  LOCATION   PIC  9999 VALUE O.
01  LOC  REDEFINES LOCATION.
    05  ROW   PIC 99.
    05  COL1  PIC 99.
01  REPORT-HEADING.

    05    PIC X(44) VALUE
            "   SSN           LAST           FIRST    ".
    05    PIC X(38) VALUE
            " STREET        CITY        STATE    ZIP".
    05    PIC  X(51)  VALUE SPACES.


01  LABEL-LINE1.
    05    FIRST-NM-LBL  PIC  X(12).
    05    FILLER        PIC  XXX.
    05    LAST-NM-LBL   PIC  X(12).


01  LABEL-LINE2.
    05    STREET-LBL   PIC  X(10).


01  LABEL-LINE3.
    05    CITY-LBL    PIC  X(10).
    05    FILLER      PIC  XXX  VALUE ",".
    05    STATE-LBL   PIC  XX.
    05    FILLER      PIC  XX.
    05    ZIP-LBL     PIC  X(5).

PROCEDURE DIVISION.


000-MAIN-LINE.
    PERFORM 100-STARTUP-MAINMENU.
    PERFORM 200-SELECT-OPTIONS UNTIL RESP = 5.
    PERFORM 300-WRAPUP.
    STOP RUN.


100-STARTUP-MAINMENU.

    MOVE O TO RESP.
    PERFORM 110-DISPLAY-MENU-ACCEPT-RESP
        UNTIL VALID-RESPONSE.
```

**EXHIBIT 10.12   (Cont.)**

```
 110-DISPLAY-MENU-ACCEPT-RESP.
*COMMENT:   THE "AT" OPTION OF THE UPON CLAUSE SHOWS A FOUR
*POSITION NUMERIC LITERAL.   THE FIRST TWO POSITIONS REFERS
*TO THE ROW LOCATION AND THE SECOND TWO POSITIONS OF THE LITERAL
*REFERS TO THE COLUMN LOCATION.   IN OTHER WORDS, 0205 MEANS
*ROW 2, COLUMN 5).

     CALL CLEAR-SCREEN.
     DISPLAY "*****************************************" UPON
     CRT AT 0105.
     DISPLAY "INTERACTIVE FILE MAKER AND LABEL MAKER" UPON CRT
     AT 0205.
     DISPLAY "*****************************************" AT
     0305.
     DISPLAY "PRESS 1 TO ADD RECORDS TO THE FILE" UPON CRT AT
     0405.
     DISPLAY "PRESS 2 TO LIST THE FILE TO THE SCREEN " UPON CRT
     AT 0605.
     DISPLAY "PRESS 3 TO LIST THE FILE TO THE PRINTER " UPON
     CRT AT 0805.
     DISPLAY "PRESS 4 TO PRINT LABELS TO THE PRINTER " UPON
     CRT AT 1005.
     DISPLAY "PRESS 5 TO QUIT                       "
      UPON CRT AT 1205.
     MOVE 0 TO RESP.
     DISPLAY "ENTER YOUR RESPONSE" UPON CRT AT 1405.
     ACCEPT RESP FROM CRT AT 1445.

 200-SELECT-OPTIONS.

     EVALUATE RESP
        WHEN 1
           PERFORM 210-ADD-RECORDS
        WHEN 2
           PERFORM 220-PRINT-THE-FILE-TO-SCREEN
        WHEN 3
           PERFORM 230-PRINT-THE-FILE-TO-PRINTER
        WHEN 4
           PERFORM 240-PRINT-LABELS
        WHEN OTHER
           CALL CLEAR-SCREEN
           DISPLAY "BAD RESPONSE" UPON CRT AT 1605
           DISPLAY "PRESS ANY KEY TO CONTINUE " UPON CRT AT 1705

     END-EVALUATE.
     MOVE 0 TO RESP.
     PERFORM 110-DISPLAY-MENU-ACCEPT-RESP UNTIL VALID-RESPONSE.
```

**EXHIBIT 10.12   (Cont.)**

```
210-ADD-RECORDS.

    CALL CLEAR-SCREEN.
    OPEN EXTEND LABEL-FILE.
    PERFORM 211-PRESENT-ADD-MENU
                UNTIL  RESP > 0 AND RESP < 3.

    PERFORM  212-ADD-A-SINGLE-RECORD
                        UNTIL RESP = 2.

    CLOSE LABEL-FILE.

211-PRESENT-ADD-MENU.
    CALL CLEAR-SCREEN.
    DISPLAY "*******************************" UPON CRT AT 0405.
    DISPLAY "ADD RECORDS TO FILE MENU" UPON CRT AT 0605.
    DISPLAY "*******************************" UPON CRT AT 0805.


    DISPLAY "TO ADD RECORD TO FILE, PRESS 1 " UPON CRT AT 1005.
    DISPLAY "TO EXIT THE ADD MENU, PRESS 2 " UPON CRT AT 1205.
    DISPLAY "WHAT IS YOUR RESPONSE? " UPON CRT AT 1305.
    MOVE SPACE TO RESP-BLANK.
    ACCEPT RESP FROM CRT AT 1345.


    IF RESP < 0 OR RESP > 3
       THEN
          DISPLAY "INVALID RESPONSE, PLEASE TRY AGAIN " UPON
             CRT AT 1505
          ACCEPT RESP FROM CRT AT 1345
    END-IF.

212-ADD-A-SINGLE-RECORD.
   MOVE SPACES TO SSN, LAST-NM, FIRST-NM, STREET, CITY
       STATE, ZIP.
   CALL CLEAR-SCREEN.
   DISPLAY "WHAT IS THE SSN? " UPON CRT AT 1210.
   ACCEPT SSN FROM CRT AT 1240.
   DISPLAY "LAST NAME? " UPON CRT AT 1310.
   ACCEPT LAST-NM FROM CRT AT 1340.
   DISPLAY "FIRST NAME? " UPON CRT AT 1410.
   ACCEPT FIRST-NM FROM CRT AT 1440.
   DISPLAY "STREET? " UPON CRT AT 1510.
   ACCEPT STREET FROM CRT AT 1540.
   DISPLAY "CITY? " UPON CRT AT 1610.
   ACCEPT CITY FROM CRT AT 1640.
   DISPLAY "STATE? " UPON CRT AT 1710.
   ACCEPT STATE FROM CRT AT 1740.
   DISPLAY "ZIP? " UPON CRT AT 1810.
   ACCEPT ZIP FROM CRT AT 1840.
   WRITE LABEL-REC.
   DISPLAY "RECORD ADDED TO LABEL FILE " UPON CRT AT 2005.
```

**EXHIBIT 10.12   (Cont.)**

```
    DISPLAY "PRESS ANY KEY TO CONTINUE " UPON CRT AT 2105
    ACCEPT ANY-KEY FROM CRT AT 2140.
    MOVE 0 TO RESP.
    PERFORM 211-PRESENT-ADD-MENU
            UNTIL RESP > 0 AND RESP < 3.


220-PRINT-THE-FILE-TO-SCREEN.

    MOVE "NO" TO END-FLAG.
    OPEN INPUT LABEL-FILE.
    CALL CLEAR-SCREEN.
    DISPLAY "***************************" UPON CRT AT 0405.
    DISPLAY "SEQUENTIAL LISTING OF LABELS FILE" UPON CRT AT 0605.
    DISPLAY "***************************" UPON CRT AT 0805.
    MOVE 5 TO LN-CT.
    MOVE 1205 TO LOCATION.
    DISPLAY "SSN        LAST NAME     FIRST NAME   STREET    CITY
-   "     STATE    ZIP" UPON CRT AT 1001.


    PERFORM 222-READ-LABEL-FILE.
    PERFORM    UNTIL  END-FLAG = "YES"
       MOVE 5 TO COL1
       ADD 1 TO ROW
       PERFORM 221-BOTTOM-SCREEN-CHECK
       DISPLAY SSN UPON CRT AT LOCATION
       ADD 12 TO LOCATION
       DISPLAY LAST-NM UPON CRT AT LOCATION
       ADD 12 TO LOCATION
       DISPLAY FIRST-NM UPON CRT AT LOCATION
       ADD 12 TO LOCATION
       DISPLAY STREET UPON CRT AT LOCATION
       ADD 10 TO LOCATION
       DISPLAY CITY UPON CRT AT LOCATION
       ADD 7 TO LOCATION
       DISPLAY STATE UPON CRT AT LOCATION
       ADD 5 TO LOCATION
       DISPLAY ZIP UPON CRT AT LOCATION
       ADD 1 TO LN-CT
       PERFORM 222-READ-LABEL-FILE
    END-PERFORM.
    CLOSE LABEL-FILE.

    MOVE SPACES TO ANY-KEY.
    DISPLAY "PRESS ANY KEY TO CONTINUE " UPON CRT AT 2520.
    ACCEPT ANY-KEY FROM CRT AT 2550.
```

**EXHIBIT 10.12    (Cont.)**

```
221-BOTTOM-SCREEN-CHECK.
    IF LN-CT > 15
        THEN DISPLAY "PRESS ANY KEY TO CONTINUE " UPON CRT
                     AT 2520
            ACCEPT ANY-KEY FROM CRT AT 2550
            MOVE 5 TO LN-CT
            CALL CLEAR-SCREEN
            MOVE 1005 TO LOCATION
    END-IF.


222-READ-LABEL-FILE.
    READ LABEL-FILE AT END MOVE "YES" TO END-FLAG.


230-PRINT-THE-FILE-TO-PRINTER.
    MOVE "NO" TO END-FLAG.
    OPEN INPUT LABEL-FILE.
    OPEN OUTPUT REPORT-FILE.
    MOVE O TO LN-CT.
    WRITE REPORT-REC FROM REPORT-HEADING AFTER ADVANCING PAGE.
    MOVE SPACES TO REPORT-REC.
    WRITE REPORT-REC.
    PERFORM 222-READ-LABEL-FILE.
    PERFORM    UNTIL END-FLAG = "YES"
        PERFORM 233-BOTTOM-PAGE-CHECK
        MOVE SSN TO SSN-O
        MOVE FIRST-NM TO FIRST-O

        MOVE LAST-NM TO LAST-O
        MOVE STREET TO STREET-O
        MOVE CITY TO CITY-O
        MOVE STATE TO STATE-O
        MOVE ZIP TO ZIP-O
        WRITE REPORT-REC AFTER ADVANCING 1 LINES
        ADD 1 TO LN-CT
        PERFORM 222-READ-LABEL-FILE
    END-PERFORM.
    CLOSE LABEL-FILE.
    MOVE SPACES TO ANY-KEY.
    DISPLAY "PRESS ANY KEY TO CONTINUE " UPON CRT AT 2020.
    ACCEPT ANY-KEY FROM CRT AT 2050.


233-BOTTOM-PAGE-CHECK.

    IF LN-CT > 40
        THEN    WRITE REPORT-REC FROM REPORT-HEADING AFTER PAGE
                MOVE O TO LN-CT
    END-IF.
```

**EXHIBIT 10.12 (Cont.)**

```
240-PRINT-LABELS.

    MOVE "NO" TO END-FLAG.
    OPEN INPUT LABEL-FILE.
    OPEN OUTPUT REPORT-FILE.
    PERFORM 222-READ-LABEL-FILE.
    PERFORM    UNTIL END-FLAG = "YES"
        MOVE LAST-NM TO LAST-NM-LBL
        MOVE FIRST-NM TO FIRST-NM-LBL
        MOVE STREET TO STREET-LBL
        MOVE CITY TO CITY-LBL
        MOVE STATE TO STATE-LBL
        MOVE ZIP TO ZIP-LBL
        MOVE SPACES TO REPORT-REC
        WRITE REPORT-REC
        WRITE REPORT-REC FROM LABEL-LINE1
        WRITE REPORT-REC FROM LABEL-LINE2
        WRITE REPORT-REC FROM LABEL-LINE3
        MOVE SPACES TO REPORT-REC
        WRITE REPORT-REC
        WRITE REPORT-REC
        PERFORM 222-READ-LABEL-FILE
    END-PERFORM.

    CLOSE LABEL-FILE.

300-WRAPUP.
    CALL CLEAR-SCREEN.
    DISPLAY "END OF PROGRAM" UPON CRT AT 0505.
    DISPLAY "PRESS ANY KEY TO CONTINUE" UPON CRT AT 1212.
    ACCEPT ANY-KEY FROM CRT.
    CALL CLEAR-SCREEN.
```

**EXHIBIT 10.13   QBASIC Interactive Program for Sequential File Creation and Label Generation**

```
'*********************************************************************
'*                      PROGRAM-IDENTIFICATION                      *
'*********************************************************************
'* PROGRAM NAME:  CH10I2NW                                          *
'*********************************************************************
'* INTERACTIVE LABEL CREATION, INQUIRY, AND PRINT                   *
'*************************************************                   *
'*  THIS IS AN INTERACTIVE MENU DRIVEN PROGRAM THAT PERMITS         *
'*  THE USER TO CREATE A SEQUENTIAL FILE FOR MAILING LABELS.DAT     *
'*  THE USER MAY ALSO ELECT TO LIST THE FILE TO THE SCREEN          *
'*  PRINT A LISTING OF THE RECORDS TO A REPORT, OR PRINT LABELS.DAT *
'*********************************************************************


'*********************************************************************
'*                          MAIN-LINE                               *
'*********************************************************************

MAIN.LINE:
      GOSUB STARTUP
      DO UNTIL RESP = 5
            GOSUB SELECT.OPTIONS
      LOOP
      GOSUB WRAPUP
      END


      '*********************************************************************
      '*                          STARTUP                                 *
      '*********************************************************************

STARTUP:
      RESP = 0
      DO UNTIL RESP > 0 AND RESP < 6
         GOSUB DISPLAY.MENU.ACCEPT.RESPONSE
      LOOP
      RETURN

      '*********************************************************************
      '*                 DISPLAY-MENU-ACCEPT-RESPONSE                     *
      '*********************************************************************

DISPLAY.MENU.ACCEPT.RESPONSE:
      COLOR 7, 9
      CLS
      LOCATE 4, 10: PRINT "*******************************"
      LOCATE 5, 10: PRINT "INTERACTIVE FILE MAINTENANCE"
      LOCATE 6, 10: PRINT "*******************************"
      LOCATE 8, 10: PRINT "PRESS 1 TO ADD RECORDS TO THE FILE"
      LOCATE 10, 10: PRINT "PRESS 2 TO LIST THE FILE TO THE SCREEN"
      LOCATE 12, 10: PRINT "PRESS 3 TO PRINT A HARD COPY OF THE FILE"
      LOCATE 14, 10: PRINT "PRESS 4 TO PRINT LABELS.DAT"
      LOCATE 16, 10: PRINT "PRESS 5 TO QUIT"
      LOCATE 17, 10: INPUT "ENTER YOUR RESPONSE :", RESP
      RETURN
```

**EXHIBIT 10.13    (Cont.)**

```
'*****************************************************************
'*                      SELECT.OPTIONS                          *
'*****************************************************************
SELECT.OPTIONS:
     SELECT CASE RESP
        CASE 1
           GOSUB ADD.RECORDS
        CASE 2
           GOSUB PRINT.THE.FILE.TO.SCREEN
        CASE 3
           GOSUB PRINT.THE.FILE.TO.PRINTER
        CASE 4
           GOSUB PRINT.LABELS.DAT
        CASE ELSE
           CLS
           PRINT TAB(20); "BAD RESPONSE"
           PRINT "PRESS ANY KEY TO CONTINE"; RESPX
        END SELECT
        RESP = 0
        DO UNTIL RESP > 0 AND RESP < 6
              GOSUB DISPLAY.MENU.ACCEPT.RESPONSE
        LOOP
        RETURN


'*****************************************************************
'*                      ADD-RECORDS                             *
'*****************************************************************

ADD.RECORDS:
        CLS
        COLOR 7, 9
        OPEN "A", #2, "LABELSFL.DAT"
        RESP = 0
        DO UNTIL RESP > 0 AND RESP < 3

              LOCATE 5, 10: PRINT "****************************"
              LOCATE 7, 10: PRINT "ADD RECORDS TO FILE MENU"
              LOCATE 9, 10: PRINT "****************************"
              LOCATE 12, 10: PRINT "TO ADD RECORD TO FILE, PRESS 1"
              LOCATE 14, 10: PRINT "TO EXIT THE ADD MENU,  PRESS 2"
              LOCATE 16, 10: INPUT "WHAT IS YOUR RESPONSE"; RESP
              IF RESP < 1 OR RESP > 2 THEN
                  LOCATE 18, 10: PRINT "INVALID RESPONSE..TRY AGAIN"
                  LOCATE 16, 10: INPUT "WHAT IS YOUR RESPONSE"; RESP
              END IF
        LOOP
        DO UNTIL RESP = 2
              GOSUB ADD.A.SINGLE.RECORD
        LOOP
        CLOSE #2
        RETURN
```

**EXHIBIT 10.13    (Cont.)**

```
'***********************************************************************
'*                  ADD-A-SINGLE-RECORD                  *
'***********************************************************************

ADD.A.SINGLE.RECORD:

    CLS
    LOCATE 12, 10: INPUT "WHAT IS THE SSN "; SSN$
    LOCATE 13, 10: INPUT "WHAT IS THE LAST NAME "; LAST.NAME$
    LOCATE 14, 10: INPUT "WHAT IS THE FIRST NAME "; FIRST.NAME$
    LOCATE 15, 10: INPUT "WHAT IS THE STREET "; STREET$
    LOCATE 16, 10: INPUT "WHAT IS THE CITY "; CITY$
    LOCATE 17, 10: INPUT "WHAT IS THE STATE "; STATE$
    LOCATE 18, 10: INPUT "WHAT IS THE ZIP "; ZIP$

    WRITE #2, SSN$, LAST.NAME$, FIRST.NAME$, STREET$, CITY$, STATE$, ZIP$
    LOCATE 19, 10: PRINT TAB(5); "THE RECORD WAS ADDED TO THE LABELS.DAT FILE"
    PRINT "PRESS ANY KEY TO CONTINUE "
    ANYKEY$ = INPUT$(1)
    RESP = 0
    DO UNTIL RESP > 0 AND RESP < 3
         CLS
         LOCATE 5, 10: PRINT "****************************"
         LOCATE 7, 10: PRINT "ADD RECORDS TO FILE MENU"
         LOCATE 9, 10: PRINT "****************************"

         LOCATE 12, 10: PRINT "TO ADD RECORD TO FILE, PRESS 1"
         LOCATE 14, 10: PRINT "TO EXIT THE ADD MENU,  PRESS 2"
         LOCATE 16, 10: INPUT "WHAT IS YOUR RESPONSE"; RESP
         IF RESP < 0 OR RESP > 3 THEN
              LOCATE 18, 10: PRINT "INVALID RESPONSE ", RESP
              LOCATE 16, 10: INPUT "WHAT IS YOUR RESPONSE", RESP
         END IF
    LOOP
    RETURN

'***********************************************************************
'*                  PRINT-THE-FILE-TO-SCREEN                  *
'***********************************************************************

PRINT.THE.FILE.TO.SCREEN:

    CLOSE #2
    OPEN "I", #2, "LABELSFL.DAT"
    CLS
    PRINT "                         SEQUENTIAL LISTING OF LABELS.DAT FILE"
    PRINT
    LN.CT = 0
    PRINT TAB(2); "SSN"; TAB(12); "LAST NAME"; TAB(28); "FIRST NAME"; TAB(40);
    LPRINT "STREET"; TAB(55); "CITY"; TAB(70); "STATE"; TAB(75); "ZIP"
    DO WHILE NOT EOF(2)
       GOSUB BOTTOM.SCREEN.CHECK
       INPUT #2, SSN$, LAST.NAME$, FIRST.NAME$, STREET$, CITY$, STATE$, ZIP$
       PRINT TAB(2); SSN$; TAB(12); LAST.NAME$; TAB(28); FIRST.NAME$; TAB(40);
       LPRINT STREET$; TAB(55); CITY$; TAB(70); STATE$; TAB(75); ZIP$
       LN.CT = LN.CT + 1
```

**EXHIBIT 10.13    (Cont.)**

```
        LOOP
        PRINT
        PRINT
        CLOSE #2
        PRINT "PRESS ANY KEY TO CONTINUE"
        ANYKEY$ = INPUT$(1)
        RETURN
        '*********************************************************************
        '*                       BOTTOM-SCREEN-CHECK                        *
        '*********************************************************************
BOTTOM.SCREEN.CHECK:
        IF LN.CT > 16 THEN
            PRINT "PRESS ANY KEY TO CONTINUE WITH LISTING"
            ANYKEY$ = INPUT$(1)
            LN.CT = 0
        END IF
        RETURN


        '*********************************************************************
        '*                     PRINT-THE-FILE-TO-PRINTER                    *
        '*********************************************************************

PRINT.THE.FILE.TO.PRINTER:

        CLOSE #2
        LN.CT = 0
        OPEN "I", #2, "LABELSFL.DAT"
        CLS
        LPRINT TAB(34); "SEQUENTIAL LISTING OF LABELSFL.DAT FILE"
        LPRINT
        LPRINT TAB(2); "SSN"; TAB(15); "LAST NAME"; TAB(28); "FIRST NAME";
        LPRINT TAB(40); "STREET"; TAB(55); "CITY"; TAB(70); "STATE"; TAB(77); "ZIP"
        DO WHILE NOT EOF(2)
           GOSUB BOTTOM.PAGE.CHECK
           INPUT #2, SSN$, LAST.NAME$, FIRST.NAME$, STREET$, CITY$, STATE$, ZIP$
           LPRINT TAB(2); SSN$; TAB(15); LAST.NAME$; TAB(28); FIRST.NAME$; TAB(40);
           LPRINT STREET$; TAB(55); CITY$; TAB(70); STATE$; TAB(75); ZIP$
           LN.CT = LN.CT + 1
        LOOP
        PRINT : PRINT
        CLOSE #2
        PRINT "PRESS ENTER TO CONTINUE"
        ANYKEY$ = INPUT$(1)
        RETURN
        '*********************************************************************
        '*                       BOTTOM-PAGE-CHECK                          *
        '*********************************************************************
BOTTOM.PAGE.CHECK:
        IF LN.CT > 45 THEN
           LPRINT CHR$(12)
           LN.CT = 0
        END IF
        RETURN
```

**EXHIBIT 10.13 (Cont.)**

```
'**********************************************************************
'*                       PRINT-LABELS-DAT                           *
'**********************************************************************

PRINT.LABELS.DAT:

        CLOSE #2
        OPEN "I", #2, "LABELSFL.DAT"
        DO WHILE NOT EOF(2)
           INPUT #2, SSN$, LAST.NAME$, FIRST.NAME$, STREET$, CITY$, STATE$, ZIP$
           PRINT
           LPRINT TAB(3); FIRST.NAME$; TAB(15); LAST.NAME$
           LPRINT TAB(3); STREET$
           LPRINT TAB(3); CITY$; TAB(15); ","; TAB(17); STATE$; TAB(20); ZIP$
           LPRINT
           LPRINT
           LPRINT
        LOOP
        RETURN


'**********************************************************************
'*                          WRAPUP                                   *
'**********************************************************************

WRAPUP:
        CLS
        PRINT "END OF PROGRAM"
        PRINT "PRESS ENTER TO CONTINUE"
        ANYKEY$ = INPUT$(1)
        RETURN
```

```
                    SEQUENTIAL LISTING OF LABELS FILE

SSN            LAST NAME    FIRST NAME   STREET        CITY          STATE   ZIP

111111111      RUSSELL      JACK         HCR 51        STEPHENVILLE  TX      76401
222222222      RUSSELL      BARBARA      STONE CUTOFF  STEPHENVILLE  TX      76401
333333333      RUSSELL      JENNY        STONE CUTOFF  STEPHENVILLE  TX      76401
444444444      ALBORN       AL           WASHINGTON    RESTON        VA      77777
888888889      BAKER        CHARLIE      111 LEVITA    LEVITA        TX      33333
555555555      DONALDSON    SAM          222 EAST      WASHINGTON    DC      33333
393939394      COOPER       DAMON        333 RANGE     ARLINGTON     TX      33333
110101017      LAMBETH      CHARLIE      222 HELM      FORT WORTH    TX      44444
191919199      HILL         BOBBY        333 WEST      JONESBORO     TX      33333
888888888      STRICKER     ROBERT       333 MAXWELL   WARREN        MI      22222
202020222      MUSSON       BETTY        222 NORTH     WARREN        MI      33333
676767673      DOBSON       DAVE         333 OAK       FT WORTH      TX      44444

PRESS ENTER TO CONTINUE
```

**EXHIBIT 10.13** (Cont.)

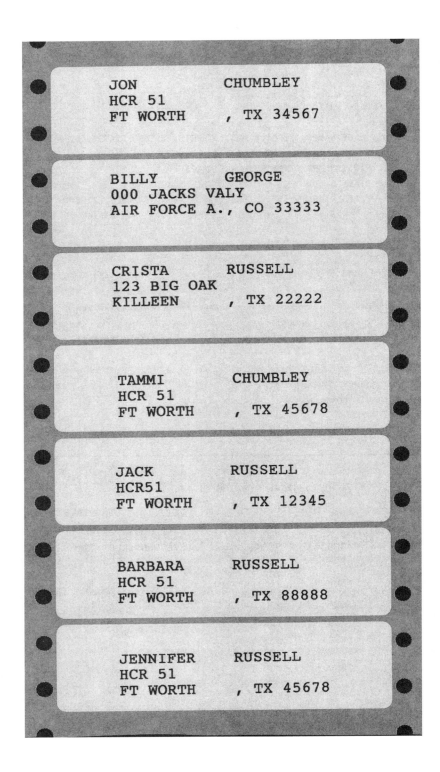

```
        JON           CHUMBLEY
        HCR 51
        FT WORTH      , TX 34567


        BILLY         GEORGE
        000 JACKS VALY
        AIR FORCE A., CO 33333


        CRISTA        RUSSELL
        123 BIG OAK
        KILLEEN       , TX 22222


        TAMMI         CHUMBLEY
        HCR 51
        FT WORTH      , TX 45678


        JACK          RUSSELL
        HCR51
        FT WORTH      , TX 12345


        BARBARA       RUSSELL
        HCR 51
        FT WORTH      , TX 88888


        JENNIFER      RUSSELL
        HCR 51
        FT WORTH      , TX 45678
```

## SUMMARY

Interactive programs allow the user to access data more freely and to dialogue with the computer to make better decisions. Interactive programs are constantly connected to the files they process and access, while batch programs are connected only temporarily. A major advantage of interactive systems is that they allow the user rather than the programmer the power of processing and accessing information. A major limitation is that interactive programs are more tedious and lengthy, thus more costly.

Interactive systems are typically menu-driven. The menu should contain a heading that clearly describes the function or purpose of the program. The selections should be clear and concise with numeric options. Validation loops (or error traps) should be utilized to avoid invalid data entry. Application 10.1 illustrates a simple dialogue with a computer program that is able to compute the areas of a circle, triangle, rectangle, or trapezoid. Application 10.2 provides file creation for mailing labels. Menu selection allows data entry for the label file, file display and printing, and label generation.

## VOCABULARY

interactive programming
batch programming
response time
menu-driven interactive dialogue
user prompt
user response
error trap
validation loop
CRT Layout Form
valid response
DISPLAY-MENU-ACCEPT-RESP module
SELECT-OPTIONS module

---

## PROBLEMS

**10–1.** An investment company wishes to have the capability of playing "what if" games with clients regarding possible investment amounts. Often clients want to know maturity amounts for given principal investments at a specific interest rate. To keep it uncomplicated for this first problem, suppose the company wants the ability to compute either simple interest or annual compound interest on various investment amounts and time periods. The screens below illustrate the main menu and sub-menus for this problem. The user should be able to initially choose between simple and compound interest. The sub-menu allows the user to key in the principal amount, interest rate as a decimal fraction, and the rate in whole years. Also, for the sake of simplicity, assume a maximum of nine years so all the output can print on a single screen. The next problem expands on this idea to include a fifty-year maximum, which is more realistic.

An error trap should be used to validate only the main menu responses for this first problem.

Simple interest is calculated as the product of the principal times the interest rate.

$$\text{COMPOUND INTEREST} = (\text{PRINC} * (1 + \text{RATE}))^{\text{YRS}}$$

What is compound interest? The interest accrued on a principal amount is calculated, then the interest is added to the old principal to yield a new principal prior to recalculating the interest for the next period. For example, The note for 10,000 at 8 percent for one year is worth 10,800. The 10,800 becomes the new principal in calculating its worth at the same interest rate for the second year, and so on.

Design the Screen Layout Form, draw the flow-chart, and write the pseudocode for the problem.

```
*************************************************
INTERACTIVE INTEREST CALCULATOR
*************************************************

PRESS 1 FOR SIMPLE INTEREST CALCULATION
PRESS 2 FOR COMPOUND INTEREST CALCULATION

PRESS 3 TO QUIT


ENTER YOUR RESPONSE :□
```

```
******************************************
SIMPLE INTEREST CALCULATOR
******************************************

WHAT IS THE PRINCIPAL?      :10000
WHAT IS THE RATE?      :.08
WHAT IS THE TIME IN YEARS?      :? 5
A MAXIMUM OF 9 YEARS CAN BE SPECIFIED
THE PRINCIPAL FOR 10000 AT .08 FOR 1 YEARS YIELDS 10800
THE PRINCIPAL FOR 10000 AT .08 FOR 2 YEARS YIELDS 11600
THE PRINCIPAL FOR 10000 AT .08 FOR 3 YEARS YIELDS 12400
THE PRINCIPAL FOR 10000 AT .08 FOR 4 YEARS YIELDS 13200
THE PRINCIPAL FOR 10000 AT .08 FOR 5 YEARS YIELDS 14000


PRESS ANY KEY TO CONTINUE□
```

```
***********************************************
COMPOUND INTEREST CALCULATOR
***********************************************

WHAT IS THE PRINCIPAL?      :10000
WHAT IS THE RATE?      :.08
WHAT IS THE TIME IN YEARS?      :? 5

THE PRINCIPAL FOR 10000 AT .08 FOR 1 YEARS YIELDS 10800
THE PRINCIPAL FOR 10000 AT .08 FOR 2 YEARS YIELDS 11664
THE PRINCIPAL FOR 10000 AT .08 FOR 3 YEARS YIELDS 12597.12
THE PRINCIPAL FOR 10000 AT .08 FOR 4 YEARS YIELDS 13604.89
THE PRINCIPAL FOR 10000 AT .08 FOR 5 YEARS YIELDS 14693.28
```

**10–2.** Expanding from problem 10.1, suppose management liked the program so well that they want us to expand on it to include more main menu choices. They want the ability to choose either simple interest, monthly interest compounding, quarterly interest compounding, and annual interest compounding. If the user enters, say, ten years and the compounding period is quarterly, this means that the program needs to multiply the number of years by four to get the number of periods for compounding purposes. The same is true for monthly compounding. Simply multiply the number of years by 12 to get the number of compounding periods.

The user also wants the ability to display a report similar to that of 10.1 except it should handle up to fifty-year investment periods.

---

**10–3.** ACE Computers is getting tired of having to provide individual cost estimates to every customer who walks into the store. It is very time consuming, because each person wants a computer tailored to their needs. Some want a 286. Some want a 386. Some want a 486. Some are even asking about the 586. Some want small hard drives and some want large hard drives. Some want Super VGA monitors while others want VGA. The amount of RAM needed by customers varies widely. The kinds of peripherals vary widely from customer to customer.

What this company needs is an on-line interactive program that lets users step through a set of hierarchical menus to tailor-select the computers they want. The output screen is an itemized invoice and final price for the microcomputer. The various menus and screens are presented below. Tables of data related to the prices of the computer components are also presented. You can use the constant price values in your calculations—in other words, you can hard code the assignment statements in your program using the actual prices.

On the other hand, you can take a more realistic approach and use your knowledge from Chapters 7 and 8 to build these tables in memory so that the response number agrees by position with the table value. In other words, if the main menu response of 3 relates to a 486–33, make sure the price for the 486–33 is the third element in the table. Subsequently, access the price from the main-board table subscripted by the response (1, 2, or 3).

```
              ACE COMPUTERS
      ON-LINE MICROCOMPUTER PRICE ESTIMATOR

  1. DO YOU WANT A PRICE QUOTE ON AN ENTIRE COMPUTER?

  2. DO YOU WANT A PRICE QUOTE ON AN INDIVIDUAL
     COMPONENT?

  3. QUIT
```

```
            INFORMATION NEEDED TO PERFORM
              PRICE QUOTE FOR ENTIRE COMPUTER

  WHAT KIND OF MAINBOARD ARE YOU INTERESTED IN?

  1.   386 — 33MHZ
  2.   386 — 40MHZ
  3.   486 — 33MH
```

```
            INFORMATION NEEDED TO PERFORM
              PRICE QUOTE ON ENTIRE COMPUTER

               486–33 MHZ MAIN BOARD OPTIONS

  How much main memory do you want?

  1.   4 mb
  2.   8 mb
  3.  16 mb

  Enter your choice
```

```
┌──────────────────────────────────┐   ┌──────────────────────────────────┐
│     INFORMATION NEEDED FOR PRICE  │   │     INFORMATION NEEDED FOR PRICE  │
│      QUOTE ON ENTIRE COMPUTER     │   │      QUOTE ON ENTIRE COMPUTER     │
│                                   │   │                                   │
│  How much hard disk space do you  │   │  What kind of monitor do you want?│
│  want?                            │   │                                   │
│                                   │   │    1.   VGA                       │
│    1.    80 mb                    │   │    2.   Super VGA                 │
│    2.   200 mb                    │   │    3.   Monochrome                │
│    3.   400 mb                    │   │                                   │
└──────────────────────────────────┘   └──────────────────────────────────┘
```

Use the tables below to perform the calculations for the various categories:

MAIN BOARD / CASE / POWER SUPPLY

386-33 . . . . . . . . . 500.00
386-40 . . . . . . . . . 540.00
486-33 . . . . . . . . . 670.00

MEMORY COSTS . . . 17 NS

 4 MB . . . . . . . . . . 200.00
 8 MB . . . . . . . . . . 380.00
16 MB . . . . . . . . . . 700.00

HARDDRIVE COSTS

 80 MB . . . . . . . . . 360.00
200 MB . . . . . . . . . 540.00
400 MB . . . . . . . . . 730.00

MONITOR COSTS

MONACHROME . . . .  60.00
VGA . . . . . . . . . . . . . 245.00
SUPER VGA . . . . . . . 300.00

```
┌──────────────────────────────────┐
│     PRICE QUOTE: ENTIRE COMPUTER  │
│                                   │
│   486-33 . . . . . . . . $670.00  │
│   16 MB . . . . . . . . . $700.00 │
│   200 MB H.D. . . . .$540.00      │
│   SUPER VGA . . . . . .$300.00     │
│                                   │
│      Total is . . . .$2210.00     │
│                                   │
└──────────────────────────────────┘
```

**10.4.** (Advanced problem) Ace Auto Parts wants to develop an online information center for its customers. A customer can find out what a part costs for an auto by making a few selections from a terminal. The customer should be able to determine the cost of, say, an oil filter by choosing the make of the auto, the year, and the engine size. The same would apply for other categories of auto parts.

Required: Draw a flowchart and write the pseudocode for this problem. Develop only the logic that relates to OIL FILTERS and SPARK PLUGS. Teachers may design other problem statements that may include other menu choices. You may use hard-coded assignment statements or set up hard-coded tables and use positional addressing to access the type and price. If you use RESPONSE codes of 1 or 2, the RESPONSE can be the subscript into the individual tables. Reference positional addressing from Chapter 7 or 8.

The main menu and sub-menus might appear as follows:

```
╭──────────────────────────────────────────╮
│ WELCOME TO ACE AUTO PARTS INFORMATION CENTER│
│                                            │
│ WHAT AUTO PART CATEGORY ARE YOU INTERESTED IN?│
│                                            │
│    1.   OIL FILTERS                        │
│    2.   GAS FILTERS                        │
│    3.   SPARK PLUGS                        │
│    4.   MISCELLANEOUS                      │
│    5.   QUIT                               │
╰──────────────────────────────────────────╯
```

```
╭──────────────────────────────────────────╮
│        OIL FILTER INFORMATION MENU          │
│                                            │
│ WHAT MAKE OF AUTO?                         │
│                                            │
│    1.    CHEVY                             │
│    2.    FORD                              │
│    3.    QUIT                              │
│                                            │
│ (WE SUPPLY ONLY CHEVY AND FORD PARTS)      │
╰──────────────────────────────────────────╯
```

**Screen**

```
            CHEVY FILTERS

WHAT YEAR?

      1.   60–78
      2.   79–87
      3.   88–92
```

**Screen**

```
            FORD FILTERS

WHAT YEAR?

      1.   60–78
      2.   79–85
      3.   86–92
```

**OIL FILTERS FOR CHEVY**

**Table**

| YEAR | TYPE | PRICE |
|------|------|-------|
| 60–78 | HR 234 | $4.56 |
| 79–87 | HR 345 | $5.87 |
| 88–92 | HR 456 | $3.45 |

**OIL FILTER FOR FORD**

**Table**

| YEAR | TYPE | PRICE |
|------|------|-------|
| 60–78 | PH13 | 3.45 |
| 79–85 | PH14 | 4.56 |
| 86–92 | PH2345 | 5.67 |

**Output Screen:**

```
            PRICE AND FILTER TYPE FOR A:

**** FORD, 86–92, . . . . . TYPE:  PH2345,   PRICE:   $5.67
```

**Screen**

```
         SPARK PLUG INFORMATION MENU

WHAT MAKE OF AUTO?

   1.    CHEVY
   2.    FORD
   3.    QUIT

(WE SUPPLY ONLY CHEVY AND FORD PARTS)
```

**Screen**

```
            CHEVY PLUGS

WHAT YEAR?

   1.    64–79
   2.    80–89
   3.    90–92
```

**Screen**

```
            FORD PLUGS

WHAT YEAR?

   1.    60–78
   2.    79–89
   3.    90–92

Output Screen
```

**Output Screen:**

```
         PRICE AND SPARK PLUG TYPE FOR A:

**** FORD, 90–92, . . . . . TYPE:  PH15,   PRICE:   (8) $5.67
```

**SPARK PLUGS FOR CHEVY**

**Table**

| YEAR | TYPE | PRICE |
|------|------|-------|
| 64–79 | HR 234 | $4.56 |
| 80–89 | HR 345 | $5.87 |
| 90–92 | HR 456 | $3.45 |

**SPARK PLUGS FOR FORD**

**Table**

| YEAR | TYPE | PRICE |
|------|------|-------|
| 60–78 | PH13 | 3.45 |
| 79–89 | PH14 | 4.56 |
| 90–92 | PH15 | 5.67 |

# 11

# Sorting Data

## OBJECTIVES

After completing this chapter, the student will be able to:

1. Define the terms *sorting* and *sort key*.

2. Discuss the difference between ascending sequence and descending sequence.

3. List the two major sorting categories.

4. List three basic internal sorting methods.

5. List three major exchange sorting techniques.

6. Identify one important selection sort.

7. Compare and contrast the bubble, exchange, and Shell sorting techniques.

8. Describe the bubble sorting procedure with reference to the number of passes and compares per pass.

9. Describe the exchange sorting procedure with reference to the number of passes and compares per pass.

10. Describe the Shell sorting procedure with regard to the number of passes, comparison intervals, forward compares, and propagation of backward compares.

11. Develop the hierarchy charts, structured flowcharts, and pseudocodes for the bubble, simple exchange, selection-with-exchange, and Shell sorting methods.

## SORTING CONCEPTS

**Sorting** is the process of ordering a file or table and is one of the primary functions in the processing of information. Before useful results can be obtained from the computer, a file or table normally must be prearranged into an acceptable sequence according to a field or a set of fields found in the records. A **sort procedure** is a program routine, or module, that performs this function.

### The Sort Key

The field, or set of fields, that is used to order the file is called the **sort key**. For example, if a sales analysis report similar to Figure 6.1 in Chapter 6 is needed by management, the file must be arranged by store number to allow for control break totals. In this case, the store number is the sort key.

### Sort Key Sequencing

The Sales Analysis Report in Figure 6.1 shows the records sorted into **ascending sequence** by store number; this means the records are ordered from the record with the smallest sort key to the record with the largest sort key. The ordering of data in ascending sequence is the usual arrangement; however, sometimes a report is needed that lists the records in **descending sequence**, that is, from the highest sort key toward the lowest sort key. In the first case (an ascending sort), for example, a sales manager might want a sales analysis report that summarizes sales by date of sale rather than by store number. The report would print sales records in ascending order by date, that is, from the first of the month toward the end of the month. Figure 11.1 shows such a report.

## Major Sorting Techniques (External/Internal)

The two major techniques used for sorting data are 1) internal and 2) external.

**Internal Sort.** An **internal sort** arranges data found in main memory. A file (or partial file) is first loaded to a memory table, and then the elements are sorted into either ascending or descending order according to the sort key. Each record is located in a separate table element. The contents of the elements are rearranged into a prescribed as-

cending or descending sequence depending on user specifications. The key point to note here is that with internal sorting methods *the data to be sorted is first placed into main memory in the form of a table and subsequently ordered.* The internal sort is a much faster sorting technique, since the data elements are swapped at electronic speeds. The only read/write access of the disk is to initially load the data to the memory table. After the loading process is complete, all subsequent ordering is handled internally in memory.

**External Sort.** An **external sort** is a technique normally used with very large files that are best handled outside of main memory, usually with files that would take up too much space in main mem-

---

**FIGURE 11.1** **Single-Level Control Break Report Sorted in Ascending Sequence by Date**

```
                MONTHLY SALES ANALYSIS REPORT
                      BY DATE OF SALE

      DATE      STORE NUMBER    QUANTITY   PRICE      SALES

    93/10/01        005            10      10.00     1000.00
    93/10/01        005             5      10.00       50.00
    93/10/01        005             1      20.00       20.00
    93/10/01        007             2      50.00      100.00
    93/10/01        007             5     100.00      500.00
    93/10/01        007             5     200.00     1000.00
    93/10/01        007             5      10.00       50.00
    93/10/01        007            10       5.00       50.00
    93/10/01        007             5       5.00       25.00

                    TOTAL SALES 93/10/01   2,795.00

    93/10/02        005             1      10.00       10.00
    93/10/02        005             5      10.00       50.00
    93/10/02        005            10      10.00      100.00
    93/10/02        005            20       5.00      100.00
    93/10/02        007            50      10.00      500.00
    93/10/02        007           100       5.00      500.00

                    TOTAL SALES 93/10/02   1,260.00 *

    93/10/03        001             1      10.00       10.00
    93/10/03        001             5      20.00      100.00
    93/10/03        005             2      25.00       50.00

                    TOTAL SALES 93/10/03    160.00 *

    93/10/04        001             5      10.00       50.00
    93/10/04        001             2      20.00       40.00

                    TOTAL SALES 93/10/04     90.00 *

    93/10/31        001             5      20.00      100.00
    93/10/31        001             5      10.00       50.00
    93/10/31        001             5      20.00      100.00
    93/10/31        005            10      10.00      100.00
    93/10/31        005            20     100.00     2000.00
    93/10/31        005            10      50.00      500.00

                    TOTAL SALES 93/10/31   2,850.00 *
                    TOTAL COMPANY SALES    7,155.00 **
```

ory. The **ANSI COBOL sort feature** is an example of an external sort. Most major computer vendors supply a good external sort-merge package, and an application programmer rarely has to write an external sort. On the other hand, the application programmer will very likely need to write an internal sort for dynamic table data for which sorting speed is extremely important.

## Basic Internal Sorting Types

The three basic sorting types are (1) **selection**, (2) **exchange**, and (3) **insertion**. In each particular processing situation, one of these types is preferable over the others. Exchange sorting is the most frequently used in the business programming environment, and three of the most popular types are 1) **bubble**, 2) **simple exchange**, and 3) **Shell**. A sorting method belonging to the selection sort category called the *selection-with-exchange* sort will also be discussed. When extremely fast sorting times are required for files holding more than one thousand records, the programmer should consider other techniques, such as the quick sort, radix exchange sort, address calculation sort, or heap sort.

### Why Study the Internal Sorts?
When processing speeds are critical, external sorts are seldom efficient. For small- and medium-scale files, when ample memory space is available, an internal exchange sort is usually more efficient. In interactive programs where one- or two-second response times are needed, a rapid internal sort is a must! If the time interval between a user's response to a prompt on a terminal screen and his or her actually receiving the report is, let's say, two seconds, then the appropriate file must be sorted during this time interval. In some instances, an external sort could take several seconds to complete and would, therefore, be prohibitively slow. The better choice would be an internal sort, which might take only an infinitesimal fraction of a second.

### Commonly Used Exchange Sorts.
The three most commonly used exchange sorting methods are the bubble, the exchange, and the Shell.

## THE BUBBLE SORT

One of the most common exchange sorts, as mentioned, is called the *bubble sort*, since this algorithm causes records to move up into position through a table much as bubbles move up through water. The bubble sort compares successive pairs of records in a table and swaps them if necessary. The process of comparing and conditional swapping occurs for N - 1 passes through the table, where N represents the number of elements (or records) in the table. The number of comparisons made for the first pass through the table is also N - 1. Figure 11.2 illustrates the comparison of adjacent record pairs and their swapping where appropriate for one pass. For each successive pass through the table, the number of comparisons required for the pass decreases by one. The required number of comparisons for adjacent pairs of elements decreases by 1 after each pass because the largest value is pulled to the end of the table and the smallest value is pulled one element closer to the beginning of the table. This is true for an ascending sort. For a descending sort, the lowest value is pushed to the end, and the highest is pulled one element closer to the beginning of the table.

Figure 11.3 illustrates the procedure for performing a bubble sort to an array of five records. The squiggly line beside each sort key symbolizes the remaining fields of the record. Panel A of the figure demonstrates the swapping of elements for each successive pass through the table whenever the first element of the adjacent pair is larger than the second. The first five adjacent records represent the elements of the *original* unsorted table. The second set of adjacent records is the resultant set of partially sorted elements *after* the *first pass* of the bubble sort is complete. Here, the record with the sort key 20 has been swapped with the record with the sort key 17, since 20 is greater than 17. Also, the record with the sort key 42 was exchanged with the record with the sort key 9, since 42 is greater than 9. At the end of pass 1, the largest value is the very last element of the table (its proper position), and the smallest value is now fourth instead of fifth—one element closer to the beginning of the table.

In the *second pass*, the record with a sort key 31 was swapped with the record with a sort key 9, since 31 is greater than 9. At the end of pass 2, the next-to-largest value (31) has been pushed into the fourth element of the table (its final position), and the smallest value (9) is now one position closer to the beginning of the table.

In the *third pass*, the second element was swapped with the third, since the sort key 20 is greater than the sort key 9. The record with the sort key 20 is now in its proper position in the table, and the record with a sort key 9 has moved one element closer to the beginning.

In the *fourth pass*, only one remaining pair of values requires comparison. In this case, the two records are swapped since the sort key 17 is greater than 9. At the end of pass 4, the result is an ordered table of records (see the SORTED TABLE at the end of the figure).

Each successive pass through the table reduces by one the number of remaining comparisons to be made, since the net result of each pass is to push the next larger value to the end of the table. Panel B of Figure 11.3 illustrates the reduction in the number of required comparisons per pass. Where N represents the number of elements (records) in the table, for pass 1 the number of element pairs to be compared is N - 1; pass 2 requires N - 2; pass 3 requires N - 3; and pass 4 requires N - 4. The notation for expressing the number of comparisons per pass is:

$$\text{Pairs to be compared} = N - L$$
$$\text{where } N = \text{number of elements}$$
$$L = \text{current pass number}$$

For example, in pass 1, the number of pairs to be examined is N - 1, since L = 1; pass 2 requires N - 2, since L=2, and so on.

## Swapping the Contents of Adjacent Element Pairs

Figure 11.4 illustrates the process of swapping adjacent elements. When it becomes necessary to swap the contents of adjacent element pairs (record x and record y), an element-hold area is needed to hold record x while record y is transferred to the element location previously occupied by record x. Panel A of Figure 11.4 illustrates this process. Step 1 shows the contents of record x being transferred to the element-hold area. Once the first transfer is complete, step 2 shows the contents of the second element (record y) being stored into element 1. Now element 1 contains record y. Step 3 shows the contents of the element-hold area being stored into the sec-

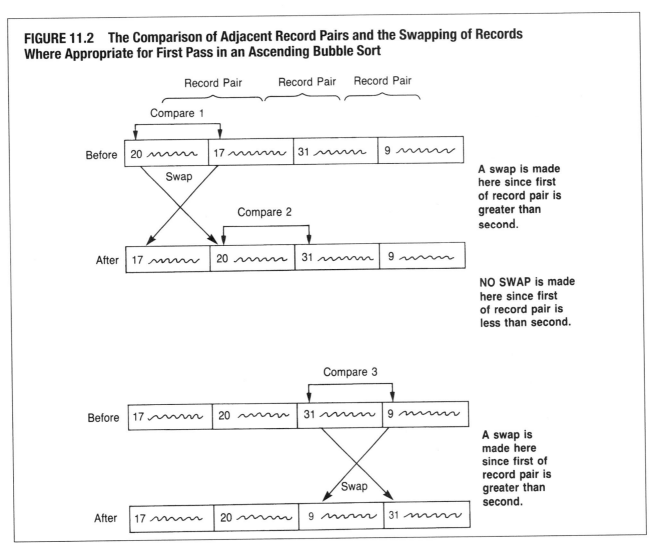

**FIGURE 11.2   The Comparison of Adjacent Record Pairs and the Swapping of Records Where Appropriate for First Pass in an Ascending Bubble Sort**

## FIGURE 11.3   The Bubble Sort Process

### Panel A—Swapping of Records for Each Successive Pass Through the Table

**Pass 1**

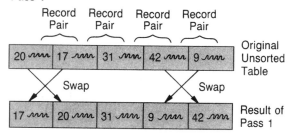

**Pass 2**

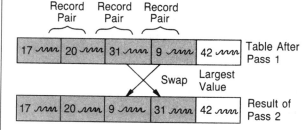

**Pass 3**

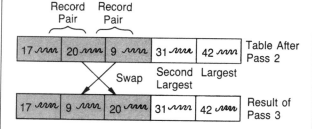

**Pass 4**

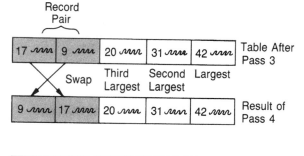

### Panel B—Number of Comparisons for Each Successive Pass

| Pass Number | Number of Element Pairs to Be Compared (N − L) | | |
|---|---|---|---|
| | No. of Elements | Value of L | |
| 1 | N − | 1 | = 4 compares |
| 2 | N − | 2 | = 3 compares |
| 3 | N − | 3 | = 2 compares |
| 4 | N − | 4 | = 1 compare |

Since there are five elements from panel A above, there will be a maximum of four passes.

For each successive pass there will be one less required comparison of adjacent pairs.

(N) = Number of elements in table
(L) = Pass number

ond element. A temporary intermediate hold area must be set up for the swapping operation. (As an example, in order to swap two books on a shelf, one of the books must be temporarily set aside while the other book is placed in the space previously occupied by the first. Then the first book can be retrieved from the temporary hold area and placed in the slot previously occupied by the second book.) Now the content of element 1 is record $y$, and the content of element 2 is record $x$. Panel B of Figure 11.4 shows the result of the swapping process. The swap is now complete.

## Bubble Sort Logic

Figure 11.5 illustrates the flowchart logic, and Figure 11.6 depicts the pseudocode to perform an ascending bubble sort to the original (unsorted) table in panel A of Figure 11.3. This logic includes a control variable (SWAP-OCCURRED-SWITCH) that allows early escape from the bubble sort routine in case the table is already sorted or becomes sorted at the end of any given pass. One important advantage of the bubble sort is its ability to escape from the sort process when no exchange occurs during any given pass. The bubble sort is normally used when the table file size does not exceed 50 records and the file is *not* initially grossly out of order. The more ordered the initial file, the sooner the bubble sort will escape from the sorting process. It is the best of all sorts for table files that are in nearly perfect order prior to sorting.

## The BUBBLE-SORT-MAIN Module

The BUBBLE-SORT-MAIN module controls the number of passes made in a sort. For the table of data in Figure 11.3, this number can vary from one to four, depending upon whether the table is sorted at the end of any given pass. First, the SWAP-OCCURRED-SWITCH is initialized to "YES," which forces completion of at least one pass (this is discussed in more detail later). Previously, it was explained that a variable is needed to control the number of comparisons of adjacent element pairs for each pass. The MAX-COMPARES variable is initially set to the number of records in the table. For the table in Figure 11.3, for example, it would be set to five—the number of records. The manipulation of this variable will be discussed later. The PASSES module will be invoked a maximum of N - 1 times; however, if the table is ordered during an earlier pass (SWAP-OCCURRED-SWITCH = "NO"), the program will simply return to the routine that called the BUBBLE-SORT-MAIN module. When BUBBLE-SORT-MAIN is first invoked, SWAP-OCCURRED-SWITCH is compared with the constant, NO. Since the switch is initially set equal to "YES," it forces at least one iteration through the PASSES module. In this first entrance to the BUBBLE-SORT-MAIN module, the comparison result of DoWhile is of course false; therefore, the PASSES module is invoked.

## The PASSES Module

The basic functions of the PASSES module are to control the number of times the COMPARE-ELEM-PAIR module is performed and to increase the subscript that controls the current element pointer. The current element pointer is called SUB and points to the first of the element pairs. The first command in the module decreases the MAX-COMPARES variable by one. Since the content of MAX-COMPARES

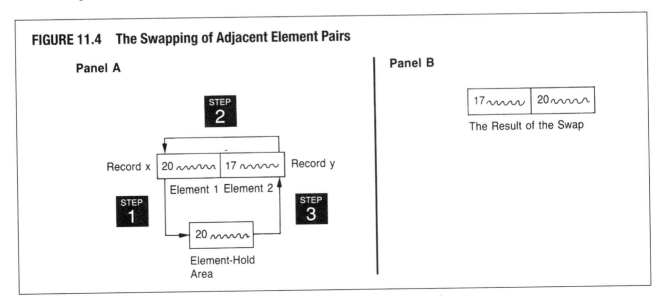

**FIGURE 11.4  The Swapping of Adjacent Element Pairs**

**Panel A**

STEP 2

Record x  | 20 ~~~ | 17 ~~~ |  Record y

Element 1  Element 2

STEP 1

STEP 3

| 20 ~~~ |

Element-Hold Area

**Panel B**

| 17 ~~~ | 20 ~~~ |

The Result of the Swap

**FIGURE 11.5    Flowchart Logic of an Ascending Bubble Sort**

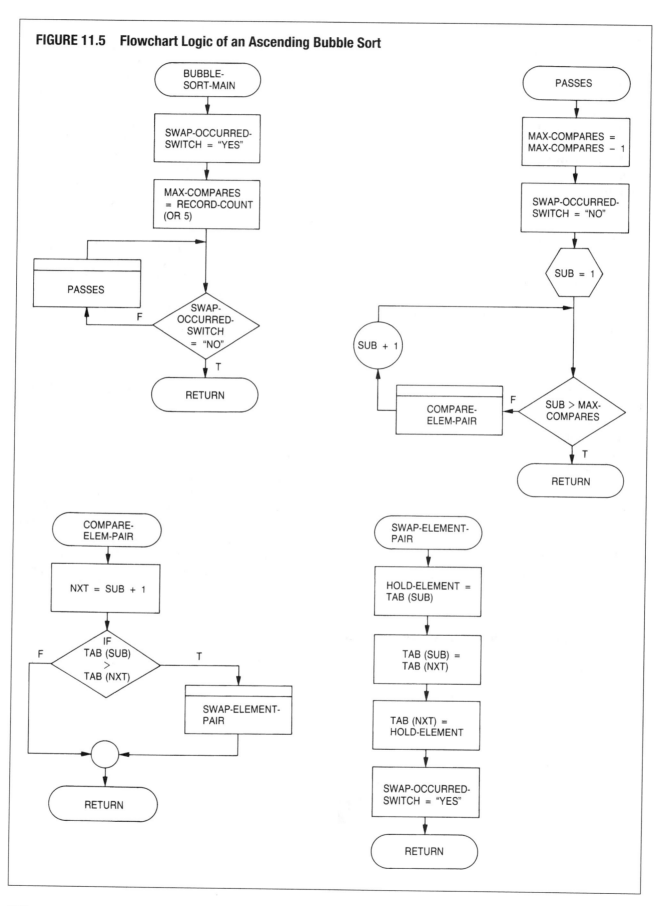

was initially set equal to the number of records in the table, the reduction of this variable by one establishes the proper N - 1 needed comparisons for the first pass. Second, the SWAP-OCCURRED-SWITCH is set to "NO" each time through the PASSES module. This switch is reset each time the SWAP-ELEMENT-PAIR routine ends. In the SWAP-ELEMENT-PAIR below, the "tripping" of the switch (SWAP-OCCURRED-SWITCH = "YES") is a message to BUBBLE-SORT-MAIN that an exchange was made. Third, the definite iteration structure in the PASSES module resembles that of a table search module in that a logic mechanism steps down through the table one element at a time.

## The COMPARE-ELEM-PAIR Module

The COMPARE-ELEM-PAIR module's function is to compare the sort key of the current record with the sort key of the adjacent record. In order to track the adjacent record in the table, a variable, NXT, will contain one more than SUB (NXT = SUB + 1). Any record referenced as TAB (NXT) is adjacent to the record referenced by TAB (SUB). Where ascending sequencing of the records is required, if the sort key of the current record is greater than the sort key of the adjacent record in the pair, then the *two records are swapped*.

## The SWAP-ELEMENT-PAIR Module

The SWAP-ELEMENT-PAIR module has the function of exchanging the record pair (see Figure 11.4). The first step—moving the first of the pair (record *x*) to the element-hold-area—is accomplished by

the notation HOLD-ELEMENT = TAB (SUB). The second step transfers the adjacent element's contents (record *y*) to the first element of the pair; this is accomplished by the notation TAB (SUB) = TAB (NXT). The third step moves the contents of the element-hold area (record *x*) to the second element of the element pair [TAB (NXT) = HOLD-ELEMENT]. At this point, the swapping process is complete. Next, the fourth step sets SWAP-OCCURRED-SWITCH on by moving YES to it. This switch setting indicates that a swap has occurred. The following RETURN sends back control to the RETURN at the bottom of the COMPARE-ELEM-PAIR module. This RETURN then transfers control to the SUB + 1 block back in the PASSES module. This causes the subscript SUB to be increased by one in order to establish the record pointer of the next record pair.

The definite iteration loop in the PASSES module is repeated. As long as SUB is not greater than the MAX-COMPARES variable, COMPARE-ELEM-PAIR is again invoked. The process of comparing the next adjacent pair of records continues until SUB is greater than MAX-COMPARES. When this condition is true, the subsequent RETURN in the PASSES module sends control back to the DoWhile condition test in the BUBBLE-SORT-MAIN module. At this point, a pass is complete. As long as a swap was made in the preceding pass, the PASSES module is reinvoked. If stopped when the SWAP-OCCURRED-SWITCH setting is equal to NO, the PASSES module is *no longer* invoked. Instead, the program control passes back to the module that invoked BUBBLE-SORT-MAIN.

---

### FIGURE 11.6    Pseudocode for an Ascending Bubble Sort

```
*bubble-sort-main                                          *compare-elem-pair
    swap-occurred-switch = "yes"                                nxt = sub + 1
    max-compares = record-count [the number of records in      if tab (sub) > tab (nxt)
    table]                                                          swap-element-pair
    dowhile swap-occurred-switch = "yes"                       endif
        passes                                                 return
    enddo                                                  *swap-element-pair
    return                                                     hold-element = tab (sub)
*passes                                                        tab (sub) = tab (nxt)
    max-compares = max-compares - 1                            tab (nxt) = hold-element
    swap-occurred-switch = "no"                                swap-occurred-switch = "yes"
    sub = 1                                                    return
    dowhile sub < or = max-compares
        compare-elem-pair
        sub = sub + 1
    enddo
    return
```

## A Monthly Summary Sales Report Using a Bubble Sort

### Program Requirements

Acme Company wishes to produce two reports, (1) a monthly sales analysis report by date of sale in ascending sequence (the sales file is already in ascending order by date of sale) and (2) a day sales summary. For the monthly sales analysis report, the date, store number, quantity, price, and sales for each sales record is to print. A subtotal is taken for each sales date. A company total is to print at the end of the report as well. *Management is also interested in determining which sales dates have generated the most sales. The second of the two reports is to provide this information.* This *second* listing prints an ordered summary of the daily sales according to their magnitude. The *highest* sale is listed first, followed by the next highest—a *descending listing*. The date of sale and sales amount print on the detail line. From this report, a manager can easily detect the dates with the highest and lowest sales amounts in order to analyze sales trends.

### Output Design

Exhibits 11.1 and 11.2 illustrate the sample reports to be produced. Exhibit 11.3 (Panel A and Panel B) illustrates the associated printer spacing charts.

---

**EXHIBIT 11.1   Sample Output for First Report in Ascending Sequence by Date**

```
                         MONTHLY SALES ANALYSIS REPORT
                               BY DATE OF SALE

          DATE      STORE NUMBER    QUANTITY    PRICE      SALES

         93/10/01       005            10       10.00     1000.00
         93/10/01       005             5       10.00       50.00
         93/10/01       005             1       20.00       20.00
         93/10/01       007             2       50.00      100.00
         93/10/01       007             5      100.00      500.00
         93/10/01       007             5      200.00     1000.00
         93/10/01       007             5       10.00       50.00
         93/10/01       007            10        5.00       50.00
         93/10/01       007             5        5.00       25.00

                             TOTAL SALES 93/10/01   2,795.00

         93/10/02       005             1       10.00       10.00
         93/10/02       005             5       10.00       50.00
         93/10/02       005            10       10.00      100.00
         93/10/02       005            20        5.00      100.00
         93/10/02       007            50       10.00      500.00
         93/10/02       007           100        5.00      500.00

                             TOTAL SALES 93/10/02   1,260.00 *

         93/10/03       001             1       10.00       10.00
         93/10/03       001             5       20.00      100.00
         93/10/03       005             2       25.00       50.00

                             TOTAL SALES 93/10/03     160.00 *

         93/10/04       001             5       10.00       50.00
         93/10/04       001             2       20.00       40.00

                             TOTAL SALES 93/10/04      90.00

         93/10/31       001             5       20.00      100.00
         93/10/31       001             5       10.00       50.00
         93/10/31       001             5       20.00      100.00
         93/10/31       005            10       10.00      100.00
         93/10/31       005            20      100.00     2000.00
         93/10/31       005            10       50.00      500.00

                             TOTAL SALES 93/10/31   2,850.00 *
                             TOTAL COMPANY SALES    7,155.00 **
```

## Input Design

The input record format of the sales records is depicted in Exhibit 11.4. The sales record contains the date of sale, customer number, register number, salesperson code, store number, quantity, and price.

## Tables

To print a summary listing of the sales in descending magnitude, it is necessary to store the control total for the daily sales and the date of sale into a single-dimensional table. After all detail processing has occurred, this table should be sorted with a

---

**EXHIBIT 11.2  Sample Output for Day Sales Summary Report**

```
            DAY SALES (ORDERED BY SALES) SUMMARY
                      DESCENDING SEQUENCE

              DATE                      SALES

            93/10/31                   2850.00
            93/10/01                   2795.00
            93/10/02                   1260.00
                *                         *
                *                         *
                *                         *
```

---

**EXHIBIT 11.3  Printer Spacing Charts for Monthly Sales Analysis Report**

**Panel A**

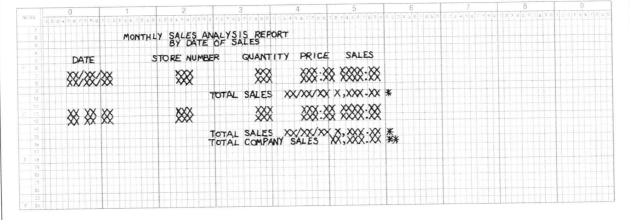

**Panel B**

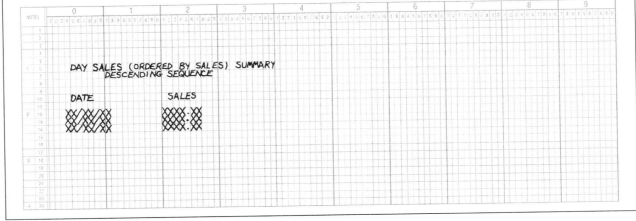

bubble sort, as previously explained. The table should be defined to accommodate up to 31 entries, one element for each day of the month. Here, the maximum table size of 31 also accommodates a month with only 30 days (or even February, with 28 or 29). The table is established as an *empty* table. Exhibit 11.5 describes the empty sales summary table called SUMMARY-SALES-TAB. In COBOL, the sub-elements are called SUMMARY-SALES-DATE-TAB and SUMMARY-DAY-SALES-TAB. In BASIC language, the sub-element names would be the two table names.

## Test Data

Exhibit 11.6 depicts a set of sales transaction records to be used in testing this program.

## Logic Considerations

The monthly sales analysis report by date of sale is a detail-printed control break report with sub-totals for each sale date. The record processing logic is simply a single-level control break check; however, at the control break interval, the sales amount and the date of sales are saved into SUMMARY-SALES-TAB. The only significant aspect of this logic is the necessary *bubble sort* of SUMMARY-SALES-TAB once all detail records have been processed. After the table is sorted into descending sequence by sales amount, the sorted contents are printed as a summary report.

## Program Design

**Hierarchy Chart.**　Exhibit 11.7 illustrates the general design of the sales analysis and summary reports (with bubble sort) in hierarchy chart form. The MAIN-LINE module appears as always. The START-UP module includes the usual commands to initialize required variables and open files. The PRINT-HEADINGS, READ-SALES-FILE, and SET-UP-PREVIOUS-DATE modules appear in that order. The RECORD-PROCESS module consists of a CONTROL-BREAK-CHECK module, a DETAIL-CALCULATION module for calculating the sales amount, an ACCUMULATE module that must appear in a control break program to add the sales to the subtotal (DAY-SALES-TOT), DETAIL-PRINT module, and a READ-SALES-FILE (post-read module.

**The WRAP-UP Module.**　The WRAP-UP module looks significantly different from those in previously designed control break reports. The MINOR-TOTAL module is invoked so that the subtotal is printed and rolled forward into the company total. The company total is then printed and the files are closed. Then, the BUBBLE-SORT-SALES module is followed by the PRINT-SORTED-SALES-FILE routine.

**Structured Flowchart.**　Exhibit 11.8 illustrates the structured program flowchart for this problem. Since you are now familiar with single-level control break logic, you need only review and study the modules pertaining to the subject of control breaks. Only the MINOR-TOTAL module of CONTROL-BREAK-CHECK and the WRAP-UP module need further explanation.

**The MINOR-TOTAL Module.**　In the MINOR-TOTAL module, the next-to-last step is to perform a LOAD-SALES-AND-DATE module, which stores the con-

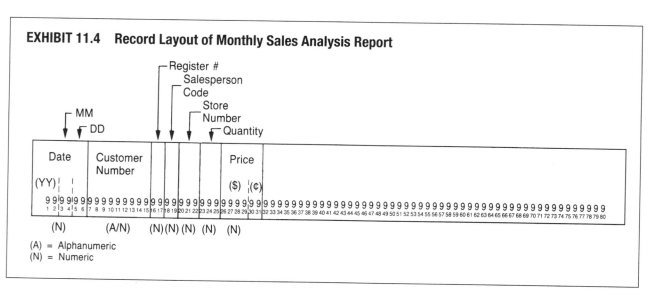

**EXHIBIT 11.4　Record Layout of Monthly Sales Analysis Report**

**EXHIBIT 11.5    Empty Table Defined to Accommodate 31 Possible Day Sales and Associated Date of Sale**

SUMMARY-SALES-TAB*

| | SUMMARY-SALES-DATE-TAB | SUMMARY-DAY-SALES-TAB |
|---|---|---|
| 1 | | |
| 2 | | |
| 3 | | |
| 4 | | |
| 5 | | |
| 6 | | |
| 7 | | |
| 8 | | |
| 9 | | |
| 10 | | |
| 11 | | |
| 12 | | |
| 13 | | |
| 14 | | |
| 15 | | |
| 16 | | |
| 17 | | |
| 18 | | |
| 19 | | |
| 20 | | |
| 21 | | |
| 22 | | |
| 23 | | |
| 24 | | |
| 25 | | |
| 26 | | |
| 27 | | |
| 28 | | |
| 29 | | |
| 30 | | |
| 31 | | |
| | YYMMDD | XXXX.XX |

*As conceptualized for the COBOL language, each element is subdivided into two parts.

For BASIC and many other languages, two separate tables are defined to accomplish the same thing. The elements of one table are associated with the elements of the other. For example, the first element of SUMMARY-SALES-DATE-TAB corresponds to the first element of SUMMARY-DAY-SALES-TAB and so on.

tents of PREVIOUS-DATE and DAY-SALES-TOT into respective subelements of SUMMARY-SALES-TAB. PREVIOUS-DATE is stored into the SUM-MARY-SALES-DATE-TAB subelement, and the DAY-SALES-TOT is stored into the SUMMARY-DAY-SALES-TAB subelement. Once the element is loaded, the MAX-ELEMENTS-LOADED counter is increased by one. Once all detail processing is complete, this counter contains one more than the number of entries loaded into the table, because the MAX-ELEMENTS-LOADED module was first initialized to the value 1 back up in the START-UP module; thus when the increment is made after an element is loaded, it contains one more than the total number of elements loaded. The last step of the MINOR-TOTAL module performs the SET-UP-PREVIOUS-DATE module.

**The Function of the WRAP-UP Module.** After the MINOR-TOTAL module is invoked and the company sales total is printed, the WRAP-UP module then invokes the BUBBLE-SORT-SALES module. The BUBBLE-SORT-SALES module performs as in the previous discussion regarding the logic of the bubble sort. One addition: The MAX-COMPARES variable in the BUBBLE-SORT-SALES main module is initialized to one *less* than the contents of MAX-ELEMENTS-LOADED. Remember that MAX-ELE-MENTS-LOADED contains one *more* than the number of elements loaded; therefore, at this point, MAX-COMPARES contains a value exactly *equal* to the number of elements in the table.

The SORTED-SALES-FILE module moves the sorted elements one by one from the table into the print line and writes the summary print lines. The logic here resembles that of a table-load module from Chapter 7 or Chapter 8. A definite loop iteration structure is used to step down through the sorted table one element at a time and load the respective subelements (SUMMARY-SALES-DATE-TAB and SUMMARY-DAY-SALES-TAB) of the table element into the print line. The number of loops through the definite iterations structure will be controlled by the contents of MAX-ELEMENTS-LOADED reduced by one. After reducing MAX-ELEMENTS-LOADED by one, it contains exactly the number of elements found in the table to be printed.

**Pseudocode.** Exhibit 11.9 depicts the associated pseudocode for this problem.

**Programs.** Exhibits 11.10 and 11.11 depict the COBOL and BASIC programs for the program design.

---

**EXHIBIT 11.6   Test Data for Monthly Sales Analysis Report**

```
COLUMN    1         2         3         4         5         6         7         8
          12345678901234567890123456789012345678901234567890123456789012345678901234567890
- - - - - - - - - - - - - - - - - - - - - - - - - - - - - - - - - - - - - - - - - - - - - -
871001|8888888888|01|02|005|010|010000
871001|7777777777|01|02|005|005|001000
871001|6666666666|01|02|005|001|002000
871001|5555555555|01|02|007|002|005000
871001|4444444444|02|03|007|005|010000
871001|3333333333|02|03|007|005|020000
871001|2222222222|02|03|007|005|001000
871001|1111111111|02|03|007|010|000500
871001|1999999999|02|03|007|005|000500
871002|1888888888|02|03|005|001|001000
871002|1777777777|02|03|005|005|001000
871002|1666666666|02|03|005|010|001000
871002|1555555555|02|03|005|020|000500
871002|1444444444|02|03|007|050|001000
871002|1333333333|02|03|007|100|000500
871003|2999999999|02|04|001|001|001000
871003|2888888888|02|03|001|005|002000
871003|2777777777|02|03|005|002|002500
871004|3999999999|02|03|001|005|001000
871004|3888888888|02|03|001|002|002000
871031|4999999999|02|03|001|005|002000
871031|4888888888|02|03|001|005|001000
871031|4777777777|02|03|001|005|002000
871031|4666666666|02|03|005|010|001000
871031|4555555555|02|03|005|020|010000
871031|4333333333|02|03|005|010|005000
```

**EXHIBIT 11.7 Hierarchy Chart for Monthly Sales Analysis Report**

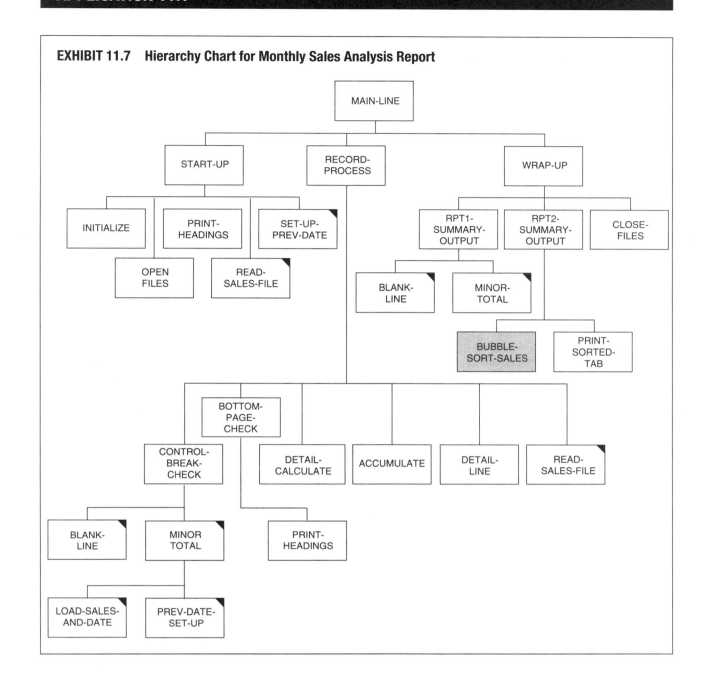

**EXHIBIT 11.8   Structured Flowchart for Monthly Sales Report**

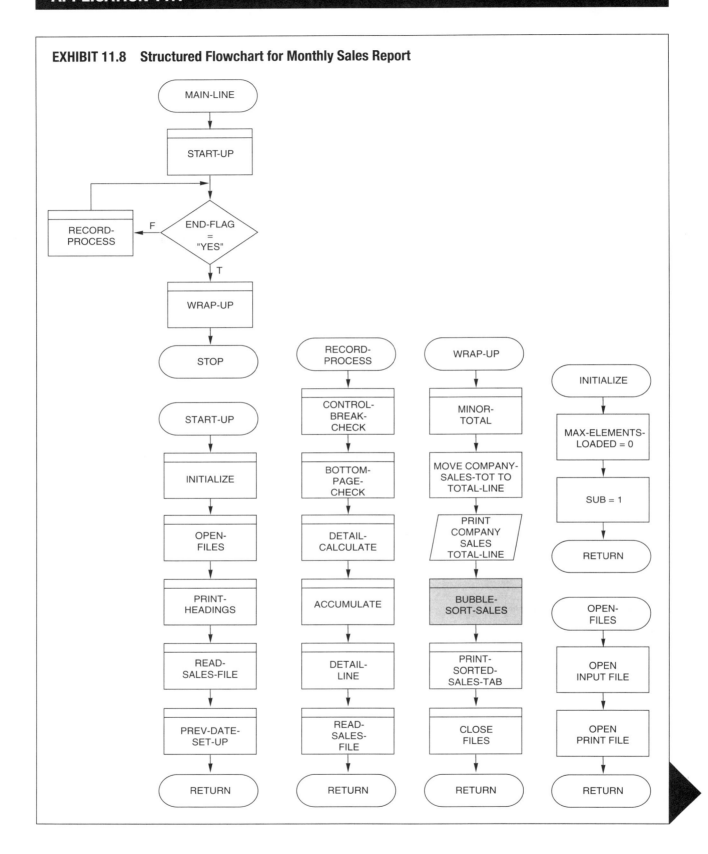

**EXHIBIT 11.8    (Cont.)**

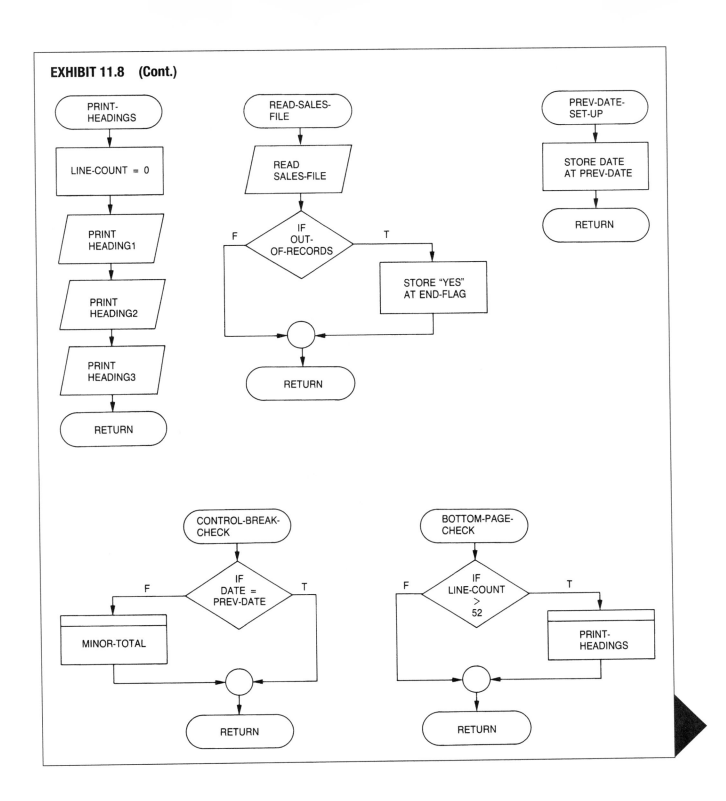

**EXHIBIT 11.8   (Cont.)**

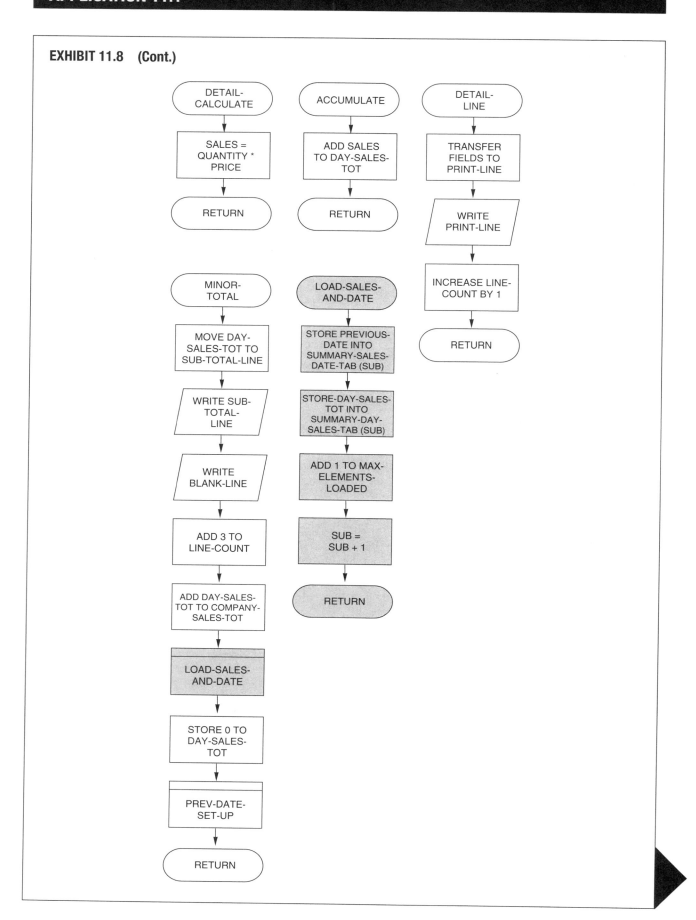

**EXHIBIT 11.8    (Cont.)**

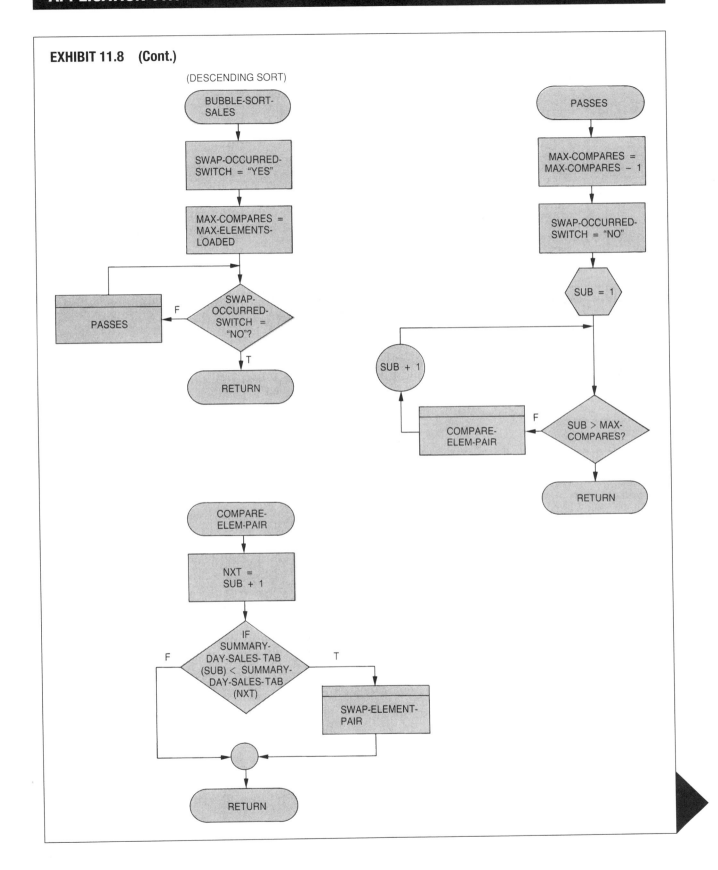

**EXHIBIT 11.8   (Cont.)**

For COBOL Only

For BASIC Only

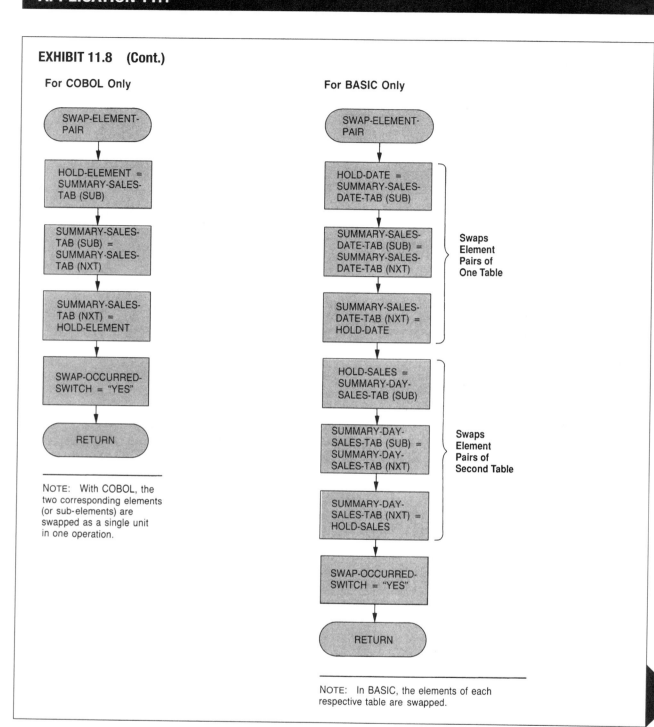

NOTE:   With COBOL, the two corresponding elements (or sub-elements) are swapped as a single unit in one operation.

NOTE:   In BASIC, the elements of each respective table are swapped.

**EXHIBIT 11.8    (Cont.)**

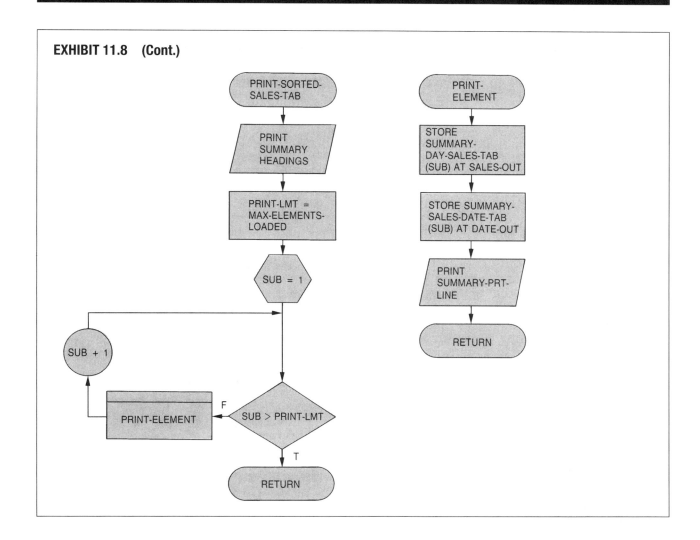

## APPLICATION 11.1

**EXHIBIT 11.9   Pseudocode for Illustration 11.1 (Monthly Summary Sales Analysis Report)**

```
*main-line
    start-up
    do while end-flag = "no"
        record-process
    enddo
    wrap-up
    stop
*start-up
    initialize
    open-files
    print headings
    read-sales-file
    prev-date-set-up
    return
*initialize
    max-elements-loaded = 1
    end-flag = "no"
    day-sales-tot = 0
    company-sales-tot = 0
    sub = 1
    return
*open-files
    open sales-file, tab-file
    open report-file
    return
*record-process
    control-break check
    bottom-of-page-check
    detail-calculate
    accumulate
    detail-line
    read-sales-file
    return
*print-headings
    print heading1
    print heading2
    return
*read-sales-file
    read sales-file
        if out of records
            store "yes" at end-flag
        endif
    endread
    return
```

```
*prev-date-set-up
    store date at prev-date
    return
*control-break-check
    if date = prev-date
        null
    else
        blank-line
        minor-total
        blank-line
    endif
    return
*bottom-of-page-check
    if line-count > 52
        headinigs
    endif
    return
*detail-calculate
    sales = quantity * price
    return
*accumulate
    add sales to day-sales-tot
    return
*detail-line
    transfer appropriate fields to print line
    write print-line
    line-count = line-count + 1
    return
*minor-total
    move day-sales-tot to sub-total-line
    print sub-total-line
    add day-sales-tot to company-sales-tot
    store 0 at day-sales-tot
    load-sales-and-date
    prev-date-set-up
    return
*load-sales-and-date
    store previous-date into summary-sales-date-tab (sub)
    store day-sales-tot into summary-day-sales-tab (sub)
    add 1 to max-elements-loaded
    sub = sub + 1
    return
```

**EXHIBIT 11.9    (Cont.)**

*bubble-sort-sales
    swap-occured-switch = "yes"
    max-compares = max-elements-loaded
    do while swap-occured-switch = "yes"
        passes
    enddo
*passes
    max-compares = max-compares - 1
    swap-occured-switch = "no"
    sub = 1
    do while sub < or = max-compares
        compare-elem-pair
        sub = sub + 1
    enddo
    return
*compare-elem-pair
    nxt = sub + 1
    if summary-pay-sales-tab (sub) < summary-day-sales-tab
    (nxt) then
        swap-element-pair
    endif
    return
*swap-element-pair
    hold-element = summary-sales-tab (sub)
    summary-sales-tab (sub) = summary-sales-tab (nxt)
    summary-sales-tab (nxt) = hold-element
    swap-occured-switch = "yes"
    return
*print-sorted-sales-tab
    print-lmt = max-elements-loaded (*see note below)
    sub = 1
    do while sub not > print-lmt
        print-element
        sub = sub + 1
    enddo
    return

*Note: max-elements-loaded will contain one more than the
        number of values added to the table. See the load-sales-
        and-date module for details.
*print-element
    store summary-day-sales-tab (sub) at sales-out in print line
    store summary-sales-date-tab (sub) at date-out in print line
    print summary-prt-line
    return
*wrap-up
    report1-summary-output
    report2-summary-output
    close-files
    return
*report1-summary-output
    minor-total
    store company-sales-tot at total-line
    store prev-date at total-line
    print company sales total-line
    return
*report2-summary-output
    bubble-sort-sales
    print-sorted-sales-tab
    return
*close-files
    close sales-file
    close tab-file
    close report-file
    return
*blank-line
    move spaces to summary-prt-line
    write summary-prt-line
    return

**EXHIBIT 11.10    COBOL 85 Program and Output for Application 11.1 (Bubble Sort)**

```
 1  2       IDENTIFICATION DIVISION.
 2           PROGRAM-ID. CH11NEW-BUBBLE-SORT.
 3           DATE-WRITTEN. NOVEMBER,10, 1992.
 4           DATE-COMPILED. 1993-06-24.
 5
 6
 7          *REMARKS:   COBOL 85
 8           *              THIS PROGRAM PRODUCES A MONTHLY SALES ANALYSIS
 9           *              REPORT BROKEN DOWN BY DATE OF SALE FROM A ORDERED
10           *              SALES FILE BY DATE.  A SUMMARY REPORT OF DAY SALES
11           *              ORDERED BY SALES IN DESCENDING SEQUENCE IS TO PRINT.
12           *              THIS IS HANDLED BY SAVING THE VARIOUS GROUP TOTALS
13           *              AND THE ASSOCIATED DATE INTO A SINGLE DIMENSIONAL
14           *              TABLE, SORTING IT IN DECENDING SEQUENCE USING THE
15           *              BUBBLE SORT AND PRINTING THE TABLE OUT.
16
17           ENVIRONMENT DIVISION.
18           CONFIGURATION SECTION.
19           SOURCE-COMPUTER. CYBER.
20           OBJECT-COMPUTER. CYBER.
21           INPUT-OUTPUT SECTION.
22           FILE-CONTROL.
23               SELECT SALES-FILE ASSIGN TO CH11I1DTA.
24               SELECT OUTPUT-FILE ASSIGN TO OUTFILE.
25
26           DATA DIVISION.
27           FILE SECTION.
28
29           FD SALES-FILE.
30           01 SALES-RECORD.
31               05 SALES-DATE.
32                   10 SALES-YEAR          PIC 99.
33                   10 SALES-MONTH         PIC 99.
34                   10 SALES-DAY           PIC 99.
35               05 CUSTOMER-NUMBER         PIC X(9).
36               05 REGISTER-NUMBER         PIC 99.
37               05 SALESPERSON-CODE        PIC 99.
38               05 STORE-NUMBER            PIC 999.
39               05 QUANTITY                PIC 999.
40               05 PRICE                   PIC 9(4)V99.
41
42           FD OUTPUT-FILE.
43           01 OUTPUT-RECORD               PIC X(133).
44
45           WORKING-STORAGE SECTION.
46
47           01 END-FLAG                    PIC XXX VALUE "NO".
48           01 SWAP-OCCURED-SWITCH         PIC XXX VALUE "NO".
49           01 MAX-ELEMENTS-LOADED         PIC 999 VALUE ZERO.
50           01 MAX-COMPARES                PIC 999 VALUE ZERO.
51           01 LINE-COUNT                  PIC 99 VALUE ZERO.
52           01 PRINT-LMT                   PIC 999 VALUE ZERO.
53           01 SUB                         PIC 999 VALUE ZERO.
54           01 NXT                         PIC 999 VALUE ZERO.
55           01 PREV-DATE                   PIC 9(6) VALUE ZERO.
56           01 SALES                       PIC 9(4)V99.
57           01 DAY-SALES-TOT               PIC 9(4)V99 VALUE ZERO.
58           01 COMPANY-SALES-TOT           PIC 9(5)V99 VALUE ZERO.
59           01 HOLD-ELEMENT                PIC X(13).
60
61           01 SUMMARY-SALES-DATE-TABLE.
62               05 SUMMARY-ELEMENT-TAB OCCURS 31 TIMES.
63                   10 SUMMARY-SALES-DATE-TAB      PIC 9(6).
64                   10 SUMMARY-DAY-SALES-TAB       PIC 9(5)V99.
65
```

EXHIBIT 11.10    (Cont.)

```
66          01 HEADING-1.
67              05                          PIC X(24) VALUE SPACES.
68              05                          PIC X(108) VALUE
69                  "MONTHLY SALES ANALYSIS REPORT".
70
71          01 HEADING-2.
72              05                          PIC X(32) VALUE SPACES.
73              05                          PIC X(100) VALUE
74                  "BY DATE OF SALE".
75
76          01 HEADING-3.
77              05                          PIC X(14) VALUE SPACES.
78              05                          PIC X(15) VALUE "DATE".
79              05                          PIC X(16) VALUE "STORE NUMBER".
80              05                          PIC X(10) VALUE "QUANTITY".
81              05                          PIC X(8) VALUE "PRICE".
82              05                          PIC X(69) VALUE "SALES".
83
84          01 PRINT-LINE.
85              05                          PIC X(13) VALUE SPACES.
86              05 PRINT-YEAR               PIC Z9/.
87              05 PRINT-MONTH              PIC Z9/.
88              05 PRINT-DAY                PIC 99.
89              05                          PIC X(12) VALUE SPACES.
90              05 PRINT-STORE-NUMBER       PIC 999.
91              05                          PIC X(11) VALUE SPACES.
92              05 PRINT-QUANTITY           PIC 999.
93              05                          PIC X(5) VALUE SPACES.
94              05 PRINT-PRICE              PIC ZZ9.99.
95              05                          PIC X VALUE SPACE.
96              05 PRINT-SALES              PIC ZZZ9.99.
97              05                          PIC X(68) VALUE SPACES.
98
99          01 SUB-TOT-LINE.
100             05                          PIC X(39) VALUE SPACES.
101             05                          PIC X(13) VALUE "TOTAL SALES".
102             05 SUB-TOT-DATE             PIC Z9/99/99.
103             05 SUB-TOT-DATE-R  REDEFINES SUB-TOT-DATE PIC X(8).
104             05                          PIC X VALUE SPACES.
105             05 SUB-TOT-SALES            PIC Z,ZZ9.99.
106             05                          PIC X(62) VALUE " *".
107
108         01 TOTAL-LINE.
109             05                          PIC X(39) VALUE SPACES.
110             05                          PIC X(21) VALUE
111                 "TOTAL COMPANY SALES".
112             05 TOTAL-COMPANY-SALES      PIC ZZ,ZZ9.99.
113             05                          PIC X(63) VALUE " **".
114
115         01 SUMMARY-HEADING-1.
116             05                          PIC X(3) VALUE SPACES.
117             05                          PIC X(129) VALUE
118                 "DAY SALES (ORDERED BY SALES) SUMMARY".
119
120         01 SUMMARY-HEADING-2.
121             05                          PIC X(9) VALUE SPACES.
122             05                          PIC X(123) VALUE
123                 "DESCENDING SEQUENCE".
124
125         01 SUMMARY-HEADING-3.
126             05                          PIC X(3) VALUE SPACES.
127             05                          PIC X(16) VALUE "DATE".
128             05                          PIC X(113) VALUE "SALES".
129
```

**EXHIBIT 11.10   (Cont.)**

```
130         01 SUMMARY-PRT-LINE.
131             05                              PIC X(2) VALUE SPACES.
132             05 DATE-OUT                     PIC 99/99/99.
133             05 DATE-OUT-R REDEFINES DATE-OUT PIC X(8).
134             05                              PIC X(8) VALUE SPACES.
135             05 SALES-OUT                    PIC ZZZ9.99.
136             05                              PIC X(107) VALUE SPACES.
137         /
138         PROCEDURE DIVISION.
139
140         000-MAIN-LINE.
141             PERFORM 100-START-UP.
142             PERFORM 200-RECORD-PROCESS UNTIL END-FLAG = "YES".
143             PERFORM 300-WRAP-UP.
144             STOP RUN.
145
146         100-START-UP.
147             PERFORM 102-INITIALIZE
148             PERFORM 105-OPEN-FILES.
149             PERFORM 110-PRINT-HEADINGS.
150             PERFORM 120-READ-SALES-FILE.
151             PERFORM 130-PREV-DATE-SET-UP.
152
153         102-INITIALIZE.
154             MOVE 1 TO MAX-ELEMENTS-LOADED.
155             MOVE 1 TO SUB.
156
157         105-OPEN-FILES.
158             OPEN INPUT SALES-FILE
159             OUTPUT OUTPUT-FILE.
160
161         110-PRINT-HEADINGS.
162             MOVE ZERO TO LINE-COUNT.
163             WRITE OUTPUT-RECORD FROM HEADING-1 AFTER PAGE.
164             WRITE OUTPUT-RECORD FROM HEADING-2.
165             WRITE OUTPUT-RECORD FROM HEADING-3 AFTER 2.
166             MOVE SPACES TO OUTPUT-RECORD.
167             WRITE OUTPUT-RECORD.
168
169         120-READ-SALES-FILE.
170             READ SALES-FILE AT END MOVE "YES" TO END-FLAG.
171
172         130-PREV-DATE-SET-UP.
173             MOVE SALES-DATE TO PREV-DATE.
174
175         200-RECORD-PROCESS.
176             PERFORM 210-CONTROL-BREAK-CHECK.
177             PERFORM 240-BOTTOM-PAGE-CHECK.
178             PERFORM 250-DETAIL-CALCULATE.
179             PERFORM 260-ACCUMULATE.
180             PERFORM 270-DETAIL-LINE.
181             PERFORM 120-READ-SALES-FILE.
182
183         210-CONTROL-BREAK-CHECK.
184             IF SALES-DATE = PREV-DATE
185                 THEN NEXT SENTENCE
186                 ELSE
187                     PERFORM 215-BLANK-LINE
188                     PERFORM 220-MINOR-TOTAL
189                     PERFORM 215-BLANK-LINE
190             END-IF
191
192         215-BLANK-LINE.
193             MOVE SPACES TO PRINT-LINE.
194             WRITE OUTPUT-RECORD FROM PRINT-LINE.
195
```

**EXHIBIT 11.10** (Cont.)

```
196          220-MINOR-TOTAL.
197              MOVE DAY-SALES-TOT TO SUB-TOT-SALES.
198              MOVE PREV-DATE TO SUB-TOT-DATE.
199              WRITE OUTPUT-RECORD FROM SUB-TOT-LINE.
200              ADD DAY-SALES-TOT TO COMPANY-SALES-TOT.
201              PERFORM 230-LOAD-SALES-AND-DATE.
202              MOVE 0 TO DAY-SALES-TOT.
203              PERFORM 130-PREV-DATE-SET-UP.
204
205          230-LOAD-SALES-AND-DATE.
206              MOVE PREV-DATE TO SUMMARY-SALES-DATE-TAB (SUB).
207              MOVE DAY-SALES-TOT TO SUMMARY-DAY-SALES-TAB (SUB).
208              ADD 1 TO MAX-ELEMENTS-LOADED.
209              ADD 1 TO SUB.
210
211          240-BOTTOM-PAGE-CHECK.
212              IF LINE-COUNT > 52
213                  THEN PERFORM 110-PRINT-HEADINGS
214              END-IF.
215
216          250-DETAIL-CALCULATE.
217              COMPUTE SALES ROUNDED = QUANTITY * PRICE.
218
219          260-ACCUMULATE.
220              ADD SALES TO DAY-SALES-TOT.
221
222          270-DETAIL-LINE.
223              MOVE SALES-YEAR TO PRINT-YEAR.
224              MOVE SALES-MONTH TO PRINT-MONTH.
225              MOVE SALES-DAY TO PRINT-DAY.
226              MOVE STORE-NUMBER TO PRINT-STORE-NUMBER.
227              MOVE QUANTITY TO PRINT-QUANTITY.
228              MOVE PRICE TO PRINT-PRICE.
229              MOVE SALES TO PRINT-SALES.
230              WRITE OUTPUT-RECORD FROM PRINT-LINE.
231              ADD 1 TO LINE-COUNT.
232
233          300-WRAP-UP.
234              PERFORM 305-RPT1-SUMMARY-OUTPUT.
235              PERFORM 307-RPT2-SUMMARY-OUTPUT.
236              PERFORM 309-CLOSE-FILES.
237
238          305-RPT1-SUMMARY-OUTPUT.
239              PERFORM 215-BLANK-LINE.
240              PERFORM 220-MINOR-TOTAL.
241              MOVE COMPANY-SALES-TOT TO TOTAL-COMPANY-SALES.
242              WRITE OUTPUT-RECORD FROM TOTAL-LINE.
243
244          307-RPT2-SUMMARY-OUTPUT.
245              PERFORM 310-BUBBLE-SORT-SALES.
246              PERFORM 350-PRINT-SORTED-TAB.
247
248           309-CLOSE-FILES.
249              CLOSE SALES-FILE
250                      OUTPUT-FILE.
251
252           310-BUBBLE-SORT-SALES.
253              MOVE "YES" TO SWAP-OCCURED-SWITCH.
254              SUBTRACT 1 FROM MAX-ELEMENTS-LOADED.
255              MOVE MAX-ELEMENTS-LOADED TO MAX-COMPARES.
256              PERFORM 320-PASSES UNTIL SWAP-OCCURED-SWITCH = "NO".
257
```

**EXHIBIT 11.10   (Cont.)**

```
258          320-PASSES.
259              SUBTRACT 1 FROM MAX-COMPARES.
260              MOVE "NO" TO SWAP-OCCURED-SWITCH.
261              PERFORM 330-COMPARE-ELEM-PAIR VARYING SUB FROM 1 BY 1 UNTIL
262                  SUB > MAX-COMPARES.
263
264          330-COMPARE-ELEM-PAIR.
265              COMPUTE NXT = SUB + 1
266              IF SUMMARY-DAY-SALES-TAB (SUB) <
267                      SUMMARY-DAY-SALES-TAB (NXT)
268                  THEN PERFORM 340-SWAP-ELEMENT-PAIR
269              ELSE NEXT SENTENCE.
270
271          340-SWAP-ELEMENT-PAIR.
272              MOVE SUMMARY-ELEMENT-TAB (SUB) TO HOLD-ELEMENT.
273              MOVE SUMMARY-ELEMENT-TAB (NXT) TO
274                      SUMMARY-ELEMENT-TAB (SUB).
275              MOVE HOLD-ELEMENT TO SUMMARY-ELEMENT-TAB (NXT).
276              MOVE "YES" TO SWAP-OCCURED-SWITCH.
277
278          350-PRINT-SORTED-TAB.
279              WRITE OUTPUT-RECORD FROM SUMMARY-HEADING-1 AFTER PAGE.
280              WRITE OUTPUT-RECORD FROM SUMMARY-HEADING-2.
281              WRITE OUTPUT-RECORD FROM SUMMARY-HEADING-3 AFTER 2.
282              MOVE SPACES TO OUTPUT-RECORD.
283              WRITE OUTPUT-RECORD.
284              COMPUTE PRINT-LMT = MAX-ELEMENTS-LOADED.
285              PERFORM 360-PRINT-ELEMENT VARYING SUB FROM 1 BY 1 UNTIL
286                  SUB > PRINT-LMT.
287
288          360-PRINT-ELEMENT.
289              MOVE SUMMARY-DAY-SALES-TAB (SUB) TO SALES-OUT.
290              MOVE SUMMARY-SALES-DATE-TAB (SUB) TO DATE-OUT.
291              WRITE OUTPUT-RECORD FROM SUMMARY-PRT-LINE.
```

**EXHIBIT 11.10** (Cont.)

```
              MONTHLY SALES ANALYSIS REPORT
                    BY DATE OF SALE

   DATE         STORE NUMBER     QUANTITY   PRICE    SALES

93/10/01           005             010      100.00  1000.00
93/10/01           005             005       10.00    50.00
93/10/01           005             001       20.00    20.00
93/10/01           007             002       50.00   100.00
93/10/01           007             005      100.00   500.00
93/10/01           007             005      200.00  1000.00
93/10/01           007             005       10.00    50.00
93/10/01           007             010        5.00    50.00
93/10/01           007             005        5.00    25.00

                   TOTAL SALES   93/10/01  2,795.00  *

93/10/02           005             001       10.00    10.00
93/10/02           005             005       10.00    50.00
93/10/02           005             010       10.00   100.00
93/10/02           005             020        5.00   100.00
93/10/02           007             050       10.00   500.00
93/10/02           007             100        5.00   500.00

                   TOTAL SALES   93/10/02  1,260.00  *

93/10/03           001             001       10.00    10.00
93/10/03           001             005       20.00   100.00
93/10/03           005             002       25.00    50.00

                   TOTAL SALES   93/10/03    160.00  *
```

```
   DAY SALES (ORDERED BY SALES) SUMMARY
          DESCENDING SEQUENCE

   DATE          SALES

93/10/31        2850.00
93/10/01        2795.00
93/10/02        1260.00
93/10/03         160.00
93/10/04          90.00
```

### EXHIBIT 11.11    QUICKBASIC Program for Application 11.1 (Bubble Sort)

```
'*********************************************************************
'*                        PROGRAM-IDENTIFICATION                    *
'*********************************************************************
'*QUICK BASIC
'* PROGRAM NAME: CH11NEW.BAS                                         *
'* REMARKS: THIS PROGRAM PRODUCES A MONTHLY SALES ANALYSIS REPORT    *
'*          BROKEN DOWN BY DATE OF SALE FROM A ORDERED SALES FILE BY *
'*          DATE. A SUMMARY REPORT OF DAY SALES ORDERED BY SALES IN  *
'*          DECENDING SEQUENCE IS TO PRINT. THIS IS HANDLED BY SAVING*
'*          THE VARIOUS GROUP TOTALS AND THE ASSOCIATED DATE INTO A  *
'*          SINGLE DIMENSIONAL TABLE, SORTING IT IN DECENDING SEQUENCE*
'*          USING THE BUBBLE SORT AND PRINTING THE TABLE OUT.        *


'*********************************************************************
'*                           MAIN-LINE                              *
'*********************************************************************

MAIN.LINE:

    GOSUB START.UP                    '* PERFORM START-UP
    DO UNTIL END.FLAG$ = "YES"
       GOSUB RECORD.PROCESS           '* PERFORM RECORD-PROCESS
       LOOP
    GOSUB WRAP.UP                     '* PERFORM WRAP-UP
    END


    '*********************************************************************
    '*                           START-UP                              *
    '*********************************************************************

START.UP:

    DIM SUMMARY.SALES.DATE.TAB(31): DIM SUMMARY.DAY.SALES.TAB(31)
    GOSUB INITIALIZE
    GOSUB OPEN.FILES
    GOSUB PRINT.HEADINGS              '* PERFORM PRINT-HEADINGS
    GOSUB READ.SALES.FILE            '* PERFORM READ-SALES-FILE
    GOSUB SET.UP.PREV.DATE           '* PERFORM PREV-DATE-SET-UP
    RETURN
    '*************************************************************
    '*                    INITIALIZE                           *
    '*************************************************************

INITIALIZE:

    PRINT.LINE$ = "        \\/\\/\ \         \ \       ###    ###.## ####.##"
    SUBTOTAL.LINE$ = "                            TOTAL SALES  \\/\\/\ \ #,###.## *"
    TOTAL.LINE$ = "                            TOTAL COMPANY SALES   #,###.## *_*"
    SUMMARY.PRT.LINE$ = "  \\/\\/\ \         ####.##"
    END.FLAG$ = "NO"
    MAX.ELEMENTS.LOADED = 1
    SUB1 = 1
    RETURN
```

**EXHIBIT 11.11    (Cont.)**

```
'*****************************************************************
'*                      OPEN-FILES                      *
'*****************************************************************

OPEN.FILES:

    OPEN "I", #1, "CH11IL1.DAT"
    RETURN

    '*****************************************************************
    '*                    PRINT-HEADINGS                    *
    '*****************************************************************

PRINT.HEADINGS:

    LINE.COUNT = 0
    LPRINT CHR$(12)
    LPRINT TAB(25); "MONTHLY SALES ANALYSIS REPORT"
    LPRINT TAB(33); "BY DATE OF SALE"
    LPRINT
    LPRINT TAB(15); "DATE"; TAB(30); "STORE NUMBER"; TAB(46); "QUANTITY"; TAB(56); "PRICE"; TAB(64); "SALES"
    LPRINT
    RETURN
    '*************************************************************************
    '*                        READ-SALES-FILE                        *
    '*************************************************************************

READ.SALES.FILE:

    INPUT #1, DAATE, CUSTOMER.NUMBER$, REGISTER$, SALESPERSON$, STORE.NUMBER$, QUANTITY, PRICE
    IF CUSTOMER.NUMBER$ = "EOF" THEN
        END.FLAG$ = "YES"
    END IF
    RETURN


    '*************************************************************************
    '*                      SET-UP-PREV-DATE                      *
    '*************************************************************************


SET.UP.PREV.DATE:

    PREVIOUS.DATE = DAATE
    RETURN


    '*************************************************************************
    '*                        RECORD-PROCESS                        *
    '*************************************************************************


RECORD.PROCESS:

    GOSUB CONTROL.BREAK.CHECK        '* PERFORM CONTROL-BREAK-CHECK
    GOSUB BOTTOM.PAGE.CHECK          '* PERFORM BOTTOM-PAGE-CHECK
    GOSUB DETAIL.CALCULATE           '* PERFORM DETAIL-CALCULATE
    GOSUB ACCUMULATE                 '* PERFORM ACCUMULATE
    GOSUB DETAIL.LINE                '* PERFORM DETAIL-LINE
    GOSUB READ.SALES.FILE            '* PERFORM READ-SALES-FILE
    RETURN
```

**EXHIBIT 11.11    (Cont.)**

```
'**********************************************************************
'*                      CONTROL-BREAK-CHECK                          *
'**********************************************************************

CONTROL.BREAK.CHECK:

    IF DAATE <> PREVIOUS.DATE THEN
        GOSUB BLANK.LINE
        GOSUB MINOR.TOTAL
        GOSUB BLANK.LINE
    END IF
    RETURN


    '**********************************************************************
    '*                        MINOR-TOTAL                               *
    '**********************************************************************

MINOR.TOTAL:

    LPRINT
    PREV.DATE$ = STR$(PREVIOUS.DATE)
    YY$ = LEFT$(PREV.DATE$, 3)
    MM$ = MID$(PREV.DATE$, 4, 2)
    DD$ = RIGHT$(PREV.DATE$, 2)
    LPRINT USING SUBTOTAL.LINE$; MM$; DD$; YY$; DAY.SALES.TOT
    LPRINT
    COMPANY.SALES.TOT = COMPANY.SALES.TOT + DAY.SALES.TOT
    GOSUB LOAD.SALES.AND.DATE             '* PERFORM LOAD-SALES-AND-DATE
    DAY.SALES.TOT = 0
    GOSUB SET.UP.PREV.DATE                '* PERFORM PREV-DATE-SET-UP
    RETURN

    '**********************************************************************
    '*                     LOAD-SALES-AND-DATE                          *
    '**********************************************************************

LOAD.SALES.AND.DATE:

    SUMMARY.SALES.DATE.TAB(SUB1) = PREVIOUS.DATE
    SUMMARY.DAY.SALES.TAB(SUB1) = DAY.SALES.TOT
    MAX.ELEMENTS.LOADED = MAX.ELEMENTS.LOADED + 1
    SUB1 = SUB1 + 1
    RETURN
```

**EXHIBIT 11.11** **(Cont.)**

```
'**********************************************************************
'*                       BOTTOM-PAGE-CHECK                            *
'**********************************************************************

BOTTOM.PAGE.CHECK:

     IF LINE.COUNT > 52 THEN
         GOSUB PRINT.HEADINGS        '* PERFORM PRINT-HEADINGS
     END IF
     RETURN



     '**********************************************************************
     '*                       DETAIL-CALCULATE                            *
     '**********************************************************************

DETAIL.CALCULATE:

     SALES = QUANTITY * PRICE
     RETURN


     '**********************************************************************
     '*                         ACCUMULATE                                *
     '**********************************************************************

ACCUMULATE:

     DAY.SALES.TOT = DAY.SALES.TOT + SALES
     RETURN
     '**********************************************************************
     '*                         DETAIL-LINE                               *
     '**********************************************************************

DETAIL.LINE:
     DAATE$ = STR$(DAATE)
     YY$ = LEFT$(DAATE$, 3)
     MM$ = MID$(DAATE$, 4, 2)
     DD$ = RIGHT$(DAATE$, 2)

     LPRINT USING PRINT.LINE$; MM$; DD$; YY$; STORE.NUMBER$; QUANTITY; PRICE; SALES
     LINE.COUNT = LINE.COUNT + 1
     RETURN


     '**********************************************************************
     '*                         BLANK-LINE                                *
     '**********************************************************************

BLANK.LINE:
     LPRINT
     RETURN
```

**EXHIBIT 11.11   (Cont.)**

```
        '*******************************************************************
        '*                           WRAP-UP                              *
        '*******************************************************************

WRAP.UP:

    GOSUB RPT1.SUMMARY.OUTPUT
    GOSUB RPT2.SUMMARY.OUTPUT
    GOSUB CLOSE.FILES
    RETURN


        '*******************************************************************
        '*                     RPT1-SUMMARY-OUTPUT                        *
        '*******************************************************************

RPT1.SUMMARY.OUTPUT:
    GOSUB BLANK.LINE
    GOSUB MINOR.TOTAL                       '* PERFORM MINOR-TOTAL
    LPRINT USING TOTAL.LINE$; COMPANY.SALES.TOT
    RETURN
        '*******************************************************************
        '*                     RPT2-SUMMARY-OUTPUT                        *
        '*******************************************************************

RPT2.SUMMARY.OUTPUT:

    GOSUB BUBBLE.SORT.SALES          ' * PERFORM BUBBLE-SORT-SALES
    GOSUB PRINT.SORTED.TAB           ' *  PERFORM PRINT-SORTED-SALES
    RETURN


        '*******************************************************************
        '*                         CLOSE-FILES                            *
        '*******************************************************************

CLOSE.FILES:
    CLOSE #1
    RETURN


        '*******************************************************************
        '*                      BUBBLE-SORT-SALES                         *
        '*******************************************************************

BUBBLE.SORT.SALES:

    SWAP.OCCURED.SWITCH$ = "YES"
    MAX.ELEMENTS.LOADED = MAX.ELEMENTS.LOADED - 1
    MAX.COMPARES = MAX.ELEMENTS.LOADED
    DO UNTIL SWAP.OCCURED.SWITCH$ = "NO"
        GOSUB PASSES                         '* PERFORM PASSES
    LOOP
    RETURN
```

**EXHIBIT 11.11** **(Cont.)**

```
'*****************************************************************
'*                         PASSES                               *
'*****************************************************************
PASSES:
    MAX.COMPARES = MAX.COMPARES
    SWAP.OCCURED.SWITCH$ = "NO"
    FOR SUB1 = 1 TO MAX.COMPARES
        GOSUB COMPARE.ELEM.PAIR          '* PERFORM COMPARE-ELEM-PAIR
    NEXT SUB1
    RETURN
    '*****************************************************************
    '*                    COMPARE-ELEM-PAIR                         *
    '*****************************************************************

COMPARE.ELEM.PAIR:

    NXT = SUB1 + 1
    IF SUMMARY.DAY.SALES.TAB(SUB1) < SUMMARY.DAY.SALES.TAB(NXT) THEN
        GOSUB SWAP.ELEMENT.PAIR
    END IF
    RETURN



    '*****************************************************************
    '*                   SWAP-ELEMENT-PAIR                          *
    '*****************************************************************

SWAP.ELEMENT.PAIR:


    HOLD.ELEMENT = SUMMARY.DAY.SALES.TAB(SUB1)
    SUMMARY.DAY.SALES.TAB(SUB1) = SUMMARY.DAY.SALES.TAB(NXT)
    SUMMARY.DAY.SALES.TAB(NXT) = HOLD.ELEMENT
    HOLD.ELEMENT = SUMMARY.SALES.DATE.TAB(SUB1)
    SUMMARY.SALES.DATE.TAB(SUB1) = SUMMARY.SALES.DATE.TAB(NXT)
    SUMMARY.SALES.DATE.TAB(NXT) = HOLD.ELEMENT
    SWAP.OCCURED.SWITCH$ = "YES"
    RETURN


    '*****************************************************************
    '*                   PRINT-SORTED-SALES-TAB                     *
    '*****************************************************************
PRINT.SORTED.TAB:
    LPRINT CHR$(12)
    LPRINT TAB(4); "DAY SALES (ORDERED BY SALES) SUMMARY"
    LPRINT TAB(10); "DESCENDING SEQUENCE"
    LPRINT : LPRINT
    LPRINT TAB(4); "DATE"; TAB(20); "SALES"
    LPRINT
    PRINT.LMT = MAX.ELEMENTS.LOADED
    FOR SUB1 = 1 TO PRINT.LMT
        GOSUB PRINT.ELEMENT              '* PERFORM PRINT-ELEMENT
    NEXT SUB1
```

**EXHIBIT 11.11    (Cont.)**

```
    RETURN

        '**********************************************************************
        '*                         PRINT-ELEMENT                              *
        '**********************************************************************

PRINT.ELEMENT:
    PREVDT = SUMMARY.SALES.DATE.TAB(SUB1)
    PREV.DATE$ = STR$(PREVDT)
    YY$ = LEFT$(PREV.DATE$, 3)
    MM$ = MID$(PREV.DATE$, 4, 2)
    DD$ = RIGHT$(PREV.DATE$, 2)

    LPRINT USING SUMMARY.PRT.LINE$; MM$; DD$; YY$; SUMMARY.DAY.SALES.TAB(SUB1)
    RETURN
```

```
                    MONTHLY SALES ANALYSIS REPORT
                         BY DATE OF SALE


        DATE            STORE NUMBER    QUANTITY  PRICE     SALES

      10/01/ 93             005            10     100.00  1000.00
      10/01/ 93             005             5      10.00    50.00
      10/01/ 93             005             1      20.00    20.00
      10/01/ 93             007             2      50.00   100.00
      10/01/ 93             007             5     100.00   500.00
      10/01/ 93             007             5     200.00  1000.00
      10/01/ 93             007             5      10.00    50.00
      10/01/ 93             007            10       5.00    50.00
      10/01/ 93             007             5       5.00    25.00


                      TOTAL SALES  10/01/ 93   2,795.00 *


      10/02/ 93             005             1      10.00    10.00
      10/02/ 93             005             5      10.00    50.00
      10/02/ 93             005            10      10.00   100.00
      10/02/ 93             005            20       5.00   100.00
      10/02/ 93             007            50      10.00   500.00
      10/02/ 93             007           100       5.00   500.00


                      TOTAL SALES  10/02/ 93   1,260.00 *


      10/03/ 93             001             1      10.00    10.00
      10/03/ 93             001             5      20.00   100.00
      10/03/ 93             005             2      25.00    50.00


                      TOTAL SALES  10/03/ 93     160.00 *
```

**EXHIBIT 11.11   (Cont.)**

| 10/31/ 93 | 001 | 5  | 20.00  | 100.00  |
|-----------|-----|----|--------|---------|
| 10/31/ 93 | 001 | 5  | 10.00  | 50.00   |
| 10/31/ 93 | 001 | 5  | 20.00  | 100.00  |
| 10/31/ 93 | 005 | 10 | 10.00  | 100.00  |
| 10/31/ 93 | 005 | 20 | 100.00 | 2000.00 |
| 10/31/ 93 | 005 | 10 | 50.00  | 500.00  |

```
             TOTAL SALES  10/31/ 93  2,850.00 *
```

```
DAY SALES (ORDERED BY SALES) SUMMARY
      DESCENDING SEQUENCE
```

| DATE      | SALES    |
|-----------|----------|
| 10/31/ 93 | 2850.00  |
| 10/01/ 93 | 2795.00  |
| 10/02/ 93 | 1260.00  |
| 10/03/ 93 | 160.00   |
| 10/04/ 93 | 90.00    |

# THE SIMPLE EXCHANGE SORT

The exchange sort is a commonly used sorting method for relatively small tables (less than 50 records) in which the records are grossly out of order. This sorting method is simply an alternative to the bubble sort. It will never outperform the bubble, since it requires the same number of passes and compares per pass, but it might be slightly easier to design and code. As mentioned, if the table is sufficiently out of order to require N – 1 passes in the bubble sort, the simple exchange works just as well. The bubble sort, as you recall, works optimally with tables that are only slightly out of order— ones, for instance, with no more than ten elements away from their true positions—since the bubble

sort algorithm allows for early escape as soon as the table becomes sorted after a pass.

Figure 11.7 illustrates the sorting process of the simple exchange sort. The exchange sort requires N – 1 passes, where N represents the number of records in the table. The first pass through the table will necessitate N – 1 comparisons; the second pass will require N – 2 comparisons; and so on. The number of comparisons for each successive pass decreases by one each time. Figure 11.7 depicts each pass by two separate representations of the same table. The first of the pair of tables in each case represents the original table (for pass 1) or the table as it would appear after a *previous pass* (pass 2 through pass 4). The second of the pair represents the *result of the table* after the *current pass*.

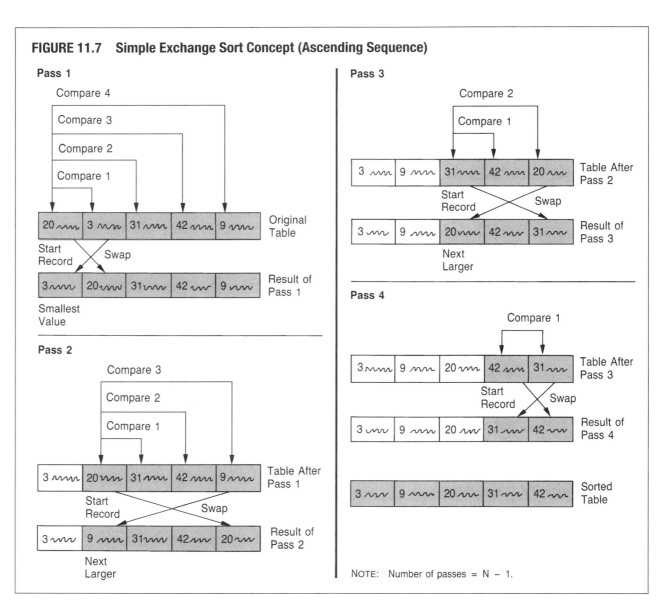

FIGURE 11.7 Simple Exchange Sort Concept (Ascending Sequence)

The sorting process starts by comparing the sort key of the first record shown in the original table of pass 1 (20) with the sort key (3) of the adjacent record (record 2). Since ascending sequence has been specified, the two records are exchanged. Now the first record of the table has a sort key of 3 and the second record has a sort key of 20. The second comparison of pass 1 compares the first record's sort key with the third; the third comparison compares the first with the fourth; the fourth comparison compares the first with the fifth. No exchanges occur for the second, third, and fourth comparisons since the first record's sort key of 3 is smaller than all the rest. The result of the pass is to place the record with the smallest key in record position number one.

For pass 2, the comparison process starts by comparing record 2 (20) with record 3 (31), then record 2 with record 4 (42), and record 2 with record 5 (9). Since record 2 is less than records 3 and 4, no exchange takes place; however, in the last comparison of pass 2, an exchange takes place. Pass 2 of Figure 9.7 illustrates the comparison process for the second pass and the resultant exchange of record 2 with record 5. Now the order of the array is 3, 9, 31, 42, and 20.

In pass 3, the comparison starts by comparing record 3 with successive records (record 4 and record 5) and exchanging them where appropriate. In this pass, record 3 (31) is swapped with record 5 (20). Now the order of the table is 3, 9, 20, 42, and 31.

In the final pass 4, record 4 (42) is compared with record 5 (31). Since 31 is less than 42, the two records are exchanged. Now the order of the table is 3, 9, 20, 31, and 42.

In each successive pass through the table, the new record used for comparison purposes is always the one adjacent to the record used in the last pass. The comparisons for any given pass are between this beginning record and successive adjacent records. Note how different this comparison method is from that of the bubble sort, in which adjacent pairs are compared for each pass.

There is one major difference between the *ascending* exchange sort and the bubble sort: The exchange sort pulls the record with the smaller sort key to the beginning of the table, while the bubble sort pushes the record with the larger key to the end. Both starting methods improve their performance by reducing the number of comparisons by one in each successive pass, because there is no need to compare a record if it has already been placed in its true position in the table.

Figure 11.8 illustrates the structured flowchart logic of the simple exchange sort. The original

unsorted table of records shown in pass 1 of Figure 11.7 will be the test data for the purpose of explanation.

The flowchart for the simple exchange strongly resembles that of the bubble sort, since both algorithms contain a PASSES module, a COMPARES module, and an EXCHANGE module. The purpose of the EXCHANGE-SORT-MAIN module is to control the number of passes to be performed. Since the number of passes is N – 1, the PASSES module is executed until PASS-PTR is greater than MAX-PASSES (one less than the number of records). A definite iteration structure is used to perform the PASSES module and also to increase PASS-PTR to accommodate the establishment of the next comparison *start record* position.

### The PASSES Module

The function of the PASSES module is to (1) establish the pointer to the record with which all others in the pass will be compared (that is, to PASS-PTR or the current comparison start record), (2) determine the successive record with which the comparison start record will be compared, and (3) perform the COMPARES module until the pointer of the successive record (variable K) is greater than the record count (RECCOUNT).

### The COMPARES Module

The function of the COMPARES module is to compare the first record (the comparison start record) with the next calculated successive record. If the start record is greater than the successive record, an EXCHANGE module is invoked.

### The EXCHANGE Module

The function of the EXCHANGE module is to swap the comparison start record with the appropriate successive record. The exchange (or swap) procedure is the same as the one explained in the preceding bubble sort discussion.

## THE SHELL SORT

The previously described sorting methods are adequate for short tables only. However, there is one sorting method that, for larger tables, significantly outperforms the others, and it's called the Shell sort. It's named for D. L. Shell, who first described it in 1959. The Shell sort belongs to the exchange sort category, but it contains two important refinements: (1) a **comparison interval** (called **distance**)

# FIGURE 11.8  Structured Flowchart of Simple Exchange Sort

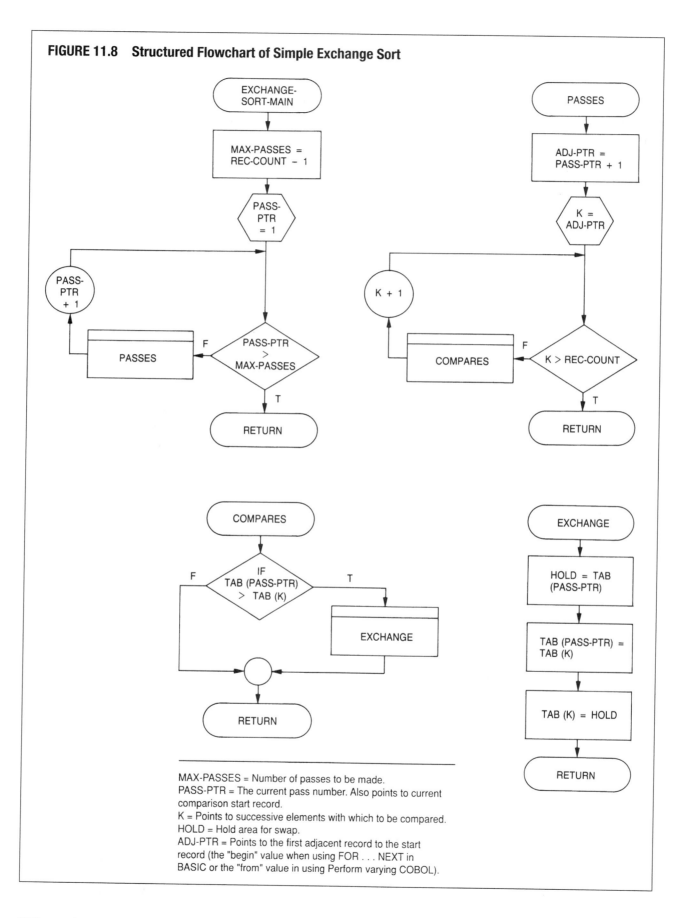

MAX-PASSES = Number of passes to be made.
PASS-PTR = The current pass number. Also points to current comparison start record.
K = Points to successive elements with which to be compared.
HOLD = Hold area for swap.
ADJ-PTR = Points to the first adjacent record to the start record (the "begin" value when using FOR . . . NEXT in BASIC or the "from" value in using Perform varying COBOL).

that diminishes in almost a binary fashion from pass to pass, and (2) a **backup comparison** that occurs at an exchange.

## Number of Passes

With the Shell sort, the number of passes required to sort a list that is greatly out of order are far fewer than with the previous sorting methods. For each pass, a *comparison interval (distance)* is calculated that determines which records are compared during the pass. Once the pass is complete, the comparison interval is first distance is equal to 3 (7 / 2 = 3). The comparison interval (d = 3) for the first pass compares the first record of the original list with the fourth record. To locate the second of the two records being compared, the distance is simply added to the record location of the first. For example, the second of the pair is found at record position 4 (the beginning record position 1 + the distance 3 = 4). For pass 2 in panel B, the distance is recalculated to be 1 (the previous distance 3 / 2 = 1).

## Forward Comparisons per Pass

The number of forward compares for the first pass is computed as N – D (7 – 3 = 4). For panel A there are four successive forward comparisons (see the first four of the five columns in panel 1). For the second pass (panel B), there are six forward compares, represented by the six arrows that move progressively downward. In panel A for pass 1, the 7 is compared with the 4 in the first forward comparison. Since this is an ascending sort and 7 is greater than 4, the two records are swapped. The forward comparison process continues for the first pass by moving down by one record in the list for each subsequent forward comparison. The second forward comparison compares 6 with 3. Since 6 is greater than 3, the two are swapped. The successive comparisons and resulting swaps occur for columns 3 and 4 also.

## Backup Comparisons

During the sorting process, when an exchange is made between two records in the list, an efficiency built into the Shell sorting process called *backup* is triggered. This backup process occurs only when a forward comparison indicates that a swap is necessary and if the forward comparison and resultant swap occur far enough down the list to permit backup. There must be a backward comparison interval equivalent to the forward comparison interval before a backward comparison can be made. Once the swap is complete, the procedure looks

back a *d* (current distance) interval in the list to determine if the first of the records being swapped can actually be placed farther back up the list to its true position. If so, an exchange occurs back up the list between the records being compared. In larger lists, several backward compares may be necessary. Backward comparisons continue until no exchange takes place or the top of the table is reached. *At the end of the backward compare process, a record will be in its true position.*

Column 5 of panel A in Figure 11.9 illustrates for the first time the backup procedure. Here, the first and fourth records are compared. Since 4 is less than 1, the two records are swapped, thus placing the record with a sort key 1 into its true position in the table. In panel B for pass 2, the backup occurs in the third and seventh columns. A backward compare is made in both cases; but as luck would have it, the records are already in order and no swap is necessary.

## The Logic of the Shell Sort

Figure 11.10 illustrates the structured flowchart logic of the Shell sort. The function of SHELL-SORT-MAIN is to compute the first comparison interval (distance) and to perform the PASSES module until the distance is reduced to zero or less than one.

## The PASSES Module

The function of the PASSES module is threefold: first, it determines the number of forward compares to be made (FWD-CMP-LMT = N – DISTANCE); second, it executes the FORWARD-COMPARE module as many times as indicated by the variable FWD-CMP-LMT (this variable contains the number of forward compares for this pass), and third, it causes a *step down* that starts the comparison with the next record down in the list. When the comparison loop has been executed the proper number of times, it then calculates a new comparison interval (distance) for the next pass.

## The FORWARD-COMPARES Module

The function of the FORWARD-COMPARE module is to compare the *first* and *last* records of the comparison interval. FIRST-PTR is saved in NEW-FIRST-PTR to preserve its contents. The reason for this preservation step becomes more obvious in the BACKWARD-COMPARE module, where the contents of the first and last pointers are adjusted to allow backup comparisons.

# FIGURE 11.9 The Shell Sort Concept

## Panel A — Pass 1

| Compare 1 | | Compare 2 | | Compare 3 | | Compare 4 | | Compare 5 | |
|---|---|---|---|---|---|---|---|---|---|
| Before | After | Before | After | Before | After | Before | After | Before | After |
| 7 | 4 | 4 | 4 | 4 | 4 | 4 | 4 | 4 | 1 |
| 6 | 6 | 6 | 3 | 3 | 3 | 3 | 3 | 3 | 3 |
| 5 | 5 | 5 | 5 | 5 | 2 | 2 | 2 | 2 | 2 |
| 4 | 7 | 7 | 7 | 7 | 7 | 7 | 1 | 1 | 4 |
| 3 | 3 | 3 | 6 | 6 | 6 | 6 | 6 | 6 | 6 |
| 2 | 2 | 2 | 2 | 2 | 5 | 5 | 5 | 5 | 5 |
| 1 | 1 | 1 | 1 | 1 | 1 | 1 | 7 | 7 | 7 |
| (1) | | (2) | | (3) | | (4) | | (5) | |

**Original List** (under column 1)  
**BACKUP COMPARE** (under column 5)

```
First Distance  =  N / 2
        D       =  7 / 2
        D       =    3
Forward Compares =  N – D
                 =  7 – 3
                 =    4
```

---

## Panel B — Pass 2

| Compare 1 | | Compare 2 | | Compare 3 | | Compare 4 | | Compare 5 | | Compare 6 | | Compare 7 | | Compare 8 | |
|---|---|---|---|---|---|---|---|---|---|---|---|---|---|---|---|
| Before | After | Before | After | Before | After | Before | After | Before | After | Before | After | Before | After | Before | After |
| 1 | 1 | 1 | 1 | 1 | 1 | 1 | 1 | 1 | 1 | 1 | 1 | 1 | 1 | 1 | 1 |
| 3 | 3 | 3 | 2 | 2 | 2 | 2 | 2 | 2 | 2 | 2 | 2 | 2 | 2 | 2 | 2 |
| 2 | 2 | 2 | 3 | 3 | 3 | 3 | 3 | 3 | 3 | 3 | 3 | 3 | 3 | 3 | 3 |
| 4 | 4 | 4 | 4 | 4 | 4 | 4 | 4 | 4 | 4 | 4 | 4 | 4 | 4 | 4 | 4 |
| 6 | 6 | 6 | 6 | 6 | 6 | 6 | 6 | 6 | 6 | 6 | 5 | 5 | 5 | 5 | 5 |
| 5 | 5 | 5 | 5 | 5 | 5 | 5 | 5 | 5 | 5 | 5 | 6 | 6 | 6 | 6 | 6 |
| 7 | 7 | 7 | 7 | 7 | 7 | 7 | 7 | 7 | 7 | 7 | 7 | 7 | 7 | 7 | 7 |
| (1) | | (2) | | (3) | | (4) | | (5) | | (6) | | (7) | | (8) | |

**BACKUP COMPARE** (under column 3)  
**BACKUP COMPARE** (under column 7)

```
Second Distance = First Distance / 2
        D       =     3 / 2
        D       =       1
Forward Compares =    7 – 1
                 =       6
```

Note: Backward comparisons happen as long as swaps are made.

# FIGURE 11.10 Structured Flowchart for Shell Sort

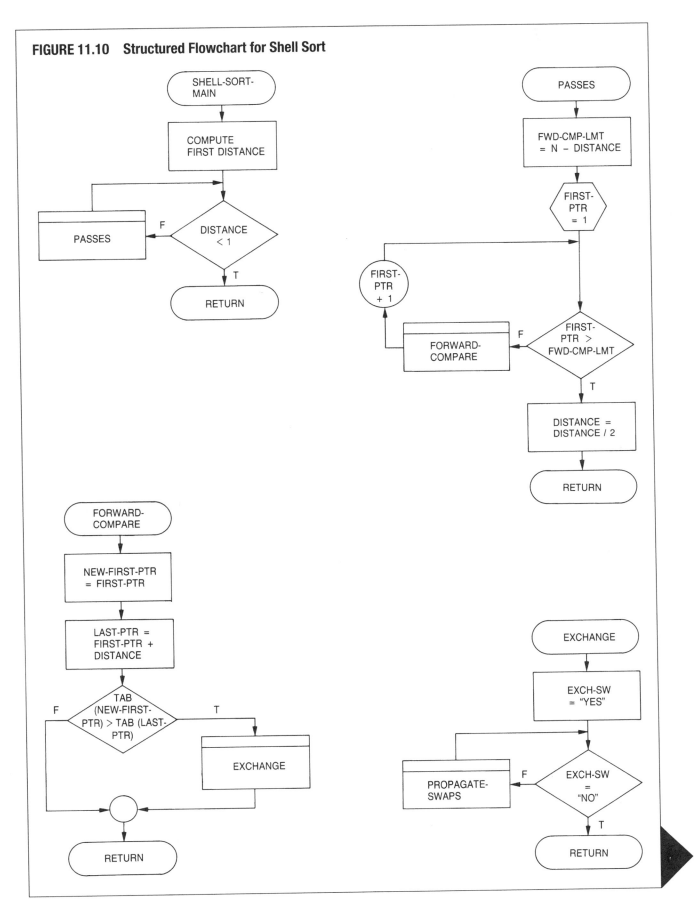

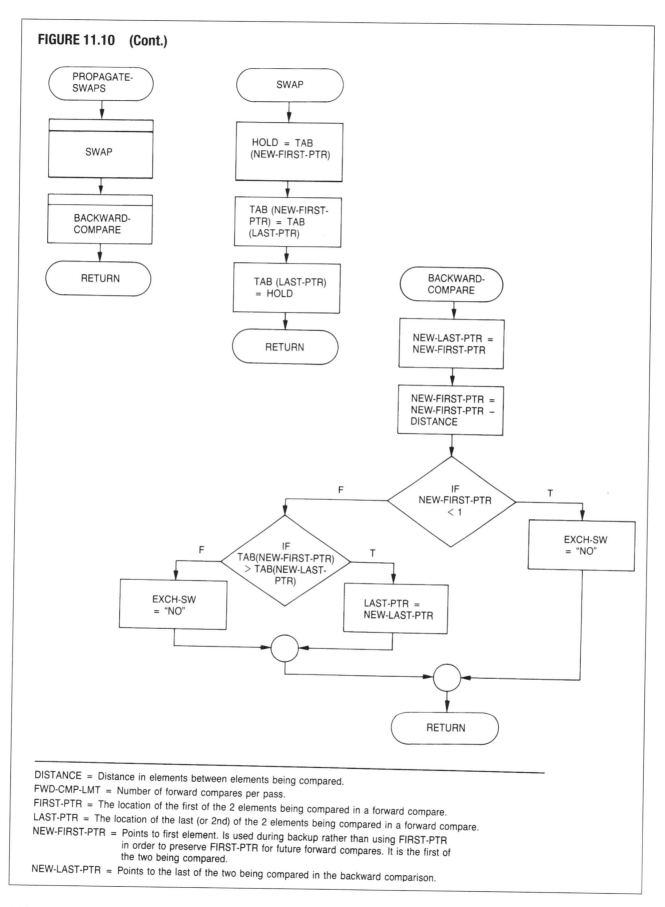

**FIGURE 11.10   (Cont.)**

DISTANCE = Distance in elements between elements being compared.

FWD-CMP-LMT = Number of forward compares per pass.

FIRST-PTR = The location of the first of the 2 elements being compared in a forward compare.

LAST-PTR = The location of the last (or 2nd) of the 2 elements being compared in a forward compare.

NEW-FIRST-PTR = Points to first element. Is used during backup rather than using FIRST-PTR in order to preserve FIRST-PTR for future forward compares. It is the first of the two being compared.

NEW-LAST-PTR = Points to the last of the two being compared in the backward comparison.

The comparison test determines if the first record of the comparison interval is greater than its last record. If the result of the condition test is true, the EXCHANGE module is executed.

## The EXCHANGE Module

The function of the EXCHANGE module in the Shell sort is a little more complex than in the other sorts. Since an exchange results in a propagation of backward compares and possible associated swaps, the procedure must allow for repeated execution of a module that will handle this propagation back up the table. A simple exchange cannot be made. The EXCHANGE module must invoke a PROPAGATE-SWAPS module until there is no need for another exchange (until EXCH-SW = "NO").

## The PROPAGATE-SWAPS Module

The PROPAGATE-SWAPS module performs two tasks: it swaps the records and performs the BACKWARD-COMPARE module to determine if a propagation of swaps will be necessary back up the list.

## The SWAP and the BACKWARD-COMPARE Modules

The SWAP module looks very much like any of the other swap modules. The BACKWARD-COMPARE module first adjusts NEW-LAST-PTR so that it will point to where NEW-FIRST-PTR was pointing. Second, it adjusts NEW-FIRST-PTR so that it will point to the record back up the list at a comparison interval away (NEW-FIRST-PTR = NEW-FIRST-POINTER – DISTANCE). The next step is a condition block that provides escape in case the comparison interval is beyond the beginning boundary of the table (if NEW-FIRST-PTR < 1). If the condition is true, the EXCH-SW is turned off (EXCH-SW = "NO") so that a subsequent execution of the EXCHANGE module will return control to the bottom of the FORWARD-COMPARE module.

If, on the other hand, a backward comparison interval does exist [the comparison (NEW-FIRST-PTR < 1) tests *false*], then a nested comparison is made to determine if a subsequent swap is needed. If this second condition is true, the contents of NEW-LAST-PTR is stored into LAST-PTR. Why is this done? Since the SWAP module can be ultimately invoked from either the BACKWARD-COMPARE module or the FORWARD-COMPARE module, a common parameter must be used (that is, LAST-PTR).

## SUMMARY

Sorting—the process of ordering a file or a table—is one of the primary functions of data processing. The field, or set of fields, used to order the file is called the sort key. Tables can be ordered in either ascending or descending order. There are two major sorting categories—internal and external. The internal sort is performed entirely in main memory, while the external sort uses auxiliary storage.

The three basic internal sorting types are exchange, selection, and insertion. Internal sorting methods are extremely fast compared to external sorting methods. The most commonly used exchange sorts are (1) the bubble, (2) the simple exchange, and (3) the Shell. The bubble sort works well with tables having up to 50 records that are not badly out of order. The simple exchange is simply an alternative for the bubble sort. The Shell sort is normally used with large tables whose records are grossly out of order. The Shell outperforms the bubble and exchange sorts on tables with more than 50 elements. The selection-with-exchange sort is a modification of the simple exchange sort and is useful for small tables that are badly ordered.

## VOCABULARY

| | |
|---|---|
| sorting | selection sort |
| sort procedure | exchange sort |
| sort key | insertion sort |
| ascending sequence | bubble sort |
| descending sequence | simple exchange |
| internal sort | Shell sort |
| external sort | comparison interval (or |
| ANSI COBOL sort | distance *d*) |
| feature | backup comparison |

## EXERCISES/QUESTIONS

1. What is a sort?
2. What is a sort key?
3. What is meant by an ascending sort? A descending sort?
4. What are the two major sorting categories?
5. What is the basic characteristic of an internal sort? An external sort?
6. Why are internal sorts used when vendors supply sort/merge packages?

7. Name and describe the basic exchange sort methods.

8. When should the bubble sort be used?

9. When should the Shell sort be used?

10. What particular capability does the Shell sort have that is not present in the bubble or exchange sort algorithms?

11. For the bubble sort with a table size of 42, what is the maximum number of passes? Minimum number of passes?

12. With a table size of 42, how many compares will be needed in the bubble sort for the first pass through the table? The second time through the table?

13. Under certain conditions, the bubble sort outperforms all the other sorts. What is this condition?

14. What advantage is there to the selection-with-exchange sort? Why is it better than the bubble sort for sorting lists that are greatly out of order?

## PROBLEMS

**11–1.** Brown Petroleum Co. wants to produce two reports: (1) a listing of their producing oil wells in ascending alphabetical order by county and (2) a listing of the well holdings in descending order by barrels production. Samples of these reports follow.

The file is normally kept in alphabetical order by county; however, due to recent updates, new wells have simply been added to the end of the file. Create a structured flowchart and pseudocode for this problem. Use the *bubble sort*.

### INPUT RECORD FORMAT:

| Field | Location | Type |
|-------|----------|------|
| County | 1–10 | A/N |
| State | 11–12 | A/N |
| Well number | 13–18 | N |
| Well-depth | 19–23 | N |
| Barrels production | 24–25 | N |
| Well-date | 26–31 | N |

### OUTPUT REQUIRED:

```
                      BROWN PETROLEUM CO.
                   OIL WELL HOLDINGS BY COUNTY

    COUNTY        STATE     OIL WELL #     DEPTH     BARRELS     DRILL
                                           (FT)      PER DAY     DATE

    BRAZOS         TX       RT-3030        4300        77      03/30/73
    COLLIN         TX       GH-1234        8900        86      06/16/66
    CORYELL        TX       AK-5678       10000        34      02/12/77
    DALLAS         TX       MC-9889        3000        55      08/19/70
    DICKENS        TX       AJ-2123        9000        55      02/12/76
    EASTLAND       TX       MD-4567        9000        67      02/23/79
    ERATH          TX       MD-3456        8800        44      03/24/67
    FLOYD          TX       MM-4456        8500        34      02/12/24
    HUTCHINSON     TX       AA-3345        6700        93      05/30/77
        "
        "
        "
```

```
                      BROWN PETROLEUM CO.
             OIL WELL HOLDINGS BY BARRELS PRODUCTION
                 (FROM HIGHEST TO LOWEST PRODUCING)

    COUNTY        STATE     OIL WELL #     DEPTH     BARRELS     DRILL
                                           (FT)      PER DAY     DATE

    KENT           TX       LL-4545        8000        98      04/05/67
    FLOYD          TX       MM-4456        8500        94      02/12/24
    HUTCHINSON     TX       AA-3345        6700        93      05/30/77
        "
        "
        "
```

**11–2.** The weather bureau wants a report to list the mean and median temperature highs and lows for the month. The daily temperature record consists of the date (yymmdd), low reading, and high reading. The differential is simply the difference between the high and low temperatures. The monthly file is to be first sorted using the *simple exchange* in ascending sequence by date. Once the file is sorted by date, print a detail line for each record in the file as shown in the following report. The test data are also presented here. At the end of the report, print the median low, median high, mean low, and mean high.

The mean is simply the arithmetic average of the temperatures. Assuming the low temperatures are in ascending order, the median is the middle value (N/2). The same process is also done using the high temperatures for the month. Use the *selection with exchange* sort to order the low and high temperatures. Create a structured flowchart, hierarchy chart and pseudocode for this problem.

## INPUT RECORD FORMAT:

| Field | Column | Type |
|-------|--------|------|
| TR-Date | 1–6 | N |
| TR-Low-temp | 7–8 | N |
| TR-High-temp | 9–11 | N |

TR = Temperature recorded

## TEST DATA:

```
COLUMN      1         2         3         4         5
1234567890123456789012345678901234567890123456789 0
- - - - - - - - - - - - - - - - - - - - - - - - - - - - - - - - - - - -
93/01/21 30 45
93/01/23 40 65
93/01/24 40 64
93/01/26 50 75
93/01/12 28 68
93/02/13 32 70
93/02/14 35 75
93/01/27 51 77
93/01/28 52 78
93/01/15 30 60
93/01/16 40 70
93/01/22 35 55
93/01/25 50 75
93/01/17 20 40
93/01/18 15 30
93/01/19 12 26
93/01/20 20 35
93/01/31 45 60
93/01/29 50 70
93/01/30 55 75
```

## OUTPUT REQUIRED:

```
                    THE WEATHER BUREAU
                  TEMPERATURE STATISTICS

      DATE      LOW TEMP    HIGH TEMP    DIFFERENTIAL

   93/01/12       28          68             40
   93/01/13       32          70             38
   93/01/14       35          75             40
   93/01/15       30          60             30
   93/01/16       40          70             30
        "          "           "              "
        "          "           "              "
        "          "           "              "

   MEAN MONTHLY LOW          XXX
   MEAN MONTHLY HIGH         XXX
   MEDIAN MONTHLY LOW        XXX
   MEDIAN MONTHLY HIGH       XXX
```

**11–3.** A teacher requires two reports. One lists the test results for her class of 150 students. The other lists the students with the top test averages. The first report is to contain each student's number, name, 11 test scores, mean test score, and median score. The 11 test scores for each student should be in ascending sequence on the report so as to allow the teacher to evaluate student progress as well as to calculate the median score. The median score is simply the middle test grade when the scores are rearranged in sequence. Use a *simple exchange sort* to sort the 11 test scores. This sorting procedure will be repeated for each record.

The second report simply lists the students' names and mean test scores in descending order. Use a *Shell sort* to order the 150 student names and associated test means. A test file of 20 records represents the actual student file. The sample reports and test data are as follows. Create a hierarchy chart, structured flowchart, and pseudocode for this problem.

## INPUT RECORD FORMAT:

| Field | Location | Type |
|---|---|---|
| SSN | 1–9 | N |
| First-name | 10–19 | A |
| Last-name | 20–30 | A |
| Test 1 | 31–33 | N |
| Test 2 | 34–36 | N |
| Test 3 | 37–39 | N |
| Test 4 | 40–42 | N |
| Test 5 | 43–45 | N |
| Test 6 | 46–48 | N |
| Test 7 | 49–51 | N |
| Test 8 | 52–54 | N |
| Test 9 | 55–57 | N |
| Test 10 | 58–60 | N |
| Test 11 | 61–63 | N |

## TEST DATA:

```
COLUMN     1         2         3         4         5         6
123456789012345678901234567890123456789012345678901234567890123
111111111BOB       JOHNSON   100100100100100100100100100100100
222222222MARY      JOHNSON   100090080070060050040030020010000
333333333DONNA     DOLITTLE  000000000000000000000000000000000
444444444SUSAN     SMART     100100100100100100100100100100100
555555555BOB       DRAKE     010020030040050060070080090100100
666666666JON       CLARKE    000010020030040050060070080090100
777777777DON       BROWN     010100020090030080050060040070075
888888888DONALD    JONES     025034067078045034055066078098055
999999999BILLY     ROBERTS   020030044055066077077022033044055
122222222DICK      SMITH     011022033044055066044033033033033
133333333ELLEN     DICKSON   078077077066077088099078067098100
144444444GARY      DONALDSON 100100100100100100100090090090090
155555555MARY      MARTIN    100020060070070060060050040050070
166666666BARBARA   THOMPSON  100100100090090090090090090090090
177777777JIMMY     THOMPSON  010020030090090090090080070080080
188888888DAMON     COOPER    100100100100100100100100090090080
199999999FRANCIS   WALKER    090090070060070080090100100100100
211111111LINDA     RODRIGUEZ 100100100100100100100100100100100
233333333NANCY     SULLIVAN  100090090070090090090090090100100
244444444MIKE      HILLIARD  100030060070090090090090100100100
```

## OUTPUT REQUIRED:

```
                            TEST RESULTS REPORT

      SSN     NAME    TST  TST  TST  TST  TST  TST  TST  TST  TST  TST  TST  MEAN MDN
                       1    2    3    4    5    6    7    8    9    10   11

  XXXXXXXXX   X    X  XXX  XXX  XXX  XXX  XXX  XXX  XXX  XXX  XXX  XXX  XXX  XXX  XXX
  XXXXXXXXX   X    X  XXX  XXX  XXX  XXX  XXX  XXX  XXX  XXX  XXX  XXX  XXX  XXX  XXX
  XXXXXXXXX   X    X  XXX  XXX  XXX  XXX  XXX  XXX  XXX  XXX  XXX  XXX  XXX  XXX  XXX
     "
     "
     "
```

```
            TOP 20 GRADES

      NAME              TEST AVERAGE

  XXXXXXXXXXXXXXXXXXXXX      XXX
  XXXXXXXXXXXXXXXXXXXXX      XXX
  XXXXXXXXXXXXXXXXXXXXX      XXX
  XXXXXXXXXXXXXXXXXXXXX      XXX
```

Note: Test Average = MEAN

# 12

# Sequential File Maintenance

## OBJECTIVES

After completing this chapter, the student will be able to:

1. Define the terms:
   sequential file
   indexed file
   random file
   master file (master record)
   transaction file (transaction record)
   record key
   transaction key
   backup (grandfather, father, son concept)
   update; add; delete; change

2. Recognize the advantages and disadvantages of sequential file update.

3. Discuss the updating procedure in a sequential file update.

4. Specifically discuss the technique of using a master and a transaction file to create a *new* master file, using sequential file update.

5. Develop the hierarchy chart, structured flowchart, and pseudocode for a sequential file update.

## ORGANIZING AND MAINTAINING FILES

### The Importance of File Maintenance

Data processing functions require the extensive use of files for data storage. Selecting the appropriate file organization and choosing the maintenance methodology are two of the most important concerns of the systems analyst or programmer/analyst. The success or failure of any system may often be linked to how well or poorly the files are designed and maintained.

### Organization Methods

The three basic file organization methods are (1) sequential, (2) indexed, and (3) random (or direct). A **sequential file** contains a series of records stored one after another. In order to access, say, the seventh record, the first six records must be read. A sequential file can be created on either tape or disk. An **indexed file** is a file that is accessed via an index, or directory; and a **random (direct) file** is a file that allows access to a record via a disk record address calculation. Indexed and direct files, discussed further in Chapter 13, are powerful tools when performing interactive processing since they permit rapid updating at the time of a transaction. Sequential access to large files is too slow for use in an interactive environment. Both indexed and random files must be stored on disk. Each of the three methods offers advantages over the others in particular processing situations. Chapter 13 will detail those advantages.

## Sequential Files

Figure 12.1 illustrates a sequential file. Panel A depicts an unblocked sequential file, and panel B shows the same file in a blocked format. An unblocked sequential file contains inter-record gaps (spaces between the records). To preserve file space and to create input/output efficiency, records are often *blocked*. Blocking separates a number of contiguous records with an interblock gap. Regardless of whether the file is blocked or unblocked, logically the program design is the same.

### Advantage and Limitations of Sequential Files.

Sequential files are *limited* by the fact that to get to the 1045th record requires reading past the first 1044 records, regardless of whether any of the first 1044 records are processed. When rapid access or update is required for any *specific record,* sequential access is a poor technique. On the other hand, sequential access has several major *advantages:* (1) the programmer can always use this access method since it is supported on any system; (2) a sequential file can be reassigned from tape to disk (or vice versa) with no effect on the computer program; (3) with large files where a large percentage of the records of a file must be updated at any single time, the sequential access method is usually better; and (4) since sequential files can be assigned to tapes, the cost may be much less than disk storage. A tape reel costs only a few dollars, while a disk may cost several hundred.

## The File Maintenance Process

**Updating.** **Updating** is the process of making a file current. This involves (1) *adding new records* to the existing file, (2) *deleting record* from the file, and (3) *changing* the contents of fields on existing records. For example, in a payroll system, when an employee moves to a new address, the employee master payroll record will require a change in the address field as well as possible modification of the phone number. If an employee resigns or is fired, his or her record will have to be deleted. In the case of a new hire, a new master record will need to be added to the file.

## Backup Files

File security is a very important part of file maintenance. It doesn't do much good to keep a file up to date if we permit it to be sabotaged or inadvertently damaged. One security technique in data processing known as **backup** ensures that files are properly backed up. Backup usually means the copying of the current version of the file (called the *son*) into what is called the *father file*. For good measure, a second backup file called the *grandfather file* may also be established. At the end of a processing period (usually one day), the father file is copied to the grandfather file, and the son file is stored on the father. This rotational process reduces the risk of losing the file with all its updates. At most, the programmer (and user) will lose only the current day's updates. Of course, the backup interval depends on file activity and volatility, which in turn depend on

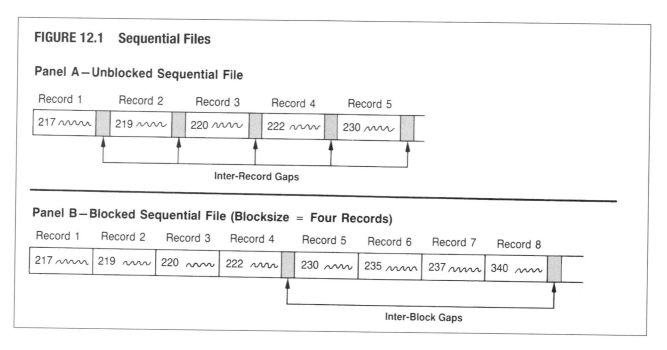

**FIGURE 12.1   Sequential Files**

**Panel A—Unblocked Sequential File**

| Record 1 | | Record 2 | | Record 3 | | Record 4 | | Record 5 | |
|---|---|---|---|---|---|---|---|---|---|
| 217 ~~~ | | 219 ~~~ | | 220 ~~~ | | 222 ~~~ | | 230 ~~~ | |

Inter-Record Gaps

**Panel B—Blocked Sequential File (Blocksize = Four Records)**

| Record 1 | Record 2 | Record 3 | Record 4 | | Record 5 | Record 6 | Record 7 | Record 8 | |
|---|---|---|---|---|---|---|---|---|---|
| 217 ~~~ | 219 ~~~ | 220 ~~~ | 222 ~~~ | | 230 ~~~ | 235 ~~~ | 237 ~~~ | 340 ~~~ | |

Inter-Block Gaps

the kind of application in use. In some cases, files are backed up much more or much less frequently than once a day. While no programming logic is presented for this copying process, the topic is too important to ignore. Normally, system utility copy programs are available to handle the backup procedure.

## File Activity and Volatility

**File activity** is frequently considered in determining the file organization method and backup interval. File activity is the number of transaction records in relation to the size of the master file, often expressed as the ratio of the number of transactions over the total number of master records.

**File volatility** is the ratio of the total number of additions and deletions to a file in a *given time period* over the total master file size.

File activity and volatility are two important criteria in determining file organization, backup, or particular access techniques. Usually, sequential file updating is used with high file activity. The choice of file organization is sometimes more complex when considering volatility. If the additions and deletions can be collected in a batch processing environment, then sequential access is the proper choice. Often, however, the update process must occur in an interactive mode, which usually makes sequential access to file records too slow.

## UPDATING FILES

### Simple Update Process

**Sequencing of Master and Transaction Files.**    As stated in Chapter 1, to update a master file in batch processing mode, the records must first be sorted

into sequence by a unique identifier called the **record key.** Then a second file, called the **transaction file,** provides the medium by which the update process can take place. It contains the needed data to carry out the update process and must be in the same order as the master file (as Figure 12.2 illustrates). For a change or deletion to be made, a transaction record must contain the same key value as the master record. This key value on the transaction record is the **transaction key,** with which a program locates the master record with the same key. The transaction record must also specify what kind of update operation will be performed, once the master record is located, by supplying an additional field called a **transaction update identification code.** This update identification code field contains a specific value that is used to tell the computer which update procedure to follow. A standard code for adding a record is A; deleting a record is usually D; and changing a record is denoted by C. If the value in the update code is D, for example, the program deletes from the file the master record with the same key as in the transaction record. Figure 12.3 illustrates a transaction record with an update code for changing a record in the master file.

### Sequential File Update

**Creating a *New* Sequential Master File as a Result of Updating.**    The sequential file update procedure that has been used since the heyday of the computer card and magnetic tape provides for the creation of a new master file. Neither computer cards nor magnetic tape permitted records in the old master file to be overwritten. The only way an existing record can be overwritten (or rewritten) is on disk.

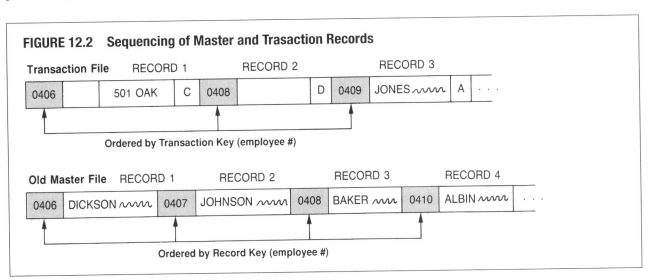

### FIGURE 12.2    Sequencing of Master and Trasaction Records

**Transaction File**    RECORD 1    RECORD 2    RECORD 3

| 0406 | | 501 OAK | C | 0408 | | D | 0409 | JONES ∿∿∿ | A | . . . |

Ordered by Transaction Key (employee #)

**Old Master File**    RECORD 1    RECORD 2    RECORD 3    RECORD 4

| 0406 | DICKSON ∿∿∿ | 0407 | JOHNSON ∿∿∿ | 0408 | BAKER ∿∿∿ | 0410 | ALBIN ∿∿∿ | . . . |

Ordered by Record Key (employee #)

Since magnetic tape applications still abound, programmers must be able to update sequential files so that a *new* master file is created. An advantage of this method is that it can be used to update either tape or disk files. Figure 12.4 illustrates the procedure of updating an existing master file and producing a *newly updated version in a different file*. The process requires a transaction file that contains the records to be affected and the kinds of update operations to be performed (panel A), the previously mentioned existing master file (panel B), and the output of the sequential file update called the new master file (panel C). In this simplified illustration, only one field on the master record will be changed if a change is required. The only information specifically presented in the various transaction records is the transaction key, the change field contents (if a change), and the transaction code. The master record is shown with only the master record key and the change field. A squiggly line is used to represent other fields that would normally be present but whose inclusion is not necessary to present the concept. In an actual update operation, a number of fields on the master record would probably need to be brought up to date. This is considered later in the application.

**Changing a Field.** Panel C of Figure 12.4 indicates that three different update operations have occurred. Since the first transaction record instigates a change operation with a matching master record

(the key 0406 appears in both the transaction and the old master files), the old master record and the new change field contents are written to the new master file (panel C–1).

**Copying the Old Master to the New Master When the Old Master is Smaller.** Since the second transaction record affects the old master record with a key of 0408, the master record with a key of 0407 is simply copied to the new master file. This will be a common operation, since there will usually be more master records than transaction records. When the transaction key is larger than the master key, the process copies the old master to the new master and reads another master record. The term "playing catch-up" is often used to refer to the copying of old records to the new file while attempting to "catch up" to the master record that is equal to or greater than the transaction key (panel C–2).

**Deleting a Master Record.** The catching-up process occurs very quickly with our small master file. The second transaction record (0408) matches the third old master record (0408). Since the transaction code is D, the third old master record is deleted by intentionally *not copying* the old master to the new master. Here the program will bypass writing to the new master file.

To delete or change a master record requires that both a transaction record and master record must

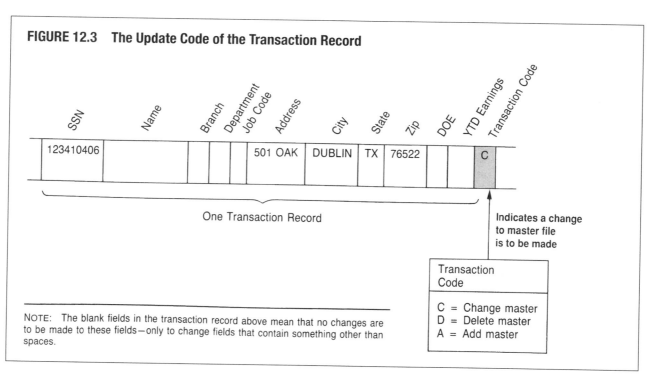

FIGURE 12.3   The Update Code of the Transaction Record

NOTE:   The blank fields in the transaction record above mean that no changes are to be made to these fields—only to change fields that contain something other than spaces.

exist with the same key. When the update process is over, *both a master and a transaction record are read*. The currently read transaction record is 0409, and the current master is 0410.

**Adding a Master Record.** Since the transaction record (0409) is less than the master (0410) and it is an addition (transaction code = A), the contents of the transaction record is copied to the new master file (panel C–3).

The remaining transactions are carried out in a similar manner.

## An Alternate Update Procedure—Updating a Sequential File in Place

With the disk file, it is possible to perform a similar update procedure. Instead of creating a new master file, however, the changes will be made to the existing master record. An advantage of this method is that it saves disk space. A limitation is that it takes longer to complete an update session, since the additions must be handled separately. This is a *less popular* technique, but one that may be used when there are severe limitations on the capacity of mass storage and update time is not critical. A deletion is made to the file by simply flagging the record with a special character in a field reserved for this pur-

pose (in COBOL, a DELETE command handles this and actually physically deletes it). As the file is processed, a record that has been flagged as deleted is bypassed. After a number of deletions have occurred, the good records must be transferred to a second file anyway—which partially explains its lack of popularity.

Additions are handled by grouping the transaction "add" records together at the end of the file. When all other updates (changes and deletions) have occurred, the master file is opened as AP-PEND so that the current record pointer is positioned at the end of the file. Any writing that is done to the file appends the records to the end.

The appending of records to the end of the file creates a new problem. How do we merge these newly added records into their appropriate physical places in the file? This involves sorting the file in ascending sequence using the record key as the sort key. Once the sort is complete, the added records find their true positions in the file.

This method was discussed so that you would be aware of the complete updating procedure. But this technique of updating a sequential file is used much less frequently than the other method. For this reason, the following illustration employs the more popular method of creating a new master file.

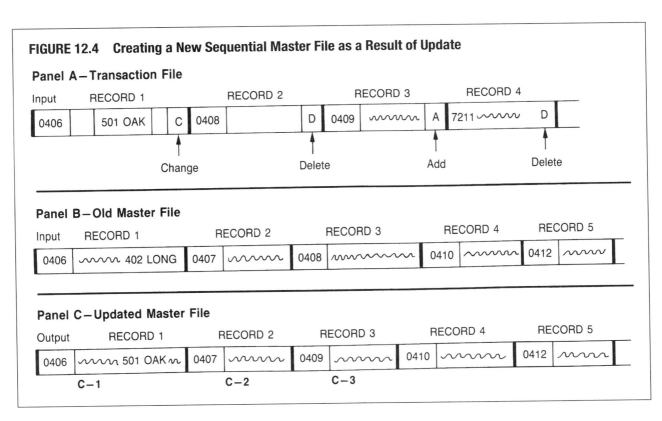

**FIGURE 12.4    Creating a New Sequential Master File as a Result of Update**

## Updating a Sequential Payroll File

## PROGRAM REQUIREMENTS

Acme Company wants to update its master payroll file in a batch mode. The payroll data is a sequential file. A program is needed that will perform the sequential update to the master file using a sequential transaction file of changes, deletions, and additions. The output to the update procedure is a *new master payroll file*. The new master payroll file will be used for future payroll processing.

The program must be able to:

1. Add new records to the master pay file.
2. Delete a record from the master pay file.
3. Change various fields on any master pay record. The program must be able to modify any of the master pay file fields except the SSN (the record key). The program is to check for the presence of spaces in the various fields of the transaction record. If the field of the transaction record contains anything other than spaces, the program writes this field on the new master record. The presence of spaces in a field of the transaction record indicates that the associated master record does *not* require a change.
4. Generate an update report (Exhibit 12.1) that shows the various updates.
5. Once the file is updated, as a verification that the file was in fact updated, simply print a listing of the new master file records with a record count at the end of the report.

## Output Design

Exhibits 12.1 and 12.2 depict the two reports to be produced. The associated printer spacing chart, illustrated in Exhibit 12.3, depicts the format for both reports. In the update report, an X in the appropriate column indicates the kind of update operation performed. There are columns in the report for RECORD ADDED, RECORD DELETED, RECORD CHANGED, and FIELD CHANGES. The specific field references shown under the FIELD CHANGES heading will contain an X only if the transaction record contains an update code of C. An X in this second part of the report allows the user (and programmer) to keep track of the fields of the master record that were actually changed.

Three different error messages can print on the report. When a record is added to the file, a duplicate record is not permitted; if a duplication attempt should occur, the error message is printed, as shown in the update report. Or a transaction record may be prepared that has no matching master record. If this is the case, in either a change or delete situation, the appropriate message is printed, as shown in the report.

Once the sequential file update process is complete, the report shown in Exhibit 12.2 is printed. This report is a simple listing of the updated master file and a record count.

## Input Design

Exhibit 12.4 presents the record layout of both the payroll transaction records and the payroll master file records.

## Test Cases

Exhibit 12.5 depicts a set of test cases for both files.

## Logic Considerations

There are three main logic considerations for this problem.

*First*, the programmer must order both the transaction file and the master file by SSN.

*Second*, the programmer must provide for catchup when the master key is less than the transaction key. The new master records are copied to the new file until a master record is read with a key that is either equal to or greater than the transaction key.

*Third*, in case the two keys are equal, the program must provide either for changes to the master record or for deletion of the record itself. If the transaction code is C, a change process occurs. If the field on the transaction record contains spaces, then no change is made to this respective field in the master file. However, if the field contains anything other than spaces, the content of the transaction record is moved to the respective field of the new master record. This is most easily handled by first storing a copy of the old master record into the new master record and subsequently transferring the non-space fields from the transaction record to the respective fields of the new master record. If the transaction code is D, the old master record is not copied to the new master file. Once a change or delete operation is performed, both a master and transaction record are read.

*Fourth*, if the key of the current transaction record being read is less than the current master and the transaction code indicates that the record is to be added, the transaction record is copied to the new master file and another transaction record is read.

## Program Design of Payroll Master File Sequential Update

**Hierarchy Chart.** Exhibit 12.6 illustrates the general program logic in hierarchy chart form. The MAIN-LINE module appears as always. The START-UP-UPDATE module is broken down into (1) SORT-FILES, (2) OPEN FILES, (3) HEADINGS, (4) READ-OLD-MASTER, and (5) READ-TRANS-FILE. The UPDATE-PROCESS module is decomposed into (1) COPY-OLD-MAST-TO-NEW-MAST, (2) CHANGE-OR-DELETE, (3) ADD-NEW-MASTER, and (4) BAD-TRANS-MESSAGE. The WRAP-UP-UPDATE module is decomposed into (1) CLOSE-NEW-MASTER, (2) OPEN-NEW-MASTER, (3) READ-NEW-MASTER, (4) PRINT-NEW-MASTER-LISTING, and (5) CLOSE-FILES. The function of the PRINT-NEW-MASTER-LISTING is to print the up-dated master payroll file once updating is complete.

The purpose of the SORT-FILES module is to sort both the old master pay file and the transaction file into ascending sequence by social security number. The SORT-FILES module of START-UP-UPDATE uses a sort/merge utility to input the un-sorted master and transaction files, sort the two files, and write the sorted versions of the two files to their respective output files.

COPY-OLD-MAST-TO-NEW-MAST will handle the writing of the old master records to the new master file as long as the master key is less than the transaction key.

The function of the CHANGE-OR-DELETE module is to change or delete appropriate master records when the transaction key is matched with a master record key. The transaction key and the master key must be equal.

The ADD-NEW-MASTER routine adds the con-tents of the old master record to the new master record. For an addition to occur, the transaction key must be less than the master key, and the transac-tion code must be A. This condition means that no duplicate master exists and the transaction code in-dicates that the record is to be added. This is an ap-propriate condition upon which an addition is to occur. The program should never permit an addi-tion if the record is found in the master file, since duplicate master records would result.

The function of the BAD-TRANS-MESSAGE module is to provide for the printing of appropriate

---

**EXHIBIT 12.1    Sample Update Report for Sequential File Update**

```
                  ACME  UPDATE  OF  MASTER  PAY  FILE

                                    **FIELD CHANGES**
SSN         RECORD    RECORD    RECORD
            ADDED     DELETED   CHANGED   NM   ADDR   BR    DEP   JOB   DOE   YTD

090909090   RECORD NOT CHANGED..MASTER RECORD NOT FOUND
101010101   RECORD NOT ADDED..DUPLICATE
101022033             X
212121212                         X           X            X     X
456741129                         X           X
888888888   X
911111111   RECORD NOT DELETED..MASTER RECORD NOT FOUND
999199923   X
```

---

**EXHIBIT 12.2    Sample Report Listing of Updated Master Records**

```
            SEQUENTIAL  LISTING  OF  UPDATED  MASTER  FILE

SSN          NAME      BRANCH   DEPT   JOB   ADDRESS       DOE        STATE
             (LAST)

XXXXXXXXX    XXXXXXXXX   XXX     XXX    XX    XXXXXXXXXX    XX/XX/XX    XX
XXXXXXXXX    XXXXXXXXX   XXX     XXX    XX    XXXXXXXXXX    XX/XX/XX    XX
XXXXXXXXX    XXXXXXXXX   XXX     XXX    XX    XXXXXXXXXX    XX/XX/XX    XX
XXXXXXXXX    XXXXXXXXX   XXX     XXX    XX    XXXXXXXXXX    XX/XX/XX    XX

NUMBER OF RECORDS = XXX
```

error messages. If the transaction key is less than the master key and the transaction code is something other than A, this indicates a master record was not located with a key equal to the transaction key when either a change or delete was attempted. One other possibility does exist; the code on the transaction record may be invalid. Generally, some kind of validity checking program is run to take care of invalid codes, but an error check is always an excellent idea.

**Structured Program Flowchart.** Exhibit 12.7 illustrates the detailed program logic in structured and modular form. One important difference is the manner in which the MAIN-LINE-SEQ-UPDATE module controls the invoking of the UPDATE-PROCESS module. The condition found here is to execute the UPDATE-PROCESS module until both END-FLAG-MAST and END-FLAG-TRANS are turned on. The processing cannot terminate until all the records of both files have been read.

In addition to the previously discussed module, the START-UP module indicates that both the master and the transaction records are read initially. In the UPDATE-PROCESS module the SSN from the master record (MAST-KEY) and the SSN from the transaction record (TRANS-KEY) are compared. If MAST-KEY is less than TRANS-KEY, then the COPY-OLD-MAST-TO-NEW-MAST routine is performed; otherwise, MAST-KEY is compared with TRANS-KEY to determine equality. If the two are equal, it means that the CHANGE-OR-DELETE module is invoked. If the test for equality is not true, it then determines whether the transaction

## EXHIBIT 12.3    Printer Spacing  Charts for Sequential File Update

**Panel A**

```
ACME UPDATE OF MASTER PAYFILE

SSN         RECORD    RECORD    RECORD     **FIELD CHANGES**
            ADDED     DELETED   CHANGED    MM  ADDR  BR  DEP  JOB    DOE  YTD
XXXXXXXX      X         X
                              X          X   X    X   X    X    X    X
XXXXXXXX    RECORD NOT ADDED --DUPLICATE
XXXXXXXX    RECORD NOT DELETED -- MASTER RECORD NOT FOUND
XXXXXXXX    RECORD NOT CHANGED -- MASTER RECORD NOT FOUND
```

**Panel B**

```
SEQUENTIAL LISTING OF UPDATED MASTER FILE

SSN         NAME      BRANCH DEPT   JOB  ADDRESS      DOE     STATE
XXXXXXXX    XXXXXXXX   XXX   XXX     XX   XXXXXXXX   XX/XX/XX  XX

NUMBER OF RECORDS = XXX
```

code contains an A. If so, the ADD-NEW-MASTER module is executed.

The COPY-OLD-MASTER-TO-NEW-MAST simply writes the OLD-MASTER to the NEW-MASTER and reads another OLD-MASTER.

The CHANGE-OR-DELETE module directs traffic by invoking the CHANGE-REC module when the transaction code contains a C or by invoking the DELETE-REC routine when the transaction code is D. If the transaction code is A, because of some data entry error, then the DUPLICATE-ADD-MSG module is called. If the transaction code is valid (either a, c, or d), then both a master and a transaction record are read. If the code is invalid, the program must read another transaction record only.

An important module for discussion is CHANGE-REC. To allow any or all of the fields in the master record to be changed (except the key), this technique stores spaces in any corresponding field of the transaction record that does not require changing. The fields for change contain the new data. The very first command in the CHANGE-REC routine is to store the entire contents of the old master record into the new master record. Then, as

deemed appropriate, the "change" data from the transaction record is stored into the respective fields in the new master record. The rather lengthy case structure checks one field of the transaction record at a time until it encounters a field with contents other than spaces. Subsequently, it moves the contents of the transaction record to the respective master record.

Another important point to note is the handling of end-of-file. The READ-OLD-SRT-MASTER and READ-SORTED-TRANS submodules contain something not shown in previous chapters. If end-of-file is sensed in the master file, then the *ten-position* MAST-KEY is filled with 9999999999 (ten 9s). What significance does this have? When the master file is depleted before the end of the transaction file is reached, the MAST-KEY is now set to a maximum amount. Therefore, during the execution of the UPDATE-PROCESS module, the MAST-KEY will always be larger than any nine-digit social security number in TRANS-KEY. Assuming the key is valid and the transaction code is A, all additional transaction records will be added to the end of the new master file. If the transaction file is depleted before running out of master records, the TRANS-

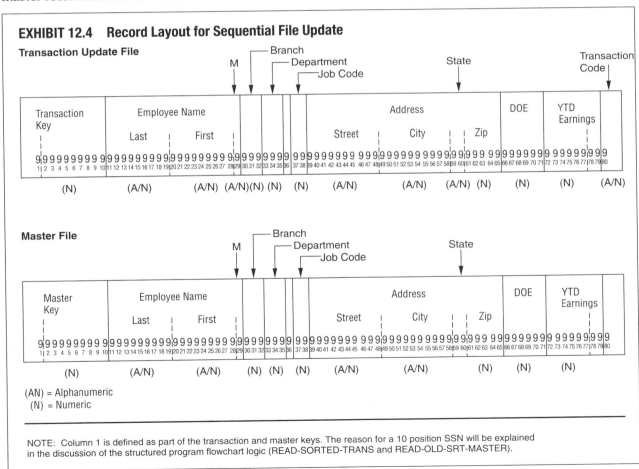

**EXHIBIT 12.4   Record Layout for Sequential File Update**

NOTE:  Column 1 is defined as part of the transaction and master keys. The reason for a 10 position SSN will be explained in the discussion of the structured program flowchart logic (READ-SORTED-TRANS and READ-OLD-SRT-MASTER).

KEY is stored with ten nines. The first condition (if MAST-KEY is less than TRANS-KEY) will always be true for the remaining master records. For all remaining iterations, COPY-OLD-MAST-TO-NEW-MAST is executed. This causes all the remaining old master records to be written to the new master file. (The TRANS-KEY and MAST-KEY fields were designed as ten-position fields even though a social security number occupies only nine. Since the SSN is numeric, the leading position of the ten-position field is zero. To reiterate, when end-of-file is sensed in either file, the appropriate key is filled with *ten* nines, making it larger than any possible nine-digit SSN. This process can be alleviated in COBOL by moving HIGH-VALUE to the appropriate key when the end of the file is reached. HIGH-VALUE eliminates the need to make the key ten positions in length. Since HIGH-VALUE represents the highest possible value in the collating sequence, then the content of the field in EBCDIC code of FFFFFFFFFFFFFFFFFF will always be larger than the decimal value F9F9F9F9F9F9F9F9F9 in EBCDIC code. These two character strings are shown in half-byte form. (Refer to Appendix D for clarification of the EBCDIC code for numeric values and the COBOL figurative constant, HIGH-VALUE.) HIGH VALUE is a figurative constant and is an IBM extension. It does not work on some architectures.

**Pseudocode.** Exhibit 12.8 depicts the associated pseudocode for this problem.

**Programs.** Exhibits 12.9 and 12.10 illustrate the COBOL and BASIC programs for this design.

---

### EXHIBIT 12.5   Test Cases for Sequential File Update

**Panel A—Test Cases for Master File**

```
COLUMN   1         2         3         4         5         6         7         8
1234567890123456789012345678901234567890123456789012345678901234567890123456789012345678901234567890
--------------------------------------------------------------------------------
0101010101JOHNSON    DANNY     D001001 09WEST GREENSTEPHENVILTX76401092345
0456741129RUSSELL    JACK      P001001 01STAR ROUTESTEPHENVILTX76401081945
0222222222BAKER      BOB       D001003 03CEDAR SPR DALLAS     TX44444051265
0333333333DICKSON    MARY      G002001 05CEDAR     ARLINGTON TX45555101067
0444444444CARLTON    BILL      E002001 04PINE      FT WORTH  TX55555091355
0212121212EVANS      SUSAN     D002002 06 SPRUCE   KELLER    TX45666111157
0555555555GREEN      DONNA     J002002 07LILLIAN   STEPHENVILTX76401112367
0666666666HILLARD    HAROLD    H002002 08VANDERBILTSTEPHENVILTX76401091272
0234254456THOMPSON   JIM       D002002 07s SUN VLY GATESVILLETX76528050647
0555556666JOHNSON    JOHN      J003001 09GREEN     STEPHENVILTX76401091373
0676767676NORTON     NATHAN    N003001 05DODGE     JONESBORO TX76528050559
0767676766MILLER     BOB       B003001 05BUICK     FLAT      TX76528050748
0777777777KRAMER     KAREN     K003001 10COLLEGE   STEPHENVILTX76401090867
0484848484ROBERTS    ROB       R003002 06CANYON    HICO      TX99999060759
0393838444JOHNSTON   JOHN      J003003 05BUMPY     LEVITA    TX99999060460
0101022033SIMPSON    CHARLES   C003004 06N OLLIE   STEPHENVILTX76401050547
0404040404DONALD     DON       D003004 1071555J4444BLUFF DALETX88888060647
```

---

**Panel B—Test Cases for Transaction Records**

```
COLUMN   1         2         3         4         5         6         7         8
1234567890123456789012345678901234567890123456789012345678901234567890123456789012345678901234567890
--------------------------------------------------------------------------------
0456741129                           BUS. BLDG STEPHENVILTX76401              C
0212121212                    003 07PLEASANT  KELLER    TX44444              C
0090909090                    003                                            C
0888888888ZIMMERMANLANCE    A001001    06PARROT   WACO      TX7777708087600000000A
0999199923DONALDSONFRANK    M002002    05MONROE   GRANBURY  TX7733309097500000000A
0101022033SIMPSON  CHARLES                                                   D
0101010101JOHNSON  DANNY     D001001    09XXXXXX   HAMILTON  TX2020203038500000000A
0911111111DOLITTLE JIMMY                                                     D
```

**EXHIBIT 12.6    Hierarchy Chart for Sequential File Update (Payroll File)**

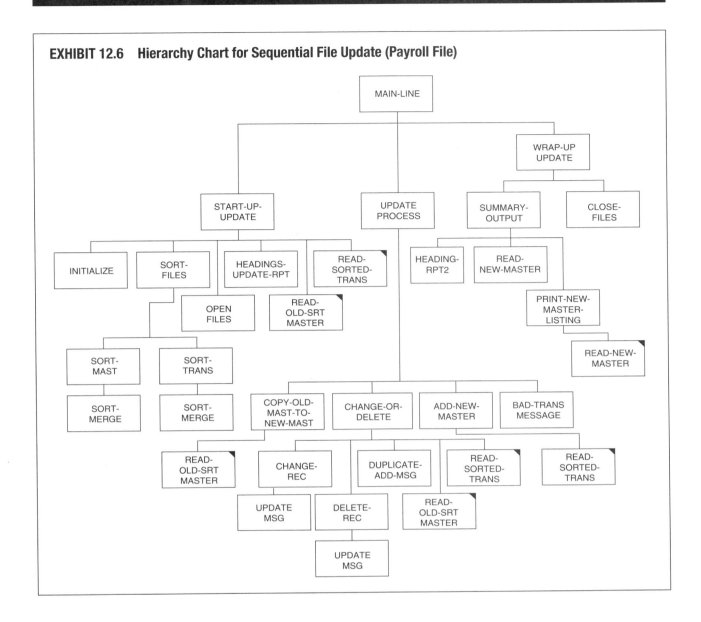

**EXHIBIT 12.7    Structured Flowchart for Sequential File Update (Payroll File)**

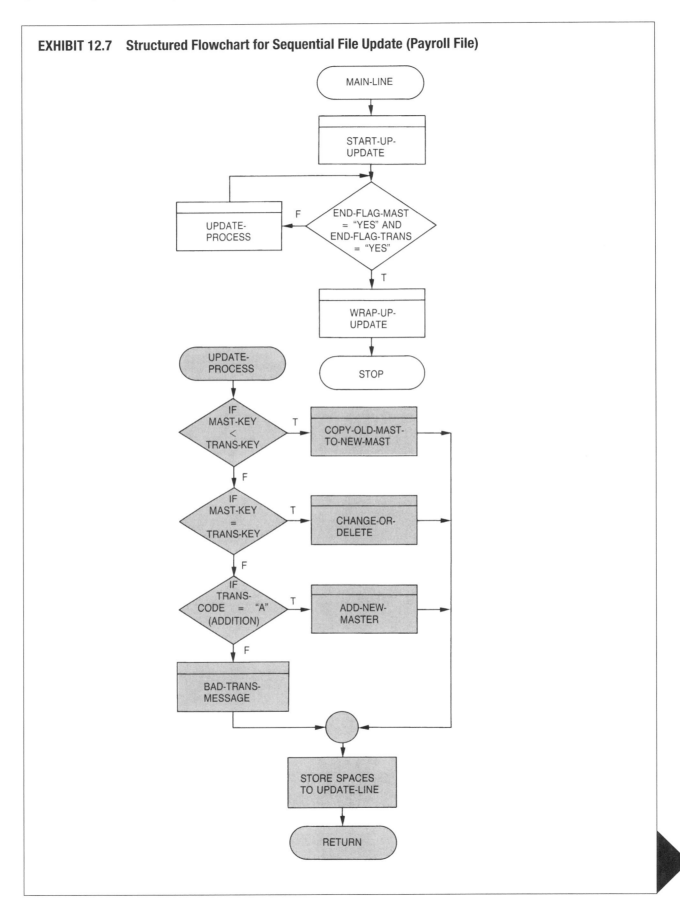

**EXHIBIT 12.7 (Cont.)**

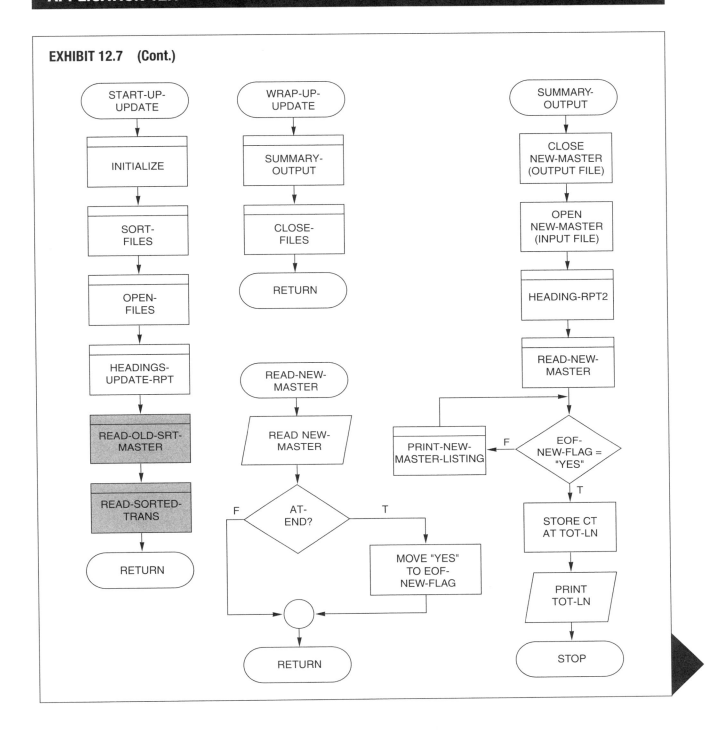

**EXHIBIT 12.7    (Cont.)**

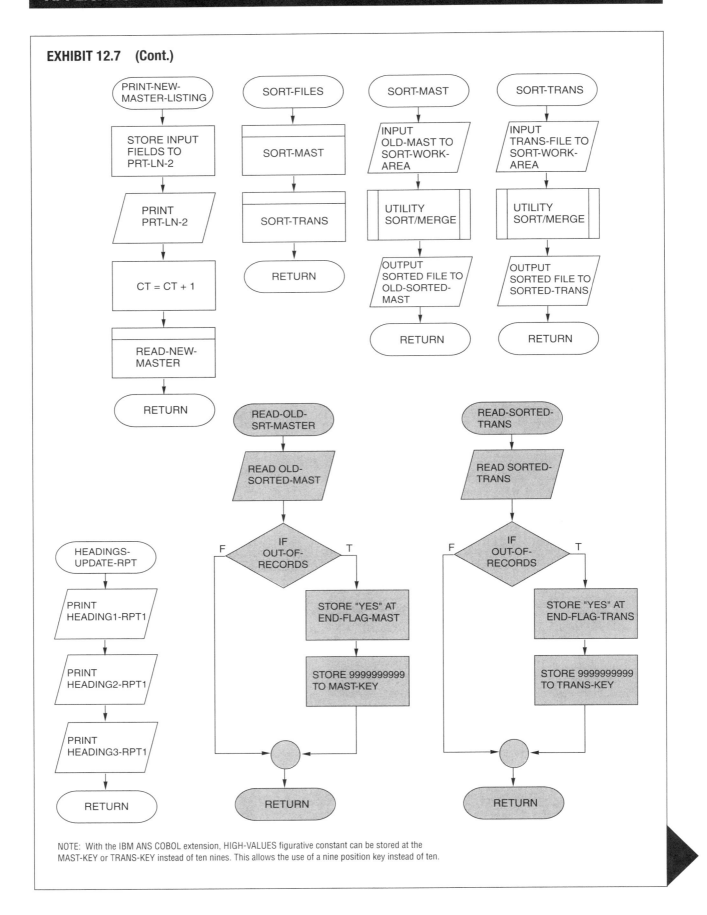

NOTE: With the IBM ANS COBOL extension, HIGH-VALUES figurative constant can be stored at the
MAST-KEY or TRANS-KEY instead of ten nines. This allows the use of a nine position key instead of ten.

**EXHIBIT 12.7** (Cont.)

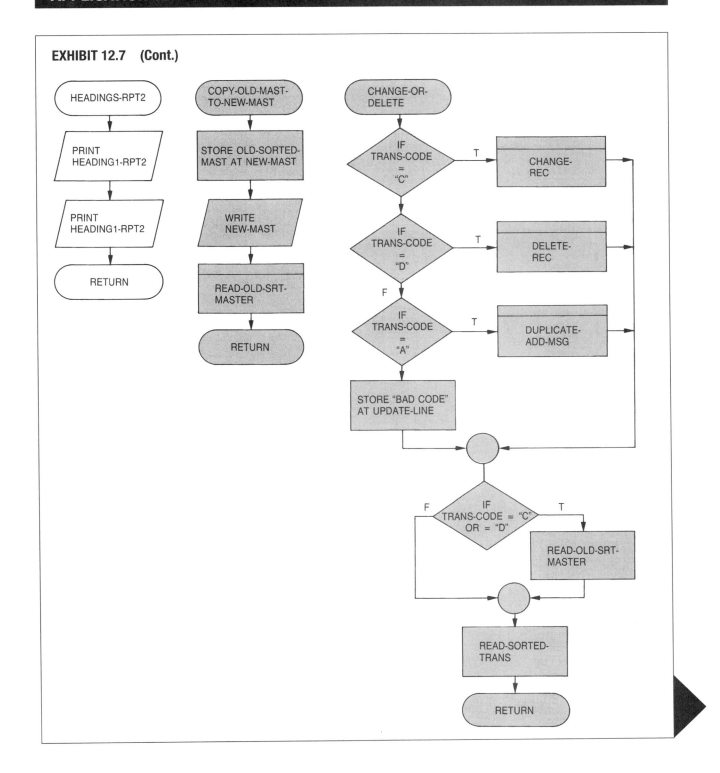

**EXHIBIT 12.7   (Cont.)**

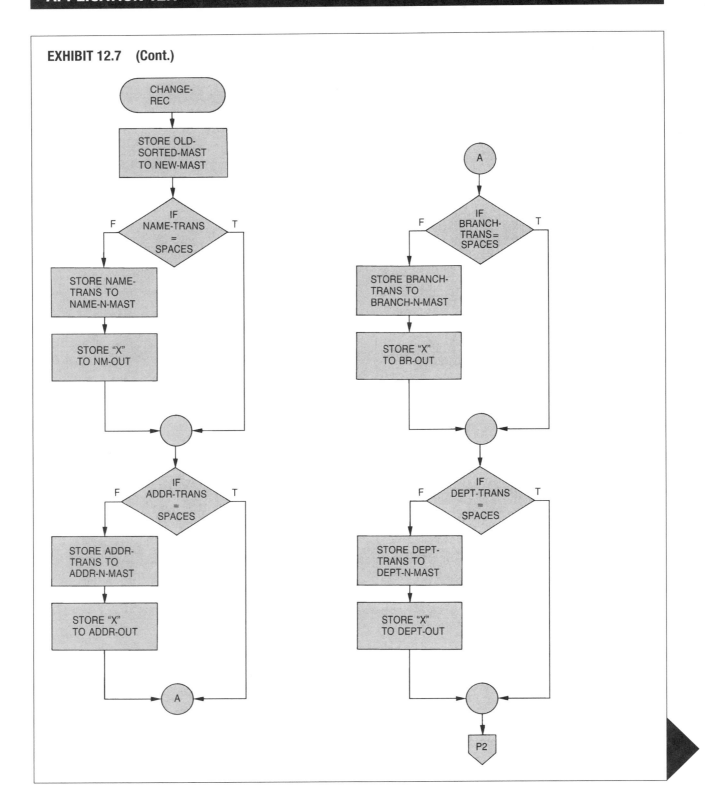

**EXHIBIT 12.7    (Cont.)**

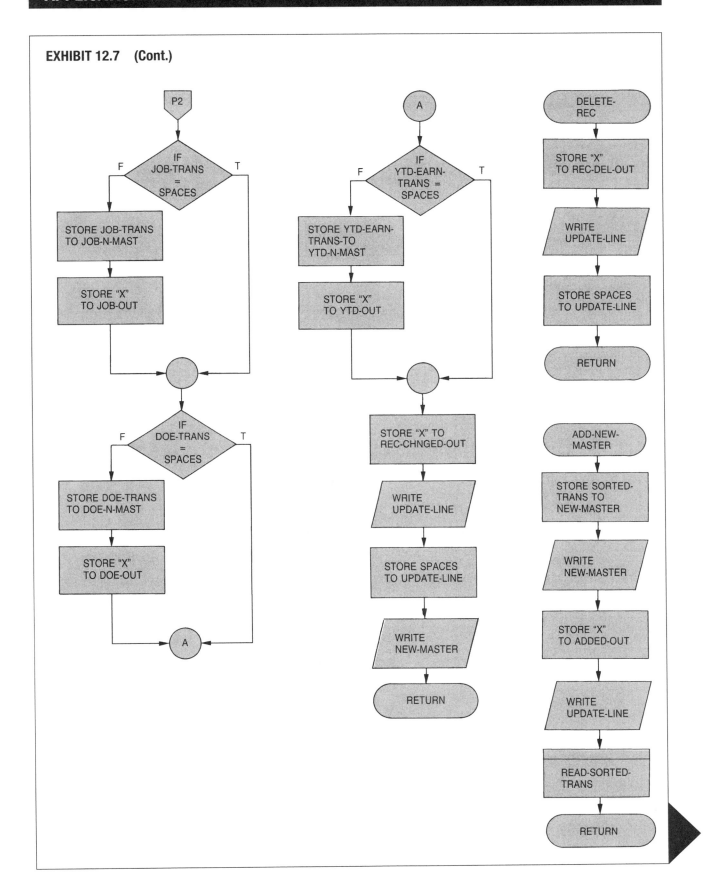

**EXHIBIT 12.7    (Cont.)**

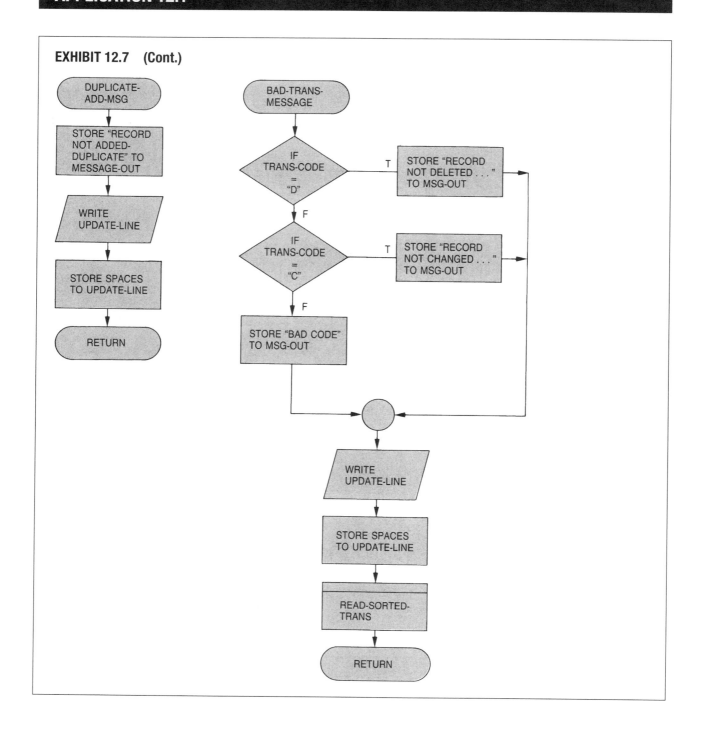

**EXHIBIT 12.8  Pseudocode for Sequential File Update (Payroll File)**

```
*main-line
    start-up-update
    do while end-flag-mast = "no" or end-flag-trans = "no"
    (***until end-flag-mast = "yes" and end-flag-trans =
         "yes")
         update-process
    enddo
    wrap-up-update
    stop
*start-up-update
    initialize
    sort-files
    open-files
    headings-update-rpt
    read-old-srt-master
    read-sorted-trans
    return
*initialize
    end-flag-mast = "no"
    end-flag-trans = "no"
    return
*sort-files
    sort-mast
    sort-trans
    return
*sort-mast
    input old-mast to sort-work-area
    utility sort/merge operation
    output sorted file to old-sorted-mast
    return
*sort-trans
    input trans-file to sort-work-area
    utility sort/merge operation
    output sorted file to sorted-trans
    return
*open-files
    open input old-sorted-mast
    open input sorted-trans
    open input new-master
    open output update-report
    open output report-of-new-recs
    return
*headings-update-rpt
    print heading1-rpt1
    print heading2-rpt1
    print heading3-rpt1
    return
*read-old-srt-master
    read old-sorted-mast
    if out of records
         store "yes" at end-flag-mast
         store 9999999999 to mast-key
    endif
    endread
    return
```

```
*read-sorted-trans
    read sorted-trans
    if out of records
         store "yes" at end-flag-trans
         store 9999999999 to trans-key
    endif
    endread
    return
*update-process
    if mast-key < trans-key then
         copy-old-mast-to-new-mast
    else
    if mast-key = trans-key
         change-or-delete
    else
    if trans-code = "A" then
         add-new-master
    else   bad-trans-message
    store blanks at update-line
    return
*copy-old-mast-to-new-mast
    store old-sorted-mast to new-mast
    write new-mast
    read-old-srt-master
    return
*change-or-delete
    if trans-code = "c" then
         change-rec
    else
         if trans-code = "d" then
              delete-rec
         else
              if trans-code = "a" then
              duplicate-add-msg
                   else
                        store "bad code" at update-line
                   endif
         endif
    endif
    if trans-code = "c" or "d" then
         read-old-srt-master
    endif
    read-sorted-trans
    return
```

**EXHIBIT 12.8   (Cont.)**

```
*change-rec
    store old-sorted-mast to new-mast
    if name-trans = blanks
        null
    else store name-trans to name-n-mast
        store "x" to nm-out
    endif
    if addr-trans = blanks
        null
    else store addr-trans to addr-n-mast
        store "x" to addr-out
    endif
    if branch-trans = blanks
        null
    else store branch-trans to branch-n-mast
        store "x" to br-out
    endif
    if dept-trans = blanks
        null
    else store dept-trans to dept-n-mast
        store "x" to dept-out
    endif
    if job-trans = blanks
        null
    else store job-trans to job-n-mast
        store "x" to job-out
    endif
    if doe-trans = blanks
        null
    else store doe-trans to doe-n-m
        store "x" to doe-out
    endif
    if ytd-earn-trans = blanks
        null
    else store ytd-earn-trans to ytd-n-mast
        store "x" to ytd-out
    endif
    store "x" to rec-chnged-out
    write update-line
    store spaces to update-line
    write new-master
    return
*delete-rec
    store "x" to rec-del-out
    write update-line
    store spaces to update-line
    return
*duplicate-add-msg
    store "record not added — duplicate" to message-out
    write update-line
    store spaces to update-line
    return
```

```
*add-new-master
    store sorted-trans to new-master
    write new-master
    store "x" to added-out
    write update-line
    read-sorted-trans
    return
*bad-trans-message
    if trans-code = "d"
        store "record not deleted..mast not found" to
            msg-out
    else
    if trans-code = "c"
        store "record not changed..mast not found" to
            msg-out
    else
    store "bad code" to msg-out
    write update-line
    store spaces to update-line
    read-sorted-trans
    return
*wrap-up-upate
    summary-output
    close-files
    return
*summary-output
    close new-master (output file)
    open new-master (input file)
    heading-rpt2
    read-new-master
    do until eof-new-flag = "yes"
        print-new-master-listing
    enddo
    store ct at tot-ln
    print tot-ln
    return
*print-new-master-listing
    store input fields to prt-ln-2
    print prt-ln-2
    ct = ct + 1
    read-new-master
    return
*read-new-master
    read new-master
        when out of records store "yes" at eof-new-flag
    endread
    return
```

**EXHIBIT 12.9  COBOL 85 Program and Output for Application 12.1 (Sequential File Update)**

```
1          IDENTIFICATION DIVISION.
2          PROGRAM-ID. CH12NWAPL1.
3          DATE-WRITTEN. JUNE 12, 1992.
4          DATE-COMPILED. 1993-06-24.
5         *AUTHOR:  JACK RUSSELL.
6         *REMARKS:    THIS PROGRAM UPDATES A SEQUENTIAL MASTER PAY
7         *            FILE FROM A TRANSACTION UPDATE FILE.  A NEW
8         *            MASTER PAY FILE IS PRODUCED.  ADDING, DELETING,
9         *            AND CHANGING OF MASTER RECORDS ARE PROVIDED FOR.
10        *            AN UPDATE REPORT IS PRODUCED WHICH INDICATE WHICH
11        *            UPDATE OPERATIONS OCCURED FOR SPECIFIC MASTER
12        *            RECORDS.
13
14         ENVIRONMENT DIVISION.
15         CONFIGURATION SECTION.
16         SOURCE-COMPUTER. CYBER.
17         OBJECT-COMPUTER. CYBER.
18         INPUT-OUTPUT SECTION.
19         FILE-CONTROL.
20             SELECT OLD-MASTER ASSIGN TO OLDMAST.
21             SELECT OLD-SORTED-MAST  ASSIGN TO OLDSRT.
22             SELECT TRANS-FILE       ASSIGN TO TRANS.
23             SELECT SORTED-TRANS     ASSIGN TO SRTTRAN.
24             SELECT NEW-MASTER       ASSIGN TO NEWMAST.
25             SELECT WORK-FILE        ASSIGN TO WRKFILE.
26             SELECT UPDATE-RPT       ASSIGN TO OUTFILE.
27             SELECT RPT-OF-NEW-RECS  ASSIGN TO OUTFIL2.
28
29         DATA DIVISION.
30         FILE SECTION.
31         FD OLD-MASTER.
32         01 OLD-MASTER-RECORD.
33             05 OM-SSN            PIC 9(10).
34             05 OM-NAME.
35                 10 OM-LAST       PIC X(9).
36                 10 OM-FIRST      PIC X(9).
37                 10 OM-MI         PIC X.
38             05 OM-BRANCH         PIC 9(3).
39             05 OM-DEPT           PIC 9(3).
40             05 FILLER            PIC X.
41             05 OM-JC             PIC 99.
42             05 OM-ADDR.
43                 10 OM-STREET     PIC X(10).
44                 10 OM-CITY       PIC X(10).
45                 10 OM-STATE      PIC XX.
46                 10 OM-ZIP        PIC 9(5).
47             05 OM-DOE.
48                 10 OM-MONTH      PIC 99.
49                 10 OM-DAY        PIC 99.
50                 10 OM-YEAR       PIC 99.
51             05 OM-YTD            PIC 9(6)V99.
52             05 FILLER            PIC X.
53
54         FD OLD-SORTED-MAST.
55         01 OLD-SORTED-MAST-RECORD.
56             05 MAST-KEY          PIC 9(10).
57             05 OS-NAME.
58                 10 OS-LAST       PIC X(9).
59                 10 OS-FIRST      PIC X(9).
60                 10 OS-MI         PIC X.
61             05 OS-BRANCH         PIC 9(3).
62             05 OS-DEPT           PIC 9(3).
63             05 FILLER            PIC X.
64             05 OS-JC             PIC 99.
```

**EXHIBIT 12.9   (Cont.)**

```
65                05 OS-ADDR.
66                    10 OS-STREET     PIC X(10).
67                    10 OS-CITY       PIC X(10).
68                    10 OS-STATE      PIC XX.
69                    10 OS-ZIP        PIC 9(5).
70                05 OS-DOE.
71                    10 OS-MONTH      PIC 99.
72                    10 OS-DAY        PIC 99.
73                    10 OS-YEAR       PIC 99.
74                05 OS-YTD            PIC 9(6)V99.
75                05 FILLER            PIC X.
76
77            FD TRANS-FILE.
78            01 TRANS-OLD-REC.
79                05 OT-SSN            PIC 9(10).
80                05 OT-NAME.
81                    10 OT-LAST       PIC X(9).
82                    10 OT-FIRST      PIC X(9).
83                    10 OT-MI         PIC X.
84                05 OT-BRANCH         PIC 9(3).
85                05 OT-DEPT           PIC 9(3).
86                05 FILLER            PIC X.
87                05 OT-JC             PIC 99.
88                05 OT-ADDR.
89                    10 OT-STREET     PIC X(10).
90                    10 OT-CITY       PIC X(10).
91                    10 OT-STATE      PIC XX.
92                    10 OT-ZIP        PIC 9(5).
93                05 OT-DOE.
94                    10 OT-MONTH      PIC 99.
95                    10 OT-DAY        PIC 99.
96                    10 OT-YEAR       PIC 99.
97                05 OT-YTD            PIC 9(6)V99.
98                05 OT-CODE           PIC X.
99
100           FD SORTED-TRANS.
101           01 SORTED-TRANS-RECORD.
102               05 TRANS-KEY         PIC 9(10).
103               05 NAME-TRANS.
104                   10 TR-LAST       PIC X(9).
105                   10 TR-FIRST      PIC X(9).
106                   10 TR-MI         PIC X.
107               05 BRANCH-TRANS      PIC 9(3).
108               05 DEPT-TRANS        PIC 9(3).
109               05 FILLER            PIC X.
110               05 JOB-TRANS         PIC 99.
111               05 ADDR-TRANS.
112                   10 STREET-TRANS  PIC X(10).
113                   10 CITY-TRANS    PIC X(10).
114                   10 STATE-TRANS   PIC XX.
115                   10 ZIP-TRANS     PIC 9(5).
116               05 DOE-TRANS.
117                   10 TR-MONTH      PIC 99.
118                   10 TR-DAY        PIC 99.
119                   10 TR-YEAR       PIC 99.
120               05 YTD-EARN-TRANS    PIC 9(6)V99.
121               05 YTD-EARN-TRANS-REDF REDEFINES YTD-EARN-TRANS PIC X(8).
122               05 TRANS-CODE        PIC X.
123
124           FD NEW-MASTER.
125           01 NEW-MASTER-RECORD.
126               05 SSN-N-M           PIC 9(10).
127               05 NAME-N-M.
128                   10 LAST-N-M      PIC X(9).
129                   10 FIRST-N-M     PIC X(9).
130                   10 MI-M-N        PIC X.
```

**EXHIBIT 12.9    (Cont.)**

```
131              05 BRANCH-N-M        PIC 9(3).
132              05 DEPT-N-M          PIC 9(3).
133              05 FILLER            PIC X.
134              05 JOB-N-M           PIC 99.
135              05 ADDR-N-M.
136                  10 STREET-N-M    PIC X(10).
137                  10 CITY-N-M      PIC X(10).
138                  10 STATE-N-M     PIC XX.
139                  10 ZIP-N-M       PIC 9(5).
140              05 DOE-N-M.
141                  10 MONTH-N-M     PIC 99.
142                  10 DAY-N-M       PIC 99.
143                  10 YEAR-N-M      PIC 99.
144              05 YTD-EARN-N-M      PIC 9(6)V99.
145              05 FILLER            PIC X.
146         SD WORK-FILE.
147         01 WORK-RECORD.
148              05 WRK-SSN           PIC 9(10).
149              05 WRK-NAME.
150                  10 WRK-LAST      PIC X(9).
151                  10 WRK-FIRST     PIC X(9).
152                  10 WRK-MI        PIC X.
153              05 WRK-BRANCH        PIC 9(3).
154              05 WRK-DEPT          PIC 9(3).
155              05 FILLER            PIC X.
156              05 WRK-JC            PIC 99.
157              05 WRK-ADDR.
158                  10 WRK-STREET    PIC X(10).
159                  10 WRK-CITY      PIC X(10).
160                  10 WRK-STATE     PIC XX.
161                  10 WRK-ZIP       PIC 9(5).
162              05 WRK-DOE.
163                  10 WRK-MONTH     PIC 99.
164                  10 WRK-DAY       PIC 99.
165                  10 WRK-YEAR      PIC 99.
166              05 WRK-YTD           PIC 9(6)V99.
167              05 WRK-CODE          PIC X.
168
169         FD UPDATE-RPT.
170         01 UPDATE-RPT-RECORD      PIC X(133).
171
172         FD RPT-OF-NEW-RECS.
173         01 RPT-OF-NEW-RECS-RECORD  PIC X(133).
174
175         WORKING-STORAGE SECTION.
176
177         01 END-FLAG-MAST    PIC XXX VALUE "NO".
178         01 END-FLAG-TRANS   PIC XXX VALUE "NO".
179         01 EOF-NEW-FLAG     PIC XXX VALUE "NO".
180         01 CT               PIC 999 VALUE ZERO.
181
182         01 HEADING1-RPT1.
183             05                    PIC X(9) VALUE SPACES.
184             05                    PIC X(29) VALUE "ACME UPDATE OF MASTER
185         -           " PAYFILE".
186             05                    PIC X(94) VALUE SPACES.
187
188         01 HEADING2-RPT1.
189             05                    PIC X(11) VALUE "SSN".
190             05                    PIC X(9) VALUE "RECORD".
191             05                    PIC X(10) VALUE "RECORD".
192             05                    PIC X(11) VALUE "RECORD".
193             05                    PIC X(17) VALUE "**FIELD CHANGES**".
194             05                    PIC X(73) VALUE SPACES.
195
```

**EXHIBIT 12.9   (Cont.)**

```
196          01 HEADING3-RPT1.
197              05                      PIC X(11) VALUE SPACES.
198              05                      PIC X(9) VALUE "ADDED".
199              05                      PIC X(10) VALUE "DELETED".
200              05                      PIC X(11) VALUE "CHANGED".
201              05                      PIC X(4) VALUE "NM".
202              05                      PIC X(5) VALUE "ADDR".
203              05                      PIC X(4) VALUE "BR".
204              05                      PIC X(5) VALUE "DEP".
205              05                      PIC X(6) VALUE "JOB".
206              05                      PIC X(4) VALUE "DOE".
207              05                      PIC X(3) VALUE "YTD".
208              05                      PIC X(60) VALUE SPACES.
209
210          01 UPDATE-LINE.
211              05 SSN-OUT               PIC 9(9).
212              05                      PIC X(4) VALUE SPACES.
213              05 MESSAGE-OUT.
214                  10 ADDED-OUT         PIC X.
215                  10                  PIC X(9) VALUE SPACES.
216                  10 REC-DEL-OUT       PIC X.
217                  10                  PIC X(9) VALUE SPACES.
218                  10 REC-CHNGED-OUT    PIC X.
219                  10                  PIC X(8) VALUE SPACES.
220                  10 NAME-OUT          PIC X.
221                  10                  PIC X(4) VALUE SPACES.
222                  10 ADDR-OUT          PIC X.
223                  10                  PIC X(2) VALUE SPACES.
224                  10 BR-OUT            PIC X.
225                  10                  PIC X(3) VALUE SPACES.
226                  10 DEPT-OUT          PIC X.
227                  10                  PIC X(5) VALUE SPACES.
228                  10 JOB-OUT           PIC X.
229                  10                  PIC X(5) VALUE SPACES.
230                  10 DOE-OUT           PIC X.
231                  10                  PIC X(3) VALUE SPACES.
232                  10 YTD-OUT           PIC X.
233                  10                  PIC X(61) VALUE SPACES.
234
235          01 HEADING1-RPT2.
236              05                      PIC X(11) VALUE SPACES.
237              05                      PIC X(41) VALUE "SEQUENTIAL LISTING OF
238          -            " UPDATED MASTER FILE".
239              05                      PIC X(80) VALUE SPACES.
240
241          01 HEADING2-RPT2.
242              05                      PIC X(11) VALUE "SSN".
243              05                      PIC X(10) VALUE "NAME".
244              05                      PIC X(7) VALUE "BRANCH".
245              05                      PIC X(7) VALUE "DEPT".
246              05                      PIC X(5) VALUE "JOB".
247              05                      PIC X(14) VALUE "ADDRESS".
248              05                      PIC X(6) VALUE "DOE".
249              05                      PIC X(5) VALUE "STATE".
250              05                      PIC X(88) VALUE SPACES.
251
252          01 RPT2-LINE.
253              05 SSN-RPT2              PIC 9(9).
254              05                      PIC X(2) VALUE SPACES.
255              05 LAST-RPT2            PIC X(10).
256              05                      PIC X(2) VALUE SPACES.
257              05 BRANCH-RPT2          PIC X(3).
258              05                      PIC X(2) VALUE SPACES.
259              05 DEPT-RPT2            PIC X(3).
260              05                      PIC X(5) VALUE SPACES.
261              05 JOB-RPT2             PIC X(2).
```

EXHIBIT 12.9    (Cont.)

```
262                05                        PIC X(2) VALUE SPACES.
263                05 STREET-RPT2            PIC X(10).
264                05                        PIC X    VALUE SPACES.
265                05 MONTH-RPT2             PIC 99/.
266                05 DAY-RPT2               PIC 99/.
267                05 YEAR-RPT2              PIC 99BB.
268                05 STATE-RPT2             PIC X(2).
269                05                        PIC X(71) VALUE SPACES.
270
271          01 TOT-LN.
272                05                        PIC X(20) VALUE "NUMBER OF RECORDS = ".
273                05 TOT-CT                 PIC Z99.
274                05                        PIC X(109) VALUE SPACES.
275       /
276        PROCEDURE DIVISION.
277        000-MAIN-LINE.
278            PERFORM 100-START-UP-UPDATE.
279            PERFORM 200-UPDATE-PROCESS UNTIL END-FLAG-MAST = "YES" AND
280                END-FLAG-TRANS = "YES".
281            PERFORM 300-WRAP-UP-UPDATE.
282            STOP RUN.
283
284        100-START-UP-UPDATE.
285      *    INITIALIZE-VARIABLES (WS)
286            PERFORM 105-SORT-FILES.
287            PERFORM 110-OPEN-FILES.
288            PERFORM 120-HEADINGS-UPDATE-RPT.
289            PERFORM 130-READ-OLD-SRT-MASTER.
290            PERFORM 140-READ-SORTED-TRANS.
291
292        105-SORT-FILES.
293            PERFORM 112-SORT-MAST.
294            PERFORM 114-SORT-TRANS.
295
296
297        110-OPEN-FILES.
298            OPEN INPUT   OLD-SORTED-MAST
299                         SORTED-TRANS
300                  OUTPUT NEW-MASTER
301                         UPDATE-RPT
302                         RPT-OF-NEW-RECS.
303
304
305        112-SORT-MAST.
306            SORT WORK-FILE
307                ASCENDING KEY WRK-SSN
308                USING OLD-MASTER
309                GIVING OLD-SORTED-MAST.
310
311        114-SORT-TRANS.
312            SORT WORK-FILE
313                ASCENDING KEY WRK-SSN
314                USING TRANS-FILE
315                GIVING SORTED-TRANS.
316
317        120-HEADINGS-UPDATE-RPT.
318            WRITE UPDATE-RPT-RECORD FROM HEADING1-RPT1 AFTER PAGE.
319            WRITE UPDATE-RPT-RECORD FROM HEADING2-RPT1 AFTER 2.
320            WRITE UPDATE-RPT-RECORD FROM HEADING3-RPT1 AFTER 1.
321
322        130-READ-OLD-SRT-MASTER.
323            READ OLD-SORTED-MAST AT END MOVE "YES" TO END-FLAG-MAST
324                                         MOVE 9999999999 TO MAST-KEY.
325
326        140-READ-SORTED-TRANS.
327            READ SORTED-TRANS AT END MOVE "YES" TO END-FLAG-TRANS
```

**EXHIBIT 12.9** (Cont.)

```
328                                              MOVE 9999999999 TO TRANS-KEY.
329
330          200-UPDATE-PROCESS.
331              IF MAST-KEY < TRANS-KEY
332                  THEN PERFORM 210-COPY-OLD-MAST-TO-NEW-MAST
333                  ELSE IF MAST-KEY = TRANS-KEY
334                          THEN PERFORM 220-CHANGE-OR-DELETE
335                          ELSE IF TRANS-CODE = "A"
336                                  THEN PERFORM 260-ADD-NEW-MASTER
337                                  ELSE PERFORM 270-BAD-TRANS-MESSAGE.
338              MOVE SPACES TO MESSAGE-OUT.
339
340          210-COPY-OLD-MAST-TO-NEW-MAST.
341              MOVE OLD-SORTED-MAST-RECORD TO NEW-MASTER-RECORD.
342              WRITE NEW-MASTER-RECORD.
343              PERFORM 130-READ-OLD-SRT-MASTER.
344
345          220-CHANGE-OR-DELETE.
346              IF TRANS-CODE = "C"
347                  THEN PERFORM 230-CHANGE-REC
348                  ELSE IF TRANS-CODE = "D"
349                          THEN PERFORM 240-DELETE-REC
350                          ELSE IF TRANS-CODE = "A"
351                                  THEN PERFORM 250-DUPLICATE-ADD-MSG
352                                  ELSE MOVE "BAD-CODE" TO MESSAGE-OUT
353                          END-IF
354                  END-IF
355              END-IF
356
357              IF TRANS-CODE = "C" OR TRANS-CODE = "D"
358                  THEN PERFORM 130-READ-OLD-SRT-MASTER
359              END-IF.
360              PERFORM 140-READ-SORTED-TRANS.
361
362          230-CHANGE-REC.
363              MOVE OLD-SORTED-MAST-RECORD TO NEW-MASTER-RECORD.
364              IF NAME-TRANS = SPACES
365                  THEN NEXT SENTENCE
366                  ELSE MOVE NAME-TRANS TO NAME-N-M
367                       MOVE "X" TO NAME-OUT
368              END-IF.
369
370              IF ADDR-TRANS = SPACES
371                  THEN NEXT SENTENCE
372                  ELSE MOVE ADDR-TRANS TO ADDR-N-M
373                       MOVE "X" TO ADDR-OUT
374              END-IF.
375
376              IF BRANCH-TRANS = SPACES
377                  THEN NEXT SENTENCE
378                  ELSE MOVE BRANCH-TRANS TO BRANCH-N-M
379                       MOVE "X" TO BR-OUT
380              END-IF.
381
382              IF DEPT-TRANS = SPACES
383                  THEN NEXT SENTENCE
384                  ELSE MOVE DEPT-TRANS TO DEPT-N-M
385                       MOVE "X" TO DEPT-OUT
386              END-IF.
387
388              IF JOB-TRANS = SPACES
389                  THEN NEXT SENTENCE
390                  ELSE MOVE JOB-TRANS TO JOB-N-M
391                       MOVE "X" TO JOB-OUT
392              END-IF.
393
```

**EXHIBIT 12.9    (Cont.)**

```
394            IF DOE-TRANS = SPACES
395                THEN NEXT SENTENCE
396                ELSE MOVE DOE-TRANS TO DOE-N-M
397                     MOVE "X" TO DOE-OUT
398            END-IF.
399
400            IF YTD-EARN-TRANS-REDF = SPACES
401                THEN NEXT SENTENCE
402                ELSE MOVE YTD-EARN-TRANS TO YTD-EARN-N-M
403                     MOVE "X" TO YTD-OUT
404            END-IF.
405
406            MOVE "X" TO REC-CHNGED-OUT.
407            MOVE TRANS-KEY TO SSN-OUT.
408            WRITE UPDATE-RPT-RECORD FROM UPDATE-LINE.
409            WRITE NEW-MASTER-RECORD.
410
411        240-DELETE-REC.
412            MOVE "X" TO REC-DEL-OUT.
413            MOVE TRANS-KEY TO SSN-OUT.
414            WRITE UPDATE-RPT-RECORD FROM UPDATE-LINE.
415
416        250-DUPLICATE-ADD-MSG.
417            MOVE "RECORD NOT ADDED -- DUPLICATE" TO MESSAGE-OUT.
418            MOVE TRANS-KEY TO SSN-OUT.
419            WRITE UPDATE-RPT-RECORD FROM UPDATE-LINE.
420
421        260-ADD-NEW-MASTER.
422            MOVE SORTED-TRANS-RECORD TO NEW-MASTER-RECORD.
423            WRITE NEW-MASTER-RECORD.
424            MOVE "X" TO ADDED-OUT.
425            MOVE TRANS-KEY TO SSN-OUT.
426            WRITE UPDATE-RPT-RECORD FROM UPDATE-LINE.
427            PERFORM 140-READ-SORTED-TRANS.
428
429        270-BAD-TRANS-MESSAGE.
430            IF TRANS-CODE = "D"
431                THEN MOVE "RECORD NOT DELETED -- MASTER RECORD NOT FOUND"
432                     TO MESSAGE-OUT
433                ELSE IF TRANS-CODE = "C"
434                        THEN MOVE "RECORD NOT CHANGED -- MASTER RECORD NOT
435     -                       " FOUND" TO MESSAGE-OUT
436                        ELSE MOVE "BAD CODE" TO MESSAGE-OUT.
437            MOVE TRANS-KEY TO SSN-OUT.
438            WRITE UPDATE-RPT-RECORD FROM UPDATE-LINE.
439            PERFORM 140-READ-SORTED-TRANS.
440
441        300-WRAP-UP-UPDATE.
442
443            PERFORM 303-SUMMARY-OUTPUT.
444            PERFORM 305-CLOSE-FILES.
445
446        303-SUMMARY-OUTPUT.
447
448            CLOSE NEW-MASTER.
449            OPEN INPUT NEW-MASTER.
450            PERFORM 310-HEADINGS-RPT2.
451            PERFORM 320-READ-NEW-MASTER.
452            PERFORM 330-PRINT-NEW-MASTER-LISTING UNTIL EOF-NEW-FLAG =
453                "YES".
454            MOVE CT TO TOT-CT.
455            WRITE RPT-OF-NEW-RECS-RECORD FROM TOT-LN AFTER 2.
```

**EXHIBIT 12.9** (Cont.)

```
457        305-CLOSE-FILES.
458            CLOSE NEW-MASTER
459                  SORTED-TRANS
460                  OLD-SORTED-MAST
461                  RPT-OF-NEW-RECS
462                  UPDATE-RPT.
463
464        310-HEADINGS-RPT2.
465            WRITE RPT-OF-NEW-RECS-RECORD FROM HEADING1-RPT2 AFTER PAGE.
466            WRITE RPT-OF-NEW-RECS-RECORD FROM HEADING2-RPT2 AFTER 2.
467            MOVE SPACES TO RPT-OF-NEW-RECS-RECORD.
468            WRITE RPT-OF-NEW-RECS-RECORD.
469
470        320-READ-NEW-MASTER.
471            READ NEW-MASTER AT END MOVE "YES" TO EOF-NEW-FLAG.
472
473        330-PRINT-NEW-MASTER-LISTING.
474            MOVE SSN-N-M TO SSN-RPT2.
475            MOVE LAST-N-M TO LAST-RPT2.
476            MOVE BRANCH-N-M TO BRANCH-RPT2.
477            MOVE DEPT-N-M TO DEPT-RPT2.
478            MOVE JOB-N-M TO JOB-RPT2.
479            MOVE STREET-N-M TO STREET-RPT2.
480            MOVE MONTH-N-M TO MONTH-RPT2.
481            MOVE DAY-N-M TO DAY-RPT2.
482            MOVE YEAR-N-M TO YEAR-RPT2.
483            MOVE STATE-N-M TO STATE-RPT2.
484            WRITE RPT-OF-NEW-RECS-RECORD FROM RPT2-LINE.
485            ADD 1 TO CT.
486            PERFORM 320-READ-NEW-MASTER.
```

```
          ACME UPDATE OF MASTER PAYFILE

SN        RECORD    RECORD    RECORD       **FIELD CHANGES**
          ADDED     DELETED   CHANGED   NM  ADDR BR   DEP    JOB     DOE YTD
90909090    RECORD NOT CHANGED -- MASTER RECORD NOT FOUND
01010101    RECORD NOT ADDED -- DUPLICATE
01022033              X
12121212                        X              X    X      X
56741129                        X              X
88888888    X
11111111    RECORD NOT DELETED -- MASTER RECORD NOT FOUND
99199923    X
```

**EXHIBIT 12.9** (Cont.)

```
          SEQUENTIAL LISTING OF UPDATED MASTER FILE

  SN         NAME       BRANCH DEPT   JOB   ADDRESS        DOE      STATE

  01010101   JOHNSON     001   001    09    WEST GREEN  09/23/45    TX
  12121212   EVANS       002   003    07    PLEASANT    11/11/57    TX
  22222222   BAKER       001   003    03    CEDAR SPR   05/12/65    TX
  34354456   THOMPSON    002   003    07    S SUN VLY   05/06/47    TX
  33333333   DICKSON     002   001    05    CEDAR       10/10/67    TX
  93838444   JOHNSTON    003   003    05    BUMPY       06/04/60    TX
  04040404   DONALD      003   004    10    71555J4444  06/06/47    TX
  44444444   CARLTON     002   001    04    PINE        09/13/55    TX
  56741129   RUSSELL     001   001    01    BUS.BLDG    08/19/45    TX
  84848484   ROBERTS     003   002    06    CANYON      06/07/59    TX
  55555555   GREEN       002   002    07    LILLIAN     11/23/67    TX
  55556666   JOHNSON     003   001    09    GREEN       09/13/73    TX
  66666666   HILLARD     002   002    08    VANDERBILT  09/12/72    TX
  76767676   NORTON      003   001    05    DODGE       05/05/59    TX
  67676766   MILLER      003   001    05    BUICK       05/07/48    TX
  77777777   KRAMER      003   001    10    COLLEGE     09/08/67    TX
  88888888   ZIMMERMAN   001   001    06    PARROT      08/08/76    TX
  99199923   DONALDSON   002   002    05    MONROE      09/09/75    TX

  NUMBER OF RECORDS =   18
```

**EXHIBIT 12.10 QUICKBASIC Program and Output for Application 12.1 (Sequential File Update)**

```
'**********************************************************************
'*                         PROGRAM IDENTIFICATION                     *
'**********************************************************************
' PROGRAM NAME: CH12NEW.BAS                                           *
'**********************************************************************
' REMARKS:   THIS PROGRAM UPDATES A SEQUENTIAL MASTER PAY
'            FILE FROM A TRANSACTION UPDATE FILE.  A NEW
'            MASTER PAY FILE IS PRODUCED.  ADDING, DELETING,
'            AND CHANGING OF MASTER RECORDS ARE PROVIDED FOR.
'            AN UPDATE REPORT IS GENERATED THAT INDICATES WHICH
'            UPDATE OPERATION HAS OCCURED FOR A SPECIFIC MASTER
'            RECORD.
'**********************************************************************
'*                       MAIN-LINE-SEQ-UPDATE                         *
'**********************************************************************

MAIN.LINE:

    GOSUB START.UP.UPDATE                   ' PERFORM START-UP-UPDATE
    DO UNTIL END.FLAG.MAST$ = "YES" AND END.FLAG.TRANS$ = "YES"
        GOSUB UPDATE.PROCESS                '* PERFORM UPDATE-PROCESS

    LOOP
    GOSUB WRAP.UP.UPDATE                    '* PERFORM WRAP-UP-UPDATE
    END

        '**********************************************************************
        '*                        START-UP-UPDATE                            *
        '**********************************************************************

START.UP.UPDATE:

    GOSUB INITIALIZE
    GOSUB SORT.FILES
    GOSUB OPEN.FILES
    GOSUB HEADINGS.UPDATE.RPT               '* PERFORM HEADINGS-UPDATE-RPT
    GOSUB READ.OLD.SRT.MASTER               '* PERFORM READ-OLD-SRT-MASTER
    GOSUB READ.SORTED.TRANS                 '* PERFORM READ-SORTED-TRANS
    RETURN
        '**********************************************************************
        '*                           INITIALIZE                              *
        '**********************************************************************
INITIALIZE:

    UPDATE.LINE$ = "\        \ \ \      \ \      \ \     \ \ \ \\\ \ \   \ \   \ \ \ \"
    ERROR.LINE$ = "\        \ \                                              \"
    RPT.OF.NEW.RECS$ = "\        \\        \ ###  ###     ## \        \   \     \ \ \"
    END.FLAG.MAST$ = "NO": END.FLAG.TRANS$ = "NO": DONE.FLAG$ = "NO"
    RETURN
```

**EXHIBIT 12.10    (Cont.)**

```
'*********************************************************************
'*                           SORT-FILES                          *
'*********************************************************************

SORT.FILES:

    GOSUB SORT.MAST                    '* PERFORM SORT-MAST
    GOSUB SORT.TRANS                   '* PERFORM SORT-TRANS
    RETURN

OPEN.FILES:

    OPEN "I", #1, "CH12C.DAT":    '* OPEN SORTED MASTER FILE
    OPEN "I", #2, "CH12D.DAT":    '* OPEN SORTED TRANS FILE
    OPEN "O", #3, "CH12E.DAT":    '* OPEN NEW MASTER FILE
    RETURN




    '*********************************************************************
    '*                           SORT-MAST                          *
    '*********************************************************************

SORT.MAST:

    SHELL "SORT < CH12A.DAT > CH12C.DAT"
    RETURN


    '*****************************************************************
    '*                     SORT-TRANS                          *
    '*****************************************************************

SORT.TRANS:

    SHELL "SORT < CH12B.DAT > CH12D.DAT"
    RETURN


    '*****************************************************************
    '*                   HEADINGS-UPDATE-RPT                     *
    '*****************************************************************

HEADINGS.UPDATE.RPT:

    LPRINT CHR$(12)
    LPRINT TAB(9); "ACME UPDATE OF MASTER PAYFILE"
    LPRINT
    LPRINT "SSN        RECORD    RECORD    RECORD    **FIELD CHANGES**"
    LPRINT "           ADDED     DELETED   CHANGED   NM  ADDR BR  DEP  JOB   DOE YTD"
    LPRINT
    RETURN
```

**EXHIBIT 12.10    (Cont.)**

```
'***********************************************************************
'*                     READ-OLD-SRT-MASTER                            *
'***********************************************************************

READ.OLD.SRT.MASTER:

    INPUT #1, MAST.KEY$, OS.LAST$, OS.FIRST$, OS.MI$, OS.BRANCH, OS.DEPT, OS.JC, OS.STREET$, OS.CITY$, OS.STATE$, OS.ZIP, OS.DOE$, OS.YTD
    IF OS.LAST$ = "EOF" THEN
         END.FLAG.MAST$ = "YES"
         MAST.KEY$ = "9999999999"
    END IF
    RETURN


    '***********************************************************************
    '*                     READ-SORTED-TRANS                              *
    '***********************************************************************

READ.SORTED.TRANS:

    INPUT #2, TRANS.KEY$, TR.LAST$, TR.FIRST$, TR.MI$, TR.BRANCH, TR.DEPT, TR.JC, TR.STREET$, TR.CITY$, TR.STATE$, TR.ZIP, TR.DOE$, TR.YTD, TRANS.CODE$
    IF TR.LAST$ = "EOF" THEN
        END.FLAG.TRANS$ = "YES"
        TRANS.KEY$ = "9999999999"
    END IF
    RETURN



    '***********************************************************************
    '*                       UPDATE-PROCESS                               *
    '***********************************************************************

UPDATE.PROCESS:

    IF MAST.KEY$ < TRANS.KEY$ THEN
         GOSUB COPY.OLD.MAST.TO.NEW.MAST
    ELSE
       IF MAST.KEY$ = TRANS.KEY$ THEN
            GOSUB CHANGE.OR.DELETE
       ELSE
           IF TRANS.CODE$ = "A" THEN
                GOSUB ADD.NEW.MASTER
           ELSE
                GOSUB BAD.TRANS.MESSAGE
           END IF
       END IF
    END IF
    RETURN



    '***********************************************************************
    '*                     COPY-OLD-MAST-TO-NEW-MAST                      *
    '***********************************************************************
COPY.OLD.MAST.TO.NEW.MAST:

    SSN.N.M$ = MAST.KEY$
    LAST.N.M$ = OS.LAST$
    FIRST.N.M$ = OS.FIRST$
    MI.N.M$ = OS.MI$
    BRANCH.N.M = OS.BRANCH
    DEPT.N.M = OS.DEPT
    JOB.N.M = OS.JC
    STREET.N.M$ = OS.STREET$
    CITY.N.M$ = OS.CITY$
    STATE.N.M$ = OS.STATE$
    ZIP.N.M = OS.ZIP
    DOE.N.M$ = OS.DOE$
    YTD.N.M = OS.YTD
    WRITE #3, SSN.N.M$, LAST.N.M$, FIRST.N.M$, MI.N.M$, BRANCH.N.M, DEPT.N.M, JOB.N.M, STREET.N.M$, CITY.N.M$, STATE.N.M$, ZIP.N.M, DOE.N.M$, YTD.N.M
    GOSUB READ.OLD.SRT.MASTER              ' PERFORM READ-OLD-SRT-MASTER     *
    RETURN
```

**EXHIBIT 12.10    (Cont.)**

```
      '************************************************************************
      '*                         CHANGE-OR-DELETE                            *
      '************************************************************************
CHANGE.OR.DELETE:
     IF TRANS.CODE$ = "C" THEN
         GOSUB CHANGE.REC
     ELSE
        IF TRANS.CODE$ = "D" THEN
            GOSUB DELETE.REC
        ELSE
           IF TRANS.CODE$ = "A" THEN
                GOSUB DUPLICATE.ADD.MSG
           ELSE
                MESSAGE.OUT$ = "BAD-CODE"
           END IF
        END IF
     END IF
     IF TRANS.CODE$ = "C" OR TRANS.CODE$ = "D" THEN
         GOSUB READ.OLD.SRT.MASTER
     END IF
     GOSUB READ.SORTED.TRANS              '* PERFORM READ-SORTED-TRANS
     RETURN




      '************************************************************************
      '*                            CHANGE-REC                               *
      '************************************************************************
 CHANGE.REC:
      SSN.N.M$ = MAST.KEY$
      LAST.N.M$ = OS.LAST$
      FIRST.N.M$ = OS.FIRST$
      MI.N.M$ = OS.MI$
      BRANCH.N.M = OS.BRANCH
      DEPT.N.M = OS.DEPT
      JOB.N.M = OS.JC
      STREET.N.M$ = OS.STREET$
      CITY.N.M$ = OS.CITY$
      STATE.N.M$ = OS.STATE$
      ZIP.N.M = OS.ZIP
      DOE.N.M$ = OS.DOE$

      YTD.N.M = OS.YTD
      IF TR.LAST$ = "" THEN
          LAST.N.M$ = LAST.N.M$
      ELSE
          LAST.N.M$ = TR.LAST$
          NAME.OUT$ = "X"
      END IF

      IF TR.FIRST$ = "" THEN
          FIRST.N.M$ = FIRST.N.M$
      ELSE
          FIRST.N.M$ = TR.FIRST$
          NAME.OUT$ = "X"
      END IF
```

**EXHIBIT 12.10** (Cont.)

```
IF TR.MI$ = "" THEN
    MI.N.M$ = MI.N.M$
ELSE
    MI.N.M$ = TR.MI$
    NAME.OUT$ = "X"
END IF

IF TR.STREET$ = "" THEN
    STREET.N.M$ = STREET.N.M$
ELSE STREET.N.M$ = TR.STREET$
    ADDR.OUT$ = "X"
END IF

IF TR.CITY$ = "" THEN
    CITY.N.M$ = CITY.N.M$
ELSE
    CITY.N.M$ = TR.CITY$
    ADDR.OUT$ = "X"
END IF

IF TR.STATE$ = "" THEN
    STATE.N.M$ = STATE.N.M$
ELSE
    STATE.N.M$ = TR.STATE$
    ADDR.OUT$ = "X"
END IF

IF TR.ZIP = O THEN
    ZIP.N.M = ZIP.N.M
ELSE
    ZIP.N.M = TR.ZIP
    ADDR.OUT$ = "X"
END IF

IF TR.BRANCH = O THEN
    BRANCH.N.M = BRANCH.N.M
ELSE
    BRANCH.N.M = TR.BRANCH
    BR.OUT$ = "X"
END IF

IF TR.DEPT = O THEN
    DEPT.N.M = DEPT.N.M
ELSE
    DEPT.N.M = TR.DEPT
    DEPT.OUT$ = "X"
END IF

IF TR.JC = O THEN
    JOB.N.M = JOB.N.M
ELSE
    JOB.N.M = TR.JC
```

**EXHIBIT 12.10** (Cont.)

```
            JOB.OUT$ = "X"
    END IF

    IF TR.DOE$ = "" THEN
        DOE.N.M$ = DOE.N.M$
    ELSE
        DOE.N.M$ = TR.DOE$
        DOE.OUT$ = "X"
    END IF

    IF TR.YTD = 0 THEN
        YTD.N.M = YTD.N.M
    ELSE
        YTD.N.M = TR.YTD
        YTD.OUT$ = "X"
    END IF

    REC.CHNGED.OUT$ = "X"
    SSN.OUT$ = TRANS.KEY$
    LPRINT USING UPDATE.LINE$; SSN.OUT$; ADDED.OUT$; REC.DEL.OUT$; REC.CHNGED.OUT$; NAME.OUT$; ADDR.OUT$; BR.OUT$; DEPT.OUT$; JOB.OUT$; DOE.OUT$; YTD.OUT$
    WRITE #3, SSN.N.M$, LAST.N.M$, FIRST.N.M$, MI.N.M$, BRANCH.N.M, DEPT.N.M, JOB.N.M, STREET.N.M$, CITY.N.M$, STATE.N.M$, ZIP.N.M, DOE.N.M$, YTD.N.M
    SSN.OUT$ = "": ADDED.OUT$ = "": REC.DEL.OUT$ = "": REC.CHNGED.OUT$ = "": NAME.OUT$ = "": ADDR.OUT$ = "": BR.OUT$ = "": DEPT.OUT$ = "": JOB.OUT$ = "": DOE.OUT$ = "": YTD.OU
    RETURN

        '******************************************************************
        '                       DELETE-REC                   *
        '******************************************************************
DELETE.REC:

    REC.DEL.OUT$ = "X"
    SSN.OUT$ = TRANS.KEY$
    LPRINT USING UPDATE.LINE$; SSN.OUT$; ADDED.OUT$; REC.DEL.OUT$; REC.CHNGED.OUT$; NAME.OUT$; ADDR.OUT$; BR.OUT$; DEPT.OUT$; JOB.OUT$; DOE.OUT$; YTD.OUT$
    SSN.OUT$ = "": ADDED.OUT$ = "": REC.DEL.OUT$ = "": REC.CHNGED.OUT$ = "": NAME.OUT$ = "": ADDR.OUT$ = "": BR.OUT$ = "": DEPT.OUT$ = "": JOB.OUT$ = "": DOE.OUT$ = "": YTD.OU
    RETURN

        '******************************************************************
        '*                  DUPLICATE-ADD-MSG                 *
        '******************************************************************

DUPLICATE.ADD.MSG:
    SSN.OUT$ = TRANS.KEY$
    MESSAGE.OUT$ = "RECORD NOT ADDED -- DUPLICATE"
    LPRINT USING ERROR.LINE$; TRANS.KEY$; MESSAGE.OUT$
    RETURN




        '******************************************************************
        '*                  ADD-NEW-MASTER                    *
        '******************************************************************
ADD.NEW.MASTER:
    SSN.OUT$ = TRANS.KEY$
    SSN.N.M$ = TRANS.KEY$
    LAST.N.M$ = TR.LAST$
    FIRST.N.M$ = TR.FIRST$
    MI.N.M$ = TR.MI$
    BRANCH.N.M = TR.BRANCH
    DEPT.N.M = TR.DEPT
    JOB.N.M = TR.JC
    STREET.N.M$ = TR.STREET$
    CITY.N.M$ = TR.CITY$
    STATE.N.M$ = TR.STATE$
    ZIP.N.M = TR.ZIP
    DOE.N.M$ = TR.DOE$
    YTD.N.M = TR.YTD
    WRITE #3, SSN.N.M$, LAST.N.M$, FIRST.N.M$, MI.N.M$, BRANCH.N.M, DEPT.N.M, JOB.N.M, STREET.N.M$, CITY.N.M$, STATE.N.M$, ZIP.N.M, DOE.N.M$, YTD.N.M
    ADDED.OUT$ = "X"
    LPRINT USING UPDATE.LINE$; SSN.OUT$; ADDED.OUT$; REC.DEL.OUT$; REC.CHNGED.OUT$; NAME.OUT$; ADDR.OUT$; BR.OUT$; DEPT.OUT$; JOB.OUT$; DOE.OUT$; YTD.OUT$
    SSN.OUT$ = "": ADDED.OUT$ = "": REC.DEL.OUT$ = "": REC.CHNGED.OUT$ = "": NAME.OUT$ = "": ADDR.OUT$ = "": BR.OUT$ = "": DEPT.OUT$ = "": JOB.OUT$ = "": DOE.OUT$ = "": YTD.OU
    GOSUB READ.SORTED.TRANS          ' PERFORM READ-SORTED-TRANS
    RETURN

        '******************************************************************
        '*                  BAD-TRANS-MESSAGE                 *
        '******************************************************************

BAD.TRANS.MESSAGE:

    IF TRANS.CODE$ = "D" THEN
        MESSAGE.OUT$ = "RECORD NOT DELETED -- MASTER RECORD NOT FOUND"
    ELSE
        IF TRANS.CODE$ = "C" THEN
            MESSAGE.OUT$ = "RECORD NOT CHANGED -- MASTER RECORD NOT FOUND"
        ELSE MESSAGE.OUT$ = "BAD CODE"
        END IF
    END IF
    SSN.OUT$ = TRANS.KEY$
    LPRINT USING ERROR.LINE$; TRANS.KEY$; MESSAGE.OUT$
    GOSUB READ.SORTED.TRANS       '* PERFORM READ-SORTED-TRANS
    RETURN
```

**EXHIBIT 12.10    (Cont.)**

```
'**********************************************************************
'*                           WRAP-UP                                  *
'**********************************************************************
WRAP.UP.UPDATE:
    GOSUB SUMMARY.OUTPUT
    GOSUB CLOSE.FILES
    RETURN


SUMMARY.OUTPUT:
    CLOSE #3
    OPEN "I", #3, "CH12E.DAT":                '* OPEN NEW MASTER FILE
    GOSUB HEADINGS.RPT2                        '* PERFORM HEADINGS-RPT2
    DO UNTIL END.NEW.FLAG$ = "YES"
         GOSUB PRINT.NEW.MASTER.LISTING    '* PERFORM PRINT-NEW-MASTER-LISTING :
    LOOP

    LPRINT
    LPRINT "NUMBER OF RECORDS = "; CT


CLOSE.FILES:

    CLOSE #1
    CLOSE #2
    CLOSE #3
    RETURN


    '**********************************************************************
    '*                       HEADINGS-RPT2                                *
    '**********************************************************************

HEADINGS.RPT2:

    LPRINT CHR$(12)
    LPRINT TAB(11); "SEQUENTIAL LISTING OF UPDATED MASTER FILE"
    LPRINT
    LPRINT "SSN          NAME        BRANCH DEPT   JOB  ADDRESS        DOE    STATE"
    RETURN
```

**EXHIBIT 12.10 (Cont.)**

```
'*****************************************************************
'*                      READ-NEW-MASTER                         *
'*****************************************************************
READ.NEW.MASTER:
    INPUT #3, SSN.N.M$, LAST.N.M$, FIRST.N.M$, MI.N.M$, BRANCH.N.M, DEPT.N.M, JOB.N.M, STREET.N.M$, CITY.N.M$, STATE.N.M$, ZIP.N.M, DOE.N.M$, YTD.N.M
    IF EOF(3) THEN
        END.NEW.FLAG$ = "YES"
    END IF
    RETURN


'*****************************************************************
'*                  PRINT-NEW-MASTER-LISTING                    *
'*****************************************************************

PRINT.NEW.MASTER.LISTING:

    GOSUB READ.NEW.MASTER                 'PERFORM READ-NEW-MASTER
    LPRINT USING RPT.OF.NEW.RECS$; SSN.N.M$; LAST.N.M$; BRANCH.N.M; DEPT.N.M; JOB.N.M; STREET.N.M$; DOE.N.M$; STATE.N.M$
    CT = CT + 1
    RETURN
```

```
        ACME UPDATE OF MASTER PAYFILE


SSN         RECORD    RECORD    RECORD    **FIELD CHANGES**
            ADDED     DELETED   CHANGED   NM  ADDR BR  DEP  JOB   DOE YTD


090909090   RECORD NOT CHANGED -- MASTER RECORD NOT FOUND
101010101   RECORD NOT ADDED -- DUPLICATE
101022033             X
212121212                       X         X        X    X
456741129                       X         X
888888888   X
911111111   RECORD NOT DELETED -- MASTER RECORD NOT FOUND
999199923   X
```

```
            SEQUENTIAL LISTING OF UPDATED MASTER FILE


        SSN          NAME        BRANCH DEPT  JOB  ADDRESS        DOE     STATE
        101010101    JOHNSON        1     1    9   WEST GREEN     092345  TX
        212121212    EVANS          2     3    7   PLEASANT       111157  TX
        222222222    BAKER          1     3    3   CEDAR SPR      051265  TX
        234354456    THOMPSON       2     3    7   S SUN VLY      050647  TX
        333333333    DICKSON        2     1    5   CEDAR          101067  TX
        393838444    JOHNSTON       3     3    5   BUMPY          060460  TX
        404040404    DONALD         3     4   10   71555J4444     060647  TX
        444444444    CARLTON        2     1    4   PINE           091355  TX
        456741129    RUSSELL        1     1    1   BUS.BLDG       081945  TX
        484848484    ROBERTS        3     2    6   CANYON         060769  TX
        555555555    GREEN          2     2    7   LILLIAN        112367  TX
        555556666    JOHNSON        3     1    9   GREEN          091373  TX
        666666666    HILLARD        2     2    8   VANDERBILT     091272  TX
        676767676    NORTON         3     1    5   DODGE          050559  TX
        767676766    MILLER         3     1    5   BUICK          050748  TX
        777777777    KRAMER         3     1   10   COLLEGE        090867  TX
        888888888    ZIMMERMAN      1     1    6   PARROT         080876  TX
        999199923    DONALDSON      2     2    5   MONORE         090975  TX


        NUMBER OF RECORDS =  18
```

## SUMMARY

The very heart of data processing focuses on file maintenance. Selection of the appropriate file maintenance technique is critical if the data processing function is to succeed. Three basic file organization methods that are normally considered when establishing file maintenance and processing procedures are 1) sequential access, (2) indexed, and (3) random. For updating large numbers of records in a batch environment, sequential access is normally the most appropriate. But when frequent and interactive access is needed within a file, then the sequential access method is inefficient. Either the random or the indexed technique would be more appropriate.

Updating is the process of bringing a file up to date by (1) adding new records, (2) deleting records, and/or (3) changing the contents of fields in existing records. File activity refers to the ratio of transaction records to master records; file volatility is the size of additions and deletions to the size of the file. These factors should be considered when choosing an appropriate file maintenance technique.

To update a file sequentially, a transaction file is needed that contains the necessary data to affect the content of the master record. To change or delete a master record, the transaction key from the transaction record must match the record key from the master record. To add a record to the master file, the transaction record must contain the precise data to be added, and the transaction key should be less than the master key. A transaction identification code informs the program that a certain kind of update operation is to be performed. The most common procedure for performing sequential file update creates a new sequential master file as a result of updating. This update process essentially provides for four major activities: (1) changing the old master file and writing newly altered data into a new master record, (2) copying unaffected old master records into the new master file, (3) deleting records, and (4) adding new ones.

## VOCABULARY

| | |
|---|---|
| sequential file | file volatility |
| indexed file | record key |
| random (direct) file | transaction file |
| updating | transaction key |
| backup | transaction update |
| file activity | identification code |

## EXERCISES/QUESTIONS

1. What are the advantages of a sequential file update? The limitations?

2. Explain the process of updating a sequential file using a transaction file and a master file when a new master file is created as a result of the update.

3. What is the purpose of the transaction key? The record key? The transaction code?

4. Explain the general backup operation in data processing.

5. In the update process, what happens if the master key is less than the transaction key? If the master key is equal to the transaction key? If the master key is greater than the transaction key?

## PROBLEMS

**12–1.** Irwin Electronics Inc. keeps a sequential customer file. A file maintenance program is needed to add new customers, delete inactive customers, and change various fields on the customer record.

The program should produce two reports. The first of the reports is a list of the various updates, and the second is a listing of the updated master file. The update report should allow easy reference to the kind of update operation that occurred and the respective field(s) affected by the update. Design the necessary print charts, hierarchy chart, structured flowchart, and pseudocode for the solution to this problem.

The master and transaction record layouts are shown in Figure 12.5.

**12–2.** Alter the program in problem 12–1 so that it will accommodate a multiple number of transaction records per master. This means that a single update operation to a master record might involve more than one transaction record. For instance, one transaction record might change a master record while a subsequent transaction record with the same key made delete the record. The program theoretically should permit an add, a change, and a subsequent delete. This means that the transaction records must also be in order by transaction code as well as by SSN. How can this be handled? Assume that the record format for this problem includes the transaction key adjacent to the transaction key (that is, in col 11). Then this 11-byte field can be sorted as one. The result will be that all records with the same SSN will be in order by transaction code. Now, the transactions with an A will precede transactions with a C and transactions with a C will precede transactions with a D. The master file format must also be adjusted to allow the TR-code in the eleventh byte (even though it is left blank). The logic for this problem is straightforward in most places but gets tricky in others. This is an advanced application for the student who likes a challenge.

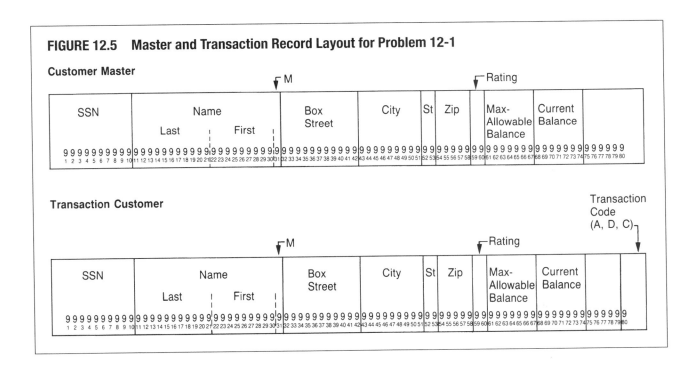

FIGURE 12.5 Master and Transaction Record Layout for Problem 12-1

# 13

# Interactive Programming and File Maintenance

## OBJECTIVES

After completing this chapter, the student will be able to:

1. Differentiate between batch and interactive processing involving ordered files.

2. List the advantages of interactive processing.

3. List the kinds of files used in interactive file maintenance.

4. Explain the concept of menu-driven systems.

5. List three important considerations in the design of an interactive system.

6. List the three nonsequential file organization methods normally used with interactive systems and discuss each method.

7. Draw the hierarchy chart and structured program flowchart for an interactive file maintenance system.

## METHODS OF PROCESSING

Chapter 10 offered a basic introduction to interactive programming and the use of sequential files. This chapter discusses the processing considerations and program logic surrounding interactive processing and file maintenance of indexed files. In review, to help you visualize the difference between batch and interactive processing, the following overview of the two methods is presented.

### Batch Processing

Chapters 2 through 9 and 11 through 12 dealt with computer applications that utilized batch processing. Chapter 1 defined batch processing as the process of collecting records over a period of time to create a file that is processed periodically. Chapter 12 showed the update of a sequential file with transaction data collected over time. Each transaction becomes a transaction *record*; a collection of transaction records becomes a transaction file. At regular intervals, the transaction file is read, one record at a time, in order to update the master file in specific ways. This technique is often the most effective one to use when a file needs periodic update and when the ratio of transactions to master records is high.

### Interactive Processing

As previously discussed in Chapter 10, with interactive (or on-line) processing, the computer has constant access to the file and allows a conversational dialogue between the user and the computer program at all times. The user is constantly connected with the computer and the interactive program that is monitoring the dialogue and can access specific files via the computer terminal. This dialogue is often presented in the form of menus and submenus on the terminal screen. These menus offer the user a choice of files to update. They also present alternative kinds of update operations. The use of menus and submenus is discussed in greater detail later. Normally, interactive processing and file update are used for applications requiring frequent access to current data, such as airline reservation systems, perpetual inventory systems, automatic customer order entry systems, and financial and marketing systems—to name a few.

## Interactive vs. Batch Processing

In practically every major computer application today, both batch and interactive processing play important roles. Few systems exist that use only one or the other of the processing modes. Especially in larger-scale processing environments, interactive processing occurs while batch processing is also in progress. Since interactive systems utilize so many of the computer's resources and depend on the human element for ongoing data collection, file update, and periodic inquiry, the interactive system is generally utilized during the business operation. Batch systems run predominantly when the business is not open, when human intervention is minimal. Interactive methods are especially suitable for:

1. Entering small amounts of data in the computer.
2. Making frequent inquiries about the status of certain records.
3. Making updates to a small number of records.
4. Information retrieval of records that satisfy some criteria of selection.

Sometimes batch systems serve the purpose of the system much better. Situations where batch processing may be preferred include:

1. Generating formal business reports with large numbers of records.
2. Printing business documents such as payroll registers and paychecks.
3. Printing summary reports.
4. Printing bills to customers.
5. Backing up computer files.
6. Making a large number of updates to a file within a short span of time.

## Advantages and Disadvantages of Interactive systems

In this chapter, the payroll system example similar to Chapter 12 becomes Application 13-1. If you compare the design of this payroll system file maintenance with the one from Chapter 12, you will observe several definite advantages of interactive file maintenance. Here are some of those *advantages:*

1. A drastic reduction in paperwork often results, since there is no need for the various documents associated with data entry and record update that are associated with batch update.
2. Selective record inquiry can eliminate piles of batch reports.
3. Menu-driven update provides an almost foolproof method for making changes to files. Errors often occur when update is handled in a batch mode, since an operator is concerned with entering data in specific positions of the record; whereas with interactive update, the prompt normally highlights the area in which the data is to be entered.
4. An important advantage of an interactive system is that the user is often able to understand the system better than the same system handled in batch mode. In batch systems, users are often baffled by data processing terms such as "data validation" and "file sorting." All the functions of data processing become transparent to the user in an interactive mode.
5. Since files are affected immediately, the data produced is more useful. Managers are able to use timely data to make decisions.

While users of information systems usually agree that an interactive design is generally better, the method is not without drawbacks. Here are some commonly identified *disadvantages* of interactive systems:

1. They tend to be more expensive since they normally require expensive communications equipment, such as computer terminals, and skilled personnel, such as programmers adept at interactive program design.
2. Interactive systems are more difficult to write and therefore require more software development time than batch systems do.
3. The computer must always be available to accept incoming data.
4. For frequent, large update operations in a multi-user environment, interactive systems are often slow.

## Kinds of Files in an Interactive System

The primary basis of all business decisions is the information derived from a computer file or data base. Providing accurate and up-to-date information to management in an interactive mode often requires many files.

**Master File.** A master file contains records of relatively permanent information about a certain entity. A master payroll record contains fields that are essential to the creation of payroll documents such as paychecks, payroll registers, and W-2 forms. The concept of the master file here is no different from that in Chapter 12. Later, in the discussion about file organization methods, the master file will be organized so that faster access can be made to specific records.

**Audit-Trail file.** An **audit-trail file** consists of records that represent various changes, additions, and deletions made to the master file from a terminal in an interactive mode. Without an audit-trail file, there would be no means of determining who made a transaction, when the transaction was made, or what field was affected. This file serves as a trace of the actual dialogue between user and computer. Preserving the history of this dialogue is essential to protect file security and file integrity.

**Transaction Files.** Sometimes interactive computer applications require that a sequential transaction file be created as output from the user's responses. The resultant sequential transaction file then becomes the input to a batch processing update operation. A formal transaction file is not illustrated in this chapter. Instead, this text focuses on the user response in interactive dialogue with the computer program.

**Backup Files.** Without an adequate file backup system, the security of the computer system and integrity of the various files would certainly be at risk. The file backup procedure could be handled very easily as a choice in the main menu of a file maintenance system. The user could select the FILE BACKUP option from the menu, and the file would be copied to a backup file. This would propagate subsequent backups to father and grandfather files to complete the backup procedure.

## Menu-Driven Interactive File Maintenance

**Main Menus and Subordinate Menus.** The vast majority of interactive systems use **menu-driven dialogue.** This hierarchical approach to interactive dialogue allows the user great flexibility while, on the other hand, harnessing him or her to the program's rules for accessing files and programs. The main program-processing menu shows the computer programs or program modules available to be run. The user has a multiple choice of functions that can be performed. Figure 13.1 illustrates a typical program-processing main menu for an interactive file maintenance system. The title of the main menu is PAYROLL FILE MAINTENANCE.

Once the user selects a main option from the **main menu,** the program invokes the appropriate program module or subroutine that carries out that particular function. The second-level module presents the user with a **subordinate menu.** For example, if the user responds with a 2 in the main menu, the UPDATE program prompts the user with a subordinate menu. Figure 13.2 depicts the options for file update. The user's choice of one of the options given in the second-level subordinate menu will trigger the invoking of a module that performs the respective function. For example, if the user chooses 1 (CHANGE A PAYROLL RECORD), program linkage is gained at a submodule that presents a third-level submenu. This submenu will allow the user to return to the next higher menu.

Figure 13.3 (panel A) shows such a menu screen. In some systems, especially in those used extensively by inexperienced data entry users, the menu allows a user to change his or her mind and abort the dialogue if he or she did not mean to press a certain key. If no "abort" provision is coded into the menu, the user might have to make some change to a file just to get back to the previous menu. While abort options are often a nuisance for the experienced file maintenance user, the technique avoids an unnecessary system failure because a panic-stricken, inexperienced user indiscriminately presses keys in an attempt to escape from the system. The option allows a user either to go ahead with the change operation or to return to the update menu (that is, choice 2). An option, or choice, of 2 allows the user to exit the process altogether. If the user chooses 1, then panel B of Figure 13.3 prompts the user for the SSN of the record to be changed. For example, the user might key in 444555666. Figure 13.4 illustrates the next stage of the CHANGE menu. Here the user is prompted with the statement SELECT THE FIELD YOU WISH TO CHANGE. A series of options are then shown representing the various fields in the record. If the user responds with a 1, the screen reads ENTER LAST NAME _____ (Figure 13.5). Once the user keys in the new name, then program control passes to the previous menu

(Figure 13.4). The user can change as many fields as necessary before returning to the UPDATE menu.

At every hierarchical level of the various menus, one of the choices allows a way to exit from the module and return to the invoking module. Every submenu should include one option for a return to the previous higher-level menu; and the main menu always provides for an exit to the operating system itself, which terminates the interactive dialogue entirely.

## User Prompts and Responses

**Provisions.** When presenting the user with a prompt in the form of a menu, the programmer should provide:

1. A major heading that clearly describes the function of the processing program.

2. Clear concise options. Use as few words as possible to describe the function, but do not sacrifice clarity for brevity.
3. A choice that allows escape from the module back to the immediate calling module.
4. Numeric options (1, 2, 3, 4, 5, etc.). Avoid using alphabetic options such as I, C, U, H, Q.
5. A program that traps any errors keyed in by the user and requires the user to rekey the data. This technique of requiring the user to reenter the data until the program recognizes it as good data utilizes what are often called *validation loops* or *error traps*. The technique repeatedly presents the user with the same menu and checks his or her responses until a given response is valid.

**FIGURE 13.1    Main Program Processing Menu**

```
            PAYROLL FILE MAINTENANCE
                   MAIN MENU



     1.....ADD NEW RECORDS TO PAYROLL FILE
     2.....UPDATE PAYROLL FILE
     3.....INQUIRY
     4.....HELP
     5.....END FILE MAINTENANCE SESSION
```

**FIGURE 13.2    Update of Payroll File Menu**

```
            UPDATE MENU (PAYROLL FILE)



       1.....CHANGE A PAYROLL RECORD
       2.....DELETE A PAYROLL RECORD
       3.....RETURN TO MAIN MENU
```

## Data Validation Loops / Error Traps

**Data validation loops (error traps)** are extremely important; they ensure that the user enters only valid data. They are the only means of validity checking in an interactive environment. In a batch processing environment, a built-in data validity checking program or an independent edit program can be written to eliminate invalid records and the subsequent printing of messages on exception reports (see Chapter 5). However, since the responses in an interactive environment are on-line, the validity of the fields cannot be tested later. Instead, *they must be tested for validity as they are keyed.* If the field is determined to be invalid, then the *menu prompt is presented again,* and the user is asked to reenter the field. Of course, this process is repeated until the user gives a valid response.

## Response Time

One of the main parameters in the design of interactive systems is an acceptable **response time**—the time the system takes to respond to a given input. In real-time systems, it is critical that both the prompt by the program and the ensuing user response be accomplished within a time frame that allows the data to be processed fast enough for results to affect the process. This is referred to as *real time.* For example, consider a simple inquiry such as one concerning the status of an airline flight. A prospective passenger asks for an aisle seat in the nonsmoking section. A quick computer response is needed if the transaction is to occur. If the response is too slow, the prospective passenger may decide to check with another airline instead! Response time is especially critical in multi-user environments. More than two or three seconds is usually unacceptable. A slow response to an inquiry at just one terminal may shut down all the others that need access to the same record.

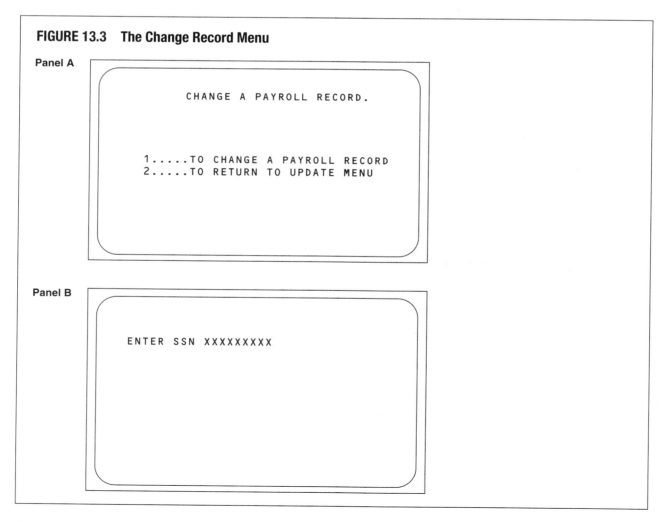

**FIGURE 13.3   The Change Record Menu**

Panel A

```
            CHANGE A PAYROLL RECORD.



    1......TO CHANGE A PAYROLL RECORD
    2......TO RETURN TO UPDATE MENU
```

Panel B

```
    ENTER SSN XXXXXXXX
```

A major consideration in designing multi-user, interactive systems is the method by which files are organized, because it affects response time.

## FILE ORGANIZATION IN INTERACTIVE SYSTEMS

Certainly, sequential file organization does not allow fast access to any given record, since the searching process starts at the beginning of the file and continues one record at a time until that particular record is located. This process could take minutes to locate the proper record rather than an acceptable two- or three-second response time. The two major categories of data organization in an interactive mode are (1) **data base** and (2) **non-sequential files.**

### Data Base Access

A number of data base packages are available for both microprocessor and mainframe computer systems. Access to relational data base systems is possible from computer languages such as COBOL. Access to the data base is also possible from fourth-generation (query) languages. Both methods of interfacing with a data base have their advantages and limitations. Sometimes accessing large data bases gives the user great power of query, but interactive response time can be prohibitively slow.

**FIGURE 13.4    Change Fields "Check Value" Menu**

```
         CHANGE FIELDS (PAYROLL RECORD)

In order to change a specific field,
select the field you wish to change.

1.....NAME
2.....ADDRESS
3.....CITY
4.....STATE
5.....ZIP
6.....JOB CODE
7.....RETURN TO THE UPDATE MENU
```

**FIGURE 13.5    Data Entry for Payroll Fields**

```
RECORD:   SSN 444555666

ENTER LAST NAME    ------------------
      FIRST NAME   ------------------
      MI
```

## Nonsequential Files

Three types of file organization methods often used when designing interactive systems are (1) **indexed files,** (2) **relative files,** and (3) **direct files.**

**Indexed Files.** Access to indexed files is gained through **directories,** or **indexes.** Each element in a directory consists of a key field and a location field. A directory, or index, is a list (usually ordered) of these elements that has one of the following relationships with a file.

1. The key field points directly to the record for which the search is made.
2. The key field points to the beginning of a sublist of the record for which the search is made.
3. The key field point to the location of a subdirectory associated with a segment of the file that contains the record for which the search is made.

Indexed files are created sequentially and can be accessed either randomly or sequentially. Random access locates the specific record or records via the directories.

Since indexed files are ordered initially, they offer reasonably fast access to records using directories and, at the same time, allow sequential access in order to produce reports in sequence by the record key (primary key). Indexed files cannot be stored on tape; they are always stored on magnetic disk. In many cases, once interactive update is complete, a report generation module is executed to produce one or more reports. The detail output of the report usually must be in order by one or more keys. An indexed file can be treated almost like a sequential file for this purpose; and this is the reason that so many interactive applications in the business world use indexed files.

Indexed file access methods give the user a relatively fast update and retrieval capability through directories (or indexes) and easy report generation capability due to its sequential access mode. The COBOL program example (Figure 13.6) uses indexed files. BASIC does interface with an indexed file method, but a programmer must create his or her own directories as memory tables within the program itself.

**Relative Files.** Relative files are accessed by a record's **relative record location** in a file. A relative file can be described as a series of slots into which records can be written. The slots are numbered from relative record location 1 to the last record in the file. Relative files can be accessed sequentially or ran-

domly. Relative access is one of the fastest access methods and is often used when very rapid response time is a must. One disadvantage of relative files is that, over time, new records are added to old slots in the file while other records are deleted, leaving empty slots in the file. Although sequential access to relative files is possible, it is somewhat slower on average than to indexed files, since the relative access method must read past the empty slots to find the next available record. Another disadvantage of relative files is that the programmer is responsible for keeping track of each record's relative location. This requirement is unrealistic and would be prohibitive in many applications with large files. Computer languages using relative files will not automatically move a record from one slot to another, nor will the language software keep track of the locations of records. If the programmer plans to delete, say, a specific record, he or she must know its relative record number to do so. The programmer can improvise by creating his or her own directory table to contain a unique record key and an associated relative record number. The computer program's ability to accept a unique record key from the user and subsequently locate the entry in the directory with the same key saves the user from having to manually determine a record's relative record location. The program can extract the corresponding record location and supply it to the relative key in the update program. While this technique works, the addition of a directory renders the technique no more efficient than the indexed file method.

Both COBOL and BASIC make use of the relative organization of data. *This is the only nonsequential file organization that can be handled with BASIC.*

**Direct Files.** Direct file organization uses a randomizing formula for the placement of records in a file. Records are placed into an available slot in the file as a result of a calculated record location or address. This method of determining record placement is often called **hashing.** A hashing algorithm or formula provides an available record address in the file. This method is very fast, since the only time delay in writing the record in the file is the execution of a few calculations. The hashed address may actually take less than a millionth of a second to locate on a mainframe—much faster than the indexed file method of searching directories. A common hashing technique used by IBM is to take the record key and divide it by 19. The integer remainder of this calculation becomes the surface address of the record. Why divide by 19? Since there are typically 19 read/write surfaces on most IBM disk drives, the surface addresses run from address 0 to address 18. Since the integer remainder will always be between 0 and 18, it provides an appropriate surface address on which a given record is stored. IBM utilizes the term *track* to denote surface (cylinder/track concept).

If a record can be stored using a hashing formula, then the same record can be retrieved or updated by using the same hashing method to locate it once again.

COBOL can effectively handle this type of file organization, but BASIC cannot. Some BASIC texts refer to the term "direct access," but it is a misnomer. BASIC readily accesses only relative files. The user must know the relative location of a given record before it can be retrieved. Direct file hashing is not easily done in BASIC.

# GENERAL PROGRAM LOGIC DESIGN OF FILE UPDATE

The general programming logic for each type of update operation is explored in this section, with the main-line module discussed first. Figure 13.6 illustrates the overall general logic in hierarchy chart form.

## The MAIN-LINE Module

The main-line module for an interactive system closely follows that of a batch system. Figure 13.8 illustrates the main-line, start-up, and main-menu modules. In the main-line the titles of the three

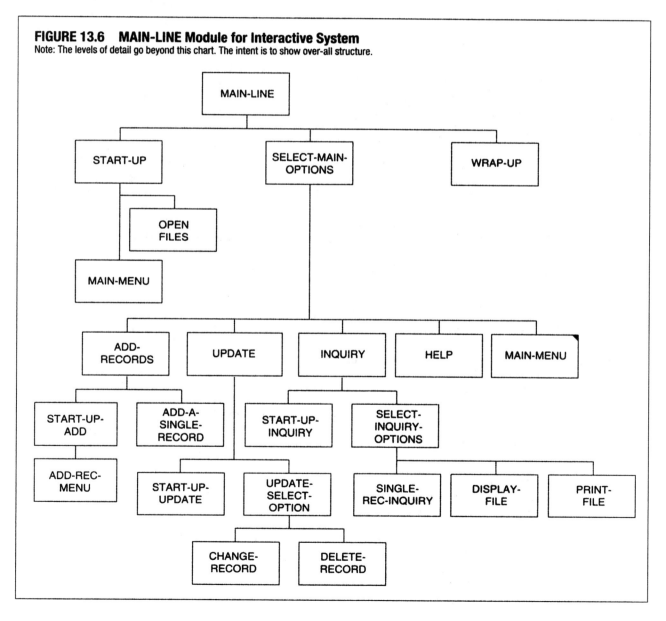

**FIGURE 13.6 MAIN-LINE Module for Interactive System**
Note: The levels of detail go beyond this chart. The intent is to show over-all structure.

main modules are modified a little to reflect a menu-oriented system.

## The START-UP Module

The function of the START-UP module is to present MAIN-MENU and accept the associated user's response. Figure 13.7 depicts the main menu on the screen, and Figure 13.8 illustrates the flowchart logic for the START-UP module. If the user response is not valid, the routine will again present the main menu until a valid response is obtained. This initial DoWhile displays the main menu and accepts a response. It equates somewhat to a pre-read in a batch environment, except that the computer does not read a transaction record; instead it attempts to begin dialogue with the user. If the user gives a valid response to the main menu, the program allows the dialogue to continue and the option response to be used in the SELECT-MAIN-OPTIONS module. Appropriate files are then opened.

The MAIN-LINE module then repeatedly performs the SELECT-MAIN-OPTIONS module until the user responds with the appropriate option that ends the interactive dialogue and returns control to the operating system of the computer.

## The SELECT-MAIN-OPTIONS Module

Figure 13.9 describes the SELECT-MAIN-OPTIONS module. The function of the SELECT-MAIN-OPTIONS routine is twofold. The first subfunction is to determine from the option response which module is to be invoked and subsequently performed, that is, 1 = ADD-RECORDS, 2 = UPDATE 3 = INQUIRY, 4 = HELP, 5 = END-SESSION. As long as the user enters a 1, 2, 3, or 4, the respective module is executed and control is regained at the bottom of the CASE structure. The second subfunction presents the main menu again for a new response from the user. This subfunction invokes the MAIN-MENU module until a valid response is entered by the user. The repetition of the module continues until the user terminates the session. Once the user responds to end the interactive session by pressing the 5 (END-SESSION), SELECT-MAIN-OPTIONS passes control to the WRAP-UP module.

## The ADD-RECORDS Module

The function of the ADD-RECORDS module is twofold. First, the submenu for adding records must be presented (Figure 13.10) and a valid response accepted before anything else happens. Second, as long as the user presses a 1 (PROCEED TO ADD A RECORD), the ADD-A-SINGLE-RECORD module is invoked. If the user presses 2 (RETURN TO MAIN MENU), the process of adding records ceases and control passes to the main menu. The submenu in the ADD-RECORDS modules *allows the user to add a multiple number of records without having to return to the main menu* after each record is added. It also serves as a safety valve in case the user inadvertently invokes the ADD-RECORDS module. In this case, the user can press the 2 and escape from the ADD-RECORDS module back to the main menu. Figure 13.11 represents the flowchart logic of the ADD-RECORDS module and the associated START-UP-ADD and ADD-MENU routines.

---

**FIGURE 13.7  Payroll File Maintenance Main Menu**

```
              PAYROLL FILE MAINTENANCE
                      MAIN MENU


     1.....ADD NEW RECORDS TO PAYROLL FILE
     2.....UPDATE PAYROLL FILE
     3.....INQUIRY
     4.....HELP
     5.....END FILE MAINTENANCE SESSION
```

## The ADD-A-SINGLE-RECORD Module

Figure 13.12 illustrates the flowchart logic of the ADD-A-SINGLE-RECORD module. The function of the module is, of course, to add a single record to the file. The module must accomplish four major tasks in order for a given record to be successfully added to a file.

1. The module looks for the record in the master file with the same key. This is done to determine if the record already exists. If the record already exists, no duplicate is added.

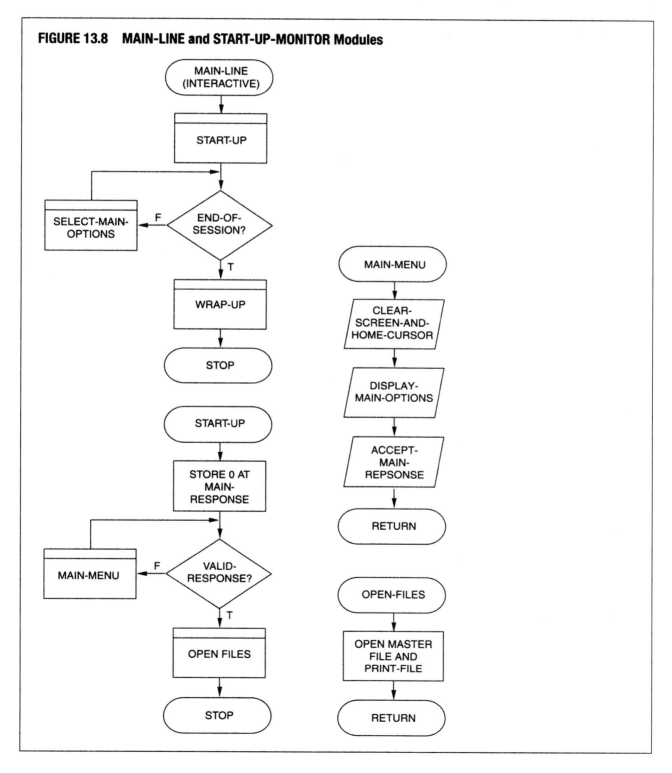

FIGURE 13.8    MAIN-LINE and START-UP-MONITOR Modules

2. If the record is not found, the data fields are validated as they are entered, and the newly formed record is written to the master file.
3. The appropriate messages appear and remain on the screen until the user presses any key.

If this is not done, the contents of the screen will vanish in a fraction of a second.
4. It presents ADD-MENU again and accepts the user response so that additional record additions can be made without returning to the main menu.

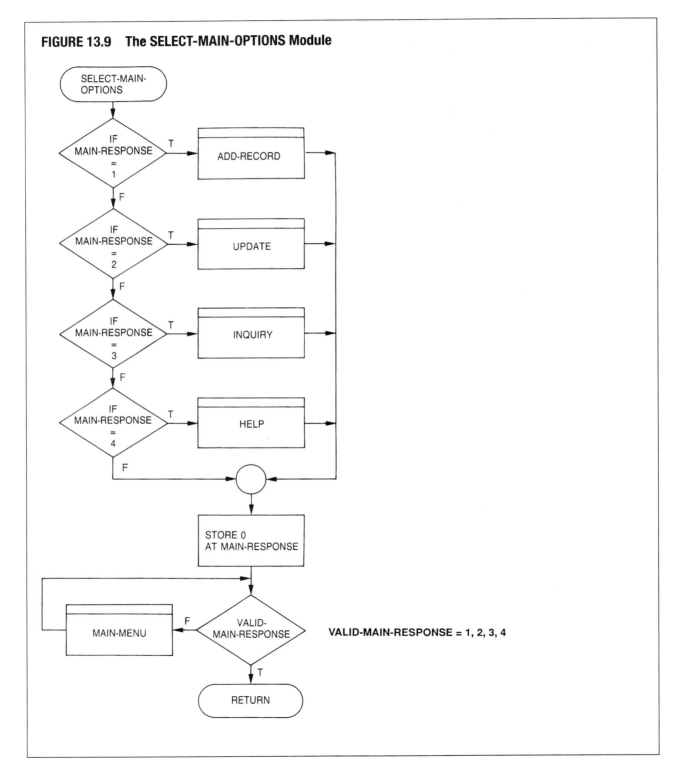

FIGURE 13.9    The SELECT-MAIN-OPTIONS Module

## The LOOK-FOR-MASTER-RECORD Module

The purpose of the LOOK-FOR-MASTER-RECORD module (Figure 13.13) is to determine if the record already exists. This module is also used by the change, delete, and inquiry modules. Its two major tasks are:

1. To accept and validate the transaction key entered by the user.
2. To read the nonsequential file until a record is located that has the same key as the transaction key. If a record in the nonsequential file is found, then a FOUND-SWITCH is set on. See the discussion of table searches in Chapters 7 and 8.

## The UPDATE Module

The purpose of the UPDATE module is to allow changes and deletions to the master file. Figure 13.14 illustrates the update menu that results from executing the UPDATE module. The UPDATE module has two major tasks:

1. To present the UPDATE menu initially and gain a response from the user regarding the update procedure that is to be executed.
2. To execute the UPDATE-SELECTION module repeatedly until the user has finished all updates to the master file. The UPDATE module invokes a module that decides which update module is to be performed (CHANGE-RECORD or DELETE-RECORD).

Figure 13.15 depicts the UPDATE module in flowchart form. It is broken down into two distinct submodules: STAR-UP-UPDATE and UPDATE-

SELECT-OPTION. START-UP-UPDATE obtains the user's first valid response. UPDATE-SELECT-OPTION directs program control to either the CHANGE-RECORD or the DELETE-RECORD module, according to the user's response. Also, just as was the case with the ADD-A-SINGLE-RECORD module, the representation of the UPDATE menu is made at the bottom of the UPDATE-SELECT-OPTION module until the user keys in a valid response (1, 2, or 3). Once the UPDATE-SELECT module is complete, control briefly returns to the UPDATE module, where the condition test of the DoWhile determines if the user will make more updates. If the user enters a 3, it means that he or she will return to the main menu. As long as the user enters a 1 (CHANGE) or a 2 (DELETE), program control returns to the UPDATE-SELECT-OPTION module. The process of directing the user to the appropriate update module is repeated until the user enters a 3 (RETURN TO MAIN MENU).

## The CHANGE-RECORD Module

To change a record in a nonsequential file, the record must first be located in the file. Next, the various fields to be changed on the master record must be identified. In order to identify which fields must be changed, a CHANGE menu is presented to the user. Figure 13.16 depicts a typical CHANGE menu. The menu gives the user a choice of which field(s) he or she wants to change. Figure 13.17 illustrates the logic necessary to change a record.

The CHANGE-RECORD module's function is, of course, to make the appropriate changes to any given record in the file. This function is broken down into three distinct tasks:

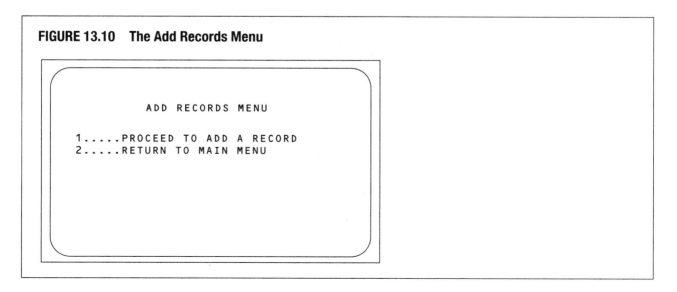

**FIGURE 13.10    The Add Records Menu**

```
              ADD RECORDS MENU

    1......PROCEED TO ADD A RECORD
    2......RETURN TO MAIN MENU
```

1. The START-UP-CHANGE submodule locates the specific record to be changed (invokes the LOOK-FOR-RECORD module) and also makes the initial presentation of a CHANGE menu.

2. Once the specific record is located in the master file and the particular field on the record is identified for change, then the CHANGE-SELECT module directs program control to the appropriate FLD-X-INPUT module. There

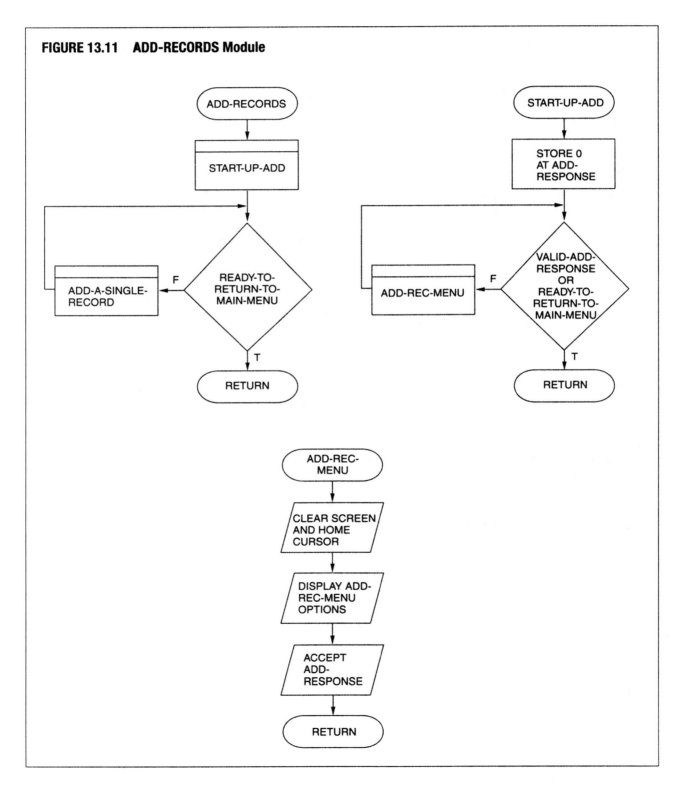

**FIGURE 13.11    ADD-RECORDS Module**

will be a FLD-X-INPUT module for every input field in the record. The "X" is a generic entry used to denote a specific field name or an abbreviation for a specific field name.

Once a given field is changed, the CHANGE-WHICH-FIELD-MENU is again presented to the user. This allows multiple fields per record to be changed without the user's having to return to the main menu. User response then indicates which field is to be changed next. The field changes made by the user are still resident only in the record area of memory. At this point they have not become a permanent part of the master record on disk.

3. The third major task is to *physically rewrite* the master record to incorporate the current changes. If the record was found and the user indicates no more changes are to be made, then the record is rewritten.

Notice that the FLD-CHANGE-xxxxxxx module contains a command that first prompts the user to enter a specific field and then requires the user of the computer to enter this field. If the user incorrectly enters the data, the program prompts the user to retry. This validation loop continues until the data entered is valid.

## The DELETE-RECORD Module

The function of the DELETE-RECORD module is to permit the user to delete a single record from the master file. First, to avoid the inadvertent deletion of a record, a DELETE menu is presented that gives the user an option to simply return to the UPDATE menu without actually deleting a record. Figure 13.18 illustrates DELETE menu, and Figure 13.19 depicts the flowchart logic for the DELETE-RECORD module. First, the logic takes care of the possibility of the user mistakenly pressing a 2 from the UPDATE menu and accidentally deleting a record. But the prompt, "ARE YOU SURE YOU WANT TO DELETE A RECORD? (Y/N)," gives the user an early out by responding with N (NO). If the user responds with N, a NO RECORD DELETED message should be displayed. Otherwise, the LOOK-FOR-RECORD module is called. If a master record is found that matches the transaction key (entered by the user), then an appropriate command is entered to delete the record. (In COBOL, the command is "DELETE file name." For the command in another language, consult the appropriate programmer's manual.) If the record is not found in the master file, a message is displayed that indicates the update operation cannot be completed

(RECORD NOT DELETED, RECORD NOT FOUND IN MASTER FILE).

## The INQUIRY Module

The INQUIRY module allows a user to make multiple inquires into a master file without having to return to the main menu. An inquiry causes a single record (or more) to be located and retrieved to the user screen. From the MAIN menu, the user responds with a 3 (INQUIRY). As a result of this choice, the SELECT-MAIN-OPTIONS routine directs program control to the INQUIRY module.

Figure 13.20 illustrates the INQUIRY menu, and Figure 13.21 depicts the logic of the INQUIRY module and its associated subordinate modules. To carry out a single inquiry, the modules must accomplish the following:

1. The INQUIRY menu (Figure 13.20) is initially presented to the user and a response (START-UP-INQUIRY module) is obtained. The possible responses are (1) INQUIRE ABOUT A SINGLE RECORD, (2) DISPLAY FILE, (3) PRINT FILE (HARD COPY), and (4) RETURN TO MAIN MENU. This process is handled by the START-UP-INQUIRY module.
2. The next step is to determine which option the user wishes to perform. The SELECT-INQUIRY-OPTIONS module handles this determination and gives control to the appropriate routine (either SINGLE-REC-INQUIRY or FILE-DISPLAY).
3. The third step is to present the INQUIRY menu again and gain another response. This will be repeated if necessary to obtain a valid response.

**SINGLE-REC-INQUIRY.** The function of SINGLE-REC-INQUIRY is to locate a single record in the master file. First, the user must enter the transaction key. Second, the program attempts to locate a master record with a record key that is the same as the user-supplied transaction key. To accomplish this, the LOOK-FOR-MASTER-RECORD module is called. If the master record is found, then the various fields are displayed to the screen; else, an error message, MASTER RECORD NOT FOUND, is displayed to the screen. The subsequent Display and Accept command retains the message on the screen until a response (pressing return) is gained.

**DISPLAY-FILE AND PRINT FILE Modules.** The function of DISPLAY-FILE is to display the entire file, one record per line, to the user screen. The PRINT-FILE module is the same except the output is

## FIGURE 13.12 The ADD-A-SINGLE-RECORD Module

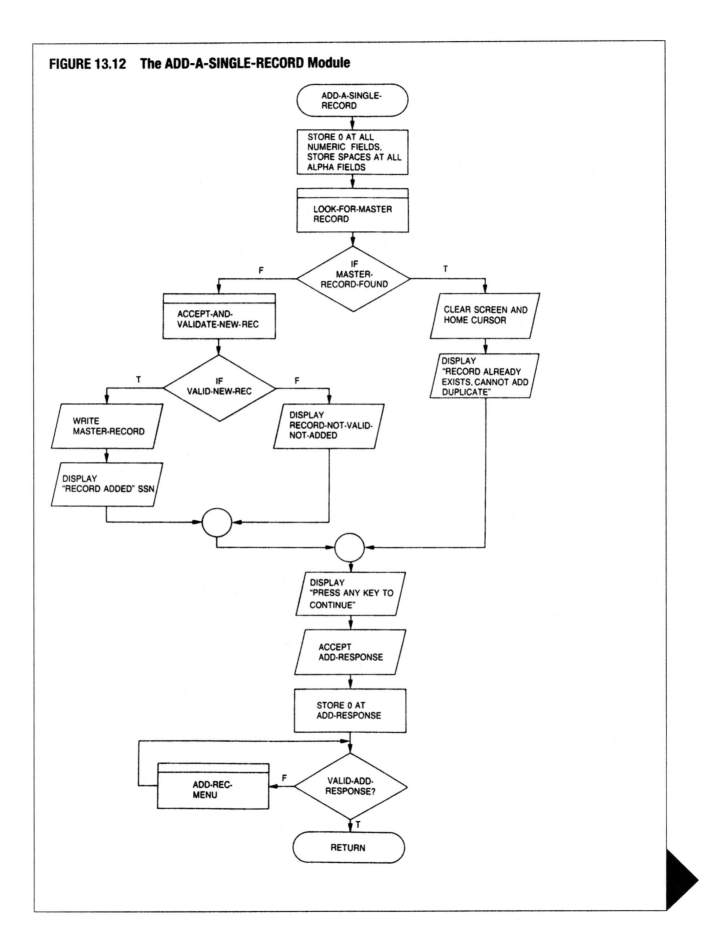

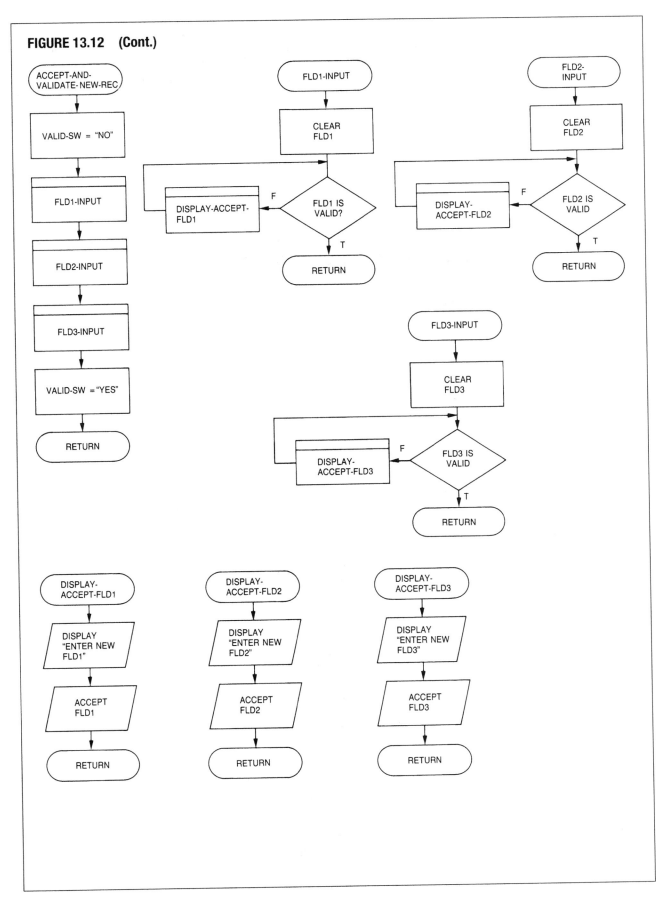

**FIGURE 13.12** (Cont.)

printed to paper copy. Since the master file is opened as I/O, the file must be closed and re-opened as *input* in order to sequentially access the master file for record printing purposes (consult programming language reference). The reexecution of DISPLAY-LINE UNTIL END-FLAG = "YES" should be self-explanatory. After the records are displayed the information is held on the screen by the display and accept commands (as previously discussed). In order to allow random access to the master file, once again the master file must now be closed as input and reopened as I/O. This sequence of opens and closes applies to both modules.

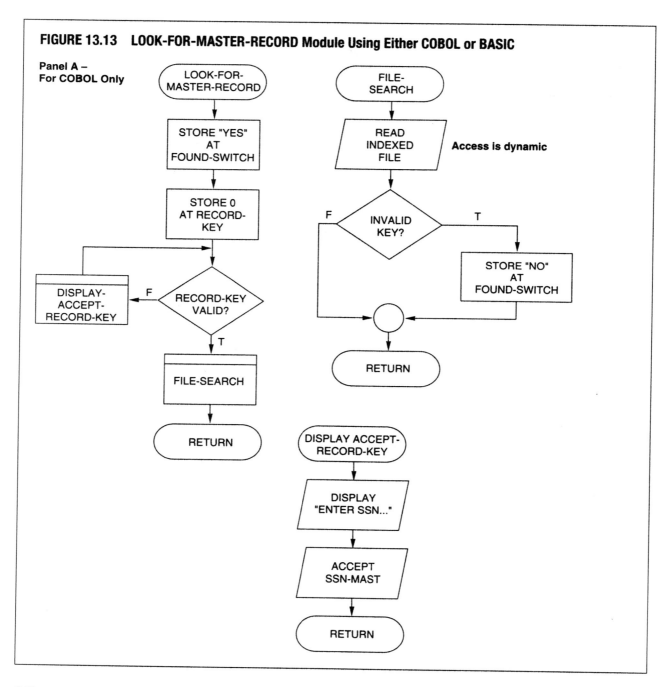

**FIGURE 13.13    LOOK-FOR-MASTER-RECORD Module Using Either COBOL or BASIC**

## FIGURE 13.13 (Cont.)

**Panel B—For BASIC Only**

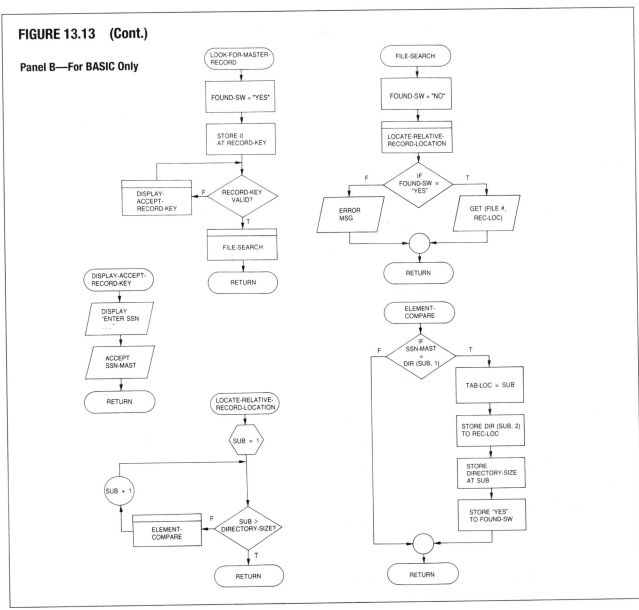

## FIGURE 13.14 The Update Menu

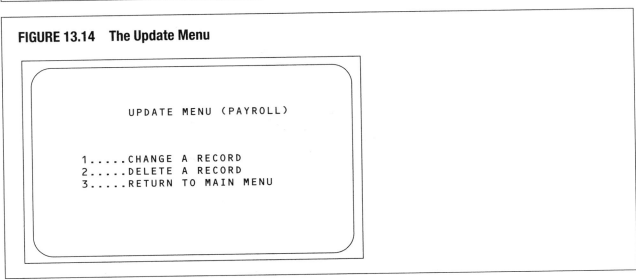

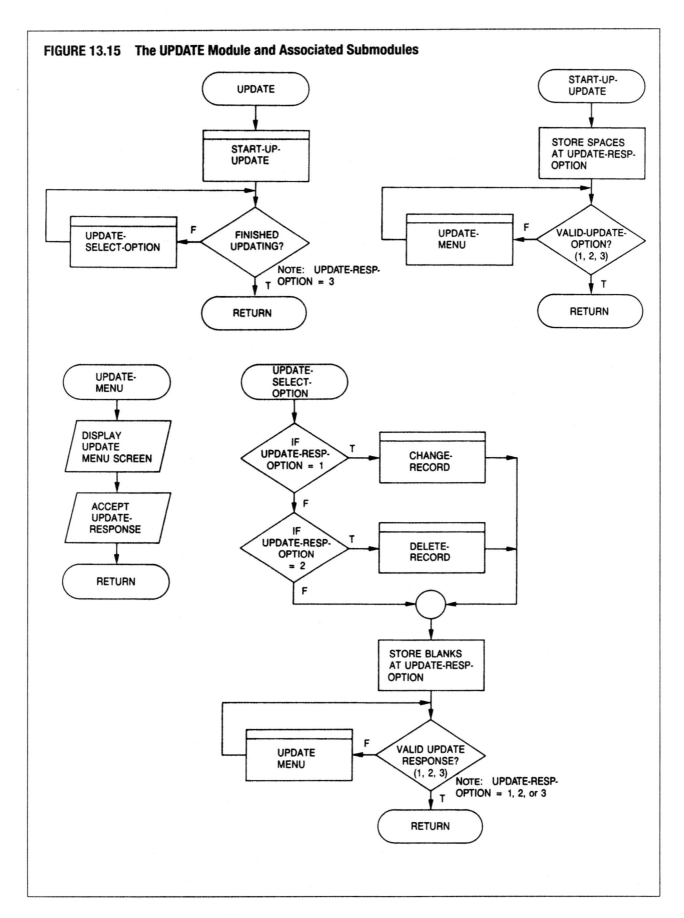

**FIGURE 13.15   The UPDATE Module and Associated Submodules**

FIGURE 13.16　The Change Record Menu

```
                    CHANGE RECORD MENU

        Which fields of the record do you
        wish to change?

             1.....NAME
             2.....ADDRESS
             3.....CITY
             4.....STATE
             5.....ZIP
             6.....JOB CODE
             7.....RETURN TO UPDATE MENU
```

**FIGURE 13.17　CHANGE-RECORD Module and Subordinate Submodules**

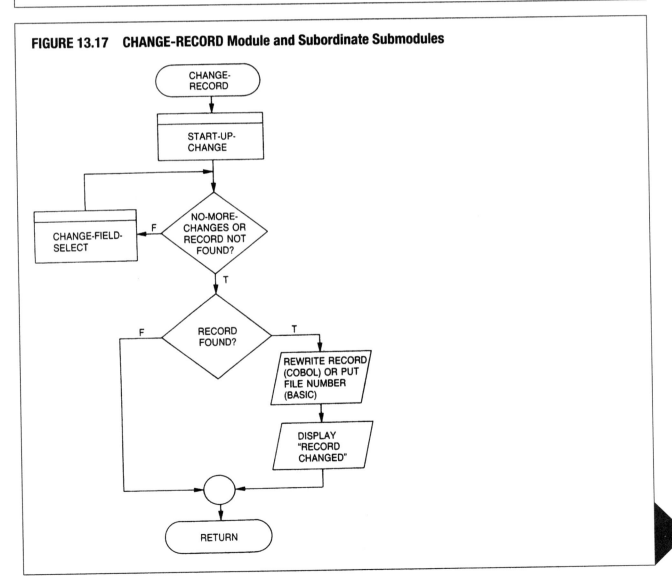

**FIGURE 13.17   (Cont.)**

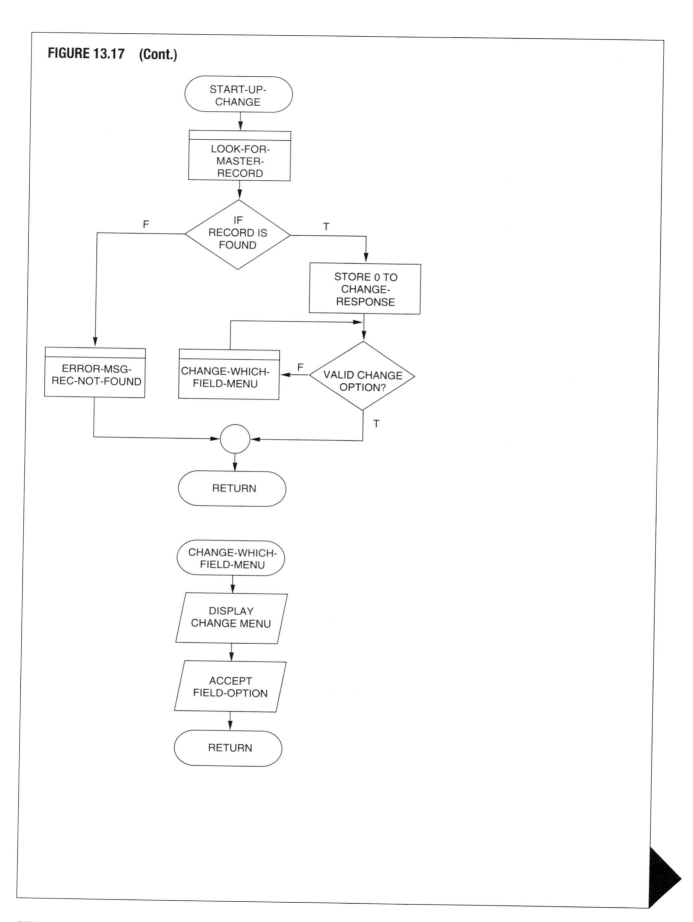

**FIGURE 13.17 (Cont.)**

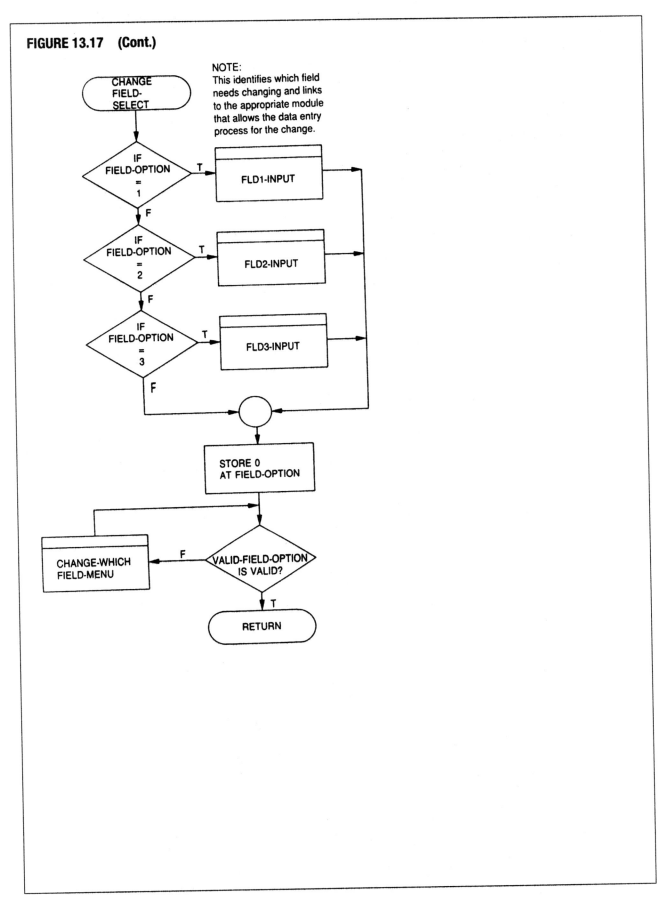

**FIGURE 13.18 The Delete Record Menu**

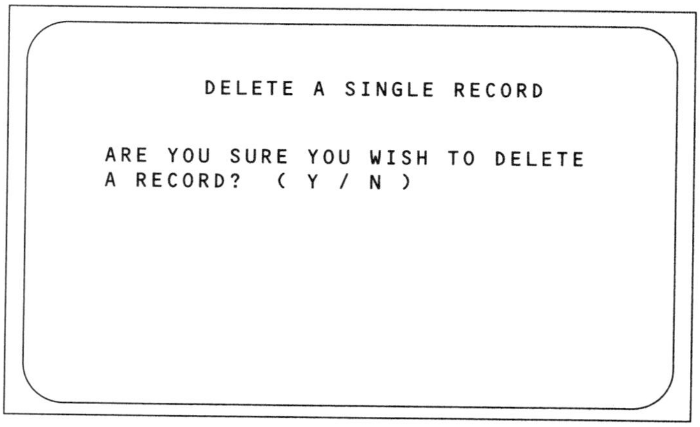

```
              DELETE A SINGLE RECORD

   ARE YOU SURE YOU WISH TO DELETE
   A RECORD?   ( Y / N )
```

# FIGURE 13.19 DELETE RECORD Module

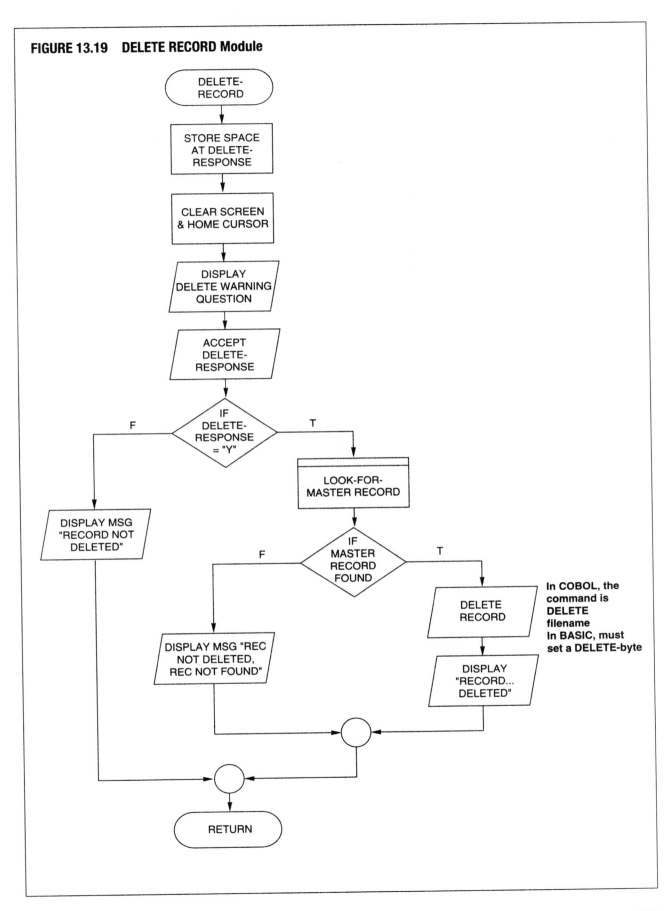

**FIGURE 13.20    The Inquiry Menu**

```
                    INQUIRY   MENU


        1.....INQUIRE ABOUT A SINGLE RECORD
        2.....DISPLAY FILE
        3.....PRINT FILE (HARD COPY)
        4.....RETURN TO MAIN MENU
```

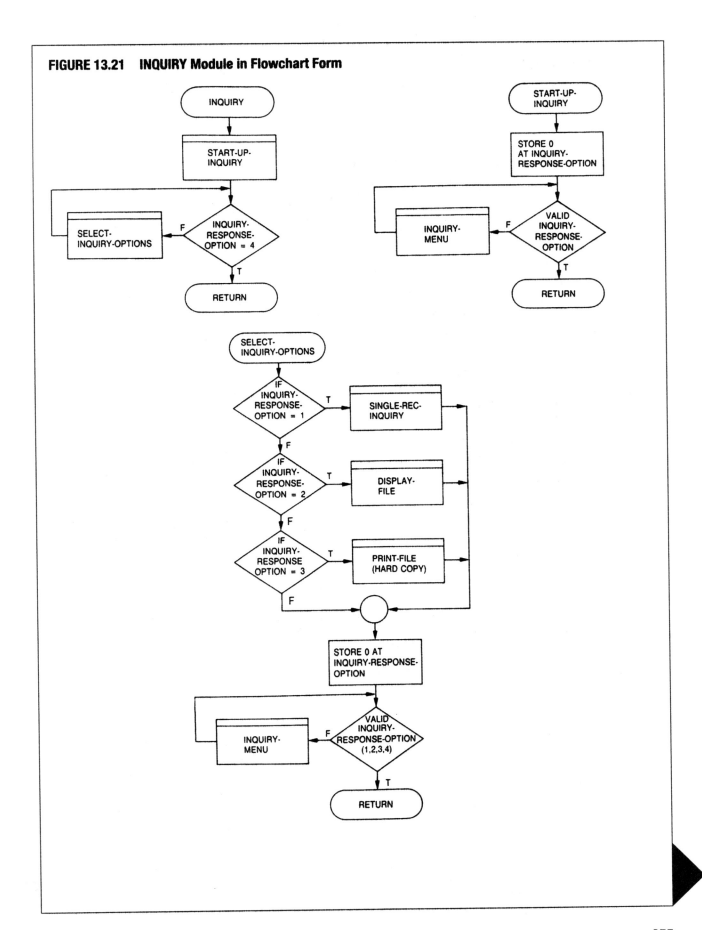

**FIGURE 13.21    INQUIRY Module in Flowchart Form**

**FIGURE 13.21  (Cont.)**

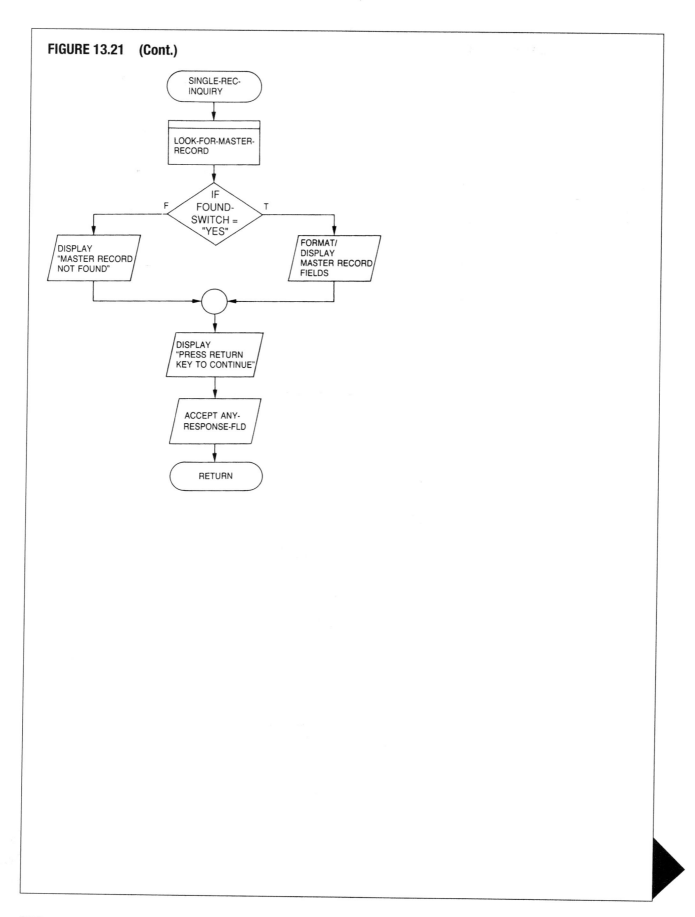

FIGURE 13.21    (Cont.)

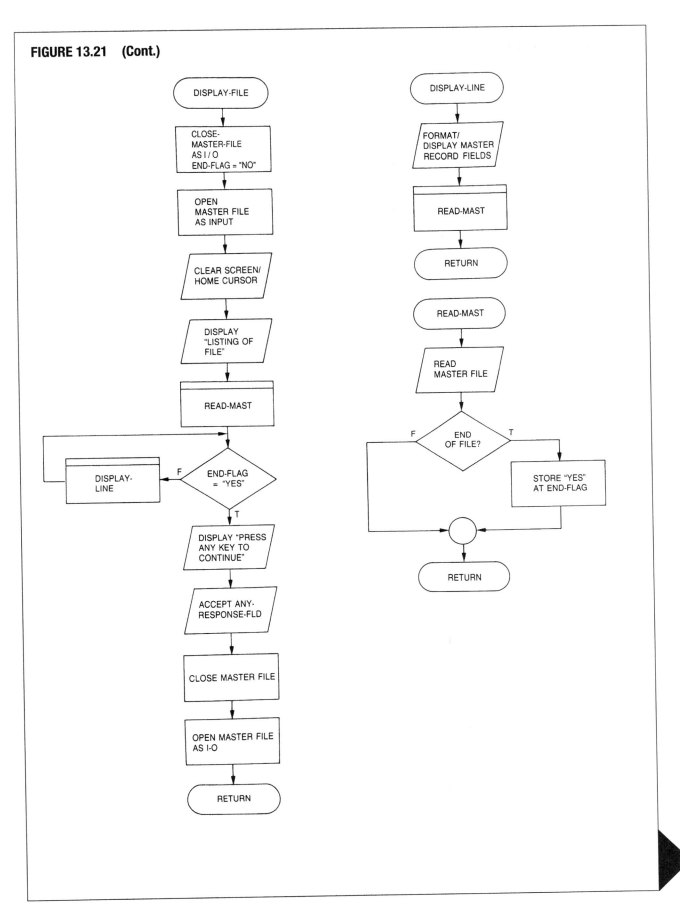

**FIGURE 13.21    (Cont.)**

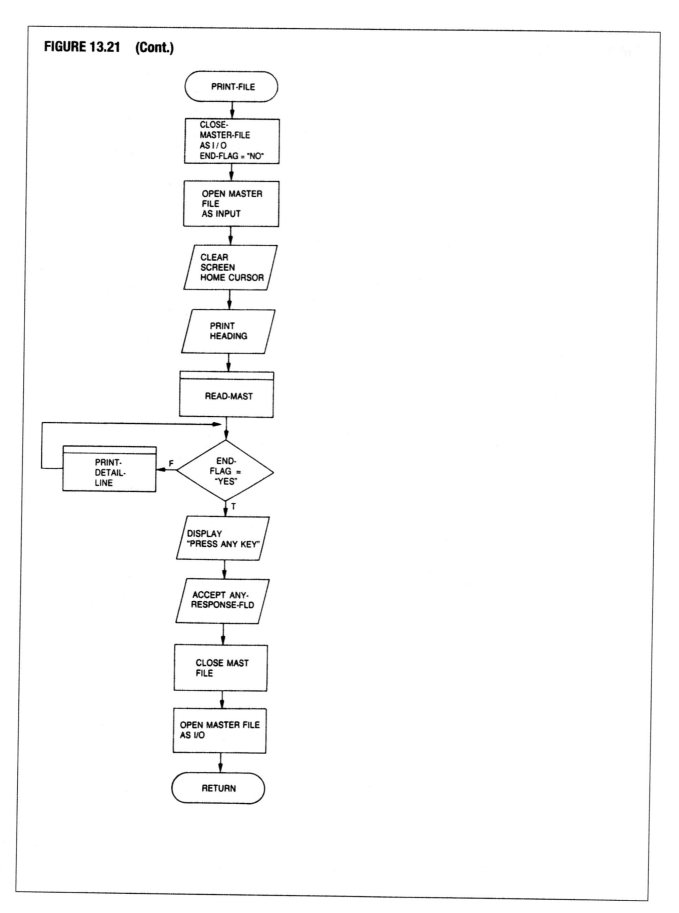

# Interactive File Maintenance of a Payroll Application

## Program Requirements

Acme Industries wants to convert their payroll system from a batch operation to interactive. The batch system works relatively well as long as a payroll maintenance programmer is available. In the programmer's absence, file maintenance of the master payroll file cannot be accomplished. This problem, coupled with the other problems inherent in batch update, necessitates a stronger on-line user interface with the system.

The new interactive payroll system should allow the user to add new records, delete existing ones, and make changes. The system should allow for record or file inquiry. The computer program should be able to do the following:

1. Supply interactive screens (menus) that give easily understood prompts that will elicit valid responses from the user.
2. Provide validation loops (error traps) that acquire only responses that are valid according to prescribed criteria for each field.
3. Provide a main menu that elicits responses from the user to add, update, and inquire.
4. Provide submenus where appropriate for each function: (1) ADD menu, (2) UPDATE menu (change or delete), and (3) INQUIRY.
5. Permit one or several records to be added during a dialogue session without leaving the ADD module. It is unrealistic to return to the main menu for each add. Often, data entry personnel will need to add records for several new employees during a single session.
6. The UPDATE module must provide for both changing and deleting records. Only one record at a time may be deleted or changed before the user is returned to the UPDATE menu. From there, the user may opt to delete or change another.
7. Provide for an inquiry of a single record or a listing of the entire file from the screen or printer.

## Output Design (Screen and Printer)

Exhibit 13.1 illustrates the various menus or screens presented to the user in an interactive dialogue session. The actual screen design may be done using a CRT layout sheet. Panel J illustrates how the main menu would be designed using a CRT layout sheet.

## Input Design

Exhibit 13.2 depicts the record layout for the master payroll file, state table, and job table. The state table consists of the state abbreviation code followed by the state name. There are 51 entries in this table, which includes the District of Columbia. The job table consists of 10 entries, each consisting of a job code followed by a job title. The various fields and their value domains (permissible values) are shown below.

| Field Description | Value |
| --- | --- |
| SSN | any numeric value |
| Last name | alphabetic |
| First name | alphabetic |
| MI | alphabetic |
| Branch | 001–003 |
| Dept | 001–005 |
| Job Code | 01–10 |
| Street | must have one letter |
| City | alphabetic |
| State | must be validated by locating a matching code in a state table |
| Zip | numeric |
| DOE | 450101—current date in form YYMMDD* |
| YTD earnings | numeric with leading zeros |

Note: 450101 means Jan. 1, 1945, so the range is between Jan. 1, 1945 and current date.

## Test Cases

Any interactive system is tested by the way the user responds to its various menus and screens. Also, each module should be tested by using invalid responses as well as valid ones. For instance, the user might enter alphabetic data into fields that require numeric data or enter unreasonable values into various variables. The error-trap logic should present the menu again if the response is invalid.

Many times, programmers prepare a formal test plan document that contains the user prompt, the user response, and the expected result. Theoretically, the test plan should provide for every conceivable response and the corresponding expected result. A formal discussion of testing programs, however, is beyond the scope of this text.

## Logic Considerations

The program should be developed in close adherence with the interactive file maintenance logic previously discussed. The only main logic consideration is the handling of data validation loops

**EXHIBIT 13.1   Screen and Report Design**

**Panel A**
**The MAIN Menu**

```
        ACME INDUSTRIES PAYROLL FILE MAINTENANCE
                    MAIN MENU

        1.......ADD A RECORD
        2.......UPDATE (CHANGE/DELETE)
        3.......INQUIRY
        4.......HELP
        5.......END FILE MAINTENANCE SESSION
```

**Panel B**
**The ADD Menu**

```
               ADD MENU (PAYROLL FILE)

        1.......ADD A RECORD
        2.......RETURN TO MAIN MENU
```

**Panel C**
**The UPDATE Menu**

```
               UPDATE MENU (PAYROLL)

        1.......CHANGE A RECORD
        2.......DELETE A RECORD
        3.......RETURN TO MAIN MENU
```

**EXHIBIT 13.1   (Cont.)**

**Panel D**
**The DELETE Menu**

```
                    DELETE MENU (PAYROLL)

          1.......DELETE A RECORD
          2.......RETURN TO UPDATE MENU
```

**Panel E**
**The CHANGE Menu**

```
              CHANGE MENU (MODIFY A RECORD)

  SELECT THE FIELD LISTED BELOW THAT YOU WISH TO CHANGE.

          1.......NAME
          2.......BRANCH
          3.......DEPARTMENT
          4.......JOB CODE
          5.......STREET
          6.......CITY
          7.......STATE
          8.......ZIP
          9.......DOE
          10......YTD GROSS
          11......RETURN TO UPDATE MENU
```

**Panel F**
**The INQUIRY Menu**

```
                 INQUIRY MENU (PAYROLL)

          1.......INQUIRE ABOUT A SINGLE RECORD
          2.......LIST PAYROLL FILE (SCREEN OUTPUT)
          3.......PRINT A HARD COPY OF PAYROLL FILE
          4.......RETURN TO MAIN MENU
```

**EXHIBIT 13.1    (Cont.)**

**Panel G**
**Example Screen**
**Messages**

```
        ATTEMPTED TO ADD RECORD XXXXXXXX, BUT RECORD ALREADY EXISTS
                          ......CANNOT DUPLICATE THIS RECORD...
```

```
        RECORD XXXXXXXX ADDED TO FILE
```

```
        RECORD XXXXXXXX NOT FOUND IN MASTER FILE..NO CHANGE MADE
```

```
        RECORD XXXXXXXX CHANGED
```

**Panel H**
**Prompts for**
**Adding**
**One Record**

```
        ENTER LAST NAME ■-------
        ENTER FIRST NAME ■------
        ENTER MI ■-------
        ENTER BRANCH NUMBER (001-003 ARE ALLOWED) ■---------
        ENTER DEPARTMENT NUMBER (001-005 ARE ALLOWED) ■-----
        ENTER STREET ■-----
        ENTER CITY ■------
        ENTER STATE (TWO CHARACTER CODE) ■-
        ENTER ZIP (5 POSITIONS) ■-----
        ENTER DATE (MMDDYY) ■-----
        ENTER YTD GROSS (DO NOT ENTER DECIMAL POINT ITSELF) ■-------
```

**EXHIBIT 13.1    (Cont.)**

**Panel I
INQUIRY Screen
(Retrieval of
One Record)
Screen Output**

```
                    INQUIRY OF SINGLE RECORD
    SSN:XXXXXXXX              NAME: XXXXXXXXXX  XXXXXXXXXXX  X.

    BRANCH: XXX              DEPARTMENT XXX

    JOB DESCRIPTION: XXXXXXXXXXXXXXX

    STREET ADDRESS: XXXXXXXXXXXX
          CITY: XXXXXXXXXX   STATE: XX  ZIP XXXXX

    DOE XX/XX/XX

    YTD GROSS PAY $ XX,XXX.XX
```

**Panel J—An Example of the Design of a Menu Using
a CRT Layout Form**

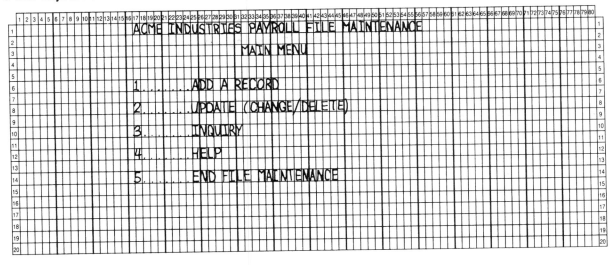

```
         ACME INDUSTRIES PAYROLL FILE MAINTENANCE

                      MAIN MENU

    1.......ADD A RECORD

    2.......UPDATE (CHANGE/DELETE)

    3.......INQUIRY

    4.......HELP

    5.......END FILE MAINTENANCE
```

**Panel K
INQUIRY Screen (Retrieval of Payroll File) Hard Copy**

```
        PAYROLL PERSONNEL REGISTER

 SSN          NAME        STREET      CITY    STATE   ZIP    DEPT   BR    JC     YTD

XXXXXXXX   XXXXXXXXXX   XXXXXXXXX   XXXXX     XX    XXXXX    XXX   XXX    X    XXXXX.XX
XXXXXXXX   XXXXXXXXXX   XXXXXXXXX   XXXXX     XX    XXXXX    XXX   XXX    X    XXXXX.XX
XXXXXXXX   XXXXXXXXXX   XXXXXXXXX   XXXXX     XX    XXXXX    XXX   XXX    X    XXXXX.XX
```

(error traps). The program will continue to ask the user to rekey a response whenever one is entered incorrectly.

The testing of the street address is a little tricky since the field must contain at least one letter of the alphabet. In COBOL, the programmer cannot simply test for a "NOT NUMERIC" condition, since any special character would also trigger this condition. A table lookup operation will be necessary to determine if a single letter or more exists in the street address.

## Program Design

Exhibit 13.3 illustrates the general program logic in hierarchy chart form, and Exhibit 13.4 depicts the structured program flowchart for the various file maintenance modules. The logic shown in the program closely resembles the various modules previously discussed. The only noteworthy difference is observed in the ACCEPT-AND-VALIDATE-NEW-REC submodule of the ADD-A-SINGLE-RECORD module. The number of fields to be validated is obviously greater than before.

The associated pseudocode and the COBOL program are shown in Exhibits 13.5 and 13.6. Since data validation is much more complex in BASIC than in COBOL, the flowcharting differences for the validation process in the BASIC language is found in Appendix E. Since there is no class test in BASIC (If . . . numeric and If . . . alphabetic), a special routine is needed to accept and validate the characters as they are keyed in from the keyboard. See Appendix C for more information about how this is handled. Also, observe how the street address is validated. The field is treated as a table with SINGLE character elements. The table is searched for a letter A–Z (i.e., alphabetic and not space).

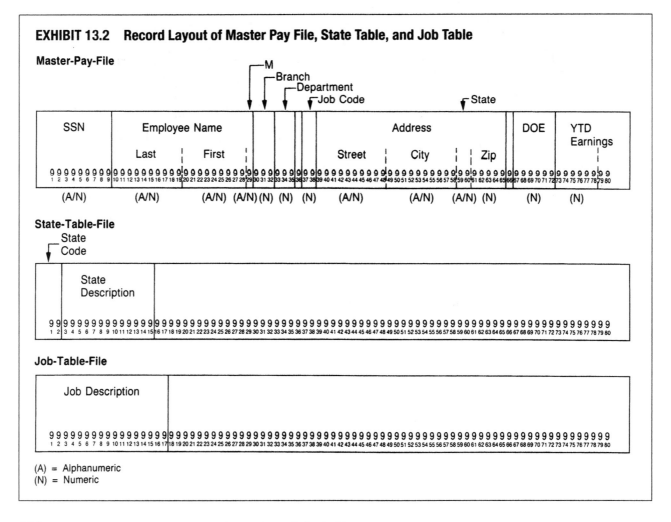

**EXHIBIT 13.2    Record Layout of Master Pay File, State Table, and Job Table**

(A) = Alphanumeric
(N) = Numeric

**EXHIBIT 13.3   Hierarchy Chart for Interactive Payroll System**

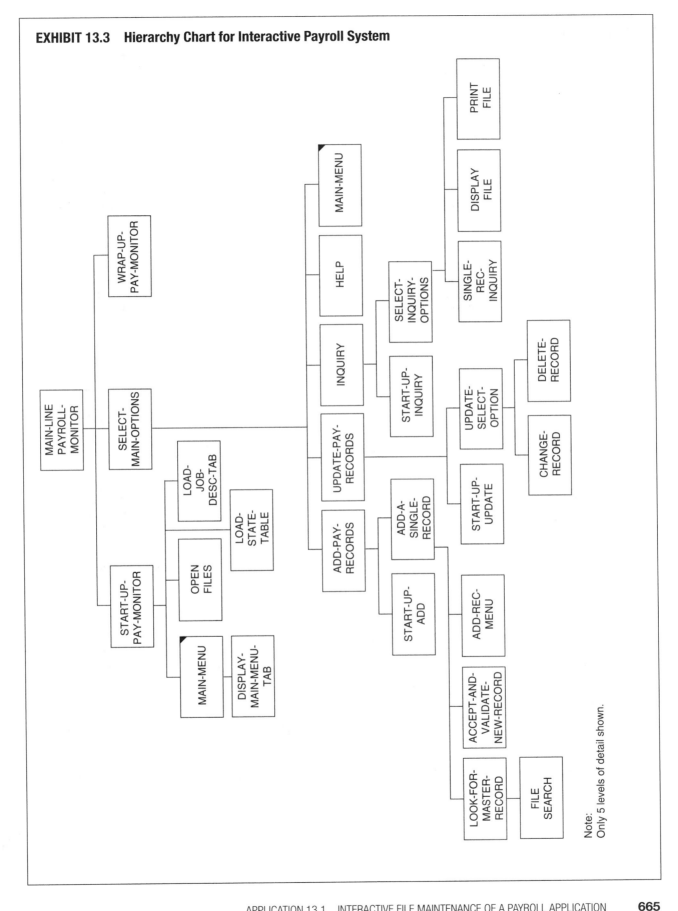

Note:
Only 5 levels of detail shown.

EXHIBIT 13.4 Structured Flowchart for Interactive Payroll

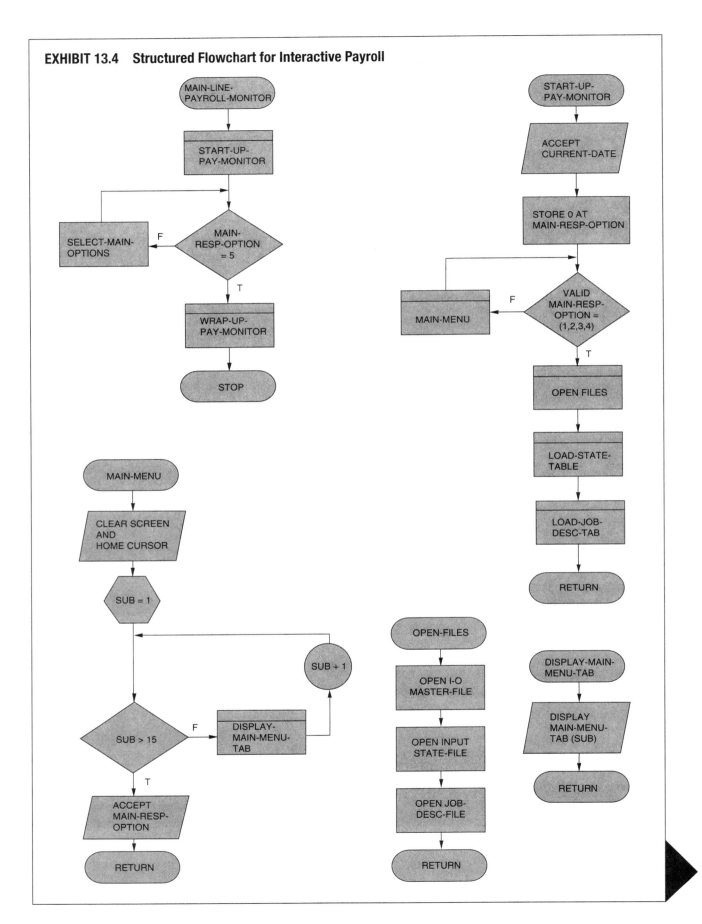

EXHIBIT 13.4    (Cont.)

**Use of the nested ELSE
to represent CASE STRUCTURE.
The matching code of the COBOL 85
program is shown in Exhibit 13.6
with multiple END IFs to represent
each connector below.  This is
shown to represent an alternative
flowcharting method**

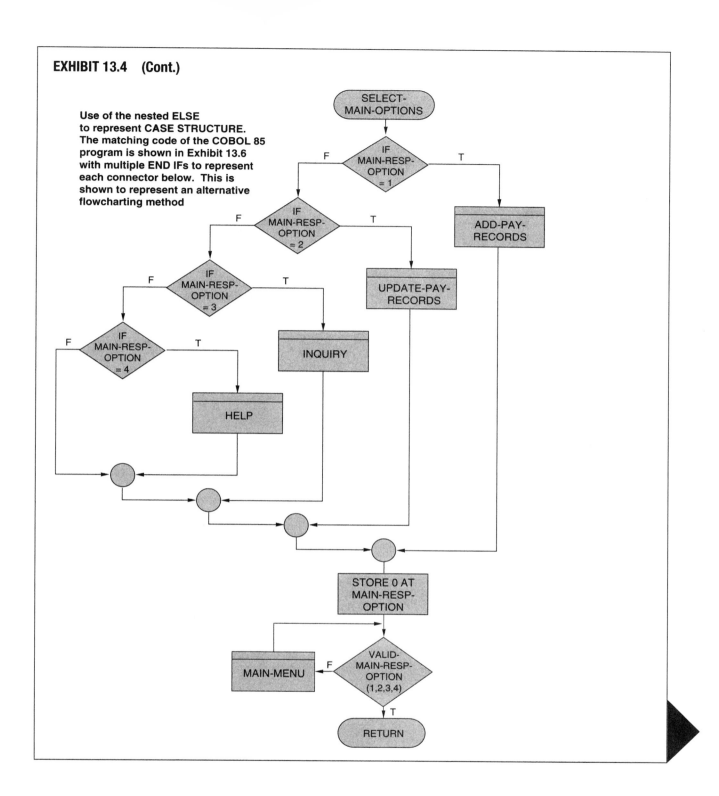

**EXHIBIT 13.4    (Cont.)**

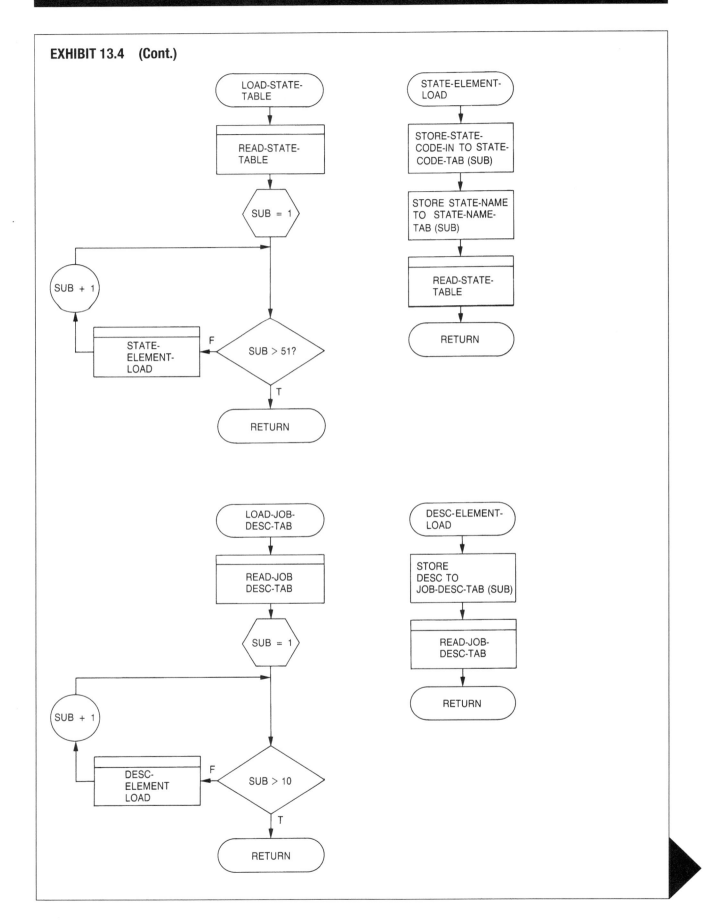

**EXHIBIT 13.4** (Cont.)

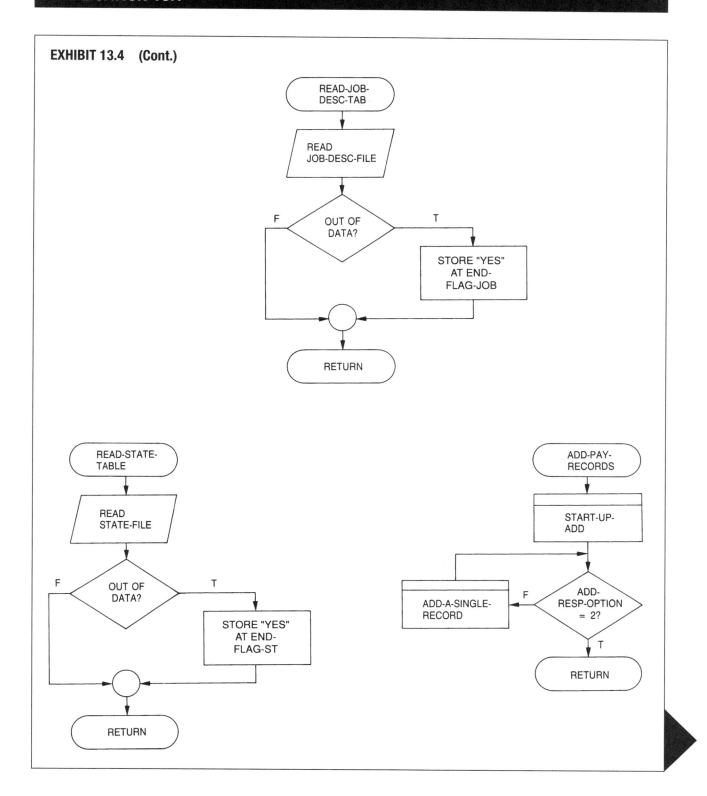

**EXHIBIT 13.4  (Cont.)**

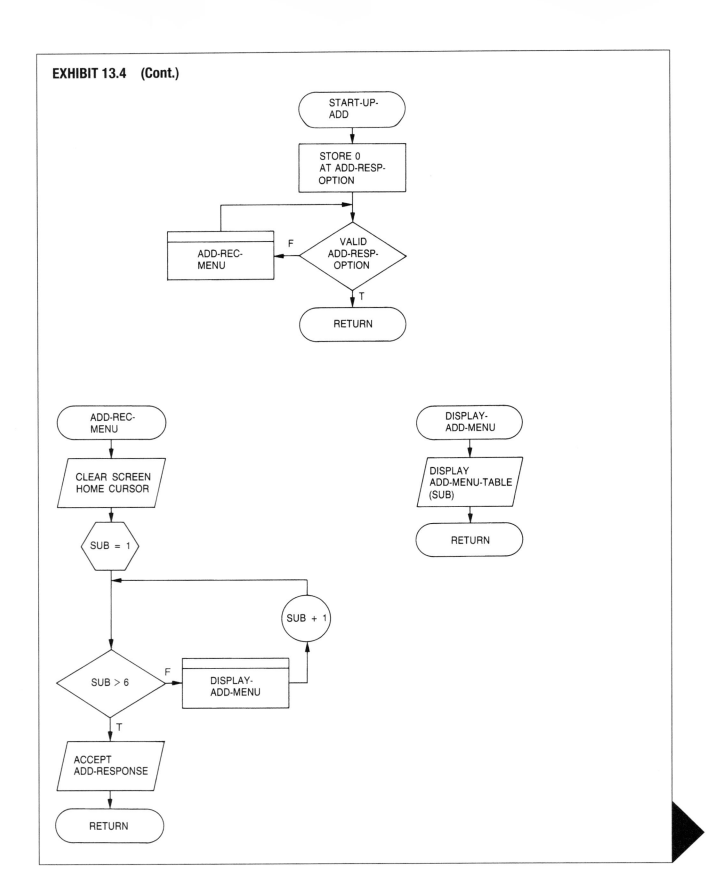

**EXHIBIT 13.4    (Cont.)**

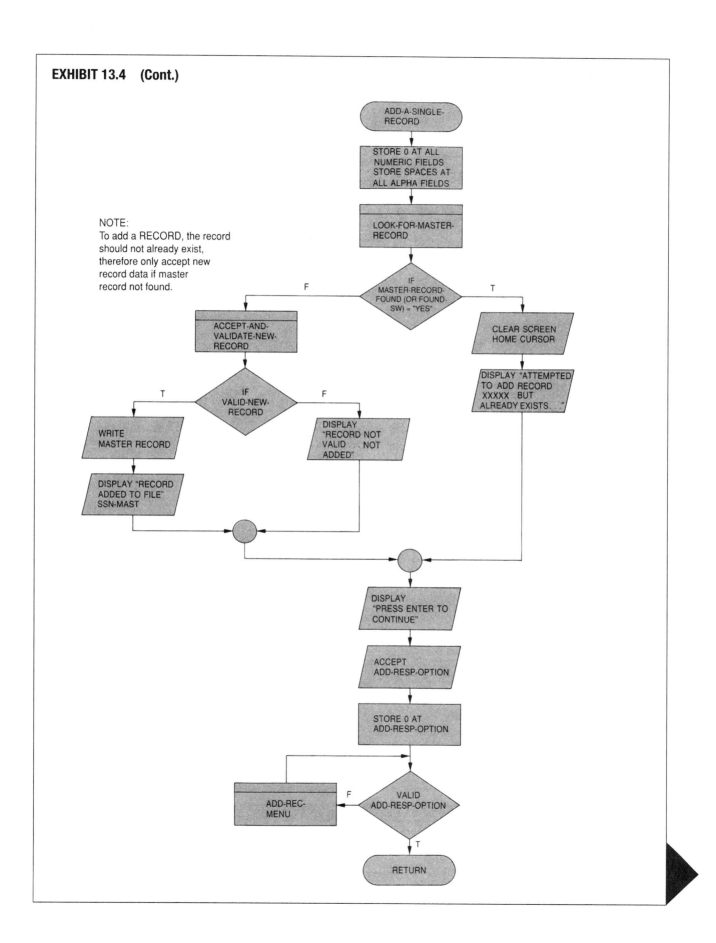

**EXHIBIT 13.4 (Cont.)**

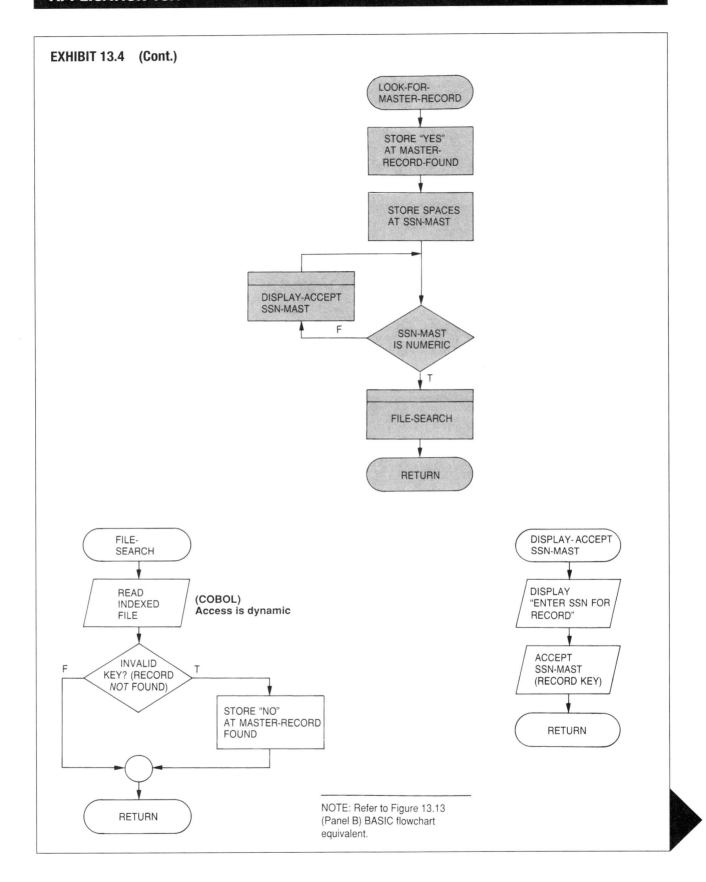

NOTE: Refer to Figure 13.13
(Panel B) BASIC flowchart
equivalent.

**EXHIBIT 13.4    (Cont.)**

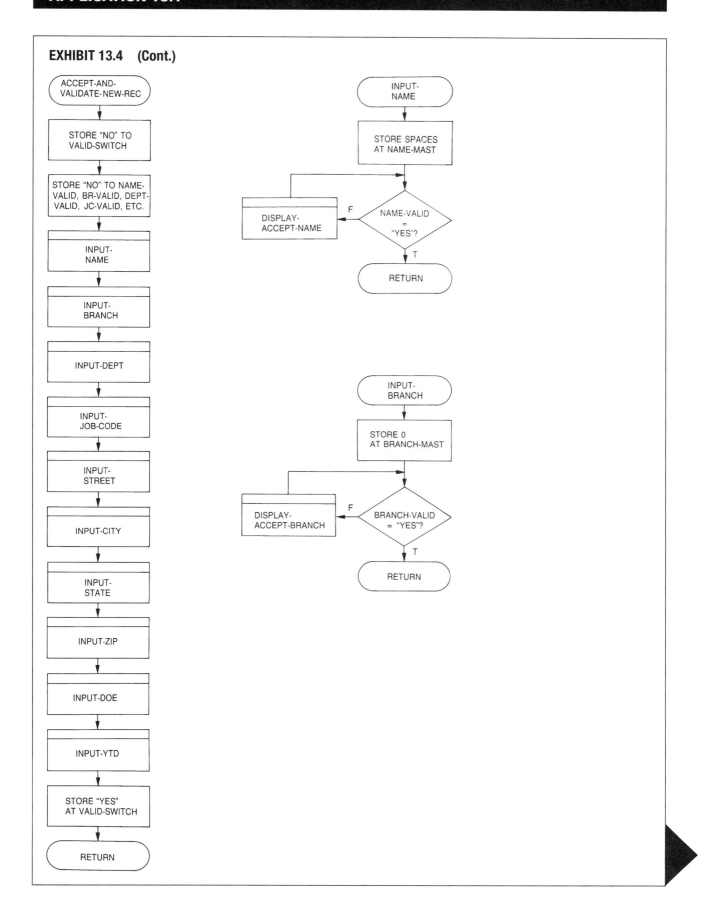

**EXHIBIT 13.4    (Cont.)**

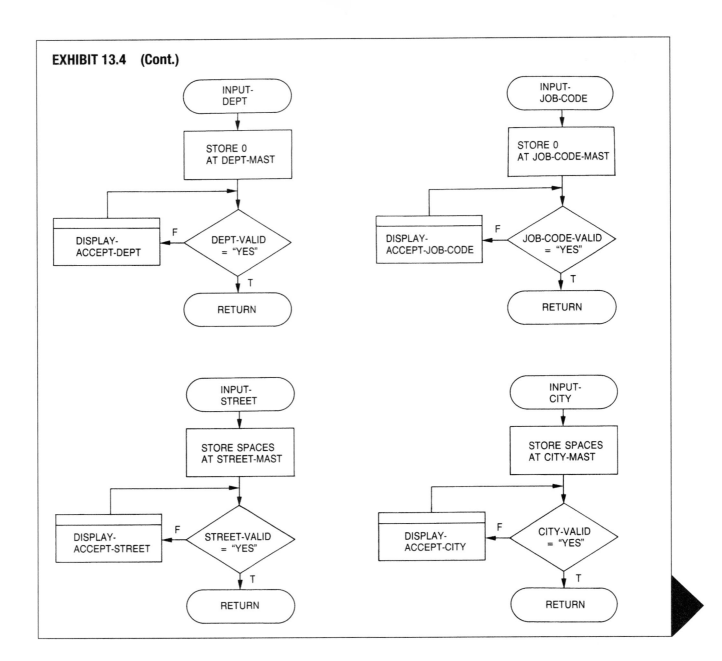

**EXHIBIT 13.4    (Cont.)**

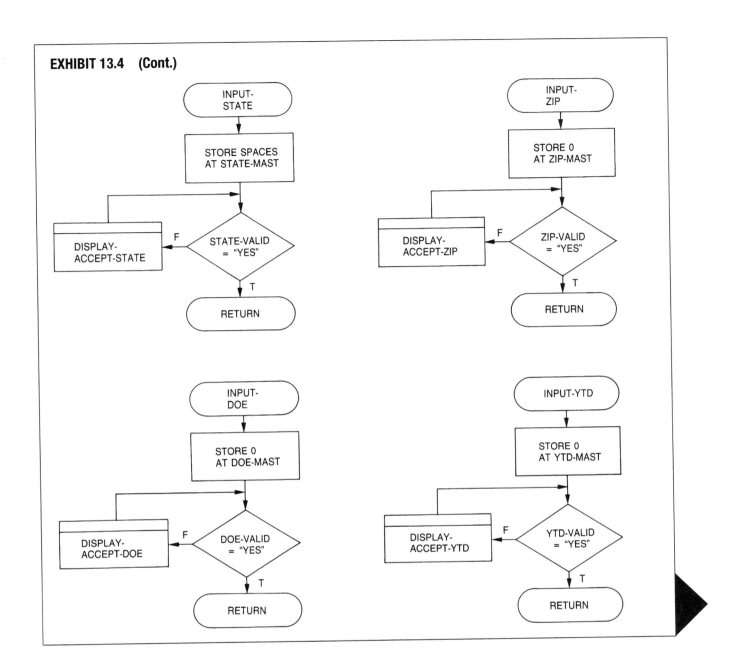

**EXHIBIT 13.4    (Cont.)**

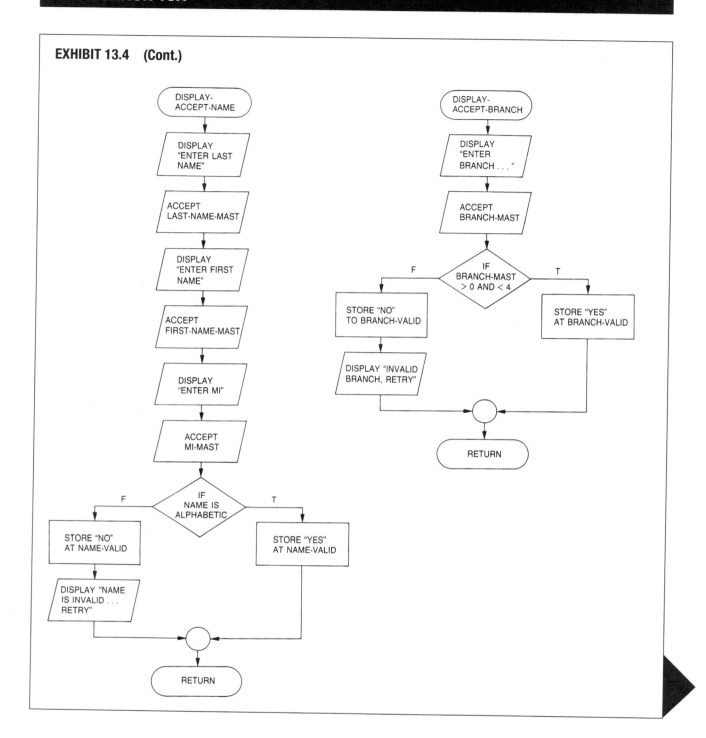

**EXHIBIT 13.4    (Cont.)**

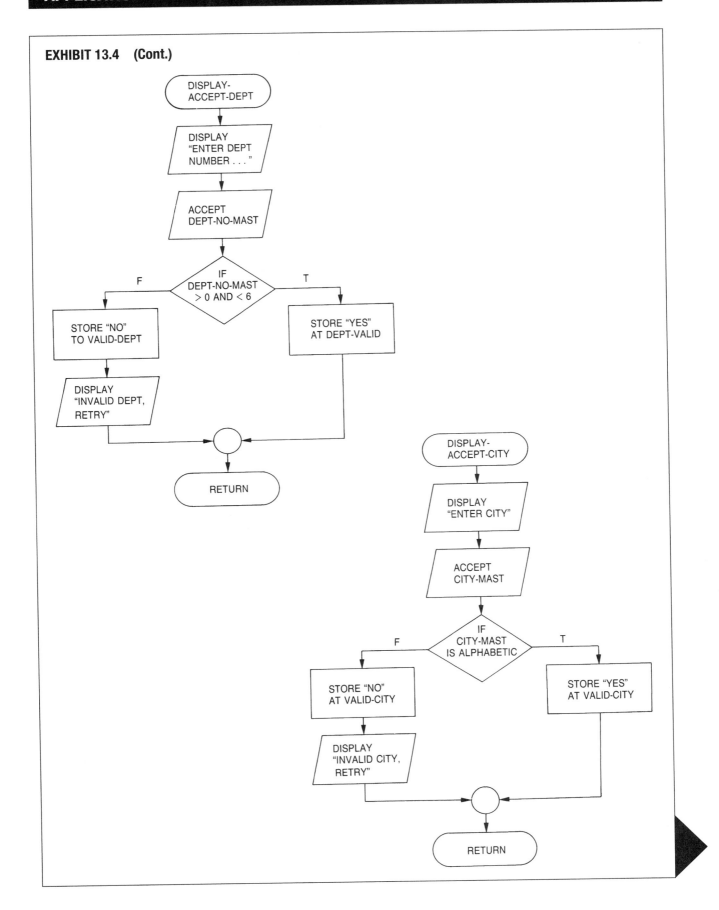

**EXHIBIT 13.4   (Cont.)**

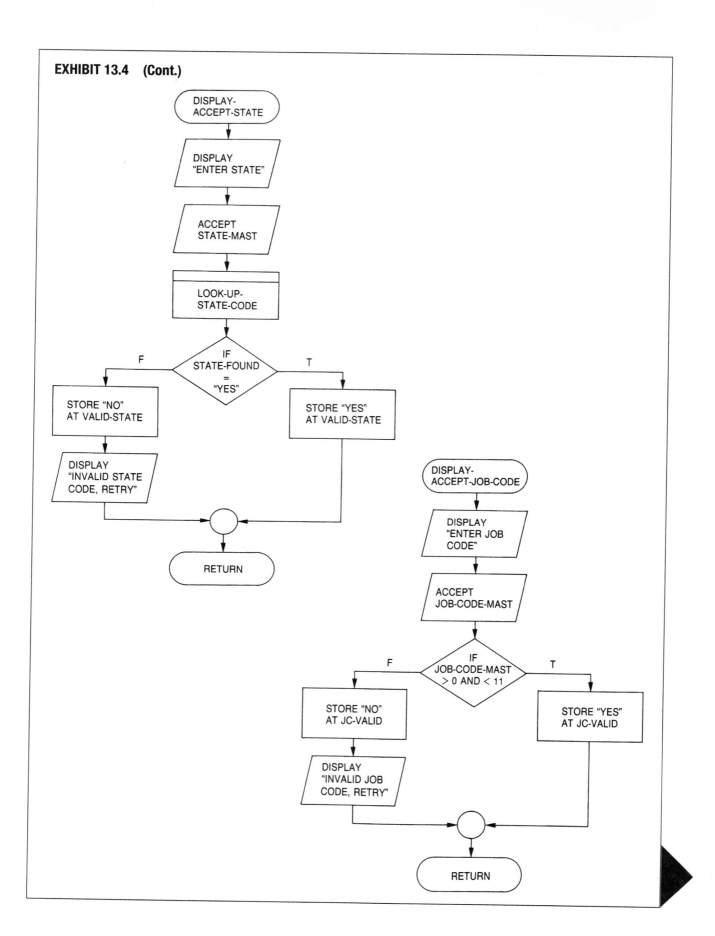

**EXHIBIT 13.4** **(Cont.)**

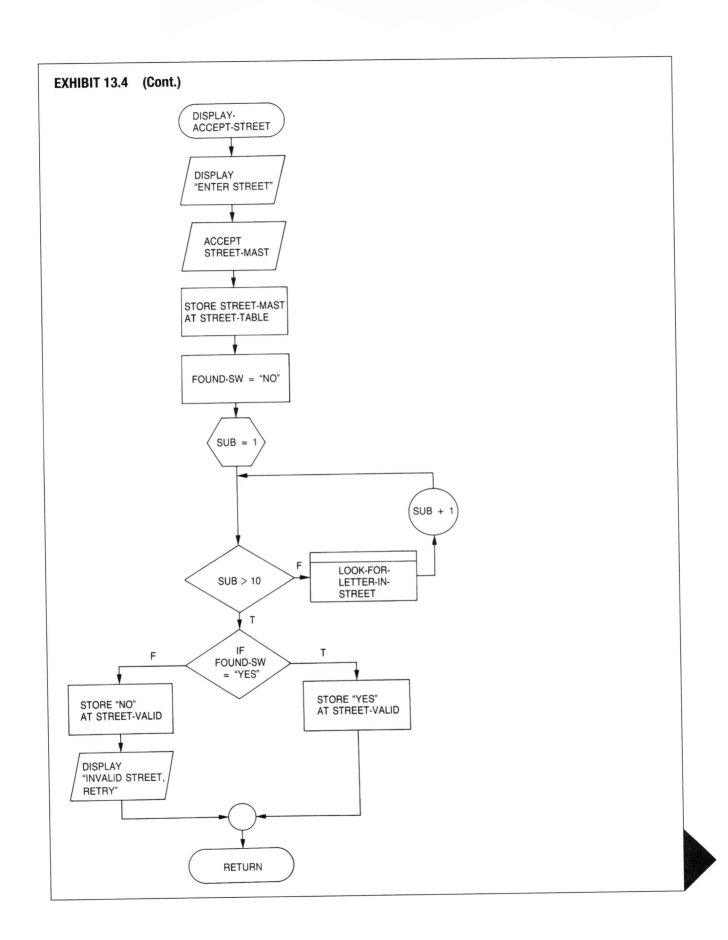

**EXHIBIT 13.4    (Cont.)**

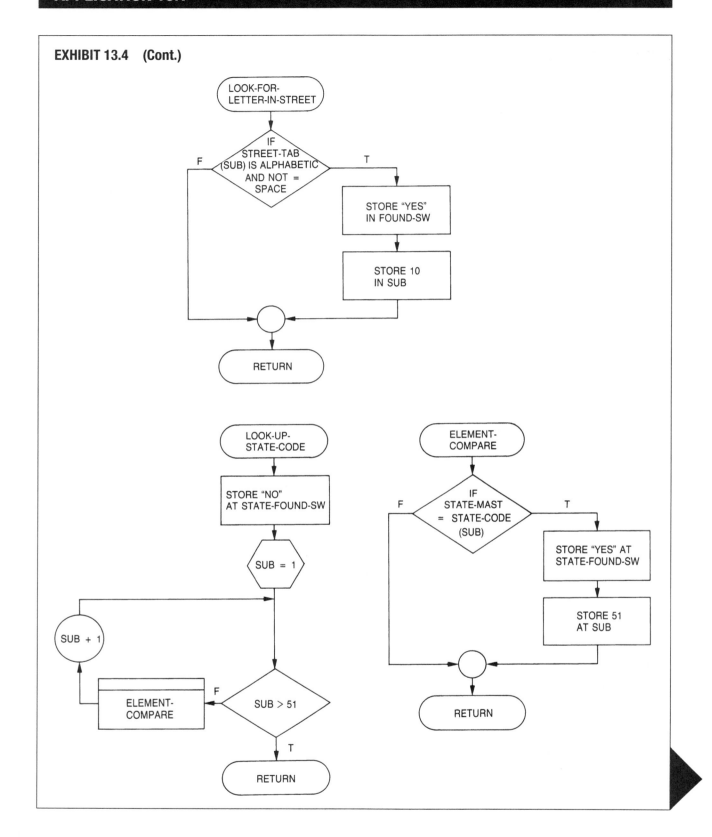

**EXHIBIT 13.4 (Cont.)**

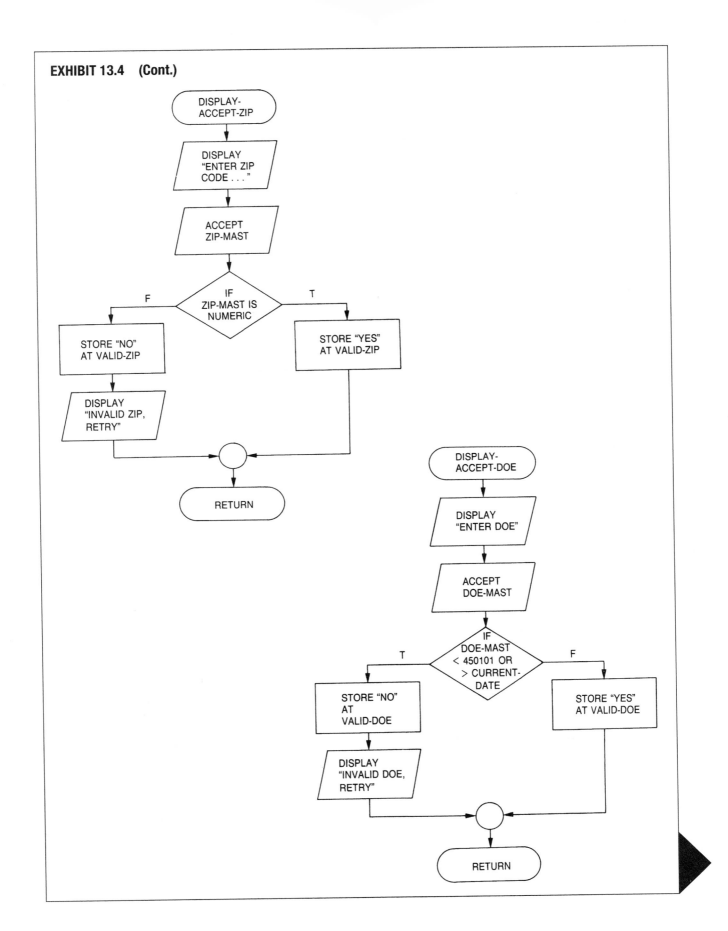

**EXHIBIT 13.4 (Cont.)**

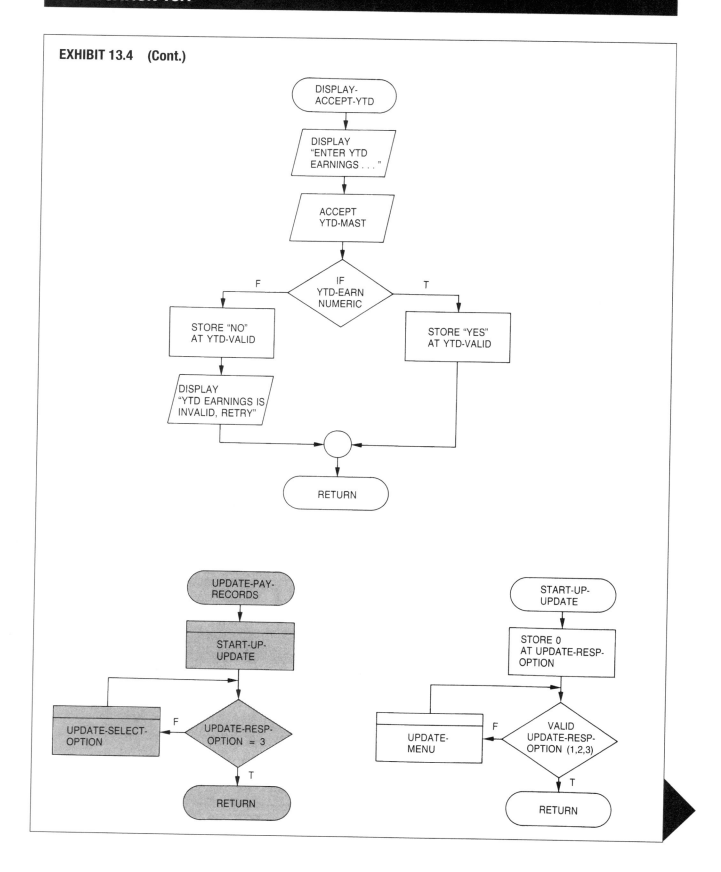

**EXHIBIT 13.4    (Cont.)**

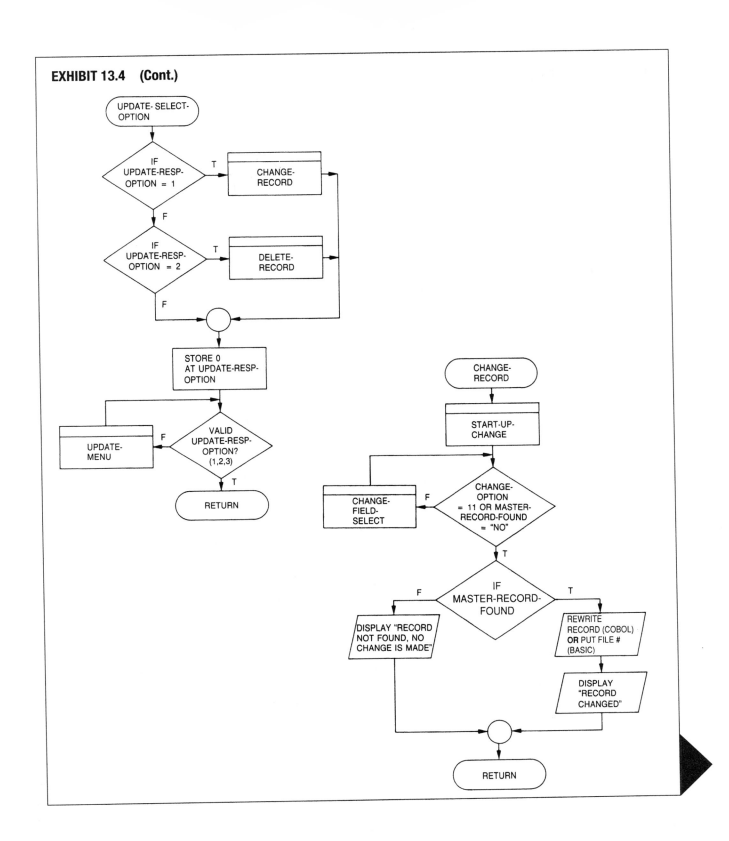

EXHIBIT 13.4   (Cont.)

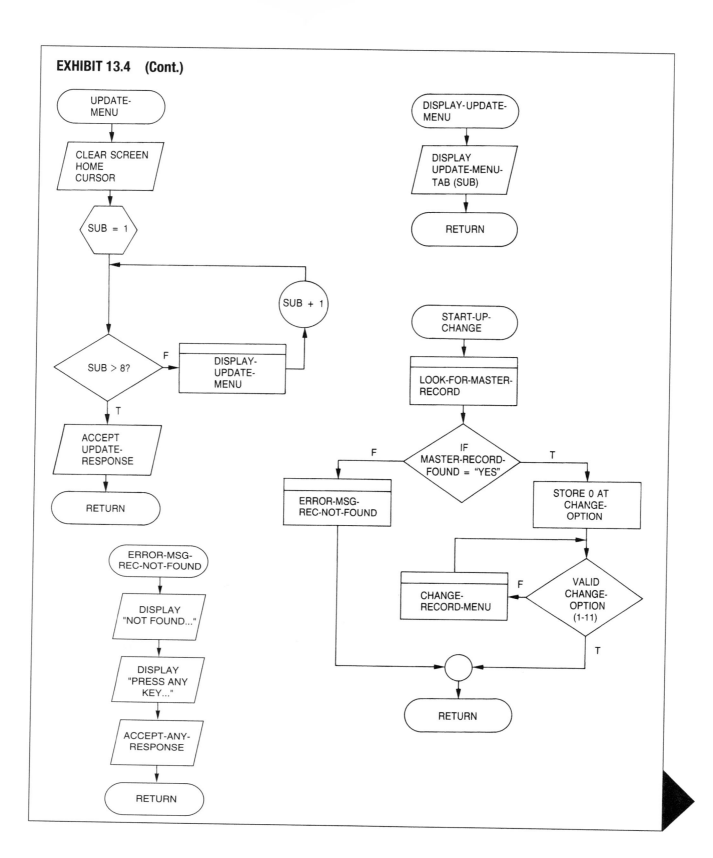

**EXHIBIT 13.4    (Cont.)**

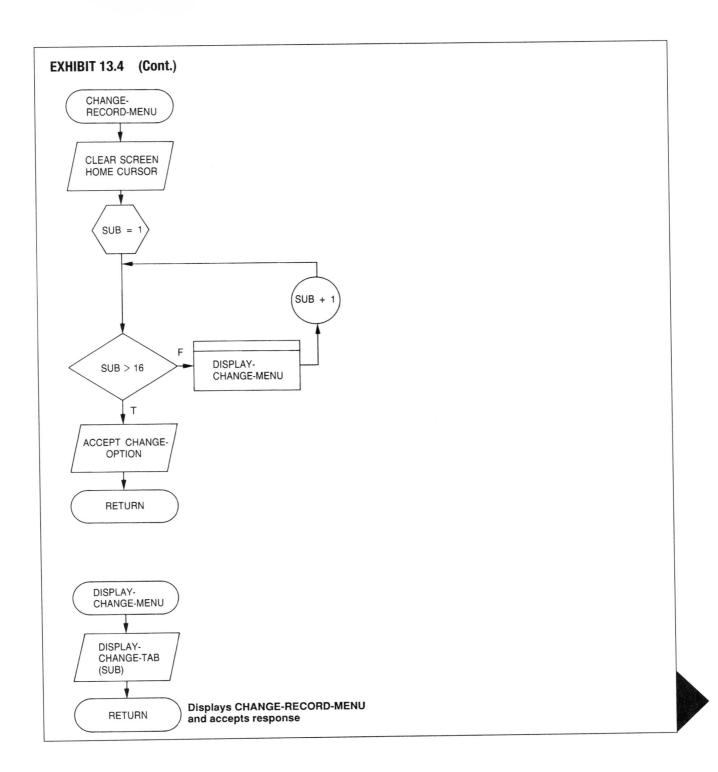

Displays CHANGE-RECORD-MENU
and accepts response

**EXHIBIT 13.4** (Cont.)

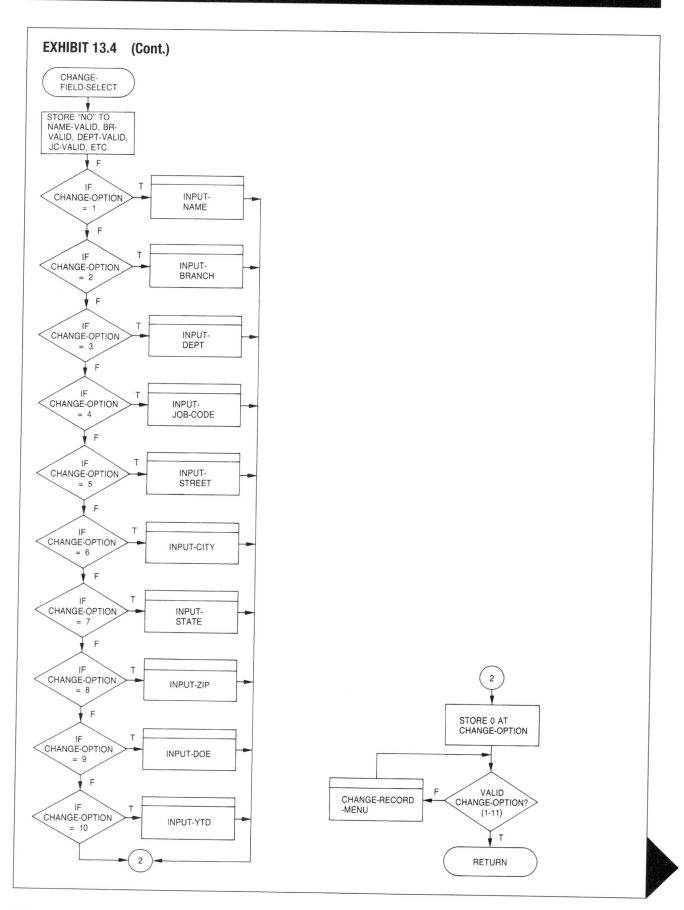

**EXHIBIT 13.4   (Cont.)**

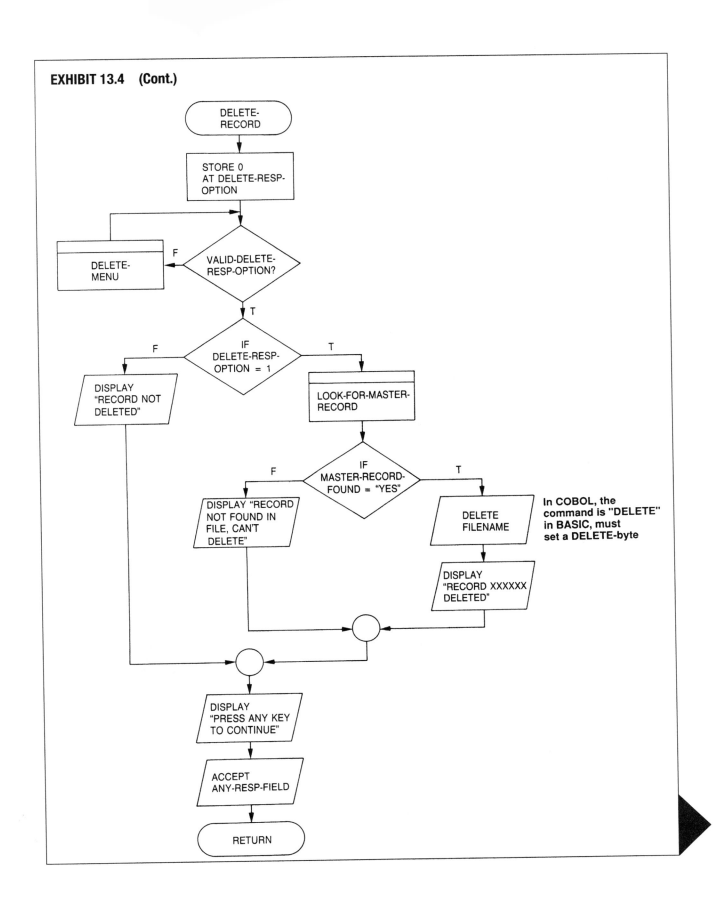

**EXHIBIT 13.4   (Cont.)**

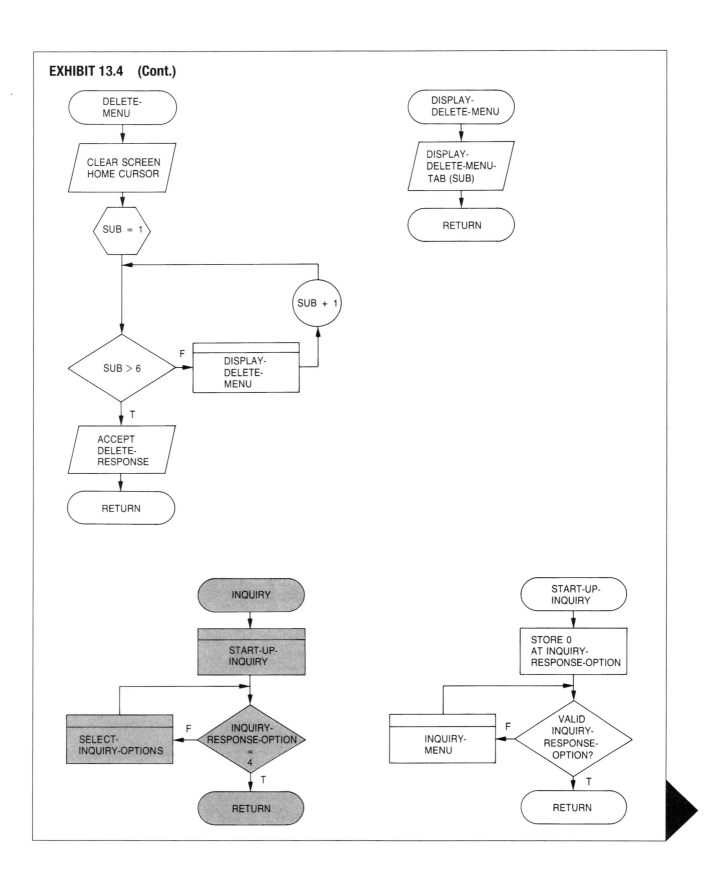

**EXHIBIT 13.4 (Cont.)**

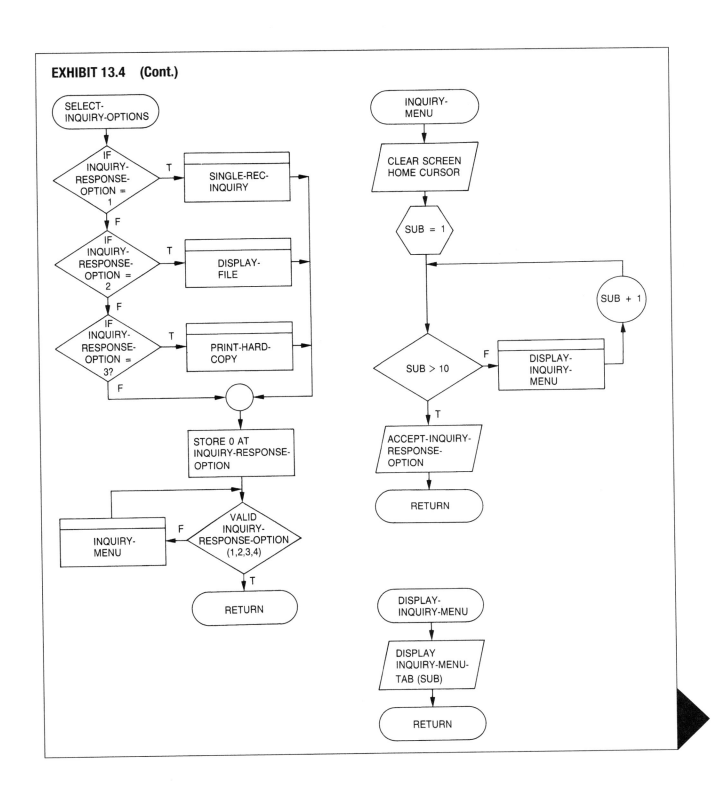

**EXHIBIT 13.4    (Cont.)**

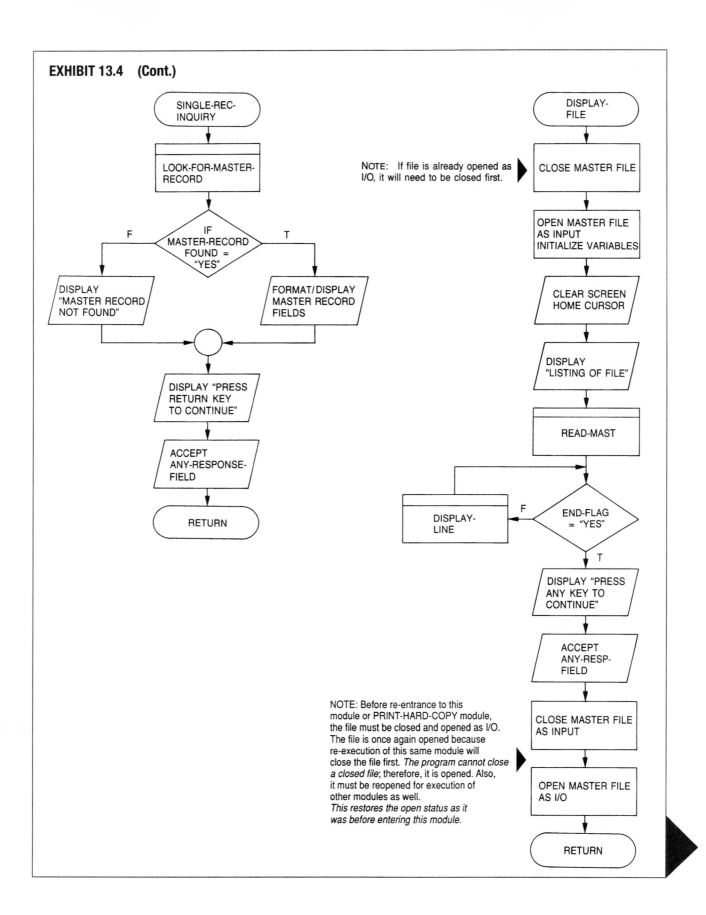

NOTE:   If file is already opened as I/O, it will need to be closed first.

NOTE: Before re-entrance to this module or PRINT-HARD-COPY module, the file must be closed and opened as I/O. The file is once again opened because re-execution of this same module will close the file first. *The program cannot close a closed file*; therefore, it is opened. Also, it must be reopened for execution of other modules as well.
*This restores the open status as it was before entering this module.*

**EXHIBIT 13.4** (Cont.)

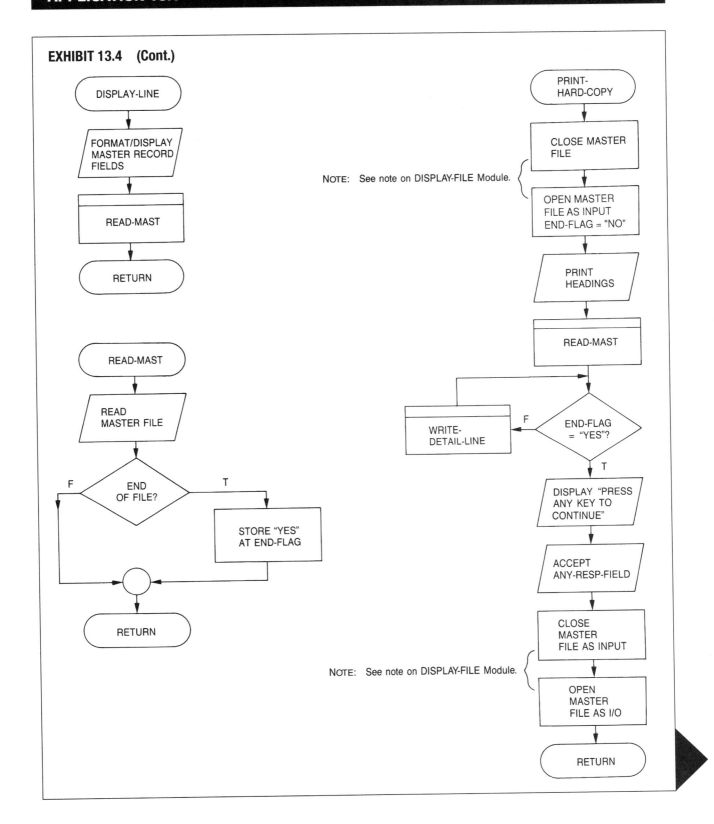

**EXHIBIT 13.4** **(Cont.)**

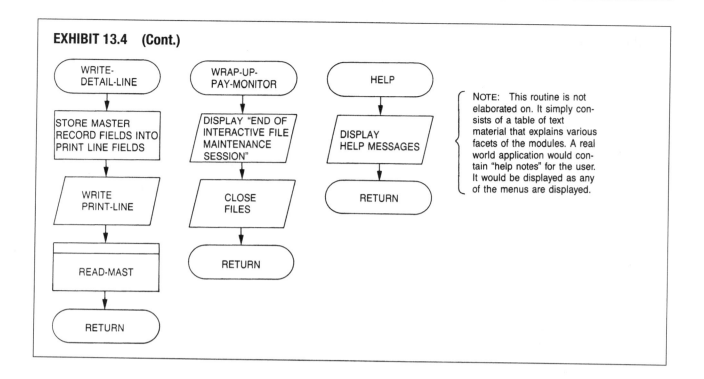

NOTE: This routine is not elaborated on. It simply consists of a table of text material that explains various facets of the modules. A real world application would contain "help notes" for the user. It would be displayed as any of the menus are displayed.

## EXHIBIT 13.5 Pseudocode for Interactive Payroll System

*main-line-payroll
    start-up-pay-monitor
    dountil main-resp-option = 5
        select-main-options
    enddo
    wrap-up-pay-monitor
    stop
*start-up-pay
    accept current-date
    store 0 at main-resp-option
    dowhile main-resp-option not (1,2,3,4)
        main-menu
    enddo
    open-files
    load-state-table
    load-job-desc-tab
    return
*main-menu
    clear screen
    sub = 1
    dowhile sub < 16
        display main-options
    enddo
    return
*display-main-options
    display main-menu-tab (sub)
    accept-main-resp-option
    return
*open-files
    open I-0 Master-file
    open input job-desc-file
    open input job-desc-file
    open state-file
    open output file
    return
*load-state-table
    read-state-table
    sub = 1
    dowhile sub < 52
        state-element-load
        increase sub by 1
    enddo
    return
*read-state-table
    read state-table-file
        when out of records
            store "yes" at end-flag
    end-read
    return
*state-element-load
    store state-code-in to state-code-tab (sub)
    store state-name to state-name-tab (sub)
    read-state-table
    return

*load-job-desc-tab
    read-job-desc-tab
    sub = 1
    do while sub < 11
        desc-element-load
        sub = sub + 1
    enddo
    return
*read-job-desc-tab
    read job-desc-tab-file
        when out of records
            store "yes" at end-flag-job
    end-read
    return
*desc-element-load
    store desc to job-desc-tab (sub)
    read-job-desc-tab
    return
*select-main-options
    if main-resp-option = 1
        add-pay-records
    else
    if main-resp-option = 2
        update-pay-records
    else
    if main-resp-option = 3
        inquiry
    else
    if main-resp-option = 4
        help
    else null
    store 0 at main-resp-option
    dowhile main-resp-option not (1,2,3,4)
        main-menu
    enddo
    return
*add-pay-records
    start-up-add
    dowhile add-resp-option not = 2
        add-a-single-record
    enddo
    return
*start-up-add
    store 0 at add-resp-option
    dowhile add-resp-option is invalid (valid option = 1 or 2)
        add-rec-menu
    enddo
    return

## EXHIBIT 13.5    (Cont.)

```
*add-rec-menu
    clear screen and home cursor
    sub = 1
    dowhile sub < 7
        display-add-menu
        increase sub by 1
    enddo
    accept add-resp-option
    return
*display-add-menu
    display add-menu-tab (sub)
    return
*add-a-single-record
    store 0 at all numeric fields
    store blanks at all alphabetic fields
    look-for-master-record
    if master-record-found = "yes"
        clear screen/home cursor
        display "attempted to add record . . . but already
        exists"
    else
        accept-and-validate-new-record
        if valid-switch = "yes"
            write master record in file
            display "record added to file," ssn-mast
        else display "record not valid . . . not added"
        endif
    endif
    display "press enter to continue"
    accept any-key
    store 0 at add-resp-option
    dowhile add-resp-option not valid (valid options are: 1 or 2)
        add-rec-menu
    enddo
    return
*look-for-master-record
    store "yes" at master-record-found
    store spaces at ssn-mast
    dowhile ssn-mast is not numeric values
        display-accept-ssn-mast
    enddo
    file-search
    return
*display-accept-ssn-mast
    display prompt
    accept ssn-mast
    return
*file-search
    read indexed master file (access is dynamic)
        invalid key (record not found)
            store "no" at master-record-found
    endread
    return
```

```
*accept-and-validate-new-rec
    store "no" to valid-switch
    store "no" to name-valid, br-valid, dept-valid, jc-valid,
        zip-valid, ytd-valid, doe-invalid
    store 0 to br-mast, dept-mast, jc-mast, zip-mast
    input-name
    input-branch
    input-dept
    input-job-code
    input-street
    input-city
    input-state
    input-zip
    input-doe
    input-ytd
    store "yes" at valid-switch
    return
*input-name
    store spaces at name-mast
    dowhile name-valid not = "yes"
        display-accept-name
    enddo
    return
*input-branch
    store spaces to branch-mast
    dowhile branch-valid = "no"
        display-accept-branch
    enddo
    return
*input-dept
    store spaces to dept-mast
    dowhile dept-valid = "no"
        display-accept-dept
    enddo
    return
*input-job-code
    store 0 at job-code-mast
    dowhile job-code-valid = "no"
        display-accept-job-code
    enddo
    return
*input-street
    store spaces at street-mast
    dowhile street-valid = "no"
        display-accept-street
    enddo
    return
*input-city
    store spaces at city-mast
    dowhile city-valid = "no"
        display-accept-city
    enddo
    return
```

**EXHIBIT 13.5    (Cont.)**

```
*input-state
      store spaces at state-mast
      dowhile state-valid = "no"
            display-accept-state
      enddo
      return
*input-zip
      store 0 at zip-mast
      dowhile zip-valid = "no"
            display-accept-zip
      enddo
      return
*input-doe
      store 0 at doe-mast
      dowhile doe-valid = "no"
            display-accept-doe
      enddo
      return
*input-ytd
      store 0 at ytd-mast
      dowhile ytd-valid = "no"
            display-accept-ytd
      enddo
      return
*display-accept-name
      display "enter last name"
      accept last-name-mast
      display "enter first name"
      accept first-name-mast
      display "enter MI"
      accept mi-mast
      if name is alphabetic characters
                  store "yes" at name-valid
      else
            store "no" at name-valid
            display "name is invalid, retry"
      endif
      return
*display-accept-branch
      display "enter branch . . . "
      accept branch-mast
      if branch-mast > 0 and < 4
            store "yes" at branch-valid
      else
            store "no" to branch-valid
            display "invalid branch, retry"
      endif
      return
*display-accept-dept
      display "enter dept number . . . "
      accept dept-no-mast
      if dept-no-master >0 and < 6
            store "yes" at dept-valid
      else
            store "no" to valid-dept
            display "invalid dept, retry"
      endif
      return
```

```
*display-accept-city
      display "enter city"
      accept city-mast
      if city-mast is alphabetic characters
            store "yes" at valid-city
      else
            store "no" at valid-city
            display "invalid city, retry"
      endif
      return
*display-accept-state
      display "enter-state"
      accept state-mast
      look-up-state-code
      if state-found = "yes"
            store "yes" at valid-state
      else
            store "no" at valid-state
            display "invalid state code, retry"
      endif
      return
*display-accept-job-code
      display "enter-job-code"
      accept job-code-mast
      if job-code-mast > 0 and < 11
            store "yes" at jc-valid
      else
            store "no" at jc-valid
            display "invalid job code, retry"
      endif
      return
*display-accept-street
      display "enter street"
      accept street-mast
      store street-mast at street-table
      store "no" at found-sw
      sub = 1
      dowhile sub < 11
            look-for-letter-in-street
            increase sub by 1
      enddo
      if found-sw = "yes"
            store "yes" at valid-street
      else
            store "no" at valid-street
            display "invalid street, retry"
      endif
      return
*look-for-letter-in-street
      if street-tab (sub) is alphabetic & not-space
            store "yes" at found-sw
            store 10 at sub
      endif
      return
```

**EXHIBIT 13.5    (Cont.)**

```
*look-up-state-code
    store "no" at state-found-sw
    sub = 1
    dowhile sub < 52
        element-compare
        increase sub by 1
    enddo
    return
*element-compare
    if state-mast = state-code (sub)
        store "yes" at state-found-sw
        store 51 at sub
    endif
    return
*display-accept-zip
    display "enter zip code . . . "
    accept zip-mast
    if zip-mast is numeric characters
        store "yes" at valid-zip
    else
        store "no" at valid-zip
        display "invalid zip, retry"
    endif
    return
*display-accept-doe
    display "enter date of employment (YYMMDD)"
    accept doe-mast
    if doe-mast < 450101 or > current date
        store "no" at valid-doe
        display "invalid date of employment, retry"
    else
        store "yes" at valid-doe
    endif
    return
*display-accept-ytd
    display "enter ytd earnings . . . "
    accept ytd-mast
    if ytd-mast is numeric characters
        store "yes" at ytd-valid
    else
        store "no" at ytd-valid
        display "ytd earnings is invalid, retry"
    endif
    return
*update-pay-records
    start-up-update
    dowhile update-resp-option not = 3
        update-select-option
    enddo
    return
*start-up-update
    store zero at update-resp-option
    dowhile update-resp-option is not (1,2,3)
        update-menu
    enddo
    return
*update-menu
    clear screen/home cursor
    sub = 1
    dowhile sub < 9
        display-update-menu (sub)
        sub = sub + 1
    enddo
    accept-update-resp-option
    return
*update-select-option
    if update-resp-option = 1
        change-record
    else
        if update-resp-option = 2
            delete-record
        endif
    store zero at update-resp-option
    dowhile update-resp-option not (1,2,3)
        update-menu
    enddo
    return
*change-record
    start-up-change
    dowhile change-option not = 11
    or mast-rec-found not = "yes"
        change-field-select
    enddo
    if mast-rec-found = "yes"
        rewrite record (for COBOL) or PUT file# (for BASIC)
        display "record changed"
    else
        display "record not found, no change is made"
    endif
    return
*start-up-change
    look-for-master-record
    if mast-record-found = "yes"
        store 0 at change-option
        dowhile change-option not (1 through 11)
            change-record-menu
        enddo
    else
        error-msg-rec-not-found
    endif
    return
*change-record-menu
    store spaces at change-option
    home cursor/clear screen
    sub = 1
    dowhile sub < 17
        display change-menu (sub)
        sub = sub + 1
    enddo
    accept-change-option
    return
```

**EXHIBIT 13.5    (Cont.)**

```
*error-msg-rec-not-found
    display "record not found"
    display "press any key to continue"
    accept any-response
    return
*change-field-select
    store "no" at name-valid, br-valid, dept-valid, etc.
    if change-option = 1
        input-name
    else
    if change-option = 2
        input-branch
    else
    if change-option = 3
        input-dept
    else
    if change-option = 4
        input-job-code
    else
    if change-option = 5
        input-street
    else
    if change-option = 6
        input-city
    else
    if change-option = 7
        input-state
    else
    if change-option = 8
        input-zip
    else
    if change-option = 9
        input-doe
    else
    if change-option = 10
        input-ytd
    endif
    store 0 at change-option
    dowhile change-option is not valid
            change-record-menu
    enddo
    return
```

```
*delete-record
    store 0 at delete-option
    dowhile not valid-delete-response-option
        delete-menu
    enddo
    if delete-resp-option = 1
        look-for-master-record
        if master-record-found = "yes"
            delete filename (COBOL)
            or set delete byte in BASIC
            display "record xxxxxxxxx deleted"
        else
            display "record not found in file, cannot delete"
            endif
    else
        display "record not deleted"
    endif
    return
*delete-menu
    clear screen/home cursor
    sub = sub + 1
    dowhile sub < 7
        display delete-menu (sub)
        sub = sub + 1
    enddo
    return
*inquiry
    start-up-inquiry
    dowhile inquiry-response not equal 4
        select-inquiry-options
    enddo
    return
*start-up-inquiry
    store 0 at inquiry-response-option
    dowhile inquiry-response-option not valid
        inquiry-menu
    enddo
    return
*inquiry menu
    clear/home
    sub = 1
    dowhile sub < 11
        display-inquiry-menu (sub)
        sub = sub + 1
    enddo
    accept inquiry-response
    return
```

## EXHIBIT 13.5    (Cont.)

*select-inquiry-options
    if inquiry-response-option = 1
        single-rec-inquiry
    else
    if inquiry-response-option = 2
        display-file
    else
    if inquiry-response-option = 3
        print-hard-copy
    endif
    store 0 at inquiry-response-option
    dowhile inquiry-response-option not = (1,2,3,4)
        inquiry-menu
    enddo
    return
*single-rec-inquiry
    look-for master-record
    if master-record-found = "yes"
        format and display master record fields
    else
        display "master record not found"
    endif
    display "press return key to continue"
    accept any-response-fld
    return
*display-file
    close master file
    open master file as input
    initialize variables
    clear screen/home cursor
    display "listing of master pay file"
    read-mast
    dowhile end-flag not = "yes"
        display-line
    enddo
    display "press any key to continue"
    accept any-resp-field
    close master file
    open master file as I/O
    return

*display-line
    format/display master record fields
    read-mast
    return
*read-mast
    read master-pay-file
        when out of records store "yes" at end-flag
    endread
    return
*print-hard-copy
    close master file
    open master file as input
    print headings
    read-mast
    dowhile end-flag = "no"
        write-detail-line
    enddo
    display "press any key to continue"
    accept any-resp-field
    close master file
    open master file as I/O
*write-detail-line
    move input fields to output fields
    write detail-line
    read-mast
    return
*wrap-up-pay-monitor
    display "end of interactive file maintenance session"
    close files
    return
*help
    display help messages
    return

**EXHIBIT 13.6   COBOL 85 Program for Interactive Payroll System**

```
1           IDENTIFICATION DIVISION.
2           PROGRAM-ID. CH13APL1.
3           DATE-WRITTEN. DEC.4, 1992.
4           DATE-COMPILED. 1993-06-24.
5       *   REMARKS: COBOL 85 PROGRAM
6       *               THIS PROGRAM IS AN INTERACTIVE (ON-LINE) MENU-
7       *               DRIVEN FILE MAINTENANCE PROGRAM FOR A PAYROLL
8       *               SYSTEM.  THE PROGRAM PRESENTS A MAIN MENU THAT
9       *               PROVIDES THE USER THE OPTION OF ADDING NEW
10      *               RECORDS, UPDATING RECORDS (CHANGING AND DELETING), &
11      *               INQUIRING ABOUT THE STATUS OF A RECORD.  THE INQUIRY
12      *               MENU GIVES THE USER THE OPTION OF INQUIRING ABOUT A
13      *               SINGLE RECORD, LISTING THE ENTIRE FILE TO THE SCREEN,
14      *               AND PRINTING A HARD COPY OF THE FILE.  THE INTERACTIVE
15      *               LOGIC PROVIDES ERROR TRAP ROUTINES THAT INSURE VALID
16      *               UPDATE INFORMATION IS BEING ENTERED BY THE USER. EVERY
17      *               MENU PROVIDES A RETURN BACK TO THE PREVIOUS MENU.
18      *
19      *               THE LOGIC IN THIS INTERACTIVE PROGRAM CLOSELY ADHERES
20      *               TO THE LOGIC PREVIOUSLY USED FOR BATCH SYSTEMS WITH
21      *               SOME NECESSARY DIFFERENCES.  SINCE THE USER IS INPUTTING
22      *               RESPONSES AND DATA FROM A TERMINAL THE "PRE-READ" AND
23      *               "POST-READ" LOGIC OF BATCH PROGRAMS ARE REPLACED WITH
24      *               ERROR TRAPS (DATA VALIDATION LOOPS).
25
26         ENVIRONMENT DIVISION.
27         CONFIGURATION SECTION.
28         SOURCE-COMPUTER. CYBER.
29         OBJECT-COMPUTER. CYBER.
30         INPUT-OUTPUT SECTION.
31         FILE-CONTROL.
32             SELECT MASTER-FILE ASSIGN TO PAYFIL6
33                 ACCESS IS DYNAMIC
34                 ORGANIZATION IS INDEXED
35                 RECORD KEY IS SSN-MAST.
36             SELECT STATE-FILE ASSIGN TO STFILE.
37             SELECT JOB-DESC-FILE ASSIGN TO JOBFILE.
38             SELECT OUT-FILE ASSIGN TO OUTFIL6.
39         DATA DIVISION.
40         FILE SECTION.
41         FD MASTER-FILE.
42         01 MASTER-RECORD.
43             05 SSN-MAST              PIC X(9).
44             05 NAME-MAST.
45                     10 LAST-NAME-MAST   PIC X(10).
46                     10 FIRST-NAME-MAST  PIC X(9).
47                     10 MI-MAST          PIC X.
48             05 BRANCH-MAST          PIC 9(3).
49             05 DEPT-MAST            PIC 9(3).
50             05 FILLER               PIC X.
51             05 JOB-CODE-MAST        PIC 99.
52             05 STREET-MAST          PIC X(10).
53             05 CITY-MAST            PIC X(10).
54             05 STATE-MAST           PIC X(2).
55             05 ZIP-MAST             PIC 9(5).
56             05 DOE-MAST.
57                     10 MONTH-MAST       PIC 99.
58                     10 DAY-MAST         PIC 99.
59                     10 YEAR-MAST        PIC 99.
60             05 YTD-MAST         PIC 999999V99.
61             05 FILLER               PIC X.
62
63         FD STATE-FILE.
64         01 STATE-RECORD.
65             05 STATE-RECORD-CODE         PIC XX.
66             05 STATE-RECORD-NAME         PIC X(20).
```

**EXHIBIT 13.6**   **(Cont.)**

```
67
68          FD  JOB-DESC-FILE.
69          01  JOB-DESC-RECORD              PIC X(17).
70
71          FD  OUT-FILE.
72          01  OUT-REC                      PIC X(133).
73
74          WORKING-STORAGE SECTION.
75
76          01  SWITCHES.
77              05  MASTER-RECORD-FOUND      PIC X(3) VALUE "YES".
78              05  STATE-FOUND              PIC X(3) VALUE "YES".
79              05  FOUND-SW                 PIC X(3) VALUE "YES".
80              05  END-FLAG                 PIC X(3) VALUE "YES".
81              05  VALID-SWITCH             PIC X(3) VALUE "YES".
82                  88  VALID-NEW-RECORD              VALUE "YES".
83
84          01  MISC-VARIABLES.
85              05  CURRENT-DATE.
86                  10  CURRENT-YEAR         PIC 99.
87                  10  CURRENT-MONTH        PIC 99.
88                  10  CURRENT-DAY          PIC 99.
89              05  SUB                      PIC 99 VALUE ZERO.
90
91          01  VALIDATION-VARIABLES.
92              05  NAME-VALID               PIC X(3) VALUE "YES".
93              05  BRANCH-VALID             PIC X(3) VALUE "YES".
94              05  DEPT-VALID               PIC X(3) VALUE "YES".
95              05  JOB-CODE-VALID           PIC X(3) VALUE "YES".
96              05  STREET-VALID             PIC X(3) VALUE "YES".
97              05  CITY-VALID               PIC X(3) VALUE "YES".
98              05  STATE-VALID              PIC X(3) VALUE "YES".
99              05  ZIP-VALID                PIC X(3) VALUE "YES".
100             05  DOE-VALID                PIC X(3) VALUE "YES".
101             05  YTD-VALID                PIC X(3) VALUE "YES".
102
103         01  RESPONSE-OPTION-VARIABLES.
104             05  MAIN-RESP-OPTION         PIC 9 VALUE ZERO.
105                 88  VALID-MAIN-RESP-OPTION    VALUE 1 THRU 5.
106             05  ADD-RESP-OPTION          PIC 9 VALUE ZERO.
107                 88  VALID-ADD-RESP-OPTION     VALUE 1 THRU 2.
108             05  UPDATE-RESP-OPTION       PIC 9 VALUE ZERO.
109                 88  VALID-UPDATE-RESP-OPTION  VALUE 1 THRU 3.
110             05  CHANGE-RESP-OPTION       PIC 99 VALUE ZERO.
111                 88  VALID-CHANGE-RESP-OPTION  VALUE 01 THRU 11.
112             05  DELETE-RESP-OPTION       PIC X VALUE SPACE.
113                 88  VALID-DELETE-RESP-OPTION  VALUE 1 THRU 2.
114             05  INQUIRY-RESP-OPTION      PIC 9 VALUE ZERO.
115                 88  VALID-INQUIRY-RESP-OPTION VALUE 1 THRU 4.
116             05  ANY-RESP-FIELD           PIC 9 VALUE ZERO.
117
118         01  MENU-MAIN.
119             05          PIC X(70) VALUE "                        ACME INDUSTRIE
120         -   "S PAYROLL FILE MAINTENANCE".
121             05          PIC X(70) VALUE SPACES.
122             05          PIC X(70) VALUE "
123         -   "MAIN MENU".
124             05          PIC X(70) VALUE SPACES.
125             05          PIC X(70) VALUE SPACES.
126             05          PIC X(70) VALUE
127             "                                1........ADD A RECORD".
128             05          PIC X(70) VALUE SPACES.
129             05          PIC X(70) VALUE
130             "                                2........UPDATE (CHANGE/DELETE) ".
131             05          PIC X(70) VALUE SPACES.
132             05          PIC X(70) VALUE
```

**EXHIBIT 13.6 (Cont.)**

```
133                      "                        3........INQUIRY".
134            05        PIC X(70) VALUE SPACES.
135            05        PIC X(70) VALUE
136                      "                        4........HELP".
137            05        PIC X(70) VALUE SPACES.
138            05        PIC X(70) VALUE
139                      "                        5........END FILE MAINTENANCE SESSI
140       -         "ON".
141            05        PIC X(70) VALUE SPACES.
142
143        01 MAIN-MENU REDEFINES MENU-MAIN.
144            05 MAIN-MENU-TABLE OCCURS 15 TIMES PIC X(70).
145
146        01 MENU-ADD.
147            05        PIC X(70) VALUE
148                      "                          ADD MENU (PAYROLL FILE)".
149            05        PIC X(70) VALUE SPACES.
150            05        PIC X(70) VALUE SPACES.
151            05        PIC X(70) VALUE
152                      "                        1........ADD A RECORD".
153            05        PIC X(70) VALUE SPACES.
154            05        PIC X(70) VALUE
155                      "                        2........RETURN TO MAIN MENU    ".
156
157        01 ADD-MENU REDEFINES MENU-ADD.
158            05 ADD-MENU-TABLE OCCURS 6 TIMES PIC X(70).
159
160        01 MENU-UPDATE.
161            05        PIC X(70) VALUE
162                      "                          UPDATE MENU (PAYROLL)".
163            05        PIC X(70) VALUE SPACES.
164            05        PIC X(70) VALUE SPACES.
165            05        PIC X(70) VALUE
166                      "                        1........CHANGE A RECORD        ".
167            05        PIC X(70) VALUE SPACES.
168            05        PIC X(70) VALUE
169                      "                        2........DELETE A RECORD        ".
170            05        PIC X(70) VALUE SPACES.
171            05        PIC X(70) VALUE
172                      "                        3........RETURN TO MAIN MENU    ".
173
174        01 UPDATE-MENU REDEFINES MENU-UPDATE.
175            05 UPDATE-MENU-TABLE OCCURS 8 TIMES PIC X(70).
176
177        01 MENU-DELETE.
178            05        PIC X(70) VALUE
179                      "                          DELETE MENU (PAYROLL)".
180            05        PIC X(70) VALUE SPACES.
181            05        PIC X(70) VALUE SPACES.
182            05        PIC X(70) VALUE
183                      "                        1........DELETE A RECORD        ".
184            05        PIC X(70) VALUE SPACES.
185            05        PIC X(70) VALUE
186                      "                        2........RETURN TO UPDATE MENU  ".
187
188        01 DELETE-MENU REDEFINES MENU-DELETE.
189            05 DELETE-MENU-TABLE OCCURS 6 TIMES PIC X(70).
190
191        01 MENU-INQUIRY.
192            05        PIC X(70) VALUE
193                      "                          INQUIRY MENU (PAYROLL)".
194            05        PIC X(70) VALUE SPACES.
195            05        PIC X(70) VALUE SPACES.
196            05        PIC X(70) VALUE
197                      "                        1........INQUIRE ABOUT A SINGLE REC
198       -         "ORD".
```

**EXHIBIT 13.6** (Cont.)

```
199            05          PIC X(70) VALUE SPACES.
200            05          PIC X(70) VALUE
201               "                      2........LIST PAYROLL FILE (SCREEN
202        -         "OUTPUT)".
203            05          PIC X(70) VALUE SPACES.
204            05          PIC X(70) VALUE
205               "                      3........PRINT A HARD COPY OF PAYRO
206        -         "LL FILE".
207            05          PIC X(70) VALUE SPACES.
208            05          PIC X(70) VALUE
209               "                      4........RETURN TO MAIN MENU    ".
210
211      01 INQUIRY-MENU REDEFINES MENU-INQUIRY.
212            05 INQUIRY-MENU-TABLE OCCURS 10 TIMES PIC X(70).
213
214      01 MENU-CHANGE.
215            05          PIC X(70) VALUE
216               "                          CHANGE MENU (PAYROLL)".
217            05          PIC X(70) VALUE SPACES.
218            05          PIC X(70) VALUE SPACES.
219            05          PIC X(70) VALUE
220               "              SELECT THE FIELD LISTED BELOW THAT YOU
221        -         "WISH TO CHANGE".
222            05          PIC X(70) VALUE SPACES.
223            05          PIC X(70) VALUE
224               "                      01........NAME".
225            05          PIC X(70) VALUE
226               "                      02........BRANCH".
227            05          PIC X(70) VALUE
228               "                      03........DEPARTMENT".
229            05          PIC X(70) VALUE
230               "                      04........JOB CODE".
231            05          PIC X(70) VALUE
232               "                      05........STREET".
233            05          PIC X(70) VALUE
234               "                      06........CITY".
235            05          PIC X(70) VALUE
236               "                      07........STATE".
237            05          PIC X(70) VALUE
238               "                      08........ZIP".
239            05          PIC X(70) VALUE
240               "                      09........DOE".
241            05          PIC X(70) VALUE
242               "                      10........YTD GROSS".
243            05          PIC X(70) VALUE
244               "                      11........RETURN TO UPDATE MENU   ".
245
246      01 CHANGE-MENU REDEFINES MENU-CHANGE.
247            05 CHANGE-MENU-TABLE OCCURS 16 TIMES PIC X(70).
248
249      01 STATE-TAB.
250            05 STATE-TABLE OCCURS 51 TIMES.
251               10 STATE-CODE     PIC XX.
252               10 STATE-NAME     PIC X(20).
253
254      01 STREET-TABLE.
255            05 STREET-TAB OCCURS 10 TIMES  PIC X.
256               88 LETTER-CHECK VALUES ARE "A" THRU "Z".
257
258      01 JOB-DESC-TABLE.
259            05 JOB-DESCRIPTION OCCURS 10 TIMES PIC X(17).
260
261      01 HEADING-LINE-1.
262            05                    PIC X(15) VALUE SPACES.
263            05                    PIC X(26) VALUE "PAYROLL PERSONNEL REG
264        -            "ISTER".
265
```

**EXHIBIT 13.6    (Cont.)**

```
266         01 HEADING-LINE-2.
267             05                      PIC X(2) VALUE SPACES.
268             05                      PIC X(11) VALUE "SSN".
269             05                      PIC X(24) VALUE "NAME".
270             05                      PIC X(12) VALUE "STREET".
271             05                      PIC X(10) VALUE "CITY".
272             05                      PIC X(7) VALUE "STATE".
273             05                      PIC X(5) VALUE "ZIP".
274             05                      PIC X(6) VALUE "DEPT".
275             05                      PIC X(5) VALUE "BR".
276             05                      PIC X(4) VALUE "JC".
277             05                      PIC X(3) VALUE "YTD".
278
279         01 DETAIL-LINE.
280             05                      PIC X(2) VALUE SPACES.
281             05 SSN-DETAIL           PIC X(9).
282             05                      PIC X(2) VALUE SPACES.
283             05 LAST-NAME-DETAIL     PIC X(10).
284             05                      PIC X VALUE SPACE.
285             05 FIRST-NAME-DETAIL    PIC X(9).
286             05                      PIC X VALUE SPACE.
287             05 MI-DETAIL            PIC X.
288             05                      PIC X(2) VALUE SPACES.
289             05 STREET-DETAIL        PIC X(10).
290             05                      PIC X(2) VALUE SPACES.
291             05 CITY-DETAIL          PIC X(10).
292             05                      PIC X(2) VALUE SPACES.
293             05 STATE-DETAIL         PIC X(2).
294             05                      PIC X(2) VALUE SPACES.
295             05 ZIP-DETAIL           PIC 9(5).
296             05                      PIC X(2) VALUE SPACES.
297             05 DEPT-DETAIL          PIC 9(3).
298             05                      PIC X(2) VALUE SPACES.
299             05 BRANCH-DETAIL        PIC 9(3).
300             05                      PIC X(2) VALUE SPACES.
301             05 JOB-CODE-DETAIL      PIC 9(2).
302             05                      PIC X(2) VALUE SPACES.
303             05 YTD-DETAIL           PIC 9(6).99.
304             05                      PIC X(44) VALUE SPACES.
305         /
306          PROCEDURE DIVISION.
307
308          0000-MAIN-LINE.
309             PERFORM 0100-START-UP-PAY.
310             PERFORM 0200-SELECT-MAIN-OPTIONS UNTIL MAIN-RESP-OPTION = 5.
311             PERFORM 5000-WRAP-UP-PAY.
312             STOP RUN.
313
314          0100-START-UP-PAY.
315             ACCEPT CURRENT-DATE FROM DATE.
316             MOVE 0 TO MAIN-RESP-OPTION.
317             PERFORM 0110-MAIN-MENU UNTIL VALID-MAIN-RESP-OPTION.
318             PERFORM OPEN-FILES.
319             PERFORM 0102-LOAD-STATE-TABLE.
320             PERFORM 0107-LOAD-JOB-DESC-TABLE.
321
322          OPEN-FILES.
323             OPEN I-O MASTER-FILE
324                  INPUT STATE-FILE
325                  INPUT JOB-DESC-FILE
326                  OUTPUT OUT-FILE.
327
328          0102-LOAD-STATE-TABLE.
329             PERFORM 0104-READ-STATE-TABLE.
330             PERFORM        VARYING SUB FROM 1 BY 1
331                 UNTIL SUB > 51
```

EXHIBIT 13.6 (Cont.)

```
332
333                     MOVE STATE-RECORD-CODE TO STATE-CODE (SUB)
334                     MOVE STATE-RECORD-NAME TO STATE-NAME (SUB)
335                     PERFORM 0104-READ-STATE-TABLE
336              END-PERFORM.
337
338        0104-READ-STATE-TABLE.
339           READ STATE-FILE AT END MOVE "YES" TO END-FLAG.
340
341        0107-LOAD-JOB-DESC-TABLE.
342           PERFORM 0109-READ-JOB-DESC-TAB.
343           PERFORM       VARYING SUB FROM 1 BY 1
344             UNTIL SUB > 10
345
346                     MOVE JOB-DESC-RECORD TO JOB-DESCRIPTION (SUB)
347                     PERFORM 0109-READ-JOB-DESC-TAB
348              END-PERFORM.
349
350        0109-READ-JOB-DESC-TAB.
351           READ JOB-DESC-FILE AT END MOVE "YES" TO END-FLAG.
352
353
354        0110-MAIN-MENU.
355           DISPLAY ":I +".
356           PERFORM 0111-DISPLAY-MAIN-OPTIONS VARYING SUB FROM 1 BY 1
357              UNTIL SUB > 15.
358           ACCEPT MAIN-RESP-OPTION.
359
360        0111-DISPLAY-MAIN-OPTIONS.
361           DISPLAY MAIN-MENU-TABLE (SUB).
362
363
364        0200-SELECT-MAIN-OPTIONS.
365           IF MAIN-RESP-OPTION = 1
366              THEN PERFORM 1000-ADD-PAY-RECORDS
367           ELSE
368           IF MAIN-RESP-OPTION = 2
369              THEN PERFORM 2000-UPDATE-PAY-RECORDS
370           ELSE
371           IF MAIN-RESP-OPTION = 3
372              THEN PERFORM 3000-INQUIRY
373           ELSE
374           IF MAIN-RESP-OPTION = 4
375              THEN PERFORM 4000-HELP
376           ELSE NEXT SENTENCE.
377           MOVE 0 TO MAIN-RESP-OPTION.
378           PERFORM 0110-MAIN-MENU UNTIL VALID-MAIN-RESP-OPTION.
379
380        1000-ADD-PAY-RECORDS.
381           PERFORM 1100-START-UP-ADD.
382           PERFORM 1400-ADD-A-SINGLE-RECORD UNTIL ADD-RESP-OPTION = 2.
383
384        1100-START-UP-ADD.
385           MOVE 0 TO ADD-RESP-OPTION.
386           PERFORM 1200-ADD-REC-MENU UNTIL VALID-ADD-RESP-OPTION.
387
388        1200-ADD-REC-MENU.
389           DISPLAY ":I +"
390           PERFORM 1300-DISPLAY-ADD-MENU VARYING SUB FROM 1 BY 1
391              UNTIL SUB > 6.
392           ACCEPT ADD-RESP-OPTION.
393
394        1300-DISPLAY-ADD-MENU.
395           DISPLAY ADD-MENU-TABLE (SUB).
396
```

**EXHIBIT 13.6** (Cont.)

```
397        1400-ADD-A-SINGLE-RECORD.
398            MOVE SPACES TO SSN-MAST.
399            MOVE SPACES TO NAME-MAST.
400            MOVE 0 TO BRANCH-MAST.
401            MOVE 0 TO DEPT-MAST.
402            MOVE 0 TO JOB-CODE-MAST.
403            MOVE SPACES TO STREET-MAST.
404            MOVE SPACES TO CITY-MAST.
405            MOVE SPACES TO STATE-MAST.
406            MOVE 0 TO ZIP-MAST.
407            MOVE 0 TO DOE-MAST.
408            MOVE 0 TO YTD-MAST.
409            PERFORM 1500-LOOK-FOR-MASTER-RECORD.
410            IF MASTER-RECORD-FOUND = "YES"
411                THEN DISPLAY ":I +"
412                    DISPLAY "ATTEMPTED TO ADD RECORD " SSN-MAST " BUT RE
413    -               "CORD ALREADY EXISTS"
414                    DISPLAY "                        ......CANNOT DUPLIC
415    -               "ATE THIS RECORD...."
416            ELSE PERFORM 1600-ACCEPT-N-VALIDATE-RECORD
417                IF VALID-NEW-RECORD
418                    THEN WRITE MASTER-RECORD
419                        DISPLAY "RECORD " SSN-MAST " ADDED TO FILE"
420                    ELSE DISPLAY "RECORD " SSN-MAST " NOT VALID..NOT
421    -                   " ADDED".
422            DISPLAY "PRESS ENTER TO CONTINUE".
423            ACCEPT ADD-RESP-OPTION.
424            MOVE 0 TO ADD-RESP-OPTION.
425            PERFORM 1200-ADD-REC-MENU UNTIL VALID-ADD-RESP-OPTION.
426
427        1500-LOOK-FOR-MASTER-RECORD.
428            MOVE "YES" TO MASTER-RECORD-FOUND.
429            MOVE SPACES TO SSN-MAST.
430            PERFORM 1550-DISPLAY-ACCEPT-SSN-MAST
431                UNTIL SSN-MAST IS NUMERIC.
432            PERFORM 1575-FILE-SEARCH.
433
434        1550-DISPLAY-ACCEPT-SSN-MAST.
435            DISPLAY "ENTER SSN FOR RECORD".
436            ACCEPT SSN-MAST.
437
438        1575-FILE-SEARCH.
439            READ MASTER-FILE
440                INVALID KEY
441                    MOVE "NO" TO MASTER-RECORD-FOUND.
442
443        1600-ACCEPT-N-VALIDATE-RECORD.
444            MOVE "NO" TO VALID-SWITCH.
445            MOVE "NO" TO NAME-VALID.
446            MOVE "NO" TO BRANCH-VALID.
447            MOVE "NO" TO DEPT-VALID.
448            MOVE "NO" TO JOB-CODE-VALID.
449            MOVE "NO" TO STREET-VALID.
450            MOVE "NO" TO CITY-VALID.
451            MOVE "NO" TO STATE-VALID.
452            MOVE "NO" TO ZIP-VALID.
453            MOVE "NO" TO DOE-VALID.
454            MOVE "NO" TO YTD-VALID.
455            PERFORM 1700-INPUT-NAME.
456            PERFORM 1710-INPUT-BRANCH.
457            PERFORM 1720-INPUT-DEPT.
458            PERFORM 1730-INPUT-JOB-CODE.
459            PERFORM 1740-INPUT-STREET.
460            PERFORM 1750-INPUT-CITY.
461            PERFORM 1760-INPUT-STATE.
462            PERFORM 1770-INPUT-ZIP.
```

**EXHIBIT 13.6    (Cont.)**

```
464                PERFORM 1790-INPUT-YTD.
465                MOVE "YES" TO VALID-SWITCH.
466
467          1700-INPUT-NAME.
468              MOVE SPACES TO NAME-MAST.
469              PERFORM 1705-DISPLAY-ACCEPT-NAME UNTIL NAME-VALID = "YES".
470
471          1705-DISPLAY-ACCEPT-NAME.
472              DISPLAY "ENTER LAST NAME".
473              ACCEPT LAST-NAME-MAST.
474              DISPLAY "ENTER FIRST NAME".
475              ACCEPT FIRST-NAME-MAST.
476              DISPLAY "ENTER MI".
477              ACCEPT MI-MAST.
478              IF NAME-MAST IS ALPHABETIC
479                  THEN MOVE "YES" TO NAME-VALID
480                  ELSE MOVE "NO" TO NAME-VALID
481                      DISPLAY "NAME IS INVALID..RETRY".
482
483          1710-INPUT-BRANCH.
484              MOVE ZERO TO BRANCH-MAST.
485              PERFORM 1715-DISPLAY-ACCEPT-BRANCH UNTIL BRANCH-VALID =
486                  "YES".
487
488          1715-DISPLAY-ACCEPT-BRANCH.
489              DISPLAY "ENTER BRANCH NUMBER (001-003 ARE ALLOWABLE)".
490              ACCEPT BRANCH-MAST.
491              IF BRANCH-MAST > 0 AND BRANCH-MAST < 4
492                  THEN MOVE "YES" TO BRANCH-VALID
493                  ELSE MOVE "NO" TO BRANCH-VALID
494                      DISPLAY "INVALID BRANCH..RETRY"
495              END-IF.
496
497          1720-INPUT-DEPT.
498              MOVE ZERO TO DEPT-MAST.
499              PERFORM 1725-DISPLAY-ACCEPT-DEPT UNTIL DEPT-VALID = "YES".
500
501          1725-DISPLAY-ACCEPT-DEPT.
502              DISPLAY "ENTER DEPT NUMBER (001-005 ARE ALLOWABLE)".
503              ACCEPT DEPT-MAST.
504              IF DEPT-MAST > 0 AND DEPT-MAST < 6
505                  THEN MOVE "YES" TO DEPT-VALID
506                  ELSE MOVE "NO" TO DEPT-VALID
507                      DISPLAY "INVALID DEPT..RETRY"
508              END-IF.
509
510          1730-INPUT-JOB-CODE.
511              MOVE ZERO TO JOB-CODE-MAST.
512              PERFORM 1735-DISPLAY-ACCEPT-JOB-CODE UNTIL JOB-CODE-VALID =
513                  "YES".
514
515          1735-DISPLAY-ACCEPT-JOB-CODE.
516              DISPLAY "ENTER JOB CODE (01-10 ARE ALLOWABLE)".
517              ACCEPT  JOB-CODE-MAST.
518              IF JOB-CODE-MAST > 0 AND JOB-CODE-MAST < 11
519                  THEN MOVE "YES" TO JOB-CODE-VALID
520                  ELSE MOVE "NO" TO JOB-CODE-VALID
521                      DISPLAY "INVALID JOB CODE..RETRY"
522              END-IF.
523
524          1740-INPUT-STREET.
525              MOVE SPACES TO STREET-MAST.
526              PERFORM 1745-DISPLAY-ACCEPT-STREET UNTIL STREET-VALID =
527                  "YES".
528
```

**EXHIBIT 13.6 (Cont.)**

```
529          1745-DISPLAY-ACCEPT-STREET.
530             DISPLAY "ENTER STREET".
531             ACCEPT STREET-MAST.
532             MOVE STREET-MAST TO STREET-TABLE.
533             MOVE "NO" TO FOUND-SW.
534             PERFORM 1747-LOOK-FOR-LETTER-IN-STREET VARYING SUB FROM 1 BY
535                1 UNTIL SUB > 10.
536             IF FOUND-SW = "YES"
537                THEN MOVE "YES" TO STREET-VALID
538                ELSE MOVE "NO" TO STREET-VALID
539                    DISPLAY "INVALID STREET..RETRY".
540
541          1747-LOOK-FOR-LETTER-IN-STREET.
542             IF STREET-TAB (SUB) ALPHABETIC
543                THEN MOVE "YES" TO FOUND-SW
544                    MOVE 10 TO SUB.
545
546          1750-INPUT-CITY.
547             MOVE SPACES TO CITY-MAST.
548             PERFORM 1755-DISPLAY-ACCEPT-CITY UNTIL CITY-VALID = "YES".
549
550          1755-DISPLAY-ACCEPT-CITY.
551             DISPLAY "ENTER CITY".
552             ACCEPT CITY-MAST.
553             IF CITY-MAST IS ALPHABETIC
554                THEN MOVE "YES" TO CITY-VALID
555                ELSE MOVE "NO" TO CITY-VALID
556                    DISPLAY "INVALID CITY..RETRY"
557             END-IF.
558
559          1760-INPUT-STATE.
560             MOVE SPACES TO STATE-MAST.
561             PERFORM 1765-DISPLAY-ACCEPT-STATE UNTIL STATE-VALID = "YES".
562
563          1765-DISPLAY-ACCEPT-STATE.
564             DISPLAY "ENTER STATE (TWO CHARACTER CODE)".
565             ACCEPT STATE-MAST.
566             PERFORM 1767-LOOK-UP-STATE-CODE.
567             IF STATE-FOUND = "YES"
568                THEN MOVE "YES" TO STATE-VALID
569                ELSE MOVE "NO" TO STATE-VALID
570                    DISPLAY "INVALID STATE..RETRY"
571             END-IF.
572
573          1767-LOOK-UP-STATE-CODE.
574             MOVE "NO" TO STATE-FOUND.
575             PERFORM 1768-ELEMENT-COMPARE VARYING SUB FROM 1 BY 1 UNTIL
576                SUB > 51.
577
578          1768-ELEMENT-COMPARE.
579             IF STATE-MAST = STATE-CODE (SUB)
580                THEN MOVE "YES" TO STATE-FOUND
581                    MOVE 51 TO SUB
582             END-IF.
583
584          1770-INPUT-ZIP.
585             MOVE ZERO TO ZIP-MAST.
586             PERFORM 1775-DISPLAY-ACCEPT-ZIP UNTIL ZIP-VALID = "YES".
587
588          1775-DISPLAY-ACCEPT-ZIP.
589             DISPLAY "ENTER ZIP CODE (5 POSITIONS)".
590             ACCEPT ZIP-MAST.
591             IF ZIP-MAST IS NUMERIC
592                THEN MOVE "YES" TO ZIP-VALID
593                ELSE MOVE "NO" TO ZIP-VALID
594                    DISPLAY "INVALID ZIP CODE..RETRY"
595             END-IF.
```

**EXHIBIT 13.6   (Cont.)**

```
596
597         1780-INPUT-DOE.
598             MOVE ZERO TO DOE-MAST.
599             PERFORM 1785-DISPLAY-ACCEPT-DOE UNTIL DOE-VALID = "YES".
600
601         1785-DISPLAY-ACCEPT-DOE.
602             DISPLAY "ENTER DOE (YYMMDD FORMAT)".
603             ACCEPT DOE-MAST.
604             IF DOE-MAST > 450101 AND DOE-MAST < CURRENT-DATE
605                 THEN MOVE "YES" TO DOE-VALID
606                 ELSE MOVE "NO" TO DOE-VALID
607                     DISPLAY "INVALID DOE..RETRY"
608             END-IF.
609
610         1790-INPUT-YTD .
611             MOVE ZERO TO YTD-MAST.
612             PERFORM 1795-DISPLAY-ACCEPT-YTD UNTIL YTD-VALID = "YES".
613
614         1795-DISPLAY-ACCEPT-YTD.
615             DISPLAY "ENTER YTD EARNINGS (8 POSITIONS,NO DECIMAL POINT)".
616             ACCEPT YTD-MAST.
617             IF YTD-MAST IS NUMERIC
618                 THEN MOVE "YES" TO YTD-VALID
619                 ELSE MOVE "NO" TO YTD-VALID
620                     DISPLAY "INVALID YTD-EARNINGS..RETRY"
621             END-IF.
622
623         2000-UPDATE-PAY-RECORDS.
624             PERFORM 2010-START-UP-UPDATE.
625             PERFORM 2040-UPDATE-SELECT-OPTION UNTIL UPDATE-RESP-OPTION =
626                 3.
627
628         2010-START-UP-UPDATE.
629             MOVE 0 TO UPDATE-RESP-OPTION.
630             PERFORM 2020-UPDATE-MENU UNTIL VALID-UPDATE-RESP-OPTION.
631
632         2020-UPDATE-MENU.
633             DISPLAY ":I +".
634             PERFORM 2030-DISPLAY-UPDATE-REC-MENU VARYING SUB FROM 1 BY 1
635                 UNTIL SUB > 8.
636             ACCEPT UPDATE-RESP-OPTION.
637
638         2030-DISPLAY-UPDATE-REC-MENU.
639             DISPLAY UPDATE-MENU-TABLE (SUB).
640
641         2040-UPDATE-SELECT-OPTION.
642             IF UPDATE-RESP-OPTION = 1
643                 THEN PERFORM 2100-CHANGE-RECORD
644             ELSE,
645             IF UPDATE-RESP-OPTION = 2
646                 THEN PERFORM 2300-DELETE-RECORD.
647             MOVE ZERO TO UPDATE-RESP-OPTION.
648             PERFORM 2020-UPDATE-MENU UNTIL VALID-UPDATE-RESP-OPTION.
649
650         2100-CHANGE-RECORD.
651             PERFORM 2110-START-UP-CHANGE.
652             PERFORM 2200-CHANGE-FIELD-SELECT UNTIL CHANGE-RESP-OPTION =
653                 11 OR MASTER-RECORD-FOUND = "NO".
654             IF MASTER-RECORD-FOUND = "YES"
655                 THEN REWRITE MASTER-RECORD
656                         INVALID KEY
657                             DISPLAY "AN ERROR WAS DETECTED, RECORD NOT
658       -                         "CHANGED"
659                     DISPLAY "RECORD " SSN-MAST " CHANGED"
660                 ELSE PERFORM 2140-ERROR-MSG-REC-NOT-FOUND.
661
```

**EXHIBIT 13.6   (Cont.)**

```
662        2110-START-UP-CHANGE.
663            PERFORM 1500-LOOK-FOR-MASTER-RECORD.
664            IF MASTER-RECORD-FOUND = "YES"
665                THEN MOVE ZERO TO CHANGE-RESP-OPTION
666                    PERFORM 2120-CHANGE-RECORD-MENU UNTIL
667                        VALID-CHANGE-RESP-OPTION
668                ELSE PERFORM 2140-ERROR-MSG-REC-NOT-FOUND
669            END-IF.
670
671        2120-CHANGE-RECORD-MENU.
672            DISPLAY ":I +".
673            PERFORM 2125-DISPLAY-CHANGE-RECORD-MENU VARYING SUB FROM 1 BY
674                1 UNTIL SUB > 16.
675            ACCEPT CHANGE-RESP-OPTION.
676
677        2125-DISPLAY-CHANGE-RECORD-MENU.
678            DISPLAY CHANGE-MENU-TABLE (SUB).
679
680        2140-ERROR-MSG-REC-NOT-FOUND.
681            DISPLAY "RECORD " SSN-MAST " NOT FOUND IN MASTER FILE..NO CHA
682      -        "NGES MADE".
683
684        2200-CHANGE-FIELD-SELECT.
685            MOVE "NO" TO NAME-VALID.
686            MOVE "NO" TO BRANCH-VALID.
687            MOVE "NO" TO DEPT-VALID.
688            MOVE "NO" TO JOB-CODE-VALID.
689            MOVE "NO" TO STREET-VALID.
690            MOVE "NO" TO CITY-VALID.
691            MOVE "NO" TO STATE-VALID.
692            MOVE "NO" TO ZIP-VALID.
693            MOVE "NO" TO DOE-VALID.
694            MOVE "NO" TO YTD-VALID.
695            IF CHANGE-RESP-OPTION = 01
696                THEN PERFORM 1700-INPUT-NAME
697            ELSE
698            IF CHANGE-RESP-OPTION = 02
699                THEN PERFORM 1710-INPUT-BRANCH
700            ELSE
701            IF CHANGE-RESP-OPTION = 03
702                THEN PERFORM 1720-INPUT-DEPT
703            ELSE
704            IF CHANGE-RESP-OPTION = 04
705                THEN PERFORM 1730-INPUT-JOB-CODE
706            ELSE
707            IF CHANGE-RESP-OPTION = 05
708                THEN PERFORM 1740-INPUT-STREET
709            ELSE
710            IF CHANGE-RESP-OPTION = 06
711                    PERFORM 1750-INPUT-CITY
712            ELSE
713            IF CHANGE-RESP-OPTION = 07
714                    PERFORM 1760-INPUT-STATE
715            ELSE
716            IF CHANGE-RESP-OPTION = 08
717                    PERFORM 1770-INPUT-ZIP
718            ELSE
719            IF CHANGE-RESP-OPTION = 09
720                THEN PERFORM 1780-INPUT-DOE
721            ELSE
722            IF CHANGE-RESP-OPTION = 10
723                THEN PERFORM 1790-INPUT-YTD
724            END-IF.
725            MOVE 0 TO CHANGE-RESP-OPTION.
```

**EXHIBIT 13.6    (Cont.)**

```
726                PERFORM 2120-CHANGE-RECORD-MENU UNTIL
727                    VALID-CHANGE-RESP-OPTION.
728
729        2300-DELETE-RECORD.
730            MOVE SPACE TO DELETE-RESP-OPTION.
731            DISPLAY ":I +"
732            PERFORM 2310-DELETE-MENU UNTIL VALID-DELETE-RESP-OPTION.
733            IF DELETE-RESP-OPTION = 1
734                THEN PERFORM 1500-LOOK-FOR-MASTER-RECORD
735                    IF MASTER-RECORD-FOUND = "YES"
736                        THEN DELETE MASTER-FILE
737                            DISPLAY "RECORD " SSN-MAST " DELETED"
738                        ELSE DISPLAY "RECORD " SSN-MAST " NOT FOUND IN F
739        -                    "ILE, CAN'T DELETE"
740            ELSE DISPLAY "RECORD NOT DELETED".
741            DISPLAY "PRESS RETURN KEY TO CONTINUE".
742            ACCEPT ANY-RESP-FIELD.
743
744        2310-DELETE-MENU.
745            PERFORM 2320-DISPLAY-DELETE-MENU VARYING SUB FROM 1 BY 1
746                UNTIL SUB > 6.
747            ACCEPT DELETE-RESP-OPTION.
748
749        2320-DISPLAY-DELETE-MENU.
750            DISPLAY DELETE-MENU-TABLE (SUB).
751
752        3000-INQUIRY.
753            PERFORM 3010-START-UP-INQUIRY.
754            PERFORM 3100-SELECT-INQUIRY-OPTIONS UNTIL INQUIRY-RESP-OPTION
755                = 4.
756
757        3010-START-UP-INQUIRY.
758            MOVE 0 TO INQUIRY-RESP-OPTION.
759            PERFORM 3020-INQUIRY-MENU UNTIL VALID-INQUIRY-RESP-OPTION.
760
761        3020-INQUIRY-MENU.
762            DISPLAY ":I +".
763            PERFORM 3030-DISPLAY-INQUIRY-MENU VARYING SUB FROM 1 BY 1
764                UNTIL SUB > 10.
765            ACCEPT INQUIRY-RESP-OPTION.
766
767        3030-DISPLAY-INQUIRY-MENU.
768            DISPLAY INQUIRY-MENU-TABLE (SUB).
769
770        3100-SELECT-INQUIRY-OPTIONS.
771            IF INQUIRY-RESP-OPTION = 1
772                THEN PERFORM 3200-SINGLE-REC-INQUIRY
773            ELSE
774            IF INQUIRY-RESP-OPTION = 2
775                THEN PERFORM 3300-DISPLAY-FILE
776            ELSE
777            IF INQUIRY-RESP-OPTION = 3
778                THEN PERFORM 3400-PRINT-HARD-COPY
779            ELSE NEXT SENTENCE.
780            MOVE 0 TO INQUIRY-RESP-OPTION.
781            PERFORM 3020-INQUIRY-MENU UNTIL VALID-INQUIRY-RESP-OPTION.
```

**EXHIBIT 13.6   (Cont.)**

```
782
783         3200-SINGLE-REC-INQUIRY.
784             PERFORM 1500-LOOK-FOR-MASTER-RECORD.
785             IF MASTER-RECORD-FOUND = "YES"
786                 THEN DISPLAY ":I +"
787                     DISPLAY "          INQUIRY OF SINGLE RECORD"
788                     DISPLAY "SSN:" SSN-MAST "                    NAME:"
789                         LAST-NAME-MAST " " FIRST-NAME-MAST " " MI-MAST
790                     DISPLAY " "
791                     DISPLAY "BRANCH:" BRANCH-MAST "             DEPARTM
792     -               "ENT:" DEPT-MAST
793                     DISPLAY " "
794                     DISPLAY "JOB DESCRIPTION:"
795                         JOB-DESCRIPTION (JOB-CODE-MAST)
796                     DISPLAY " "
797                     DISPLAY "STREET ADDRESS:" STREET-MAST
798                     DISPLAY " "
799                     DISPLAY "                CITY:" CITY-MAST "   STATE:"
800                         STATE-MAST " ZIP:" ZIP-MAST
801                     DISPLAY " "
802                     DISPLAY "DOE:" MONTH-MAST "/" DAY-MAST "/" YEAR-MAST
803                     DISPLAY " "
804                     DISPLAY "YTD GROSS PAY $" YTD-MAST
805                 ELSE DISPLAY "MASTER RECORD NOT FOUND".
806             DISPLAY "PRESS RETURN TO CONTINUE".
807             ACCEPT ANY-RESP-FIELD.
808
809         3300-DISPLAY-FILE.
810             CLOSE MASTER-FILE.
811             OPEN INPUT MASTER-FILE.
812             MOVE "NO" TO END-FLAG.
813             DISPLAY ":I +".
814             DISPLAY "LISTING OF FILE".
815             DISPLAY "SSN          NAME       STREET    CITY        STATE ZIP
816     -           " DEPT BR JC YTD"
817             PERFORM 3310-READ-MAST.
818             PERFORM 3320-DISPLAY-LINE UNTIL END-FLAG = "YES"
819             DISPLAY "PRESS RETURN TO CONTINUE".
820             ACCEPT ANY-RESP-FIELD.
821             CLOSE MASTER-FILE.
822             OPEN I-O MASTER-FILE.
823
824         3310-READ-MAST.
825             READ MASTER-FILE NEXT AT END MOVE "YES" TO END-FLAG.
826
827         3320-DISPLAY-LINE.
828             DISPLAY SSN-MAST " " LAST-NAME-MAST STREET-MAST
829                 CITY-MAST " " STATE-MAST " " ZIP-MAST " " DEPT-MAST
830                 BRANCH-MAST JOB-CODE-MAST  YTD-MAST.
831             PERFORM 3310-READ-MAST.
832
833         3400-PRINT-HARD-COPY.
834             CLOSE MASTER-FILE.
835             OPEN INPUT MASTER-FILE.
836             MOVE "NO" TO END-FLAG.
837             PERFORM 3405-PRINT-HEADINGS.
838             PERFORM 3310-READ-MAST.
839             PERFORM 3420-PRINT-LINE UNTIL END-FLAG = "YES"
840             DISPLAY "PRESS RETURN TO CONTINUE".
841             ACCEPT ANY-RESP-FIELD.
842             CLOSE MASTER-FILE.
843             OPEN I-O MASTER-FILE.
844
845         3405-PRINT-HEADINGS.
846             WRITE OUT-REC FROM HEADING-LINE-1 AFTER PAGE.
847             WRITE OUT-REC FROM HEADING-LINE-2 AFTER 2.
```

**EXHIBIT 13.6    (Cont.)**

```
848
849        3420-PRINT-LINE.
850            MOVE SSN-MAST TO SSN-DETAIL.
851            MOVE LAST-NAME-MAST TO LAST-NAME-DETAIL.
852            MOVE FIRST-NAME-MAST TO FIRST-NAME-DETAIL.
853            MOVE MI-MAST TO MI-DETAIL.
854            MOVE STREET-MAST TO STREET-DETAIL.
855            MOVE CITY-MAST TO CITY-DETAIL.
856            MOVE STATE-MAST TO STATE-DETAIL.
857            MOVE ZIP-MAST TO ZIP-DETAIL.
858            MOVE DEPT-MAST TO DEPT-DETAIL.
859            MOVE BRANCH-MAST TO BRANCH-DETAIL.
860            MOVE JOB-CODE-MAST TO JOB-CODE-DETAIL.
861            MOVE YTD-MAST TO YTD-DETAIL.
862            WRITE OUT-REC FROM DETAIL-LINE AFTER 1.
863            PERFORM 3310-READ-MAST.
864
865        4000-HELP.
866            DISPLAY ":I +"
867            DISPLAY "                    ACME INDUSTRIES PAYROLL FILE MAINTE
868     -        "NANCE".
869            DISPLAY " ".
870            DISPLAY "                        HELP FOR ONLINE FILE MAINTENANC
871     -        "E".
872            DISPLAY " ".
873            DISPLAY " ".
874            DISPLAY "  THIS PROGRAM IS A SIMPLE ONLINE FILE MAINTENANCE P
875     -        "ROGRAM USED FOR   ".
876            DISPLAY " ".
877            DISPLAY "  THE MAINTENANCE OF A PAYROLL FILE FOR THE ACME IND
878     -        "USTRIES. THE MENUS".
879            DISPLAY " ".
880            DISPLAY "  THAT APPEAR ARE TO HELP GUIDE YOU THROUGH THE PROG
881     -        "RAM. TO PERFORM THE".
882            DISPLAY " ".
883            DISPLAY "  TASK YOU WISH TO DO, SIMPLY TYPE THE NUMBER BESIDE
884     -        " THE TASK AND PRESS".
885            DISPLAY " ".
886            DISPLAY "RETURN. "
887            DISPLAY " ".
888            DISPLAY "PRESS RETURN TO RETURN TO MAIN MENU".
889            ACCEPT ANY-RESP-FIELD.
890
891        5000-WRAP-UP-PAY.
892            DISPLAY "END OF INTERACTIVE FILE MAINTANCE SESSION".
893            CLOSE MASTER-FILE
894                STATE-FILE
895                OUT-FILE
896                JOB-DESC-FILE.


LEVEL SUMMARY
   ****   1   non-standard diagnostic(unlisted)
total cp time (in microsec) = 6446484     5388880     1057604
```

```
          PAYROLL PERSONNEL REGISTER

SSN         NAME              STREET      CITY        STATE  ZIP    DEPT  BR   JC   YTD
000000000   RUSSELL  JENNIFER B  HCR 51      STEPHENVIL  TX    76401  001   001  02   000000.00
111111111   RUSSELL  JACK     P  112 NORTH   STEPHENVIL  TX    77777  002   001  03   000555.55
222222222   RUSSELL  BARBARA  A  222 WEST P  STEPHENVIL  TX    77777  003   002  05   777777.77
333333333   RUSSELL  JENNY    B  444 OAK     STEPHENVIL  TX    77777  002   001  06   444444.44
444444444   GEORGE   TAMMI    B  111 STONE   STEPHENVIL  TX    77777  003   002  03   666666.66
555555555   GEORGE   WILLIAM  K  112 AIR FO  COLORADO S  CO    33333  002   003  08   666666.66
```

# SUMMARY

The use of interactive processing is growing in popularity in business today because it provides the user a much stronger interface for the maintenance and use of data bases and files. Batch and interactive processing are now being used jointly in practically every major computer application. Interactive systems are especially suitable for entering small amounts of data to the computer, updating only a small percentage of the total number of records at one time, or making frequent inquiries of the file. However, a major limitation of interactive processing is that it is often more expensive to develop than are batch systems.

The files used in interactive systems are (1) master files, (2) audit-trail files, (3) transaction files, and (4) backup files. Today's interactive systems often utilize either the audit-trail file or the transaction file, but not both.

Modern interactive systems use a menu-driven concept that permits a user to choose from a main menu of processing options. This choice normally leads to a submenu of choices. For example, choosing the update option from the main menu screen will lead to a submenu that allows the user to opt for the change function, the delete function, or return to the main menu. Every submenu should allow return to the calling menu.

The key to a successful interactive system is threefold. First, the various menus must be clear and complete, in order to elicit a correct response from the user. Second, the response from the user must be checked for validity; as the user enters a response to the system prompt, the program must trap invalid data. Error traps are sometimes referred to as validation loops, since their logic repeatedly asks the user for another response if the previous one was invalid. Third, the response time itself must be short enough so that the user has the data as soon as it's needed for the task at hand. Some experts think a response time longer than two seconds in unacceptable. Response time is often a function of the kind of data base or file organization method used.

Interactive systems can be developed using either a data base management system or application files. Normally, where very large files are handled, a nonsequential access to data is required. For interactive systems, the types of files may be indexed, relative, or direct. Indexed files are accessed through the use of directories. Relative files are accessed with reference to a record's relative location in the file. Direct files are both created and accessed using calculated (hashed) record locations, or addresses.

Several factors will influence the programmer/analyst's choice of a file method. Where the user frequently requests lists of preordered files, the indexed file technique is often superior. A drawback to the indexed method is that it is usually a bit slower in accessing data than either the relative or direct access methods. Where extremely fast response time is needed, either the direct or the relative method is often used. A drawback to these file organization methods is that they do not afford the user the ability to retrieve records easily in a predetermined sequence. Where reports are frequently needed, the indexed file organization method is often chosen due to its middle-of-the-road capability.

# VOCABULARY

| | |
|---|---|
| batch processing | nonsequential file |
| interactive processing |   access |
| audit-trail file | indexed files |
| menu-driven dialogue | relative files |
| main menu | direct files |
| subordinate menu | directories |
| data validation loops | indexes |
|   (or error traps) | relative record location |
| response time | hashing |
| data base access | real time |

# EXERCISES/QUESTIONS

1. What are two fundamental methods of processing data? Compare and contrast them.

2. How is an audit-trail used in an interactive system? Why is it necessary?

3. Why have menu-driven interactive file maintenance systems become so popular?

4. Compare and contrast the organization methods of indexed, relative, and direct files.

## PROBLEMS

Prepare the structured flowcharts and pseudocode for the problems below.

**13–1.** Mr. Donaldson currently keeps a sequential master customer file on tape and uses a sequential transaction file to update the master file. However, Mr. Donaldson would like to be able to perform record addition and update to the customer file from an on-line terminal. He would like to inquire about any given customer's record, list the file itself, delete any record, or change any field on the customer record except the customer number (record key). The computer program should trap any invalid data entries that the user inputs.

The state table file consists of the following:

| Field | Location | Type |
|---|---|---|
| State-code | 1–2 | A/N |
| State-name | 3–22 | A/N |

This table contains 51 entries to cover all 50 states and the District of Columbia. This file can be copied from your teacher's ancillary materials.

The customer file consists of the following fields:

Create screen formats using the screen CRT form at the end of this chapter (you are permitted to copy this sheet and make as many as needed).

| Field Description | Column Location | Type |
|---|---|---|
| Customer number | 1–9 | N |
| Last name | 10–20 | A |
| First name | 21–29 | A |
| MI | 30 | A |
| Street | 31–40 | A/N |
| City | 41–49 | A/N |
| State | 50–51 | A/N |
| Zip | 52–56 | N |
| Phone | 57–63 | N |
| Balance Due | 64–70 | N ($$$$$.$$) |
| Credit code | 71 | (1–5) |
| Credit limit | 72–78 | N ($$$$$.$$) |

**13–2.** Modify the flowchart and pseudocode in problem 13–1 so that the user can request a listing of customers in descending order by balance due.

Remember that with relatively large files, the kind of sorting algorithm used may be critical for acceptable response time. Use the Shell sort.

# 14

# C. A. S. E. (Computer-Aided Systems Engineering) and Action Diagrams

## OBJECTIVES

1. Be able to define Computer-Aided Systems Engineering

2. Be able to list advantages of C.A.S.E.

3. Be able to list the limitations of C.A.S.E.

4. Be able to justify the use of C.A.S.E. in the systems development process.

5. Be able to identify and explain the four main workstations of C.A.S.E.

6. Be able to explain the rationale of each workstation.

7. Be able to list the major tools of each C.A.S.E. workstation.

8. Be able to identify the main structures in Action Diagrams.

9. Be able to draw a simple Action Diagram.

The previous chapters have dealt with the design of computer programs for both batch and interactive systems. Chapter 1 alluded to the software development revolution. It was discussed how traditional programming philosophies and methods are rapidly being challenged by those who believe that systems can be engineered. While the need for programming logic and design tools will always be needed (that is why I wrote this book), the manual process of developing systems from a systems analysis and design perspective is rapidly fading. The reason is that companies are demanding that computer systems be developed much quicker and on time, within budgeted costs, and tailored around corporate goals and critical success factors. The idea is also to develop these systems so that they are very accessible to corporate leaders as well as lower-echelon users. Management should be able to identify problem areas quickly with the system as it is being developed. This means that the system should have a robust set of documentation about the corporate data and processes.

## WHAT IS COMPUTER-AIDED SYSTEMS ENGINEERING

Computer-Aided Systems Engineering (C.A.S.E.) is a systems development method that uses systems development software technology to drastically improve the way we engineer computer applications in the business community. C.A.S.E. is based on the idea that computer applications can be engineered in a very structured manner using these automated tools to significantly improve software development productivity.

The methodology uses a structured approach and an information engineering approach. (More will be said about the information engineering approach later.) The method utilizes an intelligent encyclopedia or repository with a multi-user tool set including graphics and a window-based user interface. The encyclopedia is the heart of the C.A.S.E. package. Here is where all entities (or records), relationships between the entities, and processes (the activities using the data) are held.

## PROBLEMS WITH TRADITIONAL SYSTEMS DEVELOPMENT

One of the problems with traditional systems development is that there was no central place where information about the data and processes were kept. The process was strictly manual, and if programs were modified, rarely did this change ever get made back in the documentation (that is, data flow diagrams, flowcharts, pseudocode, and so on were rarely changed since this took backseat to new development). Often project leaders thought that data dictionaries, Entity-Relations diagrams, dataflow diagrams, program flowcharts could be worked on during slow development periods (or lulls). Anyone who has programmed in a "pressure cooker" environment would say, "Yea, sure!" Realistically, there never is a good time to go back and "do documentation." The real value of CASE is to let users help develop the documentation so that it will reflect a system that will truly be used by users.

## SURVIVAL OF THE FITTEST

Business applications always require change. The method for carrying out a given business function can be the difference in a company's surviving and being profitable or going bankrupt. Competition has never been greater within business today, and the computer is needed more than ever to provide that difference.

In the past, the average time to develop a business system was six months to a year.[1] This does not include the four to six months the user request sits on someone's desk. From request to delivery, users often wait almost two years for a major business application to be delivered in a ready-to-use status. Managers who must analyze everything on a cost-benefit basis will no longer accept the standard two-year delay in providing their company with decision-support business systems that could provide an edge over the competition. They want it now, if not yesterday! Nevertheless, the staff needed to develop these systems will be declining rapidly by the year 2000. The baby boom population, which occupies a large part of the programming population, will be retiring by the years 2000 through 2007. Moreover there are fewer entering the systems development field. According to research done in 1987 by John Rossmeisel, an application-enabling consultant at the IBM Application Enabling Marketing Center in Cary, North Carolina, there were 9 million fewer teenagers in the United States from a decade ago. This may sound great to some but not to U.S. business—or to the computer information systems development profession. Compound this with the fact that computer-related curriculum is just not being taken by as many students—in fact, computer-related curriculums are in decline in many universities. Students are just not interested in classic computer science curricula with teachers who think "programming is an art—not a science." Students are not interested in instruction that is perceived to be baffling and irrelevant. The 1987 study found that "computer science" curricula fell from 8.6 percent of the student population in 1980 to a 3.2 percent of the student population by 1987.[2] This simply tells us that with a great rise in demand for business systems that address the needs and interests of the company as a whole and with a decline in the information systems department's ability to produce business systems, there is a tremendous need for an automated, engineering approach to develop these future systems.

Traditional, manually developed systems on pieces of paper with errors lurking around every corner are just not adequate any more to management. Management wants a part in the systems development process as well. This means that systems must be planned first using C.A.S.E. tools. Company goals, strategies, objectives, and critical success factors will become a part of our C.A.S.E. encyclopedia or repository. We will be able to, say, trace a processing activity or piece of data to a specific goal or objective. Systems will be more cost-effective as they will functionally support what the company considers to be important.

Linda Taylor, President of Taylor and Zeno Systems, Inc., notes that the software crisis can only be

[1]Nolan, Richard, "Managing the Crisis in Data Processing," *Harvard Business Review,* vol. 57, no. 2 (Mar.–Apr. 1979): 115–126.

[2]CIO, "Getting a Handle on CASE," (April 1990) 89.

solved by using C.A.S.E.[3] She indicates that systems must achieve competitive advantage, must meet user's needs, must be delivered on time, and must be easily maintained.

## INFORMATION ENGINEERING

In order to achieve the four requirements proposed by Taylor, an information engineering approach to systems development is needed. This means that we must use an integrated set of methodologies involving fourth- and fifth-generation software, and we must use fully normalized data models (data that have been reduced to their simplest form, thus avoiding redundancy). Workstations must be used to build applications through the use of graphics, encyclopedias, and prototyping. Prototyping is the building of small mock samples of the real system and letting the user interface with the mock system. The prototype essentially works like the real system except the prototype has limited capability and normally can work with only small amounts of data. The modeling of data using a tool called "Entity-Relationship diagrams" becomes a primary focus of information engineering. The attention is on the design of data rather than solely processes. A small part of an Entity-Relationship diagram is illustrated later.

## OTHER MAJOR ADVANTAGES OF C.A.S.E.

The entire methodology embodies information engineering thus streamlining the thought process for each designer. The method replaces typing and templates, pencils, erasures with key strokes, mouse movement, and default settings. The tool becomes a common ground for communication between the analyst and the user. It provides an easy-to-grasp communication tool for sharing among analysts, planners, executives, and end-users. It allows project members to exchange ideas and integrate their separate components of work with precision. This is certainly not the case in the traditional systems development process where there is maximum chaos stemming from their inability to provide other team members with up-to-date documentation. Because C.A.S.E. provides a real-time update during its utilization, the development team may experience for the first time a global picture of how an entire system works, what the data

mean, and how the pieces are related. Moreover, the entire team can work jointly with the tool and with precision.

## JUSTIFICATIONS FOR C.A.S.E.

As previously mentioned, the emphasis is on productivity. Middle management is shrinking rapidly because computers can now do what they were doing but much better in most cases. With a renewed interest in code generators and expert systems and with a shrinking programmer supply, it seems clear that C.A.S.E. will be the future.

## LIMITATIONS OF C.A.S.E.

Although Computer-Aided Systems Engineering is the wave of the future, it does carry with it some limitations. C.A.S.E. workstations are still very expensive. Today a full set of integrated C.A.S.E. software for only one microcomputer (and one systems developer) can cost roughly $50,000. Multiplied by the average number of systems developers in an organization, the cost can easily run into the hundreds of thousands or even millions. Moreover, the hardware requirements for RAM and hard drive space are great. A typical environment might require 16 mb of RAM and 200 mb of hard drive spaces just to get started. Qualified data administrators versed in C.A.S.E. are scarce; thus, their potentially high salaries are a consideration. Development groups must be trained in data modeling as well as process modeling. Management can become disenchanted because they do not see immediate benefits. The learning curve is great and training costs are very high; a single, one week training session for learning one workstation such as Planning Workstation can cost $1000 or more. (Multiplying this figure by the total number of systems analysts and workstations in the company provides an idea of cost.) It is difficult to convince management to invest in the planning and analysis phases of the systems development process. Too often management simply wants the programs written to get the business system functional. They do not often recognize the pitfalls of such narrow thinking until their business system fails or is not what users wanted. Only then does management wonder why the project team does not have better documentation.

---

[3]Taylor, Linda, "CASE Review and Implementation Issues", 91, Taylor and Zeno.

## The C.A.S.E. Tool should be Considered in spite of its Limitations

Linda Taylor's 1988 research reveals that the demand for new applications far outpaces the ability to deliver them. Business and systems requirements change rapidly. Companies must go to market with new products within 30 to 60 days in some cases, and computer systems must be developed to support the new products. It makes sense to drastically reduce the development time through the use of C.A.S.E. A fully integrated C.A.S.E. tool can do that by allowing the analyst to spend much more time on the planning, analysis, and design phases of the development process.

After the appropriate design diagrams have been finished, the entire computer program can be automatically generated through the use of code generators. Systems are changed by changing the information in the various C.A.S.E. diagrams, *not* by changing code. The code is simply regenerated within a few seconds or minutes.

## STAGES OF SYSTEMS DEVELOPMENT

In a C.A.S.E. development environment, there are typically four stages in the development of a business system: Planning, Analysis, Design, and Construction. **Planning** is the phase where initial data gathering occurs. Developing a hierarchical understanding of the company structure is often identified. The process of defining company objectives, strategies, and objectives are often clarified or made at this stage. Analysts assist in the definition of the elements of data called entities during this first phase. This means that the needed data is identified and how the various entities relate to each other. To develop adequate data bases or possibly files, it is critical that we understand the relationship of data. Many interviews are often made with users to find out what their problems are with the current system so that corrective actions can be taken to create better business systems. Understanding how various *problems* relate to various business *functions* is important. For example, does a problem with billing relate to problems in the purchasing department? Do computer applications cross over functional boundaries? They invariably do. Outlining the company functions and processes in a hierarchical fashion is often helpful.

Figure 14.1 illustrates a small entity-relationship diagram. The diagram is incomplete but does show how one would be developed. Each box symbolizes a kind or class of data. An example is CUSTOMER. Another example is the ORDERS that a customer will place. The entity-relationship diagram shows the data at rest. Entities that we describe are also naturally related to each other. These relationships are symbolized by connecting lines between the entity boxes. The relationships between entities can be *one to one*. This means that one occurrence of an entity can be associated with only one occurrence of another. The relationship can be *one to many*, which means that one occurrence of one entity (such as CUSTOMER) can be related to one or many of another entity (such as ORDERS). In other words, a CUSTOMER can place 0, 1, or many ORDERS. Also, the relationship can be *many to many*. This means that one occurrence of entity type A can be related to one or many of another entity type B. And, a single occurrence of entity type B is associated with one or many occurrences of entity type A. In Figure 14.1, we see that a CUSTOMER places 0, 1, or many ORDERS. An ORDER contains one or many PRODUCTS. A PRODUCT is contained in 0, 1, or many ORDERS, and so on. Understanding these relationships is crucial to the creation of the proper data base. The crow's feet symbol is the "many" side of the relationship. The single bar crossing the relationship line is the "one" side.

The **analysis** phase is the process of determining what processes are needed to carry out the new business system. Understanding how data flows from one process to another is important. The sequence of the processes that occur must be determined. What is called a Data Flow Diagram is often drawn for this purpose.

Figure 14.2 shows an excerpt of a Data Flow Diagram. This diagram contains four kinds of symbols. The external agent, the process, the data store, and the data flow. The external agent symbol represents the tangible, outside world. They are capable of sending and receiving data to and from processes. The process symbol (box with round corners) represents the manipulation of data. The processes of validating, updating, sorting, and reporting are carried out using this symbol. The symbol can represent an entire lower level data flow diagram. This works similar to a predefined process symbol in a flowchart symbolizing the code found elsewhere. In other words, the process block explodes into an entire data flow diagram that carries out that high level process. The data store symbol (open-ended rectangle) is used to represent the storage of data. The symbol can depict a data file, data table, data base, or even a manual filing cabinet. The data flow line represents the data in motion. It represents a packet of data that is moving between either an external agent or data store and a process block. It is the input or the output of a process.

The **design** phase is the process of first developing screen layouts and reports. With an understanding of what the user wants from the computer, the analyst can develop a more detailed view of the data. Figure 14.3 illustrates a screen layout for an order entry process. The screen layout process is often done first. The programmer/analyst can then develop a structural, hierarchical outline of the computer programs that must be written to produce the screens and reports that have been designed. The Structure Chart shows the modules of the system and the kinds of module calls from one module to another. Figure 14.4 shows the Structure Chart that accomplishes this phase of development. Notice its similarity to the hierarchy chart.

The detailed logic is often developed using a tool called **ACTION DIAGRAMS.** The detailed program logic for each module shown in the Structure Chart is carried out using a Module Action Diagram. Figure 14.5 depicts this diagram. It is from this diagram that an integrated CASE package is able to automatically generate code. Notice its similarity to both the flowchart and pseudocode. In some ways, it possesses characteristics of both

flowcharts and pseudocode. Since this text deals with programming logic, we will focus on the use of the action diagram as a program design tool.

## ACTION DIAGRAMS

Action Diagrams are also rapidly increasing in popularity as a result of the heightened interest in Computer-Aided Systems Engineering (C.A.S.E.) The Action Diagram seems to be the choice for developing detailed procedural logic when using C.A.S.E. products such as KnowledgeWare's Application Development Workbench or Texas Instrument's Information Engineering Workbench.

While Structure Charts, IPO diagrams, and Warnier-Orr Diagrams depict the overall program design, they fail to show the needed detail for easy code development, whether hand coded or automatically generated by a code generator.

### How to Draw Action Diagrams

A program module or procedure is drawn as a bracket. All the statements within the bracket con-

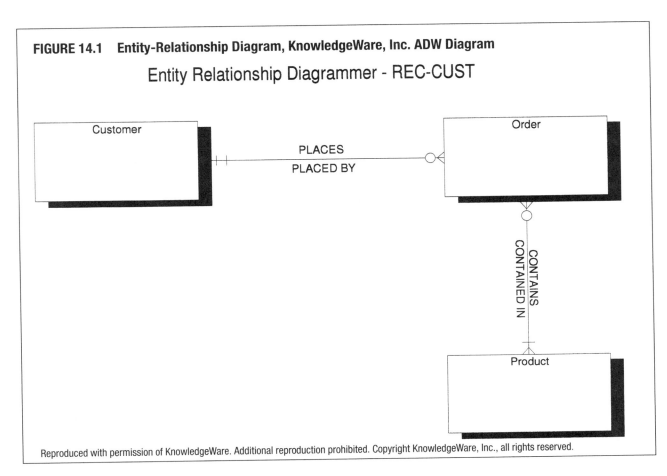

**FIGURE 14.1    Entity-Relationship Diagram, KnowledgeWare, Inc. ADW Diagram**

stitute a procedure. Brackets become the building blocks of Action Diagrams. A sequence of operations is found inside the brackets.

Some of the different types of brackets are shown in Figure 14.6. The repetition, selection, & C.A.S.E. structures are illustrated. Figure 14.7 illustrates a simple hierarchy chart with three main processes (P1, P2, and P3). The process P1 is decomposed into three processes called P1.1, P1.2, and P1.3 The process P2 is further subdivided into three processes, P2.1, P2.2, and P2.3.

The Action Diagram shown in Panel B of Figure 14.7 illustrates how the modules of the hierarchy chart would be organized within the brackets.

Notice that the major process P1 is immediately followed by the minor process activities that belong to it.

To depict a module "CALL" using an Action Diagram, the symbol is illustrated in Figure 14.8. The use of the module "call" symbol along with other Action Diagramming techniques are illustrated in Figure 14.9. This figure shows the design logic for Application 4.2 (Chapter 4) in Action Diagram format. Notice the use of the repetition structure in the main-line module. Observe that the start-up module utilizes a series of module calls, as done in the flowchart logic in Chapter 4. Also observe that the use of the C.A.S.E. structure in the

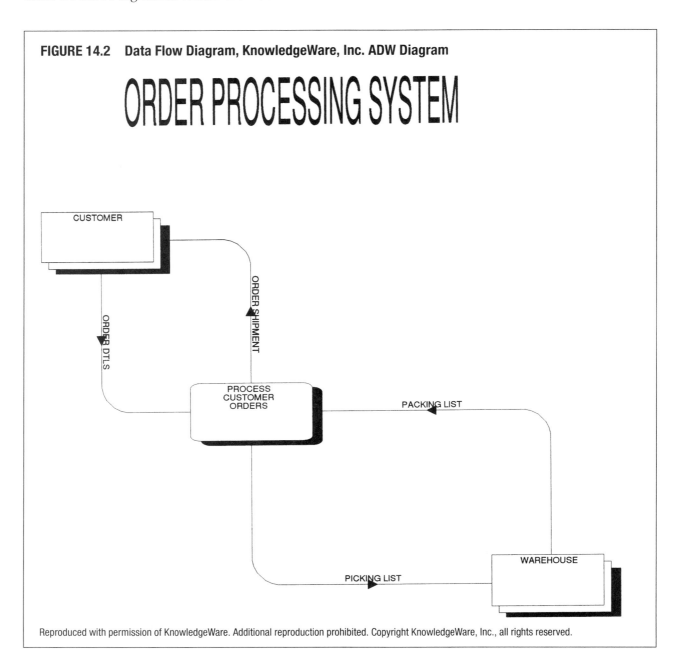

**FIGURE 14.2    Data Flow Diagram, KnowledgeWare, Inc. ADW Diagram**

detail-calculation module. The braces and the cross bar division symbolizes the "when" in the C.A.S.E. structure with great precision.

Figure 14.10 illustrates an interactive program (Application 10.1) from Chapter 10. Notice the similarities of the main-line procedure to the previous batch programs. The start-up module uses the "do until" structure to capture a valid response from the user. The select-options module uses the C.A.S.E. to determine which module is to be executed depending upon the contents of the RESP variable. Much of the remaining Action Diagramming logic has been adequately explained in Chapter 10. Since the calculation modules are simply sequence structures with fall-through code, they require little explanation.

## SUMMARY

Computer-Aided Systems Engineering (C.A.S.E.) is the technology based on the premise that computer applications can be engineered in a very structured manner. C.A.S.E. is the use of automated tools to improve software productivity during the entire systems development life cycle. The methodology uses both a structured and information engineering frame of reference. C.A.S.E. enhances and shortens the software development process; thus, allowing businesses to go to market with products faster. (With a decline in the number of expected computer professionals in the next two decades, C.A.S.E. arrived just in time.) C.A.S.E. enables a fewer number of systems analysts and program-

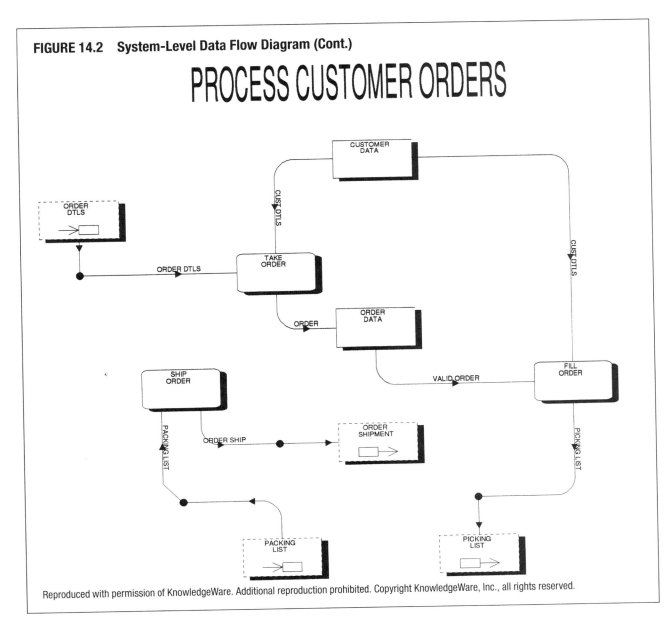

**FIGURE 14.2    System-Level Data Flow Diagram (Cont.)**

## PROCESS CUSTOMER ORDERS

mers to be more productive by allowing them to share information about entities, processes, functions, company goals, and so on using a common repository. With the use of code generators, the systems development team can spend more time ensuring that the documentation correctly reflects the kind of computer system the user wants.

The C.A.S.E. workstations consist of planning, analysis, design, and construction. The planning workstation allows the capturing of strategic goals, objectives, and critical success factors. The entities and their relationships are illustrated in an entity relationship diagram. The general data model is developed in the planning workstation. (The analysis workstation helps further define the data model and develop a process model.) A data flow diagram is developed that shows the flow of data through the system and the movement of data from the outside world (external agents) to various processes. Data stores are illustrated that show the storage of data. The data flow line illustrates the movement of the data from either an external agent or a process.

The design workstation's purpose is to further refine the data structure, and to design both the general program structure (structure chart) and the detailed programming logic (action diagram). The construction workstation takes the action diagram logic and generates code.

**FIGURE 14.3   Screen Layout, KnowledgeWare, Inc. ADW Diagram**

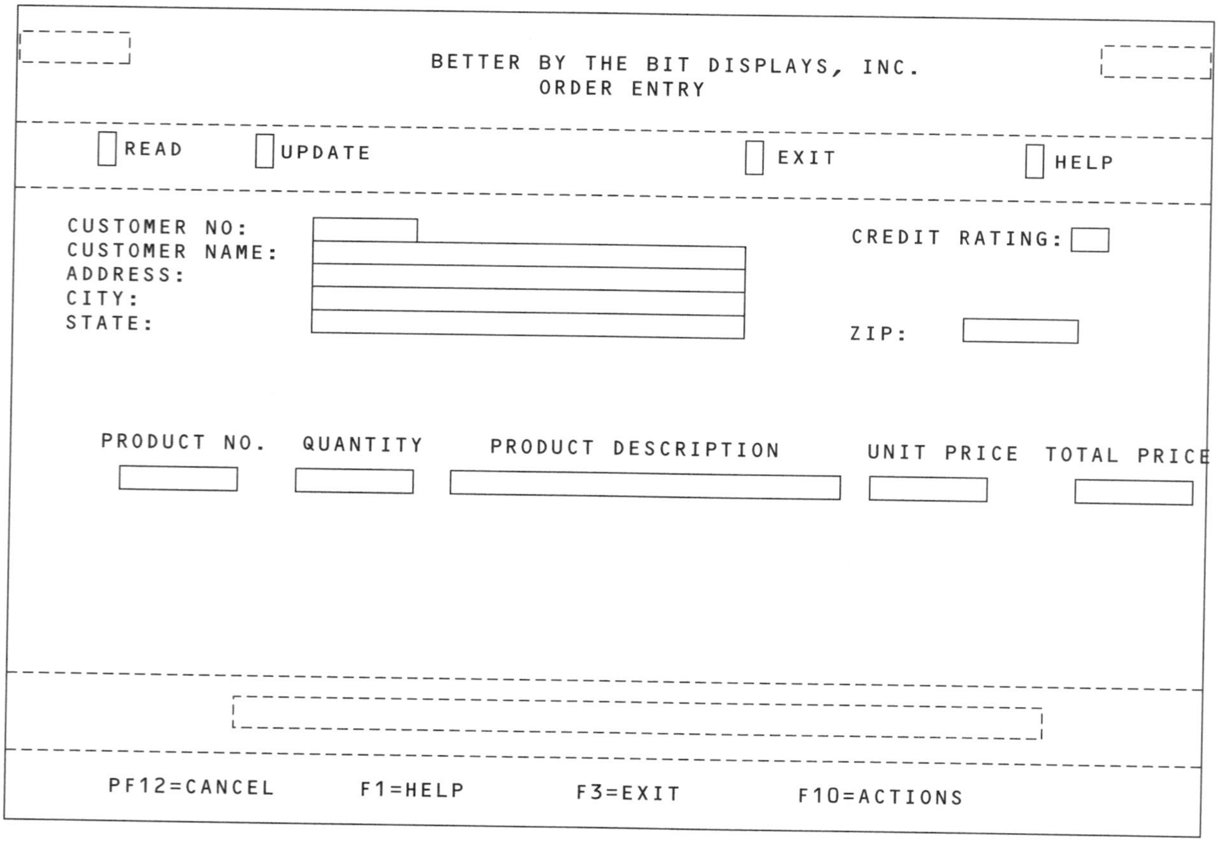

BETTER BY THE BIT DISPLAYS, INC.
ORDER ENTRY

READ     UPDATE                    EXIT         HELP

CUSTOMER NO:
CUSTOMER NAME:                              CREDIT RATING:
ADDRESS:
CITY:
STATE:                                      ZIP:

PRODUCT NO.    QUANTITY    PRODUCT DESCRIPTION    UNIT PRICE   TOTAL PRICE

PF12=CANCEL      F1=HELP        F3=EXIT        F10=ACTIONS

**FIGURE 14.4    Structure Chart, KnowledgeWare, Inc. ADW Diagram**

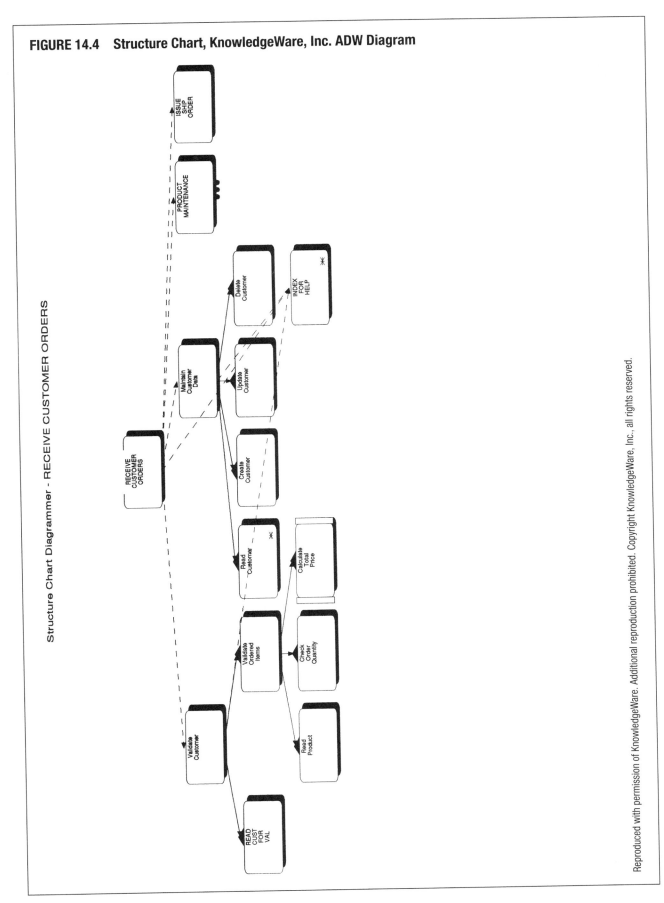

Structure Chart Diagrammer - RECEIVE CUSTOMER ORDERS

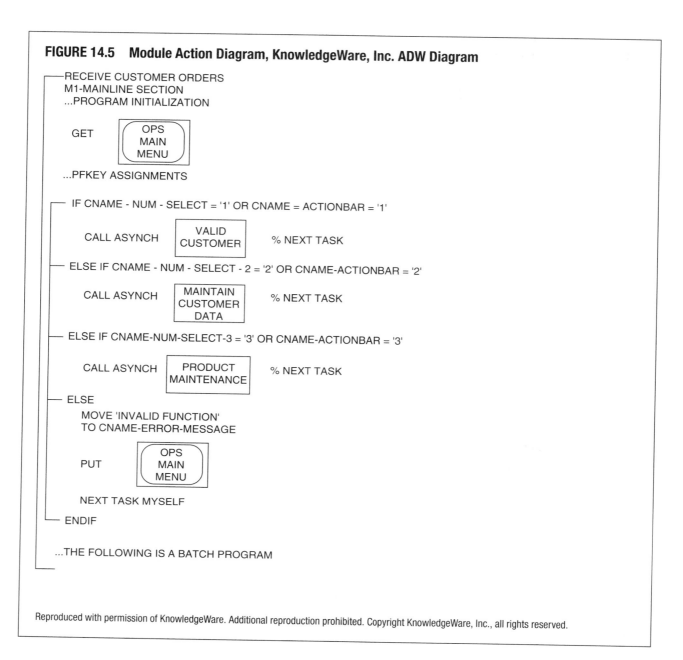

**FIGURE 14.5    Module Action Diagram, KnowledgeWare, Inc. ADW Diagram**

RECEIVE CUSTOMER ORDERS
M1-MAINLINE SECTION
...PROGRAM INITIALIZATION

GET [ OPS MAIN MENU ]

...PFKEY ASSIGNMENTS

IF CNAME - NUM - SELECT = '1' OR CNAME = ACTIONBAR = '1'

CALL ASYNCH [ VALID CUSTOMER ]    % NEXT TASK

ELSE IF CNAME - NUM - SELECT - 2 = '2' OR CNAME-ACTIONBAR = '2'

CALL ASYNCH [ MAINTAIN CUSTOMER DATA ]    % NEXT TASK

ELSE IF CNAME-NUM-SELECT-3 = '3' OR CNAME-ACTIONBAR = '3'

CALL ASYNCH [ PRODUCT MAINTENANCE ]    % NEXT TASK

ELSE

MOVE 'INVALID FUNCTION'
TO CNAME-ERROR-MESSAGE

PUT [ OPS MAIN MENU ]

NEXT TASK MYSELF

ENDIF

...THE FOLLOWING IS A BATCH PROGRAM

**FIGURE 14.6   Action Diagram Structures/Brackets**

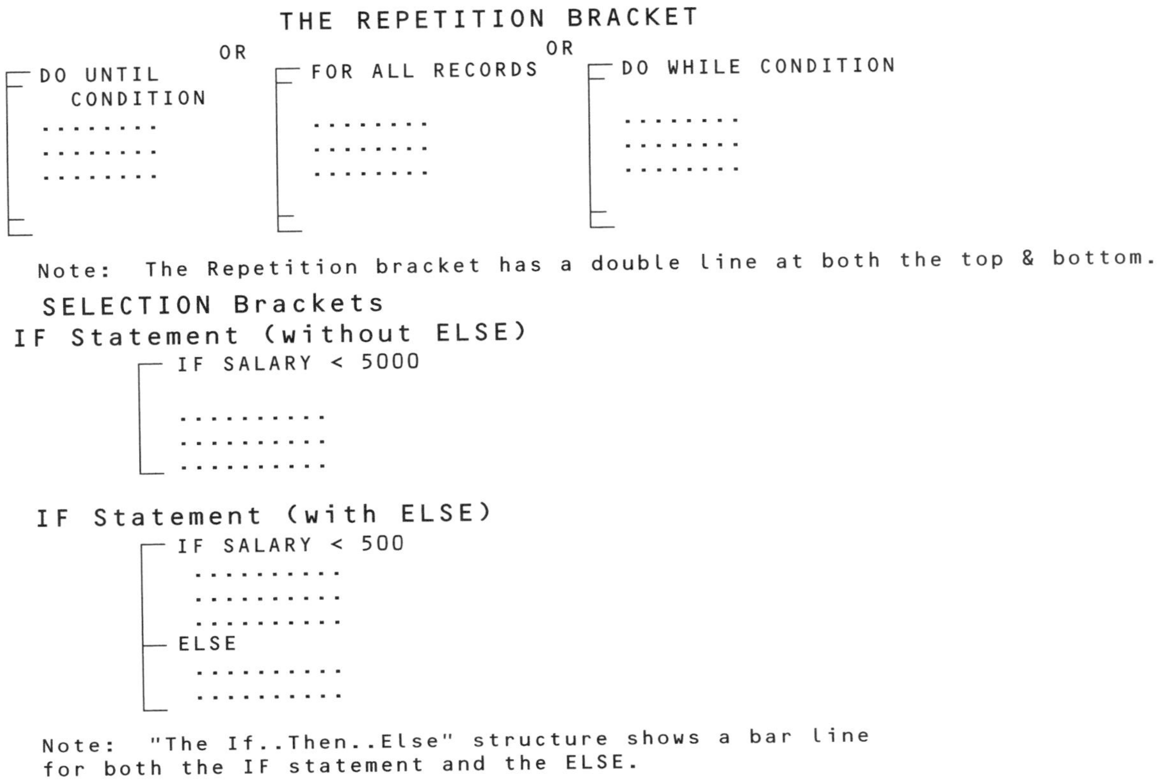

```
                    THE  REPETITION  BRACKET
              OR                    OR
  ┌ DO UNTIL         ┌ FOR ALL RECORDS      ┌ DO WHILE CONDITION
  │   CONDITION      │                      │
  │  ........        │  ........            │  ........
  │  ........        │  ........            │  ........
  │  ........        │  ........            │  ........
  │                  │                      │
  └                  └                      └

    Note:  The Repetition bracket has a double line at both the top & bottom.
    SELECTION  Brackets
  IF  Statement  (without  ELSE)
           ┌─ IF SALARY < 5000
           │
           │  ..........
           │  ..........
           └  ..........


  IF  Statement  (with  ELSE)
           ┌─ IF SALARY < 500
           │  ..........
           │  ..........
           │  ..........
           ├─ ELSE
           │  ..........
           └  ..........

  Note:  "The If..Then..Else" structure shows a bar line
  for both the IF statement and the ELSE.
```

**FIGURE 14.6 (Cont.)**

```
CASE  SUBSTRUCTURE

┌──── WHEN CLASS-STATUS = 1
│       . . . . . . . . . .
│       . . . . . . . . . .
├──── WHEN CLASS-STATUS = 2
│       . . . . . . . . . .
│       . . . . . . . . . .
├──── WHEN CLASS-STATUS = 3
│       . . . . . . . . . .
│       . . . . . . . . . .
├──── WHEN CLASS-STATUS = 4
│       . . . . . . . . . .
│       . . . . . . . . . .
└═══ END-CASE
```

One and only one of the divisions in the brackets above is executed. The CASE structure has a single bar line at the top of the CASE and a double bar line at the end of the structure.

**FIGURE 14.7   Relationship Between Hierarchy Chart and Action Diagram**

PANEL A    HIERARCHY CHART (OR STRUCTURE CHART)

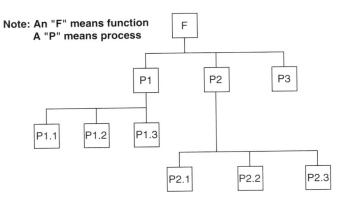

Note: An "F" means function
A "P" means process

PANEL B    ACTION DIAGRAM

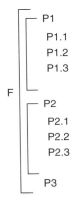

F
P1
P1.1
P1.2
P1.3

P2
P2.1
P2.2
P2.3

P3

**FIGURE 14.8   Module "Call" Symbol**

**Module CALL**

MODULE NAME

Note: This symbol indicates that a module with name specified in the block is to be executed or performed.

**FIGURE 14.9   Action Diagram for Test Results Program (Application 4.2)**

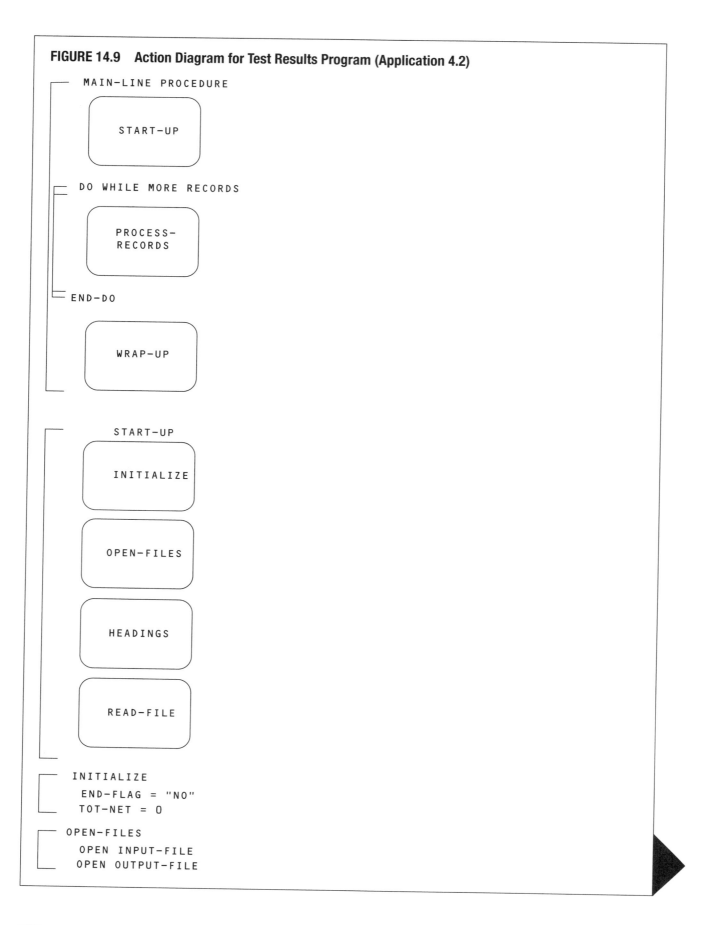

**FIGURE 14.9   (Cont.)**

```
┌─  HEADINGS
│
│     WRITE PAGE HEADING
│     WRITE COLUMN HEADING
│
└─
┌─  READ-FILE
│     READ SALES-FILE
│        WHEN OUT-OF-RECORDS
│           SET END-FLAG ON
│     END-READ
└─
┌─  PROCESS-RECORDS
│
│     ┌─────────────────────┐
│     │      DETAIL-        │
│     │    CALCULATION      │
│     └─────────────────────┘
│
│     ┌─────────────────────┐
│     │                     │
│     │     ACCUMULATE      │
│     │                     │
│     └─────────────────────┘
│
│     ┌─────────────────────┐
│     │                     │
│     │      DET-LINE       │
│     │                     │
│     └─────────────────────┘
│
│     ┌─────────────────────┐
│     │                     │
│     │     READ-FILE       │
│     │                     │
│     └─────────────────────┘
│
└─
┌─  DETAIL-CALCULATION
│
│   CASE
│   ┌─ WHEN SALES < 200
│   │        STORE    AT PCT
│   │
│   ├─ WHEN SALES < 500
│   │        STORE .01 AT PCT
│   │
│   ├─ WHEN SALES < 1000
│   │        STORE .02 AT PCT
│   │
│   ├─ WHEN OTHER
│   │        STORE .03 AT PCT
│   │
│   └─ END-CASE
│
│   DISCOUNT = SALES * PCT
│   NET = SALES - DISCOUNT
└─
```

**FIGURE 14.9   (Cont.)**

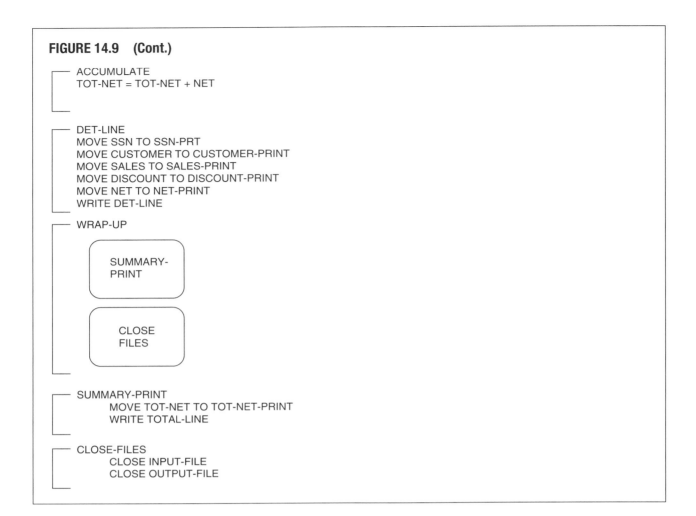

```
    ┌─── ACCUMULATE
    │    TOT-NET = TOT-NET + NET
    │
    └───


    ┌─── DET-LINE
    │    MOVE SSN TO SSN-PRT
    │    MOVE CUSTOMER TO CUSTOMER-PRINT
    │    MOVE SALES TO SALES-PRINT
    │    MOVE DISCOUNT TO DISCOUNT-PRINT
    │    MOVE NET TO NET-PRINT
    └───  WRITE DET-LINE

    ┌─── WRAP-UP
    │
    │       ╭──────────────╮
    │       │  SUMMARY-    │
    │       │  PRINT       │
    │       ╰──────────────╯
    │
    │       ╭──────────────╮
    │       │  CLOSE       │
    │       │  FILES       │
    └───    ╰──────────────╯


    ┌─── SUMMARY-PRINT
    │        MOVE TOT-NET TO TOT-NET-PRINT
    │        WRITE TOTAL-LINE
    └───

    ┌─── CLOSE-FILES
    │        CLOSE INPUT-FILE
    │        CLOSE OUTPUT-FILE
    └───
```

**FIGURE 14.10  Action Diagram for Interactive Program (Application 10.1)**

```
┌─  MAIN-LINE PROCEDURE
│   ╭───────────────────╮
│   │                   │
│   │    START-UP       │
│   │                   │
│   ╰───────────────────╯
│ ┌─ DO WHILE RESP ≠ 5
│ │ ╭───────────────────╮
│ │ │    SELECT-         │
│ │ │    OPTIONS         │
│ │ ╰───────────────────╯
│ └─ END DO
│   ╭───────────────────╮
│   │                   │
│   │    WRAP-UP         │
│   │                   │
│   ╰───────────────────╯
│
└─

┌─  START-UP
│   STORE 0 AT RESP
│ ┌─ DO UNTIL VALID-RESP (1,2,3,4, OR 5)
│ │ ╭───────────────────╮
│ │ │ DISPLAY-          │
│ │ │ MENU-             │
│ │ │ ACCEPT-RESP        │
│ │ ╰───────────────────╯
│ └─ END-DO
└─

┌─  DISPLAY-MENU-ACCEPT-RESP
│   CLEAR SCREEN
│   DISPLAY MAIN-MENU SCREEN
│   ACCEPT RESP
└─
```

**FIGURE 14.10    (Cont.)**

```
┌── SELECT-OPTIONS
│   CASE
│   ┌── WHEN RESP IS 1
│   │   ╭─────────────╮
│   │   │   AREA-OF-   │
│   │   │    CIRCLE    │
│   │   ╰─────────────╯
│   ├── WHEN RESP IS 2
│   │   ╭─────────────╮
│   │   │   AREA-OF-   │
│   │   │  TRIANGLE    │
│   │   ╰─────────────╯
│   ├── WHEN RESP IS 3
│   │   ╭─────────────╮
│   │   │   AREA-OF-   │
│   │   │  RECTANGLE   │
│   │   ╰─────────────╯
│   ├── WHEN RESP IS 4
│   │   ╭─────────────╮
│   │   │   AREA-OF-   │
│   │   │  TRAPEZOID   │
│   │   ╰─────────────╯
│   ╘══ END-CASE
│   RESP = 0
│   ╔══ DO UNTIL VALID-RESPONSE (1,2,3,4, OR 5)
│   │   ╭─────────────╮
│   │   │  DISPLAY-    │
│   │   │  MENU-       │
│   │   │  ACCEPT-RESP │
│   │   ╰─────────────╯
│   ╚══ END-DO
└──
```

**FIGURE 14.10** (Cont.)

```
AREA-OF-CIRCLE
   CLEAR SCREEN
   HOME CURSOR
   DISPLAY SCREEN TITLE
   DISPLAY "What is the diameter of circle?"
   ACCEPT DIAMETER
   AREA = 3.14 * (DIAMETER / 2)²
   DISPLAY AREA
   DISPLAY "Press any key"
   ACCEPT ANY-RESP

AREA-OF-TRIANGLE
   CLEAR SCREEN
   HOME CURSOR
   DISPLAY "What is base?"
   ACCEPT BASE
   DISPLAY "What is height?"
   ACCEPT HEIGHT
   AREA = (BASE X HEIGHT) / 2
   DISPLAY AREA
   DISPLAY "Press any key"
   ACCEPT ANY-KEY

AREA-OF-RECTANGLE
   CLEAR SCREEN
   HOME CURSOR
   DISPLAY MENU TITLE
   DISPLAY "What is the length?"
   ACCEPT LENGTH
   DISPLAY "What is width?"
   ACCEPT WIDTH
   AREA = LENGTH X WIDTH
   DISPLAY AREA
   DISPLAY "Press any key"
   ACCEPT ANY-RESP

AREA-OF-TRAPEZOID
   CLEAR SCREEN
   HOME CURSOR
   DISPLAY MENU TITLE
   DISPLAY "What is bottom base?"
   ACCEPT BASE1
   DISPLAY "What is top base?"
   ACCEPT BASE2
   DISPLAY "What is height?"
   ACCEPT HEIGHT
   AREA = (BASE1 + BASE2) / 2 X HEIGHT
   DISPLAY AREA
   DISPLAY "Press Any Key"
   ACCEPT ANY-RESP

WRAP-UP
   CLEAR SCREEN
   DISPLAY "END OF PROGRAM"
```

## VOCABULARY LIST

Computer-aided
 Systems Engineering
C.A.S.E.
Traditional Systems
 development
Information
 Engineering
CASE encyclopedia
Prototyping
Prototype
CASE advantages
CASE disadvantages

Stages of Systems
 Development
Planning phase
Analysis phase
Design phase
Construction phase
Entity-relationship
 diagram
Data flow diagram
Screen Layout form
Action diagram
Structure chart

## EXERCISES

1. What is C.A.S.E.?

2. List four advantages to the use of C.A.S.E.

3. List four disadvantages to C.A.S.E.

4. List three justifications to the use of C.A.S.E.

5. What is the general rationale for companies changing over to a C.A.S.E. methodology?

6. In spite of C.A.S.E. tool limitations, what would you tell a circumspect corporate executive to win him over to the use of C.A.S.E.?

7. What are the four stages of systems development when using C.A.S.E.?

8. What is the purpose of the planning workstation?

9. What is the purpose of the analysis workstation?

10. What is the purpose of the design workstation?

11. What is the purpose of the construction workstation?

12. What is the purpose of the entity-relationship diagram?

13. What is the purpose of the decomposition diagram?

14. What is the purpose of the data flow diagram?

15. What is the purpose of the structure chart?

16. What is the purpose of the screen layout?

17. What is the purpose of the action diagram?

18. Draw the symbol used to denote a procedure for an action diagram.

19. Draw the symbolic notation used to denote a procedure call for an action diagram.

20. Draw the symbolic notation used to denote a repetition structure for an action diagram.

21. Draw the symbolic notation used to denote a selection structure with an else for an action diagram.

22. Draw the symbolic notation used to denote a C.A.S.E. structure for an action diagram.

23. Using the flowcharting logic for Application 4.5, develop the action diagram for this identical logic.

24. Using the flowcharting logic for Application 6.2, develop the action diagram for this identical logic.

25. Using the flowcharting logic for Application 8.2, develop the action diagram for this identical logic.

26. Using the pseudocode logic for Application 8.2, develop the action diagram for this identical logic.

27. Using the flowcharting logic for Application 10.2, develop the action diagram for this identical logic.

# Appendix A

# IPO Chart

Developed by the IBM Corporation, the IPO Chart is both a logic development tool and a documentation aid. The concept on which the IPO chart is based was first called HIPO (Hierarchical-Input Process-Output). The HIPO technique emphasized the use of modular design and showed the hierarchical decomposition of modules into submodules. The HIPO method has since been expanded into what is now referred to as IPO (Input-Process-Output).

Figure A.1 illustrates the use of an IPO chart to solve a sales commission problem. An IPO chart assumes that all problems are divided into three distinct areas: (1) inputs required, (2) processing steps to be accomplished, and (3) output to be produced. The rules for developing an IPO chart are quite simple. A large rectangle is subdivided into three parts—(1) input, (2) process, and (3) output—one part for each segment of the processing cycle.

The first step is to name the module to be developed. Second, the function of the module must be carefully identified. Third, the OUTPUT column of the IPO chart must be filled in. Here the programmer must determine the output required to meet the module's function. Fourth, the input file, field names, tables, and so on, are entered in the first column, labeled INPUT. Any input that will be used by this specific module is included. Fifth, the processing steps necessary to carry out the module's function are entered in the center column, labeled PROCESS.

The top portion of Figure A.1 depicts the program name, programmer, date written, *module name*, and module function. The column headings INPUT, PROCESS, and OUTPUT are then shown. Under the INPUT column, "sales transaction file" is listed. The three main modules of any program (START-UP, PROCESS, and WRAP-UP) are listed under the PROCESS heading. The words "sales commission report" are listed under OUTPUT.

Subsequent IPO charts are then used to represent the further decomposition of the three main modules. Figure A.2 shows the START-UP module in IPO chart form. Since START-UP contains a command to read a sales record, the sales transaction file is shown in the INPUT column. The four pseudocode commands in the PROCESS segment are (1) initialize variables, (2) open files, (3) print headings, and (4) read sales transaction file. The only output generated as a result of the execution of the START-UP module is the printing of a heading lines.

Figure A.3 illustrates the PROCESS-COMMISSION module in IPO chart format. While some of these activities could be established as separate functions, in this example they are treated as a single module for the sake of brevity. However, in order to follow modularity more closely, each of the five coding segments could be broken down into a separate module. The sales amount is calculated by multiplying quantity by unit price (1). If the sales amount is greater than 500, then it is multiplied by five percent to determine the commission; otherwise the commission is computed at a four percent rate (2). Next, the sales and commission are accumulated into their respective counters (3), the detail line is written (4), and the next record is read (5). It is implied that the code in the PROCESS column is to be repeated for as many times as there are records. The output for this module is to print the detail line.

Figure A.4 depicts the WRAP-UP module. This module requires no input, since all inputs have been accepted and processed. The three commands in the PROCESS column are (1) print the total sales, (2) print total commission, and (4) close the files.

As the reader can detect, a slightly relaxed form of pseudocode is used to represent the processing steps for the various modules. The IPO charting method does make use of the three main structures of structured programming. The DoWhile (iteration) structure can be either implicitly or explicitly shown. As the author has explained earlier, there are two different ways of handling the iteration logic structure— implicit and explicit. One method is to assume that iteration occurs in the first PROCESS module (implicit) and subordinate modules should show a Repeat . . . Until (DoWhile) at the top of the commands that are to be repeated. In the other method, the Repeat . . . Until is used at all module levels of the program. Figure A.1 shows the latter. The scope of the Repeat . . . Until ends with an End-Repeat.

## Advantages of the IPO Chart

These are the major advantages of the IPO chart:

1. No special symbols are needed.
2. No specific syntax is required. The placement of either data or instructions is informal.
3. Because of its English-like syntax, it is easy to read.
4. The technique emphasizes the use of modularity.
5. The programmer can easily determine what input is needed for any given module and what output it produces. This may be its best feature.

**FIGURE A.1   The MAIN-LINE Module**

| IPO CHART | | |
|---|---|---|
| PROGRAM Sales-Comm | PROGRAMMER J. Russell | DATE 10/12/93 |
| MODULE NAME mainline | MODULE FUNCTION driver | |
| INPUT | PROCESS | OUTPUT |
| sales transaction file | 1. start-up module<br>2. repeat until eof<br>   process-comm<br>   end-repeat<br>3. wrap-up | sales commission report |

**FIGURE A.2   The START-UP Module**

| IPO CHART | | |
|---|---|---|
| PROGRAM | PROGRAMMER | DATE |
| MODULE NAME start-up | MODULE FUNCTION initiate report | |
| INPUT | PROCESS | OUTPUT |
| sales transaction file | 1. initialize variables<br>2. open files<br>3. print headings<br>4. read transaction file | heading lines |

## Disadvantages of the IPO Chart

These are the basic limitations of the IPO chart:

1. Complex problems are sometimes difficult to represent in a single column of an IPO chart.
2. Module decomposition is not readily observable. The program hierarchy is hidden away in the stack of IPO sheets. One cannot see the structure as easily as one can with hierarchy charts.
3. The iteration (DoWhile) structure is not easily represented.

**FIGURE A.3   The PROCESS-COMM Module**

| IPO CHART | | |
|---|---|---|
| PROGRAM | PROGRAMMER | DATE |
| MODULE NAME process-commission | MODULE FUNCTION generate-report | |
| INPUT | PROCESS | OUTPUT |
| salesman-no<br>salesman-name<br>quantity<br>price/unit | 1. calculate sales = quantity * price<br>2. if sales > 500<br>    calculate comm = sales * .05<br>    else<br>    endif calculate comm = sales * .04<br>3. accumulate sales and comm into<br>    respective counters<br>4. print detail line<br>5. read sales line | detail<br>line |

**FIGURE A.4   The WRAP-UP Module**

| IPO CHART | | |
|---|---|---|
| PROGRAM | PROGRAMMER | DATE |
| MODULE NAME wrap-up | MODULE FUNCTION print totals | |
| INPUT | PROCESS | OUTPUT |
| none | 1. format total lines<br>2. print total sales<br>3. print total commission<br>4. close files | total lines |

# Appendix B

# Data Representation in Computer Memory

The *byte* is the smallest addressable unit of storage in many computers. Two main computer codes are the Extended Binary Coded Decimal Interchange Code (EBCDIC) and American Standard Code for Information Interchange (ASCII). The EBCDIC code is widely used by IBM mainframes, and the ASCII code is rapidly being accepted as the standard in industry today since it is the universal code for data transmission.

## Extended Binary Coded Decimal Interchange Code (EBCDIC)

EBCDIC uses eight bits to store a letter, number, or special character. Together, the eight bits make up a byte. Normally, a single character of data is read into a single byte of memory. The EBCDIC byte is divided into two parts, the zone portion and the digit portion. Each portion consists of four bits.

Figure B.1 illustrates the general makeup of the byte in EBCDIC form. The place values of each bit of the byte are displayed. The place values of 8 4 2 1 are shown for both the zone and digit portions of the byte. To store a number in a byte, all zone bits are turned on; in other words, each position in the zone portion is a 1. When all zone bits are turned on, it is equivalent to the decimal value 15. The digit portion of the byte contains the necessary bits (or the appropriate assemblage of bits) to represent the values 0 through 9. Figure B.2 shows the EBCDIC form of the value 1.

To store a letter of the alphabet, a proper configuration of bits must be placed in the zone portion. To represent the letters A through I, the decimal value 12 is placed in the zone portion (1100). The

letters J through R equate to the zone value of 13, and the letters S through Z use the 14 zone value.

Figure B.3 illustrates the assemblage of bits for the letter A. Figure B.4 depicts the EBCDIC code in binary and hexadecimal notation.

## Data Types

On IBM mainframes, data is read into memory in the EBCDIC (or zoned-decimal) form. For input and output operations, the data must be in this form; however, for performing arithmetic and logical operations upon numeric data, the data must be translated into one of the following data types: (1) packed-decimal, (2) binary, or (3) floating-point. The simplest to understand is the packed-decimal format. Figure B.5 illustrates the reading of data into memory in EBCDIC form and its conversion into packed-decimal.

After the data is read and placed into the bytes in EBCDIC form, the illustration shows the F in the left half of the rightmost byte being flipped into the rightmost half of the rightmost byte. Is that baffling? And, the 6 is flipped back into the left half (that is, the two half bytes exchange places). The zone portions of the bytes are ignored (or stripped away). Remaining digits in the EBCDIC bytes are stored in adjacent half bytes of the packed decimal field. Any empty bytes or half bytes are zero-filled. The only valid signs that the byte may have are C, D, E, and F. When doing arithmetic or numeric comparisons, the machine must find a valid sign or it will abort the program execution with a "data exception." The machine refuses to perform these operations with invalid numeric data. The C and F signs are positive, and the D and E signs are negative. The binary and floating-point data types will not be discussed here.

## American Standard Code for Information Interchange

The American Standard Code for Information Interchange (ASCII) was developed by the International Standards Institute and is published by the American National Standards Institute. ASCII utilizes seven bits to represent letters, numbers, and special characters. Figure B.6 lists the characters along with their equivalent bit configuration in ASCII.

**FIGURE B.1 Computer Byte in EBCDIC**

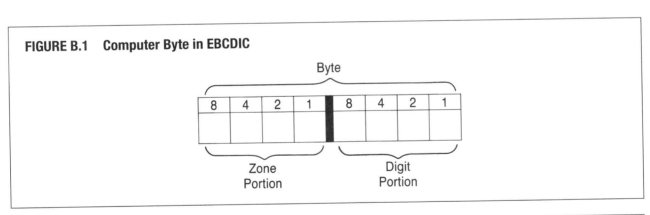

**FIGURE B.2 The EBCDIC Bit Configuration for the Digit 1**

| | 8 | 4 | 2 | 1 | 8 | 4 | 2 | 1 |
|---|---|---|---|---|---|---|---|---|
| 1 = | 1 | 1 | 1 | 1 | 0 | 0 | 0 | 1 |

**FIGURE B.3 The EBCDIC Bit Configuration for the Letter A**

| | 8 | 4 | 2 | 1 | 8 | 4 | 2 | 1 |
|---|---|---|---|---|---|---|---|---|
| A = | 1 | 1 | 0 | 0 | 0 | 0 | 0 | 1 |

## FIGURE B.4    EBCDIC Codes in Binary and Hexadecimal Notation

| Value or Constant | Binary<br>8 4 2 1 8 4 2 1 | Hexadecimal |
|---|---|---|
| *EXTENDED BINARY CODES DECIMAL INTERCHANGE CODE* | | |
| 0 | 1 1 1 1 0 0 0 0 | F 0 |
| 1 | 1 1 1 1 0 0 0 1 | F 1 |
| 2 | 1 1 1 1 0 0 1 0 | F 2 |
| 3 | 1 1 1 1 0 0 1 1 | F 3 |
| 4 | 1 1 1 1 0 1 0 0 | F 4 |
| 5 | 1 1 1 1 0 1 0 1 | F 5 |
| 6 | 1 1 1 1 0 1 1 0 | F 6 |
| 7 | 1 1 1 1 0 1 1 1 | F 7 |
| 8 | 1 1 1 1 1 0 0 0 | F 8 |
| 9 | 1 1 1 1 1 0 0 1 | F 9 |
| A | 1 1 0 0 0 0 0 1 | C 1 |
| B | 1 1 0 0 0 0 1 0 | C 2 |
| C | 1 1 0 0 0 0 1 1 | C 3 |
| D | 1 1 0 0 0 1 0 0 | C 4 |
| E | 1 1 0 0 0 1 0 1 | C 5 |
| F | 1 1 0 0 0 1 1 0 | C 6 |
| G | 1 1 0 0 0 1 1 1 | C 7 |
| H | 1 1 0 0 1 0 0 0 | C 8 |
| I | 1 1 0 0 1 0 0 1 | C 9 |
| J | 1 1 0 1 0 0 0 1 | D 1 |
| K | 1 1 0 1 0 0 1 0 | D 2 |
| L | 1 1 0 1 0 0 1 1 | D 3 |
| M | 1 1 0 1 0 1 0 0 | D 4 |
| N | 1 1 0 1 0 1 0 1 | D 5 |
| O | 1 1 0 1 0 1 1 0 | D 6 |
| P | 1 1 0 1 0 1 1 1 | D 7 |
| Q | 1 1 0 1 1 0 0 0 | D 8 |
| R | 1 1 0 1 1 0 0 1 | D 9 |
| S | 1 1 1 0 0 0 1 0 | E 2 |
| T | 1 1 1 0 0 0 1 1 | E 3 |
| U | 1 1 1 0 0 1 0 0 | E 4 |
| V | 1 1 1 0 0 1 0 1 | E 5 |
| W | 1 1 1 0 0 1 1 0 | E 6 |
| X | 1 1 1 0 0 1 1 1 | E 7 |
| Y | 1 1 1 0 1 0 0 0 | E 8 |
| Z | 1 1 1 0 1 0 0 1 | E 9 |
| LOW-VALUE* | 0 0 0 0 0 0 0 0 | 0 0 |
| HIGH-VALUE* | 1 1 1 1 1 1 1 1 | F F |
| space | 0 1 0 0 0 0 0 0 | 4 0 |

*COBOL figurative constant

## FIGURE B.5    Conversion to Packed Decimal

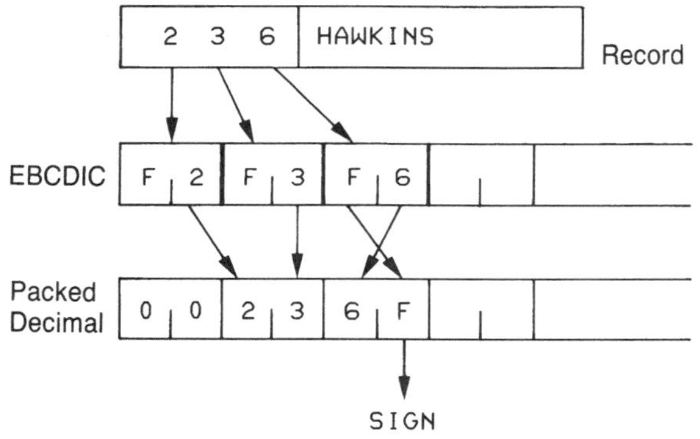

**FIGURE B.6    ASCII Codes**

| Character | Bit Representation (Place Values) | | | | | | |
|---|---|---|---|---|---|---|---|
| | 64 | 32 | 16 | 8 | 4 | 2 | 1 |
| 0 | 0 | 1 | 1 | 0 | 0 | 0 | 0 |
| 1 | 0 | 1 | 1 | 0 | 0 | 0 | 1 |
| 2 | 0 | 1 | 1 | 0 | 0 | 1 | 0 |
| 3 | 0 | 1 | 1 | 0 | 0 | 1 | 1 |
| 4 | 0 | 1 | 1 | 0 | 1 | 0 | 0 |
| 5 | 0 | 1 | 1 | 0 | 1 | 0 | 1 |
| 6 | 0 | 1 | 1 | 0 | 1 | 1 | 0 |
| 7 | 0 | 1 | 1 | 0 | 1 | 1 | 1 |
| 8 | 0 | 1 | 1 | 1 | 0 | 0 | 0 |
| 9 | 0 | 1 | 1 | 1 | 0 | 0 | 1 |
| A | 1 | 0 | 0 | 0 | 0 | 0 | 1 |
| B | 1 | 0 | 0 | 0 | 0 | 1 | 0 |
| C | 1 | 0 | 0 | 0 | 0 | 1 | 1 |
| D | 1 | 0 | 0 | 0 | 1 | 0 | 0 |
| E | 1 | 0 | 0 | 0 | 1 | 0 | 1 |
| F | 1 | 0 | 0 | 0 | 1 | 1 | 0 |
| G | 1 | 0 | 0 | 0 | 1 | 1 | 1 |
| H | 1 | 0 | 0 | 1 | 0 | 0 | 0 |
| I | 1 | 0 | 0 | 1 | 0 | 0 | 1 |
| J | 1 | 0 | 0 | 1 | 0 | 1 | 0 |
| K | 1 | 0 | 0 | 1 | 0 | 1 | 1 |
| L | 1 | 0 | 0 | 1 | 1 | 0 | 0 |
| M | 1 | 0 | 0 | 1 | 1 | 0 | 1 |
| N | 1 | 0 | 0 | 1 | 1 | 1 | 0 |
| O | 1 | 0 | 0 | 1 | 1 | 1 | 1 |
| P | 1 | 0 | 1 | 0 | 0 | 0 | 0 |
| Q | 1 | 0 | 1 | 0 | 0 | 0 | 1 |
| R | 1 | 0 | 1 | 0 | 0 | 1 | 0 |
| S | 1 | 0 | 1 | 0 | 0 | 1 | 1 |
| T | 1 | 0 | 1 | 0 | 1 | 0 | 0 |
| U | 1 | 0 | 1 | 0 | 1 | 0 | 1 |
| V | 1 | 0 | 1 | 0 | 1 | 1 | 0 |
| W | 1 | 0 | 1 | 0 | 1 | 1 | 1 |
| X | 1 | 0 | 1 | 1 | 0 | 0 | 0 |
| Y | 1 | 0 | 1 | 1 | 0 | 0 | 1 |
| Z | 1 | 0 | 1 | 1 | 0 | 1 | 0 |

# Appendix C

# The Input Validation Routine for BASIC

In Application 13.1 of Chapter 13, it was pointed out that the BASIC language does not have a data class condition test as does COBOL. In COBOL, we can say IF FLDX IS ALPHABETIC . . . , but in BASIC there is no command equivalent to this one. Condition testing can be handled in one of two ways with BASIC; (1) the entire field can be accepted by the program as the user keys in the data on a keyboard, and, after it has been entered, the program can go back and check one character at a time to determine if they are all of a certain class (numeric or alphabetic), or (2) each character of data can be immediately validated as it is entered from the keyboard.

From a programming perspective, the second method has been found to be easier—validating each character immediately as it is keyed in—with a technique involving the use of For . . . Next loops and While . . . Wend structures. The flowcharting module for this validation procedure follows (Figure C.1). Four variables are used in the routines that validate the data from the keyboard, (1) LENGTH, (2) X, (3)Y, and (4) ITEM$. The four variables are set to the values required for that field. X

and Y are used to determine the row and column positions on the screen. LENGTH is used to determine the maximum length of the field to be input. ITEM$ is used to place a message on the screen to identify the field that is being input.

After these variables are set to the proper values, a particular subroutine is called for each type of variable to be entered. If the field is alphabetic, program control passes to the alphabetic input routine. In the routine that tests for alphabetic characters, as each key is pressed, the ASCII character code for that key is checked to see if it is in the range of 64 (the letter A in ASCII) through 91 (the letter Z in ASCII). If it is within this range, it will be then accepted as alphabetic; otherwise, the key will be ignored and the user will be asked to retry.

When the user keys in the maximum number of characters for a particular field (a number controlled by the variable, LENGTH), control will automatically pass to the next field validation check. If the data in the field is shorter than the maximum field size (LENGTH), then pressing return (or enter) will automatically cause control to pass to the next field validation check.

# FIGURE C.1  Data Validation Routine for BASIC

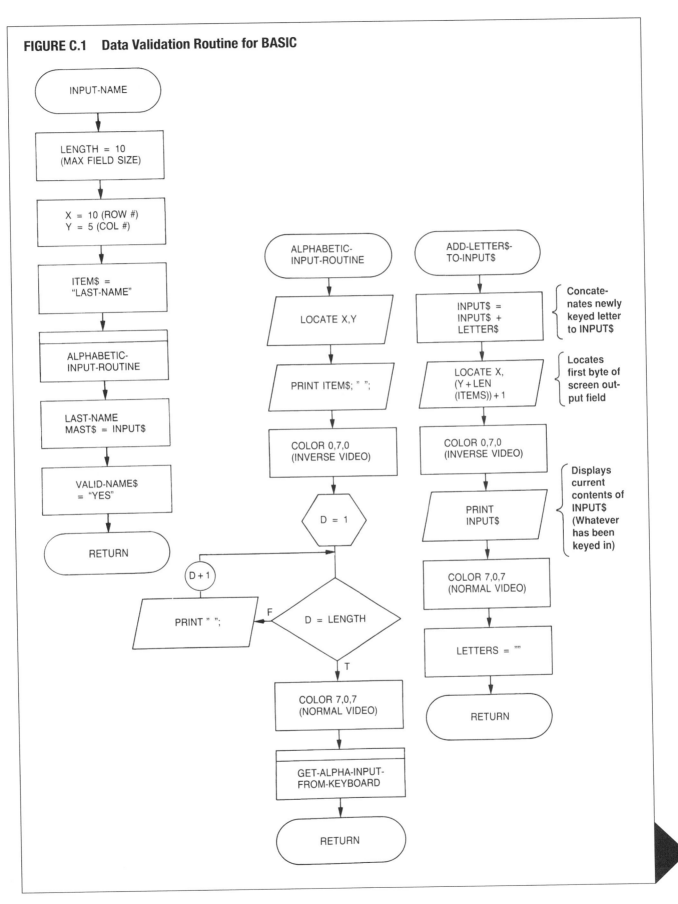

**FIGURE C.1 (Cont.)**

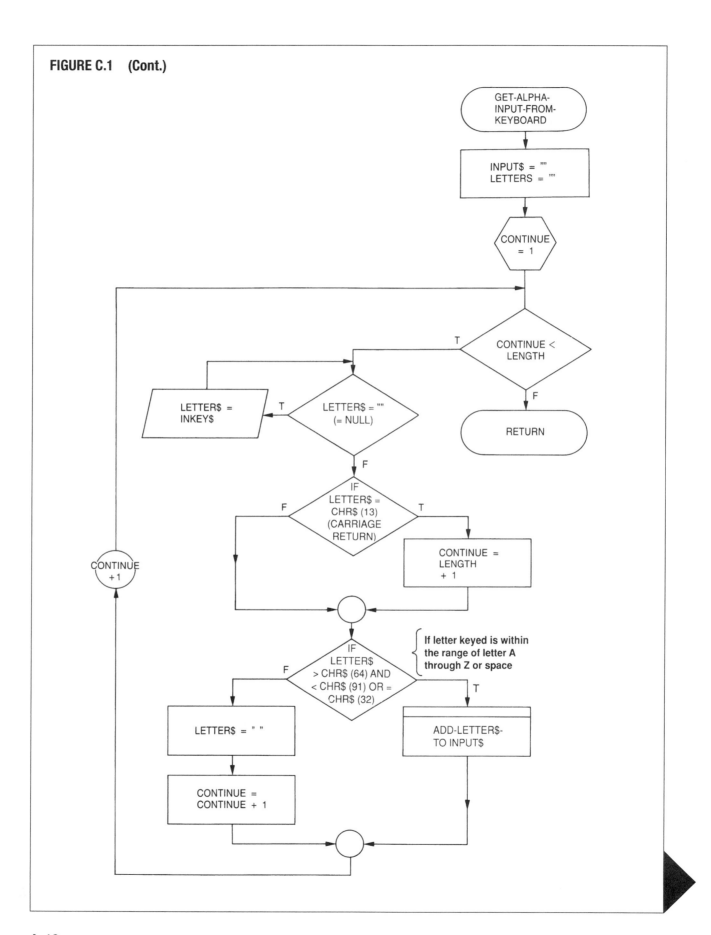

FIGURE C.1 (Cont.)

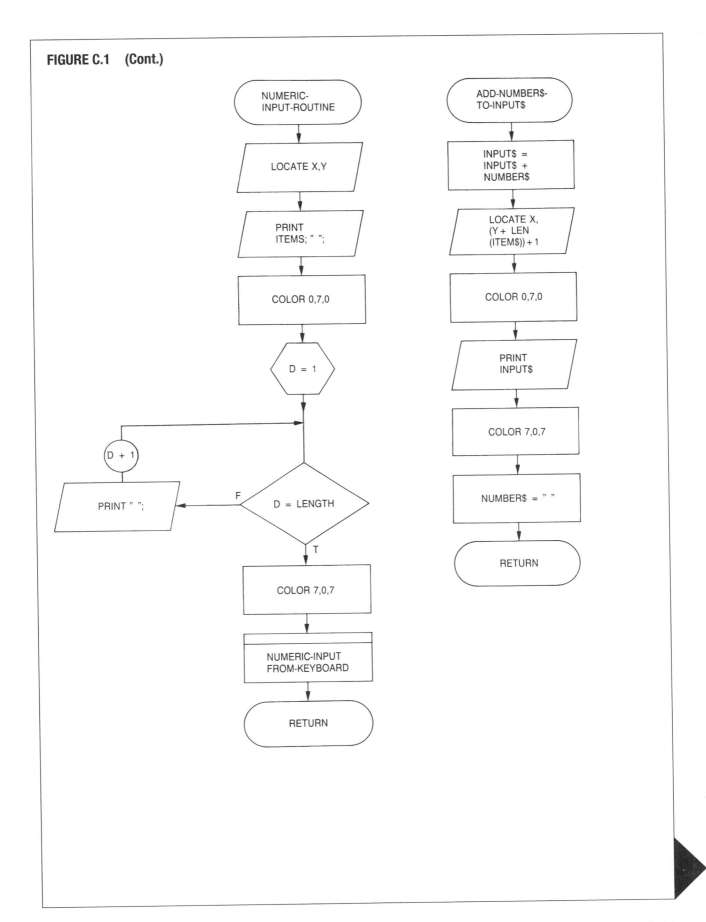

**FIGURE C.1    (Cont.)**

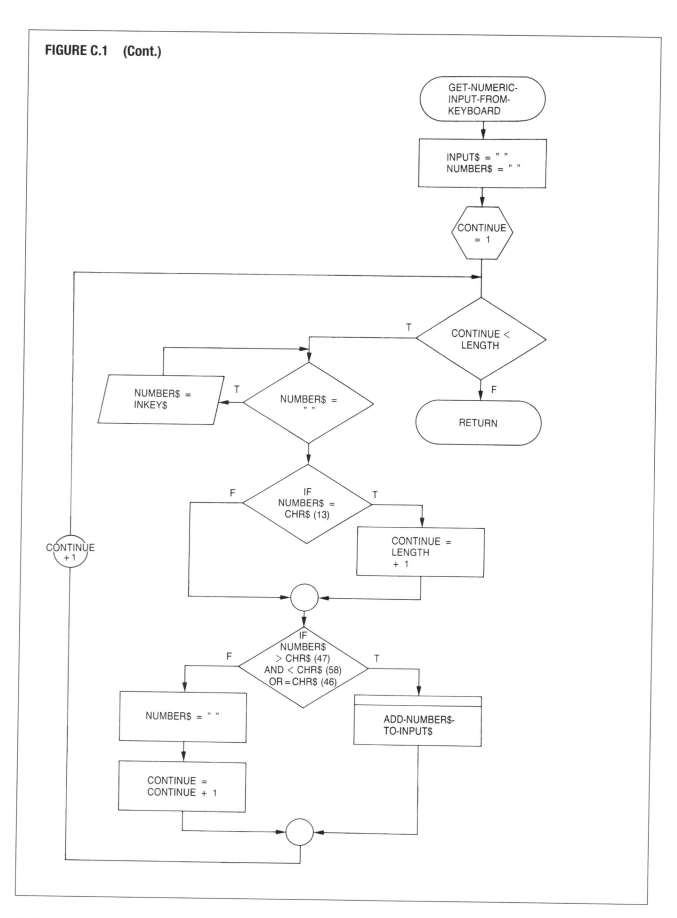

A-12

# Glossary

**accumulation** the process of adding an incoming number to a counter or accumulator and replacing the contents with the sum.

**accumulator** (also counter) a memory area set aside for the purpose of performing add operations. *See* accumulation.

**Action Diagram** a program design tool for developing program logic that can be used as input by code generators in a CASE environment. The action diagram uses brackets to make programming structures highly visible.

**address** a label, name or number, that identifies an exact storage location in main memory and enables the computer to manipulate the byte of data stored there.

**alphabetic data** data consisting of only the letters of the alphabet. In COBOL, alphabetic data also includes the space character.

**alphanumeric data** data consisting of any combination of digits, letters, and special characters such as the symbols on the keyboard.

**array** *See* table.

**ascending sequence** arrangement from smallest to largest (numerical) or from first to last (as in alphabetical sequence). *See* sort.

**assembly language** set of computer instructions that resemble the actual machine language and are therefore "machine dependent," i.e., varying from one computer to another. *See* low-level language, machine language.

**Association Matrix** a tool used in information engineering and with CASE technology for analyzing relationships between processes and entities, between goals and functions, etc.

**attribute** *See* field.

**audit-trail file** records of the changes made to a master file from a computer terminal operating in interactive mode, a trace of the actual dialog between user and computer.

**automatic destroy read-in** the replacing (or overlaying) of a data record or variable by a new record or variable.

**backup** a copy of the current version of a file, made as a safeguard against its loss or as a security measure; also, to copy a file or group of files.

**backup file** *See* backup.

**batch processing** collecting records over a period of time to create a file and then periodically processing the entire file.

**binary table search** a method of searching a table in which the table is first sorted into ascending sequence; then the midpoint of the table is found and compared with the search key. Successive divisions and comparisons are made until the values match. *Compare* sequential search.

**bottom-of-page checking** computer instructions based on If . . . Then . . . Else logic that enable the computer to determine when the printer is printing the last line on a page so that it can cause the printer to advance to the top of the next page.

**bubble sort** a technique for ordering records that causes them to move up into position through a table much as bubbles move up through water; it compares successive pairs and swaps them if necessary. *See* simple exchange sort.

**built-in validity checking** a validity-checking routine that is written into a processing program rather than written separately as an editing program. *See* validity checking.

**byte** a particular location—or "pigeonhole"— in memory where a character (letter, digit, or symbol) needed for either instructions or data is stored. *See* address.

**C.A.S.E.** (Computer-Aided Systems Engineering) a methodology of using the computer to assist in the systems development process. A central repository is used for storing both data and metadata. The basic rationale of CASE is to build information systems around the enterprise rather than around the function with automated modeling tools. Normally, code generators allow automatic code generation from the action diagrams developed.

**calculating** performing arithmetic operations on data in order to generate useful information. *See* reporting.

**CASE structure** a special type of If . . . Then . . . Else structure used when several consecutive comparisons to a single variable must be made; furthermore, dependent code may be executed, after which program control passes to the end of the series of comparison blocks or operations.

**central processing unit** *See CPU.*

**class test** a routine that determines if the content of a field is numeric or alphabetic data. *See* validity checking.

**code** (1) programming language instructions; (2) to write such instructions; (3) a field on a record (I.D. code).

**code test** (valid code test) a routine that ensures that the content of the identification code field contains one of the valid codes. *See* validity checking.

**coding** writing a computer program in a specific programming language, such as COBOl, BASIC, Pascal, etc.

**cohesion** the relationship between commands in a single module. Ideally, a module should have strong cohesion, i.e., relate only to the achievement of the function at hand.

**comparison** a logical operation in which a data item is determined to be greater than, less than, or equal to another data item. *See* If . . . Then . . . Else, selection structure.

**compile** to translate, using a special computer program, high-level instructions into machine language instructions for execution by the computer. *See* compiler.

**compiler** a computer program for translating a high-level program into a machine language program or object program.

**compound expression** a conditional expression made up of two simple conditional expressions that are either in an OR relationship or an AND relationship. For an AND compound conditional expression, both simple conditions must be true for the compound condition to be true. For an OR compound conditional expression, either of the two simple conditions can be true for the compound conditional to be true.

**computer instruction** machine language instruction. *See* operation code, operand.

**computer program** a set of instructions given to a computer to solve a specific problem or a set of problems.

**connector symbol** a flowcharting symbol that (1) serves as a focal point to show that two or more flowlines are merging and (2) shows the continuation of a flowchart module on the same page.

**control break** a program that is used to print subtotals or various items of intermediate information whenever there is a change in the control field value of the records, e.g., from one department to another in a store.

**control break report** printout that includes control totals, i.e., subtotals for various groups or subgroups of records. *See* control break.

**control coupling** one module's dependence on another that is based on their mutual access to a variable. Normally we are looking for weak coupling where one module is not dependent upon another.

**control field** unique identifier used by a programmer to distinguish between groups of records.

**control variable** *See* program switch.

**counter** the term for an accumulator that is used to count the occurrences of something. *See* accumulator.

**coupling** the relationship of program modules to each other. Ideally program modules are loosely coupled, i.e., they can stand by themselves without dependence upon the output from other modules.

**CPU** abbreviation for central processing unit, one of the four main units of a computer. *See* processor.

**CRT** abbreviation for cathode ray tube, a screen for viewing computer output. Together with a keyboard, it makes up a terminal.

**data** formalized facts, grouped in specific patterns, about a person, place, or thing.

**data base** a set of interrelated data records stored on a direct-access storage device in a structure designed to allow multiple applications to access the data usually in an interactive mode.

**data entry** the process of transferring data from a source document to a computer record.

**data validation** checking recorded data to ensure that it satisfies certain validity criteria, i.e., that the data is numeric if used in calculations or that it falls within a prescribed range of acceptable values.

**data validation edit program** an independent edit program or validity checking program that checks for invalid fields in records.

**data validation edit report** (exception report) a listing of the data records that, following a validity check, have been found to be in error.

**data validation loop** an on-line "error trap" routine for testing the validity of data in an interactive environment, i.e., as it is keyed in by a user. Invalid data causes reprompt and a recheck, i.e., looping.

**debug** to correct errors in a program.

**decision symbol** the diamond-shaped flowcharting symbol that denotes that two values are being compared.

**decomposition diagram** a tool used in information engineering and structured analysis to decompose functions, processes, and other kinds of business objects.

**definite iteration structure** a program with four basic steps that causes a loop to be executed a predefined number of times. A modification of the DoWhile structure that shows automatic initialization of a subscript, a condition text, a module call, and a subscript increment. The FOR . . . NEXT in BASIC and the Perform . . . Varying in COBOL are examples of the definite iteration structure.

**descending sequence** numerical arrangement from the largest to the smallest value or alphabetical arrangement from Z to A. *See* sort, ascending sequence.

**detail-calculation module** the module into which all calculation activities related to the record itself (except for accumulation of final totals) will be placed. Usually results go to the detail-line module for output.

**detail-line module** the module that prints the detail line.

**detail-printed control break report** a control break report that prints the control field as a part of every detail line. *Compare* with group printed control break report.

**Dijkstra** His work led to the development of structured programming and "GOTOless" programming.

**direct file** a file organized by using a randomizing formula ("hashing") for placement of records in a file. The same formula is used to update or retrieve the records.

**documentation** a collection of written descriptions and procedures that provide information about and guidance in using or maintaining a program or computer system; a user's manual, procedures manual, flowchart, etc.

**element** a subcompartment, or subset, of a table in which one or more values are placed.

**end-flag** (or end-of-file switch; EOF switch) a variable in the process-file module that, when equal to some predetermined value (e.g., "YES"), signals that all the records in a particular file have been processed, thus stopping the looping process.

**end user** the ultimate user of output produced by a program or system.

**Entity-Relationship Diagram** a diagramming method for modelling data and the relationships between various entities. The cardinality (1:1, 1:M, and M:N) of the relationships are also shown.

**entry point** the address of the first instruction in a program, routine, or subroutine where execution begins.

**error message** printed description of an error in a program or data that causes the computer to abort the execution of the program.

**error trap** *See* data validation loop.

**exception report** *See* data validation edit report.

**execute** run a program.

**exit point** the address of an instruction in a program that transfers control to a subroutine or back to the mainline module.

**explicit table argument** a value used in a table in order to locate the desired element. An actual table search is needed to locate this value. In a two-dimensional table, it is used to locate the row or column where an appropriate range of values or a specific value may be found. *Compare* positional addressing.

**external sort** arrangement of data used with very large files, in which work areas outside the main memory are used. *Compare* internal sort.

**field** (also called attribute) a specific area on a record reserved for storage of a specific category of data about a person, place, or thing.

**file** a collection of logically related records that can be dealt with as a unit.

**final total** a total that prints at the end of a report and that represents the summation of calculated values or values input from the record.

**flowchart**   a representation of computer instructions in the form of a block diagram, using specially shaped symbols, that shows the program logic in detail.

**flowline**   straight lines, usually with arrowheads, that connect the symbols on a flowchart and show the execution path of a computer program.

**For . . . Next**   a statement in BASIC language that causes looping. Equivalent in some ways to the development iteration structure.

**GOTOless programming**   a programming methodology advocated by Dijkstra that enables the programmer to write programs that do not use the GOTO command.

**group-printed control break report**   a report in which control fields print only on the first detail line of a group.

**hierarchy chart**   a diagram of the modules in a computer program that shows the general relationship of major to minor modules, without detail.

**high-level language**   a set of instructions to the computer that is very English-like, or "machine independent," requiring little or no interpretation in order to be intelligible to a programmer. *Compare* low-level language, assembly language, machine language.

**identification code**   code used to classify data according to some variable, saving record storage space and reducing the chance of keying error (i.e., a class code of "3" means the student is a junior).

**If . . . Then . . . Else**   a program statement that compares two values and based on the results of the comparison, provides for alternative processing operations. *See* selection structure.

**independent edit program**   *See* data validation edit program.

**indexed file**   a file that is accessed via an index or directory. It must be stored on disk. *Compare* sequential file, random file.

**information**   data organized into a usable form, i.e., data that has been processed by a computer and is output in a form meaningful to a user.

**input**   (1) data entered or to be entered into the computer for processing; (2) to enter such data. *Compare* output.

**input area**   a portion of memory used to temporarily store data that have been input to the computer system and are waiting to execute. Also called input buffer.

**input/output symbol**   (I/O symbol) a flowcharting symbol (parallelogram) used to indicate the reading of a record or the writing of the contents of variables.

**interactive processing**   (on-line processing) mode of computer operation in which the user can access any given file at any moment through an ongoing dialog with the computer via menus and submenus on the terminal screen. *Compare* batch processing.

**interactive update**   using interactive processing to update files.

**internal sort**   arrangement of data by placing it in main memory in the form of a table and subsequently ordering it. *Compare* external sort.

**left-justified**   the positioning of alphabetic and alphanumeric data from left to right in a field. Remaining positions are filled with spaces. Compare right-justified.

**literal subscript**   the use of a numeric constant as a subscript (e.g., Tab (3)).

**looping**   (1) repetition of the basic steps of the processing cycle—input, process, and output; (2) the iteration of any set of program commands.

**low-level language**   a set of instructions for the computer that are in a form very near the language of the machine itself. *See* assembly language, machine-dependent language.

**machine language**   *See* low-level language.

**mainline module**   the starting point of program logic from which the three main submodules are called and to which control is returned after the submodule has been executed. It consists of three parts: (1) START-LT module, (2) PROCESS-FILE module, and (3) WRAP-UP module.

**main memory**   storage within the computer for programs and their data while they are executing; it is composed of a number of locations, each of which has a unique address and can store a specified number of bits. *See* address, byte, read-write memory.

**master file**   a file of records containing relatively permanent information about a person, place, or thing.

**master record**   *See* master file.

**master record key**   a unique identifier used to sort the records into sequence in a master file.

**memory**   *See* main memory.

**memory table**   *See* table.

**menu**   a multiple-choice list of computer functions presented to the user for selection on the terminal screen.

**menu-driven file maintenance**   updating of files through an interactive dialog between user and computer via a hierarchical system of menus.

**Mills, Harlan**   a pioneer in the use of modular programming.

**modular design** program design with a top-down approach, in which modules are often broken down into functional segments.

**module** a sequence of instructions for performing a single task in a computer program.

**Module Action Diagram** diagram that uses brackets and pseudocode to show various program logic structures. The diagramming method is the accepted program design method when using CASE tools that support Information Engineering.

**nested comparison** (or nested IF) a comparison that is dependent upon the outcome of a previous comparison.

**nested IF** *See* nested comparision.

**nonautomatic destroy read-out** when data is moved or transferred from one place to another, the end result is a copy of the original. The data is not really moved. It remains in the original area as well. *See* automatic destroy read-in.

**numeric data** data consisting of only the digits 0 through 9.

**on-line processing** a method by which the computer constantly has access to the file and the processing is ongoing. Changes may be made immediately to the file at any time.

**op code** *See* operation code.

**operand** the part of the machine language instruction that contains the necessary information about the location or address of the data upon which the operation will be performed. *Compare* operation code.

**operation code** the part of the machine language instruction that tells the computer what operation or function it is to perform. *Compare* operand.

**output** (1) display or printout of the results of computer processing, or (2) devices for displaying or printing such results.

**peripheral unit** one of four main units of the computer; it stores data permanently on tape or disk.

**perform varying** a COBOL language command that is used to code the definite iteration structure; it is usually used in manipulating tables.

**positional addressing** using a subscript, usually a field on a record, to locate a value in a table without actually searching it.

**predefined process** a programming segment found elsewhere in the program; a callable module.

**predefined process symbol** a flowcharting symbol used to call, or invoke, a segment of the program (or module) that is defined elsewhere.

**previous-number variable** a work variable into which a control field is stored so that subsequent control field values can be compared to the contents of the previous number variable. When the values are unequal a control break exists.

**printer spacing chart** a chart filled in by a programmer to show the actual positions that data will occupy on the printed page.

**problem definition** the first step in writing a computer program. A statement defining the problem that must be solved.

**process-file module** the module that represents the processing steps—detail calculations, accumulation detail-line, and read-file—that are to occur for each and every record in the file.

**processing cycle** the three basic steps in computer operation: (1) input, (2) processing, and (3) output of data. *See* looping.

**processor** the main unit of the computer, consisting of the CPU and memory. *See* CPU.

**process symbol** a flowcharting symbol rectangle used to represent processing steps such as computations and data movement; it may also be used to initialize a variable to a particular value.

**program** *See* computer program.

**program switch** (control variable) controls the execution path of the program. *See* end-flag, for example.

**prompt** on-screen menu or message from the computer to the user.

**pseudocode** an intermediate step between flowcharting and coding, consisting of short commands in English, that allows a programmer to concentrate on the problem rather than on the programming language.

**random file** a file that allows access to a record via a disk record address calculation. It must be stored on disk. *Compare* sequential file, indexed file.

**range-step table** a table that is searched to find an appropriate range of values rather than a specific value.

**range-step value** a table argument that allows an element to be located based on a range of values rather than a specific value.

**read-file module** the module responsible for reading a record.

**reasonableness test** (limit test) a check to determine whether a value is within a prescribed range of reasonable values. *See* validity checking.

**record** a group of logically related fields treated as a unit; a group of records that make up a file.

**record layout**   the document that describes the input format to the computer; it is also used to design the data entry form for keying in records.

**relative file**   a file organized like a series of slots into which records can be written; they are accessed—either sequentially or randomly—by their relative position in the file.

**repetition structure**   the part of computer program logic that executes a module repeatedly while a condition is true. Also called the DoWhile.

**reporting**   outputting on printer or terminal screen the results of computer calculations or input.

**response**   user's answer to a computer prompt: choosing a menu option or keying in data.

**response time**   the time the interactive computer system takes to respond to a given response by the user.

**right-justified**   the positioning of numeric data in a field as far to the right as possible or aligned by a decimal point. Unfilled positions are marked with zeros. *Compare* left-justified.

**selection structure**   the part of structured programming logic that deals with the comparison of two values and the alternative processing that takes place based on the result of the comparison.

**selection-with-exchange sort**   a sorting method that uses successive comparisons, as in the simple exchange sort, in which the records are selected, or "flagged" but not physically exchanged until the end of each pass.

**sequence structure**   the serial execution of imperative commands, such as add, subtract, move, compute, etc.

**sequential file**   a serial placement of records. To access the fifth record, the first 4 records must be read. It may be created on either tape or disk. *Compare* index file random file.

**sequential table search**   the simplest method of searching a table, one record at a time, for the table element key that corresponds to the input record key. The search starts with the first element and progresses serially (one element at a time) until either a match is found or the end of the table is reached. *Compare* binary search.

**Shell sort**   a variation on the exchange sort that requires fewer passes to sort a large list that is grossly out of order, since the comparison interval diminishes from pass to pass in almost a binary fashion.

**sign test**   a routine that determines whether a value is positive or negative. *See* validity checking.

**simple exchange sort**   a commonly used sorting method using successive comparisons and exchanges that works well for relatively small tables in which the records are grossly out of order. An alternative to the Bubble sort.

**single-dimensional table**   a table where data elements are referenced using a single subscript. A linear list.

**single-level control break**   the point at which a single control field of the current record is unequal to the control field of the previous record. *See* control break.

**sort**   (1) a technique for arranging in order alphabetically, numerically, or according to control code-records in a file; (2) to arrange records in some logical order.

**sorting**   (1) the process of arranging or alphabetizing records in a file according to one or more selected key fields; (2) arranging records in some logical order. *See* sort key field.

**sort key field**   a unique identifier on a record that differentiates the record from any other record within the file and is used for sorting the records.

**span of control**   the number of submodules for which a single module is responsible.

**standard program design**   a design defined by the author that uses a mainline module with three major submodules—START-UP, PROCESS, and WRAP-UP. (The PROCESS module is normally segmented into the CALCULATIONS, ACCUMULATIONS, DETAIL-LINE, and READ-FILE submodules.)

**startup module**   the first module in a computer program to be called by the mainline module. It initializes the values of certain variables, opens files, prints headings, sometimes sorts files and loads tables, invokes the read-file routine, and then returns control to the mainline module.

**stepwise refinement**   the process of writing code in a horizontal manner. In other words, develop the logic a layer at a time avoiding the introduction of programming detail too soon.

**Structure Charts**   A tool used to decompose programs into functional, callable modules. The diagram shows the hierarchy of the modules within the program and the kind of program call used to invoke the module.

**structured programming**   a programming discipline that uses the three main structures—iteration, selection, and repetition. The discipline also uses the top-down approach, or modular design methodology.

**submenu**   a subordinate menu, a secondary set of options that appear on a terminal screen when a user selects an option from the main menu.

**subscript**  in a table, either a constant or variable symbol that is placed in parentheses after the table name that denotes the relative location of a value within the table. *See* literal subscript, variable subscript, element.

**table**  (also memory table, array) a list of related items with common attributes that is placed into main memory for fast access during record processing.

**table loading**  entering or placing data in a table prior to the actual processing of the input records.

**table lookup**  *See* table search.

**table of corresponding values**  a table that has elements that are normally subdivided. The subelements correspond to each other in some way.

**table search**  (table lookup) the process of scanning a table for a value based on a search key from a record.

**terminal symbol**  the flowcharting symbol that indicates the beginning (name) and end (STOP or RETURN) of programming segments or modules.

**three-level control break**  a point in the processing where the major of three control field keys is not equal to the previous record's major control key.

**top-down design**  the subdividing of modules into submodules until each submodule performs a single function.

**total line(s)**  usually represents the summation of one or more variables. The variables may be either input or calculated.

**transaction file**  a file of records containing the necessary data to update a master file.

**transaction key**  a key value on a transaction record that is used to locate (match) the key value on a particular master record for updating purposes.

**transaction record**  *See* transaction file.

**transaction update code**  (identification code) a code on a transaction record that specifies the kind of updating operation the computer is to perform on the master record.

**two-dimensional table**  (also chart or matrix) a table with two subdivisions or points of reference—rows and columns.

**two-level control break**  a processing point where the major of two control field keys is not equal to the previous record's major control key.

**updating**  changing, adding, and deleting data records in a file to correct it and/or bring it up to date.

**valid code test**  *See* code test.

**validity checking**  a program routine that determines whether the data entered in certain important fields is valid, i.e., meets certain prescribed criteria. *See* data validation edit program, built-in validity checking.

**validity switch**  a control variable in a validity checking program that flags the presence or absence of a valid record.

**valid switch**  *See* validity switch.

**variable**  the memory field into which data is read, or stored, and whose contents can vary during the execution of a computer program.

**variable name**  the name, or label, by which a variable is referenced in a programming command.

**variable subscript**  a subscript in a table that is specified as a variable (e.g., Tab(Sub)).

**wrap-up module**  the module responsible for functions normally related to the output (printing) of total or summary information and for closing any files.

# Index